Literature Criticism from 1400 to 1800

Guide to Gale Literary Criticism Series

For criticism on	Consult these Gale series
Authors now living or who died after December 31, 1999	*CONTEMPORARY LITERARY CRITICISM (CLC)*
Authors who died between 1900 and 1999	*TWENTIETH-CENTURY LITERARY CRITICISM (TCLC)*
Authors who died between 1800 and 1899	*NINETEENTH-CENTURY LITERATURE CRITICISM (NCLC)*
Authors who died between 1400 and 1799	*LITERATURE CRITICISM FROM 1400 TO 1800 (LC)* *SHAKESPEAREAN CRITICISM (SC)*
Authors who died before 1400	*CLASSICAL AND MEDIEVAL LITERATURE CRITICISM (CMLC)*
Authors of books for children and young adults	*CHILDREN'S LITERATURE REVIEW (CLR)*
Dramatists	*DRAMA CRITICISM (DC)*
Poets	*POETRY CRITICISM (PC)*
Short story writers	*SHORT STORY CRITICISM (SSC)*
Black writers of the past two hundred years	*BLACK LITERATURE CRITICISM (BLC)* *BLACK LITERATURE CRITICISM SUPPLEMENT (BLCS)*
Hispanic writers of the late nineteenth and twentieth centuries	*HISPANIC LITERATURE CRITICISM (HLC)* *HISPANIC LITERATURE CRITICISM SUPPLEMENT (HLCS)*
Native North American writers and orators of the eighteenth, nineteenth, and twentieth centuries	*NATIVE NORTH AMERICAN LITERATURE (NNAL)*
Major authors from the Renaissance to the present	*WORLD LITERATURE CRITICISM, 1500 TO THE PRESENT (WLC)* *WORLD LITERATURE CRITICISM SUPPLEMENT (WLCS)*

ISSN 0740-2880

Volume 82

Literature Criticism from 1400 to 1800

Critical Discussion of the Works of Fifteenth-, Sixteenth-, Seventeenth-, and Eighteenth-Century Novelists, Poets, Playwrights, Philosophers, and Other Creative Writers

Michael L. LaBlanc
Project Editor

GALE®

THOMSON
GALE

Detroit • New York • San Diego • San Francisco • Cleveland • New Haven, Conn. • Waterville, Maine • London • Munich

Literature Criticism from 1400 to 1800, Vol. 82

Project Editor
Michael L. LaBlanc

Editorial
Jenny Cromie, Kathy D. Darrow, Elisabeth Gellert, Madeline S. Harris, Edna M. Hedblad, Jelena O. Krstović, Michelle Lee, Ellen McGeagh, Jessica Menzo, Thomas J. Schoenberg, Lawrence J. Trudeau, Maikue Vang, Russel Whitaker

Research
Nicodemus Ford, Sarah Genik, Tamara C. Nott, Tracie A. Richardson

Permissions
Debra Freitas, Lori Hines, Sue Rudolph

Imaging and Multimedia
Dean Dauphinais, Robert Duncan, Leitha Etheridge-Sims, Mary K. Grimes, Lezlie Light, Dan Newell, David G. Oblender, Christine O'Bryan, Kelly A. Quin, Luke Rademacher

Composition and Electronic Capture
Carolyn Roney

Manufacturing
Stacy L. Melson

LIBRARY OF CONGRESS CATALOG CARD NUMBER 94-29718

ISBN 0-7876-5996-7
ISSN 0740-2880

Contents

Preface vii

Acknowledgments xi

Literary Criticism Series Advisory Board xiii

Preface

*L*iterature Criticism from 1400 to 1800 (*LC*) presents critical discussion of world literature from the fifteenth through the eighteenth centuries. The literature of this period is especially vital: the years 1400 to 1800 saw the rise of modern European drama, the birth of the novel and personal essay forms, the emergence of newspapers and periodicals, and major achievements in poetry and philosophy. *LC* provides valuable insight into the art, life, thought, and cultural transformations that took place during these centuries.

Scope of the Series

LC provides an introduction to the great poets, dramatists, novelists, essayists, and philosophers of the fifteenth through eighteenth centuries, and to the most significant interpretations of these authors' works. Because criticism of this literature spans nearly six hundred years, an overwhelming amount of scholarship confronts the student. *LC* organizes this material concisely and logically. Every attempt is made to reprint the most noteworthy, relevant, and educationally valuable essays available.

A separate Gale reference series, *Shakespearean Criticism,* is devoted exclusively to Shakespearean studies. Although properly belonging to the period covered in *LC*, William Shakespeare has inspired such a tremendous and ever-growing body of secondary material that a separate series was deemed essential.

Each entry in *LC* presents a representative selection of critical response to an author, a literary topic, or to a single important work of literature. Early commentary is offered to indicate initial responses, later selections document changes in literary reputations, and retrospective analyses provide the reader with modern views. The size of each author entry is a relative reflection of the scope of the criticism available in English. Every attempt has been made to identify and include the seminal essays on each author's work and to include recent commentary providing modern perspectives.

Volumes 1 through 12 of the series feature author entries arranged alphabetically by author. Volumes 13-47 of the series feature a thematic arrangement. Each volume includes an entry devoted to the general study of a specific literary or philosophical movement, writings surrounding important political and historical events, the philosophy and art associated with eras of cultural transformation, or the literature of specific social or ethnic groups. Each of these volumes also includes several author entries devoted to major representatives of the featured period, genre, or national literature. With volume 48, the series returns to a standard author approach, with some entries devoted to a single important work of world literature and others devoted to literary topics.

Organization of the Book

An *LC* entry consists of the following elements:

- The **Author Heading** cites the name under which the author most commonly wrote, followed by birth and death dates. Also located here are any name variations under which an author wrote, including transliterated forms for authors whose native languages use nonroman alphabets. If the author wrote consistently under a pseudonym, the pseudonym will be listed in the author heading and the author's actual name given in parenthesis on the first line of the biographical and critical information. Uncertain birth or death dates are indicated by question marks. Topic entries are preceded by a **Thematic Heading,** which simply states the subject of the entry. Single-work entries are preceded by the title of the work and its date of publication.

- The **Introduction** contains background information that introduces the reader to the author, work, or topic that is the subject of the entry.

- A **Portrait of the Author** is included when available.

- The list of **Principal Works** is ordered chronologically by date of first publication and lists the most important works by the author. The genre and publication date of each work is given. In the case of foreign authors whose works have been translated into English, the title and date (if available) of the first English-language edition is given in brackets following the original title. Unless otherwise indicated, dramas are dated by first performance, not first publication. Lists of **Representative Works** by different authors appear with topic entries.

- Reprinted **Criticism** is arranged chronologically in each entry to provide a useful perspective on changes in critical evaluation over time. The critic's name and the date of composition or publication of the critical work are given at the beginning of each piece of criticism. Unsigned criticism is preceded by the title of the source in which it appeared. All titles by the author featured in the text are printed in boldface type. Footnotes are reprinted at the end of each essay or excerpt. In the case of excerpted criticism, only those footnotes that pertain to the excerpted texts are included. Criticism in topic entries is arranged chronologically under a variety of subheadings to facilitate the study of different aspects of the topic.

- Critical essays are prefaced by brief **Annotations** explicating each piece.

- A complete **Bibliographical Citation** of the original essay or book precedes each piece of criticism.

- An annotated bibliography of **Further Reading** appears at the end of each entry and suggests resources for additional study. In some cases, significant essays for which the editors could not obtain reprint rights are included here. Boxed material following the further reading list provides references to other biographical and critical sources on the author in series published by Gale.

Indexes

A **Cumulative Author Index** lists all of the authors that appear in a wide variety of reference sources published by the Gale Group, including *LC*. A complete list of these sources is found facing the first page of the Author Index. The index also includes birth and death dates and cross references between pseudonyms and actual names.

A **Cumulative Nationality Index** lists all authors featured in *LC* by nationality, followed by the number of the *LC* volume in which their entry appears.

A **Cumulative Topic Index** lists the literary themes and topics treated in the series as well as in *Nineteenth-Century Literature Criticism, Twentieth-Century Literary Criticism,* and the *Contemporary Literature Criticism* Yearbook, which was discontinued in 1998.

An alphabetical **Title Index** accompanies each volume of *LC*. Listings of titles by authors covered in the given volume are followed by the author's name and the corresponding page numbers on which the titles are discussed. English translations of foreign titles and variations of titles are cross-referenced to the title under which a work was originally published. Titles of novels, dramas, nonfiction books, and poetry, short story, or essay collections are printed in italics, while individual poems, short stories, and essays are printed in roman type within quotation marks.

In response to numerous suggestions from librarians, Gale also produces an annual paperbound edition of the LC cumulative title index. This annual cumulation, which alphabetically lists all titles reviewed in the series, is available to all customers. Additional copies of this index are available upon request. Librarians and patrons will welcome this separate index; it saves shelf space, is easy to use, and is recyclable upon receipt of the next edition.

Citing *Literature Criticism from 1400 to 1800*

When writing papers, students who quote directly from any volume in the Literary Criticism Series may use the following general format to footnote reprinted criticism. The first example pertains to material drawn from periodicals, the second to material reprinted from books.

Eileen Reeves, "Daniel 5 and the *Assayer*: Galileo Reads the Handwriting on the Wall, " *The Journal of Medieval and Renaissance Studies,* 21, no. 1 (Spring 1991): 1-27; reprinted in *Literature Criticism from 1400 to 1800,* vol. 45, ed. Jelena Krstović and Marie Lazzari (Farmington Hills, Mich.: The Gale Group, 1999), 297-310.

Margaret Anne Doody, *A Natural Passion: A Study of the Novels of Samuel Richardson* (Oxford University Press, 1974), 17-22, 132-35; excerpted and reprinted in *Literature Criticism from 1400 to 1800,* vol. 46, ed. Jelena Krstović and Marie Lazzari (Farmington Hills, Mich.: The Gale Group, 1999), 20-2.

Suggestions are Welcome

Readers who wish to suggest new features, topics, or authors to appear in future volumes, or who have other suggestions or comments are cordially invited to call, write, or fax the Project Editor:

Project Editor, Literary Criticism Series
The Gale Group
27500 Drake Road
Farmington Hills, MI 48331-3535
1-800-347-4253 (GALE)
Fax: 248-699-8054

Acknowledgments

The editors wish to thank the copyright holders of the excerpted criticism included in this volume and the permissions managers of many book and magazine publishing companies for assisting us in securing reproduction rights. We are also grateful to the staffs of the Detroit Public Library, the Library of Congress, the University of Detroit Mercy Library, Wayne State University Purdy/Kresge Library Complex, and the University of Michigan Libraries for making their resources available to us. Following is a list of the copyright holders who have granted us permission to reproduce material in this volume of *LC*. Every effort has been made to trace copyright, but if omissions have been made, please let us know.

Literary Criticism Series Advisory Board

The members of the Gale Group Literary Criticism Series Advisory Board—reference librarians and subject specialists from public, academic, and school library systems—represent a cross-section of our customer base and offer a variety of informed perspectives on both the presentation and content of our literature criticism products. Advisory board members assess and define such quality issues as the relevance, currency, and usefulness of the author coverage, critical content, and literary topics included in our series; evaluate the layout, presentation, and general quality of our printed volumes; provide feedback on the criteria used for selecting authors and topics covered in our series; provide suggestions for potential enhancements to our series; identify any gaps in our coverage of authors or literary topics, recommending authors or topics for inclusion; analyze the appropriateness of our content and presentation for various user audiences, such as high school students, undergraduates, graduate students, librarians, and educators; and offer feedback on any proposed changes/enhancements to our series. We wish to thank the following advisors for their advice throughout the year.

Jane Barker
1652-1732

English novelist and poet.

The following entry provides an overview of Barker's life and works. For additional information on her career, see *LC*, Volume 42.

INTRODUCTION

Barker is an important figure in the emergence of the novel in the early decades of the eighteenth century. She is best remembered for the "Galesia Trilogy" of novels she published between 1713 and 1726, but she also composed occasional verse and constructed a devotional manual from materials she translated from the works of French cleric François Fénelon. Barker was little known during her lifetime, although her novels did enjoy a modest success upon initial publication, marking her as one of the first women to enter the expanding literary marketplace. Feminist scholars in the late twentieth century began to show interest in Barker's life and work because of the insights they provide into women's literary history and self-portrayal. Barker was an unmarried woman who dabbled in commercial medicine and was a staunch supporter of the exiled Stuart court, and her writing draws heavily on these and other autobiographical elements of her life.

BIOGRAPHICAL INFORMATION

The particulars of Barker's life are the subject of some controversy. Because her fictional works have elements of autobiography, earlier scholars reconstructed her biography based on events described in her novels and verse. Later critics have contended that the earlier reconstructions were inaccurate and have sketched a new biography based on historical records; but the details of her life remain murky. Barker was born in May, 1652 in Northamptonshire, England, the only daughter of Thomas and Anne Barker. Barker's parents, while not landed gentry or aristocracy, enjoyed modest prosperity, and were staunch supporters of the royal House of Stuart. Barker received almost all of her education from her elder brother, Edward, who attended Oxford and Leyden Universities. He taught her Latin, philosophy, and medicine. When her brother died around 1675, it came to a blow as Barker, and she continued to mourn his early death in her prose and verse as late as 1723. In 1681 Barker's father died, and shortly thereafter she and her mother moved to London. In 1685 her mother died, and Barker continued to live on the inheritance she had received from her father.

Sometime during the reign of the Roman Catholic monarch James II (1685-1688), Barker converted to Catholicism. In 1688 her collection of poems, *Poetical Recreations,* appeared. She likely fled to France early the next year, following James's flight at the time of the Glorious Revolution. Although she was not in the upper ranks of exile society, she moved in distinguished circles, and her verse probably circulated among James's followers. While in France, Barker developed cataracts, and although she had an operation to help the problem, she became functionally blind.

Barker returned to England around 1704 (some accounts say as late as 1713), where she took up the management of her family farm in Wilsthorpe. It is likely that she had financial difficulties during this time. In 1713 the novels she worked on in the 1680s and in France began to be published. Little more is known of her life. She apparently suffered a serious illness in 1726, and may have gone back to France in 1727. After this nothing is recorded about her. She died either in France or in England in 1732.

MAJOR WORKS

Barker's first published work was *Poetical Recreations,* a collection of about 55 pieces of occasional verse written by Barker in the 1670s and 1680s, along with a number of works by others. Many of Barker's poems are familiar epistles to friends and acquaintances, including a number of learned men at Cambridge, and there are others on medical themes. What emerges from these poems is a portrait of a woman concerned with her self-image as a person of education and intellectual attainment. Barker's later verse, written during her exile in France, was circulated in manuscript but not published. The poems, written to support the Jacobite cause, are preserved in the first two parts of a manuscript in the library of Magdalen College, Oxford (a third part consists of "corrected" versions of her earlier poems).

Love Intrigues, the first novel in Barker's so-called Galesia Trilogy was published in 1713. It is a romance in which a mature Galesia looks back on her days as a young lady, when she was pursued by her cousin, Bosvil. The work departs from the conventional romantic fiction of its day, as it offers a cynical view of love and considers the difficulties of choosing to be an unmarried, educated woman with literary aspirations. The second and third novels in the trilogy, *A Patch-Work Screen for the Ladies* (1723) and *The Lining of the Patch-Work Screen* (1726) reiterate some of the themes of the earlier novel. These works are an interesting mix of fiction, philosophy, poetry, recipes, and hymns woven together by a number of narrators (including Galesia), much like a patchwork quilt, that tell interrelated stories of political and domestic life.

The heroic romance *Exilius: or, The Banish'd Roman,* published in 1715, was written as an imitation of Archbishop François Fénelon's *Telemaque.* The long, episodic narrative has an intense moral purpose: to show the proper behavior of young ladies in various real-life situations. Each of the several simultaneous plots is designed to place its heroine in a situation that tests her resilience, trains her into the proper way of conformity to social expectations, or punishes her for transgressions against accepted norms. Some critics have suggested that the titular "Banish'd Roman," a man of impeccable virtue, courage, and wisdom, is a reference to the exiled Stuart monarch James. Barker also translated works by Fénelon in the collection of meditations, *The Christian Pilgrimage* (1718), which, according to some scholars, was an attempt by Barker to make Catholicism more accessible to those schooled in the Protestant faith.

CRITICAL RECEPTION

Although she was not well known in her lifetime, Barker was paid for her writing, making her one of the first professional female writers in Britain. Although she claimed that *Poetical Recreations* was published without her consent, and she professed a disdain for commercial publication, she sought to have her fiction published, in part because she had financial difficulties. Two of her novels were published by the infamous Edmund Curll (who, during his career was sued for literary piracy and was tried and convicted for publishing obscene books); he actively marketed her works to an expanding reading public, labeling them "novels" rather than "romances," a term increasingly unfashionable.

Very little mention was made of Barker after her death, but feminist scholars began to show interest in her work in the 1980s, seeing her as a central figure in the rise of the woman novelist. The autobiographical nature of her fictions, and what they said about female authorship in the eighteenth century, was also of interest. As research into Barker's life and work has expanded, critics have examined more closely the connection between autobiography and fiction in her work, the self-image she projects in her novels and verse, her relationships with literary and learned men, her attitude toward her own education and literary achievement, her entry into the literary marketplace, and her political ideology as revealed in her writing.

PRINCIPAL WORKS

Poetical Recreations: Consisting of Original Poems, Songs, Odes, &c. with Several New Translations. In Two Parts, Part I. Occasionally Written by Mrs. Jane Barker. Part II. By Several Gentlemen of the Universities, and Others [editor and contributor] (poetry) 1688

†*Love Intrigues; or, the History of the Amours of Bosvil and Galesia, As Related to Lucasia, in St. Germains Garden* (novel) 1713

Exilius: or, The Banish'd Roman. A New Romance in Two Parts: Written After the Manner of Telemachus, For the Instruction of Some Young Ladies of Quality (novel) 1715

The Christian Pilgrimage: or a Companion for the Holy Season of Lent: being meditations upon the Passion. Death, Resurrection and Ascension of . . . Jesus Christ [translator; from works by François Fénelon] (meditations) 1718

*The Entertaining Novels of Mrs. Jane Barker. 2 vols. (novels) 1719

†*A Patch-Work Screen for the Ladies, or Love & Virtue Recommended in a Collection of Instructive Novels. Related After a Manner intirely New, and Interspersed with Rural Poems, describing the Innocence of a Country-Life* (novel) 1723

†*The Lining of the Patch-Work Screen: Design'd for the Father Entertainment of the Ladies* (novel) 1726

*This work contains revised versions of *Exilius* and *Love Intrigues.*

†These three works comprise the "Galesia Trilogy."

CRITICISM

Jane Spencer (essay date 1983)

SOURCE: Spencer, Jane. "Creating the Women Writer: The Autobiographical Works of Jane Barker." *Tulsa Studies in Women's Literature* 2, no. 2 (fall 1983): 165-81.

[*In the following essay, Spencer claims that Barker's main concerns were to define herself as a woman and as a writer and to create for herself and her audience an acceptable self-image. Spencer also states that Barker's works are especially important to those interested in the history of women's writing and women's self-definition because they seem to be largely autobiographical.*]

To some extent, the autobiographer's problem with the meaning of the self is shared by all writers. "For all literary artists," write Sandra Gilbert and Susan Gubar, "self-definition necessarily precedes self-assertion"; and the problems of self-definition have been particularly acute for the female artist, as their study of nineteenth-century women writers demonstrates.[1] If women had difficulty in defining themselves as writers in the nineteenth century when there were many successful women poets and novelists, the problem was worse in the seventeenth when writing for publication was a most unusual and generally unacceptable occupation for a woman. Margaret Cavendish, Duchess of Newcastle, publishing her *Poems, and Fancies* in 1653, wrote, "I imagine I shall be censur'd by my owne *Sex; and Men* will cast a *smile* of *scorne* upon my *Book,* because they think thereby, *Women* incroach too much upon their *Prerogatives*." Dorothy Osborne, herself a woman of some literary talent, greeted Cavendish's work with amazed disapproval. "Sure, the poor woman is a little distracted, she could never be so ridiculous else as to venture at writing books, and in verse too. If I should not sleep this fortnight I should not come to that," she wrote. Professional women writers like Aphra Behn, Delariviere Manley, Catherine Trotter and Mary Pix were usually bolder in self-definition and self-assertion; but even Behn, who led the way in this respect, tended to think of her literary skill as a masculine attribute. She wanted "the Priviledge for my Masculine Part the Poet in me . . . to tread in those successful Paths my Predecessors have so long thriv'd in."[2] By the early eighteenth century, the reading and theater-going public had at least been alerted to the idea of women's writing, but the woman writer had not gained widespread acceptance. To the fear that a woman's writing could be criticized as a presumptuous abandonment of the proper feminine role was added the fear of gaining the reputation for immorality associated with writers like Behn and Manley. It was still by no means easy for a woman to claim or justify a literary vocation.

In the works of Jane Barker, a little-known author of late seventeenth-and early eighteenth-century England, we can observe one attempt to overcome the problems facing women writers in this period. Barker produced a variety of literary work. She began with poetry, her first publication being *Poetical Recreations* in 1688. *Love Intrigues: Or, The History of the Amours of Bosvil and Galesia* (1713) marked her entry into the expanding literary market for prose narrative. *Exilius* (1715) is a romance dealing with the intertwined adventures of several pairs of heroic lovers. A translation from Fénelon appeared as *The Christian Pilgrimmage* in 1718. Her last two publications, *A Patch-Work Screen for the Ladies* (1723) and *The Lining of the Patch-Work Screen* (1726), continued Galesia's story. In the long gap between the publications of the poems and the first narrative, she wrote a number of poems which are extant in manuscript.[3] Barker's achievements deserve more recognition than they have so far received. Some of the manuscript poems show her to be of great historical interest as a Jacobite poet. Her contribution to the development of the novel is even more important. My main interest here, however, is the "anxiety of authorship" which colors her poems and her Galesia narratives.[4] I hope to show that one of her most pressing concerns was to define herself as a woman and a writer, and to create a self-image that would be acceptable to herself and to her public.

Jane Barker's work is especially pertinent to the question of the woman writer's self-definition because it appears to be largely autobiographical. Very little is known of her life apart from what can be gathered from her writings. They tell us of her childhood in Wiltsthorp, her close relationship with her brother who studied medicine and instructed her in the subject, and her grief at his early death.[5] The deaths of her parents are recorded in her narratives and poems.[6] Jane Barker converted to Roman Catholicism. She

left England soon after James II and lived for some years in the court-in-exile at St. Germain.[7] After her return to England she was patronized by the Countess of Exeter, to whom she dedicated *Exilius.* Nothing is known of her after the publication of *The Lining.* From the frequent correspondences between statements Jane Barker makes about herself, and evidence about her which can be gathered from the publication details of her books, it seems that we are safe in assuming her works to be autobiographical.[8] Further details of her life have been found in external sources using her works as the starting point. G. S. Gibbons identifies the Uncle, Colonel C—, mentioned in *Poetical Recreations,* as William Connock, who served with James II's army in Ireland. He finds Jane Barker of Wiltsthorp, spinster, who has an estate of £47 10s. annual value, mentioned in a list of Roman Catholic nonjurors in 1715.[9] Thus we gain more details for the picture of Barker as a woman whose family espoused the Stuart cause, who became a Catholic, and who was living in England on a small income in the early eighteenth century.

This does not mean, of course, that Barker offers an entirely factual account of her life. It would be hard to ascertain to what extent the stories of the love affair in *Bosvil and Galesia* and the problems with various suitors in *A Patch-Work Screen* are based on true events. Some of the interpolated tales in *A Patch-Work Screen* and *The Lining* are certainly fictional, but this does not destroy the autobiographical significance of the narratives. In his work on autobiography, Georges Gusdorf emphasizes that it can never offer us the "truth" of a life but constructs a life from what the writer creates, as well as what she or he remembers and distorts in the act of remembering. The autobiography shows what the writer "believes and wishes himself [sic] to be and to have been. What is in question is a sort of revaluation of individual destiny."[10] On the basis of this theoretical assumption, I intend to approach Jane Barker as a writer who offers us, in the way of autobiographers, not so much the facts of her life as her creation of "the meaning of [her] own mythic tale."[11] I hope to show that the meaning of the tale in Barker's case is the presentation and explanation of a life which deviates in many ways from the norm prescribed for women. It is the life of a spinster, a healer, an intellectual, a writer. All are significant parts of Barker's image of herself, but the image of the writer is of key importance because on this image depends the articulation of all the others.

In creating her autobiography, Barker chooses to fictionalize her identity in the pseudonyms Galesia (sometimes spelled Galecia or Galaecia) and Fidelia. The two personae are used to present her experiences in different ways. Fidelia, as her name implies, represents fidelity—to Jacobitism and to her chosen religion—and she is used in poems dealing mainly with religious and political topics. Galesia is used for poems and narratives dealing with Barker's life before her journey to France and after her return. Poems addressed to Barker sometimes call her Mrs. Jane Barker, and sometimes Galesia, suggesting how clearly she was identified by her friends with her pseudonym.[12] One question to be considered about Barker, then, is how this use of a persona affects her work as autobiography.

The adoption of the romantic name Galesia was one of many ways in which Barker wrapped her life-story in the conventions of romance. She was both protecting herself, and offering the public the kind of work it wanted, by disguising her autobiography as a "diverting Novel."[13] The central reason for the self-disguise, however, may be that by calling herself Galesia, Barker immediately became, in her own and her readers' eyes, a heroine like the heroines of romance and pastoral. This meant that the significance of her life-story was established at the outset and that her conduct could be explained by being related to the conduct of other literary heroines. By making her autobiography into a romance about a version of herself called Galesia, Barker gained all the advantages of a heroine's identity.

One advantage of being a heroine was that it made it easier to define herself as a woman writer. There was already a tradition linking the two identities. In the seventeenth-century romances produced in the world of the French salons, the characters were often based on men and women known to the writer, and part of the appeal of a romance for members of these select circles was to recognize their friends and themselves transformed into idealized heroes and heroines.[14] In this transference of the status of literary heroine to women in a literary circle, we see the beginnings of the implication that a literary woman is a heroine. Romances frequently included epistles written by the heroines who could thus become models for the woman writer. English women who, often inspired by the *précieuses,* corresponded under literary pseudonyms taken from pastorals and romances, contributed to the identification of woman writer with literary heroine. Katherine Philips, as "Orinda," corresponded with a number of friends who also adopted pastoral pseudonyms. Jane Barker in her youth had a circle of literary friends to whom she was known as Galesia. When women writers known as "Orinda" or "Astrea" (Aphra Behn) began to publish their work, the idea that a woman writer was somehow akin to a heroine in romance gained wider currency. For these reasons, Barker's Galesia could simultaneously serve as the heroine of a romance and as a representation of herself as a writer.

Barker represents herself as Galesia the writer in *Poetical Recreations* and in a number of the manuscript poems, and some poems from these collections are inserted into the first two Galesia narratives, *Bosvil and Galesia* and *A Patch-Work Screen.* Her use of poems written in her youth about her poetic vocation to help in the construction of Galesia's story many years later shows that Barker was preoccupied with this subject over a long period. Sometimes the changed context of the poems within the narratives alters their significance. Here, I am concerned with the poems only as elements of the later narratives, contributing to Barker's creation of the heroine-writer of the autobiographical romance.

Bosvil and Galesia, A Patch-Work Screen, and *The Lining* are successive creations of Galesia's identity as heroine-writer through the account of various stages of her life. *Bosvil and Galesia* is the story of the failed love affair of her youth, told by Galesia to her friend Lucasia years after the event. Galesia falls in love with Bosvil and manages to conceal her feelings while puzzling to understand his. He sometimes appears as an enthusiastic lover and sometimes, for no apparent reason, he ignores her. On one occasion, when Bosvil explains his long absence as a result of illness and produces a marriage license to back up his proposals, Galesia's belief in his love seems justified; but this is followed by a three-weeks' absence after which Bosvil reappears, cold and indifferent again. Eventually he marries another woman, and so ends a relationship that Galesia sums up as "one continu'd Act of Folly on the one side, and Treachery on the other" (*Bosvil and Galesia,* p. 64).

This definition of the heroine's relationship with her lover in terms of her folly and his treachery is one indication that Galesia's story is a variant of what Nancy K. Miller calls "the heroine's text": that is, "the text of an ideology that codes femininity in paradigms of sexual vulnerability."[15] Miller sees the feminocentric novels of the eighteenth century as expressions of the period's obsession with womanhood and with the inscription of feminine destiny in terms of sexuality. "In *Moll Flanders, La Vie de Marianne, Pamela,* and *Fanny Hill* . . . the fundamental structuring sequence is set in motion by a confrontation between feminine virtue and illicit masculine desire."[16] The typical heroine's text is a story of seduction suffered or avoided.

Galesia's story does not fit this description exactly, for Bosvil neither seduces nor attempts to seduce her. The idea of the seduction tale nevertheless haunts Galesia throughout their acquaintance and offers her a means of interpreting his enigmatic behavior. From the beginning she suspects him of masculine treachery. Bosvil visits Galesia while she is staying in London under her aunt's protection and openly declares his love; but she, wary of town libertinism and fearful of losing her reputation, has "the Cunning to conceal [her] Passion, and pretend not to believe his" (p. 8). Her mistrust seems justified by his altered behavior when he visits her after her return home. Though he later resumes the role of lover, he does not make his intentions known to her parents, and this in itself makes the courtship an illicit one. Galesia eventually avoids any slur on her reputation only at the cost of losing Bosvil altogether. When he is at his most eager as a lover, he complains that her reserve has convinced him that she cannot love him. Though she now believes herself to be on the verge of matrimony, Galesia does not confess her love, but resolves that next time she sees him she will be "no longer cruel to my self, and him; but let him know what mighty Sums of Love I had been hoarding up for him, since the Moment of our first Interview" (p. 37). It is too late. Bosvil never returns in the posture of a lover again.

Galesia's story ends with neither of the alternatives (seduction, leading to catastrophe, or avoided seduction, leading to marriage) usual to eighteenth-century heroines. Her failure to marry appears an oddity to critics who do not take the autobiographical nature of the narratives into account.[17] *Bosvil and Galesia* has to be understood both as a "heroine's text" and as autobiography because Barker has superimposed the literary convention of the heroine's sexual and social initiation onto the structure of her own single life. Galesia is not, like the typical heroine-narrator, recalling her pre-marital life or excusing a sexual lapse; instead, she is explaining the lack of a sexual relationship in her life. She attributes to herself the characteristics of heroines whose destiny she does not share in order to make her single life seem equally valid as another kind of heroine's destiny.

The failure of the Bosvil-Galesia relationship can be attributed to Galesia's pride and her vulnerability, both of which are explained in terms of her identity as heroine. She admits that it was pride that prevented her from telling Bosvil that she loved him, and from confiding in her mother, who might have been able to bring about a happy conclusion to the affair. Such pride is explicable as the characteristic of a romance heroine. In the French heroic romance of the seventeenth century, the position of the heroine is one of despotic power over her lover. He is expected to serve her for years for the reward only of kissing her hand or hearing that she is so gracious as not to hate him. Galesia the narrator portrays her younger self as a vain imitator of the romance heroine: "I pleased my self to think how [one of her suitors, Brafort] wou'd be balk'd, who, I thought, had been very remiss in his Devoirs towards such a Goddess, as the World's Flatterers had made of me," she reports (p. 10). Galesia acts the goddess when Bosvil declares his love. His dedication of "every Action of his Life to love, please and serve" her is met with the haughty command to "Cease . . . these Asseverations" (p. 27). He declares he will die if she does not return his love, and she offers not love but friendship, though her heart has a secret fondness for him. This is strictly virtuous according to the conventions of romance, but as narrator, Galesia interprets this failure to be frank as pride, which leads to the loss of Bosvil.

The mockery of the heroine's pride, however, reveals the vulnerability behind it. Galesia is not the powerful heroine she believes herself to be, and Bosvil certainly will not die without her love. The theme of the vulnerability behind the heroine's pride is developed through the use of other literary idioms. Bosvil proposes a friend of his to Galesia's father as a husband for Galesia. In her anger about this, Galesia changes from heroine of romance to the passionate woman of heroic drama. She is thwarted in her love and intent on revenge, and her language and actions are appropriate to heroic tragedy:

> I went towards the Place of his Abode, supposing a Rapier in my hand, and saying to my self, The false *Bosvil* shou'd now disquiet me no more, nor any other of our Sex; in him I will end his Race, no more of them shall come to disturb, or affront Womankind; this only Son, shall dye by the hands of me an only Daughter.
>
> (p. 43)

In this passage, the rapier exists only in Galesia's fancy, but in the second edition of *Bosvil and Galesia* (1719), Galesia actually seizes "a Steel Rapier, which stood in the Hall."[18] However, instead of carrying out her intention, she bursts into tears and turns her anger against herself. Galesia the narrator comments on this as an example of female weakness: "if the Feebleness of our Hands did not moderate the Fury of our Heads, Woman sometimes would exceed the fiercest Savages, especially when affronted in her Amours" (p. 44). This undercuts the former Galesia's heroic stance and ranks her rather with the ridiculed cast-off mistresses of Restoration comedy who fail in their attempts to attack their ex-lovers.[19] The younger Galesia, revealed like these characters as a weak woman behind her heroic posture, is viewed with some mockery. At the same time there is sympathy for her as a victim who, in the revised version of the story, laments "Why was I born, or why a Female born" (2nd ed., p. 40).

At times, Galesia even justifies her pride as the necessary effect of female vulnerability and thus offers a different interpretation of the love affair. Her behavior towards her early suitor, Brafort, is haughtiness masquerading as modesty, but she excuses herself because "as the World now rolls, we are under a Kind of Constraint to follow its Byass" (p. 10). Her behavior with Bosvil can also be seen as dictated by convention. Thus there is a wide difference between Bosvil's reticence about his feelings and her silence about her love for him. Given the restrictive code of feminine behavior that makes an admission of love tantamount to a loss of chastity, a woman must be careful not to "betray [her] Weakness by a too ready Compliance" (pp. 21-22). It is the man's duty to make his feelings clear, and Galesia has the right to complain of Bosvil that "his Tongue was the only part silent in the Declaration of a violent Passion" (p. 18). The failure of their love, then, is Bosvil's fault more than Galesia's: he fails to understand and allow for her vulnerability as a woman.

The paradox of this heroine's text is that because Galesia behaves like a proper heroine, she is prevented from fulfilling a heroine's destiny. Thus the story contains an implicit criticism of the conventions governing women "as the World now rolls." At the same time, underlying the surface narrative of self-justification in the face of failure, is the tale of a different kind of success. The thwarted romance-heroine becomes the heroine-poet.

It is during the first of Bosvil's recurrent periods of coldness towards her that Galesia first identifies herself as a poet. On one of her melancholy, solitary walks she composes a poem, elsewhere referred to as her "contract with the muses," in which she dedicates herself to poetry:

> Methinks these Shades, strange Thoughts suggest,
> Which heat my Head, and cool my Breast;
> And mind me of a Laurel Crest.

Methinks I hear the Muses sing,
And see 'em all dance in a Ring;
And call upon me to take Wing.

We will (say they) assist thy Flight,
Till thou reach fair *ORINDA*'s Height,
If thou can'st this World's Follies slight.

We'll bring thee to our bright Abodes,
Among the Heroes and the Gods,
If thou and Wealth can be at Odds.

Then gentle Maid cast off thy Chain,
Which links thee to thy faithless Swain,
And vow a Virgin to remain.

Write, write thy Vow upon this Tree,
By us it shall recorded be;
And thou enjoy Eternity.

(p. 14)[20]

The choice is clear. Married life has been renounced in exchange for the promise of literary achievement. In the reference to Orinda we notice the importance of real-life heroines, as well as literary models, for creating the woman writer's sense of identity. Katherine Philips is, in Gilbert and Gubar's terms, the "female precursor" who makes Galesia's assumption of poetic identity possible.[21] Galesia also appeals, like other women writers of her time, to the example of Sappho: "I imagin'd myself the *Orinda,* or *Sapho* of my time," she explains (p. 15).

Galesia becomes a healer as well as a poet. She decides to imitate "the Faithful Shepperdess in the Play" (Clorin, in Fletcher's *Faithful Shepherdess*) in perpetual chastity and in practicing medicine with herbal remedies. Her two vocations are neatly united in the identity of "*Apollo*'s Darling Daughter," Apollo being god of poetry and of medicine (p. 15). However, there is something of a sarcastic tone in this description of her early ambitions, or "thousand vain Conceits" (p. 15), which led her into "Pride, with all its vile Adherents" (p. 17); and the intellectual life is described as a mere substitute for Bosvil's love: "I, finding my self abandoned by *Bosvil,* and thinking it impossible ever to love again, resolved to espouse a Book, and spend my Days in Study" (p. 15).

As narrator, Galesia criticizes her dedication to study, medicine, and poetry; but she leaves no doubt that these vocations are the most important parts of her life. Although the vow to the muses is presented as a reaction to the loss of love, Galesia's readiness to make such a vow contrasts with her careful avoidance of making any promises to her lover. It is significant that one very important image of Galesia as poet is found when the love affair appears to be on the point of success. After Bosvil has played devoted romance hero to her haughty romance heroine, Galesia's thoughts are "in a Sea of Joy," as she believes their marriage to be a certainty (p. 32). At this high point of happiness, she falls asleep in the garden and dreams that an "angry Power" makes her climb a high mountain

(evidently the poets' mountain, Parnassus). Then he takes her to the tree on which she wrote her contract with the muses. He warns her that there is no escaping the poet's fate now: "Since, since thou hast the Muses chose, / *Hymen* and Fortune are thy Foes" (p. 33). According to this "uncouth Guardian," Galesia's poetic vocation is to lose her Bosvil's love and the chance of marriage, but the choice has been hers. The opposition between poetry and love is intensified in the second edition of *Bosvil and Galesia,* in which, when Galesia climbs Parnassus, Bosvil attempts to "tumble [her] down," but is prevented by the guardian (2nd ed., p. 29). The sexual implication in this encounter befits Galesia's identification of poetry with chastity. There is a covert suggestion in this that Galesia's reserve towards Bosvil was adopted not just from fear of being seduced but from fear of being seduced away from her vocation. The dream as a whole implies that her contract with the muses was not merely a reaction to Bosvil's behavior but an expression of her preference for an unmarried life of study and poetry.

Barker's later narratives continue to develop the picture of Galesia established in *Bosvil and Galesia.* The narrator of *A Patch-Work Screen for the Ladies* is Galesia after her return from France. Her narrative deals with the events following Bosvil's desertion, but thematically it re-enacts the same struggle between poetry and love. Once Bosvil has gone, Galesia devotes herself to the study of Orinda:

I began to emulate her Wit, and aspired to imitate her Writings; in doing of which, I think, I deserved *Arachne*'s Fate, or at least to be transform'd into one of the lowest of *Mack-Fleckno*'s Followers: Her noble Genius being inimitable . . . each line [of her poetry] was like a Ladder to climb, not only to *Parnassus*, but to Heaven: which I (poor Puzzle as I was!) had the Boldness to try to imitate, 'till I was dropped into a Labyrinth of Poetry, which has ever since interlac'd all the Actions of my Life.

(*A Patch-Work Screen*, p. 3)

This attitude to the poetic vocation is typical of *A Patch-Work Screen* as a whole. Admiration of the model woman writer is combined with self-mockery and self-depreciation of Galesia's own attempts to write. At the same time there is a sense of pride for having embraced the fate of a poet, whatever the effects on the rest of her life.

In fact, the idea that poetry is Galesia's fate is even stronger in *A Patch-Work Screen* than in *Bosvil and Galesia.* Love has much less power to disturb the poetic life for instead of the long drawn out emotional turmoil of the relationship with Bosvil, this narrative presents a series of suitors, briefly sketched and rapidly dismissed, whom neither Galesia nor the reader can take seriously. While Galesia's entry into the labyrinth of poetry is sometimes dated after the loss of Bosvil, as in the above quotation, at other times it is claimed that the poet's fate was sealed in her childhood. One poem in the narrative which makes this claim, **"The Necessity of Fate,"** was first published in Barker's 1688 collection. Having described her failure to cast off the "Chain" of poetry, the poet laments,

All this, my *Fate*, all this thou didst fore show,
   Ev'n when I was a Child,
   When in my *Picture*'s Hand,
   My Mother did command,
There should be drawn a *Lawrel Bough.*
Lo! then my *Muse* sat by, and smil'd. . . .

(p. 94)[22]

The muse smiled because she knew Galesia would forsake

   Soaring Honours, vain Persuits of Pleasure,
   And vainer Fruits of worldly Treasure,
     All for the Muses *melancholy Tree,*
     E'er I knew ought of its *great Mystery.*

(p. 95)

Reflecting on this, the poet reconciles herself to her fate and asks for the reward appropriate to her dedication to poetry—to be crowned with the laurel: "Since, O my Fate! thou needs wilt have it so, / Let thy kind Hand exalt it to my Brow" (p. 95). Galesia's mother's comment on this poem provides the comic deflation that Barker is always ready to give after an exaltation of her poetic identity. "I think, *Fate* would be more kind to set a Basket, or a Milk-pail on thy Head; thereby to suppress those foolish Vapours that thus intoxicate thy Brain" (p. 95). However, her mother also adds, "I shall no more oppose thy Fancy [for poetry] but comply and indulge so innocent a Diversion" (p. 95).

Her acceptance of Galesia as poet is important, for up to this point she has been opposing this identity with her own recommendation that Galesia should get married, "This being the Business for which you came into the World," as she tells her (p. 80). Galesia cannot oppose what she believes to be the truth of this, but she retains her "secret Disgust against Matrimony" (p. 80), and her preference for poetry.

Fortunately, the many suitors who appear on the scene all justify Galesia's rejection of them by proving unworthy. One young gentleman who offers marriage is mistrusted by her from the start because he is known to have been a rake. Even when all the correct procedures have been followed, with his father making a formal proposal to hers, she suspects him of intending to seduce her. Luckily she is saved from either compliance or rebellion when her would-be lover is hanged for a robbery committed in a frolic. Those she describes as "Pretenders to my Person" after her father's death has left her fortune in her own power (p. 40) are easily dismissed as mercenary, and "These Amours affected me but little, or rather not at all," she reports (p. 42). It is harder to reject a worthier character who does not appeal to her because he is "a little in Years" (p. 49), but she manages to discourage him. Later, her reputation for virtue threatens to trap her when the mother of profligate young Lysander asks her to marry and thereby reform him. However, Lysander has put his fortune into the hands of an adulteress who paid his debts for him, and she refuses to let him marry, so he shoots himself. Despite Galesia's laments that some devil has been

allowed "to persecute me in the Persons of all that pretended to love or like me" (p. 89), she is obviously relieved at his disappearance: "you cannot imagine, that his Death affected me much as a Lover, there being but little of that in the Story" (p. 88).

It is not only her own experience that convinces Galesia that she is right to reject sexual involvement. The stories interpolated in her narrative often serve the purpose of further demonstrating the dangers both of illicit sexuality and of marriages entered into from a sense of duty. In her capacity as physician, Galesia is consulted by a girl who has been seduced and is suffering from a venereal disease (pp. 51-54). Soon afterwards she hears the story of a nurse who made the mistake of marrying according to her father's "prudent" wishes, and was reduced to poverty while the lover she had been forced to give up as unsuitable for an heiress himself became rich (pp. 59-63).

No wonder, on the whole, that Galesia decides in favor of **"A Virgin Life,"** as she calls one of her poems. She explicitly links such a life with poetic achievement:

   Since, O good Heavens! you have bestow'd on me
   So great a Kindness for *Virginity,*
   Suffer me not to fall into the Powers
   Of Man's almost Omnipotent Amours.
   But let me in this happy State remain,
   And in chaste Verse my chaster Thoughts explain.

(p. 90)[23]

To Galesia, chastity means poetry. Orinda's example is important in sustaining this link. Although Katherine Philips, a married woman, could not serve as a model for Jane Barker's "Virgin Life," her reputation as "chaste Orinda" was a useful one to set against the common belief that to be a woman writer was proof in itself of sexual looseness.

Galesia does not receive any such accusation. On the contrary, she is criticized for her love of the single life. Her mother fears that her "idle Dreams on *Parnassus,* and foolish Romantick flights, with *Icarus*" (p. 79) will give her a bad reputation for folly and the eccentricity of a solitary life, not for sexual misconduct. Nevertheless, Galesia's continual insistence on the chastity of poetry perhaps suggests that the bad reputation of some women writers disturbs her. Fears about a possible connection between poetry and sexuality are perhaps expressed in the story of Galesia's adventure in the garret-closet. While she and her mother are lodging in London, Galesia escapes from the noisy world into "a Closet in my Landlady's Back-Garret which I crept into, as if it had been a Cave on the Top of *Parnassus*" (p. 64). She adds that "this Hole was to me a kind of Paradise" (p. 65). Here she resumes her intellectual life and her poetry. The closet is both a retreat from the world and a vantage-point from which she can survey it, giving free play to her intellect:

   Out of this Garret, there was a Door went out to the
   Leads; on which I us'd frequently to walk to take the
   Air . . . here I was alone, or, as the Philosopher says,

never *less alone*. Here I entertain'd my Thoughts, and indulg'd my solitary Fancy. Here I could behold the *Parliament-House, Westminster-Hall,* and the *Abbey,* and admir'd the Magnificence of their Structure, and still more, the Greatness of Mind in those who had been their Founders.

(p. 67)

As usual, Galesia wavers between acceptance and rejection of her muse. She writes two poems within a few days of each other, one a warning against poetry, the other ending with a welcome to the muse. The turmoil of her mind as she considers this question is interrupted by "a hasty Knocking on the Door of the Leads" (p. 73). She opens the door to find a distressed young woman, Belinda. Her story is the familiar one of eighteenth-century narrative: she has been seduced and abandoned and is pregnant. She was fleeing across the rooftops of London to avoid the parish officers when she found Galesia's garret. This incident, Galesia explains, "prov'd a Misfortune to me; for hereupon my Mother prohibited me my Garret-Closet, and my Walk on the Leads; lest I should encounter more Adventures, not only like this, but perhaps more pernicious" (p. 78). Galesia's solitary retreat has become a source of danger. When she is up in her innocent poetic paradise, a seduced woman appears at the door. Poetry and intellectual interests it seems, however innocent Galesia's intentions, will lead her to pernicious adventures.

In *A Patch-Work Screen* Galesia is surrounded by various arguments against her poetic and intellectual vocation. However, her bitter feelings that a learned woman may be "at best but like a Forc'd Plant, that never has its due or proper Relish" (p. 11) are counteracted, not only by her mother's change of heart towards the end, but by the attitude of the lady to whom her story is related. When Galesia tells her about being forbidden her garret-closet, the lady flatteringly compares her to Ovid in banishment (p. 78). When Galesia apologizes for her poems, the lady tells her, "I like them all so well, I will not have *One* lay'd aside" (p. 21). This appreciative listener plays an important part in *A Patch-Work Screen* for she helps Galesia to reconcile her writing career with her feminine identity. When Galesia goes to stay with the lady, she finds her employed on a patch-work "most curiously compos'd of rich Silks, and Silver and Gold Brocades: The whole Furniture was completed excepting a SCREEN, which the Lady and her Maids were going about" (Introduction, sig. a5r-a5v). Galesia is invited to contribute to this typically feminine endeavor, but the unconventional life she has led has left her with no silks or brocades to offer. They open Galesia's trunks and boxes, but "alas! they found nothing but Pieces of *Romances, Poems, Love-Letters,* and the like" (sig. a5v). However, Galesia's new friend smiles at this. She is happy to accept these pieces of writing instead of more feminine patches, and it is from them that the patch-work screen is composed. Galesia's story of her writing career is therefore set in a framework which justifies it by relating it to feminine accomplishments.

The Lining of the Patch-Work Screen is written to a similar plan. One side of the screen has been covered, and now the screen must be lined. Interpolated tales fill up much of the narrative. Galesia in this work is Jane Barker's self-portrait in her old age. Though she has a much less prominent position here than in the previous narratives, she reveals a good deal about Barker's attitude to literature and to women's writing. Galesia looks to the past for her inspiration, treating the present as a time of lamentable moral decay in literature:

> Those honourable Romances of old *Arcadia, Cleopatra, Cassandra,* &c. discover a Genius of Vertue and Honour, which reign'd in the time of those Heroes, and Heroines, as well as in the Authors that report them; but the Stories of our Times are so black, that the Authors, can hardly escape being smutted, or defil'd in touching such Pitch.[24]

The celebration of the woman writer's abilities is similarly confined to the past. Her praise is given, as usual, to Katherine Philips, who died in 1664, not to any woman writer living in the eighteenth century. This is shown in a dream within the narrative. A young man calling himself her "good Genius" leads Galesia up Parnassus where they find "*Orinda* seated on a Throne, as Queen of Female Writers, with a Golden Pen in her Hand for a Scepter, a Crown of Laurel on her Head" (*The Lining,* p. 174). A bard sings Orinda's praises. Like other contemporary eulogists of women's poetry, he sees in it a unity of masculine and feminine qualities:

> As in Angels, we
> 　Do in thy Verses see
> Both improv'd Sexes eminently meet,
> They are than Man more strong, and more than
> 　Woman sweet.

(p. 175)

There is something wistful in the description of Galesia's appearance on this occasion. She arrives "somewhat late; so that the grand Ceremonies were over," and sits inconspicuously "in a Corner, where she might see and hear all that pass'd" (p. 174). This perhaps expresses Barker's feelings late in her life that she has survived into a new and uncongenial age when the great tributes to the poet she admires are over, and that she herself has failed in her ambition to "reach fair *ORINDA*'s Height." However, she does claim the right to celebrate the achievement of her model woman poet and through her the abilities of women as writers.

Jane Barker's allegiance may have been to the past, but her autobiographical narratives point to plots of the future. Barker loved the seventeenth-century romances, old fashioned by the early eighteenth century. *Exilius: or, The Banish'd Roman* (1715) is modelled on them, and it concludes with the marriages of numerous pairs of lovers. In the Galesia narratives, however, Barker's consideration of her own life makes her search for an alternative to this literary convention. Literary sources, as we have seen, helped Barker create Galesia, but the plots of fiction offer Galesia no conclusion satisfactory to Barker. While other writers were just beginning to establish the feminocentric novel of the heroine's journey to identity through marriage, Jane Barker was offering an alternative pattern for the novel far in advance of her time. Her unmarried heroine achieves her identity through study, the practice of medicine, and writing. This important innovation results from Jane Barker's blend of fictional conventions with autobiographical plot, a blend made because of her need as a woman writer to create an identity for herself.

Galesia is the portrait of a woman writer offered by one woman writer to the early eighteenth-century reading public. Her emphasis on the chastity of the female writer is important not only to her personally, but to the history of women writers. In Barker's time leisured women who wrote poetry were considered respectable, while mercenary women writers were often thought of as immoral women combining illicit sexual behavior in their lives with bawdry in their writings. Jane Barker is careful to place herself on the side of the reputable woman writer. Katherine Philips is contrasted with Aphra Behn, and Barker's disapproval of the type of writer Behn represents is made clear. In **A Patch-Work Screen** Galesia reports that a lady she met, "asked me, if I lik'd Mrs. *Phillips,* or Mrs. *Behn* best? To whom I reply'd, with a blunt Indignation, that *they ought not to be nam'd together*" (p. 44). This is a very different attitude from that taken by writers like Mary Pix, Catherine Trotter, and Delariviere Manley in the late seventeenth century. They compared each other to both Astrea and Orinda, seeing both as shining examples of the woman writer's power. Manley called Catherine Trotter the successor to "*Orinda,* and the Fair *Astrea,*" and she herself was described by Mary Pix as "Like Sapho Charming, like Afra Eloquent, / Like chaste *Orinda,* sweetly Innocent."²⁵ For Jane Barker only Sappho and the chaste Orinda can be acceptable models.

Jane Barker was one of the earliest "respectable" women novelists, uniting the mercenary motive of the professional woman writer and the chastity associated with the leisured poetess. In a century when women writers increased significantly in numbers and gained some acceptance from the general public, she contributed to the growing idea that a woman writer—even when she wrote novels—could be chaste, moral, and respectable. This meant that the woman writer's role in the eighteenth century was a narrow one, for her life and her works were usually judged on the basis of the chastity, or lack of it, displayed there. However, this belief in the chaste female writer did help create a climate in which a number of women writers achieved popular success and public respect.

Jane Barker's work, then, is of great importance to everyone interested in the history of women's writing. Her Galesia narratives contain perhaps the first attempt to make a woman's literary talent the central interest of a story. In them we witness Barker's personal struggle to come to terms with her literary ambitions, and we also gain insight into the creation of the woman writer as a publicly acceptable figure.

Notes

1. Sandra Gilbert and Susan Gubar, *The Madwoman in the Attic: The Woman Writer and the Nineteenth Century Literary Imagination* (New Haven: Yale University Press, 1979), p. 17.

2. Margaret Cavendish, *Poems, and Fancies* (London, 1653; Facsimile Reprint, Scholar Press, 1972), Introduction, n. pag.; Dorothy Osborne, *Letters of Dorothy Osborne to Sir William Temple 1652-54,* ed. Kingsley Hart (Folio Society, 1968), p. 53; Aphra Behn, *The Lucky Chance* (London, 1687), Preface, n. pag.

3. In one manuscript, "A Collection of Poems Refering to the times" (British Library Add. Ms 21, 621), Barker, as "Fidelia," discusses public affairs in the years 1685-1700 from a Jacobite point of view. There is also a three-part manuscript volume, the first part comprising these "Fidelia" poems, the second containing some unpublished poems and some which are printed (with alterations) in the later narratives, and the third part being a revised version of the 1688 poems. This volume is in the library of Magdalen College, Oxford (MS 343). I am indebted to Mr. F. W. J. Scovil of Magdalen College for his kind help and to the President and Fellows of the College for permission to quote from this volume.

4. The term comes from Gilbert and Gubar's revision of Harold Bloom: "the 'anxiety of influence' that a male poet experiences is felt by a female poet as an even more primary 'anxiety of authorship'—a radical fear that she cannot create, that because she can never become a 'precursor,' the act of writing will isolate or destroy her" (*The Madwoman in the Attic,* pp. 48-49).

5. Wiltsthorp is mentioned in *Poetical Recreations: Consisting of Original Poems, Songs, Odes, &c. With Several New Translations* (London: Benjamin Crayle, 1688), Part I, p. 19. Her tuition in medicine by her brother is referred to in *Love Intrigues: Or, The History of the Amours of Bosvil and Galesia* (London: E. Curll and C. Crownfield, 1713), pp. 52-53. It is also described in *A Patch-Work Screen for the Ladies* (London: E. Curll and T. Payne, 1723), pp. 10-11, and in *Poetical Recreations,* Part I, pp. 31-32. A poem "On the Death of my Brother" appears in *Poetical Recreations,* Part I, p. 107, and his death is mentioned in *A Patch-Work Screen,* p. 12. Biographical accounts of Jane Barker can be found in Karl Stanglmaier, *Mrs. Jane Barker. Ein Beitrag zur Englischen Literaturgesichte* (Berlin, 1906), and in W. H. McBurney, "Edmund Curll, Mrs. Jane Barker, and the English Novel," *Philological Quarterly,* 37 (1958), 385-99.

6. See "Poems Refering to the Times," p. 1, and *A Patch-Work Screen,* p. 39 and p. 126.

7. "Poems Refering to the Times," *passim.* For her decision to leave England see p. 58; for her decision to become a Catholic see the poetic dialogues on pp. 31-44.

8. For example, in *A Patch-Work Screen,* pp. 22-23, Galesia refers to friends in Cambridge colleges who encouraged her to write; this is corroborated by the appearance of her poems in 1688 together with some poems addressed to her by Cambridge men. Her own reference to Wiltsthorp is corroborated by the title page of *A Patch-Work Screen,* which identifies her as "Mrs. Jane Barker, of Wiltsthorp, near Stamford, in Lincolnshire." The long gap between the 1688 poems and the publication of her narratives fits in with the account she gives of spending years in France.

9. G. S. Gibbons, "Mrs. Jane Barker," *Notes and Queries* ser. XI, No. 12 (1922), 278.

10. Georges Gusdorf, "Conditions and Limits of Autobiography," in *Autobiography: Essays Theoretical and Critical,* ed. James Olney (Princeton: Princeton University Press, 1980), p. 45.

11. Gusdorf, p. 48.

12. The first part of *Poetical Recreations,* which contains Barker's poetry, is prefaced by poems in her praise. Three of these address her as Jane Barker and one as "the Incomparable Galaecia." The second part, containing poems by a number of people, includes more poems to Barker. Two of these refer to her by her pseudonym: "On the most charming Galecia's Picture," Part II, p. 190, and "The Young Lover's Advocate: being an Answer to a Copy of Verses: Written by Galaecia to her Young Lover on his Vow," Part II, p. 192.

13. See *Bosvil and Galesia,* p. 2. The title pages of both first and second editions of the work call it a novel.

14. T. P. Haviland, *The roman de longue haleine on English soil* (Philadelphia, 1931), p. 15.

15. Nancy K. Miller, *The Heroine's Text: Readings in the French and English Novel, 1722-1782* (New York: Columbia University Press, 1980), p. ix.

16. Miller, p. 4.

17. P. M. Spacks, for example, writes that "One might expect *A Patch-Work Screen* to bring its heroine to a more satisfactory conclusion, educating her to achieve happiness in wedlock. . . . Galesia never manages to marry, the book ends *in medias res* with her mother's death and a series of poetic meditations on religious subjects, and the heroine's failure to unite herself to a man has come to seem oddly like a triumph." *Imagining a Self: Autobiography and Novel in Eighteenth-Century England* (Cambridge, Mass.: Harvard University Press, 1976), pp. 66-67.

18. *The Amours of Bosvil and Galesia, As related to Lucasia in St. Germain's Garden. A Novel.* 2nd ed., corrected (London: A. Bettesworth and E. Curll, 1719), p. 39.

19. For example, Termagant in Shadwell's *Squire of Alsatia* (1688) tries to stab and to shoot her ex-lover Belford, and Lady Touchwood in Congreve's *Double Dealer* (1694) tries to attack her ex-lover, Maskwell, with a dagger. For the treatment of these and other deserted mistresses in Restoration comedy, see Candace Brook Katz, "The Deserted Mistress Motif in Mrs. Manley's *Lost Lover,* 1696," *Restoration and Eighteenth-Century Theatre Research,* XVI, No. 1 (May, 1977), 27-39.

20. This poem is found in "part the second" of Magdalen MS 343, p. 37, and is given the title "The contract with the muses writ on the bark of a shady ash-tree" in the list of contents to this volume. There are some differences, mainly in spelling, between the two versions. In the manuscript this poem is placed within a long narrative poem, "the lover's Elesium." In a dream Galesia meets a youth killed in the Battle of Sedgemoor, who reports that the "fools paradice" to which he has been sent, and which Galesia is visiting in her dream, is a place where romantic love has replaced religion. Galesia decides she cannot stay in such a place, and she is taken away from it by an "angry power" who makes her climb a "stupendious mountain." *Bosvil and Galesia* also contains the prophecy of the "angry power" (see p. 33), but placed in the context of the affair with Bosvil, instead of in the political and religious context of "the lover's Elesium."

21. See Gilbert and Gubar, p. 49.

22. The earlier published version of this poem is in *Poetical Recreations,* Part I, pp. 38-40.

23. The earlier published version of this poem is in *Poetical Recreations,* Part I, pp. 12-13.

24. *The Lining of the Patch-Work Screen; Design'd for the Farther Entertainment of the Ladies* (London: A. Bettesworth, 1726), p. 129.

25. Delariviere Manley, "To the Author of Agnes de Castro," in prefatory material to Catherine Trotter, *Agnes de Castro, A Tragedy* (London, 1696); Mary Pix, "To Mrs. Manley, upon her Tragedy called *The Royal Mischief,*" in prefatory material to Delariviere Manley, *The Royal Mischief. A Tragedy* (London, 1696).

Jane Spencer (essay date 1986)

SOURCE: Spencer, Jane. "Jane Barker." In *The Rise of the Woman Novelist: From Aphra Behn to Jane Austen,* pp. 62-70. Oxford: Basil Blackwell, 1986.

[*In the following excerpt, Spencer claims that, throughout her work, Barker is concerned with the creation of her self-portrait as a woman and a writer.*]

Like Delariviere Manley, Jane Barker presented herself as her own heroine, but a very different kind of heroine. Virginity, instead of eroticism, was the keynote of her self-portrait. Autobiographical elements take a central place in Barker's work, none of her writings being free of them, and in fact much of what is known about her life comes from her own account. Born in Wiltsthorp, Lincolnshire, in 1660, she grew up in the country and was taught Latin and medicine by her brother, whose early death had a profound effect on her. Her family was royalist in the Civil War and later supported James II. Jane Barker converted to Catholicism, and in 1689 she followed James II into exile in France. She went blind by 1700, but continued to write. It seems to have been while she was in France that she wrote the account of her early life eventually published as *Love Intrigues: or the Amours of Bosvil and Galesia* in 1713, some years after her return to England. *Bosvil and Galesia,* like the later narratives which appeared in 1723 and 1726, uses material from the poetry she wrote much earlier, some of which was published as *Poetical Recreations* in 1688. Barker's career covers a long period, then, but one concern remained constant throughout: the creation of her self-portrait as woman and as writer.

Barker adopted two personae in different places in her writing, Fidelia and Galesia (sometimes spelt Galecia or Galaecia). Fidelia is the name she gives herself when proclaiming her fidelity—to Jacobitism and to her chosen faith—in a number of poems extant in the manuscript '**A Collection of Poems Refering to the Times**' (*c.*1700).[1] It is in the person of Galesia, though, that she examines her literary vocation. Galesia appears many times in her work—not directly in the 1688 poems, but in the praise of them written by men from Cambridge colleges, whom Jane Barker had apparently got to know through her brother. This suggests that the pseudonym was originally acquired, like Katherine Philips's Orinda, in the course of correspondence with a circle of Platonic friends. In *Exilius: or, the Banished Roman,* an imitation of the French heroic romance begun early in life but not published until 1715, Galesia makes a brief appearance, transformed into a princess for the occasion. In *Bosvil and Galesia* Galesia is both narrator and heroine. In the later narratives, *A Patch-Work Screen for the Ladies* and its sequel *The Lining to the Patch-Work Screen,* Galesia's story continues, interspersed with a number of fictional tales. Because all three narratives use some of the early poems and attribute them to Galesia, it is clear that Galesia in the narratives is intended as a self-portrait of Jane Barker the writer. In contrast to Aphra Behn's insistence on her descent from masculine predecessors, Barker confines her claims to a place in the tradition of Orinda. In fact her poems often seem closely modelled on Cowley's odes, but she does not mention him as her inspiration or mentor. Like most women writers of her time, she sees her work as part of a feminine tradition, and in her case she emphasizes this because of her deep fears that writing is itself an unfeminine pursuit.

In her poems and her prose Galesia always shows herself concerned about her role as a woman. She is an intellectual woman who studies Latin and medicine, she is a prac-

tising healer, and she is a poet: so she is bound to seem unwomanly to many of her contemporaries, and this worries her. On the other hand she, unlike Delariviere Manley, can lay claim to that virtue most required of women, chastity. Barker did not marry, and her Galesia narratives were written at a time when it must have been clear that she never would do. So she emphasizes her identity as virginal spinster, and uses it to defend her literary life, just as Manley laid stress on her own sexual experience in order to portray herself as the writer Rivella.

In her Galesia narratives Barker not only provides herself with a romantic pseudonym, but wraps her life story in the conventions of romance. The first-person narrative of *Bosvil and Galesia* is prefaced by a short framing account, signed 'J. B.', introducing Galesia and the friend, Lucasia, who is supposed to be listening to her story. In *A Patch-Work Screen* and *The Lining,* Galesia is referred to in the third person, though within the narrative of *A Patch-Work Screen* Galesia tells her own story to a lady she meets. In each of these last two works there is an introduction signed by Jane Barker, who claims to have met Galesia. Thus Barker distances herself from her persona, freeing 'Galesia' to be like a heroine of romance. By transforming the autobiographical story she has to tell into the life of a romance-like heroine, she is able to claim that Galesia's story is significant and to justify Galesia's actions according to romance convention. Turning her own life story into what she calls a 'diverting Novel',[2] she is offering her public the kind of work it wants; and she is also protecting herself and liberating her imagination.

The first of the narratives, *Bosvil and Galesia,* is the story of a failed courtship, told by Galesia to Lucasia years after the event. As a young girl, Galesia loves her cousin Bosvil and believes he loves her, but her maidenly decorum and his erratic behaviour—veering from enthusiastic devotion to cold indifference—prevent them from reaching an understanding, and eventually he marries another woman. Galesia's narrative is a subtle variation on an important theme in eighteenth-century narration—seduction, which, whether the heroine suffers or avoids it, is nearly always central to her story.[3] In fact Bosvil neither seduces nor attempts to seduce Galesia, but the idea of seduction haunts her and provides her with a way of interpreting his enigmatic behaviour. Is his clandestine and interrupted courtship a sign that he is unsure of his own feelings, or of hers; or does it indicate a plan to seduce her? As she recreates and analyses her youthful experiences in narrative, Galesia is unable to decide.

Galesia accuses herself of a heroine's pride: flattered during her youth, she thinks herself a 'goddess' to her lover, like a heroine of romance. She keeps Bosvil at a distance, and her haughty behaviour, which makes him think she cannot love him, is one explanation offered for the failure of their relationship. On the other hand, her narrative shows that behind a heroine's pride lies vulnerability. She has to conceal her feelings because if a woman should 'betray [her] Weakness by a too ready Compliance' with even an honourable proposal, her purity might be questioned (***Bosvil and Galesia,*** pp. 21-2). A young girl's reserve towards her suitor is made necessary by the society she lives in: 'as the World now rolls, we are under a Kind of Constraint to follow its Byass' (p. 10). The way the world rolls is implicitly criticized in the narrative. The young Galesia acted like a proper heroine in being proud and punctilious; yet this helped to deprive her of the virtuous heroine's proper destiny, marriage.

Galesia's story, ending in neither of the usual alternatives—'ruin' or marriage—open to the eighteenth-century heroine, seems an oddity to those who do not take the autobiographical nature of the narrative into account.[4] Barker has superimposed the literary convention of the heroine's social and sexual initiation onto the story of her own single life, attributing to herself as 'Galesia' the characteristics of heroines whose destiny she does not share, in order to make the single life a new kind of heroine's destiny.

On the surface, Galesia's narrative is an explanation of her failure to marry; but underlying this is a tale of success, when the thwarted heroine of romance becomes a poet.

During the first of Bosvil's recurrent periods of coldness towards her, Galesia composes verses dedicating herself to poetry:

> Methinks these Shades, strange Thoughts suggest,
> Which heat my Head, and cool my Breast;
> And mind me of a Laurel Crest.
>
> Methinks I hear the Muses sing,
> And see 'em all dance in a Ring;
> And call upon me to take Wing.
>
> We will (say they) assist thy Flight,
> Till thou reach fair *ORINDA*'s Height,
> If thou can'st this World's Follies slight.
>
> We'll bring thee to our bright Abodes,
> Among the Heroes and the Gods,
> If thou and Wealth can be at Odds.
>
> Then gentle Maid cast off thy Chain,
> Which links thee to thy faithless Swain,
> And vow a Virgin to remain.
>
> Write, write thy Vow upon this Tree,
> By us it shall recorded be;
> And thou enjoy Eternity.
>
> (p. 14)[5]

The choice she is offered is clear: the hope of married life or the promise of literary achievement. By inscribing the verses on the tree as the muses suggest, Galesia has taken their offer: henceforth she (like so many women writers of her time) will try to emulate Orinda.

Here, then, is an alternative explanation for the heroinely pride that kept the lovers apart. Galesia actually preferred to remain unmarried and dedicate herself to poetry. Her other ambition, to be a healer, is mentioned immediately afterwards and linked to the literary aspirations in her description of herself as 'Apollo's Darling Daughter', Apollo being god of poetry and of medicine (p. 15). The sarcastic tone here expresses Galesia's typical uncertainty about the value of the choice she has made. On the one hand, she describes her intellectual life as merely a substitute for Bosvil's love: 'I, finding my self abandoned by *Bosvil,* and thinking it impossible ever to love again, resolved to espouse a Book, and spend my Days in Study' (p. 15). On the other hand, her readiness to make vows to the muses contrasts with her care never to promise anything to her lover, and even when her thoughts are in 'a Sea of Joy' at the thought of marrying Bosvil soon, her choice of poetry haunts her. In a dream she is made to climb a high mountain, evidently the poet's mountain, Parnassus, and she is warned by a mysterious 'angry Power' that:

> Since, since thou hast the Muses chose,
> *Hymen* and Fortune are thy Foes.
>
> (p. 33)

The opposition between poetry and love is intensified in the second edition of ***Bosvil and Galesia,*** in which, when Galesia climbs the mountain, Bosvil attempts to 'tumble [her] down', but is prevented by the angry power.[6] The sexual implication in this encounter befits Galesia's identification of poetry with chastity, and it suggests that the young Galesia's apparently unwarranted fears that Bosvil will try to seduce her arise from her unacknowledged dread that, if he marries her, he will seduce her away from her literary vocation.

Barker's later narratives continue to develop the picture of Galesia established here. The speaker of most of ***A Patch-Work Screen for the Ladies*** is Galesia after her return from France. She tells the story of her life after Bosvil's desertion, which contains further struggles between poetry and marriage. Once Bosvil has gone, Galesia devotes herself to the study of Orinda:

> I began to emulate her Wit, and aspired to imitate her
> Writings; in doing of which, I think, I deserved
> *Arachne*'s
> Fate, or at least to be transform'd into one of the lowest
> of *Mack-Fleckno*'s Followers: Her noble Genius being
> inimitable . . . each line [of her poetry] was like a
> Ladder
> to climb, not only to *Parnassus,* but to Heaven: which
> I
> (poor Puzzle as I was!) had the Boldness to try to imitate,
> 'till I was dropped into a Labyrinth of Poetry, which
> has ever
> since interlac'd all the Actions of my Life.[7]

Galesia's praise of Orinda is mixed with typical self-mockery, but there is a sense of pride in having embraced the fate of a poet, whatever the effects on the rest of her life.

In *A Patch-Work Screen* Galesia's commitment to poetry and the single life is opposed by her mother, who tells her that marriage is 'the Business for which [she] came into the world' (p. 80). Fortunately, however, Galesia's numerous suitors justify her rejection of them by their evident unworthiness, and they soon disappear from the scene. One is hanged for robbery and another, who has led a profligate life, shoots himself. Galesia's rejection of sexual involvement receives further support from the reported experiences of the women she meets, including one who is suffering from a venereal disease after being seduced, and another who, marrying according to her father's wishes, was reduced to poverty and misery. Dutiful marriage and illicit sexuality seem equally to carry danger, and Galesia understandably celebrates 'A Virgin Life' in one of her poems, which explicitly links virginity with poetic achievement:

> Since, O good Heavens! you have bestow'd on me
> So great a Kindness for *Virginity,*
> Suffer me not to fall into the Powers
> Of Man's almost Omnipotent Amours.
> But let me in this happy State remain,
> And in chaste Verse my chaster Thoughts explain.
>
> (p. 90)

Galesia's verse opposes the common belief that to be a woman writer suggests sexual looseness. Not that Galesia receives any such accusation herself: it is her dedication to virginity that worries her mother. Nevertheless the continual insistence on the chastity of poetry in Barker's work suggests that the sexual reputation of some women writers disturbs her. One incident in *A Patch-Work Screen* seems to be an expression of her fears that poetry will unleash the dangers of sexuality. While she and her mother are lodging in London, Galesia escapes from the noisy world into 'a Closet in my Landlady's Back-Garret which I crept into, as if it had been a Cave on the Top of *Parnassus*' (p. 64). The closet is both a retreat from the world and a vantage-point from which she can survey it, giving free play to her intellect:

> Out of this Garret, there was a Door went out to the Leads; on which I us'd frequently to walk to take the Air . . . Here I entertain'd my Thoughts, and indulg'd my solitary Fancy. Here I could behold the *Parliament-House, Westminster-Hall,* and the *Abbey,* and admir'd the Magnificence of their Structure, and still more, the Greatness of Mind in those who had been their Founders.
>
> (p. 67)

On one occasion, though, Galesia's thoughts are interrupted by 'a hasty Knocking on the Door of the Leads' (p. 73). She opens the door to find a distressed young woman, Belinda, whose story is a familiar one in eighteenth-century narrative: she has been seduced and abandoned, and is pregnant. She was fleeing across the roof-tops of London to avoid the parish officers when she found Galesia's garret. After this Galesia's mother forbids her to use her garret closet, in case, Galesia explains, she should

'encounter more Adventures, not only like this, but perhaps more pernicious' (p. 78). Galesia cannot find an innocent poetic retreat without having her peace shattered by the appearance of a seduced woman, and it seems that her intellectual interests, however pure in themselves, carry with them the danger of contact with impurity.

In *A Patch-Work Screen* Galesia is surrounded by various arguments against her vocation, but her bitter feeling that a learned woman may be 'at best but like a Forc'd Plant, that never has its due or proper Relish' (p. 11) are counteracted by the attitude of the lady to whom she relates the story. This appreciative listener praises Galesia's verses, and allays her fears that her writing is an unfeminine activity. She is working on a patch-work 'most curiously compos'd of rich Silks, and Silver and Gold Brocades: The whole Furniture was completed excepting a SCREEN' (Introduction, sig. a5r-a5v). Galesia is invited to contribute to this typically feminine endeavour, but her unconventional life has left her with no silks or brocades to offer. They open her trunks and boxes, but 'alas! they found nothing but Pieces of *Romances, Poems, Love-Letters,* and the like' (sig. a5v). However, the lady is happy to accept these pieces of writing as Galesia's version of silk patches, and it is from them that the screen is composed. Galesia's story of her writing career is thus set in a framework which justifies it by relating it to feminine accomplishments.

The Lining of the Patch-Work Screen is written to a similar plan. One side of the screen has been covered, and now the screen must be lined. Interpolated tales fill up much of the narrative. Galesia in this work is Jane Barker's self-portrait in her old age. She looks to the past for her inspiration, finding a lamentable moral decay in the literature of the present.

> Those honourable Romances of old *Arcadia, Cleopatra, Cassandra,* &c. discover a Genius of Vertue and Honour, which reign'd in the time of those Heroes, and Heroines, as well as in the Authors that report them; but the Stories of our Times are so black, that the Authors, can hardly escape being smutted, or defil'd in touching such Pitch.[8]

Praise is given, as usual, to Katherine Philips, long dead by this time, and not to any woman writing in the eighteenth century. In a dream within the narrative, a young man calling himself her 'good Genius' leads Galesia up Parnassus, where they find '*Orinda* seated on a Throne, as Queen of Female Writers, with a Golden Pen in her Hand for a Scepter, a Crown of Laurel on her Head' (***The Lining,*** p. 174). Part of Cowley's poem 'Upon Mrs. K. Philips her Poems' is recited by 'a Bard' (p. 175). There is something wistful in the description of Galesia's appearance on this occasion. She arrives 'somewhat late; so that the grand Ceremonies were over', and sits inconspicuously 'in a Corner, where she might see and hear all that pass'd' (p. 174). This perhaps expresses Barker's feelings, late in her life, that she has survived into a new and uncongenial age, when the tributes to the poet she admires are over; and that she herself has failed in her ambition to 'reach fair *ORINDA'*s Height'.

Jane Barker's allegiance may have been to the past, but her autobiographical narratives point to plots of the future. In her romance, *Exilius,* she concludes conventionally with the marriages of numerous pairs of lovers, but in the Galesia narratives her focus on her own life leads her to modify literary conventions. Various literary heroines contributed to the creation of Galesia, but the plots of fiction offered her no conclusion satisfactory to her author. While other writers were just beginning to experiment with the novel as the story of the heroine's journey to identity through marriage, Jane Barker was already offering an alternative pattern for the novel, with the creation of an unmarried heroine who achieves her identity through study, the practice of medicine, and writing.

Jane Barker, like Delariviere Manley, defined her authorial position by suggesting connections between her own character and situation and the kind of writing she produced. While Manley argued from her sexual life to her sexy writing, Jane Barker linked her virgin life to her pure and moral work. Manley's self-portrait encouraged others to adopt her image, whereas Barker, never so well-known a writer, was less influential in herself.[9] Yet she is the one who represents the winning side in the eighteenth-century debate about the woman writer. Choosing the famously pure Katherine Philips for her model, she rejected the other precursor with whom Philips had previously been associated—Aphra Behn. In *A Patch-Work Screen,* Galesia reports that a lady she met, 'asked me, if I lik'd Mrs. *Philips,* or Mrs. *Behn* best? To whom I reply'd, with a blunt Indignation, that *they ought not to be nam'd together*' (p. 44). This is a very different attitude from that taken by Manley, Pix and Trotter in the 1690s. Whereas they saw both Philips and Behn as shining examples of the woman writer's power, Barker could only acknowledge Sappho and the chaste Orinda as her models, even though Behn's novels probably provided some material for her narratives.[10]

Jane Barker was never a best-selling novelist, but her Galesia narratives and *Exilius* did provide something for her support when she was spending her later years in England on a small income.[11] She was one of the earliest women novelists to unite the mercenary motive of the professional writer with a prominent display of the 'chaste Verse . . . chaster Thoughts' associated with the leisured poetess; so she has a significant place in the history of women's writing. Her work, unlike Behn's and Manley's, would always remain respectable even to the later eighteenth-century reader. Her Galesia narratives give a fascinating picture of a woman wanting to be accepted as a writer, explaining what is unconventional about her life, anxiously insisting on her own purity. In her self-portrait we begin to see hints of something that will be much in evidence in the writing of other eighteenth-century women: the cost of becoming acceptable.

Notes

1. The MS 'A Collection of Poems Refering to the Times' is in the British Library (Add. MS 21,621). Another MS copy of these poems comprises the first part of a three-part MS volume of Jane Barker's poems in the library of Magdalen College, Oxford (MS 343). The second part of this contains some unpublished poems, and some which are printed (with alterations) in her later narratives. The third part is a revised version of the poems published as *Poetical Recreations: Consisting of Original Poems, Songs, Odes, &c. With Several New Translations* (London: Benjamin Crayle, 1688).

2. See *Love Intrigues: Or, The History of the Amours of Bosvil and Galesia* (London: E. Curll and C. Crownfield, 1713), p. 2. The title page of both first and second editions of this work call it a novel.

3. Miller, *The Heroine's Text, Readings in the French and English Novel 1722-1782* (New York: Columbia University Press, 1980), p. 4.

4. Patricia M. Spacks writes that 'One might expect *A Patch-Work Screen* to bring its heroine to a more satisfactory conclusion [than the one in the earlier narrative], educating her to achieve happiness in wedlock . . . Galesia never manages to marry, the book ends *in medias res* . . . the heroine's failure to unite herself to a man has come to seem oddly like a triumph.' *Imagining a Self: Autobiography and Novel in Eighteenth-Century England* (Cambridge, Mass.: Harvard University Press, 1976), pp. 66-7.

5. This poem is found in 'part the second' of Magdalen MS 343, and is given the title 'The contract with the muses writ on the bark of a shady ash-tree', in the list of contents to the volume.

6. *The Amours of Bosvil and Galesia, As related to Lucasia in St. Germain's Garden. A Novel,* 2nd edn, corrected (London: A. Bettesworth and E. Curll, 1719), p. 29.

7. *A Patch-Work Screen for the Ladies* (London: E. Curll and T. Payne, 1723), p. 3.

8. *The Lining of the Patch-Work Screen: Design'd for the Father Entertainment of the Ladies* (London: A. Bettesworth, 1726), p. 129.

9. Some success for Barker's narratives may be inferred from the appearance of second editions of *Bosvil and Galesia* and *Exilius* together as *The Entertaining Novels of Mrs. Jane Barker* in 1719, and the further edition of *Entertaining Novels* in 1736. Barker's name, however, rarely if ever appears in eighteenth-century discussions of the novel, while Manley's and Haywood's appear very frequently.

10. One of the interpolated stories in *The Lining of the Patch-Work Screen* appears to be modelled on Behn's *The History of the Nun: or, the Fair Vow-Breaker* (1689). See W. H. McBurney, 'Edmund Curll, Mrs. Jane Barker, and the English Novel', *PQ* 37 (1958), pp. 385-99.

11. Jane Barker is mentioned in a 1715 list of Roman Catholic nonjurors as holding an estate of £47-10s. annual value: see G. S. Gibbons, 'Mrs. Jane Barker',

Notes and Queries ser. XI, no. 12 (1922), p. 278. Presumably she also benefited from the patronage of the Countess of Exeter, to whom she dedicated *Exilius.*

Marilyn L. Williamson (essay date 1990)

SOURCE: Williamson, Marilyn L. "Orinda's Daughters and Providence: Barker, Penelope Aubin (ca. 1685-1731), Rowe." In *Raising Their Voices: British Women Writers, 1650-1750,* pp. 244-53. Detroit: Wayne State University Press, 1990.

[*In the following excerpt, Williamson discusses Barker's novels and their themes of heroic love, parental authority about marriage, and the woman rescuer.*]

Jane Barker . . . contributed four major pieces to this fiction [of the waning of parental authority]: *Love Intrigues* (1713), *Exilius* (1715), *A Patch-Work Screen for the Ladies* (1723), and *Lining for the Patch-Work Screen* (1726). *Love Intrigues* is the closest of her works—or any of the fiction by this group—to the Behn tradition. It is clearly written to represent a young woman's predicament as she is courted by a man who toys with her emotions, attempts to get her to agree to a hasty marriage, swears everlasting devotion and urgent desire, but then leaves her for long periods and finally never asks her parents for her hand in marriage. The writer of a poem of praise for the novel suggests its monitory function; the novel describes,

> The Charms of Nature, and those painted true.
> By what strange Springs our real Passions move,
> How vain are all Disguises when we Love;
> What Wiles and Stratagems the Men secure,
> And what the tortur'd Female Hearts endure;
> Compell'd to stifle what they feign would tell,
> While Truth commands, but Honour must rebel.[1]

Galesia is indeed constrained by her sense of propriety in not revealing her passion for Bosvil, either to him or to her mother, but the reader has a sense that the revelation would have made little difference to the inconstant Bosvil. When he presses Galesia for a "speedy Marriage," she rebukes him for treating her like a mistress, and he responds passionately but with patent hypocrisy:

> Sure, dear Cousin, said I, (with a Tone wholly confus'd) you forget in whose Company you are, and believe your self with fair Mrs. *Lowland:* if such an amorous Slumber has cast you into this *Delerium,* pray awake, and behold before you, your Cousin *Galesia* with whom I converse at present: her reserv'd Behaviour, with which she treats me her faithful Lover, is a sufficient Demonstration, that it is the prudent, vertuous, chast *Galesia!* It is this reserved Mein, Madam, which has often deter'd me, and commanded my Tongue to a respectful Silence; whilst my poor Heart, over-charg'd with Passion, only eas'd with Sighs, and my Looks were the only Language whereby to express my interiour Thoughts.
>
> (p. 28)

Here Barker anticipates Haywood in demonstrating the ways men blame their perfidy on women. Although Galesia is the stereotypically innocent young woman, she is responsible for her involvement with Bosvil and her survival after the relationship: both occur because of Orinda. As Margaret Doody has said, modeling on Orinda went on throughout Jane Barker's fiction: *Love Intrigues* is "related to Lucasia," for example (Sig. B).[2] As the story opens, the reader is aware that Galesia has been made very vulnerable to fantasies of love by her reading, which also has made her equally eager to imitate Orinda in writing poetry and to write her commitment to single life upon a tree, the old pastoral lover's gesture:

> Then gentle Maid cast off thy Chain,
> Which links thee to thy faithless Swain,
> And vow a Virgin to remain.
>
> Write, write thy Vow upon this Tree,
> By us it shall recorded be;
> And thou enjoy Eternity.
>
> (p. 14)

When she is actually abandoned by Bosvil, Galesia

> resolved to espouse a Book, and spend my Days in Study: This Fancy having once taken Root, grew apace, and branch'd it self forth in a thousand vain conceits. I imagined my self the *Orinda,* or *Sapho* of my Time, and amongst my little Reading, the Character of the Faithful Shepperdess in the Play pleas'd me extreamly; I resolved to imitate her, not only in perpetual Chastity, but in learning the Use of Simples for the Good of my Country Neighbors. Thus I thought to become *Apollo's* Darling Daughter, and Maid of Honour to the Muses. In order to do this I got my Brother (who was not yet return'd to *Oxford*) to set me in the way to learn my Grammar, which he willingly did, thinking it only a Vapour of Fancy.
>
> (p. 15)

Literature has a double meaning for Galesia: it feeds her fantasies of love and models her behavior in life, but it also changes the meaning of Bosvil's desertion. Writing gives Galesia a means of surviving her abandonment: like the Portuguese nun, Galesia has a voice, in part, because her relationship to Bosvil does not culminate in marriage. The relationship has ended, but the emotions remain to be explored and analyzed.

Throughout the process of the novel, which is, of course, narrated by Galesia, both she and Bosvil appear to be imitating romances, largely because of Galesia's innocence of the world. Thus the text is a mirror of the social transaction of amatory fiction: a female reader, largely without access to the world, learns about it and models her behavior through reading. We feel for Galesia as she tries to cope with Bosvil's actions, in this case, informing a friend that he will not introduce him to Galesia because "he design'd his Cousin *Galesia* for himself":

> This Transaction, tho' coming to me by a third hand, gave me a strong Belief of *Bosvil's* Sincerity; and made me interpret every little dubious Word, which he some-

times mix'd with his fond Actions, to be Demonstrations of a real Passion; not doubting but a little time wou'd ripen the same into an open Declaration to my Parents, as well as formerly to me, and now lately to young *Brafort*. In the mean time attributing this Delay to his Prudence, in acquainting himself with my Humour, and Inclinations, before he gave himself irrevocably to me; which made me regulate my Behaviour with discreetest Precautions my poor inexperienced Thoughts cou'd dictate. My Grammar Rules now became harsh Impertinences, for I thought I had learnt *Amo* and *Amor,* by a shorter and surer Method; and the only Syntax I studied, was how to make suitable Answers to my Father, and him, when the long'd-for Question shou'd be propos'd; that I might not betray my Weakness.

(p. 21)

Here Barker clearly presents the central function of amatory fiction: to teach its readers the complex codes of the grammar of love, to provide in Foucault's terms, a discourse of sexuality in which any subject may find a syntax. Although the narrative frequently implies that Galesia's prudence with Bosvil is a cause of his cooling toward her, the reader can only conclude that her reserve has saved Galesia from being ruined and that she is blaming herself as a victim. The novel is a fascinating and complex representation of a woman's predicament, in which she escapes the fate of a Haywood heroine because of the particular literary models she has chosen. Barker is simply more explicit than her contemporaries in showing how her characters model their behavior on what they read.

Exilius or, the Banish'd Roman (1715) was Jane Barker's reply to tales of gallantry. As her subtitle informs the reader, Barker wrote "for the Instruction of Some Young *Ladies* of Quality," to stem the tide of libertinism with a concept of heroic love that would fulfill itself in marriage:

> Thus it has far'd with this kind of Heroick Love of late; it has been as it were rallied out of Practice, and its Professors laughed out of Countenance, whilst Interest and loose Gallantry have been set up in its Place, and monopolized all its Business and Effects. How far this has been an Inlet to that Deluge of Libertinism which has overflow'd the Age, the many unhappy Marriages and unkind Separations may inform us, and at the same time show how proper an Ingredient Love is, towards the making of a happy Marriage: for where Love is not the Cement, as well as Interest the Foundation, the Superstructure of Conjugal Faith, seldom stands long, the first Wind that blows . . . will go near to shake, if not quite overthrow the Fabrick.[3]

Romances, Barker tells her reader, are therefore justified in demonstrating how heroic love is to be achieved. To represent the value of heroic love, four sets of Roman mates—Cordiala and Scipio, Clelia and Marcellus, Clarinthia and Asiaticus, and Scipiana and Exilius—have complicated and farflung adventures that culminate in their unions. *Exilius* is written "after the Manner of Telemachus," which implies that it celebrates the manly

virtues Odysseus's son defended in his scenes with Penelope. Thus, drawing on the epic sources of romance, Barker makes marriage of the four couples into their destinies, like the founding of Rome or the conquest of Jerusalem. For example, Clelia has the approval of Jupiter's oracle for her love of Marcellus. In these stories men and women are allies as they struggle against obstacles to their destined mates. Their commitment to one another does not begin with marriage, for it has already been amply demonstrated. Interest and marriage bonds are no longer the enemies of love but, with it, support the ideal relationship.

Another important theme in *Exilius* is obedience to parental authority and its relation to heroic love. *Exilius* overtly and repeatedly condemns filial disobedience. Daughters who defy their fathers end up married to monsters or fish: "In this I could not but again admire the exact justice of Heaven, in thus punishing her Lewdness and Disobedience to her Parents. She that refus'd the honest Esposals provided by her Father, became Wife to a monster; she that disgrac'd herself and her Friends by unlawful Lust, was a Prostitute to a Fish" (2:72). Still, as Doody points out, the woman's predicament as a fish's spouse is not as bleak as one might expect: "There are delicate ambiguities to the moral fable; although the author seems officially to present the undersea world as the domain of the inhumane and lustful, the world under water has its attractions and advantages. The comic, the grotesque, and the beautiful combine in a manner that complicates interpretation and resists simple moral exemplification."[4] And, paradoxically, *Exilius* leaves the reader skeptical of parental authority in relation to genuine heroic love of the sort experienced by the four central couples. If parents become tyrannical in opposing a destined heroic love, as they invariably do, then children are justified by the romance in opposing them. Parents do not come off very well in this novel: at least they are blind to the destined loves of their children, and at worst they oppose them because of incestuous longings. The children's relationships are only unsuitable, but never adulterous or lustful; and so the effect on the reader is to inspire skepticism about parental authority in filial marriage choices, which should be left to providential design, sensed and understood only by the children. Just as Barker's fantasies support and interrogate social structures, so the narrative is more subtle than first appears about both supporting and subverting parental authority.

A Patch-Work Screen for the Ladies (1723) continues Galesia's story from ***Love Intrigues***. Barker proves herself a true daughter of Orinda by using undoing generously in the address to the reader. She has chosen a patchwork screen as a metaphor for her narratives, she says, "the better to recommend it to my Female Readers, as well in their Discourse, as in their Needle-Work," for "whenever one sees a Set of Ladies together, their Sentiments are as differently mix'd as the Patches in their Work."[5] Then she exclaims, characteristically, "Forgive me, kind Reader, for carrying the Metaphor too high; by which means I am out of my Sphere, and so can say nothing of the *Male Patch-*

Workers" (p. vi). Barker's fiction is that Galesia has become a virgin recluse who passes her time in retreat, reading, writing poetry, telling stories, and rescuing women in distress. Barker records the stories in a work that gives the appearance of fragmentation, "but in a *Patch-Work* there is no Harm done" (p. viii).

The patches present Galesia's story as well as those she tells the narrator. Both Galesia and the narrator are personae for Barker. We learn that Galesia has been engaged to a young man whom she did not greatly fancy but who was much favored by her parents. At the last minute, he was arrested for robbery, and so she escaped that union. Galesia and her mother move to the city, and a friend tries to persuade Galesia to marry an old man; but she is now too wise for that (p. 54). Her mother also urges Galesia to marry, but her "Reflections on Bosvil's Baseness, gave me a secret Disgust against Matrimony" (p. 79). Later, when another suitor has committed suicide after a violent argument with his mistress, Galesia wonders if fate is persecuting her; but at this time, as at all other moments of despair, she is comforted by thoughts of Katherine Philips and her poem, **"A Virgin Life."** Galesia concludes that fate has designed her for a single life (p. 89).

Orinda, then, is the inspiration for Galesia, as she writes poetry in her garret, eschewing ambition or wealth for the sake of virtue:

> The Pleasure of [retreat] was greatly improv'd by reading Mrs. *Phillips*. I began to emulate her Wit, and aspir'd to imitate her Writings; in doing of which, I think, I deserv'd *Arachne's* Fate, or at least to be transform'd into one of the lowest of Mack-Fleckno's Followers: Her noble Genius being inimitable; especially in Praise of a Country-Life, and Contempt of human Greatness . . . Her Poetry I found so interwoven with Vertue and Honour, that each Line was like a Ladder to climb, not only to Parnassus, but to Heaven.
>
> (p. 3)

Galesia becomes a learned woman (she is interested in Harvey's theories of circulation of the blood, for example). Although her brother, like Barker's, humors Galesia's interests, the rest of the world finds her unfit company, "for the Unlearned fear'd and the Learned scorn'd my Conversation; at least, I fancy'd so: a Learned Woman, being at best but like a Forc'd Plant, that never has its due or proper Relish, but is wither'd by the first Blast that Envy or Tribulation blows over her Endeavours" (p. 11). Barker portrayed Galesia and her mother as further internalizing this view of learned women, who are not made attractive by learning, "but live in a Stoical Dulness or humersome Stupidity" (p. 79). Again there is tension between the values Barker herself held and those she represented in her fiction. In the early eighteenth century, to be sure, a learned woman was often regarded as an oddity, but Orinda was certainly not rejected by society because of her achievements.

A Patch-Work exhibits parents in very much the way they appeared in *Exilius*: lacking in understanding of their children's welfare. Galesia's parents favored her marriage to the robber, for example, and her mother favored her marriage to the suicide. In a telling example of Galesia's stories, a father forces his daughter to marry a man other than the lawyer she desires. The husband goes bankrupt, whereas the lawyer grows to fame. Wherever parents set their judgment ahead of the inclination of their children, the outcome in both the short and long run is bad for the children.

Another important pattern in Barker's fiction is the woman rescuer. One of Galesia's stories tells of a goldsmith who seduces an innocent girl and then denies her. Galesia gets her into a hospital and thence to a plantation (p. 54). Belinda is a similar example. A married man preaches to her of platonic love, but she soon finds herself pregnant; and when he deserts her, Galesia and her landlady come to her rescue. The culmination of this theme is the story of **"The Unaccountable Wife,"** which paradoxically conforms to and violates all contemporary codes for female behavior. It begins with a wife's toleration of her husband's open affair with their servant. When the husband tries to get rid of the servant, however, the wife does the servant's work, much to the disapproval of their friends. Both wife and servant finally leave for the servant's hovel in the country. There the neighbors try to get rid of them "to prevent a Parish charge" (p. 103). A lady of quality sees them being driven from town and shelters them in her house. They return to the husband because he is ill, and he soon dies. The queen eventually offers the wife a pension, but she refuses it and ends her life a beggar. The narrator attributes the "unaccountable" actions to infatuation, yet to a reader familiar with women's discourses, the story is full of resonances about women's predicament, and one of its points is the lack of social understanding of contradictions in codes of behavior. For example, the women live out the opening line of Mary Chudleigh's famous poem "Wife and Servant are the same." One also recalls the many pleas in advice books for wives to tolerate their husbands' extramarital affairs, rather than disturb their marriages. The problem with social acceptance of these terms is that the women, as in a comedy, have followed them to their logical extreme and thereby expose the social system. The husband wanted to cast off only the awkward member of the triangle, not both women. The social system (i.e., the Poor Law) will not tolerate two unattached, unemployed women in the servant's former village. The wife's refusal of the pension is a rejection of her social station and illuminates the condition of all less fortunate women. Unaccountable in contemporary terms is the fact that the wife calls the servant the only friend she has. Women wooed by the same man and bonding across class lines are simply not to be understood. The story is a powerful indictment of the status of women in Barker's society, but it is presented without rancor: rather, its effect is to interrogate the social structure through irony, not anger.

The Lining of the Patch-Work Screen: Designed for the Farther Entertainment of the Ladies (1726) extends the reader's sense that women help women. Barker creates this impression partly by having a group of women who listen to Galesia and contribute stories to the text, but her most effective device is to use several stories of the Behn tradition for new purposes. The Portuguese nun reappears, as does Behn's fair vow-breaker, but she now accidentally sews her first husband's shroud to the second husband's coat. The old stories from the libertine tradition refined and set in a moral framework impress the reader with the scope of the female community and its strong internal bonds. . . .

Notes

1. S. G., "To the Author," *Love Intrigues: Or, The History of the Amours of Bosvil and Galesia* (London: E. Curll and C. Crownfield, 1713; facsimile, ed. Josephine Grieder [New York: Garland, 1973]), Sig. A^v.

2. Margaret A. Doody, "Jane Barker," *British Novelists, 1660-1800,* ed. Martin C. Battestin (Detroit, Mich.: Gale, 1985), pp. 27-28. For analysis of the dreams in *Love Intrigues,* see also Doody's "Deserts, Ruins and Troubled Waters: Female Dreams in Fiction and the Development of the Gothic Novel," *Genre* 10 (Winter 1977): 529-72.

3. Jane Barker, *Exilius or, the Banished Roman* (London: E. Curll, 1715; facsimile, ed. Josephine Grieder [New York: Garland, 1973]), Sig. A2-A2^v.

4. Doody, "Barker," p. 26.

5. Jane Barker, *A Patch-Work Screen for the Ladies; or, Love and Virtue Recommended: In a Collection of Instructive Novels* (London: E. Curll, 1723; facsimile, ed. Josephine Grieder [New York: Garland, 1973]), pp. iv-v.

Kathryn R. King and Jeslyn Medoff (essay date 1997)

SOURCE: King, Kathryn R. and Medoff, Jeslyn. "Jane Barker and Her Life (1652-1732): The Documentary Record." *Eighteenth-Century Life* 21, no. 3 (November 1997): 16-38.

[*In the following essay, King and Medoff offer an account of the life of Barker that contrasts with the biography that has been erroneously reconstructed from her fictional works.*]

Jane Barker's time has come. That this poet, novelist, lay physician, Catholic convert, exile, and Jacobite is an immensely intriguing figure has been an open secret among specialists for the past fifteen years. Now that much of her best work is finally available in modern editions, Barker's stock as a writer in the larger scholarly community is almost certain to rise. The 1996-97 academic year alone saw the publication of a paperback edition of three of her novels and a selection of her verse; the inclusion of her work in two important anthologies, one of which claimed for her first novel "nearly canonical" status; and an extended

discussion of her poems in a critical study.[1] Since this recent spate of scholarship will surely generate further interest in an author whose life and personal circumstances have been, until quite recently, deeply shadowed, we offer here for the first time an extended, archivally based account of the life of Jane Barker.

To date, accounts of the life have relied heavily on Barker's own writings, especially the three seemingly autobiographical Galesia fictions (1713-26).[2] Their relationship to the actualities of the life has been more often invoked than investigated, however. A 1983 article that has been the starting point for much subsequent work on Barker asserts, for example, that readers are "safe in assuming her works to be autobiographical"—when, as Jane Spencer was the first to admit, almost nothing was then known about Barker.[3] Critics since have been content to operate in a near vacuum so far as real biographical information goes. Less excusably, so have biographers, who regularly resort to the fictions for at least some portion of their biographical "fact." Such incautiousness is not hard to understand. The novels certainly *seem* to be "about" their author: not only is Galesia's interior life rendered with a psychological complexity well in advance of anything then available in novelistic discourse, but as a heroine she behaves in ways unheard of in narratives of the time.[4] Add to this the fact that details from the fictions could be seen to match what little was known about the life and it becomes only too easy to see why some biographers would permit themselves to quarry the novels as if they constituted alternate versions of the documentary record. Our research suggests, however, that this uncritical reliance on Barker's self-representations has distorted our understanding of the life and has blinded us to some of the more interesting features of the novels, as well.

The present account makes available biographical information that has come to light in the decade or so since Spencer wrote. Much of it was excavated by Jeslyn Medoff in connection with research on seventeenth-century women poets for the anthology *Kissing the Rod* (1989).[5] She has since been joined in the archives by others, among them Carol Barash, Carol Shiner Wilson, and Kathryn King,[6] whose endeavors make it at last possible to tell the story of the life independent of Barker's own accounts.[7] Barker was not a public figure and was only indirectly involved in affairs of state; she belonged to the minor gentry; she never married; and from 1685 or thereabouts she belonged to an outlawed church. Much of her life, in other words, was played out on the edges of the official system of record-keeping. Nonetheless, a good deal of documentation is now available for analysis.

Our account relies mainly on four classes of evidence. First, materials drawn from a variety of local archives, as these permit more informed speculation about the social and economic standing of the Barker family. Second, a recently discovered Chancery case from 1717, which sheds light on Barker's personal circumstances during the period when she began publishing her novels. Third, two extraordinary letters by Barker, the only correspondence by her known to have survived, which offer glimpses of her involvement in the Jacobite network and illustrate in macabre detail or thinly veiled code her steadfast devotion to a lost cause. Fourth, the Magdalen Manuscript, a substantial volume of original verse produced by Barker while an exile at St. Germain at the turn of the century. The volume, now in the library of Magdalen College, Oxford, casts an invaluable light on Barker's circumstances during a hitherto obscure period of her life and contains besides an important conversion narrative in the voice of Fidelia, her Jacobite and Roman Catholic persona.[8] Since we seek to sift fact from fiction, however, we generally refrain from using either the Fidelia or the Galesia narratives as biographical evidence, except as they suggest avenues for further investigation or illustrate Barker's tendency to recast personal experience in mythic or politicized terms.

Our aim is to supply materials for more informed readings of Barker's novels and for closer study of her purposes and strategies as an autobiographer, as well as to lay the groundwork for further biographical investigations. We do not seek to tease out the complex interplay of fact and fiction in Barker's novels, still less to theorize the link between life-writing and fiction in Barker's or early modern women's fiction more generally. This we must leave to others. But the gap between the "life-writing" and the "life" that our research exposes argues for more complicated understandings of the autobiographical tendency of her work.[9] Barker was unquestionably a self-regarding writer, mindful always of her singularity and insistent on her otherness; her narratives exhibit a strong desire to "write the self." But this self-fashioning impulse is bound up in a web of political and religious commitments whose threads we are only now coming to recognize. This much is clear: in Barker's hands life-writing is anything but unmediated life-story. It is, among other things, a vehicle for projecting the experience of the Catholic and Jacobite oppositional communities with which she strongly identified, and serves novelistic purposes that originate, paradoxically, in a retreat from the modernity with which her fictions are most often associated. If, then, the following account warns against undue confidence in the factual reliability of the Galesia and Fidelia narratives, it also challenges the received image of Jane Barker as exemplar of emerging bourgeois respectability and suggests that critics would do well to look beyond the coming-to-writing themes that have attracted virtually all commentary on the novels,[10] and begin to explore the links between her novelistic experiments and her conservative political agenda.

Family and Friends

The family Jane Barker was born into is invariably described as staunchly royalist, but not a great deal is known about either side beyond her own accounts, which tend to cast family history in terms of a mythology of loyal sufferings. On her mother's side, "many Heroes" (of the Connock family) "had shed their dearest Blood" during the civil wars;[11] on her father's, some "were in Battle

slain, and some in Prison died; some were ruin'd in their Estates, some in their Persons."[12] The oft-told story of gallant sacrifice and loss in the king's cause is rehearsed with full royalist panache in one of the manuscript poems:

> My father and his brother Cavaliers,
> Stuck to their king as did their ancestors,
> Wives portions, and paternal means they spent
> To serve the King against the Parliment,
> Thus for their Loyalty being both undone,
> Were forc'd to quit the court, the camp, and town,
> They sold their swords and other warlike things,
> As did their wives, their petycotes and rings,
> And therwithal, bought equipage for plows,
> Betook themselves, to mannage sheep and cows,
> Instead of scarlet, Russet now they wore,
> And sheep-hooks were the leading staves they bore,
> Free from court factions, and the discontents,
> Which dayly rise in Rebell Parliaments. . . .
> And for their Loyal losses, never felt regrett.[13]

This is just one of many places where, in the absence of external evidence, it is impossible to disentangle biographical truth from royalist mythology.

What can be established from external sources is quickly summarized. Her mother, Anne, was a Connock (or Connoch), a Cornish gentry family that produced a number of army officers,[14] a scattering of members of parliament—not all of them staunchly pro-Stuart,[15] and, in the eighteenth century, members of the Jacobite baronetage.[16] The particulars of Anne's birth remain untraced, but it seems likely she was descended from an unlanded branch of the family. She was related to the noted Whig physician, Richard Lower (1631-91), who is made to address Jane Barker as "dear Cousin" in one of her published poems.[17] Of Thomas Barker's family even less is known. It seems to have been armigerous, for the seal on his will bears a coat of arms; he is identified as a gentleman in most surviving documents. Barker tells us that her father "lost a very honourable and profitable Place" at the court of Charles I (BG, p. 3), a claim that might seem to owe more to royalist convention than fact. It is corroborated, however, by the entry recording Barker's burial (in St. Germain 29 March 1732) describing her as the daughter of the "Secretaire du grand sceau d'Angleterre"—meaning, perhaps, that Thomas had been one of the secretaries to the lord keeper of the Great Seal of England.[18]

By the late 1640s, Thomas and Anne Barker were living in Blatherwick, Northamptonshire, a village not far from Stamford, Lincolnshire.[19] Here Jane was born in May 1652, the only daughter and second of three surviving children.[20] It is not clear what brought the Barkers to Blatherwick, but we do know that by the early 1660s Thomas was working in some capacity for (or with) Robert Clayton, the London "money-scrivener" who, with his partner John Morris, helped invent modern banking. (Described by his recent biographer as a "self-made Midas," Clayton would be knighted in 1671 and in 1679-80 serve as lord mayor of London; but during the period of his association with Thomas Barker he was still an obscure figure, just beginning to build his immense fortune.)[21] A signed letter of 14 July 1661 would seem to indicate that Thomas was acting as Clayton's agent in an area that included parts of Rutland, Lincolnshire, and Northamptonshire. The letter, addressed to Clayton at the Flying Horse (the shop in Cornhill that until 1666 was the site of Clayton's and Morris's bank), is signed "you ʳ Loving ffrind," implying a personal as well as professional relationship (NRO, Clayton MS 16). A bond signed by Clayton and Morris in May 1663 and countersigned by "Tho. Barker" suggests Barker may have been working at least part of the time in London, since in the early 1660s Clayton and Morris used their own employees to witness documents signed at the Flying Horse.[22]

By August 1662 Thomas held the lease to the manor house and land in Wilsthorpe, Lincolnshire, a village six miles northeast of Stamford, just west of the low-lying region called "the Fens," granting him use of some eighty acres of arable land, several acres of water meadow, a number of enclosed fields, and an orchard.[23] The hearth tax returns of 1665 charge "Mr. Barker" of "Wilstropp" with five hearths.[24] It was in the Wilsthorpe manor house that Jane lived, with intervals in London and St. Germain, from the 1660s until at least 1717.

Like other families of only moderate prosperity, the Barkers pinned their ambitions and concentrated their limited resources on the eldest son and heir. Edward's academic career witnesses to the minor gentry's pursuit of advancement through the channels of elite education: when nearly thirteen he was sent to the prestigious Merchant Taylors' School in London;[25] he matriculated five years later (on 3 July 1668) at St. John's College, Oxford,[26] receiving a B.A. in 1672 and an M.A. from Christ Church on 8 March 1675.[27] (He may have changed colleges in order to become eligible for one of the Christ Church Studentships reserved for students pursuing medical studies.)[28] It is possible that he considered a career in law at one time, for on 9 March 1670 he was admitted a student at Gray's Inn, although he may instead have been following custom in cultivating the social connections offered by a stint at one of the inns of court.[29] In the poetry and novels the Edward-figure is consistently represented as a medical student.

By the fall of 1675 Edward Barker was almost certainly dead. The precise date and circumstances are unknown, though in **"On the Death of my Brother"** Jane explains in heroic couplets that he died of a "Feavour" in spite of the efforts of his medical colleagues (PR, p. 48). His death probably occurred between March, when he received his M.A., and November, for a new lease to the Wilsthorpe property dated 2 December names Jane Barker as "a life": it was to be valid for Thomas Barker, "his Exec ʳˢ adm ʳˢ & assigns" for a "tenure of ffour score and nineteen years from these next ensuing if so be Jane Barker daughter to the s[ai]d Thomas Barker shall so long live."[30] Were Edward still alive and healthy, Jane Barker would hardly be

named as a life. Edward died, we may conclude, at twenty-five; Jane would have been twenty-three.[31] She continued to lament his early death in verse and fiction published as late as 1723.

In at least one respect Edward's place in Jane's literary life has been exaggerated, however. He is often credited with introducing her to the university men with whom she exchanged much of her early verse (some of it printed in 1687 in **Poetical Recreations**), but whom we now know to have been students at St. John's College, Cambridge—not Oxford, where Edward took his bachelor's degree. Her prominent place in a Cambridge literary-exchange coterie gives evidence of her ability to forge intellectual friendships with young men, as perhaps does her friendship with the London bookseller Benjamin Crayle, who published **Poetical Recreations** when he was just twenty-seven. The younger son of a Newark gentleman, Crayle had university and inns of court connections and fancied himself something of a poet in the genteel amateur mode. Barker seems to have formed her Cambridge friendships through one John Newton, a man ten years her junior, who lived in the nearby village of Uffington. Newton is the St. John's Fellow who as "J. N." and "Philaster" wrote commendatory verse for **Poetical Recreations** [**PR**] and who may have played a key role in getting her earliest verse into print.[32] No evidence has emerged to support the claim, first made by William McBurney and since often repeated, that her earliest work was "written for a rural literary circle, which continued the tradition of the 'Society of Friendship'" associated with Katherine Philips ("Orinda").[33]

A PATRIARCHAL PUZZLE

Some of the most puzzling bits of information about the family come from Thomas Barker's will.[34] Even the circumstances of his death are mysterious. Thomas composed his brief and hasty will in a quavering hand on 27 September 1681 in Shingay, Cambridgeshire, a parish located just west of the Old North Road leading from London to Stamford. Four days later he was buried in the Shingay chapel. In the will and burial register he is designated "Thomas Barker Gentleman of Shingay in the County of Cambridge."[35] Shingay? What brought him to a parish of no more than six or seven households, some fifty miles from Wilsthorpe? Why was he buried in the chapel, a privilege generally reserved for persons of some standing in the community? We have found nothing to indicate the existence of family or property in or around Shingay, but we do know from one of Jane's poems that she spent time there herself: to a poetic correspondent she apologizes that her *Epistles* grow on every Bow, / O'th' multitude of *Shin-gay* Trees" (**PR,** p. 95), and Shingay was, in fact, heavily wooded in the seventeenth century.[36] The highly generalized account of Galesia's father's death in **A Patch-Work Screen,** however, offers no clues.[37]

The will itself contains one piece of information startling to anyone who comes to the Barker family history through the Galesia fictions: a younger brother, Henry. Nowhere do the fictions hint at the existence of this second brother, whereas the figure corresponding to Edward is highly visible, and the subject of a number of grief-stricken poems as well.[38] That Henry might have been something of a *persona non grata* in the family is a possibility his father's will does little to counter. Thomas leaves the Wilsthorpe manor house and land; property in nearby King's Cliffe, Northamptonshire;[39] and all other goods and chattels, both personal and real, to "my loving wife" Anne Barker and "my daughter" Jane Barker.[40] Wife and daughter are also named joint executors of his will. To his "sonne Henry Barker," said to be "of Newgate Streete in London," he leaves the sum of ten pounds.

Before speculating on the meaning of this bequest, it is best to set down such information as can be gathered about Henry. Of his first twenty-four years nothing is known beyond the date of his baptism. The archives of the sites of male learning that record so clearly the stages in Edward's educational progress—Merchant Taylors', St. John's College, Gray's Inn, Christ Church—register no trace of Henry. This is not too surprising, given his status as younger son in a family that appears never to have been wealthy. He was doubtless expected to follow a less expensive path to a career, perhaps by serving an apprenticeship in one of the London companies, a route not at all uncommon for younger sons of the gentry in the seventeenth century.[41] However, one document identifies him as a gentleman, an unlikely designation had he entered a trade. His situation and standing in London remain shadowy.

The first trace of Henry in adulthood is a marriage allegation of 28 February 1679 between Henry Barker of the parish of Christchurch Newgate Street and Anne Phipps, daughter of William Phipps, of the parish of St. Andrew Holborn.[42] Both the parish and the age of twenty-four given on the allegation fit what is known about Jane's brother Henry. Henry and Anne were married the next month in the parish of St. Mary Margaret Fish Street.[43] From 1679 to 1681 Henry Barker paid poor taxes in Christchurch Newgate St. parish, assessed in the middle ranges.[44] Two children are known to have been born to the couple,[45] including a daughter Mary, who will prove an important player later in the story: in 1717 she will take legal action against her aunt Jane.[46]

We may now return to Henry's inheritance. Ten pounds was a considerable sum those days, for some laborers a year's wages; but compared with an inheritance in land it was a mere pittance. It was certainly odd for a daughter to come into land in these circumstances;[47] but it may mean no more than that Thomas settled money and property on his son when he turned twenty-one, some five years earlier, which was not uncommon at this time, or upon his marriage. Support for this possibility comes from a parish register entry identifying him in 1688 as "Henry Barker Gent."[48] Complicating the picture, however, is his daughter's later claim that as a teenager she could have gone into service at four pounds a year: she "could have gott a

Sufficient Livelyhood for her self and was offered four pounds a Year Wages in case she would have gone to Service" (Chancery Deposition, PRO, C11 237/28). Girls of genteel upbringing did, in fact, go into service, generally into elite "upper servant" positions, but this may be an indication that "Henry Barker Gent" was not exactly thriving.[49] Henry's ten pounds may be evidence of family antagonism or of a previous settlement—although, as has been pointed out to us, if the former, Thomas is more likely to have cut him off with the proverbial shilling.[50]

London, Revolution, and Exile

The decade that began with Thomas Barker's death was a momentous one for Jane, now in her thirties. In the 1680s she lost her father, removed to London, lost her mother, was received into the Catholic Church, saw a large body of her verse published in the unauthorized *Poetical Recreations,* watched the fall of her beloved House of Stuart, and, in 1689, fled to France in the violent (for Catholics) aftermath of the so-called Bloodless Revolution.[51] In the *Patch-Work Screen* version of the events following the death of the father, Barker places Galesia and her mother in lodgings near Westminster Abbey, a site chosen for its gentility and political resonance, one suspects, rather than for biographical veracity. Indeed, there is some evidence to suggest that Jane and Anne Barker took up residence in the City in the considerably less fashionable parish of Christchurch Newgate Street, presumably to be near Henry and his wife.[52] Corroboration of her presence in London in the mid-1680s comes from a poem by her publisher Benjamin Crayle, whose bookshop at the west and of St. Paul's Churchyard was not far from Newgate Street. He claims in a 1687 poem to have known Barker ("Cosmelia") for three years.[53]

A Crayle publication from this period casts a tantalizing glimmer on Barker's London medical practice. In a book he brought out in 1685 he inserted a notice that at his shop was to be had, for the sum of five shillings a roll, something called Dr. Barker's Famous Gout Plaister, which "infallibly takes away the pain in Twelve Hours time, with the Paroxysm of the Distemper, and in time may effect a perfect Cure."[54] It seems at first improbable that a country gentlewoman as mindful of decorum as Jane Barker would be selling a "Famous Gout Plaister" under the name "Dr. Barker," but internal evidence for her involvement in such a scheme is fairly convincing. Crayle's "Cosmelia" poem indicates he and Barker were acquainted by this time. Though she never refers in her writings to Crayle, his bookshop, or her selling of medicines, in *A Patch-Work Screen* [*PWS*] she does ascribe to Galesia some reputation as a lay physician in London. In the *Poetical Recreations* verse "On the Apothecaries Filing my Recipes amongst the Doctors," the speaker boasts of her ability as a "fam'd *Physician*" to "overcome" the "sturdy Gout" (*PR,* Pt. I, p. 31). When Barker reprints this same poem nearly four decades later, she appends a footnote indicating she had possessed "a particular Arcanum for the Gout" (*PWS,* p. 57).

That Barker converted to Catholicism during the reign of James II (1685-88) seems almost certain, but our only source is the "Fidelia" poems from the Magdalen MS.[55] These poems, along with others on affairs of state—such as "Fidelia weeping for the Kings departure at the Revolution"—register (in ways that remain to be explored) Barker's response to political and religious events in London during the troubled years of James' short reign. They suggest also that she fled to France early in 1689.[56] A poem written to accompany a gift to the Prince of Wales on his first birthday establishes her as part of the community of exiles at St. Germain-en-Laye by 10 June 1689.[57] She would live in St. Germain until 1704, when she returned to Wilsthorpe.

Though Barker sought notice and patronage from members of the royal family—she addressed poems to Queen Mary of Modena, Arabella FitzJames (the illegitimate daughter of James II and Arabella Churchill), and Princess Louise Maria (the younger sister of the Prince of Wales), and dedicated an entire volume of scathingly anti-Williamite political verse to the twelve-year-old Prince of Wales (the future "Old Pretender")[58]—nothing has emerged to suggest she had personal access to court circles, still less a position there, as has been claimed. Her name appears in none of the surviving court-in-exile lists, and the only documentary trace of her presence in St. Germain is the parish register recording her appearance as godmother to Christine Winiffe, born to Dorothy (née Ford) and George Winiffe, a London lawyer.[59] The fact that her co-sponsor was Robert Brent, a leading lawyer in the pre-Revolution Catholic world and an important figure at St. Germain until his death in 1695,[60] suggests that, although not part of the upper ranks of exile society, she did move through fairly distinguished circles. We know, too, that her verse circulated in manuscript among the exiles.[61] A bound volume of her work would eventually come into the possession of Anne-Charlotte de Crussol de Florensac, duchesse d'Aiguillon, a member of one of the most eminent families in France.[62]

From a marginal note in the Magdalen Manuscript we know that in 1696, when Barker was forty-three, she had an operation to have her cataracts couched.[63] (Couching involved the insertion of a needle into the eye; the needle was then used to work the clouded lens down out of the line of vision.) In the years following the operation, Barker represented herself as "a blind person"—and for good reason.[64] A person not fully blinded by the infections introduced by such an operation would afterwards be able to read and write, but only barely, and would require the assistance of a powerful magnifying glass. This explains why in 1700 she enlisted the services of her cousin, Colonel William Connock, to help her prepare the presentation volume of her verse. The presentation copy, or a prototype of it, is almost entirely in Connock's hand (BL Add. MS 21, 621).

CHANCERY

A rich body of information about Barker's life in Wilsthorpe after the turn of the century is found in deposi-

tions submitted in a Chancery case of 1717. They tell us that "sometime" early in 1704 Barker returned to England, "having been abroad beyond the Seas for a considerable time," evidently with the intention of taking up management of the Wilsthorpe farm.[65] She arranged for her niece Mary, Henry's daughter, to return with her. Mary, then sixteen, may have welcomed an opportunity to live apart from her family; while Jane, nearly fifty-two and semiblind, would almost certainly have required help. Mary would be "extreemly serviceable to her in managing her house and upon other Occasions," she is reported to have said. By May 1704, Mary was installed with her aunt on the farm in Lincolnshire, and there began the sequence of events—two marriages, two births, and a funeral—that culminated in legal action in 1717, when aunt and niece went to court against each other. To the Chancery documents we owe a glimpse of the aging Barker in her private, domestic existence and of a largely female household and its rather sordid family politics.

In the summer of 1717 Barker went to Chancery to stop proceedings initiated against her by Mary and her second husband, John Staton. The Statons were pressing for the return of money (about forty pounds) and household goods (worth an additional five pounds), which they claimed Barker owed her niece. Barker counterclaimed that she was holding the money and goods in trust for Mary's daughters by a previous marriage. (Mary's first husband, William Henson, had died intestate in 1710 when the elder daughter was only a year old. By law one-third of Henson's estate would go to his children.) In Barker's bill of complaint, dated 10 July 1717, she speaks as "next friend" of two grandnieces, whom she raised almost from birth. She charges the Statons with attempting to defraud the girls of their proper inheritance, and asks the court to stop their attempt to recover the money and goods. She was temporarily successful. The court issued a stay of injunction against John and Mary Staton on 23 July 1717. Shortly thereafter, however, the Statons submitted a long, detailed, and, it must be said, damaging answer to Barker's accusations. On 6 August the court found for the Statons and gave them permission to proceed. And there, so far as we know, the official documentation ends.[66] The outcome of the Statons' action is not known, but the extant evidence does not favor Barker.

Mary is a remarkable figure in this conflict. She was born 21 December 1687 and presumably lived with her father (no trace of her mother has survived) in London until May 1704, when she removed to Wilsthorpe.[67] For the next three years Mary lived in Wilsthorpe with her aunt. Concerning her life in the Barker household during those years we have only her statement, obviously biased, that she worked "in the nature of a Servant," though without wages. In 1707, Mary, now nineteen, married William Henson, a yeoman from nearby Carlby, a village not three miles from Wilsthorpe.[68] By him she had two daughters, Mary and Anne, the grandnieces whom Barker would name as coplaintiffs in the 1717 proceedings. In the months after William died late in January 1710, aged thirty-four, Mary undertook to settle his affairs with what appears to have been uncommon energy and admirable resourcefulness.[69]

By June 1710, some five months later, Mary, a twenty-two-year-old widow with two infant daughters, was once again living in the manor house at Wilsthorpe. At some point—when and why are at the heart of the dispute—she turned over to Barker the forty-odd pounds and household goods that may or may not have been part of William Henson's estate and may or may not have constituted her daughters' inheritance. In January 1714 she eloped with a craftsman from the nearby village of Irnham, John Staton, leaving behind her two young daughters.[70] She married "without your said oratrix Jane's knowledge," Barker's bill charges. Indeed she did, Mary retorts, "nor do these Def[endants] know that either of them were obliged" to "ask her consent." John Staton, her second husband, was either a cobbler (Barker's version) or a shoemaker (the Statons' version); either "a person of very meane and necessitous Circumstances" (Barker) or one who lived with his wife "comfortably in the world" (Staton). In any case, from 1714 Barker took over care of the two Henson girls, her grandnieces (they would have been about four and five at the time), and maintained them at Wilsthorpe for at least the next three years.[71]

The Statons began pressing Barker for the money—they "oftentimes" and "in a friendly manner" requested its return, as they would have it—but Barker steadily refused. At one point, if the Staton account can be relied upon, she directed a Mr. Newton to inform the Statons "she would sooner live a constant Prisoner to her house or leave the Kingdome rather than these Def[endants] should have Either money or Goods from her." (The utterance *does* sound like Barker.) Eventually the Statons went to court. In July 1717 a "John Stayton" is named on a summons to appear in the midsummer Kesteven Quarter Sessions.[72]

Even allowing for exaggeration on the Statons' part, the picture of Barker that emerges from the Chancery documents is of a woman hard driven by economic need. According to Mary, by 1714 she was "in necessitous Circumstances"; she was "in trouble" and involved in law suits; her "present wants" were many. Of course, Mary had good reason to construct her aunt as impecunious, and it might be argued that Barker's willingness to initiate a potentially costly Chancery case suggests some command of financial resources. It should be remembered, however, that Chancery was not especially expensive in its initial stages. Barker may have spent little more than a pound to obtain a stay against the Statons' action at law.[73] Against the forty-plus pounds the Statons were demanding, a pound may have seemed a good gamble, especially if Barker's circumstances were anything like as exigent as the Statons claimed and as other evidence does nothing to deny. It is certainly suggestive that she seems not to have pursued legal action beyond the relatively inexpensive initial stages. Her recourse to Chancery in summer 1717 may suggest not so much economic reserves as desperation.

Further light on her financial difficulties comes from another document from 1717, a deposition in response to the 1715 statute requiring papists to register their names and real estates.[74] (Barker registered her leasehold estate on 15 October 1717, the last Roman Catholic in the Kesteven division of Lincolnshire to do so.) In addition to confirming information from the 1675 lease,[75] her deposition tells us of the existence of a tenant, one Robert Arden, who sublet a portion of the estate, paying an annual rent of £24 17s. 8d. for the approximately forty acres that he farmed. This means that Barker did not actually pay a "sizable annual rent of £47.10s.," as has been asserted;[76] she paid £22 12s. 4d., a more manageable sum, especially as it was offset by Arden's yearly payment. Nonetheless, her financial difficulties may have been formidable. The strain of the heavy taxation required to finance the wars on the Continent, exacerbated by a series of bad harvests, had left many small landholders straitened. As a Roman Catholic she was subject to double land tax, and the 1715 registration was intended to make possible an additional special charge on two-thirds of any Catholic estate.[77]

Ignorance of Barker's economic circumstances during the period when she published her fictions has resulted in erroneous speculations about the supposedly "leisured" character of her writing career. Especially misleading is the oft-repeated claim that she inherited a comfortable income in the form of a royal grant or pension, amounting in some versions to as much as eighty pounds a year—a version of events that gives the impression of a writer freed from economic necessity and thus able to turn her energies chiefly to writing.[78] The evidence of the Chancery case challenges such a picture; there is, moreover, nothing in the documentary record to indicate the existence of a royal grant or pension of any kind.[79] The evidence, admittedly fragmentary and, in the case of the Staton testimony, subject to bias, points quite clearly away from the life of rural quiet and modest independence envisioned by some commentators toward one marked by financial anxieties and the struggle of a middle-aged woman to keep the Wilsthorpe household going.

There can be little doubt necessity played a role in Barker's decision to take up professional authorship in the eighteenth century. Novel writing was poorly paid, however, and there is no reason to suppose she garnered more than the five or ten guineas that a writer of prose fiction might expect for the sale of copy, especially as she was publishing with Edmund Curll, a bookseller not known for princely generosity. The need for income might explain why she sought aristocratic patronage for her earliest works. *Bosvil and Galesia* (1713) and *Exilus* (1715) were dedicated to the countess of Exeter, the former Elizabeth Brownlow of Belton, Lincolnshire.[80] Barker was evidently acquainted with both the countess and her youngest child and only daughter, Elizabeth, for the dedication ends with the hope that "my Young Lady," who was then seven and "the Darling of Your Ladyship's Heart," may "never intangle her Noble Person in those Levities and Misfortunes the ensuing Treatise describes me unhappily to have struggled with."[81] Barker's translation of *The Christian Pilgrimage* (1718), a collection of Lenten meditations from the French of François Fénelon made "to speak *English* in the Dialect of the Church of *England*,"[82] was dedicated to the countess of Nottingham, who lived at this time at Burley-on-the-Hill, near Oakham, Rutland, less than twenty miles from Wilsthorpe. It is not clear whether Barker was personally acquainted with Lady Nottingham; in seeking her patronage, she may have been influenced by her dedicatee's reputed Roman Catholic sympathies.[83]

"OUR HOLY KING"

Jane Barker's Jacobitism still awaits full investigation, but that she was a committed Jacobite is beyond dispute. During the 1690s she composed a considerable body of loyalist verse; and the volumes in the Galesia trilogy, especially the final *The Lining of the Patch Work Screen*, make it clear she never wavered in her devotion to the Pretender's cause. Two further documents indicate involvement in Jacobite politics and even conspiracy during the Hanoverian era. Each is sensational in itself and foregrounds a side of Barker that will come as a surprise to many admirers of her writing.

The first is an abstract in French of a letter intercepted in 1718 by the government's anti-Jacobite intelligence machine.[84] Dated 19 March, the letter was sent by Barker from London[85] to James Butler, second duke of Ormonde (1665-1745), who had been forced to flee to France in August of 1715. Using the thinly veiled language beloved of Jacobite correspondents, she informs Ormonde that swelling support for his "jeune amy"—the Old Pretender, "James III"—made the time ripe for an invasion. (Ormonde did, in fact, help organize an invasion effort that ended disastrously in March of the next year with the destruction of a fleet off Cadiz.) Barker's letter, in literal translation, reads as follows:

> It has been a long time that we have been without letters from you. Mr. Hutchesson [Archibald Hutcheson][86] is your strong supporter. He is ashamed of his past errors, and he disavows them publicly. Several of his friends who were not yours now place themselves in your party, the number of your friends increases every day. They strongly wish to see you with your young friend, and [wish] that he could dispossess those who unjustly withhold his goods; for it is very sad to see him thus wandering in foreign countries. But I must tell you that if you wish to find inexpensive houses here, you ought to come after the end of the session of Parliament, when everyone goes to the country.[87] I would never advise you to come during the session everything then being too expensive.[88]

This letter is the basis for the claim, first made by McBurney (p. 390) and repeated by Moira Ferguson (p. 171), that Barker "engaged in clandestine correspondence with the exiled Jacobite peer, James Butler, Duke of Ormonde." No further correspondence with Ormonde has come to light, and a note on the abstract indicates that the letter's signatory was a stranger to the Hanoverian authorities: "on ignore qui est Barker." There can be no doubt, however, that Barker was engaged in Jacobite intrigue. It

seems probable that she was used as an amanuensis to pass on information from plotters whose names and handwriting would be known to the authorities, perhaps information regarding Hutcheson's change of political sympathies ("He is ashamed of his past errors").[89] There is, moreover, some reason to believe her name might have been known to Ormonde through her Connock relations.[90] It may seem a bit sensationalizing to call Barker a "Jacobite spy," but active Jacobite she manifestly was, and willing to assist those seeking to overthrow the British government of George I.[91]

The second is an autograph letter, probably dating from 1730, to an unnamed woman she addresses as "Madam" and "your Ladyship."[92] The letter, which testifies to the healing power of the blood of the late James II, who died in 1701, appears to be Barker's contribution to one of several Jacobite efforts during her lifetime to secure James' canonization,[93] and suggests that she continued to support the Stuart cause long after any real hopes of a restoration had passed. It begins, remarkably enough, by offering the unidentified lady "so od a present," a cancer from Barker's own breast (the "cancer" may have been a cyst of some kind) and goes on to rehearse its emergence and progress:

> The first appearance of it, was in form of a grain of oatmeal, with great iching and between whiles, pricking and shooting, by which Symtoms I knew it to be a cancer, and therfore looked upon it as a deaths head, and so resolved to let it work its will, or rathe[r] the will of god, only addressd, my prayrs, to our holy King, touching it with his blood which I had on a little rag, but instead of deminiching, it grew to the bigness you see, see [*sic*], which was in the space of some years, still iching and pricking by fits, at last it seem'd to put its head out (as it were) from under its little mole-hill, by degree[s] put out farther, till its whole vile body came quite out, hanging by a little string like a white thred, of which there are divers witnesses. . . .

She names as witnesses her father confessor (still unidentified) and "my little neece [one of the Henson girls?], and Coll connocks neece," and testifies that the cancer, through the agency of the king's blood, worked free of her breast with "no soar or any manner of corruptio[n] appearing." She also attests to the efficacy of James's blood in curing "my little neeces eye," which had been subject to a "bloodshed" since infancy:

> I kneelld doun and touched it with the Kings blood in form of a cross, saying The Kings blood touch, God heal, the Eye retir'd into its place, the nose and face became well and and [*sic*] never had any return since, much nor little. . . .

Barker leaves the disposal of her "od" gift entirely to the discretion of the lady, but mentions sending on the evidence either to Lewis Sabran (1652-1732), rector of the Jesuit college at St. Omers, or Lady Nithsdale (d. 1749), both notable Roman Catholic Jacobites. She concludes by suggesting that the addressee—probably Lady Nithesdale's sister, Mother Lucy Theresa Joseph, Superior of the Augustinian Convent at Bruges—inform "our friends at Rome" of these miracles.

Two final glimpses of Jane Barker come from a pair of letters written from St. Germain by her cousin William Connock. On 14 January 1726 he reports receiving word that "Cos. Barker" was "very ill & had receivd the Blessed Sacrament." On 26 May 1727 she is said to be on her way to France: "I expect every day a lettre from Cosin Barker of her beeing arived at Diep" (BL Add. MS 21, 896, f. 1; f. 11v.). Thereafter silence, save the canonization letter discussed earlier, until 1732, when an entry of 29 March in the parish register of St. Germain records her burial. In two more months she would have been eighty.

"JANUS" BARKER

These, then, are the facts as they can now be established. More doubtless remains to be discovered, but enough is known to permit some thoughts about Barker's practices as an autobiographer. First, and most obviously, the self projected in the autobiographical novels is an invention, and the narratives are idealized recastings of a life; they are not "the life." In the novels the father is a virtuous gentleman-farmer, to take a single example, and the family lives in happy rural innocence. The archives tell another story, however. They give glimpses of a father associated with a City money-scrivener; a brother of uncertain occupation living in Newgate Street, London; a niece who may have cheerfully contemplated going out to service at four pounds a year and who married first a yeoman of modest means and later a shoemaker or cobbler. External sources point toward a range of middle-aged experience that goes unrecorded in the novels: conversion to an outlawed religion, life as an exile during a prolonged residence in France, and struggle in England to raise two grandnieces and to keep the Wilsthorpe household going. The novels give no hint of the bookshop in St. Paul's Churchyard where she may have offered for sale the Famous Gout Plaster; and they fail to recount her business dealings in her sixties and seventies with Edmund Curll, whose name, then as now, was a byword for piracy and salaciousness. They do not tell of the despair that must have accompanied her failing eyesight or the anxieties engendered by what she believed was breast cancer. If these omissions suggest a measure of status insecurity and doubtless some female anxieties of authorship as well,[94] they also suggest that at this moment the novel as a genre had not yet learned to accommodate the bodily and economic experiences of women no longer ingenues.

Information that has come to light regarding her political involvements suggests the need for a reassessment of her novelistic aims and strategies. That Barker—famously moral, decorous, and above all respectable—was attached to an insurrectionary politics certainly complicates the prevailing picture of her as "the new, moral woman writer, acceptable to later generations"[95]—and not simply because her idiosyncratic novels failed to inspire imitations or even, for that matter, to find a wide readership, at least so far as we can tell. Barker, born during the Interregnum and living well into the Age of Walpole, continued all her life to inhabit a mental universe shaped by the political and religious crises of the seventeenth century. The texts she wrote exhibit that century's refusal to separate private and national, personal and public history. Though associated—rightly—with "the rise" of a genre that laid claim to and in part invented domesticity, interiority, female subjectivity, and the private sphere; though committed to exploration of the intensely individuated life; though displaying the self-consciously experimental attitude toward genre and form and multiple voicings that we think of as distinctively modern, Barker was herself looking in the other direction. Her fictions resist precisely those public/private disjunctions that have come to dominate our own thinking about the eighteenth century and the early novel. Considered historically, then, the current image of Barker as exemplar of the novelistic shift toward respectable privatized domestic fiction is almost comically wrongheaded. Not only does it assign Barker a role she would have found baffling at best, but it fails signally to take account of the specifically political aims and purposes of the novels, consistently ignoring or misrepresenting their Jacobite elements in favor of what is "pious," "didactic," "pure," and "respectable" and contributing thereby to what we might call the dulling down of Jane Barker, with the further result that we miss much of what is most distinctive in her ambiguous, oblique, alienated and in some ways deeply reactionary texts.

All of this has implications for the growing body of revisionist work devoted to seeking new approaches to early eighteenth-century narrative—the Novel Before. Serious attention to the political underpinnings of Barker's novels will, we believe, compel a rethinking of our paradigms of female authorship in this period. Barker is almost invariably placed in the so-called pious school of female novel-writing (with, among others, Penelope Aubin and Elizabeth Rowe) as part of the habitual separation of women into the opposing camps of "daughters of Behn" (scandalous, outspoken, sexually explicit) and the "daughters of Orinda" (moral, ladylike, modest)—a good girl/bad girl split that, remarkably, remains largely unchallenged, even in feminist literary histories. A close look at Barker's practices would go a long way toward dismantling a dichotomy that may have outlived its usefulness. We suggest that as a maker of fictions of political opposition Barker practices "a complex form of (auto)-biographizing" that shares much with the aims and strategies of the amatory writers analyzed by Ros Ballaster,[96] and that in her politicized use of a variety of highly crafted authorial self-images she has much in common with Aphra Behn and Delarivière Manley, two "scandalous" women writers to whom she is habitually (and misleadingly) opposed.[97] Barker chooses, however, not to eroticize her autobiographical personae, but to construct them as figures of the alienated Other, so shaped as to express the disaffection of a whole range of people marginalized in Hanoverian Britain—among them a tiny Roman Catholic minority, a more widespread community of Jacobite dissidents, and an assortment of odd women. Like Behn and Manley—and a host of male poets, as well, among them her coreligionist Pope—Jane Barker does not so much "write the self" as use the materials of her own life to create myths and stories for readers estranged from the new political order. That in her hands the novel was a reactionary instrument, written in resistance to the very modernity it expressed, is just one of the paradoxes of her strange, and compelling, art.

Notes

1. Carol Shiner Wilson, ed., *The Galesia Trilogy and Selected Manuscript Poems by Jane Barker* (N.Y. & Oxford: Oxford Univ., 1997); Robert DeMaria, Jr., ed., *British Literature (1640-1789): An Anthology* (Oxford & Cambridge, Mass.: Blackwell, 1996); Paula R. Backscheider and John J. Richetti, eds., *Popular Fiction by Women (1660-1730): An Anthology* (Oxford: Clarendon, 1996), p. xix; Carol Barash, *English Women's Poetry, 1649-1714: Politics, Community, and Linguistic Authority* (Oxford: Clarendon, 1996).

2. The Galesia trilogy—so called because the narratives recount different phases in the life of their narrator and protagonist, Galesia, before and after her residence in France—comprises *The Amours of Bosvil and Galesia, As related to Lucasia in St. Germain's Garden. A Novel* (1713, under the title *Love Intrigues: Or, The History of the Amours of Bosvil and Galesia*, rev. 1719); *A Patch-Work Screen for the Ladies* (1723), and *The Lining of the Patch Work Screen: Design'd for the Farther Entertainment of the Ladies* (1726).

3. "Creating the Woman Writer: The Autobiographical Works of Jane Barker," *Tulsa Studies in Women's Literature* 2 (Fall 1983): 166. It is a measure of Barker's obscurity that the only biographical source in English available to Spencer in 1983 was a notice from the 1920s where the "what-is-known"—much of it speculative, and much of that wrong—filled all of five paragraphs. See G. S. Gibbons, "Mrs. Jane Barker," *Notes and Queries* ser. 11, no. 12 (30 Sept. 1922): 278-79. A German dissertation contains some biographical information, but it appears to have been derived entirely from Barker's writings. See Karl Stanglmaier, *Mrs. Jane Barker: Ein Beitrag zur Englischen Literaturgeschichte* (Berlin, 1906), available on microfilm from Research Publications (New Haven).

4. Myra Reynolds, *The Learned Lady in England 1650-1760* (Gloucester, Mass.: Peter Smith, 1964), comments, for example, "Galesia's recourse to hard study and responsible farm management as a cure for a wounded heart sets her as a heroine in a class by herself. She is so sensible and reasonable as to seem out of place in a romance" (pp. 164-65).

5. Some of these findings were summarized by Margaret Doody in "Jane Barker," *British Novelists, 1660-1800*, vol. 39, pt. 1 of *Dictionary of Literary Biography*, ed. Martin C. Battestin (Detroit: Gale Research, 1985). Their documentary basis was recorded in the headnote to the Barker selections in *Kissing the Rod: An Anthology of Seventeenth-Century Women's Verse*, ed. Germaine Greer, Susan Hastings, Jeslyn Medoff, & Melinda Sansone (N.Y.: Farrar, Straus & Giroux, 1989).

6. We are grateful to Barash and Wilson for allowing us to read unpublished versions of their work, and to Wilson for generously making available to us information from the documents she uncovered. King is in the final stages of a book on Barker's texts and literary career that emphasizes her political engagements.

7. Barker's published work includes the verse printed in Part One of *Poetical Recreations* (1687; title page has 1688), the Galesia fictions (see n. 2), *Exilius* (1714; the title page has 1715), and a translation from the French of Lenten meditations by Bishop Fénelon, *The Christian Pilgrimage* (1718). A revised version of *Bosvil and Galesia* was published with *Exilius* in 1719 as *The Entertaining Novels of Mrs. Jane Barker*.

8. Magdalen MS 343. The three-part volume, completed probably by 1704, incorporates poems composed over a period of at least a quarter century, as well as what may be later revisions. Parts Two and Three are in Barker's quirky hand, Part One in the more finished hand of her cousin, William Connock. The Part One poems are copied into a volume now in the British Library, Add. MS 21,621, also in Connock's hand. For a detailed discussion of the two volumes, see Kathryn R. King, *The Poems of Jane Barker: The Magdalen Manuscript*, Magdalen College Occasional Paper No. 3, forthcoming 1998.

9. Movement in this direction can be seen in Wilson (see n. 1), who has discovered a brother absent from Barker's writings and argues partly on this basis for a consideration of the "selective silences" in the Galesia narratives. Wilson's biographical account is weakened, however, by its tendency to conflate the fictions and the documentary record.

10. The inaugural text is Spencer (see n. 3); but see Kristina Straub, "Frances Burney and the Rise of the Woman Novelist," in *The Columbia History of the British Novel*, ed. John Richetti (N.Y.: Columbia Univ., 1994), pp. 203-5, for a perceptive rereading of Spencer.

11. Barker, *A Patch-Work Screen for the Ladies* (London, 1723), p. 112. Subsequent refs. will be cited parenthetically as PWS. A Colonel Connock was among the conspirators led by Colonel John Gerard, whose plans to assassinate Cromwell in May 1654 were quickly thwarted (Thomas Newcomb, *A True Account of the Late Bloody and Inhuman Conspiracy Against His Highness the Lord Protector* [1654]; rpt. *The Harleian Miscellany* in 10 vols. [1808-13], 10:248). We are grateful to Sharon Valiant for drawing this information to our attention.

12. Barker, *Bosvil and Galesia* (London, 1713), p. 3. Subsequent refs. will be indicated parenthetically as BG. The only Barker who turns up in P. R. Newman's *Royalist Officers in England and Wales, 1642-1660: A Biographical Dictionary* (N.Y. & London: Garland, 1981) is a Lt. Col., either a George or a Daniel Barker, who was acting commander of Col. Henry Bard's Horse in May of 1645; of his background nothing is known (p. 16).

13. "A dialogue between Fidelia and her little nephew, Martius, as they walk in Luxembourg. disguis'd as a shepherdess or country maid," Magdalen MS 343, Pt. II, 25v. Subsequent refs. will be cited parenthetically as Mag. MS.

14. The military branch of the Connocks descends from Captain George Connock (b. 1575). Letters dated 1726 and 1727 from his grandson, the exiled Jacobite Colonel William Connock (d. 1738), to his son, Timon, an aide-de-camp to Philip V of Spain (d. ca. 1731), refer to Barker as "cosin" (BL Add. MS 21, 896, ff. 1 and 11v). According to his burial notice, which was made available to us by Edward Corp, William served with Sir Toby Bourke in the Nine Years' War; from Barker's verse it appears he fought in the Irish campaign. He is probably the addressee of the poem, "To My dear cosen Coll—at his return out of Irland into France," which describes "Connocks battery" at the seige of Limerick in 1690 (Mag. MS 343, Pt. II, 8-9). He may be the father of the Major William Connock (d. 1704) who served in the earl of Pemboke's regiment of foot, one of six regiments of the Anglo-Dutch Brigade stationed in Holland. In the summer of 1685, the regiments were summoned back to England to assist James in crushing Monmouth's rebellion; in "Fidelia alone lamenting her parents lately dead, and her relations gone into the west against Monmoth," Fidelia fearfully imagines her "aged Uncles dying groans" and "his grandson's shattered bones," as well as "a cousin wounded, brother dy" (Mag. MS 343, Pt. I, 1). Early in 1688, a Catholic Major William Connock was one of forty officers who voluntarily gave up their commissions in the Anglo-Dutch regiments and returned to England to join newly formed (but short-lived) regiments of foot, composed almost entirely of Roman Catholics, in the pay of Louis XIV (Charles Dalton, ed. *English Army Lists and Commission Registers 1661-1714,* 6 vols. [1892-1904], 2:155 & 2:230). G. S. Gibbons' claim in *Notes and Queries* (see n. 3) that Barker's mother was sister to the Col. William Connock who fought for James II in Ireland cannot be substantiated.

15. John Connock (ca. 1654-1730), of Tweworgy, Cornwall, who gained the seat for Liskeard in 1679, initially supported the Whig side in the Exclusion crisis, voting for the first exclusion bill. He sat also during James II's Parliament, and is known to have accepted the Revolution (Basil Duke Henning, *The History of Parliament: The House of Commons 1660-1690*, 3 vols. [London: Secker & Warburg, 1983], 2:117).

16. See marquis of Ruvigny and Raineval, *The Jacobite Peerage, Baronetage, Knightage, and Grants of Honour* (Edinburgh, 1904), p. 37-38. For the Connock family more generally, see C. S. Gilbert, *An Historical Survey of the County of Cornwall,* 2 vols. (London, 1817-20), 2:79, and John Lambrick Vivian, *The Visitations of the County of Cornwall . . . 1530, 1573, and 1620* (Exeter, 1887), p. 93.

17. "A Farewell to Poetry, with a Long Digression on Anatomy," *Poetical Recreations* (London, 1688), p. 104. Subsequent refs. will be cited parenthetically as PR. Though he spent most of his life in London, Richard Lower was Cornish, born and buried at Tremeer, in the parish of St. Tudy, near Bodmin. His wife, Elizabeth (Billing) Lower, was grandaughter to Elizabeth (Connock) Billing, sister of Captain George Connock (see ns. 14 & 16). Since Lower's mother was also a Billing, he may be been related to his wife, and therefore related to the Connocks and Jane Barker, by blood as well as marriage. See Vivian, *Visitations,* pp. 32, 93, 302.

18. Carol Shiner Wilson, intro., *The Galesia Trilogy and Selected Poems by Jane Barker* (N.Y. & Oxford: Oxford Univ., 1997), p. xviii. The persons filling these positions prior to the disruptions of the Civil War remain unidentified. According to G. E. Aylmer, *The King's Servants: The Civil Service of Charles I, 1625-1642* (London: Routledge & Kegan Paul, 1961), p. 470, the lord keeper's personal staff consisted of two chief secretaries and two other secretaries.

19. The Hearth Tax of 1662 charges "Mr Thos Barker" with four hearths; the returns show thirty households in Blatherwick (PRO [Public Record Office], E179 254/11).

20. Jane was baptised 17 May 1652. A son George was baptized 8 Oct. 1648 and buried five months later, on 18 Mar. 1649. Edward, the oldest known surviving son, was baptized 16 Apr. 1650; Henry on 31 July 1655 (NRO [Northamptonshire Record Office], Blatherwick Parish Register, 1621-1689 [Blatherwycke 34 P/1]).

21. Frank T. Melton, *Sir Robert Clayton and the Origins of English Deposit Banking, 1658-1685* (Cambridge: Cambridge Univ., 1986), p. 5.

22. Melton, p. 74. Melton briefly discusses Barker's services on Clayton's behalf, calling him Clayton's "commissioner" (p. 80). The bond is in the Osborn Collection, Clayton Papers (1589-1664), Yale Univ. Beinecke Library. Additional information about Thomas Barker's relationship with Sir Robert Clayton may turn up. Among the many lots of Clayton corre-

spondence sold at Sotheby's on 20 Mar. 1940 was an autograph letter signed by Thomas Barker dated 1660, lot 699, sold to Maggs (for someone designated "Ry") and now unlocated. For an account of the vast and widely dispersed Clayton archives, see Frank T. Melton, "The Clayton Papers," *Bulletin of the Institute of Historical Research* 52 (May 1979): 91-99.

23. A covenant not to assign the lease without written permission of the owner, John Cecil, fourth earl of Exeter, dated 30 Aug. 1662 and signed by Thomas Barker, is preserved among other estate papers at Burghley House, Ex 62/74. We are grateful to Lady Victoria Leatham for granting access to the Burghley Archives and to Felix Pryor for his generous help in locating and interpreting relevant documents.

24. PRO, E179 140/754. Five hearths would place the Barker household just below the gentry level; of the eighteen or so households in Wilsthorpe, most had one or two hearths. Thomas appears again in the Wilsthorpe hearth tax records in 1670 (PRO, E 179 [140/791]); in 1672 he was a signatory in the bishop's transcripts of the parish register of Gretford-cum-Wilsthorp.

25. Charles J. Robinson, ed., *A Register of the Scholars Admitted into Merchant Taylors' School, From A.D. 1562 to 1874,* 2 vols. (Lewes: Farncombe & Co., 1882-83), 1:264; E. P. Hart, ed., *Merchant Taylors' School Register 1561-1934,* 2 vols. (London & Reading: for the Merchant Taylors' Co., 1936).

26. The Subscription Register, SP 41, Oxford Univ. Archives shows his signature for 3 July 1668 next to an entry that reads, "Edwardus Barker e Coll: Di: Jo: Bapt: gen: filius." It is the only example of Edward's hand known to survive.

27. Joseph Foster, *Alumni Oxonienses: The Members of the University of Oxford, 1500-1714,* 4 vols. (Nendeln/Liechtenstein: Kraus Reprint, 1968), 1:70.

28. These studentships did not carry the obligation to enter holy orders. We are grateful to Mark Curthoys, archivist of Christ Church, for this suggestion. He adds, however, that there is no indication of Edward's having been nominated to a studentship among the "extremely sparse" records surviving from the mid-17th century. The fictionalized brother in the Galesia narratives is said to have studied medicine in Paris and the Univ. of Leiden (PWS, p. 2; BG, p. 23). Edward's name does not appear in R. W. Innes Smith's thorough *English-Speaking Students of Medicine at the University of Leyden* (London & Edinburgh: Oliver & Boyd, 1932), though it is possible he may have studied there informally. We have not examined the records of the Univ. of Paris.

29. Joseph Foster, ed., *The Register of Admissions to Gray's Inn, 1521-1889* (London: Hansard, 1889), p. 309.

30. The lease, drawn up between Thomas Barker and John Cecil, fourth earl of Exeter, is dated 2 Dec. 1675 (NRO, S[T] 674).

31. In PWS Galesia describes herself as "little more than Twenty" when her brother died (p. 27).

32. For more on Newton and the Cambridge circle, see Kathryn R. King, "Jane Barker, Poetical Recreations, and the Sociable Text," *ELH* 61 (1994): 551-70.

33. "Edmund Curll, Mrs. Jane Barker, and the English Novel," *Philological Quarterly* 37 (1958): 389.

34. The registered copy of the will is in the PRO, PROB 11/367; the original, signed by Thomas and possibly bearing his seal, is PROB 10/1124.

35. Thomas Barker's burial is recorded in the register of the neighboring parish of Croyden-cum-Clopton. The Shingay chapel was later pulled down.

36. When she revised the poem ("To my brother, on my frequent writing to him, a sort of borlesk") for the Mag. MS, *"Shin-gay,"* was changed to "Willsthorp." The man playfully named "brother," elsewhere identified as George P., remains untraced.

37. Galesia recalls "that I had the real Affliction of losing my dear and indulgent Father; and so was left the only Consolation of my widow'd Mother. I shall not mention the Grief, Care, and Trouble which attended this great Change; these Things being natural and known to every-body" (p. 39).

38. The manuscript poem "Fidelia alone lamenting her parents lately dead, and her relations gone into the west against Monmoth" may contain a reference to Henry: "I see a cousin wounded, brother dy" (Mag. MS, Pt. I, 1). If read literally, the reference places Henry at the Battle of Sedgemoor; it is possible she is fictionalizing, however.

39. A Latin court roll dated 6 Oct. 1670 held at the NRO (LB 35) indicates that Thomas Barker was then admitted tenant to property (mainly arable and meadow land) in the manor of King's Cliffe that had previously been conditionally surrendered to him by two copyhold tenants, as security for loans of £144 4s. and £61 18s. Curiously, he is identified as "situate in Blatherwick in the county of Northampton." Our thanks to Peter Beal for locating this document, and to Mrs. J. A. Minchinton for translating and helping us to interpret it.

40. The will at once glosses and obliquely confirms Galesia's statement: after her "Affairs [were] adjusted," following her father's death, the "World knew what Fortune I had to depend upon, and that in my own Power" (PWS, p. 40).

41. Peter Earle, *The Making of the English Middle Class: Business, Society and Family Life in London 1660-1730* (London: Methuen, 1989), pp. 6-7. According to Alan Everitt, large numbers of Northamptonshire

younger sons "became merchants, goldsmiths, grocers, stationers, chandlers, ironmongers, or gunsmiths; whilst their numerous daughters more frequently married London merchants than local Northamptonshire gentry" ("Social Mobility in Early Modern England," *Past & Present* 33 [1966]: 68).

42. Lambeth Palace Library, Faculty Office Marriage Allegations. According to the International Genealogical Index, an Anne Phipps, daughter of William and Katherine Phipps, was christened 18 Nov. 1660 in Holburn St. Andrew.

43. Society of Genealogists, Boyd's Marriage Index.

44. Henry was a rated occupier of the parish's second precinct; see the Christchurch Poor Rate Ledger, Guildhall Library, MS 9, 163. He also appears during these years in the Farringdon Ward Within Assessments in the Corporation of London Record Office; see, for example, Assessment Box 7, MS 7 (6 Months Tax for 1680).

45. A daughter Catharine, of whom no more is heard, was christened in Christchurch Newgate Street parish on 8 Apr. 1680 (Willoughby A. Littledale, ed., *The Registers of Christ Church, Newgate, 1538 to 1754*, Harleian Society, vol. 21 [London: Harleian Society, 1895], p. 49). The parish register was destroyed in World War II.

46. She was born 21 Dec. 1687 and christened 9 Jan. 1688 in St. Giles Cripplegate (Guildhall Library, St. Giles without Cripplegate General Register, MS 6419/10).

47. Fathers seldom left land to daughters when they had sons. Of 41 cases in Lincoln-shire and Sussex studied by Amy Louise Erickson (*Women and Property in Early Modern England* [London & N.Y.: Routledge, 1993]), only two left land to daughters (p. 61). The fact that Jane and her mother were named coexecutors was not unusual, however. In "appointing executors from among their children," she finds, "both married men and widowers were more than twice as likely to choose daughters or youngers sons, or a combination thereof, in preference to the heir" (p. 71).

48. Guildhall Library, St. Giles without Cripplegate General Register, MS 6419/10.

49. According to Bridget Hill, "upper servant" positions—waiting women, ladies' maids, and companions—were "to be occupied only by those of genteel upbringing who had enjoyed a 'polite education'" (*Women, Work, and Sexual Politics in Eighteenth-Century England* [Oxford: Basil Blackwell, 1989], p. 132).

50. Barbara Todd, letter of 30 Aug. 1995.

51. See J. C. H. Aveling, *The Handle and the Axe: The Catholic Recusants in England from Reformation to Emancipation* (London: Blond & Briggs, 1976), esp. pp. 240-45.

52. The same Christchurch Poor Ledgers (Guildhall Library, MS 9, 163) that record Henry's presence in Christchurch parish for the years 1682 through 1685 record the presence of a "Widow Barker" and, for 1684 and 1685, a "Mdm Barker" as well. No female Barkers appear in subsequent years. According to *The Registers of Christ Church, Newgate* on 24 Apr. 1685, an Ann Barker was buried in the parish (Harl. Soc. 21, p. 299). It is impossible to be certain that the "Widow Barker" who paid the poor rate between 1682 and 1685 and the Ann Barker who died in 1685 are the same person, or that either or both are Jane Barker's mother; but their identity is consistent with Barker's fictional account of Galesia's removal to London with her mother. The only difference is that the novel places them within sight of Westminster Abbey (St. Margaret's parish, Westminster). The St. Margaret's Overseers Accounts for 1685 (Westminster Archives, E193) names a "Madame Barker" as a rated occupier of Ship Yard in Petite France. There is no record of the death of an Anne Barker in the St. Margaret's parish register.

53. PR, Pt. II, p. 180. The poem is "On His Secret Passion for Cosmelia."

54. The advertisement appears in the anonymous *Delightful and Ingenious Novels: Being Choice and Excellent Stories of Amours, Tragical and Comical* (1685).

55. See esp. "Fidelia having seen the Convent at St. James's," "Fidelia and her friend on her becoming a Catholick," and "Fidelia arguing with her self on the difficulty of finding the true Religion." In the last she concludes her spiritual struggle with a resolution to reject all "worldly joys" along with "Benit's sons," that is, the Benedictines, who evidently received her into the Church.

56. She left one highly mythologized account of her own exile and wanderings in "A dialogue between Fidelia and her little nephew, Martius," which depicts Fidelia as driven from her homeland by "curssed Orange": "Thus helpless, friendless, destitute forlorn, / 'Twixt debters, creditors, and lawyers torn, / I wander'd on, in hopes of better chance, / Till curssed Orange drive us all to France, / And here we wander vagabons alone, / Not knowing any, or to any known, / And all methinks do our acquaintance shun. / But honour, conscience, vertue brought us here, / We cannot sink, since they the vessel steer" (Mag. MS, Pt. II, 27v).

57. "To His Royal Highness the Prince of Wales, on His birth day 1689: or 99: The author having presented him a Calvary set in a vinyard" (Mag. MS 343, Pt. II, 40-41v).

58. BL Add. MS 21,621. A group of twenty "Poems Refering to the times" arranged to tell the story of the trials of the Stuarts and their followers from the accession of James II to the defeat of his troops in Ireland in 1691 (followed by a joyful coda occa-

sioned by events in Nov. 1700), they were prepared at Barker's direction for presentation to the prince by way of wishing him "a happy new Century."

59. 29 Jan. 1691 (*The Parochial Registers of St. Germain-en-Laye: Jacobite Extracts of Births Marriages and Deaths,* ed. C. E. Lart, 2 vols. [London: St. Catherine, 1910-12], 1:137).

60. Paul Hopkins (letter of 18 June 1995) informs us that Brent was head of the commission of "regulators" who in 1687-88 attempted to pack Parliament in a pro-Catholic direction.

61. "At the sight of the body of Our late gracious sovereign Lord King James As it lys at the English Monks" (Mag. MS 343, Pt. II, 20-21v) appears with only a few significant variants in BL Add. MS. 10, 118, ff. 410v-411, a history of James drafted by the Benedictine monks in Paris. "A rough first draught of the History of England's late . . . King James II" (1706) is attributed in the BL catalog to Joseph Johnston, prior of the English Benedictines of St. Edmund in Paris; but Dom Geoffrey Scott identifies the author as Ralph Benet Weldon, one of Johnston's monks (*"Sacredness of Majesty": The English Benedictines and the Cult of King James II,* Royal Stuart Papers 23 [Huntingdon: Royal Stuart Soc., 1984], pp. 5-6).

62. BL Add. MS 21,621. A modern pencil note beneath the bookplate identifies the arms represented in it as those of Armand-Louis du Plessis-Richelieu, the duc d'Aiguillon (1683-1750). In fact the dual arms are those of his wife, after their marriage in 1718. The volume was later sold for 19s. at Sothebys, on 21 Nov. 1856, lot 255, described in the catalog as belonging to a library formed by a collector "during his residence abroad."

63. The note beside "To Her Majesty the Queen, on the Kings going to Callis this carnival 1696" indicates her eyes were then "bound doun" as a result of a cataract operation. King James was in Calais by 7 Mar. (Historical Manuscripts Commission, *Calendar of the Stuart Papers,* 7 vols. [London: HMSO, 1902], 1:113).

64. Mag. MS 343. The dedication (from late 1700) opens with a reference to "blindness and misfortunes"; a preface (also from late 1700) attributes "slips of the pen, and defects in the English" to "long absence and blindness"; an undated preface "to the Reader" (probably no later than 1704) asks that the poems be "consider'd as the work of a blind person."

65. The information in this paragraph comes from a statement submitted by the defendants (PRO, C11 237/28).

66. Records of this case are in the PRO. We are indebted to Carol Shiner Wilson for uncovering the Statons' undated answer, which is now bound with Jane Barker's bill of complaint, dated 10 July 1717, in C11/237/28. The court's order in response to Barker's Bill is recorded in an entry for 23 July 1717 in Chancery Decrees and Orders (C33/327 f. 382); the court's response to the Staton answer dated 6 Aug. 1717 is recorded in C33/329 f. 23.

67. According to her Chancery statement, at the age of "seventeen" she was living with and maintained by her father.

68. William Henson was christened 12 Nov. 1675, according to the International Genealogical Index. In 1709, the year before he died, he was churchwarden of the Carlby parish (LAO [Lincolnshire Archive Office], Ch. P. 1709, Box 4/14b). William appears to have been the eldest son of Robert Henson of Carlby, yeoman, and Ann Figge, of Wilsthorpe, who married in 1672 (LAO, Gretford-cum-Wilsthorp parish register). In 1683 Robert was named one of the constables of the wapentake of Ness (LAO, Kestevan Session Bundle 49). He died in Feb. 1706, leaving his estate to his wife, whom he named his sole executrix, providing that she pay off all his debts and "save harmless & indemnified my son William Henson from a bond for five pound in which he is bound with me to the Overseers of the Poor of Carlby" (LAO, LCC Will 1707/141). Robert's signature to the will, dated 1 Jan. 1705, suggests the barest ability to write.

69. An inventory of his goods preserved in the Lincolnshire Archives estimates the value of his estate at the time of his death as £101 14s. 8d. (LAO, LCC Admon 1710/62). It shows him possessing, in addition to household goods, considerable livestock (including horses, eleven head of cattle, fifteen pigs, and over a hundred sheep), and twenty-one acres of land, at least seven of them arable. This would place him somewhat below the level of a substantial yeoman. David Cressy found that the mean probate estate of an English yeoman in 1640 was £195 (*Coming Over: Migration and Communication Between England and New England in the Seventeenth Century* [Cambridge: Cambridge Univ., 1987], p. 121).

70. There is irony in Staton's coming from Irnham. This village, some eleven or twelve miles north of Stamford (and about the same distance from Wilsthorpe), was site of the highest concentration of Roman Catholics in Lincolnshire, though Staton was not one of them, and in the 17th century a hotbed for Roman Catholic women writers. See the Thimelby entries in Virginia Blain, Isobel Grundy, and Patricia Clements, *The Feminist Companion to Literature in English: Women Writers from the Middle Ages to the Present* (New Haven & London: Yale Univ., 1990). It is likely Barker would have attended mass at the chapel at Irnham Hall, home of the Thimelby family. The Compton Census of 1676 shows 149 recusants over the age of sixteen in Kesteven; fifty-six were in Irnham, with a total population of only 137. Wilsthorpe, with a population of 95 in 1665 (based

upon the Hearth Tax Return), had none. See Appendix A of vol. 25 of The Publications of the Lincoln Record Society, esp. p. cxxxiii. For the Compton Census, see Anne Whiteman, ed., *The Compton Census of 1676: A Critical Edition,* Records of Social and Economic History n.s. 10 (London: Oxford Univ. for The British Academy, 1986).

71. No trace of the Henson girls beyond 1717 has been found.

72. The summons, from July 1717, appears to be all that has survived from the Staton proceedings in the Kesteven Quarter Sessions (LAO, Kesteven Sessions Bundles, 1717, KQS A/2/32).

73. According to Erickson (see n. 47), in the 17th century *The Country-Man's Counsellor* reckoned the cost of an injunction to stay proceedings at £1s. 6d. (p. 117).

74. The Lincolnshire Archives Office holds two documents relating to Barker's registration of her estate. "Schedules and Letters of Attorney, 1717" is a statement she prepared (although not in her own hand) describing her estate; it bears her signature. "Kesteven Quarter Sessions. Papists' Estates. Rolls. 1717," also bearing her signature, is an official enrollment of the information provided above. The same information is recorded in documents in the PRO: FEC 1/1200 (Abstracts of Papists Estates) and FEC 1/1201 (Returns). The LAO "Schedules" document, in what is surely a scribal error, refers to Barker as a "Widow." The only reference to her as something other than "spinster" on any official record, it is corrected on the "Rolls" document.

75. That is, she holds land subject to a rent of £22 12s. 4d. (as it was in her father's time) by virtue of a lease from the earl of Exeter, deceased, made to her father, gentleman, from 22 Dec. 1675 for 80 years. On this latter point the documentary record is discrepant: the lease preserved in the NRO (S[T]674) is for 99 years and dated 2 Dec. 1675.

76. This corrects the account offered in *Kissing the Rod* (see n. 5), p. 354.

77. For the 1715 statute and registration, see Edgar E. Estcourt and John Orlebar Payne, *The English Catholic Nonjurors of 1715: Being a Summary of the Register of their Estates* (London: Burns & Oates, [1885]).

78. Various biographical entries have Thomas Barker living on a royal grant or pension. Moira Ferguson makes Thomas the recipient of "an annual grant of eighty pounds from Charles I from 1675 onward" (*First Feminists: British Women Writers 1578-1799* [Bloomington: Indiana Univ.; Old Westbury, N.Y.: Feminist Press, 1985], p. 171); Janet Todd implies that Barker was spared the necessity of marrying when "a small income from a royal grant made to her father" gave her the "option of spinsterhood"

(*British Women Writers: A Critical Reference Guide,* ed. Janet Todd [N.Y.: Frederick Ungar/Continuum, 1989], p. 42); John T. Shawcross, in an especially error-ridden account, says of Barker that after 1685 she "continued to live on the inheritance from her father" (*Dictionary of Literary Biography,* vol. 131: *Seventeenth-Century British Nondramatic Poets,* 3rd ser., ed. M. Thomas Hester [Detroit: Bruccoli Clark Layman, 1993], p. 3). Alison Shell's more reliable entry in the recent *Dictionary of National Biography: Missing Persons,* ed., C. S. Nicholls [Oxford Univ., 1993], p. 43) still repeats the story of the fictive royal grant.

79. This error originated with McBurney (see n. 33, p. 390), who claimed on the basis of a misreading of Gibbons (see n. 3) that in 1715 Jane Barker possessed "a small annual income which had been granted to her father, Thomas Barker, for eighty years by Charles I." Gibbons had said that in 1715 Barker had "an estate of annual value £47 10s., which was granted to Thomas Barker, gent., for eighty years from Dec. 2, 1675." Thomas had been granted lease of the Wilsthorpe estate by the earl of Exeter, not the king.

80. Elizabeth Brownlow, daughter of Sir John Brownlow of Belton, Lincs., married John Cecil, sixth earl of Exeter, in 1699 and lived at the family seat, Burghley House, near Wilsthorpe, until her death in Nov. 1723.

81. Barker revised and substantially expanded the dedication for the 2nd edn. of *Bosvil and Galesia,* which appeared in the 2nd vol. of *The Entertaining Novels of Mrs. Jane Barker* (1719). Elizabeth Cecil (1706-33), daughter of the sixth earl of Exeter and Elizabeth Brownlow, married William Aislabie, son and heir of John Aislabie of York, the chancellor of the exchequer, in 1724, soon after her parents' deaths and a few months before her 18th birthday. See Oswald Barron, ed., *Northamptonshire Families. Victoria History of the Counties of England,* 2 vols. (London: Archibald Constable, 1906), 1:35.

82. *The Christian Pilgrimage: Or, A Companion for the Holy Season of Lent* (London: E. Curll & C. Rivington, 1718), pp. ii-iii. The original is evidently an unidentified work by Fénelon, the Archbishop of Cambrai.

83. The Countess was Anne Hatton, second wife of Daniel Finch, second earl of Nottingham, and a kinswoman of the Cecil family (earls of Exeter). Though not herself Roman Catholic, she was reputed to be devoted "to the forms and ceremonies thought to be 'papist' by less rigid Anglicans" (*Poems on Affairs of State: Augustan Satirical Verse, 1660-1714,* ed. William J. Cameron et al., 7 vols. [New Haven & London: Yale Univ., 1963-75], 5:206). It may also be relevant that two years earlier, in 1716, her husband was dismissed from office when he tried unsuccessfully to dissuade King George I from executing the Scottish lords captured in the 1715 Jacobite rising.

84. BL Stowe 232, f. 93. In 1718 a Secret Office was established to open, search, and reseal all foreign correspondence. For more on the anti-Jacobite intelligence system, see Paul S. Fritz, *The English Ministers and Jacobitism between the Rebellions of 1715 and 1745* (Toronto & Buffalo: Univ. of Toronto, 1975), esp. pp. 51-58.

85. Though Barker appears on the title page of *A Patch-Work Screen* (1723) as "of Wilsthrop," the preface, dated Candlemas Day, 1722/3, i.e., 2 Feb. 1723, places her in Richmond. The preface to *The Lining of the Patch Work Screen* (1726), gives no place. Barker may have left Wilsthorpe after 1717, perhaps to reside in London or its outskirts, or even to return to St. Germain. Timon Connock, the son of Barker's cousin William, wrote in 1720 to Brigadier John Hay (later titular earl of Inverness) in Rome, thanking him for his kindness to Timon's "poor Ant," but described himself as "very much mortifyed [that] shee has taken the desperate resolution to go so far to starve," wishing that she had remained at St Germain (Windsor Castle, Royal Archives, Stuart Papers 46/14). If indeed Barker is the "poor Ant" of this letter, this would indicate she traveled to St. Germain and then on to Rome at this time. We are grateful to Edward Corp for bringing the Connock letter to our attention.

86. Hutcheson (ca. 1659-1740)—lawyer, economist, and maverick Whig M.P.—was Ormonde's "man of business" after he went into exile (Romney Sedgwick, ed., *The History of Parliament: The House of Commons 1715-54*, 2 vols. [London: HMSO, 1970], 2:163).

87. According to Sedgwick the parliamentary session ran until 21 Mar. in 1718.

88. The original reads: "Il y a longtems que nous sommes sans lettres de vous. m r. Hutchesson vous est fort devoüé. Il a honte de ses et Erreurs passèes, Et il les desavoüe publiquement, Plusieurs de ses amis qui n'ont pas essè des vostres se rangent à present à vostre party, le nombre de vos amis s'augmente tous les jours. Ils souhaitent fort de vous voir avec vostre jeune Amy, et qu'il puisse deposseder ceux qui luy retiennent injustem[ant] son bien; Car il est bien triste de le voir ainsy errer dans les Païs estrangers. mais je dois vous dire que si vous voulez trouver icy des maisons à bon marché, il y faut venir apres la fin de la session du parlem[ent], lors que chacun va à la Campagne. je ne vous conseilleray jamais de venir pendant la session tout estant alors trop cher." Our thanks to Lindsay Kaplan for assisting with the translation.

89. John Menzies, a London-based Jacobite intelligence agent, reported in a letter of 28 Feb. 1718 to Lewis Innes that "Mr. Hu[t]chi[n]son, a great friend personally to the late D[uke] of Orm[onde] from whom he had received signal obligations" is "at present a mal-content, for he was not enough considered, and so sides highly with the Prince." Previously he had been "a mighty man for the Government" (Historical Manuscripts Commission, *Calendar of the Stuart Papers*, 7 vols. [London: HMSO, 1912], 5:524).

90. A letterbook of the duke of Ormonde in the British Library, Add. MS 33,950, contains copies of eighteen letters written by Ormonde in 1719 to Sir Timon Connock, son of Barker's cousin William. On 20 May 1720, Timon wrote from Spain that he expected a visit from "the Duke of O." that night (Royal Archives, Windsor Castle, Stuart Papers 47/3) and in 1732 Timon's widow, Mary, acknowledged to "James III" that the duke of Ormonde was prompted by his "friendship" for Timon to solicit a baronetcy for Timon's father, William, which would devolve to Timon's then-underage son upon William's death (Royal Archives, Windsor Castle, Stuart Papers, 152/81). According to Micheline Kerney Walsh, "Toby Bourke, Ambassador of James III at the Court of Philip V, 1705-13" (*The Stuart Court in Exile and the Jacobites*, ed. Eveline Cruickshanks & Edward Corp [London & Rio Grande: Hambledon, 1995]), Timon [whose name she misspells Simon], figured prominently in Bourke's reports from the Spanish court; he "became brigadier-general, officer of the king's guards, and later governor of the infante, son of Philip V" (p. 151). For more information on the Connocks, see ns. 14 and 16.

91. We are grateful to Paul Hopkins for helping us interpret this document. He observes (in a letter of 18 June 1995) that Barker would hardly be one of those accustomed to receiving letters from Ormonde—"but she might hold the pen for those who did."

92. Royal Archives, Windsor Castle, Stuart Papers 208/129, misdated 1738. The letter is difficult to date. The date reads "Aug 14:73 0." which may mean [17]13 0—the "7" possibly being a 1. Internal evidence suggests, however, that the correct interpretation is [1]730. The letter is reprinted in Henrietta Tayler, *Lady Nithsdale and Her Family* (London, Lindsay Drummond, [1939]), pp. 239-40, misdated 1739 and attributed to an "I. Barker." Tayler thinks it was written to Lady Nithsdale's sister, Mother Lucy Theresa Joseph, Superior of the Augustinian Convent at Bruges, and forwarded by her to Lady Nithsdale in Rome.

93. More than forty miraculous cures occurring through James' intercession were verified as part of a commission to consider James' canonization. Many of the cured were women, and women were active in promoting the canonization effort. The Visitation nuns at Chaillot distributed relics, mostly fragments of cloth that had touched the king's coffin or had been placed under his heart. One Ursuline nun claimed, as Barker did, to have been cured by a rag that had been dipped in the king's blood by officials present at the embalming (Scott, "*Sacredness of Maj-*

esty" [see n. 61], pp. 3-4; correspondence from Dom Scott, 12 May 1986). Most of the attested cures date from 1701 and 1702, but Barker's must have occurred later: her letter indicates that the cure took place "over the space of some years."

94. They may also express the discomforts of writing for money. It is notable that in the fictions Galesia consistently identifies herself as writer with the 17th-century poet Katherine Philips ("Orinda") and the nostalgic world of literary amateurism and virtuous rural retirement over which Orinda symbolically presided. The prefaces are another matter: those to *A Patch-Work Screen* and *Lining* in particular offer richly ambivalent representations of "Jane Baker"—another of the author's fashioned self-images—as marketplace professional.

95. Jane Spencer, *The Rise of the Woman Novelist: From Aphra Behn to Jane Austen* (Oxford & N.Y.: Basil Blackwell, 1986), p. 42. An earlier and no less influential formulation of this view is found in John Richetti's characterization of Barker as maker of "pious polemics" whose work represents a "deliberate attempt to sell female fiction to a wider audience by making it impeccably respectable" (*Popular Fiction Before Richardson: Narrative Patterns: 1700-1739* [1969; Oxford: Clarendon, 1992], p. 239).

96. *Seductive Forms: Women's Amatory Fiction from 1684 to 1740* (Oxford: Clarendon, 1992), p. 3.

97. Some of the most interesting recent work on the relationship between gender and the early novel has stressed the political dimensions of women's amatory fiction. Ballaster is especially good on Behn and Manley; for another view of Manley, see Paula McDowell, *The Women of Grub Street: Press, Politics and Gender in the London Literary Marketplace 1678-1730* (Oxford: Clarendon, forthcoming); for suggestive work on Eliza Haywood, see Toni O'Shaughnessy Bowers, "Sex, Lies, and Invisibility: Amatory Fiction from the Restoration to Mid-Century," in *The Columbia History of the British Novel*, ed. John Richetti (N.Y.: Columbia Univ., 1994). We would like to see a downgrading of the status of "scandal" in their work so as to permit us to see the shared political commitments that link these writers and their so-called decorous or "Orindan" counterparts.

Toni Bowers (essay date 1997)

SOURCE: Bowers, Toni. "Jacobite Difference and the Poetry of Jane Barker." *ELH* 64, no. 4 (winter 1997): 857-69.

[*In the following essay, Bowers examines the poetry of Barker, a staunch Jacobite, to argue against the myth of Jacobite certainty, as the poet shows disappointment, uncertainty, and dark regret in her political choices despite her loyalty to the royalist cause.*]

The more I learn about the partisan politics of Augustan England, the more difficult it becomes to trust what once seemed stable points of demarcation among the categories of players, and especially between Jacobites and Tories. "Tory" and "Jacobite" once seemed clearly distinct alternatives. But recent scholarship has complicated this view by arguing that political identities and affiliations were less than exclusive or stable in the century following the fall of King James II in 1688.[1] Augustan English men and women, it turns out, were capable of moving between camps according to shifting circumstance, even of holding dissonant positions simultaneously. Toryism and Jacobitism tend now to be seen as shifting, relational functions rather than fixed identities. The revision is important: it forces us to more complicated and historically nuanced understandings of Augustan culture, and it challenges us to define our investments there.

Despite this advance, unexamined assumptions remain, especially when it comes to our understandings of Jacobitism. My purpose here is to contribute to current explorations into the varieties of sensibility within Jacobitism by drawing attention to one assumption that has remained largely unquestioned throughout the process of revision and by testing that assumption against the work of an important and neglected Jacobite writer, the poet and novelist Jane Barker (1652-1732).

To begin, it seems appropriate to offer some account of how I understand the much-contested terms under discussion. As traditionally understood, "Jacobites" were those who continued to support the monarchical claims of King James II and his male heirs even after the Glorious Revolution of 1688-89, when the king went into exile and Parliament decided to replace him. Jacobites, in this view, are defined as those who accompanied the fallen king in his banishment or who actively plotted and fought for his reinstatement at home; they were uncompromising, unquestioningly loyal, and necessarily Roman Catholic. It has recently been pointed out, however, that this way of defining "Jacobitism" may be unnecessarily rigid: it leaves us unable to recognize Jacobitism as part of the sensibility of the many English men and women who compromised with the new government but who nevertheless continued to feel sympathy and connection with the dethroned king, to regret late seventeenth-century political developments, or to consider their participation in the new regime provisional—those, in short, who withheld full ideological commitment, or whose commitment mutated over time.[2]

And then we have Toryism, hardly a simpler category. Like Jacobites, Tories were royalists who found themselves out of sympathy with the prevailing directions of late seventeenth-century politics and uncomfortable with the implications of dethroning a reigning monarch. They too held staunchly traditionalist views: Tories tended, for instance, to share with Jacobites a belief in the sanctity of hereditary kingship and in the necessary subordination of subjects to the will of the monarch. But as a party, Tories have usually been distinguished from Jacobites by their personal hostility to James II and their commitment to the Anglican Church. Though loyal to the *idea* of divinely ordained, hereditary monarchy, Tories tended to be deeply distrustful of its particular personification in James—distrustful enough to lend support (however anxious and passive) to efforts that eventually dislodged the king in 1689, even though those efforts were profoundly at odds with Tory principles. Because of this, Tories have traditionally been distinguished from Jacobites not only by their religion and detestation of James, but also according to their willingness to compromise. I shall return to this idea in a moment.

Identifying particular individuals as Tory or Jacobite has proven to be a difficult enterprise, not only because people tended to cover their tracks and measure their language, but also because there were many more shades of difference within each category, and indeed within individuals over time, than such classificatory projects presume. Though vocal Tories often represented their party as the bastion of the Anglican Church, for instance, individual Tories were not, in fact, unanimously Anglican or even necessarily Protestant, any more than every Jacobite was Roman Catholic.[3] While it may be true that Tories as a group were revolted by James, it is demonstrably not true that every Jacobite revered him and though many of those who emigrated with King James sacrificed everything rather than compromise ideologically, others who might also fairly be called Jacobites stayed at home, paid taxes, even took the sacraments and oaths necessary for participation in government. There were Jacobites in Parliament, Tory Nonjurors, and many other such hybrids not adequately accounted for by traditional definitions. In short, an individual's religion and/or opinion of King James have proven unreliable as litmus tests for Jacobitism and Toryism.

For this reason, scholars have lately resorted to the third strategy I've mentioned: distinguishing between Tories and Jacobites on the basis of each camp's differing capacity for ideological compromise. The argument, briefly stated, is that Tories inhabited a self-consciously duplicitous position in relation to the fall of the king, but Jacobites operated without such duplicity. Unlike Tories, we have assumed, Jacobites did not compromise ideologically; so whatever else they may have endured after 1689, Jacobites did not suffer the pangs of self-reproach that necessarily characterized Tory existence. So powerful has this assumption grown that it hardly seems worth examining, even among those most alert to differences within Augustan ideological camps. Szechi, for instance, a meticulous and insightful scholar of Jacobitism, takes it for granted that though the price of loyalty was high there was never a question among Jacobites themselves as to whether it was worth paying. "All Jacobites," he declares, "felt themselves to be following the path of rectitude toward a certain end."[4] In contrast to this definitive Jacobite certainty, we have come to believe, stood the troubled Tory position. Whole books have been written about a *specifically Tory* crisis over the dissonant claims of principle and practical survival, but no such crisis has been identified among Jacobites.[5]

But if indeed the effort definitively to separate Jacobites from Tories is as reductive an enterprise as contemporary discussion suggests, if recent reexaminations have revealed not so much fixed and opposed ideological identities as complex, changing political organisms, then one likely result is that Toryism will begin to lose not only its presumed distance from Jacobitism, but also its monopoly on "agony of spirit."[6] Perhaps Jacobites were not immune to the kinds of bitter misgivings and sense of personal compromise we have learned to associate with Tory sensibilities.

The point of making such a suggestion, of course—and indeed the point of the broader reconsiderations of Jacobitism now taking place—is not to reduce Jacobite radicalism or to deny any distinction between Jacobites and Tories. Eighteenth-century English men and women themselves distinguished between Tory and Jacobite ideologies and behaviors; they made personal and political alignments according to those distinctions, and not always from cynical or interested motives. For this reason, we cannot understand Augustan political history, including the writing that forms part of that history, without understanding how Tories and Jacobites defined and distinguished themselves. But what recent scholarship suggests is that these political camps cannot be—and never could be—distinguished simply or finally; the boundaries between Jacobites and Tories in Augustan England, though real enough, were permeable and changing. There can be no single, reliable point of demarcation, not even the contrast between Tory misgivings and Jacobite certainty.

As a first step toward supporting and specifying this suggestion, we might do worse than to listen carefully to the voice of Jane Barker, one of the most dyed-in-the-wool and unequivocal of Jacobites. Having followed James into exile at St. Germains, where she remained until 1704, Barker wrote a number of poems in honor of the exiled king and his queen, Mary of Modena.[7] In 1700, Barker presented her manuscript poems to their son James Edward—the Jacobites' Prince of Wales. In 1701, she was among the loyal mourners at James II's funeral, and commemorated the event with a poem in which she extolled the departed as "Hero, saint, and King."[8] Financially strapped but still loyal to the cause, Barker returned to England a few years later to manage a family farm. There she continued an active Jacobite and a known Roman Catholic. In 1718 she corresponded secretly with the Duke of Ormonde, encouraging a Jacobite invasion. And in 1731, a year before her death, Barker was among those who petitioned Rome for James's canonization. In short, Barker seems to embody the very image of uncompromising Jacobite certainty, to epitomize our stereotype of the convinced and unequivocal Jacobite.

Though a devout Catholic who occasionally retreated to a convent for periods of contemplation, Barker was never a nun. Nor was she a wife, though she seems to have been pursued for many years by at least one suitor. Instead, Barker was at pains to construct herself as a kind of elective poet-virgin: she seems to have considered poetry to be a vocation requiring an almost monastic vow, at once a commitment to virginity and a kind of marriage contract, a sacred and costly calling. Moreover, as is well known, much of Barker's poetry and fiction seem directly autobiographical: her heroine Galesia, who figures in both Barker's poetry and her prose, is clearly based on the poet herself and seems designed to be recognized as such. For Barker more than for most other writers of her generation, then, writing was a process of self-definition, and that definition was largely achieved through three central delineations: single woman, Christian poet, and loyal Jacobite.

For all these reasons, it is especially telling that representations of the Jacobite cause in Barker's poetry, and indications of her own hopes for that cause's success, are by no means confident and unhesitating. On the contrary, many of Barker's most overtly Jacobite poems are charged with anxiety about the outcome of the struggle for the restoration of the Catholic Stuarts, and suggest a level of self-doubt and negative expectation quite different from what we might expect from a Jacobite of her stripe.

Now, not all of Barker's poems display agony of spirit. In the relatively early poem **"To His Royal Highness, the Prince of Wales, on his birth day,"** the tone is bright and confident (292-94).[9] To the dispossessed prince the poet inscribes commonplaces that exemplify the self-righteous optimism Szechi uses to define Jacobitism:

> though cross accidents your merits wrong,
> Tis but like weight to make the arch more strong. . . .
> Then let's rejoyce, sing, love, and with you smile
> Forgeting friends, estates, or native soyle,
> For having you we're here in full content,
> Tis they in England suffer banishment.
>
> (ll. 14-15, 23-26)

Even allowing for an element of wishful thinking and a certain poignant suggestion that the speaker is most of all convincing herself, the upbeat tone of this tribute to the young prince remains palpable—especially when contrasted with the tone of another, slightly later, poem, **"The lovers Elesium, Or Foolls Paradice: a dream"** (320-25). Here, as in Barker's novels, we see a much darker representation of the life of virginity and poetry for which she has "contracted" with the Muses, described in language that invites us to recall the other form of exile this poet has chosen.

The poem's speaker, in a dream, finds herself lost in a "pleasant labrinth" representative of "my fate, / How my lives steps, shou'd be all introcate."[10] Many others also wander in this bizarre, mazelike landscape "strew'd with flaming darts, / Knots, chains, devices, verses, [and] bleeding hearts" (ll. 9-10). The speaker strikes up a conversation with a "gentle youth," only to discover that he is in fact the ghost of a young man who died at the battle of Sedgemore, James II's great military triumph of 1685.[11] The ghost ruefully recalls that he had been fighting on the wrong side of the battle, and for the most predictable of reasons,

> I lov'd . . . a shee false and ingrate:
> Who having promis'd me her faith and love,
> Like all her sex, did most unconstant prove.
> Then to devert my griefs, I took the field,
> And at Sedge-more deservedly was killed.
>
> (ll. 21-25)

Fortunately, however, he came to see the light just before the end: "E'er I dy'd, I did in mercy trust, / I saw my guilt, and pray'd for James the Just" (ll. 26-27).

Together this converted Jacobite shade and the dreamer enter "a statly bower" called Fools' Paradise, a jostling, cacophonous realm between Heaven and Hell where those who made love their religion during life now wander in their own peculiar purgatory.

> All who live here, are given up to folly,
> Some mad with mirth, and some with melancholy
> Some read Romances, some love-letters writ,
> Some curss'd their chain, and some were fond of
>   it. . . .
> All was confusion here, they'd but one rule,
> That none must enter, but must play the fooll. . . .
> I ask'd em, what Religion they had there,
> And if there any priests, or alters were,
> 'Twas answer'd; lovers, to each other pray'd,
> The brightest altar, was the fairest maid.
>
> (ll. 37-40, 61-62, 64-67)

Filled with disdain for such heresy, the speaker is about to leave when "an angry power" snatches her away and makes her climb a "stupendious" mountain from whose peak she views, "ith' retrospect of time," a climactic moment in her own past—"that very place, that seat, that pleasant shade, / Where I a contract, with the muses made" (ll. 75-77). From her present, mature vantage point, the dreamer looks on as her younger self chooses to follow a poetic vocation at the cost of renouncing earthly love and material wealth, and hears again the muses' promises of rewards for her self-denial.

> We will, say they, assist thy flight
> Till thou reach fair Orindas height,
> If thou canst this worlds follys slight.
>
> We'll bring this to our bright aboads,
> Amongst the Heroes, and the Gods
> If thou and wealth, can be at odds,
>
> Then gentle maid, cast off thy chain,
> Which links thee to thy faithless swain,
> And vow a virgin to remain.
>
> Write, write thy vow upon this tree,
> By us it shall recorded be
> And thou fam'd to eternity.
>
> (ll. 91-102)[12]

After the chaotic and heretical scene she has just witnessed, we might expect this review of her long-ago vow to art and chastity to bring the dreamer joy and confirm her feelings of superiority to those in the "foolls Paradice" whose lives (indeed, whose afterlives) are consumed by a foolish pursuit of romantic love. But such is distinctly not the case. Surveying the scene now, the speaker realizes that the promises the Muses made on that long-ago day, promises of glory and eternal fame in exchange for the poet's renunciation of her lover, have turned out to be false. None of the rewards mentioned has materialized for the poet, despite her faithfulness and sacrifice. Though she renounced "all things" for the Muses, the "bough" of poetry has turned out to be, as she observes bitterly, "frutless" (l. 78).

What is more, on the heels of this realization, certainly bad enough, comes the belated revelation that the poet's bargain was doomed from the start. The dreamer's "uncouth guardian"—the "angry power" who snatched her from the fools' paradise to the mountaintop—utters a curse on her idealistic younger self, a curse that, I want to suggest, extends not only to her condition as virgin poet, but also to her position as political exile. "Unluckey maid," the guardian says,

> Since, since thou has the muses chose,
> Hymen and fortune are thy foes,
> Thou shalt have Cassandras fate,
> In all thou sayst unfortunate,
> The god of wit, gave her this curss
> And Fortune gives thee, that and worse,
> In all thou doest, though ne'er so good,
> By all the world misunderstood.
> In best of actions, be dispis'd,
> And foolls and knaves, above thee pris'd. . . .
> Thy youth and fortune, vainly spend,
> And in thy age, have not a friend,
> Thy whole life pass in discontent,
> In want, and wo, and banishment.
>
> (ll. 106-15, 122-25)

"The lovers Elesium," in short, exemplifies what would be a major theme of Barker's work—confusion and disappointment over the choice of renunciation, whether the renunciation of marriage for poetry, or that of her homeland for political and religious principle, both of which have led to thankless "banishment."[13]

A similar connection between Barker's disappointment in poetry and in Jacobitism may be found in an intensely moving poem, **"The Miseries of St. Germains"** (302-7). Staunch Jacobite though she remained, Barker argues here that the devastating famine that plagued the St. Germains court in 1694 and '95 constituted a "curss" (l. 4) on the exiled loyalists, the delayed punishment for generations of blasphemy and pride. (The judgments once "deverted" by the "humility and prayer" of the Ninnevites, she says, "were hoorded up, and executed here" [ll. 10-12].) In the very palace of the court-in-exile, she laments, one encounters not "a courtly throng," but

> poor widows, with their wretched train,
> Crying their parents, were at Achrim slain,
> My husband was at Limerick kill'd says one,
> And mine in prison dy'd at lost Athlone
> My father rais'd a troop, and so lost all,
> And I have prisoner been e'er since the fall
> Of my unhappy friends, and now am come,
> To seek in Flanders, or Savoy a tomb. . . .
> Some with lost armes, and some with leggs of wood,
> Crying they lost those limbs because they stood,
> When others fled, at Boyn's unluckey flood.
>
> (ll. 51-57, 59-61)

Even worse is reserved for the deposed and impoverished King and Queen, who discover—"with what regret, none but themselves can know"—that they have "nought but pitty to bestow" on these faithful petitioners, having lost practical potency with their fiscal supply (ll. 82-83). But worst of all is the condition of the "poor virgins" who, like Barker herself, have both "their fortunes and their lovers lost" for the Cause. These last suffer most for, "though both for the King were lost or slain, / Still modesty forbids them to complain" (ll. 64-67).

What is perhaps most striking about **"The Misery of St. Germains"** in light of **"The lovers Elesium,"** however, is the tolerant spirit it shows toward the foolishness of lovers. What was insupportable "folly" in the first poem is clearly preferable to the miserable returns of faithful stoicism in the second. Taking a final view of the bedraggled court-in-exile, the dreamer laments, in the poem's last lines, that

> Instead of lovers meetings, assignation,
> Ogling, laughing, talking of new fassions,
> Whether this Borgoin lookss best plain or lace'd,
> Which patch the pocket-glass says is best place'd
> which periwigg does which face best befit,
> the cavalier, the bobb, Hispaniolet,
> The only study is, where one shou'd dine,
> At least to get a crust, or glass of wine.
> Thus are we more contemptible by far,
> Then old wives tale, old maid, old cavalier.
>
> (ll. 116-25)

The point is not that old wives, old maids, and old cavaliers are *not* contemptible, but that the starving loyalists, who expected to be blest for high principles, faithfulness, and sacrifice, are more contemptible still. Likewise in **"The lovers Elesium,"** the dreamer shows no hesitation in deriding the foolishness of the amorous inhabitants of lovers' purgatory; but the poem's dark, even cynical, point is merely that the young woman who contracts instead for a life of virtuous renunciation and "banishment" is even more foolish than the lovers.

Perhaps none of Barker's poems more clearly reveals the degree of ambivalence and doubt that could mark the sensibility of a to-the-core Jacobite than another dream poem, **"The Virgins paradise: a dream"** (326-29). This time, Barker's speaker dreams that while flying "above the spheres," she comes to a place of joy not for lovers, but for virgins. Entrance to the palace there requires both humility (the first of seven porches is "arch'd so very low, / that to get in, one very much must bow" [ll. 26-27]) and vows of virgin chastity. Significantly, the latter "choice" is presented here as brutally overdetermined. The veil of virginity is offered by an "old portress" who, according to Barker's own note, represents "the church":

> She told me if I'd not be veil'd by her,
> Nothing so certain but I'd grossly err.
> Not only so, but I shou'd swallow'd be,
> In that three corner'd gulph I there might see,
> Then looking in, I saw the gulph turn round,
> And saw withall I cou'd not scape be'ing drownd,
> Then I resing'd me to her as I ought,
> And through the porches, and the gate was brought.
>
> (ll. 32-39)[14]

Caught between the portress and the deep blue sea, the dreamer "resigns" herself to virginity, with a good grace but something less than a freely willing heart.

After taking the vow to remain a virgin, Barker's speaker is allowed into the palace, where she beholds angels singing in "vast raptures" and "strong extasies," dancing on clouds embroidered with stars. Above the dancers are "curling lambent flames," from which the angels "take importall fire, / When with gods love, they mortall hearts inspire" (ll. 41-51). These "wond'rous joys," however, like the fantastic scene where they take place, are nourished by fountains and springs "made of virgins tears" (l. 54). And the place is decorated with carvings that tell the stories not of rejoicing angels, but of unfortunate women forced unwillingly to remain virgins.

> Amongst whome, Jepthas daughter makes her moans,
> And many who in monesterys dy'd,
> Not for devotion, but their mothers pride.
> Who hide their daughters to hide their own age,
> Mean time spend what shou'd make their marriage.
> Large were the streams, which helpless orphans
>   mourn,
> Betwixt false guardians, and fals Lawyers torne,
> But that stream was the greatest of them all
> Which from balk'd lovers, took original.
>
> (ll. 64-72)

The speaker finds, in other words, a phantasmogorical world of rapture maintained by the misery of defrauded, commodified, and abandoned women whose "choice" to remain virginal is exposed as the result of force.

It is at this point that the connection between virginity, poetry, and Jacobitism becomes explicit. The dreamer, approaching a door "which opens to the virgins Room of state," finds it flanked by banners on which depictions of "heavn's conquest" are embroidered. These represent "Sedge-more fight, and how Gray ran away / How the Kings guards, made there the Rebells bleed"—and realistically, too: "One wou'd have thought the blood ran down indeed" (ll. 92-94). Once again, as in **"The lovers Elesium,"** the reference is to the Battle of Sedgemoor, where the then newly—crowned King James had gloriously defended his throne against Monmouth's rebels. ("How Gray ran away" is Jacobite shorthand for the famous cowardice of Forde Grey, Earl of Werke, the only nobleman to lead troops on Monmouth's side of that rebellion.[15]) For decades, James's rout of the Protestant bastard and his followers held an honored place in Jacobite collective memory: for the exiles at St. Germains, Sedgemoor represented their beleaguered king's defining triumph and the last instance of God's just distribution of rewards to virtue. But that was just the trouble. By the time Barker wrote **"The Virgins paradise,"** the victory at Sedgemoor was long past. Further, it must have seemed more than a little ironic that the Jacobites' most glorious victory had taken place before the Glorious Revolution had even created "Jacobitism" as an oppositional category, and before the long years of misery and privation that category had entailed ever since.

It is perhaps not surprising, then, that although the dreamer genuflects to the story of Sedgemoor as one for which "due thanksgiving" should be made, the tapestry representing the battle holds little interest for her: "All the rest which at that place befell," she says, "I not minded 'cause I knew it well" (ll. 90, 95-96). What interests her more, indeed what she is "longing" for, is final entrance to the "virgins Room of state" (l. 87), where she hopes to glimpse not past but future heavenly conquests. That reassuring glimpse, however, is denied; in the poem's final lines the speaker is rebuffed for the desire to see "what can't enter human thought."

> They briskly shut the door against my face,
> Saying that mortals there cou'd have no place,
> At this repulse, dispite so fill'd my brest,
> That I awak'd, and so lost all the rest.
>
> (ll. 98-102)

The future remains unknown, victory cannot be assured. The speaker is left unsatisfied and alone, an exile even from her own dream of a land of joyful virginity and triumphant Jacobitism. And both virginity and Jacobitism are presented, as in **"The Lovers' Elesium,"** as forced choices made under terrible duress and accompanied by bitterness, banishment, and loss.

Among early eighteenth-century writers, Jane Barker's view of her own poetic vocation was inflected in unique ways by Catholicism and Jacobitism. For Barker, poetry is a sacred calling that requires virginity, poverty, and loyalty to the fallen king. But in the poems I've discussed as in much of the rest of her writing, Barker's language reveals bitterness over the circumstances of that calling, and over the results of "choices" in which she retrospectively feels she had very little choice. Remembering the Muses' promise of poetic grandeur, the older poet is overcome with "grief" (325, l. 128); surveying the ragged supplicants at the court of the impotent king, she concludes that "mutual kindness, mutual griefs create, / As lovers who love most, are most unfortunate" (306, ll. 92-93); and when, longing for reassurance about the future, she finds the door to "the virgins Room of state" shut against her, her heart is so filled with "dispite" that both the rest of the dream and dreamer's own rest are forever "lost" (329, ll. 102-3).

The example of Barker's work provides evidence to undermine scholarship's continued *de facto* subscription to the myth of Jacobite certainty, ideological clarity, and unquenchable optimism, perhaps among the few remaining descriptors still assumed to distinguish reliably between Jacobites and their conscience-stricken Tory contemporaries. Where we might expect an unequivocal celebration of the Jacobite poet's chosen path of poetry and loyalty, we find instead disappointment, uncertainty, and dark regret. In Barker we confront a Jacobite not true to type, at once wholly committed and deeply equivocal. Hers constitutes a discordant voice capable of broadening the current discussion about Jacobitism precisely because it challenges our efforts at making a difference.

Notes

1. The work that most powerfully established this revisionary argument is Geoffrey Holmes's *British Politics in the Age of Anne,* rev. ed. (1967; London: Hambledon, 1987). Holmes's influence has been enormous, and continues to exert itself in recent scholarship. See for example Daniel Szechi, *Jacobitism and Tory Politics, 1710-14* (Edinburgh: John Donald, 1984); Paul Monod, *Jacobitism and the English People, 1688-1788* (Cambridge: Cambridge Univ. Press, 1985), 4-6; J. C. D. Clark, *English Society, 1688-1832* (Cambridge: Cambridge Univ. Press, 1985), *Samuel Johnson: Literature, Religion and English Cultural Politics from the Restoration to Romanticism* (Cambridge: Cambridge Univ. Press, 1994), 6-8, 43-45; and John Cannon, *Samuel Johnson and the Politics of Hanoverian England* (Oxford: Clarendon Press, 1994), 51-52, 62-67.

2. For a recent example of criticism that relies on this kind of complexity within Jacobitism, see Clark. Clark offers a portrait of Johnson as what we might call a "Jacobite Tory" who nevertheless, over the course of his career, went from uneasy accommodation with the Hanoverian solution to a belief in its practical legitimacy.

3. Szechi, 1-3, 35, 53-54. Szechi provides a nuanced understanding of the various competing factions within Jacobitism.

4. Szechi, 53.

5. See G. V. Bennett's *The Tory Crisis in Church and State, 1688-1730* (Oxford: Clarendon, 1975).

6. Bennett, 10.

7. *The Galesia Trilogy and Selected Manuscript Poems of Jane Barker,* ed. Carol Shiner Wilson (New York: Oxford Univ. Press, 1997), xxvi. Hereafter cited parenthetically in the text by page and line number.

8. "At the sight of the body of Our late gracious sovereign Lord King James 2d As it lys at the English Monks" (310).

9. There is some question about the date of this poem. The full title reads, "To His Royal Highness the Prince of Wales, on His birth day 1689: or 99:, The author having presented him a Calvary set in a vineyard." The recipient is James Francis Edward Stuart (1688-1766), later called the Old Pretender, but it is unclear why two dates appear in the title. See Prof. Shiner Wilson's note, 192.

10. "The lovers Elesium, Or foolls Paradece: a dream" (320-325, ll. 2-6).

11. At Sedgemoor, James decisively put down the popular rebellion led by James Scott, Duke of Monmouth (1649-85), Charles II's beloved Protestant bastard. For excellent modern histories of the event, see W. MacDonald Wigfield, *The Monmouth Rebels, 1685* (Somerset: Somerset Record Society, 1985) and David G. Chandler, *Sedgemoor 1685: an account and an anthology* (New York: St. Martin's Press, 1985). Chandler reprints King James II's own account of the battle (110-18); Wigfield includes a contemporary account from the other side, the prison confession of Nathaniel Wade, a soldier who fought with Monmouth (149-71).

12. Orinda is most likely a reference to the poet Katherine Philips (1632-1664), known to contemporaries as "the Matchless Orinda."

13. These lines appear tellingly in Barker's most famous work, *Love Intrigues* (1713). See *Galesia Trilogy,* 25.

14. In addition to the note, Barker identifies this lady iconographically. The portress is "Of looks devine, in wond'rous garments dress'd, / Crowns on her head, and crosses on her brest" (ll. 30-31).

15. A fascinating figure, Grey led one of the most scandalous lives of a scandalous era. Along with other distinctions, he did indeed flee the scene of one battle—though not Sedgemoor—and was the real-life model for the incestuous title character of Aphra Behn's racy political novel, *Love-Letters Between a Nobleman and His Sister* (1684-87).

Kathryn R. King (essay date 1998)

SOURCE: King, Kathryn R. Introduction to *The Poems of Jane Barker: The Magdalen Manuscript,* pp. 1-23. Oxford: Magdalen College, 1998.

[*In the following essay, King claims that the Magdalen manuscript of Barker's poems is particularly important for the glimpse it affords into Barker's writing life and her evolution as a artist; for the light it sheds on seventeenth-*

century English Catholicism, early Jacobitism, spiritual autobiography, and women's writing; and for the oppositions it discloses between public/private and political/ domestic in writings about politics and affairs of state.]

The Magdalen Manuscript and its Significance

One of the most important, and intriguing, figures to emerge in the current recovery of early women writers is Jane Barker (1652-1732), of Wilsthorpe, Lincolnshire. Barker was the author of three partly autobiographical novels (1713-26) and a politically encoded romance (1715), as well as a translation of a long devotional work by Fénelon (1718); and she led a long, active, and diverse life as a gentlewoman leaseholder and sometime farm manager, a London medical practitioner, a convert to Roman Catholicism, and a fervent Jacobite supporter who followed the Court of James II into exile at St Germain and continued throughout her life actively to support the Stuart cause. She also wrote a substantial body of poems, of which some 118 are known to exist.

By far the most important single text of her poems is MS 343 in Magdalen College, Oxford. This is a 272-page collection of eighty poems prepared directly under her supervision during her residence in St Germain.[1] This source can be supplemented by two other principal known texts of her verse: one, a collection of twenty poems prepared as a New Year's gift to the Prince of Wales in 1700, now in the British Library (Additional MS 21,621);[2] the other, a collection of fifty-three poems printed as Part I of the miscellany *Poetical Recreations* (London, 1688).[3] All twenty of the poems in the BL manuscript are represented in the Magdalen manuscript, as are thirty-two of those printed in 1688. In addition there are versions of some forty poems—seventeen of which are represented in the Magdalen manuscript—scattered throughout the prose fictions.

The eighty poems in the Magdalen manuscript bear a general title-page, 'Poems on several occasions. in three parts', which is preceded by a preface 'to the Reader' asking indulgence for the inclusion of 'a little, idle love poem or so' and followed by a table of contents at the end. Each of the three distinct 'Parts' of the volume has its own title-page, the first preceded by a Dedication to the Prince of Wales and its own preface 'To the Reader'.

Part One, 'Poems Refering to the times', is a group of twenty poems on Roman Catholic and Jacobite themes, some of them composed at St German where Barker resided on the fringes of the Stuart court-in-exile. The poems are arranged to tell the story of the trials of the Stuarts and their followers in the years following the accession of James II in 1685 and to condemn Williamite England for its stupidity, disloyalty, and treachery. Interbraided with this chronicle-cum-excoriation is a conversion narrative in which 'Fidelia', a Roman Catholic persona invented by Barker for these poems (and found nowhere outside the manuscript verse), traces the stages in her awakening to the errors of the Church of England and her embracing of Catholicism. It is this group of twenty poems which, late in 1700, Barker duplicated in a fair copy prepared for presentation to the twelve-year-old Prince of Wales (James Francis Edward Stuart, the Old Pretender) by way of wishing him 'a happy Century' (see further below).

Part Two consists of twenty-seven pieces of verse, chiefly occasional, including elegies on the death in 1700 of John Cecil, fifth Earl of Exeter, and King James II, who died in September 1701.[4] Many of the poems are addressed to people in and around St Germain, including Queen Mary of Modena, Arabella FitzJames (the illegitimate daughter of James II and Arabella Churchill), and Princess Louise Maria, the younger sister of the Prince of Wales. Nearly all the poems in Part Two were written, according to a note in Barker's hand, 'since the author was in France,' that is, since 1689 or so.

Part Three is a selection of thirty-two of the fifty-three poems that had been printed in 1688 as Part I of *Poetical Recreations,* where, according to a note in Barker's hand, they had appeared 'without her consent'. They are 'now corrected by her own hand'. Many are indeed substantially altered.

The hitherto little-studied Magdalen manuscript of Barker's poems is of considerable interest to students of English Catholicism, Jacobitism in its early phases, and spiritual autobiography, as well as students of women's writing. By any reckoning, the manuscript represents a remarkably large and varied body of poetry by a woman in the late seventeenth century, and the revisions alone provide a wealth of materials for investigation of women's poetic practices at this time. The collection is an extremely important source for investigation of a woman's role, and the role of manuscript exchange, within different writing communities, two of which can be partly reconstructed: a Cambridge poetic-exchange coterie of the 1680s (Part Three) and an exiled Jacobite community in France in the 1690s (Parts One and Two). We can watch Barker-the-poet evolve from an occasional versifier engaged in witty and sometimes high-spirited exchange with a circle of young men into a writer of fiercely partisan religio-political verse written, during the decade or so following the trauma of 1688-89, to strengthen bonds within an inward-looking minority community proudly aware of its oppositionality. The collection contains, then, two quite distinct bodies of coterie verse illustrative of both the sociable and the communal functions of such poetry. The strenuous engagement with politics and affairs of state that is so marked a feature of much of this verse deserves close study, not least because it calls into question the oppositions between public and private, political and domestic that are commonplace in many accounts of women's literary history.

The Magdalen manuscript is also an indispensable source of biographical information about Jane Barker herself, casting light on a period of her life—from the mid-1680s through roughly the turn of the century—for which very little documentary evidence exists. Barker is not named in the surviving lists of the court-in-exile, and, save a single appearance in 1691 in the parish register (as witness to a christening), the Magdalen manuscript is our only record of her life in St Germain at this time. From it we learn of her conversion to Catholicism, her association with the Benedictines, her flight to France, her attachment to the Connock relations who fought for James in Ireland, her failing eyesight, and her operation in 1696 for cataracts. We sense something of the way Barker used verse to bring notice to herself within the community at St Germain, as well.

The discussion that follows looks at features of the Magdalen manuscript as they enable us to reconstruct some of the history of the volume and its place in Barker's writing life. For now it may be noted that the volume, which appears to have begun as a kind of personal poetic archive, became in time a working manuscript, subject to fresh revision. As such it affords a rare glimpse of an early modern woman writer actually at work. On the heavily marked, sometimes sloppy pages of the Magdalen manuscript we can watch Barker modernizing her spelling (sensitive, perhaps, to the ridicule routinely heaped on female orthography), adjusting her word choices, adding fresh lines in her clear but quirky hand, spilling ink, and smudging the pages—and leaving, midway through the volume, her fingerprint.

There is always something moving about the traces of a writer in the act of composing, but it is especially evocative to come upon this fingerprint: a trace, in ink, of the material body, possibly of the writing hand. And when we discover that the poet who left this imprint was nearly blind and almost certainly obliged to peer at these pages through a crude magnifying glass, her eye close to the paper, the poignancy sharpens. That fingerprint is a reminder of how awkward the physical process of writing must have been for Barker, who, stubbornly insistent, continued writing all the same. It is also a fitting emblem of a woman whose sense of her own singularity was always acute and whose desire to see her life and work honoured, if only within the covers of a personal manuscript volume, was one of the forces motivating all of her writing. It is a pleasure to reproduce the fingerprint here three hundred years later.

THE MANUSCRIPT: PHYSICAL DESCRIPTION AND PROVENANCE

The Magdalen manuscript is a quarto volume comprising 136 leaves in all (each measuring *c.* 220 × 159 mm), with seven remaining stubs at various points denoting leaves excised, probably by Barker herself to eliminate botched copy. It is bound in contemporary calf (measuring *c.* 227 × 171 mm), its spine decorated in gilt in compartments. All the leaves save a few versos are filled with writing except for a single leaf (fol. 133) where the title only of a poem already copied in the volume was entered by mistake and

then cancelled. It appears that Part One was originally bound, after writing, perhaps as a separate volume, but was later disbound and amalgamated with Parts Two and Three, at which time Barker inserted a preface (fol. 1), general title-page (fol. 2), and a title-page to Part One (fol. 7) and gave the whole a table of contents at the end, making what might have been two (or three) separate collections of verse into a fresh unified volume.

The handwriting in the Magdalen manuscript has never been described accurately. The brief account in the pioneering anthology *Kissing the Rod* (1988) has the volume written entirely in Barker's hand (p. 354). There can be no doubt it is in two hands, however, G. S. Gibbons, describing the manuscript in the 1920s,[5] notices that the first part was 'written in a stronger, different hand to the rest of the book', but incorrectly assigns the writing of Part One to Barker herself, speculating that failing eyesight may have required her to turn to an amanuensis. The conjecture is reasonable given several internal references to the author's 'blindness', but from manuscript sources unknown to Gibbons, it is now possible not only to confirm the presence of two hands in the Magdalen manuscript, but also to establish their correct identity.

One is certainly that of Jane Barker herself. She is entirely responsible—not for Part One, as Gibbons supposed—but for Parts Two and Three. In addition, in Part One, written chiefly by an amanuensis, she makes the occasional small revision in her own hand (ranging from a single word to a whole line), and, in two instances, copies or rewrites substantial passages of eight lines or more. The identification of her hand can be confirmed chiefly by comparison with the one extant letter written and signed by Barker, dating probably from 1730, now preserved among the Stuart Papers in the Royal Archives at Windsor Castle.[6]

The second hand is the 'stronger' one responsible for Part One. This is the amanuensis also responsible for BL Add. MS 21,621, the quarto volume prepared by Barker (possibly) for presentation to the Prince of Wales on 1 January 1701. The BL manuscript is entirely in the hand of the amanuensis, except for some five small alterations in Barker's hand, including expansions of two titles and three single-word additions, such as that on fol. 35, where the word *nam'd,* partly lost in the binder's cropping, has been replaced above the line in her clumsy hand.[7] All the evidence suggests that BL Add. MS 21,621 was prepared under Barker's supervision.

The amanuensis can now be identified as her cousin William Connock. His clear, upright, distinctive, rounded script can be found in three letters from 1726-27, now in the British Library as part of Add. MS 21,896, fols. 1, 5, 11. William Connock appears to have been a distinguished figure at St Germain. He was created a baronet by James 'III' in 1732 and, according to the parish register recording his death in December 1738 at the age of eighty-nine, he had been an infantry colonel who served with Sir Toby Bourke's regiment in the Nine Years War.[8] From Barker's verse it would appear that her 'dear cosen' had also fought for James in Ireland, seeing action at the siege of Limerick in August 1690 (see, in Part Two, **'To My dear cosen Coll—at his return out of Ireland into france',** which claims that 'the bold Rebells, did at Limerick fall / By Connocks battery, rais'd within the wall'). The scant evidence to survive suggests that the cousins had been close. Our two last glimpses of Barker in England before her final removal to St Germain come from a pair of letters written by William to his son Timon (the 'little Martius' of the Magdalen verse). On 14 January 1726 William reports receiving word that 'Cos. Barker' was 'very ill & had receivd the Blessed Sacrament'. On 26 May 1727 she is said to be on her way to France: 'I expect every day a letter from Cosin Barker of her beeing arived at Diep' (Add. MS 21, 896, fols. 1, 11ᵛ).

Gibbons's speculation that failing eyesight prompted Barker to use an amanuensis seems right. The Magdalen manuscript refers in several places to vision problems. The Dedication from late 1700 opens with a reference to 'blindness and misfortunes'; a preface from the same time attributes 'slips of the pen, and defects in the English' to 'long absence and blindness'; an undated preface 'to the Reader' (probably no later than 1704) asks that the poems be 'consider'd as the work of a blind person'. From these references and a marginal note to a 1696 poem in Part Two (**'To Her Majesty the Queen, on the Kings going to Callis this carnival 1696:'**) indicating that her eyes were then 'bound doun' as a result of a cataract operation, we can reconstruct some of the history of the author's deteriorating eyesight. It appears that one or both of her eyes suffered from cataracts and that by 1696, when she was forty-three, her vision was sufficiently poor that she decided to have them couched. Couching was an ancient surgical procedure, dangerous, uncertain, and, to the modern mind at least, intensely distressing to contemplate. A needle was inserted into the eye and then used to work the clouded lens downward out of the line of vision or, in some cases, to cut the lens into small pieces to settle into the bottom of the eye. (It was the middle of the eighteenth century before cataracts would be extracted.) The eyes were anointed with something to prevent infection and then bound up. The procedure has been described as 'painless', but it is hard to believe that the prospect of the cataract needle, even in those less squeamish times, could have been anything but disquieting.

From what we know about the results of this operation, it is probable that Barker would thereafter have good reason to regard herself as 'a blind person'. Assuming that it did not result in full blindness (from sepsis or injury to the eye), a person whose lens had been couched would afterwards be able to read and write, but only barely, and only with the assistance of a powerful magnifying glass. Awareness of this goes a long way towards explaining the sloppy appearance of many pages of Parts Two and Three of the Magdalen manuscript, where ink-blots and smudges, heavy deletions and messy overwriting testify to Barker's difficulties managing pen and ink. Barker's semi-blindness

may also explain some of the peculiarities of her actual handwriting—the large, careful but often quavery letters, for example—and may even account for one of the more eccentric features of her punctuation, namely her tendency to double up terminal punctuation, as in the frequent use of a comma followed by a full-stop (',.'), which might conceivably result from her uncertainty as to whether she had actually used an end-stop or not. Another striking feature of her punctuation is the form of her commas, which are inverted, tailing to the right. It is possible (though this is speculation) that in addition to having vision problems Barker was left-handed, but, as was common in her time, had been constrained by her childhood teachers to write with her right hand—hence the occasional unwitting aberration, which went, as it were, visually unchecked.

The actual presentation copy to the Prince, which Part One of the Magdalen manuscript closely duplicates, must have been ready in late December 1700 or very early in January 1701, for the Dedication wishes the Prince 'not only a happy new year, but a happy new Century', the century commencing in January 1701 (according to the New Style calendar in use in France). Moreover, the reference to the 'coming Felicity' that follows in the Dedication alludes to what Barker and other Jacobites hoped—devoutly but, as it proved, wrongly—would be a Stuart restoration.⁹ Jacobite hopes were soon quashed: in June 1701 the Act of Settlement established the Hanoverian succession.

Nevertheless, it is impossible to date the writing of Part One of the Magdalen manuscript with precision or even to be certain of its relationship to the actual presentation copy. Indeed, even the general assumption that the volume in the British Library is the one actually presented to the Prince admits of doubts. That BL Add. 21,621 was the presentation copy itself has marginal support from the French provenance of the manuscript, since it came into the library of the Duchesse d'Aiguillon, a French noblewoman of considerable eminence (see n. 2), though of course it might have shared the same distinguished provenance had it been retained by another highly placed member of the exile community. That it was instead either a prototype or a retained copy of the presentation copy has some support from its imperfect nature, for it includes two sections on inserted leaves subsequently bound-in (as an afterthought or replacement), a thin layer of additions, the cropping of some words too close to the margins, and a few lines whited out—the effect of which, taken together, is to leave open the possibility that the BL manuscript was not quite of sufficiently prestigious a standard to be the manuscript actually given to the heir of the Stuart throne.

Whatever its relationship to BL Add. 21,621 and whatever its original purpose—whether for circulation among the St Germain exiles or for Barker's private use—Part One of the Magdalen manuscript became in time a working book. She returned to the verse at some point to make corrections and revisions, adding marginal glosses and explanatory notes as well. The most interesting alteration is the restoration of an 'athe[i]stical' passage omitted from the presentation copy. A marginal note below the restored passage—which is written on a slip of paper literally sewn into place with white silk thread over heavily worked lines—explains that 'these athestical lines were not given to the Prince, but being in the original, they are here incerted'. The lines deemed unsuitable for the Prince accuse providence of almost malignant mismanagement:

> Thus Providence cheats fools, and fool the wise
> Lulling us into stupid letergies,
> Till worthless fools the worthiest men dispise.

> (fol. 36)

In the presentation version, as represented in BL Add. 21,621, the harsh reflection on the workings of providence is softened into a question: 'If Heav'n be just, and good, O tell me then, / Why are the just made preys to wicked men?' (**'Fidelia walking the Lady Abess comes to her,'** fol. 52ᵛ).

The poems in Parts Two and Three were entered by Barker no earlier than 1701. They too were subsequently corrected and revised, in some places quite heavily. It is evident that she came to regard the volume as work-in-progress, for she continued to tinker with the poems in all three parts, many of which would later be printed with yet further revisions in the first two autobiographical fictions, *Love Intrigues* [*LI*] (1713) and *A Patch-Work Screen for the Ladies* [*PWS*] (1723). It is impossible to know when or how often she returned to these copies.

Though Barker's revisions cannot be dated, it is possible, on the basis of internal evidence, to arrive at some probabilities regarding dates of composition. If, as it seems reasonable to assume, she began a poem not long after the event it depicts, then the verse in Part One, which chronicles the misfortunes of the House of Stuart from the Battle of Sedgemoor (1685) to the collapse of the Irish campaign (1691), was composed between 1685 and 1691 or 1692—with one exception. The final poem dates from November 1700, and provides a triumphant coda to a sequence chiefly concerned with rehearsing the 'madness and mallice which concluded the old [century]'. The poem, **'Hell's Regret, for the peace & unity like to ensue the Duke of Anjou's accession to the Crown of Spain,'** gives exaltant voice to the jubilation that broke out in Jacobite quarters early in November, when news reached Paris that the Duke of Anjou had been named successor to the Spanish crown—the death of Carlos II thus affording Barker materials to bring an otherwise surpassingly gloomy sequence to a happy ending. That the poem was an afterthought is evidenced by the fact that it is present in BL Add. 21,621 as an inset, a folio sheet folded into two quarto leaves and bound-in after the main body of verse (fols. 54-55ᵛ).

Internal evidence suggests that the verse in Part Two dates from 1689-1701, which accords with the note in Barker's hand on the title-page saying that most of the Part Two poems were written 'since the author was in France', the word *since* suggesting the author was still in France when she prepared the title-page. This would date the unrevised contents of the volume as a whole to no later than 1704, when Barker is known to have returned to England. The earliest poem in Part Two appears to be a birthday poem addressed to the Prince of Wales (who was born 10 June 1688), entitled **'To His Royal Highness the Prince of Wales, on His birth day i689: or 99.'**—the dates suggesting the possibility that this was composed in 1689 then revised, or updated, for 1699. Corroborating the 1689 date is a marginal note next to a passage about soldiers dying in defence of the Prince saying 'this was writ at the time of the first battell in Ireland' (fol. 41). She may be referring to fighting that broke out around Enniskillen and Londonderry in April 1689. Another poem to her 'dear cosen Coll————' (William Connock, presumably) addresses him on his arrival in France, having returned after 'Irlands loss', that is, in 1691 or early 1692.

The poems in Part Three are the earliest in composition. All had been printed late in 1687 (the title-page says 1688) in *Poetical Recreations.* If the elegies on her brother were composed at the time of his death, then some of these poems can be dated as early as 1675.

We can conclude, then, that the verse copied into the Magdalen manuscript was composed over a period of roughly a quarter of a century, from 1675 through 1701 or 1702: Part One between 1685 and 1700, with all but the final poem having been begun probably by 1692; Part Two between 1689 and 1701 (or so); Part Three between 1675 (or earlier) and 1687 at the outside. Given that Part One was probably prepared near the end of 1700 and that Parts Two and Three were probably copied while Barker was still in France, it seems likely that the preparation of the Magdalen manuscript occurred in at least two stages between late 1700 and 1704, when Barker returned to England, presumably taking the volume with her.

The first recorded appearance of the volume is in the library of the Rev. Thomas Corser (1793-1876), the distinguished editor and book collector, of Stand Rectory near Manchester, as part of the 'magnificent collection of early English poetry which [Corser] had begun to form at an early age' (*DNB*). Corser was editor of the *Collectanea Anglo-Poetica* for the Chetham Society, of which he was a founder-member. His labours on the *Collectanea,* an alphabetized selection of extracts from, and biographical and bibliographical accounts of the early English poets, were taken over by the author and book collector James Crossley (1800-83), who acquired the Barker volume when it was sold, as part of the 'seventh portion' of the Corser library, by Sotheby's on 10 July 1871 (lot 204). In 1884 it was purchased by a dealer, Salkeld, for 15*s*. He in turn sold it for £1 1*s*. in February 1886 to W. D. Macray (1826-1916), librarian and historian of the Bodleian. It was Macray, evidently, who gave the volume to Magdalen College. Macray was associated with Magdalen for the better part of his long academic life, taking an undergraduate degree in 1848, serving as chaplain from 1856 to 1870, and preparing a calendar of the muniments at Magdalen College from 1864 to 1878. In 1891 he was elected to a research fellowship and for the next twenty years worked on bringing to completion the eight volumes of the college register. The inside front cover of the Barker volume bears Macray's signature and the date 1886, and his MS notes, some on the provenance of the manuscript, are tipped into the front of the volume.[10]

A Life 'Interlac'd' with Verse

Galesia, the fictionalized persona Barker used throughout her writing life, describes herself in one of the autobiographical fictions as having been 'dropp'd' while still a girl into a 'Labyrinth of Poetry, which has ever since interlac'd all the Actions of my Life' (***PWS*** 3). This next section traces the outlines of Barker's life as a poet as it can be reconstructed from documentary sources, printed self-representations, and the manuscript verse, focusing on the life up to the turn of the century when the Magdalen manuscript was begun.

Little is known of Barker's family beyond her own accounts. She was related on her mother's side to the Connocks, a Cornish gentry family. Anne, her mother, appears to have come from an unlanded branch of the family, many of whose male members made careers in the military, including the 'uncle' and 'cosen' honoured in the Magdalen verse. Barker may have had her Connock relations in mind when she commended James II's support of the army and navy, for by means of this kingly generosity 'younger brothers had their bread' and were spared being a shame or burden to the 'elder house', and 'many familys, which had not lands, / Were dayly fed' (**'Fidelia in a Convent garden'**, fol. 31ᵛ). It is not clear how Anne Connock met her future husband Thomas Barker, whose background is even more obscure. Even the county of his birth is unknown. Thomas may have had a minor position at court prior to the civil wars, possibly as a member of the staff or household of the Keeper of the Great Seal, since, as Carol Shiner Wilson reports, the 1732 entry in the St Germain parish register recording Jane's death describes her father as having been 'Secretaire du grand sceau d'Angleterre'. Other parish records indicate that by autumn of 1648 Thomas and Anne, now married, were living in Blatherwick, a hamlet in Northamptonshire, not far from Stamford, Lincolnshire. An entry for 8 October 1648 in the Blatherwick register records the birth of what may have been their first child, a son, George, who would die five months later. The same register records the baptisms of Edward, 16 April 1650; Jane, 17 May 1652; and Henry, 31 July 1655.

Blatherwick appears to have been Jane's home for the first ten years of her life. The family was comfortable enough, it would seem, for they leased a house with four hearths, and by the early 1660s Thomas was serving as an agent for the London financier Robert Clayton. Edward, the oldest son, was sent to London in March 1663 to enter the Merchant Taylors' School, and then matriculated at St

John's College Oxford, taking a BA in 1672 and an MA from Christ Church on 8 March 1675. He died, not long after, of a fever, aged twenty-five. His sudden death was a stunning blow to Jane. She continued lamenting in print his death for the next half century. . . . Of Henry, the younger son, no trace is to be found in the academic registers surviving from the period, an indication, perhaps, of the family's limited resources.

In 1662, when Jane was ten, the family moved to Wilsthorpe, Lincolnshire, Thomas Barker having taken a lease on the manor house and surrounding farmland from the Earl of Exeter. (Jane would later inherit the ninety-nine year lease.) At Wilsthorpe she pursued a remarkable course of self-education that included Latin, classical poetry, and academic medicine. She read widely. Her texts suggest familiarity with a range of belletristic writings, mostly from the seventeenth century, and all royalist. She cites or alludes to Cowley, Katherine Philips, and Dryden (her favourites, it would appear), but also Butler, Otway, Rochester, Denham, and Beaumont and Fletcher; among the classical poets she seems to have preferred Horace and, with reservations, Ovid. More surprisingly, she refers to a variety of medical writers—Aristotle, Galen, Hippocrates, and, from her own century, Richard Lower (to whom she was related on her mother's side), William Harvey, and Thomas Willis. She also read in religion. One of her early printed poems thanks the man who can be identified as George Hawen, the rector of the local parish, for supplying her with religious tracts. A circle of 'witty and youthful' friends at Cambridge, students at St John's College in the 1680s, provided her with pamphlets, poems, and other items of current interest (***PWS*** 23, 26). To them she addressed a number of the poems found in the Magdalen manuscript, including **'An Invitation to my Learned Friends at Cambridge'** and, **'To my Friends'**, a tribute to their camaraderie and support, both printed below. The latter swells with affection for the 'band of gallant youths' who 'teach me how to sing, then praise my song', but the representation of the female poet as Daphne-as-a-tree encircled by these same admiring youths hints at ambiguities.

Barker was fortunate in her older brother, who helped her learn Latin, classical poetry, botany, herbal medicine, anatomy, and physiology. At first, according to an account offered in one of the fictions, he mocked her enthusiasm for Latin grammar as a 'Vapour of Fancy, to be blown away with the first Puff of Vanity, or new Mode' (***LI*** 16-17), but he assisted all the same. She was an apt pupil. Using his medical textbooks she undertook the study of scientific medicine, declaring herself (in the person of Galesia) especially pleased by the writings of William Harvey, his 'Circulatio Sanguinis' in particular (***LI*** 52), and indicating that in time she 'made such Progress in *Anatomy,* as to understand *Harvey*'s Circulation of the Blood, and *Lower*'s Motion of the Heart' (***PWS*** 10). Barker's medical learning and her grief for the loss of her brother are reflected in one of her most interesting poems, entitled in the Magdalen manuscript 'She begining to study phisick, takes her leave of poetry, so falls into a long degression on anatomy'. Versions of this poem can be found, annotated, in both *Kissing the Rod* and the new Wilson edition of Barker's autobiographical writings.

Sometime after 1681, when her father died, and probably no later than 1685, Barker removed from Wilsthorpe to London. Evidence from **Poetical Recreations** indicates that while in London she continued to exchange verse with members of the Cambridge circle and that she became the friend and possibly the object of the amatory attentions of a City bookseller, then in his twenties, Benjamin Crayle. It was Crayle who brought out **Poetical Recreations** in 1687. In 1685 Crayle included on the advertisement page of one of his publications a notice informing readers that they might purchase at his shop, for five shillings a roll, something called Dr Barker's Famous Gout Plaister, which 'infallibly takes away the pain in Twelve Hours time, with the Paroxysm of the Distemper, and in time may effect a perfect Cure'. But beyond this little can be said with assurance of Barker's goings on in the 1680s except that, on the evidence of the manuscript verse, she increasingly sought her identity in the Roman Catholic Church and, after the Revolution of 1688-89, in the Jacobite community in France. Her conversion to Catholicism in London under the direction of 'Benit's sons'— the Benedictines—may have occurred as early as 1685. (Relevant are a couple of Part One poems . . . , **'Fidelia arguing with her self on the difficulty of finding the true Religion'** and **'Fidelia having seen the Convent at St James's'**.) One of her poems, **'Fidelia weeping for the Kings departure at the Revolution'**, includes an account of a cat crucifixion in London in one of the outbreaks of anti-Catholic violence that occurred after James's flight to France. Barker must have fled herself not long after. A poem written to accompany a birthday present to the Prince of Wales suggests she was established in St Germain by 10 June 1689.

In the group of twenty poems 'Refering to the times' of Part One Barker writes as a member of the St Germain community. Although these poems contain quietly reflective moments, mostly touching on the dubieties of her new identity, they are more often uncompromisingly partisan— bitter, self-righteous, relentless in their indictment of English perfidy under William and Mary. Her Dedication describes this verse as representing 'the frenzie, mallice, and madness' of the years since 1685 and declares her hope that it might 'fright the future from the like proceedings even in thought', thereby 'cut[ting] off troops of unborn Rebells'. In addition to expressing political loyalties, these poems are vehicles for fashioning a new identity as a Roman Catholic convert and religio-political exile, an identity understood in terms of a mythology of the virtuous but persecuted outsider, at once alone in the world and part of a wandering community. (A poem from Part Two recounts how she 'wander'd on' from Wilstrope to London and then tells how, driven on by 'cursed orange', that is William III, she and others fled from England to France, where now they 'wander vagabons alone'.) Part conversion nar-

rative, part semi-mystical Stuart propaganda, and part political jeremiad, the poems 'Refering to the times' are an outstanding example of Jacobite myth-making.

If verse-writing enabled Barker to construct an identity and a place for herself within her new community, it also, and perhaps even more fundamentally, constituted a means of self-documentation. Her female predecessor Margaret Cavendish, Duchess of Newcastle, wrote famously that it was the anonymity of women's lives that drove her to set down her life story. For, Cavendish remarks, poignantly, in the final passage of her autobiography, 'my Lord having had two Wives, I might easily have been mistaken, especially if I should dye and my Lord Marry again'. Barker was haunted by the awareness that hers too was a life easily mistaken. She came from an undistinguished family, never married or bore children, never achieved public acclaim or notoriety; hers was an 'obscure Corner of the World' (**PWS** iv). One senses that verse-writing presented her with a means to commemorate her own otherwise disregarded existence and at the same time to honour political loyalties that were increasingly the object of disregard, if not suspicion, in the post-Revolutionary world. The body of verse she accumulated over the years, the record of a poet in exile in her own country and abroad, came to constitute a kind of personal archive from which to draw when, remarkably, in the second and third decades of the eighteenth century, this aging and unrepentant Jacobite, now in her sixties and seventies, undertook to fictionalize the story of her early years, constructing around the poems of her youth and middle age the autobiographical Galesia narratives for which she is known today. The bound volume that is now Magdalen manuscript 343 may have been a central document in this process—perhaps her most comprehensive collection. It is certainly a repository of the many voices, self-constructions, and poetical practices of Jane Barker.

THE MAGDALEN POEMS

The Magdalen poems are of various kinds: religio-political polemics, amatory lyrics, elegies, poems-against-marriage, odes, verse epistles, verses of poetic vocation. Some originate within a matrix of predictably 'feminine' relationships and situations—the bereaved sister, affectionate niece, disprized victim of male perfidy—while others draw upon areas of experience and construct poetic roles largely without precedent in seventeenth-century women's verse-writing: the student of anatomy, the prescribing lay-physician, the chronicler of the Stuart cause. Some speak in the oppositional, even subversive tones that feminist criticism has taught us to hear: the beloved object talking back; the impassioned, perhaps homoerotic female friend. Much of the interest of these poems—their ironies, anger, complexities, poignancy—results from Barker's willingness to enter into and probe the oddities of her position as a spinster whose allegiance to elite male learning, an ambiguous (for women) poetic heritage, an outlawed religion, and an increasingly discredited political ideology took her well outside the ordinary sphere of the country gentle-woman.

Those seeking moments of resistance to patriarchal values or constricting constructions of 'Woman' will find plenty to work with in the Magdalen manuscript. **'Fidelia in st Germains garden, lamenting her misfortunes'** flaunts its feminine abjection, raising self-pity to the level of the high heroic; **'On the Apothecaries filing my bills amongst the Doctors'** constructs a boastful female warrior-physician triumphing over the puny he-doctors. Poems such as these show Barker experimenting with modes of feminine excess, creating an almost campy 'larger-than-lifeness' that laughs at lesser understandings of female nature. Other poems achieve radical effects simply by translating established (male) poetic codes into female terms. The retirement poem takes on startling implications when it is recognized that the withdrawal from distraction and empty business it valorizes is at base a refusal of romance, love, marriage, and reproduction—of the whole business of heterosexual obligation. Her anti-carpe-diem poems disrupt the standard equation of love, youth, sexual pleasure, and feminine desirability, implicitly proposing modes of female worth less dependent on male approval. **'A Virgin Life'**, perhaps Barker's best-known poem, is an outstanding example. A more ambiguous one, is **'A song'** (**'When poor Galæcia aged grew'**), in which an abject female speaker likens herself and, grotesquely, her hymen to an overblown flower. Poems such as these take a jaundiced view of a sexual economy based upon male control over definitions of female value and point toward the need for alternative sexual economies. Barker's poems of female community hint at one form such an alternative might take.

Also of interest are the poems of poetic vocation. Barker is unusual among early modern women writers in having left a detailed account of her coming to poetry, a process memorialized in a number of verses, including **'The contract with the muses writ on the bark of a shady ash-tree'** and **'The Necessity of Fate'**. The difficulties of fashioning a feminine poetic identity are the subject of **'The contract,'** a poem that plays upon Barker's oft-expressed admiration for the poet Katherine Philips (1632-64), whose acclaim as the 'matchless Orinda' was an inspiration to many women in Barker's generation. Dedication to poetry is shown not only to be incompatible with the ordinary feminine destiny of romance, marriage, and motherhood but also to visit upon the woman poet loneliness, alienation, hostility, and contempt. The giddy dreams of fame and adoration, associated early in the poem with the iconic figure of Orinda, are exposed as delusions: in reality the woman poet shares in Cassandra's fate. This bleak, but also, it must be said, somewhat callow poem, replete with what one hopes are calculated sillinesses, should be read in dialogue with **'Necessity of Fate'**, which employs the 'contract with the muses' topos to strikingly different effect. **'Necessity of Fate'** assumes the same opposition between the poet's identity as a writer and her identity as a woman, and puts into play many of the same elements— the muses, the contractual vow, the symbolic tree, the needful renunciation of the things of this world—but re-

casts them in the form of an elegantly controlled Pindaric ode. Where **'The Contract'** swings from the glorious Orindan heights to the bitterness of Cassandra's fate, **'Necessity of Fate'** records the mysterious rewards to be found in acceptance of an exile's destiny with its renunciation of conventional worldly—and womanly—success. It concludes with a stanza that sums up and transforms the dedicatory vow-upon-the-tree of **'The Contract'** into something deeper and more enigmatic:

> For fate at my initiation
> In the muses congregation,
> As my responsor promis'd then for me
> I shou'd forsake those three,
> Soaring honours, and vain sweets of pleasure
> And vainer fruits of worldly treasure,
> All for the muses melancholy tree,
> E're I knew ought of its great mistery,
> Ah gentle fate since thou wilt have it so,
> Let thy kind hand exalt it to my brow.

(fol. 113)

Notes

1. I have counted 'The contract with the muses writ on the bark of a shady ash-tree' (fol. 76) as a separate poem.

2. This is a quarto volume of ninety pages of poetry (each page measuring *c.* 176 × 234 mm), a title-page, dedication, preface, and table of contents. The volume appears to be in original early eighteenth-century boards (measuring *c.* 187 × 240 mm), later rebound with a new gilt spine spliced-in and with new paste-downs and end-papers. It bears the book-plate of Anne-Charlotte de Crussol de Florensac, Duchesse d'Aiguillon, engraved by the Parisian engraver Antoine Aveline (1691-1743) after her marriage in 1718 with Armand-Louis du Plessis-Richelieu (1683-1750). The volume was sold at Sothebys 21 November 1856 as lot 255 for 19*s.*, where it was described as belonging to a library formed by a collector 'during his residence abroad'.

3. An alternative method of counting would yield fifty-one poems. 'The Prospect of the Landskip' is listed on the title-page of *Poetical Recreations* as a single poem, but is split into three poems in the body, as it is in the Magdalen manuscript. I have counted it as three separate poems in both.

4. Cecil died in Issy-les-Moulineaux, just outside Paris. A nonjuror and anti-Williamite, he was head of the leading landowning family in the Stamford area of Lincolnshire, and Barker's landlord. A copy of this poem, ascribed to 'J. Barker', appears in a commonplace book kept by Charles Caesar of Great Grandsen, Huntingdonshire (fol. 160). The volume, dated 1705, is now in the British Library (Add. MS 43,410). Caesar was then living in Stamford, where he died in 1707. An unattributed copy of the elegy on the death of James II is found in BL Add. MS 10,118 (fols.

410^v-11), a collection of materials for a history of James II brought to completion in 1706 by the Benedictine historian Ralph Benet Weldon (1674-1713), 'y^t nothing may perish coming to my hand y^t sounds forth ye praises of this Royall Victime of ye True Faith' (fol. 410). The volume is attributed in the BL catalogue to Joseph Johnston, Prior of the English Benedictines of St Edmund in Paris, but was actually the work of Weldon, one of Johnston's monks. I am indebted to Jeslyn Medoff for both references.

5. 'Mrs. Jane Barker', *Notes & Queries,* ser. 11, no. 12 (1922), 278.

6. Royal Archives, Windsor Castle, Stuart Papers 208/129, misdated 1738 (Barker died in 1732). The letter, from Jane Barker to an unidentified woman whom she addresses as 'Madam' and 'your Ladyship', is difficult to date. The date reads 'Aug 14:73^0', which may mean [17]13^0—the '7' possibly being a 1—or [1]730. Internal evidence supports the latter. The letter is printed in Henrietta Taylor, *Lady Nithsdale and Her Family* (London: Lindsay Drummond, 1939), 239-40, misdated 1739. Tayler thinks it was written to Lady Nithsdale's sister, Mother Lucy Theresa Joseph, Superior of the Convent of the Augustinian Nuns at Bruges, and forwarded by her to Lady Nithsdale in Rome. Barker's signature can be found elsewhere on two 1717 documents in the Lincolnshire Archives Office—'Schedules and Letter of Attorney, 1717' and 'KQS. Papists' Estates. Rolls. 1717'. According to Carol Shiner Wilson her signature is also to be found in the 1691 St Germain parish register.

7. See fols. 34, 35, 36, 39, and 47. On folios 36 and 39 she supplies the words 'on the Revolution' to the title. The others are single syllables or words, to restore letters lost in cropping or in anticipation of their loss, since they jutted out into the margin.

8. I am grateful to Edward Corp for this information.

9. Two recent events contributed to the ebullience in St Germain. The first was the death in late July of Anne's last surviving heir, the Duke of Gloucester, raising hopes among the Jacobites that Anne's nephew, the Prince of Wales, would be named successor. The second was the naming in November of Louis XIV's grandson, Philip of Anjou, as the successor to the Spanish Crown.

10. Mary Clapinson, 'W. D. Macray (1826-1916) Historian of the Bodleian', *Bodleian Library Record,* 15, no. 4 (1996), 300-7. Above his signature at the very top are two lines in a hand not found elsewhere in the volume (it may be early eighteenth century). They read: 'Curst is that kingdome where there Reigns a man / that can not ere he will, wills what he can.' Above that, in tiny characters in the top right corner, is what looks like 'o/o/o Br'.

James Fitzmaurice (essay date 1998)

SOURCE: Fitzmaurice, James. "Barker and the Tree of Knowledge at Cambridge University." *Renaissance Forum* 3, no. 1 (spring 1998): 1-15.

[*In the following essay, Fitzmaurice examines the 1723 version of Barker's poem "An Invitation to my friends at Cambridge" to show that later in life the author was not as enamored of the opinions of academic men as she had been as a younger woman, because she saw the limitations of worldly knowledge and no longer felt she needed to justify her lack of formal education.*]

Jane Barker is perhaps most widely known these days as a writer of novellas who was active during the early eighteenth century. The 1997 Oxford University Press paperback edition of three of these pieces is testimony to considerable scholarly interest in her, particularly as a woman author who published her fiction and who was much read during her own lifetime. (Barker 1997) She is often mentioned in conjunction with Mary Manley and Eliza Haywood, but John Richetti argues that in the more precise view she falls into a group of women writers for whom the 'public image of the lady novelist' was, contrary to the cases of Manley and Haywood, without blemish. The reputation for rectitude that marked Barker's group, according to Richetti, also contributed to publishing successes for men like the 'unscrupulous but astute' Edmund Curll. (Richetti 1969, 230) Richetti, unsurprisingly, finds Barker's fiction itself rigorously 'moral and free of erotic detail', though I would argue that her moral sense is more complicated and nuanced than might appear to be the case at first glance. Jane Spencer, in the influential monograph *The Rise of the Woman Novelist,* notes the same sort of difference between Manley and Barker as is to be found in Richetti: 'Virginity, instead of eroticism, was the keynote'. (Spencer 1986, 62) Spencer, however, is as much interested in Barker as an autobiographer as in her as a novelist, and Spencer contends that the fiction routinely is intended to reveal aspects of Barker's life as a writer, a woman who devoted herself to pen and ink rather than to marriage. Spencer's view makes sense and is widely held, but Kathryn R. King and Jeslyn Medoff warn that Barker's biographers should use make use of archival material and not confine themselves to interpretation or overinterpretation of the fiction. (King and Medoff 1997, 16-38) Barker's fiction may strike the modern reader as slightly odd, for it often appears to be rambling and sometimes contains snippets of verse that seem pointless beyond being homespun. At the same time, her narratives frequently explore issues of sex and gender in ways that appeal to the modern sense of life's complexities and of the difficulties in drawing easy, clear-cut moral judgments.

While Barker wanted her novellas to be published, she did not seek print for her poetry except as it is sometimes found revised and interspersed in the fiction. If her verse has received less attention than her prose, it is by no means ignored and plays a prominent part in Carol Barash's recent study of women poets. (Barash 1996, 174-198) Barash finds strong connections between Barker's poetry and verse by Katherine Philips, though Spencer believes Cowley's odes to be the main influence. (Spencer 1986, 63) An essay by Kathryn R. King corrects the common misapprehension that Barker had little interest in the world of men. (King 1994, 551-70) Rather, many of her friends were male academics. Barker's poetry, itself, treats a broad range of topics including medicine and religion. It, like the fiction, deals with the complexities of various aspects of sex and gender, and it, too, suggests the difficulties involved in making easy, clear-cut moral judgments.

In a poem titled **'An Invitation to my Friends at Cambridge',** a poem among those printed without her permission in *Poetical Recreations* in 1688, Barker advanced a claim for a special relationship with the exclusively male academy. The male friends of the poem's title, she suggested, should come to visit her home in Lincolnshire, for the area was a haven of rural solitude and beauty. Barker was very much under the spell of academics in general and of Cambridge men in particular when this first version of the poem was published. She had not had an opportunity to pursue a university education because she was a woman. Nevertheless, she found herself being treated, she said, as a 'copartner'[1] in writing by a group that included at least one fellow of St. John's College.[2] These same men, individually and taken as a group, clearly had devoted a good deal of time to discussing with her a wide variety of serious and lighthearted subjects. Serious dialogue between a member of Cambridge University and an intelligent woman, of course, was not without precedent, for Anne Finch, Countess of Conway, not long before had enjoyed a fruitful correspondence with Henry More. Nevertheless, Barker was delighted both with the respect accorded to her by well-educated men and by the attendant opportunities for what amounted to informal tuition. She was able to learn from learned men. When a second and heavily revised version of the poem appeared in 1723 as part of the novella *A Patch-Work Screen,* Barker was some thirty years older and not quite so dewy-eyed about what university men might have to offer. Indeed, the full title of the book is *A Patch-Work Screen for the Ladies,* and domestic issues, as well as observations regarding the dangers of associating with young men and old, are paramount. University men drift towards the background of this later book and males of genteel upbringing, educated or not, are rarely admirable. Rather, such a man is likely to seduce an unwary woman, to be hanged for committing robbery as part of a 'frolick' (Barker 1997, 104) or to end up as a suicide. (Barker 1997, 138)

It would be a mistake to say that Barker had seen the error of her infatuation with academe when she published the 1723 version of **'To My Friends'** in *A Patch-Work Screen.*[3] After all, she only revised the poem and did not exclude it. Nevertheless, she did leave out many others of her academically oriented poems and instead chose to include such homespun domestic verse as **'A Receipt for making Welsh Flummery'** and **'The Czar's Receipt to make Punch'**. *A Patch-Work Screen* is, then, quite definitely a book for women, written by a woman, though this is not to say that it is relentless in its depictions of men as seducers and corrupters. A man, like a woman, can be a victim, a dupe who falls prey to those who are unscrupulous. (Barker 1997, 134ff) The book also is professedly 'a patch work', that is, a collection of odds and ends that in its structure recalls other collections including Margaret Cavendish's *The World's Olio* (1655) and *Nature's Pictures* (1656).

The version of **'To My Friends'** included in *A Patch-Work Screen* leaves out two sections, one of six and the other of eight lines. These sections, taken in context, cast a good deal of light on the feelings that were generated just prior to the 1688 publication of *Poetical Recreations* in an intelligent and talented woman who had a great many male academics as friends. While she clearly was delighted to be taken seriously by these men, she also understood that there was a large gap between the kind of life she found herself obliged to lead as a genteel woman and many aspects of existence in the world in which they resided. She apparently envied them their knowledge derived from this world but knew that as a genteel woman she could not quite live the kind of life that would open it up to her fully. Indeed, in other poems she shows that she was not entirely convinced that she really wanted the knowledge that she seems to envy in **'To My Friends'**. The world of academe, unlike the world of rural Lincolnshire, was sophisticated but also a little sullied. While academe concerned itself with serious ethical questions that might have been discussed after dinner at Barker's home in Wilsthorp, academe did so in a very different environment, one where intelligent and well-educated men actually tested the limits of morality. Such men sometimes tried out precepts derived from their 'Father Hobbs' on 'Orange-wenches'. (Barker 1688, 5) They drank alcohol beyond what was moderate, they swore, and they 'Kick[ed] Tavern boys'. (Barker 1688, 5) Bad behaviour of this sort was certainly to be found in Lincolnshire, but most of the men—and women—who practised it were not likely to have pondered questions derived from *The Leviathan.* Not all Cambridge academics were so worldly, of course, but many had experience of this environment, if not as participants then as direct observers. Any considerable time spent in such observation itself might have been repugnant to Barker. At the same time, she was unabashed about claiming direct knowledge, or learning, not requiring experiences that were of dubious morality.

The 1688 *Poetical Recreations* version of **'To My Friends'** offers men from the academy not merely solitude and beauty but innocence—a characteristic denied to a person, male or female, with too much worldly knowledge. After a brief introduction, the poem continues as follows.

Hail, Solitude, where Innocence do's shroud
Her unvail'd Beauties from the cens'ring Croud;
Let me but have her Company, and I
Shall never envy this World's Gallantry:
[The following lines were dropped in 1723 *Patch-
   Work Screen*:]
We'll find out such inventions to delude
And mock all those that mock our solitude
That they for shame shall fly for their defence
To gentle Solitude and Innocence.
Then they will find how much they've been deceiv'd,
When they the flatt'ries of this World believ'd.

(Barker 1688, 1 and 2)

Barker is so concerned with getting across the importance of innocence that she overworks the word a little, an artistic weakness not to be found in the 1723 **Patch-Work Screen** version. In this later version, the first 'Innocence' is replaced with 'Peace and Vertue', though the line is not otherwise changed. The last six lines of the passage quoted above, however, are simply dropped. One reason they might have been removed is that Barker, who had just turned seventy, no longer felt the need to justify her lack of worldly knowledge to anyone, least of all to herself. She did not fear being mocked nor did she want to take the time to point out what must have been obvious to her, that one should not believe the flatteries of the world in general and of Cambridge academics in particular.

Both versions continue with a description of the natural beauties of Lincolnshire and both condemn 'Emulation', the petty rivalries for power and honour that beset men at Cambridge. Barker does not deny the complexities of the situation, however, for she ends each version with an admission of what is lacking for women like her in rural Lincolnshire:

But that the Tree of Knowledge won't grow here:
Though in its culture I have spent some time,
Yet it disdains to grow in our cold Clime,
Where it can neither Fruit nor Leaves produce
Good for its owner, or the public use.
[Eight-line section left out of 1723 *Patch-Work
   Screen*:]
How can we hope our Minds then to adorn
With any thing with which they were not born;
Since we're deny'd to make this small advance,
To know their nakedness and ignorance?
For in our Maker's Laws we've made a breach,
And gather'd all that was within our reach
Which since we ne're could touch; Altho' our Eyes
Do serve our longing Souls to tantalize,
[text resumed in 1723 *Patch-Work Screen*:]
Whilst kinder fate for you do's constitute
Luxurious Banquets of this dainty Fruit.
Whose Tree most fresh and flourishing do's grow,
E'er since it was transplanted amongst you;
And you in wit grow as its branches high,
Deep as its Root too in Philosophy;
Large as its spreading Arms your Reasons grow,
Close as its Umbrage do's your Judgments show
Fresh as its Leaves your sprouting fancies are,
Your Vertues as its Fruits are bright and fair.

(Barker 1688, 3 and 4; Barker 1997, 94 and 95)

Knowledge is what is in short supply in Lincolnshire, but it is knowledge associated with the experience of evil as well as good, knowledge of the sort that had to be obtained by eating the forbidden fruit and that was involved in the expulsion from the Garden of Eden. Barker begins the biblical metaphor early in the poem when she says that the beauty which she offers to Cambridge men is 'unveil'd', beauty such as was naked with Adam and Eve before the fall. This beauty, she writes, is protected from criticism by innocence. Innocence was seen as a substantial if not always successful protector of beauty in Barker's day, and in another poem she writes that she needs no guard for her heart 'but its own innocence, / Under which Fort, it could fierce storms endure'.[4] 'Peace and Virtue', substituted for 'Innocence', in the revision of 'To my Friends' don't work quite so well as guardians. Peace, in particular, is more a pleasant state of being than a protector. The threat against beauty, however, is less serious in the revised than in the 1688 **Poetical Recreations** version of the poem.

The set of eight deleted lines from the earlier version quoted above makes another interesting point about the complexities of gender relationships. Innocent people often do not have full knowledge about their innocence as regards the opposite sex.

. . . we're deny'd to make this small advance,
   To know [our Minds'] nakedness and ignorance.

It is an observation that Aphra Behn, Margaret Cavendish, and others had already made in slightly different circumstances. When innocent people fall in love, they do not at first recognize that they are in love.[5] They understand that they are full of emotion, but do not have knowledge of the cause or of possible courses of action. It takes someone who is experienced in love, often someone who is himself or herself a little sullied, to point out to them what is happening. With Barker, writing **'An Invitation'** prior to 1688, certain sorts of important knowledge are always out of reach for the innocent, if they remain innocent. These people may want to pluck fruit from the Tree of Knowledge but 'ne're could touch' and the effort merely 'serve[s] [their] longing Souls to tantalize'. Barker, recasting the same poem for **A Patch-Work Screen,** feels far less desire to know more about the worldly side of Cambridge life.

The second version of the poem, curiously, does leave in some small reference to the less than laudable world of university—or, perhaps, of college—life in lines which originally were:

Whilst kinder fate for you do's constitute
Luxurious Banquets of this dainty Fruit.

There is only a minor change in the revision, which follows:

Whilst God and Nature for you do's constitute
Luxurious Banquets of this dainty Fruit.

In the first version with the undeleted eight lines, 'Luxurious Banquets of this dainty Fruit' can refer to the sexual adventurism of fellows and students among 'Orange-wenches'. That interpretation is not impossible in the re-written poem, but the removal of the eight lines taken together with the change of 'fate' to 'God and Nature' strengthens a reading that stresses the enjoyment of college feasts and of such activities as philosophical discussion. A little overeating was a failing, but a trivial one, among academics.

The revision of **'To my Friends'** also offers an opportunity to fine tune the interpretation of the first version of the poem offered here. Two footnotes in *A Patch-Work Screen* provide interesting information concerning what Barker may have thought about the earlier version. 'Our' (preceding 'cold Clime') is glossed by Barker as 'A Female Capacity', and 'you' (in the phrase 'you do's constitute') she explains as 'The Men'. Thus, the problem of knowledge and innocence in **'To my Friends'** in *Poetical Recreations,* if we figure in the footnotes of thirty years later, becomes less general and more specific. That is, men have certain sorts of worldly knowledge, and women, in their 'capacity' as women, do not. 'Capacity' here probably means something like 'force of mind' or 'mental ability'.[6] 'What', it might be asked, 'of 'fallen women'? Do they have 'female capacity' or have they lost it?' Jane Spencer believes that Barker's heroine and alter ego, Galesia, is fearful that poetry will 'unleash the dangers of sexuality' that will, in turn, lead to Galesia's own seduction. (Spencer 1986, 67 and 68) Whether or not Spencer is right, there is, finally, good reason to believe that the footnotes from the revised version of the poem may be used in a legitimate fashion to explain the poem as it was printed in 1688. It makes sense to argue that the first versions of all the poems were intended for an educated and sophisticated coterie readership. When the poems were revised and printed in 1723, Barker no doubt expected that they would be seen by a less educated and more general audience. Thus, in the 1723 version, we find Orinda glossed as 'Mrs. Katherine Philips'. (Barker 1997, 127) A footnote of this sort would have been unnecessary for Barker's Cambridge friends, who also may not have needed the explanations for 'The Men' and 'A Female Capacity'.

Whatever Barker may have thought about 'fallen women' in 1723, she certainly was interested in knowledge generated by the dubious behaviour of Cambridge men when she wrote prior to 1688. The second poem in *Poetical Recreations* is **'To Mr. Hill, on his Verses to the Duchess of York, when she was at Cambridge'.** In **'To Mr. Hill',** Barker praises the addressee, who is able to 'induce the Gallants to forsake / Their dear-lov'd Town' and draw them to listen to eloquence in the service of the Royal Household. Her praise, however, does not keep her from taking a careful look at the intellectual and dissolute life from which she is excluded.

> And for their Father Hobbs [they] will talk so high,
> Rather than him they will their God deny:
> And lest their wit should want a surer proof,
> They boast of crimes they ne're were guilty of.

> Thus hellish cunning drest in Masquerade
> Of Wit's disguise, so many have betray'd,
> And made them Bondslaves, who at first did fly
> Thither Wit's famine only to supply.
> But now I hope they'll find the task too great,
> And think at last of making a retreat:
> Since here's a Pisgah-Hill whereon to stand
> To take a prospect of Wit's holy Land,
> Flowing with Milk of Christian innocence,
> And Honey of Cic'ronian Eloquence.

> (Barker 1688, 5 and 6)

Barker points out the irony that those who pretend to greater wit because they have greater knowledge of dissolute life are liable to have lied about whom they have seduced or what brawls they have experienced. Further, these 'Machavillians in a Coffee-house' have as their master someone, who, while possessing a reputation for intellect, was often seen as a promoter of amorality if not immorality. Barker's biblical metaphor of the addressee, Mr. Hill, as the hill from which Moses saw the Promised Land fits nicely because Cambridge is 'such a foggy level place' both morally and geographically. Nevertheless, Barker betrays an infatuation with some aspects of the life she condemns. Despite what might seem to be an angry and sarcastic tone found in phrases like 'dear-lov'd Town' and 'Father Hobbs', the poem is full of wit of the sort that those who frequented taverns would have appreciated, and it is Mr. Hill's 'witticisms' as well as his 'innocence' that she praises.

What appears to be a bad rhyme, 'surer proof' and 'guilty of' may simply be another example of wit—if the rhyme was, indeed, as bad at the time as it is now. Barker may use this poem to redirect the academy's attention away from the tavern but she does so in a poetic style that would not be uncongenial to a public house wit. For somebody who could not 'lead the life', she nevertheless was able to duplicate some of the writing that it generated.

Barker goes on to flirt with actual participation in bad behaviour by using slightly off-colour puns in **'To my Friend Exillus, on his persuading me to Marry Old Damon',**[7] a piece that might seem at first glance to be a 'virginity' poem and a poem that Elaine Hobby cites as a serious attack on the institution of marriage. (Hobby 1988, 160) While the serious import is certainly there, it is found in the context of slightly dubious jollity. This is another poem with Cambridge connections, for Exillus (Exilius in *A Patch-Work Screen*) was at St. John's in some capacity prior to 1688.[8] Barker, or her speaker, teasingly says she is not entirely averse to the marriage. The reasons for deciding against the union are, in the end, two, the first almost purely comic and the second at once comic and serious. First, Barker, or her speaker, will have to sleep with Old Damon, and, second, he later on mistakenly will think her guilty of adultery.

> Thou [Exillus] with Idolatry mak'st me adore,
> And homage do to the proud Conqueror [Damon],
> Now round his Neck my willing Arms I'd twine,

And swear upon his Lips, My Dear, I'm thine,
But that his kindness then would grow, I fear,
Too weighty for my weak desert to bear.
. . .
. . . after all my kindness to him shown,
My little Neddy, he'll not think't his own:
Even thou my Dear Exillus he'll suspect
If I but look on thee, I him neglect.

(Barker 1688, 14; Barker 1997, 111)

Barker, or her speaker, might go so far as to kiss Damon but will not proceed to 'bear' his weight. It is not her 'desert' to become his 'dessert', that is his 'fruit or sweetmeats'. Further the 'thine' of the section has an ambiguous antecedent. Perhaps Damon is to be told that Exillus is loved. These are instances of word play that might be included in the speech of a character from a play by Aphra Behn, someone like Hellena from *The Rover*, but they are probably a little risqué for a woman taken to be a rigorously moral poet, one who denies that she has the ability to touch the Tree of Knowledge. If nothing else, the lines are more examples of the wit that Barker displayed in the poem on Mr. Hill. It is a little surprising, then, that when Barker revised the poem and included it in *A Patch-Work Screen* she let the puns stand as they were, for she certainly was not interested in impressing the Cambridge University community with her daring in 1723. On the other hand, she had no desire to be labelled a 'prude', and there was heightened danger of that for 'old maids' after the publication of *Rape of the Lock* some ten years earlier. Perhaps most important, even in old age she occasionally seems to have liked to attach a crude label. One finds 'old Whoreson' and 'impudent Slut', used to tag characters in *A Patch-Work Screen.* (Barker 1997, 113 and 114) Barker did drop the lines about twining her willing arms around Damon and about swearing 'My Dear' upon his lips from the 1723 version of the poem. She may have preferred witty puns and crude labels to a mildly salacious image. The second reason given for the rejection of Damon is that he would be a jealous old fool in the tradition of Shakespeare's Leontes, a man who seriously damaged his family life and lost a male heir due to 'horn madness'. Nevertheless, male jealousy was as often comic as serious on the Restoration stage and finds itself expressed in unforgettable characters like Wycherley's Pinchwife. Barker is just a little arch when she suggests that Damon will suspect that Exillus has fathered a son on the poem's speaker—or perhaps on Barker, herself.

If Barker indulges her fondness for wit in **'To my Friend Exillus'** by including only one slightly less than 'ladylike' image, she is considerably less restrained in **"A Bachanalian Song"**, printed in *Poetical Recreations* and not included in *A Patch-Work Screen.* An observation made by Katheryn R. King about Barker's character Galesia, might be applied to Barker herself at this point: she 'writes as if male, using the language and discourses of university . . . men.' (King 1993, 95) This poem, which could pass for the product of an undergraduate evening at the Pope's Head Tavern in Cambridge (an institution with which she was familiar presumably by reputation)[9] begins with an obvious pun and in the process seems to strain after wit.

Troy had a Breed of brave stout Men,
Yet Greece made shift to rout her;
'Cause each Man drank as much as Ten,
And thence grew Ten times stouter.

It is tempting to speculate that Barker wrote **'A Bachanalian Song'** just to show her coterie audience that she could mimic undergraduate writing style and subject matter. Indeed, the poem may be intended to be silly in the way that some of Rochester's poems are silly. Rochester, for example, produced the double rhyme 'his bone' and 'Lisbon'—if tradition has it right—for Charles II extempore. Barker has no trouble with doggerel of this sort when she combines double rhyme with bathroom humour thus:

Though Hector was a Trojan true,
As ever Piss'd 'gen Wall, Sir;
Achilles bang'd him black and blue, For he drank
    more than all, Sir.

The poem does return to Barker's interest in the problem of knowledge, or at least of the sources of wit, for she notes that a drunken Grecian, 'was ne'er asham'd on's Writing'.

He that will be a Souldier then,
Or Witt, must drink good Liquor;
It makes base Cowards fight like Men,
And roving Thoughts fly quicker.

Barker's own thoughts were probably given to a tamer sort of roving, and it is unlikely that she admired a drunk in actuality any more than she wanted to be a soldier.

'On my Mother and my lady W——— who both lay sick at the same time under the Hands of Dr. Paman' is a far more serious effort than **'A Bachanalian Song',** and one that begins with an unexpected, almost Metaphysical, comparison. The women are likened to two naked boys who foolishly think to swim in the ocean, perhaps about to act on a dare.

Like two sweet Youths strip'd naked on the Strand,
Ready to plunge, in consternation[10] stand,
Viewing the dimples of that smiling Face,
Whose frigid Body they design t'imbrace,
Till by their Guardian Angel's care, some friend
Snatches them from the danger they intend:
So did these Pious Souls themselves prepare,
By putting off the Robes of worldly care.
Thus fitted (as they were) in each degree,
To lanch into a bless'd Eternity.

(Barker 1688, 42, Dropped from the Magdalen manuscript.)

If the poem begins with an unexpected comparison, it continues in an odd direction. Barker loses interest in the women's sickness and preparation for 'making a good end'. Instead she uses the occasion to give medical advice to Dr. Paman, who had been Public Orator at Cambridge University between 1674 and 1681 and who had been elected, in the 1640s, a fellow of St. John's.[11]

> Ah happy Paman, mightily approv'd,
> Both by thy Patients, and the Poor belov'd.
> Hence[12] let no Slander light upon the Fame
> Of thy great Art, much less upon thy Name:
> Nor to bad Druggs let Fate thy Worth expose,
> For best Receipts are baffl'd oft by those:
> Nor let no Quack intrude where thou do'st come,
> To crop thy Fame, or haste thy Patients doom;
> Base quackery to Sickness the kind Nurse,
> The Patient's ruine, and Physicians curse.
>
> (Barker 1688, 42)

Barker's praise for the doctor in the first two lines is generous, but she does Paman no favour when she says that she hopes there will be no slander on his professional reputation. Specifically she warns him not to allow 'bad Druggs' to be used in the preparation of his prescriptions. Her attitude is a little like that of a gifted undergraduate who feels knowledgeable enough to offer advice to a senior, indeed an elderly, professor. She felt qualified to discuss the topic of drugs, no doubt because her own prescriptions were being filled by pharmacists. Indeed, she openly takes pleasure that she, as a woman, was treated as if she were a physician in **'On the Apothecary's Filing my bills amongst the Doctor's'**.

> I Hope I shan't be blam'd if I am proud,
> That I'm admitted 'mongst this Learned Croud.
> . . . . .
>
> The sturdy gout, which all Male power withstands,
> Is overcome by my soft Female hands.
> No Deb'ra, Judith, or Semiramis
> Could boast of Conquests half so great as this.
>
> (Barker 1688, 31-4)

The poem on Dr. Paman does not appear in *A Patch-Work Screen*. Paman, who died in 1695, was a matter of history rather than of current events when the book was published in 1723. More importantly, the poem is a little too irreverent in what might have seemed, thirty years later, to be a silly way. Barker, however, continued to be proud of her medical learning, in part because it was not derived from the Tree of Knowledge. The poem on apothecaries, unsurprisingly, is included in *A Patch-Work Screen*. (Barker 1997, 116-119)

Barker is considerably more respectful of her addressee in 'To my Honoured Friend, Mr. E. S——t'. Mr. E. S——t has not been identified but he seems to have been a serious poet and may have been one of her less worldly Cambridge friends.

> I often read your Lines, and oft admire,
> How Eloquence and Fancy do conspire,
> With Wit and Judgment to make up a Quire,
> And grace the Music, of Apollo's Lire.

> But that which makes the Musick truly sweet,
> Virtue and Innocence in Chorus meet.

As with the poem on Mr. Hill, Barker here chooses to praise her subject using the word 'innocence'. She goes on to consider worldly verse by what may be Mr. E. S——t's Cambridge associates.

> If I with other Authors them [Mr. E. S——t's writ-
>   ings] compare,
> Methinks their Modish wit to me do's shew,
> But as an Engyscope to view [his] through:
> Nor do [his] Writ'ngs only smoothly glide,
> Whilst [his] whole life's like some impetuous tide,
> But both together keep a gentle pace,
> And each other do each other grace.

It is not just the man's verse that partakes of innocence, but also his entire existence. His lack of worldly knowledge, in something of an oxymoron, may be the source of 'perfection' in his poetry and his life, that is both the source of incomplete (or innocent) completeness and of unmatched quality. If so, then Barker could scarcely find a more complicated way to praise the man's status regarding gender. He is at once a whole man and one who is thoroughly lacking in forbidden knowledge. The image of the engyscope, or microscope, is interesting, for it suggests that the verse of 'Modish', of more worldly, wits is large, obvious, and even 'gross'. With John Donne, Mr. E. S——t may not need 'half-acre tombs' in which to enshrine his art.

Mr. E. S——t is probably the subject of **'A Second Epistle. To my Honoured Friend Mr. E. S'**. E. S., like Mr. E. S——t, has persuaded Barker to continue writing after she decided to 'banish' her muse. It is tempting to speculate that E. S. gave her encouragement and boosted her self-confidence when she was full of doubts, but the cause of Barker's reasons for deciding to give up writing is not made explicit.[13] She does, however, take a lighthearted approach to the situation and indicates that she has sent her muse packing more than once.

> Oft has my Muse and I fall'n out,
> And I as oft have banish'd her my Breast;
> But such, alas, still was her interest,
> And still to bring her purposes about;
> So great her cunning in insinuation,
> That she soon gain'd her wish'd-for restoration.
>
> (Barker 1688, 70-72)

Barker then puts the muse to a 'Violent Death', but E. S. uses his 'All-pow'rfull Pen' to raise '[the muse] from the Dead again'. This levity would suggest that Barker now looks back on her previous self-doubts and finds them to be a little comic. Nevertheless, she shows genuine gratitude to E. S. for his taking the time to persuade her to return to writing.

> And now, alas, what can she [the muse] doe,
> Or speake or shew,
> How very much she is oblig'd to you?

> For where the Boon's so great, it were a rude
> Presumption to pretend to Gratitude;
> And a mad project to contrive to give
> To you, from whom she do's her All receive.

While Barker's professions of gratitude may seem a little overblown by modern standards or at least somewhat conventional in their use of the inability topos, there is absolutely no reason to question her sincerity. E. S. convinced Barker to continue writing and she, under the name of her muse, owes him a debt. More importantly, the muse in some way has been given her 'All' by E. S. Again Barker is not explicit, but it seems likely that she uses the phrase 'her All receive' to allude to tuition that she, Barker, received in the writing of poetry. Elsewhere she alludes to receiving instruction in medicine from what appears to be a Cambridge man.[14] She goes on to say:

> Yet if she [the muse] Traffick on your Stock, and
>   thrive,
> 'Tis fit, how e'er the Principal be spent,
> To pay the Int'rest of Acknowledgment.

If the metaphor begins in the world of business and commerce, it ends with what is, at least today, a word with literary associations, 'acknowledgment'. It is, of course, possible that Barker thanks E. S. for his praise of her poetry rather than for his instruction in writing. Chances are that she thanks him for both.

> And with her [the muse] I [Barker] must acknowledge
>   too,
> The honour which you did on me bestow.

It seems likely that the muse, Barker as poet, offers thanks for instruction and that Barker the person says 'thank you' for praise. The learning involved, of course, is far removed from undergraduate taverns in Cambridge and the fatal tree.

A poem contained in a manuscript at Magdalen College, Oxford, and not found in **Poetical Recreations** is more specific about tuition and praise. Its lengthy title seems to connect this poem to both universities and to a variety of learned and witty men: **'To my friends who prais'd my Poems and at the beginning of the little printed book placed this motto—pulcherrima virgo Icedit, magna juventum stipante caterva.'**[15] Barker did not authorize the printing of her poems, but neither was she altogether unhappy that the book had appeared. As with her poem to E. S., she offers thanks both for tuition and for praise.

> This band of gallant youths, bears me along,
> Who teach me how to sing, then praise my song.

It is in this poem that Barker claims to be 'copartner' with a group of learned and witty men, but even in her somewhat breathless self-congratulation she does not forget the problem of worldly knowledge.

> 'Twas not for beauty, learning, eloquence
> No, 'twas your vertue, lov'd my innocence,

My rural muse, which never higher aimes
Than to discourse of shepherds and their lambs,

Innocence is once again brought forward, even if a few of Barker's verses in **Poetical Recreations** are a little more suited to undergraduates in a tavern than to shepherds tending their sheep.

'What', one might ask, 'did Cambridge academics think of Barker?' Did they treat letters and conversations connected with her as a pleasant diversion from time spent in more difficult and sophisticated pursuits, or did they take her seriously? Was she just a mascot or, as she thought, a 'copartner'? Benjamin Crayle, her publisher, does Barker no favour when he writes in his preface that genteel men and women will treat her verses with respect out of civility.

> [Barker's poems] are the effects of a Ladies Wit, and I
> hope all the Courtly will (though out of a Complement)
> allow them for valuable.

Gerard Langbaine offers similar dubious praise for the plays of Margaret Cavendish on the same 'Courtly' basis, and other women writers were likewise treated to male condescension.[16] Barker may well allude to Crayle's words when she writes the following lines in 'To my friends who prais'd my Poetry'.

> . . . these young sons of Phoebus dance around
> And sing the praise of her themselves have crown'd
> Not like those Idole-makers heretofore
> Who had no right to praise, much less adore.
> No, justly I a poet's honour claim.

Crayle—like Curll some thirty years later—may turn Barker into an 'Idole' by publishing her writing, but, since Crayle is less than convinced about the poetry's quality, he is in no position to praise it. Further, this hypocrite should not 'adore' the author. Crayle offers a set of love poems directed to Barker at the end of **Poetical Recreations,** poems that might have caused her some annoyance.

The men who are clearly identified both with Barker and with Cambridge in the 1688 volume, however, offer a vastly different set of attitudes from Crayle's. Perhaps most interesting is an ode by Exillus, the unidentified man associated with St. John's. Rather than offer stock praise of the sort directed by gentlemen to ladies, he couches his lines on her poetry in a sophisticated religious metaphor. Exillus, while twisting around the beginning of the gospel of St. John, says that God created order out of chaos not by thought but by action.

> Nothing of Beauty did appear,
> But all was a continu'd boundless space,
> Till the Almighty's powerfull Command,
> Whose Action ev'r more quick than thought,
> The Infant World out of confusion brought.
>
> (Barker 1688, sig A7v)

Barker, like God acting upon chaos, takes the thoughts of Exillus and gives them form by the act of writing.

So where my [Exillus'] Thoughts, if Thoughts can be
Design'd from Wit, and Poetry,
Nothing but Ignorance appear'd,
Dull ignorance, and folly too,
With all that Crew,
And home-bred Darkness held the regencie,
Till your Almighty Pen
This Chaos cleared,
And of old arm'd Men,
Strange Miracles rose out o' th' Earth

(Barker 1688, sig. A8)

Exillus, as is the case with Barker elsewhere, is just a little Metaphysical in his comparison. Barker is not likened to the Virgin Mary, a kind of comparison attacked by Johnson in comments on Donne's poem on the death of Elizabeth Drury. Nevertheless, the likening of Barker to God is not much more restrained. More importantly for the purposes of this essay, Exillus admits of something like a collaboration between himself and Barker. He provides the material for composition, and she produces the finished product. Barker went on to publish this romance some years later as ***Exilius or the Banish'd Roman*** (1715). (See McBurney 1958, 338 and 389) The collaboration would have constituted a sort of tutorial for her, but one in which she was an active participant rather than a passive auditor. Exillus is probably the author of a second and more conventional poem, specifically on the topic of 'Scipina'. The second poem is far less accomplished and is considerably less revealing of their interactions. (Barker 1688, [part II] 35)

The first poem, as it turns out, can be interpreted as something of an effort at seduction. Exillus continues as follows:

And as the Heav'ns, to which we all things owe,
Scarce own those Bounties which they do bestow:
So you're as kind as they,
Submit your kinder influence,
To be by us determin'd, us obey,
And still from them
Give us ev'n for our weakness a reward,
Without regard
To Merit. . . .

The reward is not specified, but Old Damon, of **'To My Friend Exillus',** would have had his suspicions.[17] The 'us' is quite clearly Exillus, himself. Although seduction poems were quite conventional, Barker actually may have needed recourse to her innocence when dealing with Exillus. While her life fits with Richetti's 'public image of the lady novelist' as morally upright, the life of at least one close friend does not appear to have been so unspotted.

A poem by John Newton, fellow of St. John's College, is less sophisticated and complex than the verses by Exillus concerning Barker, God, and chaos. Nevertheless, 'To Mrs. Jane Barker, on her most Delightful and Excellent Romance of Scipina, now in the Press.'[18] contains further indications of what Cambridge men thought about her.

Thy Lines may pass severest Virtue's Test,
More than Astrea's soft, more than Orinda's chast.
Young Country Squires may read without offence,

Nor Lady Mothers fear their debauch'd Innocence.
Only beware, Incautious Youths beware,
Lest when you see such lovely Pictures there;
You, as of old the Fair Enamour'd Boy,
Languish for those feign'd Beauties you descry,
And pine away for Visionary Joy.
Then if by day they kindle noble Fire,
And with gay thoughts your nightly Dreams inspire
Bless, Bless the author of your soft desire.

(Barker 1688, [Part II] 32)

The suggestion that Barker's poetry manages to combine the 'softness' of Aphra Behn's (Astrea's) verse with the virtue of Katherine Philips' (Orinda's) poetry is fairly obvious as a compliment and one that might have been offered to many woman poets of the time. Newton is more revealing of his, and perhaps other Cambridge men's views of Barker, in suggesting that young men may read her verse without offense. When he goes on to write that the 'Lady Mothers' of rural England need not 'fear' that Barker will corrupt the innocence of their sons, he obviously is having a little joke. He teases her about the poems she had written concerning the taking of young lovers. These poems are innocent enough, and love poems in which the speaker pretends to a substantial age difference with the beloved were not unusual.[19] Since there seems to be the evidence of an actual romantic attachment between Exillus and Barker and since Exillus could have been an undergraduate, the joke might have been just a tiny bit cruel.[20] If so, Barker could take the ribbing. In **'To my friends who prais'd my Poems',** she says that her friends are 'of all your Reverend mothers sons the prime'. (Barker 1997, 308) The point, finally, is that Newton is comfortable enough with Barker to tease her and in doing so treats her as something like a 'copartner'. Further, the final line of 'To Mrs. Jane Barker' shows that her poetry's evocation of 'soft desire' in a young man, that is her affinity with Behn, struck Newton as more important than her poetry's chaste content. In this case, Barker's moral rectitude did not preclude a bit of teasing from friends on amorous topics.

If Fidelius was another Cambridge man, and his coterie name would suggest that such is the case, then 'To the Incomparable Galaecia, on the Publication of Her Poems' shows that the academy was well aware of Barker's interest in the Tree of Knowledge. The poem begins with an ordinary comparison: Barker is like a new star in the sky. The poem continues as 'The Sons of Art' are amazed by the star's 'Noveltie'. Barker was new and unusual as a woman poet, a novelty, and she was also a star that was very bright, a 'nova'. The Sons of Art, then would want to admire her 'theory', her 'spectacle' in a now obsolete sense of the word 'theory', and would have to come to terms with her 'theory' in a second and more modern sense: the system of her thought. Fidelius concludes the poem by paying metaphorical tributes to Barker's beauty and her unreflected brilliance.

And may your piercing Wit shine always bright
As th' Ev'ning Star in a clear frosty Night,
Unrival'd by the Moon's faint borrow'd light.

(Barker 1688, sig a2v)

Barker is beautiful as Venus, the evening star, and does not give off light at second hand, as does the moon. It is with a reference to her specific interests rather than in such stock compliments that the poem ends, however.

> But may your Rhimes be still imploy'd to tell,
> What satisfaction do's in Knowledge well;
> And as you have begun, so yet go on,
> To make coy Nature's secrets better known;
> And may we learn in purest Verse, from thee,
> The Art of Physick, and Anatomie.

Fidelius understands that Barker aspires to knowledge—medicine in particular—but he also knows that she does not want to write in a worldly way.

Not all of Barker's Cambridge friends were so genteel. One such man, who went by the initials S. C., may be identified with Cambridge only on the basis of the content of his poem.

> 'Tis true, at Ten, we're sent to th' whipping fry,
> To tug at Clasick Oars, and trembling lye
> Under Gill's heavy lash, or Buzby's Eye.
> At Eighteen, we to King's or Trinity are sent,
> And nothing less than Laureate will content.

> (Barker 1688, sig. a)

According to S. C., Cambridge undergraduates do not aspire so much to ancient learning as to being included as wits in this or that miscellany of verse.

> We search all Sects, (like Systematick Fools)
> And sweat o'er Horace for Poetick rules.
> Yet all these Mountain-throes and din,
> At length drops out some poor crude Sooterkin,
> And makes ——cob Tonson vex'd he e'er put in.

S. C. is given to the sort of comparison that was to be made in Cambridge's Pope's Head tavern and not at the dinner table in Wilsthorp. Indeed, his crude punning goes beyond what Barker was likely ever to have written. A 'sooterkin' was an imperfect literary composition, but it was also, literally, an 'afterbirth'. Tonson, the publisher, was according to S. C., a 'cob', that is a 'lumpish person' but also a 'testicle'. The string of sexual puns concludes with Tonson sorry that he included poetry from the boys at King's and Trinity in his collection and also sorry that he 'put in' in another sort of way. It is, of course, possible that Barker had read S. C.'s poem in private and acceded to its undergraduate wit in those circumstances. She might not have been so happy to have the piece used as a commendatory poem in an anthology that introduced her to the literary world in print for the first time.

In *A Patch-Work Screen,* Barker explicitly claims Katherine Philips as a poetic model and at the same time is careful to put a good deal of distance between herself and Aphra Behn. Philips, after all, was known for her modesty and Behn was taken to be a brazen woman. (Barker 1997, 108) It is as if Barker were saying in 1723 to the likes of S. C., 'I am no longer interested in your

academic world with its dubious knowledge'. Jacqueline Pearson observes that the heroine of *A Patch-Work Screen* and Barker, too, exemplify the eighteenth-century ideal of 'chaste, domestic, unassertive authorship'. (Pearson 1993, 241) Barker apparently had put her Cambridge days behind her. In a general sort of way, such is the case. Nevertheless Barker borrowed freely from the fiction of Behn for many of the plots in her last book *The Lining of the Patch Work Screen* (1726) and seems in temperament more tolerant of the worldliness of Behn than committed to replicating exactly any supposed modesty of Philips.[21] A sentence from Barker's first novella, *Love's Intrigues* (1713), helps to sum up Barker's position on academe late in life: 'But let the World confine, or enlarge Learning as they please, I care not; I do not regret the time I bestow'd in its Company, its having been my good Friend . . . though I am not so generous, by way of Return to pass my word for its good Behaviour in our Sex always, and in all persons'. (Qtd from Greer et al. 1984, 355) Barker's Cambridge days and their connections to undergraduates of dubious morality were indeed behind her, but she was by no means ready to turn her back on the 'Friend' that they had provided for her.

Notes

1. The word comes from a manuscript poem, 'To my friends who prais'd my Poetry,' discussed later in this essay.

2. King (1994, 555) identifies this man, who carried the coterie name of Philaster and the initials of J. N. He was John Newton, first a student (1678-1685) and then a fellow (1685-1700) of St. John's. Another member of college, who carried the coterie name Exillus has not been identified but is discussed by King (1994, 568).

3. Revisions of the 1688 poems contained in the 1723 volume are often the same as what is to be found in the Magdalen College, Oxford manuscript.

4. 'To my Friend Exillus, on his persuading me to marry old Damon' (Barker 1688 14; Barker 1997, 111). The lines are identical in both printings.

5. Isabella in Behn's 'The Nun or the Fair Vow Breaker' needs to ask a confidant about her feelings, and Deletia in Cavendish's 'The Contract' is similarly unable to explain her emotions to herself.

6. OED

7. Barker uses the name Exillus in *Poetical Recreations* and changes it to Exilius in *Exilius or the Banish'd Roman* (1715).

8. See note 1.

9. See 'Absence for a Time' (Barker 1688, 87), for Barker's reference to this establishment:

> I Dread this tedious time more than
> A Fop to miss a Fashion,

Or the Pope's Head Tavern can
Dread the long Vacation.

10. Amazement and terror.

11. Henry Paman, who took an M.D. degree in 1658, was for a time professor of physic at Gresham College. He was an important fellow at St. John's at the time when Barker was composing the poems that were printed in *Poetical Recreations.* Along with gaining other powerful positions, he became bursar and held the Linacre lectureship in medicine. Another very slim possibility would be Dr. Clement Paman, who published verse in *Poems by Several Hands,* Dublin, 1663. Clement Paman's death around the time of the publication of *Poems by Several Hands,* would seem to make him an unlikely candidate for a connection with Barker's poem. I would like to thank Mr. Underwood, archivist, at St. John's for providing me with access to biographical information contained in the Rent Books of St. John's for the 1670s and 1680s.

12. The Cambridge University Library copy of *Poetical Recreations* was used for all transcriptions in this essay. There is, however, a hole in the paper where 'Hence' should appear in that copy. The emendation comes from the University Microfilms copy.

13. In the Magdalen manuscript, number 47, it is titled 'To my friend mr—on his perswading me to poetry'.

14. Her early understanding of her medical conversations with 'Strephon' seems to have been that such talk would lead to a long-term relationship, probably marriage. Apparently Strephon lost interest in his association with her, and she later came to believe that she had avoided the 'sottish ease' of a housewife and instead had acquired knowledge in an important profession. 'On the Apothecary's Filling my Bills,' (Barker 1688, 32; Barker 1997, 117).

15. The Latin is translated in *The Galesia Trilogy*: 'The most beautiful virgin goes [to the temple] with a vast company of youths thronging about her' (Barker 1997, 307).

16. 'Sure I am, that whoever will consider well the several Epistles before her Books, and the General Prologue to all her Plays, if he have any spark of Generosity, or Good Breeding, will be favourable in his Censure'. Langbaine does praise the originality of her plots. (Langbaine 1691, 391) Katherine Philips specifically attacks such false gentility in letter 42 to Sir Charles Cotterell. (Philips 1705, 206).

17. Exilius also hints at a romantic connection between Exillus and Barker. Scipiana (Scipina in the unpublished version) seems to be another alter ego of Barker and is loved by Exilius in the romance. See McBurney (1958, 301).

18. If the book was printed before 1715 when it appeared as *Exilius,* all trace of it has been lost.

19. See Rochester's speaker in 'Ancient Lover of My Heart'.

20. See also notes 15 and 18 [17?—Technical Editor] for other evidence of romantic attachment.

21. Philips, in her letters to Sir Charles Cotterell, is far more ambitious for public recognition as a writer than she was given credit for being at the end of he seventeenth century. In letter 21, she is, for instance, very impatient that the duchess of York see her translation of Corneille's *Pompey* while it is in manuscript. (Philips 1705, 99). Janet Todd sees Barker as 'decorous' in comparison with Behn, Manley, and Haywood, but Todd also writes that *A Patch-Work Screen* has 'an uneasy, unsettling nature reminiscent of the short tales of Behn'. (Todd 1989, 50)

List of Works Cited

Barash, Carol. 1996. *English Women's Poetry 1649-1714.* Oxford: Clarendon Press.

Barker, Jane. 1997. *The Galesia Trilogy.* Edited by Carol Shiner Wilson. Oxford: Oxford University Press.

Greer, Germaine, et al. Eds. 1984. *Kissing the Rod.* New York: Noonday.

Hobby, Elaine. 1988. *Virtue of Necessity: English Women's Writing, 1649-88.* Ann Arbor: University of Michigan Press.

King, Kathryn R. 1993. 'Galesia, Jane Barker, and a Coming to Authorship.' In *Anxious Power: Reading. Writing, and Ambivalence in Narrative by Women,* edited by Carol J. Singley and Susan Elizabeth Sweeney. Albany: State University of New York Press.

King, Kathryn R. 1994. 'Jane Barker, *Poetical Recreations,* and the Sociable Text'. *ELH* 61 (fall): 551-70.

King, Kathryn R. and Jeslyn Medoff. 1997 'Jane Barker and Her Life (1652-1732): The Documentary Record.' *Eighteenth Century Life* 21: 16-38.

Langbaine, Gerald. 1691. rpt. 1973. *An Account of the English Dramatick Poets.* Oxford. [New York: Garland].

McBurney, William H. 1958. 'Edmund Curll, Mrs. Jane Barker, and the English Novel,' *Philological Quarterly* 37: 388 and 389.

Pearson, Jacqueline. 1993. 'The History of *The History of the Nun.*' In *Rereading Aphra Behn.* Edited by Heidi Hutner. Charlottesville: The University Press of Virginia.

Philips, Katherine. 1705. *Letters from Orinda to Poliarchus.* London.

Richetti, John. 1969. *Popular Fiction Before Richardson.* Oxford: Clarendon Press.

Spencer, Jane. 1986. *The Rise of the Woman Novelist.* Oxford: Basil Blackwell.

Todd, Janet. 1989. *The Sign of Angellica.* London: Virago.

Kathryn R. King (essay date 2000)

SOURCE: King, Kathryn R. "A Jacobite Novelist." In *Jane Barker, Exile: A Literary Career 1675-1725,* pp. 147-79. Oxford: Clarendon Press, 2000.

[*In the following essay, King tells the story of Barker as a Jacobite novelist, showing the connections between the plots of her novels and the political activities and ideologies of the Stuart court.*]

Barker is in fact a supremely self-regarding writer, mindful of her gendered singularity and fascinated with the many ways to tell her own story; and it seems undeniable, if hard to prove, that her heroine, Galesia—poet, healer, virgin, *femme savante,* and odd woman—is in many ways a self-portrait. However, when the complex self-fashionings of the prose fictions, the Galesia trilogy in particular,[1] are read in relation to their own political moment, these narratives emerge as complex elegiac responses to the declining fortunes of the exiled Stuarts and their followers in England.[2]

That Barker's career as a market-place novelist overlaps closely with the reign of the first of the Hanoverians, George I (1714-27) is no coincidence. These were years of intense Jacobite, or anti-Hanoverian, activity—the two were never easily distinguishable—protests, plots, conspiracies, alarms, riots, abortive and actual invasions, including in 1715-16 a full-fledged uprising, the Fifteen, one of the most serious of several attempts in the first half of the century to overthrow the Hanoverian government. With its ongoing unrest over the question of the succession, the period from 1714 to 1723 was the 'most widespread and the most dangerous' of the 'three great waves' of Jacobite agitation that threatened the English government between 1689 and 1754.[3] (It was during the first of these waves, 1689-96, that Barker composed much of [her] St-Germain verse. . . ..) The failure of the Fifteen, as will be seen, had disastrous consequences for the English Catholic community: from this point on Jacobite political activism would be largely a Protestant phenomenon. Barker remained stalwart, however. A former inhabitant of St-Germain, kin to ex-officers in James's army and at least one officer presently in the service of Philip V of Spain, a person whose name was known to the exiled duke of Ormonde, she evidently had connections with the Jacobite underground. A 1718 letter to Ormonde demonstrates she was implicated in Jacobite plotting at high levels, and it is possible she lent covert assistance to the Pretender in ways no longer discoverable. She continued to write with a Jacobite purpose, but starting in 1714 she began publishing in the literary market-place and would require strategies of indirection to advance her Catholic-Jacobite programme.

Critics have shown little interest in the political dimensions of the novels and until recently have failed to recognize their deep immersion in a Jacobite world-view,[4] while studies of the links between women, politics, and the novel

such as those provided by Ros Ballaster, Catherine Gallagher, and Paula McDowell omit Barker from consideration. Yet Barker was, arguably, England's leading producer of Jacobite fiction. The discussion that follows focuses upon her career as a Jacobite novelist, beginning with *Exilius* in 1714, published just weeks after the death of Queen Anne, and ending in 1725 with *The Lining of the Patch Work Screen,* a work that wrestles with the implications for English Jacobites of the failure of the Jacobite cause. (Her first published prose fiction, *The Amours of Bosvil and Galesia* (1713), better known as *Love Intrigues,* presents a special case. . . .) Barker was no propagandist; she did not attempt political interventions in the manner of Tory party-writer Delarivier Manley. Although she shared her predecessor's anti-Whig animus as well as her appreciation of the political possibilities of market-place fiction, Barker wrote quite, realistic stories far removed in tone and intent from the lurid sex-and-scandal allegories that brought Manley infamy but also contributed, it has been thought, to the fall of the Whig ministry in 1710.[5] None the less, the plots and central situation of the Galesia stories, even the heroine's identity as a spinster, would have carried strong political resonances for contemporary readers attuned to Jacobite interpretative codes. Read through these codes and against the backdrop of the ongoing crisis over the succession—a sustained conflict that constitutes, it seems to me, a crucial context for everything Barker published between 1714 and 1725—her prose fictions present themselves as highly allusive political meditations designed to express the hopes and anxieties of politically disaffected readers, Catholics and Jacobites especially, in ways we are only now beginning to recognize.

EXILIUS; OR, THE BANISH'D ROMAN

Although the title-page reads 1715, *Exilius; or, The Banish'd Roman,* an old-fashioned heroic romance, appeared in August 1714 during the interval between the death of Queen Anne, the last of the Stuarts, and the arrival of George I from Hanover.[6] (The post-dating is typical of its publisher, Edmund Curll, who found it expedient to prolong thus a work's claim to currency.)[7] The weeks and months following Anne's death saw a flood of pro-Stuart writing as fears about the Hanoverian succession and the change of ministry gave rise to pro-Jacobite riots and demonstrations. Throughout the kingdom, according to historian Kathleen Wilson, political anxieties found expression in a Tory-Jacobitism that would provide the 'dominant idiom of protest in the extra-parliamentary nation between 1715 and 1722'.[8] In its own way *Exilius* frames a fittingly pro-Stuart response to the succession crisis of 1714. Turning on a bewildering array of returns from exile, its plot organized around crises of obligation and authority displaced onto a variety of father—child relationships, *Exilius* develops the themes of loyalty, constancy, and obligation beloved of Stuart supporters in the seventeenth century and their Jacobite successors in the next. In the manner of the French heroic romance of the previous century, Madeleine de Scudéry's *Clélie* (1654-61) for example, she used Roman history to comment on present affairs of state;[9] as with the royalist dramas of the 1680s to which it is related, the extravagantly heroic plot inscribes codes of loyalty and obligation shown to be inviolable even under the most egregious conditions, including attempted rape and incest.[10] By reaffirming these old-fashioned royalist virtues and celebrating a determination to remain faithful at all costs, Barker offers in *Exilius* a fiction designed, it would seem, to strengthen Jacobite resolve to resist the House of Hanover and bring home the true king.

Readers are right to feel there is something retro about *Exilius,* however. Parts had in fact been written much earlier, as far back perhaps as the early 1680s in response to the Exclusion Crisis.[11] Commendatory verses printed in **Poetical Recreations** reveal that an earlier version of *Exilius,* then entitled *Scipina,* was 'in the Press' in 1687—why it failed to appear is unknown—and that the romance had been read in manuscript by members of the Cambridge circle, two of whom wrote under names shared by characters in the romance ('Exilius' and 'Fidelius'), suggesting its coterie origins.[12] It seems reasonable to speculate, then, that the episode in which the princess Galecia runs her lover through with a sword was written with a view toward amusing the Cambridge friends, who would have been all too familiar with Barker's obsession with Strephon/Bosvil (called Boccus in *Exilius*), the unreliable suitor whose perfidy was evidently the subject of verse exchanged within this circle. A further example of coded, in-group humour may be found in John Newton's tongue-in-cheek observation that 'Young *Country Squires*' may read *Scipina* 'without *offence,* | Nor *Lady Mothers* fear their debauch't *Innocence*' (*PR* 2. 32), a mischievous gender reversal that suggests he and Barker may have been enjoying a private joke.

We do not know whether Barker had a hand either in initiating or in stopping publication of *Scipina* or why publication was delayed nearly three decades. One of the first hints the romance had resurfaced under a new title comes on 14 August 1714 in the *Post Boy* (No. 3006): 'Next Thursday will be publish'd, in a neat Pocket-Vol. **Exilius; or, The Banish'd Roman: A new Romance, in Two Parts**'. Curll may have rushed the book through the press to take advantage of the political moment. (On 5 August, just days after Anne died, he published a pamphlet on her death: he 'must have been first in the field', his biographer comments.)[13] In any event *Exilius* came out at last in the context of widespread apprehensions about the Hanoverian succession. Fitted out with a topical, politically allusive title, this high-minded story of constant love and banished Romans, a piece of coterie fiction dating back to the Restoration and begun in response to a different Stuart crisis, emerged a deeply (if in a sense inadvertently) Jacobite work. It seems right Barker should assume the role of market-place writer at the precise moment of the passing of the Stuart era.

She did not consider herself a market-place author, however, not yet anyway. She seemed rather to imagine herself as writing in the tradition of aristocratic sixteenth- and seventeenth-century royalist romance,[14] if a dedication dated 10 June 1715 is any indication.[15] She casts herself in the role of a latter-day Sir Philip Sidney, 'whose steps with awful Distance, I now take Leave to trace', and calls attention to the affinities between her own '*Roman* Heroes' and 'his *Arcadians*'.[16] Perhaps she saw *Exilius* as providing the present generation of Stuart loyalists with what, according to Annabel Patterson, Sidney's *Arcadia* gave royalists in the seventeenth century: pro-Stuart commentary in the guise of romance, 'a key to class solidarity, a language in which to express and assess their own recent history'.[17]

Exilius is in many ways an angry work, filled with a Jacobite's contempt for the credulity of the lower orders, ready to fall for the absurdity of the fiction of the warming-pan birth, and fury at the fear-mongering tactics of those with an illegitimate hold on power,[18] but it remains Barker's most sanguine fiction. The multiple weddings with which it closes exhibit the triumph of 'unfashionable Constancy', as the dedication puts it, and proclaim faith in the power of loyalty, honour, moral integrity, and steadfast love—sacred ideals in the Jacobite constellation of virtues—to triumph over adverse circumstance. Such faith would fade in the novels to come. *A Patch-Work Screen for the Ladies* and *The Lining of the Patch Work Screen,* written after the spectacular failure of the Fifteen and the collapse of other lesser Jacobite restoration attempts, deliberately reject the affirmations of marriage in order to explore the uncertain circumstances of the woman never-married, a spinster and an exile who never quite makes it home. If *Exilius* uses romance, exalted love, and a heroic idiom to project Jacobite faith, the more pessimistic patch-work novels for which she is better known turn away from love, marriage, and the heroic possibilities of the past to confront instead the gritty, here-and-now experience of loss, disappointment, loneliness, and compromised loyalty in early Georgian Britain.

THE CHRISTIAN PILGRIMAGE

Her next publication was not a fiction at all, however, but a translation of Lenten meditations by the French prelate and man of letters François de Salignac Fénelon (1651-1715), the archbishop of Cambrai. The octavo volume, advertised in the *Post Boy* on 18 February 1718 (No. 4456) as 'This Day' published, came out under the auspices of Curll and Charles Rivington as *The Christian Pilgrimage,*[19] dedicated to the countess of Nottingham. She was a High Anglican reputed to have Catholic sympathies; her husband had recently been dismissed from office for his opposition to the government in the aftermath of the Fifteen.[20] The Catholic devotional manual was obviously intended for a Protestant audience: Barker sought to make Fénelon 'speak *English,* in the Dialect of the Church of England' ('Dedication', ii-iii).[21]

Given Fénelon's strong market value at this time Curll's part in the venture is not difficult to understand. The decade witnessed a veritable outpouring of Fénelon titles from mainstream (that is, non-Catholic) presses. The previous year, 1717, Curll had brought out a highly successful new translation by John Ozell of Fénelon's *Telemachus* (1699), said to have established 'the cult for the Archbishop of Cambrai'.[22] By 1720 it had gone into a third edition. Though little read today *Telemachus*—part didactic romance, part political theory, part mirror-for-princes treatise, and part *cause scandale* for what was universally thought to be its attack on the absolutism of Louis XIV— was extraordinarily influential in its time, the 'most notorious, then the most renowned book of the early eighteenth century'.[23] Barker sought to draw upon its prestige when on the title-page she described *Exilius* as 'Written After the Manner of TELEMACHUS, For the Instruction of Some Young LADIES of Quality', although in fact the two books are not much alike.

If Curll's involvement in the publication of **The Christian Pilgrimage** requires little explanation, Barker's motives are more complicated and are, as usual, bound up in her Catholic-Jacobite agenda. To understand why she might want to translate a French Roman Catholic devotional manual at this particular juncture, and publish it through the auspices of a Protestant publisher,[24] we need to recall the crisis in which hard-line Jacobite members of the English Catholic community found themselves early in 1716 when government forces managed successfully to quash the Jacobite rebellion. Catholics had been heavily involved in the Fifteen and faced severe reprisals from a government determined to crush all future Catholic opposition. Prominent members of the Catholic aristocracy and gentry were imprisoned and in some cases executed—the hapless young earl of Derwentwater lost his head—and many priests were forced into hiding. Catholic landowners of all ranks and regions were threatened with additional charges on estates already subject to double land taxes; some faced forfeitures. As a known papist Barker was herself obliged by a 1715 statute to register her estate in Wilsthorp; documents preserved in the Lincolnshire Archives Office show that she submitted a deposition on 15 October 1717, just before the government's deadline.[25] The English Catholic community was deeply shaken by these events. Indeed, as Colin Haydon has observed, 'for contemporary Catholics the aftermath of the uprising had the potential to develop into one of the greatest crises for their church since Elizabethan times'.[26] Leading members of the gentry and nobility renounced their faith in order to hold onto their property; those who did not looked for ways to assure the authorities of their political loyalty. To the consternation of many Catholic Jacobites a group of churchmen, led by Bishop John Talbot Stonor and Dr Thomas Strickland, went so far as to draft for the community's use an oath that would enable Catholics anxious to protect their estates to swear allegiance to George I.[27] In short, government measures designed to sap Catholic opposition to the established order largely succeeded. Historians Geoffrey Holmes and Daniel Szechi report that from 1716 Catholic support of Jacobite plots was 'minimal': the 'dwindling Catholic élite was no longer prepared to risk what it had left by rebelling' while the larger Catholic community 'was forced

into quietism to protect itself'.[28] Hereafter the impetus for Jacobite conspiracy would come principally from Protestants, as evidenced by the Atterbury plot exposed in 1722, named after one of the central conspirators, the Anglican bishop Francis Atterbury: it was a plan for a foreign invasion hatched at the very highest levels of the Church of England.

Catholics who retained their commitment to Jacobite activism were compelled to adopt strategies of accommodation to pursue their political ends. **The Christian Pilgrimage,** which seeks to reframe Anglican understandings of Catholicism in such a way as to secure greater toleration for the Catholic community, represents one such strategy. Barker makes Fénelon speak 'in the Dialect of the Church of *England*' so that the volume might be 'universally beneficial', to which end she expunges a few Catholic bits, some Hail Marys for example, in order *'to prevent any sudden Disgust the Protestant Reader might take at the Sight of it'*.[29] Barker's translation is an instance of 'protestantization', that is to say, a kind of sanitizing process whereby 'Catholic publications, especially works of devotion' were deliberately 'purged of all-too Catholic elements, and provided with an introduction warning the Protestant reader'.[30] But Barker's purposes went beyond making Catholic materials palatable to non-Catholic readers and beyond extending the common ground between Catholics and Anglicans, important though these were to her greater aim, which was, to soften resistance to the notion of a Catholic monarch on the English throne.

For such a project Fénelon was ideal. Why? To begin with, he was a revered figure not only in English Jacobite circles, where his role as counsellor to the Pretender would have been well known, but in broader circles as well—for reasons wrapped up, ironically, in British xenophobia and anti-French prejudice. At the turn of the century Louis XIV, infuriated by certain passages in *Télémaque,* had banished Fénelon from Versailles to the remote frontier diocese of Cambrai: ill-treatment at the hands of the French king counted for much among Barker's contemporaries. For another thing, Fénelon's particular brand of Catholicism, quietist and mystical, appealed to Anglicans of a highly spiritual turn of mind. The compilers of *English Catholic Books* include his devotional writings (along with those of Thomas à Kempis) in a select category of 'spiritual classics' destined to remain 'popular across the denominational divide throughout the century'.[31] But even more importantly, perhaps, Fénelon—famously mild, gentle, urbane, tolerant, universalist, even in a sense anti-French—offered an effective counterbalance to English stereotypes of 'superstitious' and 'tyrannical' papists, an answer of sorts to the anti-Catholic propaganda churned out by government writers nothing loath to whip up support for George I and the Whig ministry around longstanding fears of Catholic atrocities.[32] In such a papiphobic climate the benign example of Fénelon and his devotional writing would offer reassurance to an English public all too inclined to assume Catholics capable of the worst kind of militancy and superstition and in this way, perhaps, diminish antipathy toward the notion of a Catholic Stuart on the English throne.

Barker's use of a conciliatory, ostensibly universalizing stance that at once masks and advances her Jacobite purposes associates her with such well-known Stuart adherents as Thomas Southcott (1670-1748) and his friend Andrew Michael Ramsay (1686-1743), the former a Benedictine monk with close links to the Stuart court-in-exile, the latter the Scots Catholic convert who edited Fénelon and published the first biography. Although there is no evidence that Barker knew Southcott or Ramsay, it is clear they all appreciated Fénelon's tactical importance to the restoration cause. In 1723 Andrew ('Chevalier') Ramsay published a deeply sympathetic *Life of Fénelon* in the hope, according to Geoffrey Scott, that non-Catholic readers 'would be impressed' by Fénelon's willingness to suffer 'for his principles' and to 'distinguish essential elements of Catholicism from its trappings'.[33] (As Ramsay put it, somewhat disingenuously, in the *Life,* 'Pure Love and humble Faith are the whole of the Catholick Religion'.)[34] Southcott vigorously promoted Ramsay's *Life,* Scott argues, because he was persuaded that Fénelon's teachings on 'disinterested love' would draw Anglicans of a particularly spiritual turn of mind closer to Catholicism.[35] From 1723, in other words, Fénelon would be a key element in the British Catholic-Jacobite programme. At a time when many of the Pretender's Protestant supporters urged him to renounce his religion, Catholic Jacobites such as Southcott and Ramsay chose for obvious reasons to devise strategies for cultivating greater popular acceptance of his Catholicism, a tolerance which would in turn remove from the minds of many Britons what amounted to the chief obstacle to a Stuart Restoration, the Pretender's repugnant religion. Historians would do well to consider that five years earlier Barker had embarked upon much the same project.

The Patchwork Narratives

Five years would pass before Barker brought out a new work, possibly because she had once more gone to live abroad.[36] About these years nothing is known beyond the fact that, in 1718, only a month after the publication of **Christian Pilgrimage,** Barker wrote a letter to the exiled Ormonde passing on information regarding a proposed invasion scheme. (We know about this letter only because it was intercepted and duly copied into a letterbook by the bemused authorities: 'On ignore qui est Barker'.)[37] *A Patch-Work Screen for the Ladies* was published in June 1723,[38] the same month Bishop Atterbury went into exile and just one month after the hanging of the Jacobite conspirator Christopher Layer. The sequel, *The Lining of the Patch Work Screen,* appeared in the autumn of 1725.[39] The preceding decade had been disastrous for Jacobites. Starting with the reprisals following the failure of the Fifteen, these years brought one hardship after another. Imprisonments and executions, the threat of new taxes, renewed vigour in the enforcement of the penal laws, and increased surveillance made life perilous for Catholics and

suspected Jacobites, while the exposure of the Atterbury plot brought new severities, including in 1723 Walpole's imposition on the Catholic community of a levy of 100,000 pounds.[40] Jacobitism was 'at a low ebb, with its morale so shaken that another spontaneous rising like the '15 was unthinkable'.[41] Even among the hard-core faithful restoration began to seem a lost cause. Barker never ceased working for the cause, however, lending it her support up to the last years of her life, as we saw earlier in her contribution of the 'od present' to the newly resurgent movement to canonize 'our holy King'. Perhaps she was able to keep alive her belief in the ultimate triumph of Jacobite hopes. But the post-Atterbury fictions suggest otherwise, or more accurately perhaps, suggest a struggle to accommodate her faith in the transcendent virtue of the Stuart cause to the bleak events of recent history, to negotiate what has aptly been termed a 'crisis over the dissonant claims of principle and practical survival'.[42] Read through the lens of this crisis, *Patch-Work Screen* can be seen to register a complex elegiac response to the collapse of Jacobite political ambitions while its sequel, *Lining of the Patch Work Screen,* can be seen to explore the dilemma of the Jacobite subject in a time of defeat, when she or he is torn between rival claimants to the throne and forced into positions of ideological compromise.

This is not to say that the patchwork narratives are Jacobite works in an overt, systematic, or even sustained way. First and foremost they are studies of a singular woman whose life takes shape on the boundaries of ordinary female existence, as feminist scholars have long recognized. My claim is rather that the courtship plot that is an important thread of Galesia's life-story would have been politically allusive for Barker's contemporaries in ways likely to go unnoticed today. In a ground-breaking essay that asks whether there was a rhetoric of Jacobitism, Howard Erskine-Hill answers affirmatively by detailing a distinctively Jacobite use of the image of rape, used to signify William's conquest but also various other violations of political legitimacy.[43] He does not discuss a related counter-image that reverberates through a range of somewhat later Jacobite discourses and furnished Barker with her central political trope: marriage (or sexual union) as an image of wished-for political legitimacy.[44] In many Jacobite contexts the marriage trope tended to be eroticized, as if to convey the immense pain of separation or the intense desire for a union endlessly deferred. Its most characteristic expression is the image of the dashing 'lost lover' pervasive in representations of James Francis Stuart from 1715.[45] Against this background Barker's use of the marriage trope in the two patchwork narratives emerges as wholly her own. In place of the erotically charged Stuart romance favoured by other Jacobite writers she uses spinsterhood and a failure-of-marriage plot to explore by way of analogy the situation of the loyal subject when the 'lost lover' is truly, perhaps irretrievably lost.

Long before she began to make political use of the figure of the spinster, Barker had been fascinated by the literary possibilities of the image of the celibate woman. In *Exilius,* the virgin-princess Galecia belongs to the tradition of female martial valour which in the second half of the seventeenth century inspired the heroic self-fashionings of aristocratic women in France and England.[46] The heroic model of the *femme forte* continued to shape the otherwise more realistically conceived Galesia of *Amours of Bosvil and Galesia,* [*BG*] as when Galesia at one point fancies herself the champion of her sex, 'rank'd in the Catalogue of Heroines', for 'ridding the World' of the monstrous Bosvil (*BG* 31). But by the time Barker wrote *A Patch-Work Screen for the Ladies* [*PWS*] the heroic virgin had undergone a change of key to become the diminished figure of the spinster, slightly peculiar, out-of-step; an odd woman. Read in the context of the Stuart romance of the 'lost lover', her unmarriedness suggests by analogy a country separated from its ruler/husband; and we begin to understand why an author not notably enamoured of the possibilities of conjugal union should permit an otherwise independent-minded heroine, a character more attuned to the muses than to men,[47] to rue the collapse of one marriage proposal after another.

For Galesia's uncharacteristic regrets, so at odds with the 'secret Disgust against Matrimony' (*PWS* 133) expressed elsewhere in the narrative, are meant to supply a kind of allegorical shorthand for the trials and disappointments of the Jacobites since the period of wandering and exile began in 1688. 'I could *hope* nothing, *propose* nothing, but I was cross'd or disappointed therein, e'er I could arrive at Accomplishment', Galesia muses sadly, 'I began to believe Providence had ordain'd for me a *Single Life*' (*PWS* 139). She speaks here, I suggest, less as a woman than as a study in exemplary Jacobite quietism, a follower of Fénelon perhaps, passively resigned to an acceptance of God's will. As her auditor puts it, underscoring the Fénelonian point, Galesia has been granted a 'Mind submissive and resign'd' and in spite of her losses can 'hope for more prosperous Days for the Time to come' (*PWS* 140). She is at once repining England and Jacobite perseverance in a season of little hope.

Once their Jacobite underpinnings are recognized, elements of *Patch-Work Screen* that seem incomprehensible or even inept begin to take on meaning. Take, for example, the famous failure of the Galesia plot to achieve closure. The apparent irresolution has prompted a fair amount of commentary, both admiring and smug. The 'book ends *in media res*'; the heroine 'remains in the limbo of the unconcluded *Patch-Work Screen*'; her fate 'is not resolved; one cannot make a finished screen of the ambiguous fragments'.[48] Patricia Meyer Spacks seems uncertain whether to chalk up the 'ostentatious incoherence' of the narrative method to incompetence or to an indifference to craft that amounts to a 'disclaimer of serious intent'.[49] It is true Galesia's life-story does not have a happy ending or much of an ending at all, but there is a reason for this: the Stuart story still lacks the happy ending that will bring Galesia's to a close. Once the absence of closure is seen to be the analogue of a much greater failure of history then we are able to bring into view the ending that *is* there and

that criticism has thus far conspicuously failed to engage: the lengthy 'An *Ode* In *Commemoration* of the *Nativity* of *Christ*', the final lines of which pray for the conversion of the 'stubborn *Jews*', a people blind, sin-hardened, and in thrall to 'obstinate Delusions' (*PWS* 172). The reference would have carried a strong political charge for readers attuned to the familiar typological equation between the Jews, unconverted after seventeen hundred years, and the no less obstinate English people:

> Tho' suff'ring still, they still thy Laws despise,
> Since Seventeen Cent'ries cannot make them wise:
> Since from their rooted Sin they cannot part;
> Melt (for Thou canst!) the hardest Heart,
> And open Blindest Eyes:
> Make All on Earth, as All in Heav'n, join,
> Since All in Heav'n and Earth alike are Thine.
>
> (*PWS* 173)

It is thus with a prayer for the conversion of the Jews that Barker brings closure, of sorts, to Galesia's strangely unfinished life-story. Such an ending, bizarre at first and ignored in all commentary on the novel, is seen to be, typologically speaking, wholly fitting: in Jacobite contexts the conversion of the Jews stood for that conversion of English hearts and minds that would usher in a Stuart restoration.[50]

The Lining of the Patch Work Screen, published when Barker was 73 and Jacobitism an all but lost cause, is Barker's bleakest work. If *Patch-Work Screen* focuses upon the plight of the spinster, the loyal subject denied union with her lover/king, *Lining of the Patch Work Screen* uses a bigamy trope to express the troubles of the subject divided between *de jure* and *de facto* husbands/sovereigns and in this way to deepen her analysis of Jacobite existence in a time of defeat, compromise, and political illegitimacy. Galesia is now an old woman with no story of her own to tell; we first encounter her in the lodgings where she lives alone, deprived of even the 'Society of Friends by [her] Fire-side' (180). The narrative is an assemblage of stories of the loves, sufferings, and wanderings of survivors of the Jacobite diaspora, men and women of exemplary virtue who end up in Galesia's London lodgings where they reminisce about better days. The stories they tell, many of them set in Catholic countries, are concerned to a remarkable degree with convents, priests, nuns, conversions, and the happiness to be found in the 'Society of holy Virgins' (201); several recur to memories of St-Germain, a kind of Jacobite imaginary where 'Inferiours are humble, Superiours are affable, the Women vertuous, the Men valiant, the Matrons prudent, Daughters obedient, Fathers obliging, Sons observant, Patrons readily assisting, Supplicants gratefully accepting' (222). (In view of the neglect Barker evidently experienced at St-Germain one suspects that the idealized image of the reciprocal relationship between patrons and clients reflects at once long-standing irritation and self-preserving forgetting.) The battered but virtuous survivors—men and women of staunch old-fashioned virtue who with enormous patience suffer 'Poverty, Prosecution and Punishment of all sorts' (213)—seem themselves almost ghostly as they flicker in and out of the loosely connected tales, recalling a world that exists only in memory or imagination.

Indeed, *Lining* seems in some ways a study of what it means to live outside history. The distinction Marita Sturken draws between 'history' and 'cultural memory' in her work on national biography illuminates what is meant here by the phrase living outside history. History, in her usage, refers to 'narratives that have been sanctioned in some way, that often tell a self-conscious story of the nation', whereas cultural memory refers to stories 'told outside official historical discourse, where individual memories are shared, often with political intent, to act as counter-memories to history'.[51] By the time she began *Lining,* it seems to me, Barker had come to regard fiction-making as a vehicle for promulgating Jacobite 'counter-memories' meant to exist alongside and in opposition to official history, the latter increasingly used to prop up the values and world-view of the Whig regime. Both the Magdalen manuscript and the Galesia story told in *Patch-Work Screen* engage crucial moments in recent Stuart history, chronicling in direct fashion the fall of James and the early years of his exile (the Fidelia narrative) and the final years of the reign of Charles II (*Patch-Work Screen*), where Charles's death resonates with apocalyptic significance ('as if *Dooms-day* had discharg'd it self of a Shower of black walking Animals' (*PWS* 153)). *Patch-Work Screen* also projects, in coded and allusive ways, events of national history since the death of Anne, a recent past understood as a succession of failures to unite king and kingdom, true monarch and loyal subjects. But the intense nostalgia of *Lining,* the hagiographic treatment of wandering Jacobites, the characterization of Galesia as a winter's night spinster: all suggest a pronounced shift in purpose—a deliberate turning away from history toward the preservation (in Sturken's terms) of unsanctioned cultural memories, as in this final work Barker undertakes not to rewrite history so much as to devise a narrative framework capable of accommodating elements of Catholic and Jacobite experience omitted from or distorted in the stories Protestant Great Britain told about itself.

But if the narrative looks back nostalgically to an ideally virtuous world symbolized by St-Germain, it also engages in a tough-minded way problems of economic and social survival in the early Georgian England. Emblematic in this regard is the story of Mrs Goodwife, a supporter of James who took to small trading to support her husband and children after the family lost everything in the Irish campaign (218-21). But Barker is even more interested in issues of conflicted allegiance that exercised English Jacobites on an almost daily basis in the immediate post-Atterbury period. *Lining* includes a number of stories turning on bigamy (and near-bigamy), a plot vehicle that enabled her to imagine and work through the questions of legitimacy, fidelity, and troubled conscience facing those who, in rejecting the Protestant succession, were destined to be subject to one king while loyal to another. No fewer than five

inset tales use a bigamy plot, including one that offers a highly compressed retelling of Behn's 'The History of the Nun'—called by Barker '*Philinda's Story* out of the *Book*' (214)—in which the heroine arrives at the less than satisfactory solution of killing in one night two husbands.[52] As a means of giving form to the problems associated with divided loyalty two stories seem especially important. The first, the story of '*Tangerine,* the Gentleman Gypsie', is concerned with the question of how to 'come home' to the political nation after years of disaffection. The title figure, a former soldier in Charles II's army whose wife married his brother in his absence, is an ageing gypsy-outlaw tired of wandering. An updated version of the gypsies and beggars used in the seventeenth century to figure the impoverished cavalier, Barker's Gentleman Gypsy is at once a wanderer in the Jacobite diaspora and a more metaphorical exile within the British political nation.[53] A chance meeting with his newly widowed wife affords him an opportunity to bring his wanderings to an end. A storyline involving a tangle of broken promises, violated vows, vagabondage, and disguise is brought to a satisfying comedic conclusion when the Gentleman Gypsy is reunited with his wife; while a spirited girl in disguise as a gypsy, his companion in his late wanderings, is at last allowed to marry her true love, who turns out to be the Gypsy's son. Bigamy—split allegiance—is resolved into lawful marriage, and the girl's 'Extravagance in leaving her Father's House' (237) has no serious consequences. This story ends with a pair of marriages and a dissolving of disguise: a happy ending to years of concealment, wandering, and uncertain loyalty. A tale of Jacobite wish-fulfilment, it would seem.

A later tale, however, Amarantha's 'The *Story* of *Bellemien*', uses the bigamy trope to grimmer purpose as part of a plot which would seem to express an ambivalent accommodation to the Hanoverian succession. The story involves a virtuous and loving young couple who marry secretly and then allow themselves to be persuaded by family pressures and financial exigency to renounce 'their first conjugal Vows' and commit bigamy. The narrator makes it clear we are to see the 'unhappy couple' as basically good, well-meaning people forced by the pressure of circumstances into criminality. Like the virtuous but troubled Jacobites they represent, the now doubly married man and woman seek to make the best of it. They try to bear patiently the 'Yoke' of these 'new Espousals, which courted their acceptance' (256), but nothing but trouble ensues. The man longs to return to his 'true and lawful Wife' (257), but when he does, he brings heartbreak to his second wife and infamy to his first, who is universally condemned as a whore. There can be, Barker seems to be suggesting, no satisfactory arrangement for Jacobites under present conditions. The tale is a working out in pessimistic, almost tragic terms of the Jacobite dilemma in the early Hanoverian era.

In the only extended discussion to date of Barker as Jacobite poet, Toni Bowers calls attention to elements of 'disappointment, uncertainty, and dark regret' in the St-Germain verse that in her view sit oddly with Barker's identity as one of the most uncompromising of Jacobites.[54] Bowers probably underestimates the extent to which Barker deliberately mythologizes herself in this verse, most of it from the 1690s, but her observation that Jacobites in general were caught up in a 'crisis over the dissonant claims of principle and practical survival' (859) contains a valuable insight that seems to be borne out by study of Barker's late prose fictions. I would locate the acute phase of that crisis later than Bowers does, however. If Barker can be taken as representative, then the difficult process of learning to live with the ideological muddle of compromise and divided allegiance may have belonged primarily to the period from 1716, when English Jacobites, Catholics most pressingly, were compelled to come to terms with the practical failure of the cause and with the retreat of the Catholic community into quietism. It was largely for this community apart that Barker wrote her patchwork narratives. Drawing upon the materials of her own life to tell the life-story of an odd woman, she created fictions of spinsterhood and bigamy in which dissident readers could find figures not only for the failure of the Stuart romance but also for their own alienated existence in Hanoverian Britain.

ROMANCE, READERS, COMMUNITIES OF THE BOOK

Recognition that Barker's career as a novelist is tied from beginning to end to Jacobite imperatives invites us to think more closely about the role of party politics in the formation of the novel and to consider the possibility that the early novel, often regarded as the most self-consciously modern of forms, was (in some of its manifestations at least) implicated in a conservative politics. Consideration of the Jacobite dimensions of her novels throws new light on the old question of who was reading the early novel and why. For whom was Barker writing or did she think she was writing? To whom might her works be expected to appeal? Who actually read her? What cultural needs did her novels serve? In 1974 Pat Rogers remarked the 'notable lack of concrete research into the size and composition' of the audience for the emergent novel.[55] A quarter-century later, despite some important work on the sociology of the early novel, the situation has not greatly changed. The extent to which the rise of the novel is linked with the rise of the middle class and the rise of a middle-class reading public is a matter 'on which there is great interest and little definitive evidence', Michael McKeon has observed; and in spite of a host of well-aired problems with the 'triple rise' thesis, scholars continue to seek links between the emergence of the genre and the development of a bourgeois public sphere, and, less abstractly, to posit for the early novel a spectrum of urban readers new to the pleasures of reading—the semi-literate maidservants and apprentices that feature regularly in many accounts.[56] The discovery that Barker's chief publisher, Edmund Curll, targetted her prose fictions for an elite provincial audience with Tory-Jacobite leanings complicates present understandings and suggests we may need to widen considerably our angle of vision so far as the audience for the early novel is concerned.[57] Analysis of Curll's marketing of her work also confronts us with an unappreciated side of a publisher seldom noted for his relations with Jacobites, genteel lady novelists, or a gentry clientele.

Study of Curll's advertising strategies leaves no doubt that during the opening phase of her career as a novelist she was marketed as a Jacobite writer. At a time when much printed matter was sold unbound, the title-page was the bookseller's most important promotional resource, serving many of the same purposes of display as cover and dust-jacket do today. It provided copy for newspaper notices and was often posted by way of advertisement. Curll saw to it that the title-pages of Barker's earliest novels sent clear Jacobite signals. *Bosvil and Galesia* (1713), though not strictly speaking a Jacobite work, hints at the unknown author's ideological leanings with its announcement that the tale was related 'in *St*. Germains *Garden*'.[58] A reader who glanced at the first paragraph would find in its openly Jacobite references confirmation of the hint. Not only is the 'as-told-in-a-garden' frame set beside the palace of the exiled Stuarts, but the Nine Years War (as we now call it) that furnishes its backdrop is described in terms only a Stuart adherent would use—as a conflict over 'King JAMES's Affairs'.[59] *Exilius; or, The Banish'd Roman,* her next publication, could have proclaimed its Stuart allegiances more flagrantly only by entitling itself *The Exiled Pretender.*

Newspaper advertisements suggest also that Curll sought to draw Barker's first readers from the provincial gentry. One of his earliest attempts to promote Barker, a notice in the *Post Boy* of 23 May 1713 (No. 2814) for *Love Intrigues* (as it was then entitled), attributes the 'Novel' to 'a Lady': obviously Barker had yet to acquire a following or even a name. (The following year when Curll advertised *Exilius* in the *Post Boy* (14 Aug. 1714), the name of 'Mrs. JANE BARKER' would figure prominently.) In what amounts to a fascinating instance of early niche marketing, Curll emphasizes distinctions of class. *Love Intrigues* is said to be 'Dedicated to the Countess of Exeter' and, even more remarkably, the notice is given this heading: '*Advertisement to the Lincolnshire Gentry*'. The appeal is to the social sense of a very specifically targetted readership and by extension to a broader range of readers who either belonged themselves to the upper reaches of the provincial social scale or were pleased to identify with those who did.[60]

That the notice appeared in the *Post Boy,* a tri-weekly with strong Tory leanings and a large country readership, may suggest he was aiming for a politically disaffected readership as well. The *Post Boy,* under the editorship of Abel Roper, constituted the 'staple printed diet' of Tory sympathizers during the last four years of Anne's reign, according to J. A. Downie.[61] It went out with the post to the provinces, where by one estimate it would have been seen by as many as 50,000 readers, including a sizeable number of Stuart loyalists.[62] Indeed, if Paul Monod's estimates are reliable, at this time perhaps one in four members of the English landed classes would have possessed loyal sympathies.[63] Curll, always a canny interpreter of market trends, must have sensed the existence 'out there' of a considerable audience of men and women with at the very least a sentimental attachment to Jacobite principles.

This speculation finds support from the discovery that Curll marketed other Jacobite romances in the second decade of the century. In the aftermath of the Jacobite rebellion in 1715 he brought out *Irish Tales* (1716), a historical romance by Sarah Butler which a scholar of Irish literature has recently described as 'a challenging fiction of contemporary political relevance: an Irish, Roman Catholic, and Jacobite work, published in Protestant, Hanoverian England, just four months after the execution of the leading Jacobite rebels for their parts in the Rebellion of 1715'.[64] *Irish Tales* provides a superb example of Curll's use of the title-page to attract readers of Jacobite proclivities. This one names among its characters a 'Banish'd PRINCE', a 'Constant FAIR-ONE', a 'Depos'd USURPER', while the pages that follow are populated by figures sure to stir Jacobite minds and hearts: a lover-hero who takes matters like oaths and loyalty to fathers very seriously indeed; a bloody-minded virgin-heroine active in the Irish resistance. One of the heroine's finest moments comes when, the only woman in a band of 'counterfeit Ladies', she takes part in a cross-dressed massacre: she joins a 'Noble Train of suppos'd young Virgins'—stout young men really—who promise sex to gain entry to the usurper's court and then efficiently reduce the startled male courtiers to a 'purple Deluge on the Floor'.[65] This is Jacobite resistance heroics at its campiest and in some ways most characteristic, and answers to the author's stated design of showing the '*strange means by which* Ireland *was once deliver'd from the Tyranny of* Turgesius *and the* Danes, *by the Beauty of a Virgin*'.[66] For reasons that must be left to other scholars to explore, the Jacobite imagination seems to have been especially stirred by displays of female martial heroics, almost as if women were expected to enact the derring-do denied their more compromised husbands and brothers.[67]

The story, which is set in Gaelic Ireland between the late ninth and early eleventh centuries, during the time of the Danish invasions, uses events from the Irish past to recall more recent events, in particular James II's Irish expedition, here given a more satisfying conclusion than the one James provided in 1690 when he fled from the Boyne. The heroic plot celebrates resistance to tyranny and loyalty to one's lawful ruler. It focuses on the actions of the valiant 'few' who offered resistance to the slavish tyranny of an unlawful monarch, the 'few' who 'knew not how to bow their Necks in subjection to any but a lawful Prince, or stoop to any thing beneath their free Liberties, and Obedience to their own Kings . . .' (3). Historical parallels and an unmistakably Jacobite idiom must have made the politics of *Irish Tales* absolutely clear. Ross has argued otherwise, however. He thinks the Jacobite and Roman Catholic thrust of the novel would have been 'almost wholly inaccessible' to Butler's contemporaries.[68] My analysis of Curll's promotional strategies would suggest the converse, that there existed at this time a sizeable number of readers

who would have sought out *Irish Tales* precisely *for* its political aspect. If so, then it is significant that among the titles advertised on the final leaf, Curll should give top billing to Barker's heroic romance. The notice for *Exilius* fills up nearly the entire first page—evidence that it was the leading work of Jacobite popular fiction in Curll's list at this time.[69]

Another Curll-sponsored Jacobite romance from this same period offers additional insight into the appeal of these works in their political moment. This one, said to be 'Done from the *French* by a LADY', was first published in 1715 as the *German Atalantis* and was reissed in 1718 and again in 1721 with the even more pointed title *Hanover Tales*.[70] The action of this romance moves across a familiar Jacobite terrain—a kingdom in revolt, brave and noble men in exile, a haughty usurper, noble resistance to unlawful rule. Like all such politically encoded romances *Hanover Tales* offers imagined solutions to seemingly intractable political problems, but more directly than either *Exilius* or *Irish Tales* it seeks to promote acceptance of the change of state. Anxiety and confusion are displaced onto a fable in which contrasting feminine responses to thwarted love offer metaphors for responses to changes of state. Baritia (i.e. Britain) is the Jacobite figure. Torn between duty to her father and desire for a banished lover, refusing to marry without her father's (lawful) consent, she resolves to abandon herself to grief and sullen retirement. Happily, Baritia's father is eventually reconciled to the match and permits her to devote herself to her 'faithful, tender, and most constant Love' for her Fradonia (143). So far we have a fairly straightforward rendering of the Jacobite predicament brought to a satisfying wish-fulfilment conclusion. But the ideologically correct Jacobite response of Baritia in the novel's foreground is contrasted with that of Calista, who stands for accommodation to the Hanoverian regime. When her first beloved dies in battle she too devotes herself to grief, but when commanded to remarry by her parents she does so, albeit reluctantly, and to her surprise finds contentment in the new relationship. *Hanover Tales,* appropriately enough given its otherwise inexplicable title, is a fable of compromise and acceptance, permitting its conflicted readers the pleasures of identification with an uncompromisingly loyal Jacobite position while making available a respectable position of accommodation. Like other historical romances from 1715-20, and like the bigamy plots strongly featured in *The Lining of the Patch Work Screen,* the dual storyline offers a way, finally, of working through ambivalent feelings towards the Hanoverian succession.

We might now take up more fully the question of who read Jane Barker in this period and why by considering the nature of the Jacobite historical romance—*Exilius, Irish Tales,* and, in more complicated ways, *Hanover Tales.* Works such as these, coded, oblique, politically allusive, and intensely idealizing, would doubtless have supplied the 'Jacobite faithful' with the special 'pleasures of complicity and solidarity', as Valerie Rumbold has said of Mary Caesar's Jacobite writing.[71] The escapist fantasy they delivered would have appealed, it seems likely, to a broader readership as well, one consisting of overlapping groups of political and cultural dissidents. At the core would have been a 'self-sustaining, recognisable minority who rejected the social, political and religious order installed after 1688'—the Jacobite faithful—and around it a 'shifting cloud of individuals, families and connexions', not necessarily Jacobite, drawn for various reasons into opposition to the new Whig order.[72] For readers such as these Jacobite historical romances, like their precursors the heroic romances of the seventeenth century, would have delivered alternative worlds of high principle and uncompromising ideals—a retreat from the sordid realities of the compromised Hanoverian present—as well as the pleasures of imagined resistance.

Few accounts of the early novel take notice of historical romances or their readers since by no stretch of the critical imagination can they be assimilated to any strand of the evolutionary 'triple rise'. And herein, perhaps, lies part of their significance to scholars today. These romances serve to remind us that an insistent focus upon the urban middle-class reader is, in the words of Paul Hunter, a 'vast simplification of the readership spectrum'. What distinguishes novel readership in the eighteenth century, he stresses, is 'not its confinement to a particular class or group' but rather 'its social range': the appeal of the novel 'spanned the social classes and traditional divisions of readers'.[73] Yet even Hunter's examples tend to move us down the social scale, to the clerks, apprentices, and domestic servants presumed to be fairly recent recruits to the pleasures of reading. My work on Curll's marketing of Barker's novels suggests that we must also look up the scale, as well as out of London, if we are to develop a full and reliable picture of the early readership of popular fiction. The fact that Edmund Curll trafficked in Jacobite popular fiction during the opening years of the Georgian era is evidence of a robust demand for such wares.[74] With an uncertain political nation working through anxieties around the new succession, with some Jacobites and many Tories seeking face-saving ways to compromise with the new order, and with even Whigs unclear what to make of a German-speaking Lutheran monarch, Curll knew there was money to be made selling idealized nostalgic romances with a Jacobite edge. His doubtless well-calculated appeal in 1713 to 'the Lincolnshire Gentry' suggests as well that in his analysis the early market for prose fiction was more elite than many accounts would have us believe.[75]

I would like to suggest by way of speculative conclusion that Barker's Jacobite fictions may have circulated through and served to promote bonding within politically estranged communities, or what have been called 'subaltern counterpublics'.[76] If this is so, then further attention to the political orientation of early popular prose fictions might usefully complement and complicate the view of the novel as agent of *national* cultures and identities that appears to be gaining ground in recent accounts of the early novel. Deirdre Lynch and William Warner have made an intriguing case for the constitutive role of the novel in the formation of national imagined communities. Novels, they point out, are uniquely mobile. They are able to 'circulate among a diverse readership within the nation', crossing lines of gender and class and mobilizing desire by 'triggering identification with a central character and transporting readers into alternate desires'. They thus serve to promote a sense of national belonging and unity: 'When novel reading traverses the social boundaries within the nation, novels' popularity can seem an index of the nation's essential coherence'.[77] Yet in the case of Jacobite romances a different mechanism of identification seems to be at work.

The imaginative counter-worlds created in Jacobite historical romances promote identification not only with characters but also, perhaps more crucially, with other readers, making available communal recognitions serving to nourish a sense of kinship among constituents of various estranged communities—Tory, Catholic and Jacobite, male and female—and to support shared antipathies to the new order. The circulation of such romances among the disaffected may indeed have enabled the formation within the larger national community of 'subaltern counterpublics', or 'parallel discursive arenas', as Nancy Fraser puts it, in which 'members of subordinated social groups invent and circulate counterdiscourses to formulate oppositional interpretations of their identities, interests, and needs'.[78] To acquire, say, ***Exilius*** with a view toward reading and then passing it on to another of the tribe of the politically righteous was to position oneself alongside imagined others at the cultural periphery. The popularity of Jacobite romance in its own moment suggests, we might say, the existence of a reading public that understood itself less in terms of unity and coherence than of national heterogeneity—a patchwork public, if you will.

Notes

1. The Galesia trilogy, as it is coming to be known, comprises *The Amours of Bosvil and Galesia,* first published as *Love Intrigues* (1713), *A Patch-Work Screen for the Ladies* (1723), and *The Lining of the Patch Work Screen* (1725; the title-page has 1726).

2. Recent years have seen an explosion of work on Jacobitism and literature. For non-canonical Jacobite verse, see Paul Monod, *Jacobitism and the English People, 1688-1788* (Cambridge: Cambridge UP, 1989), ch. 2, and Murray G. H. Pittock, *Poetry and Jacobite Politics in Eighteenth-Century Britain and Ireland* (Cambridge: Cambridge UP, 1994). For Jacobitism in the mainstream tradition, see Howard Erskine-Hill, *Poetry of Opposition and Revolution: Dryden to Wordsworth* (Oxford: Clarendon P., 1996). For Dryden, see Alan Roper, *Dryden's Poetic Kingdoms* (New York: Barnes and Noble, 1965), 165-84; William J. Cameron, 'John Dryden's Jacobitism', in Harold Love (ed.), *Restoration Literature: Critical Approaches* (London: Methuen, 1972), 277-308. For Pope, see Douglas Brooks-Davies, *Pope's* Dunciad *and the Queen of the Night: A Study in Emotional Jacobitism* (Manchester: Manchester UP, 1985);

Howard Erskine-Hill, 'Pope: The Political Poet in his Time', *ECS* 15 (1981-2), 123-48; John M. Aden, *Pope's Once and Future Kings* (Knoxville: U. of Tennessee P., 1978); John Morillo, 'Seditious Anger: Achiles, James Stuart, and Jacobite Politics in Pope's *Iliad* Translation', *ECL* 19 (1995), 38-58. For Swift, see Ian Higgins, *Swift's Politics: A Study in Disaffection* (Cambridge: Cambridge UP, 1994). For Anne Finch, see Charles H. Hinnant, 'Anne Finch and Jacobitism: Approaching the Wellesley College Manuscript', *Journal of Family History,* 21 (1996), 496-502. For an overview of novels of the 1740s having Jacobite themes, see Jerry C. Beasley, *Novels of the 1740s* (Athens: U. of Georgia P., 1982), 13-15. Although most were anti-Stuart, they 'capitalized on the aura of romance' surrounding the 'Forty-Five' (14).

3. Monod, *Jacobitism,* 11. The third wave was from 1745 to 1754.

4. Jerry Beasley, 'Politics and Moral Idealism: The Achievement of Some Early Women Novelists', in Mary Anne Schofield and Cecilia Macheski (eds.), *Fetter'd or Free? British Women Novelists, 1670-1815* (Athens and London: Ohio UP, 1986), 216-36 (226), for example, describes *Exilus* as a 'didactic romance' with neither 'hidden partisan interest' nor reflections on 'contemporary political history'. See also William H. McBurney, 'Edmund Curll, Mrs. Jane Barker, and the English Novel', *Philological Quarterly,* 37 (1958), 385-99, esp. 390.

5. Gwendolyn B. Needham, 'Mary de la Riviére Manley, Tory Defender', *Huntington Library Quarterly,* 12 (1948-9), 253-88 (263).

6. Although the political reference of the title has been recognized, no one has attempted a political reading. The only sustained discussion of *Exilius* to dare is Eleanor Wikborg, 'The Expression of the Forbidden in Romance Form: Genre as Possibility in Jane Barker's *Exilius*', *Genre,* 22 (1989), 3-19, which examines its rendering of female sexuality within the framework of romance.

7. *The Monthly Catalogue* No. 4 for Aug. 1714 lists as published that month 'Mrs. *Barker's* New Entertaining Romance, call'd Exilius: Or, the banish'd Roman' (25). *Exilius* was advertised 14 and 21 Aug. in the *Post Man* (No. 11050), and 14 Aug. in *Post Boy* (No. 3006), where it is said to be published 19 Aug. Queen Anne died 1 Aug.

8. Kathleen Wilson, *The Sense of the People: Politics, Culture and Imperialism in England, 1715-1785* (Cambridge: Cambridge UP, 1995), 102. For ideological conflict in the post-succession years, see ch. 2.

9. Annabel Patterson, *Censorship and Interpretation: The Conditions of Writing and Reading in Early Modern England* (Madison: U. of Wisconsin P., 1984), 186, reports that de Scudéry may have used Tarquin in *Clélie* to represent Cromwell.

10. See Susan Staves, *Players' Scepters: Fictions of Authority in the Restoration* (Lincoln and London: U. of Nebraska P., 1979), and J. Douglas Canfield, 'Royalism's Last Dramatic Stand: English Political Tragedy, 1679-89', *Studies in Philology,* 82 (1985), 234-63.

11. Barker appears to have worked on the romance over a period of many years. Parts completed by 1687, when it was called *Scipina,* probably included the Egyptian episode (i. 103-14), which echoes crises from the 1680s, including the Exclusion Crisis (1678-83) and Monmouth's rebellion (1685). The history of the Queen of Egypt (i. 118-33), a monarch with secret Jewish—i.e. Roman Catholic—inclinations, may date from the 1680s as well. Vol. ii contains material suggestive of Barker's post-revolution preoccupations: the nature of cultural misrepresentations (ii. 41), the warming-pan columnies (ii. 55-6), prophecies about the triumphs of the house of Scipio (ii. 60-1), bitter reflections on the cheats and impostures practised by priests (ii. 89-90). Some of this material may have been written at St-Germain, or later.

12. The verses, printed in the second part of *PR,* are 'To Mrs. JANE BARKER, on her most Delightfull and Excellent *Romance* of SCIPINA, now in the Press' (2. 29), by J[ohn] N[ewton]; 'To the Incomparable AUTHOR, Mrs. JANE BARKER, On her Excellent ROMANCE of SCIPINA', by an unidentified '*Gentleman of* St. John's *College,* Cambridge' (2. 35), and 'To my Ingenious Friend, Mrs. JANE BARKER, on my Publishing her Romance of SCIPINA' (2. 194), by Benjamin Crayle.

13. Ralph Straus, *The Unspeakable Curll: Being Some Account of Edmund Curll Bookseller* (London: Chapman and Hall, 1927), 229. The pamphlet was entitled *The State of the Nation.*

14. For which tradition see Lois Potter, *Secret Rites and Secret Writing: Royalist Literature, 1641-1660* (Cambridge: Cambridge UP, 1989), esp. ch. 3, and Patterson, *Censorship,* esp. ch. 4.

15. The dedication to the countess of Exeter, first printed in *EN* (1719), was undated until 1736 when it appeared in the 'third edition' of *EN* (no 'second edition' has been found). It is reprinted in Wilson, 2-4, as the dedication to what the editor calls *Love Intrigues.*

16. Dedication, *EN* (1736), sig. A2.

17. Patterson, *Censorship,* 25. We can hear a particularly pointed appeal to Jacobite sentiment in the dedication to the countess of Exeter: 'It is in your Power, Madam, to dissipate all those Clouds of Tribulation which encircled these my *Roman* Lovers, from the Time of their Separation at *Rome,* 'till their Return to their Father's House in the Country' (Wilson, 3).

18. The episode of the Mauritanians, who believe dead a prince standing among them, offers a sardonic gloss on the warming-pan fiction (*Exilius,* ii. 55-6). For

other treatments of this fiction between 1688 and 1745, see Rachel J. Weil, 'The Politics of Legitimacy: Women and the Warming-pan Scandal', in Lois G. Schwoerer (ed.), *The Revolution of 1688-1689: Changing Perspectives* (Cambridge: Cambridge UP, 1992), 65-82.

19. A similar ad. *PB*, No. 4459 (25 Feb.), quotes from Barker's preface: she undertook the translation so that the 'Protestant Reader might not be depriv'd of the most Useful and Profitable Book of Devotion in the World'.

20. According to *POAS*, v. 206, the countess was reputed to be devoted 'to the forms and ceremonies thought to be "papist" by less rigid Anglicans'. She was Anne Hatton, second wife of Daniel Finch, second earl of Nottingham, dismissed from office in 1716 when he tried to dissuade the king from executing the Scottish lords; they made their home at Burley-on-the-Hill, near Oakham, Rutland, not twenty miles from Wilsthorp. The dedication may reflect political sympathy with a local powerful family that suffered for its opposition, Barker's Catholicizing programme, or (probably) both.

21. It is the only Curll publication to be listed in a bibliography of 18th-cent. Catholic publications running to nearly 3,000 items: see F. Blom, J. Blom, F. Korsten, G. Scott, *English Catholic Books 1701-1800: A Bibliography* (Aldershot, Hampshire: Scolar P., 1996), item 1039. The volume has an engraved frontispiece of the Crucifixion by Michael van der Gucht. Catholic historian and bibliographer Geoffrey Scott reports that such engravings were becoming quite rare in English Catholic books by this time, bibliographic evidence that the translation was probably destined for a Protestant readership. Barker never published under Catholic auspices or engaged in open Catholic apologetics or controversy. For the latter, see Robert Blackey, 'A War of Words: The Significance of the Propaganda Conflict Between English Catholics and Protestants, 1715-1745', *Catholic Historical Review*, 58 (1973), 534-55.

22. James Herbert Davis, Jr., *Fénelon* (Boston: G. K. Hall-Twayne, 1979), 108.

23. A. T. Gable, 'The Prince and the Mirror, Louis XIV, Fénelon, Royal Narcissism and the Legacy of Machiavelli', *Seventeenth-Century French Studies*, 15 (1993), 243-68 (244). For a summary of the impact and influence of *Télémaque* generally, see Davis, *Fénelon*, 107-10.

24. She might, for example, have published with an established Catholic bookseller such as Thomas Meighan, who the year before had published for a Catholic readership a Fénelon devotional manual, *Pious Reflections for Every Day of the Month* (1717). This and *Christian Pilgrimage* are the only Fénelon titles from the decade listed in Blom, *English Catholic Books,* out of only five for the entire century.

25. For the 1715 statute and registration, see Edgar E. Estcourt and John Orlebar Payne, *The English Catholic Nonjurors of 1715: Being a Summary of the Register of their Estates* (London: Burns and Oates, [1885]). The LAO holds two documents relating to Barker's registration of her estate: 'Schedules and Letters of Attorney, 1717' and 'Kesteven Quarter Sessions. Papists' Estates. Rolls. 1717'; both bear her signature. The same information is recorded in documents in the PRO: FEC 1/1200 (Abstracts of Papists Estates) and FEC 1/1201 (Returns).

26. Colin Haydon, *Anti-Catholicism in Eighteenth-Century England, c.1714-80: A Political and Social Study* (Manchester and New York: Manchester UP, 1993), 104. My account of the post-15 reprisals and their effects on the Catholic community draws from Haydon, 103-16.

27. For the movement to recognize the legitimacy of George I, see Haydon, *Anti-Catholicism,* 104-5, and Geoffrey Scott, *Gothic Rage Undone: English Monks in the Age of Enlightenment* (Bath: Downside Abbey, 1992), 56-7.

28. Geoffrey Holmes and Daniel Szechi, *The Age of Oligarchy: Pre-industrial Britain, 1722-1783* (London and New York: Longman, 1993), 90.

29. 'Dedication', iii; 'The Translator to the Reader', sig. Bv.

30. Blom, *English Catholic Books,* xxiv. In 1715, for example, Whitelocke Bulstrode composed a preface for some essays written by his Catholic father, Sir Richard Bulstrode, during the latter's exile at St-Germain, intended to '"soften" the Catholic nature of the work'. The collection is entitled *Miscellaneous Essays. With the Life and Conversion of St. Mary Magdalen* (London: Jonas Browne, 1715). The Anglican non-juror George Hickes attempted something similar in the previous decade in his translation of *Instructions for the Education of a Daughter, By the Author of Telemachus* (London: Jonah Bowyer, 1707). His dedication to the duchess of Ormonde stresses the absence of everything mainstream English readers might find suspect in Catholicism: one finds no 'Superstition' or 'Indiscreet Zeal', no recourse to images, saints, angels, relics, beads, or prayers for the dead.

31. Blom, *English Catholic Books,* xiii.

32. For anti-Catholicism in the early Georgian period, see Haydon, *Anti-Catholicism,* esp. chs. 3 and 4.

33. Scott, *Gothic Rage,* 129.

34. [Andrew Ramsay], *The Life of François de Salignac De la Motte Fénelon, Archbishop and Duke of Cambray* (London: Paul Vaillant and James Woodman, 1723), 241. For an account of the *Life* (which, however, underplays its Jacobite implications) see G. D. Henderson, *Chevalier Ramsay* (London: Thomas Nelson and Sons, 1952), ch. 7.

35. Scott, *Gothic Rage,* 128. See also 114-15.

36. She may have resided in St-Germain and Rome for part of these years. A letter from her nephew Timon Connock to John Hay, dated 20 Feb. 1720, Royal Archives, Stuart Papers 46/14, expresses mortification that his 'poor Ant'—unfortunately she goes unnamed—had 'taken the desperate resolution' of leaving St-Germain to starve in Rome (where the Pretender now made his court). Since Timon had at least one other aunt living at St-Germain, it is impossible to know whether the letter concerns Jane. I am grateful to Edward Corp for sharing this letter.

37. Letter of 19 Mar. 1718 from London; BL Stowe MS 232, 'Jacobite Correspondence, 1717-1719'. For a transcription and translation of the letter from the original French, see Doc. Rec. 26, 37 n. 88. During this time, when mail across the Channel was closely watched, it was standard practice to open suspected letters, copy out their contents, and send them on. See G. V. Bennett, *The Tory Crisis in Church and State, 1688-1730: The Career of Francis Atterbury, Bishop of Rochester* (Oxford: Clarendon P., 1975), 211.

38. *PWS* was advertised 13 June 1723 in the *Evening Post* (No. 2165) as 'This day . . . publish'd' and, somewhat unusually, was steadily promoted in the *EP* over the next three months, at least ten more ads appearing. *PWS* was listed in the *Monthly Catalogue* No. 4, June 1723, 2, its inset tales amusingly Curllicized as, for example, 'The Religious Adulterer', 'The Perfidious Adultress', and, my favourite, 'The Unaccountable Wife; or the Matrimonial Bawd'.

39. *Lining* was advertised in the *Monthly Catalogue* No. 30, Oct. 1725, 111, described as 'a Collection of Novels recommending virtuous Love' for the 'farther Entertainment of the Ladies'.

40. There were risings in 1708, 1715, and 1719. For a readable narrative overview, see Bruce Lenman, *The Jacobite Risings in Britain 1689-1746* (London: Eyre Methuen, 1980), and Frank McLynn, *The Jacobites* (London and New York: Routledge and Kegan Paul, 1985).

41. Lenman, *Jacobite Risings,* 195.

42. Toni Bowers, 'Jacobite Difference and the Poetry of Jane Barker', *ELH* 64 (1997), 857-69 (859). Barker's ambivalence has much in common with that of Mary Caesar, whose unpublished autobiographical writings, begun in 1724, have been described by Valerie Rumbold as a 'poignant attempt to integrate an increasingly negative experience of life with a faith in the ultimate triumph of Jacobite virtue': see 'The Jacobite Vision of Mary Caesar', in Isobel Grundy and Susan Wiseman (eds.), *Women, Writing, History 1640-1740* (Athens: U. of Georgia P., 1992), 178-98 (178).

43. Howard Erskine-Hill, 'Literature and the Jacobite Cause: Was there a Rhetoric of Jacobitism?', in Eveline Cruickshanks (ed.), *Ideology and Conspiracy: Aspects of Jacobitism, 1689-1759* (Edinburgh: John Donald, 1982), 49-69.

44. In the Mag. MS poem, 'On The kings birth-day, writ at St-Germains. 1694:' (fos. 42r-v) Barker imagines England as a wayward wife who promises to renounce her sexual crimes to ensure her husband's, i.e. James's, return.

45. Monod, *Jacobitism,* 62-9. The use of love song to address the exiled Stuart monarch can be traced back to at least 1694: see Pittock, *Poetry and Jacobite Politics,* 48. For examples of the translation of political affairs into amatory terms in contemporary poetry, see Erskine-Hill, *Poetry of Opposition,* 71-4.

46. Barash, *EWP,* esp. 32-40.

47. See, for example, the ode 'The *Necessity* of *Fate*' (*PWS* 141), to which Galesia's mother responds by saying, 143, in what reads very like a benediction, 'if there be a *fatal Necessity* that it must be so, e'en go on, and make thyself easy with thy fantastick Companions the Muses'.

48. Patricia Meyer Spacks, *Imagining a Self: Autobiography and Novel in Eighteenth-Century England* (Cambridge and London: Harvard UP, 1976), 66; Josephine Greider, 'Introd.', *A Patch-Work Screen for the Ladies,* ed. Josephine Greider (New York and London: Garland, 1973), 12; Mary Anne Schofield, *Masking and Unmasking the Female Mind: Disguising Romances in Feminine Fiction, 1713-1799* (Newark: U. of Delaware P., and London and Toronto: Associated UPs, 1990), 75.

49. Spacks, *Imagining,* 69.

50. In a discussion of her poetry John T. Shawcross, 'Jane Barker', *Seventeenth-Century British Nondramatic Poets, DLB,* 3rd ser. (Detroit, Washington, DC, London: Gale-Bruccoli Clark Layman, 1993), 131. 5, notes the reference to the conversion of the Jews but does not remark its political significance.

51. Marita Sturken, 'Memory, Reenactment, and the Image', in Mary Rhiel and David Suchoff (eds.), *The Seductions of Biography* (New York and London: Routledge, 1996), 31-41 (31).

52. For a discussion that emphasizes the differences in the two versions, see Jacqueline Pearson, 'The History of *The History of the Nun*', in Heidi Hutner (ed.), *Rereading Aphra Behn: History, Theory, and Criticism* (Charlottesville and London: UP of Virginia, 1993), 234-52. Other bigamy tales, all from *Lining,* include the story of Capt. Manly (182-202); the story of Tangerine, the Gentleman Gypsie, based on the 1698 Behn story 'The Wandering Beauty' (229-37); the story of double bigamy told by

Amarantha (254-60); and an episode of near-bigamy included in the seduction-and-abandonment history of Malhurissa (261-6). There is, finally, a rather bizarre retelling of the story of the Portuguese nun (223-6) which, while not a bigamy story as such, involves vow-breaking on the part of a nun, who on her deathbed reflects upon the story of her 'criminal Marriage' (225).

53. For 17th-cent. usages, see Potter, *Secret Rites,* 103-4.

54. Bowers, 'Jacobite Difference', 868.

55. Pat Rogers, *The Augustan Vision* (London: Weidenfeld and Nicolson, 1974), 250.

56. Michael McKeon, *The Origins of the English Novel 1600-1740* (Baltimore: Johns Hopkins UP, 1987), 51. For a good summary of the difficulties that have emerged in connection with the 'triple-rise' thesis, see J. A. Downie, 'The Making of the English Novel', *Eighteenth-Century Fiction, 9* (1997), 249-66. For an argument for the construction at around this time of an 'indeterminate but alluring "general reader"' of the novel, see William B. Warner, 'Formulating Fiction: Romancing the General Reader in Early Modern Britain', in Deidre Lynch and William B. Warner (eds.), *Cultural Institutions of the Novel* (Durham, NC, and London: Duke UP, 1996), 279-305.

57. McKeon, *Origins,* 52, makes a similar point: 'on the evidence of subscription lists, at least, a very large proportion of the readership of Defoe, the *Spectator,* and other "middle class" publications belongs to the nobility and gentry'.

58. This failed courtship tale belongs, we are told, to Galesia's 'early Years'—to the extent that the story draws upon Barker's own experience this would set it in the early 1670s—but the heroine's confusion, her inability to make sense of the changing attachments of her incomprehensible lover, may catch something of the quality that Erskine-Hill, *Poetry of Opposition,* 20, detects in the (Jacobite) dramas Dryden wrote in the decade after the Revolution, which focus 'upon people in conflict or bewildered in situations where not only values, but even the facts, are uncertain'. *BG* incorporates poems that can be dated with probability to the 1690s. It seems likely the narrative was at least partly written at St-Germain.

59. 'King JAMES's Affairs having so turn'd Things in *Europe,* that the War between *France* and the Allies was almost like a Civil War: Friend against Friend, Brother against Brother; Father against Son': *Love Intrigues: Or, the History of the Amours of Bosvil and Galesia, As Related to Lucasia, in St.* Germains *Garden. A Novel* (London: E. Curll and C. Crownfield, 1713).

60. Cf. McBurney's speculation, 'Edmund Curll', 387, that Curll's publication of *BG* may have been moti-

vated by a desire to supply high-toned reading matter for his newly opened bookshop in fashionable Tunbridge Wells.

61. J. A. Downie, *Robert Harley and the Press: Propaganda and Public Opinion in the Age of Swift and Defoe* (Cambridge: Cambridge UP, 1979), 162. He gives the circulation figures for the *PB* at 3,000 for each issue during the Harley years, describing it as oriented toward 'tory country gentlemen' (7); for the role of *PB* in the Tory propaganda machine, see 162-4. The other two tri-weeklies, the *Post Man* and George Ridpath's *Flying Post* were Whiggish. The other main Tory press organ at this time was the *Examiner,* edited for a period in 1711 by Mrs Manley. R. B. Walker, 'Advertising in London Newspapers, 1650-1750', *Business History,* 15 (1973), 112-30, distinguishes the Tory readership of the *PB* from that of the *Gazette,* the official government newspaper, on the basis of its advertising profile: the *Gazette* catered to 'the country gentry' while the 'less specialized' *PB* would have included readers of 'the more middling sort' as well (120). For circulation figures, see James R. Sutherland, 'The Circulation of Newspapers and Literary Periodicals, 1700-30', *Library,* 4th ser. 15 (1934), 110-24 (111).

62. Geoffrey Holmes, *British Politics in the Age of Anne* (London: Macmillan and New York: St Martin's, 1967), 30.

63. Monod, *Jacobitism,* 271. He arrives at these estimates by figuring that between 7 and 10 per cent of the aristocracy and gentry were Catholic and most of these loyal (on some level) to the Stuarts through the 1760s; perhaps 1 per cent were nonjurors; juring Anglicans with Stuart sympathies would have brought the number to about one in four, with great variations in different counties.

64. Ian Campbell Ross, '"One of the Principal Nations in Europe": The Representation of Ireland in Sarah Butler's *Irish Tales*', *Eighteenth-Century Fiction,* 7 (1994), 1-16 (4). According to McBurney, 'Edmund Curll', 398, it was advertised in *The Post Man,* 30 June 1716. *Irish Tales: or, Instructive Histories for the Happy Conduct of Life,* published in London for Curll and J. Hooke in 1716, was reissued in 1718 as *Milesian Tales.* The BL catalogue attributes it to Charles Gildon, who signed the dedication. Ross, 6, who so far as I know has written the only reliable modern discussion of the novel, regards Butler as an actual person but one about whom our lack of knowledge is 'nearly total'; he speculates, 7, that she was of high social rank and Catholic, but finds no evidence she was one of the Ormonde Butlers: 'All we know for certain, on the authority of Charles Gildon in his "Epistle Dedicatory" to *Irish Tales,* is that Sarah Butler was dead by 1716'.

65. Sarah Butler, *Irish Tales: or, Instructive Histories for the Happy Conduct of Life* (London: E. Curll and J. Hooke, 1716), 70, 66, 75.

66. *Irish Tales,* preface, [xix]. Cross-dressing themes as well as displays of female heroics figure importantly in Jacobite resistance lore. For Colonel Parker's escape in 1694 from the Tower in women's clothes supplied by his wife, see Jane Garrett, *The Triumphs of Providence: The Assassination Plot, 1696* (Cambridge: Cambridge UP, 1980), 48-9; for Lord Nithsdale's in 1716, see William Fraser, *The Book of Carlaverock: Memoirs of the Maxwells, Earls of Nithsdale, Lords Maxwell & Herries,* 2 vols. (Edinburgh, 1873). Accounts of the episode, which stressed the ingenuity, skill, and intrepidity of Lady Nithsdale in engineering her husband's escape from the Tower, are said to have 'created a deep sensation at the Court in London, and throughout the kingdom' (*Book,* i. 437).

67. For an early verse rendering of this theme, see Dryden's 'The Lady's Song' (written *c.*1691, published 1704), discussed by Anne Barbeau Gardiner, 'A Jacobite Song by John Dryden', *Yale University Library Gazette,* 61 (1986), 49-54. Cf. the manuscript poem from the 1690s, 'The Female Heroine. Or the Loyall Fair One's Noble Resolution', which calls upon women to take up the heroism no longer practised by men: 'Come Brisk Lasses let's unite | Arm, Arm your selves, your foes to fight, | Let us Perform Heroick Deeds | And Cast off all our Female Weeds' in order to 'redeem our Mangled Laws' and place the 'Lawfull King' on the throne. The speaker rejoices that 'our Great King by female strength, | From Exile was brought home at length' (Yale, Osborn b. 111, pp. 53, 54). Another version is found in Bod., MS Firth d. 13, fo. 43.

68. Ross, 'One of the Principle', 16.

69. Its twenty-three lines give titles for the eight interlocking tales making up *Exilius,* supplied no doubt by Curll—titles such as 'Clelia and *Marcellus*: Or, The Constant Lovers', 'The Lucky Escape: Or, The Fate of *Ismenus*', and '*Piso*: Or, The Lewd Courtier'. The one other book mentioned on the page, receiving only three lines of type, is *BG,* sporting here the title 'The *Sincere* VIRGIN: Or, The Amours of *Bosvil* and *Galesia*. A NOVEL'.

70. *The German Atlantis: Being, A Secret History of Many Surprizing Intrigues, and Adventures transacted in several Foreign Courts. Written by a Lady,* no publisher named. The *Monthly Catalogue* for Feb. 1715 advertises it as published by Curll. The unsigned author's 'advertisement' (1715) calls attention to the political charge of the title while seeming to disavow political intent: 'It is hoped no Offence will be taken at the Title, since none is intended by it, and therefore 'tis best to conclude with the Royal Motto, *Evil be to him that Evil thinks*'. Although *German Atalantis* (or *Hanover Tales*) is sometimes attributed to Mary Hearne, a signed receipt in the Upcott Collection (BL Add. MS 38,728, fo. 37r) indicates its author was one Robert Busby.

71. Rumbold, 'Jacobite Vision', 179.

72. Daniel Szechi, *The Jacobites: Britain and Europe 1688-1788* (Manchester and New York: Manchester UP, 1994), 12.

73. J. Paul Hunter, 'The Novel and Social/Cultural History', in John Richetti (ed.), *The Cambridge Companion to the Eighteenth-Century Novel* (Cambridge: Cambridge UP, 1996), 19.

74. Cheryl Turner, *Living by the Pen: Women Writers in the Eighteenth Century* (London and New York: Routledge, 1992), 50; McBurney, 'Edmund Curll', 386, writes: 'any publishing venture by Curll was a strong indication that a lucrative market for such a product existed'.

75. Pat Rogers, *Robinson Crusoe* (London: Allen and Unwin, 1979), 102, speculated that in 1710-29 the audience for popular fiction probably overlapped 'with the traditional literary public' more than we might have imagined. Subsequent work on subscription publication and dedications in the first half of the century lends support to this speculation. See W. A. Speak, 'Politicians, Peers, and Publication by Subscription 1700-50', in Isabel Rivers (ed.), *Books and their Readers in Eighteenth-Century England* (Leicester: Leicester UP and St Martin's P., 1982), 47-68; Pat Rogers, 'Book Dedications in Britain 1700-1799'. *British Journal for Eighteenth-Century Studies,* 16 (1993), 213-33.

76. The phrase is from Nancy Fraser, 'Rethinking the Public Sphere: A Contribution to the Critique of Actually Existing Democracy', in Craig Calhoun (ed.), *Habermas and the Public Sphere* (Cambridge, Mass., and London: MIT P., 1992), 109-42 (123).

77. Lynch and Warner, 'Introduction', *Cultural Institutions of the Novel,* 4.

78. Fraser, 'Rethinking', 123.

FURTHER READING

Biography

King, Kathryn R. *Jane Barker, Exile: A Literary Career 1675-1725.* Oxford: Clarendon Press, 2000, 263 p.

  The only full-fledged biography of Barker, emphasizing her writing life—her literary friendships, readers and readerships, relations with men in the book trade, and dialogue with literary conventions.

Criticism

Gibbons, G. S. "Mrs Jane Barker." *Notes and Queries* 12th Series, no. 33 (30 September 1922): 278.

Brief biography and description of the Magdalen manuscript of Barker's poems.

King, Kathryn R. "Of Needles and Pens and Women's Work." *Tulsa Studies in Women's Literature* 14 (spring 1995): 77-93.
Discusses the metonymic needles and pens in Barker's *A Patch-Work Screen for the Ladies* and Charlotte Smith's *The Old Manor House.*

————. "Jane Barker, Mary Leapor and a Chain of Very Odd Contingencies." *English Language Notes* 33 (March 1996): 14-27.
Examines the poem "Catharina's Cave," attributed to John Newton and adapted and preserved by the working-class poet Mary Leapor, which the author says has a great deal to tell readers about Barker's virginal self-image.

Medoff, Jeslyn. "Dryden, Jane Barker, and the 'Fireworks' on the Night of the Battle of Sedgemore (1685)." *Notes & Queries* 35 (June 1988): 175-76.
Observes that phrases in poems by Barker and John Dryden indicate that the two described the same phenomenon.

Shiner Wilson, Carol. Introduction to *The Galesia Trilogy and Selected Manuscript Poems of Jane Barker,* edited by Carol Shiner Wilson, pp. xv-xliv. Oxford: Oxford University Press, 1997.
Reconstructs Barker's life from a variety of contemporary records and emphasizes the way Barker's works have forced scholars to rethink literary history by shedding new light on eighteenth-century authorship, political identity, sexuality, the literary marketplace, and social class.

Additional coverage of Barker's life and career is contained in the following sources published by the Gale Group: *Dictionary of Literary Biography,* **Vols. 39, 131;** *Literature Criticism from 1400 to 1800,* **Vol. 42**

Captivity Narratives

INTRODUCTION

Captivity narratives emerged with the settlement of North America and continued as a significant genre in American literature until the closing of the frontier at the end of the nineteenth century. The first captivity narratives may have been created by Native Americans who were captured by early Spanish explorers. However, the genre commonly refers to the accounts written by European settlers who were abducted by Native Americans.

Many scholars cite Captain John Smith's *Generall Historie of Virginia, New-England, and the Summer Isles* (1624) as containing the first American captivity narrative. The genre began to take on greater significance in Puritan society, where fiction, plays, and poetry were prohibited. Captivity narratives served the community as a form of entertainment as well as a means of promoting the Puritan theology. Early Puritan captivity narratives, such as Mary Rowlandson's *The Sovereignty and Goodness of God Together, with the Faithfulness of His Promises Displayed* (1682) and John Williams's *The Redeemed Captive, Returning to Zion* (1707), were written in the first person by the victims of the abduction. The authors focused on details of the attack, forced marches, torture, life among the Native Americans, and return to Puritan society. Increasingly, the authors framed their narratives around the ideology that God was punishing a wayward people through capture, and showing his ultimate forgiveness and mercy to the faithful through rescue and return. Such writers as Cotton Mather made use of the narratives to urge social conformity. As the genre developed, first-hand victim accounts were replaced by professional authors' renderings and stock material about the practices of Native Americans, thus decreasing the immediacy and accuracy of the accounts. During times of war against the French and Native Americans, the captivity narratives increased in popularity; many works were reprinted dozens of times. As popular tastes in the United States shifted and sentimental fiction became more popular, captivity narratives began to reflect these changes. The moral tone of the novels and the anti-Native American themes remained prominent, but the stories became more sensational. Authors focused on male heroes who were bringing society to the frontier and building a nation, and women played less of a role. By the nineteenth century, the popular dime novel created a forum for the captivity narrative.

Literary scholars largely ignored the popular genre of captivity narratives until the mid-twentieth century. In the late 1940s Roy Harvey Pearce undertook the first significant study, in which he argued that the body of captivity narratives spread over three centuries was too fragmented and disparate to be classified as a single genre. He posited that captivity narratives were significant, not because they provided historical fact about Native American practices, as earlier scholars had implied, but because the accounts provided modern readers with a window on changes in popular mass culture. Unlike Pearce, Richard Vanderbeets has claimed that captivity narratives comprise a unified, single genre; and later scholars have emphasized the continuity in the genre, particularly the demonization and villainization of Native Americans. Gary L. Ebersole has explored the relationship between captivity narratives and the sentimental novel, while David T. Haberly has considered the influence of captivity narratives on literary works such as James Fenimore Cooper's *The Last of the Mohicans*. Critics including Alden T. Vaughan, Edward W. Clark and Lorrayne Carroll have explored the connections between Puritanism and captivity narratives; and Colin Ramsey has analyzed the influence of Puritanism on the demonization of Native Americans in captivity narratives.

REPRESENTATIVE WORKS

Ann Eliza Bleeker
The History of Maria Kittle (1790)

Charles Brockden Brown
Edgar Huntly (1799)

Thomas Brown
A Plain Narrative of the Uncommon Sufferings and Remarkable Deliverance of Thomas Brown, of Charleston, in New England (1760)

Jonathan Dickenson
God's Protecting Providence Man's Surest Help and Defense (1699)

John Gyles
Memoirs of the Odd Adventures, Strange Deliverances, etc., in the Captivity of John Gyles, Esq. (1736)

Elizabeth Hanson
God's Mercy Surmounting Man's Cruelty, Exemplified in the Captivity and Redemption of Elizabeth Hanson (1728)

Edward Kimber
The History of the Life and Adventures of Mr. Anderson. Containing His Strange Varieties of Fortune in Europe and America (1754)

Cotton Mather
Humiliations Follow'd with Deliverances (1697)

John Norton
The Redeemed Captive (1748)

Mary Rowlandson
The Sovereignty and Goodness of God Together, with the Faithfulness of His Promises Displayed; Being a Narrative of the Captivity and Restoration of Mrs. Mary Rowlandson (1682)

John Gilmary Shea, editor
Captivity of Father Isaac Jogues, of the Society of Jesus, among the Mohawks (1697)

James Smith
An Account of the Remarkable Occurrences in the Life and Travels of Col. James Smith, during His Captivity with the Indians (1799)

Captain John Smith
Generall Historie of Virginia, New-England, and the Summer Isles (1624)

John Williams
The Redeemed Captive, Returning to Zion: or a Faithful History of the Remarkable Occurrences in the Captivity and the Deliverance of Mr. John Williams (1707)

Peter Williamson
French and Indian Cruelty; Exemplified in the Life and Various Vicissitudes of Fortune, of Peter Williamson, a Disbanded Soldier (1757)

OVERVIEWS

Roy Harvey Pearce (essay date 1947-48)

SOURCE: Pearce, Roy Harvey. "The Significances of the Captivity Narrative." *American Literature* 19 (1947-48): 1-20.

[*In the following essay, Pearce examines the evolution of the style and intent of captivity narratives, from religious confessional to pulp thriller, and argues that they provide a window into American popular culture.*]

The narrative of Indian captivity has long been recognized for its usefulness in the study of our history and, moreover, has even achieved a kind of literary status. Generally it has been taken as a sort of "saga," something which somehow is to be understood as expressive of the Frontier Mind—whatever that may be.[1] But this is to make of the captivity narrative a kind of composite, abstracted thing; this is to make a single genre out of the sort of popular form which shapes and reshapes itself according to varying immediate cultural "needs." Certainly there is a natural basic unity of content in the many narratives which we have; but variation in treatment of content, in specific form, and in point of view is so great as to make for several genres, for several significances. Here matters of pure historical fact (a purity which is often suspect, as we shall see) and ethnological data—that is, of content abstracted from treatment—are beside the point; what is important is what the narrative was for the readers for whom it was written. The significances of the captivity narrative vary from that of the religious confessional to that of the noisomely visceral thriller. The distance between the two sorts of narratives is great; over that distance can be traced the history of the captivity narrative taken as a popular genre—or, more properly, genres. As popular genre, or genres, it comes to have a kind of incidental literary value, enters literary history proper in *Edgar Huntly,* and functions as a popular vehicle for various historically and culturally individuated purposes. And it is as such that I propose to consider it here.[2]

I

The first, and greatest, of the captivity narratives are simple, direct religious documents. They are for the greater part Puritan; and their writers find in the experience of captivity, "removal," hardships on the march to Canada, adoption or torture or both, the life in Canada which so often seemed to consist in nothing but resisting the temptations set forth by Romish priests, and eventual return (this is the classic pattern of the captivity), evidences of God's inscrutable wisdom. Thus Increase Mather in the *Essay for the Recording of Illustrious Providences* (1684) prefaces Quintin Stockwell's story of his captivity with these words:

> Likewise several of those that were taken Captive by the *Indians* are able to relate affecting Stories concerning the gracious Providence of God, in carrying them through many Dangers and Deaths, and at last setting their feet in a large place again. A Worthy Person hath sent me the Account which one lately belonging to *Deerfield* (his name is *Quintin Stockwell,*) hath drawn up respecting his own Captivity and Redemption, with the Providence attending him in his distress, which I shall here insert in the Words he himself expresseth. . . .[3]

Thus too, John Williams, in dedicating his *Redeemed Captive Returning to Zion* (1707) to Joseph Dudley, indicates that he tells his story because "The wonders of divine mercy, which we have seen in the land of our captivity, and been delivered therefrom, cannot be forgotten without incurring the guilt of blackest ingratitude."[4] The Puritan narrative is one in which the details of the captivity itself are found to figure forth a larger, essentially religious experience; the captivity has symbolic value; and the record is made minute, direct, and concrete in order to squeeze the last bit of meaning out of the experience.

The Stockwell and the Williams narratives, along with Jonathan Dickenson's Quaker *God's Protecting Providence Man's Surest Help and Defense* (1699), are in the pattern of the best known (and deservedly so) of the narratives, Mrs. Rowlandson's *Soveraignty and Goodness of God* (1682). Here, it will be recalled, there is the fusion of vivid immediacy and religious intensity. At the very beginning Mrs. Rowlandson writes: "Now away we must go with those barbarous creatures, with our bodies wounded and bleeding, and our hearts no less than our bodies." And later she pictures the Indians' triumphant celebrations: "This was the dolefullest night that ever my eyes saw. Oh the roaring and singing and dancing and yelling of those black creatures in the night, which made the place a lively resemblance of hell. . . ." Constantly she prays and considers her life one long terrifying religious adventure.[5] There is even in the Rowlandson narrative, as in the others which I have instanced, a certain aesthetic quality which derives from the freshness and concreteness of detail with which the narrator explores her experience. Here we have the quality of the diary and that of, say, Edwards's *Personal Narrative* at their best. Here we have the captivity as a direct statement of a frontier experience, an experience which is taken as part of the divine scheme.

Such narratives were popular in their appeal when they first appeared and so continued.[6] But gradually the quality of directness, of concern with describing an experience precisely as it had affected the individual who underwent it, of trying somehow to recapture and put down what were taken as symbolic psychic minutiae, began to disappear. Other interests predominated. The propagandist value of the captivity narrative became more and more apparent; and what might be termed stylization, the writing up of the narrative by one who was not directly involved, came to have a kind of journalistic premium.

Cotton Mather propagandizes. He presents in the *Magnalia* (1702) the direct, religiously intense narratives of Hannah Swarton and Mrs. Duston (Book VI, Chapter II, and Book VII, Appendix, Article XXV) and four "Relations" of "*The Condition of the* Captives *that from time to time fell into the Hands of the* Indians; with some very Remarkable Accidents" (Book VII, Appendix, Article VII). He concludes the "Relations" thus:

> In fine, when the *Children* of the *English Captives* cried at any time, so that they were not presently quieted, the manner of the *Indians* was to dash out their Brains against a *Tree*.
>
> And very often, when the *Indians* were on or near the Water, they took the small *Children,* and held 'em under Water till they had near Drowned them, and then gave 'em unto their Distressed Mothers to quiet 'em.
>
> And the *Indians* in their Frolicks would Whip and Beat the small *Children,* until they set 'em into grievous Outcries, and then throw 'em to their amazed Mothers for them to quiet 'em again as well as they could.
>
> This was *Indian Captivity!*

If the *Magnalia* is the record of godly New England's triumph over the wilderness, part of that record is of a triumph over the evil dwellers in the wilderness. Even as

Mather rejoices over Christianizing the Indian (Book VI, Chapter VI), so he promotes hatred of the Indian. And in the *Magnalia* the captivity begins to become explicitly a vehicle of Indian-hatred.

The development of variant texts of *God's Mercy surmounting Man's Cruelty, Exemplified in the Captivity and Redemption of Elizabeth Hanson* (1728) indicates clearly the pattern of what I have termed stylization of the captivity narrative. The edition of 1728 is direct and colloquial, in the pattern of Mrs. Rowlandson's narrative. The nominal reprint of this (1754) is somewhat more "correct." And the *Account of the Captivity of Elizabeth Hanson* which first appeared (so far as I have been able to discover) in 1760 as "Taken in Substance from her own Mouth, by Samuel Bownas," although it still is in the first person, is made into something even more acceptably "literary"; freshness and direct emotional value have all but disappeared. The beginnings of the three versions will illustrate satisfactorily this matter of stylization:

1728:

> As soon as they discovered themselves (having as we understood by their Discourse, been sculking in the Fields some Days watching their Opportunity when my dear Husband, with the rest of our Men, were gone out of the way) two of the barbarous Salvages came in upon us, next Eleven more, all naked, with their Guns and Tomahawks came into the House in a great Fury upon us, and killed one Child immediately, as soon as they entered the Door, thinking thereby to strike in us the greater Terror, and to make us more fearful of them.
>
> Then in as great Fury the Captain came up to me; but at my Request, he gave me Quarter; there being with me our Servant, and Six of our Children, two of the little Ones being at Play about the Orchard, and my youngest Child but Fourteen Days old, whether in Cradle or Arms, I now mind not: Being in that Condition, I was very unfit for the Hardships I after met with, which are briefly contained in the following Pages.

1754:

> As soon as the Indians discovered 'emselves (having as we afterwards understood, been sculking in the fields some days watching their opportunity when my dear husband, with the rest of our men, were gone out of the way) two of them came in upon us, and then eleven more, all naked, with their guns and tomahawks, and in a great fury killed one child immediately as soon as they entered the door, thinking thereby to strike in us the greater terror, and to make us more fearful of them.
>
> After which, in like fury the captain came up to me; but at my request, he gave me quarter. There was with me our servant, and six of our children; two of the little ones being at play about the orchard, and my youngest child but fourteen days old, whether in cradle or arms, I now remember not; being in this condition, I was very unfit for the hardships I after met with, which I shall endeavor briefly to relate.

1760:

> On the 27th of the Sixth Month, called August, 1725, my husband and all our men-servants being abroad, eleven Indians, armed with tomahawks and guns, who had some time been skulking about the fields, and watching an opportunity of our mens absence, came furiously into the house. No sooner had they entered, than they murdered one of my children on the spot; intending no doubt, by this act of cruelty, to strike the greater degree of terror into the minds of us who survived. After they had thus done, their captain came towards me, with all the appearance of rage and fury it is possible to imagine; nevertheless, upon my earnest request for quarter, I prevailed with him to grant it.
>
> I had with me a servant-maid and six children; but two of my little ones were at that time playing in the orchard. My youngest child was but fourteen days old; and myself, of consequence, in a poor weak condition, and very unfit to endure the hardships I afterwards met with, as by sequel will appear.

And so it goes throughout the entire narrative. Bownas, as a traveling, ministering Quaker, has reworked the Hanson narrative into something which, although its main intent is still to illustrate "the many deliverances and wonderful providences of GOD unto us, and over us," is essentially a journalistic piece, and as such prefigures the stylistic form of the later captivity narrative.[7]

II

What one sees developing in Cotton Mather's use of the captivity narrative and in Bownas's version of the Hanson narrative became formally characteristic of the genre by the mid-eighteenth century. Religious concerns came to be incidental at most; the intent of the typical writer of the narrative was to register as much hatred of the French and Indians as possible. In order to accomplish this, he produced a blood-and-thunder shocker. Hence the captivity narrative was shaped by the interests of the popular audience towards which it was directed; French and Indian cruelty, not God's Providences, was the issue. The writing of the hack and the journalist, not the direct outpourings of the pious individual, became the standard of, and the means to, this new end. By 1750 the captivity narrative had become the American equivalent of the Grub Street criminal biography. To say all this is not to deny the fact of suffering and hardship and tremendous courage on the part of captives. It is only to record the cultural significance of what the captives had to say about their experiences and of the way in which they said it.

So William Fleming in his *Narrative of the Sufferings and Surprizing Deliverances of William and Elizabeth Fleming* (1750) records in adventurous detail how he was taken captive on his Pennsylvania farm and was forced by the Indians to guide them to his wife, how she was taken captive, and how after seeing others tortured and killed, the two of them managed to escape. For all of this, he is willing to exculpate the Indians; hence the subtitle of the Narrative reads: "A NARRATIVE necessary to be read by all

who are going in the Expedition [against the French], as well as by every BRITISH subject. Wherein it fully appears, that the Barbarities of the *Indians* is owing to the *French,* and chiefly their Priests." The French, their priests, and the French-inspired Indians are the objects of the hatred of many others, among them Nehemiah How (*A Narrative of the Captivity of Nehemiah How* [1748]), John Gyles (*Memoirs of the Odd Adventures, Strange Deliverances, &c. in the Captivity of John Gyles, Esq.* [1736]), Joseph Barlett (*A Narrative of the Captivity of Joseph Bartlett among the French and Indians* [1807, written *ca.* 1754]), Robert Eastburn (*The Dangers and Sufferings of Robert Eastburn* [1758]), and Thomas Brown (*A plain Narrative of the Uncommon Sufferings, and Remarkable Deliverance of Thomas Brown* [1760]).

The natural shift from this sort of narrative is to the out-and-out sensational piece. Here the problem for the historian who would wish to make use of such information as the narratives contain would be one of verification. For these stories are truly wild and woolly. One of the best is the immensely popular *French and Indian Cruelty Exemplified, in the Life and Various Vicissitudes of Fortune, of Peter Williamson* (1757). According to his narrative, Williamson was kidnaped "when, under the years of pupillarity" and taken from his native Scotland to America. There he was sold as a bond servant and eventually, falling into all sorts of good fortune, acquired a wife, a wealthy father-in-law, and a fine frontier Pennsylvania farm. But then came captivity.

He recounts in great and gory detail his struggles, his marches with his captors, and his being tortured. But he adds: ". . . yet what I underwent was but trifling, in comparison to the torments and miseries which I was afterwards an eye-witness of being inflicted on others of my unhappy fellow creatures." As the Indians proceed, they murder and pillage and scalp; such prisoners as they take they torture mercilessly. Then Williamson makes his point:

> From these few instances of savage cruelty, the deplorable situation of these defenceless inhabitants, and what they hourly suffered in that part of the globe, must strike the utmost horror to a human soul, and cause in every breast the utmost detestation, not only against the authors of such tragic scenes, but against those who through perfidy, inattention, or pusillanimous and erroneous principles, suffered these savages at first, unrepelled, or even unmolested, to commit such outrages and incredible depradations and murders: For no torments, no barbarities that can be exercised on the human sacrifices they get into their power, are left untried or omitted.

He continues, giving a simple illustration of what he means. He describes three persons whom the Indians decided to torture. They were tied to a tree "where one of the villains, with his scalping knife, ript open their bellies, took out their entrails, and burnt them before their eyes, whilst others were cutting, piercing, and tearing the flesh from their breasts, hands, arms, and legs with red hot irons, till they were dead." Since one was still alive, however, he was buried so that only his head remained above ground; then he was scalped, still alive, and fire put to his head so that "his brains were boiling." Then, "inexorable to all his plaints, they continued the fire, whilst, shocking to behold! his eyes gushed out of their sockets; and such agonizing torments did the unhappy creature suffer for near two hours, till he was quite dead." On such details Williamson lovingly dwells. Later he even points out that it is an Indian custom to let children train themselves for warfare by beating out the brains of the useless old people of the tribe!

Williamson continues his own story in this vein. Eventually he escapes, enlists to fight the French and the Indians, records his rejoicing when the soldiers were "cutting, hacking, and scalping the dead Indians" and when they quarreled over possession of Indian scalps. Williamson says that he fought all over the colonies in the middle fifties; he seems to have been in on every major campaign; one wonders how he got around so handily. At any rate, the bulk of his story exists only to exemplify French and Indian cruelties. And its significance here is mainly vulgar, fictional, and pathological.[8]

Other narratives of the type of Williamson's seem also to be mélanges of fact and fiction. To point this out is not to indulge in a kind of historical sophistication, not to forget that captivity and torture and death were hard facts of frontier life. Rather it is to suggest that the writers of these later narratives are not concerned with working up accurate records of their (or others') captivities, but with the salability of penny dreadfuls. Thus the blood-and-thunder *History of the Life and Sufferings of Henry Grace* (1764) records a ten-year captivity in which Grace was carried back and forth from Canada to the Mississippi country and saw all tribes from the St. John's Indians to the Cherokees. *A Brief Narration of the Captivity of Isaac Hollister* (1767) has as its high point Hollister's detailing how he cut off five or six pounds of a recently dead fellow-prisoner; one is left to assume that Hollister was thus kept from starving. The *Narrative of Mr. John Dodge* (1779), in which hatred is shifted from the French- to the British-inspired Indian, is marked by a minute description of the "thoughts that must have agitated the breast of a man, who but a few minutes before saw himself surrounded by Savages," and who now was being saved in proper melodramatic style. Thus, too, finally, it is with *A Narrative of the Capture of certain Americans* (1780?), with William Walton's *Captivity and Sufferings of Benjamin Gilbert and His Family* (1793), and with *The Remarkable Adventures of Jackson Johonnot* (1793); all are most likely at bottom true, but are built up out of a mass of crude, sensationally presented details.

The journalistic extremity of language and style of these later narratives is typified by that of *A True Narrative of the Sufferings of Mary Kinnan* (1795). Here, however, it is sensibility which takes over. She begins thus:

> Whilst the tear of sensibility so often flows at the unreal tale of woe, which glows under the pen of the poet

and the novelist, shall our hearts refuse to be melted with sorrow at the unaffected and unvarnished tale of a female, who has surmounted difficulties and dangers, which on a review appear to be romantic, even to herself?

In this vein she goes on, relating how her captivity broke the pattern of her happy, pastoral life in Virginia: "Here I would mark nature progressing, and the revolutions of the season; and from these would turn to contemplate the buds of virtue and of genius, sprouting in the bosoms of my children." In the Indian attack her children and her husband were killed:

> Gracious God! What a scene presented itself to me! My child, scalped and slaughtered, smiled even then; my husband, scalped and weltering in his blood, fixed on me his dying eye, which, though languid, still expressed an apprehension for my safety, and sorrow at his inability to assist me; and accompanied the look with a groan that went through my heart. Spare me the pain of describing my feelings at this scene, this mournful scene, which racked my agonizing heart, and precipitated me on the verge of madness.[9]

Nevertheless, throughout the narrative she continues to dwell on Indian horror and cruelty and on her own torn sensibilities.

Tales of barbarity and bloodshed, however true at base and however "serious" in intent, were everywhere the thing. Hugh Henry Brackenridge, one of our great Indian haters, edited and caused to be published in the 1780's the garish narratives of Knight and Slover (*Narrative of a Late Expedition*, 1783). These are particularly interesting because of their verifiable authenticity. Knight and Slover describe their adventures as members of Crawford's expedition into the Ohio country in 1782. The story of their capture and of Crawford's being horribly tortured while Simon Girty looked on is too well known to require retelling here. It is sufficient to note that the narratives are printed mainly to point up Brackenridge's firm belief in the necessity of eliminating entirely those "animals, vulgarly called Indians." The purpose of the publication of the narratives is put straightforwardly in the prefatory note "To the Public":

> . . . these Narratives may be serviceable to induce our government to take some effectual steps to chastise and suppress them; as from hence they will see that the nature of an Indian is fierce and cruel, and that an extirpation of them would be useful to the world, and honorable to those who can effect it.

So, too, the *Affecting History of the Dreadful Distresses of Frederic Manheim's Family* (1793?) is a hodgepodge of journalistic horrors aimed at proving that the Indians exercise "dreadful cruelties" on "persons so unfortunate as to fall into their hands." The *Affecting History* is actually a little anthology of choice bits of captivity narratives, each bit selected for its blood-chilling potentialities. In the edition of 1794, issued by commercially wise Matthew Carey, there is a crude engraving, portraying Manheim's daughters, nude at the stake, while Indians dance madly about them. And even such narratives as Luke Swetland's *Narrative (ca.* 1780) and James Smith's *Account of Remarkable Occurrences* (1799), although they contain little of Indian horrors (their authors indeed were admittedly rather well treated), are aimed at giving Americans some practical ways of dealing with the Indian on the frontiers.

The various states of the narrative of Mercy Herbeson will sum up the fate of the captivity narrative towards the end of the eighteenth and at the beginning of the nineteenth century. Mrs. Herbeson's captivity came as an aftermath of the failure of St. Clair's expedition against the Indians of the Ohio country, who were now dangerously self-confident and daring. They had waited until her husband and the other men of the neighborhood were gone, awakened her in her sleep, murdered one of her children as they left the cabin, and killed another as they journeyed. She managed to escape on the third day out and, after great suffering, finally reached a settlement, almost naked, starving, with thorns driven all the way through her un-shod feet. And the next morning, as she writes, "a young man employed by the magistrates of Pittsburgh came for me to give in my deposition, that it might be published to the American people."

We have two versions of the deposition, both dated 1792; one of these (*Capture and Escape of Mercy Harbison*) is a direct, semi-literate narrative in the first person, the quality of which reminds one of the earliest captivity narratives; the other is a third person recounting of this, virtually a summary. This last forms one of the choice bits which is included in the Manheim *Affecting History,* described above. Then in 1825 the narrative was published as *A Narrative of the Sufferings of Massy Harbison.* Here the 1792 deposition is expanded into something like the Kinnan narrative. The editor ("J. W.") points out in his introduction that Mrs. Herbeson is now a poor widow, that she has suffered heroically, and that it is the duty of every good American to keep her memory green. The narrative proper is still in the first person, but it is shot through with pleasantly sentimental bits. Mrs. Herbeson is made to make such comments as this: "Some seem to pass over the seasons of life, without encountering those awfully agitating billows which threaten their immediate destruction; while to others, the passage to the tomb is fraught with awful tempests and overwhelming billows." Generally sensibility and melodrama take the place of simplicity and directness. Much miscellaneous material on the nature of the savage and on the Indian wars is added. And in the fourth edition (1836) of this version, the "editor's" name, John Winter, appears, the miscellaneous material has practically smothered the original narrative, and there is little or no pretense at authenticity. The publication of a captivity narrative had become an occasion for an exercise in blood and thunder and sensibility.

Moreover, it becomes apparent that towards the end of the eighteenth century American readers were not taking the captivity narrative very seriously. Even for a popular genre,

it was quite old and quite tired. In 1796 Mrs. Susannah Willard Johnson felt it necessary to apologize for the publication of her recollections of her captivity in 1749:

> Our country has so long been exposed to Indian Wars, that recitals of exploits and sufferings, of escapes and deliverances have become both numerous and trite.— The air of novelty will not be attempted in the following pages; simple facts, unadorned, is what the reader must expect; pity for my sufferings, and admiration at my safe return, is all that my history can excite.

If this prefatory note is genteel, Mrs. Johnson's *Narrative* is not. Taken captive while pregnant, giving birth to her child while on the march, adopted into an Indian family, and finally sold to the French and then ransomed by her family—she still cannot expect that her experiences will be taken as seriously as they should be.

And something analogous to this also seems to have been the experience of Mrs. Jemima Howe. For, objecting to the polished-up and hence commercially acceptable version of her captivity published by David Humphreys in his *Essay on the Life of the Honourable Major-General Israel Putnam* (1788), she allowed the Reverend Bunker Gay to edit a *Genuine and Correct Account* of her captivity in 1792; truth was more important than the journalistic appeal demanded by American readers. And later, to take another sort of example, Matthew Bunn, apparently finding that his *Narrative* (1806) was not being swallowed whole, appended a truth-swearing affidavit to editions of his story appearing after 1826. By 1800, then, the captivity narrative had all but completed its decline and fall.

III

It is as the eighteenth-century equivalent of the dime novel that the captivity narrative has significance for the history of our literature. We have already seen how in the latter half of the eighteenth century it had become more and more customary to work up the narrative into something exciting and journalistically worth while by stylizing and by adding as much fictional padding as possible. There are, of course, narratives which are out-and-out fakes—for example, *A Surprizing Account of the Captivity and Escape of Philip M'Donald & Alexander M'Leod* (1794), "Abraham Panther's" *A Very Surprising Narrative of a Young Woman Discovered in a Rocky Cave* (1788?), *The Surprising Adventures and Sufferings of John Rhodes* (1799), and "Don Antonio Descalves's" *Travels to the Westward* (1794?). But these narratives differ from such as those of Peter Williamson and Mrs. Kinnan only in the degree of their absurdity; and they are published as genuine and authentic accounts. What I should like to consider here are two specifically "literary" pieces, Ann Eliza Bleecker's *History of Maria Kittle* (1793) and Charles Brockden Brown's *Edgar Huntly* (1799), both of which were intended to achieve much of their effects as they related to the captivity genre of the 1790's.

The History of Maria Kittle is simply a captivity narrative turned novel of sensibility. This, Mrs. Bleecker says, is a "true" story:

However fond of novels and romances you [she is addressing the novel to a Miss Ten Eyck] may be, the unfortunate adventures of one of my neighbours, who died yesterday, will make you despise that fiction, in which, knowing the subject to be fabulous, we can never be so truly interested.

The "unfortunate" adventures are the stock materials of the captivity, conditioned, as I have indicated, by female sensibility. Horror is piled on horror. The Indian raiders come, shoot Maria's brother-in-law (her husband is away, of course), tomahawk that brother-in-law's pregnant wife, and tear Maria's infant son from her arms and "dash his little forehead against the stones." Her daughter hides herself in a closet and is burned alive when the Indians set fire to the house. Maria and another brother-in-law are taken prisoner; and the march begins. On all this she soliloquizes:

> O barbarous! surpassing devils in wickedness! so may a tenfold night of misery enwrap your black souls as you have deprived the babe of my bosom, the comfort of my cares, my blessed cherub, of light and life—O hell! are not thy flames impatient to cleave the center and engulph these wretches in thy ever burning waves? are there no thunders in Heaven—no avenging Angels—no God to take notice of such Heaven defying cruelties?[10]

Pitched thus, the *History* goes on through suffering, struggling, and bloodshed to eventual rescue, ransom, and reunion. Mrs. Bleecker delights in gruesomeness—in, as she says, opening the sluice gates of her readers' eyes. She is interested, most of all, in—and this again is her phrasing—the luxury of sorrow. And she finds that this is to be achieved by actualizing the potentialities of the captivity narrative as novel of sensibility. Still, the distance between the two was, as we have already seen, really not very great.

Charles Brockden Brown similarly is interested in the luxury of horror and, perhaps more seriously, in the workings of a mind under abnormal stress. This American Gothicism he points up in *Edgar Huntly* by making marauding Indians representative of the terrors of existence on the frontier, thus attempting to domesticate the English genre from which his novel stems:

> One merit the writer may at least claim: that of calling forth the passions and engaging the sympathy of the reader by means hitherto unemployed by preceding authors. Puerile superstitions and exploded manners, Gothic castles and chimeras, are the materials usually employed for this end. The incidents of Indian hostility, and the perils of the Western wilderness, are far more suitable; and for a native of America to overlook these would admit of no apology.

This, of course, is from Brown's famous preface. If English writers were to use medieval materials for their romances, American writers were to tap native Gothic sources.

It will be recalled that in Chapter XVI Huntly finds himself in an underground pit, with no knowledge of how he got there or how he is to get out. After a series of storm-and-stress adventures, he does find his way to a cave which will lead him out; but the cave is occupied by a party of raiding Indians with a girl captive. Huntly manages to kill the Indian sentinel and to escape with the girl to the deserted hut of an Indian crone whom he calls Queen Mab. Indians come to the hut, and Huntly kills them, meantime being wounded himself. When a rescue party arrives, Huntly is thought to be dead and is left alone. But his Indian adventures continue. And in the process of these adventures he kills another Indian, gets lost trying to make his way home through the wilds, is mistaken for an Indian and pursued, and finally discovers that the Indian raiders have killed the uncle with whom he has lived.

Brown does not reproduce the captivity narrative as such; but he capitalizes on all that such narratives had come to mean for American readers—a meaning which rose out of emphasis on physical terror, suffering, and sensationalism. He is careful to account exactly for Huntly's fascination by and fear of the Indians: They had murdered his parents. As he has Huntly say:

> Most men are haunted by some species of terror or antipathy which they are, for the most part, able to trace to some incident which befell them in their early years. You will not be surprised that the fate of my parents, and the body of this savage band, who, in the pursuit that was made after them, was overtaken and killed, should produce lasting and terrific images in my fancy. I never looked upon or called up the image of a savage without shuddering.[11]

Brown was thus doing little that was new. He was simply legitimatizing much that was part of the captivity narrative and its sensational offshoots in the 1790's.[12]

IV

The captivity narrative continued to be a popular journalistic, terroristic vehicle through the first three quarters of the nineteenth century. New episodes came with new frontiers; yet patterns and themes were reproduced again and again. There is little need of detailing these, I think; for they simply define and redefine the captivity as we have seen it produced in the 1780's and 1790's. I have seen some forty narratives printed between 1813 and 1873, all of which seem to stem from real enough experiences, but all of which have been worked up into something terrible and strange. Their language is most often that of the hack writer gone wild. Even when they appear to be genuine productions of the nominal narrator, they tend to be formed according to the pattern of the captivity narrative as pulp thriller.[13]

As is to be expected, the problem of authenticity in some of the narratives of the first half of the nineteenth century is hopelessly confused. Thus the *Narrative of the Captivity and Extreme Sufferings of Mrs. Clarissa Plummer* (1839) seems to be worked up from *A Narrative of the Captivity of Mrs. Horn* and the *Narrative* of Mrs. Rachel Plummer, both of the same year. The writer of the first of these three simply put together the best (and wildest) parts of the second and third. The *Narrative of the Capture and Providensial Escape of Misses Frances and Almira Hall* (1832) is basically true, but the captives' names were Sylvia and Rachel and the details of the actual captivity have been highly colored in the narrative.[14] And in *An Affecting Narrative of the Captivity and Sufferings of Mrs. Mary Smith* (1818), which is a tale of the Creek War and of Mrs. Smith's being rescued by a detachment of Jackson's army, the torture episode is lifted verbatim from the title narrative in the *Affecting History of the Dreadful Distresses of Frederic Manheim's Family* (1793).[15] Faced with such a confusion of fact and fiction, the twentieth-century reader can only wonder.

Already, however, the captivity narrative had been looked on from something of a scholarly point of view. Certainly, if the coming of a document into the province of antiquarian scholarship and pseudo scholarship means that that document is no longer immediately vital, that its vitality has to be recovered, as it were—then the captivity narrative as a significant popular form was all but dead in the second quarter of the nineteenth century. The problem now was to "use" the captivity narrative, to see what it revealed about the frontier and the frontiersman, to broaden the scope of the American historical imagination.

In short, such narratives were collected and anthologized for what their editors (rather self-consciously, to be sure) insisted were scholarly reasons. The earlier collections seem to be equally sensational, propagandist, and academic. Archibald Loudon calls his two-volume collection (1808) *A Selection of Some of the Most Interesting Narratives of Outrages Committed by the Indians in Their Wars, with the White People.* He is proud that his is the first genuinely scholarly collection of such narratives and intends it for historians: "The historian, will here find materials to assist him in conveying to after ages, an idea of the savages who were the primitive inhabitants of this country; and to future generations of Americans, the many difficulties, toils, and dangers, encountered by their fathers, in forming the first settlement of a land, even at this day so fair, so rich, in every kind of cultivation and improvement." And beyond this: "The philosopher who speaks with delight, of the original simplicity, and primitive innocence of mankind, may here learn, that man, uncivilized and barbarous, is even worse than the most ferocious wolf or panther of the forest." Finally, Loudon quotes, approvingly of course, Brackenridge on the ignoble savage.[16]

Significantly, Loudon includes in his collection only narratives and anecdotes which support his thesis; but all these, he indicates, are "compiled from the best authorities." Included are the Knight and Slover narratives, the whole of the Manheim *Affecting History* compilation, the narrative of Mrs. Herbeson, and many another such. Here Loudon

sets the pattern for three other editors who follow him, Samuel Metcalf (*A Collection of Some of the Most Interesting Narratives of Indian Warfare in the West* [1821]), Alexander Withers (*Chronicles of Border Warfare* [1831]), and John A. M'Clung (*Sketches of Western Adventure* [1832]).

Later collections are somewhat more objective than these. So Samuel Gardner Drake refrains from comment when he includes two New England captivity narratives in his vastly popular *Indian Biography* (first printed in 1832 and reprinted many times thereafter in various versions under various titles). His large-scale work with the captivity narrative, however, is to be found in his *Indian Captivities* (1839), a collection which may be called truly scholarly in intent. As Drake indicates, he prints only "entire Narratives," and he has not "taken any liberties with the language of any of them, which would in the remotest degree change the sense of a single passage. . . ." He realizes that these narratives will shock some of his readers, but he reminds them that the stories are only "pages of Nature"; and the fashion of studying those pages "has now long obtained, and pervades all classes." And he points out that there is much to be learned incidentally about the Indian and his nature and customs in these narratives. Thus they are worth the study of historians and scientists.[17]

Interestingly enough, Drake takes time out to attack other "collections of Indian Narratives of a similar character to this." They are similar in title only, he insists; for their editors tamper with the original texts. Drake will let the captives speak for themselves and thus preserve the integrity of their narratives. And then he presents his narratives, some twenty-nine of them, including those of Mrs. Rowlandson, Mrs. Hanson, Mrs. Howe, How, Williamson, Colonel Smith, and Manheim. Others he prints from manuscripts which he apparently obtained from local historical societies. He offers little comment on the individual narratives. He takes his task as editor very seriously.

So, too, one J. Pritts, following largely Withers's *Chronicles* of 1831, published in 1839 his *Incidents of Border Life, Illustrative of the Times and Conditions of the First Settlements in Parts of the Middle and Western States.* He indicates that he is publishing this collection as the result of a

> determination on our part to collect as many of the printed fragments of that part of our country's history as a diligent research might enable us to procure; and from the collection, and such additional resources as might fall within our reach, to compile a volume embracing whatever might seem interesting and suitable to the design and scope of the desired work.[18]

Although this collection is localized, in form and intent it closely parallels that of Drake.

Finally, even the great Schoolcraft appended to his much reprinted *The American Indians, their History, Condition, and Prospects* (first issued in 1844-1845 under the title

Onéata, or The Red Race of America) an "Appendix, containing Thrilling Narratives, Daring Exploits, Etc. Etc." And there is serious editorial treatment of single captivity narratives in Edwin James's *A Narrative of the Captivity and Adventures of John Tanner* (1830) and in Lewis Henry Morgan's notes to editions of Seaver's *Narrative of the Life of Mary Jemison* appearing after 1847 (which, incidentally, contrast greatly with the materials and manner of the narrative itself). Thus, even as sensational narratives were being produced, the older narratives—sensational or not—were being considered for their possible historical and ethnological value.

V

From Mrs. Rowlandson through Williamson and Mrs. Kinnan and Mrs. Smith to Dr. Drake is indeed a long, long way. The captivity narrative as a popular genre varies with the quality of the cultural milieu in which it is produced; it comes finally into the province of historical scholarship, for the immediate cultural "need" for it is gone, or almost gone. Certainly, so long as the narrative continues to be produced, the experience which it records is at core vital; but to say this is only partially to describe both experience and narrative. For an experience and a narrative, as we have seen, can be vital for many different reasons. And the captivity narrative is interesting and valuable to us, I submit, not because it can tell us a great deal about the Indian or even about immediate frontier attitudes towards the Indian, but rather because it enables us to see more deeply and more clearly into popular America culture, popular American issues, and popular American tastes. As religious confessional, as propaganda, and as pulp thriller, the captivity narrative gives us sharp insight into various segments of popular American culture. Only a properly historical view, a consideration of form, impact, and milieu as well as of content, will enable us to see what the captivity narrative really was and came to be.

Notes

1. This thesis has most recently and most fully been worked out by Phillips D. Carleton, "The Indian Captivity," *American Literature*, XV, 169-180 (May, 1943).

2. I base this study on an examination of the great collection of captivity narratives in the Ayer Collection of the Newberry Library and of various narratives, not in the Ayer Collection, which I have seen at the Library of Congress and the Huntington Library. Generally I have cited the narratives by short titles, quoting, when possible, from modern reprints which are relatively easy of access. I have not been concerned with problems of small-scale textual variants in those narratives which were widely reprinted; nor have I attempted, except incidentally, to make this a bibliographical study. This last is the enormous task on which Mr. R. G. W. Vail has been engaged for some years; completion of it will mean that it will be possible to write a satisfactorily detailed history of

the narrative. Meantime, I have been able to see at least one exemplar of each of the great bulk of the known narratives; and I have attempted to consider each for its significance at the point of its publication. Finally, I should note that this essay is at once tangential and supporting to a much larger (and, I hope, comprehensive) study on which I am now engaged, a study of the impact of the Indian on the American mind and creative imagination from 1607 to *ca.* 1850.

3. P. 39.

4. I cite the edition of Springfield, Mass., 1908 (which reprints the text of the sixth edition, 1795), p. 2.

5. *The Narrative of the Captivity and Restoration of Mrs. Mary Rowlandson* (Boston, 1930), pp. 9-10.

6. The Rowlandson narrative, for example, had gone through fifteen editions by 1800.

7. It is worth noting here that all versions of the Hanson narrative seem heretofore to have been attributed to Samuel Bownas. Actually there appear to be two basic versions of the narrative, those stemming from the 1728 text *(God's Mercy)* and those stemming from the 1760 text *(Account of the Captivity)*. Although Sabin (30264) adds Bownas's name to the 1754 edition of *God's Mercy,* the name does not appear on the title-page, as it does in editions deriving from the 1760 *Account.* Bownas himself, in his posthumously published journal (*An Account of the Life, Travels, and Christian Experiences in the Work of the Ministry of Samuel Bownas* [London, 1756]), notes that he visited Mrs. Hanson in 1726 and took down an account of her captivity "from her own Mouth." Then he presents a summary, of about 250 words, of her narrative and follows it with this postscript: "The incredible and severe Trials the poor Woman and her Children went through during their Captivity, I cannot here describe to the full. . . . After my return to Europe, I saw at Dublin a Relation of this extraordinary Affair in a printed Narrative, which was brought over by a Friend from America" (*Account of the Life* [Philadelphia, 1759], pp. 179-180). Since Bownas was in Dublin in 1740 (*Account of the Life,* p. 215) and since he died in 1753, it would seem that he saw the 1728 edition of *God's Mercy* (which was printed at New York and Philadelphia) and later polished it up for the reading public and retitled it *An Account of the Captivity of Elizabeth Hanson.* One bibliographical problem remains: How can one account for the fact that the first known version of *An Account* was published in London in 1760, after Bownas's death? For this problem I can offer no solution except to point out that Bownas's journal was published (in a polished-up version too?) three years after his death; perhaps he left other religiously useful papers. Finally, I should note that I have seen editions of *God's Mercy* dated 1728, 1754, 1803, and 1824 (this last called *The Re-*

markable Captivity and Surprising Deliverance of Elizabeth Hanson) and editions of *An Account* dated 1760, 1782, 1787, and 1815. The editions of *God's Mercy* are all American; those of *An Account* all English. Such, I might piously add, is the sort of problem which one prays that Mr. Vail can solve!

8. I have quoted here from the edition of Edinburgh, 1792, pp. 19, 24, 25. Incidentally, the Williamson narrative offers another very troublesome bibliographical problem. In such late editions as I have seen there are various complex appendices and many textual variants.

9. *A True Narrative* (Elizabethtown, 1795), pp. 3, 4, 5.

10. I quote from *The History of Maria Kittle* (Hartford, 1797), pp. 3, 21-22.

11. I quote from the edition of New York, 1928, ed. D. L. Clark, pp. xxiii, 219.

12. It is worth noting here that the captivity narrative finds poetic expression in *The Returned Captive, A Poem Founded on a Late Fact* (1787). Here poetic and subject matter are nicely complementary; both are gruesome. Too, Andrew Coffinberry's *Forest Rangers* (1842), as a poetic account of Wayne's campaign, derives much of its epical strength from its relation to the popular captivity narrative.

13. For examples of such narratives, see *Narrative of the Captivity and Sufferings of Ebenezer Fletcher, of New-Ipswich* (1813?); *An Affecting Account of the Tragical Death of Major Swan, and of the Captivity of Mrs. Swan and infant Child by the Savages, in April Last* (1815); *Narrative of Henry Bird* (1815); Zadock Steele, *The Indian Captive* (1818); James E. Seaver, *A Narrative of the Life of Mary Jemison* (1824); Charles Johnston, *A Narrative of the Incidents Attending the Capture, Detention, and Ransom of Charles Johnston* (1827); Ewel Jeffries, *A Short Biography of John Leeth* (1831); *Narrative of the Captivity and Providential Escape of Mrs. Jane Lewis* (1833); *Captivity and Sufferings of Mrs. Mason, with an account of the Massacre of her Youngest child* (ca. 1836); *Narrative of the Captivity and Extreme Sufferings of Mrs. Clarissa Plummer* (1838); *Narrative of the Massacre, by the Savages, of the Wife and Children of Thomas Baldwin* (1835); *A Narrative of the Captivity of Mrs. Horn and Her two Children with Mrs. Harris, by the Camanche Indians* (1839); Hiram Hunter, *Narrative of the Captivity and Sufferings of Isaac Knight from Indian Barbarity* (1839); *Narrative of the Extraordinary Life of John Conrad Shafford, Known by Many by the Name of the Dutch Hermit* (1840); four narratives by Josiah Priest; *The Low Dutch Prisoner* (1839), *A True Narrative of the Capture of David Ogden* (1840), *The Fort Stanwix Captive* (1841), and *A True Story of the Extraordinary Feats, Adventures, and Sufferings of Matthew Calkins* (1841); *Indian Battles, Murders, Sieges, and Forays in the South-West* (1853); Nelson Lee, *Three Years among the Camanches* (1859); Ann Coleson, *Miss Coleson's Narrative of her Captivity among the Sioux Indians!* (1864); Fanny Kelly, *Narrative of my Captivity among the Sioux Indians* (1871); *The True Narrative of the Five Years' Suffering & Perilous Adventures, by Miss Barber, Wife of "Squatting Bear," A Celebrated Sioux Chief* (1873). Interesting in this light too are *Indian Anecdotes and Barbarities* (1837), which was reprinted virtually verbatim as *Indian Atrocities! Affecting and Thrilling Anecdotes* (1846).

14. See *Narratives of Captivity among the Indians of North America,* Publications of the Newberry Library, No. 3 (Chicago, 1912), pp. 67-68.

15. Cf. the Smith narrative (Williamsburgh, 1818), pp. 13-14, with the Manheim narrative, ed. 1794, reprinted in the *Magazine of History,* Extra No. 152 (1929), pp. 169-170.

16. I quote from the reprint of Harrisburg, 1888, p. iv.

17. I have seen reprints of this collection, with variant titles, dated 1841, 1846, 1850, 1851, and 1870. I quote from the first edition (1839), pp. v-vii.

18. (Chambersburg, Pa., 1839), p. iii. This was reprinted with additional material in Abingdon, Va., 1849, as the *Mirror of Olden Time Border Life.*

Richard Vanderbeets (essay date 1972)

SOURCE: Vanderbeets, Richard. "The Indian Captivity Narrative as Ritual." *American Literature* 43, no. 4 (January 1972): 548-62.

[*In the essay below, Vanderbeets urges readers to view captivity narratives as a unified genre built upon common rituals.*]

All civilized peoples have recognized the value of tempering their joys with a play or story chronicling the misfortunes and tragedies of others. Because the earliest Americans countenanced neither play-acting nor the unhealthy influences of the novel, they wrote and read true tales of tragedy and horror in the form of disasters, plagues, and shipwrecks—and of Indian massacres and captivities. As the frontier pushed westward under continuing conflict the tales of Indian captivity accompanied it, gradually becoming our first literature of catharsis in an era when native American fiction scarcely existed. The immense popularity of the Indian captivity narratives in their time is unquestionable. First editions are rare today because they were quite literally read to pieces, and most narratives went through a remarkable number of editions: there are over thirty known editions of the Mary Rowlandson narrative; John Dickenson's account went to twenty-one, including translations into Dutch and German; there are twenty-nine editions of the Mary Jemison captivity, and the popularity of Peter Williamson's narrative carried it through forty-one editions.[1]

Over twenty-five years ago, Phillips Carleton made the point that the vast body of Indian captivity narratives was known mostly to historians, anthropologists, and collectors of Americana.[2] Regrettably, that observation is as true today as then. And in the rare instances where informed scholarship has turned its attention to the narratives, emphasis has been upon the historical and cultural rather than the literary value of the tales. In a pioneering and widely influential study, Roy Harvey Pearce in 1947 conceived of the Indian captivity narrative as but a thread in the loose fabric of American cultural history; consequently he discerned not a single genre but rather several "popular" subliterary genres ranging from the religious confessional to the noisomely visceral thriller, their several significances shaped and differentiated largely by the society for which the narratives were intended.[3] This approach places the narratives almost exclusively within the province of historical scholarship, and an unfortunate corollary to this conception holds that the captivity narratives have but "incidental literary value" and enter literary history proper only with the Indian episodes in Charles Brockden Brown's *Edgar Huntly* (1799).

This fairly states the general view that has stood for over twenty-three years. The present intention is not so much to overturn that view as to effect an accommodation of its apprehension of several popular genres by considering the entire range of captivity narratives as a single genre—developing and demonstrating variations of cultural application—but nonetheless a single genre in terms of the shared literary, as opposed to historical and narrow cultural, significances of the narratives. The discrete historical and cultural significances of the Indian captivity narrative, however illuminating they may be in their religious, propagandistic, and visceral applications, are subordinate to the fundamental informing and unifying principle in the narratives collectively: the core of ritual acts and patterns from which the narratives derive their essential integrity. The variable cultural impulses of the narratives of Indian captivity are then but a part of their total effect, and the narratives are more than the simple sum of their parts. The result is a true synthesis. The shared ritual features of the captivity narratives, manifested in both act and configuration, provide that synthesis.

I

Unrelated to a particular time yet found in particular records of human experience, certain acts tend to have a common meaning and serve similar functions. Recurring acts recorded in the narratives of Indian captivity, given their underlying beliefs, can be seen as ritual reenactments of practices widely separated in time and place. Principal among these are cannibalism and scalping. Cannibalism, a practice rather more widespread among American Indians than is commonly understood, is reported in captivity narratives from the seventeenth to the nineteenth centuries and involves a geographical span of tribes ranging from New England forest Indians to tribes of the Great Lakes to the Plains and Southwest Indians: Mohawks, Delawares,

Chippewas, Miamis, Ottawas, Shawnees, Chickasaws, and Comanches. For tribes that practiced it, cannibalism was a ritual of war, like their purification rites. The practice of eating the flesh of an enemy derived from the belief that the eater could acquire the courage and strength of his victim, a belief that is part of a primitive system of sympathetic or homoeopathic magic. This belief and consequent practice are reported among Indians not only of North America but of Ecuador and Brazil, among bushmen of Central Africa, East Africa, and Southeastern Australia, and even in the Norse Legends.[4] In this connection, Northrop Frye observes that the metaphorical identification of vegetable, animal, human, and divine bodies has "the imagery of cannibalism" for its demonic parody, citing particularly Dante's Ugolina and Spenser's Serena.[5] Further, the imagery of cannibalism is seen to involve images of torture and mutilation. American Indian cannibal practices tend to reinforce this imagery.

Jesuit missionary-captive Father Isaac Jogues reports the sacrifice of a woman captive to a Mohawk "demon" god: she was first burnt all over her body and thrown onto a pyre; the body was then cut up, sent to various other villages, and devoured. On another occasion, Jogues's captors lamented not having eaten their most recent Huron captives and resolved, in a prayer to the demon-god, "if we shall ever again capture any, we promise thee to devour them."[6] Father Francis Bressani substantiates Jogues's observations on Mohawk cannibalism: the body of one of his slain Huron companions was dismembered—feet, hands, and "most fleshy parts of the body to eat, as well as the heart." Bressani also witnessed an act of cannibalism when the burnt body of another slain Huron was brought into his cabin: "Before my eyes, they skinned and ate the feet and hands."[7] Alexander Henry's account of cannibalism among his Chippewa captors illustrates the customary rather than culinary significance of the act for most tribes: of seven dead white men, the Indians took the fattest, cut off the head and divided the rest into five parts; these were put into five kettles over as many fires. Henry's "master" ate a hand and a large piece of flesh, remarking that while he did not relish it, the custom among Indian nations when returning from war was to make a feast from among the slain. This is done, Henry was told, to inspire warriors with courage. On another occasion, he was informed that, in preparation for returning to the siege of Detroit, it was proposed that he should be killed in order to give the warriors "a mess of English broth to raise their courage."[8] In most tribes, eating of human flesh was acceptable only as ritual. John Tanner tells of an Ottawa who had eaten his dead wife because of hunger; the tribe considered him unworthy to live and wanted to put him to death.[9] Yet, other tribes appeared to enjoy the practice. Charles Johnston's fellow captive, William Flinn, was burned at the stake and then devoured by Shawnees, one of whom later remarked to Johnston that Flinn's flesh was "sweeter than any bear's meat."[10] During Rachel Plummer's captivity, her Comanche captors engaged in a battle with Osages and, victorious, boiled and ate the dead Osage warriors. Rachel was offered the foot of one, but declined.[11]

Blood-drinking was among many tribes considered generally salutary and often specifically medicinal. Charles Johnston tells of a fellow captive wounded in the attack that led to their capture. The wound was washed by a squaw who caught the bloody water in a cup and forced the injured man to drink it, saying it would hasten the cure (p. 47). Mary Kinnan witnessed Delawares "quaff with extatic pleasure the blood of the innocent prisoner" undergoing torture.[12] Jonathan Carver reports that during the massacre of men, women, and children at Fort William Henry, "many of these savages drank the blood of their victims, as it flowed warm from the fatal wound."[13] Alexander Henry observed at the massacre at Fort Michilimackinac that "from the bodies of some, ripped open, their butchers were drinking the blood, scooped up in the hollow of joined hands, and quaffed amid shouts of rage and victory" (p. 291). Cannibalism, as practiced among American Indians, was essentially a ritual enactment and, even in those instances where tribes developed a taste for human flesh, had its origins in deeply rooted primitive systems of sympathetic magic. Other Indian barbarities have equally primitive foundations.

The taking of scalps, a practice popularly thought to have originated with the American Indian, was in part a manifestation of far older beliefs ascribing magical powers to the hair. Anthropology attests the widespread primitive belief in the hair as the seat of the soul, and the hair is also a principal feature of the primitive and pagan conception of the external or separable soul: "The idea that the soul may be deposited for a longer or shorter time in some place of security outside the body, or at all events in the hair, is found in the popular tales of many races. It . . . is not a mere figment devised to adorn a tale, but is a real article of primitive faith which has given rise to a corresponding set of customs."[14] American Indians, like many other primitive peoples, attributed special powers to the hair and believed the scalp to be somehow connected with a person's fate. Consequently, the scalp often symbolized life itself. The practice of scalping scarcely requires elaboration and documentation here, and the narratives of captivity—like all other Indian histories, relations, and accounts—are replete with descriptions and commentaries upon it. It should be noted, however, that scalps were generally desired in a diameter of approximately two inches (although more than that was often taken in haste[15]), a fact that tends to substantiate the symbolic as opposed to merely evidential significance of the practice.

These ritualized acts—cannibalism and scalping—are themselves significant ritual features of the Indian captivity narrative; yet they but surround and support the primary unifying and informing pattern that lies at the heart of the narratives, the configuration of greatest meaning that binds them collectively into a coherent whole: that of the Hero embarked upon the archetypal journey of initiation. The quest, or ancient ritual of initiation, is a variation of the fundamental Death-Rebirth archetype and traditionally involves the separation of the Hero from his culture, his undertaking a long journey, and his undergoing a series of excruciating ordeals in passing from ignorance to knowledge. In the Monomyth, this consists of three stages or phases: separation, transformation, and enlightened return.[16] The pattern of the Indian captivity experience, in its unfolding narrative of abduction, detention/adoption, and return, closely follows this fundamental configuration.

II

"Ah, poor man, Rip Van Winkle was his name, but it's twenty years since he went away from home with his gun, and never has been heard of since . . . whether he shot himself, or was carried away by the Indians, nobody can tell." That such separation from one's culture was symbolic death, and return (from either cave in the Kaatskills or captivity in the forest) a symbolic rebirth is implicit in Irving's tale. Those who were literally torn from their homes and carried into Indian captivity were for the most part dead to their families and friends. In one narrative after another, the returning captive is met in an affecting scene by relatives who confess that they had never expected to see him alive again. But it is in the captivity experience itself—the transformation by immersion into an alien culture accompanied by ritualized adoption into that culture—that constitutes the initiatory process and prepares for the enlightened return or rebirth of the initiate. This process of transformation in the captivity experience involves first a ritual initiatory ordeal, followed by a gradual accommodation of Indian modes and customs, especially those relating to food, and finally a highly ritualized adoption into the new culture.

The ritual ordeal faced by almost all captives was the gauntlet, the initiation into captivity that Heckewelder in his early Indian *History* gives name to and describes: "On entering the village, [the new captive] is shewn a painted post at the distance from twenty to forty yards, and told to run to it. . . . On each side of him stand men, women, and children, with axes, sticks, and other offensive weapons, ready to strike him as he runs, in the same manner as is done in the European armies when soldiers, as it is called, run the gauntlet. . . . Much depends upon the courage and presence of mind of the prisoner."[17] The Indian gauntlet ritual pervades captivity accounts from the mid-seventeenth to the mid-nineteenth century and was practiced by tribes of wide geographical divergence. Fathers Jogues and Bressani attest the Mohawk ordeal. Jogues describes being required to run the gauntlet in 1642 and being beaten senseless to the ground by clubs, noting that the Indians forming the gauntlet are called "saluters" (p. 31). In 1644 Bressani endured a similar experience to which was added the refinement of a knife-wielding brave who cleft open the Jesuit's hand between two fingers (p. 109). Thomas Brown, taken upon capture in 1757 to an Indian village near Montreal, was met by a crowd of men and women who stripped him naked and told him to run toward a wigwam: "They beat me with sticks and stones all along the way" (p. 16). Henry Grace describes his having to "run the Gantlope" between two rows of Indians, "some beating me with Sticks, and some with their Hands, while others flung any Thing they could lay their Hands on. . . ."[18] John Slover tells of captives running the ritual gauntlet and having loads of powder fired on their bodies as they ran.[19] Daniel Boone ran a Shawnee gauntlet in 1778, but by ducking, zigzagging, and bowling over some of the Indians on the line, emerged with only bruises and the admiration of his captors.[20] Jackson Johonnot reported that all captives entering a new Kickapoo Indian village immediately underwent initiation to the camp by beating.[21] Major Moses Van Campen ran an Iroquois gauntlet in 1781.[22] James Smith was told by his Delaware captors that his gauntlet ordeal was "an old custom, like saying how do you do."[23] And, as late as 1866, Frank Buckelew was forced to run a gauntlet of whips and clubs wielded by his captors, Lipan Indians in Texas.[24]

Having suffered this initial ordeal and introduction to captivity, the captive then underwent the second phase of transformation by a gradual accommodation to Indian practices and modes. The most striking and consistently recorded of these accommodations is at once the most fundamental: that of food. In narrative after narrative, captives describe an initial loathing of Indian fare, then a partial compromise of that disgust under extreme hunger, and ultimately a complete accommodation and, in many cases, even relish of the Indian diet. Captives, of course, were given very little to sustain them (Quintin Stockwell reports, for example, that he and four others subsisted on one bear's foot a day among them[25]), and the food was loathsome to the white palate ("what an Indian can eat is scarcely credible to those who have not seen it," observed Thomas Morris, a captive during Pontiac's Conspiracy in Ohio[26]).

After several months' captivity, Father Jogues found rotten oysters, whole frogs (unskinned and uncleaned), and deer intestines full of blood and half-putrified excrement to be "I will not say tolerable, but even pleasing" (p. 54). Mary Rowlandson's experience was typical: during the first two weeks of her captivity she ate hardly anything, disdaining the Indians' "filthy trash"; but thereafter, "though I could think how formerly my stomach would turn against this or that, and I could starve before I could eat such things, yet they were sweet and savoury to my taste." Among Indian dishes she ultimately found "savoury" were partially cooked horse liver ("as it was, with the blood about my mouth, and yet a savoury bit it was to me"); boiled bear meat ("that was savoury to me that one would think was enough to turn the stomach of a brute creature"); and boiled horses' feet and pieces of "small guts" ("the Lord made that pleasant refreshing, which another time would have been an abomination").[27] Elizabeth Hanson considered want of food "the greatest difficulty, that deserves the first to be named" in her captivity account. Many times she had nothing to eat other than pieces of beaver-skin cut into strips, laid on fire until the hair had been singed away, and then eaten "as a sweet morsel, experimentally knowing that 'to the hungry soul every bitter thing is sweet.'" Mrs. Hanson lived largely on nuts, tree bark, and roots, though occasionally her captors caught a beaver and gave

her "the guts and the garbage," which she found tolerable even though she was not allowed to clean and wash the offal. Like Mrs. Rowlandson some fifty years before, Elizabeth Hanson knew the extent of her accommodation, that what she had to eat "became pretty tolerable to a sharp appetite, which otherwise could not have been dispensed with. . . . none knows what they can undergo until they are tried; for what I had thought in my own family not fit for food, would here have been a dainty dish and sweet morsel."[28]

Henry Grace relates that it was five days before he could bring himself to stomach the "filthy and wretched" diet of his Indian masters (raw or quarter-done meat "with the Hairs sticking about it"), but ultimately confesses that "Hunger will make a Man eat what he could not think on" (p. 17). Charles Johnston describes eating the flesh of bear cubs during his captivity. The entrails were taken out, the hair singed from the carcasses, and they were roasted whole: "To me it was excellent eating, although it would hardly suit a delicate taste" (p. 56). On the first day of his capture by the Northwest Nootkas, John Jewitt found his meal of clams and whale oil unpalatable: "Both the smell and taste were loathsome to me." After several months of captivity, he was able to boil whale blubber in salt water and nettles and think it "quite tolerable."[29] Oliver Spencer was given hawk meat and boiled leaves when first captured, but could not eat it ("the taste was not only insipid, but sickening"). Gradually, however, Spencer accommodated and survived.[30] Fanny Kelly, offered a slab of raw buffalo flesh, declined it "thinking then it would never be possible for me to eat uncooked meat"; some days later, though still "painful to contemplate," Indian food was at least palatable. Subsequently, during a sustained Sioux flight from pursuing cavalry, she subsisted for a week on leaves and grass.[31] Frank Buckelew's accommodation to Indian fare seemed complete: "The raw liver which had been so detestable to me, I soon learned to crave and could eat with as much relish as the savages themselves" (p. 35).

The final phase of transformation, as represented in the captivity experience, is that which effects the deepest immersion into the alien culture and completes the initiation of the Hero: symbolically "becoming" an Indian by ritualized adoption into the tribe. As Leslie Fiedler has accurately perceived, archetypal tensions tend to translate the tale of captivity into one of adoption;[32] and it is this stage of the captivity that holds the greatest transforming significance. For some captives, adoption and immersion into Indian culture were so complete that they chose to remain, refusing redemption or release when offered. Most of these captives were, of course, taken at a very early age and quickly forgot their own culture. One of the earliest recorded instances of complete immersion is in the example of Anne Hutchinson's daughter, who was captured by Pequots in Connecticut in 1643 at the age of eight. She was four years in captivity and had forgotten how to speak English; when ransomed she refused to be taken from the Indians and was eventually returned to white civilization against her will.[33] The later but more widely known case

1857 wood engraving depicting Mary Rowlandson and her children being transported by their Native American captors.

of John Williams's daughter Eunice is even more compelling. Williams, in the narrative of his own captivity, relates his initial attempt to redeem his daughter but ultimately must tell the reader very simply, "she is there still; and she has forgotten to speak English."[34] John Slover, taken into his first captivity in 1761 at the age of eight, spent twelve years with Delawares and Shawnees and gave up the life of a savage, he confesses, "with some reluctance—this manner of life had become natural to me" (p. 9). Frances Slocum, taken at the age of five, concealed for fifty years her white identity because she feared that her relatives, of whom she still had recollection, would come and take her away if they knew she was alive. When finally discovered by her surviving sister and brothers, she refused to go with them: "I cannot," she said. "I am an old tree. . . . I was a sapling when they took me away. It is all gone past."[35] She died in 1847 at the age of seventy-four. John Tanner seemed all his life torn between both worlds. Captured at the age of nine, he lived with Chippewas and Ottawas in Ohio until 1817 when he emerged from the wilderness at age thirty-seven. In 1846 he disappeared without a trace and, though his end is a mystery, was believed to have re-

turned to the Indians. It is with the other captives, however, those who came back and whose captivity experience can be regarded in the context of the separation, transformation, and return pattern of the Hero's initiation, that the ritual of adoption effects its archetypal significance.

As Father Jogues noted during his captivity, it was the custom of savages "when they spare a prisoner's life, to adopt him into some family to supply the place of a deceased member" (p. 36). Jogues's fellow captive-missionary Father Bressani was himself given to an old Mohawk couple to replace a relative killed by Hurons. Bressani does not describe the ritual attending his adoption, but does say that it took place "with all the usual ceremonies" (p. 116). John Tanner was adopted by an Ottawa whose youngest son had recently died and whose wife had complained that unless he "brought her son back," that is, brought her a captive whom she might adopt, she could not go on living (p. 55). Charles Johnston's experience among the Shawnees reveals another function of Indian adoption—not only to replace the lost or dead but also as payment for killing a member of the tribe. Johnston relates that it was the custom of the Shawnees, as well as many other tribes, that when a man took the life of another he was obliged to make amends to the dead man's family either by payment or by furnishing a substitute for him. In this manner, Johnston was given to a Mingo to be substituted for a slain Wyandot (pp. 87-88). For whatever reasons, adoption was a widespread, almost universal practice among American Indians, a practice that involved elaborate ceremony and ritual.

Alexander Henry, saved from death even as the tomahawk flashed in his face because one brave decided to adopt him to replace a lost brother, underwent such a ceremony. First his head was shaved except for a spot on the crown. Then his face was painted red and black. Two bead collars were placed about his neck, and his arms were decorated with bands of silver. Finally, a red blanket was given him to complete the ritual (p. 305). Nelson Lee was stripped of his clothes and outfitted in Comanche dress, was required to paint his face daily, and took part in a "covenant" ritual with the chief wherein he opened a vein on his hand and marked in blood his bond to that sachem.[36] The adoption ceremony accorded James Smith was even more elaborate. Every hair was pulled out of his head except for a three-inch scalp-lock, which was then decorated Indian fashion. Holes were bored in his ears and nose, and he was given rings and nose jewels. After his head, face, and body were painted, the ceremony was completed by three squaws who dipped him into a river. By this last part of the ritual, Smith was told, "every drop of white blood was washed out of your veins" (pp. 185-186). John M'Cullough's adoption ceremony began by repeated immersion into a river. After being pulled out and told that he "was then an Indian," he was given the Indian name "Isting-go-weh-hing."[37] Daniel Boone, adopted by Shawnees because the chief wanted him for his son, was dressed in Indian garb, given the name "Sheltowee" (Big Turtle), and had all his hair plucked out except for the traditional scalp-lock (pp. 64-65). Frances Slocum's adoption by Delawares as daughter to a couple who had lost their own child included Indian clothes and an Indian name, as did the ceremony of Hugh Gibson during his five-year captivity.[38] Mary Jemison was stripped, taken into a river and washed, and dressed in Indian clothes. This was followed by ritual weeping for the deceased relative whose place she was taking and, finally, bestowing of the Indian name "Dickewamis" (Handsome Girl).[39] Robert Eastburn's adoption was also accompanied by a ritualized weeping, after which his adoptive mother "dried up her tears and received me for her son."[40] Some ritual adoptions included the practice of tattooing. After Thomas Brown was stripped, had his hair entirely cut off and his face and body painted, the back of his hand was pricked with needles and Indian ink to make a tattoo (p. 18). The adoption of the Oatman girls into the Mohave tribe was effected by the ritual of facial tattooing, after the fashion by which female Mohaves were marked: "They pricked the skin in small regular rows on our chins with a very sharp stick, until they bled freely. Then they dipped these same sticks in the juice of a certain weed that grew on the banks of the river, and then in the powder of a blue stone . . . and pricked this fine powder into the lac-

erated parts. They told us that this could never be taken from the face."[41] Olive Oatman bore these marks the rest of her life.

By whatever means and ceremonies, ritual adoption into the tribe and symbolically becoming a member of the new culture was the ultimate transforming experience of Indian captivity. It remained only for the captive to return to his former culture and complete the journey-adventure. Most captives, having been given up for dead or at best considered "lost" after capture, were received on their return by relatives and friends in the sense of having come from the grave, reborn to the world from which they had passed by means of symbolic death. Robert Eastburn arrived home to be told by his wife and family that they had "thought they should never see me again, till we met beyond the grave" (p. 69). When redeemed, Mrs. Rowlandson stayed for three months with Reverend and Mrs. Thomas Shepard, who, to the reborn captive, seemed "a Father and Mother" to her (p. 163). Peter Williamson was transformed by his captivity to the extent that, after escaping and reaching the home of an old friend, he was not recognized and was even taken for an Indian.[42] And Charles Johnston, in a remarkable statement that could not be more to the point here, relates that he was ransomed from captivity "by a singular coincidence" on exactly the day he reached the age of twenty-one; in Johnston's own words, "It might be truly and literally denominated my second birth" (p. 98).

The journey of the archetypal initiate, then, proceeds from Separation (abduction), Transformation (ordeal, accommodation, and adoption), and Return (escape, release, or redemption). This ritual passage, one of the most fundamental of all archetypal patterns, finds expression in the narratives of Indian captivity to an extent that renders this configuration an essential structuring device of the tales. This basic pattern, when viewed in the light of such ritual practices as cannibalism and scalping, demonstrates the degree to which elements of distinctly archetypal nature have pervaded and informed the captivity narratives throughout their development. Further, these elements account in large measure for the remarkable pull the captivities have exercised upon readers, an appeal that transcends sectarian religious feeling, narrow chauvinism, or morbidity—the several "popular" subliterary significances. The narratives of Indian captivity are more than cultural indices or curiosities; they touch upon fundamental truths of experience. It is in this that the Indian captivity narratives collectively constitute a single and literary whole, and it is by this that they belong with those expressions of man which draw and shape their materials from the very wellsprings of human experience.

Notes

1. For assistance in acquiring primary materials for this study, grateful acknowledgment is here made to the Special Collections Division, The Newberry Library (Edward E. Ayer Collection); the Reference Department of the Huntington Library; the State Library and Archives, Sacramento, California; and the Docu-

ments and Loan Department of the San Jose State College Library. For a valuable compilation of titles and editions of captivity narratives published before 1800, see "Appendix" to R. W. G. Vail's *The Voice of the Old Frontier* (Philadelphia, 1949).

2. "The Indian Captivity," *American Literature,* XV (May, 1943), 169-180. Carleton draws a parallel between the narratives and the Icelandic Sagas in their treatment of violent periods of first settlement, although unlike the Sagas the captivity narratives had no oral tradition.

3. "The Significances of the Captivity Narrative," *American Literature,* XIX (March, 1947), 1-20.

4. Sir James George Frazer, *The Golden Bough* (New York, 1959), pp. 132-133, 178 ff.

5. *Anatomy of Criticism* (New York, 1967), pp. 148 ff.

6. *Captivity of Father Isaac Jogues, of the Society of Jesus, Among the Mohawks,* in *Perils of the Ocean and Wilderness: or, Narratives of Shipwreck and Indian Captivity,* ed. John Gilmary Shea (Boston, 1857), pp. 58-59. Subsequent references will appear in parentheses following quotations.

7. *Captivity of Father Francis Joseph Bressani, of the Society of Jesus,* in Shea, *Perils of the Ocean and Wilderness,* pp. 106, 119.

8. *Travels and Adventures in Canada and the Indian Territories Between the Years 1760 and 1776* (New York, 1809), in Samuel Gardner Drake, ed., *Indian Captivities* (Auburn, 1850), pp. 301, 322.

9. *A Narrative of the Captivity and Adventures of John Tanner, U.S., During Thirty Years Residence Among the Indians in the Interior of North America* (New York, 1830), p. 90.

10. *A Narrative of the Incidents Attending the Capture, Detention, and Ransom of Charles Johnston* (New York, 1827; reprinted, Cleveland, 1905), p. 104.

11. *Narrative of the Perilous Adventures, Miraculous Escapes and Sufferings of Rev. James W. Parker, To Which is Appended a Narrative of the Capture and Subsequent Sufferings of Mrs. Rachel Plummer, His Daughter* (Louisville, 1844), p. 27. Some captives were themselves almost driven to cannibalism by hunger. Thomas Brown, for example, escaped from Canada with a friend who subsequently died from starvation; Brown, near dead from hunger himself, cut off as much flesh from the body as he could tie up and carry, resolving to eat it if necessary. He was relieved of the need when he managed to kill three birds (*A Plain Narrative of the Uncommon Sufferings and Remarkable Deliverance of Thomas Brown, of Charleston, in New-England,* Boston, 1760, pp. 20-21).

12. *A True Narrative of the Sufferings of Mary Kinnan* (Elizabethtown, N. J., 1795), p. 9.

13. *Captain Jonathan Carver's Narrative of His Capture, and Subsequent Escape from the Indians,* in Drake, *Indian Captivities,* p. 174.

14. Frazer, p. 599.

15. Rev. John Corbly, for example, relates that his two daughters were scalped alive, one "on whose head they did not leave more than one inch round, either of flesh or skin." Miraculously, both survived and were living at the time Corbly wrote his account (*The Sufferings of John Corbly's Family,* in *Affecting History of the Dreadful Distresses of Frederic Manheim's Family,* Philadelphia, 1794, pp. 7-8).

16. Joseph Campbell, *The Hero With a Thousand Faces* (New York, 1960), pp. 58-80, *passim*; p. 246. The first stage of the journey, separation, signals the fact that destiny has called the Hero and transferred his spiritual center from his own society to a zone unknown; one manifestation of this fateful region, among others such as a distant land or underground kingdom, is the forest or wilderness. Further, the Hero can go forth of his own volition or he may be carried off by some malignant agent. Once having crossed the threshold of his adventure, the Hero must survive a succession of trials. At the nadir of the mythological round the Hero undergoes a supreme ordeal and is transformed by the experience. The final work is that of the return, and the Hero reemerges from the kingdom of dread (return, resurrection).

17. Rev. John Heckewelder, *An Account of the History, Manners, and Customs, of the Indian Nations,* in *Transactions of the Historical and Literary Committee of the American Philosophical Society* (Philadelphia, 1819), I, 212.

18. *The History of the Life and Sufferings of Henry Grace* (Reading, Pa., 1764), p. 13.

19. *Narratives of a Late Expedition Against the Indians; with an Account of the Barbarous Execution of Col. Crawford; and the Wonderful Escape of Dr. Knight and John Slover from Captivity in 1782* (Philadelphia, 1783), p. 22.

20. John Filson, *The Discovery, Settlement, and Present State of Kentucke . . . To Which It Added, An Appendix, Containing I. The Adventures of Col. Daniel Boon* (Wilmington, Del., 1784), p. 64.

21. *The Remarkable Adventures of Jackson Johonnot, of Massachusetts, Containing an Account of his Captivity, Sufferings, and Escape from the Kickapoo Indians* (Boston, 1793), p. 34.

22. *A Narrative of the Capture of Certain Americans at Westmoreland, by Savages; and the Perilous Escape which they Effected, by Surprizing Specimens of Policy and Heroism* (New-London, Conn., 1784), p. 8.

23. *An Account of the Remarkable Occurrences in the Life and Travels of Col. James Smith, During his Captivity with the Indians* (Lexington, Ky., 1799), in Drake, *Indian Captivities,* p. 183.

24. Lillie M. Ross, *Life of an Indian Captive* (Philadelphia, 1965), p. 55.

25. Increase Mather, *An Essay for the Recording of Illustrious Providences, Wherein an Account is Given of Many Remarkable and Very Memorable Events* (Boston, 1684), in Drake, *Indian Captivities,* p. 63.

26. *Journal of Captain Thomas Morris of His Majesty's XVII Regiment of Infantry,* in Thomas Morris, *Miscellanies in Prose and Verse* (London, 1791), p. 15.

27. *The Soveraignty and Goodness of God, Together With the Faithfulness of His Promises Displayed; Being a Narrative of the Captivity and Restauration of Mrs. Mary Rowlandson.* "The second Addition Corrected and amended" (Cambridge, 1682), reprinted in *Narratives of the Indian Wars,* ed. C. H. Lincoln (New York, 1913), pp. 131-37, *passim*; p. 149.

28. *An Account of the Captivity of Elizabeth Hanson, Now or Late of Kachecky, in New England . . . Taken in Substance from her own Mouth, by Samuel Bownas* (London, 1760), p. 6-7, 15-16.

29. *The Adventures and Sufferings of John R. Jewitt; Only Survivor of the Crew of the Ship Boston, During a Captivity of Nearly Three Years Among the Savages of Nootka Sound* (Middletown, Conn., 1815), pp. 9, 58.

30. *Indian Captivity: A True Narrative of the Capture of the Rev. O. M. Spencer by the Indians, in the Neighbourhood of Cincinnati, Written by Himself* (*New York,* 1835), p. 69.

31. *Narrative of My Captivity Among the Sioux Indians* (Hartford, 1871), pp. 76, 103.

32. *The Return of the Vanishing American* (New York, 1968), p. 90. Fiedler's apprehension of the mythos of Indian captivity, however, is shaped largely by his characteristic critical stance, e.g., seventeenth-century captive-turned-avenger Hannah Duston, tomahawk raised aloft, is seen to embody "the standard Freudian dream of a castrating mother," an early avatar of "the Great WASP Mother of Us All" (pp. 91-95). In the light of such narrow formulae, Fiedler finds the "insufferably dull and pious journal of Mrs. Mary Rowlandson" quite irrelevant (p. 51).

33. Samuel Gardner Drake, *The Aboriginal Races of North America* (New York, 1880), p. 133.

34. *The Redeemed Captive Returning to Zion: or, a Faithful History of the Remarkable Occurrences in the Captivity and Deliverance of Mr. John Williams* (1707; 6th ed., Boston, 1795), p. 36. Eunice later took an Indian husband, a development especially dismaying to her Indian-hating uncle, Cotton Mather.

35. John F. Meginness, *Biography of Frances Slocum* (Williamsport, Pa., 1891), p. 182.

36. *Three Years Among the Comanches, the Narrative of Nelson Lee the Texas Ranger; Containing a Detailed Account of His Captivity among the Indians* (1859; reprinted, Norman, Okla., 1957), pp. 115, 122.

37. *A Narrative of the Captivity of John M'Cullough, Esq., Written by Himself* in Archibald Loudon, *A Selection of Some of the Most Interesting Narratives of Outrages, Committed by the Indians, in Their Wars, with the White People,* 2 vols. (Carlisle, Pa., 1808-1811), II, 322.

38. *An Account of the Captivity of Hugh Gibson among the Delaware Indians,* in *Collections of the Massachusetts Historical Society,* Third Series, VI (Boston, 1837), 206.

39. James E. Seaver, *A Narrative of the Life of Mrs. Mary Jemison* (Canandaigua, N. Y., 1824), p. 153.

40. *A Faithful Narrative of the Many Dangers and Sufferings, as well as Wonderful and Surprizing Deliverances of Robert Eastburn* (Boston, 1758), p. 47.

41. R. B. Stratton, *Life Among the Indians, or: The Captivity of the Oatman Girls Among the Apache and Mohave Indians* (San Francisco, 1857; reprinted, San Francisco, 1935), p. 134.

42. *French and Indian Cruelty; Exemplified in the Life and Various Vicissitudes of Fortune, of Peter Williamson, a Disbanded Soldier* (London, 1759), p. 30.

David L. Minter (essay date 1973)

SOURCE: Minter, David L. "By Dens of Lions: Notes on Stylization in Early Puritan Captivity Narratives." *American Literature* 45, no. 3 (November 1973): 335-47.

[*In the following essay, Minter considers changes in the purpose and tone of captivity narratives over time, particularly focusing on the narrative of Mary Rowlandson.*]

The "Indian Captivities" of the New England Puritans were, during the first several years of their existence, deeply devout. Born as they were, however, in the late seventeenth century, in what was for the Puritan way an era of fundamental transformation, the captivity narratives soon changed drastically. First, they became instruments of propaganda against Indian "devils" and French "Papists."[1] Later, after need for inspiring hatred of the French had subsided, the narratives played an important role in encouraging government protection of frontier settlements. Still later they became pulp thrillers, always gory and sensational, frequently plagiaristic and preposterous.[2]

Popular in each of these three different modes, as religious tale, as propagandistic tract, and as sensational thriller, Indian captivity narratives spread well beyond the borders of New England and lasted well into the nineteenth century. About 1875, when people stopped reading them, scholars began studying them. Moses Coit Tyler (1878) viewed them as records of Indian "conflict" and as pictures of Indian "cruelty."[3] In an effort to generalize the significance of the narratives, Phillips Carleton interpreted them as accounts of *the* frontier experience and as expressions of *the* frontier mind.[4] Later, in a far more searching essay, "The Significances of the Captivity Narrative" (1947), Roy Harvey Pearce reoriented study of the form.

Pearce insists, and establishes beyond doubt as it seems to me, that there are different captivity narratives expressive of different minds. Distinguishing the "religious" narratives from the "propaganda" narratives and both from the sensational "thrillers," Pearce argues that they vary fundamentally, that they differ, to borrow Francis Fergusson's appropriate if grand term, in "spiritual motive."[5]

Concerned mainly with tracing the changes that overtook the captivity narrative, Pearce contents himself with describing the early narratives as "religious" (as "simple, direct religious documents") and as "individual" (as accounts of direct experience apprehended by an individual mind).

> gradually the quality of directness, of concern with describing an experience precisely as it had affected the individual who underwent it, of trying to recapture and put down what were taken as symbolic psychic minutiae, began to disappear. Other interests predominated. The propagandistic value of the captivity narrative became more and more apparent; and what might be termed stylization, the writing up of the narrative by one who was not directly involved, came to have a kind of journalistic premium.[6]

By tracing the changes in the text of *God's Mercy surmounting Man's Cruelty, Exemplified in the Captivity and Redemption of Elizabeth Hanson,* from the more colloquial 1728 version to the more "correct" 1754 version to the even more "correct" 1760 edition, Pearce defines, in relation to the later narratives, the process he terms *stylization.* The purpose of this essay is to examine, with particular reference to the work of Mary Rowlandson, a different but equally significant kind of stylization in the early narratives.[7]

In the process I hope to revise our notion of them as predominantly individual; to recast our understanding of the quality of the changes that took place as the narratives spread and developed; and to redefine the basis for our regarding the early narratives as superior.

I

Drawing on an established conception of history and established doctrinal traditions, the Indian captivity narratives of the Puritans place a familiar story (of providential deliverance) in a new setting (the American Indian frontier). In telling "affecting Stories concerning the gracious Providence of God,"[8] the narratives follow a clear, recurring pattern of action: attack and capture lead to a several-stage forced march or journey, then to detention in one place or sale or trade, and finally to either ransom or escape. The pattern allows for only slight variations, except in the last stage, where the protagonist's role is far larger and more dramatic in escape. But behind the narra-

tives lie two traditions: a providential theory of history that interpreted the design and action of God as ruling even "the most unruly"[9]; and a doctrine of afflictions that welcomed suffering and adversity by defining them as corrective, instructive, profitable.[10] In *The Soveraignty and Goodness of God, Together With the Faithfulness of His Promises Displayed; Being a Narrative of the Captivity and Restauration of Mrs. Mary Rowlandson,* the author simply assumes that the Indians, whom she characteristically terms "hell-hounds" (p. 121) are actors in a divine drama. Unwilling and unwitting though they be, they are instruments of her chastisement, participants in God's plan for calling one of "his dear ones" (p. 115), the elect, back to obedient service (see pp. 158-167). What her code required of her, in response to chastisement and adversity, she also well understood; "Patient bearing of the crosse, with profit" was after all one of the accepted "signes of salvation."[11] Rowlandson accordingly not only bears suffering without flying out in wrath against God; she also specifies the failings that have preceded chastisement. Prior to the experience of captivity, she discovers a period of complacency:

> I then remembered how careless I had been of Gods holy time, how many Sabbaths I had lost and mispent, and how evily I had walked in Gods sight; which lay so close unto my spirit, that it was easie for me to see how righteous it was with God to cut off the thread of my life, and cast me out of his presence for ever.

> (p. 124)

God, of course, does not cast her out: as he wounds her "with one hand," so he heals her "with the other" (p. 124). Her suffering proves profitable precisely because it leads to new reliance upon God. Bereft of husband, friends, and relations, of "House and home and all our comforts within door, and without," indeed of everything "except my life," and not knowing "but the next moment that might go too," completely vulnerable and precarious, she rediscovers God's presence. "In a wonderfull manner," he provides for her, "carrying" her along and "bearing up" her spirit (pp. 122-123). In response to her patient suffering (see p. 141), God shows her a double mercy: he protects her life and draws her back from the edge of despair. Chastisement becomes not a sign of judgment only but of love. Since "whom the Lord loveth he chasteneth," captivity, affliction, and suffering become signs of election (see pp. 166-167).

What we see here is one of the ways a familiar conception of life functions for Rowlandson. Christians of the sixteenth and seventeenth centuries were still accustomed to viewing the whole of human existence under the aspect of imprisonment. From the "welbelov'd imprisonment" of the womb man entered the "lower prisons" of this "fallen world" only to find in his body a visible and sensual prison of his soul. Envisioning hell as a "horrible dungeon full of fier," and heaven as an "open place," a "spatious plesantnes," Christians defined the life of sin as a terrible enslavement and the life of faith in a fallen world as servitude, a "sweet captivitie" to God.[12] What the language of captivity most forcibly did, however, was more specific and limited: it made any particularly dramatic experience of captivity a sign of judgment and any dramatic deliverance a sign of grace. For Rowlandson, accordingly, deliverance from this particular "grievous Captivity" (p. 121) to the Indians marks both her return to her society and her restoration to a larger sweet captivity to God. But it also functions as a sign prefiguring final deliverance to the spacious pleasantness of heaven.[13]

It is in this last capacity, as token or sign, that Mary Rowlandson's deliverance from the Indians becomes immensely significant. To the Puritans, for each of whom the question of whether "my self was one" of those whose name appeared on the list of "the Elect" was ever "the question," such signs were altogether necessary.[14] But since pride and complacency were to them signs not of salvation but of its opposite, Puritans knew too that assurance must always be imperfect.[15] Rowlandson, accordingly, is careful not to overstate the significance of her deliverance. Temporal deliverance, she clearly assumes, may prefigure but cannot guarantee eternal salvation.

Like other early Puritan "captivities," Rowlandson's narrative speaks directly to the two great dangers that haunted the Puritans: pride and complacency born of excessive confidence of election; anxiety and despair born of failure of confidence of election. By reminding her of dependency and unworthiness, the experiences she recounts in the narrative make her incapable of complacency. To the very end, beyond deliverance, in the act of writing itself, as the writer of the Preface is careful to make clear, Mary Rowlandson is moved not by smugness and self-satisfaction but by "gratitude unto God," who is in fact the final protagonist of her narrative. Repeatedly we move in the narrative from near-despair to hope and back again. As the Indians begin, with "outragious roaring and hooping" and with "hideous insulting and triumphing," to celebrate another victory and to count the scalps of those "they had destroyed," Mary Rowlandson's spirits sink. At this particularly "melancholy time," God mercifully sends her a Bible. With hope reviving she opens the Bible only to find in Deuteronomy 28 not relief but new darkness. "But the Lord helped me still to go on reading till . . . I found, There was mercy promised again . . ." (pp. 127-128). The basic rhythm as well as the total structure of the work thus obliterates complacency, self-satisfaction, and self-reliance and yet teaches, not despair, but hope of salvation. The "grievous Captivity" the teller experiences is more than tamed; it is made representative and necessary, a sign of all dangers that have been, are, and will be, but a sign, too, of an encompassing hope. The "solemn sight" of seeing "so many Christians lying in their blood . . . like a company of Sheep torn by Wolves, All of them stript naked by a company of hell-hounds" (pp. 120-121), however terrible, does not teach terror. For it is placed in the larger context of a divine scheme that reclaims even the deepest affliction.

> But now I see the Lord had his time to scourge and chasten me. The portion of some is to have their afflic-

tions by drops, now one drop and then another; but the dregs of the Cup, the Wine of astonishment, like a sweeping rain that leaveth no food, did the Lord prepare to be my portion.

The drinkers of such wine knew better than to take pride in their afflictions and astonishment, but knowing, too, that the Lord chasteneth all whom He loveth "and scourgeth every Son whom he receiveth," they could say, with David, "It is good for me that I have been afflicted" (pp. 166-167).

Rowlandson's narrative thus operates, in a very traditional way, as a story, as an "ensample," of God's salvific activity. Like Puritan conversion narratives, the captivity stories trace "the noble Operations of the blessed Spirit" in a particular soul.[16] For the Puritans, the requirement that they live in a state of imperfect assurance intensified two needs at once: the need to read or hear accounts of the work of the spirit so as to find models by which to judge one's own experience; and the need to produce one's own record, the need to tell one's own story, as a sign that one's own name too was listed among the Elect. By making the writing and telling as well as the reading or hearing of such accounts extensions of living in imperfect certainty, however, the Puritan way made writing and telling moments in the drama of salvation, the drama they were so remarkably given to retelling and reexamining.[17] In short, writing and reading were for them continuations of the drama written of and read about. For the Puritans in fact had no sense of an ending to that drama, this side of death. In it living, writing, and reading played similar roles and were informed by the same basic rhythm.

What we accordingly sense at every point in Rowlandson's narrative is a curious and double present-mindedness. The narrative engages a past experience. But by presenting what has happened to her as representative, Rowlandson wants to make her story useful to others. Implicit in the act of writing itself is the conviction, shared with the friend who writes the preface, that for others her story can be exemplary, that it can enter their ongoing struggles with salvation. But since her own struggle, too, is ongoing, she wants the act of writing to be for her what the act of reading will be for others: a quieter scene continuing the drama the narrative records. Writing and publishing an account "of her affliction and deliverance" will continue the basic rhythm of the narrative, will mark new moments in the dialectic between despair and assurance that informs the work itself.[18]

Puritans were of course also concerned with "the noble Operations of the blessed Spirit" in historical "Reformation."[19] Like biographical writings, historical writings seemed to them useful as records of God's activity. Given the Puritans' "covenant theology," which gave an individual's drama of salvation social and historical analogues, and given the way Indian captivity represented individual involvement in historical conflict, captivity narratives came, almost inevitably, to serve not only as stories prefiguring an individual's eternal fate, but also as paradigms of the larger society's story. Both Rowlandson and her prefacing friend view her story as a warning to other individuals grown complacent or desperate, and to a society. In this context Rowlandson's story of tamed tribulations suggests that New England's present troubles are both justified and temporary, that her God is a God of wrath and judgment but also of deliverance.[20]

To expand her narrative's range of reference, Rowlandson repeatedly uses the very familiar Puritan device of introducing Biblical references and allusions that link the experience and fate of an individual to the experience and fate of a people. She also makes the lives of other sufferers exemplary. Her sister's life, for instance, recalls a pattern that pervades the personal literature of the Puritans. "In her younger years she lay under much trouble upon spiritual accounts, till it pleased God to . . . take hold of her heart" and make known his grace to her. For "More then twenty years" she has lived to "tell how sweet and comfortable" God's grace has proved. "I hope she is reaping the fruit of her good labours, being faithfull to the service of God in her place" (p. 120). Even the sister's death becomes a sign of deliverance: hearing of the deaths of some, witnessing the agony of others, the sister cries out, "Lord, let me dy with them; which was no sooner said, but she was struck with a Bullet" (p. 120). What we see in the narrative, in short, is not only an encompassing providential design, but such specific deliverances as the sister's death and Mary Rowlandson's being saved from rape. In each episode or event Rowlandson focuses, not on experience per se, but on experience as sign; she finds parallels, examples, analogues, prefigurings—familiar patterns—at every turn. Yet because she takes the reading of experience, its interpretation, seriously, she is attentive to its details.

What she finds in event enables her to add to her primary role, of wayward child of God duly chastised and delivered, another very different role, that of prophetess. She speaks repeatedly to the children of New England of the danger of divine wrath. Having been "One hour . . . wanting nothing: But the next hour . . . having nothing but sorrow and affliction," as one who knows what affliction means and who has "seen the extrem vanity of this World," she is prepared to speak, beyond her own adversity and deliverance, both of "the awfull dispensation of the Lord towards us" and of "his wonderfull power and might, in carrying of us through so many difficulties" (p. 166). With David she says, "It is good for me that I have been afflicted"; and to all New Englanders she says, "I have learned to look beyond present and smaller troubles, and to be quieted under them . . ." (p. 167).

Mary Rowlandson thus finds in the Bible, as William Tyndale had hoped that she would, "true and faithful ensamples" of how God has and will deal with man "in all infirmities"; repeatedly she turns to its "stories and lives . . . for sure and undoubted ensamples" not only of the ways of God with man but also of the role she must play

and the message she must utter, almost as a kind of Lazarus come back to tell us all.[21] Her captivity and deliverance become representative of God's providential activity on a large historical stage and become, in particular, paradigmatic of New England's story.

It is this last expansion that so obviously preoccupies the writer of "The Preface to the Reader," a piece signed *Ter Amicam* and probably written by Increase Mather.[22] Two years later, in 1684, Mather was to provide not only clues to the social significance but a providential framework for understanding the far more secular narrative of Quentin Stockwell.[23] Still later Cotton Mather would find, in the work of such writers as Hannah Swarton and Mrs. Duston, personal experiences to be put to social purposes, and the move toward propaganda would become dominant.[24] Rowlandson's friend merely highlights points she comes to late and touches lightly. The *Narrative,* we are told, was written out of "gratitude unto God," not pride. Although "it is not [the friend's] business to dilate" on such noble work, that is precisely what he does. He urges readers to attend what she has to say who has been "captivated, and enslaved" to atheistical and diabolical creatures; he reminds them that the God of Mary Rowlandson is the God both of New England and of Israel's deliverance; and he assures them that for God's "dear ones" the "worst of evils" will work "together for the best good." New Englanders accordingly are charged to "lay by something from the experience of another": namely, that if they are children of God they will gain "by all this affliction" (pp. 114-117). A story of affliction "now made Publick . . . for the benefit of the Afflicted" (p. 112), Mary Rowlandson's narrative comes to us as experience apprehended (and to be read) in terms provided by a highly developed intellectual context which defined experience as representative and instructive on several levels at once.

II

The American Puritans, we have long delighted in remarking, were limited men, repressive and dogmatic. Disciples of learning, they were uneasy with art, even suspicious of it, as their meager production suggests. Yet we know from the examples of Milton and Bunyan that the Puritans possessed a force of very considerable potential for literature. Though confining, their ideology and their traditions gave meaning to history and heroic proportion to individual experience.[25] American Puritans, of course, produced nothing comparable to Milton's epic and colossal imagination, nor any vision of Paradise so fleshly and abundant as his. They were uneasy with talk of rich groves, "odorous gumms and balme," of hyacinthine locks, fair forms, and "umbrageous grots and caves." Even in their finer flights their world was less copious than his. In accounts of disasters—of the shipwrecks, massacres, plagues, and captivities we repeatedly meet in their writings—they were, if still no match for Milton, nevertheless on more familiar ground. "All our way to Heaven lies by Dens of Lions and the Mounts of Leopards," Cotton Mather once wrote; "We are poor travellers in a world which is as well the Devil's Field, as the Devil's Gaol. . . ."[26]

Some such conception provides the radical principle of the early captivity narratives, the principle that controls both the apprehension and the uses of the experiences recounted. The Puritans were in fact nothing if not acquainted with sorrow and misfortune, and they did nothing if not make, particularly in their accounts of Indian captivity, remarkable images of human existence in its aspect of adversity. Like Mather they conceived the world as fallen, and they associated heaven with both Eden (temporarily lost) and a Promised Land (ever more about to be). But the primary lesson of the Bible for the life they lived was other, and it too was double: the stories of Egypt and Babylon spoke to them of institutionalized slavery, of the world become the devil's jail, of society used by men to enslave God's chosen, a condition they associated with the Old World; and the story of the forty years' sojourn suggested that the forces of darkness could also inhabit the caves of lions and the mounts of leopards, a condition they associated with the New World and its wildernesses. The captivity narratives accordingly combine focus on nature with concern for society and culture. Given a society like their own, however, in which enemies of God were either dispatched or silenced, the Puritans saw nature, the vast, desolate, howling wilderness that so horrifies Mary Rowlandson, and nature's child, the Indian as "hellhound," as most formidably the devil's own (see pp. 122, 126, 132). Accordingly, in the captivity narratives the Puritan imagination is intensely adverse, not in its address to society, whose deliverance it anticipates, but in its address to nature, whose bondage it describes and fears.

In the particular way that they combine focus on nature (as sinister captivity) and society (as lesser prison of this lower world, but also as man's proper home, as scene of saintly pilgrimage), the early captivity narratives embody one of the primary tensions in Puritan life—tension between the urge toward unification and interdependence and the urge toward separation and independence.[27] As an ecclesiastical solution to the problems of the Reformation, Congregationalism represented a move toward separatism and individualism, and thus participated in what historians, at least since Burckhardt, have seen as one of the defining characteristics of the Renaissance. But the Congregational solution, in tension between separating and non-separating forms of it, embodied one version of the problem it was devised to resolve, and this familiar fact of Puritan intellectual history held significant implications for the Puritan imagination as well as for the Puritan mind.

At their most successful, in Mary Rowlandson's work, for example, the captivity narratives do something like justice to both the personal and the social significances of the experiences they recount. But even in Rowlandson's narrative, which Pearce sees as individual (as concerned "with describing an experience precisely as it had affected the individual"), there is clearly present a fundamental Puritan need and habit: the turning of private emotion and personal experience into emotion and experience approved by public code and ideology.[28] In the providential theory of history, in the doctrine of afflictions, in the literature of

personal witness, in the conception of life as pilgrimage through prisons to freedom, and in the notion of salvation as continuous drama—in the presence of these, together with countless biblical allusions, we see the shaping influence of the Puritan code. And it is precisely in that influence that we can discover the kind of achievement Rowlandson's narrative represents. For what we see in Mary Rowlandson is something very close to what every Puritan desired—a state of being in which mind so controlled emotion, in which sanctioned modes of interpretation so controlled perception and response, that there was total harmony between self and established pattern, between individual experience and accepted form. We may at times feel something like the presence of "raw" emotion in Rowlandson's narrative. But what we are most aware of is harmony in which mind, idea, form are preeminent, harmony in which the self finds expression, not in freedom, spontaneity, and individuality, but under severe restriction and constraint and in accord with accepted formulas.

In short, there is in Rowlandson no weakness of the impulse, through careful stylization, to conform private experience to public code, personal apprehension to social model. Rather, what we see in her, at least as she comes to us in her narrative, is a nearly perfect internalization of a social code which possessed, despite its distinct social bias, a capacity for giving heroic proportion and definite meaning to individual adventure.

As we move from Rowlandson (1682) through Duston and Swarton (1702) to Hanson (1728, 1754, 1760), we observe the displacement of one code, with its formulas and needs, by another with different formulas and needs. That displacement represents, among other things, progressive secularization and adaptation of a literary mode, a process at work as early as Quentin Stockwell's narrative (1684) and perhaps dominant as early as John Williams (1707).[29] Internal turmoil, disputes with England, pressures of war and frontier conflicts made that adaptation, however, the opposite of individualistic. What secularization meant, in this case, was propaganda and sensationalism, and what propaganda and sensationalism meant was increasing exploitation—increasing disregard for the particularities of the experience recounted as well as for the language of its appropriation. What we observe in the later narratives is experience that remains socially useful, as propaganda and as entertainment, and yet becomes centerless as expressing self is lost. But what we observe in the early narratives is the work not simply of an individual but of a radically socialized individual, an individual who feels a deep need to conform experience to socially sanctioned patterns and no longer feels any deep resistance to such restriction.

Notes

1. See, for example, the "Narrative of Hannah Swarton," in Cotton Mather, *Magnalia Christi Americana* (London, 1702), Book VI, Chapter II.

2. This essay contains a minimum of bibliographical data. For a very useful compilation of titles and editions of narratives published in the seventeenth and

eighteenth centuries, see the "Appendix" to R. W. G. Vail, *The Voice of the Old Frontier* (Philadelphia, 1940). See also the article of Carleton cited in note 4 below and the article of Pearce cited in note 5. Pearce lists examples of each of the types of narratives I mention.

3. Moses Coit Tyler, *History of American Literature during the Colonial Period* (New York, 1878), p. 138.

4. Phillips D. Carleton, "The Indian Captivity," *American Literature,* XV (May, 1943), 169-180.

5. Roy Harvey Pearce, "The Significances of the Captivity Narrative," *American Literature,* XIX (March, 1947), 1-20. For a recent revision of Pearce, concerned not with discriminating among the captivity narratives but with treating them as "a single genre," see Richard VanDerBeets, "The Indian Captivity Narrative as Ritual," *American Literature,* XLIII (Jan., 1972), 548-562. VanDerBeets views the narratives as a single genre whose "fundamental informing and unifying principle" is a ritualistic journey of an archetypal initiate from separation through transformation to return or rebirth. Thus, whereas VanDerBeets is interested in the very broad pattern that unites the narratives, I am interested in defining the precise spirit and distinguishing character of the very early narratives.

6. Pearce, p. 3.

7. Rowlandson's is deservedly the best known of the narratives (see Pearce, p. 3); and it has the added advantage of being the most widely available. Although the kind of "stylization" I am interested in is very different from the kind Pearce traces, it is interesting to note the role Increase Mather played in the writing and publishing of the Rowlandson piece. In an unpublished Yale College Honors Thesis, *The Memorable Preservations: Narratives of Indian Captivity in the Literature and Politics of Colonial New England, 1675-1725* (1967), David A. Richards argues persuasively that Mather encouraged the writing of the narrative (probably in 1676), sponsored its publication (in 1682), and probably supplied the Preface for it. See Richards, pp. 20-30.

8. Increase Mather, *Essay for the Recording of Illustrious Providences* (Cambridge, Mass., 1684), p. 39.

9. Mary Rowlandson, *The Soveraignty and Goodness of God, Together With the Faithfulness of His Promises Displayed; Being a Narrative of the Captivity and Restauration of Mrs. Mary Rowlandson,* in Charles H. Lincoln, ed., *Narratives of the Indian Wars, 1675-1699* (New York, 1913), p. 117. All page references in the text of this essay are to this edition of the Rowlandson narrative, which has the advantage of wide availability and is more than adequate for a study not concerned with minor textual variations. Of the first edition of the Rowlandson narrative (Samuel Green, Boston, 1682) only four pages of one copy are extant; of the two issues of the second edition, corrected and amended (Samuel Green, Cambridge, Mass., 1682), several copies survive, and it is this edition that Lincoln follows; a third edition, less reliable, followed in 1682 (London), and a dozen more by 1800. For further information, see Vail, pp. 31-34.

10. For a brief discussion of the providential interpretation of history, see Douglas Bush, *English Literature in the Early Seventeenth Century* (New York, 1945), pp. 209-213. See also Increase Mather, *The Doctrine of Divine Providence Opened and Applyed* (1684); and *As Essay for the Recording of Illustrious Providences* (1684). On the doctrine of afflictions, familiar to readers of *Job,* St. Augustine, and Bunyan, see Louis L. Martz, *The Poetry of Meditation* (New Haven, 1954), pp. 159-170; and William Haller, *The Rise of Puritanism* (New York, 1938), pp. 143-145.

11. Arthur Dent, *The Plaine-Mans Path-way to Heauen. Wherin euery man may cleerly see whether he shall be saued or damned* (London, 1609), pp. 31-32.

12. The quoted phrases are from the works of John Donne, St. Ignatius, Luis de la Puente, and Robert Southwell, but they could be found in many places. For useful discussions see Haller, pp. 145-146; Martz, pp. 28-48; and Helen C. White, *English Devotional Literature [Prose], 1600-1640* (Madison, Wisc., 1931), pp. 55-57.

13. On the tendency to see society as man's proper place, see John Gyles, *Memoirs of odd adventures, strange deliverances, etc. in the captivity of John Gyles* (Boston, 1736).

14. John Bunyan, *Grace Abounding to the Chief of Sinners* (Cambridge, 1907), p. 22. Compare the title of the work by Dent, note 11 above.

15. Edmund S. Morgan, *Visible Saints* (New York, 1963), p. 91.

16. Richard Baxter, Introduction, *Life and Death of . . . Joseph Allaine* (1672), quoted in Haller, p. 101. See the useful discussion in Haller, pp. 100-101.

17. Compare St. Augustine's *Confessions.* Most of the emphases we find in the Puritan conversion narratives are anticipated in Augustine. But because Augustine's assurance is purer his purpose is simpler—persuasion and conversion of others. For the Puritans the act of writing stands in significantly different relation to the drama described.

18. What is implicit here is consonance between the rhythm of the narrative, the spirit of its writing, and the character of the action of God—his wounding with one hand and healing with the other. See Rowlandson, p. 124.

19. Baxter quoted in Haller, p. 101.

20. Richards (note 7 above) is particularly useful in showing how the New England clergy used works such as the captivity narrative in efforts to influence magistrates. See his discussion, pp. 14-15.

21. William Tyndale, "Prologue to the Prophet Jonas" (1531) in *Doctrinal Treatises and Introductions to Different Portions of the Holy Scriptures* (Cambridge, Mass., 1848), pp. 451, 464.

22. See the discussion in note 7 above.

23. Pearce sees Stockwell's narrative as fitting the Rowlandson pattern (pp. 2-3). But Stockwell's piece is very short on biblical quotation and allusion and is not much concerned with God's providential activity. Most of its "religious" framework was supplied by Increase Mather, in whose *Essay for the Recording of Illustrious Providences* (1684) Stockwell's narrative first appeared.

24. The Swarton narrative can be found in Cotton Mather's *Magnalia Christi Americana* (1702), Book VI, Chapter II; the Duston narrative in Appendix, Article XXV.

25. See Allen Tate, "Emily Dickinson," *The Man of Letters in the Modern World: Selected Essays, 1928-1955* (New York, 1955), pp. 212-213.

26. Cotton Mather, *Wonders of the Invisible World* (Boston, 1693), p. 63.

27. See Perry Miller, *Orthodoxy in Massachusetts 1630-1650* (Boston, 1959), pp. 53-101.

28. See Robert Middlekauff's fine article, "Piety and Intellect in Puritanism," *William and Mary Quarterly*, Third Series, XXII (1965), 457-470.

29. John Williams, *The Redeemed Captive Returning to Zion* (Boston, 1707).

June Namias (essay date 1993)

SOURCE: Namias, June. "White Men Held Captive." In *White Captives: Gender and Ethnicity on the American Frontier*, pp. 49-83. Chapel Hill: The University of North Carolina Press, 1993.

[*In the following excerpt, Namias explores the changing images of males in captivity narratives from 1608 through the nineteenth century.*]

In the first and most famous captive story of an Englishman on the North American continent, Captain John Smith spent a month among the native people of tidewater Virginia. Admitting to some difficulties, Smith wrote of his experiences: "Yet hee so demeaned himselfe amongst them, as he not only diverted them from surprising the Fort: but procured his owne liberty, and got himself and his company such estimation amongst them, that those Savages admired him as a demi-God."[1]

Were men's experiences, behavior, perceptions, and story-telling style on the various American frontiers different from women's? The answer is yes. On the New England

frontier, many more males than females were captured. Of captives taken by French, by Indian and French, and by Indian forces between 1675 and 1763, 771 were males and 270 were females. Men were also at risk because, as in most of human history, men made up the fighting forces. Men were the warriors and the shock troops. They were the leaders of the onslaught onto Indian lands. The codes for prisoners of native capture differed, but a male at adolescence or older might be subject to torture, death, or a combination of the two. Of 1,187 known male captives of French, Indians, and French-Indians in the various New England hostilities between 1675 and 1763, 132 (11 percent) of the male captive population died of all causes; of 392 women, only 16 (4.1 percent) died. Yet 18 males (1.5 percent) were killed as were 33 females (8.4 percent). For infants and children to age six, there was little numerical differentiation between the sexes for those who died or were killed by Indians. For adult males over fifteen, 119 (10 percent) died and 9 were killed; only 12 women (3 percent) died, while 14 (3.5 percent) were killed.[2]

The white male experience ranged from one extreme of torture and death to the other of adoption and acceptance. Torture was nearly always reserved for men, but accounts of torture are also related to religion and ethnicity. The most horrific spectacles of torture were reported by French Catholics. Father Isaac Jogues, a Jesuit, was captured with a group of Hurons and three other Frenchmen by the Mohawks in Quebec in 1642. Three were killed and twenty-two marched south through three Iroquois towns on the Mohawk River. Jogues's report is filled with the burning, biting, and ripping off of flesh; running gauntlet after gauntlet; nails being plucked out; thumbs and fingers cut and bitten off; and ashes and live coals thrown at French captives. The Huron chief and French convert Ahatsistari (Eustace) suffered the worst abuse, "burned in almost every part of his body and then beheaded." On being rescued by the Dutch at Rensselaerswyck, Jogues wrote his observations back to Paris. Unfortunately, he returned to his mission in 1646 and was killed.[3]

There is certainly no lack of torture stories among the English and Americans of the new republic; which are true and which exaggerated is hard to know. The worst tortures seem to have occurred in times of war. The French reports appear to contain the most brutality, and one wonders whether the Catholic ideal of martyrdom or the need for continual financial support from the orders back home for further missionary activity might not account for the brutality detailed in the Jesuit sources. Certainly, men able to stand up under torture won both sympathy and heroic, if not martyr, status.[4]

White male behavior in captivity was not uniform. Age, time, place, and capturing Indian group were significant determinants. Surveying the captivity literature from the period 1608-1870 reveals two critical factors that shaped white male captives: the length of their stay among native people and their age at capture.[5] As was true for women, the younger the age and the longer the stay with the Indi-

1607 illustration depicting the capture of Captain John Smith by Native Americans.

ans, the more likely it was that the male captive would become a "white Indian." For some men and boys, adoption meant discovering a new world and new ways of understanding themselves, but to gain these perspectives, one was subjected to harsh tests.

The range of experience and the plight of male captives is reflected in the accounts of John Gyles, Quentin Stockwell, and James Smith. The first two were late seventeenth-century New England captives. Gyles was ten years old when he was captured along with his father, mother, and three other siblings at Pemaquid, Maine, in August 1689. He was held prisoner for nine years—six among the Abenakis, three with the French. When his brother James (held captive for three years) was caught deserting with an Englishman, both were recaptured "and carried back to Penobscot Fort, where they were both tortured at a stake by fire for some time; then their noses and ears were cut off and they were made to eat them, after which they were burned to death at the stake." When captives were taken or deserters retaken, Gyles saw the Indians dance and "torture the unhappy people who fall into their hands." Gyles himself was beaten with an ax and forced to dance around fellow captive James Alexander, "a Jersey man who was taken from Falmouth in Casco Bay." In the third winter of his captivity Gyles watched as John Evans, a "most intimate and dear companion," was given "a heavy burden . . . even though he was extreme[ly] weak with long fasting." While walking, Evans broke through the ice, cut his knee, and was eventually left to freeze to death.[6]

Unlike Gyles's firsthand account, Quentin Stockwell's story entered the colonial war and propaganda literature in reports from Increase Mather. Captured at Deerfield September 19, 1677, Stockwell described being brought together with a group of Hatfield captives. He and they were "pinioned and led away in the night over the mountains in dark and hideous ways about four miles further before we took up our place for rest. . . . We were kept bound all that night." They were spread out on their backs. "Our arms and legs stretched out were staked fast down and a cord about our necks so that we could stir no ways." He was told that it was the custom to fasten captives for the first nine nights of travel to prevent their escape. Over the northern New England winter, Stockwell, like Mary Rowlandson, had his taste of bear's foot and horse meat. He nearly died of frostbite before being cured by a French surgeon; he finally escaped.[7] Robert Rogers, a captive from Salmon Falls, New Hampshire, in 1690, was not so lucky. He was tortured and burned to death.[8]

Along with death, torture, and escape, adoption was a common experience, especially for young male captives. The first favorable account of this experience appeared after the close of the French and Indian wars. Colonel James Smith (ca. 1737-1814) was captured in Bedford, Pennsylvania, in 1755 and kept journals during his nearly six years of captivity. Smith observed that male captives, whether white or Indian, could undergo identical perils or ultimate good fortune. Smith was eighteen and on a road-building expedition in western Pennsylvania for General

Edward Braddock just before the Battle of the Wilderness. He and other Indian enemies of the French were captured by Caughnawagas (Mohawks). Marched back to the Indian village, he was forced to run the gauntlet, flogged, had sand thrown in his eyes, and was beaten. He was then adopted and treated like a son.[9]

The violence and torture inflicted on male captives contrasts sharply with the experience of women. In the Northeast some women appear to have been tormented, and women and children were forced to march over miles of rough terrain and were tied down. But with the exception of a few reported cases in the seventeenth century, women were seldom killed except at the time of attack or occasionally, as in the case of John Williams's wife, Eunice, if they were sick and unable to make the required trek.[10] Several captivity stories, however, tell of women or small children carried by Indian men. John Dunn Hunter indicates that the pattern of saving women and children and torturing men continued into the early nineteenth century in the central and western states. In his experience, women and children were "treated well," but "the warriors, who were so unfortunate as not to fall in battle, were nearly all tortured to death" unless they were thought to be very brave, in which case they were allowed to live with their captors. Hunter and others discuss the socialization process that tried to mold stoic boys who, if captured, would go to their death singing, even if hot coals were applied to their genitals and skin stripped from their bodies.[11]

In general, in the captivity literature for the period 1608 to 1870 white Anglo-American males appear to fall into two categories: the Hero and the White Indian.

THE HEROIC MODE

Male captives in the Heroic Mode came to the frontier to spread "civilization." They were there to uplift "mankind," bring the true God to the heathen, help the empire or the nation, and protect white women. Rarely, if ever, did they dwell on the advantages of their quest for their own personal gain; still, their exploits usually brought them the benefits of fame, fortune, and gratitude. Out of their capture by and contact with native peoples came a recognition of their own historic mission. Amusement, disdain, or contempt often accompanied the contact of these men with Indians; little appreciation or understanding of the other resulted.

"Heroes" of this type further subdivide into those who were inspired by God and those for whom empire, country, or "civilization" were the motivating force—along with occasionally saving women in distress. Captives in the Heroic Mode include Father Isaac Jogues, John Williams, Captain John Smith, Daniel Boone, and their dime novel spin-offs.

HEROES FOR GOD

The first Heroes for God in the North American wilderness were the Black Robes—Jesuit priests who moved through Quebec and New France and into New York and the Mississippi Valley. In the eyes of men like Father Isaac Jogues, no suffering was too great for himself or others to sustain for the glory of God. When the Hurons and fellow Frenchmen in his party were captured by the Iroquois (1642) one Frenchman was "stripped naked, all his nails torn out, his very fingers gnawed, and a broad-sword driven through his right hand." Jogues wrote to his superior: "Mindful of the wounds of our Lord Jesus Christ, he bore, as he afterward told me, this pain, though most acute, with great joy." Suffering blows to his own person, Jogues was no less willing to serve his God: when he entered a second Iroquois village gauntlet, "blows were not spared." Even though they were struck "constantly on the shins to our exquisite pain," Jogues comforted himself with a comparison between the work of the French Catholics and that of God's "apostle, who glories that he was thrice beaten with rods." In the worst of times Jogues saw his mission keenly. Rather than escape torture and misery, he was happy to serve the French captives. To do so might inspire "the christened Huron of his duties." Jogues found it "a peculiar interposition of divine goodness" to have "fallen into the hands of these Indians." During his stay he "baptized seventy, children, young and old, of five different nations and languages, that of every tribe, and people, and tongue, they might stand in the sight of the Lamb."[12]

Father Louis Hennepin, a Franciscan, was one of many French priests to go among the North American Indians. In April 1680, he and two other Frenchmen were captured by Mdewakanton Dakotas, probably on the Mississippi near the junction of the Illinois River. The recollect found it especially difficult to say his breviary and was told by one of the other Frenchmen to watch out or they would all be killed. He tried going into the woods, but the Indians followed him. "I chanted the Litany of the Blessed Virgin in the canoe, my book opened." He got away with it because the Dakotas thought the breviary "a spirit which taught me to sing for their diversion, for these people are naturally fond of singing." Hennepin was luckier than Jogues on several counts. First, though full of his mission to God, he could see his captors. They in turn gave him a large robe made of beaver skins and trimmed with porcupine quills. When he was sick, they fed him fish and brought him naked into a sweat lodge with four Indians. There in the "cabin covered with buffalo skins" around red-hot stones the Dakotas sang and placed their hands on him, "rubbing me while they wept bitterly." He continued this regimen of sweats three times a week and soon "felt as strong as ever." Finally, he was rescued by explorer Sieur Duluth not long after his capture. Duluth saw the treatment of Hennepin in a more negative light than apparently the recollect himself, whose memoirs some say underestimated his cruel treatment as "a captive and a slave." Duluth says he told the recollect they must leave or else hurt the French nation "to suffer insult of this sort without showing resentment of it."[13] Hennepin, although a Hero for God, did not altogether spurn the Indian life, having something in common with both adventurous heroes for empire and White Indians.

Not so John Williams, an English Hero for God. Queen Anne's War began in the colonies in 1703 with an attack on Wells, Maine. Soon the two-hundred-mile area from Maine into western Massachusetts had become a battlefield. In late February 1704 a party of Abenaki and Caughnawaga Indians, with some Frenchmen, attacked Deerfield. John Williams (1664-1729) was minister of the Deerfield, Massachusetts, congregation, a Harvard College graduate (class of 1683), husband of Eunice Mather (niece of Increase), and father of ten children. During the attack, thirty-eight members of the Deerfield community were killed and about a hundred were captured. When the war party struck Deerfield, two of Williams's sons were killed. Williams and the rest of his family were among those taken prisoners. His wife died on the forced march to Canada.[14]

Williams's losses were considerable. Besides grieving over family deaths, he felt great anguish for his congregation. He tried to get protection for them before the attack, but the Massachusetts government ignored his pleas. After his nearly three-year captivity and return, he went back to Canada and worked to negotiate the release of captives from Deerfield and other New England towns. At the end of his narrative he gave thanks to God, "who has wrought deliverance for so many," and asked for prayers "to God for a door of escape to be opened for the great number yet behind," which amounted to nearly one hundred. He lamented that among the children, "not a few among the savages having lost the English tongue, will be lost and turn savages in a little time unless something extraordinary prevent." Among those children was his ten-year-old daughter, Eunice.[15]

Williams's narrative is in the heroic mold because he turns captivity into a religious trial and holy crusade. Captivity is a matter of Divine Providence. It has lessons to teach. Rowlandson's and Mather's narratives assume this. Williams goes one step further by turning the captivity into a jeremiad and a personal crusade. Williams's twin enemies were the Indians and the French. He feared "popish country." On the trek to Canada he was allowed to preach on the Sabbath, but on arrival in New France, he wrote, "we were forbidden praying one with another or joining together in the service of God," and some captives had their Bibles taken from them by the French priests "and never re-delivered to them, to their great grief and sorrow."[16]

Williams's heroism was most actively displayed in his struggles to get back his daughter Eunice and his son Samuel, the first from Indian, the second from Jesuit clutches. *The Redeemed Captive, Returning to Zion* (1707), Williams's narrative of the events, is given over to what today reads as esoteric religious debate. For Williams and the Puritan world, this debate was nothing if not a fight for the immortal souls of himself, his sons and daughter, and his flock. "All means," he wrote, "were used to seduce poor souls." Jesuits told him of wanting to baptize any of the unbaptized English, offering that, "if I would stay among them and be of their religion, I should have a great

and honorable pension from the king every year." He would also get all his children back with "'enough honorable maintenance for you and them.'" Again and again he rebuffed them, although he admitted that their efforts "to seduce" him "to popery were very exercising to me."[17]

More than a quarter of Williams's account consists of his correspondence with his son Samuel. Williams claimed that the boy was threatened continually by the priests, who sent him to school to learn French and then "struck him with a stick" when he would not cross himself. Williams "mourned" just thinking of this boy of fifteen or sixteen and a younger boy of six, both in Montreal being "turned to popery." One letter admonished Samuel and prayed that he might be "recovered out of the snare you are taken in." The father's letters were long and very specific on the subject of the apostles, the Virgin Mary, saints, and prayer. Repeatedly Williams declared that "the Romanists" answers were "a very fable and falsehood." The business of the letters is minute textual analysis, and in each Williams cites chapter and verse of the Scriptures. In one letter, after fourteen long paragraphs, Williams writes, "Again, if you consult Acts 15 where you have an account of the first synod or council, you will find. . . ." The father appears to overlook that Samuel was not a theological student but a *son* whose mother and two brothers had recently died. The rest of his family were in an unknown state and place. Now his father wanted him to follow a very complex line of theological debate. At the close of another letter, Williams momentarily realized he might be overwriting his case: "There are a great many other things in the letter [you sent] that deserve to be refuted, but I shall be too tedious in remarking all of them at once." But after a "yet" the minister continued in the same vein.[18] That Williams saw fit to print these personal letters filled with biblical citations shows that to him they were not just private writings to his son but part of a greater crusade against Catholicism.

Williams's narrative went through six editions between 1707 and 1795. *The Redeemed Captive, Returning to Zion* was first printed in Boston in 1707 and was issued four more times, including one by his son Stephen Williams, published in Northampton in 1853. John Williams's heroism in the service of God was widely read about and much admired in New England. A children's version, *The Deerfield Captive: An Indian Story, Being a Narrative of Facts for the Instruction of the Young,* complete with a print of the Deerfield house in flames on the title page, went through several nineteenth-century editions.[19]

HEROES OF THE EMPIRE

John Williams, religious hero, was atypical of male captives even in British colonial America; he was more typical perhaps of some of his theological counterparts in New France and New Spain. But Williams, like Mary Rowlandson, became a popular and heroic figure to the Puritan community. Among the first English settlers, the adventurous, death-defying hero predated the religious one and is popular to our own day. As a swashbuckling Elizabethan, a world traveler, a man who was patronized by many women but married to none, an explorer, adventurer, historian, scientist, and weaver of tales, John Smith still cuts a heroic figure. It is to him that the heroic tradition of gunslinger, Indian fighter, and twentieth-century western hero hark back. He is a man alone, full of bravado, meeting with strange men and exotic women.[20]

The text of Smith's work and the stories of his life are well known. But let us begin by looking at the pictures. Following in the tradition of his earlier exploits in the Middle East, Smith provides vivid illustrations of his North American exploits. His earlier works show knights jousting on horseback and Smith killing a man by battering him over the head with a club, whereas the six-part foldout of illustrations to *The Map of Virginia* (1612) portrays Smith among the Indians. In the top right and bottom left corners Smith is manfully confronting individual Indian men. In one he has a gun, in the other a large sword. In both cases *he* is taking Indians prisoner. In both cases the Indian is a *big* Indian, at least a head taller than the Elizabethan. In the two pictures that show him taken prisoner (bottom right and center left in the original) Smith is a smaller figure among many Indians; they overpower him with their numbers. These two renditions of his capture are much less distinct and take up less space than those of his exploits. "How they tooke him prisoner" is the smallest action shot of the group.[21] "Their triumph about him" (top left) after he is captured is the same size as the drawing of him capturing Opechancanough, the king of Pamunkey (or Pamunkee), which shows him "bound to a tree to be shott to death," but larger and more central is Smith surrounded by what appear to be dancing Indians, who, although carrying weapons, look more like figures out of Greek mythology. The top center picture shows Smith enjoying himself around a camp fire with several semiclad Indians, including a seated woman and a man wearing antlers. It all looks like a good deal of fun.[22]

In the top right picture of Smith taking the king captive, Smith points a gun at the Indian's head. Sunflowers are growing below Smith's "peece." Smith's left leg is close to the Indian's, almost in a fighting (or dance) pose. Each man has a long weapon pointing down and to the right, a sword in Smith's case, an arrow in the Indian's. The Indian's size and stature, plus his broad and seminaked physical frame, claim the center of the print. In comparison, Smith looks almost doll-like. He is pulling the king's braid, on one hand an ineffectual gesture, on the other one of mockery—something that a man might do to a woman, perhaps implying the "womanliness" of this tall, very masculine-looking bigger man. The "peece" becomes the great leveler. In the background, the English armies in two settings fire weapons at the Indians. In one case, the natives are wounded and run away; in the other, a few Englishmen fire on a larger number of Indians with many more in the background. The gun is thus an instrument of physical and sexual power. In the bottom right frame, we see how "Pokahontas beggs his life."

From the first, Smith wants us to see him "admired" as a "demi-God." Traditional Indian practice has something to do with his success, but the true causes for their hospitality escape him. In *A True Relation* (1608), he gives more detail but is hardly more modest. First, he traveled upriver with a barge, two of his men, and two Indian guides. They stopped to eat. He then headed off with one Indian to test soil. Within fifteen minutes he heard "a loud cry, and a hollowing of Indians." Figuring the Indian guide "betraid us," he grabbed him and bound his arms, his pistol "ready bent to be revenged on him." Smith was then hit in the right thigh with an arrow but was not hurt. So began a tradition in American literature, later picked up in film: a white man is in the wild with his men and an untrustworthy Indian, and he gets hurt. Some other men may die, but the Hero is fine—he can make it through. Smith spied two Indians "drawing their bowes" but made short work of them by "discharging a french pistoll." He then fired again. (Where was the rest of his party?) After a moment twenty or thirty arrows flew toward him. Miraculously, they all fell short! He was then surrounded by the "king of Pamaunch" and two hundred men, who drew their bows but then laid them on the ground—the scene referred to in the illustration of dancing Indians with bows and arrows. The Indians demanded his arms and told him his other men were dead: only him "they would reserve: The Indian importuned me not to shott." The Indian in question was the same one Smith had aimed a gun at and taken prisoner.[23]

Once captured, Smith turned on the charm—or as he would say, "I resolved to trie their mercies," hoping to buy his way to freedom by presenting the chief "with a compasse daill." He then gave the man "a discourse on the roundness of the earth" with a discussion of the stars and the moon—no doubt one of the first English science lessons in the New World.[24]

In Smith's subsequent travels though the wondrous kingdoms of Virginia, he charms us with complete descriptions of his captive but (according to him) honored guest status. The intercession by a young Indian princess and the lavish treatment he received will be discussed later, but his descriptions of men with "white Beads over their shoulders," of emperors sitting upon "tenne or twelve Mattes" with chains of pearls around their necks and covered with raccoon skin furs, of men who "have as many weomen as they will," must have tantalized the Elizabethans. They strike a twentieth-century reader as fare for movie moguls. Smith's captivity is the first big western without the silver screen.[25]

It is too bad that no Chesapeake natives wrote down their stories of Smith's escapades. Certainly self-aggrandizement helped the captain to construct the most abiding captivity narrative, which, significantly, is not recalled as a captivity narrative at all. Smith's expert storytelling gives his European and later American audiences all they want to hear: an exotic but primitive culture meets the European representative, is completely awestruck by him, and falls at his feet. There are many adventures with new food, drink, women, and battle, and there are harrowing experiences, but in the end, he wins and there are few real losses, no reconsideration of the worth of the colonizing project, and no thoughts of what might be the personal consequences for the other.

A second figure among male captive heroes for the empire is Daniel Boone. Both Smith and Boone are well-recognized American folk heroes, but neither is known as a captive. Richard Slotkin has documented the impact of the Boone legend on shaping the American mythic hero. Boone's origins, however, appear to be well grounded in the English adventure traditions personified by Smith, and Boone's significance as folk hero, like Smith's, involves his three stints as an Indian captive. There he outsmarts the enemy and "opens" the continent west of the Appalachians. In two instances, Boone himself was captured; in a third, one of his daughters was captured and then rescued by Boone.[26]

Between his introduction in 1784 as a bit player in the appendix of John Filson's *Discovery, Settlement and Present State of Kentucke . . . The Adventures of Col. Daniel Boon,* to his 1856 starring role in Timothy Flint's *First White Man of the West, or the Life and Exploits of Col. Dan'l. Boone,* the persona of Boone undergoes a transformation. Its effect is important for showing how male and female roles on the frontier became more stereotyped in the nineteenth-century captivity literature than they had been in the colonial period.[27] Of the thirty-two pages devoted to Boone in Filson's account, one long paragraph, taking up about a page of print, gives the first account of Boone's capture and escape in May 1769. Four pages are devoted to Boone's second capture and escape from February to July 1778 and following. Boone's daughter's captivity on July 14, 1776, gets one-half of one paragraph. Each of these exploits forms a chapter in Flint's account seventy years later.[28]

In Filson's account of the first escape, Boone and friends were enjoying the wonders of nature and admiring "a variety of flowers and fruits" when, late in the day, near the Kentucky River, "a number of Indians rushed out of a thick cane-brake upon us, and made us prisoners. The time of our sorrow was now arrived. . . . The Indians plundered of us what we had, and kept us in confinement for seven days, treating us with common savage usage." Because they did not seem anxious to escape, the Indians were "less suspicious of us" and so "in the dead of night, as we lay in a thick cane-brake by a large fire, when sleep had locked up their senses, my situation not disposing me to rest, I touched my companion and gently awoke him." They escaped. Escape and capture are not presented as major issues. One gets captured, undergoes some minor problems, uses one's wits, and outsmarts the "savages" to obtain freedom.[29]

The second capture was more difficult as Boone was taken, according to this account, by "a party of one hundred and two Indians, and two Frenchmen, on their march against

Boons-borough." The similarity to the vast numbers who confronted John Smith is not accidental. How could a "hero" go into a second captivity out of stupidity or oversight? Apparently, only overwhelming odds could convince the reader of his undisputable prowess and the inferiority of "savage" tactics. Boone became the adoptee of a Shawnee family and was introduced to Indian ways. This second capture lasted from February 7 to July 15, 1778. It began the lore of Boone's out-Indianizing the Indians. Culturally, Boone became a White Indian, with the emphasis on the *White* because Boone—like Colonel James Smith, Caughnawaga captive of the 1750s—wanted to learn Indian ways for military purposes, to use them to wipe out Indians.[30]

Besides being a hero for empire, Boone begins the romantic tradition of savior hero. Filson's account gives us the following information about Boone's rescue of his daughter Jemima from captivity: "On the fourteenth day July, 1776, two of Col. Calloway's daughters, and one of mine, were taken prisoners near the fort. I immediately pursued the Indians, with only eight men, and on the fifteenth overtook them, killed two of the party, and recovered the girls."[31] In the mid-nineteenth century, this story of paternal rescue became a popular tale of female weakness and white male prowess. In John Frost's *Daring and Heroic Deeds of American Women . . . among the Pioneer Mothers of the Western Country,* this one-sentence recapture gets the frontispiece illustration and another illustration in a related chapter—noteworthy in the context of a book about women who escaped trouble on the frontier by their own wits.

In Frost's Boone account, he first praised the father of Kentucky for his "hardihood," ability to surmount "all perils," boldness, and the like: "But whatever praise we concede to Boone, we must remember that his wife and daughters also deserve our eulogy." Why? Because he "was a bold and skillful Indian fighter, and accustomed to scenes of danger and death. They belonged to what is commonly called a 'weaker sex,' were much unaccustomed to the wilderness, and to constant alarms of savage warfare," but they went onto the frontier anyway.[32] Of the triple capture of Jemima Boone and the Calloway girls, Flint notes that all three friends, "if we may take the portraits of the rustic time," were "patterns of youthful loveliness, inexpressibly dear to their parents." But as girls will "imprudently" do, they wandered into the woods too far from the protection of "their habitations, to gather flowers with which to adorn their rustic fire-places. They were suddenly surrounded by a half-dozen Indians. Their shrieks and efforts to flee were alike unavailing. They were dragged rapidly beyond the power of making themselves heard." Once among the Indians, however, they were treated with "the utmost indulgence and decorum."[33]

Apparently, the author would not want anyone to believe that anything bad happened to these fair maidens. Flint followed with a paragraph assuring his reader that this is always the case with Indians: after their "demonic" cries and wild fighting antics they "are universally seen to treat captive women with a decorous forbearance." Why is this so, he asks? "This strange trait, so little in keeping with other parts of their character, has been attributed by some to their want of the sensibilities and passions of our race." Translation: the reason for this unusual characteristic of not raping women during or after battle is that Indians are not as sexual or masculine as white males.[34]

When the parents missed their wayward daughters, Boone declares, "By the Eternal Power that made me a father, if my daughter lives, and is found, I will either bring her back, or spill my life blood." At this point, "every individual of the males crowded round Boone and repeated it." "Seven selected persons were admitted to the oath," and the rescue mission was on. The next day a few free men came to the camp, firing their rifles, "cutting down two savages at the first shot," and sending the rest running away. In a moment, the daughters were in their fathers' arms and "in the unutterable joy of conquest and deliverance, were on their way homewards."[35]

In sum, by the Flint account of 1856, Boone was not only a great Indian fighter, scout, and hero of the future American empire but a savior of white womanhood. According to nineteenth-century norms, women needed to be saved because they were weak. Men had a sacred duty to protect them. It was an especially sacred duty for the man of the family to try to save his daughter or wife. Boone's several experiences with captivity all resulted in benefits to him and to society because they showed his agility in escaping or in mobilizing escape parties. They resulted in his befriending the Indians to learn survival skills, which proved him to be smarter than they were, tougher than they were, and able to use their own tools against them as he moved across the Appalachians and into the Northwest and South. But the importance of the Boone narratives and accompanying pictures is their assertion of a father's power as savior and preserver of the frontier family and the basic insecurity of the family without the white male protector. From Rowlandson's and Williams's dependence on the protection of God to save souls, the main lines of protection move with the Smith and Boone traditions to dependence upon weapons, "smarts," and masculine prowess to save one's self and family.

The Romantic Savior and the Market

By the mid-eighteenth century the religious figure faded as the clever, rough, and tough hero which Smith set, combined with the alleged "civilizing" and "rescuing" qualities of both Williams and Boone, emerged as the family figure that dominated the nineteenth-century male narratives of the Heroic Mode. These heroes "save" and protect the "weaker sex" and the patriarchal family. The evolution of this figure by the late nineteenth century can be observed in dime novel creations such as Edwin Eastman's narrative, *Seven and Nine Years among the Camanches and Apaches* (1873), one of many popular romantic savior stories, in which, after the capture of Eastman and his wife,

the hero moves from a "consciousness" that he was "powerless to snatch her from her relentless captors" to organizing a rescue party and lifting "the curtain of dressed buffalo hide" and, after trembling "like an aspen" before his sleeping wife, "awakened the sleeper" and in "an instant" wrapped her in a robe, headed for the mountains, and was soon with the party "in full gallop down the valley."[36]

The combination of Smith and Boone themes, "pseudo-White Indian," "hero," and "savior of white womanhood," was exaggerated in dime novels and mid- to late nineteenth-century accounts. The center of the American pantheon changed gradually but definitively. The strengthening of the male hero came at the expense of and concomitantly with the waning power of the female figure. That this shift occurred in a period that idealized the weak woman and the angel of the bourgeois household and stressed male assertiveness and national expansion is not a surprise. But why is the female heroine nearly obliterated, and how is this accomplished? Why and how does the western frontier become the ground of female trivialization and male supremacy? Certainly the unsettling nature of the process of westering itself is important here, but so is the potential challenge of others, women and Indians, who might challenge the direction of gender and national hegemony.[37]

The dime novels' mass-market approach set the mode of the rough, tough, protector, rescuer male frontier figure packaged for an ever-widening audience. Erastus Beadle picked up where the Boston firm of Gleason and Ballou had begun in midcentury. The nickel and dime stories' novelty was in their characteristic packaging, advertising, and tendency to western themes. In the words of Henry Nash Smith, there were quite a few "subliterary" writers in the dime pool. Yet these works tended "to become an objectified mass dream, like the moving pictures, the soap operas, or the comic books that are the present-day equivalents of the Beadle stories. The individual writer abandons his own personality and identifies himself with the reveries of his readers. It is the presumably close fidelity of the Beadle stories to the dream life of a vast inarticulate public that renders them valuable to the social historian and the historian of ideas."[38] Early dime novels repackaged the themes and dreams of frontier capture and rescue and sold them for big profits. *Seth Jones,* Edward S. Ellis's best-seller of the 1860s and 1870s, became the newest forum for an old frontier hero, creating a popular heroic figure as part-time captive and full-time savior of white womanhood and protector of advancing "civilization."[39]

Ellis was a twenty-year-old teacher in Red Bank, New Jersey, when he was called to New York to make the deal on the book. In a later interview he recalled that the success of the novel was based on its marketing. It was with Seth, he said, that the Beadle series really began. "It was not the merit of the book. . . . It was the ingenious way in which it was advertised."[40] The technique was to print "a rush of posters" and "painted inscriptions" all over the country asking, "Who is Seth Jones?" Ellis claimed, "Everywhere you went this query met you. It glared at you in staring letters on the sidewalks. . . . In the country, the trees and rocks and the sides of roofs of barns all clamored with stentorian demands to know who Seth Jones was." When everyone was just about fed up with the question, the answer was presented in the form of "big and little posters bearing a lithographic portrait of a stalwart, heroic-looking hunter of the Fenimore Cooper type, coon-skin cap, rifle and all. And above or below this imposing figure in large type were the words: 'I am Seth Jones.'" The book was published on October 2, 1860. When soldiers went to the front, the Beadles sent them novels by the tens of thousands.[41]

Seth Jones is a "civilizer," savior of white womanhood, and easterner turned frontiersman. The work shows how the medium may change, but the message lingers on. As Seth's story begins, we hear the sounds of an ax and see "an athletic man" swinging it, "burying his glittering blade deep in the heart of the mighty kings of the wood." The settler's cabin is soon attacked and his "beautiful blue-eyed maiden" daughter stolen from him by "dusky beings." To the rescue comes Seth Jones, mysterious woodsman, to save "that purity daughter."[42] In a comic Boone-like replay, Seth out-Indians the Indians and amuses his captors as well. As with John Smith, his "air of conscious superiority" wins the day. He escapes, returns to the white territory to organize a rescue party, and rescues the maiden.[43] In this gendered, nineteenth-century way of looking at capture, the brave, smart, and tough American white male beats out the Indians. By contrast, the frail, childlike white female must wait for her father, husband, frontier hero, or some combination of white men to save her from misery. In the triumph of the romantic savior, nineteenth-century cultural frontier history thus juxtaposes the ascendancy of white male supremacy from the mountain to the prairie, while simultaneously depicting a weak, infantilized female needing male protection against the evil of Indian wildness.

WHITE INDIANS

If the fictional models for the heroic figure in the captivities go back to the adventuring Odysseus and on to the "real" world of Captain Smith, those of the White Indian probably go back to the children raised by wolves in prehistoric Rome. Fortunately, the raising of white children by North American Indians is more easily documented. There are several narratives of adoptees who became White Indians. Those who assimilated rarely returned to write memoirs, but some did, and others recounted or dictated their stories.

Unlike the stolid, singular, and tough figures that came down in the heroic Boone and Leatherstocking lore, the male captives who lived among the Indians from an early age did not define their manhood by singularity and individual prowess but, not surprisingly, rather more in an In-

dian context of interrelationship. In many cases, that interrelationship was a bond between (Indian) mother and (white adopted) son. This was the case in two of the longest nineteenth-century captivities of white boys captured at a young age. Other elements that differentiated males in the White Indian mode from their "heroic" brothers (or fathers) was their sympathy for Indian ways and, even when they were not adopted as young children, their ability to see the group in which they found themselves, not as monsters but as people like themselves. Still another feature of these men and boys was the way in which they observed, respected, and became part of the natural world.

John Gyles became a White Indian. He was captured at about age ten on August 2, 1689, in Pemaquid, Maine, along with both of his parents and three siblings. Like many other white male captives, he experienced a good deal of beating and observed the death and torture of other white captives, both French and English. He admitted his fears; after all, he was a child. He mentioned whippings, the tossing of hot embers onto captives' chests, and the death of his brother. The difference between Gyles and almost all the female captives of the seventeenth and early eighteenth centuries was his occasional understanding of why captives were badly treated or even killed. He explained that captive James Alexander was treated badly to "revenge" the Indians "having lost some friends." This did not make Gyles happier or less fearful when they beat him, but at least he recognized the emotional intensity of the nature of war in any culture.[44]

Shortly after his capture, when he underwent some torment, a little girl took him "by the hand" and led him out of the captive circle, and an older Indian gave him a pipe to smoke. He thought he would be killed, but this was the first of many protective gestures shown him. When a plague fell upon the Abenakis, "Indians applied red ochre to my sores which by God's blessing cured me." And later, "an old squaw who was kind to captives" gave him hints as to what to beware of when watching male ceremonials and how to avoid the demons of the woods. After he watched one ceremony and came back to her, she "was glad that I returned without hurt."[45]

Gyles's approach was different from Williams's or Smith's. His writing shows an awareness of Indian humanity and an alternative way of looking at the earth. He explained how his Eastern Abenaki (Maliseet) family protected him by having him run off when he was in danger; they told him not to return until they said it would be safe. A young Indian girl jumped in the river to save him when the Indian men forced him to swim even though they knew he could not. Another time, when he suffered with severe frostbite, these Abenakis helped him. (He was about thirteen at the time.) Gyles's lengthy stay in the wilderness made him a keen observer of flora and fauna. He probably wrote his memoirs many years after his release, when he was in his late forties, and revised them in his early fifties after living with the French and becoming a hunter. Still, the earlier years affected him. He called the moose "a fine lofty creature about eight feet high with a long head and a nose like a horse, with horns very large and strong." He included detailed descriptions of the beaver, the wolverine, the hedgehog, the tortoise, and the life of the salmon.[46] He described the ceremonies of the Indians of northern Maine from marriage to mourning and threw in a myth or two. For a seventeenth-century child of the Puritans, his openness to Abenaki ways and his lack of invocation of God and Providence are atypical of Puritan men and women alike. Gyles might well be called the prototype for the White Indian: a young captive living with Indians for many years, protected and cared for by them, especially by Indian women, learning to understand and appreciate the world around him. He was not a nineteenth-century figure and did not see his captors as noble. He would call them devil worshipers. He certainly expressed no interest in staying with them even though six of his first sixteen years of life were spent with them.[47]

The two most famous White Indians of the nineteenth century were captured as children and raised as Indians. John Dunn Hunter was captured at a young age by the Kickapoo along with two other white children. He eventually wound up with (Plains) Kansas Indians and was adopted by a woman who had lost a son in a war with the Pawnees. He found that the Kansas treated him "with regard and tenderness" and that women and children captives were treated well "while every imaginable indignity was practiced on the [adult male] prisoners." In such situations, women who lost a relative were joined by children. At the defeat of the Pawnee, Hunter said children "whipped the prisoners with green briars, and hazel switches, and threw firebrands, clubs, and stones at them as they ran between their ranks, to the painted post of safety." In this particular instance, all the male Indian captives died with the exception of two Mandan chiefs. The opposing chief expected to be tortured and gave the following speech: "'I am a man: the fate of war is against me:—I die like a warrior.'"[48]

Hunter was adopted by several mothers. When he was among the Kansas, he felt a most "painful loss" when his mother drowned one day while collecting driftwood.

> I sincerely and deeply felt the bereavement; and cannot even at this late day, reflect on her maternal conduct to me, from the time I was taken prisoner by the Kansas, to her death, without the association of feelings, to which, in other respects I am a stranger. She was indeed a mother to me; and I feel my bosom dilate with gratitude at the recollection of her goodness, and care of me during this helpless period of my life. This, to those who have been bred in refinement and ease, under the fond and watchful guardianship of parents, may appear gross and incongruous. If, however, the imagination allowed scope, and a lad ten or twelve years of age, without kindred or name, or any knowledge by which he could arrive at an acquaintance with any of the circumstances connected with his being, be supposed in the central wilds of North America, nearly a thousand miles from any white settlement, a prisoner or sojourner among a people, on whom he had not the slightest claim, and with whose language, habits and

character, he was wholly unacquainted; but, who nevertheless treated him kindly; and it will appear not only natural but rational, that he should return such kindness with gratitude and affection. Such nearly was my situation. . . . I have no hope of seeing happier days than I experienced at this early period of my life, while sojourning with the Kansas nation, on the Kansas river, some hundred miles above its confluence with the Missouri.[49]

Despite his grief, Hunter said he could not show his feelings because Indians "regard tears, or any expression of grief, as a mark of weakness in males, and unworthy of the character of a warrior."[50] Hunter's spirits were revived, however, when he was adopted again, this time in Osage territory by the family of Shen-thweeh, whose wife, Hunk-hah, adopted him for her lost son and "took every opportunity . . . to engage my affections and esteem. She used to weep over me, tell me how good her son had been, how much she loved him, and how much she mourned his loss. 'You must be good . . . and you shall be my son, and I will be your mother.'" The daughter of the family was equally attentive to his needs: "The greatest care was taken to supply my wants with the choicest things they had in their power to bestow." Although he was still a boy, she made him ornamented moccasins, leggings, a beaver hat, a buffalo robe, and other clothes reserved for men. When he was wounded in a battle some time later, the "skill of our physicians and the kind attentions of my Indians mother and sister" cured him. At another point he could have returned to the Kansas but felt more kinship with his Osage "mother and sister, who were dear to me, and who loved me in return."[51] But though Hunter received much love and affection from Kansas and Osage mothers and sisters, his Kansas father showed him "little or no regard or tenderness."[52]

Hunter, like all white captive boys, was required to learn the meaning of manhood in the Indian context. The mother who was central to his care and comfort was the same woman who showed him the basic road to becoming a man and a warrior. His account shows the complex nature of the mother-son bond in those native societies in which he lived. He describes how boys at an early age were trained to withstand and inflict pain. In her rounds with the boy, the mother deliberately started fights with him, then took him home and, "placing a rod in his hand," helped him to beat up the dog "or any thing else that may come in his way." She also "teases and vexes him, creates an irritable temper, submits to the rod, and flees before him with great dread." Afterward, she beat him and pulled his hair and he responded by hitting her back, "by which her pupil has learned to bear pain without dread." These "trials of courage" were required by the mother before her son was allowed again to play with his friends.[53]

Hunter was given his name for his hunting prowess. He was neither shy nor modest. His feats included a sixteen-month trip across the plains and the Rockies and back. He compared his life to Daniel Boone's and boasted of an acquaintance with him, saying they "became strongly attached to each other."[54] But Hunter, like Gyles, demonstrates that living with the Indians helped some Euro-American men and boys find alternative ways of seeing their role as men in relation to women and living on the earth. In works like Hunter's, readers could see another way of living.

The life and work of John Tanner presents yet another example of a White Indian whose Indian mother reshaped the direction of his life. Tanner's father was a Virginia clergyman who settled on the Ohio River in Kentucky. Tanner's mother died when he was two. The family moved onto the edge of Shawnee territory, where his father's brother, with some other white men, killed and scalped an Indian. The family moved again after the father's remarriage, this time past Cincinnati "to the mouth of the Big Miami." As Tanner told the story, "The earliest event of my life, which I distinctly remember is the death of my mother. This happened when I was two years old, and many of the attending circumstances made so deep an impression, that they are still fresh in my memory." His clergyman father soon "removed to a place called Elk Horn." The boy was expected to take care of younger siblings and at one point was beaten for not doing so. "From that time, my father's house was less like home to me, and I often thought and said, 'I wish I could go and live among the Indians.'"[55] Shawnees captured him in 1785.

Tanner was first adopted by an old woman known as "'the Otter woman,' the otter being her *totem*." She treated him well, but he was happier when he was readopted over her strong objections. His second Indian mother was chief of the Ottawa "notwithstanding her sex." Her name was Net-no-kwa. She was able to use her status and "considerable whiskey" to get the young Tanner. He thought she was younger and "of a more pleasing aspect than my former mother. She took me by the hand after she had completed the negotiation with my former possessors, and led me to her own lodge which stood near." He soon learned that she would indulge him a good deal. She fed him, gave him "good clothes," and told him to play with her children. They went past Mackinac and when the corn was ripe arrived in Ottawa territory in northern Michigan. Net-no-kwa's husband was seventeen years her junior and an Ojibwa who treated Tanner "like an equal, rather than as a dependent." Net-no-kwa led an Ottawa band at Arbre Croche on the northern part of the lower peninsula.[56] Tanner said he never met an Indian of either sex "who had so much authority as Net-no-kwa."[57] He respected her understanding of the world of nature and her ability to interpret dreams. Tanner, however, was a braggart. He told of every bear and elk he killed and probably a good number he never saw. He claimed to have killed twenty-four bear and ten moose in one month and at another point, twenty moose and elk and forty-two beaver in a ten-day period.

Although he had many words of love for his mother, he could say little good about his mother-in-law, whom he claimed tried to kill him. His marriages failed one after another. He complained constantly about his Ojibwa brother. No true sibling ever met a worse rival. Tanner spent more pages trying to tell how much better he was than his brother than John Williams did on the evils of popery.[58]

Tanner lived with the Ottawa-Ojibwas for nearly thirty years. Born in 1780 and captured in 1789 by Saginaw Ojibwas, he returned with his white brother to Kentucky in about 1817. After his return, he lived in emotional turmoil, later settling in northern Michigan Territory around Sault Ste. Marie. He is thought to have married four times. Between 1837 and 1846 he was arrested several times for killing livestock, was in jail, had confrontations with various northern Michigan whites, and had his house set on fire. He became more and more disturbed and reclusive after the failure of his third marriage to an Ojibwa woman, was accused of murder, and finally disappeared and was never heard from again.[59]

A nineteenth-century captive boy who remained with the Senecas was also deeply touched and shaped by his Indian mother. Renamed White Chief, he had been taken from the Susquehanna during the French and Indian War, at the age of four. He remembered losing his mother and finding himself in an Indian woman's lap. "Looking kindly down into my face she smiled on me, and gave me some dried deer's meat and maple sugar. From that hour I believe she loved me as a mother. I am sure I returned to her the affection of a son. . . . I always had a warm place at the fire, and slept in her arms. I was fed with the best food the wigwam could afford." The boy learned to compete with the other Seneca boys with the bow "my Indian mother put into my hands." He shot birds and squirrels, which she promised to cook. "I often gave her much pleasure by bringing her game and demanding the fulfillment of her promise. She never disappointed me."[60]

Stories of white male captives point out the necessity of dealing with a new culture. Adapting demanded a reassessment of all aspects of a boy's or a man's life: male behavior, family relations, and gender relations. In redefining or at least reassessing the "normal" behavior from which they came, men and boys were confronted with contrasting or perhaps more exaggerated (in their eyes) forms of male behavior. They were not to cry, not to show pain or fear, even under torture. Some were subjected to racial and ethnic taunts. Hunter's first memory is of a little girl captive being killed for crying. Tanner remembered Indian boys taunting captives with racial and sexual slurs. They "upbraided me with being *white,* and with the whites all being *squaws*; a reproachful term used generally among the Indians, in contradistinction to that of *warrior.*"[61] This new view of cultures did not always bring an easier life. Some nineteenth-century White Indians, like Hunter and Tanner, suffered severe marital and personal difficulties when they returned to Anglo-American life.

Mathew Brayton was a child captive who, as an adult, searched for and found his brother and other family members. He went from Anglo-American childhood to Indian manhood only to rediscover his original identity. In the end, he found his white family, but in the process abandoned his Indian wife and two children, along with the extended family and tribe that raised him. These contradictions are not stated in the happy ending of his narrative, a story told by another because he could neither write nor speak English fluently. One guesses that the next chapter of Brayton's life, like that of some captives who changed cultures and crossed sexual boundaries, did not have a happy ending.[62]

The captive experience forced both men and women to confront what they had thought were roles given by God and nature. For male captives it challenged their masculine definitions of strength and endurance. It required them to use every method available to withstand violence against them and against friends and family. It forced them to assume responsibilities for the women and children in their families, which tested them both physically and psychologically. It forced them to live in new ways and in relationship to other men and other women, which, in every century, challenged their society's conceptions of men, women, family, and sexuality. There were variations in men's and boys' individual behaviors and responses, for males of different ages, between French and Anglo-Americans, and over time. Although the religious hero is a seventeenth- and early eighteenth-century phenomenon, and the adventure hero evolves from Smith to empire-building hero Boone and later dime novel romantic savior descendants, of the fourteen men discussed (and the one fictive captive), the basic typology of Hero and White Indian is more persistent than changes over time.

As is true for their female counterparts, the juxtaposition of the white male captive on a field of red brought out certain adaptive reactions based on extreme circumstances. For both men and women, age of capture was an indicator of adaptation, with younger captives being more malleable and more open to seeing the other. In both cases, however, gender and attitudes toward the Indian other were critical as well. For women, the separation from their families, homes, and traditional male "protectors" and the dangers to themselves and their children put them in touch with their vulnerability but forced them to confront their own inner resources. For most women in the centuries under consideration, capture proved a prolonged test of faith, endurance, and self-reliance. Not underestimating the ways in which many Indian societies facilitated the integration of captives into their societies, these women were, at least for the first days, weeks, and months, and for Mary Jemison, years, subject to feelings of deep loneliness. It appears that the tests for male captives were more on the battlefield of prowess, religious or physical, and that even when other tests presented themselves, these were the ways in which many defined the task of their captivity.

The mode of writing shaped the story told by both men and women. From the earliest accounts, style was shaped by period, by religious or secular orientation, and by the particular audience reading the materials. But again, gender left its mark, as has been evident. In her study of pardon tales in sixteenth-century France, Natalie Zemon Davis reports that in both style and content, women's and men's attempts to gain pardon for crimes by appeal before French kings and magistrates differed.[63] The same is true of captivity narratives and writings. With the exception of Mary Rowlandson, women in the seventeenth and much of the eighteenth centuries told their stories to others, and others wrote them. Women's written stories differ in style and content from men's (and from men's renditions of women's stories). The telling differs in the way it appeals to the reader, its emotion, its language, and its subjects. For men, adventure, trials, physical pain, and the resistance to pain, learning from, outsmarting, or becoming Indian are at the center of the accounts. This bifurcation of sentiment versus adventure was most pronounced in the period from 1830 to the end of the nineteenth century and was shaped largely by the demands of the market, along with the emerging ideology of separate spheres.[64]

But there were also physical and social realities that made capture different for each sex. For women there was the question of their physical vulnerability, the question of whether they had the stamina to go on, the mention of forced marriage to Indians, the fear of rape, and familial and psychic vulnerability. What will happen to the children? How will the woman, usually a wife and a mother, stand up under the stress? These are common questions beneath the plot and move the narration from the seventeenth century onward. Women are able to survive, though in some nineteenth-century cases they appear to revel in their frailty and vulnerability. In the Amazon stories, from Dustan and on through the nineteenth-century recountings, a few escape stories are told by these women themselves, but no violent stories or adventure narratives are written by them about their experiences. Similar stories of male prowess, from Smith to Eastman, are all written by the men themselves.

Why was this the case? To the extent that this literature served as nation-building propaganda, white male weakness always had to be both masked and overcome. Men who were too weak or could not outsmart the enemy would die. For men like Father Jogues, death meant martyrdom and the ultimate victory of Christ; for Englishmen and men of the new American nation, it meant defeat of the founding mission and of the westward expansion of that mission through the perpetuation of new families. Powerful figures of women and children could be used as backups against the Indians and fortify the courage of all. But they were also symbols of the growth and vigor of a new Zion and later a new republic.

What changes occurred over time? Female vulnerability was more salable in the nineteenth century than earlier, as were protective male heroics. The markets for fiction and nonfiction were not very different when it came to reports about the frontier.[65] But female vulnerability is a constant, a continuity embedded in all the captivity genres, even those in which women strike back. Women's generally more diminutive physical stature and role as childbearer and nurturer is used as a sign of personal and social vulnerability to evoke sympathetic response. An injured, raped, or unprotected woman (or child) calls out for help. Captive stories of women and children pointed out the vulnerability of the family and social fabric on the frontier. These stories served as cautionary tales. If mothers and children could disappear from a homestead, near a frontier fort, en route west, or in an uprising, "civilization" was precarious indeed.

Charles Johnston returned to Virginia in 1790 after five weeks with Shawnees. His family thought him dead. "The anxiety of the neighborhood, to hear the details of my capture, and of all my way-faring, brought them in great numbers, day after day, to my mother's house, and subjected me to narrations, which I was compelled so often to repeat, and which begat in me so many unpleasant recollections, that I almost dreaded the return of each succeeding day."[66]

From the earliest accounts of Smith, Rowlandson, Dustan, and Williams, Anglo-American colonists identified with the variety of struggles men and women faced on the frontiers of the New World. Their epic stories challenged listeners and readers to put themselves in the place of the captive, to ask themselves what they would have done. These stories asked, Who are you? Who might you become? What might this land become? Their answers contend that you cannot know what man you are, what woman you are, what child you are until you have seen another way, have become vulnerable, crossed boundaries. In that other land, you encounter dangers of every sort. The very social experiment of the New World is brought to the test. You will see a different world, a different self, and in the process you will reevaluate the society of which you are a part.

Notes

1. Alden T. Vaughan, *American Genesis: Captain John Smith and the Founding of Virginia* (Boston: Little, Brown, 1975), 37. For Smith's description of the events see John Smith, *A Generall Historie of Virginia, New-England, and the Summer Isles,* The Third Booke, in Edward Arber and A. G. Bradley, eds., *Travels and Works of Captain John Smith: President of Virginia, and Admiral of New England, 1580-1631,* 2 vols. (Edinburgh: J. Grant, 1910), 2:397. Also see Philip L. Barbour, ed., *The Complete Works of Captain John Smith (1580-1631) in Three Volumes* (Chapel Hill: University of North Carolina Press, 1986). For differing views on contact with Indians in Virginia see Nancy Oestreich Lurie, "Indian Cultural Adjustment to European Civilization," in *Interpreting Colonial America: Selected Readings,* ed. James Kirby Martin (New York: Harper & Row, 1973), 36-45; Helen C. Rountree, *Pocahontas's People: The Powhatan Indians of Virginia through Four Centuries* (Norman: University of Oklahoma Press, 1990).

2. Another twenty-one (2.5 percent) of the males probably died as compared to another two (1.2 percent) of the females. Eight male and three female children died or were killed. See Alden T. Vaughan and Daniel K. Richter, "Crossing the Cultural Divide: Indians and New Englanders, 1605-1763," *Proceedings of the American Antiquarian Society* 90 (Apr. 16, 1980): 66-67. On assimilation see A. Irving Hallowell, "American Indians, White and Black: The Phenomenon of Transculturalization," in *Contributions to Anthropology: Selected Papers of A. Irving Hallowell,* with introductions by Raymond D. Fogelson (Chicago: University of Chicago Press, 1976), 498-552; J. Norman Heard, *White into Red: A Study of the Assimilation of White Persons Captured by Indians* (Metuchen, N.J.: Scarecrow Press, 1973); Cornelius J. Jaenen, *Friend and Foe: Aspects of French-Amerindian Cultural Conflict in the Sixteenth and Seventeenth Centuries* (New York: Columbia University Press, 1976); William A. Starna and Ralph Watkins, "Northern Iroquois Slavery," *Ethnohistory* 38 (Winter 1991): 34-57; Richard VanDerBeets, "The Indian Captivity Narrative: An American Genre" (Ph.D. dissertation, University of the Pacific, 1973).

3. Jogues's letter was signed August 5, 1643. The work was first printed in French in 1655 and had a long print history on both sides of the Atlantic, in French and in English. Biographers report that Jogues's head was cut off and placed on a pole in a Mohawk village ("Captivity of Father Isaac Jogues, of the Society of Jesus, among the Mohawks," [1655] taken from John Gilmary Shea, *Perils of the Ocean and Wilderness* [1857] in *Held Captive by Indians: Selective Narratives, 1642-1836,* ed. Richard VanDerBeets [Knoxville: University of Tennessee Press, 1973], 3-40, esp. 4, 9-12, 19). For a comparison of savage behavior, the body of King Philip (Metacom, Metacomet) was quartered and decapitated after the 1675 war in New England. The head was placed on a pole in Plymouth and remained there for twenty-five years (Alvin M. Josephy, Jr., *The Patriot Chiefs* [New York: Viking, 1961], 61-62). One of Philip's hands was sent to Boston for display. His body was not buried but, "having been quartered, was hung upon four trees" (Samuel G. Drake, *Biography and History of the Indians of North America, from Its First Discovery* [Boston: Benjamin B. Muzzey, 1851], 227). For an analysis of the early Indian wars see Wilcomb E. Washburn, "Seventeenth-Century Indian Wars," in *Handbook of North American Indians,* gen. ed. William C. Sturtevant, vol. 15, *Northeast,* Bruce G. Trigger, vol. ed. (Washington, D.C.: Smithsonian Institute, 1978), 89-100; Washburn, "The Moral and Legal Justifications for Dispossessing the Indians," in *Seventeenth-Century America: Essays in Colonial History,* ed. James M. Smith (Chapel Hill: University of North Carolina Press, 1959), 15-32. For an analysis of the Huron people and Jogues's stay among them see Bruce G. Trigger, *The Children of Aataentsic: A History of the Huron People to 1660* (Montreal: McGill-Queen's Univer-

sity Press, 1976), 522, 541, 645-47, 654-57. Trigger also analyzes the capture and torture sequence among the Hurons. His work indicates that men, women, and children taken by the Hurons in the early and mid-seventeenth century were often taken alive and tortured. His descriptions relate primarily to Huron captures of Iroquois and other Indian enemies but also include French captives (ibid., 68-75).

4. Daniel K. Richter mentions the fund-raising issues of the Jesuits and "suggests a need for caution" in using the *Relations* as sources ("Iroquois versus Iroquois: Jesuit Missions and Christianity in Village Politics, 1642-1886," *Ethnohistory* 32 [1985]: 1-16, esp. 1).

5. Vaughan and Richter, "Cultural Divide," 66-67.

6. John Gyles, *Memoirs of Odd Adventures, Strange Deliverances* [1736], in *Puritans among the Indians: Accounts of Captivity and Redemption, 1676-1724,* ed. Alden T. Vaughan and Edward W. Clark (Cambridge, Mass.: Harvard University Press, 1981), 93, 105, 106, 109, 81-83.

7. "'Quentin Stockwell's Relation of His Captivity and Redemption' Reported by Increase Mather," in *Puritans among the Indians,* ed. Vaughan and Clark, 81-83, 89. On the literature of the pulpit as war propaganda see Richard Slotkin and James K. Folsom, eds., *So Dreadfull a Judgment: Puritan Responses to King Philip's War, 1676-1677* (Middletown, Conn.: Wesleyan University Press, 1978).

8. *Indian Captivities: Life in the Wigwam,* ed. Samuel G. Drake (New York: Miller, Orton, 1857), 109-10, 113.

9. *An Account of the Remarkable Occurrences in the Life and Travels of Colonel James Smith* [1799] in *Indian Captivities,* ed. Drake, 178-252, esp. 182.

10. W. M. Beauchamp says that cases of women (in this case enemies of the Iroquois) being burned and eaten were common in the seventeenth century. He cites Jogues's account among others ("Iroquois Women," *Journal of American Folk-Lore* 13 [1900]: 81-91, esp. 84). Frederick W. Waugh, citing sources from the *Jesuit Relations,* says that "ceremonial cannibalism" was "quite a common practice" and body parts were eaten as part of rites of sympathetic magic (*Iroquois Foods and Food Preparation* [Ottawa: Government Printing Bureau, 1916], 134). Buell H. Quain, also using Jesuit sources, stresses the "ritualistic nature" of such practice ("The Iroquois," in *Cooperation and Competition among Primitive Peoples,* ed. Margaret Mead [New York: McGraw-Hill, 1937], 253-54). William N. Fenton documents a number of cases of Indian men and women who committed suicide to escape harm from their Iroquois captors. Most of Fenton's cases are taken from the Jesuit records (*Iroquois Suicide: A Study in Stability of a Culture Pattern* [Washington, D.C.: U.S. Government Printing Office, 1941]).

11. John D. Hunter, *Manners and Customs of Several Indian Tribes Located West of the Mississippi* (1823; rpt. Minneapolis: Ross & Haines, 1957); also *Garland Library,* vol. 39 (New York: Garland, 1977), 27. For an account of the torture of an infant child reported by Rachel Plummer with the Comanches see Rachel Plummer, "Narrative of the Capture and Subsequent Sufferings of Mrs. Rachel Plummer, Written by Herself," in *Held Captive by Indians,* ed. VanDerBeets. On torture see Nathaniel Knowles, "The Torture of Captives by the Indians of Eastern North America" (Ph.D. dissertation, University of Pennsylvania, 1940).

12. "Captivity of Father Isaac Jogues," in *Held Captive by Indians,* ed. VanDerBeets, 9, 7, 38.

13. Rev. Edward V. Neill, *The History of Minnesota from the French Explorations to the Present Time,* 5th ed. (Minneapolis: Minnesota Historical Society, 1883), 128-33; Father Hennepin, *The New Discovery of a Vast Country,* 2 vols., ed. Reuben Gold Thwaites (Chicago: A. C. McClurg, 1903); "Memoir of Duluth on the Sioux Country, 1678-1682," in *Early Narratives of the Northwest, 1634-1699,* ed. Louise Phelps Kellogg (New York: Charles Scribner's Sons, 1917), 331-33, 332, n. 1. The validity of Hennepin's account is discussed in F. Sanford Cutler, "An Evaluation of Documents Useful to the Ethnohistorian: The Writings of Father Hennepin," *Proceedings of the Minnesota Academy of Science* 23 (1955): 23-28.

14. John Williams, "The Redeemed Captive Returning to Zion," in *Puritans among the Indians,* ed. Vaughan and Clark, 167; David Hawke, *The Colonial Experience* (Indianapolis: Bobbs-Merrill, 1966), 329-30. For a museum and shrine to the captives of Deerfield, see the second-floor exhibit in the museum in Historic Deerfield, Massachusetts. For comparisons of British Protestant and French Catholic successes among the Indians, see James Axtell, *The Invasion Within: The Contest of Cultures in Colonial America* (New York: Oxford University Press, 1985), 80, also chaps. 1-6. On the Deerfield experiences of Williams, Stockwell, and others see Richard I. Melvoin, *New England Outpost: War and Society in Colonial Deerfield* (New York: Norton, 1989), esp. chaps. 7-9, and the work of John Demos on Eunice Williams (forthcoming).

15. Williams, "Redeemed Captive," in *Puritans among the Indians,* ed. Vaughan and Clark, 168, 225; Edward W. Clark, *The Redeemed Captive: John Williams* (Amherst: University of Massachusetts Press, 1976), 16.

16. Clark, *Redeemed Captive,* 9; Williams, "Redeemed Captive," in *Puritans among the Indians,* ed. Vaughan and Clark, 173, 178, 180. For the language of Puritan New England's sermons see Sacvan Bercovitch, *The American Jeremiad* (Madison: University of Wisconsin Press, 1978), and Mason I. Lowance, Jr.,

The Language of Canaan: Metaphor and Symbol in New England from the Puritans to the Transcendentalists (Cambridge, Mass.: Harvard University Press, 1980).

17. Williams, "Redeemed Captive," in *Puritans among the Indians,* ed. Vaughan and Clark, 195, 197.

18. Ibid., 204, 209, 212, 215, 218; also 204-20 for correspondence.

19. The small book called itself a "narrative of facts, intended for the instruction and improvement of children and youth taken from an interesting portion of the early history of our country" (A. Phelps, *The Deerfield Captive,* 3d ed. [Greenfield, Mass.: n.p., 1837], 11-12, Newberry Library, Chicago, Illinois).

20. Vaughan, *American Genesis,* 117. Also see A. L. Rouse, *The Elizabethans and America: The Trevelyan Lectures at Cambridge, 1958* (New York: Harper & Row, 1959).

21. John Smith, "Part of the Travels of Capt. John Smith amongst Turks, Tartars and others," and "A reprint, with variations of the First Part of the *Map of Virginia,*" 1612, both in Arber and Bradley, eds., *Travels and Works,* illus. 2:821-24, and illus. 1:342.

22. See Christian F. Feest, "Virginia Algonquians," in *Handbook of North American Indians,* gen. ed. William C. Sturtevant, Vol. 15, *Northeast,* Bruce G. Trigger, vol. ed. (Washington, D.C.: Smithsonian Institution, 1978), 253-70. Richard Drinnon suggests that relationships to the sensual both attracted and frightened Euro-Americans ("The Metaphysics of Dancing Tribes," in *The American Indian and the Problem of History,* ed. Calvin Martin [New York: Oxford University Press, 1987], 106-13). Newberry Library, Chicago, Illinois photographer Ken Cain pointed out that the woman around the fire looked like a blond.

23. John Smith, *A True Relation,* in *Virginia Reader: A Treasury of Writings from the First Voyages to the Present,* ed. Frances C. Rosenberger (New York: E. P. Dutton, 1948), 77, 78, 81, 84; Barbour, ed., *The Complete Works of Captain John Smith,* 1:43-45.

24. Father Hennepin also found that the mariner's compass dazzled the Dakotas (Neill, *History of Minnesota,* 152). In the film *Dances with Wolves,* actor and director Kevin Costner succeeds in a similar feat, dazzling the Lakotas with a magnifying field glass.

25. See Vaughan, *American Genesis,* 81, 84.

26. Richard Slotkin, *Regeneration through Violence: The Mythology of the American Frontier, 1600-1860* (Middletown, Conn.: Wesleyan University Press, 1973), 294-301; Henry Nash Smith, *Virgin Land: The American West as Symbol and Myth* (New York: Vintage Books, 1959), 54-63.

27. John Filson, *The Discovery, Settlement and Present State of Kentucke . . . The Adventures of Col. Daniel Boon* (1784), *Garland Library,* vol. 14 (New York:

Garland, 1978); Timothy Flint, *The First White Man of the West* (Cincinnati: H. M. Ruilson, Queen City Publishing House, 1856).

28. Filson, *Discovery,* 51-52, 60, 63-66.

29. Ibid., 52.

30. Ibid., 63.

31. Ibid., 60.

32. Frost gave a chapter to the capture and rescue of the daughters, Elizabeth Ellet gave Mrs. Boone a chapter in *Pioneer Women of the West,* and Timothy Flint devoted a chapter to each episode of capture. See John Frost, *Daring and Heroic Deeds of American Women* (Philadelphia: G. G. Evans, 1860), 26; E[lizabeth] F. Ellet, *Pioneer Women of the West* (New York: Charles Scribner, 1852), 42-57.

33. Flint, *First White Man of the West,* 85-86.

34. Ibid., 86.

35. Ibid., 87-88, 94-95.

36. Edwin Eastman, *Seven and Nine Years among the Camanches and Apaches: An Autobiography* (Jersey City, N.J.: Clark Johnson, M.D., 1873), 210, 216-17.

37. Richard Slotkin emphasizes the role of the other in nineteenth-century narratives and history in the period of industrialization in *The Fatal Environment: The Myth of the Frontier in the Age of Industrialization, 1800-1890* (New York: Atheneum, 1985).

38. Smith, *Virgin Land,* 101 and chap. 9. Smith discusses *Seth Jones* in the first section of the chapter.

39. Edward Sylvester Ellis, *Seth Jones; or The Captives of the Frontier,* 7th ed., Beadles Half Dime Library, vol. 30, no. 60 (New York: Beadle and Adams, ca. 1878).

40. Interview, June 24, 1900, in Albert Johannsen, *The House of Beadle and Adams and Its Dime and Nickel Novels: The Story of a Vanished Literature,* 2 vols. (Norman: University of Oklahoma Press, 1950), 2:32.

41. Ibid. Edward S. Ellis's admiration for Boone is apparent in his biography, *The Life and Times of Col. Daniel Boone: Hunter, Soldier, and Pioneer* (Chicago: Union School Finishing Co., n.d.).

42. Ellis, *Seth Jones,* 3.

43. Ibid., chaps. 3 and 5.

44. Gyles, *Memoirs of Odd Adventures,* in *Puritans among the Indians,* ed. Vaughan and Clark, 93, 101-2, 105-6.

45. Ibid., 107-9, 111, 113-14.

46. Ibid., 95, 116, 103n., 116-20.

47. Gyles spent three of his nine captive years with the French. On Maliseets and Eastern Abenakis see Vincent O. Erickson, "Maliseet-Passamaquoddy,"

123-36, and Dean R. Snow, "Eastern Abenaki," in *Handbook of North American Indians,* gen. ed. William C. Sturtevant, Vol. 15, *Northeast,* Bruce G. Trigger, vol. ed. (Washington, D.C.: Smithsonian Institution, 1978).

48. Hunter, *Manners and Customs,* 26-27, 34-35. See Father Jogues on the torture of the Huron chief cited earlier. Also see Richard Drinnon's introduction to his edition of *Memoirs of a Captivity among the Indians of North America: John Dunn Hunter* [1824] (New York: Schocken, 1973).

49. Hunter, *Manners and Customs,* 34-35. My emphasis on mothers and relationship with women differs from Leslie Fiedler's, who stresses the WASP male-Indian male bond (*The Return of the Vanishing American* [New York: Stein and Day, 1968], 24 and chap. 2).

50. Hunter, *Manners and Customs,* 35.

51. Ibid., 43, 62, 64.

52. Ibid., 44.

53. Ibid., 272-73.

54. Ibid., 135.

55. Edwin James, *A Narrative of the Captivity and Adventures of John Tanner* (1830), *Garland Library,* vol. 46 (New York: Garland, 1975), 1-2.

56. John T. Fierst, "Return to 'Civilization': John Tanner's Troubled Years at Sault Ste. Marie," *Minnesota History* 50 (Spring 1986): 23.

57. Edwin James with Noel Loomis, *A Narrative of the Captivity and Adventures of John Tanner* (1830; rpt. Minneapolis: Ross and Haines, 1956), xii, 15, 16, 27.

58. Ibid., 115, 119, 120, 205, 230-32, x-xvi.

59. In 1846 he was accused of murdering James Schoolcraft, brother of Henry Rowe Schoolcraft, Indian agent and compiler of a multi-volume work on North American Indians. On Schoolcraft see Robert E. Bieder, *Science Encounters the Indian, 1820-1880: The Early Years of American Ethnography* (Norman: University of Oklahoma Press, 1986), 146-94; Bieder, "Henry Rowe Schoolcraft," in *Handbook of North American Indians,* gen. ed. William C. Sturtevant, Vol. 4, *History of Indian-White Relations,* Wilcomb E. Washburn, vol. ed. (Washington D.C.: Smithsonian Institution, 1988), 680-81; P. Richard Metcalf, "John Tanner," in *Handbook of North American Indians,* gen. ed. William C. Sturtevant, Vol. 4, *History of Indian-White Relations,* Wilcomb E. Washburn, vol. ed. (Washington D.C.: Smithsonian Institution, 1988), 689; Fierst, "Return to 'Civilization,'" 23-36. Fierst says Tanner may have had four wives and ten children (ibid., 27, n. 12).

60. The account is from Henry Sheldon of Vermont, who visited his sister Harriet Caswell at the New York Seneca Mission (Harriet Caswell, *Our Life among the Iroquois Indians* [Boston: Congregational Sunday School and Publishing Society, 1892], 51-62). Other white males who spent their youth among eastern Indians were John Slover among the Shawnees (from age eight to age twenty) in the 1760s and 1770s and John Brickell among the Delawares. John R. Swanton finds that among thirty captives, fifteen male and fifteen female, four males became chiefs and three or four females became the wives of chiefs. See Swanton, "Ethnology—Notes on the Mental Assimilation of Races," *Journal of the Washington Academy of Sciences* 16 (Nov. 3, 1926): 495-96, 501.

61. James, *Narrative of John Tanner,* 20. White Chief was also taunted for being white.

62. Matthew Brayton with John H. A. Bone, *Indian Captive: A Narrative of the Adventures and Sufferings of Matthew Brayton* (1860), *Garland Library,* vol. 76 (New York: Garland, 1977), 6-10. On the nature of as-told-to traditions among native people of the Americas see Gretchen M. Bataille and Kathleen Mullen Sands, *American Indian Women: Telling Their Lives* (Lincoln: University of Nebraska Press, 1984), 3-26.

63. Natalie Zemon Davis, "Bloodshed and the Woman's Voice: Gender and Pardon Tales in 16th Century France," paper presented at Harvard University, Mar. 6, 1987; Davis, *Fiction in the Archives: Pardon Tales of Sixteenth-Century France* (Stanford: Stanford University Press, 1987).

64. Some scholars attribute a significant part of Rowlandson's narrative to her husband, minister John Rowlandson; others claim Cotton Mather had a hand in it. I would not deny these influences, but I think she was quite capable of doing the writing herself. In any case, John's piece in her original is not as well written as hers.

65. As Leslie Fiedler says, "It is hard to tell history from myth in such accounts, though these earliest attempts to create an image of the Indian for the American imagination usually presented themselves as 'true relations' of fact. Capt. John Smith may seem to have fabricated rather than recorded the story of his encounter with Pocahontas; but his early readers took as literal truth the fanciful tale [of his rescue]" ("The Indian in Literature in English," in *Handbook of North American Indians,* gen. ed. William C. Sturtevant, Vol. 4, *History of Indian-White Relations,* Wilcomb E. Washburn, vol. ed. (Washington D.C.: Smithsonian Institution, 1988), 573).

66. Charles Johnston, *A Narrative of the Incidents Attending the Capture, Detention, and Ransom of Charles Johnston* [1827] in *Held Captive by Indians,* ed. VanDerBeets, 314.

CAPTIVITY NARRATIVES AND PURITANISM

Alden T. Vaughan and Edward W. Clark (essay date 1981)

SOURCE: Vaughan, Alden T. and Edward W. Clark. "Cups of Common Calamity: Puritan Captivity Narratives as Literature and History." In *Puritans among the Indians: Accounts of Captivity and Redemption: 1676-1724,* edited by Alden T. Vaughan and Edward W. Clark, pp. 1-28. Cambridge, Mass.: Belknap Press, 1981.

[*In the following essay, Vaughan and Clark expound on the uniquely religious characteristics and influences of the Puritan captivity narrative.*]

"It is no new thing for Gods precious ones to drink as deep as others, of the Cup of common Calamity."

—Preface to Mary Rowlandson, *The Sovereignty & Goodness of God,* 1682

"Remarkable Mercies should be Faithfully Published, for the Praise of GOD the Giver."

—Sermon by John Williams, 1706

"It would be unaccountable stupidity in me," wrote a former captive of the Indians in 1707, "not to maintain the most Lively and Awful Sense of Divine Rebukes which the most Holy GOD has seen meet . . . to dispense to me, my Family and People in delivering us into the hands of those that Hated us, who Led us into a strange Land." But the redeemed captive, Reverend John Williams of Deerfield, Massachusetts, did not dwell on the Lord's rebukes. Like so many of his contemporaries in New England, Williams emphasized instead "The wonders of Divine Mercy, which we have seen in the Land of our Captivity, and Deliverance there-from [which] cannot be forgotten without incurring the guilt of the blackest Ingratitude."[1] A staunch Puritan, Williams believed—as earlier and later generations did not—that capture by the Indians was no military happenstance or secular accident. Captivity was God's punishment; redemption was His mercy; and New England must heed the lesson or suffer anew. Many survivors of the captivity ordeal proclaimed that message in stirring narratives which tell much about Puritan prisoners among the Indians and their French allies in the late seventeenth and early eighteenth centuries and reveal even more about the Puritan mind.

Puritans, of course, did not invent the captivity narrative. It is one of America's oldest literary genres and its most unique. Soon after Europe awakened to the existence of an inhabited western continent, stories of captivity by an alien culture began to excite the public imagination. Ironically, the earliest New World captivity tales must have been told by American natives: Spaniards, not Indians, first seized hapless victims to serve as guides, interpreters,

hostages, or curiosities. But the Indians soon retaliated, and because Europeans long had a monopoly on the written word, most printed accounts related capture by Indians. Hence "captivity narrative" came to mean an account, usually autobiographical, of forced participation in Indian life. The literature of early American colonization is dotted with poignant and often gruesome tales of seizure, torture or adoption (sometimes both), and eventual escape or release. Such stories found a ready audience on both sides of the Atlantic, where they flourished, in one form or another, for three centuries.

Not until the late seventeenth century did captivity narratives emerge as a separate and distinct literary genre. Before then most captivity tales appeared as dramatic episodes in works of larger scope. That was true not only in Latin American literature—the accounts of Cabeza de Vaca and Juan Ortiz, for example—but also of North American settlement.[2] Captain John Smith's various versions of his capture by Powhatan Indians and his last-second rescue by Pocahontas is a case in point; they were embedded in Smith's chronicles of early Virginia.[3] Similarly, accounts of Father Isaac Jogues's incarceration, torture, release, recapture, and eventual death at the hands of the Iroquois were scattered through the annual Jesuit relations.[4] More than a century later, the earlier pattern of captivity narratives as a single stage in an unfolding adventure still survived: witness the stories of Daniel Boone's capture and adoption by the Shawnee.[5] But in the last quarter of the seventeenth century, writers in Puritan New England began to issue narratives of Indian captivity in separate book-length works, though usually brief and sometimes bound with other items.

The Puritans approached the new genre cautiously at first—their initial narrative appeared more than five years after the event and was privately printed. When that volume achieved instant popularity, similar works soon followed. Thereafter captivity narratives, usually as separate works, enjoyed nearly two centuries of commercial success in colonial America and the United States, although not without important changes. From unpolished but intense religious statements in the Puritan period, captivity narratives had evolved by the late eighteenth century into ornate and often fictionalized accounts that catered to more secular and less serious tastes. By the late nineteenth century the genre had lost most of its historical and autobiographical integrity. It ultimately blended with the "penny-dreadfuls" of America's Victorian-age fiction.

Puritan captivity narratives began in 1682 with Mary Rowlandson's story of capture during the later stages of King Philip's War. Her brisk *Soveraignty & Goodness of God . . . Being a Narrative of the Captivity and Restauration of Mrs. Mary Rowlandson* sold quickly; three more issues appeared within the first year, and others followed periodically throughout the Puritan era.[6] Many subsequent New England narratives had almost as impressive literary careers and were the best-sellers of their day, and they remain among the most insightful clues to the tensions and expectations of Puritan society.

These stories were immensely popular because—like any successful literature—they served readers a hearty fare of literary and psychological satisfaction, peculiar to their time and place. In a society without fiction and plays, and almost barren of poetry, real-life dramas filled a crucial cultural void. Histories and accounts of warfare only partly met the need for dramatic literature. After 1676 tales of Indian captivity offered a more personal story: they told of raids and forced marches, of the wilderness and its native inhabitants, of the chilling efforts of Indians and Frenchmen to assimilate their captives into an alien culture. But the heart of the New England narrative—the theme that made it truly Puritan and infused it with unusual dramatic force—was its introspective concentration on God's role in the life of the individual and the collective community. As Rowlandson's title proclaimed, she wrote only incidentally about deliverance from misery and potential death. More important, she portrayed "The Sovereignty & Goodness of GOD, Together with the Faithfulness of His Promises," while an appended posthumous sermon by her husband raised "the possibility of God's forsaking a people, that have been visibly near & dear to him." In sum, the Rowlandson's publisher promised an intensely personal account of God's testing and eventual salvation of a tormented soul, and a broad hint that her experience might foretell in microcosm the fate of all Puritans. Those were compelling attractions to the deeply pietistic people of seventeenth-century New England, who sought desperately to comprehend their preordained roles in God's awesome universe.

Puritan authors wove the captivity narrative from several existing literary strands. One strand was spiritual autobiography; numerous seventeenth and early eighteenth-century New Englanders described their search for salvation to edify their children and other kin and occasionally to inspire the community at large. John Winthrop's "Christian Experience," Thomas Shepard's "My Birth & Life," Anne Bradstreet's "To My Dear Children," and Edward Taylor's "Spiritual Relation" are notable examples of an abundant theo-literary form.[7] The literary use of a representative life reaches much further back, to be sure, at least to the Reformation when Martin Luther developed the *exemplum fidei,* which stressed the spirit of Christ's life rather than his deeds.[8] That notion found congenial soil in Tudor-Stuart England, where the Puritans gave it added prominence and eventually carried it to their American Zion. The New England branch of the Puritan movement, and still later the Quakers in Pennsylvania, encouraged spiritual autobiography as a vital expression of the search for personal salvation. The principal authority on this early American literary form observes that "the spiritual autobiographer is primarily concerned with the question of grace: whether or not the individual has been accepted into divine life, an acceptance signified by psychological and moral changes which the autobiographer comes to discern in his past experience."[9] But the search for salvation was fraught with torments, doubts, and relapses, in almost perfect parallel to the experiences reported in the captivity narratives. In spiritual autobiogra-

phies, God and Satan wrestled for the sinner's soul; in captivity autobiographies, the captive, with God's help, battled Satan's agents. In both cases, of course, God eventually prevailed: the weary pilgrim survived the ordeal because his faith wavered but did not break, and because God's mercy was stronger than His wrath.

During and after his captivity by Indians, the victim pondered how his own experience coincided with God's plan. A redeemed captive usually saw his ordeal, and even the ordeal of his loved ones, as punishment for his past sins or present impiety. The survivor often concluded that he had gained measurably from the chastisement, and he almost invariably offered his experience as a lesson to neighbors of the ephemeral security of this world and the awesomeness of God's sovereignty. Mary Rowlandson, for one, came to appreciate God's omnipotence: "I then remembered how careless I had been of Gods holy time: how many Sabbaths I had lost and mispent, and how evily I had walked in Gods sight; which lay so close unto my spirit, that it was easie for me to see how righteous it was with God to cut off the threed of my life, and cast me out of his presence forever. Yet the Lord still showed mercy to me, and upheld me; and as he wounded me with one hand, so he healed me with the other."[10] "Redemption," a frequent term in captivity titles and texts, thus had a double meaning—spiritual as well as physical. Similarly, captivity stories combined individual catharsis and public admonition. Implicitly, at least, they exhorted the reader to find his or her own spiritual redemption. Rowlandson's title page explains that her story is directed "Especially to her dear Children and Relations." God would not have subjected her to such an ordeal had He not intended her spiritual pilgrimage to enlighten her family and neighbors. Everything had a purpose. As Reverend John Williams insisted after his own harrowing ordeal, the Lord "has enjoyned us, to shew forth His praises in rehearsing to others the Salvations, and Favours we have been the Subjects of."[11]

Astute ministers such as Cotton Mather made sure the lesson was not missed. Serving as Hannah Swarton's amanuensis, Mather wrote an epitome of the abasement-salvation theme which offered hope and courage to those in doubt of their own fate. Swarton laments, "I was neither fit to live nor fit to die; and brought once to the very Pit of Despair about what would become of my Soul." But she found in her Bible the account of Jonah's troubles and resolved to pray as her biblical prototype had: "In the Meditation upon this Scripture the Lord was pleased by his Spirit to come into my Soul, and so fill me with ravishing Comfort, that I cannot express it."[12] And in *Humiliations Followed With Deliverances* Mather related the now-legendary story of Hannah Dustan's escape from the Indians after tomahawking her sleeping captors. In his initial recitation of the episode, Mather addressed a congregation in which she sat; he observed that "there happens to be at this very Time, in this Assembly, an *Example,* full of Encouragement unto these *humiliations,* which have been thus called for."[13] Presumably Hannah Dustan served many New Englanders as a living example of Christian piety and courage. In the same vein, Reverend John Williams wrote an extensive account of his own captivity and redemption; it went through several editions and ranks as one of the most forceful Puritan statements.[14]

A second source of inspiration for early New England captivity narratives was the sermon, that quintessential Puritan expression to which several generations of congregational preachers and settlers were addicted. In addition to the usual two Sunday sermons, there were Lecture Day sermons (usually on Thursday evening), election day sermons, fast and humiliation sermons, thanksgiving sermons, artillery company sermons, funeral sermons, even execution sermons. Most were delivered by clergymen, but occasionally laymen indulged as well.[15] John Winthrop's shipboard "Model of Christian Charity" is the most famous lay sermon, but there were many others, and they formed an important, if smaller, part of the same rhetorical type. And while most sermons—lay or clerical—were never published, an impressive number were put into print and widely read. Moreover, many parishioners took notes on sermons for later meditation, and schoolchildren were required to discuss Sunday's sermon in Monday morning's class. Not surprisingly, Puritan captivity narratives borrowed liberally from sermon themes and language. Especially evident are their emphasis on moral lessons and their extensive use of biblical citations to bolster almost every argument. At root, captivity narratives were lay sermons (or, when recited secondhand by an Increase or Cotton Mather, clerical sermons) in the guise of adventure stories.

Third, and perhaps most significant, the Puritan captivity narrative owed much of its tone and content to "jeremiads"—those peculiar laments by Puritan clergymen (and, again, sometimes by laymen) that accused New England of backsliding from the high ideals and noble achievements of the founders, of God's evident or impending wrath, and of the need for immediate and thorough reformation.[16] That theme emerged as early as the 1650s, sometimes in the pronouncements of the founding generation itself, but not until the 1660s and 1670s did the jeremiad become a literary cliché. Usually it appeared in sermons, but it also took other forms, such as Michael Wigglesworth's poetic *God's Controversy with New England* and the report of the Reforming Synod of 1679, which epitomized the jeremiad genre. (Even Cotton Mather's *Magnalia Christi Americana,* a massive ecclesiastical history of New England, is part jeremiad.) In 1662, Wigglesworth, the lugubrious Massachusetts minister-poet, interpreted a prolonged drought as a clear sign of God's growing wrath:

> For thinke not, O Backsliders, in your heart,
>   That I shall still your evill manners beare:
> Your sinns me press as sheaves do load a cart,
>   And therefore I will plague you for this geare
> Except you seriously, and soon, repent,
>   Ile not delay your pain and heavy punishment.[17]

The impetus for such harangues came partly from an exaggerated sense of New England's "Golden Age" and

chiefly from the Puritans' extreme biblicism. From close scrutiny of the Bible, Puritan divines drew parallels or types between the Old and New Testaments on which they based much of their religious and social doctrine. They used this typological system, for example, to justify their rejecting the corruptions of Old England for the wilderness of New England, thus reenacting the Israelites' flight from Egypt to the milk-and-honey land of Canaan. The ramifications of Puritan typology are too complex for adequate discussion here, but among them was the belief that God, in return for the colonists' suffering in the wilderness and establishing a new Zion, would protect and prosper His newly chosen people—*if* they remained true to His laws and steadfast in their faith.[18] Puritan enthusiasts such as Increase and Cotton Mather searched relentlessly for evidence of God's favor to New Englanders, which they duly published under titles such as *Illustrious Providences, Wonderful Works of God,* and *Remarkable Judgements of God.*[19] Predictably, the Mathers and their fellow seventeenth-century colonists found what they were looking for: miraculous deliverances from danger for the godly, divine retribution for the godless.

This search for the Lord's guiding hand had implications far beyond individual rewards and punishments. Sins—especially a persistent flouting of the true faith—brought punishment to the entire community because of the Puritans' compact with the Lord; as John Williams explained, "the great God . . . hath taken us into *Covenant Relation* to Himself."[20] Accordingly, the righteous must suffer along with transgressors when He punished his flock for its accumulated wrongs. Mary Rowlandson was only the first of the Puritan captivity narrators to identify Indian depredations with God's retribution against the entire community: "It is said, *Psal. 81. 13. 14. Oh that my People had hearkned to me and* Israel *had walked in my ways, I should soon have subdued their Enemies, and turned my hand against their Adversaries.* But now our perverse and evil carriages in the sight of the Lord, have so offended him, that instead of turning his hand against them, the Lord feeds and nourishes them up to be a scourge to the whole Land."[21] Two decades later, John Williams opened his narrative with essentially the same message: "The History I am going to Write, proves, That Days of *Fasting & Prayer,* without REFORMATION, will not avail, to Turn away the Anger of God from a Professing People."[22]

Williams's contemporaries had frequently witnessed God's anger at incomplete reformation. In the 1670s and after, New England suffered a frightful series of major and minor calamities. The worst came in 1675-1676 when the region's most devastating Indian war claimed the lives of nearly a tenth of its adult colonial males—the highest mortality rate in American military history, before or since—and took a correspondingly heavy toll in property: twelve thousand homes burned, eight thousand head of cattle destroyed, innumerable farmlands laid waste. And the destruction did not end in 1676 with the death of Metacomet (King Philip); rather, it shifted to the relatively vulnerable northern frontier in Maine, New Hampshire, and western Massachusetts where Indians, often accompanied by their French allies, continued to raid isolated farms and villages. No wonder the Reforming Synod of Puritan ministers and lawyers concluded in 1679 that "God hath a Controversy with his New-England People"; the Indians, they believed, were His principal rod of chastisement.[23] No wonder too that Puritan captives looked inward for signs of their own shortcomings. Most captives found convincing evidence; others acknowledged their failings but also recognized that even the innocent and the saintly must suffer when God punished an errant flock. "It is no new thing," wrote the anonymous author of the preface to Mary Rowlandson's narrative, "for Gods precious ones to drink as deep as others, of the Cup of common Calamity."[24]

Puritan readers responded enthusiastically to the captivity genre not only because it fused the prominent features of spiritual autobiography, lay sermon, and jeremiad with those of the secular adventure story. In its descriptions of the forced rending of Puritan families, the narratives unintentionally added an element of pathos that appealed profoundly to a society which placed unusual emphasis on family ties and responsibilities. This fundamental social unit was often revered in Puritan tracts and sermons and was frequently the subject of governmental legislation and proclamations. The importance Puritans gave to the family undoubtedly touched a universal chord among readers of the narratives and made more poignant their grief over the death of loved ones that so often accompanied captivities. Accounts of the murder of a husband, wife, or child are numerous, and the understated descriptions of their deaths helped the narrators weave their fascinating and sometimes horrifying tapestry of despair and salvation. A modern reader—like readers in the seventeenth and eighteenth centuries—cannot resist deep sympathy for Mary Rowlandson when her six-year-old daughter dies in her arms or for John Williams when he learns of his wife's death by an Indian tomahawk after she fell through a frozen river.

Despite the importance a Puritan attached to family love and security, he knew that these affections were ultimately temporal and must not supersede the love of God. Had not Jesus said that a true Christian should follow Him (Luke 14:26) and if necessary forsake his family? And Puritans were familiar with the lesson of Bunyan's *Pilgrim's Progress*: every Christian must turn his back on spouse and family, shoulder his burden of sins, and start out for the Celestial City. This ultimate reliance on the self and its relation to God often conflicted with the family communal bond. A Puritan whose family had been dispersed after capture suffered an enormous sense of loss and guilt, tempered only slightly by the dictates of religion. The narratives of Mary Rowlandson, John Williams, and Elizabeth Hanson bear witness to the depth of such heart-wrenching experiences. Puritan captivity narratives have interest for modern readers beyond their poignant expression of religious fervor and individual anguish. As anthropological records they recount unique individual and group experiences; as observations of native tribes, many of which no

longer exist, they provide rare descriptions of northeastern Indian life; and as ethnological histories they shed light on conflicts between disparate cultures—New England's against Algonquian-Iroquoian and, in some cases, New England's against French Canadian.

Modern readers of an Indian captivity narrative are likely to see what anthropologists term a rite of passage, or, more specifically, an initiation process by which a person moves from one set of perceptions to another. Several scholars have isolated the initiation process as a vital element in the captivity experience.[25] There is, however, a danger in focusing too intently on the initiation ordeal and overlooking the significance of the much longer and equally profound captivity experience itself. The day-to-day struggle with an alien culture is the mainspring of the experience and the driving force of the captive's attempt to understand the change he has undergone.

Anthropologist Victor Turner provides an explanation of the initiation process that permits a broader focus on the three stages of *rites de passage,* or transitions from one social position to another—separation, margin, and reaggregation.[26] Turner's analysis can be applied to captivity narratives. First, captives began to gain new knowledge about their own culture and American Indian culture when they were separated from their natal environment—in Puritan narratives, a New England town or frontier settlement. They then entered a "margin" (or "liminal") phase where they lost the security they had enjoyed as English subjects and usually suffered servitude in a culture they considered grossly inferior to their own. With their world in psychological as well as physical disarray, the captives initially saw their new social relationships and consequent obligations as punishment and humiliation; unfamiliarity with Indian language kept them from understanding even nonthreatening remarks. Later they became more flexible and began to comprehend, perhaps even to appreciate, their captors' beliefs and manner of living.[27] Finally, in the third stage, they were redeemed and reintegrated ("reaggregated") into their own culture.

During the liminal phase the captive witnessed the bulk of what he recorded in his narrative, for in that stage—the actual captivity—he was relatively free from the social strictures and cultural values of his previous life. His natal culture's values were called into question; he must adapt to foreign ways or starve or be killed. Cut loose from his normal guideposts of language and social relationships, he entertained ideas and values that colonial New England did not allow. Old patterns were abandoned and new ones acquired. Just to keep alive, for example, all captives had to eat food they previously considered inedible. Mary Rowlandson drank broth boiled from a horse's leg and ate bark from trees, and found them palatable; Hannah Swarton ate "*Groundnuts, Acorns, Purslain, Hogweed,* Weeds, Roots, and sometimes *Dogs Flesh*"; Elizabeth Hanson scavenged "Guts and Garbage" of the beavers her masters had eaten.[28] And virtually every captive, even in time of war, eventually admired the Indians' ability to accommode harsh conditions. A captive's admiration usually extended only to Indian clothing and housing or to personal stamina and ingenuity; he rarely appreciated the complexities of Algonquian spiritual life or the Indians' approach to social and political organization. But at least the captives' earlier prejudices lost some of their rigidity when confronted by the realities of Indian life.

Rarely was a captive taken singly. Usually he was part of a group, often survivors of the same attack. Seeing the death of a parent or sibling sometimes left him in a psychological trauma, too shocked to rebel. When captives shared such a crisis, a small community of sufferers emerged. Turner calls the resulting *esprit de corps* "communitas"—the group identity created by those in the same liminal experience.[29] Communitas can be seen in the New England narratives when captives gathered for group prayer. By praying together, Puritan hostages gained comfort from familiar religious rites and values while simultaneously restating their cultural separateness from their Indian or French captors. Both Indians and Frenchmen recognized the cohesive strength of group prayer and its detriment to acculturation, and both usually proscribed it.

Although collective activities strengthened common identity, Indian retribution against all captives when one of them escaped probably did more to cement communal bonds. When an English prisoner ran away, the captors usually threatened to kill one or more of those remaining. Few captives risked the responsibility, and the ensuing guilt, for such retaliation against their compatriots. John Williams reported one situation: "In the Night an *English* Man made his escape: in the Morning I was call'd for, and ordered by the General to tell the English, That if any more made their escape, they would burn the rest of the Prisoners."[30] Sometimes the Indians vented their wrath on those who escaped and were recaptured. John Gyles described his brother's fate: "My unfortunate Brother who was taken with me, after about three Years Captivity, deserted with an Englishman who was taken from *Casco-Bay,* and was retaken by the Indians at *New-Harbour* and carried back to *Penobscot Fort,* where they were both tortured at a Stake by Fire for some time; then their Noses and Ears were cut off, and they made to eat them; after which they were burned to Death at the Stake."[31] Such intimidating events worked paradoxically on a surviving captive: on one hand they forced him to endure, even to cooperate with his captors; on the other hand they heightened his resentment of the captors' culture and raised psychological barriers to acculturation.

Each captivity narrative was written during the postliminal period, usually soon after redemption, and reflects the profound impact of the liminal experience on the writer. And whatever the depth and variety of the impact, redeemed captives seemed compelled, like Coleridge's ancient mariner, to recite their tales. Among the scores of narratives that spanned the centuries and the continent, several distinct categories emerge.

First, some writers give the impression that they had not substantially changed, although former captives were obvi-

ously not quite the same psychologically as they had been before their ordeals. After redemption, once again in familiar surroundings, captives still vividly remembered their months in the wilderness. Mary Rowlandson, for one, could not forget: *"I can remember the time, when I used to sleep quietly without workings in my thoughts, whole nights together, but now it is other wayes with me. When all are fast about me, and no eye open, but his who ever waketh, my thoughts are upon things past."*[32]

For women especially, the return to New England society posed problems of readjustment and reacceptance. Although no ethnological evidence indicates that northeastern Indians ever raped women prisoners, as Plains Indians sometimes did, female captives sometimes felt a need to defend their sexual conduct. Rowlandson, for example, assured her readers that *"not one of them ever offered me the least abuse of unchastity to me, in word or action.* Though some are ready to say I speak it for my own credit, *But I speak it in the presence of God, and to his Glory."*[33] Similarly, Elizabeth Hanson insisted that the Indians were "very civil toward their captive Women, not offering any Incivility by any indecent Carriage (unless they be much overgone in Liquor[)]," and implied that no intoxicated Indians had molested her.[34]

Under captivity, when many undreamed-of things could occur, both fear and its opposite—temptation—were omnipresent. There was always the suspicion that redeemed captives had, consciously or unconsciously, found Indian ways irresistible, and that they had to some degree "gone savage." Such suspicions came easily in a culture that interpreted the form of God's displeasure as a reflection of its cause. "Christians in this Land, have become too like unto the Indians," the Reforming Synod declared, "and then we need not wonder if the Lord hath afflicted us by them."[35] Thus community group pressure urged captives to reaffirm their natal culture's values more fervently than ever and to deny the attractions of "savage" life. On the other hand, it was acceptable to admit, as Hannah Swarton repeatedly does, that she strayed from God's path so long as it was a torment of the soul, not the passions. Mather, Swarton's mouthpiece, defends her honor while steadily guiding her toward conversion.[36] Most New England narrators did not need such help. John Williams's *Redeemed Captive* and Mary Rowlandson's *Sovereignty & Goodness of God* emphatically reaffirm the Puritans' errand into the wilderness. It may not be coincidental that Williams was a clergyman and Rowlandson a clergyman's wife. The clerical class had the deepest commitment to Puritan values.

Narrators who gained empathetic insight into Indian culture constitute a second group. Although they reaffirm their natal ways, they acknowledge some Indian virtues. John Gyles is a good example. He admired the Indians' skill in hunting moose as well as the powwow's ability to forecast the hunt's success through dream visions; yet he considered Indian myths of no more value than fairy tales. Similarly, Gyles praised the Indians' adaptation to their environment but believed them too influenced by the unpredictable elements of nature and too addicted to feasting to plan for future needs. On the whole, adult Puritan captives successfully resisted efforts at assimilation by the French and Indians. Puritan indoctrination had been thorough, and a pervasive sense that an omniscient God kept close eye on His chosen flock was real enough to shield most adult New Englanders from cultural innovation.[37]

A third group of narratives was written by those who had difficulty adjusting to their natal culture after long exposure to Indian life. The number of such accounts is small and includes none of the New England captivities. However, as a matter of illustration, James Smith's *Account of the Remarkable Occurences in the Life and Travels of Col. James Smith* reflects a substantial assimilation of Indian habits.[38] Captured in 1755 on the Pennsylvania frontier by a Caughnawaga and two Delawares, Smith lived for four years with Indians in the Ohio territory. He did not publish his narrative until 1799 because he felt that "at that time [1760] the Americans were so little acquainted with Indian affairs, I apprehended a great part of it would be viewed as fable and romance." Although Smith returned to white America, he sympathetically described his life among the Indians and so thoroughly absorbed their military tactics that he taught them to settlers on the Ohio frontier.[39] A more difficult adjustment is illustrated in John Tanner's narrative, published in 1830. Tanner spent over thirty years among the Ojibway tribe and, not surprisingly, his account offers a more accurate picture of Indian life than narratives by those who lived only briefly with their captors. When Tanner attempted to return to "civilized" society, he was rejected, and he probably rejoined the culture he had so thoroughly absorbed.[40]

Another category of narratives, this one hypothetical, could have been written by those who never returned to their natal culture. If captives who entirely forsook their original environment—who completely transculturated—had written of their experiences, we would have a still more sympathetic and knowledgeable portrayal of Indian life. This category would be filled mainly by those who had been captured as children; in most cases they forgot their mother tongue and hence could not easily have written their narratives. The Indians and the French were well aware, of course, that children did not have the physical or psychic strength to resist acculturation and had not yet acquired the political and cultural loyalties of adulthood. Although a captive child was not exactly a Lockean *tabula rasa* for his Indian captors, he readily learned a new language and new values. (By the same token, English missionaries made special efforts to indoctrinate Indian children into Christianity and European customs.) The most famous example of an unredeemed Puritan youngster's assimilation into Indian and French ways was Eunice Williams, daughter of John Williams. Aged seven when captured, Eunice remained in custody long after the rest of her family returned to New England, and she eventually succumbed to the alien culture. She was converted to Catholicism by Canadian nuns, married an Indian, and refused all subsequent efforts to reunite her with her Puritan family.[41] The fact that many children captives chose not to return to their families must have shaken New England's confidence. Perhaps these youthful expatriots are a bittersweet symbol of the failure of the concept of "progress," a notion to which the Puritans firmly subscribed and which became almost universal among nineteenth-century Americans.

Despite the relative brevity of the captivity period for most captives (usually a few months to a few years), the narratives collectively provide a fascinating glimpse of Indian culture. It is only a glimpse; Puritan society had abundant legal and social structures against imitating or admiring the Indians' "prophane course of life."[42] Indian ways were to be shunned, not emulated; "savagery" was feared and despised, not appreciated or respected. Hence captives had little incentive, save their own curiosity or a desire for dramatic detail, to describe native customs, and the few exceptions are marred by pervasive ethnocentricity.

Even if the captives had been willing and unbiased, the task of description would have been formidable. Most raiding parties probably had warriors from several tribes, each with a slightly—sometimes markedly—different cultural heritage; the same was often true of the villages to which the captives were taken. And although most Indian captors were from the northeastern Algonquian linguistic group, a significant minority were from the linguistically and culturally distant Iroquois Confederacy. Especially important among the latter were Mohawks who had converted to Roman Catholicism, nominally at least, and had moved to the Caughnawaga missionary settlement near Montreal. (Many Puritan captives, including Eunice Williams, were thus simultaneously confronted by Indian and French cultural pressures.) Most New England prisoners were taken to southeastern Canada, where French, Algonquian, and Iroquoian cultural influences were gradually but unevenly blending. Bewildered captives could scarcely have comprehended the complex and ever-changing Franco-Indian world of the late seventeenth and early eighteenth centuries, but we can wish they had tried harder to describe, even if they could not understand or appreciate, their new surroundings.

When ethnographic material does appear in the captivity narratives, it is valuable and fascinating. Mary Rowlandson, for example, included a lively if not entirely sympathetic description of the ceremonial preparations for an attack on Sudbury, Massachusetts.[43] Elizabeth Hanson explained (unsympathetically) Indian eating customs.[44] John Gyles told much about Indian hunting and farming practices, methods of preserving food, and burial and marriage rites. Gyles, in fact, came closest of the Puritan narrators to providing comprehensive ethnographic information. Although he appears to have been a member in good standing of the Puritan community, his account is conspicuously less pietistic than the others; his relatively secular turn of mind allowed him to describe Indian and French customs more fully and even to devote several pages to the curious habits of the beaver.[45]

Several Puritan narrators dwelled on Indian maltreatment of captives—especially Quentin Stockwell and John Gyles, who were apparently handled more harshly than most New England captives. Gyles twice was saved from torture ceremonies, once by his master and once by a squaw and an Indian girl. In each instance, Gyles's savior pledged a gift to the tribe to reprieve him. Gyles later explained that "A Captive among the Indians is exposed to all manner of Abuse, and to the utmost Tortures, unless his Master, or some of his Master's Relations, lay down a Ransom, such as a Bag of Corn, or a Blanket, or such like: by which they may redeem them from their Cruelties." When Gyles's kindly master later traveled to Canada and left him with less friendly guardians, Gyles fell into the hands of Cape Sable Indians who inflicted the torture that he had earlier avoided.[46]

Perhaps because he wrote his narrative long after the era of intense Puritan piety, Gyles attributed Indian compassion or cruelty to human inclination, Earlier captives saw the Indians as God's pawns, at least when it came to kindness. John Williams epitomized this aspect of the Puritan perspective: among "Passages of Divine Providence," he reported that "God hath made such . . . characters . . . as delighted in cruelty, to pity and compassionate such who were led into captivity by them. Made them bear on their Arms, and carry on their Shoulders our *Little Ones,* unable to Travel, Feed the Prisoners with the best of their Provisions: Yea, sometimes pinch themselves, as to their daily food, rather than their Captives."[47] Similarly, Cotton Mather attributed the Indian men's reluctance to molest female captives to "a wonderful Restraint from God upon the Bruitish Salvages."[48] But whether God or man got the credit, New England narratives clearly reveal that some Indians were kind, some were cruel, and that generally the treatment of women and children was as humane as wartime conditions allowed.

Puritan perceptions of how Indians treated captives may be partly explained by the narrators' norms for family structure and its responsibilities. The New England family centered on the conjugal relationship of husband, wife, and children. Servants who resided under the roof of a Puritan home were treated almost as family members. They called the patriarchal head of the family "master" and owed him loyal and industrious service. Masters, in turn, were obliged by law and custom to treat their servants humanely and to provide them with adequate food, shelter, clothing, education, and religious training. Master and servant, in short, had almost the same relationship as father and child.[49] (A sharp increase in African and Indian slaves in the eighteenth century helped to undermine the earlier master-servant relationship.) A Puritan captive of the Indians usually referred to his principal captor as master, which not only implied the captive's inferior status but also suggested that, in the captive's eyes, each had reciprocal obligations. In many of the Puritan narratives, captives—unconsciously thinking in terms of their culture alone—complain bitterly of the failure of Indian masters to provide them with enough food or comfort. Yet a captive often re-

alized, as he grew more accustomed to Indian ways, that he usually ate as well or as poorly as his captors; the ill treatment of Elizabeth Hanson and her children in the 1720s was an exception, not the rule.

The Puritan family centered primarily on the relationship of husband, wife, and children in what anthropologists call a cognatic descent group: all descendants, both male and female, are emphasized equally. Northeastern Indians, on the contrary, employed a complex mixture of unilineal descent groups, both matrilineal and patrilineal. The lineage groups of a particular clan of a tribe could be traced through either husband or wife. Thus, an Indian child could inherit a distinct group of rights and responsibilities from his mother and quite a different set from his father.[50] Moreover, in many tribes a man might have two or three wives, which not only offended the English captive but added to his bewilderment over the intricate matrix of Indian social bonds. In Elizabeth Hanson's narrative, for example, when her master ordered his son to beat her child, "the Indian boy's [maternal] grandmother, would not suffer him to do it." Hanson's protectoress later became so upset with her son-in-law's behavior that she moved out of his wigwam.[51]

Because all captives were prisoners of war, some animosity toward Indians or French captors was inevitable, whatever the treatment accorded the prisoners and whatever the reasons for it. Perhaps inevitable too was the combination of war-bred enmity with latent contempt for Indians that gradually shifted the New England captivity narrative from an essentially religious tract, with occasional insights into Indian culture, to what Roy Harvey Pearce has aptly called a "vehicle of Indian-hatred."[52] That motif had first appeared in the preface to Rowlandson's narrative—though significantly not in the narrative itself—in an assertion that "none can imagine what it is to be captivated, and enslaved to such atheisticall proud, wild, cruel, barbarous, bruitish (in one word) diabolicall creatures as these, the worst of the heathen."[53] But not until Cotton Mather's accounts, especially those published in *Decennium Luctuosum* (1699) and repeated in *Magnalia Christi Americana* (1702), did the anti-Indian and anti-French themes become blatant. Late in the seventeenth century Mather lashed out at "those Ravenous howling *Wolves,*" and "these cursed Blood-Hounds"; by the turn of the century, Mather was ranting about "those *Dragons of the Wilderness,*" and "the *Dark places* of *New-England,* where the *Indians* had their Unapproachable *Kennels . . . of Cruelty.*"[54] That atrocities took place is undeniable; the point to be made here is that Mather began the transformation of captivity narratives into a new sub-genre. By 1740, as Pearce notes, "religious concerns came to be incidental at most; the intent of the typical writer of the narrative was to register as much hatred of the French and Indians as possible . . . The captivity narrative had become the American equivalent of the Grub Street criminal biography."[55] By then it had also ceased to be Puritan.

Most New England narratives before mid-eighteenth century praised the French for tempering the Indians' cruelty, providing material comfort, and arranging prisoner exchanges. That did not prevent Puritan writers from venting their contempt for the "Popish" or "Romish" religion, as can best be seen in the narratives by Williams and Swarton. Both accounts record extensive debates between the authors and their Catholic hosts, which forcefully illustrate how the Puritan mind continued to battle what it considered the regressive doctrines of Roman Catholicism. The Puritans' antagonists were seldom the Canadian laity, whom the narrators often thanked explicitly and abundantly, but rather the Jesuits and other clerics who assumed a God-directed edict to convert English captives—just as the Puritans assumed the opposite. Puritan captivity narratives thus suggest a cultural hostility between Canada and New England that in some ways paralleled the cultural chasm between English and Indians.

In style as well as substance, Puritan captivity narratives reflect the dominant characteristics of early New England. The narratives are distinguished not only by their religious fervor but (not surprisingly) by the clergy's close involvement in their composition, which gives them a distinct tone. Of the best New England narratives before 1750, only a few can be considered purely lay products. Several were written by clerics or their immediate kin; others were transcribed and embellished by clergymen, especially Cotton Mather. Even John Gyles, the most secular of the Puritan narrators, may have leaned heavily on a local chaplain for stylistic guidance.

Authors with clerical affiliation or assistance were not reluctant to arouse the reader's emotions, though they were less inclined to sensationalism than were later writers. Cotton Mather especially employed attention-grabbing devices usually suited for oral delivery, such as alliteration, exaggerated emphasis, and exclamations. And because of his concern with communal rather than individual experience, Mather often resorted to generalized diction. This tendency is evident in his attempts to deal with the physical landscape. When Mather writes of Mary Plaisted's journey into captivity, his description is not tactile but mental, filtered through a mind more concerned with spiritual than with physical reality. "But she must now Travel many Days," he wrote, "thro' Woods, and Swamps, and Rocks, and over Mountains, and Frost and Snow, until she could stir no farther."[56] By contrast, John Williams had experienced captivity firsthand. Although his diction too is often general, he can recall physical details precisely; he writes, for instance, "Each night I wrung blood out of my stockings," and "My shins also were very sore, being cut with crusty snow."[57]

Although Mary Rowlandson cited biblical sources more than Williams did, she balanced spiritual generalities with precise observations. For example, in her chilling description of the attack on Lancaster, she and other victims were "standing amazed, with the blood running down to our heels."[58] Williams was more concerned with the Canadian Jesuits' attempts to convert his flock to Roman Catholicism than with an accurate rendering of the physical details of his wilderness experience. His narrative, in fact, is more precise in its Canadian than its New England portions. Rowlandson, on the other hand, displayed an acute understanding of the psychology of her Indian captors. She described with keen insight the second wife of her Indian master. Weetamoo, she tells us, was "a severe and proud Dame . . . bestowing every day in dressing her self neat as much time as any of the Gentry of the land: powdering her hair, and painting her face, going with necklaces, with Jewels in her ears, and Bracelets upon her hands: When she had dressed her self, her work was to make Girdles of *Wampum* and *Beads*." Rowlandson thus reveals her mistress's preoccupation with cosmetic baubles; Weetamoo's vanity becomes obvious.[59]

Gyles, too, presents his observations more carefully than his clerical counterparts. He can be meticulous in his description, even excruciating in detail. For example, Gyles contracted a severe case of frostbite, and wrote: "Soon after the Skin came off my Feet from my Ankles whole like a Shoe, and left my Toes naked without a Nail, and the ends of my great Toe-Bones bare, which in a little time turn'd black, so that I was obliged to cut the first Joint off with my Knife."[60] Later writers of captivity narratives would strive for such sensational effects, but Gyles does not indulge in gory detail for its own sake. His narrative unfolds with honesty and simplicity—no pious ejaculations nor infants with bashed-in skulls. He does not see his Indian companions through Rousseau-colored glasses; rather he identifies with them, often using "we" and "our" when referring to his captors.

Gyles's structural form also sets his narrative apart from earlier New England captivity accounts. Although it follows the usual chronological sequence, some of its chapters interrupt the narrative flow. Chapter VI, for example, presents a "description of several creatures commonly taken by the Indians on St. John's River." That Gyles would pause in his story to include such an account suggests a subtle shift in author-audience relations. It is difficult to imagine Mather, Williams, or Rowlandson succumbing to such a natural history urge. Thus, by the time Gyles published his story, captivity narratives were in the process of becoming a sub*literary* genre; its audience expected not only a truthful tale but information about Indians, the landscape, and animals of which most townsfolk had no firsthand knowledge. Perhaps such pressure encouraged editors to "improve" the narratives for better reception.

Although Elizabeth Hanson was Quaker, her story belongs within the New England captivity narrative framework. The writer of the three-paragraph preface to her narrative of *God's Mercy Surmounting Man's Cruelty* alludes to biblical themes as well as contemporary historians, including, apparently, Cotton Mather. Hanson was captured in Maine and she, like other New Englanders, was bought from her captors by the Canadian French.[61] When compared to another famous Quaker captivity narrative, Jonathan Dickinson's *God Protecting Providence,*

Hanson's account—with its focus on New England terrain, on family trials, and on the moral lesson of the "kindness and goodness of God"—is clearly within the New England mold. Dickinson's narrative, published in 1699, is set in East Florida and Carolina. Moreover, Dickinson is more properly considered an Englishman than an American, and he does not conclude his narrative in the usual New England manner by asking the reader to see in the captive experience evidence of God's over-arching plan. Dickinson merely hopes "that I with all those of us that have been spared hitherto, shall never be forgetful nor unmindful of the low estate we were brought into."[62]

Hanson's work, however, stands at the end of the New England school and at the beginning of a more personal and secular response to Indian captivity. Her narrative illustrates an increasingly conscious literary attempt to arouse the reader's sentiments. The drama of her family's ordeal and her husband's death while trying to redeem one of their children proved too tempting for later editors, who liberally embellished her story.[63]

As the narratives progress chronologically over the years, biblical quotations—another evidence of Puritan piety and clerical influence—decrease. John Gyles's book (1736) has few. Instead Gyles quotes *The Odyssey*, Dryden's *Virgil*, and even Mather's *Magnalia Christi Americana*. Elizabeth Hanson's narrative (1724) contains no biblical citations. Although religious tracts and sermons remained popular literary forms well into the eighteenth century, the focus of New England captivity narratives shifted from communal to personal, from religious to secular. Later, in narratives published during the Revolution and the early national period, the emphasis shifted again to a combination of personal experiences and national spirit. Puritan narratives, like Puritanism itself, had given way to new modes of expression.

Embellishment and diffusion marked the narratives' subsequent career. Beginning in the latter half of the eighteenth century, publishers of captivity narratives increasingly exercised a heavy editorial hand. Often they sought to imitate the sentimental fiction in vogue in England; sometimes they merely heightened the drama and polished the prose. The earlier narratives, especially those in Puritan New England, had exhibited a simple, unadorned style. Authors were not overly concerned with careful sentence patterns or orchestration of tone. Most narrators told their stories in chronological order and in a sparse, vital style that effectively conveyed the immediacy of the author's life-and-death struggle. Even when an editor's ghostly hand seemed to hover over the narrative, its emphasis remained substantive rather than rhetorical.

In the second half of the eighteenth century, the literary image of women captives also underwent significant alteration. Mary Rowlandson, Hannah Swarton, and Elizabeth Hanson achieved fame during their lifetimes as resilient and resourceful women. The gothic vogue of the late eighteenth and early nineteenth centuries stereotyped female captives: the woman became a passive mother who witnessed the murder of her baby and the abduction of her older children by a cruel man-monster. Although the actual experience of captive women often justified a more assertive image, the usual picture in the public mind was of a frail woman submissively kneeling before her Indian captor, waiting for a death stroke from a raised tomahawk. Various components of this icon may be found in the woodcut depictions of later narratives and ultimately in Horatio Greenough's massive sculpture, "The Rescue Group."[64]

In the early nineteenth century, captivity narratives presented fewer unadorned firsthand experiences and more rhetorical flourishes, often verging on fantasy. Even then, however, some of the captivity accounts contained important ethnographic detail, as in the narrative of John Tanner (1830) on which Longfellow drew extensively for his epic poem *Hiawatha*. But Tanner was exceptional. More representative of the later genre were dime novels such as *Nathan Todd; or The Fate of the Sioux' Captive* (1860), which catered to an audience more interested in sensation than verisimilitude.[65] Even though authentic narratives about life among the western Plains Indians appeared as late as 1871, when Fanny Kelly's *My Captivity among the Sioux Indians* was published, popular fiction had largely absorbed the genre years before.[66]

In the 1830s Andrew Jackson's removal policy transplanted most eastern Indians permanently beyond the Mississippi River. As aggressive white farmers and land speculators moved onto confiscated Indian lands, the Indian, no longer viewed as a serious threat by easterners, became the sympathetic subject of popular dramas and novels. In 1829, King Philip, having lain silent for a century and a half, was resurrected by John Augustus Stone in *Metamora, or the Last of the Wampanoags*. The lead role secured Edwin Forrest an enduring fame and a small fortune as well; he played the part for forty years. In 1855 the stage Indian was so noble and so ethereal that John Brougham aimed a satiric arrow at pompous portrayals of Indians by actors such as Forrest; his burlesque *Po-ca-hon-tas* also made fun of James Nelson Barker's early drama *The Indian Princess* (1808) and George Washington Custis's *Pocahontas* (1830).[67]

The themes, imagery, and language of the captivity narrative occurred frequently in the more serious realms of American literature. As Richard Slotkin has pointed out, eighteenth-century works such as Jonathan Edwards's evangelical sermon, "Sinners in the Hands of an Angry God," employed the captivity rhetoric.[68] In the early nineteenth century, when writers in the young republic increasingly turned their attention to American topics, the captivity genre helped to create a new national mythology. Here was the stuff of New World experience, something that contemporary Europe could not offer. Charles Brockden Brown's novel *Edgar Huntly* (1799) employed the capture-escape-flight theme so congenial to an audience familiar with captivity narratives. Brown's application of the wilderness landscape to reflect the tangled battle between reason and emotion in his hero's psyche parallels the Puritan's use of the wilderness to symbolize the struggle between the spiritual and physical worlds. Other early American novelists used the captivity theme more explicitly: by 1823 at least fifteen American novels included a captivity episode.[69]

Poets as well as prose writers responded to the quickening pace of American interest in Indian material in the early decades of the nineteenth century. The extremely popular *Yamoyden, a Tale of the Wars of King Philip* (1820), a long narrative poem written by James W. Eastburn and Robert C. Sands, focused on the plight of a fictional Nipnet chieftain and his white wife, Nora. With its shopworn imagery, sentimental description, and well-established romantic conventions, the poem nevertheless illustrates the sympathy which writers of imaginative literature then extended toward the Indian. The captivity theme and its underlying drama of the clash between Indian and European cultures reached its zenith, however, in the writer who first systematically exploited the myth of the American frontier, James Fenimore Cooper. The five volumes of the Leatherstocking tales delighted the American public: the initial novel of the series, *The Pioneers* (1823), sold 3,500 copies in its first day of publication.[70] Although Cooper killed off his hero, Natty Bumppo, in *The Prairie* (1827), the wilderness theme was so effective that he resurrected the hunter and wrote three more novels about Bumppo's youth. Cooper's portrayal of the inevitable demise of his Noble Savage, Chingachgook, was more than lively reading; it was grist for the mills of those who cried Manifest Destiny in the 1830s and after, and thus encouraged American expansion as well as American literary themes. Cooper was not the only prominent writer of the early nineteenth century whose work reflected America's perception of the taming of the wilderness. Southern novelists such as William Gilmore Simms, most notably in *The Yemasee* (1835), echoed Cooper's message.

Later writers also exploited the metaphors of the hunter and the hunted that were central to captivity narratives. Nathaniel Hawthorne reconstructed the famous Hannah Dustan story, making the husband the hero. Mather's account of the tomahawk-wielding frontierswoman also intrigued Henry David Thoreau. In *A Week on the Concord and Merrimack Rivers* (1849), Thoreau underscores the ambiguities of Indian-European relations; the climactic moment of the "Thursday" section of the book retells the Dustan story differently: "The family of Hannah Dustin all assembled alive once more except the infant whose brains were dashed out against the apple tree, and there have been many who in later times have lived to say that they have eaten of the fruit of that apple tree."[71] Thoreau's most famous work, *Walden* (1854), chronicles a mid-nineteenth-century American's attempt to confront nature on a level parallel to the Indians of earlier centuries. Herman Melville's first novel, *Typee* (1846), is based on the captivity-escape plot in which Toby, the main character, flees not from Indians but from South Sea islanders he

suspects of cannibalism. Melville's awareness of the cruelties of both frontiersmen and Indians is found in its most mature form in *The Confidence-Man* (1857) in a perceptive chapter called "Metaphysics of Indian-Hating."[72]

By mid-nineteenth century the captivity narrative had become fully integrated into American literature. If it had largely lost its standing as a reliable and introspective autobiographical account, and had wholly lost its religious fervor, it had nonetheless assumed an important role in the minds of America's most prominent authors. Through the voluminous and popular works of Cooper, Melville, Simms, Thoreau, and many others, the setting if not always the plot and substance of wilderness captivities had entered the mainstream of American literature.

Notes

1. John Williams, *The Redeemed Captive Returning to Zion: A Faithful Narrative of Remarkable Occurrences in the Captivity and the Deliverance of Mr. John Williams* (Boston, 1707), A2v.

2. For bibliographic details see R. W. G. Vail, *The Voice of the Old Frontier* (Philadelphia, 1949), 90-91.

3. Edward Arber and A. G. Bradley, eds., *Travels and Works of Captain John Smith . . . 1580-1631,* 2 vols. (Edinburgh, 1910), I, 14-22; II, 395-401, 911-912.

4. Reuben Gold Thwaites, ed., *The Jesuit Relations and Allied Documents,* 73 vols. (Cleveland, 1896-1961), XXXI, 17-137. This version is in Fr. Jerome Lalemont's "Relation of 1647" and includes Jogues's death. Father Jogues also wrote an account of his first captivity (1642) in a letter of 1643 to Father Jean Filleau, which has been reprinted several times. In 1646 Jogues was recaptured by the Iroquois and killed.

5. Boone was a captive for seven days in 1769 and for several months in 1778. See John Filson, *The Discovery, Settlement and Present State of Kentucke* (Wilmington, Del., 1784; facs. repr. Ann Arbor, Mich., 1966), 51-53, 63-66.

6. For bibliographic details see Vail, *Voice of the Old Frontier,* 167-169. A case could be made for John Underhill as the author of the first Puritan captivity narrative. Though not autobiographical, his account of the captivity and release of two girls from Wethersfield, Connecticut, in 1637 has many of the characteristics that later appear in Cotton Mather's secondhand accounts: drama, moral lessons, and pious rhetoric. See Underhill, *Newes from America . . .* (London, 1638; repr. in *Massachusetts Historical Society Collections,* 3rd ser., 6[1837]), 12-13, 17-23.

7. Some Puritan autobiographies were published; most remained in manuscript. For discussions of the genre see Daniel Shea, *Spiritual Autobiography in Early America* (Princeton, N.J., 1968), and Owen C.

Watkins, *The Puritan Experience: Studies in Spiritual Autobiography* (New York, 1972). Winthrop's account is in Massachusetts Historical Society, *Winthrop Papers,* 5 vols. (Boston, 1929-1947), I, 154-161; Shepard's is best consulted in Michael McGiffert, ed., *God's Plot: The Paradoxes of Puritan Piety, Being the Autobiography and Journal of Thomas Shepard* (Amherst, Mass., 1972), 33-77; Bradstreet's is in *The Works of Anne Bradstreet in Prose and Verse,* ed. John Harvard Ellis (Charlestown, Mass., 1867; repr. Gloucester, Mass., 1962), 3-10; and Taylor's is reprinted in Donald Stanford, ed., "Edward Taylor's 'Spiritual Relation,'" *American Literature,* 35 (1963-1964), 467-475.

8. Sacvan Bercovitch, *The Puritan Origins of the American Self* (New Haven, 1976), 9-10.

9. Shea, *Spiritual Autobiography,* xi.

10. Mary Rowlandson, *The Soveraignty & Goodness of God,* 2nd ed. (Cambridge, Mass., 1682), 9.

11. Williams, "Reports of Divine Kindness," appended to *Redeemed Captive,* 97.

12. Cotton Mather, *Magnalia Christi Americana: or the Ecclesiastical History of New-England, from . . . 1620. unto . . . 1698* (London, 1702), Bk. VI, 13.

13. *Humiliations,* 40.

14. Williams, *Redeemed Captive.* The best modern version is edited by Edward W. Clark (Amherst, Mass., 1976). For bibliographic details on the early editions see Vail, *Voice of the Old Frontier,* 201-202, 209, 265, 296, 300, 304, 387, 407-410.

15. Puritan sermons have been studied from diverse perspectives. Suggestive if not always convincing analyses include John Brown, *Puritan Preaching in England* (New York, 1900); Babette M. Levy, *Preaching in the First Half Century of New England History* (Hartford, Conn., 1945); Bruce A. Rosenberg, *The Art of the American Folk Preacher* (New York, 1970); Horton Davies, *Worship and Theology in England,* vols. I-II (Princeton, N.J., 1970-1975); and Emory Elliott, *Power and the Pulpit in Puritan New England* (Princeton, N.J., 1975). Convenient anthologies of Puritan sermons include Phyllis M. Jones and Nicholas R. Jones, eds., *Salvations in New England: Selections from the Sermons of the First Preachers* (Austin, Tex., 1977); and A. W. Plumstead, ed., *The Wall and The Garden: Selected Massachusetts Election Sermons, 1670-1775* (Minneapolis, 1968). Many sermons are reprinted in the Arno Press, "Library of American Puritan Writings: The Seventeenth Century," selected by Sacvan Bercovitch (New York, 1979).

16. The best discussion of the jeremiad is Sacvan Bercovitch, *The American Jeremiad* (Madison, Wis., 1978), chaps. 1-2. Important earlier analyses include Perry Miller, *The New England Mind: From Colony to Province* (Cambridge, Mass., 1953; repr. Boston, 1968), *passim*; and Bercovitch, "Horologicals to Chronometricals: The Rhetoric of the Jeremiad," *Literary Monographs,* III (Madison, Wis., 1970).

17. Wigglesworth, "God's Controversy with New England," *Massachusetts Historical Society Proceedings,* 12 (1871-1873), 89.

18. Among several modern studies of Puritan typology, see especially Sacvan Bercovitch, ed., *Typology and Early American Literature* (Amherst, Mass., 1972).

19. Increase Mather, *An Essay for the Recording of Illustrious Providences . . . Especially in New England* (Boston, 1684); Cotton Mather, *The Wonderful Works of God Commemorated . . .* (Boston, 1690); Cotton Mather, *Terribilia Dei: Remarkable Judgements of God, on Several Sorts of Offenders . . . among the People of New England . . .* (Boston, 1697). For additional works by the Mathers on the same subject see Thomas J. Holmes, *Increase Mather, A Bibliography of His Works,* 2 vols. (Cleveland, 1931); and Holmes, *Cotton Mather, A Bibliography of His Works,* 3 vols. (Cambridge, Mass., 1940).

20. Williams, "Reports of Divine Kindness," 97.

21. Rowlandson, *Soveraignty & Goodness of God,* 62.

22. Williams, *Redeemed Captive,* 1.

23. On King Philip's War see Douglas Edward Leach, *Flintlock and Tomahawk: New England in King Philip's War* (New York, 1958). The quote from the Reforming Synod is in [Increase Mather], *The Necessity of Reformation . . .* (Boston, 1679), 1.

24. Rowlandson, *Soveraignty & Goodness of God,* A2v.

25. See, for example, Richard Slotkin, *Regeneration through Violence: The Mythology of the American Frontier, 1600-1860* (Middletown, Conn., 1973), 103-104. Because this work relies so heavily on Joseph Campbell's monomyth theory (*Hero with a Thousand Faces* [New York, 1949]), it should be used with discretion; it does, however, contain provocative ideas and a valuable bibliography. See also James Axtell, "The White Indians of Colonial America," *William and Mary Quarterly,* 3rd ser., 32 (1975), 55-88; and Richard VanDerBeets, "The Indian Captivity Narrative as Ritual," *American Literature,* 43 (January, 1972), 562.

26. Turner, *Dramas, Fields, and Metaphors: Symbolic Action in Human Society* (Ithaca, N.Y., 1974), 231-232. Turner expands and modifies Arnold Van Gennep's terms of separation, margin, and reaggregation.

27. Psychologists and other students of human behavior have long recognized the tendency of captives—whether they are taken by kidnappers, terrorists, or military forces—to develop sympathy for their captors. In some instances, the sympathy reflects a new

awareness of the captors' viewpoint or culture—a true learning experience. But in other instances, captives admire, even emulate, captors who abuse and threaten them. The essential mechanism in this ostensibly illogical identification with the enemy is the captive's utter dependence on the captor for every necessity, even for life itself. For some widely diverse but highly suggestive writings on this matter, see Bruno Bettelheim, "Individual and Mass Behavior in Extreme Situations," *Journal of Abnormal and Social Psychology,* 38 (1943), 417-452; William Sargant, *Battle for the Mind: A Physiology of Conversion and Brainwashing* (New York, 1957); Dorothy Rabinowitz, "The Hostage Mentality," *Commentary,* 63 (June 1977), 70-72; and Walter Reich, "Hostages and the [Stockholm] Syndrome," *New York Times,* Jan. 15, 1980.

28. Rowlandson, *Soveraignty & Goodness of God,* 18-19, 21-22, 33; Swarton in Cotton Mather, *Magnalia Christi Americana,* Bk. VI, 10; Hanson, *God's Mercy Surmounting Man's Cruelty* (Philadelphia, 1728), 13.

29. Turner, *Dramas, Fields, and Metaphors,* 231-232.

30. Williams, *Redeemed Captive,* 7. For a similar threat see "Quentin Stockwell's Relation" in Increase Mather, *An Essay for the Recording of Illustrious Providences* (Boston, 1684), 45-46.

31. John Gyles, *Memoirs of Odd Adventures, Strange Deliverances, etc., in the Captivity of John Gyles, Esq. . . .* (Boston, 1736), 11-12.

32. Rowlandson, *Soveraignty & Goodness of God,* 71.

33. Rowlandson, *Soveraignty & Goodness of God,* 64.

34. Hanson, *God's Mercy,* 35-36.

35. Increase Mather, *Necessity of Reformation,* 5.

36. Cotton Mather, *Magnalia Christi Americana,* Bk. VI, 10-14 *passim.*

37. For a discussion of Puritan captives' attraction to Indian life and the reasons why most resisted it, see Alden T. Vaughan and Daniel K. Richter, "Crossing the Cultural Divide: Indians and New Englanders, 1605-1763," *American Antiquarian Society Proceedings,* 90 (1980), 23-99, especially 81-83. At most, about twelve percent of the captives who spent the last part of their captivities with the Indians, rather than with the French, remained permanently among them.

38. For bibliographic details see Vail, *Voice of the Old Frontier,* 447.

39. James Smith, *Scoouwa: James Smith's Indian Captivity Narrative,* ed. John J. Barsotti (Columbus, Ohio, 1978), 16.

40. Tanner, *A Narrative of the Captivity of John Tanner* (New York, 1830).

41. For a discussion of captives from all parts of British America who were assimilated by Indians, see Axtell, "White Indians of Colonial America." The demographic aspects of Puritan captives—numbers, age, sex, and length of captivity—are analyzed in Vaughan and Richter, "Crossing the Cultural Divide." Eunice Williams's story is best followed in John Williams's narrative and Alexander Medlicott, Jr., "Return to the Land of Light: A Plea to an Unredeemed Captive," *New England Quarterly,* 38 (1965), 202-216. A valuable examination of the legends that accumulate around famous unredeemed captives, especially Eunice Williams, is Dawn Lander Gherman, "From Parlour to Teepee: The White Squaw on the American Frontier" (Ph.D. diss., University of Massachusetts, 1975), 70-91. The most famous narrative of a captive who remained with her captors is the semi-autobiographical account by Mary Jemison of Pennsylvania. In 1755, at age twelve, she was taken by the Seneca, with whom she lived until her death in 1833. Her career was described by James Everett Seaver, who interviewed her in 1823, in *A Narrative of the Life of Mrs. Mary Jemison* (Canandaigua, N.Y., 1824). Many subsequent editions have been issued, some of them entitled *Deh-he-wa-mis . . . the White Woman of the Genessee.*

42. For example, J. Hammond Trumbull, ed., *The Public Records of the Colony of Connecticut . . . ,* 15 vols. (Hartford, 1850-1890), I, 78.

43. Rowlandson, *Soveraignty & Goodness of God,* 50-52.

44. Hanson, *God's Mercy,* 12-13, 15-17, 22, 24.

45. Gyles, *Memoirs of Odd Adventures, passim,* especially 24-27. Gyles was a captive from 1689 to 1695, but his narrative did not appear until 1736. By the later date the old Puritan enthusiasm had severely waned, and the new enthusiasm of the Great Awakening had yet to make its full impact. That may account for Gyles's secular tone; it may also reflect an editor's influence. For a summary of the ethnographic information to be found in captivity narratives throughout North America and over the span of three centuries, see Marius Barbeau, "Indian Captivities," *American Philosophical Society Proceedings,* 94 (1950), 522-548, especially 531-543.

46. Gyles, *Memoirs of Odd Adventures,* 5. For a comprehensive but somewhat muddled analysis of cruelty to captives, see Nathaniel Knowles, "The Torture of Captives by the Indians of Eastern North America," *American Philosophical Society Proceedings,* 82 (1940), 151-225.

47. Williams, *Redeemed Captive,* 98.

48. Cotton Mather, *Good Fetch'd Out of Evil* (Boston, 1706), 33-34.

49. For a valuable general account of the Puritan family, see Edmund S. Morgan, *The Puritan Family: Religion and Domestic Relations in Seventeenth Century*

New England, rev. ed. (New York, 1966). Of special relevance is the final chapter on Puritan tribalism. Among the most extensive Puritan statements are Cotton Mather, *A Family Well-Ordered . . .* (Boston, 1699), and Benjamin Wadsworth, *The Well-Ordered Family . . .* (Boston, 1712).

50. For a general introduction to the complexities of kinship, see two chapters in Robin Fox, *Encounter with Anthropology* (New York, 1968), "Comparative Family Patterns" (85-94) and "Kinship and Alliance" (95-112). Useful also for its information on tribes in northern New England and southern Canada is *Handbook of North American Indians,* XV, *Northeast,* ed. Bruce G. Trigger (Washington, D.C., 1978).

51. Hanson, *God's Mercy,* 26-28.

52. "The Significances of the Captivity Narrative," *American Literature,* 19 (1947), 5.

53. Rowlandson, *Soveraignty & Goodness of God,* A3v.

54. Cotton Mather, *Souldiers Counselled and Comforted* (Boston, 1689), 28; *Fair Weather. Or, Considerations to Dispel the Clouds . . . of Discontent . . .* (Boston, 1691), 90; *Good Fetch'd Out of Evil* (Boston, 1706), 4; *Magnalia Christi Americana,* Bk. VII, 69.

55. Pearce, "Significances of the Captivity Narrative," 6-7.

56. Cotton Mather, *Magnalia Christi Americana,* Bk. VII, 71.

57. Williams, *Redeemed Captive,* 16.

58. Rowlandson, *Soveraignty & Goodness of God,* 4.

59. Rowlandson, *Soveraignty & Goodness of God,* 47-48.

60. *Memoirs of Odd Adventures,* 16-17.

61. For full bibliographic information see Vail, *Voice of the Old Frontier,* 216-218, 248, 272, 274, 309, 313, 336, 362-363.

62. For full bibliographic information on Dickinson's narrative, see ibid., 192-194, 207-208, 223, 225-226, 244, 267, 292, 335, 350, 360, 370-372. The quote is from Jonathan Dickinson, *Journal or, God's Protecting Providence, Being the Narrative of a Journey from Port Royal in Jamaica to Philadelphia between August 23, 1696 and April 1, 1697,* ed. Evangeline Walker Andrews and Charles McLean Andrews (New Haven, Conn., 1961), 78.

63. Compare, for example, the early American and English editions. The latter is conveniently reprinted, with frequent comparative passages from the 1754 American edition, in Richard VanDerBeets, *Held Captive by Indians: Selected Narratives, 1642-1836* (Knoxville, Tenn., 1973), chap. 4.

64. Slotkin, *Regeneration through Violence,* 94. See also Gherman, "From Parlour to Teepee," which successfully counters the prevailing image of the American white woman on the frontier as a genteel carrier of Western culture. For a vivid example of the nineteenth century's image of the woman captive as submissive mother, see John Mix Stanley's oil painting, "Osage Scalp Dance" (1845), reproduced in *Smithsonian,* 9, no. 4 (July 1978), 52-53.

65. Henry Nash Smith, *Virgin Land: The American West as Symbol and Myth* (New York, 1950), 99-135.

66. It is indicative of the "degenerate" state of the captivity narrative that Fanny Kelly's publishers felt compelled to verify her experience by appending several affidavits from United States military officers who rescued Mrs. Kelly. See Fanny Kelly, *My Captivity among the Sioux Indians* (1871; repr. Secaucus, N.J., 1962).

67. *Metamora* and *Po-ca-hon-tas* are included in Richard Moody, ed., *Dramas from the American Theatre, 1762-1909* (Boston, 1966), 199-228, 397-422.

68. Slotkin, *Regeneration through Violence,* 103-106.

69. Dorothy Forbis Behan, "The Captivity Story in American Literature, 1577-1826" (Ph.D. diss., University of Chicago, 1952), *passim.*

70. For the popular reception of the Leatherstocking Tales see James D. Hart, *The Popular Book: A History of America's Literary Taste* (New York, 1950), 80. One of Cooper's lesser known novels (*The Wept of Wish-Ton-Wish: A Tale,* 2 vols. [New York, 1829]) focused directly on Puritan New England and the dilemmas of captivity and assimilation, and one of his better known (*The Last of the Mohicans*) was strongly influenced by the captivity theme.

71. *A Week on the Concord and Merrimack Rivers* (Boston, 1896), 426-427. For an interesting and provocative analysis of the Hannah Dustan story and how it fits into the American literary canon, see Leslie A. Fiedler, *The Return of the Vanishing American* (New York, 1968), 98-108.

72. *The Confidence-Man: His Masquerade,* ed. Elizabeth S. Foster (New York, 1954), 163-171.

Lorrayne Carroll (essay date 1996)

SOURCE: Carroll, Lorrayne. "'My Outward Man': The Curious Case of Hannah Swarton." *Early American Literature* 31, no. 1 (winter 1996): 45-73.

[*In the following essay, Carroll investigates Cotton Mather's underlying message in his account of Hannah Swarton's abduction, comparing it to Mary Rowlandson's narrative.*]

> Properly an instrument is an efficient cause moved by the principal to an effect above its proper virtue.
>
> *Oxford English Dictionary*[1]

Writing begins with an awareness of the person, not as an individual but rather as a social category.

Jonathan Goldberg, *Writing Matter*

In the conjunction of images of captivity, gender, and authorship found in women's captivity narratives, representations of power, powerlessness, and social authority exist in a dynamic relationship to one another. For example, Increase Mather endorses Mary Rowlandson's narrative,[2] *The Sovereignty and Goodness of GOD . . . ,*[3] to give evidence of divine "dispensation" and thereby asserts his prerogative as minister to grant legitimacy (his "dispensation") to her suspect undertaking, publication. However, it is Rowlandson herself, moving across the New England landscape, and finally encountering King Philip, who earns the experiential authority to speak to the public—to publish—the particulars and the consequences of her captivity. Divine and ministerial authority depend on the singular female who recounts her exceptional tale to spread the news of providence at work in the New England wilderness. Increase Mather's "Preface" therefore seeks to recontain Rowlandson's authority under the rubric "dispensation" and place her safely back within the fold.

It is important to note that Rowlandson's journey begins and ends within the pale of Puritan practices. Although Lancaster is an outpost settlement, Rowlandson's husband is the minister for the community. And Rowlandson returns to Boston, where her story is published.[4] Thus, with all her removes, Mary Rowlandson's journey terminates in the heart of New England Puritan culture.[5] She spent the entire captivity among the Narragansetts in the wilderness, and her captivity had lasted approximately three months, an excruciatingly long time for her, but not nearly as long as other captivities. And Rowlandson was never installed in a French Canadian household, a fate that befell many subsequent captives. We may view her text as the preeminent example of the genre because, not only is it the first of its type and relatively long, but also its dramatic rendering of physical hardship and mental anguish produces rich images of the conditions of captivity. However, an examination of those captivity narratives published in the last years of the seventeenth century reveals that *The Sovereignty and Goodness of God* offers later writers not so much a model to emulate as a template against which to measure differences.

In these differences, stresses in Puritan culture reveal themselves. Reading for the ways that subsequent female captivity narratives vary from Rowlandson's (and on occasion echo it), we can recognize several cultural preoccupations. The texts address prescribed gender roles (and their corollary, the fashioning of a "reputation") as well as fears concerning the vulnerability of northern borders to Indian and French attack. Variations and circumstances of publication—including date of publication, accompanying or embedding texts, attributions of authorship, and contemporary contextualizing documents—demonstrate that the female captivity narratives depict an array of issues: shrinking spheres of Puritan influence (and lax practices in the

spheres purported to be properly constituted congregations), control of historiography (especially the writing of New England history), and the wars against the French (with the implicit threats of "papistry"). This catalogue of dread illustrates the broad context of the Puritan "errand into the wilderness."

Understanding the importance of gender in these narratives allows us to examine the "errand," especially as it attempted to construct a coherent society by instruction. Since instructional texts were crucial to shaping the culture, authorship offered a powerful instrument to those, like the Mathers, who held positions of authority. Authorship represented both a great burden—truthfully to display working providence—and a great avenue to power as a participant in cultural formation. That power in the hands of the traditionally quiescent female sector of the congregation posed specific problems for the ministers who saw the instructional potential in captivity but also the danger in allowing a woman to assert a public authority.[6]

Circumscriptions governing female authorship permitted spiritual leaders to reconfigure the female author, from *subject* of her narrative to *object* used for instructional purposes. This reconfiguration is achieved through the concepts of dispensation and reputation, terms that provide flexibility in dealing with the problem of the public, published woman. A goodwife superseding the bounds of home and hearth requires explanation and exculpation; thus Increase Mather preemptively defends Mary Rowlandson's propriety: "and therefore though this gentlewoman's modesty would not thrust it into the press, yet her gratitude unto God made her not hardly persuadable to let it pass, that God might have his due glory, and others benefit by it as well as herself" (320). He first emphasized that captivity can only be appreciated thoroughly by those who have suffered it and then goes on to argue that such captivity indicates divine dispensation. Through Mather's interpretation, the personal experience is transformed into a providential sign for all to read, or at least for all to understand. Here lies the justification for publication: because the text dramatizes God's mercy, specifically the spectacular form it takes in the New England forests, it warrants dissemination as example. This fact precedes all others, including the sex of the author. The dual definitions of dispensation, in its Puritan construction, allow for such elasticity. As both a system of divine ordering and a license for exceptional cases, dispensation provides a sense of God's plan, albeit not completely revealed, coupled with the concept that the plan is made (partially) visible through the unique experience of the individual, especially if the experience is itself unusual.[7] Thus ministers like Mather can control the persuasive power of an author both personally exorbitant and with a unique story to tell, making her an instrument of their ends.

This combination of divine and ministerial authority, turning on the concepts of dispensation and reputation, can be found operating in subsequent captivity narratives attributed to women. When both God and a Mather interest themselves in a woman's text, there is certainly much at stake for Puritan culture. The instrumentality of the female author provides unique opportunities for lessons that exceed spiritual instruction and encompass larger issues of political and social import.[8] Thus the figure of the woman captive who returns to write her story demonstrates not only the means by which Puritan ideologies can refashion the geographical/political frontiers but also the cultural frontiers demarcating private/public discourse. In this way the female author disrupts the conventional scene of public witness: the previously silenced woman not only testifies to personal salvation, but she does it in the broadest possible manner, the printed text.

Emerging into the public realm, a woman relies on her reputation, as well as a minister's testament, to grant her publication a *nihil obstat*. In Rowlandson's case, her reputation derives not only from her husband's position in Lancaster but also, as Teresa A. Toulouse indicates, from her own socially privileged family, the Whites.[9] If a woman's dispensation to publish depends, at least initially, on the theological project of interpreting God's plan, then attestations to her good reputation clearly signal the much more temporal issue of class distinction. The two concepts are manipulated by the sponsoring clergy to fashion an apt instructional instrument legitimized by providential and secular authority.

This authority, indeed cultural prominence, of the Mathers throughout the seventeenth and early eighteenth century arises from several factors that include their position as leading clergymen, practical politicking, longevity, and, not least, their prolific publication. The topics of these publications vary, from printed execution sermons to treatises on comets or the efficacy of inoculations against smallpox; both Increase and Cotton Mather wrote on a range of issues that extended beyond particular theological concerns. Diary entries by Cotton Mather testify to his almost obsessive concern with his own authorial practices and with publication; they indicate that Mather saw himself as an instrument and his writing as a means to further the work of Providence on earth.

Some of Mather's diary entries illustrate the collapse of distinctions between "private" writing—such as redactions of sermons made by congregants and brought home to be read to the family—with "public" writing—understood as the publication by printing press of texts meant for wide circulation. Particularly, emphasis on the trope of instrumentality confounds a reading of strictly bound realms of private and public. In the long entry for 20 August 1697, Mather records a day "sett apart, for the Exercises of a secret THANKSGIVING before the Lord" (Cotton Mather, *Diary* 1:226). Having first confessed his "horrible Sinfulness," he writes: "I then solemnly declared unto the Lord, that I made *Choice* of this, as my *chief Happiness,* to bee a Servant of my Lord JESUS CHRIST, and an Instrument of His Glory" (*Diary* 1:227). He follows this declaration with a catalogue of reasons for thanksgiving. The "one special Article" is God's support for finishing what will

become the (never published) *Biblia Americana,* here called "my CHURCH-HISTORY": "I will in this Place, transcribe a few Lines of my Introduction to that History" (*Diary* 1:229). Thus the private diary receives a transcription of the (proposed) public document, and its introduction is embedded within the personal accounts of Mather's daily life where he records his determination to act on God's behalf. Writing, both private and public, represents an essential instrumentality, an exalted endeavor in which Christ is coauthor and for which Mather acts as both author and publisher.[10]

Authorship, for Mather, is simultaneously the act of an instrument and the instrument itself.[11] So, the public document signed at Mather's behest by the contentious members of the Watertown church represents both the means and the sign of reconciliation:

> I did endeavour to do service, (especially, at miserable *Watertown,* bringing the People in the east part of that poor Town, to sign an Instrument, wherein they confessed the Errors of their late Actions, and promised by the Help of Christ, a regular Behaviour; and otherwise helping the Council that mett there).
>
> (*Diary* 1:235)

This doubled function of the authorial instrument—tool and testament—collapses the public and private realms. With divine guidance, Mather expresses his interior life to provide teachings and models for the public. Although all authors convert private thought into public expression, Mather's conception of instrumentality *conflates* his private thoughts with divine intention. The provenance of these expressions—his sermons, histories, biographies, and reportage of current events—explicitly appears as God, the First Author, with Mather as temporal author/instrument. Authorship therefore is the public rendering of a providential agenda privately revealed to Mather as willing recipient of divine favor—"His favouring mee, with the *Liberty of the Press*" (*Diary* 1:228).

Among the stratagems Mather chose in publishing his divinely inspired texts were anonymity and pseudonymity. In *To the People of New England,* the opening address of *Decennium Luctuosum,* Mather argues for his own anonymity as the author of his history of the ten-year-war with Northeast tribes. However, the text includes a sermon delivered by him the previous September. He then elaborates on the conceit of anonymity by aligning his hand with God's, effectively making himself the instrument of divine revelation:

> I pray, Sirs, Ask no further; Let this Writing be, like that on the Wall to Belshazzar, where the Hand only was to be seen, and not who'se it was. The History is compiled with Incontestable Veracity; and since there is no Ingenuity in it, but less than what many Pens in the Land might Command, he knows not why his Writing Anonymously may not Shelter him from the Inconveniencies of having any Notice, one way or other, taken of him.
>
> (*Decennium* 181)

The purposes of this (false) anonymity, couched in terms of reticence and, especially, humility, are obscured by claims of "Incontestable Veracity," an assertion that "the Author pretends that the famous History of the Trojan War it self comes behind our little History of the Indian War" and most directly by the invocation of the Biblical hand of God as a simile for the authorial hand. Thus the instrument and the power which it serves become one, and given Mather's strongly idiosyncratic style the authorship could hardly be in question for most who read this "anonymous" history, even had they been absent from the original sermon.

Mather's convoluted approach to authorship—his alternate claims, denials, and demurrals—achieves its most peculiar form in the captivity narrative of Hannah Swarton. Appended to his 1697 printed sermon *Humiliations follow'd by Deliverances,* the Swarton narrative stands at the end of a work detailing the tribulations of captives from the continuing skirmishes with the tribes along the frontiers. It is textually distinct from the body of the sermon, literally designated an appendix; like Mary Rowlandson's *The Sovereignty and Goodness of God,* the Swarton narrative is written in the first person. The story portrays a Hannah Swarton whose startling—and suspicious—capacity for theological debate indicates her exceptional grasp of subtle doctrinal positions, noteworthy in a frontier woman. And the curious dialogue this narrative conducts with the larger text that precedes it (and, to some extent, with Rowlandson's narrative) demonstrates some uses of the female author both within the Mather canon and within the broader sphere of New England Puritan literature. In these respects, the Swarton narrative avoids the tensions resulting from what Tara Fitzpatrick calls the "dueling textual voices" of the narrator and "the established ministers, who vied with the returned captives for authorial control of their narratives." As she convincingly argues, "The women captives' ministerial sponsors sought, with decreasing success, to interpret the individual experiences of the captives as lessons directed at the entire community, regardless of the captives' own implicit resistance to such appropriation."[12] But Mather's complete authorial appropriation of Hannah Swarton's "I" produces a new set of tensions, ambiguities, and images that speak more to *representations* of female authorship and the author's reputation than to the exceptional condition of the returned captive and her need to tell her own story.

Hannah Swarton left no personal records apart from the alleged narrative of her captivity. Her name appears in the list of redeemed captives presented by Mathew Cary to the Council of the Massachusetts Bay Province in October of 1695.[13] There, she is named "Johana Swarton" from the town of York. As Emma Coleman notes, there are several errors in the hometown ascriptions of the various captives, and from the *Narrative* we know that Hannah Swarton resided in Casco ([now Portland, Maine] Coleman 1:74). Margaret Stilson, who was "in the same house with

[Swarton]" was redeemed by Cary as well, although Col. Tyng and Mr. Alden, mentioned as part of the displaced English in Quebec, were not on the list of redeemed captives.[14]

The historical record of Hannah Swarton,[15] then, exists in the Cary list and the appendix to Cotton Mather's 1697 text, *A Brief Discourse On the MATTER and METHOD, Of that HUMILIATION which would be an Hopeful Symptom of our Deliverance from Calamity. Accompanied and Accommodated with A NARRATIVE, of a Notable Deliverance lately Received by some English Captives, From the Hands of Cruel Indians. And some Improvement of that Narrative. Whereto is added A Narrative of Hannah Swarton, containing a great many wonderful passages, relating to her Captivity and Deliverance.*[16] According to the testimony of the "Narrative," Hannah Swarton moved to the Casco settlement from Beverly, and as such, lived outside the "public ordinances" of Puritan polity. This lack of ministerial control differentiated most Maine settlers from other captives, who, exposed though they were in the frontier towns such as Haverhill and Lancaster, had benefit of established congregations (Ulrich 175-80). Indeed, the inhabitants of the Province of Maine historically had been a thorn in the side of the Massachusetts Province, not only aligning themselves with the Crown in the uprising of 1688 but then also petitioning King William for "assistance and protection" against the Massachusetts rebels.[17] Maine had a bad reputation as a region of outlaws, "ungospelized plantations"[18] and, corollary to that, Catholic sympathizers—a thicket of renegade settlers requiring the firm hand of congregationalist discipline. The settlements in Maine did not function as proper frontier buffers; instead, they represented the threat of a porous, exposed, vulnerable array of backsliding or areligious English communities, established to trade with the Indians and French rather than congregated around an ordained minister (such as Lancaster was under Joseph Rowlandson). Both the political and religious concerns with these outlying settlements emerge in Mather's portrait of Hannah Swarton.

In his bibliography of Cotton Mather's works, Thomas Holmes notes that the Swarton narrative

> printed for the first time in *Humiliations,* is told, unlike the [Hannah] Dustan account, in the first person. Evidently Cotton Mather was Hannah Swarton's "ghost writer." The narrative is printed entirely without quotation marks. The story is told with rich and intimate details of Swarton's experience, but the text of it in polished prose, embellished with Biblical references, allusions, and illustrations, with occasional moralizings in the true Matherian manner, is clearly Mather's.
>
> (Holmes 2:492)[19]

Holmes notices the affiliation between the stories of the two Hannahs who appear in *Humiliations,* Duston (variously spelled, "Dustin," and "Dustan") and Swarton. Although the Swarton text

> was advertised in *Tulley's Almanack* for 1697 as a part of an intended publication entitled *Great Examples of Judgment and Mercy,* that work was probably not

printed. . . . We know that the Swarton Narrative as it appears in *Humiliations* was printed with this work and does not consist of sheets printed with and transferred from any other work, for the Narrative begins on signature E2, while the leaf E1 contains the last two pages connected with the Hannah Dustan Narrative.

(Holmes 1:498 n. 6)

Mather includes Duston's heroic escape from her captors in the primary text but appends "Swarton's" relation as a cautionary tale of the spiritual perils of frontier life in an "ungospelized plantation." Whereas Duston's experiences emphasize her divine "deliverance" and Mather celebrates her heroism, Swarton is most clearly marked out for "humiliations." As Mather's instrument for instruction, the Swarton narrative administers a warning to those choosing to live "outside the public ordinances"; more significantly, it baldly reveals Mather's use of authorial prerogatives. By "ghosting" for Hannah Swarton, Mather can become her, simultaneously representing her experiences and projecting himself *as Hannah* into the Northern wilderness and the parlors of the papists.

Diary entries for the autumn of 1696 illuminate Mather's motives for publishing Swarton's story. His entry for 2 October describes a "secret Fast" practiced "Especially to obtain Mercy for this Land in its deplorable Circumstances, and a mighty Revolution upon the Kingdomes of Great *Britain* and upon the *French* Empire" (*Diary* 1:205). Again, on 10 October he keeps a day of prayer for "Captives in the hands of cruel Enemies" with the resulting "Newes that came the Day following, of several Persons, escaped out of the Hands of the Indians" (*Diary* 1:206). Mather's interest in the captives forms part of his larger political concerns. When he prays, his personal spiritual needs often align with the Colony's more global interests: he "wrestled with the Lord" to obtain the knowledge that "a mighty Convulsion shall bee given to the *French* Empire; and that *England, Scotland,* and *Ireland,* shall bee speedily Illuminated, with glorious Anticipations of the *Kingdome of God*" (*Diary* 1:207). For Mather, indeed, the personal (and, therefore, spiritual) is the political (and, therefore, historical).

The diary notes as well Hannah Swarton's place in this expansive scheme. Eager to make use of "the terrible Disasters wherewith *some* are afflicted," Mather prepares for publication

> a *Collection* of terrible and barbarous Things undergone by some of our *English Captives* in the Hands of the *Eastern Indians.* And I annexed hereunto, a memorable *Narrative* of a good Woman, who relates in a very Instructive Manner, the Story of her own *Captivity* and *Deliverance.* . . . Yea, I could not easily contrive, a more significant Way, to pursue these Ends; not only, in respect of the *Nature* of the Book itself, which is *historical* as well as *theological*; but also, in respect of its coming into all Corners of the Countrey, and being read with a greedy Attention."

(*Diary* 1:210)[20]

The "who relates" would seem to indicate that Swarton herself composed this text, at least orally giving it some kind of narrative form, but as Holmes asserts and an examination of the text's style and content demonstrates, the printed text is Mather's composition. The emphasis on the story's instructional use and on Mather's contrivance to publish something read with "greedy Attention" reveals the value of novelty in a woman's text, particularly as a magnet for public notice. "Historical" and "theological," and purportedly produced by a captive woman, this captivity narrative provides Mather with ample opportunity to pursue his "Ends."

His choice to impersonate Hannah Swarton rather than employ the third person depends for its success on the concepts of dispensation and reputation, the same terms anchoring the Rowlandson narrative, and here reconfigured to suit the circumstances of Swarton's 1690 Maine captivity. The dispensation is formal, inhering in the narrative's function as an appendix to the sermon; the text itself requires no apologia because its publication is literally contextualized. Reputation, however, is a more complicated matter, and this key issue enables Mather to write in the first person as Hannah Swarton. Unlike Mary Rowlandson, "gentlewoman" wife of a Lancaster minister, Swarton lives in a free-floating society without the rigid hierarchies in which "reputation" has meaning. Indeed, as far as Boston is concerned, Hannah Swarton has no reputation—until Mather confers one. In impersonating Swarton, Mather chooses a castaway from the Maine woods, a woman whose personal value in the Puritan hierarchy is insignificant. The text thus recognizes conventions of both gender and class. Women—hidden in their homes, bound to obedience—and settlers without name or fortune (especially, those who are not members of established congregations) are blanks. Their invisibility in Puritan society makes them perfect tablets upon which ministers such as Mather can inscribe meaning and position.

If Mary Rowlandson tries in her narrative to recuperate her social "credit" by publishing her sufferings, the Swarton text never addresses the anxieties Rowlandson displays, especially about returning to Puritan society. This is because Hannah Swarton's "credit" is identical with her text, both invented by Cotton Mather. He simultaneously constructs a reliable, reputable witness *and* her narrative, one "instrument" in the conflated Matherian sense of agent and document. The fiction of her authorship succeeds because the actual Hannah Swarton is a social nonentity and her experiences produce a tale of humiliation and deliverance that dramatizes the lessons of the sermon. To that end, Mather employs the figure of Swarton to illustrate the points of his homily.

Humiliations begins appropriately with an image of Old Testament punishment, a scourging, and emphasizes the "Instrument, every stroke whereof gave *Three* Lashes to the Delinquent" (*Humiliations* 3). Close reading of the text demonstrates that Hannah Swarton performs the dual role of delinquent and instrument for the readers of the printed sermon; she is both sinner and means of redemption because, in confessing her sins and properly suffering for them, she provides a completed figure of the redemptive process by which the reader can "lay by" the lesson. As Mather asks at the outset, "What signifies confession without reformation?" (*Humiliations* 14), and the re-formed Swarton embodies deliverance—after humiliation.

The sermon was "preached at the Boston Lecture on Thursday, May 6, 1697" and a "public fast was observed a week later" (Holmes 2:488). As a jeremiad, it called for a fast to address the "*Sad Catalogue* of *Provocations*" (*Humiliations* 7) by which the population had angered the Lord and thereby drawn down his wrath. These provocations included twenty offenses, ranging from apostasy to "the woful Decay of good *Family Discipline*" (*Humiliations* 9). There is little attempt to classify the sins by degree of severity, so that the "multitudes" castigated for being unregenerate are listed along with the problems evinced by "a *Flood* of *Excessive Drinking*." *Humiliations* thereby stands as a compendium of ministerial anxieties that predictably encompass both spiritual and social issues, personal salvation and cultural conformity.

For example, in opening the text of 2 Chronicles 12:7 ("When the Lord saw, that they humbleth themselves, the Word of the Lord came unto Shemajah, saying, They have humbled themselves, I will not destroy them, but I will grant them some deliverance"), the second lesson describes the necessity of regular fasting, a duty not practiced "often enough" by the Church in New England. "Like Silly Children we know not when to *Feed,* and when to Forbear *Feeding.* But our Good God, in His Word ha's taught us!" (*Humiliations* 23). This theme is retrieved in the Swarton appendix with an ironic twist.

> For the first Times while the Enemy feasted on our English Provisions, I might have had some with them: but then I was so filled with *Sorrow* and *Tears,* that I had little *Stomach* to Eat; and when my *Stomach* was come, our English Food was spent, and the Indians wanted themselves, and we more: So that then I was pined with want.
>
> (*Humiliations* 52)

Swarton, "Like a Silly Child," represents not only the extreme of enforced fasting, but also the wilful behavior of someone who succumbs to her emotions rather than attending to her needs. As well, Swarton's "want of Cloathing" and insufficient covering so that she is "pinched with Cold," aggressively answers the sermon's call to put aside "Gay Cloaths" for "*Sober, Modest, Proper, and very Humble*" attire and symbolizes the chastisement due to "*Churches* [who] fall asleep till they are stript of their Garments" (*Humiliations* 26, 34).

The preeminent icon of *Humiliations* is the *Judea capta* motif. As Annette Kolodny notes, "New England divines were quick to seize upon the emblematic, *typick* features inherent in the increasing incidence of captivity" (Kolodny 20). Mather recalls a tradition of coins made in commemoration of the Roman conquest of Israel, then contextualizes it with one of his favorite scriptural representations of womanhood, the Daughter of Zion: "*She being Desolate, shall sit upon the Ground*" (*Humiliations* 31). As in Mather's 1692 sermon-cum-conduct book, *Ornaments for the Daughters of Zion,* the Church (here, synonymous with "*New-England*") is again "figured by a woman."[21] Translated from Israel to the northern woods, Judea no longer leans against a palm tree:

> Alas, If poor *New-England,* were to be shown upon her old Coin, we might show her *Leaning* against her Thunder-struck *Pine tree, Desolate, sitting upon the Ground.* Ah! *New England!* Upon how many Accounts, mayst thou say with her, in Ruth 1.13. *The Hand of the Lord is gone out against me!*
>
> (*Humiliations* 31)

Mather reprises the woman/tree figure in the appendix, creating the image of Hannah Swarton, "pined with want," "pined to Death with Famine," and exhausted to the point of utter resignation, "so that many times I thought I could go no further, but must ly down, and if they would kill me, let them kill me."

Yet Swarton "held out with them," sturdily marching, outlasting poor John York who, weakening under duress, was killed by the Indians. Significantly, the only people who die in this narrative are men; women prevail throughout. The absence of men in the Indian captivity section of the Swarton text echoes their absence from the sermon (excepting the brief allusion to Thomas Duston's escape from the Haverhill attack). Mather closes the theological section of the sermon with a question: "Now, who can tell, how far one *Humble Soul,* may prevail, that shall put in Suit, the *Sacrifice for the Congregation?*" (*Humiliations* 39). The answer sat in front of him at the lecture in the person of Hannah Duston. Her trials readily provide the conclusion to the sermon proper and her actions and experiences, in many ways, determine the figuration of Hannah Swarton.

The relationship of the two Hannahs is crucial to an understanding of what is at stake in the authorship of the Swarton narrative. In dialogue with the sermon, the Swarton text recontains the image of a woman superseding her role, that depicted by the heroic, yet murderous, Duston, who killed and scalped her captors. The entire "Appendix" immediately follows the Duston passage, which is itself part of the sermon but distinctly bound within quotation marks. As well as creating a passive counter to the active Duston, the first-person Swarton text purports to be Hannah's version of her own experiences, a simultaneous claim to authenticity and immediacy. The Duston story, however, is removed from this immediacy graphically, by the quotation marks (that reveal it to be someone else's version of the events), and grammatically, by its third-person narration.

Indeed, the title-page of *Humiliations* refers to the Duston escape tale as "A NARRATIVE, Of a Notable Deliverance lately Received by some English Captives, From the Hands of Cruel Indians, And some *Improvement* of that *Narrative.*"[22] Hannah Duston may have initiated her own escape, but at the Boston Lecture she heard her own exploits narrated back to her, recontextualized—"improved"—by Mather, her exceptional behavior reconfigured for the purposes of the sermon. Hannah Swarton, captured, sold to the French, and ransomed back to Boston, represents not only the more common fate of the captive, but also the value of passivity. That is, Duston is transformed from an active subject to a passive object, while Swarton, passive sufferer, becomes the narrator of her own story, the speaking subject. Female resistance in any form must be contained: Swarton is ascribed the unusual role of author precisely because she is a nonresisting woman, humiliated by her sins, whose reputation is manufactured then manipulated for its instructional value. The image of the passive woman, even one writing her own story, is the example that really closes the printed version of the sermon.

* * *

The juxtaposition of Hannah Duston and Hannah Swarton speaks to the problem of redeeming the captive woman from her position out of bounds, again a question of dispensation and reputation. Duston's dispensation for her lethal actions relies both on her extraordinary deliverance and on her position outside the law: "and being where she had not her *own Life* secured by any *Law* unto her, she thought she was not forbidden by any *Law,* to take away the *Life* of the *Murderers,* by whom her *Child* had been butchered" (*Humiliations* 46), and her reputation is made upon her return by the acclaim she receives.[23] The repetition of "Law" and emphasis on her child's murder surely means to justify Duston's actions. But for those in the congregation who recall the trial of 1693, the line reverberates with the fate of Duston's sister Elizabeth Emerson, who was executed for killing her illegitimate infant. Mather's personal connection to Emerson is noteworthy because he not only preached the sermon on her execution day, but he later published that sermon with "a pathetical *Instrument*" "obtained from the young Woman."[24] Although one was punished and the other praised, the significant characteristic shared by the sisters is a capacity for violence, indeed, murder. In light of Elizabeth Emerson's story, Mather's transformation of Duston from active deliverer to passive listener becomes more urgent: Duston's killings require exculpation, divorcing her (frighteningly similar) behavior from her sister's.

Symbolically, however, Hannah Duston's exorbitant actions are redeemed through the representation of the later Hannah, Swarton. Referring to a Biblical figure, the sermon asserts that Duston and her companion Mary Neff, "do like another *Hannah,* in *pouring out their Souls before the Lord*" (*Humiliations* 45). The concatenation of Hannahs creates an affiliation, from the Old Testament to Duston to Swarton, with Duston set off by the figures who "pour out their souls." The Hannah of *I Samuel* supplicates the priest Eli, and Swarton asks forgiveness while recounting her wilderness experiences: they reach out to the elders for de-

liverance. Thus an implicit comparison is set up between the two New England Hannahs. The "Improvement" following Duston's story, directed at Duston, Neff, and Lennardson, makes it clear that none of the escapees had publicly confessed the *spiritual* experience of redemption.[25] So, Mather admonishes them, "You will seriously consider, *What you shall render to the Lord for all His Benefits?*" (*Humiliations* 49); Hannah Swarton's narrative, which contains her testimony of spiritual redemption, concludes with that same text. Swarton therefore recuperates the as yet unregenerate Duston by providing the image of a woman who undergoes conversion during her captivity, thus making her first-person narrative worthy of dispensation and producing her new reputation. That is, if Duston's experience is noteworthy because it represents divine intercession resulting in her physical redemption, Swarton's story displays the greater providence of a religious conversion. So, female captivity permits a broad range of behaviors as long as the woman ends firmly ensconced in the ministerial text, recaptured for Puritan instruction.

In this respect, the Swarton text improves on previous captivity stories, particularly Mary Rowlandson's. Cotton Mather authorizes his own work by obviously alluding to the popular 1682 text introduced by Increase Mather. Mather goes one better than his father, however, not merely writing a preface, but actually composing the entire text. And, in following Rowlandson, Mather concludes the Swarton narrative with the same scripture (Psalms 116.12) Increase Mather uses in his Preface:

> To conclude: whatever any coy fantasies may deem, yet it highly concerns those that have so deeply tasted, how good the Lord is, to enquire with David, *What shall I render to the Lord for all his benefits to me.* Psalms 116.12.
>
> (*Rowlandson* 321)

On several levels, "A Narrative of Hannah Swarton" becomes a condensed version of *The Sovereignty and Goodness of God,* with language and images abbreviated, telescoped, and combined in a rush to get to the crucial encounter with French Catholics. For example, Mary Rowlandson's twenty "Removes" reduce to Swarton's "Thus I continued with them, hurried up and down the Wilderness, from *May* 20, till the middle of *February*" (*Humiliations* 52-53). Where Rowlandson remained in the wilderness with the Indians from February 1675/6 to May 1676, Swarton's captivity lasted five years, from May 1690 to November 1695, largely spent in Canada. (She arrived "in sight of some French houses" in February 1690/91). Yet the Rowlandson narrative is a book-length text, running to seventy-three pages in its 1682 Cambridge edition, while the Swarton "Appendix" is only twenty-one pages long.

The popularity of Rowlandson's narrative may have been reason enough for Mather's translation of some of its elements into his own publication. In recalling many features of the Rowlandson text, Mather at once asserts the primacy of *The Sovereignty and Goodness of God* and establishes the female captivity narrative as a genre with standard images: privation in the woods, loss of kin, spiritual conversion. Mather's reiteration of his father's scriptural quotation both in the Duston section and the Swarton appendix signals another, less obvious but potent, component of the emerging form: whether the text is prefaced by a minister or actually written by one, the (purported) authors depend on the sponsoring ministers for the dispensation to publish. The Rowlandson text, with Increase Mather's preface and Joseph Rowlandson's closing sermon, gives Cotton Mather a model for ministerial publication that he quite capably wholly inhabits.[26]

Both indirectly and directly quoting Rowlandson's narrative, Mather provides a shorthand, recognizable digest of wilderness suffering en route to Quebec. But Indian captivity is not the focus of the Swarton narrative. Hannah Swarton's main adversaries are not her captors, the murderers of her husband and son, but the French who imperil her immortal soul. The distinction between Swarton's relationship with the Indians and that with the French can even be traced in the narrative's disposition of pronouns: at times "we" refers to the English captives, at times to Swarton and her Indian captors, but "we" never comprehends the French. Unlike Mary Rowlandson, who resented her Indian mistress, and Hannah Duston, who killed two men, two women, and six children, Hannah Swarton seems sometimes even to appreciate her captors. She is often left alone with her Indian mistress, and the two fend for themselves, subsisting on a maggoty moose liver or contacting a canoe of squaws who give Swarton a roasted eel. The spiritual bond she will later form in Quebec with Margaret Stilson is foreshadowed in this earlier connection with the Indian women who tend to her mortal needs.

The brevity of the Indian captivity section allows Mather to acknowledge the physical dangers of life on the frontier on his way to the real matter at hand: emphasizing the spiritual traps awaiting English settlers placed in proximity to French Catholics. As well, the narrative exposes the failures of the English missionary project when Swarton's "Indian Mistress" declares "That had the English been as careful to instruct her in our Religion, as the French were, to instruct her in theirs, she might have been of our Religion" (*Humiliations* 55). But the problem of proselytizing Indians is only incidental to Mather's immediate project of castigating, and besting, the French.

His "Appendix" consists of nine paragraphs, and by the third, Swarton has arrived in Quebec. The majority of scriptural quotations occur in the French section of the narrative. For example, only three short passages, from Ezekiel, Jeremiah, and Job, appear in the text until the narrative approaches Swarton's first encounter with the French. As if bolstering her faith in preparation for that "trial," lengthier interpolations from Psalms and Job remind Swarton of her spiritual and physical humiliation, and the paragraph ends with an attestation of their efficacy: "And by many other Scriptures, that were brought to

my Remembrance, was I instructed, directed and comforted" (*Humiliations* 59). These quotations presage Swarton's remarkable facility in recalling scripture during religious debate, where she parries with the French Catholics who besiege her soul.

This passage reveals just how far Mather will stretch the captivity conventions to suit his agenda. Whereas the Rowlandson text, in general, confined itself to Rowlandson's personal spiritual and psychological matters, Mather uses the Swarton narrative to address contemporary social and political concerns. Removed from the wilderness, safe from the Indian captors, Swarton finds herself serving in a French household but under pressure "to Turn *Papist.*" She is threatened with deportation to France, where she would be burned; this threat serves Mather's aim of demonizing the French and increases the dramatic effect when Swarton challenges her captors on their own theology:

> For their Praying to *Angels,* they brought the History of the *Angel,* that was sent to the Virgin *Mary,* in the First of *Luke.* I answered them, from *Rev.* 19.10 and 22.9. They brought *Exod.* 17.11 of *Israels* prevailing, while *Moses* held up his Hands. I told them, we must come to God only by Christ, Joh. 6[.] 37, 44. For *Purgatory,* they brought Mat. 5.25. I told them, To agree with God while here on *Earth,* was, to *Agree with our Adversary in the way*; and if we did not, we should be Cast *into Hell,* and should not come out until we *Paid the utmost Farthing,* which could never be paid.

> (*Humiliations* 63-64)

Surprisingly adept at arguing doctrinal subtleties, "Hannah Swarton" functions most obviously here as Mather's instrument, proving the superiority of Puritan doctrine and practices over Catholic. The text itself nods toward the improbability of an unconverted frontier woman triumphing in theological argument with "the Nuns, the Priests, Friars, and the rest" (*Humiliations* 62). After this breathtaking scholarly fusillade from both sides, the narrator confesses "But it is bootless for me, a poor Woman, to acquaint the World, with what Arguments I used, if I could now Remember them; and many of them are slipt out of my memory" (*Humiliations* 64). Hannah Swarton triumphs because she has God (and Cotton Mather) on her side. Her French adversaries are doomed to fail in the face of such truth and power. That she is "a poor Woman" only makes the victory more compelling because she excels in a man's realm, with the sanction—and considerable scriptural knowledge—of a Puritan divine.

However, the indictment of Hannah Swarton's memory after so sharp a demonstration of its facility—literally citing chapter and verse to counter the Catholics—subverts the debate's authenticity and, ultimately, the very authority for the text, her remembrances. The authorial—and authoritative—voice falters here, perhaps retreating from that frightening Hutchinsonian image of the woman preacher, and reveals the fiction of the historical Hannah Swarton's authorship. From the description of her arrival in Quebec, we know that Hannah could not speak French, yet her skills improve dramatically so that she can hold forth against her enemies. This, and the relentless interpolations of Mather's interests should give the game away for later commentators. However, Fitzpatrick ascribes authorship to both Mather *and* Hannah Swarton, contending that, although "Swarton's narrative conveyed the most absolute submission to the will of God, . . . [it] again conflicted with Mather's interests in transcribing her story" (Fitzpatrick 17).[27] It is difficult to see a conflict of interests, given that the narrative produces not only a redeemed soul, but also representations of religious declension, missionary failure, French coercion, Indian brutality, the dangers of life outside Puritan polity: all images and themes Mather consistently employed to critique the political and religious establishments in Boston for administrative laxity in Maine.[28]

A redemption occurring without benefit of the "public ordinances" might seem to certify the exceptionalism of Hannah Swarton.[29] However, in captivity, Swarton does find a "congregation" among the other captives in Quebec. In the midst of spiritual despairs over her own regeneracy, the narrator states "I had gotten an *English Bible,* and other Good Books, by the Help of my Fellow Captives" (*Humiliations* 66). By means of this Bible and meditation, she achieves an understanding of her own salvation and describes it in the conventional language of conversion, noting the "Ravishing Comfort" that fills her and harkening to her previous sinfulness.[30] The group of captured English provides an impromptu reconstruction of basic Puritan practice:

> I found much Comfort, while *I* was among the *French,* by the Opportunities *I* had sometimes to *Read* the Scriptures, and other Good Books, and *Pray* to the Lord in Secret; and the *Conference* that some of us Captives had together, about things of God, and *Prayer* together sometimes; especially, with one that was in the same House with me, *Margaret Stilson.* Then was the Word of God precious to us, and they that *feared the L O R D, spake one to another* of it, as we had Opportunity. And Colonel *Tyng,* and Mr. *Alden,* as they were permitted, did speak to us, to confirm and Strengthen us, in the wayes of the Lord.

> *(Humiliations* 68)

Although neither Tyng nor Alden is an ordained minister, they function as representatives of the ministry in their exhortations to spiritual strength. The women pray together at home, but in the "public" world of the captive congregation, men lead. When the French finally prohibit the gathering, Alden sends a message *"That this was one kind of Persecution, that we must suffer for Christ"* (*Humiliations* 68-69). Thus, as Fitzpatrick notes, captivity "relocat[es] the central experience of trial and redemption" (Fitzpatrick 17), but this narrative does so by reconstituting Puritan community in the "wilderness" of French homes and churches: the text explicitly refers to Swarton's "Captivity, among the *Papists*" (*Humiliations* 69).

In Quebec Swarton is treated well by the French woman from whom she begs provisions and is finally bought by the *"Lady Intendant."* Emphasizing female community reinscribes proper domestic roles, which in themselves render Swarton properly passive. The first part of the narrative depicts Swarton obeying her Indian master and mistress, as when she aids them by gathering berries. When she arrives in Canada, however, this replaying of the Puritan domestic gives way to the pressing concerns of spiritual contest; once in a functioning household, the role changes. As Laurel Thatcher Ulrich notes, Boston ministers saw the threat of Catholicism more deeply troubling than the Indian menace, especially where the captives were women, because "twice as many females as males remained with the [French] enemy." She attributes this behavior to "the primacy of marriage, the influence of religion, and the supportive power of female networks" (Ulrich 208). These networks, explicitly portrayed in the scenes with her Indian mistress and the squaws, disappear once Swarton's captivity with the French becomes the focus of the narrative. Her only female friend in Canada is the Puritan Margaret Stilson.[31]

Indeed, the relatively condensed account of Indian captivity comes to a remarkable conclusion with a spectacular image. When Swarton visits the first European home she has seen in nine months to beg for food, she is given beef, bread, and pork and is expected to return to her captors. "But the Snow being knee deep, and my Legs and Hams very sore, I found it very tedious to Travel; and my sores bled, so that as I Travelled, I might be Tracked by my Blood, that I left behind me on the Snow" (*Humiliations* 60). Immediately after this sentence, Swarton asks to spend the night at the French house, and she never returns to the Indians. Here, the transformation in circumstances that the narrative characterizes as a "Change, as to my *Outward man*" opposed to the *"Inward man"* is marked in blood. In the forest, suffering from scant cover, Swarton bleeds; once in French hands, she is brought to the hospital where she is "Physicked and Blooded" (*Humiliations* 62). The move from external to internal, registered in blood, signals the beginning of her greatest trial. Previously, Swarton's emblematic suffering resonated with other accounts of wilderness captivity. Her blood on the landscape writes the recognizable tale of survival as seen in Rowlandson; in this respect, it metaphorizes female authorship, the fiction of a teller and her (salvational) tale, the marks on the page. The shift from outward to inward "man" actually represents a shift from passive female captive to active male debater; more precisely, Swarton's blood marks the end of Swarton's story and the initiation of Mather's theological *tour de force.*

In this, the Swarton narrative's value as an Indian captivity tale is superseded by the powerful image of English Protestantism conquering French Catholicism. As we have seen, the narrative emphasizes the French aspect of the captivity, not only in the amount of text dedicated to French, as opposed to Indian, captivity, but also in the reconstructed Puritan congregation in the heart of Canada. Swarton's transformation, from passive Indian captive to aggressive theological warrior, indicates that this story, although initially echoing previous captivity narratives, has a different agenda. It is indeed a tale of suffering, conversion, and return. And as a conversion narrative, it reinforces the concept that the greatest battles occur internally, spiritual wrestling in the privacy of the soul. Yet this wrestling is then externalized in the theological debates. Hannah Swarton's fictive authorship thus channels the flow of Puritan instruction, into "Hannah Swarton" then out again to the French, an instrument of Mather in the Canadian wilderness.

As J. M. Bumstead notes in his study of colonial captivity narratives, "Because of the emphasis on the Indian, it is frequently overlooked that most of the captivity accounts [between 1680 and 1760] record contact with the French" and the frequency of French contact can be seen in Emma Coleman's two-volume study of Canadian captives.[32] Mather's "Appendix" to *Humiliations follow'd with Deliverances* was the first published account of a captive brought to Canada. As I have noted, Swarton's narrative is indebted to the Rowlandson text, but the Swarton account, in turn, dramatizes the concerns of a specifically French captivity that surface in subsequent narratives set in Canada. In so doing, it shifts away from the Indian captivity's focus on the exigencies of wilderness survival. Indeed, no actual wilderness threatens Swarton once she arrives in Quebec, and the anxiety about physical suffering gives way to spiritual turmoil. Civilization (albeit French) offers a test of faith as demanding as the thickets of the north woods. Ardent Puritans like John Williams remain steadfast until deliverance. Others, such as Williams's daughter Eunice and, apparently, Swarton's own daughter, succumb to French influence.[33] Later captivities, particularly those published after the Revolutionary War, negotiated the difficult task of recounting a time when the French, contemporary allies of the new Republic, represented a great threat. Jemima Howe's captivity narrative (1792), for example, is notable for its delicate, even sentimentalized, portrayal of her French captors and was used later as anti-British propaganda.[34]

By 1792, women's publications were more common than in the days of Hannah Swarton. Mather's impersonation relied on the historical and cultural forces shaping gender roles and authorship in 1697. But use of the captivity narrative as anti-French polemic persisted throughout the wars between France and Britain waged during the eighteenth century. The endangered soul, snared by Catholicism, remained a potent icon in the ideological battles fought in the colonies. Cotton Mather, in the guise of Hannah Swarton, established captivity as a genre that not only attacked Indians as brutish heathens but reached into the refined parlors of Quebec to find horrific threats there as well.

"THE WONDERFUL DISPENSATIONS OF HEAVEN"

When Mather turns to history to chronicle ten years of debilitating Indian warfare, he constructs thirty "articles" to illustrate the awful depredations endured by English set-

tlers throughout New England. *Decennium Luctuosum* is a catalogue of horrors, graphically informing readers about scalpings, eviscerations, immolations, and hatchetings. A series of captivity stories appears in the text, including "Article XXV," "*A Notable Exploit; wherein Dux Femina Facti*," the tale of Hannah Duston. Published only two years after *Humiliations,* however, *Decennium* does not include the Swarton text. Mather used his own material from other sources to bolster the book, and the opening "articles" detail early skirmishes on the eastern frontier. It would seem that Hannah Swarton's story, beginning with the attack on Casco, would fit naturally into this scheme. But *Decennium Luctuosum* emphasizes Indian brutality, not French religious coercion. In fact, the final pages of the book portray the fallacies of Quakerism rather than the importunities of French Catholicism. Therefore, although the "Narrative of Hannah Swarton" purports to be an Indian captivity narrative, a personal account of suffering in the hands of the tribes, it is more accurately characterized as a French captivity narrative and theological exercise. As such, Mather rightly excludes it from this historical text, keeping his antipathies focused on the "Nations of Indians."

As self-professed historiography, *Decennium Luctuosum* moves away from earlier homiletic tracts employing current events to demonstrate providential displeasure. The text's obsessive classicism, interpolating more Latin and Greek than scripture, secularizes the project. Here is no sermon to instruct readers in the path of salvation but rather a highly sensationalized register of relentless misery and occasional relief.[35] As history, it required the omniscient authority of third-person narration. In the self-effacing tone adopted at the outset of *Decennium,* Mather states:

> In Truth, I had rather be called a Coward, than undertake my self to Determine the Truth in this matter; but having Armed my self with some good Authority for it, I will Transcribe Two or Three Reports of the matter, now in my Hands, and Leave it unto thy own Determination.

> (*Decennium* 186)

He includes accounts from "a Gentleman of Dover" and "a Gentleman of Casco" that indict not only the Indians but particularly Governor Andros for their roles in fomenting the hostilities. The language of both accounts replicates Mather's own perfervid prose in the introduction and the text following; when he appends a third account, "which was published in September, 1689," it is an excerpt from his own sermon, "Souldiers Counselled and Comforted" (Boston, 1689 [Editor's Note, *Decennium* 190]). Significantly, the "Gentlemen" whose reports are embedded in this Mather text produce an entirely different discourse from the Swarton narrative. Theirs is literally named "Authority" and represents public witness to political events, not personal (and spiritual) experience. So although Mather "transcribes" male authors to support his history, this purloined authorship is contextualized as historical, public, and authoritative: an admitted transcription, not a fictionalized first-person relation.

Mather's final rendition of the "Narrative of Hannah Swarton" appears in 1702 with the publication of *Magnalia Christi Americana*. Having begun its literary life intended for a text never printed, then appearing as an appendix to a sermon, the Swarton passage finally rests among some of Mather's stranger productions. Reprinted in chapter 2 of the sixth book of *Magnalia*, the narrative seems to come full circle. From the unpublished *Great Examples of Judgment and Mercy*, Swarton's story moves to the section designated "Illustrious Discoveries and Demonstrations of The Divine Providence in Remarkable Mercies and Judgments on Many Particular Persons." There are minor, but telling variants between the two versions; for example, the word "them" is more often rendered "'em" in the *Magnalia*, approximating a frontier women's conversation more than the formal discourse of the printed sermon.

The strangest variant occurs near the end of the text where Swarton, having bested the Catholics, resumes her retrospection of scriptural comfort,

> I often thought on the History of the man *Born Blind*; of whom Christ, when His Disciples asked, *Whether this man had Sinned, or his Parents?* answered, *Neither this man, nor his Parents; but this was, that the works of God might be made manifest in him.* So, tho' I had deserved all this, yet I knew not but one Reason, of Gods bringing all these Afflictions and Miseries upon me, and then Enabling me to bear them, was, *That the Works of God might be made manifest.*
>
> (*Humiliations* 70)

Within the Puritan calculus of sins accounted and punished, Swarton "deserved" the miseries she incurs. In *Magnalia,* the word "deserved" becomes "desired" (*Magnalia* 360), signalling a shift from passive suffering to active atonement and utility. If the first version suits Mather's reliance on the required passivity of a woman author as instrument, the second version ups the ante. That is, in moving from a deserving subject to a desiring subject, the instrument becomes a more fit vessel for the lessons offered. The variant represents Hannah Swarton as a *willing* instrument, a self-aware subject for the manifestation of divine providence. Although this would seem to subvert the passivity of the *Humiliations* narrator, the *Magnalia* text offers a Swarton utterly complicit in her abjection. This odd rendition of Swarton's spiritual self-evaluation aptly illustrates a powerful figuration of the female author: one conscious of, and acceding to (indeed, craving), the redemptive use of her publicized figure.

Magnalia recontextualizes Hannah Swarton's story once more. Clearly not of historical value—or it would have been included in the voluminous *Decennium*—the narrative assumes the status of a curiosity, an "extraordinary salvation." *Magnalia*'s Swarton follows descriptions of miraculous rescues and "rare cures," where Mather recounts the tale of dropsical Sarah Wilkinson:

> When she was open'd, there were no bowels to be found in her, except her heart, which was exceeding small, and as it were perboil'd. . . . Other bowels, none could be found: yet in this condition she liv'd a long while, and retain'd her senses to the last.

But we will content ouselves with annexing to these things a narrative of a woman celebrating the wonderful *dispensations* of Heaven.

(*Magnalia* 356)

Proceeding from the amazing hollow woman to Hannah Swarton, the segue seems quirky at best. Yet relegation of the narrative to a passage of "Believe It or Not" sensationalism reveals its oddity even in Mather's estimation. By 1702, over thirty years of intermittent, sometimes acute, Indian battle had made captivity commonplace. Gory, horrific tales fill *Decennium Luctuosum,* and women constitute the majority of sufferers. Without fierce anti-Indian rhetoric, the Swarton narrative cannot perform the ideological work that a story like Duston's can. Nor can its highly stilted version of religious contest, which actually portrays the French as kind, if zealous, missionaries, suffice for the scathing criticisms the continuing warfare requires. Reduced to a conventional spiritual conversion account, the "Narrative of Hannah Swarton" provides insufficient propaganda to warrant reprinting as history or jeremiad. Subject of a text without social utility except as an exhibit in Mather's freak show of remarkables, Hannah Swarton, who never wrote her own story, is an appropriate emblem of his use of female authorship: a hollow woman, filled in by Mather's (divinely directed) hand.

Laurel Thatcher Ulrich describes Hannah Swarton as "the ideal captive" (Ulrich 180). Indeed, Swarton represents the *idealized* captive, Mather's extension into the theological thickets of Catholic Canada, whose "means of . . . Deliverance, were by reason of Letters" (*Humiliations* 71). In staging Hannah Swarton's conversion not in the wild forests of northern New England but the civilized venue of the French Lord-Intendant's home, Cotton Mather literally domesticates the captivity narrative and extends its utility as a device for propaganda against both the French and the Indians. Alluding to the familiar imagery of deprivation, he moves quickly to the more important business of conversion in the face, not of physical suffering, but of religious antagonism. Although she has suffered the grueling journey of winter travel through northern Maine forests and lost her family in the attack, Swarton's gravest concern is arrival in Canada, "for fear lest I should be overcome by them, to yield to their Religion" (*Humiliations* 59). The horrors of Indian attack and near-starvation fade in comparison to the "greater snare" of Catholicism.

Mather both cannily taps popular images of suffering and invents fresh ones like *Judea capta* to assemble his own version of captivity's humiliations. Adopting a woman's voice, he elaborates on the figure of the virtuous woman, extending the instrumental potential for this usually silent segment of the Church. Mather's own complicated engagement with the vicissitudes of authorship allows him to invoke certain expectations about female authors in his readers while simultaneously creating a new use for woman's publication, as a variation on pseudonymity and anonymity. In this, he relies on what Michel Foucault characterizes as the author's "classificatory function." "Such a name," here, the woman's name, Hannah Swarton, "permits one to group together a certain number of texts, define them, differentiate them from and contrast them to others. In addition, it establishes a relationship among the texts" (Foucault 107). Although Hannah Swarton's name appears only once as author, the scarcity of women's texts in the period affiliates "her" relation with Mary Rowlandson's and so claims authenticity only from an extraordinary experience like captivity. This *authenticity* is the prerequisite for female authorship and is differentiated from the *authority* of the male accounts Mather interpolates into *Decennium*; women's publication can only signalize the private experience of deliverance as opposed to the public function of the male writer as historian and reporter.[36] This distinction accounts for the Swarton narrative's absence from Mather's historical productions and its final home in a series of curiosities. "A Narrative of Hannah Swarton" had outlived its usefulness by 1702; as instrument in the vast project of ecclesiastical and secular history, which *Magnalia* attempts to unite, the woman's story remains much too personal, even idiosyncratic, to serve as an entry into the public spectacle of Puritan progress. Appended to the tale of the hollowed-out woman, Hannah Swarton's narrative represents the limits of female authorship's utility for Mather. He never published as a woman again.

Notes

1. From *Baxter's Catholic Theology,* an entry from 1675, in the *Oxford English Dictionary* for "instrument."

2. Increase Mather's authorship of the preface remains unproved. However, several scholars believe that textual evidence supports the premise that Mather was indeed "Ter Amicam" and wrote it (Minter 343 n.; and Derounian 85). Although there is no absolute confirmation for this assumption, I am persuaded by Derounian et al. that Increase Mather is the likely author and, as my argument will demonstrate, his authorship influences Cotton Mather's foray into the captivity narrative form. However, even if Increase Mather were not the author, the Rowlandson Preface stands as a kind of editorial practice whose emphasis on dispensation and reputation recurs in Cotton Mather's works discussed here.

3. I use *The Sovereignty and Goodness of God, together with the Faithfulness of His Promises Displayed; Being a Narrative Of the Captivity and Restoration of Mrs. Mary Rowlandson . . .* in Slotkin and Folsom, because, unlike the *True History,* which was published in London, *Sovereignty* was published and circulated in the Colony.

4. "Our family being now gathered together (those of us that were living) the South Church in Boston hired an house for us: then we removed from Mr. Shepards, those cordial friends, and went to Boston, where we continued about three-quarters of a year: still the Lord went along with us, and provided graciously

for us. I thought it somewhat strange to set up housekeeping with bare walls; but as Solomon says, *Money answers all things*; and that we had through the benevolence of Christian friends, some in this town, and some in that, and others: and some from England, that in a little time we might look, and see the house furnished with love" (364). It is clear from the list of "friends" that the Rowlandsons enjoyed a great deal of support after their trials. The breadth of support, from various towns and from England, speaks to the relative importance of the Rowlandson and White families.

5. The Rowlandson family then moved from Boston to Wethersfield, Connecticut.

6. The Biblical authority derives in part from the Pauline proscription against women speaking in Church in 1 Timothy: 11, 12. The notorious, more proximate, example of the problem is, of course, Anne Hutchinson.

7. In *The Doctrine of Divine Providence,* Increase Mather offers theodicy couched in terms of the exceptional. He cautions readers not to rely too much on their own understanding or reason. "To make things depend chiefly upon the decrees and wills of man, is to place Man in the Throne and to dethrone him that sitteth in Heaven. We must therefore know, that all Events of Providence are the issues and executions of an Ancient, Eternal, Unchangeable decree of Heaven" (8). Explicitly, the verb "to dispense" speaks to both this "decree" and the interpretation of the exceptional: "There are also extraordinary mercies and extraordinary judgements, which the Providence of God does sometimes dispense towards the children of men" (47).

8. Increase Mather notes the "atheistical, proud, wild, cruel, barbarous, brutish (in one word) diabolical creatures" (321) who captured her and the folly of a premature determination "that the army should desist the pursuit, and retire" (318) in their battle against the Narragansetts. Thus, Mather's preface places Rowlandson's tale within a broader range of Puritan concerns, from the diabolical provenance of the Narragansetts to the ill-executed military strategies of "the forces of Plymouth and the Bay."

9. Toulouse argues that it is precisely the anxiety of a captive woman to redeem her social value within the "hierarchical social discourse" of Puritan New England that characterizes the Rowlandson narrative. She notes that Rowlandson's father, John White, was "Lancaster's wealthiest citizen" (670).

10. The *Diary* contains many references to Mather's visitations among his congregation in which he disseminates his own work.

11. "When I have readd thro' a Book, at any time, I would make a Pause; and first, give Thanks to the Father of Lights, for whatever Illumination He has

by this Book bestow'd upon me. Secondly, If the Author be in his Book an useful Servant of the Church, I would give Thanks to God, for His Raising up such an Instrument, and Inclining and Assisting of him to this Performance . . ." (*Diary* 2:226).

12. Fitzpatrick characterizes the "dueling textual voices of the captives and their ministerial sponsors" as "palimpsests, engraved by authors whose exegeses are in dialogical relation to one another." Acknowledging "the clergy's attempts to impose a socially and doctrinally unified and orthodox interpretation of the captives' experiences," Fitzpatrick reads in the tensions between these voices a "gendered site of . . . narrative formation" (2). The subversive effect of the woman's voice, noticed by many scholars, including Fitzpatrick, in studies of Mary Rowlandson's narrative, meets an unusual obstacle in Cotton Mather's treatment of Hannah Swarton's story.

13. See "INSTRUCTIONS TO MATTHEW CARY ABOUT BRINGING PRISONERS FROM CANADA; INFORMATION OBTAINED BY HIM IN QUEBEC, AND LISTS OF THE PRISONERS REDEEMED AND LEFT IN CANADA—1695."

14. Edward Tyng was commander of Casco fort until 1688 when he was appointed Governor of Annapolis by Phips. He was returning to Maine when he was captured on board John Alden's sloop. Alden was in the service of the Colony "to provide provisions and clothes for the force at Falmouth." Both Tyng and Alden were carried to France, and Tyng died in prison there. Alden returned, only to be charged in the 1692 witchcraft trials (when he was 70 years old). He escaped from a Boston jail and hid until the furor passed (Coleman 1:70 n., 215-16). Another, less reliable, source for Swarton, Tyng, and Alden's stories is Willis, who relies unquestioningly on Mather's text.

15. Coleman has traced a history of John Swarton ["spelled on Canadian records: Soarre, Shiard, Shaken, Soüarten, Sowarten, Schouarden, Souard"]: "John Swarton of Beverly received a fifty acre grant in North Yarmouth. In his petition he said he had fought with Charles II in Flanders." "Church mentions 'One Swarton, a Jersey man' whose language he could hardly understand" (Coleman 1:204).

16. Because my concern with the Swarton narrative includes its publication history, I use two versions of the text. The first, hereafter referred to as *Humiliations,* was published in 1697 and the second version, "A Narrative of Hannah Swarton," appeared in Mather's *Magnalia*. The variants are discussed below.

17. The petition accuses the Massachusetts Bay leaders of dragging their heels in dispatching aid to Maine during the Indian attacks waged in the summer of 1688. It not only praises the work of Gov. Andros in providing relief to the Province upon his return from New York and getting a full report of the depradations, but it indicts the "Change of Government" (after the insurrection of April 1688) with supplying the Indians "with stores of Warr and Amunition by vessels sent by some in Boston to trade with them, and thereupon [the Indians] took new Courage and resolution to Continue the Warr; and having got to their assistance other Indians, who before were unconcerned they presently burnt and destroyed the several Fortifications which the Forces had deserted. . . ." The petition was signed 25 January 1689, almost a year after the anti-Andros uprising in Boston, and shortly before the attack on Casco.

18. Mather later wrote specifically about the dangers of living without benefit of a minister in his 1702 *Letter to Ungospelized Plantations.*

19. Holmes asserts that "Cotton Mather wrote this Narrative some time between November, 1695, the month of Hannah Swarton's return, and November, 1696—probably nearer the latter date—when he wrote his advertisement for *Great Examples,* the work in which he first intended to print the Swarton Narrative" (2:493).

20. Holmes discusses the trajectory of the Swarton text at length (1:452-53). It was advertised as part of the forthcoming *Great Examples of Judgment and Mercy,* which was never printed.

21. Mather explicitly metaphorizes female virtue as the Church itself: "Indeed, there are more women than men in the Church and the more virtuous they prove, the more worthy will the Church be to be figured, by a woman that fears the Lord" (*Ornaments* 9).

22. Holmes initially states that the Duston Narrative "as it now stands is almost certainly of Cotton Mather's authorship or editing" (2:491). However, in a longer consideration of the timing of the sermon and Mather's other attempts at fact-gathering, he concludes, "We are inclined to believe, therefore, that the original of the Hannah Dustan Narrative was written by the Rev. Benjamin Rolfe of Haverhill, but that its statements were confirmed by Cotton Mather's interview with the principals, and that the printed text received his editorship" (2:492). This view is supported by the title page's presentation of the story as an "*Improvement.*"

23. The variant reading of the Duston episode in *Decennium Luctuosum* provides information about the specific rewards received by Duston, Neff, and Lennardson.

24. See Holmes (3:1198-1200) for notes on the sermon *Warnings from the Dead* (Boston, 1693). Emerson's "Instrument" was reprinted in Mather's *Pillars of Salt* and in the *Magnalia*. Ulrich reports that Emerson was severely beaten by her father and indicates that this abuse could account for her "rebellion" (Ulrich 197-98).

25. Duston (1657-c. 1735) did not become a member of the Church until March 1727, almost exactly thirty years after the captivity. See Taylor 182.

26. Comparing Rowlandson's captivity narrative with *Life Among the Indians,* the 1857 account of Olive and Mary Ann Oatman's captivity (and its subsequent editions), Derounian-Stodola argues that the two texts are "complementary examples of intertextual continuity and narrative evolution" (33); she sees continuity in the works' function as "political guises" (43) but distinguishes them through their respective authorial voices. So, because "Mary Rowlandson's voice and style still dominate her narrative . . . we might identify her text as 'factive,' that is, told in the first person and tending toward veracity" (43). However, the Oatman narratives, which Derounian-Stodola argues are "constructed—indeed, *created*" (35) by a Methodist minister, Royal B. Stratton, seem to her "'fictive,' that is, tending toward fiction and using narrative strategies appropriate to that genre" (43). If one were to argue continuity along the lines of "ministerial involvement," as Derounian-Stodola does, the Swarton narrative provides much more evidence of ministerial manipulation, especially in terms of the purported/purloined authorial voice. Swarton's is indeed "fictive" in Derounian-Stodola's terms.

27. Fitzpatrick argues that Swarton was "converted at the hands of apostates, whose challenges to the 'true religion' prompted Swarton's profession of Puritan faith." She sees this as a subversion of the notion that conversion should occur within "the communal covenant," which would offer nurturance within Puritan social order, the congregation.

28. See the controversy surrounding the publication of *Publick Occurrences,* an anonymously published criticism of the government's campaign on the eastern frontier, and Mather's "slippery" disavowal of his authorship in Silverman, *The Life and Times of Cotton Mather* 75-76. Mather's dodging is evident in his letter to John Cotton (October 17, 1690) protesting that "the publisher had not one line of it from me, only as accidentally meeting him in the highway, on his request, I showed him how to contract and express the report of the expedition at Casco and the east" in Silverman, *Selected Letters of Cotton Mather* 27. These are the expeditions that should have prevented the attack on Casco that resulted in Swarton's capture.

29. Mather reminds his audience in the sermon that "Words that are spoken in an *Ordinance* of the Lord Jesus Christ, carry with them a peculiar Efficacy and Authority" (*Humiliations* 48).

30. "I desired to see all my Sins, and to Repent of them all, with all my Heart, and of that Sin which had been especially a Burden to me, namely, *That I Left the Publick Worship and Ordinances of God, to go to Live in a Remote Place, without the Publick Ministry . . ."* (*Humiliations* 67-68).

31. According to church records, Swarton's daughter, whose whereabouts were unknown at the end of the narrative, remained in Canada and converted. See Levernier and Cohen 31-32.

32. Bumstead states that Mrs. Sarah Gerish was "the first Canadian captive whose narrative was printed" because it was included in Cotton Mather's *A History of Remarkable Occurrences in the Long War* (1699) [see note below]. Since Swarton's text appeared in 1697, hers was certainly the first. Although Bumstead's article contains other errors, it is a useful overview of British responses to French Canadian captivity. He argues that French attitudes toward Protestant captives changed from "efforts at complete cultural assimilation of the captive" to a more detached and "regularized" practice of incarceration. So, where Swarton and other earlier captives lodged with French families as house servants or farm workers, later captives were treated as conventional prisoners-of-war and passed their captivities in "formal prison buildings" (87). Some of the language that appears for the first time in the Swarton text is reiterated in later narratives, such as the differentiation figured by the "inward man" threatened by French Catholics and the "outward" man provided for by them. Bumstead does not mention the Swarton narrative in his study.

33. Bumstead argues that "The real dramatization of the ambiguities and anxieties of the English was done by John Williams . . ." (82). See his discussion (82-84) of Williams's *The Redeemed Captive.*

34. See "Jemima Howe—Background" in Kestler 139-42. There are several versions of Howe's narrative, as Kestler notes; I refer to "A Genuine and Correct Account of the Captivity, Sufferings and Deliverance of Mrs. Jemima Howe, of Hinsdale in New-Hampshire." "Taken from her own mouth, and written, by the Reverend Bunker Gray [*sic*]," in Washburn.

35. The story of seven-year-old Sarah Gerish, "a very Beautiful and Ingenious Damsel" foreshadows the sensationalism of later captivity narratives in its sentimental rendering of the little child imprisoned in a wilderness with a "Dragon" for a master. The Gerish account is notable, too, for its representation of sexual threat when Sarah's master commands her to "loosen som of her upper-Garments." "God knows what he was going to do . . ." the account continues, but no harm comes to the child and she is eventually restored to her family (*Decennium* 200).

36. Derounian-Stodola notes that "by the mid-nineteenth century, the Indian captivity narrative was no longer primarily an autobiographical literary construct but was often an exploitative political vehicle to facilitate genocide [of Native Americans]" (44). As my ar-

gument demonstrates, the construct and the vehicle were conflated as early as 1697. This political aspect of the texts appears precisely because women's stories were private matters. They therefore depend for publication on ministers, who can offer both dispensation and certification of good reputation, because the Church is a *public* institution that shapes and ministers to the *private* soul.

Works Cited

Bumstead, J. M. "'Carried to Canada!': Perceptions of the French in British Colonial Captivity Narratives, 1690-1760." *American Review of Canadian Studies* 13 (1983): 79-96.

Coleman, Emma Lewis. *New England Captives Carried to Canada.* 2 vols. Portland, Maine: The Southworth Press, 1925. Vols. 1-2.

Derounian, Kathryn Zabelle. "Puritan Orthodoxy and the 'Survivor Syndrome'" in Mary Rowlandson's Indian Captivity Narrative." *Early American Literature* 22 (1987): 82-93.

Derounian-Stodola, Kathryn Z. "Indian Captivity Narratives of Mary Rowlandson and Olive Oatman: Case Studies in the Continuity, Evolution, and Exploitation of Literary Discourse." *Studies in the Literary Imagination* 27 (1994): 33-46.

Fitzpatrick, Tara. "The Figure of Captivity: The Cultural Work of the Puritan Captivity Narrative." *American Literary History* 3 (1991): 1-26.

Foucault, Michel. "What Is an Author?" *The Foucault Reader.* Ed. Paul Rabinow. New York: Pantheon Books, 1984.

Goldberg, Jonathan. *Writing Matter: From the Hands of the English Renaissance.* Stanford, Calif.: Stanford Univ. Press, 1990.

Holmes, Thomas J. *Cotton Mather: A Bibliography of His Works.* 3 vols. Cambridge, Mass.: Harvard Univ. Press, 1940. Vols. 1-3.

"INSTRUCTIONS TO MATTHEW CARY. . . ." *New England Historical and Genealogical Register* 24 (1870): 286-91.

Kestler, Frances Roe. *The Indian Captivity Narrative: A Woman's View.* New York: Garland Press, 1990.

Kolodny, Annette. *The Land Before Her: Fantasy and Experience of the American Frontiers, 1630-1860.* Chapel Hill, N.C.: Univ. of North Carolina Press, 1984.

Levernier, James A., and Hennig Cohen, eds. *The Indians and Their Captives.* Westport, Conn.: Greenwood Press, 1977.

Mather, Cotton. *Diary of Cotton Mather.* 2 vols. New York: Frederick Unger Publishing Co., 1957. Vols. 1-2.

———. *Decennium Luctuosum. Narratives of the Indian Wars.* Ed. Charles H. Lincoln. New York: Charles Scribner's Sons, 1913.

———. *Humiliations follow'd With Deliverances.* 1697. New York and London: Garland Publishing Inc., 1977.

———. *Magnalia Christi Americana.* 2 vols. 1852. New York: Russell and Russell, 1967.

———. *Ornaments for the Daughters of Zion or the Character and Happiness of a Virtuous Woman by Cotton Mather: A Facsimile Reproduction.* Delmar, N.Y.: Scholars' Facsimiles & Reprints, 1978.

Mather, Increase. *The Doctrine of Divine Providence.* Boston, 1684. Evans 371.

Minter, David L. "By Dens of Lions: Notes on Stylization in Early Puritan Captivity Narratives." *American Literature* 45 (1973): 335-47.

"Petition of the Inhabitants of Maine." The Andros Tracts. Boston: The Prince Society, 1868.

Silverman, Kenneth. *The Life and Times of Cotton Mather.* New York: Columbia Univ. Press, 1985.

———. *Selected Letters of Cotton Mather.* Baton Rouge, La.: Louisiana State Univ. Press, 1971.

Slotkin, Richard, and James K. Folsom, eds. *So Dreadfull a Judgment: Puritan Responses to King Philip's War, 1676-1677.* Middletown, Conn.: Wesleyan Univ. Press, 1978.

Taylor, E. W. B. "Hannah Dustin of Haverhill." *The Granite Monthly* 43 (1911): 177-83.

Toulouse, Teresa A. "'My own Credit': Strategies of (E)valuation in Mary Rowlandson's Captivity Narrative." *American Literature* 64 (1992): 655-76.

Ulrich, Laurel Thatcher. *Good Wives: Image and Reality in the Lives of Women in Northern New England, 1650-1750.* New York: Oxford Univ. Press, 1983.

Washburn, Wilcomb E., ed. *Narratives of North American Indian Captivities.* 111 vols. New York: Garland, 1977.

Willis, William. *The History of Portland.* Portland, Maine: Bailey and Noyes, 1865. [facs. rpt., Portland, Maine: Maine Historical Society, 1972.]

CAPTIVITY NARRATIVES AND NATIVE AMERICANS

Colin Ramsey (essay date 1994)

SOURCE: Ramsey, Colin. "Cannibalism and Infant Killing: A System of 'Demonizing' Motifs in Indian Captivity Narratives." *Clio* 24, no. 1 (fall 1994): 55-68.

[*In the essay below, Ramsey links captivity narratives with the demonizing of Native Americans during the Puritan era.*]

The Puritan phase of the Indian captivity narrative, both in its binary "good vs. evil" oppositions and in its imagery, established the paradigm for much of the subsequent development of the Indian captivity narrative form—helping to fix particular (and ethnocentric) views of the Indian in the American imagination, and thereby making those same images and motifs readily available for political and ideological manipulation. This paper will examine two such captivity narrative motifs, ubiquitous in Puritan captivities but by no means limited to them, namely, the motifs of Indian cannibalism and infanticide. I will discuss these motifs within Indian captivity narratives as a "demonology," defined by Phillips Stevens, Jr., as

> an elaborate body of belief about an evil force that is inexorably undermining the society's most cherished values and institutions. The evil it describes may be embodied in and perpetrated by a specific group, a minority which becomes the scapegoat. . . . Examples of such persecuted minorities in Western history are the Jews, over and over again; or Bolsheviks; or Japanese-Americans. . . . [And also] late medieval heresies, including witchcraft. . . .[1]

I will add to those "demonized" groups the Native Americans, and consider the corresponding cultural results of such "demonology." To do so, I will examine the history of the above motifs, cannibalism and infanticide, positing them within a tradition of demonizing imagery and folklore which pre-dates the Puritans considerably, and, finally, I will identify the same "demonizing" motifs within contemporary folklore, offering through the comparison a partial explanation for the pervasiveness of the motifs in captivity narratives, and more broadly, American culture, despite strong evidence that Indians are not and never were "cannibals" or "baby killers," at least not in any systematic and culturally sanctioned way. Indeed, reports of cannibalism and infanticide, without basis in significant rational or empirical evidence, have regularly demonized many groups of people throughout Western history; as this paper will demonstrate, the motifs can be seen as a standardized means for characterizing any group which the dominant culture finds threatening as animalistic barbarians, as dehumanized and "other."

Among the most important factors in the standardization of the motifs of cannibalism and infanticide within the Puritan version of the captivity narrative was the particular relationship of those narratives to the Puritan world view. From its beginnings, the Puritan captivity narrative worked as a myth which, according to Richard Slotkin, "reduced the Puritan state of mind . . . along with the events of colonization and settlement, into archetypal drama," and which demanded that the Puritans reject the Indian "cannibal Eucharist."[2] Most scholars echo Slotkin's assessment of the relation of the "Puritan mind" to Indian captivity narratives. William S. Simmons, for instance, argues that the Puritans ultimately saw the world as the scene of a continuing battle between the forces of light and darkness, saints and devils, and that this mental framework provided Puritans with a ready-made theory for interpreting cultural

differences between themselves and the Native Americans—that the Indians were "cannibals" who "worshipped devils" and who themselves were "bewitched" or "witches." Moreover, these beliefs were so pervasive that they became "matter of fact assumptions in the vocabulary of all the New English who wrote about Indian culture."[3]

Robert Berkhofer further argues that the Puritan clerical and intellectual elite "picked up this method [the captivity narrative] for impressing the power of the Lord and the sinfulness of His people."[4] Moreover, Berkhofer argues that the early New England captivity narrative's best-seller status led to the "retention of its basic premise of the horror Whites suffered under Indian 'enslavement'" (84-85). Thus the "horrors" of Indian captivity, as represented in Puritan captivity accounts, became the standard "horrors" of subsequent Indian captivity narratives. Puritan clerical authorities, such as the Mathers, seized upon the Indian captivity narrative as an instrument of manipulation; Indian captivity was cast as a trial of the spirit. Such narratives were designed to highlight God's great protecting providence. To help demonstrate the important role of the divine, these narratives portrayed the Indians as incalculably evil, cannibals and baby killers, creatures so evil that only by God's help could a Puritan survive captivity in their hands. In addition, the sensationalism of such narratives ensured a steady readership, and the Puritan clerics encouraged and contributed to their circulation. As long as the Indians were portrayed as barbarians, the narratives were a perfect template for religious instruction according to Puritan doctrine.

Mary Rowlandson's captivity narrative[5] was the first in a long succession of Puritan captivity accounts that painted Indians as Satanic cannibalistic infant-killers. Rowlandson's language conveys this message implicitly: she describes the Indians as "a company of hellhounds" (2), who smash out the brains of some children and shoot others. "Thus we were butchered," she writes, and all the while the Indians were "roaring, singing, ranting and insulting,"—the scene looked to Rowlandson like "a company of sheep torn by wolves" (3). Later in the narrative, the motifs of cannibalism and infanticide are blended together when Rowlandson inquires after her son. She writes:

> I had not seen my son a pretty while, and here [sic] was an Indian of whom I made inquiry after him, and asked him when he saw him: he answered me, that such a time his master roasted him and that himself did eat a piece of him, as big as his two fingers, and that he was very good meat.
>
> (15)[6]

Although Rowlandson later expresses disbelief at this story, attributing it to the Indian's "horrible addictedness to lying,"[7] the motifs stuck, ready as the Puritans were to believe any story about the "devilish" Indians. Not surprisingly, given the Puritan's particular world view, the threat of cannibalism and the more overt accounts of the murder of children are picked up by, and amplified in, subsequent

Puritan narratives, maximizing their de-humanizing effect. Cotton Mather, for example, in *Decennium Luctuosum* writes that during the march to Indian villages on the Kennebec following the so called "Salmon Falls Massacre," a woman named Mary Plaisted complained that she could not march quickly because of the infant she carried in her arms. An obliging brave dashed out the child's brains against a tree (an extremely popular way of killing babies in the narratives), and told her to "walk faster than she did before."[8] Mather further relates that this was customary treatment of infants in Indian hands. Later in Mather's *Decennium Luctuosum,* the cannibalistic Indians are seen working in concert with the Quakers—who are after souls. The Indians eat the left-overs:

> the Quakers have chosen the very same Frontiers and Outskirts, of the province [as the Indians] for their more Spiritual Assaults; . . . and have been Labouring [*sic*] incessantly . . . to Poison the Souls of poor people, in the very places, where the Bodies and Estates of the people have presently after been devoured by the Salvages.
>
> (162)

As the political context shifted, so did the target of the demonization in the Puritan captivity narratives. In Reverend John Norton's *The Redeemed Captive,* published during the French and Indian War, the French are portrayed as cannibals along with the Indians:

> After some time the Indians seemed to be in a Russle; and presently rushed up into the Watch-Box, bro't down the dead Corpse, carried it out of the Fort, scalpt it, and cut off the Head and Arms: A young Frenchman took one of the Arms and Flay'd it, roasted the Flesh, and offere'd some of it . . . to eat.[9]

During the Revolutionary War, captivity narratives paint the British along with, as always, the Indians as brutal infant killers. In *A Narrative of the Capture and Treatment of John Dodge,* Dodge reports that "the British governor of Detroit, Henry Hamilton, gave Indians a bounty for American Scalps, ordering both Indians and British soldiers alike 'not to spare man, woman or child.'"[10] Importantly, though Indian cannibalism and infanticide in the above narratives are depicted in association with various and shifting other groups, the Indian role remains the same. Thus with the help of a politically and religiously motivated clergy and a public "primed," so-to-speak, by their own cultural baggage, the motifs of Indian cannibalism and infanticide so prevalent in Puritan captivities became standardized in captivity accounts and in American culture.

Nevertheless, one is moved to consider, if for no other reason than the very regularity with which the motifs appear, whether Native Americans ever did systematically kill children and/or eat people. Though it would be impossible to argue that no Native American ever killed a child or consumed human flesh, a brief review of current events shows that individual aberrations of that kind exist even

today in virtually all cultures. Furthermore, when one takes into account both the social contexts from which captivity narratives arose and the dubious nature of their authorship, and compares the motifs in the narratives to the long tradition of inaccurate "demonizing" characterizations of "out" groups—based at best on misunderstandings and at worst on conscious political manipulation—one has considerable reason to doubt the accuracy of the reported incidents of cannibalism and infanticide in Indian captivity narratives.

For instance, all the narratives cited above were published either during, or right after, wars, and were propagandistic in nature. Mary Rowlandson's narrative was published during King Philip's War, which coincided with the rise of Increase Mather, and later, of his son Cotton: both were enormously influential in the formation and mytho-political use of the captivity narrative and had an interest in demonizing Native Americans. Indeed, the Rowlandson narrative underwent several subsequent surges of popularity during later wars. Greg Sieminski argues that the renewed popularity of Rowlandson's narrative during the 1770s was due to the narrative's very great effectiveness *as* propaganda. The colonists named the riots in Boston in March of 1770 the "Boston Massacre"; the Rowlandson narrative had supplied the images "they knew best: an Indian raid on a frontier settlement."[11] The British forces involved in the riots became, by implication, cannibals and baby killers—they were effectively demonized. During the French and Indian War, as has been demonstrated above, the French were similarly "demonized," and, as European expansion brought Whites into increasing conflict with Native Americans, the established demonology continued to offer ready excuses for the destruction of Native Americans and their cultures. Cannibals and infant killers deserved no better than to be "exterminated"—which would also conveniently free the land for White settlement. Clearly, the captivity narrative was an effective way of making an opponent in war, or later, a competitor for land, into a non-human, particularly through painting him as an infant killer and cannibal. As Levernier and Cohen argue, many captivities were *designed* to "horrify audiences into hating" the Indian, who "is painted as so irredeemably brutish that he deserves to be deprived of his lands."[12]

In addition, and despite much recent revisionist scholarship, the historical record remains colonial in nature. Mainstream American history is still a history written by the conqueror; thus, negative stereotyping of the conquered remains largely unchallenged. Indeed, many early historians of colonial North America advanced, even expanded, such demonizing racial stereotypes. For example, Cotton Mather, who situated himself as the principal chronicler and historian of the Puritan experience in America, "elaborated this myth [the captivity narrative] as *the* historical framework for summarizing Indian-White relationships throughout the seventeenth century."[13] David Stannard argues, even more strongly, that *all* American history is "colonialist history," written from a Eurocentric perspective which implies there was no history before Columbus.

It sees the 30,000-year, or more, history of Native Americans prior to Columbus' arrival as inconsequential. These notions amount to a "political mythology" which reinforces the views held by the dominant culture—that, among other things, Native Americans were "primitive savages"[14] living in darkness who were infant-killers and cannibals.

And not surprisingly, the genesis of the demonization of Native Americans as infant-killers and cannibals lies with Columbus. He reported that on an island called "Carib" there were people who were "very fierce" and who ate "human flesh." Thus began the "line of savage images of the Indian as not only hostile but depraved."[15] Significantly, Columbus was informed of these inhuman natives through the Arawaks, who describe the people on the islands to the south as having "one eye and dogs' noses, who ate men, and when they took a man, they cut off his head and drank his blood and castrated him."[16] Columbus probably had little trouble believing this sort of thing; it reinforced many of the cultural notions already existent in Europe for hundreds of years—not just as a familiar demonology but as part of broader cultural notions of the Wild Man of folklore. Thus, "the depraved nature of man eaters captured the imagination of Europeans. . . . they were truly wild men of the lowest order, clearly beyond the pale of civilization" (45). Just so, reports of cannibalism and infanticide in the native inhabitants of the "New World" insured a readership and popularity back in Spain, and "served as a pretext for their [Indians'] enslavement to swell the labor supply in the new Spanish colonies" (46).

Though W. Arens' study *The Man Eating Myth* is controversial, if valid, it further discredits Columbus' accounts of cannibalism, and points to the kind of political motivation which greatly contributed to the stubborn recurrence of the motifs of Indian cannibalism and infanticide in captivity narratives. According to Arens, the Arawaks had every reason to provide a believing Columbus with demonizing stories about the Caribs. The Arawaks and the Caribs, the native inhabitants first encountered by Columbus, were two distinct groups with separate world views. Included in the world view of the Arawaks was fear and hatred of the more aggressive people on the southern islands in the Caribbean, and thus they were "eager to fill him [Columbus] in on the gossip about their enemies to the south."[17] In reality, when Columbus landed the following year to colonize the southern islands, the Caribs "ran from their villages at the sight of the Spaniards." As Arens wryly puts it, "perhaps they too had heard of the existence of man eaters on distant islands" (46). One can only assume from Columbus' silence on the subject that the fleeing Caribs had human noses and two eyes apiece.

As with the Puritans, the political convenience of such a demonology, combined with the sometimes dubious nature of the sources for such stories and the colonizing cultures' predisposition to believe them, throws doubt on whether the Native Americans encountered by Columbus were really cannibals. What is not in doubt is that Europeans, and the West in general, have a long tradition of demonizing groups of people through accounts of cannibalism and baby-killing. That these characterizations often stem from misunderstandings of the groups being demonized is of little importance to the groups doing the demonizing since, if the demonization does not serve some overt political end, it seems always to, at least, reinforce the cultural assumptions of the dominant group.

That cannibalism and infanticide are an effective means to demonization is supported by the regularity with which the motifs have appeared in association with various scapegoat minority groups. For instance, while the origins of the cannibalism motif may be impossible to trace, Herodotus in the fifth century BC wrote of a people across the desert who lived lawlessly and "devoured human flesh" (10). In the second century after Christ, the Christian communities in the Roman Empire "were the object of strange suspicions and accusations"—Minucius Felix related the then popular belief about Christian religious rites: a child, covered in dough, would be stabbed by new initiates, who were unaware of what they were doing; the rest would then drink the child's blood and compete for his limbs.[18] There are two plausible explanations for these presumably erroneous beliefs. First, the demonization served the political and economic ends of the Roman Senators. Marcus Aurelius and the Senate made it possible for local notables to purchase condemned criminals, such as the cannibalistic baby-killing Christians, for use in the gladiatorial games, at a much lower cost than to hire a gladiator. Even more expediently, the demonization of the Christians such that they could be executed in the games would reduce "an alien and potentially troublesome group." Second, the Christian Eucharist *is* a kind of symbolic cannibalism and thus could easily be misinterpreted as the real thing by a society already suspicious of this strange new group in their midst (7-10). Though the above pattern proves nothing directly about reports of cannibalism and infanticide on the part of Native Americans, the motif patterns are strikingly similar. Certainly, the motifs have a long history as part of European "demonologies" and appear quite regularly throughout European history. The list of those demonized in this manner reads like an honor roll of European out groups: of so-called medieval heretics it was said "They cut their [babies', what else?] tender flesh all over with sharp knives and catch the stream of blood in basins"; of the Knights of the Templars when they began to threaten the power of King Philip of France, "[the Templars'] idol was anointed with the fat of roasted infants"; of the so-called "witches" of the fifteenth, sixteenth, and seventeenth centuries, "according to some writers of the time, to kill, cook, and eat a baby which had not yet been baptized was a witch's greatest pleasure" (19, 88, 100). Each of the above demonologies follows largely the same motif pattern and arises out of similar social contexts. As in the Indian captivity narrative, the groups being demonized are seen as threatening to the society doing the demonizing; and with each successive demonology, European culture became more bound to those same motifs. Is it any wonder that the Puritans decided the Native Americans, who were quite different and seemingly strange, were cannibals and baby killers?

The above demonology surrounding "witches" is especially pertinent to Puritan captivity accounts. In fact, what is essentially the demonology of the captivity narratives had become such a part of the Puritan consciousness at the end of King Philip's War that the Witch Trials were the direct result: "the strain and anxiety of revolutionary times culminated in the witchcraft delusion of 1692-93, in which Cotton Mather and his reworkings of the captivity mythology played a conspicuous part."[19] Mercy Short, a returned captive from the Salmon Falls "Massacre," who was reportedly "possessed by devils," helped Cotton Mather, who was working on his "history" of New England, "discover the common pattern" in each of the "assaults on pious New England—Indians and paganism, ministerial frauds and heretics, the assaults of the Quakers, the assaults of the royal governor on colonial prerogatives, and the final assault of the witches and the Invisible Kingdom in 1692" (129). As demonstrated earlier in this paper, all of the above groups were accused of cannibalism and infanticide at one time or another, and, as might be expected, Mather saw in all of the above groups a *threat* to "pious Puritan society." The fears associated with Indians, notably, cannibalism and infant killing, were carried forward into the Witch Trials.

Mather, then, used Mercy Short as a symbol; the witch trials, as Slotkin notes, became none other than a Puritan attempt to exorcise from within themselves what they feared most: that they, as they imagined the Indians, were cannibalistic, baby-killing, primitive devils. In this instance, the tropes of demonology became not just damaging cultural stereotypes, but community wide, even cultural, psychotic delusions; the Puritans, under stress, framed the world in terms of the traditional motifs of demonology with which they were all too familiar; thus they saw cannibals and baby killers in their own midst, as they had "seen" the same qualities in the Indian, and as the Romans had "seen" them in the early Christians.

A further testament to the peculiar power of the motifs of cannibalism and infanticide, many folklore narratives, particularly those loosely categorized under the heading Contemporary Legend, often contain many of the same demonizing motif patterns as the Indian captivity narratives. Jeffrey Victor, for instance, has outlined the growth of satanic cult rumors in Jamestown, New York. He reports that the rumors of a "satanic cult" in the vicinity accumulated over time, gaining wider and wider circulation and force. The main rumor story, though there were countless variations, was that the "Satanists" were planning to "kidnap and sacrifice a blond, blue-eyed virgin."[20] The community's responses to such rumor stories were massive: at school board meetings parents, worried over rumors of "ritual sacrifice" and fearing their children would be kidnapped for use in such sacrifices, demanded the speedy apprehension of the "Satanists" at all costs. Victor argues that a "symbolic interactionist" interpretation is the best explanation for the eruption of such rumor-panics:

The key insight of symbolic interactionism is that people interact with their environment through symbolic cultural meanings. The stories of rumor-panics embody cultural symbols, which a group of people can use to give meaning to their social reality. The rumor stories become "real" through the interaction process of the consensual validation of reality. . . . [It] is best understood as . . . a group's fearful reaction to collectively shared stories about immediately threatening circumstances.

(60)

There are some interesting similarities: the Puritans, reinforced by their clergy, saw the very possibility of Indian captivity as both extremely fearful and immediately threatening. It thus might be reasonably argued that the Puritans' culture, under increasing economic and cultural stress as time moved on, created the "reality" of cannibalistic infant-killing Indians through the "consensual validation of reality." In other words, a similar mechanism of symbolic interaction could easily have produced narratives about cannibalistic Indians within the Puritan communities of the seventeenth and eighteenth centuries, just as such a mechanism produced the Satanic rumor-panic narratives in the modern communities of upstate New York. Moreover, the role of the Puritan clergy in the development, dissemination, and validation of such narratives resembles the role of the secular police "authorities" to Satanism rumor narratives in the modern context; both the Puritan clerics and the police positioned themselves as experts, and their interpretations of events were accepted with little or no empirical scrutiny. Such "experts" helped to bolster the believability of both sets of narratives, and contributed to their circulation.

And in fact, the symbolic outlines of the Satanist rumor-panic stories closely match those of the Puritan captivity narratives and other earlier demonologies, that children are "kidnapped and murdered" and their blood and body parts are used in cannibalistic rituals. Victor argues that these very motifs are the symbolic way that communities express anxieties about their future (52). Predictably, the "evil strangers" in these stories are usually people from some widely despised group in society.

The comparisons between these "urban belief tales" and the Western historical tradition of demonizing imagery are tantalizing. Bill Ellis notes that the current "urban-legend" of "The Castrated Boy," a particularly nasty infanticide narrative, was widely believed in ancient Rome, "*Non nova sed ingenita,* . . . what we see today as our modern folklore may in fact be only universal human hates and anxieties in a contemporary cloak."[21] Jan Harold Brunvand cites in *The Vanishing Hitchhiker* a narrative called "The Hippie Baby Sitter." In this legend, a young couple (evocative of the same scene of domestic happiness which is likewise shattered by the Indian raid in captivity narratives) hire an unknown "hippie" baby sitter. When they call to check up on the girl, she is almost incoherent ("on drugs" like all "wild-haired" hippies) but assures them all is well as she has placed their turkey in the oven.

The couple rushes home "to find their baby roasting in the oven."[22] Compare this to a scene from the Fanny Kelly captivity *Narrative of My Captivity Among the Sioux Indians*:

> One day, the Indians went into a house where they found a woman making bread. Her infant child lay in the cradle, unconscious of its fate. Snatching it from its little bed they thrust it into the heated oven, its screams torturing the wretched mother.[23]

The similarities are striking: the "hippie" being demonized in the baby sitter narrative symbolizes the same fears that the "Indian" does in the Kelly narrative, i.e., "wildness," nature (hippies are often "tree-huggers" and the environmental movement suffers under the same demonizing imagery), licentiousness (the "free-love" movement associated with "hippies"), in a word, *everything* which the Indian has come to symbolize in American culture. Even the form of the story in the Kelly narrative conforms to traditional folklore narratives: the "one day" beginning is ubiquitous in them. Again, the similarities are suggestive; the cultural tradition of demonization motifs in the captivity narratives, themselves influenced by cultural antecedents, might very easily have influenced the "Hippie Baby Sitter" narrative.

Nor are more scholarly works free from these culturally and mythologically driven motif patterns. Indeed, even the work of some contemporary scholars remains influenced by them; reports of Indian cannibalism and infanticide are still often taken at face value. Richard VanDerBeets writes that "cannibalism . . . [is] a practice more widespread among American Indians than is commonly understood."[24] He cites as evidence for this generalization the *same* Fanny Kelly narrative as cited above, which is highly propagandistic in nature and which contains folkloristic accounts of babies being roasted. He approaches the Kelly narrative as utterly factual, assuming the barbarian nature of the Indian as a given. Yet VanDerBeets' assumptions are in direct conflict with recent studies, like that of W. Arens, which suggest that cannibalism and murder as ritual customs—including such "common knowledge" notions as that the Aztecs committed systematic and widespread human sacrifice or that South Pacific Islanders were cannibals—are extremely rare in any part of the world. All this points to, as Victor puts it, "how internalized legends easily create believability."[25]

And it is the internalized nature of these motifs which has made them such powerful tools for the creation of demonologies, not just in reference to the "scapegoating" of Native Americans via the Indian captivity narrative, but for a vast number of marginalized groups over the centuries. Though it is problematic to argue that cannibalism and infanticide motifs are human universals, univocal in interpretation as demonizing stereotypes, certainly they appear over and over again in very much the same form: the less-than-human and evil "other" (fill in any number of marginalized groups) kidnap and thoughtlessly torture and kill our children, and then proceed to dismember and eat their body parts and/or drink their blood. These motifs are not limited to Western sources; as Stevens points out, such motif patterns have been found in the Islamic world, in Asia, and in the traditional narratives of tribal cultures around the globe (129). Nor are these motifs limited to conquering or dominant cultures. As Arens reports in his study, Western anthropologists have been demonized by many of the cultures they were studying, according to the same motif pattern, as have colonial governments by the colonized peoples.[26] In any case, regardless of the groups involved, such demonologies seem always to develop within "situations of prolonged, unrelenting and often unexplainable social stress."[27] Such socio/political stresses have been commonplace throughout world history, and the recurrence of the motif pattern within such historical contexts points to a great need for further research into their deeper symbolic significance. The political impact of such demonologies seems clear—they place whatever group is being demonized "beyond the pale of civilization"—but important questions remain: why do human cultures respond to particular kinds of stress in this way? Why are such motifs so easily internalized, and why do they remain so stubbornly pervasive, even into contemporary times, as a narrative pattern?

Although this does not absolutely prove that no Native American ever killed a child, we must remember that examples of such aberrant behavior exist, on an individual basis, in White culture. The point is, the belief that such things are sanctioned by other cultures less "civilized" than our own is what is truly erroneous. Furthermore, that belief is a mistake with *terrible* consequences. Thus, culturally determined misunderstandings and the political and ideological exploitation of such misunderstandings, in concert with an ever-growing cultural tradition that picks up on the motifs produced and transforms them into symbols—thereby forming the unconscious assumptions of a culture over the centuries—create a willingness to believe in the notion that there are "barbarous cannibalistic baby killers" at the gates. This is a powerful demonology, and the history and current status of the European culture's interaction with Native American cultures shows how devastating such a demonology can be. Further research and the continual re-examination of assumptions will help to reduce the commonalty of such "demonizing" motifs and the need to see others as barbarous cannibals—so that we might deal more rationally with "inner demons," the "wild men within."

Notes

1. Phillip Stevens, Jr., "'New' Legends: Some Perspectives from Anthropology," *Western Folklore* 49 (1990):128.

2. Richard Slotkin, *Regeneration through Violence: The Mythology of the American Frontier, 1600-1860* (Middletown, CT: Wesleyan UP, 1973), 94.

3. William S. Simmons, "Cultural Bias in the New England Puritans' Perception of Indians," *William and Mary Quarterly* 42 (1981):56.

4. Robert F. Berkhofer, *The White Man's Indian* (New York: Knopf, 1978), 81.

5. All quotations are from Mary Rowlandson, *A True History* (London: J. Poole, 1682), the fourth edition of her narrative. This edition is generally considered to be the closest to the now lost first edition. Mary White Rowlandson, "A True History of the Captivity and Restoration of Mrs. Mary Rowlandson," (rpt. of 1682 London ed.) in *Narratives of Indian Captives,* vol. 1 (New York: Garland, 1977).

6. The "roasting" children motif is a stable element in many types of folklore, from "Hansel and Gretel" to "The Hippie Baby Sitter" in Jan Harold Brunvand's, *The Vanishing Hitchhiker: American Urban Legends and Their Meanings* (New York: Norton, 1981).

7. Rowlandson, 15.

8. Cotton Mather, *"Decennium Luctuosum,"* (rpt. of 1699 ed.) in *Narratives of Indian Captives,* vol. 3 (New York: Garland, 1978), 56-57.

9. John Norton, *The Redeemed Captive,* (rpt. of 1748 ed.) in *Narratives of Indian Captives,* vol. 6 (New York: Garland, 1978), 10.

10. James A. Levernier and Hennig Cohen, eds., *The Indians and Their Captives* (Westport, CT: Greenwood, 1977), 50.

11. Greg Sieminski, "The Puritan Captivity Narrative and the Politics of the American Revolution," *American Quarterly* 42 (1990):36-37.

12. Levernier and Cohen, xxii.

13. Slotkin, 71.

14. David E. Stannard, "Recounting the Fables of Infanticide and the Functions of Political Myth," *Journal of American Studies* 25 (1991):381-83.

15. Berkhofer, 7.

16. Stanley L. Robe, "The Wild Men and Spain's Brave New World," in *The Wild Man Within: An Image in Western Thought from the Renaissance to Romanticism,* ed. Edward Dudley and Maximilliam E. Novak (Pittsburgh: U of Pittsburgh P, 1973), 44.

17. W. Arens, *The Man Eating Myth* (New York: Oxford UP, 1979), 45. According to Arens, in a further irony of cultural misunderstandings, the Spanish mispronounced "Carib"—making it into "canib" and thus the word for man-eater is now "cannibal" and not "arawakibal" because it was the Arawaks whom Columbus encountered first (45-46).

18. Norman Cohn, *Europe's Inner Demons* (New York: Basic Books, 1975), 10.

19. Slotkin, 117.

20. Jeffrey Victor, "Satanic Cult Rumors as Contemporary Legend," *Western Folklore* 49 (1990):52.

21. Bill Ellis, "De Legendis Urbis: Modern Legends in Ancient Rome," *Journal of American Folklore* 96 (1983):206.

22. Brunvand, 65.

23. Fanny Kelly, *Narrative of My Captivity Among the Sioux Indians* (Hartford: Mutual Publishing Company, 1871), 117.

24. Richard VanDerBeets, "The Indian Captivity Narrative as Ritual," *American Literature* 43 (1972):550.

25. Victor, 70.

26. See Arens, (1979).

27. Stevens, 129.

Robin Riley Fast (essay date 1999)

SOURCE: Fast, Robin Riley. "Resistant History: Revising the Captivity Narrative in 'Captivity' and *Blackrobe: Isaac Jogues*." *American Indian Culture and Research Journal* 23, no. 1 (winter 1999): 69-86.

[*In the following essay, Fast examines the modern poetry of Native Americans Louise Erdrich and Maurice Kenny, which attempts to re-read the captivity narratives written by Europeans.*]

Many contemporary American Indian writers are engaged in the shared project of complicating and revising the received history of the Americas. Kimberly Blaeser reminds us that survival is at stake here when she says that "the creation and interpretations of histories have . . . functioned directly as the justifications for possession or dispossession." In "Captivity" and *Blackrobe: Isaac Jogues* respectively, Louise Erdrich and Maurice Kenny reread histories of captivity among the Indians recorded by the colonizers. Their revisionary agendas necessarily foreground interpretive conflicts and draw attention to cultural and linguistic dialogism. As Blaeser observes regarding Gerald Vizenor's writings about history, these poems "force recognition of the already embattled visions all readers bring to the text[s]."[1] In doing so, the poems become implicitly ironic, as their Native authors turn to colonizers' writings about Indians as sources of inspiration for their own work. As they imagine alternative readings of the European-written accounts, they both highlight the fact that written American history still belongs almost entirely to non-Natives and resist that domination.

Erdrich begins with a story that is virtually a cornerstone of popular American history. Mary Rowlandson, a Puritan minister's wife, was captured in the Narragansett attack on Lancaster, Massachusetts, on February 1, 1675-76, in what became known as King Philip's War, after the English name of its Wampanoag leader, Metacomet. She traveled with her captors for almost twelve weeks, until she was ransomed and returned to Boston. Her account of her ordeal, first published in 1682, went through numerous editions into the middle of the nineteenth century (and has been republished several times in the twentieth). Its full title conveys Rowlandson's intent and some of the impact her story must have had on early readers: *The Sovereignty and Goodness of God Together, with the Faithfulness of His Promises Displayed; Being a Narrative of the Captivity and Restoration of Mrs. Mary Rowlandson.* Later American editions (and the 1682 London edition) modified the title to deemphasize the "sovereignty . . . of God" and foreground the dangers encountered by the captive; thus several editions from the late eighteenth century are entitled *A Narrative of the Captivity, Sufferings and Removes of Mrs. Mary Rowlandson, Who Was Taken Prisoner by the Indians with Several Others; and Treated in the Most Barbarous and Cruel Manner by Those Vile Savages: With Many Other Remarkable Events during her Travels.*[2]

Not only, as its titles suggest, did Mrs. Rowlandson's narrative serve important cultural purposes for generations of European Americans, but it was the first publication in English of what was to become an enormously popular genre of American writing, right up to and beyond the "closing of the frontier" in the 1890s. The genre produced numerous true accounts, which fostered the fascination with "Indian captivity" that has marked American fiction since its beginnings.[3]

In her poem "Captivity," Louise Erdrich draws on Rowlandson's language to reinterpret not just this narrative—it is not absolutely necessary to read the poem's voice as that of Rowlandson herself—but possibilities perhaps inherent in many such experiences and accounts. While retaining the point of view of a white woman, Erdrich creates an alternative version of the captivity narrative, a version that, among other differences, contrasts to Rowlandson's as it replaces assertions of moral and theological certainty (Rowlandson's bulwark against the nearly total physical uncertainty she faced—and perhaps also against skeptics in the New England community) with a pervasive, destabilizing uncertainty. The poem makes transparently clear a contemporary Indian writer's dialogue with diverse traditions and heightens the reader's awareness of the generally suppressed dialogic potential of Rowlandson's account; these effects simultaneously multiply the layers of meaning in Erdrich's own text.

Erdrich's poem begins with an epigraph attributed to Mary Rowlandson: "'*He [my captor] gave me a bisquit, which I put in my pocket, and not daring to eat it, buried it under a log, fearing he had put something in it to make me love him.*'"[4] This sentence refers to one of Rowlandson's most constant concerns—food—and introduces a theme that surfaces only rarely in the *Narrative,* sexual fear. She twice expresses wonder and gratitude that she was never imposed upon sexually. In the ninth Remove,[5] a little less than halfway through the account, she remarks upon "the goodness of God to me, in that, though I was gone from home, and met with all sorts of Indians, and those I had no knowledge of, and there being no Christian soul near

me, yet not one of them offered the least imaginable miscarriage to me" (p. 33). And again, in the twentieth Remove, near her book's end: "I have been in the midst of those roaring lions and savage bears that feared neither God nor man nor the devil, by night and day, alone and in company, sleeping all sorts together, and yet not one of them ever offered me the least abuse of unchastity to me in word or action. Though some are ready to say, I speak it for my own credit; But I speak it in the presence of God, and to his Glory" (pp. 70-71).

In short, the epigraph does not appear in Rowlandson's *Narrative.*[6] Even the epigraph, then, raises questions about history, truth, and their uses (just as seventeenth- and eighteenth-century changes in the title draw attention to interpretive questions). Of course it is possible that this sentence is attributed to Mary Rowlandson in some source other than the *Narrative.* It seems more likely that Erdrich, who plays freely in the poem itself with incidents and language from the *Narrative,* is beginning with an intentionally ironic invention: ironic in that, if we accept the epigraph at face value (as most readers must), then we have begun our reading by replicating earlier readers' likely acceptance of Rowlandson's assumptions. Further, our subsequent recognition of ironic complexity in the poem itself must be shadowed by our having granted credence to a questionable text. The questions thus raised by the epigraph parallel questions that the poem differently raises about Rowlandson's and Erdrich's accounts; the epigraph itself becomes part of the poem's project of destabilizing received history.

From the beginning to the end of her *Narrative,* Mary Rowlandson maintains that her ordeal was a punishment and a test sent to her by God, and thus a sign of God's goodness and concern for "his people" who, so chastised, might be moved to accept divine grace. In this scheme of things, the Indians become agents of the devil, and even though she describes many individual kindnesses to her, her account never really breaks free of this conviction. Even her many references to Quannopin, her master, "the best friend that I had of an Indian, both in cold and hunger" (p. 37), are always in tension with all-encompassing references to "the heathen," "pagans," and "our enemies." Thus a major change in Erdrich's rendition is to focus the captive's attention on one particular individual and to trace the developing complexity of her response to him. The poem's first incident establishes this focus as it revises one from the *Narrative.* In Rowlandson's text, the sixteenth Remove begins as follows: "We began this remove with wading over Baquag river. The water was . . . very swift and so cold I thought it would have cut me in sunder. . . . The Indians stood laughing to see me staggering, but in my distress the Lord gave me experience of the truth and goodness of [His] promise" (p. 49). In contrast, Erdrich's poem begins with the recollection of being rescued from the icy stream by an Indian man.

The poem's second verse paragraph illustrates the frightening disorientation that the captive experiences. It first displays the dichotomous thinking fundamental to Puritan theology and animosity toward indigenous peoples: the speaker characterizes the unknown pursuers of the Indians and their captives either as "God's agents" (colonial troops) or "pitch devils" (another party of Indians). The dichotomy may be slightly blurred when she tells that her child was fed by an Indian woman. That this action has at least jostled her assumptions is implied in the section's final line: "The forest closed, the light deepened." This ambiguity forecasts the pained ambivalence of the poem's ending.

The sexual theme introduced in the epigraph culminates in the middle of the poem. The speaker recalls that although she intended to starve rather than accept food from her captor, when he killed a pregnant deer, he shared the meat of the fawn with her:

> It was so tender,
> the bones like the stems of flowers,
> that I followed where he took me.
>
> After that the birds mocked.
> He did not notice God's wrath.

In the empty white space between verse paragraphs, something unspeakable happens. In the *Narrative* Rowlandson, always hungry, does not resolve to starve; she does fear God's wrath, but for her own earlier failings. The *Narrative* does include this passage in the fourteenth Remove: "As we went along they killed a deer with a young one in her. They gave me a piece of the fawn and it was so young and tender that one might eat the bones as well as the flesh, and yet I thought it was very good" (p. 47). Within the poem, revision proceeds as the captive apparently realizes that sin fails to produce its expected consequences, that what she sees as obvious signs of divine wrath has no effect on the Indian. The certainties on which she has relied for emotional and spiritual survival are crumbling (the same certainties that were used to justify the expansion of the English colonies and later of the United States). And this, not the implied sexual transgression, is what is most devastating.

The captive is rescued, but unlike the historical Rowlandson, she does not claim to find in Scripture the assurance that would sanctify her experience and reinforce her belief. She prays, but her prayer is to no orthodox avail: rather than being reassured of her place within the Puritan community, at night she recalls her exclusion from the Indians' "circle." Here is the worst of this captive's experience: she has been rescued into the knowledge of unremitting loneliness. (Perhaps this depiction of loneliness implies, too, something of what led a considerable number of white captives to remain by choice with the Indians, even when offered "redemption."[7]) She continues, remembering how he "led his company in the noise / until I could no longer bear / the thought of how I was." Beating with a stick on the earth, she "begg[ed] it to open / to admit me / . . . and feed me honey from the rock." These, the poem's final lines, reveal a terrible ambivalence. Twice the words seem to invite one reading, then imply another,

and this seeming invitation reveals the cultural heteroglossia and dialogism of the poem: what the speaker can "no longer bear" is not the "noise," but her isolation; she begs the earth not to swallow her (and her presumed sin), but to unite her with "him"—and to "feed [her] honey from the rock."

The allusion to Psalm 81 echoes Rowlandson's reflection on her experience, near the end of her *Narrative*. "I remember in the night season how the other day I was in the midst of thousands of enemies and nothing but death before me. It was hard work to persuade myself that ever I should be satisfied with bread again. But now we are fed with the finest of the wheat, and (as I may say) with *honey out of the rock*" (p. 78—emphasis in the original). In Rowlandson's account, the allusion implies that God has rewarded her submission to his ways. In the poem, it is virtually blasphemous, a fitting culmination to the subversive potential Erdrich has detected in the captive's response.

Having lived with the "enemy" and returned to Christian civilization, Erdrich's captive knows herself to be effectively excluded from both worlds, her former certainties undone, the possibility of a new way of seeing and being decisively cut off. Perhaps a similar intimation stirs below the surface, as Rowlandson continues, after the passage just quoted, "O the wonderful power of God that mine eyes have seen, affording matter enough for my thoughts to run in, that when others are sleeping mine eyes are weeping" (p. 78). Both Susan Howe and Mitchell Breitwieser suggest that such lines adumbrate an estrangement similar to that imagined in "Captivity," though not grounded in sexual experience as Erdrich implies.

Howe emphasizes Rowlandson's status as a Puritan woman and implies that she might have told a different story had she not been subject to the requirements of the New England theocracy. On the day of the Narragansetts' attack she finds Rowlandson "look[ing] out at the absence of Authority and see[ing] that we are all alone"; "abducted from the structure of experience[,] Rowlandson wraps herself in separateness for warmth," and to defend herself against "[l]imitlessness, where all illusion of volition, all individual identity may be transformed—assimilated." Back in the English colony, "Perhaps she told her story to assure herself and her community that she was a woman who feared God and eschewed evil." Such persuasion would have been necessary if, in her memory, "captives and captors . . . [were] walking together beyond . . . Western culture."[8]

In a similar vein, Breitwieser finds Rowlandson's *Narrative* an "intense and unremitting representation . . . of experience as a collision between cultural ideology and the real," a "narrative . . . which fails to annul the powers of anomaly." For Rowlandson, he argues,

> experience came to mean disconnection from enclosing contexts, not only from the life she enjoyed before the war and the Algonquian life amidst which she survived,

but also from the social reality constructed in the aftermath of the war, a labor of construction to which her narrative was supposed to be an important contribution.

He argues that "despite her best intentions," in the course of her writing "things get loose or come forward that . . . signal the vitality of a distinctly non-Puritan view of her experience," and thus her text "allows various anomalous glimpses, not only of her own emotions, but also of her captors." Rowlandson's narrative thus becomes, "an account of experience that breaks through or outdistances her own and her culture's dominant means of representation."[9]

Howe's and Breitwieser's readings complement Erdrich's poem by arguing that Rowlandson's text reveals traces of suppressed doubt and a disruptive vision. As Erdrich, Howe, and Breitwieser look through the surface of Puritan didacticism, they illuminate the dialogism hidden in the *Narrative*. Prompted by their insights, we can recognize that even the Biblical quotations expose heteroglossia and dialogic potential, as Rowlandson struggles to bring her experiences into line with her culture's most authoritative language.[10]

Erdrich cannot have read the *Narrative* without noting Rowlandson's unending search for food and for shelter against the cold and dark; her poem depicts the captive as engaged in a parallel search for spiritual and emotional shelter. One of the poem's most powerful dialogic reversals is its suggestion that she might have been able to find such shelter in the alien world of the Indians. Further, Erdrich recognizes that the need for shelter is the need for inclusion, for community. The historic Mary Rowlandson sought inclusion by reading the Bible she'd been given by an Indian, searching out opportunities to see her children and other English captives, and anticipating her eventual rescue. Perhaps prompted in part by passages in Rowlandson's text that record changes in attitude—toward food, tobacco, herself—Erdrich envisions for the captive an elusive opportunity for integration with a Native community (perhaps prompted too, as Breitwieser suggests, by evidence of Rowlandson's economic integration, as she knits and sews and is paid for her work).

The history Erdrich constructs, in dialogic response to Rowlandson's *Narrative*, is one not of rescue and return, however problematical that might have been, to the colonists' community; rather she tells of a lost opportunity for a new vision of relationship and community. One might ask whether Erdrich's history is too easy—what about the terrible suffering that Rowlandson and other captives endured? But Erdrich does not deny them. Once Rowlandson's name appears in the epigraph, the story she told is unavoidably part of the poem's dialogical struggle, even the focus of that struggle, grounded as it is in the question whether the history might reveal more truths than those Rowlandson could see or acknowledge.

In *Blackrobe: Isaac Jogues*, Mohawk poet Maurice Kenny, too, exposes the contested nature of history and vision. Like Erdrich's poem, Kenny's poetic sequence engages

multidimensional language in dialogic discourse that recreates the political and interpretive conflicts recorded and embodied in historical accounts. Kenny complicates the project and its effects further by recounting his history through the diverse voices of French and Dutch colonists in North America, the Jesuit missionary Isaac Jogues, and Mohawks who encountered him. The history thus becomes a web of stories in dialogue across cultural, geographic, and temporal borders, as Kenny shows us how diverse voices created meanings and realities in the past and continue to do so now as well.

Isaac Jogues' story (documented in his own *Narrative* and letters, as well as by others) may not be as widely known as Mary Rowlandson's. However, it is evidently quite familiar to Mohawk people. "For generations now," Joseph Bruchac says, "the Mohawk people have been told they must feel guilty about killing this holy man and approaching that story is like cauterizing an old wound for Kenny."[11] Like Rowlandson's story, Jogues' represents that major theme in European American versions of the history of North America, the colonizers' dedication to a transcendent mission, and their sufferings at the hands of indigenous aliens. Indeed, the pervasive piety of both Rowlandson and Jogues affords Erdrich and Kenny alike an opportunity to expose the Europeans' sense of divinely established prerogative, and to contest the Christian construction of colonial experience as a conflict between "saints" and "savages."

Jogues arrived in New France in 1636 and joined a mission to the Hurons in southern Ontario. In June 1642 he was sent to Quebec to obtain supplies, and in August, on their return trip, he and his party of forty, mostly Hurons, were attacked by a larger force of Mohawks. Jogues' account of his subsequent captivity graphically details the tortures he witnessed and endured, while it reveals his dedication to his priestly work of instructing, baptizing, absolving, and comforting both the Huron and the French captives and his readiness for martyrdom. In the course of this captivity he may have been adopted into the Wolf clan; in any case, he was sheltered by an older woman of that clan who had recently lost a son and whom he called "aunt."[12] Brought eventually into the vicinity of the Dutch colony at Renselaerwyck (Albany, New York), he became the object of unsuccessful Dutch efforts to ransom him; finally, after Jogues had persuaded himself that by fleeing he could better serve God, the Dutch helped him to escape. He returned to France, but only to recover his strength and secure permission to return to Canada, which he did in the spring of 1644.

Back in Montreal, he accepted an assignment to establish a mission among the Mohawks, with whom a tenuous peace agreement had recently been made. He set out in May 1646 as an ambassador from the French. The Mohawks "welcomed [him] as a friend"; he dispatched his ambassadorial duties by exchanging greetings and gifts, then "turned to his spiritual avocations,"[13] but the Indians pressed him to leave, and he turned back to Canada in mid-June. Eager to return to the Mohawks, he was delayed until September by rumors that the peace had failed. On this final journey, Jogues, his assistant, Jean de La Lande, and Otrihoure, a Huron envoy, were captured by a Mohawk war party and taken to Ossernenon, the town where Jogues had previously been a captive. As had happened before, he was told that he would die. Though the Turtle and Wolf clans were opposed, members of the Bear clan were determined to kill the missionaries. (Kenny describes the Bear clan as "holding a strong religious persuasion" [p. 68], perhaps suggesting an additional motive.) On October 18, 1646, while a council of Mohawk leaders was meeting in another town to determine the prisoners' fate, he was summoned to eat in a lodge of the Bear clan and was killed on the way. De La Lande was killed within a day. A letter from the Dutch governor indicates that some of the Mohawks believed that religious paraphernalia left behind by Jogues in June had blighted their corn.[14] Jogues was canonized in 1930.

Kenny's *Blackrobe* tells not only of Jogues' life and death, but also of the French in North America and the Mohawk people—and of the rifts among the Mohawks perhaps occasioned, or at least aggravated, by European colonization, trade, and proselytizing. The sequence is framed with history and prophecy. Two poems, titled "Peacemaker" (pp. 3, 5) and "Aiionwatha" (p. 6), tell of the establishment of the Iroquois confederacy for peace and protection. An ominous note is sounded, though, by the first "Wolf" poem (p. 4), in which the forest is "trampled" by "heavy footsteps." "Little People" (p. 7) seems to identify the intruder as a Christian priest who enters the woods and fails to acknowledge the presence of the little people, protectors and benefactors of the Iroquois. The poem which follows, "Wolf (Snakes)" (p. 8), intensifies the sense of foreboding as it alludes to "the Mohawk Prophecy" of two devouring snakes, Canada and the United States (p. 67). These first poems, then, both establish the context of traditional values and ways of life, and foreshadow the impending cultural disruptions.

In the body of the work, Kenny creates direct speech, journal entries, letters, commentaries, and accounts by Jogues, individual Mohawks, and observers of or participants in the French colonial effort. Thus we read statements by Cardinal Richelieu, the explorer La Salle, and the Jesuit Father Superior of New France, Vimont, as well as letters from Jogues to his mother and an assessment of the missionary by a Dutch official, Arendt Van Corlear; there are also recollections from Jean de La Lande and Hoantteniate, "Jogues' Adopted 'Wolf Brother.'" Kenny follows a basically chronological order, from Jogues' eager but somewhat fearful first voyage to Canada ("how happy I am . . . that now / I will have the opportunity / of saving these lost souls for God" [p. 10]; "I shall / manage this boat! This storm! / This fear! God is in my heart." [p. 11]) to his death. However, he condenses and somewhat conflates Jogues' several sojourns and two captivities so that the sequence not only tells the French priest's story but also evokes cultural conflicts and explores the mean-

ings of Jogues' entry into the Native world. A number of poems dramatize a difference in views and feelings between "Bear" and "Wolf 'Aunt'"; far from simply illuminating the Jesuit's impact, these poems deepen the depiction of the Mohawk people, whom he wished to convert.

The sequence concludes as Kenny completes the frame of history and prophecy: first, two later historical Mohawk converts speak, in poems that bear their names. "Tekakwitha (Kateri)" (p. 57) combines full commitment to the new faith with alienation from the earth, the Mohawk community, and the flesh; "Aroniateka" (p. 58), who also speaks in "Hendrik" (p. 59) using his European name, suggests a return, perhaps after death, to older ways. Then "Turtle" (p. 60) offers a prophecy about the colonizers' descendants. This poem is somewhat ambivalent, yet it represents, I think, an effort to be hopeful: "Someday they will come / to learn . . . not to teach" (Kenny's ellipsis). However, it is followed by "Rokwaho" (p. 61), dated 1978, which returns to history and grief:[15]

> From his prayers flowed death
> of salmon and trout in mercury pools.
> . . . settlers followed
> soldiers behind hooded priests.
>
> In his pouch he carried raisins
> to cure the influenza his people
> brought to the shores of the lake.
> My hair and tongue are cut!

Only after so painfully testifying to the ongoing consequences of colonialism can Kenny bring his book to end with serenity and unambiguous hope. He does so in a poem dated 1979 (p. 62), in which Rokwaho speaks directly to Kenny, reminding him that though "we do not speak [the Peacemaker's] name / in an act of respect," still

> His thought moves among us
> through the pine,
> and his power.[16]

This final poem reveals most clearly Kenny's commitment not only to historical reclamation, but also to continuity and survival.

The struggle for survival is embodied in the dialogic contests of the poems that make up the book's core, particularly those that juxtapose French and Indian voices and the differing perspectives of Wolf "Aunt" and Bear. A number of poems tellingly counterpoint Jogues' voice to those of Indians with whom he came into contact. In "First Meeting with Kiotsaeton" (p. 19), Jogues responds (inwardly) to the Mohawk chief sent both to welcome the Jesuits as visitors and persuade them not to stay (p. 67). The poem begins in the vein of exoticism with which Kenny has already had Jogues, in his journal, describe the Hurons ("Les Hures," p. 14). "Like some marvelous bird," Kiotsaeton "stood on the river bank in plummage [*sic*], . . . in rainbow colors." The Natives' physical presence is powerful: Kiotsaeton's "air of royalty stunned my sensibilities"; and

Jogues fears the motives of his warriors, "whose faces—on which I can discern / paint!—margin the woods."[17] Jogues "exchange[s] gifts of food" with Kiotsaeton, but he resists recognizing Native prerogative: "I / represent the French crown! / and shall not be . . . denied my route"; secure in his knowledge that he is "son of God and priest / of Christ's blood," he comes away from this meeting determined to prevail. The following poem, "Kiotsaeton," gives us the Mohawk's speech to Jogues (p. 20). He counters European claims with indigenous authority when he begins, "through my lips / the Nation speaks." He offers Jogues reassurance and hospitality, but also defines his people's terms: they "will respect your customs / and invite you into the lodge / if you maintain respect for ours." Placing this poem after the preceding one throws into relief Jogues' failure to accept the requirement of mutual respect. These two poems together highlight his (and the Church's) breach of the rules of the traditional culture, and prepare us for his part in the fulfillment of the prophecy of "Wolf" (p. 8) when he becomes in effect an accessory to the devouring snake.

Jogues' perspective is next voiced in "Approaching the Mohawk Village," an excerpt from his "Journal" (p. 24). Defying advice, he "enter[s] the village" holding his "silver cross . . . upright" before him.[18] The rest of this "journal" entry demonstrates that converting the Indians would in essence mean possessing them:

> Iroquois, give me your children,
> . . .
> Iroquois give me your chieftains.
> Give me your pride and arrogance.
> Give me your wildness.
> Give me your souls for God
> and your sins for hell.

Further, a "Marginal Note" implies material wealth to be had, if not by Jogues then by others, for he comments on the "Richly furred / beaver pelts" at the lodge entrances.

Using the church's language in such a compromised circumstance, Kenny has already drawn attention to its heteroglossia and conveyed his own dialogic intention. In "Bear" (p. 25), the poem that immediately follows (and the first of five so titled), he draws attention to the dialogic struggle between Jogues and the Indians. The priest had offered "French raisins / to cure your influenza" (p. 24); now Bear begins angrily, "What do I want with his raisins!" His challenge continues as he claims that "[t]here is blood on that cross he wears" and that Jogues' rosary "beads are / the spittle of a snake." That the Mohawk's objection is political, too, is apparent: "Didn't he come / from Huron country[?]" Bear seems to demonstrate a limitation analogous to Jogues' when he questions the humanity of one who doesn't conform to his own cultural expectations: "What kind / of human is this who does not hunt for his own food[?]" Then he voices his primary concern, one certainly not limited to his own culture: "If he would leave / the children alone . . . children make men . . . / I would not interfere" (Kenny's ellipses). In fact, Jogues'

Narrative indicates that another French captive, Rene Goupil, was killed precisely because, "taking off the cap of a child in the hut where he lived, he made him make the sign of the cross on his breast and forehead" (pp. 30-31). An act of piety and love to a devout young European Catholic, this gesture evidently conveyed dreadful possibilities to the child's Mohawk grandfather; Goupil might be said to have died of cultural heteroglossia.

Bear, I think, can be read as one member of the Bear clan or as several speaking in succession; he might perhaps be read as speaking for his clan. The five "Bear" poems give this voice an importance almost matching that of Jogues. Bear speaks next in two consecutive pairs of poems that juxtapose his words to those of Wolf "Aunt" (the name Kenny gives to the Wolf clan elder who sheltered Jogues). In the first pair, the speakers justify their actions: Wolf "Aunt," her "adoption" of "Blackrobe" ("I had the right to choose. / It is customary," p. 37), and Bear, his anticipated killing of Jogues ("Our corn withers! . . . We will starve / if this Blackrobe remains," p. 38).

In the second pair, each tells the story of Jogues' death. Wolf "Aunt" speaks from inside her lodge (pp. 39-41). She describes her efforts to persuade the priest to leave the village and to instruct him in propriety and respect, her hope that "he would learn our ways," his obstinacy, and finally the moment of his death: "they came to the door, / called him by name," he stepped out of the lodge, and she "heard a thump and . . . knew / his body crumpled under the club." Bear (pp. 43-45) recounts Jogues' offenses, focusing on "his preaching, / his determined wish to change, . . . his power to strike out a past / that has taken centuries to build"; he also admits his own dislike of "the hook of his nose," an ironic echo of Jogues' "journal" description of the Hurons (p. 14) and further evidence that Kenny sees these figures as complex and flawed—there are no paragons in *Blackrobe*. After affirming that the Mohawks had "carr[ied] out the law" by offering "sanctuary" and "hospitality . . . to satisfy the demands / of the Seneca," Bear recalls the night of Jogues' death: his own preparations, how he and two friends summoned Jogues and heard "his aunt's . . . arguments," her last effort to protect the priest. "Then the clubs rained upon his head." Afterwards, Bear "returned to [his] lodge," where "the doctors purged [his] flesh / with burning cedar smoke," and he "awaited the Seneca runners." Mentioning the Senecas again, Bear alludes to the dissension not only among the three Mohawk clans, but also among the peoples of the Iroquois League over how to deal with the French; Kenny thus silently reminds us that by killing Jogues, the Bear clan members preempted the right of the council to decide on an appropriate, communal resolution. These paired poems spoken by Wolf "Aunt" and Bear powerfully demonstrate the dialogism of history. Both accounts are true, and both Bear and Wolf "Aunt" justify their attitudes and actions in terms of their culture's traditional expectations, yet obviously their emphases and implications differ, even while each leads to the same conclusion, Jogues' death.

If Wolf "Aunt" and Bear reveal a dialogics of conflict within Mohawk culture, an analogous dialogic tension is evident within European culture, for Kenny gives us not only poems from Jogues' perspective, but others in the voices of more secularly oriented Europeans. "The French Informal Report" (p. 51) is representative. It shares the Natives' assessment of Jogues as a fool; it also shares with the fourth "Bear" poem (p. 50), which precedes it, a view of the commercial-political agenda as primary for the French in North America. Bear states that "The French . . . demand retribution, / but will settle for beaver pelts, . . . and an opened gate to the Mohawk / Valley." And the "Informal Report" rages that Jogues "foiled our plans. The Dutch laugh / in our face, and the English frigates / approach New Amsterdam harbor." Ironically, Bear is the speaker who most unambiguously honors the courage of La Lande and Jogues. In the fifth "Bear" poem (p. 52), his last word, he acknowledges that "It is that very courage, bravery / in men that I fear most."

In *Blackrobe: Isaac Jogues,* Maurice Kenny revises the documentary record in a number of significant ways, each of which foregrounds the inherent heteroglossia and intensifies the dialogism of the history—or histories—and the telling. He does so, perhaps most importantly, by giving voice to Native speakers who've been "heard," if at all in writing, in records written by the French and their successors; in so doing, he implicitly counterpoints and revalues the oral and the written. Conversely, he barely alludes to a major theme of Jogues' *Narrative,* the excruciating tortures suffered by the Mohawks' Indian and French prisoners. This may have been a choice he felt necessary if he was to lead his audience to think beyond stereotypes; it may also be appropriate to his focus on his Mohawk characters' (and ancestors') motives.

Kenny also complicates the position and characterization of Isaac Jogues by suggesting his implication in worldly motives. First, there is the suggestion that Jogues may not have escaped complicity in the French pursuit of wealth. His "journal" note delightedly describing the "[r]ichly furred / beaver pelts" in the Mohawk village (p. 24) and his statement in a "letter" to his mother that the pelts "will make handsome chapeaux for our French / gentlemen and the grandees of China" (p. 29) might imply such complicity. That he was expected not to interfere with commercial interests and, if only by deferring, to promote them, is implied in the "French Informal Report." That he in effect served the larger European agenda of conquest foretold in "Wolf" (p. 8) is the claim of the sequence's penultimate poem: "Out of his black robe came Kraft, / feedmills, blight, Benson Mines" (p. 61). Ironically, perhaps tragically (and even if unwittingly), the man who would be a tool of God became a tool of commerce, and worse.[19]

More difficult to assess are the passages in which Kenny attributes sexual interests to the priest. Sexual fear—somewhat akin to that implied in Rowlandson's *Narrative* and directly attributed to Rowlandson in Erdrich's epigraph—is evident in the first such passage from Jogues' "letter" to the Jesuit Father Superior in France:

> . . . I hardly dare
> speak of the danger there is
> . . . amongst
> the improprieties of these
> savages. I understand adultery
> flourishes throughout their country.

> (p. 11)

This passage might echo one from near the end of Jogues' account of his first captivity: "Purity is not, indeed, endangered here by delights, but is tried, amid this promiscuous and intimate intercourse of both sexes, by the perfect liberty of all in hearing and doing what they please; and, most of all, in their constant nakedness" (p. 45).[20] Kenny gives Jogues himself only one other expression of sexual interest. It comes in the "journal" passage entitled "Les Hures" (p. 14), which focuses on the exotic physicality of "[n]aked, reddish-brown bodies" and concludes (the ellipsis is Kenny's):

> It is exciting to be
> here among these fetching
> people . . . rogues which we Jesuits
> will change into angels and saints.

This poem's evident fascination with the Indians' bodies and its language (exciting, fetching, rogues) make the more directly stated suspicions of Bear and Wolf "Aunt," that Jogues is unusually interested in boys, seem not implausible. Bear objects that "[h]is eye / is always either on pelts or dis- / tracted by the boys" (p. 25); after Jogues' death, Bear elaborates:

> he could not bear the sight
> of naked flesh, nor two people
> coupling in the shadows of the lodge.
> Chastity, he called, chastity!
>
> . . .
> . . . Yet, he stared
> at the young boys swimming nude
> in the river. And flew to make signs
> over their heads.

> (p. 43)

Wolf "Aunt," concerned for Jogues' safety, fears that "one day . . . some boy would resent his stares" (p. 41). And in "Hoantteniate" (p. 53), "Jogues' Adopted 'Wolf Brother'" remembers "trembl[ing] / when his warm hand touched / my bare shoulder"; Hoantteniate says that he

> . . . will miss the touch of his fingers
> and his whispering through the corn fields
> while reading his book, and the sweet
> raisins he offered the boys and myself. . . .

These passages don't lend themselves to a clear, singular conclusion about the meanings of the characters' (including Jogues') statements, suspicions, and memories. Each is entangled in her or his own needs and commitments. Would Bear, for example, condemn a homoerotic interest as such? Another passage (p. 44) might suggest that he would. Is he rather objecting to the possibility of an adult's exploiting the young? His earlier statement that if Jogues "would leave / the children alone" he, Bear, would "not interfere," might suggest that interpretation. Could these objections of Bear's actually be ironic, revealing his own intolerance? And is Hoantteniate remembering Jogues' seduction, or the seductiveness of unfamiliar sensory experiences? These questions, I think, are unanswerable. Two things do seem clear. First, by inviting such questions Kenny again undercuts the image of Jogues as a purely religious person, one who transcended worldly needs and desires. Second, he may be responding critically and ironically to the Europeans' sexualization of the American landscape and of Native peoples as "parts of" the landscape, which converted land and people into objects to be enjoyed and exploited by outsiders.[21] (Erdrich, too, may respond to the implications of such a view; in "Captivity," though, the dread that follows from sexualization is subverted, as the captive's perception is transformed.)

Another possibility is that implying Jogues' perhaps homoerotic interest in the boys might be a way for Kenny, a gay poet, obliquely to signal sympathy for him. Walter Williams includes the Iroquois among "aboriginal American cultures [that] did not recognize berdaches" (men who do not conform to standard men's roles, usually blending men's and women's work and roles) "as a respected status."[22] Kenny himself, in his essay "Tinselled Bucks: A Historical Study in Indian Homosexuality," does not refer specifically to Mohawk or Iroquois attitudes, though he maintains that "[h]omosexuality was found in all American Indian tribes." A young man, he says, who had "forfeit[ed] his right to masculine privilege" by choosing not to take the warrior's path, "possibly exposed himself to insulting ridicule and abuse though rarely would he have been castigated, ostracized, or expelled."[23] His poem "Winkte" emphasizes the respect accorded berdaches in Sioux, Cheyenne, Crow, and Ponca cultures, contrasting such acceptance with the intolerance that, it implies, gay Indians and berdaches meet elsewhere—and perhaps met even in some traditional communities.[24] Bear's words about Jogues, then, could anticipate and echo scornful words that gay and lesbian Indians have heard even from within Native communities.[25] If so, Bear's remarks might veil Kenny's own engagement in dialogic discourse with tribal forebears and contemporaries.

Jogues has his last word in "His Visions" (pp. 47-48), which follows the accounts of his death. Here Kenny alludes to visions that may allow us more directly to sympathize with Jogues. In the poem itself, Kenny only implies the import of these visions, but their significance becomes clear if we read this poem's tone and language in the context of words earlier attributed to Jogues. The most important element of the visions is contained in these lines (emphasis added):

> What greater sacrifice can I
> make for God and the salvation

> of these *brothers* who I shall
> and must lead to God.
>
> . . .
>
> I will example my life for Jean
> and for these *innocents*
> who are in need of God's love

No longer do we hear him speaking of "lost souls," "savages," "rogues," or the "wildness" of exotic and dangerous warriors, for he has had a vision of the Natives' humanity. Kenny makes this clear when he responds to Bruchac's observation that his picture of Isaac Jogues is "almost sympathetic." He reveals his own ambivalence when he responds at first, "No, it's not really sympathetic at all. . . . I try to show him in the round as much as possible." However, as he speaks of the visions, Kenny seems to modify his position:

> But what did happen with Isaac was that he had two visions when he came to this land . . . totally believing the bilge that Indian people were just plain wild savages. . . . he had his first vision in which was told, and he came to understand and accept, that the Indian people . . . were his brothers and sisters. . . . That's a lesson we can all still learn, not just about Indian people but about each other. . . . And his second vision told him that because he had finally accepted the people as his brothers and sisters that he must remain with them and die.[26]

As Kenny describes them here, the visions offer a way of imagining a sympathetic potential in Jogues. The Jogues of "His Visions" has already moved beyond the insistent preacher who "openly refute[d the Indians'] foolish tales / that the world was built on a turtle's back" (p. 36). But Kenny sees in these visions the potential for further growth, foreclosed though it was by Jogues' death: in accepting the need to remain with his "brothers and sisters," Kenny believes, Jogues

> was throwing The Crown away. He would eventually, I am sure, have fought against The Crown . . . it would have been a different story. But because of Isaac Jogues the state of New York . . . and . . . the United States of America is a different place. . . . He was the first missionary to come to this area and survive for any length of time. . . . So it is directly upon his head. So you see where I might favor him a little bit. . . . had he lived longer, it might have been different.[27]

Like Erdrich, it seems, Kenny sees at least the intimation of a different relationship between Europeans and Indians. Though in each case the possibility is cut off, perhaps simply suggesting an alternative (albeit a tenuous one) to stark animosity may be taken as a hopeful consequence of reinterpreting history. Or perhaps not.

"What should we make of this man-priest . . . [?]" Kenny has the Dutch official Arendt Van Corlear ask (p. 31). In the poems of *Blackrobe* and his comments to Bruchac, he demonstrates his knowledge that we do *make* something of Jogues, and of history, and that history is susceptible to revision. The successive monologues, speeches, journal entries, letters, and recollections of *Blackrobe* illuminate each other, complicating and deepening the meanings of the parts and the whole. In doing so they demonstrate the vitality of history and show that true history, or history that approaches being adequate to lived experience, must be polyvocal and dialogic. Early on, Kenny allows the explorer La Salle to assert confidently that "we have all plotted our places in history" (p. 9), but he proceeds to show that the stability La Salle takes for granted is illusory. Every voice, every piece, in *Blackrobe* implies dialogic struggle in some sense, even if only (as is probably so for La Salle's) in the relationship between a voice or a poem and its contexts.

Like Erdrich, then, Kenny shows us that the still-contested histories and interpretations of colonization demand, even create, dialogic discourse. As they write against such colonialist impositions as the "saints-vs.-savages" construction of colonial history, both poets complicate received history and raise questions about the meanings and limits of documentary truth. Erdrich does so by revising Rowlandson's *Narrative*; Kenny, through the proliferation of invented "documents" in *Blackrobe,* as well as by indirectly responding to published accounts of Jogues' life. Directly confronting and reimagining the victors' accounts, they offer resistant alternatives, imply the possibility of reclaiming other stories, and implicitly challenge their readers to respond.

Notes

1. Kimberly M. Blaeser, *Gerald Vizenor: Writing in the Oral Tradition* (Norman: University of Oklahoma Press, 1996), 84, 85.

2. The first title is from the second edition published in Cambridge, Massachusetts in 1682 by Samuel Green. The second title is from the 1773 edition, printed in Boston by John Boyle. I quote from the 1930 "Lancaster Edition," based on the 1682 Cambridge edition: Mary Rowlandson, *The Narrative of the Captivity of Mrs. Mary Rowlandson,* Lancaster Edition (Boston: Houghton Mifflin, 1930).

3. See Alden T. Vaughn, *Narratives of North American Indian Captivity, A Selective Bibliography* (New York: Garland, 1983). Vaughn lists narratives published into the 1890s and even some publications of new accounts, as well as re-publications, into the 1940s. Continuing popular interest in captivity narratives is evident in Frederick Drimmer, ed., *Scalps and Tomahawks: Narratives of Indian Captivity* (New York: Coward McCann, 1961), and in movies like *Little Big Man* and *Dances with Wolves,* to cite just a few examples. For other examples, see Raymond William Stedman, *Shadows of the Indian: Stereotypes in American Culture* (Norman: University of Oklahoma Press, 1982). For another poetic reimagining of the meanings of captivity, see Mary Oliver's "The Lost Children," in *American Primitive* (Boston: Little, Brown, 1983), 12-15. Among recent studies of captivity narratives are those by Annette

Kolodny, in *The Land Before Her: Fantasy and Experience of the American Frontiers, 1630-1860* (Chapel Hill: University of North Carolina Press, 1984), 17-89, and Richard Slotkin, in *Regeneration Through Violence: The Mythology of the American Frontier, 1600-1860* (Middletown, CT: Wesleyan University Press, 1973), especially 94-145.

4. Louise Erdrich, *Jacklight* (New York: Holt, Rinehart, Winston, 1984), 26-27. All subsequent quotations from Erdrich's poem are from this text.

5. *Remove* is the term Rowlandson uses to designate chapters, each of which recounts one leg of her journey with the Indians.

6. I've consulted photocopies of the first London and the second American editions (the earliest extant), both published in 1682, as well as two other editions taken from the latter.

7. See, for example, Kolodny, *The Land Before Her,* 68-81.

8. Susan Howe, *The Birth-mark: Unsettling the Wilderness in American Literary History* (Hanover: Wesleyan University Press/University Press of New England, 1993), 94, 96, 123, 124.

9. Mitchell Breitwieser, *American Puritanism and the Defense of Mourning: Religion, Grief, and Ethnology in Mary White Rowlandson's Captivity Narrative* (Madison: University of Wisconsin Press, 1990), 4, 6, 8-9, 10. Slotkin's assertions about Rowlandson's "insights" probably overstate matters; still, like Howe and Breitwieser, he reads her text as undermining the Puritan community's expectations (*Regeneration Through Violence,* 111-12). I mention him here especially because he is the one of these critics whose book could have been available to Erdrich before she wrote "Captivity."

10. See, for example, Howe, *The Birth-mark,* 97 and 124.

11. Joseph Bruchac, "New Voices from the Longhouse: Some Contemporary Iroquois Writers and Their Relationship to the Tradition of the Ho-de-no-sau-nee," in *Coyote Was Here: Essays on Contemporary Native American Literature and Mobilization,* ed. Bo Schöler (Aarhus, Denmark: Seklos, 1984), 158.

12. For information on Jogues' life and death see Francis Talbot, *Saint Among Savages: The Life of Isaac Jogues* (New York: Harper and Brothers, 1935); see also Isaac Jogues, *Narrative of a Captivity Among the Mohawk Indians, and A Description of New Netherland in 1642-3,* with John Gilmary Shea, *A Memoir of the Holy Missionary* (New York: Press of the Historical Society, 1856; rpt. New York: Garland, 1977). See also the other documents published in the same volume: the *Memoir* by Shea, letters from Jogues to various people, and letters from others announcing his death.

Regarding the "adoption" of Jogues, Shea refers to his having been "incorporated" into the Wolf "tribe" (*Memoir,* 10); Talbot says that when he visited the Mohawks as an ambassador, he was welcomed into the Wolf clan's "special protection and their adoption" (*Saint Among Savages,* 389). Describing his first captivity, Jogues himself refers to "a good old woman, who from her age and her care of me, as well as from her compassion for my sufferings, called me her nephew, as I called her aunt" (48). Kenny states that this elder woman "did not legally, in ceremony, adopt Isaac Jogues, but simply took him into her protective house." Obviously, *adoption* is a term rife with the contending intentions of heteroglossia. See Maurice Kenny, *Blackrobe: Isaac Jogues* (Saranac Lake, NY: North Community College Press, 1982), 68. Unless otherwise noted, all quotations from *Blackrobe* and Kenny's notes on that work are from this edition; page numbers will be noted parenthetically in the text.

13. Shea, 10.

14. Jogues, 68.

15. The name, Kenny tells us, means "Wolf-robe" (69); it is also the name of a younger Mohawk poet and artist, one of the people Kenny acknowledges in the dedication of *Between Two Rivers: Selected Poems, 1956-1984* (Fredonia, NY: White Pine Press, 1987).

16. Discussing Kenny's first "Peacemaker" poem, Bruchac illuminates "that dominant Iroquois image of the great pine (under whose four white roots the weapons of war were buried and at whose top an eagle always perches, vigilant, watching for any disturbance of the peace)." "New Voices," 158.

17. I quote these two lines from the poem as it appears in the selections from *Blackrobe* included in *Between Two Rivers* (109) because I think Kenny has not so much improved as corrected the lines printed in the original: "whose faces margin the woods / on which I can discern paint."

The descriptive words Kenny attributes to Jogues at the beginning of this poem ("some marvelous bird . . . in plummage") may ironically echo Talbot's description of "Kiotsaeton and the Mohawk leaders, sharp featured and barbaric in their head-dress of brilliant plumage" (*Saint Among Savages,* 386-87).

18. The Algonquian who advised Jogues not to wear his habit when he visited the Mohawks as an ambassador explained that "'nothing [is] more repulsive at first, than this doctrine, that seems to exterminate all that men hold dearest,'" and the habit "preach[ed the doctrine] as strongly as your lips'" (Jogues, 9).

19. In a note Kenny says, "There is definite thought that Jogues was sent as a pawn by the French government . . . to keep a keen eye out for beaver pelts and other valued furs. Jogues may well have been duped in the veils of his religious ardor and zeal" (68).

20. Kenny's lines are even closer to words Talbot attributes to Jean de Brébeuf, Jogues' mentor at the Huron mission: "'I hardly dare speak of the danger there is of ruining oneself among the impurities of these savages, in the case of one whose heart is not sufficiently full of God to resist firmly this poison'" (*Saint Among Savages,* 69). Recognizing such a likely source increases our sense of Kenny's complex dialogism.

21. See Annette Kolodny, *The Land Before Her* and *The Lay of the Land: Metaphor as Experience and History in American Life and Letters* (Chapel Hill: University of North Carolina Press, 1975).

22. Walter Williams, *The Spirit and the Flesh: Sexual Diversity in American Indian Culture* (Boston: Beacon, 1986; 1992), 39.

23. Maurice Kenny, "Tinselled Bucks: A Historical Study in Indian Homosexuality," in *Living the Spirit: A Gay American Indian Anthology,* ed. Will Roscoe (New York: St. Martin's Press, 1988), 18, 20.

24. Kenny, *Between Two Rivers,* 61-62.

25. Chrystos alludes to such tensions within Indian communities in "Askenet, Meaning 'Raw' in My Language," in *Inversions: Writing by Dykes, Queers, and Lesbians,* ed. Betsy Warland (Vancouver, BC: Press Gang, 1991), 237-47.

26. Joseph Bruchac, *Survival This Way: Interviews with American Indian Poets* (Tucson: University of Arizona Press, 1987), 153-54.

27. Ibid., 154.

INFLUENCE ON AMERICAN LITERATURE

David T. Haberly (essay date 1976)

SOURCE: Haberly, David T. "Women and Indians: *The Last of the Mohicans* and the Captivity Tradition." *American Quarterly* 28, no. 4 (autumn 1976): 431-44.

[*In the essay below, Haberly outlines the influence of captivity narratives on James Fenimore Cooper's creation of* The Last of the Mohicans.]

Despite considerable new interest in narratives of Indian captivity, this large genre remains somewhat isolated within American literary history—more interesting to bibliographers and ethnohistorians than to critics.[1] Some recent studies of captivity narratives have ably elaborated basic ideas first presented by Roy Harvey Pearce a generation ago; new and highly imaginative approaches to the captivities have also been attempted, but the critics' eagerness to fit one or more narratives into universal mythic structures or into psychosexual theories of American culture has often distracted them from the fundamental question about the captivities—the specific influence of this vast and enormously popular genre upon the development of literature in the United States.[2]

Yet it is only logical that such influence must have existed. Bibliographers have catalogued more than a thousand separate captivity titles, published fairly steadily from the sixteenth century to the first decades of the twentieth; many of the best-known narratives were reprinted in dozens of editions.[3] For roughly a hundred years, from 1750 to 1850, the Indian captivity was one of the chief staples of popular literary culture; as Phillips D. Carleton noted, such narratives "took the place of fiction, of what might be called escape literature now."[4]

The frontier between fact and fiction, moreover, was often very vague indeed, and it is sometimes difficult today to separate the authentic accounts of redeemed captives from the works of writers eager to make a quick buck by milking a well-established market—Ann Eliza Bleecker's *History of Maria Kittle* is a notable example—or dimly conscious of the fictional possibilities inherent in the totally violent and alien reality of Indian captivity—as in the cryptic narrative of "Abraham Panther"[5] or Charles Brockden Brown's *Edgar Huntly*.

These fictional captivities, however, are at best of marginal interest. I would suggest, rather, that an important and neglected aspect of the captivity tradition is its influence upon major works of nineteenth-century American fiction.[6] And my purpose here is to define and analyze the impact of that tradition upon James Fenimore Cooper's *The Last of the Mohicans*—for several generations one of the most popular of all American novels and a work which created an idea of America which put down deep and permanent roots in Europe, in Latin America, and in the recesses of our own minds.

I believe, further, that a number of the most controversial aspects of the structure and the thematics of Cooper's novel are only tangentially related, at best, to such generalities as the theory and practice of myth-making or the suggested homoeroticism of American literature. These aspects, rather, flow directly from the very concrete difficulties Cooper faced in adapting the traditional and clearly-defined captivity narrative to his new and very different purposes.

By 1825, Cooper had tried his hand at a range of novelistic genres, seeking to identify his own strengths and weaknesses and to find a way to use fiction to foster America's "mental independence," a goal he was to describe—in a letter of 1831—as his chief object.[7] He had written a novel of manners (*Persuasion*, 1820); two patriotic historical novels (*The Spy*, 1821, and *Lionel Lincoln*, 1825); a sea

story (*The Pilot,* 1824); and a semicomic, semi-autobiographical novel of the local gentry (*The Pioneers,* 1823). It was natural that, in shuffling through the available genres, he should attempt a fictionalized captivity. A concrete link between parallel incidents in Cooper's fiction and in one authentic captivity has only recently been established,[8] but his passionate interest in the American past and the ready availability of such narratives—some dealing specifically with his own area of upstate New York—would inevitably have led him to the captivities.

And *The Last of the Mohicans,* despite the shift in narration away from the traditional first person, is above all a captivity narrative—more exactly, as we shall see, it is two separate captivity narratives. First, however, it is important to look back at the tradition those narratives had created, the tradition Cooper necessarily inherited when he sought to use the genre.

The purpose of many captivities, by 1825, was often frankly commercial. Rescued captives not infrequently found themselves without family or funds, and their accounts of life in Indian hands served both to bring in a little cash and to advise their neighbors—as well as generous readers throughout America—of their heroism, their suffering, and their present need. There must also have been, for many returned captives, a kind of therapy in the recounting of their adventures, a way to exorcise their darkest memories—particularly by Cooper's time, when the changing stylistic conventions of the narrative had placed a barrier of verbal commonplaces between experience survived and experience described.[9]

In the early narratives of Puritans like Mary Rowlandson, captivity, suffering, and final redemption were all part of God's plan, and the publication of these events was a Christian duty.[10] By the nineteenth century, that sort of easy metaphoric structure had disappeared; what remained, in its essence, was violence—the total and almost incomprehensible violence of captives scalped and beaten, women starved or tortured to death, babies drowned or bashed against blood-spattered rocks, children with faces burned into unrecognizable scars.

The physical environment of the captivity narratives linked all of this violence and suffering to the frontier; one wonders anew that Americans moved westward in the face of these tracts, the most readily obtainable and believable accounts of the fate that might await them there. And the captivity narratives were filled with raw and burning hatred of the Indian—a hatred so intense that the motives and even the reciprocal violence of the Indian-hater seem understandable and even, for a moment, wholly justified.

Cooper's own ideas, as he sat down to write his fictionalized captivity, were very different indeed. He was conditioned by his background and by his nationalism to idealize the frontier—the endless forests that appear in *The Last of the Mohicans* as the image of all of the American West. As George Dekker has noted, ". . . in Cooper's mind American nationhood and the Westward Movement . . . were intimately connected; each new clearing furnished a sign of the increasing temporal greatness of the nation. . . ."[11] Further, Cooper's ethnological readings and a patriotic fervor that transcends chronology and even race both determined him to idealize the American Indian.

Cooper's problem, then, was to reconcile his own ideals—the beauty of the American wilderness, the glory of the Westward Movement, and the native heroism and goodness of at least a part of Indian America—with the powerful captivity tradition of horrendous barbarities committed on the western frontier by Indians unspeakably vile. The key to the fictional resolution of these antitheses, I believe, lay for Cooper in a basic feature of the captivity narratives—the role of women.

A large proportion of the authentic narratives of captivity were written by women; deprived by Indian violence of the protection of husbands or family, female captives were often more pressingly in need of the financial support a successful narrative might provide. But women captives were also central figures in many of the captivities produced by males, and by Cooper's time had become preeminent in the increasingly popular anthologies of captivities and in the fictional offspring of the tradition.

In these works, women suffered the cruelest torments, and it was those torments which most sorrowed and enraged readers. Beyond this, however, female-centered captivity narratives had a special interest for readers—and for potential romancers—because they were inherently more suspenseful than the stories of males taken by Indians. For quite apart from the common perils of torture and death, three important additional dangers might await female captives.

There was, first, the possibility that a white woman captured by Indians might be defeminized; that is, that her suffering and her separation from civilization might lead her into patterns of behavior suitable only for males. This danger had not greatly preoccupied the Puritans, who applauded Hannah Dustin's massacre of her captors, but it did worry nineteenth-century readers. Bravery, quickness of action, mental and physical independence—and even the shedding of blood—were totally at odds with the ideal of the sentimental heroine. Leslie Fiedler has documented the hostile reactions of Hawthorne and Thoreau to Hannah Dustin's heroics; Hawthorne's attitude was the more important and more typical. While Thoreau was concerned that Hannah had axed Indian children, Hawthorne was merely distressed that she had acted as a man, shoving her husband into the background.[12]

Similar reservations about unfeminine reactions to even the most horrifying situations were expressed by the editors of nineteenth-century captivity anthologies. John Frost, for example, in his *Thrilling Adventures among the Indians,* criticized and even ridiculed some acts of heroism by white women, since he found such tales "little pleasing or amiable. Woman, as an Amazon, does not appear to advantage. Something seems to be wanting in such a character; or, perhaps, it has something too much."[13]

Considerably more frightening for the readers of captivity narratives was the possibility that a white woman might be raped—or, more genteelly, forced into marriage with an Indian. The factual evidence on Indian sexual abuse of captive women in the East is contradictory. Mary Rowlandson declared that during her captivity, ". . . by night and by day, alone and in company: sleeping all sorts together, and yet not one of them [the Indians] ever offered me the least abuse of unchastity to me, in word or action."[14] Elizabeth Hanson hedged a little, writing that ". . . the Indians are seldom guilty of any indecent carriage towards their captive women, unless much overtaken in liquor."[15]

Cooper clearly did not believe that Indians were as chaste as was claimed,[16] and it is likely that his readers had serious doubts as well. It was hardly to be expected, after all, that redeemed female captives would openly confess the loss of their virtue. And the genteel disclaimers of seventeenth-and eighteenth-century captives are repeated, during a later western expansion, in the accounts of women captured by tribes for whom rape appears to have been an established practice.[17] One Mrs. Horn, for example, wrote, "In conclusion, perhaps I ought to say, that with reference to a point, of all others of the most sacred importance to a captive female, (with gratitude to my Maker I record it.) my fears were in no part realized."[18] But, as a modern scholar notes, ". . . most white women redeemed from captivity in the West charged that sexual abuse of their fellow captives was common but claimed that because of some unusual circumstance they, themselves, had been spared the ordeal."[19]

Female captives might not only lose their femininity and their virtue; they might also lose their very whiteness. The Indianization process has been of great interest to twentieth-century anthropologists and psychologists,[20] but it also troubled thoughtful students of America, like Franklin, who feared that the rapid Indianization of large numbers of white captives—in sharp contrast to the pitifully few recorded cases of Indians civilized by white society—bore some worrisome lesson about the comparative value and permanence of two very different cultural systems.[21]

The Indianization of white females, however, posed a particular problem, since it suggested willing acceptance of Indian sexual mores and of an Indian spouse. The chief characters in many of the most popular captivity narratives—Eunice Williams, Mary Jemison, Frances Slocum, and Cynthia Ann Parker, for example—were Indianized white women who declined to be redeemed and who established enduring relationships with Indian males;[22] other captive white females struggled desperately to flee their rescuers and return to their Indian husbands and children.[23] The existence of such Indianized female captives did not merely raise doubts about the values of white civilization; it could also imply the far more disturbing possibility that white women might find Indian men sexually superior.

When Cooper began his fictional captivity, therefore, he quite naturally chose to focus the book on the perilous adventures of white women in the wilderness. In order to describe and discuss a full range of possible reactions to captivity, Cooper used the fictional technique that Henry Nash Smith—in his study of the Leatherstocking character—called "doubling."[24] The two sisters, Alice and Cora Munro, represent two very different types of captivity heroine, and two divergent reactions to captivity.

The doubling process, however, is not confined to the Munro sisters; it also defines the structure of the novel, for *The Last of the Mohicans* is composed of two separate captivity narratives. The first captivity—the happy captivity, to borrow the title of a seventeenth-century Chilean example of the genre[25]—ends with the safe arrival of Alice and Cora at Fort William Henry, at the close of Chapter XIV; it derives from the simplest and most pleasant of the captivity narratives, those in which the captive or captives return safely to the bosom of family and friends. After two intercalary chapters, the second narrative begins with the Fort Henry Massacre in Chapter XVII; this captivity—the tragic captivity—represents another, grimmer tradition.

The first, happy captivity, as Donald Darnell has pointed out, takes place between forts, within the outer limits of the white world.[26] The violence it contains is almost always potential rather than actual—shouted threats, a drop of blood on a leaf, the loss of a few of Alice's tresses. The purpose of this narrative is not to describe blood-baths—those follow later on in the novel; through this recreation of one type of captivity, Cooper sets out to define and differentiate the characters of Cora and Alice, before they enter the second captivity and the dark, alien world that belongs to the Indian alone.

Cooper begins this process when fair Alice and dark Cora first appear, using the established equation of complexion and character as a kind of novelistic shorthand, suggesting to his readers exactly where their fullest sympathies should lie.[27] This cosmetic characterization is immediately reinforced as Cooper gets down to the business of defining the disparate "gifts" the sisters possess—"gifts" as different as those of Natty Bumppo and David Gamut. Alice is lighthearted, weak, and innocent; she is the ideal sentimental heroine of a captivity narrative, weeping and fainting as she confronts a series of purely physical dangers. Cora, however, is prey to the three important moral perils—defeminization, rape, and Indianization—and the "gifts" that expose her to these dangers are made clear in her first reactions to Magua. The sudden appearance of the Indian startles Alice, but she quickly recovers to banter coyly with Duncan. Cora, on the other hand, gazes at Magua with "an indescribable look of pity, admiration, and horror, as her dark eye followed the easy motions of the savage." (21) In Cora's pity lies her "gift" for unwomanly serious-

ness and strength of character; her horror foreshadows the rape motif; and her admiration for "the easy motions of the savage" reveals a sensuous miscibility that will lead to her relationship with Uncas and the gradual Indianization that relationship implies.

Cora's unfeminine "gifts" of courage, logic, and self-reliance are more fully developed as the first captivity progresses; even Duncan comes, rather grudgingly, to admire these traits: ". . . your own fortitude and undisturbed reason," he tells her, "will teach you all that may become your sex." (104) By the time the captives reach the security of the fort, Cora actually longs for adventure—like a seasoned trooper. "I sicken at the sight of danger that I cannot share," she proclaims; Natty welcomes her as an equal, "with a smile of honest and cordial approbation," and wishes for "a thousand men, of brawny limbs and quick eyes, that feared death as little as you!" (179)

Cora is also far more sensual than Alice, as her "rather fuller and more mature" figure suggests (21); Magua's threats to her virtue are the direct result of this "gift." She is threatened by rape—in Cooper's terms, forced marriage and sexual submission to Magua—in large part because she is conscious of its possibility. Thus, in the cave scene in the first captivity, the two sisters react in very different ways when suddenly awakened by Duncan. Alice murmurs in her sleep: "No, no, dear father, we were not deserted; Duncan was with us!" Cora's dreams, however, are not those of innocence: ". . . the motion caused Cora to raise her hand as if to repulse him. . . ." (81-82)

When the captivity begins, Alice and Cora appear "to share equally in the attentions of the young officer" (21), but it gradually becomes clear that Duncan belongs to Alice alone. While some critics have seen Cora as a case of unrequited love, pining after Heyward, this seems a misreading of the novel. Cora is disappointed that she is not Duncan's choice, but she is also increasingly attracted to Indian men, as her thoughtful contemplation of Magua first suggests. In the cave, when the captives first see Uncas in all his glory, Alice's reaction is that of an art student gazing upon a Greek statue; Duncan considers the young brave a remarkable anthropological specimen; but Cora sees Uncas as a man, without consideration for race and color—and that perception embarrasses her white companions (65-66).

And Cora must have a potential mate, as Alice has Duncan. Natty might seem a reasonable candidate, but Cooper clearly felt that the scout—while suited to Cora by character and by color—was too much her social inferior. Natty's dialect would have made this class distinction obvious to contemporary readers, and Cooper drives the point home, towards the end of the book, when he describes the scout's "deference to the superior rank of his companions, that no similarity in the state of their present fortune could induce him to forget." (373)

Social class, then, is more important than race, and Cooper provides Cora with two suitors of equal rank—a chief of the Mingoes, Magua; and the last prince of the Mohicans.

If we ignore, for a moment, the fact that both Uncas and Magua are Indians, a perfectly commonplace sentimental triangle emerges. Cora is sought after by two suitors of her class—one a handsome and good nobleman of long and illustrious ancestry; one a violent and lecherous type, born a chief but more recently a drunken servant. In these terms, it is only natural that Cora should prefer Uncas.

Because Uncas is an Indian, however, the progress of the Cora-Uncas romance necessarily implies her Indianization. It is Cora who adopts the Indian techniques of leaving a trail, and the full development of the relationship with Uncas is symbolized in a passage at the very end of the first captivity; as the party approaches the fort, "Duncan willingly relinquished the support of Cora to the arm of Uncas, and Cora as readily accepted the welcome assistance." (183)

During the Fort William Henry interlude, Cooper takes pains to reassure readers worried and perplexed by Cora's "gifts." "Gifts," in Cooper, are not the result of conscious choices, but are preordained by genetics or by environment; even the satanic Magua's character is the result of his tribal ancestry and his sufferings among the whites. Cora, as we discover in Chapter XVI, is of African descent, the daughter of a West Indian mulattress with whom Colonel Munro formed a connection and whom he later married; the future mother of pure Alice, of course, was still in Scotland, "a suffering angel [who] had remained in the heartless state of celibacy twenty long years. . . ." (201-02) This background immediately explains Cora's "gifts," assures us that she is not really a bad person after all, and makes her relationship with Uncas seem both natural and permissible.

The established characters of Cora and Alice are not altered in any important way during the second captivity, deep in the Indian world. Alice is ever more dependent, a tear-stained and insensible bundle dragged from place to place by her male protectors. Cora is still self-reliant, fatally attractive, and increasingly Indianized—as her adoption of Indian oratory shows. In her plea to Tamenund, in fact, Cora strongly identifies the curse of her ancestors—African slavery—with the sufferings of the Indians, like her the victims of white racism (386).

Cooper finally gives Uncas a forced and tightly-structured opportunity to choose between two worlds—between his love for Cora and his respect for Indian traditions. Uncas cannot overcome the force of tradition and environment; he allows Magua to take Cora away once again, and by that choice all hope for a conventional happy ending is destroyed. Cora's Indianization is complete with her death; she receives an Indian burial, beside Uncas, while the native maidens sing prophecies of a marriage consummated in heaven—a standard resolution of the miscegenation issue in novels from other New World cultures.[28]

Through this juxtaposition of two kinds of captivity narrative and through the development of the different "gifts" of his two captivity heroines, Cooper explores the multiple fictional possibilities of the genre. The deaths of Uncas and Cora, moreover, allow the novelist to make several self-righteous but highly comforting statements about race. First, he can claim to be free from the racial prejudice he describes as a Southern trait, since he admits the possibility of interracial love. Miscegenation, however, is still an impossibility, precluded by unalterable barriers of culture and tradition. This reassured white Americans worried about the development of mixed races and cultures, like those found in other parts of the Americas, and about the possible miscibility of the two victimized races—the Indians and those of African descent.

Cooper's exposition of the disparate "gifts" of his characters explains *what* happens in the novel; but it does not explain *why* such things occur. And his fundamental problem remains: how to reconcile his idealized vision of the frontier with the violence implicit in the captivity tradition and explicit in this, the most violent of the Leatherstocking tales.

The gap between idealism and the reality of violence could be bridged only by an explanation based upon immutable "nature," not upon the deterministic "gifts" of individuals. And Cooper therefore took the central role of white females in the captivity tradition and in his own novel, and subtly changed the focus in order to provide such an explanation. It is not mere chance and coincidence that women appear as the chief objects of captivity violence; that violence does not flow from the realities of frontier life or from the evil lusts of Indian males. White women, rather, are the direct cause of all the violence that surrounds their passage through a world in which they do not belong; it is their "nature."

Cooper and his contemporaries believed that the power of white women was the result of their powerlessness; as he wrote in *The Sea Lions,* most of their ". . . real power and influence . . . arises from their seeming dependence. . . ."[29] And *The Last of the Mohicans* is above all a study of the enormous, ironic power of those consistently described as "tender blossoms" and "harmless things."

This power, while interesting and perhaps amusing in the drawing rooms of civilization, becomes immensely destructive when transferred to the frontier wilderness. White men and red, Cooper believed, could sublimate their different genetic and environmental "gifts" and exist in something approaching harmony in the haven of the American wilderness; the very presence of white women makes such harmony impossible. As Natty says, in one of the novel's most significant speeches, ". . . it would not be the act of men to leave such harmless things to their fate, even though it breaks up the harboring place for ever." (55)

White women have this effect because it is their "nature" to excite passion among men—all sorts and kinds of men. No matter how superficially civilized in dress and speech, no matter how sharply their different "gifts" are defined, Cora and Alice are both inherently and potentially sexual, designed above all else for procreation—a point Cooper makes obliquely through his description, in the lines just before our introduction to the sisters in all their finery, of the "low, gaunt, switch-tailed mare," whose foal is "quietly making its morning repast, . . ." (20) As soon as Cora and Alice appear, they artlessly exhibit their charms; such is their "nature," as it is the "nature" of males to react. And such brief moments of exhibitionism in fact become a kind of predictable motif in the novel, inevitably introducing violence.[30]

This inherent power of attraction upsets the balance between man and nature, between white and Indian. To preserve and to please white females, the harboring places are broken up; horses are trained to ungainly and unnatural paces (154-55); and the decorative creatures of the wilds are slaughtered (378). And men of both races willingly take enormous and totally irrational risks in order to possess or to defend the virtue of white women.

Thus, merely because these "flowers, which, though so sweet, were never made for the wilderness" (55) have presumed against all advice to travel where they do not belong, violence will replace harmony and death will come to Cora, to Magua, and to Uncas—the last of the Mohicans, the last hope in Tamenund's vision for a rebirth of Indian America. No less is the natural culpability of Alice and Cora.

In the first captivity, Alice and Cora are only intuitively conscious of their power. Of the male characters, only Magua fully understands the potential of white women—the power, as he expresses it, to make white men their dogs. He seeks to possess Cora because he is attracted to her, but he also comprehends her importance as a symbol and as a means to control the actions and reactions of other men.

Magua's expectations are realized. Duncan becomes so distraught at the thought of "evils worse than death" (100), of a fate "worse than a thousand deaths" (138), that he is almost incapable of rational thought and action. Uncas too becomes, in Magua's terms, a dog to the women, providing menial services for the two sisters and amazing and amusing the others (69). By the mere presence of white women, Uncas is led to deny "his habits, we had almost said his nature, . . ." (145); his contact with Cora and Alice has "elevated him far above the intelligence, and advanced him probably centuries before the practices of his nation." (146) In fact, Natty complains that Uncas' behavior, in his eagerness to rescue the girls, has been "more like that of a curious woman than of a warrior on his scent." (152)

Once the women are safe within Fort William Henry, Cooper suggests the deep cultural roots of their power. Alice coyly calls Duncan to task—in terms of the chivalric tradition: ". . . thou truant! thou recreant knight! he who abandons his damsels in the very lists!" (189) She is surprised when Heyward is deeply wounded by the accusation. References to chivalry continue to crop up in these intercalary chapters—and it is this tradition which forms the powerless power of Cora and Alice and all other white women.

Just as the first captivity began with the mare-foal image and with the sisters' artless display of their charms, the tragic captivity begins with women and children—the latter serving as symbols of the sexual nature and purpose of women. An Indian is attracted by a shawl one of the women wears and tries to grab it. "The woman, more in terror than through love of the ornament, wrapped her child in the coveted article, and folded both more closely to her bosom." The Huron then grabs the child, teases the woman with it, and dashes the head of the infant against a rock; he then kills the mother. At that point the massacre of the innocents and the second captivity commence; once again women appear as the cause of violence as well as its object (221-23).

Magua seizes Alice—"he knew his power, and was determined to maintain it" (225)—and the two girls disappear with him into the forest. Their power remains, however, affecting their rescuers. Uncas is uncharacteristically excited by the discovery of Cora's veil, and begins to act "as impatient as a man in the settlements. . . ." (235) Duncan embarks on the insane and dangerous adventure as a sham witch doctor: "I too can play the madman, the fool, the hero; in short, any or everything to rescue her that I love," he declares (288). Natty is amazed by Heyward's irrational daring, but such is the power of the women that the young officer for the first time takes command: "But Duncan, who, in deference to the other's skill and services, had hitherto submitted somewhat implicitly to his dictation, now assumed the superior, with a manner that was not easily resisted." (288)

Natty continues to ponder this power, and tries to define it. "I have heard," he muses, "that there is a feeling in youth which binds man to woman closer than the father is tied to the son. It may be so. I have seldom been where women of my color dwell; but such may be the gifts of nature in the settlements. You have risked life, and all that is dear to you, to bring off this gentle one, and I suppose that some such disposition is at the bottom of it all." (336)

The power of Cora and Alice increases in its scope as the second captivity progresses. Magua loses his cool, cunning appreciation of the symbolic and strategic value of his captives, and begins himself to be controlled. Natty too falls under the influence of the power he cannot explain, and offers Magua an increasingly illogical set of bargains in exchange for Cora. While the scout knows that ". . . it would be an unequal exchange, to give a warrior, in the prime of his age and usefulness, for the best woman on the frontier," he is nonetheless prepared to sacrifice himself when all else fails. Magua, with equal irrationality, refuses the trade (397-98). Even David Gamut, the pacifist hymnmaster, is overpowered, and prepares to go to war for Cora, reminded "of the children of Jacob going out to battle against the Shechemites, for wickedly aspiring to wedlock with a woman of a race that was favored of the Lord." (413)

When the last battle begins, Cora challenges Magua—confident that he too is now her "dog." He tries to kill her, but cannot: "The form of the Huron trembled in every fibre, and he raised his arm on high, but dropped it again with a bewildered air, like one who doubted. Once more he struggled with himself and lifted the keen weapon again. . . ." (426) As he hesitates, another Huron kills Cora—and Magua delays his escape and slays one of his own men to avenge her death. Magua and Uncas then struggle; Uncas allows himself to be killed—since Cora is dead. Magua makes a mad, suicidal attempt to escape, and Natty kills him.

The final victory of the Delawares over the Hurons is itself yet another example of Cooper's doubling. Magua consistently refers to the Delaware-Mohican tribes as "women"—a pejorative epithet that Cooper took from Heckewelder's writings, but which fully conforms to his own cultural prejudices. As Paul Wallace has demonstrated, Cooper's use of this epithet was conditioned by a misunderstanding of the complex intertribal relationships of Indian America. The Delawares were defined as "women" in their agreements with the Five Nations; that role, however, was one of honor and of power.[31] For Cooper, however, women were necessarily dependent and inferior. But the concept of the natural powerless power of white women is transferred, in the novel, to the Delawares and Mohicans. Like Cora and Alice, they cannot escape violence, and cannot control their own destinies; but they do retain the power to destroy.

The ending Cooper chose for the novel is a direct result of his transmutation of the captivity tradition. White women and their intrusive, destructive power must be removed before the ideal harmony of the frontier can exist once again; Cora is buried, and Alice departs for civilization, sobbing in the seclusion of her litter. With her go her white "dogs," like her the creatures of the civilized world. Natty and Chingachgook must stay behind, since the harmony of their grief for Uncas represents all that is possible in the absence of white women. The crude woodsman and the drunken Indian of *The Pioneers* are no longer merely local color, quaintly useful in forcing philosophical discussions about the nature of government; they are the final proof of Cooper's reconciliation of his idealized frontier with the tradition of the captivity narratives. And from this artificial, novelistic pairing—from these "two childless womanless men of opposite races," in Lawrence's phrase[32]—issue Huck and Jim, the Lone Ranger and Tonto, and all the other offspring, cultured or popular, of *The Last of the Mohicans.*

Notes

1. Major bibliographical sources for the captivities include: the Newberry Library's list of books in the Edward E. Ayer Collection (Chicago: Newberry Library, 1912) and Clara A. Smith's supplement to that list, *Narratives of Captivity among the Indians of North America* (Chicago: Newberry Library, 1928); R. W. G. Vail, *The Voice of the Old Frontier* (Philadelphia: Univ. of Pennsylvania Press, 1949); and C. Marius Barbeau, "Indian Captivities," *Proceedings of the American Philosophical Society,* 94 (1950), 522-48. Also see Dwight L. Smith, "Shawnee Captivity Ethnography," *Ethnohistory,* 2, No. 1 (Winter 1955), 29-41.

2. To date, by far the most interesting response to this question is Richard Slotkin's massive and always stimulating study of the captivities, *Regeneration Through Violence* (Middletown, Conn.: Wesleyan Univ. Press, 1973).

3. Four captivity narratives—those of Mary Rowlandson, John Williams, Jonathan Dickinson, and Mary Jemison—are listed among the great bestsellers of American publishing by Frank Luther Mott, *Golden Multitudes* (New York: Macmillan, 1947), pp. 20-22 and 303-05.

4. Phillips D. Carleton, "The Indian Captivity," *American Literature.* 15 (1943-44), 170.

5. R. W. G. Vail, "The Abraham Panther Indian Captivity," *The American Book Collector* 2 (1932), 165-72.

6. The importance of the captivity tradition in the formation and popularization of the figure of the Indian-hater—in Bird's *Nick of the Woods,* Melville's *Confidence Man,* and elsewhere—has not yet been fully studied. The captivity theme also crops up elsewhere within Cooper's Leatherstocking novels, notably in *The Deerslayer,* and is central to his *Wept of Wishton-Wish.* However, its first and most forceful appearance, in Cooper's works, is in *The Last of the Mohicans.*

7. Cited by Robert E. Spiller, *James Fenimore Cooper* (Minneapolis: Univ. of Minnesota Press, 1965), p. 8.

8. Richard VanDerBeets, "Cooper and the 'Semblance of Reality': A Source for *The Deerslayer*" *American Literature,* 40 (1971), 544-46.

9. See Roy Harvey Pearce, "The Significances of the Captivity Narrative," *American Literature,* 19 (1947-48), 4-5; and Richard VanDerBeets, "A Surfeit of Style: The Indian Captivity Narrative as Penny Dreadful," *Research Studies,* 39 (1971), 297-306.

10. Pearce, "The Significances," pp. 2-3; and David L. Minter, "By Dens of Lions: Notes on Stylization in Early Puritan Captivity Narratives," *American Literature,* 45 (1973), 335-47.

11. George Dekker, *James Fenimore Cooper* (New York: Barnes and Noble, 1967), p. 65.

12. Leslie A. Fiedler, *The Return of the Vanishing American* (New York: Stein and Day, 1968), pp. 95-108.

13. John Frost, *Thrilling Adventures among the Indians* (Philadelphia: J. W. Bradley, 1851), p. 84.

14. Mary Rowlandson, from *The Sovereignty and Goodness of God,* in *Held Captive by Indians,* ed. Richard VanDerBeets (Knoxville: Univ. of Tennessee Press, 1973), p. 84.

15. Samuel Bownas, ed., *An Account of the Captivity of Elizabeth Hanson,* from the English edition of 1760, in *Held Captive by Indians,* p. 147.

16. Natty claims, at one point, that not "even a Mingo would ill-treat a woman, unless it be to tomahawk her," but this statement is contradicted by Magua's insistence that Cora become his squaw and by the reactions of Heyward and of Natty himself. J. F. Cooper, *The Last of the Mohicans* (New York: W. A. Townsend, 1859), p. 273. All page references in the text are to this, the Darley edition.

17. See Dee Alexander Brown, *The Gentle Tamers* (New York: Putnam, 1958); Carl Coke Rister, *Border Captives* (Norman, Okla.: Univ of Oklahoma Press, 1940); and J. Norman Heard, *White into Red* (Metuchen, N.J.: Scarecrow Press, 1973).

18. From Mrs. Horn's narrative, in Carl Coke Rister, *Comanche Bondage* (Glendale, Calif.: A. H. Clark, 1955), p. 197. The punctuation is Mrs. Horn's.

19. J. Norman Heard, *White into Red,* p. 101.

20. A. Irving Hallowell, "American Indians, White and Black: The Phenomenon of Transculturalization," *Current Anthropology,* 4 (1963), 519-31.

21. See Franklin's famous letter of May 9, 1753, to Peter Collinson, in Alfred Owen Aldridge, "Franklin's Letter on Indians and Germans," *Proceedings of the American Philosophical Society,* 94 (1950), 392-93; and J. Hector St. John Crèvecoeur, *Letters from an American Farmer* (New York: Fox, Duffield, 1904), Letter XII, pp. 304-08.

22. John Williams, *The Redeemed Captive* (Boston: Printed by B. Green for S. Phillips, 1707); *A Narrative of the Life of Mrs. Mary Jemison* (Canandaigua, N.Y.: J. D. Bemis, 1824); John Todd, *The Lost Sister of the Wyoming* (Northampton, Mass.: J. H. Butler, 1842)—the first account of the Frances Slocum captivity, subsequently retold by a number of other authors; *Narrative of the Perilous Adventures, Miraculous Escapes and Sufferings of Rev. James W. Parker* (Louisville: Morning Courier, 1844), which includes Cynthia Ann Parker's story.

23. Heard, *White into Red,* pp. 2-4.

24. Henry Nash Smith, *Virgin Land* (Cambridge, Mass.: Harvard Univ. Press, 1950), p. 69.

25. Francisco Nuñez de Pineda y Bascuñán, *Cautiverio feliz* (Santiago, Chile: Imp. de El Ferrocarril, 1863).

26. Donald Darnell, "Uncas as Hero: The *Ubi Sunt* Formula in *The Last of the Mohicans.*" *American Literature,* 37 (1965), 261-62.

27. The best general discussion of Cooper's female characters and his use of cosmetic symbolism is Nina Baym's "The Women of Cooper's Leatherstocking Tales," *American Quarterly,* 23, No. 5 (Dec. 1971), 696-709.

28. For a very similar example from Brazil, see José de Alencar's *O Guarani* (Rio de Janeiro. Tip. do Diário do Rio de Janeiro, 1857).

29. Cited by Kay Seymour House, *Cooper's Americans* (Columbus, Ohio: Ohio State Univ. Press, 1966), p. 27.

30. See, for example, p. 110.

31. Paul A. W. Wallace, "Cooper's Indians," in *James Fenimore Cooper: A Re-Appraisal* (Cooperstown, N.Y.: New York State Historical Association, 1954), pp. 63-77.

32. D. H. Lawrence, *Studies in Classic American Literature* (New York: T. Seltzer, 1923), p. 86.

Gary L. Ebersole (essay date 1995)

SOURCE: Ebersole, Gary L. "Capturing the Audience: Sentimental Literature and the New Reading Covenant." In *Captured by Texts: Puritan to Postmodern Images of Indian Captivity,* pp. 98-128. Charlottesville: University of Virginia Press, 1995.

[*In the excerpt below, Ebersole traces the emergence of the sentimental novel format in eighteenth-century captivity narratives, focusing on Edward Kimber's novel* The History of the Life and Adventures of Mr. Anderson.]

> Though our brother is upon the rack, as long as we ourselves are at our ease, our senses will never inform us of what he suffers. They never did, and never can, carry us beyond our own person, and it is by the imagination only that we can form any conception of what are his sensations. . . . By the imagination we place ourselves in his situation, we conceive ourselves enduring all the same torments, we enter as it were into his body, and become in some measure the same person with him, and thence form some idea of his sensations.
>
> —Adam Smith

Puritan captivity narratives—part confessional, part meditational text, and part jeremiad—were dominant for two generations. By the early eighteenth century the Puritan divines' monopoly over publication in America had ended, while the American book trade saw ever-increasing imports of works, both nonfictional and fictional, from England and Europe.[1] Captivity was to remain a popular literary theme, but it was to be narratively cast in a different fashion and consumed to different effect. The most significant development in terms of literary form was the emergence and tremendous popularity of the sentimental novel.

Most studies have overemphasized the discontinuities between the Puritan works of the seventeenth century and the fictional captivities of the eighteenth century while ignoring important elements of continuity. Drawing upon the recent work of J. Paul Hunter, G. J. Barker-Benfield, and others, I will suggest that the sentimental novel developed out of the increased emphasis in the eighteenth century on the affections of the heart—"sentiments"—as the locus of morality. With the appropriation and adaptation of features of earlier genres, the sentimental novel represented a newly emergent social reality.

The reading practices discussed in the preceding chapters were adapted to new ends. The sentimental novel was both a product and a producer of a new reading community, based on a shared understanding (which I shall call a new "reading covenant") of epistemology, human nature, and the moral significance of the transaction between author, text, and audience. Only after tracing the outlines of this emergent worldview, with its emphasis on the moral significance of one's affective responses to the existential situations of other human beings in the real world and in literature, will we be able to appreciate the cultural role the captivity topos played at this time.

The sentimental novels that appeared in great numbers from the 1740s onwards, beginning most especially with Samuel Richardson's *Pamela,* were very different from the earlier sorts of texts we have seen, even as they shared certain elements. The captivity narratives produced in this period were not limited to sentimental works, but a large number were cast in this mode. Moreover, Pamela, the paradigm of virtue-in-distress, was herself a captive of a sort, suggesting an early link between sentimental fiction and the captivity topos.[2] In this chapter, two eighteenth-century works—Edward Kimber's *The History of the Life and Adventures of Mr. Anderson* (1754) and Ann Eliza Bleeker's *The History of Maria Kittle* (1797)—will illustrate both the general assumptions operative in sentimental literature and the way scenes of Indian captivity functioned therein. Kimber's is one of the earliest sentimental novels to include a captivity episode, while Bleeker's work represents a famous example of a fictional captivity narrative presented to the reader as a factual account. Not limiting our purview to works written or published in America may also remind us that the book market of the late eighteenth and early nineteenth centuries was transatlantic in nature, since many works of fiction published in Europe were readily available in America.

It must be said immediately, however, that the distinction commonly drawn between fictional and nonfictional captivities is problematic. Some of the fictional narratives are based, however loosely, on an actual captivity (e.g., the many stories of Jane MacRea), while many so-called non-fictional works have been embellished (some a little bit, others to a much greater extent) with events and scenes that did not happen. Moreover, narrative stylization in these works often functioned to shape disparate events into similar tales. The intertextual relations among works were complex—works of fiction constantly borrowed descriptions and even whole action scenes from earlier travel or journal accounts, while factual accounts were similarly in-

fluenced by fictional descriptions. Many students of the captivity narratives have despaired over the hybrid character of so many of these texts, preferring plain, first-person, historical accounts above all others. Yet as Cathy Davidson has reminded us in a different context, this approach to works of fiction from this period is wrongheaded; works of fiction helped to create events in history through the very act of narrative representation, which always included interpretation.[3]

Unfortunately, most fictional captivities have received short shrift from literary critics and historians. Some critics have been quick to dismiss many novels as penny dreadfuls, hardly worthy of critical attention. Richard Van Der Beets, voicing a common prejudice, suggests that "for all practical purposes and with few exceptions, the two-hundred-year development of the narratives of Indian captivity culminates in the travesty of the Penny Dreadful." Thirty-five years earlier Roy Harvey Pearce had stated as an obvious and indisputable fact, "The first, and greatest, of the captivity narratives are simple, direct religious documents," while many of the later narratives were, to his mind at least, "mainly vulgar, fictional, and pathological."[4] Many other critics have found most of the popular novels to be bad literature and the products of the hack writer gone wild. These novels are characterized as being filled with cardboard characters, impossible plot twists, absurd coincidences, and heavy-handed moralism. Moreover, most modern readers find the plots of sentimental novels to be both predictable and redundant, much as are the story lines of modern romance novels. Such judgments, though, finally tell us more about the different reading structures and expectations of modern readers than they tell us anything of significance about the meaning of these texts in the lives (imaginary and real) of earlier readers.

In 1794 Susanna Haswell Rowson, one of the most successful American novelists of her generation, wrote, "I wonder that the novel readers are not tired of reading one story so many times, with only the variation of its being told in different ways."[5] While Rowson was speaking of the sentimental novel, the genre in which she worked, her comment is equally relevant to captivity narratives. Rowson's puzzlement is instructive, for she rightly sees that the fact that a familiar plot remains popular over time is a problem requiring explanation. To her credit, unlike some modern scholars, she does not take the shared general plot to be an adequate explanation of the popularity of the texts. The pleasure readers found (and find) in reading basically the same story again and again was (and is) a function of the specific reading practices and expectations readers bring to them. In this regard, we may recall that many types of narrative, from myths and folktales to children's bedtime stories, are consumed not for their novelty but for their familiarity. As Wendy Doniger O'Flaherty has rightly noted, "People listen to the stories not merely to learn something new (communication), but to relive, together, the stories that they already know, stories about themselves (communion). Where communication is effective, communion is evocative."[6]

The consequences of failing to reconstruct the reading practices of earlier generations while projecting one's own back onto texts are evident in many studies. For example, in a generally excellent study of the literary representations of the American Indian, Louise K. Barnett's discussion of fictional captivities is marred by her uncritical acceptance of the long-standing negative evaluation of sentimental and romantic fiction. "Although the captivity narrative continued to be published successfully during the first three quarters of the nineteenth century," she writes, "by 1800, according to Roy Harvey Pearce, it 'had all but completed its decline and fall.' Its vitality passed at this time into overt fiction in which the horrors and travails of the frontier experience were combined with a complicated romantic plot of English origin. In this amalgam, a set of foreign and artificial conventions was superimposed on the basically real and indigenous captivity events." Jay Fliegelman, in his masterful study *Prodigals and Pilgrims,* slips into this same characterization of the history of captivity narratives as one of progressive degeneration.[7]

This evaluation of the history of the captivity narrative is unacceptable for a number of reasons. First, by privileging the plain first-person Puritan accounts as the paradigm and norm against which all other captivities are to be measured, the fictional narratives inevitably emerge as distorted or corrupt. Moreover, the assumption that the Puritan first-person accounts were objective reports, uncolored by any stylistic or genre conventions is untenable. Barnett mistakenly assumes that at this time in history English literature and American literature were neatly and meaningfully separated. This allows her to assume that romantic conventions were alien to America, while American writers had ready at hand their own separate cultural idioms and conventions with which they could narratively represent "the basically real and indigenous captivity events." She implies that while it may be acceptable that romantic conventions were imposed on the historical reality of captivity from a distance by foreign writers, this is unforgivable in American literature, which, in order to be authentic, should capture and represent the historical reality. To put this another way, Barnett shares the broadly held assumption that early American literature—or at least the best of it—is realistic. Yet for readers in the eighteenth century, *Pamela, Clarissa, Tristram Shandy,* and other similar works were all held to be realistic. Indeed, realism was understood to be one of the hallmarks of the novel.

For their part, historians of religions have tended to focus their attention almost exclusively on those texts that are explicitly religious, ignoring others that are not. Thus, Puritan captivity narratives, with their informing theological interpretive frame and explicit biblical citations, have been considered appropriate objects of study, while works of fiction (and most especially sentimental novels) have not. Yet we can learn something about the social function of religion and of the history of religion in Europe and America by paying attention to what replaced an explicitly religious interpretive frame in the narration and reception of essentially the same event or existential situation. Thus,

if we find that the Puritan interpretive frame had largely disappeared from most captivity narratives by the mid-eighteenth century while captivity tales continued to be generated in great numbers, then we need to explore the significance of this fact and to investigate what replaced the earlier interpretive frame and see how this shift affected the reception of the captivity story line. Moreover, we need to understand the continuing attraction of captivity as a narrative topos in different types or genres of literature, as well as to understand the new questions and concerns that people brought to these texts. In pursuing this task, we will once again explore issues of generative occasion and authorial intention, as well as the reading practices and expectations brought to bear on captivities.

THE MORAL SIGNIFICANCE OF SENTIMENTS

An appreciation of the socioeconomic and historical developments contributing to the emergence of a "culture of sensibility" in the eighteenth century, of the reading structures brought to the sentimental novel, and of the horizon of expectations of the readers of such texts will prove much more important in increasing our understanding of the cultural work of the captivities from this period than will a facile appeal to the congenial nature of the theme or to archetypalism. We ignore to our peril the significance of what some scholars have called a paradigm shift in cultural discourse in the decades following the publication of Mary Rowlandson's narrative in 1682, resulting from a convergence of developments in science, physiology, epistemology, and religion.

A number of recent studies have greatly increased our knowledge of the origins and development of sentimental literature. Several important cultural developments in the late seventeenth and the early eighteenth centuries deserve mention here, since they led to the emergence of new epistemological assumptions and new compositional and reading practices. Newton's *Principia* (1687) and his *Opticks* (1704) changed the scientific view of the world. Newton's work had an important impact on the religious worldview of many and affected the literary sphere as well. For our immediate purposes, it is enough to recall that Newton's great intellectual prestige led many to take his work on sensory perception seriously.[8]

In his research into how human beings come to know anything about the world around them, Newton argued for the existence of an organ in the body called the sensorium, the node of all the nerves in the brain. Already in 1675 he had argued that the nerves were solid, rather than hollow, and transmitted sense impressions through vibrations carried to the brain, where they were registered by the sensorium. Significantly, Newton's sensational psychology was promulgated along with an implicit religious worldview. He argued that the human sensorium was a part of God's "boundless uniform Sensorium." Linking these two was to have important consequences. For Newton, the world was a divine book to be read by man, who could know God and his grandeur by discovering the laws at the foundation of the universe. By identifying the sensorium in each individual with the boundless uniform sensorium of God—and by invoking the metaphor of reading nature—Newton was to open the way for a revisioning of human nature, divine providence, and the significance of human affective responses to external stimuli.

The Puritan literature of the seventeenth and early eighteenth centuries was replete with reports of the great variety of wonders, miracles, and instances of God's direct intervention in the world known as "special providences." The Puritans also spoke of God's "general providence," which ordered and structured the universe and maintained its regularity and, thus, functionally was roughly equivalent to Newton's natural laws. In general, however, the Puritans were more interested in appealing to the agency of special providence in order to explain events in history than in proving God's general providence through scientific experimentation. While many seventeenth-century texts besides the captivity narratives regularly invoked special providence as an interpretive frame, such appeals declined noticeably in the literature of the early eighteenth century, the writings of Cotton Mather notwithstanding.

Moreover, at the same time—first among the Cambridge Platonists and then more broadly—the predominant conception of God shifted from that of the excoriating and afflicting God of the Old Testament to that of a more benevolent God. Concomitantly, human nature was also reconceptualized from the earlier emphasis on the fallen and corrupt state of humanity to a more positive view of humans as innately compassionate beings.[9] For our purposes it is most important to note that the new sensational psychology led to a revaluation of the moral significance of human emotional and somatic responses and, by extension, to a revaluation of audience responses to nature, art, and narrative activity.

While this history cannot be rehearsed in any detail here, we can say that Newton's ideas were quickly picked up and extended by many others, including Locke, whom Newton christened "the first Newtonian philosopher." In his *Essay concerning Human Understanding* (1690), Locke dismissed Descartes's idea that humans were born with innate ideas; instead, he characterized the infant as a tabula rasa. All human knowledge, Locke maintained, was gained through sensory perceptions. This sensationalist epistemology was then translated into a pedagogical program by Locke in *Some Thoughts concerning Education* (1693), "a volume whose influence on eighteenth-century English culture and especially eighteenth-century English literature can hardly be overemphasized."[10] Other thinkers and authors soon accepted Locke's views in whole or in part, either extending his ideas or challenging them, but no one could ignore them. Many of the major questions that were to occupy thinkers in the eighteenth century came to cluster around the status and implications of Newtonian-Lockean thought, most especially on the relationship of reason and affect. Discussions of human understanding necessarily led to reconsiderations of human nature, hu-

man faculties, the bases of moral systems, and issues related to religious experience.

The major shift in cultural episteme that occurred in the first half of the eighteenth century involved not only a reconceptualization of divinity but also of human nature, familial relations, and education. All of these developments were tied together by a focus on models of sensory perception and the relationship of human sentiments, reason, and morals. George Cheyne (1671-1743), a well-known English physician, is typical of the general acceptance among men of science of Locke's argument that all knowledge was based on experience of the world and, most especially—building on Newton's corpuscular theory of light—that sensory experience was based on motion caused by objects. In 1733 Cheyne wrote, "Feeling is nothing but the Impulse, Motion or Action of Bodies, gently or violently impressing the Extremeties or Sides of the Nerves, of the Skin, or other parts of the Body, which . . . convey Motion to the Sentient Principle in the Brain."[11]

Cheyne is a historically significant figure insofar as he served as an intermediary between the medical and the literary worlds. As Richardson's physician and confidant, he made the latest medical and physiological knowledge immediately available to this novelist. Most importantly, this knowledge informed the early novel, which became a major means of transmitting to the general public an epistemology and moral system based primarily on affect rather than reason. In this cultural milieu, "sentimental fiction, next to the religion with which it overlapped, was to become the most powerful medium for the spread of popular knowledge of sensational psychology."[12]

The Scottish commonsense movement, which I will return to later, represented at once an extension and a challenge to Lockean thought. The figures associated with this school, including Adam Ferguson, Francis Hutcheson, and Thomas Reid, shared Locke's views concerning the moral necessity for parents to educate their children in a proper manner. They differed from Locke, however, insofar as they denied that the newborn child was a complete tabula rasa. Rather, they believed that humans were born with an innate moral sense or affection. As the first edition of the *Encyclopaedia Britannica* said in defining the subject matter and goal of moral philosophy, "Its object is to shew whence our obligations arise and where they terminate. Moral philosophy is concerned not with what he may be, by education, habit or foreign influence come to be or do, but what by his nature or original constituent principles he is formed to be and do, what conduct he is obliged to pursue."[13]

This is a crucial difference between Locke and the Scottish philosophers. Locke emphasizes the agency of early education as determinative in forming an individual's moral character, whereas the Scottish commonsense philosophers assume a moral sense to be a part of human nature. Yet by accepting Locke's sensational psychology, these philosophers were driven to posit a sixth sense in human beings, the affections, but now with an innate, if undeveloped, moral component. This linkage of morality, first with the affective rather than the rational side of humans, had important implications. Among other things, it meant that moral education was to be realized through the affections rather than through reason alone. It is this implication that the writers of the eighteenth century were to take up and run with. The novel was to emerge as a vehicle of rational entertainment and moral edification in two ways—first, by illustrating the cultivation of the main characters' sensibilities in a variety of difficult and trying situations and, second, by evoking a sympathetic affective response in the reader.[14] (This latter fact helps to explain the prevalence of the term *pathetic* in so many titles of the day.)

A few names and titles will suggest the extent to which "sensibility," "sentiment," and "affection" characterized the discourse of the eighteenth century: Francis Hutcheson, *An Essay on the Nature and Conduct of the Passions and Affections with Illustrations on the Moral Sense* (1728); David Hume, *A Treatise of Human Nature* (1739-40); Richardson, *Pamela: or, Virtue Rewarded* (1740) and *Clarissa* (1744); Edmund Burke, *The Philosophical Origins of the Sublime and the Beautiful* (1757); Laurence Sterne, *Tristram Shandy,* (vol. 1, 1759) and *A Sentimental Journey through France and Italy* (1768); Albrech von Haller, *De Partibus Corporis Humani Sensibilus et Irritabilius* (1753), published in English in 1775 as *A Dissertation on the Sensible and Irritable Parts of Animals*; Adam Smith, *The Theory of Moral Sentiments* (1759); Rousseau, *La Nouvelle Héloïse* (1761); and Henry Mackenzie, *The Man of Feeling* (1771).

For many people in the early eighteenth century, physiological sensibility and moral sensibility were intertwined or one-and-the-same. This was so because they assumed that the sensorium or the human faculties, however these were understood, had been created by God precisely so that humans might be morally responsible for their behavior. After the Restoration, the Cambridge Platonists had sought to soften various aspects of Puritan theology and thought. Rather than stressing man's sinful nature, they began with the assumption that humans were essentially benevolent beings. These thinkers influenced in turn the Latitudinarians, who also argued that human nature was instinctively sympathetic and that humans were, thus, naturally inclined to virtuous actions. This nature was to be reinforced by self-discipline, however, or refined through education and cultivation. Even Hume, the supreme skeptic, held that all human virtues flowed from sympathy.

Eighteenth-century thinkers and writers differed in their precise evaluations of human moral capabilities and of human nature in general, of course. They also had to address the issues of the great differences that were evident among individuals and peoples; in addition, many people began to address gender differences and in so doing sought to naturalize these. In general, these explanations ascribed differences to environmental factors or innate differences, or to some combination of these. On the one hand, some writers, following Locke, stressed that education and training in morals from an early age was essential. Other persons, however, proffered their own varieties of Calvinist determinism by suggesting, for instance, that individual differences were in large part the results of the endowments God had given each person at birth. Cheyne belonged to the latter camp. He wrote:

> There are as many and as different Degrees of Sensibility or of Feeling as there are Degrees of Intelligence and Perception in human Creatures; and the Principle of both may be perhaps one and the same. One shall suffer more from the Prick of a Pin, or Needle, from their extreme Sensibility, than others from being run thro' the Body; and the first sort, seem to be of the Class of these Quick-Thinkers I have formerly mentioned; and as none have it in their Option to choose for themselves their own particular Frame of Mind nor Constitution of Body; so none can choose his own Degree of Sensibility. That is given him by the Author of his Nature, and is already determined.[15]

Not surprisingly, perhaps, the new sensational physiologies and moral philosophies could be (and were) extended to the social sphere and used to justify and legitimate social hierarchies, class distinctions, gender roles, and even racism. Yet the significance of the scientific evidence was unclear, so that the same fact could be used to argue for both sides of a question. For instance, reports of the ability of American Indians to bear great pain and deprivation were cited by some authors as proof of their relative inhumanity; others, however, used the same reports to cast the Indians as stoics with a developed moral sense.

It is in light of these developments that we can better understand the tremendous upsurge in interest in the eighteenth and nineteenth centuries in recording the manners, customs, and beliefs of peoples around the world, including the American Indians. Gathering and ordering these objective facts, it was believed, would allow one to determine the degree of humanity these people possessed (or lacked). Moreover, the diverse societies provided case studies of the effects of different environmental situations and educational practices on human development. When the third earl of Shaftesbury (1671-1713), often called "the father of sentimental ethics," published a collection of his essays as *Characteristicks of Men, Manners, Opinions, Times,* he was participating in a broad-based discourse of moral philosophy that included subject matter we would now divide among psychology, anthropology, sociology, pedagogy, and politics.

Such investigations into human nature, however, were not limited to works of science, theology, or philosophy. Works of literature also imaginatively (yet realistically) explored the nature of men and women, familial and sexual relations, and the consequences of different socioeconomic systems and situations, and in so doing served as vehicles of moral instruction. For many persons in the eighteenth century, sentimental literature functioned as an adjunct of these fields. *Pamela,* for instance, was sometimes read from the pulpit; others report that people who would never have deigned to read mere novels read *Clarissa* with the same care and in the same contexts that they read the Bible.[16] Richardson's works served as moral guides for generations of readers. In 1755, no doubt in response to market demands, he published a handbook entitled *A Collection of the Moral and Instructive Sentiments, Maxims, Cautions and Reflections Contained in the Histories of "Pamela," "Clarissa," and "Sir Charles Grandison," Digested under Proper Heads.* This instructional manual was extremely influential in the second half of the century. Similar works appeared during the century drawing from the novels of Sterne, Fielding, and others. In fact, Sterne's fictional character Parson Yorick became so popular that Sterne took to publishing volumes of his own sermons under the guise of *The Sermons of Mr. Yorick.*

Because sentimental novels were consumed in this way, informing the religious lives of many persons in the eighteenth and nineteenth centuries, they are important documents for the work of historians of religions, as well as literary critics. In the following pages we will work toward understanding how a work like *Pamela* came to be read from church pulpits and how tears and sighs came to be viewed as "natural revelations" of God's moral expectations for human beings. It was no accident that the sentimental novel, John Wesley's "heart religion," and the Great Awakening in America all appeared in the same decade; all of these developments were a result of, and further contributed to, the heightened value placed on the religious or moral affections.[17]

In chapter 1 we saw how tears and affliction worked in Mary Rowlandson's text. By comparing these and related phenomena with those found in eighteenth- and nineteenth-century sentimental works dealing with Indian captivity, we will be able to glimpse an important aspect of cultural change. Admittedly, sentimental novels do not speak to modern readers; they do not easily give pleasure to us. Instead, the characters and plots seem to be overwrought (both narratively and emotionally), if not impossible to believe as realistic. Writing about these novels in general, Jane Tompkins notes, "What all of these texts share, from the perspective of modern criticism, is a certain set of defects that excludes them from the ranks of the great masterpieces: an absence of finely delineated characters, a lack of verisimilitude in the story line, an excessive reliance on plot, and a certain sensationalism in the events portrayed."[18] Rather than accepting these modern values as normative and then imposing them on these texts, Tompkins has made a concerted effort to recover the aims and practices informing the literary activity of sentimental authors, as well as the perspectives, expectations, and reading practices the nineteenth-century audience brought to these texts. As a result of this and other recent studies, it is clear that many (though not all) works of sentimental literature functioned didactically, conveying a moral message to readers and helping them to evaluate their lives.

Kimber's *Mr. Anderson*

The History of the Life and Adventures of Mr. Anderson. Containing His Strange Varieties of Fortune in Europe and America (1754), a novel by the English writer Edward Kimber (1719-1769), may serve as an entrée into the heated cultural debate about the social responsibilities of authorship, the operative understanding of the power of narrative representation, the didacticism of sentimental literature, the role of imagination in the reader's creation of the meaning of the text, the role of the cult of sensibility or cultivated emotions in the composition and reception of the novel, and the topos of Indian captivity as an instance of virtue-in-distress.

With this mid-eighteenth-century work, we find the form of the sentimental novel fully developed. (*Pamela* had been published several years earlier, in 1740, and was brought out in an American edition by Benjamin Franklin in 1744.) The title page, however, is similar in layout and appearance to most of the earlier captivity narratives we have seen, thus linking it, at least visually, to those nonfictional texts. Below the title and between two heavy rules, one finds the words "Compiled from his Own Papers"—an epistolary ruse used to suggest that the work is nonfiction. Below this is an excerpt from a verse by Addison:

> —If there is a Power above us,
> And that there is, all Nature cries aloud,
> Thro' all her Works, he must delight in Virtue,
> And that which he delights in must be happy.[19]

This verse encapsulates the informing religious and moral world-view of the sentimental novel: the virtuous will be rewarded with happiness in the end, even though they suffer terribly beforehand, because divine providence has so ordered the world. At the same time, then, that Kimber's work is linked to the earlier tradition of captivity narratives, this verse marks it as also belonging to the newer genre of sentimental literature.

The title page represents this text to prospective readers through a number of key words—"history," "life and adventures," "strange varieties of fortune," "Power," "Nature," and "Virtue"—all which combine to suggest a true story of the adventures and vicissitudes in the protagonist's life in Europe and America, which, of course, ends happily. At the same time it suggests links to other forms of literature. The word *strange,* for instance, would have evoked a connection with the wide variety of popular works of surprising happenings in the world, such as Defoe's immensely popular *The Life and Strange Surprizing Adventures of Robinson Crusoe.*[20]

The title page also implies that when read, this story of virtue triumphing in the end will lead the reader to a heightened appreciation of God's goodness and providence. Absent, though, is the Puritan emphasis on the fallen, sinful nature of humankind; instead, one finds an optimism concerning the innate goodness of human beings—at least those "of the better sort." This is characteristic of sentimental literature at large and marks a significant change from the religious anthropology of the Puritans, for, as Herbert Ross Brown rightly noted, "A favorite article in the sentimental creed is the belief in the innate goodness of the heart."[21]

The eighteenth century saw a broad-based reaction against both the Puritan anthropology and that found in Hobbes. The Cambridge Platonists, Lord Shaftesbury, Francis Hutcheson, Henry More, and others argued that spontaneous affections were the true locus of all knowledge and morality. Shaftesbury, for instance, in his *Inquiry concerning Virtue* (1699) had argued, "We cannot doubt of what passes within ourselves. Our passions and affections are known to us. They are certain, whatever the objects may be on which they are employed."[22] He assumed that the sense of right and wrong was "implanted in our heart," but it had to be cultivated, as did the natural recognition of beauty and the odious. Aesthetic taste and moral sensibility were natural capacities, but they had to be cultivated through a disciplined regimen of training involving "labour and pains." More, the Cambridge Platonist, was representative of the age (and in complete agreement with Addison) when he argued that we "relish and savour what is absolutely best and rejoice in it." Moreover, he maintained that natural expressions of human emotion, such as a "lamenting tone of Voice, the dejection of the Eyes and Countenances, Groaning, Howling, Sighs, and Tears" have the power to move others to compassion and sympathy. More himself was to influence John Wesley's theology and "religion of the heart." The Great Awakening and the sentimental novel may both be seen as expressions of the increased cultural attention to the affective side of human life and religiosity.[23]

For persons of sensibility, affective exchanges participated in a moral economy within which the exchange of a shared currency of tears, sighs, swoons, and shudders created value and social relations. Moreover, since spontaneous emotive and physical responses were understood to be natural revelations of God's moral expectations of human beings, they were also signals to persons for action. In the sentimental novel, the innate potential of individuals for making proper value judgments and acting virtuously is realized through a process of education, training, and testing through adversity.

It is the last of these—the testing through a reversal of fortune or unmerited suffering—that both shares some aspects with the Puritan representation of affliction and marks a radical difference. The Puritans employed the metaphor of refining gold in a crucible to represent the positive spiritual transformation that could result if instances of divine affliction were experienced and accepted in the proper attitude of humility. In the sentimental novel, however, the characters are not radically transformed through their experience of affliction; rather, the trying experience, be it captivity or whatever, serves to bring out more clearly or to heighten their innate goodness and virtue. In the sentimental novel, the character of the protago-

nists is never in doubt and, consequently, neither is the final result. Adversity is an occasion for displaying one's virtue and sensibility to the world and to oneself.

The opening of Kimber's novel confirms the reader's expectations, generated by the title page, of the type of narrative one is about to enter into, even as the author apologizes for necessarily breaking with one of the conventions of biography: he cannot provide much detail concerning the hero's parents and family because as a child he had been "plunged into the deepest calamities of life" and denied this knowledge himself. Nevertheless, the reader is assured, Mr. Anderson's experiences proved "equally capable of affecting the head and improving the heart." The narrator then announces the purpose of this work of fiction, masquerading as historical biography:

> If the narrative I am about to present to the public, insensibly, under the guise of a rational entertainment, steals instruction upon the peruser, and produces benefit to the mind; if it should draw the hard bound tear from the eye of inhumanity; if whilst the souls "that bleed for others woes, that feel for suffering merit's deep distress," lend an attentive ear, or eye, to this strange story; it serves to mollify unfeeling, obdurate cruelty, I shall have my wish, and the trouble I have been at to fashion my friends memoirs, will be well repayed; for I am of the poet's opinion, that
>
> "One moral, or a mere well natur'd deed,
> Does all desert in sciences exceed."
>
> (*Garland* 7:1-2)

In the world of the sentimental novel (that is, among authors, readers, and the characters populating the texts), one finds a supreme confidence in both the revelatory power of emotions and the power of narrative representation to [steal moral] "instruction upon the peruser" by "affecting the head and improving the heart." Kimber's belief—that if he is successful in moving his readers, in drawing "the hard bound tear from the eye of inhumanity" through his narration, then acts of human cruelty in the world will decrease—was widely shared in the culture of sensibility. The stated goal of the act of narration is to effect a moral change in society through affecting individual readers. This authorial intention, based on this understanding of the power of literature to alter the real world, was, significantly enough, still found a century later in sentimental works such as *Uncle Tom's Cabin*.[24]

Kimber's confidence in the power of literature is such that, like Richardson, he implies that it is more efficacious than even sermons. Whereas many persons might experience the message of theological writing or preaching as heavy handed and thus resist it at some level, with fiction ("a rational entertainment") the ethical message is artfully and painlessly transmitted.

Writers of sentimental fiction played an important cultural role in promulgating this new epistemology, which privileged feeling over reason as a guide in discerning virtue and making moral decisions. Sentimental authors shared the view of Adam Smith and others that the imagination played an important role in the moral life, for only through imagining oneself into the situation of another was sympathy fully activated. The pleasure to be derived from the exercise of the sympathetic imagination, however, was twofold. On the one hand, there was the pleasure to be had in aiding another person in distress and in knowing that one had done some good. However, while the operation of the sympathetic imagination involved an element of identification with the suffering of another, at the same time (and somewhat paradoxically) it also involved an element of distancing and of contrasting one's own situation with that of the person in distress. This second pleasure was found especially in the act of reading moving tales, where leisure allowed the requisite time for comparative reflection, even if it was largely unconscious. The *Spectator* put this clearly, noting that "when we read of torments, wounds, deaths and the like dismal accidents, our pleasure does not flow so properly from the grief which such melancholy description gives us, as from the secret comparison which we make between ourselves and the person who suffers. Such representations teach us to set a just value upon our own condition, and make us prize our good fortune, which exempts us from the like calamities."[25]

We have already seen Per Amicum direct the reader of Mary Rowlandson's narrative to "read therefore, peruse, ponder, and from hence lay up something from the experience of another, against thine own turn comes." What is new here is the heightened attention to be paid to one's visceral responses to narrated scenes. In one sense, of course, this aspect of the reading practices brought to bear on works of sentimental literature was an extension and application of the imaginal activity implied in the Golden Rule. To "do onto others as you would have them do onto you" requires one to project oneself imaginatively into the situation of the other person and then to act out of that assumed position. At the same time, part of the pleasure to be found in the reflective activity the *Spectator* speaks of is a result of the recognition that "there but for the grace of God go I."

Most moral philosophers and sentimental writers concurred that morality and moral action originated in feeling rather than reason. Hume, for instance, maintained, "All morality depends upon our sentiments," not upon reason.[26] What philosophers sought to demonstrate through logical argument the writers of fiction sought to represent through the lives of the characters in their novels. It is important to recognize how developments in philosophy, theology, physiology, and psychology were brought into the real world through works of fiction. Along with sentimentally colored historical pieces, novels helped to shape the expressions of feeling of historical agents. Such works helped to locate affective responses within a moral economy. This fact was recognized by authors throughout the eighteenth and nineteenth centuries. In *Adam Bede* (1859), for instance, George Eliot says of one of her characters, "Hetty

had never read a novel . . . how then could she find a shape for her expectations?"[27]

Today we assume that an individual can (and must) learn to control and modulate his or her emotional responses, such as laughter or words spoken in anger, in ways appropriate to the specific time, place, and circumstance. Our ancestors believed the same thing, although they assumed that it was the sensorium, or the moral sense, that needed to be trained or, better, refined, so that the affective and physiological responses (tears, sighs, tremors, fainting) to specific stimuli and situations could be controlled. Once this was assumed, it was a natural next step to suggest that the emotional responses of a person to a given situation were an immediate and accurate expression of moral character.

In claiming for literature the role of inculcating moral values, Kimber participated in an increasingly influential cultural discourse in the eighteenth century that privileged examples from real life in the contemporary world over those from antiquity as effective vehicles in this exercise. Novels, as well as biographies, provided paradigmatic figures for emulation by readers seeking both entertainment and self-improvement. Just as the third generation of New England Puritans had come to accept funeral sermons, eulogies, and even biographies of members of the founding generation as vehicles for instructing others, especially youth, so too many eighteenth-century readers and commentators were willing to acknowledge factual accounts as, potentially at least, morally uplifting.

Vociferous resistance surfaced, however, when some people argued that explicitly fictional tales could also serve proper didactic purposes. They argued that the novel could serve as a vehicle of moral instruction precisely because this form was based on everyday life, not fantasy. The trials and situations faced by the characters in novels were similar, even if heightened, to those readers would encounter in their own lives. Such arguments, however, did not convince many others. One commentator, writing in the *Weekly Magazine* in 1789, expressed a concern he shared with many of his contemporaries:

> I have heard it said in favour of novels that there are many good sentiments dispersed in them. I maintain, that good sentiments being found scattered in loose novels, render them the more dangerous, since, when they are mixed with seducing arguments, it requires more discernment than is to be found in youth to separate the evil from the good . . . and when a young lady finds principles of religion and virtue inculcated in a book, she is naturally thrown off her guard by taking it for granted that such a work can contain no harm; and of course the evil steals imperceptibly into her heart.[28]

The presumption behind the "of course" here clearly demarcates the critical point on which these two camps differed: either readers could be trusted to discern the good and the moral from the seductive or seemingly good and the immoral or they could not be so trusted. Either moral instruction stole upon the reader's mind and heart in the reading of novels, or "seducing arguments" and evil did. It is clear that issues of class and gender lay behind the fears of many of those who were suspicious of the novel and other forms of popular literature. Yet both camps shared the belief that literature had the power to affect the moral fiber of the readers, even if they differed radically in their valuation of this power.

Kimber, like many of his fellow fiction writers, sought to evade the critical arrows flung at him by adversaries of fiction by assuming the pose of being merely the editor of the papers of an actual individual. Though a work of out-and-out fiction, *Mr. Anderson* was presented to the reading public as a factual account. Similarly, Bleeker's *The History of Maria Kittle* employed the same epistolary ruse. This may be merely an artful (or clumsily obvious) dodge. On the other hand, this appeal to historicity may also have been a literary device used to justify the act of narration itself, to create a narrative voice, and to heighten the reader's sense of engagement with the story by facilitating the willing suspension of disbelief or tempering skepticism.[29]

In Kimber's novel, however, unlike the Puritan texts we saw earlier, no program of ritual humiliation and spiritual reformation is offered, nor is there a heavy emphasis on the involvement of divine providence in the protagonist's captivity. Rather, the emphasis is on releasing and developing the innate goodness and powers of moral discrimination found in persons of sensibility through their encounters with both virtuous and villainous characters. At the same time, the earlier confidence, epitomized by Cotton Mather, that the deep meaning of the text of history could be spelled by human beings, is absent. Instead, Kimber cautions his reader, "We must not expect that all seeing Providence should, according to our expectations, always punish even the most degrading and abominable crimes" (*Garland* 7:9-10).

Significantly, the authoritative texts appealed to by Kimber are inevitably poetic texts, not Scripture. Moreover, the proper locus of moral attention here is the individual human heart, not the community or society at large. Through the act of reading, an increasingly private practice, the narrative "steals instruction upon the peruser, and produces benefit to the mind" by providing paradigmatic existential situations of conflict or real-life problems and their resolutions. For the modern reader, this understanding of the spiritual and moral impact of the expected narrative transaction (indeed, almost a pact) between author, text, and reader must be taken seriously in order to appreciate the cultural work such texts performed in the eighteenth and nineteenth centuries. As Davidson has noted, "Psychologically, the early novel embraced a new relationship between art and audience, writer and reader, a relationship that replaced the authority of the sermon or Bible with the enthusiasms of sentiment, horror, or adventure, all of which relocate authority in the individual response of the reading self."[30] Not surprisingly, this democratization, if you will,

of the ability to interpret texts and to judge affect was perceived by many to be a threat to the patriarchal social order and moral values.

Most important, perhaps, for the authors and readers of sentimental literature, the moral authority and the power of a text were to be measured and verified through the affective responses it elicited in readers. Given that reading was usually done individually and in private, only the reader would be in a position to note and then to evaluate these responses. This situation is in sharp contrast to that associated with the Puritan confessional narrative. There not only was the narrative of the applicant's spiritual responses to specific existential situations in the past subjected to scrutiny by an examining committee from the church, but the individual's oral responses to questions posed by this group were also judged as to their appropriateness. Although there were shaded differences in Puritan conversion narratives at different times and places, as Caldwell has demonstrated, there was nevertheless a communal consensus as to what constituted proper and improper responses to specific types of situations or scenes in life. This consensus was worked out and then reinforced through ritualized public performances as well as through the improvements of such narratives offered by the clergy in the oral delivery of sermons and in print. Both the Rowlandson and the Swarton narratives were, as we saw, circulated with accompanying texts that framed and guided their reception and proper usage.

Yet it must always be borne in mind that the sentimental author had designs on his reader, too. The author assumed that readers would learn about the proper affective responses to specific sorts of situations from his novel and then act on and out of these. Through the act of reading, readers would refine their own sensibilities and display these in their reactions to similar situations as these were encountered in their own lives. And even if many of the wildest episodes were unlikely to be found in the lives of most readers, there was still moral good to be gained through imaginatively entering into and contemplating such scenes. Here the sentimental novel clearly shares a direct continuity with Puritan assumptions and reading practices, as we saw in both Per Amicum's preface, the Rowlandson narrative proper, and the sermons of Mather. This understanding of the didactic value of narrative representation was to continue to be held by many persons down through the late nineteenth century.

In an important sense, though, the sentimental novel represented a significant challenge to the earlier cultural status quo by shifting the ultimate locus of moral authority from the clergy as a group to the individual lay person and from the Bible to secular works of rational entertainment and wisdom. This shift was in part a result of the implicit drive of Protestant understandings of the status and power of the Bible, of religious epistemology, and hermeneutics. Insofar as Protestant thought and practice stressed both the necessity and the efficacy of the individual's immediate encounter with the written revealed word of God, the relationships of reader to text and reader to author (or "Author" in the case of the Bible) were already culturally available for extension to other sorts of texts, including didactic works of fiction.

This is not to say, however, that readers were left to their own devices in reading these sorts of texts. Indeed, the opposite is the case. Readers were given explicit guidance in the novels themselves as to what constituted the proper reactions to specific scenes in real life and in narrative representations. There were, as well, negative examples, which illustrated uncultured, out-of-place, and otherwise improper responses.

The following passage from *Maria Kittle* has frequently evoked derisive comment precisely because modern readers have failed to appreciate the active manner in which the author, as part of her role as instructor and guide in moral sensibility, involved her original audience in imaginatively composing a scene and then empathetically entering into the emotional life of the characters. The husband, Henry Kittle, is returning to his frontier home, where he had left his beloved wife, Maria, and two small children, only to discover that they have fallen victim to an Indian attack:

> As he approached his late happy dwelling, his bosom dilated with the pleasing hope of soon extricating his beloved family from danger; he chid the slowness of the carriages, and felt impatient to dissipate the apprehensions of Maria, to kiss the pendant tear from her eye, and press his sportive innocents to his bosom. While these bright ideas played round his soul, he lifted up his eyes, and through an opening of the woods, beheld his farm: but what language can express his surprise and consternation at seeing his habitation so suddenly desolated! a loud exclamation of amaze burst from the whole company at so unexpected a view—the blood revolted from Mr. Kittle's cheek—his heart throbbed under the big emotion, and all aghast, spurring on his horse, he entered the inclosure with full speed.—Stop here unhappy man! here let the fibres of thy heart crack with excruciating misery—let the cruel view of mangled wretches, so nearly allied to thee, extort drops of blood from thy cleaving bosom! It did—it did. Uttering a deep groan, he fell insensible from his horse.

> (*Garland* 20:27-28)

Brown assigns most of the end of this passage to Kittle as a soliloquy, although the punctuation of the 1797 text does not justify this reading. According to him, "Henry Kittle's outburst was too self-conscious to be indicative of anything more than his own egoism."[31]

In Brown's misreading, the text seems very awkward, while the characters come off as pretentious poseurs. Yet the reading practices brought by late eighteenth- and nineteenth-century readers to texts such as this would have made this scene very effective. Brown himself seems to have sensed something of what was involved in the transaction between author, text, and reader in the sentimental novel, although he never put the various clues or pieces together and, as a result, was never able to appreciate the cultural work of such texts or to transcend a condescending bemusement with the seeming silliness of the genre. Only a few pages earlier, he had perceptively noted (although he quickly trivialized his own insight) that sentimental novels often portrayed specific emotional responses in given situations ("swoons, trances, visions, languishings, ecstasies, and a variety of emotional delirium tremens") as proof of the character's sensibility and even spiritual election, a situation not unlike that found in Puritan conversion testimonies and written accounts.[32]

Passages such as that above can only be understood if we take seriously the extent to which the early novel, in many ways seemingly so different from Puritan texts, nevertheless shared a deeper identity, for the sentimental novel developed out of the exploitation of certain shared reading structures and practices. If, for example, one recalls the meditative practice of "the composition of place"—a practice first popularized in Ignatian meditation manuals but widely adopted and adapted in Protestant circles as well in the form of "Occasional Meditation"—one can better appreciate how and why Bleeker composed this scene as she did, confident that her readers would share reading practices which would make it work. In the First Exercise of St. Ignatius's spiritual exercises, the meditator is directed to use his imagination to conjure up "a mental image of the place . . . where the object that we wish to contemplate is present." After "seeing" this place or scene "with the mind's eye," the meditator next seeks to share the "pain, tears, and suffering" of Christ in the Passion, or other emotions from the specific biblical scene. In the sentimental novel, this spiritual exercise is simply applied to nonbiblical scenes and narratives. If Bleeker knew her audience, as any successful author must, then she was cognizant of the expectations and reading practices that the reader would most probably bring to her text.[33]

After having assisted the audience in conjuring up the scene of devastation and death, one that would have been well known to most readers already from acquaintance with earlier captivity narratives and their accompanying illustrations, Bleeker then invites the reader to pause before it, to hold the scene before one's gaze, precisely in order to feel the emotional response of Henry Kittle in one's own body. Brown was more correct than he realized when he suggested that the affective response of the reader was taken to be evidence of one's spiritual condition in much the same way as in Calvinist practice.

In order to demonstrate the tradition that immediately links captivity in the sentimental novel with Puritan captivities, let us recall that a century earlier Per Amicum had also conjured up the scene of a husband (there the Rev. Joseph Rowlandson) returning to the site of his former domestic happiness, only to find it a scene of death and destruction: "At his return, he found the Town in flames, or smoke, his own house being set on fire by the Enemy . . . and all in it consumed: His precious yoke-fellow, and dear

Children, wounded and captivated (as the issue evidenced, and following Narrative declares) by these cruel and barbarous Salvages. A sad Catastrophe!" Let us recall, too, Per Amicum's claim that "the works of the Lord . . . are great, sought out of all those that have pleasure therein."

Over a century before Bleeker composed her novel, the affective power of the idyllic domestic scene suddenly shattered by Indian attack and captivity had been fully realized and employed as a didactic device by the Puritans. If Per Amicum and his friends had found the Rowlandson narrative "worthy to be exhibited to, and viewed, and pondered by all, that disdain not to consider the operation of [God's] hand," this was because they were convinced that, "forasmuch as not the general but particular knowledge of things makes deepest impression upon the affections," "those of a true Christian spirit" would necessarily find themselves moved by the account and the scenes recalled therein. That is, Per Amicum also recommended scrutinizing reader responses as a way of evaluating the spiritual condition of individuals (*Garland* 1:A2, A3, A4). The continuity in the understanding of the narrative and reading processes and the transaction between author, text, and reader found in these works by Per Amicum and Bleeker is undeniable, although the obvious differences in genre and style have heretofore kept us from realizing the full nature of this continuity. These differences, however, now appear to be less significant than the continuity in the reading structures and practices brought to bear on these texts.

The theme of captivity was widely employed in the seventeenth, eighteenth, and nineteenth centuries in diverse literary genres because it represented a striking instance of sudden reversal of fortune, whether this was understood to be divine affliction or not. The theme of the sudden reversal of fortune of the good and apparently blameless was, of course, as old as the story of Job. Yet if it was seemingly guaranteed to evoke a response, the shape and meaning of the response was determined by the then-operative reading practices, narrative conventions, and communal valuations of the expression of specific emotions in specific contexts.

Such an empathetic emotional response by the reader was the goal of sentimental authors. In a letter to one of his own readers, Laurence Sterne, a doyen of the genre, explicitly pointed to the role of the reader in generating the pleasure to be found in novels, such as his *Tristram Shandy:* "A true feeler always brings half the entertainment along with him . . . and the vibrations in him so entirely correspond with those excited [in the novel's characters], it is like reading himself and not the book."[34] Sterne understood full well that the author could only do so much in order to elicit a given response; the reader played an equally important role in bringing certain reading structures to bear on the text.

As a result of this situation, the sentimental novel worked only so long as the author and the audience shared the same practices and expectations. If such novels do not

work for us today, it is because we no longer identify with the emotional lives of the characters, not because Kimber and Bleeker were bad writers. The words on the page have not changed, but reading practices have. Puritan readers—who had already affirmed the moral imperative of observing the movements of their souls, participated in the tradition of writing spiritual autobiographies and journals, and learned to read themselves through devotional practices of intense self-scrutiny—would have readily understood the assumptions shared by the authors and readers of sentimental novels even if they finally could not have embraced them.

The sentimental novel, then, no less than the Puritan captivity narrative, provided rational entertainment insofar as the emotional responses evoked in the reader were subjected to intense scrutiny as a part of a practice of self-examination. Reading done in this manner was an efficacious path, it was held, leading to the cultivation of one's sensibilities and powers of moral discrimination. Not everyone shared this understanding of the moral benefits of novel reading, as we have already had occasion to note. Many commentators (not all of them male) doubted that the young and female readers would have the wherewithal, the reading skills, and powers of discrimination needed to distinguish corrupting literature from morally uplifting works. We have also alluded to the beginnings of a significant shift in epistemology and ethical thought in the English-speaking world related to the intellectual movement that came to be known as Scottish commonsense philosophy. This involved a shift from an explicitly Calvinist providential view of history to an increased emphasis on natural religion.

Many of those who doubted the claims made for literature as a vehicle of moral education feared that works of fiction threatened to seduce or captivate the hearts and minds of the "weaker sex" and youth. The common usage of terms such as *captivate* and *captivating* in the ongoing, sometimes boisterous, cultural discourse over the relative merits or demerits of fiction in general is worth noting in passing. In railing against novels and other forms of fiction, some opponents had appeal to imagery redolent of the Puritan rhetoric on the dangers of temptations and sin. One editor argued, for instance, that novels "are written with an intent to captivate the feelings, and do in fact lead many on to the path of vice, from an idea that they are within the pale of gallantry." Another male opponent of fiction, wrote in the *Massachusetts Magazine,* "But too many [readers], especially persons of warm passions and tender feelings [i.e., females], are too apt to be captivated with everything which drops from [Sterne's] descriptive, though loose and unguarded pen, and, in swallowing the nectar, to swallow what is enflaming and poisonous." This writer employed, no doubt unconsciously, phallic images that would seem to invite a Freudian analysis themselves, even as they hint at the sexual politics involved in this debate, often just below the surface.

Richardson presented a standard counterargument by suggesting that because the new novel was rooted in the everyday world it represented reality in ways other forms of fiction, such as romance, had not. He called the novel "a new species of writing, that might possibly turn young people into a source of reading different from the pomp and parade of romance writing, and dismissing the improbable and marvelous with which novels generally abound, might tend to promote the cause of religion and virtue." The contest between these positions was not settled quickly, however. Over a century later, in 1853, Margaret Fuller concurred with the critics who found fiction to be seductive and captivating, although she was willing to accept it if certain conditions were met. "But it is only when some effort at human improvement is robed in its captivating garb that fiction should be tolerated," she wrote.[35]

With this general introduction, let us look more closely at our two selected novels. The protagonist of Kimber's *Mr. Anderson* is Tom(my) Anderson. The novel is told in the third-person past tense, with an omniscient narrator. It opens with the editor-narrator recalling that Tommy's parents had been "above the common rank." In May 1697, as Tommy (then aged seven) waited on a doorstep in London for his father, who had gone inside on business, he was abducted by a sea captain. With this incident, Kimber invoked the fairly widespread and highly publicized incidents of child abduction in the British Isles earlier in the century. The kidnapping functions as a device to get his protagonist to America;[36] at the time it would have represented a realistic touch.

Kimber then proceeds to tell a typical sentimental tale of class and virtue denied yet triumphing in the end. We learn that onboard the ship, a slaver headed for America, Tommy was sexually abused by the captain. When they arrived in Maryland, Tommy was immediately sold to a planter, Mr. Barlow, a mean-spirited, abusive man in his own right. Mrs. Barlow, on the other hand, was "a woman of sense and humanity, of many extraordinary endowments, and a mother" (*Garland* 7:1-2).

As in so many sentimental novels, one finds maternal love, virtue, warmth, gentleness, and a nurturing nature counterposed to male brutality, insensibility, and baseness. Equally sharp contrasts are drawn between virtuous individuals and dastardly reprobates throughout the novel. Of special note, however, is the moral anthropology shared by the sentimental novelists and readers, including the belief that the character and moral fiber of individuals were ultimately a matter of temperament. The character, or mettle, of individuals was tested and tempered on the anvil of adversity and suffering. If temperament was inherited, however, it was so along lines distinct from genetic inheritance (e.g., we are told that the sweet daughter, Fanny, had her mother's temperament and nothing of her father's). Moreover, innate goodness had the power to establish bonds of affection that transcended biological relationships—Mrs. Barlow cannot help but feel maternal toward Tommy, who naturally reciprocates, while Fanny and Tommy recognize each other to be soulmates, not merely playmates. Indeed, we are told that all those with any sensibility readily dis-

cerned that Fanny and Tommy were almost "twins from the same womb," while the crude and uncultured Mr. Barlow was oblivious to any elective affinities.

The moral anthropology of the sentimental novel owed something to the Calvinist belief in predestination but was not limited to this theological understanding. Like the Calvinists, sentimental novelists and readers believed that a person's innate virtue would necessarily attract the attention of the divine (even if this was often delayed) and ultimately lead to the virtuous being blessed. Some, but by no means all, sentimental novels promised that virtue might well be rewarded in this world, rather than being withheld until the afterlife. Indeed, as we shall see shortly, Kimber claims that the natural activities of the virtuous would prove to be not only economically viable but profitable. There was an inherent economic rationality, then, in virtuous activity—men of good character and sensibility got the goods and the girl.

Persons of sensibility naturally resonated to each other, producing or evoking mutually recognizable physiological and emotional responses. Both their speech and actions disclosed their true nature, their innate goodness and virtue, to others of a similar temper or nature, while those who did not share these qualities were blind to their existence in others. As a consequence, persons of the latter sort rarely recognized the true character and value of persons of refined sensibility. As was to be expected, then, in a woman of refined sensibility and cultivated mind, Mrs. Barlow immediately recognized Tommy's "promising genius, and a softness and good nature of disposition, that would have melted any heart, but that of the villain who had him in his power." Kimber repeatedly emphasizes the innate goodness of his main character, Tommy, and then proceeds to create scenes in which this goodness is readily recognized by others of refined sensibility, no matter how low Tommy's present station or how wretched his material conditions.

We must note, though, the importance attached in the novel to literacy and education in cultivating innate qualities of mind and moral discrimination. Mrs. Barlow, for instance, ignores the express commands of her brutish husband and secretly teaches little Fanny, her daughter, and Tommy to read "prettily." After they had quickly exhausted her "female collection of the politest authors," a more substantial library was supplied by a family friend, a Scottish clergyman. The children studied with a neighbor, another Scottsman, Mr. Ferguson. In time Tom "became a proficient in the Latin and French, in all the useful branches of the mathematics, spoke and wrote correctly and elegantly, and acquired such additions to his native dignity of soul and sentiment" that everyone "stood amazed at him" (*Garland* 7:10, 26).

Education, then, was of value in developing and refining one's "native dignity of soul and sentiment." We may assume that the reading of novels of rational entertainment also was felt to contribute to this end. The seemingly minor detail of these educated gentlemen being Scottish is in fact significant, since it suggests (albeit anachronistically within the time frame or historical setting of the novel) Kimber's endorsement of Scottish commonsense philosophy. The influence of Lord Kames, whose *Principles of Morality and Natural Religion* (1751) had appeared three years before the publication of Kimber's novel, can clearly be sensed informing the moral of this tale.[37]

Kimber occasionally uses his novel as a vehicle for criticizing the moral hypocrisy of England and many Christians. For instance, in speeches by Mrs. Barlow, Tommy, Mr. Ferguson and others, he repeatedly rehearses the theme that a person's worth and character are not to be measured by financial or social status but by integrity and industry. After Tom and Fanny have grown into young adulthood, a different love appropriate to their age develops between them. Because they have been raised almost as brother and sister, they realize that they need to know how Tom came into the family and what their true relationship to each other is. They implore Mr. Ferguson to enlighten them. Instead of immediately complying, Ferguson tells the history of his own fall from a high estate into poverty and even serfdom in order to criticize those who judge people by exterior trappings rather than on their merits. He also instructs them on the morally deadening effects of the hurried life in the cities, as people scramble to make ends meet. Finally, Ferguson tells Tommy and Fanny of his father-in-law, who, through no fault of his own, had been cast into debtor's prison "through the merciless principles of revenge, of a few creditors, who yet were church goers, and every day repeated, 'Forgive us our debts, as we forgive our debtors'" (*Garland* 7:36).

This pathetic tale leaves everyone in tears. When Mrs. Barlow happens upon this scene and finds the participants all weeping, Ferguson hastens to inform her that it had been "their sensibility . . . which had cast them into such disorder." Mrs. Barlow's response reflects the shared assumption in the cult of sensibility that affective responses revealed one's character: "'I'm glad of it, cry'd the excellent woman; shedding tears for others woes, betokens a goodness and nobleness of nature, that I hope my children will never be deficient in.'"

Then a series of sudden reversals of fortune are introduced, which are each in turn turned completely around as the force of Tom's goodness overcomes all adversity. Mr. Barlow is intent on marrying his daughter to the doltish and uncouth son of a wealthy neighbor, a plan that throws everyone into the depths of despair, although he is oblivious to the entreaties and tears of his wife and daughter. Tom is exiled to a distant plantation as an overseer, but ever true to himself—hardworking, honest, diligent, kind, and considerate—the plantation is soon more profitable than it had ever been, since even the slaves love to serve him (*Garland* 7:40).

Tom is then sold to an Indian trader and seems doomed to a life in the distant wilderness, separated from Fanny and civilization. As Tom and the trader, named Matthewson,

leave the plantation on horseback, he has Tom recount his life story. Matthewson is deeply affected by it (and, thus, the reader learns he is a man of sensibility), sets Tom free, and adopts him as his own son. Tom's narrative of his sad history—like the novel itself—evokes the sentimental cycle of emotional responses that witness to the character and temper of each character. As a result, Tom wins a new relation, patron, and friend. Like Ferguson before him, Matthewson sees that Tom's innate goodness and character will ultimately lead him to success.

Sentimental characters are inevitably captivated by each other, as they are enmeshed in a social—even cosmic—world of affect, a world spun out of emotive webs of signification. Kimber expresses as much in the following passage:

> There is a certain somewhat, in certain countenances, that prepossesses us in the favour of the wearers at first sight, an openness, and ingenuity, and an amiableness, that immediately strikes the beholder—such was Tom's, and that and the many noble instances he had given of his sentiments and his fortitude, had quite captivated his master, so that he really began to look upon him as a son. The mingled starts of joy, gratitude, and love towards this generous man, which inspired Tom's breast, at the conclusion of this speech, no words can paint—it actuated his whole person, it heaved his bosom—it flushed his face, and deprived him of utterance.
>
> (*Garland* 7:99)[38]

Predictably, when Matthewson is killed, Tom inherits all of his property and quickly becomes the most successful Indian trader in the country. Indian captivity is introduced into the novel as yet another (though certainly not the last) sudden reversal of fortune precisely when the tide seems to be turning in his favor. The reader is addressed directly at this point: "Thus behold a reserve of fortune—he, who but a small space of time before, was happy, and employed in making others so, is now strip'd naked, bound with thongs, and a spectacle of triumph and reproach to a barbarous gang of savages!" (*Garland* 7:140-41).

This familiar scene of the captive being carried off to an unknown fate functions in this sentimental novel as one of many reversals that the protagonist undergoes in the course of the tale on the way to his reward—economic security, social status and respect, and domestic bliss. It is impossible to rehearse all of the vicissitudes of the hero's life thereafter as they are played out over the next hundred pages. Suffice it to say that they all follow the same pattern. One incident bears mention in passing, however, since the introduction of divine providence here is representative of its function in many works of sentimental literature. At one point, after a battle with pirates on the Atlantic, Tom discovers that one of the prisoners he has taken is none other than the man who had kidnapped him as a child years before. As Tom recounts his history to the crew, the sailors' "resentment at so base, so wicked an action, carry'd them out into exclamations against the villain, and the captain added—how just is providence—who has permitted you to see the miserable death of your persecutor! I am convinced that, in crimes of an enormous nature, heaven most commonly punishes the criminal even in this life" (*Garland* 7:156-57).

Tom eventually wins his Fanny, rescues the long-suffering Mrs. Barlow from her life with her abusive husband, and they all return to England. The novel ends with the reader being assured that "Mr. Anderson and his lovely Fanny are still living, and, tho' now in the decline of life, experience that love founded on good sense and virtue can never know decay, and that providence ever showers down blessings on truth and constancy. "Oh! never let a virtuous mind despair; / For heaven makes virtue its peculiar care" (*Garland* 7:287-88).

Notes

1. For a summary of the publishing situation, see Davidson, *Revolution and the Word*, p. 11. For background on the history of the book in America at this time, including publication, distribution, and consumption of texts, see Lehmann-Haupt, *Book in America*; Berthold, *American Colonial Printing*; Oswald, *Printing in the Americas*; Shepard, *History of Street Literature*; Hall and Hench, *Needs and Opportunities;* Resnick, *Literacy;* Joyce et al., *Printing and Society*; Hall, *Worlds of Wonder*; and J. Paul Hunter, *Before Novels*. American booksellers imported most of the fictional reading materials available in North America well into the eighteenth century or, alternatively, brought out American editions (frequently pirated) of English and European fiction. At the same time, there was a ready market in England and on the Continent for some types of American works, which were quickly reprinted there. An instance of the latter case is *A Narrative of the Captivity of Mrs. Johnson* (Walpole, N.H.: David Carlisle, Jr., 1796), which was brought out in a pirated edition the following year in Glasgow. The pirated edition included the following notice: "The Publishers of this Narrative bought it of an American Gentleman who arrived at Greenock in the Bark Hope, a few weeks ago; and as he assured them that there was not a copy of it to be procured in Europe, and that it sold in America for four shillings and sixpence, they deemed it worthy of reprinting" (*Garland* 23: n.p.).

2. This linkage of Pamela and captivity narratives has recently been made by Armstrong and Tennenhouse, *Imaginary Puritan*, pp. 200-216.

3. See Davidson, *Revolution and the Word*, p. 260.

4. Van Der Beets, *Indian Captivity Narrative*, p. 36; Pearce, "Significances," pp. 2, 9.

5. Rowson, *The Inquisitor,* cited in Herbert Ross Brown, *Sentimental Novel*, p. 166. Two useful studies of the female domestic novel and the modern romance novel are Papashvily, *All the Happy Endings*; and Radway, *Reading the Romance*.

6. O'Flaherty, *Other People's Myths,* p. 148.

7. Barnett, *Ignoble Savage,* p. 48; Fliegelman, *Prodigals and Pilgrims*, p. 144.

8. I have found the following works useful in understanding the emergence of the Newtonian-Lockean sensory psychology and epistemology, as well as the attendant developments over the next century and a half, especially the rise of a culture of sensibility: Todd, *Sensibility*; Proby, *English Fiction*; Mullan, *Sentiment and Sociability*; Brissenden, *Virtue in Distress*; Beasley, *Novels of the 1740's*; Sambrook, *Eighteenth Century;* Fliegelman, *Prodigals and Pilgrims*; McKeon, *Origins of the English Novel*; Gillian Brown, *Domestic Individualism*; Barker-Benfield, *Culture of Sensibility*; Nicolson, *Newton Demands the Muse*; Samuels, *Culture of Sentiment*; Hagstrum, *Sex and Sensibility*; Bredvold, *Natural History of Sensibility*; and Gura, *Wisdom of Words*.

9. Barker-Benfield, *Culture of Sensibility,* p. 69. See also Fiering, "Irresistible Compassion."

10. Fliegelman, *Prodigals and Pilgrims*, p. 12.

11. Cited in Brissenden, *Virtue in Distress,* p. 42, n. 60.

12. Barker-Benfield, *Culture of Sensibility,* p. 6. This form of the transmission of knowledge should not surprise us, nor should the fact that developments in science quickly affected literary forms. It is well known, for instance, that secondhand information on Einstein's theories of relativity, which Virginia Woolf gained from acquaintances at Oxford, affected the form of her novels and inspired aspects of her narrative manipulation of time.

13. "Moral Philosophy" (unsigned), *Encyclopaedia Britannica.*

14. As Brissenden has noted, concerning Richardson's works, "The sentiments in his novels were indeed 'moral and instructive' and they were intended to provide comfort as much for the reader as for the heroine during her trials" (*Virtue in Distress*, p. 100).

15. Cited in Barker-Benfield, *Culture of Sensibility*, p. 9.

16. Dr. Benjamin Slocock read *Pamela* to his congregation from the pulpit. See Beasley, *Novels of the 1740's*, pp. 134, 138.

17. For an introduction to the culture of sentiment and the moral economy of tears in France, see Vincent-Buffault, *History of Tears.*

18. Tompkins, *Sensational Designs*, p. xii.

19. *Garland* 7. The source of these lines is not cited on the title page, but we may assume that most contemporary readers would have readily recognized them as from Addison's *Cato*, 5.2.15-18.

20. In *Before Novels*, J. Paul Hunter convincingly argues that the early novel is indebted to the diverse literature of wonders and remarkable occurrences, includ-

ing the works of Puritans such as Cotton Mather, while eschewing the earlier reliance on supernatural intervention in history because of the increasing acceptability of rational scientific explanations of the world and of causality.

21. Herbert Ross Brown, *Sentimental Novel,* p. 38.

22. Shaftsbury, cited in Humphreys, "'The Friend of Mankind,'" p. 205.

23. See Fiering, "Irresistible Compassion"; Crane, "Suggestions"; and Donald Greene, "Latitudinarianism and Sensibility."

24. Stowe felt that social reformation would come about only through a spiritual conversion in the individual, which would be marked by correct emotional responses to specific situations: "There is one thing that every individual can do—they can see to it that they feel right. An atmosphere of sympathetic influence encircles every human being; and the man or woman who feels strongly, healthily and justly, on the great interests of humanity, is a constant benefactor to the human race. See, then, to your sympathies in this matter! Are they in harmony with the sympathies of Christ? or are they swayed and perverted by the sophistries of worldly policy?" (*Uncle Tom's Cabin,* p. 448).

For more on the ways in which *Uncle Tom's Cabin* participated in the cultural work of the sentimental novel, see Jane Tompkins, "Sentimental Power: *Uncle Tom's Cabin* and the Politics of Literary History," in *Sensational Designs,* pp. 122-46. In the following pages, however, I will suggest by example that the sentimental novel was not exclusively a female literary form but was a culturally available form appropriated by female authors for their own soteriological or religiopolitical purposes.

25. *The Spectator,* No. 418, cited in Barker-Benfield, *Culture of Sensibility,* pp. 62-63.

26. Hume, *A Treatise of Human Nature,* p. 569.

27. Eliot, *Adam Bede,* p. 116.

28. Cited in Davidson, *Revolution and the Word,* p. 43.

29. Thomas Berger followed in this tradition of the fictional ruse of an editor retelling "remarkable" tales in his 1964 best-selling novel *Little Big Man,* a modern fictional captivity.

30. Davidson, *Revolution and the Word,* p. 14.

31. Herbert Ross Brown, *Sentimental Novel,* pp. 86-87.

32. Ibid., p. 78.

33. On the popularization of Ignation and other meditative practices in Protestant circles, see Martz, *Poetry of Meditation,* as well as the more recent work of J. Paul Hunter, *Before Novels,* which links these practices to the novel.

34. Cited in Herbert Ross Brown, *Sentimental Novel,* p. 85. In an important sense, Sterne's understanding of the complicity of the author *and* the reader in the construction of meaning (more precisely, shared meaning) would have helped modern critics to avoid the major weakness of early reader-response and audience-oriented criticism—an overemphasis on the author's ability to channel or structure the reader's response. The reader was represented as largely passive, while the text, as an autonomous object, had the power to generate specific responses.

35. Brown notes that some sentimental authors even claimed that medical autopsies, then a new scientific advance, "proved" the refined sensibility of certain characters by revealing the delicate lines of his or her sensorium, the organ of sensibility (ibid., pp. 78-79).

36. Cited ibid., pp. 9, 76.

37. On the kidnapping of children for sale into indentured servantship, see Coldham, "'Spiriting' of London Children," and Robert C. Johnson, "Transportation of Vagrant Children."

38. On the influence of Scottish commonsense philosophy on Americans, including Jefferson and Benjamin Franklin, and American fiction, see Terence Martin, *Instructed Vision,* Gura, *Wisdom of Words,* and Fiering, *Moral Philosophy.*

Bibliography

Armstrong, Nancy, and Leonard Tennenhouse. *The Imaginary Puritan: Literature, Intellectual Labor, and the Origins of Personal Life.* Berkeley: Univ. of California Press, 1992.

Barker-Benfield, G. J. *The Culture of Sensibility: Sex and Society in Eighteenth-Century Britain.* Chicago: Univ. of Chicago Press, 1992.

Barnett, Louise K. *The Ignoble Savage: American Literary Racism, 1790-1890.* Westport, Conn.: Greenwood, 1975.

Beasley, Jerry C. *Novels of the 1740's.* Athens: Univ. of Georgia Press, 1982.

Berger, Thomas. *Little Big Man.* New York: Dial, 1964.

Berthold, Arthur Benedict. *American Colonial Printing as Determined by Contemporary Cultural Forces, 1639-1763.* New York: Burt Franklin, 1970.

Bredvold, Louis I. *The Natural History of Sensibility.* Detroit: Wayne State Univ. Press, 1962.

Brissenden, R. F. *Virtue in Distress: Studies in the Novel of Sentiment from Richardson to Sade.* New York: Harper and Row, 1976.

Brown, Gillian. *Domestic Individualism: Imagining Self in Nineteenth-Century America.* Berkeley: Univ. of California Press, 1990.

Brown, Herbert Ross. *The Sentimental Novel in America, 1789-1860.* Durham: Duke Univ. Press, 1940.

Coldham, Peter Wilson. "The 'Spiriting' of London Children to Virginia, 1684-1685." *Virginia Magazine of History and Biography* 83 (1975): 280-87.

Crane, Ronald S. "Suggestions toward a Genealogy of the 'Man of Feeling,'" *ELH: A Journal of English Literary History* 1 (1934): 205-30.

Davidson, Cathy N. *Revolution and the Word: The Rise of the Novel in America.* New York: Oxford Univ. Press, 1986.

Eliot, George. *Adam Bede.* Boston: Houghton Mifflin, 1968.

Fiering, Norman S. "Irresistible Compassion: An Aspect of Eighteenth-Century Sympathy and Humanitarianism." *Journal of the History of Ideas* 37 (1976): 195-218.

Fliegelman, Jay. *Prodigals and Pilgrims: The American Revolution against Patriarchal Authority, 1750-1800.* Cambridge: Cambridge Univ. Press, 1982.

The Garland Library of Narratives of North American Indian Captivities. 311 titles in 111 volumes. Selected and arranged by Wilcomb E. Washburn. New York & London: Garland, 1976-77.

Greene, Donald. "Latitudinarianism and Sensibility: The Genealogy of the 'Man of Sensibility' Reconsidered." *Modern Philology* 75 (1977): 159-83.

Gura, Philip F. *The Wisdom of Words: Language, Theology, and Literature in the New England Renaissance.* Middletown, Conn.: Wesleyan Univ. Press, 1981.

Hagstrum, Jean H. *Sex and Sensibility: Ideal and Erotic Love from Milton to Mozart.* Chicago: Univ. of Chicago Press, 1980.

Hall, David D. *Worlds of Wonder, Days of Judgment: Popular Religious Belief in Early New England.* Cambridge: Harvard Univ. Press, 1989.

Hall, David D., and John B. Hench, eds. *Needs and Opportunities in the History of the Book: America, 1639-1876.* Worcester, Mass.: American Antiquarian Society, 1987.

Hume, David. *A Treatise of Human Nature.* Ed. Ernest C. Mossner. London: Penguin Books, 1969.

Humphreys, A. R. "'The Friend of Mankind' (1700-[17]60)—an Aspect of Eighteenth-Century Sensibility." *Review of English Studies* 24 (1948): 203-18.

Hunter, J. Paul. *Before Novels: The Cultural Contexts of Eighteenth-Century English Fiction.* New York: Norton, 1990.

Johnson, Robert C. "The Transportation of Vagrant Children from London to Virginia, 1618-1622." In *Early Stuart Studies: Essays in Honor of David Harris Willson,* ed. Howard S. Reinmuth, Jr., pp. 137-51. Minneapolis: Univ. of Minnesota Press, 1970.

Joyce, William L., ed. *Printing and Society in Early America.* Worcester, Mass.: American Antiquarian Society, 1983.

Lehmann-Haupt, Hellmut. *The Book in America: A History of the Making and Selling of Books in the United States.* New York: Bowker, 1951.

McKeon, Michael. *The Origins of the English Novel, 1600-1740.* Baltimore: Johns Hopkins Univ. Press, 1987.

Martin, Terence. *The Instructed Vision: Scottish Common Sense Philosophy and the Origins of American Fiction.* Bloomington: Indiana Univ. Press, 1961.

Martz, Louis L. *The Poetry of Meditation: A Study in English Religious Literature of the Seventeenth Century.* New Haven: Yale Univ. Press, 1954.

Mullan, John. *Sentiment and Sociability: The Language of Feeling in the Eighteenth Century.* Oxford: Clarendon Press, 1988.

Nicholson, Marjorie Hope. *Newton Demands the Muse: Newton's Opticks and the Eighteenth-Century Poets.* Princeton: Princeton Univ. Press, 1946.

O'Flaherty, Wendy Doniger. *Other People's Myths: The Cave of Echoes.* New York: Macmillan, 1988.

Oswald, John Clyde. *Printing in the Americas.* New York: Hacker Art Books, 1968.

Papashvily, Helen Waite. *All the Happy Endings: A Study of the Domestic Novel in America, the Women Who Wrote It, the Women Who Read It, in the Nineteenth Century.* New York: Harper & Brothers, 1956.

Pearce, Roy Harvey. "The Significances of the Captivity Narrative." *American Literature* 19 (1947): 1-20.

Proby, Clive T. *English Fiction of the Eighteenth Century, 1700-1789.* London and New York: Longman, 1987.

Radway, Janice A. *Reading the Romance: Women, Patriarchy, and Popular Literature.* Chapel Hill: Univ. of North Carolina Press, 1984.

Resnick, Daniel P., ed. *Literacy in Historical Perspective.* Washington, D.C.: Library of Congress, 1983.

Sambrook, James. *The Eighteenth Century: The Intellectual and Cultural Context of English Literature, 1700-1789.* London and New York: Longman, 1986.

Samuels, Shirley, ed. *The Culture of Sentiment: Race, Gender, and Sentimentality in Nineteenth-Century America.* New York: Oxford Univ. Press, 1992.

Shepard, Leslie. *The History of Street Literature.* Detroit: Singing Tree Press, 1973.

Todd, Janet. *Sensibility: An Introduction.* London: Methuen, 1986.

Tompkins, Jane. *Sensational Designs: The Cultural Work of American Fiction, 1790-1860.* New York: Oxford Univ. Press, 1985.

Van Der Beets, Richard. "The Indian Captivity Narrative as Ritual." *American Literature* 43 (1972): 548-62.

Vincent-Buffault, Anne. *The History of Tears: Sensibility and Sentimentality in France.* London: Macmillan, 1991.

FURTHER READING

Criticism

Arner, Robert D. "The Story of Hannah Duston: Cotton Mather to Thoreau." *American Transcendental Quarterly* 18 (spring 1973): 19-23.
Discusses the ways in which various writers have incorporated the legend of Hannah Duston into their writings.

Barnett, Louise K. "The White Fantasy World of the Frontier Romance." In *The Ignoble Savage: American Literary Racism, 1790-1890,* pp. 17-142. Westport, Conn.: Greenwood Press, 1975.
Argues that frontier narratives reflect the nationalism and racism of white society.

Carleton, Phillips D. "The Indian Captivity." *American Literature* 15 (March 1943-January 1944): 169-80.
Advocates a greater respect for, and attention to, the genre of American captivity narratives.

Dondore, Dorothy A. "White Captives among the Indians." *New York History* 13 (1932): 292-300.
Surveys captivity narratives.

Hartman, James D. "Providence Tales and the Indian Captivity Narrative: Some Transatlantic Influences on Colonial Puritan Discourse." *Early American Literature* 32, no. 1 (winter 1997): 66-81.
Contends that English providence tales and Puritan Indian captivity narratives are closely related.

Heard, J. Norman. *White into Red: A Study of the Assimilation of White Persons Captured by Indians.* Metuchen, N.J.: The Scarecrow Press, 1973, 180 p.
Studies the various reactions of white captives to Native culture, ranging from rejection to assimilation. Also considers the struggle and readjustment of redeemed captives and Native children raised in white civilization.

Levernier, James and Hennig Cohen, eds. *The Indians and Their Captives.* Westport, Conn.: Greenwood Press, 1977, 291 p.
Collection of captivity narratives, ordered chronologically from the earliest narratives written during the sixteenth century through the nineteenth century.

Whitford, Kathryn. "Hannah Dustin: The Judgement of History." In *Essex Institute Historical Collections* 108, no. 4 (October 1972): 304-25.
Surveys various accounts of Hannah Dustin's captivity narrative.

Bernard Mandeville
1670-1733

English poet, satirist, and nonfiction writer.

INTRODUCTION

Described by Benjamin Franklin in his *Autobiography* as "a most facetious, entertaining companion," Mandeville is best known for his provocative writings about society, morality, and religion. In such works as *The Fable of the Bees: or, Private Vices, Publick Benefits* (1714), he used satire to convey his belief that vice as well as virtue is vital to a healthy society. Mandeville's writings were assailed by some of the most prominent thinkers of the day, though, later critics have shown, some, such as David Hume and Adam Smith, were significantly influenced by his views.

BIOGRAPHICAL INFORMATION

Little is known about Mandeville's life. He was born in the Netherlands, possibly in Rotterdam or nearby Dort (present-day Dordrecht). Public records show that he was baptized in Rotterdam in 1670. He attended the Erasmian School in Rotterdam and then studied philosophy and medicine at the University of Leyden. He received a Doctor of Medicine degree at Leyden in 1691. Shortly afterwards, he immigrated to England, where he lived for the remainder of his life. In 1693 he was charged with practicing medicine without a license; though he never applied for a license, he appears to have continued practicing medicine. In 1699 he married an Englishwoman, and the couple had two children. Mandeville published a number of medical studies and satirical works—including over thirty pieces contributed to the magazine *The Female Tatler* between 1709 and 1710—before the publication in 1714 of *The Fable of the Bees*. Although the first edition of this work attracted little attention, the second, expanded, edition in 1723 caused an uproar. The book's publisher was charged in court as a "public nuisance" for issuing such an immoral book. (It was published without Mandeville's name on it, so he was not charged.) It was attacked by such notable figures as John Dennis, Alexander Pope, Samuel Richardson, and Henry Fielding. Mandeville defended his work in *A Vindication of the Book, from the Aspersions contain'd in a Presentment of the Grand-Jury of Middlesex, and an abusive Letter to Lord C.*, which was issued as a pamphlet (now lost) in 1723 and included in the third edition of *The Fable of the Bees* the following year. In 1732 George Berkeley directed an attack on Mandeville and other freethinkers in *Alciphron; or, The Minute Philosopher*; Mandeville defended himself in *A Letter to Dion, Occasion'd by his Book call'd Alciphron, or The Minute Philosopher*, published later the same year. Mandeville died on 21 January 1733.

MAJOR WORKS

Mandeville's works cover a wide range of genres and subjects. In the poem *Typhon: or The Wars Between the Gods and Giants* (1704), he lampoons the gods and heroes in the classical epics of Homer and Virgil. In the prose work *The Virgin Unmask'd,* (1709) he offers a dialogue between an unmarried aunt and her inexperienced niece on the potential temptations and dangers a young woman faces in her encounters with men. Mandeville's contributions to the *The Female Tatler,* advanced his ideas on human nature, and his position on this subject appears in its most developed form in *The Fable of the Bees,* which demonstrates the author's belief that vices are as important as virtues if human society is to flourish, and his conviction that any attempt to create a thoroughly virtuous society would therefore be disastrous. The poem *The Grumbling Hive: or, Knaves Turn'd Honest,* which was first published in 1705, is the centerpiece of the collection. In this verse fable, Mandeville describes a hive of bees that is thriving and productive as whole, despite the fact that its individual members are given to a variety of vices analogous to those in human society. When Jove replaces the vices with virtues, the hive starts to degrade in a number of ways and eventually deteriorates completely as a functioning unit. Mandeville's other major works of social criticism include *Free Thoughts on Religion, the Church, and National Happiness* (1720), in which he condemns the excesses of organized religion throughout history; *A Modest Defence of Publick Stews* (1724), in which he wryly advocates the legalization of prostitution; and *An Enquiry into the Origin of Honour, and the Usefulness of Christianity in War* (1732), which concludes that Christian beliefs and morality have no place during a time of war.

CRITICAL RECEPTION

During his lifetime, Mandeville was viewed as a controversialist and came under repeated attacks from critics. The second edition of *The Fable of the Bees,* in particular, was denounced as blasphemous and immoral. Modern critics generally view Mandeville's works as complex responses to the social and political pressures of his time, which was witnessing the decline of absolutism and the rise of commercialism. As M. M. Goldsmith and others have argued, Mandeville shows that the health of a society based on commerce requires that virtues and vices must coexist. In such a world, these and other scholars have noted, traditional definitions of ethics and morality are overturned and even divorced from religion. It is from this starting point that much modern criticism of Mandeville proceeds. M. R. Jack has sought to delineate the conception of religion that underlies Mandeville's works. Robert H. Hopkins has proposed that Mandeville exposes the religious and ethical compromises that are made in a society based on money and commerce. E. G. Hundert has argued that *The Grumbling Hive* demonstrates that "commercial societies seem naturally to entail forms of artifice and imposture which should be understood as the moral price of commercial prosperity." J. A. W. Gunn has investigated Mandeville's view of politics in a commercial society. Other critics, including Louis Schneider, have attempted to form a clearer picture of Mandeville in the absence of substantial biographical information. Hector Monro has gone so far as to assemble multiple portraits derived from the observations of his contemporaries and their diverse reactions to his works.

PRINCIPAL WORKS

The Pamphleteers: A Satyr (poetry) 1703

Some Fables after the Easie and Familiar Method of Monsieur de la Fontaine (poetry) 1703; expanded as *Æsop Dress'd; or a Collection of Fables Writ in Familiar Verse*, 1704

Typhon: or The Wars Between the Gods and Giants; A Burlesque Poem in Imitation of the Comical Mons. Scarron (poetry) 1704

*The Grumbling Hive; or, Knaves Turn'd Honest (poetry) 1705

A Treatise of the Hypochondriak and Hysterick Passions, Vulgarly Call'd the Hypo in Men and Vapours in Women; In which the Symptoms, Causes, and Cure of those Diseases are set forth after a Method intirely new (dialogue) 1711

Wishes to a Godson, with Other Miscellany Poems (poetry) 1712

The Virgin Unmask'd: or, Female Dialogues Betwixt an Elderly Maiden Lady, and Her Niece, On several Diverting Discourses on Love, Marriage, Memoirs, and Morals, &c. of the Times (dialogue) 1709; revised as *The Mysteries of Virginity*, 1714

The Fable of the Bees: or, Private Vices, Publick Benefits (poetry and prose) 1714; enlarged in 1723 and again in 1724

The Mischiefs that Ought Justly to be Apprehended from a Whig-Government (dialogue) 1714

Free Thoughts on Religion, the Church, and National Happiness (nonfiction) 1720

A Modest Defence of Public Stews: or, an Essay upon Whoring, As it is now practis'd in these Kingdom (pamphlet) 1724

An Enquiry into the Causes of the Frequent Executions at Tyburn: and a Proposal for some Regulations concerning Felons in Prison, and the Good Effects to be expected from them (pamphlet) 1725

The Fable of the Bees. Part II. By the Author of the First (dialogues) 1729

An Enquiry into the Origin of Honour, and the Usefulness of Christianity in War (dialogue) 1732

A Letter to Dion, Occasion'd by his Book call'd Alciphron, or The Minute Philosopher (letter) 1732

The Fable of the Bees. 2 vols. [edited by F. B. Kaye] 1924

*This work was later included in *The Fable of the Bees.*

CRITICISM

Hector Monro (essay date 1975)

SOURCE: Monro, Hector. "The Two Mandevilles" and "The Real Mandeville?" In *The Ambivalence of Bernard Mandeville*, pp. 1-24; 249-67. Oxford: Clarendon Press, 1975.

[*In the following essays, Monro discusses two very contradictory but equally plausible interpretations of Mandeville and finds such ambiguity consistent with the philosophical view evident throughout his work that the world is ultimately indefinable and unknowable.*]

THE TWO MANDEVILLES

Mandeville is not an obscure writer, but it has nevertheless been found possible to interpret him in two diametrically opposed ways. On one view, he is a pious Christian, an ascetic, and an unusually austere moralist, who finds corruption even in apparently laudable or at least innocent activities. On the other, he is at best an easy-going man of the world, at worst a profligate, a cynic, a scoffer at all virtue and religion, and even (in the words of William Law, the author of *A Serious Call to a Devout and Holy Life*) a man who 'comes a missioner from the kingdom of darkness to do us harm'.[1]

In Mandeville's day, and even perhaps in ours, the second view is the commoner. The Grand Jury of the County of Middlesex, noting that the Almighty had, understandably, visited France with the plague but spared England, was afraid that the circulation of *The Fable of the Bees* might cause a change in the divine policy.[2]

John Wesley thought Mandeville even wickeder, at least in his writings, than Machiavelli or Voltaire, and as wicked as Mr. Sandeman.[3] Mandeville would have found it easy to explain why Wesley thought the opinions of a rival preacher more wicked than those of an unbeliever. In fairness, however, it should be said that the Sandemanians were commonly believed to be anti-nominas. But the coupling of Mandeville with Sandeman as well as Voltaire does leave some slight doubt as to which of the two Mandevilles roused Wesley's horror.

There is no such doubt about Fielding. Miss Matthews, in *Amelia*, says that Mandeville had taught her to regard the words 'virtue' and 'religion' as 'only cloaks under which hypocrisy may be the better enabled to cheat the world'. She is shaken a little when told that Mandeville also denied the existence of 'the best passion which the mind can possess', love: a charge also made against Mandeville by Fielding, speaking in his own person, in one of the introductory chapters in *Tom Jones*.[4]

Adam Smith has a chapter in the *Theory of Moral Sentiments* called 'Of Licentious Systems' [of Moral Philosophy]. The entire chapter is devoted to Mandeville. In the first edition, it is true, La Rochefoucauld is included as well, but Smith deleted this passage in the later editions at the request of the Duke's grandson. Only the plural remains in the chapter heading as a vestigial reminder, a kind of literary coccyx.[5]

With no titled descendants to intercede for him, Mandeville continued to be abused. Gibbon said that 'Morality as well as Religion must joyn' in applauding William Law for 'drawing his pen against the licentious doctrine' of ***The Fable of the Bees***.[6] An anonymous writer in the *Gentleman's Magazine* of 1846 remarked that 'nobody would be the better for reading Mandeville' and that he tended 'to lower the standard of virtue, and to set life on a narrow expediency footing'.[7] Sir James Mackintosh, writing on the 'Progress of Ethical Philosophy' in the *Encyclopaedia Britannica*, dismissed him with the phrase: 'not to mention Mandeville, the buffoon and sophister of the alehouse'.[8] Even Leslie Stephen said that Mandeville 'represents scepticism in its coarsest and most unlovely stage'.[9] And it would be very easy to go on quoting similar remarks: a book published in 1959 calls him 'Mandeville, a tavern character whose malice sharpened his wit'.[10]

The main exponent of the other view is probably Mandeville himself: a somewhat suspicious fact that is not inconsistent with, and might even tend to confirm, Law's opinion that he was an emissary of the Devil. But Mandeville is not alone in his presentation of himself. Francis Hutcheson conjectured: 'He has probably been struck with some old *Fanatick* Sermon upon *self-denial* in his youth, and can never get it out of his head since.'[11] Selby-Bigge thought his asceticism genuine, and his themes, when properly understood, 'the perpetual topics of the pulpit'.[12] Robert Browning put Mandeville firmly on the side of the angels, and called upon him to help refute the scepticism of Carlyle.[13] Browning, it is true, did not see Mandeville as a stern moralist, but as a kind of Pippa who sunnily insisted on seeing the Good that came unnoticed out of Evil. This was hardly Mandeville's own picture of himself; he would no doubt have preferred the writer in the *Monthly Mirror* for 1803, who said that he 'supports one of the tenets of our religion, the natural corruption of human nature, unless assisted by divine grace'.[14]

For the first of the two Mandevilles, the pious one, is a man who looks round him at a professedly Christian society, and is scandalized at what he sees. In his reply to Mandeville, Hutcheson is at pains to point out that Christianity 'no where condemns the Rich or Powerful for being so, or for desiring high Stations'.[15] True though this may be, it is the kind of remark that makes twentieth-century Christians squirm a little. Neither now nor in Mandeville's time would a visitor from another planet, observing the people among whom he found himself, suspect that they were committed to loving their enemies, turning the other cheek, renouncing the things of this world.

> When Ministers of *Christ* assure their Hearers, that to indulge them selves in all earthly Pleasures and Sensualities, that are not clashing with the Laws of the Country, or the Fashion of the Age they live in, will be no bar to their future Happiness, if they enjoy them with Moderation; that nothing ought to be deem'd Luxury, that is suitable to a Person's Rank or Quality, and which he can purchase without hurting his Estate, or injuring his Neighbour; that no Buildings or Gardens can be so profusely sumptuous, no Furniture so curious or magnificent, no Inventions for Ease so extravagant, no Cookery so operose, no Diet so delicious, no Entertainments or Way of Living so expensive as to be Sinful in the Sight of God, if a Man can afford them, and they are the same as others of the same Birth or Quality either do or would make use of, if they could: That a Man may study and be sollicitous about Modes and Fashions, assist at courts, hunt after Worldly Honour, and partake of all the Diversions of the *beau monde,* and at the same time be a very good Christian; when Ministers of *Christ* I say, assure their Hearers of this, they certainly teach what they have no Warrant for from his Doctrine. For it is in Effect the same as to assert that the strictest Attachment to the World is not inconsistent with a Man's Promise of renouncing the Pomp and Vanity of it.[16]

This is Mandeville's first charge: worldliness, self-indulgence, complacency. England (Europe, for that matter) is only nominally Christian. Its real God is Mammon. Materialistic, money-grubbing, pleasure-seeking: the indictment is familiar, and has been repeated thousands of times, both before and since. The theme of *The Fable of the Bees* is that society is built entirely upon these worldly foundations: a genuine attempt by its members to lead a life of Christian devotion would bring it crashing down at once. The bees in Mandeville's fable, it will be remembered, were hypocritical or self-deceiving enough

> Always to rail at what they loved.

That is to say, they complained of dishonesty and self-seeking in others, while practising them themselves:

> One, that had got a Princely score,
> By cheating Master, King and Poor,
> Dar'd cry aloud, *The Land must sink*
> *For all its Fraud*; And whom d'ye think
> The Sermonizing Rascal chid?
> A Glover that sold Lamb for Kid.

Jove, indignant at this duplicity, and noticing that

> . . . all the Rogues cry'd brazenly,
> *Good Gods, Had we but Honesty!*

decides to teach them a lesson by granting them their prayer. The bees become honest and virtuous: with startling results. Lawyers, turnkeys, milliners, footmen, courtiers lose their livelihoods:

> All Places manag'd first by Three
> Who watched each other's Knavery,
> And often for a Fellow-feeling
> Promoted one another's stealing,
> Are happily supply'd by One,
> By which some thousands more are gone.

With luxurious living and conspicuous consumption abandoned, trade and commerce languish:

> The Price of Land and Houses falls
> Mirac'lous Palaces, whose Walls
> Like those of *Thebes,* were rais'd by Play,
> Are to be let . . .
> . . .
> The building Trade is quite destroy'd,
> Artificers are not employ'd;
> No Limner for his Art is fam'd,
> Stone-cutters, Carvers are not nam'd.
> Those that remain'd, grown temp'rate, strive
> Not how to spend, but how to live,
> And when they paid their Tavern Score,
> Resolv'd to enter it no more:
> No Vintner's Jilt in all the Hive
> Could wear now Cloth of Gold, and thrive.
> . . .
>   The haughty *Chloe,* to live Great,
> Had made her Husband rob the State:
> But now she sells her Furniture,
> Which th' *Indies* had been ransack'd for;
> Contracts th' expensive Bill of Fare,
> And wears her strong Suit a whole Year:
> The slight and fickle Age is past,
> And Clothes, as well as Fashions, last.

Finally, the once large and prosperous community, the 'Spacious Hive well stockt with Bees', thronged with

> Millions endeavouring to supply
> Each other's Lust and Vanity

dwindles to a handful of hardy simple-lifers:

> Hard'ned with Toils and Exercise,
> They counted Ease itself a Vice;
> Which so improv'd their Temperance
> That, to avoid Extravagance,
> They flew into a hollow Tree,
> Blest with Content and Honesty.

So far, then, it is mainly luxury, self-indulgence, and self-deception that Mandeville is denouncing: the delusion (to update the clichés a little) that the affluent society, obsessed with material values, could also be a community of Christians. The real values of the fashionable world are described in the Preface to Part 2 of the *Fable.*

> Virtue . . . is a very fashionable word, and some of the most luxurious are extremely fond of the amiable sound; tho' they mean nothing by it, but a great Veneration for whatever is courtly or sublime, and an equal Aversion to every thing, that is vulgar or unbecoming. They seem to imagine that it chiefly consists in a strict Compliance to the Rules of Politeness, and all the Laws of Honour, that have any regard to the Respect that is due to themselves. It is the Existence of this Virtue, that is often maintain'd with so much Pomp of Words, and for the Eternity of which so many Champions are ready to take up Arms. Whilst the Votaries of it deny themselves no Pleasure, they can enjoy either fashionably or in Secret; and instead of sacrificing the Heart to the Love of real Virtue, can only condescend to abandon the outward Deformity of Vice, for the Satisfaction they receive from appearing to be well-bred. It is counted ridiculous for Men to commit Violence upon themselves, or to maintain, that Virtue requires Self-denial; all Court-philosophers are agreed, that nothing can be lovely or desirable that is mortifying or uneasy. A civil Behaviour among the Fair in Publick and a Deportment, inoffensive both in Words and Actions, is all the Chastity, the polite World requires in Men. What Liberties soever a Man gives himself in private, his Reputation shall never suffer whilst he conceals his Amours from all those that are not unmannerly inquisitive, and takes care that nothing criminal can ever be proved upon him. *Si non castè saltem cautè,* is a Precept that sufficiently shews, what every Body expects; and tho' Incontinence is own'd to be a Sin, yet never to have been guilty of it is a Character, which most single men under thirty would not be fond of, even amongst modest Women.[17]

There were other ways, too, in which men's actual beliefs differed from their professions. The real ideal of the English gentleman was not the Christian saint, but the Man of Honour.

> For ever since the Notion of Honour has been receiv'd among Christians, there have always been, in the same Number of People, Twenty Men of real Honour to one of real Virtue. The Reason is obvious. The Persuasions to Virtue make no Allowances, nor have any Allurements that are clashing with the Principle of it; whereas the Men of Pleasure, the Passionate and the Malicious, may all in their Turns meet with Opportunities of indulging their darling Appetites without trespassing against the Principle of Honour. A virtuous Man thinks himself obliged to obey the Laws of his Country; but a Man of Honour acts from a Principle which he is bound to think Superior to all Laws . . . A virtuous Man expects no Acknowledgments from others; and if they won't believe him to be virtuous, his Business is not to force them to it; but a Man of Honour has the Liberty openly to proclaim himself to be such, and to call to an Account Every body who dares to doubt of it; Nay, such is the inestimable Value he sets upon himself, that he often endeavours to punish with Death the most insignificant Trespass that's committed against him, the least Word, Look, or Motion, if he can find but any far-fetch'd Reason to suspect a Design in it to undervalue him, and of this No body is allowed to be a Judge but himself.[18]

There was of course a better side to the ideal of Honour, as Mandeville admitted. In one of the **'Remarks'** added to the *Fable* he tells us that the Man of Honour 'is oblig'd always to be faithful to his Trust, to prefer the publick interest to his own, not to tell lies nor defraud or wrong any Body, and from others to suffer no Affront, which is a Term of Art for every Action designedly done to undervalue him'. He adds, however, that whereas all of these rules were faithfully observed by 'the Men of ancient Honour, of which I reckon *Don Quixote* to have been the last upon Record', their modern counterparts paid little attention to any but the last of them. 'In great Families', Mandeville tells us, Honour 'is like the Gout, generally counted Hereditary, and all Lord's Children are born with it . . . there is nothing that encourages the Growth of it more than a Sword, and upon the first wearing of one, some People have felt considerable Shoots of it in four and twenty Hours.'[19]

The real point, however, is that the ideal of Honour is inconsistent with Christianity. To see this one only needs to consider duelling or war.

> The only thing of weight that can be said against modern Honour is, that it is directly opposite to Religion. The one bids you bear Injuries with Patience, the other tells you if you don't resent them, you are not fit to live. Religion commands you to leave all Revenge to God, Honour bids you trust your Revenge to nobody but your self, even where the Law would do it for you; Religion plainly forbids Murther, Honour openly justifies it: Religion bids you not shed Blood upon any account whatever: Honour bids you fight for the least Trifle: Religion is built on Humility, and Honour upon Pride . . .[20]

Mandeville denounces duelling in several places: in both parts of the **Fable** as well as in the **Origin of Honour.** That book, like Part 2 of the **Fable,** takes the form of dialogues in which Mandeville's spokesman and defender, Cleomenes, expounds Mandeville's ideas to a sceptical friend, Horatio. Horatio is 'a Man of strict Honour', who has himself fought a duel. In the **Origin of Honour,** Cleomenes' comments on duelling are given in a style worthy of Wesley or Sandeman themselves. A 'sincere follower of the Apostles, a downright Christian', he says, would first give all the obvious arguments against duelling.

> But if all these could not divert the Dueller from his Purpose, he would attack his stubborn Heart in its inmost Recesses, and forget Nothing of what I told you on the Subject in our Second and Third Conversation. He would recommend to him the Fable of the *Bees,* and, like that, he'd direct and lay open to him the Principle of Honour, and shew him, how diametrically opposite the Worship of that Idol was to the Christian Religion: the First consisting in openly cherishing and feeding that very Frailty in our Nature, which the latter strictly commands us with all our Might to conquer and destroy. Having convinced him of the substantial Difference and Contrariety of the Two Principles, he would display to him, on the one Hand, the Vanity of Earthly Glory, and the Folly of Coveting the Applause of a Sinful World; and, on the other, the Certainty of a Future State and the Transcendency of everlasting Happiness over every Thing that is perishable. From such Remonstrances as these the good, pious Man would take an Opportunity of exhorting him to a Christian Self-denial, and the Practice of real Virtue, and he would earnestly endeavour to make him sensible of the Peace of Conscience and solid Comforts that are to be found in Meekness and Humility, Patience and an entire Resignation to the Will of God.

HOR.:

> How long, pray, do you intend to go on with this Cant?

CLEO.:

> If I am to personate a Christian Divine, who is a sincere Believer, you must give me Leave to speak his Language.

HOR.:

> But if a Man had really such an Affair upon his Hands, and he knew the Person, he had to do with, to be a resolute Man that understood the Sword, do you think he would have Patience or be at leisure to hearken to all this puritanical Stuff, which you have been heaping together? Do you think (for that is the Point) it would have any Influence over his Actions?

CLEO.:

> If he believ'd the Gospel, and consequently future Rewards and Punishments, and he likewise acted consistently with what he believ'd, it would put an entire Stop to all and it would certainly hinder him from sending or accepting of Challenges, or ever engaging in anything relating to a Duel.

HOR.:

> Pray now, among all the Gentlemen of your Acquaintance, and such as you your Self should care to converse with, how many are there, do you think, on whom the Thoughts of Religion would have that Effect?

CLEO.:

> A great many, I hope.

HOR.:

> You can hardly forbear laughing, I see, when you say it; and I am sure, you your Self would have no Value for a Man whom you should see tamely put up a gross Affront: Nay I have seen and heard Parsons and Bishops themselves laugh at, and speak with Contempt of pretended Gentlemen, that had suffer'd of themselves to be ill treated without resenting it.[21]

Duelling is a test case which brings out clearly the contrast between Christian morality and the prevailing *mores.* Mandeville was not, of course, the only one to point this out. Richard Steele, for example, attacked duelling obliquely in *The Christian Hero* (1701), more forthrightly in *The Lying Lover* (1703), and quite explicitly in the *Tatler*[22] (which certainly influenced Mandeville, the contributor to the *Female Tatler*) and other periodicals. But Captain Steele, as he then was, wrote *The Christian Hero* as a soldier commending the Christian way of life to his fellow soldiers: it was left to Mandeville to suggest that war itself was also incompatible with Christianity. The bees in the *Fable,* after they had been afflicted with virtue,

> . . . have no Forces kept Abroad;
> Laugh at th' Esteem of Foreigners,
> And empty Glory got by Wars;
> They fight but for their Country's sake,
> When Right or Liberty's at Stake.[23]

In the *Origin of Honour,* however, Cleomenes (and so presumably Mandeville) goes further still: he is emphatic that 'there is Nothing contain'd in the Gospel, that can have the least Tendency to promote or justify War or Discord, Foreign or Domestick, Publick or Private; nor is there any the least Expression to be found in it, from which it is possible to excite or set People on to quarrel with, do Hurt to, or any Ways offend one another, on any Account whatever.'[24]

For all the lip-service paid to religion, the army chaplains, and the official prayers, the soldier cannot be permitted to be a genuine Christian.

> If he has but Courage, and knows how to please his Officers, he may get drunk Two or Three Times a Week, have a fresh Whore every Day, and swear an Oath at every Word he speaks, little or no Notice shall be taken of him to his Dishonour; and if he be good humour'd, and forbears stealing among his Comrades, he'll be counted a very honest Fellow. But if, what *Christ* and his Apostles would have justify'd him in and exhorted him to do, he takes a Slap in the Face, or any other gross Affront before Company without resenting it, tho' from his intimate Friend, it cannot be endured; and tho' he was the soberest and the most chaste, the most discreet, tractable and best temper'd Man in the World, his Business is done . . . and the Officers are forc'd to turn him out of the Regiment.[25]

Yet the full title of the *Origin of Honour* is *An Enquiry into the Origin of Honour and the Usefulness of Christianity in War.* It is generally believed, Horatio points out and Cleomenes concedes, that Christians make the best soldiers. This is possible, however, only through the perversion and distortion of Christianity. Morality, and 'even the Gospel', may be preached to soldiers

> at seasonable Times when they are in Winter Quarters, or in an idle Summer when there is no Enemy near, and the Troops perhaps are encamped in a Country, where no Hostilities should be committed. But when they are to enter upon Action, to besiege a large Town, or ravage a rich Country, it would be very impertinent to talk to them of Christian Virtues; doing as they would be done by; loving their Enemies, and extending their Charity to all Mankind . . . Then the Mask is flung off; not a Word of the Gospel, or of Meekness or Humility, and all Thoughts of Christianity are laid aside entirely.[26]

What is useful in war, then, is not genuine Christianity, but simply the belief that God is on one's side. Men are ready enough to believe this, especially if the outward acts of devotion are performed: frequent prayers, long and pathetic sermons, the singing of psalms, keeping the Sabbath. Mandeville demonstrates how the religious beliefs of the soldiers may be made serviceable by giving us the sermon of 'a crafty Divine':

> Provisions had been scarce for some Time; the Enemy was just a Hand; and Abundance of the Men seem'd to have little Mind to fight when a Preacher, much esteem'd among the Soldiers, took the following Method: First, he set faithfully before them their Sins and Wickedness, the many Warnings they had received to repent, and God's long Forbearance, as well as great Mercy, in not having totally destroy'd them long ago. He represented their Wants, and Scarcity of Provision, as a certain Token of the Divine Wrath, and shew'd them plainly, that labouring already under the Weight of his Displeasure, they had no Reason to think, that God would connive longer at their manifold Neglects and Transgressions. Having convinc'd them, that Heaven was angry with them, he enumerated many Calamities, which, he said, would befal them; and several of them being such, as they had actually to fear, he was hearken'd to as a Prophet. He then told them, that what they could suffer in this World, was of no great Moment, if they could but escape Eternal Punishment; but that of this (as they had lived) he saw not the least Probability, they should. Having shewn an extraordinary concern for their deplorable Condition, and seeing many of them touch'd with Remorse, and overwhelm'd with Sorrow, he changed his Note on a Sudden, and with an Air of Certainty told them, that there was still one Way left, and but that one, to retrieve all, and avert the Miseries they were threaten'd with; which, in short, was to Fight well, and beat their Enemies; and that they had nothing else for it. Having thus disclosed his Mind to them, with all the Appearances of Sincerity, he assumed a chearful Countenance, shew'd them the many Advantages, that would attend the Victory; assured them of it, if they would but exert themselves; named the Times and Places in which they had behaved well, not without Exaggeration, and work'd upon their Pride so powerfully, that they took Courage, fought like Lions, and got the Day.[27]

The distortion of Christianity to serve the worldly ambitions of priests and politicians is a favourite theme of Mandeville's. He devotes a whole book to it: his *Free Thoughts on Religion, the Church, and National Happiness.* The thesis here is really the same as in the *Fable*; Christian virtue is quite incompatible with worldly prosperity and greatness. It follows that if the Christian Church had become great and prosperous (as it undoubtedly had) it could only be by abandoning Christian virtue.

That the Church should have attained so much power and greatness was, Mandeville remarks, a very considerable achievement, considering the intractable material its priests had to work with:

> The *Pagans,* whose religion was built upon poetry and fiction, had a wretched theology, that might be turn'd to any purpose, and the priests in their contrivances

had no morals to cope with. In Mahometism there is more morality, and the notions of the Deity are better . . . but then the whole religion seems contriv'd to engage the sensual and voluptuous: in the alcoran it self many things are ludicrous and silly, and not a few that are soothing human passion. But in the Christian religion all is grave and solid; every part of it worthy of the most serious contemplation of a man, that can and dares think freely and thoroughly. The idea it furnishes us with of the Godhead is sublime, and as incomprehensible as it should be: in the doctrine of Christ there are no worldly allurements to draw the vicious, and all his followers are ty'd down to the strictest morality: the whole aim of the gospel is divine, nothing in it can possibly be construed so as to encourage priestcraft, or be serviceable to sooth any human passion, without doing the utmost violence to truth and good sense; and yet behold, what has been made of it![28]

So far Mandeville appears as a familiar figure: the prophet denouncing the wickedness of the times and the backsliding of his contemporaries. They worship false gods while blandly pretending to themselves that they are still good Christians; they pervert the most sacred things to serve worldly ends; the very clergy are bulwarks of hypocrisy and worldliness. They mistake the outward trappings of religion for true devotion and they cry peace where there is no peace, and there is no health in them.

But he goes still further. It is not merely that men are weak and sinful, and find it hard to live by what they know to be right. The truth is that the nature of man makes virtue impossible for him. Man is motivated by his passions, by self-love and by pride, the desire to think well of himself and have others think well of him. But no action is virtuous unless there is self-denial. No human actions, then, except those rare ones inspired by divine grace, are virtuous. What men mistake for virtue is something quite different: pride or self-righteousness or fear of public opinion. This is quite central to Mandeville's thought. It provides him with a theme on which he plays many variations. He is fairly light-hearted about it in *The Virgin Unmask'd*:

LUCINDA:

> . . . All is not gold that glisters; many things are done daily for which People are extoll'd to the Skies that at the same time, tho' the Actions are Good, would be blamed as highly, if the Principle from which they acted, and the Motive that first edg'd them on, were thoroughly known. When People are too Lazy, or fearful to undertake any thing, they are praised for being Contented; and the Effects of Avarice are often called Temperance and Sobriety. I know two Married People that seem to be very Loving, and never displeased with one another, and indeed they Live so well, that they are thought a very happy couple: But you would hardly guess at the Reason of all this.

ANTONIA:

> Without doubt they are both very Good Humour'd.

LUC.:

> Just the Reverse, for their present Unison is owing to no other cause, than their both being Devils alike.

AN.:

> How can that be?

LUC.:

> When they came first together, they Fell out, and Fought every Day like Dogs and Cats, and did one another abundance of Mischief. But as every one feels his own Hurt best, so both perceiving the ill conveniences they got by every quarrel, being equally Match'd, they became so terrible one to another, that at last they lived Peaceably, in Dread only of provoking one another's Anger.[29]

Mandeville's convert and spokesman, Cleomenes, is much more serious about it:

> Cleomenes seemed charitable, and was a Man of strict Morals, yet he would often complain that he was not possess'd of one Christian Virtue, and found fault with his own Actions, that had all the Appearances of Goodness; because he was conscious, he said, that they were perform'd from a wrong Principle. The Effects of his Education, and his Aversion to Infamy, had always been strong enough to keep him from Turpitude; but this he Ascribed to his Vanity, which he complain'd was in such full Possession of his Heart, that he knew no Gratification of any Appetite from which he was able to exclude it . . . He was sure, that the Satisfaction which arose from worldly Enjoyments, was something distinct from Gratitude, and foreign to Religion; and he felt plainly that, as it proceeded from within, so it center'd in himself. The very Relish of Life, he said, was accompanied with an Elevation of Mind, that seem'd to be inseparable from his Being. Whatever Principle was the Cause of this, he was convinced within himself, that the Sacrifice of the Heart, which the Gospel requires, consisted in the utter Extirpation of that Principle; confessing at the same time, that this Satisfaction he found in himself, this Elevation of Mind, caused his chief Pleasure; and that in all the Comforts of Life, it made the greatest Part of the Enjoyment.[30]

Men are not naturally good: on the contrary, they cannot be virtuous without conquering their natural impulses. And, however we may delude ourselves, this is something we very rarely do:

HORATIO:

> But are there no Persons in the World that are good by Choice?

CLEOMENES:

> Yes, but then they are directed in that Choice by Reason and Experience, but not by Nature, I mean, not by untaught Nature: But there is an ambiguity in the Word Good which I would avoid; let us stick to that of Virtuous, and then I affirm that no Action is such, which does not point at some Conquest or other, some Victory great or small over untaught Nature; otherwise the Epithet is improper.

HOR.:

> But if by the help of a careful Education this Victory is obtain'd, when we are young, may we not be virtuous afterwards voluntarily and with Pleasure?

CLEO.:

> Yes, if it really was obtain'd: But how shall we be sure
> of this, and what Reason have we to believe it ever
> was? When it is evident, that from our Infancy, instead
> of endeavouring to conquer our Appetites, we have al-
> ways been Taught, and have taken pains ourselves to
> conceal them; and we are conscious within, that what-
> ever Alterations have been made in our Manners and
> Circumstances, the Passions themselves always
> remain'd?[31]

The worldliness, the hypocrisy, the backsliding are not,
then, accidental: they are the necessary consequences of
man's nature. Virtue, it would seem, is impossible. At
least, it is impossible to corrupt and unregenerate man:
'when I say Men, I mean neither Jews nor Christians; but
meer Man, in the State of Nature and ignorance of the true
Deity.'[32] 'Devout Christians, who alone are to be excepted
here, being regenerated and preternaturally assisted by the
Divine Grace, cannot be said to be in Nature.'[33] But good
Christians, Mandeville adds, 'have always been very scarce
and there are no Numbers of them any where, that one can
readily go to'.[34]

There seems, then, to be a good deal to support
Mandeville's claim that *The Fable of the Bees* 'is a Book
of severe and exalted Morality'.[35] Mandeville himself appears as a quite uncompromising ascetic, disgusted by the
materialism, the selfishness, the lust, and the vanity of
mankind, detecting the wickedness in the hearts of even
the respectable and apparently upright, horrified at the
worldliness and hypocrisy of institutionalized religion, and
preaching spiritual regeneration as the only possible remedy.

One might expect such a man to be unpopular, especially
for what he said about the churches and about the corruption on which every powerful and prosperous state was
built. One might even expect him to be accused of cynicism, of scoffing at some of the finer things in life, of tra-
ducing good and pious men. That is what the boosters usually say about the knockers; and Mandeville was
undoubtedly a knocker. But why should he be accused of
godliness, of materialism, of licentiousness, of moral nihil-
ism? Why should he be linked, not only with Sandeman,
but with Hobbes, Machiavelli, Voltaire, Tindal, and the
Devil?

The explanation is put very neatly by Richard Whately,
Mandeville, he suggests, is merely putting forward a hypothetical argument. If virtue consisted in self-denial, as was
taken for granted by all the moralists and theologians, and
if national wealth and greatness were desirable, as was
taken for granted by everybody, then the public happiness
depended on the vices of individuals. National virtue and
national wealth must be irreconcilable. 'Of two incompatible objects we must be content to take one, or the other.
Which of the two is to be preferred he nowhere decides in
his first volume: in his second, he solemnly declares his
opinion that wealth ought to be renounced, as incompatible with virtue.'[36]

The argument, that is to say, cuts both ways. One might
draw the conclusion that the world ought to be renounced.
But one might also decide that virtue should be. Or at
least that the virtue of the theologians, which consisted in
self-denial, was not really virtue at all. Why not adopt the
utilitarian criterion, and count as virtuous any action that
contributed to the welfare of society in the long run? In
that case the 'vices' on which the national prosperity depended were really not vices, but virtues. Perhaps that was
what Mandeville was really getting at? When one then remembered that in *The Fable of the Bees* not only luxuri-
ousness and worldly enjoyment were shown to contribute
to the nation's prosperity, but also the activities of cheats
and highwaymen, this became a very shocking conclusion
indeed.

Was there anything to suggest that this was Mandeville's
real meaning, in spite of his denials? There was a great
deal.

To begin with, there was Mandeville's personality. His
early opponents accused him of dissolute habits. There is
however very little reason to believe them; Mandeville
somehow managed to sustain a medical practice as well as
writing a good many books, which could hardly have left
him much time for debauchery. Leslie Stephen says:
'Mandeville is said to have been in the habit of frequent-
ing coffee-houses and amusing his patrons by ribald conversation. The book smells of its author's haunts. He is a
cynical and prurient writer, who shrinks from no jest,
however scurrilous, and from no paradox, however grotesque . . .'[37] But Mandeville is no coarser than Swift,
who was after all a Dean, Stephen's contemporaries might
have thought Bunyan coarse, if they had read all of him.[38]
There is a different way, however, in which the quality of
Mandeville's prose tells against the view that he was a pious ascetic. His tone is too detached, too amused. When,
in *Free Thoughts on Religion,* he recounts the enormities
committed by churchmen in the name of Christianity, it is
much in the tone of Voltaire, or Gibbon, or Anatole France:

> In the time of *Theodosius* junior, they [Christians]
> enjoy'd a full liberty of conscience in *Persia,* when
> *Abdas,* a zealous bishop, had the courage to pull down
> one of the temples where the Persians worship'd the
> fire. The *Magi* made their complaints to the King, who
> sent for *Abdas,* and demanded no other satisfaction
> than the rebuilding of the temple: *Abdas* refus'd it with
> scorn, tho' that prince had declar'd to him that in case
> of disobedience he would cause all the christian
> churches to be pull'd down; which he did, and began a
> terrible persecution, in which the valiant *Abdas* fell the
> first martyr.

> The brave remainder of the faithful, that could escape
> the fury of the *Persian* priests, were not so dejected at
> their loss, but that, animated with the hopes of a noble
> revenge, they implored the assistance of the emperor,
> which kindling a long war between *Romans* and *Per-
> sians,* occasion'd a second deluge of blood in vindica-
> tion of the gospel.[39]

Or again:

> Nothing is more diverting than to read the various and noble struggles the popes have had with the princes of christendom, till *Gregory* the seventh, with the utmost intrepidity, and equal hazard and difficulties, establish'd his superiority over their temporalities: that able and stately prelate, who, in the midst of winter made an emperor barefoot wait unattended in a hall, fasting from morning till night, for three days together, before he would admit him to his presence; and was the first, who undertook to deprive his lord and master of the imperial dignity.[40]

Then there is the actual subject-matter of some of his books. One would after all be surprised to learn that Savonarola, say, had written a tract called *A Modest Defence of Public Stews* (subtitle: an Essay upon Whoring) in which he argued strongly for the establishment of state-owned brothels, and worked out all the practical details, including charges. One would be only a little less surprised if he published an attack on free schools for the poor, on the ground that education would make the poor discontented with their lot and lead to a scarcity of servants and a rise in the wages masters would have to pay. One can hardly regard the author of these works as excessively unworldly.

None of this is, of course, conclusive. Obviously Mandeville did not correspond to popular stereotypes of an austere moralist; he was certainly a wit who sometimes found men's follies amusing. It may still be true that he also found them horrifying and was sincere in denouncing them. As for the **Modest Defence** and the **Essay on Charity and Charity-Schools,** a firm belief in human corruption and the final inefficacy of any remedy short of spiritual regeneration with miraculous assistance need not rule out an interest in palliatives. Charity schools, Mandeville argued, only made social conditions worse; public brothels, as a means of regulating and controlling sexual irregularity, might make them at least a little better. Nevertheless, it is not very easy to see Mandeville as the kind of pious Christian he declares himself to be.

More significant than any of this is the equivocal note which creeps into Mandeville's most earnest preachments, and even into his very denials of the charges against him. I have already quoted one exchange between Horatio and Cleomenes:

Hor.:

> How long, pray, do you intend to go on with this Cant?

Cleo.:

> If I am to personate a Christian Divine, who is a sincere Believer, you must give me leave to speak his Language.

If Cleomenes is really Mandeville's spokesman here, we may well conclude that he, too, is merely personating a Christian. But of course Mandeville could point out in re-

ply that Cleomenes, though a convert to the ideas of **The Fable of the Bees,** is also represented as a member of the *beau monde,* along with Horatio. In a discussion between gentlemen the phrases of the pulpit would be a little out of place, and it was after all only the phraseology, and not the actual arguments, that Cleomenes was disclaiming.

There are, however, other passages less easy to explain away. 'If I have shown the way to worldly Greatness', Mandeville says in his own defence, 'I have always without Hesitation preferr'd the Road that leads to Virtue.' He then goes on to tell us how to travel along that road:

> Would you banish Fraud and Luxury, prevent Profaneness and Irreligion, and make the generality of the People Charitable, Good and Virtuous, break down the Printing Presses, melt the Founds, and burn all the Books in the Island, except those at the Universities, where they remain unmolested, and suffer no Volume in private Hands but a Bible: Knock down Foreign Trade, prohibit all Commerce with Strangers, and permit no Ships to go to Sea, that ever will return, beyond Fisher-Boats. Restore to the Clergy, the King and the Barons their Ancient Privileges, Prerogatives, and Possessions: Build New Churches, and convert all the coin you can come at into Sacred Utensils: Erect Monasteries and Alms-houses in abundance, and let no Parish be without a Charity-School. Enact Sumptuary Laws, and let your Youth be inured to Hardship: Inspire them with all the nice and most refined Notions of Honour and Shame, of Friendship and of Heroism, and introduce among them a great Variety of imaginary Rewards: Then let the Clergy preach Abstinence and Self-denial to others, and take what Liberty they please for themselves; let them bear the greatest Sway in the management of State-Affairs, and no Man be made Lord-Treasurer but a Bishop.

> By such pious Endeavours, and wholesome Regulations, the Scene would be soon alter'd; the greatest part of the Covetous, the Discontented, the Restless and Ambitious Villains would leave the Land, vast Swarms of Cheating Knaves would abandon the City, and be dispers'd throughout the Country: Artificers would learn to hold the Plough, Merchants turn Farmers, and the sinful over-grown *Jerusalem,* without Famine, War, Pestilence or Compulsion, be emptied in the most easy manner and ever after cease to be dreadful to her Sovereigns . . .

And so on, ending with a quite indubitable sneer: '. . . an harmless, innocent and well-meaning People, that would never dispute the Doctrine of Passive Obedience, nor any other Orthodox Principles, but be submissive to Superiors and Unanimous in religious Worship'.[41]

Mandeville cites this passage, or at least the sentence preceding it, about preferring the road that leads to virtue, in both the **Vindication** attached to later editions of the **Fable** and **A Letter to Dion,** in which he replies to Berkeley's attack on him. Yet it hardly reassures the reader who suspects him of scoffing at both virtue and religion. It is true that one recent defender of Mandeville finds in this passage 'proof of his ferocious seriousness'. Mandeville, he suggests, is mocking his own hopes for salvation as well as ours. The program horrifies him as much as it was calculated to horrify the newly liberated middle-class readers or us, their liberal heirs . . . We may hope for reformation within individual men . . . but if some miracle were to effect a wholesale conversion to virtue, could we bear it? It would be as hard for Mandeville as anyone; the peculiar honesty of his method requires that he be as vulnerable as his readers . . . The point is that whole-hearted Christianity is rare, to say the least, and Mandeville would not claim it for himself any more than he will allow it to most other men.[42]

This is hardly convincing. No doubt Mandeville did regard some Christian virtues as desirable, but too hard for unregenerate men; but no reader of his *Free Thoughts on Religion* can suppose that he felt that about the participation of the clergy in politics, or the doctrine of passive obedience, to say nothing of charity schools. The Utopia described in the passage we are considering seems to be a curious mixture of what, in Mandeville's view, the clergy say they want but really do not, and what they really want but say they do not. Mandeville is not only saying that real virtue would be incompatible with national power and prosperity; he is also saying that what the clergy call virtue is a sham, and a cloak for their avarice and their thirst for power.

Mandeville may well have believed both propositions. Neither is inconsistent with a genuine concern for morality and religion. But here the two are so confused that the reader can hardly escape the conclusion that it is only the sham and not the real virtue that cannot coexist with national greatness.

This impression may well be confirmed by the Preface to Part I of the *Fable,* in which Mandeville says that his object is

> to expose the Unreasonableness and Folly of those, that desirous of being an opulent and flourishing People, and wonderfully greedy after all the Benefits they receive as such, are yet always murmuring at and exclaiming against those Vices and Inconveniences, that from the Beginning of the World to this present Day, have been inseparable from all Kingdoms and States that ever were fam'd for Strength, Riches and Politeness, at the same time.[43]

It is true that Mandeville merely says here that it is inconsistent to expect a state to be opulent and virtuous at the same time. As he puts it in the *Fable* itself:

> Then leave Complaints: Fools only strive
> To make a Great an Honest Hive.

This leaves it an open question whether greatness or honesty should be abandoned. But the emphasis is on the folly of complaining about the necessary accompaniments of opulence, not on the folly of pursuing opulence in the first place. Of course this may be meant ironically; but there is at least ground for suspicion that Mandeville is really saying: 'Why make all this fuss about vice? We could not get

on without it, and, besides, those who make most fuss about it are really only trying to hoodwink us so that they can gain control of the state and set up a theocracy like Cromwell's.'

William Minto, indeed, in an *Encyclopaedia Britannica* article on Mandeville, suggested that *The Fable of the Bees,* or at least its nucleus, the poem called *The Grumbling Hive, or Knaves Turn'd Honest,* was originally published as an election pamphlet.

> It appeared during the heat of the bitterly contested elections of 1705, when the question before the country was whether Marlborough's war with France should be continued. The cry of the high Tory advocates of peace was that the war was carried on purely in the interests of the general and the men in office; charges of bribery, peculation, hypocrisy, every form of fraud and dishonesty were freely cast about among the electors.[44]

In *Free Thoughts on Religion* Mandeville tells us: 'I despise the very thoughts of a party-man and desire to touch no man's sore, but in order to heal it.'[45] But that book itself contains a fairly orthodox statement of whig political theory: he was certainly no friend to the Tories. Minto does not, however, suggest that the intention of *The Grumbling Hive* was to defend Marlborough by defending vice; he sees the poem as merely 'a political *jeu d'esprit,* full of the impartial mockery that might be expected of a humorous foreigner'. This need not prevent the *Fable* from being also 'a Book of severe and exalted Morality'; but it is at least consistent with, and perhaps tends to suggest, a quite different interpretation.

Once Mandeville was taken seriously as a defender of vice, it was easy to see his attacks on the ideal of Honour, and on duelling and war, as simply deriding the values which good citizens held dear. Horatio complains to Cleomenes that Mandeville 'ridicules War and Martial Courage, as well as Honour and everything else'.[46] Alternatively, Mandeville could be taken to be defending duelling, at least by those who read only Part 1 of the *Fable.* He says there that the practice of duelling

> polishes and brightens Society in general. Nothing civilizes a Man equally as his Fear . . . the dread of being called to an Account keeps abundance in awe, and there are thousands of mannerly and well-accomplish'd Gentlemen in *Europe,* who would have been insolent and insupportable Coxcombs without it; besides if it was out of Fashion to ask Satisfaction for Injuries which the Law cannot take hold of, there would be twenty times the Mischief done there is now, or else you must have twenty times the Constables and other Officers to keep the Peace . . . It is strange that a Nation should grudge to see perhaps half a dozen Men sacrific'd in a Twelvemonth to obtain so valuable a Blessing, as the Politeness of Manners, the Pleasure of Conversation, and the Happiness of Company in general, that is often so willing to expose, and sometimes lose as many thousands in a few Hours, without knowing whether it will do any good or not.[47]

In Part 2, Cleomenes has to tell Horatio that this passage is meant ironically.[48] He was certainly not the only reader to take it seriously. His contemporary George Bluet did, for one. Mandeville's genuine dislike of duelling does, I think, shine through the discussion in the *Origin of Honour,* but even here it might be pointed out that his chief argument is that duelling is opposed to Christian principles. It could be alleged that he was saying, *sotto voce,* so much the worse for those principles. It was, after all, claimed that in *The Fable of the Bees* Mandeville was really saying: if Christianity and national prosperity are incompatible, so much the worse for Christianity. It is true that in the *Free Thoughts on Religion* Mandeville attacked the clergy on the ground that their principles were incompatible with Christianity, and here no one doubted that it really was the clergy he was attacking. But, it might be argued, what he really objected to was their hypocrisy, not their worldliness, though it was the worldliness that he ostensibly attacked.

But it was Mandeville's views on human corruption that drew most of the fire. For what he is saying here is that it is simply not in human nature to behave in the ways commonly called virtuous. Virtue, then, is neither desirable (if national prosperity and happiness are) nor even possible. Men are bound to act from self-interest, however much they delude themselves that they have other motives. The conclusion seems irresistible: why not, then, abandon all this fuss about virtue, accept man as he is, and make the best of what we have got?

Mandeville, Leslie Stephen tells us,

> will not be beguiled from looking at the seamy side of things. Man, as theologians tell us, is corrupt, nay, it would be difficult for them to exaggerate his corruption; but the heaven which they throw in by way of consolation is tacitly understood to be a mere delusion, and the supernatural guidance in which they bid us trust, an ingenious device for enforcing their own authority. Tell your fine stories, he says in effect, to school girls or to devotees; don't try to pass them off upon me, who have seen men and cities, and not taken my notions from books or sermons. There is a part of our nature that is always flattered by the bold assertion that our idols are made of dirt; and Mandeville was a sagacious sycophant of those baser instincts.[49]

Mandeville's doctrine was, he adds a little later: 'Virtue is an empty pretence . . . To feather our own nests as warmly as may be is our only policy in this pitiless storm. Lust and pride are realities; to gratify them is to secure the only genuine enjoyment.'[50]

There is, then, a plausible case to be made for either interpretation of Mandeville. . . . Which is the right one? Which of the two Mandevilles really existed? Perhaps the best way of arriving at an answer to that question will be to forget it for a while, and look more closely at some other aspects of Mandeville's work. We may even discover more Mandevilles than two.

. . . . .

THE REAL MANDEVILLE?

What conclusions, if any, can we now reach about the question . . . : which of the representations of Mandeville is the true one?

So far we have considered only the evidence of his own writings. There is not much to be added from external evidence, which is scanty, unreliable, and sometimes conflicting. Records show that he was baptized at Rotterdam on 20 November 1670, and that he matriculated at the University of Leyden in October 1685.[51] He presented a dissertation in 1689 on the consciousness of animals, taking the Cartesian view (which he afterwards abandoned) that they were automata, and another one in 1691 on the chylification of the blood, after which he took the degree of Doctor of Medicine. He seems to have gone to England shortly afterwards. He married there in 1699. We know from his medical treatise that, in specializing in nervous disorders, he was following in the footsteps of his father, who had practised medicine in Amsterdam and Rotterdam for more than thirty-eight years.[52] He died in London on 21 January 1733. The *Gentleman's Magazine* has the briefest of entries in its list of deaths for January:[53]

> 21st. Dr. Mandeville, author of *The Fable of the Bees* and other pieces.

The traces of feminism shown by Mandeville in *The Virgin Unmask'd* and elsewhere did not extend to his will: of five hundred pounds he had in South Sea Annuities, he left one hundred to his wife and the remainder, together with the rest of his estate, to his son Michael; to his daughter Penelope he left 'twenty shillings for a Ring'.[54]

In his article on Mandeville in the *Dictionary of National Biography* Leslie Stephen says that the only personal details of Mandeville's life that have been preserved are to be found in brief references in Benjamin Franklin's *Autobiography,* Sir John Hawkins's *Life of Samuel Johnson,* and Jeremiah Whitaker Newman's *Lounger's Commonplace Book.* Of these Hawkins's account is the most circumstantial, even though most of it is contained in a footnote (to a remark about the effect on 'the moral conduct of the young and unthinking' of such writers as 'Collins, Mandeville, Morgan and Tindal; the first pair deists, and the latter infidels'). Mandeville, he tells us, 'lived in obscure lodgings in London and was never able to acquire much practice'; he made a living by writing 'sundry papers in the *London Journal* and other such publications, to favour the custom of drinking spirituous liquors, to which employment of the pen it is supposed he was hired by the distillers'; he was 'coarse and overbearing in his manners where he durst be so; yet a great flatterer of some vulgar Dutch merchants who allowed him a pension'. He adds that 'this last information comes from a clerk of a city attorney, through whose hands the money passed.'[55]

Such of this as can be checked would seem to be false: Kaye went through the files of the *London Journal* and other contemporary journals without finding the articles commissioned by the distillers.[56] Mandeville's known writings, he points out, contain vivid warnings of the evil effects of excessive drinking, notably **'Remark G'** of the **Fable.** Since Kaye's researches, Paul Bunyan Anderson, who discovered Mandeville's contributions to the *Female Tatler,* has unearthed a pamphlet called **A Dissertation upon Drunkenness,** which he also attributes to Mandeville, mainly because of its close verbal resemblance to **'Remark G'.**[57] The title-page includes the words: 'Also an Account of the Pride, Insolence and Exorbitance of Brewers, Vintners, Victuallers, Coffee-House-Keepers, and Distillers, with the various Arts and Methods by which they allure and excite People to drink and debauch themselves.'[58] It now seems established that Anderson's attribution was mistaken, and that the author of the pamphlet was not Mandeville, but someone who plagiarized freely from the **Fable.** But the mere fact that the attribution could be made, with some plausibility, tells heavily against Hawkins's story.

In his medical treatise, Mandeville extols the medicinal qualities of wine, while deploring the fact that people render themselves immune to its curative effects by drinking it when they have no need of them. He also introduces a rhetorical eulogy of it:

> . . . it is not only in the power of this Vegetable to make the Slave fancy himself to be free, the Poor to be Rich, the Old Young, and the Miserable Happy; but it likewise actually mends visible Imperfections; renders the Infirm Strong, the Decrepit Nimble, and the Stammerer Eloquent; and what neither *Circe's* nor *Medea's* Art could ever perform; turns Vices into Virtues, and by the Charm of it, the Coward, the Covetous, the Proud, and the Morose become Valliant, Generous, Affable, and good Humour'd.[59]

But, apart from the obvious irony of this, it is made quite clear that it is not meant seriously: 'I am no Critick', Philopirio adds immediately afterwards, 'but well assured that, Poetical Flights apart, the innumerable mischiefs which Wine, as it is managed, creates to Mankind, far exceed whatever *Horace,* or any body else can say in commendation of it.'[60]

This part of Hawkins's story, then, seems unlikely to be true. As for the Dutch merchants, Kaye makes the plausible conjecture that they were John and Cornelius Backer, mentioned in Mandeville's will as holding the South Sea Annuities for him, and that they were not his patrons but merely his business agents.

Kaye also thinks it unlikely that Mandeville lived in poverty. He must have made money out of the **Fable,** which was enormously successful, even if it was a success of scandal. He is known to have been an intimate friend of Lord Macclesfield, the Lord Chancellor, as Hawkins himself notes, among others. (It was at Macclesfield's house that Mandeville met Addison and later made the famous remark that he was 'a parson in a tie-wig'.)[61] Benjamin Franklin who, unlike Hawkins or Newman, actually met

Mandeville, draws a picture rather different from Hawkins's. Working as a printer in London, Franklin set up the second edition of Wollaston's *Religion of Nature Delineated,* and was moved to write an answer to it, *A Dissertation on Liberty and Necessity, and on Pleasure and Pain.*

> My pamphlet by some means falling into the hands of one Lyons, a surgeon, author of a book entitled *The Infallibility of Human Judgment,* it occasioned an acquaintance between us. He took great notice of me called on me often to converse on those subjects, carried me to the Horns, a pale-alehouse in—Lane, Cheapside, and introduced me to Dr. Mandeville, author of the Fable of the Bees, who had a club there, of which he was the soul, being a most facetious, entertaining companion.[62]

But this must have been in 1725 or 1726, during the nineteen months Franklin spent in London. The undated letter to Sir Hans Sloane, cited by Kaye as evidence of Mandeville's success in his profession, could not have been written, as Kaye himself points out, before 1716, when Sloane was made a baronet. Mandeville's will, which shows him to be in relative affluence, is dated 1729. It is quite possible, therefore, that Mandeville did have to struggle to make a living in his earlier years in London, and he may very well have spent as much time on journalism as on medicine. At least this would seem to be true for the five months between November 1709 and March 1710, during which he wrote thirty-two issues of the *Female Tatler.* If Anderson is right, the other thirty-three issues were written by Mrs. Susanna Centlivre, the playwright. Probably she and Mandeville had taken over the paper between them, which would mean editing and perhaps publishing as well as writing.

The medical treatise in 1711 was at least partly a bid for patients. Mandeville's preface suggests that he is a little on the defensive about this. It may possibly have been used against him by Bluet, who says that Mandeville's 'Vindication' of the **Fable** 'is writ in the true Spirit of a Quack Bill'.[63] Given the controversial manners of the times, however, a doctor with Mandeville's opinions would have been called a quack in any case. It is also possible that the publication of the **Treatise** had something to do with the feud between Mandeville and Dr. John Radcliffe, whose bequest to Oxford is put forward in the **Essay on Charity and Charity-Schools** as a prime example of vanity masquerading as philanthropy: 'what must we judge of his Motive, the Principle he acted from, when after his Death we find that he has left a Trifle among his Relations who stood in need of it, and an immense Treasure to an University that did not want it?'[64] Richard Fiddes, who was related to Radcliffe, devotes several pages of his preface on Mandeville to answering this attack. While admitting that the charge about leaving a trifle to his relations is 'not altogether groundless', he denies that Radcliffe's motives were unworthy ones. In reply to another comment of Mandeville's, that Radcliffe was known 'to look down with contempt on the most deserving of his Profession, and never confer with any other Physician but what will pay Homage to his Superior Genius, creep to his Humour, and never approach him but with all the slavish Obsequiousness a Court-Flatterer can treat a Prince with'[65] Fiddes says: 'If the Doctor did really look down with Contempt upon any Persons, it was upon those, and those only, who had Recourse to vile and ignoble Methods, towards opening a Way to Practice. And this might be, and I have Reason to believe was, the true Cause why he, sometimes, refused to confer with others of the same Faculty.'[66]

This may not have been a direct hit at Mandeville, but it may be significant that Mandeville seems to have changed his mind about Radcliffe some time between 1709 and 1714, when Radcliffe died, or at least before 1723, when the **Essay on Charity** first appeared. In the *Female Tatler* for 21-3 November 1709, 'Lucinda' criticizes Steele's *Tatler* for publishing scandal about real people under 'ingenious Nicknames' easily seen through, and refers unmistakably to a piece in which Radcliffe (called Aesculapius) had been ridiculed over a love-affair with a much younger woman. She imagines the delight of Steele's readers: 'Pray, Madam, did you see the Doctor in the *Tatler*; did you mind the Gold Buttons, was not that very Witty? I declare I am glad to see him exposed, because he wou'd not come to my Sister *Patty,* tho' my Father sent twice, and never yet gave him less than three Guineas for a Fee.'[67] In 1709 Mandeville is virtuously protesting against such attacks on 'a Physician famous for the Splendour of his Practice': in 1723 he is himself attacking the same physician much more severely. It is possible that all he objected to in the first place was the trivial ground of the attack: 'In Writing Scandal', he says, 'I wou'd draw the Picture of those upon whom it is design'd, not from Things that are indifferent, and have neither good nor harm in them, but from the Folly and Vices of which they are really guilty.' But he also criticizes the practice of referring to real people who can be readily identified; and in any case the *Tatler,* though mainly making fun of Radcliffe as an ageing lover, also anticipates Mandeville in mentioning his avarice: 'Love has taken place of avarice, or rather is become an avarice of another kind, which still urges him to pursue what he does not want.'[68] One thing that happened between 1709 and 1714 was the publication of Mandeville's **Treatise**: in view of Fiddes's remark, it is at least possible that it was the repercussions from that event that made him less tender of Radcliffe's reputation.

If Mandeville did have difficulty in establishing himself in practice, probably this situation did not last. Whether or not the **Treatise** brought him patients, it is likely that the **Fable,** with the celebrity that followed it, did. If the **Fable** brought him money as well as fame, he may have deliberately kept his practice small, to give himself time for his writing, and for evenings of witty talk at Lord Lansdowne's or the Horns.

Most of this is, of course, conjecture. As Kaye points out, 'there is no authoritative first-hand evidence whatever as to Mandeville's character and habits except what he himself has told us and the brief remark of one single contemporary.'[69] We come back, then, to the ground already surveyed; and to the question at the beginning of this chapter.

It is obvious, I think, that neither of the views outlined in the first chapter is wholly accurate. Mandeville was neither a Savonarola nor Law's missioner come from the kingdom of darkness to do us harm: the **Fable** is not an evangelical tract, but neither is it, as *Chambers' Encyclopedia* was still proclaiming in 1891, 'a pot-house fulminant'.[70] Any brief characterization of Mandeville is inadequate. To take one example: there is some plausibility in Wilde's suggestion that he was the mouthpiece of the diehards of the Restoration who were made uneasy by the softening of manners and the higher moral tone of the new age; but it does not survive examination. Consider Wilde's illustrations of the new moral temper: 'Attempts were made to improve and educate the poor, and charity schools were founded. Laws were enacted against gaming and cock-spitting and the more brutal amusements of all kinds were discouraged.'[71] Mandeville, as we know, opposed charity schools, and was contemptuous of the Societies for Promoting a Reformation of Manners, but he also condemned cruelty to animals. I have been unable to find the law against cock-spitting which Wilde refers to, unless he has in mind 4 & 5 William and Mary, c. 23 (1692), which forbids the burning of heath-lands to trap grouse or heath-cock. This, like other Acts for preserving game, was intended to benefit landowners rather than their prey. Another possibility is that he means cock-throwing (the practice of tying a cock to a stake and throwing stones or sharp sticks at it) though I have found no evidence that that was prohibited at this time. But whatever cock-spitting may have been, we may safely assume that the man who wrote so movingly of the death of an ox would have been opposed to it. Mandeville's attack on the cult of Honour hardly fits Wilde's thesis; and, in general, his satire is directed quite as often against rakes of the old as against moralists of the new school.

Again, it is tempting to say that Mandeville's essential characteristic is his hatred of cant and hypocrisy: his refusal to be blinded by comforting conventional fictions, and his insistence on showing men as they really are. 'You, Sir', he tells Berkeley, 'think it for the Good of Society that human Nature should be extoll'd as much as possible: I think, the real Meanness and Deformity of it to be more instructive.'[72] And, indeed, there is a suggestion in *Alciphron* that Berkeley himself regards Mandeville as a reckless and uncompromising utterer of inconvenient truths. Alciphron says in the first dialogue: 'Convenience is one thing, and truth is another. A genuine philosopher, therefore, will overlook all advantages, and consider only truth itself as such.'[73] Euphranor in reply seems to be suggesting that, when it comes to the general happiness of mankind, expediency is more important than truth: 'Might it not therefore be inferred, that those men are foolish who go about to unhinge such principles as have a necessary connexion with the general good of mankind?'[74] The same argument is used against Lysicles in the second dialogue:

EUPHRANOR:

Virtue then, in your account, is a trick of statesmen?

LYSICLES:

It is.

EUPHRANOR:

Why then do your sagacious sect betray and divulge that trick or secret of State, which wise men have judged necessary for the good government of the world?

Lysicles hesitating, Crito made answer, that he presumed it was because their sect, being wiser than all other wise men, disdained to see the world governed by wrong maxims, and would set all things on a right bottom.[75]

Probably, there is no single characteristic of Mandeville's as prominent as his hatred of hypocrisy and self-deception; yet the moment we try to set him up as the champion of candour and frankness above all, doubts begin to rush in. Why, in that case, is it so hard to take his professions of religious belief seriously? Does he not himself think it necessary to pander to the stubborn belief in an invisible cause, which is a congenital human weakness, hardly less strong than the instinctive tendency to overvalue oneself? Would an apostle of candour be quite as fond of irony as Mandeville? Would he use literary devices like the alleged answer to the **Modest Defence,** purporting to come from the Societies for Promoting a Reformation of Manners? Would he share Lucinda's weakness for treating an argument like a pot of tea, and straining the last drop out of it?

Moreover, it must be admitted that, as a controversialist, Mandeville does not always show an uncompromising devotion to strict honesty. He protests, quite rightly, against Berkeley's unfairness to Shaftesbury in ignoring 'the many admirable Things he has said against Priestcraft, and on the side of Liberty and Human Happiness'. Few of Berkeley's readers, he adds, 'among those that have read, and are not lash'd in the *Characteristicks . . .* will think that My Lord *Shaftsbury* deserves one Tenth Part of the Indignity and Contempt, which you treat Cratylus with'.[76] Yet elsewhere Mandeville himself makes capital out of the charges levelled against Shaftesbury by those who had been lashed. 'The *Characteristicks*', he makes Cleomenes say, 'have made a Jest of all reveal'd Religion, especially the Christian.'[77] He at least hints that Shaftesbury was remiss because 'he did not follow Arms when his Country was involved in War':[78] a charge one hardly expects from the author of the **Enquiry into Honour,** or the other works in which Mandeville tells us what he thinks of warfare. Similarly, any reader of **Free Thoughts on Religion,** with its plea for religious tolerance, would expect Mandeville to welcome Shaftesbury's humane policy for the treatment of heretics. They should be laughed at, he said, but not persecuted. Ridicule was a test of truth: a solemn opinion that could be punctured by a little raillery could have no substance in it. Ridicule was also a more effective way of discrediting cranks and enthusiasts than making martyrs of them.

The *Jews* were naturally a very cloudy People, and wou'd endure little Raillery in any thing; much less in what belong'd to any Religious Doctrines or Opinions. Religion was look'd upon with a sullen Eye; and Hanging was the only Remedy they cou'd prescribe for any thing which look'd like setting up a new Revelation. The sovereign Argument was, *Crucify, Crucify.* But with all their malice, and Inveteracy to our Saviour, and his Apostles after him, had they but taken the Fancy to act such Puppet-Shows in his Contempt, as at this hour the Papists are acting in his Honour; I am apt to think they might possibly have done our Religion more harm, than by all their other ways of Severity.[79]

This remark naturally scandalized the orthodox; but was it quite sincere of Mandeville to echo them?

CLEO.:

. . . Lord *Shaftsbury* takes Joke and Banter to be the best and surest Touchstone to prove the Worth of Things: It is his Opinion, that no Ridicule can be fasten'd upon what is really great and good; his Lordship has made use of that Test to try the Scriptures and the Christian Religion by, and expos'd them because it seems they could not stand it.

HOR.:

He has exposed Superstition and the miserable Notions the Vulgar were taught to have of God; but no man ever had more Sublime Ideas of the Supreme Being and the Universe than himself.

CLEO.:

You are convinc'd that what I charge him with is true.[80]

So no doubt it is; and Cleomenes' remarks (if quoted, say in *The Rationalist Annual* for 1974) might even be taken as commending Shaftesbury. But not in 1729, and in the context of a discussion in which Shaftesbury's views are fairly thoroughly demolished. Mandeville is undoubtedly making a point against Shaftesbury that he knows will tell against him with his readers. And he is probably making it tongue in cheek.

It is true that Horatio makes an able defence of Shaftesbury. This might be taken as proof of Mandeville's fair-mindedness, and his care not to do what he blamed Berkeley for, and make the characters in his dialogues mere men of straw. But Horatio's defence reminds us of another possible piece of deviousness on Mandeville's part. Cleomenes, we are told in the preface, is Mandeville's mouthpiece; yet whenever he and Horatio discuss religion, it seems (at any rate to a careful, perceptive, and sympathetic editor like Kaye) that Mandeville agrees, not with the orthodoxy of Cleomenes, but with Horatio's criticisms of it. This almost certainly applies to this exchange in the **Origin of Honour**:

HOR.:

It is better to have no Religion, than to worship the Devil.

CLEO.:

In what Respect is it better?

HOR.:

It is not so great an Affront to the Deity not to believe his Existence, as it is to believe him to be the most Cruel and the most Malicious Being that can be imagin'd.

CLEO.:

That is a subtle Argument, seldom made Use of but by Unbelievers.[81]

It was an argument made use of by Shaftesbury, as Mandeville's readers would probably know. It is also not very far removed from what Cleomenes himself says in Part 2 of the *Fable*: 'I could as soon believe, that he could cease to exist, as that he should be the Author of any real Evil.'[82]

It is hard to escape the impression that Mandeville is decrying Shaftesbury for holding opinions that he secretly shared. If there is any doubt of this, it is because of the difficulty of pinning Mandeville down; and that is enough in itself to cast doubt on the representation of Mandeville as a fearless upholder of truth and sincerity at all costs.

Shall we, then, go to the opposite extreme with Minto and (in a rather less charitable version) Wilde, and say that Mandeville is primarily a wit, who cares little for consistency as long as he can propound an ingenious paradox or score off an opponent? Mandeville has too many favourite opinions, sustained over too many books, for that to be wholly true. But it is part of the truth. Why, after all, did Mandeville make such a parade of not being a deist or an atheist? Understandable caution, in a man whose books attracted the attention of grand juries? But it did him little good: almost everyone took his godlessness for granted. Caution may have had something to do with it; but less, I think, than his pleasure at turning the believers' arguments against themselves, at gravely reminding contumacious clergymen that they are committed to 'meekness, patience, humility, peace and charity to all men',[83] their worldly parishioners that slander and back-biting are not 'less heinous in the sight of God than murder or adultery',[84] and both of them that, in a matter on which St. Paul himself could only appeal to the impenetrable mysteriousness of God's ways, 'the subtlest logician or most learned theologist . . . can have no more claim or colour to be dogmatical . . . than the simplest shepherd, or the most illiterate plowman.'[85] Mandeville is quite genuinely deploring sectarian bitterness and worldly spitefulness, and he does want to make a point about predestination; but he is also having fun. His is not the simple-minded earnestness of a man with a message. It would not quite be true to say that he prefers the booby-trap to either the rapier or the bludgeon; but it is characteristic that, when he wants Cleomenes to attack Shaftesbury, he begins by making him pretend to have been converted to Shaftesbury's

views. He enjoys an ingenious argument or an apt parallel (the parable of small beer, the analogy of the dirt in the streets of London, or the castrati, the likening of society to a bowl of punch) for its own sake. Sometimes I think he lets virtuosity take over, as when (with doubtful taste, but an undoubted gift for parody) he imagines the pious exhortations of the poor wretch being hanged at Tyburn by his improved method, and renders them in the most nauseating of evangelical styles.

Yet, if Mandeville is not earnest, he is usually serious: he does have something he wants to say. If one had to characterize him briefly, one might do worse than take as a text a sentence from *Free Thoughts on Religion*: 'My aim is to make men penetrate into their own consciences and by searching without flattery into the true motives of their actions, learn to know themselves.'[86] So put, this sounds, and is intended to sound, like the earnest preacher again, the enemy of hypocrisy; but it might also do for the psychologist. Mandeville may have been disingenuous at times; but disingenuousness and self-deception are not the same thing. He does take 'Know thyself' seriously; and he sees (and makes Cleomenes point out, with side references to weeding gardens and exterminating moles)[87] that moralizing about the passions can get in the way of understanding them. The botanist is just as interested in weeds as in the prize-winners at the garden show; and Mandeville is not so much exhorting men to repent as to understand themselves. Hutcheson's sneer: 'so dearly does he love making a very *Dispensatory of Passions*'[88] does fasten on to one truth about Mandeville. This love of his was not unrequited: his analysis of the code of Honour, or of the motives underlying politeness and good breeding, his pursuit of 'self-liking' in all its manifold disguises, his speculations on the origin of language, his insistence on the evolutionary principle in explaining human behaviour, all represent genuine achievements. Yet this is clearly not the whole truth about Mandeville either. The satirist, the novelist, and the moralist all intrude upon the dispassionate psychologist. Even after he has substituted the neutral word 'self-liking' for the tendentious 'pride' (which is in any case, he comes to realize, only one manifestation of self-liking), his thesis is still about human weakness and frailty. When he preaches the sermon of 'a crafty divine' rallying the troops before battle or gives us a character sketch of Oliver Cromwell, he is not just grappling with the problem of why men risk their lives in war, or how they maintain themselves in power: he is also writing as an anti-clerical and as a debunker.

So far, then, it seems that Mandeville cannot be characterized in a sentence or two, and that he will not fit neatly into any single pigeon-hole. He was a highly complex and sometimes inconsistent man. Like most of us.

Perhaps one should stop there and accept that, once we have looked at the satirist, the wit, the social reformer, the medical man, the theologian, the psychologist, and the moralist, and perhaps one or two others not dealt with here, such as the economist or the politician, there is nothing useful to be said further about Mandeville the whole man. Yet perhaps there is, after all, something that is fairly central to all of these: a vision of the universe and of man's place in it. It is mainly, if not entirely, a comic vision: one might perhaps call it tragicomic.

Visions are notoriously difficult to capture. Let us approach this one obliquely, by considering another vision of the universe which both resembles it and contrasts with it. In his much anthologized and uncharacteristically dithyrambic essay, 'A Free Man's Worship', Bertrand Russell asks how we are to come to terms with the universe revealed to us by modern science, in which 'Man is the product of causes which had no prevision of the end they were achieving' and 'his origin, his growth, his hopes and fears, his loves and his beliefs, are but the outcome of accidental collocations of atoms'. 'Only within the scaffolding of these truths', he tells us, 'only on the firm foundation of unyielding despair, can the soul's habitation henceforth be safely built.'[89]

We are inclined to think of this as a purely twentieth-century problem; but of course it is not. Something like it presented itself to Spinoza, who proceeded to reinterpret the traditional theological formulas so as to accommodate the view that man was a small and insignificant part of nature, and nature essentially indifferent to man. God, he suggested, was just another name for Nature, mind and matter were reverse sides of the same medal, and the Love of God the frame of mind of one who admires the neat way in which every part fits into the whole (the spider's web and the fly's delicate wing, to take Shaftesbury's example) and the laws of nature work themselves out with austere perfection, regardless of the hopes and fears of self-centred individuals who cannot see past their own noses, especially when they are dropping off with frostbite. It is the frame of mind in which a biologist might take pleasure in observing the inexorable progress of his own disease and noting how well it exemplified the laws of physiology and biochemistry, themselves exemplifications of those more general physical laws, which, by realizing all their manifold possibilities, produce a varied but unified whole, that perfection which is the sum of all being, and also its ground and sustaining cause.

Russell's solution is different. Instead of consoling himself with the reflection that this pitiless universe has its own austere beauty, man can remind himself that this beauty, like all beauty, is after all a creation of the mind of man. 'Brief and powerless is Man's life, on him and all his race the slow, sure doom falls pitiless and dark. Blind to good and evil, reckless of destruction, omnipotent matter rolls on its relentless way.' Freedom is to be found, not in the consciousness of necessity, or in prostrating oneself before it, but in man's ability to fashion his own ideals even though they are doomed to frustration: 'to worship at the shrine that his own hands have built; undismayed by the empire of chance, to preserve a mind free from the wanton tyranny that rules his outward life; proudly defiant of the irresistible forces that tolerate, for a moment, his knowl-

edge and his condemnation, to sustain alone, a weary but unyielding Atlas, the world that his own ideals have fashioned despite the trampling march of unconscious power.'[90] It is a solution that also seems to have commended itself to the existentialists.

But not to Mandeville. He too is impressed by the cruelty and indifference of nature, and by the extent to which man is the sport of forces outside his control, even when, like his own passions and appetites, they are inside him. He is sure that there is no solution to the problem of evil; in that respect Shaftesbury's optimistic deism is no better than orthodox Christianity. He is just as sure as Russell that man does not live in a cosy little world in which somehow good will be the final goal of ill: no one misinterpreted him more egregiously than Browning. Man is of very little importance in the scheme of things: if the sun's sole purpose was to warm the earth, it would not need to be so large. It must have been made 'to enlighten and cherish other Bodies besides this Planet of ours'.[91] And even on this planet Providence has 'no greater regard to our species than it has to Flies, and the Spawn of Fish'.[92] But Mandeville does not take up Russell's stance of heroic though hopeless defiance. In some ways he is nearer to Spinoza's scientific quietism: though 'quietist' would be an odd word to apply to Mandeville. But consider this snatch of dialogue:

CLEO.:

> . . . All Actions in Nature, abstractly consider'd, are equally indifferent; and whatever it may be to individual Creatures, to die is not a greater Evil to this Earth, or the whole Universe, than it is to be born.

HOR.:

> That is to make the First Cause of Things not an Intelligent Being.

CLEO.:

> Why so? Can you not conceive an Intelligent, and even a most Wise Being, that is not only exempt from, but likewise incapable of entertaining any Malice or Cruelty?[93]

Cleomenes' retort may be only a debating point: perhaps this is one of the places in which Horatio is meant to get the better of the argument, and Cleomenes to be merely evasive. I think that this is true to the extent that Mandeville meant (though he could not let Cleomenes say) that the First Cause was incapable of malice or cruelty only in the sense that it was also incapable of compassion, or fatherly love, or the other attributes of a personal god. But it is probably not just as a debating point that Mandeville makes Cleomenes deploy the argument from design:

> From the little we know of the Sun and Stars, their Magnitudes, Distances, and Motion; and what we are more nearly acquainted with, the gross, visible Parts in the Structure of Animals, and their Oeconomy it is de-

monstrable that they are the Effects of an intelligent Cause, and the Contrivance of a Being infinite in Wisdom as well as Power.[94]

Mandeville may have been a deist rather than an atheist. Most proponents of the argument from design do not take it seriously enough: they triumphantly produce the conclusion, that the universe is controlled by an intelligent being, and do not go on to ask what attributes such a being, who designed such a universe, must have. It is clear to Mandeville that the First Cause is certainly not benevolent; but he readily concedes its extraordinary ingenuity. Death is an ingenious contrivance for preventing the world from being overpopulated; and how neat the arrangement by which one animal keeps alive by eating another!

CLEO.:

. . . For the Continuance of every Species, among such an infinite Variety of Creatures, as this Globe yields; it was highly necessary, that the Provision for their Destruction should not be less ample, than that, which was made for the Generation of them; and therefore the Sollicitude of Nature in procuring Death, and the Consumption of Animals, is visibly superiour to the Care she takes to feed and preserve them.

HOR.:

Prove that pray.

CLEO.:

Millions of her Creatures are starv'd every Year and doom'd to perish for want of Sustenance; but whenever any dye, there is always plenty of Mouths to devour them. But then again, she gives all she has: Nothing is so fine or elaborate, as that she grudges it for Food; nor is any thing more extensive or impartial than her Bounty: She thinks nothing too good for the meanest of her Broods, and all Creatures are equally welcome to every thing they can find to eat. How curious is the Workmanship in the Structure of a common Fly; how inimitable are the Celerity of his Wings, and the Quickness of all his Motions in hot Weather! Should a *Pythagorean,* that was likewise a good Master in Mechanicks, by the help of a Microscope, pry into every minute part of this changeable Creature, and duly consider the Elegancy of its Machinery, would he not think it a great pity, that thousands of Millions of animated Beings, so nicely wrought and admirably finish'd, should every Day be devour'd by little Birds and Spiders, of which we stand in so little need?[95]

This is Shaftesbury's 'Animal-Order or Oeconomy', the Great One of Nature, more sardonically observed; but Mandeville does not deny the skilfulness and the intricacy of the contrivance. Nature's solicitude in procuring death has been responsible for other master-strokes of ingenuity: disease, for example, and war (including 'general Massacres, private Murders, Poyson, Sword, and all hostile Force'):[96] in order to perfect this device it was necessary to endow man with a large stock of innate aggressiveness.

For man is a part of nature: as much a puppet in her hands as the spider or the fly. And this rules out a response like Russell's. It is no use trying to console oneself with thoughts of man's indomitable spirit and his lofty ideals. Man is nature's tame lapdog like everything else, and his ideals are themselves illusions by which he is tricked into serving nature's purpose: all the swagger about national honour and martial glory, for example, is just a way of getting him to keep the population down.

The system works, of course, by means of the passions and appetites of animals: hunger, for example. And clearly man is no exception. Intent on gratifying his passions, he is constantly contributing to results he does not intend: his lust perpetuates his species, his greed keeps other animals from getting too numerous, his anger and malice perform the same service for his own kind. His fear and his weakness gradually lead him, when enough of his fellows have been eaten by wolves or lions, to stumble into society; his aggressiveness, his urge for dominance, and his unreliability make it necessary for the social bonds to be tightened, and a morality devised; his taste for luxury and display lead to the development of civilization. All this he does without knowing clearly what he is doing, or seeing where he is going: often enough he only does it because he is nursing fictions which tickle his vanity.

That is the universe, and man's place in it, as Mandeville sees it. It is not a spectacle to call forth Russell's defiant glorification of man, or Spinoza's pietistic reverence, or Shaftesbury's beaming optimism. It is on the whole a comic spectacle. It is particularly diverting to notice how everything has the opposite effect to what you might expect: how men's weakness and fear make them eventually the lords of creation, how arrogance and vanity make men invent modesty and politeness and apparent self-effacement, how the poverty and ignorance of the labouring poor create a rich, sophisticated, and luxurious civilization; how fear can make men risk their lives, and vanity lead them to mortify the flesh, and self-seeking make them contribute more to the well-being of other men than ever benevolence would: how, in short, good springs up and pullulates from evil as naturally as chickens do from eggs.[97]

In such a universe, what is to be done? Nothing very much, except to lean back and enjoy it, with a wry kind of enjoyment: noting that respectable businessmen behave very much like criminals, and that the professional devotees of humility and charity have a formidable record of rapacity, contentiousness, and readiness to persecute. One may, perhaps, try to stop some of the more obvious silliness, like whipping prostitutes to make them virtuous, when society offers them no alternative means of making a living, or allowing criminals to go to their death in an atmosphere of boozy adulation. And one may make a protest against men's cutting each other's throats in a frenzy of brotherly love. But one need not expect to achieve much:

If you ask me, why I have done all this, *cui bono*? and what Good these Notions will produce? truly, besides the Reader's Diversion, I believe none at all . . . Mankind having for so many Ages remain'd still the same, notwithstanding the many instructive and elaborate Writings, by which their Amendment has been endeavour'd, I am not so vain as to hope for better Success from so inconsiderable a Trifle.[98]

One should, of course, try to remain clear-sighted oneself, surrounded though one is by a fog of almost universal self-deception and hypocrisy. But one should not delude oneself that one can blow away the fog or be too earnest in denouncing it: better to write for the diversion of one's readers, and oneself. One might as well, then, pretend to go along with some of the delusions, and have some fun on the way, by pointing out the less comfortable conclusions that might be drawn from them, but seldom are. Besides, human knowledge really is very limited: we know practically nothing even about our own bodies, let alone about First and Last Things. With a little ingenuity, it is possible to make a plausible case for all sorts of unlikely hypotheses. And there really is something to be said for that last resort of the theologian when pushed into a corner (like St. Paul): man can hardly expect to understand fully a universe of which he is a small and insignificant part. No doubt the proper conclusion from that is that one should suspend judgement on ultimate metaphysical questions, not that one should feel free to dogmatize about them, and accept the most unlikely hypotheses without question, on the doubtful evidence of 'revelation'. But it might be amusing to ignore that from time to time and demonstrate to the theologians that theirs is a game that two can play.

Is that 'the real Mandeville'? I think that it at least represents one of his moods, and a fairly constant one; and that it may help to explain how he can be at once tough-minded and tolerant, visionary and cynical, a denouncer of deception who constantly dissimulates. In his writings, as in the bowl of punch to which he compared society, apparently incompatible ingredients combine to make a stimulating and palatable mixture. Even if it was too potent for many of his contemporaries (though they drank it avidly) the time may now have come to recommend it to connoisseurs.

Notes

1. W. Law, *Remarks upon a late Book entitled* The Fable of The Bees, 1724, ed. F. D. Maurice, Cambridge, 1845, p. 67.

2. B. Mandeville, *A Vindication of the Book, from the Aspersions Contain'd in a Presentment of the Grand Jury of Middlesex, and an Abusive Letter to Lord C.* In *The Fable of the Bees,* ed. F. B. Kaye, 1924, vol. 1, p. 384.

3. J. Wesley, *Journal of the Rev. John Wesley,* ed. Nehemiah Curnock, London, Epworth Press, 8 vols., 1909-16. Entry for 14 April 1756, vol. 4, p. 157.

4. *Amelia,* Book 3, Chapter 5; *Tom Jones,* Book 6, Chapter 1.

5. Adam Smith, *Theory of Moral Sentiments,* 1759, Part VII, Section II, Chapter 4. For the La Rochefoucauld story, see 'Short Account of the Life and Writings of Adam Smith' in *Wealth of Nations,* London, Nelson, 1864, pp. vii-viii.

6. Edward Gibbon, *Memoirs of My Life,* 1789, Chapter 1.

7. *Gentleman's Magazine,* n.s. 25 (June 1846), 484, in one of a series of articles called 'Extracts from the Portfolio of a Man of the World'.

8. Quoted by J. M. Robertson in his essay 'The Fable of the Bees', in *Essays toward a Critical Method,* London, 1889, p. 227. James Mill defended Mandeville in his *Fragment on Mackintosh,* 1835.

9. L. Stephen, 'Mandeville's *Fable of the Bees*', in *Essays on Freethinking and Plainspeaking,* London, 1907, p. 315.

10. Louis I. Bredwold, 'The gloom of the Tory Satirists', in J. Clifford, ed., *Eighteenth-Century English Literature,* New York, Oxford University Press, 1959, p. 16.

11. F. Hutcheson, *Reflections upon Laughter and Remarks upon The Fable of the Bees,* in *Collected Works,* Georg Olms, Hildesheim, 1971, vol. 7, p. 407.

12. L. A. Selby-Bigge, ed. *British Moralists,* Oxford, Clarendon Press, 1897, vol. 1, pp. xvi and xv.

13. R. Browning, *Parleyings with Certain People of Importance in their Day,* 1887.

14. Quoted in Kaye's edition of *The Fable of the Bees,* vol. 2, p. 438.

15. F. Hutcheson, op. cit., p. 148.

16. B. Mandeville, *An Enquiry into the Origin of Honour and the Usefulness of Christianity in War,* 1732, pp. 104-5 (Second Dialogue).

17. *Fable of the Bees,* ed. F. B. Kaye, vol. 2, pp. 12-13 (Preface).

18. B. Mandeville, *An Enquiry into the Origin of Honour and the Usefulness of Christianity in War,* 1732, pp. 43-4 (First Dialogue).

19. *Fable of the Bees,* ed. Kaye, vol. 1, p. 199 (Remark R).

20. *Fable of the Bees,* ed. Kaye, vol. 1, pp. 221-2 (Remark R).

21. *Origin of Honour,* pp. 77-9 (Second Dialogue).

22. See e.g. nos. 25, 29, and 31 of the *Tatler.*

23. *Fable of the Bees,* ed. Kaye, vol. 1, p. 32.

24. *Origin of Honour,* pp. 156-7 (Third Dialogue).

25. Ibid., pp. 150-1 (Third Dialogue).

26. Ibid., pp. 160-1 (Third Dialogue).

27. *Origin of Honour,* pp. 215-17 (Fourth Dialogue).

28. B. Mandeville, *Free Thoughts on Religion, the Church, and National Happiness,* 2nd ed., 1729, pp. 149-50 (Chapter 6).

29. B. Mandeville, *The Virgin Unmask'd: or Female Dialogues betwixt an elderly Maiden Lady and her Niece, on several Diverting Discourses on Love, Marriage, Memoirs, Morals, etc., of the Times,* 1709, p. 73 (Fourth Dialogue).

30. *Fable of the Bees,* ed. Kaye, vol. 2, pp. 18-19 (Preface to Part 2).

31. Ibid., p. 109 (Third Dialogue).

32. Ibid., vol. 1, p. 40 (Introduction to *An Enquiry into the Origin of Moral Virtue*).

33. Ibid., p. 166 (Remark O).

34. *Origin of Honour,* p. 56 (Second Dialogue).

35. *Fable of the Bees,* ed. Kaye, vol. 1, p. 404 (*A Vindication of the Book from the Aspersions,* etc.).

36. R. Whately, *Introductory Lectures on Political Economy,* 2nd ed., 1832 (Reprints of Economic Classics, New York, Augustus M. Kelley, 1966, p. 44).

37. L. Stephen, 'Mandeville's *Fable of the Bees*', in *Essays on Freethinking and Plainspeaking,* London, 1907, p. 279.

38. For example, his comparison of the evangelist to the father of a family ridding his children's hair of lice. See W. Y. Tindal, *John Bunyan. Mechanick Preacher,* New York, Russell & Russell, 1964.

39. *Free Thoughts on Religion,* pp. 143-4.

40. Ibid., pp. 145-6.

41. *Fable of the Bees,* ed. Kaye, vol. 1, pp. 231-2 (Remark T).

42. Thomas R. Edwards, Jr., 'Mandeville's Moral Prose', *ELH* 31 (1964), 208.

43. *Fable of the Bees,* ed. Kaye, vol. 1, p. 7 (Preface).

44. *Encyclopaedia Britannica,* 9th ed., Edinburgh, A. & C. Black, 1875-87, vol. 15 (1883), p. 472.

45. *Free Thoughts on Religion,* p. 169 (Chapter 7).

46. *Fable of the Bees,* ed. Kaye, vol. 2, p. 103 (Third Dialogue).

47. Ibid., vol. 1, pp. 219-20 (Remark R).

48. Ibid., vol. 2, p. 101 (Third Dialogue).

49. L. Stephen, *Essays on Freethinking and Plainspeaking,* 1907, pp. 281-2.

50. Ibid., p. 314.

51. *Fable of the Bees,* ed. Kaye, vol. 1, pp. xvii-xx. Most of the facts mentioned in this paragraph come from Kaye.

52. *Treatise of the Hypochondriack and Hysterick Passions,* 1711, pp. xii and 40.

53. *Gentleman's Magazine,* 3 (1733), 46.

54. *Fable of the Bees,* ed. Kaye, vol. 1, facing p. xx (reproduction of Mandeville's will).

55. Sir John Hawkins, *The Life of Samuel Johnson, LL.D.,* 1787, p. 263.

56. *Fable of the Bees,* ed. Kaye, vol. 1, p. xxiii, n. 3.

57. P. B. Anderson, 'Bernard Mandeville on Gin', *PMLA* 54 (1939), 775-84.

58. Ibid., p. 777.

59. *Treatise on the Hypochondriack and Hysterick Passions,* 1711, p. 272.

60. Ibid., p. 273.

61. S. Johnson, *Lives of the English Poets. Works,* 1823, vol. 7, p. 114; Hawkins, op. cit., p. 264.

62. B. Franklin, *Autobiography. Works.* ed. J. Bigelow, New York, Putnam's, 1904, vol. 1, p. 92.

63. [G. Bluet], *Enquiry whether . . . Virtue tends to . . . Wealth or Poverty . . . ,* 1725, p. 97.

64. *Fable of the Bees,* ed. Kaye, vol. 1, p. 263 (*Essay on Charity and Charity-Schools*).

65. Ibid., p. 263.

66. R. Fiddes, *General Treatise of Morality,* 1724, p. cxii.

67. *Female Tatler,* no. 60, 21-3 Nov. 1709.

68. *Tatler,* no. 44, 21 July 1709.

69. *Fable of the Bees,* ed. Kaye, vol. 1, pp. xxvii-xxviii.

70. *Chambers' Encyclopedia,* 1888-92, vol. 7, p. 16, under Mandeville, Bernard de.

71. N. Wilde, 'Mandeville's Place in English Thought', *Mind,* 11 (1898), 224.

72. *A Letter to Dion,* 1732, p. 48.

73. G. Berkeley, *Alciphron. Works,* ed. Luce and Jessop, vol. 3, p. 60.

74. G. Berkeley, *Alciphron. Works,* ed. Luce and Jessop, vol. 3, p. 62.

75. Ibid., p. 80.

76. *A Letter to Dion,* 1732, p. 48.

77. *Fable of the Bees,* ed. Kaye, vol. 2, p. 47 (First Dialogue).

78. Ibid., p. 332 (*Search into the Nature of Society*).

79. Shaftesbury, *Characteristics,* 2nd ed., 1714, vol. 1, pp. 29-30 (*A Letter Concerning Enthusiasm*).

80. *Fable of the Bees,* ed. Kaye, vol. 2, p. 53 (First Dialogue).

81. *Enquiry into the Origin of Honour,* 1732, p. 154.

82. *Fable of the Bees,* ed. Kaye, vol. 2, p. 252.

83. *Free Thoughts on Religion,* 2nd ed., 1729, p. 16.

84. Ibid., p. 13.

85. Ibid., p. 124.

86. *Free Thoughts on Religion,* 2nd ed., 1729, p. 11.

87. *Enquiry into the Origin of Honour,* 1732, pp. 4-5.

88. F. Hutcheson, *Reflections upon Laughter and Remarks upon* The Fable of the Bees. *Works,* G. Olms, Hildesheim, 1971, vol. 7, Opera Minora, p. 166.

89. B. Russell, 'A Free Man's Worship', in *Mysticism and Logic,* New York, Norton, 1929, pp. 47-8.

90. B. Russell, 'A Free Man's Worship', in *Mysticism and Logic,* p. 57.

91. *Fable of the Bees,* ed. Kaye, vol. 2, p. 244 (Fifth Dialogue).

92. Ibid., p. 251 (Fifth Dialogue).

93. Ibid., p. 252 (Fifth Dialogue).

94. Ibid., p. 311 (Sixth Dialogue).

95. *Fable of the Bees,* ed. Kaye, vol. 2, pp. 249-50 (Fifth Dialogue).

96. Ibid., p. 254 (Fifth Dialogue).

97. Ibid., vol. 1, p. 91 (Remark G).

98. *Fable of the Bees,* ed. Kaye, vol. 1, p. 8 (Preface).

M. R. Jack (essay date 1975)

SOURCE: Jack, M. R. "Religion and Ethics in Mandeville." In *Mandeville Studies: New Explorations in the Art and Thought of Dr. Bernard Mandeville (1670-1733),* edited by Irwin Primer, pp. 34-42. The Hague: Martinus Nijhoff, 1975.

[*In the following essay, Jack examines Mandeville's "naturalistic" view of religion and ethics as having psychological rather than theological bases.*]

At the beginning of his full-length work on religion entitled *Free Thoughts on Religion, the Church, and National Happiness,* Mandeville defines religion as "an Acknowledgment of an Immortal Power."[1] He later says that "Men of Sense, and good Logicians" have vainly wasted their time arguing about and discussing the subject since time immemorial, for knowledge of God is something "which no Language can give them the least Idea of."[2] God is ineffable, religion is mysterious, and "no Man therefore ought to be too dogmatical in Matters of Faith."[3] Mandeville has thus ruled out the possibility of religion on epistemological grounds: being a matter outside human comprehension, nothing can be known about God and nothing worthwhile can be said on this subject. He thus leaves himself free to concentrate on what really interests him in the rest of the book, namely, a general review of religious phenomena as an aspect of human behavior, an exposé of the corrupt practices of the clergy through the ages and a plea for toleration if not permissiveness.[4]

It will be my contention in this essay that it is essential to understand this point, clearly evidenced in Mandeville's works, before any meaningful discussion of his treatment of religion and ethics can take place. For in taking the position outlined above, Mandeville has declared his lack of interest in religion for its own sake. He has announced that he will not indulge in what has been called "the grand subterfuge" of the seventeenth century, that is, the fear of examining "religious emotion nakedly as an aspect of human nature."[5] At the same time there can be no doubt about his interest in the phenomenon of moral behavior, but it is an interest that is altogether divorced from the otherworldly. This divorce, I believe, can be interpreted in the light of his Calvinist background, but it has to be emphasized that Mandeville has taken the Baylian severance of religion and ethics to its extreme, so that any interpretation relying heavily on assuming a theological basis to his thinking on ethical matters is bound to be misleading. It may help us to understand the origin of the kind of distinction Mandeville makes between religion and ethics to consider the matter in terms of the Calvinist distinction between grace and nature, but it obscures his intentions as a psychologist interested in giving a naturalistic account of ethical phenomena.

My contention is, therefore, that Mandeville must be read as primarily one who is uninterested in religion for its own sake and one who is concerned with giving a naturalistic account of ethical behavior. This account is naturalistic both in the sense of its being unrelated to any transcendent theological position and in the sense of its being an explanation of morality in terms of human nature. I shall argue that most modern critical studies of these aspects of Mandeville's thought, by concentrating on elucidating his views in the light of some theological framework such as Calvinism, miss his main intention and interest. As much of this modern discussion has arisen within the framework sketched by F. B. Kaye in what is the standard modern edition of *The Fable of the Bees,* I will begin by considering this account.

II

Kaye's exposition of Mandeville's ethics depends upon accepting that there are two different standards applied by Mandeville in his assessment of the morality of actions: the first is "rigoristic" (ascetic and rational) and is applied as a criterion for judging the motives of individuals' behavior; the second is "empirical" or "utilitarian" and is applied as a criterion for judging the social consequences of such behavior. Thus for an action to be judged virtuous under the first condition, it must be disinterestedly motivated; that is, the individual must be attempting to deny his own inclination and further he must be doing this because he believes such denial to be good.[6] For an action to be judged virtuous under the second condition, it is necessary to judge the results which it led to, or, in other words, whether it was publicly beneficial. By holding to both these standards at the same time, Kaye asserts, Mandeville arrived at his paradox that public benefits arose from private vices. However, Kaye then says that in fact Mandeville's adoption of the first condition of "rigorism" was indeed disingenuous and that by insisting upon it at the same time as he insisted upon the utilitarian condition, he was achieving a *reductio ad absurdum* of rigorism. And this was entirely understandable since, according to Kaye, Mandeville's rigorism was in any case an entirely artificial addition to his thought.[7]

The confusion of Kaye's treatment of Mandeville's ethics has been clearly shown up in an important article by M. J. Scott-Taggart, entitled "Mandeville: Cynic or Fool?"[8] Scott-Taggart is concerned with rejecting both the traditional view that Mandeville's *Fable* was a testimonial for vice and Kaye's view that the adoption of two standards led Mandeville to paradox and to a *reductio ad absurdum* of rigorism. In dealing with Kaye's interpretation, Scott-Taggart holds that there may be no inconsistency in holding to the two standards as Kaye has understood them. "In a footnote," writes Scott-Taggart, "Kaye explains that he is using the terms 'rigorism' and 'utilitarianism' loosely, and intends his use of the latter term to mark 'an opposition to the insistence of "rigoristic" ethics that not results but motivation by right principle determines virtuousness."[9] Where Kaye wrote that "The paradox that private vices are public benefits is merely a statement of the paradoxical mixing of moral criteria which runs through the book,"[10] Scott-Taggart would substitute the following revision: "'The paradox that private vices are public benefits is merely a statement of the paradoxical mixing of appraisal of conduct in terms of motive and appraisal of conduct in terms of consequences.' But," adds Scott-Taggart, "there is nothing paradoxical about this mixing as such. We might analogously be interested both in the dexterity and effectiveness of an action, and discover that, although connected, the two were not exactly correlated with one another. To infer from this that one of them must be dropped as in some way impossible would be absurd: we select between them according to the purposes we want served."[11] In short, Mandeville offers to the world two competing varieties of moral principle, without overtly recommending that we adopt the one or the other.[12]

Kaye's interpretation of Mandeville as defending a substantially utilitarian ethic which defines the morality of actions in terms of their social consequences is thus confused and misleading. Mandeville was not concerned with advancing a substantive moral view when he advanced his paradox, "private vices, public benefits"; rather he was concerned with exposing the inconsistency and hypocrisy of those who in his own society did try to retain an ascetic and utilitarian ethic simultaneously. His argument showed, in a characteristically pungent manner, the absurdities which resulted from such combinations. Although we may be tempted to ascertain his own commitment to one ethic

or another, such a commitment cannot be deduced from his paradox. Moreover, a concentration on this aspect of his thought—i.e., his satirical intentions—obscures a more interesting and ambitious attempt of Mandeville's, namely, his attempt to derive an explanation of moral motivation from the psychological facts about human nature, to wit, his naturalism.

Mandeville's naturalism can be clearly seen if we examine the context of his initial definition of vice and virtue in ***An Enquiry into the Origin of Moral Virtue.*** As the title suggests, Mandeville in this work is examining the origins of morality or trying to give an account of the way in which man became a moral being. He does this by saying that "Lawgivers and other wise Men, that have laboured for the Establishment of Society," having thoroughly examined human nature, agreed upon the need for a "myth" which represented men as either angelic (if they were rational and disinterested) or brutish (if they were "passionate" and selfish).[13] This mythical division of men into those who by their behavior benefitted society at large and those who benefitted none but themselves, was the first distinction made between virtue and vice, for the former men's actions were characterized as virtuous while the latter's were characterized as vicious. According to this myth, the lawgivers relied upon the natural instinct of man to seek the esteem of his fellows to lead men to try to emulate the virtuous. Although in the second part of ***The Fable*** Mandeville shows that social norms evolved over vast epochs (that in fact the literal "invention" of morality by particular men was to be read as an allegory), the basic understanding of moral behavior as a reaction to the opinion of other men remained Mandeville's basic tenet.

Scott-Taggart explains the way in which Mandeville thereby moves from "you ought" to "I ought" as follows: "The fact that *other people* have an interest in my being moral entails that *I* have an interest in being moral, not merely to the extent that other people are able to punish me physically for not being moral, but also to the further extent that other people are able to back up their interest with approval or disapproval."[14] In the social context as a whole, Mandeville sees this motivation as making for stability; each individual, in pursuing his need for the approbation of his fellows (ultimately deriving from what Mandeville calls "self-liking"), contributes to the welfare of society as a whole. This is thus his view of the harmony of interests. Whenever there is a threat to this naturally smooth-running order of things, it is the responsibility of political leaders to suppress or control this potential disturbance.

To continue this line of discussion would be to enlarge upon Mandeville's social theory, whereas my intention has been only to establish the naturalistic basis of his ethics. It is therefore to consider his religion that I now turn.

III

To support my contention that a naturalistic interpretation also gives us a clearer idea of the place of religion in Mandeville's thought, I propose to consider his ***Free***

Thoughts on Religion, the Church, and National Happiness. Although this work, as its title implies, is concerned with religion, the Church and questions of faith and happiness, it is also, as soon becomes apparent to the reader, a plea for toleration and an end to sectarian schism. However, what might be called the political intention of the book—the strict control of the clergy in the public interest—covers up yet another aspect of the author's interest, namely, his obsession with "anatomizing" human nature.[15] Although an understanding of the theological background to his plea for toleration helps us to understand one part of the *Free Thoughts*, it does little to shed light on this really important intention—the exploration of the motives and behavior of men in religious matters.

One of the most striking features about the *Free Thoughts* is Mandeville's tendency to avoid religious controversy altogether. He does this on the grounds that the traditional controversies are too complicated for him or any man to solve. Thus it is his view that men have wasted their time in trying to solve the problem of how God can be both one and three persons at the same time. They have vainly wrestled with the complex problems of free-will and predestination, mysteries which were beyond the competence even of St. Paul to elucidate. They have taken to arguing about such matters as the symbolic function of the cross and various other rites and ceremonies of the Christian religion. Mandeville's attitude in these matters has, of course, been seen as part of what I have called the political intention of the book, that is, the aim of getting the Church entirely under the control of the state. This aim has been interpreted in the light of events and ideas in seventeenth-century Holland (which Mandeville knew well), as well as in the context of Augustan England. Thus G. S. Vichert traces the growth of toleration in Holland after the bitter sectarian struggle between the Calvinists and the Arminian Remonstrants and remarks that these events were followed closely in England.[16] In addition, Englishmen themselves had seen religious disputes cause major disruptions in their own country and were therefore well-disposed towards latitudinarianism.

While this type of explanation helps to make clear the likely considerations which gave rise to Mandeville's plea for tolerance, it does not convey the sense in which his avoidance of theological discussion is inextricably linked to his desire to pursue the subject from the point of view of a psychologist examining human actions and responses. Thus in the examples I have referred to, when discussing the problem of the trinity, Mandeville is more interested in the way men come to accept ideas contrary to their senses and to reason, than in the theological merits of the various views on this subject. He anticipates the modern school of behaviorist psychology when he speculates upon the manipulation of religious belief: ". . . were Men to be taught from their Infancy that it was a Mystery, that on a certain occasion Two and Two made Seven, with an addition to be believ'd on pain of Damnation, I am perswaded, that at least Seven in Ten would swallow the shameful Paradox. . . ."[17] In a similar manner his consideration of the

question of free will and determinism is largely taken up with an analysis of human behavior only tenuously connected with the theological problem itself. He asserts that everyone "can wish what he pleases," but not will what he pleases, for,

> was the one as Arbitrary as the other, there would be more Virtue, and not half the Misery, and what are call'd Misfortunes in the World, of what we now see Men labour under. There is hardly a Person so debauch'd, but what has often wish'd, tho' but for his Health's or Fortune's sake, that it was in his Power to lead a more regular Life: What is it hinders him, but his Appetites and Inclinations, that influence and seduce his Will, and do him the same Prejudice he could receive from a fatal and unavoidable Necessity of Sinning?[18]

Not only does such a passage reveal that Mandeville is back to his favorite pastime of scrutinizing human motives, but it confirms his treatment of moral behavior as being comprehensible in psychological terms. The other example mentioned above, that of the symbolic role of the cross in Christianity, is also discussed in the context of a psychological examination, this time into the role of rites and their impact on the human psyche.

If Mandeville's concern in the *Free Thoughts* is with a pathology of the religious instinct in man and a psychological account of religious behavior, this concern remains active in his other works on religion. The title of his last work, ***An Enquiry into the Origin of Honour and the Usefulness of Christianity in War,*** suggests that he is again investigating how men reconcile their religious beliefs with their behavior. Once again this interest can be understood in terms of a Calvinist background, but an extended treatment of his thought in terms of a doctrinal position is liable to obscure rather than clarify what he is doing. For example, Vichert observes that "Bayle's view of man is darker and sterner than Mandeville's, but the difference is only of degree. Immediately behind both of them stand the words of the Heidelberg catechism."[19] Such an approach surely obscures the fact that in Mandeville's hands the doctrine has become entirely secularized: not only has he abandoned redemption for corrupted man, but he concentrates his attention on considering in detail the behavior of fallen man. When his views come closest to Calvinism, he is being satirical or expressing cynicism. M. M. Goldsmith succinctly elucidates this point as follows:

> Rigorous Calvinism or Augustinianism can produce a condemnation of human beings so thorough that it caricatures itself. If all men sin all the time, if no man can be righteous, the distinction between good and evil seems meaningless. If men are damned for helping others because they do it as a result of their natural desire to win the approval of other men (approbativeness, a form of pride) and damned for gratifying themselves and ignoring others, damned if they do and if they don't, then, says the cynic, why not do as you please?[20]

It is the entire inability of such versions as E. Chiasson's to account for this secular, not to say wordly, tone of Mandeville's which make them so unconvincing.[21] Not only does such a strictly "doctrinal" account render his satire unintelligible, but it greatly obscures his real interests which are in the psychology of religion rather than in theology or dogma.

IV

I have argued in this paper that Mandeville's religion and ethics are best understood as naturalistic. By this I mean that they are a reflection of his worldly, as opposed to otherworldly, interests and that they derive from his psychology. The approaches taken by Kaye, Vichert, Chiasson and others to an understanding of Mandeville's ethics and religion err to the extent that each attributes to Mandeville a kind of religious concern or involvement, more or less, which results from a misreading of the general drift of his writings. Their misreadings in this area result from an unwillingness to accept the fact that his discussions of religion do not proceed upon any assumptions of the value of piety and do not aspire to advance the cause of any specific sect. This is not to say, however, that Kaye and Vichert show no appreciation of the importance of the empirical side of Mandeville; they seem not to emphasize sufficiently how committed Mandeville was to his naturalistic outlook. Religion, for Mandeville, presents social and political problems. He is not concerned with worship, redemption and so forth; he *is* concerned with keeping the different sects "tractable" or manageable from a political point of view. As for ethics, he is far more interested in analyzing the hidden springs of human behavior than in prescribing cures for the behavioral problems in society.

These were closer to his central interests. As M. M. Goldsmith put it, "By showing that prosperity and power were based on luxury and pride, Mandeville confronted the eighteenth century with a set of problems that stimulated others to attempt solutions."[22] These problems Goldsmith broadly considers as problems of moral theory, of economics and of history or evolution. They are problems of social science rather than of theology or substantive ethics. Thus Mandeville is concerned above all with a psychological theory about how men actually behave; he says little about how they ought to behave, making only a limited satirical plea for consistency. Temperamentally Mandeville is worldly, and he makes no effort to have us believe otherwise. With Walpole he would happily have joined in saying he was no saint, no Spartan, no reformer.

Notes

1. London, 1720, p. 1; all future references to his work are to this edition, the first.

2. *Ibid.,* 67.

3. *Ibid.,* 68.

4. Mandeville's anticlericalism is quite marked. He believed that since it was against their own interest, the clergy would not encourage compromise or reasonable behavior. It was also an aspect of his notion that the professions live off the vices and deficiencies of men.

5. Frank E. Manuel, *The Eighteenth Century Confronts the Gods* (Harvard Univ. Press, 1959), 21.

6. Thus he says virtue is applicable to "every Performance, by which Man, contrary to the impulse of Nature, should endeavor the Benefit of others, or the Conquest of his own Passions out of a Rational Ambition of being good." *The Fable of the Bees,* ed. F. B. Kaye (Oxford Univ. Press, 1924), I, 48-9.

7. See Kaye, I, lii-lvi. This is also the view taken by J. Viner who regarded "the advocacy, real or pretended, of unqualified rigorism in morals" as "an essential element of Mandeville's system of thought." Viner supported Kaye's view in saying that Mandeville achieved a *reductio ad absurdum* of rigorism, though unlike Kaye he insisted that this is a deliberate part of Mandeville's intention. See J. Viner, *The Long View and the Short* (Glencoe, Ill., 1958), 334.

8. In *Philosophical Quarterly,* v. 16, no. 64 (July, 1966).

9. Scott-Taggart, 228.

10. *Loc. cit.*

11. *Loc. cit.* J. C. Maxwell also takes this view in his essay "Ethics and Politics in Mandeville," *Philosophy,* XXVI (1951), 242-52.

12. Scott-Taggart, 228.

13. Kaye, I, 42.

14. Scott-Taggart, 230-31.

15. Thus Mandeville speaks of "The curious, that are skill'd in anatomizing the invisible Part of Man. . . ." Kaye, I, 145.

16. G. S. Vichert, *A Critical Study of the English Works of Bernard Mandeville (1670-1733),* Ph.D. Thesis, U. of London, 1964, 166-67.

17. *Free Thoughts,* 80.

18. *Ibid.,* 89-90.

19. Vichert, 165-66.

20. M. M. Goldsmith, Introduction to *An Enquiry into the Origin of Honour and the Usefulness of Christianity in War* (London, 1971), xvii.

21. See E. J. Chiasson, "Bernard Mandeville: A Reappraisal," *Philological Quarterly,* XLIX, 4 (October 1970), 489-519. Chiasson is concerned with refuting the view that Mandeville is to be read as an exponent of "segregation," i.e., a complete division between grace and nature. He maintains that Mandeville must be seen in the "massive but flexible" tradition of Christian humanism, as a successor to Hooker in asserting the need for grace and regeneration. Moreover, he observes, "the supposition that Mandeville could seriously propose embracing *either* the world *or* religion is a serious misunderstanding of what he means by both terms. For just as he recognizes in his

philosophy of man that grace is given to nature to re-generate it, so he recognizes, in his social philosophy, that the purely secular state is a truncated version of what the state might be if grace and revelation were permitted to perform their illuminating function" (p. 515).

There seems to be little evidence from the texts to support Chiasson's main argument and where he does quote from Mandeville to support his position, his references often seem to ignore entirely the contexts from which they are removed. Thus his reference to Mandeville's acknowledgement of the possibility of knowledge of an infinite and eternal being (Kaye, II, 208) appears in the context of Mandeville's explanation of savage man; prompted by fear, the savage begins to entertain "some glimmering Notions of an invisible Power" (Kaye, II, 207). In this passage Mandeville explores the psychological origins of the religious impulse—a factor ignored by Chiasson.

Later on, quoting from Mandeville to show his awareness of man's obligation to God, Chiasson neglects to point out that this remark is to be found in a passage dealing with the development of the religious instinct in man, once man had advanced beyond paying "his Respects to the Tree, he gathers Nuts from" (Kaye, II, 211). The type of analysis Mandeville pursues in this part of *The Fable* seems to be entirely ignored by Chiasson. Mandeville's concern here is to relate the religious impulse in men to the passions and to trace the development of the ideas man had of the supernatural as society advanced. Thus he clearly says, "Another Reason, why Fear is an elder Motive to Religion, than Gratitude, is, that an untaught Man would never suspect; that the same Cause, which he receiv'd Good from, would ever do him Hurt; and Evil, without doubt, would always gain his Attention first" (Kaye, II, 212).

When he deals with Mandeville's attitude to reason, Chiasson again seems to miss the point, for rather than reason guiding the passions, the reverse is Mandeville's stated view. According to Mandeville, ". . . we are ever pushing our Reason which way soever we feel Passion to draw it, and Self-love pleads to all human Creatures for their different Views, still furnishing every individual with Arguments to justify their Inclinations" (Kaye, I, 333). At least part of Mandeville's satire rests upon ridiculing those who pretend that this is not the case. In the end, Chiasson seems to provide his own refutation by alluding (p. 504n.) to Mandeville's "patience with the immoralities of men resulting from his tendency to look at these matters *as a sociologist* rather than a moralist . . ." [my italics] for he thereby casts doubt on the idea which he began with, that of regarding Mandeville as a Christian moralist.

22. M. M. Goldsmith, xvii.

Robert H. Hopkins (essay date 1975)

SOURCE: Hopkins, Robert H. "The Cant of Social Compromise: Some Observations on Mandeville's Satire." In *Mandeville Studies: New Explorations in the Art and Thought of Dr. Bernard Mandeville (1670-1733)*, edited by Irwin Primer, pp. 168-92. The Hague: Martinus Nijhoff, 1975.

[*In the following essay, Hopkins argues that, despite the attacks of many of his contemporaries, Mandeville in his satires was censuring many of the same things they were, stressing "how much in common Mandeville had with some of his illustrious adversaries in attacking the same satiric targets."*]

> Let any Man observe the Equipages in this Town; he shall find the greater Number of those who make a Figure, to be a Species of Men quite different from any that were ever known before the Revolution; consisting either of Generals and Colonels, or of such whose whole Fortunes lie in Funds and Stocks: So that *Power,* which, according to the old Maxim, was used to follow *Land,* is now gone over to *Money*. . . .
>
> Jonathan Swift, *The Examiner,* No. 13 (Nov. 2, 1710)

It is my belief that we must ultimately read Mandeville as a comic satirist and that we shall never fully understand him through an ossified history-of-ideas approach which in cataloging likenesses loses Mandeville's devastating sardonic tone. The current trend of dealing with Mandeville as first and last a satirist should do much to restore to him his historical identity; for if, as Edward Rosenheim insists, satire attacks "discernible, historically authentic particulars" and if the critic has an obligation to identify these particulars we shall be forced to relate Mandeville's satire to its historical context.[1] If we can show, furthermore, how *The Fable of the Bees* and *An Enquiry into the Origin of Honour* satirize certain ambiguities in Mandeville's world that have not diminished in time and that are still very much a part of our contemporary experience, these works may still be found to be very pertinent indeed. In this essay I shall focus on what one recent critic has aptly termed the "sense of the pressure of the social scene" and try to show through the study of several words and phrases occurring in Mandeville's works how this "pressure of the social scene" results in some of Mandeville's most effective satire.[2]

Only in the last several years has a critic suggested a really plausible motive for Mandeville's writing the initial verse pamphlet that led to *The Fable—The Grumbling Hive: or, Knaves Turn'd Honest* (1705). Isaac Kramnick drew attention to a number of verse pamphlets written in the 1690's-1700's attacking the corruption of English society by money and identified *The Grumbling Hive* as Mandeville's answer to this verse convention in defense of what historians now call The Financial Revolution.[3] This Financial Revolution is established by the development of long-term public borrowing, the creation of "a whole range of securities in which mercantile and financial houses could safely invest, and from which they could easily disinvest (unlike land mortgages)," and a transition from a primarily agrarian economy to a mercantile economy centered in London around urban monied interests. If Kramnick's conjecture is valid, Mandeville's initial effort in the writing of **The Fable** would seem to place him on the side of the moneyed interest as opposed to the landed interest although in a very little time the landed interest itself came to be what Raymond Williams has termed England's "first really ruthless capitalist class."[4] Mandeville felt compelled later to expound on his verses through essays and prose remarks in the 1714 first edition of **The Fable,** and then again in the 1723 edition. It was the "Essay on Charity, and Charity-Schools" added to this later edition, however, which finally exploded the time-bomb and made **The Fable** one of the most vexing works in all of eighteenth-century English literature.

It is my belief that all of the radical elements which were present in the 1714 edition were not really noticed by Mandeville's contemporaries until history itself caught up with the work. Urban capitalism with all of its ambiguities was becoming the dominating mode of life, but its implications had yet to penetrate fully into the consciousness of Mandeville's contemporaries. The sin of Mandeville's wit was that he had stated more explicitly than any other writer yet had the unstated assumptions and hypocrisies of a social compromise which his society had tacitly agreed upon in order to live with the Financial Revolution.[5] Mandeville had had the unmitigated nerve to depict these hypocrisies under the guise of traditional satire by relying on a norm of Christian rigorism which at times appears itself a target of satire. Whereas Swift clearly seemed to be writing his satire from a base of Christian value, Mandeville seemed to be using the guise of Christian value to expose the impossibility of a compromise between his affluent society and that value, only then to cast his lot with that society in all of its negative as well as positive aspects. Mandeville's contemporaries responded to his satire not by examining Leviathan's goals and priorities but by making Mandeville himself the scapegoat. (It is the classic reaction in all societies to the world's great satirists.) The amazing overresponse (overkill?) to the 1723 **Fable** by John Dennis, Richard Fiddes, William Law, George Bluet, Francis Hutcheson, and later in 1732 by George Berkeley, had the curious result of broadcasting Mandeville's satire to a much wider reading audience until it was not necessary to have read **The Fable** in order to know its central themes. This unintentional broadcasting of **The Fable** by its enemies so as to make it a central presence in the literary consciousness of the middle decades of the eighteenth century has not been stressed enough. We may also use these attacks on **The Fable** as a valuable index to those aspects of Mandeville's satire which seemed to vex most his contemporaries.

THE "STATE OF NATURE" AND THE "NATURE OF SOCIETY"

One of the most vexing phrases in **The Fable** was the "State of Nature." It is first encountered in the "Introduction" to "An Enquiry into the Origin of Moral Virtue." After complaining that "most Writers are always teaching Men what they should be, and hardly ever trouble their heads with telling them what they really are" (I, 39), Mandeville proceeds to state that men are governed primarily by their passions and that this truth is intrinsic to "a flourishing Society." Mandeville intends to discover how Man might "yet by his own Imperfections be taught to distinguish between Virtue and Vice": "*And here I must desire the Reader once for all to take notice, that when I say Men, I mean neither* Jews *nor* Christians; *but meer Man, in the State of Nature and Ignorance of the true Deity*" (I, 40).

"An Enquiry" proper begins with the thesis that "all untaught Animals" are motivated only by self-interest, that in "the wild State of Nature" only animals with the "least of Understanding" and the "fewest Appetites to gratify" are "fittest to live peaceably together in great Numbers" (I, 41). In this same "State" Man is the "Species of Animals" least capable of "agreeing long together in Multitudes" without "the Curb of Government." The social evolution of Man is accomplished by "Law-Givers and other Wise Men" who by the "artful Way of Flattery" insinuate "themselves into the Hearts of Men" and begin to "instruct them in the Notions of Honour and Shame." These leaders divide "the whole Species in two Classes," one consisting of "abject, low-minded People," always "hunting after immediate Enjoyment," and the other consisting of "lofty high-spirited Creatures," free from "sordid Selfishness," who esteem "the Improvements of the Mind to be their fairest Possessions" (I, 44). (Mandeville mimics here the patronizing snobbery of the upper classes.) These "first Rudiments of Morality, broach'd by skilful Politicians, to render Men useful to each other as well as tractable," were "contriv'd" so that "the Ambitious might reap the more Benefit from, and govern vast Numbers of them with the greater Ease and Security" (I, 47). It turns out, then, that the "lofty, high-spirited Creatures," "free from sordid Selfishness," have much to gain from the exploitation of the lower class and that "the very worst" of the ruling class "preach up Publick-spiritedness, that they might reap the Fruits of the Labour and Self-denial of others" (I, 48). Rather than defining virtue and vice in terms of an absolute morality based on Christian revelation, Mandeville proceeds to redefine these terms instrumentally according to what is beneficial or injurious to society. Immediately after this utilitarian redefining, Mandeville returns to "Man in his State of Nature":

> It shall be objected, that no Society was ever any ways civiliz'd before the major part had agreed upon some Worship or other of an over-ruling Power, and consequently that the Notions of Good and Evil, and the Distinction between *Virtue* and *Vice,* were never the Contrivance of Politicians, but the pure Effect of Religion. Before I answer this Objection, I must repeat what I have said already, that in this **Enquiry into the Origin of Moral Virtue,** I speak neither of *Jews* or *Christians,* but Man in his State of Nature and Ignorance of the true Deity. . . .
>
> (I, 49-50)

Since the "Idolatrous Superstitions of all other Nations" were "incapable of exciting Man to Virtue," Mandeville argues that it is "the skilful Management of wary Politicians" that "first put Man upon crossing his Appetites and subduing his dearest Inclinations": "Moral Virtues are the Political Offspring which Flattery begot upon Pride" (I, 51).

But politics is supposed to be a branch of ethics, not vice versa! Mandeville's satirical reversal which reflects the image of a society in which political activities are to be judged by the instrumental needs of society rather than by traditional ethical standards is prepared for by his loaded phrase, "State of Nature," which, I believe, is intentionally derived from Hobbes's famous chapter in *Leviathan,* "Of the Natural Condition of Mankind . . ." (Pt. I, ch. 13). What Mandeville is suggesting is that the dominating ethic of his competitive society is the Hobbist ethic of the marketplace rather than the Christian ethic of the cathedral.

To appreciate fully the significance of this point, C. B. Macpherson's treatment of Hobbes in his *The Political Theory of Possessive Individualism: Hobbes to Locke* (London, Oxford University Press, 1962) becomes of paramount importance. Macpherson believes that the theoretical foundations for the liberal-democratic state stem from seventeenth-century individualism and the political theories of Hobbes and Locke among others which provided the philosophical underpinning for this individualism. The "possessive" quality of this individualism developed from a concept of the individual as essentially a proprietor of his own person or capacities, owing nothing to society for them. The individual is no longer seen as part of a larger social whole, or as an intrinsically moral entity, but as an owner of himself. Society comes to consist of a series of relations of exchanges between proprietors, and political society becomes a calculated device for the protection of the property of proprietors and for the maintenance of an orderly relation of exchange. Macpherson believes that in the past Hobbes's political theory has been studied too narrowly in an analytical philosophical tradition which ignores both Hobbes's historical and cultural context and the unstated assumptions operative in his theory which are provided by a historical frame of reference. In a section entitled "Human Nature and the State of Nature," Macpherson argues persuasively for an interpretation of Hobbes's "Natural Condition of Man" not as literally to be referred to as early primitive man, but as a logical hypothesis about "men whose desires are specifically civilized . . . the hypothetical condition in which men as they now are, with natures formed by living in civilized society would necessarily find themselves if there were no common power able to overawe them" (pp. 18-19): "Natural man is civilized man with only the restraint of law removed" (p. 29). What Hobbes has done, according to Macpherson, is to construct a political theory on the model of a "possessive-market society," a society in which the market itself provides the real basis for morality in contrast to traditional society with its basis for morality stemming from Christian revelation and natural law. Men in

Hobbes's possessive-market society find themselves "subject to the determination of the market" and this determinism explains "the somewhat inhuman flavour of Hobbes's political obligation" (p. 106). Hobbes's great achievement was to penetrate into "the heart of the problem of obligation in modern progressive societies," even though, as Macpherson wryly notes, "the English possessing class . . . did not need Hobbes's full prescription" and had "some reason to be displeased with his portrait of themselves." "Before the end of the century the men of property had come to terms with the more ambiguous, and more agreeable, doctrine of Locke" (p. 106). Though Macpherson's overall treatment of Hobbes appears to be too reductive in order to support a Marxist interpretation, I would plead that his analysis of the ironies of Hobbes's "State of Nature" is sound because he has hit upon the uses of this loaded term for a literary strategy. If political scientists tend to seek only univocal meanings in Hobbes as political scientist, we as literary critics may relish the deliberate pluri-significant meanings in Hobbes as Restoration satirist.[6]

What I am suggesting is that in the 1714 editions of **The Fable** Mandeville was using "State of Nature" in the Hobbist sense. Mandeville's myth or fiction describing how clever politicians govern society by a "Flattery begot upon Pride" reflects the actual expedient ethic of an age governed increasingly by possessive individualism, one which truly needs the "Curb of Government" if men are to restrain themselves. Insofar as the actual ethic of most men is not a Christian one, but one governed by the market in a mercantile economy, virtue really is "the Political Offspring which Flattery begot upon Pride." Mandeville's genealogy-of-morals parable reflects satirically on his own society. Too many critics have unfortunately read this fiction in a literal sense, partly because Mandeville's contemporary critics deliberately chose to rebut his work by reading it literally rather than as deliberate irony (with the important exception of John Dennis). Quoting Mandeville's insistence that he meant "neither Jews nor Christians, but meer Men in the State of Nature, and Ignorance of the true Deity," Dennis shrewdly observed that it took "very little Discernment" to see "that when he [Mandeville] says Men, he means *Englishmen,* whether they are Christians, or Deists, or Atheists."[7]

Later in **"Remark (O)"** (1714) Mandeville fuses deliberately "State of Nature" in its Hobbist sense with a theological sense to taunt his readers who are, of course, all in a state of grace: "Thus I have prov'd, that the Real Pleasures of all Men in Nature are worldly and sensual, if we judge from their Practice; I say all Men *in Nature,* because Devout Christians, who alone are to be excepted here, being regenerated, and preternaturally assisted by the Divine Grace, cannot be said to be in Nature. How strange it is, that they should all so unanimously deny it!" (I, 166). The double meaning here is particularly effective in carrying the satiric thrust of the passage. Christian readers living in a state of grace need not fear Mandeville's thesis, but since society assumes that most men are really living their everyday lives as if they were in a fallen "State of Nature" Christians will not find themselves easily able to live in society and still maintain their integrity. By equating the Hobbist "natural condition of man" which reflects a possessive-individualistic market society with the Augustinian view of fallen, unregenerated man in **"Remark (O),"** Mandeville articulates a highly vexing paradox.

Mandeville's mythical "State of Nature" represents an image of early eighteenth-century London society as it really was. If the Hobbist naturalistic ethic was unacceptable to most Englishmen, John Locke's political theory provided the foundation for a more amiable compromise between the ethic of the marketplace and the traditional ethic of moral authority. Macpherson is again invaluable in his analysis of Locke's compromise. In his rejection of political theories based on paternalism, Locke devised a theory of natural right by which men were originally created equal by God and then lost this equality in history. To support this myth of natural right and equality, Locke's "State of Nature" assumes in one sense that "the natural condition of man is eminently rational and peaceable" (Macpherson, p. 245). Locke's optimistic fiction enables him to "base property right on natural right and natural law, and then to remove all the natural law limits from the property right" (*Ibid.*, p. 199). Thereby Locke is able to put men "on their own, and leave them to confront each other in the market without the protections which the old natural law doctrine upheld" (*Ibid.*, p. 245). Macpherson's deduction from this analysis is that Locke conceived "man in general in the image of rational bourgeois man, able to look after himself and morally entitled to do so" (p. 245).

Once Locke had worked out a fiction which would free society from traditional restrictions, he then had to work out an explanation for man's observable inequality. As Macpherson shows, Locke equated this inequality with the difference in men's reasoning powers, and this difference was "not inherent in men, not implanted in them by God or Nature," but rather "socially acquired by virtue of different economic positions" (p. 246). Since men are through this process unequal and possess varying degrees of rationality, a civil society with legal sanctions and a church with spiritual sanctions are necessary to maintain an orderly society. Locke's utilitarian argument for this kind of social order is really focused on what Mandeville terms the "Nature of Society." Macpherson is invaluable in showing how Locke arrives at an ambiguous compromise to accommodate a society based on possessive individualism while defending traditional political institutions. Locke will have it both ways. Unlike Hobbes, according to Macpherson, Locke "refused to reduce all social relations to market relations and all morality to market morality" or to "entirely let go of traditional natural law" (p. 269). On the other hand if Locke "did not read market relations back into the very nature of man, as Hobbes had done," he did read into the nature of society a Hobbist ethic "in the image of market man" (pp. 268-69). This ambiguity in Locke's political theory is the result of a kind of compromise, then, between the necessity for an ethic of economic and political expedience and the necessity for retaining traditional moral sanctions.[8]

If, as I have suggested, Mandeville's use of paradox is intended to highlight in public consciousness the unstated ambiguities of the compromises in a possessive individualistic society, his paradoxes are indeed the perfect vehicle for his intentions. In his 1714 edition of **The Fable** Mandeville had exploited the satirical possibilities in the Hobbist state of nature. His 1723 addition to **The Fable,** "A Search into the Nature of Society," attacks Shaftesbury and the political compromise of his tutor, John Locke, based on an amiable view of man in a state of nature. It is a logical expansion of his position in **"Remark (O),"** and to show that man is "sociable beyond other Animals the Moment after he lost Paradise" because of "the Hateful Qualities of Man, his Imperfections and the want of Excellencies which other Creatures are endued with" is to counter the tendency to see society as an extension of the natural goodness of man. The very nature of society itself is intrinsically evil and legislatures should act to harness this society through laws for the public good. In a parody of sermonizing rhapsodies of Man before the Fall, Mandeville alludes to Man "endued with consummate Knowledge the moment he was form'd," "the State of Innocence, in which no Animal or Vegetable upon Earth, nor Mineral under Ground was noxious to him," "wholly wrapt up in sublime Meditations on the Infinity of his Creator" (I, 346). "In such a Golden Age," there is no possible explanation as to why mankind should ever have formed large societies. Only when Man was fallen was there a need for society, and by implication this society by absolute moral standards must be evil although by utilitarian standards absolutely essential for survival. Mandeville's definition of society is that of "a Body Politick, in which Man either subdued by Superior Force or by Persuasion drawn from his Savage State, is become a Disciplin'd Creature, that can find his own Ends in Labouring for others, and where under one Head or other Form of Government each Member is render'd Subservient to the Whole, and all of them by cunning Management are made to Act as one" (I, 347).

Martin Price has suggested that Mandeville relies on "causal or genetic explanation" as did Hobbes because such explanation "is our stay against confusion in an essentially unknowable world, and its causal nature is the condition of its rationality."[9] But Kaye is surely correct to see Mandeville rejecting such fictions on the genesis of society and believing that civilization is "the result, not of sudden invention, but of a very slow evolution based on man's actual nature" (I, lxiv-lxvi, 46-47, fn. 1). The political-genesis myths of Hobbes and Locke become valuable reductive myths for Mandeville whose real commitment is to an empirical descriptive account of society as it actually is. When Mandeville writes that "no Societies could have sprung from the Amiable Virtues and Loving Qualities of Man," he is attacking those optimistic theories of human nature which seemingly ignored the Fall completely while retaining the Garden of Eden. It is on this point that Macpherson offers an interesting partial explanation for the rise of optimistic theories of human nature in early eighteenth-century thought. Macpherson argues that when Locke chose to depict, unlike Hobbes, an idyllic state of nature in which all men were equal, Locke was conceiving "man in general in the image of rational bourgeois man able to look after himself and morally entitled to do so": "Now when man in general is thus conceived in the image of rational bourgeois man, the natural condition of man is eminently rational and peaceable" (Macpherson, p. 245). If Macpherson is right on this point, and I believe that he is, the rise of optimistic views towards human nature and society in the essays of Addison and Steele and in the ethical theories of Shaftesbury and Hutcheson may be viewed as self-delusionary ideologies which support in all of their affirmative aspects a society committed to possessive individualism while refusing to confront the realities of such individualism in all of its negative aspects. By calling attention to some of the precedents to Mandeville's **The Fable** in Hobbes's *Leviathan* and in Locke's *Two Treatises of Government,* we may develop some genuinely new insights both into the function of Mandeville's satire and into the sociology of competing literary styles.

Mandeville's first satiric target in the 1714 version of **The Fable** was of course not Shaftesbury but Steele: "When the Incomparable Sir *Richard Steele,* in the usual Elegance of his easy Style, dwells on the Praises of his sublime Species, and with all the Embellishments of Rhetoric sets forth the Excellency of Human Nature, it is impossible not to be charm'd with his happy Turns of Thought, and the Politeness of his Expressions" (I, 52-53). Relying on the excessive alliteration of S's and P's and on the burden of meaning being carried vacuously by the adjectives, Mandeville's parody suggests that Steele often substitutes metaphors and analogies for logical exposition and often substitutes for the concrete reality of experience a glib fictitious world too easily gained by the internal coherence of style.

Mandeville's parody of Addison's *The Spectator,* No. 69, may be found, I believe, in his essay "A Search into the Nature of Society" added to the 1723 edition of **The Fable.** The impact of *The Spectator,* No. 69, on eighteenth-century ideology has been discussed by Donald F. Bond who notes that it became for "eighteenth-century Whigs one of the classic expositions of the value of the merchant class to the nation"; and, indeed, Addison's half-comic and half-serious panegyric on the Royal Exchange does seem painfully chauvinistic: "I am wonderfully delighted to see such a Body of Men thriving in their own private Fortunes, and at the same time promoting the Publick Stock; or in other Words, raising Estates for their own Families, by bringing into their Country whatever is wanting, and carrying out of it whatever is superfluous" (*The Spectator,* I, 294).[10] Mandeville, on the other hand, goes to great pains to show both the negative and the positive effects of commerce on the "labouring poor." Whereas Addison tends to rhapsodize over the products which come to England from all over the world, Mandeville dwells on the plight of the hu-

man beings who make such commerce possible: ". . . the Losses of Men and Treasure swallow'd up in the Deep, the Tears and Necessities of Widows and Orphans made by the Sea, the Ruin of Merchants and the Consequences, the continual Anxieties that Parents and Wives are in for the Safety of their Children and Husbands, and . . . the many Pangs and Heart-akes that are felt throughout a Trading Nation by Owners and Insurer at every blast of Wind . . ." (I, 361). Whereas Addison celebrated mock-heroically that romanticized image of commerce, "the single Dress of a Woman of Quality," Mandeville countered with a mock-heroic celebration of "Scarlet or crimson Cloth" (I, 356-57). Whereas Addison tends to assume that what is good for private fortunes is good for public well-being, Mandeville examines with considerable glee the conflict between manners and morals involved in an economy of conspicuous consumption:

> It is the sensual Courtier that sets no Limits to his Luxury; the Fickle Strumpet that invents new Fashions every Week; the haughty Dutchess that in Equipage, Entertainments, and all her Behaviour would imitate a Princess; the profuse Rake and lavish Heir, that scatter about their Money without Wit or Judgment, buy every thing they see, and either destroy or give it away the next Day, the Covetous and perjur'd Villain that squeez'd an immense Treasure from the Tears of Widows and Orphans, and left the Prodigals the Money to spend: It is these that are the Prey and proper Food of a full grown Leviathan. . . .
>
> (I, 355)

F. B. Kaye himself recognized the literary resemblances between Mandeville's satire and Addison's essay (**The Fable,** I, 357, fn. 1), but the clinching piece of evidence that Mandeville had *The Spectator* in mind was his attack on Addison's rhapsody of England's commercial blessings as a gift from God: Addison exclaims, "Nature seems to have taken a particular Care to disseminate her Blessings among the different Regions of the World, with an Eye to this mutual Intercourse and Traffick among Mankind, that the Natives of the several Parts of the Globe might have a kind of Dependance upon one another, and be united together by their common Interest" (*The Spectator,* I, 294-95). Writing after the South Sea Bubble and refusing to minimize "the necessary Consequence of Foreign Trade, the Corruption of Manners, as well as Plagues, Poxes, and other Diseases, that are brought to us by Shipping" (I, 360), Mandeville almost certainly refers to Addison when he asks: ". . . would it not be amazing, how a Nation of thinking People should talk of their Ships and Navigation as a peculiar Blessing to them, and placing an uncommon Felicity in having an Infinity of Vessels dispers'd through the wide World, and always some going to and others coming from every part of the Universe?" (I, 361).

It seems to me that Mandeville throughout **The Fable of the Bees** shows a more all-encompassing, genuine sympathy with the laboring poor than Addison ever does. *Spectator,* No. 69, presents an attitude which really does tend to romanticize English commerce as if God were a middle-class merchant. To counter this attitude, Mandeville uses the Hobbist "State of Nature" as a foil with which to attack the delusionary optimism in the Steele-Shaftesbury tradition. To assume that the Christian ethic and the mercantile ethic can be easily unified in an ideological compromise was repugnant to Mandeville. The Financial Revolution is an amoral secular phenomenon, Mandeville seemed to be suggesting, and requires carefully thought-out secular solutions. Within the marketplace the Christian ethic has little, if any, place, and one must not pretend that it does. Rather than reacting to the scandal of the South Sea Bubble with jeremiads in the pulpit, Englishmen should follow the lead of the Netherlands and pass good regulations and laws which will hold politicians to a strict accounting (*The Fable,* I, 190). But above all, Mandeville is saying, one must not fall back on a reactionary kind of Luddite Christianity which rejects the modern world or delude oneself with an optimistic "moral" compromise which views the world as made primarily for the affluent middle class.

"Religion is one thing, and Trade is another" (I, 356) is the vexing thesis of "A Search into the Nature of Society." Mandeville brought home to his contemporaries more dramatically than almost any other writer the intimations of a modern world with an economic soul while appearing not to condemn such a world, and for this he was made a scapegoat. Swift, too, brought home the shock of recognition with remarks in *Gulliver's Travels* to the effect that the "positive, confident, restive temper, which Virtue infused into Man, was a perpetual Clog to public Business" (III, viii) and that the failure of the Brobdingnagians to apply such secrets as the manufacture of gunpowder to affairs of state resulted from their failure to reduce "*Politicks* into a *Science,* as the more acute wits of *Europe* have done" (II, vii). But I would suggest that, unlike Swift, Mandeville is a modern who saw that to cope with the complexities of the modern secular state a political science *was* necessary.

"Charity," "Pity," and the Problem of the Poor

Mandeville's treatment of "State of Nature" and the "Nature of Society" so as to bring out into the open all of the implications of a society increasingly governed by the market-place while professing Christian values is based on his primary satiric norm which is defined in *Free Thoughts on Religion, the Church, and National Happiness* (1720): "Whoever would be happy should endeavour to be wise, and as this consists in having a diffusive Knowledge of the real worth of Things, and a Capacity of chusing on all Emergencies what to sound and unbyass'd reason would seem the most eligible, so it is by shaking of all Clogs of Prejudice, and Fetters of human Authority, by thinking freely, that Men can only mount to Wisdom. There is no better way of curing groundless Jealousy and pannick Fears, than by daring to examine and boldly look into the Face of Things" (p. 335). Unlike the genteel liberalism of Addison and Steele which tended to view society in terms

of the middle class while unintentionally patronizing the poor, Mandeville's hard-boiled acceptance of the implications of the Financial Revolution enabled him to see things as they really were and to sympathize with the laboring poor without sentimentalizing over them. The historian Charles Wilson has shown how in the late seventeenth century there developed a particular concern over the relief and employment of the poor and over the relationship of employment to the national welfare as reflected in the balance of trade and how efforts were made to find new alternatives for the relief of the poor in contrast to the passive forms of relief (alms) common in earlier periods.[11] New solutions were necessary because of the flow of population to London from the country as families sought to be nearer to the financial centers and because of the subsequent increase of urban poor, probably from the servant classes and farm workers who followed householders into the city. Organized philanthropy, supported primarily by the merchant and middle classes, was unable to ameliorate the lot of the urban poor to any great extent because of their large numbers. In the ensuing national debate over the problem of the poor which lasted for almost a century one side saw the solution to be through the charity school and the workhouse while the other side, which included Mandeville, saw the solution to be "only through an accelerated rate of economic activity in general" (p. 99). The parallel to our age seems obvious. Now that the most highly industrialized society in the twentieth century has discovered how much institutionalized welfare leaves to be desired and how in such a society as ours jobs, and access to jobs are desperately needed by the poor to sustain a living standard commensurate with human dignity, perhaps Mandeville's "Essay on Charity, and Charity-Schools" will no longer be interpreted as brutally cynical.

Mandeville's essay seems even less cynical if one is fully aware of just how much the charity schools had become a political pawn in Anglican politics. In the second decade of the eighteenth century many of the London charity schools were considered hotbeds of Jacobite sympathizers.[12] They constituted for Mandeville the symbol of the vicious repression of the Societies for the Reformation of Manners and the reactionary dogmatism of the Society for the Promotion of Christian Knowledge which had in the second decade hounded out of the charity-school movement the nonconformists. The hypocritical compromise of the charity schools was their effort to indoctrinate, rather than to educate genuinely, the children of the poor. Worse yet, this attempt to control the poor by indoctrinating their children submerged its intention under the smokescreen of helping to solve the problem of the poor by training their children for suitable jobs. Thus in *Spectator,* No. 294, Steele could plead good-naturedly with his readers to contribute to the charity schools even if for no "other Expectation than that of producing a Race of good and useful Servants, who will have more than a liberal, a religious Education" (III, 49). Steele's concluding sentence is from a charity-school sermon: "*Thus do they* [the students] *become more exalted in Goodness, by being depressed in Fortune, and their Poverty is, in Reality, their Preferment to Heaven*" (III, 50). It was just such an attitude that angered Johnson in his review of Jenyns.

The charity schools through their subscription campaigns offered the middle class the opportunity to placate its conscience, and the charity school sermon or subscription illustrates a particularly egregious form of conspicuous consumption. One such event is described in the 1720 enlarged edition of Stow's *Survey of the Cities of London*: "And here the Charity Children are brought and placed with their Masters and Mistresses, in convenient Seats, where they may be seen decently habited, sitting or standing, joining with the Publick Prayers, responding, singing the Psalms, and sometimes answering their Catechisms; *to the great Delight and Satisfaction of the better sort that see and hear them* [italics mine]" (p. 49). In later editions of Stow's *Survey,* Strype included a description of the annual gathering of London charity children at St. Andrew's Holborn Church (later held at St. Paul's) and which was one source for William Blake's "Holy Thursday" poems. From Mandeville's point of view the propaganda in favor of the charity schools was a well-meaning but totally self-deluding effort that failed to see that the long-range solution to the problem of the poor would have to be political and economic. Mandeville deliberately takes an unpopular stance on the issue of charity schools and the problem of the poor, and if a precedent is to be found in eighteenth century literature to William Blake's poetical indictment of false charity and patronizing pity, it is in Mandeville's **"Essay on Charity, and Charity-Schools."**

Genuine charity is defined at the beginning of the **"Essay on Charity"** as the "part of that sincere Love we have for our selves" which is "transferr'd pure and unmix'd to others" (I, 253). Mandeville distinguished between charity and pity: "This Virtue is often counterfeited by a Passion of ours, call'd *Pity* or *Compassion,* which consists in a Fellow-feeling and Condolence for the Misfortunes and Calamities of others: all Mankind are more or less affected with it; but the weakest Minds generally the most" (I, 254). To make his point that the response of pity is universal so that if charity were synonymous with pity even an "Highwayman, an House-Breaker, or a Murderer" would be charitable, Mandeville presents the extraordinary instance of a man locked in a room being forced to watch a "nasty over-grown Sow" devour a very young child without being able to help the child: "To see her widely open her destructive Jaws, and the poor Lamb beat down with greedy haste; to look on the defenceless Posture of tender Limbs first trampled on, then tore asunder; to see the filthy Snout digging in the yet living Entrails suck up the smoking Blood, and now and then to hear the Crackling of the Bones, and the cruel Animal with savage Pleasure grunt o'er the horrid Banquet; to hear and see all this, What Tortures would it give the Soul beyond Expression!" (I, 255). The comic exuberance of this description which is gleefully concrete—"smoking Blood," "the Crackling of the Bones"—the reversal of man eating animal to animal devouring man, and the concreteness of the immediate situation to counter the abstractions and clichés of orga-

nized philanthropy which will be present later in the essay, all conspire to vex the reader of tenderly exquisite—and phony—sensibility. If pity is a universal passion and if charity is merely pity, then such undiscriminating universal charity would be absurd and meaningless. Mandeville asserts that although pity "is the most amiable of all our Passions," no "Pity does more Mischief in the World than what is excited by the Tenderness of Parents, and hinders them from managing their Children as their rational Love to them would require" (I, 260). Mandeville's point is identical with Swift's indictment of "fondness" in Book Four of *Gulliver's Travels*: "They [the Houyhnhnms] have no fondness for their colts or foals, but the care they take in educating them proceedeth entirely from the dictates of *Reason.*" "Fondness" meaning foolish affection was meant by Swift to be pejorative in the context of the Houyhnhnms, who try to raise their offspring by rational principles.

Mandeville proceeds next to show how false charity, *i.e.,* pity, is exploited by the professional beggar and then goes on to show how conspicuous charity in the form of the Radcliffe endowment to Oxford is really a clever manifestation of pride. Finally, he reaches his main target, the charity schools, a form of organized philanthropy which promotes "Sloth and Idleness" and which destroys "Industry" (I, 267). After carefully stipulating that he believes in "sufficient Hospitals for Sick and Wounded" and in tender care for "Young Children without Parents, Old Age without Support, and all that are disabled from Working," Mandeville argues that all of the rest of the poor "should be set to Work." This unpopular position is contrary to the "Enthusiastick Passion for Charity-Schools" that has "bewitch'd the generality" so that he who "speaks the least Word against it" it branded "an Uncharitable, Hard-hearted and Inhuman, if not a Wicked, Prophane and Atheistical Wretch" (I, 269). After defining this mock-villain role in the simplistic idiom of a charity-school fanatic, Mandeville proceeds to play the role to the hilt.

The charity schools participated in the social compromise in that the middle class purported not only to teach morals to the aristocracy but to teach morals and manners to the children of the poor. Unintentionally, the London charity schools were molding a small minority of the children of the poor into the narcissistic image of the prospering urban middle class, and there can be no doubt at all that Mandeville spends much of his essay attacking the charity schools as a middle-class phenomenon and as an *urban* phenomenon.[13] When Mandeville maintains that true "Innocence and Honesty" are most generally characteristics of the "poor, silly Country People," "poor" and "silly" mimic the patronizing of country folk by the urban gentility. Mandeville refuses to patronize the laboring poor when he tartly asserts that it "is not Compliments we want" of the "Labourious Poor" but rather "their Work and Assiduity" (I, 270). Furthermore, it will not be the charity schools that will prevent crime through moral education because those poor parents who care about their children will keep their children off the streets at night and will make their children "do something or other that turns to Profit" (I, 270). There is some historical evidence to suggest, as we have noted earlier, that the rapid growth of London and the increase of urban poor was caused by the Financial Revolution and by the need of country gentry to be near the center of eighteenth-century English commerce. The urban middle class's support of charity schools to control crime is a pathetically puny attempt to cope with the symptom rather than the cause. To control the children of the urban poor by educating them just enough—but not too much—to be servants and obsequious clerks is rank hypocrisy. It would remain for Charles Dickens to show how such efforts could backfire in his portrayal of the 'umble Uriah Heep. Mandeville's satire, however, goes directly to the heart of the matter.

If the urban middle class opts for the affluence which is the result of London's rapid growth, then it will have to accept the consequences of the "enormous Crimes" which are the result of density of population: "One of the greatest Inconveniences of such vast over-grown Cities as *London* or *Paris*" is that they harbor "Rogues and Villains as Granaries do Vermin" (I, 272). Just as a sociologist would see the charity schools as an urban phenomenon designed by the middle class to cope with the large masses of children of the urban poor, so Mandeville also sees the growth of crime as stemming from the complexity of urbanization itself: "It is manifest then that many different Causes concur, and several scarce avoidable Evils contribute to the Misfortune of being pester'd with Pilferers, Thieves, and Robbers, which all Countries ever were and ever will be, more or less, in and near considerable Towns, more especially vast and overgrown Cities" (I, 274). Mandeville goes to great pains to show the middle-class origins of the charity school in a kind of mock case-history of how such a school is founded. They are started by not very successful "young Shop-keepers." In contrast, "Men of Worth, who live in Splendor" and "thriving" business men are "seldom seen among" the organizers of the charity schools. Mandeville was to write in 1724 a sarcastic dedication to the "Gentlemen" of the Societies for the Reformation of Manners,"[14] and he mingles them with the charity-school supporters when he refers to those "diminutive Patriots" who enlist the support of "stanch Churchmen" and "sly Sinners" at meetings where they declaim on "the Misery of the Times occasion'd by Atheism and Profaneness" (I, 279). The underlying motive for many who attend is "Prudentially to increase their Trade and get Acquaintance." The "Governours" of this school once it is organized are "the midling People" (I, 280), and their real motive for serving in such a capacity is for the sheer "Pleasure in Ruling over any thing"—particularly over "the Schoolmaster himself!" (I, 280-81). In a really stunning insight into the structure of his society Mandeville notes that the middle-class supporters of the charity school take particular pleasure in their vicarious ownership of 'Our Parish Church' and 'Our Charity Children' (I, 282): "In all this *there is a Shadow of Property*" [italics mine] that tickles every body that has a Right to make use of the Words, but more especially those who actually contribute and had a

great Hand in advancing the pious Work" (I, 282). Here Mandeville himself is looking at the genteel ideology of his own society and observing that it is grounded in possessive individualism. Macpherson's thesis could hardly be more effectively vindicated.

When Mandeville follows with a relatively straightforward analysis of how charity schools are a smokescreen which cover up a failure to solve the problem of the poor, there is little ambiguity in what he is saying. But when he writes that charity schools interfere with the market economy by incapacitating the children of the poor for "down right Labour" and that the "Proportion as to Numbers in every Trade finds it self, and is never better kept than when no body meddles or interferes with it" (I, 299-300), we are wrong to infer that Mandeville believed in a laissezfaire economy (a nineteenth-century development).[15] On the contrary Mandeville sees the charity schools as an ill-conceived, unilateral attempt which educates the children of the poor for jobs which are not necessarily in any real demand. Within the context of this essay Mandeville's argument is for continuation of a planned economy—the kind Walpole was running—and, indeed, he later writes that "the Conveniency of the Publick ought ever to be the Publick Care" (I, 319) and that it is "the Business of the Publick to supply the Defects of the Society, and take that in hand first which is most neglected by private Persons" (I, 321). When read within the context of the eighteenth-century debate over the problem of the laboring poor, Mandeville's essay is not cynical. In fact his proposal to solve the problem of the poor by keeping them employed was a radical one as he himself suggests: "The Fearful and Cautious People that are ever Jealous of their Liberty, I know will cry out, that where the Multitudes I speak of *should be kept in constant Pay* [italics mine], Property and Privileges would be precarious" (I, 319).[16]

Mandeville's attack on charity as a form of self-delusion founded on the passion of a pejorative kind of pity brought the economic debate over the problem of the poor into the center of literary consciousness. Fielding's concern with the true meaning of charity, Goldsmith's satire on universal benevolence, and Johnson's refusal to accept the status quo of the poor, all reflect different aspects of the same humanitarian concern. After Mandeville, no serious writer could employ "charity" without testing the meaning of the term in the realm of experience. For Fielding "charity" was a genuine virtue and not a mere empty word, but only empirically in the fictitious world of *Tom Jones* is the term reinvested with its true significance.

The most complex treatment of "Charity" and "Pity" occurs in the poetry of William Blake. Blake found pity in the form of organized, institutionalized charity to be perversely depersonalized, a "Human Abstract," and hence a way for individuals to avoid personal commitment. Jean Hagstrum finds that Blake is "one of the most unrelenting satirists of Pity and Love that England ever produced" and that in "an analysis of social 'virtues' worthy of Bernard Mandeville, Blake perceives that Urizenic pity arises from social poverty, Urizenic mercy from a lack of equal happiness."[17] It is not, I believe, by mere coincidence that Mandeville and Blake are compared. There is every reason to believe that Blake had read Isaac Watts' *Essay on Charity-Schools* (1728) which, as Vivian de Sola Pinto has shown, reflects a "characteristic dualism of thought" in that Watts sympathizes on the one hand with the children of the poor while defending on the other hand the social structure which assumed the status quo of the poor.[18] Nowhere in eighteenth-century literature is the social compromise with all its limitations so graphically shown as in the concessions which Watts makes to charity school opponents. Watts' original 1727 sermon which was expanded into the 1728 *Essay* was in fact specifically in answer to Mandeville's attack on the charity schools. Both Mandeville and Blake in his "Holy Thursday" poems are indicting the same genteel compromise, and Mandeville's influence en Blake is more complex than one of direct influence. Rather, Watts, forced by Mandeville to state explicitly all of the unstated assumptions behind the charity-school movement, revealed to Blake all of the hypocrisies of these assumptions. Mandeville's "Essay on Charity and Charity-Schools" and Watts' reply to Mandeville form a kind of eminent domain, the reverberations of which form the texture of Blake's poetic analysis of "Charity" and "Pity." Mandeville's clarification of the issues involved in these terms—even if written within the limits of the "single Vision"—must have served as a valuable catalyst to Blake's poetic imagination.

"HONOR"—THE USEFULNESS OF CHRISTIANITY IN WAR

Rachel Trickett has shown how honor "had been the ideal of a chivalric military society" and how it was being replaced in the eighteenth century by the ideal of honesty which "epitomized all that was best in a world where peace and prosperity in a well-ordered state was the common aim."[19] The attempt to redefine an aristocratic mode of secular manners by integrating it with middle-class morality was one of the professed aims of Richard Steele, and such a social compromise may be traced in his work from *The Christian Hero* to *The Conscious Lovers* (1722). Such a compromise at its worst tended toward the genteel, toward a reduction of complex tensions to a simplistic middle-class solution. Swift's contribution to the reformation of manners, *A Project for the Advancement of Religion and the Reformation of Manners* (1709), need not be interpreted as anything but straightforward, but his method of proceeding towards such a reformation is highly original. Instead of a hypocrisy which allows one to profess Christianity while expediently living by a set of secular values, Swift proposes a hypocrisy whereby nonbelievers both profess *and* practice Christian values. As Claude Rawson observes, whereas "Fielding and Chesterfield both seek to narrow the gap between morals and manners, Swift makes use of a logic which inexorably widens this gap until the whole social basis of the compromise is reduced to nullity. In an absolute morality, there can be no chartable point where gallantry ends and infamy begins."[20]

While Addison and Steele continued to rework honor in genteel terms, Mandeville proceeded to destroy its use in such a sense so that it could not easily be used as a reifying concept. **"Remark (C)"** with its conclusion that "Good Manners have nothing to do with Virtue or Religion," directly challenges the aims of the *Societies for the Reformation of Manners*. For Mandeville, like Swift, there can be no real compromise between absolute morality and gallantry: "Virtue bids us subdue, but good Breeding only requires we should hide our Appetites" (I, 72). Mandeville's satiric strategy here as elsewhere in his works is to cite illustrations of his shocking paradoxes that are "low" in subject matter. This technique of burlesque which gave his enemies the opportunity to call him "coarse" is a form of proof in its appeal to everyday experience bluntly and concretely described as well as a means of satirizing genteel insipidity which by an implicit censorship of language and content devitalizes literary discourse. Thus Mandeville demonstrates his distinction between virtue and good breeding by a ludicrous contrast between the "fashionable Gentleman" and the "brutish Fellow" who both have violent inclinations to a woman. The "fine Gentleman" by virtue of being "well bred" arrives at his goal of sexual consummation through the courtship ritual culminating in marriage. If he is "hotter than Goats or Bulls," as soon as the wedding is over he may have at it and "sate and fatigue himself with Joy and Ecstacies of Pleasure" (I, 73). Better yet, he will even have a cheering section in that "all the Women and above Nine in Ten of the Men are of his side" (I, 74). Mandeville's marvelous Rabelaisian exuberance here drives home his point that often polite marriages grounded only on sexual desire, although civilly correct, are merely a form of what Defoe termed "conjugal whoredom."

For Mandeville "Manners and good Breeding" may be merely another means of "flattering the Pride and Selfishness of others, and concealing our own with Judgment and Dexterity" (I, 77), and his habit of asserting such theses absolutely rather than conditionally is another satiric technique which serves to vex the opposition. One can trace throughout the remainder of **"Remark (C)"** Mandeville's incremental repetition of "well-bred Man" until it becomes a thoroughly pejorative phrase. The undermining of honor continues in **"Remark (R)"** when Mandeville writes: "Honour in its Figurative Sense is a Chimera without Truth or Being, an Invention of Moralists and Politicians, and signifies a certain Principle of Virtue not related to Religion, found in some Men that keeps 'em close to their Duty and Engagements whatever they be . . ." (I, 198). In this prose remark it is "Man of Honour" that becomes a key pejorative phrase. Mandeville exploits the animal analogy by comparing the aggressive behavior of men of honor to bulls and cooks in heat. Since modern man's real underlying ethic is determined by the pragmatic ethic of his society, Mandeville chooses to redefine honor as a useful social code based upon pride and fear. Though morally wrong, duelling makes men watch their manners! Mandeville knew very well of the campaign by Collier, Steele, and the Societies for the Reformation of Manners against duelling. His comic reversal which makes duelling useful in this reform can only be read satirically as an attack against the genteel compromise between morals and manners: "If every ill-bred Fellow might use what Language he pleas'd, without being called to an Account for it, *all Conversation would be spoil'd*" [italics mine] (I, 219).

The genteel attempt to have the best of both possible worlds on watered-down terms will not do for Mandeville. He insists that "modern honour" be recognized as a purely secular code and that to do otherwise is another form of self-delusion. After writing that the "*only* thing of weight that can be said against modern Honour is, that it is directly opposite to Religion" [italics mine], Mandeville lists the differences:

> Religion commands you to leave all Revenge to God, Honour bids you trust your Revenge to no body but your self, even where the Law would do it for you: *Religion plainly forbids Murther, Honour openly justifies it* [italics mine]: Religion bids you not shed Blood upon any account whatever: Honour bids you fight for the least Trifle: Religion is built on Humility, and Honour upon Pride: How to reconcile them must be left to wiser Heads than mine.

> (I, 221-22)

It should be clear from this passage that Mandeville's defense of duelling is a mock one and that in reality he condemns it as "Murther." Louis Landa has noted the similarity between Mandeville and Swift who was "contemptuous" of the "whole 'Cant of Honour'" and of efforts by Shaftesbury and others to "construct an independent or secular ethics" and to make a distinction "between true and false honour."[21] It is enough that a satirist such as Mandeville demonstrate through his paradoxes the discrepancy between secular manners and Christian morality.

Why then did Mandeville feel compelled to write his last and perhaps most neglected treatise, ***An Enquiry into the Origin of Honour, and The Usefulness of Christianity in War*** (London, 1732)? I believe that the answer is in Francis Hutcheson's refusal to accept the implications of Mandeville's satire and in fact to reify honor as a kind of moral sense in a work which cited ***The Fable of the Bees*** as an adversary in the title: *An Inquiry into the Original of our Ideas of Beauty and Virtue; in Two Treatises. In which the Principles of . . . Shaftesbury are . . . defended against . . . the Fable of the Bees* (London, 1725). Hutcheson was later to claim in 1730 that in his *Inquiry* he had provided ample "Proofs and Illustrations of a *moral Sense,* and a *Sense of Honour.*" But other than mere repetition and assertion, Hutcheson's primary proof is a circular argument that the "Determination to love *Honour,* presupposes a *Sense* of moral *Virtue,* both in the Persons who confer the Honour, and in him who pursues it" and that we possess "by NATURE, a moral Sense of virtue . . . antecedent to *Honour*" (pp. 225, 231). Hutcheson's treatment of honor explains the opening of the third dialogue in Berkeley's *Alciphron* which deals with honor for several pages

even though the dialogue is supposed to be directed towards Shaftesbury. Berkeley clears away the debris on honor created by Shaftesbury's chief disciple before he directs himself to his main target. Alciphron begins the dialogue with a definition of honor as "a noble unpolluted source of virtue, without the least mixture of fear, interest, or superstition" which is to be "found among persons of rank and breeding." When Euphranor asks if "a man of honour is a warm man, or an enthusiast," Alciphron is reduced to protesting that the "high sense of honour which distinguished the fine gentleman" was a "thing rather to be felt than explained." Unfair as Berkeley may be to both Mandeville and Shaftesbury in *Alciphron,* there can be no doubt that he sees the emphasis on "modern honour" to be pretentiously genteel.

Mandeville's ***Origin of Honour*** once and for all seeks to discredit the compromise between honor and Christian morality. Mandeville's mock defense of duelling as an aid to manners is now extended to an ironic defense of the "usefulness" of Christianity in fighting a war. As we have shown earlier in **The Fable** Mandeville had reversed the traditional relationship of ethics and politics to show that in the modern world politics and the market govern the ethical behavior of both individuals and nations. Now the pattern of reversal is repeated to claim that politicians use a "Gothic" notion of Christian honor—a contradiction in terms—to encourage soldiers to fight well in battle.

According to Jeremy Collier in his essay "Upon Duelling" duelling was not characteristic of classical civilization nor of primitive Christian culture, but was derived from the Lombards, Saxons, and Normans. This thesis was developed far more elaborately in John Cockburn's *The History and Examination of Duels, Shewing Their Heinous Nature and the Necessity of Suppressing them* (London, 1720), a book owned by Henry Fielding and to which Fielding was probably indebted in his treatment of duelling, war, and the spectrum of Gothic honor in *Tom Jones.* Cockburn identifies the custom of duelling with the Gothic custom of trial by ordeal and with the encouragement of this custom by the Church of Rome. This equation of Gothic honor with Popery forms a large part of Mandeville's ***Origin of Honor.*** Rather than merely showing the incompatibility between war and Christian virtue, Mandeville argues that by means of army chaplains quoting from the Old Testament rather than the New, Christian doctrine is useful in preparing soldiers to fight courageously in battle. Thus under the banner of "Honour" Christianity in the new society is converted from an end to a means. With this *reductio ad absurdum* Mandeville's final corrosive treatise on honor posed a formidable barrier to any future attempt to fuse honor and Christian value.

It is true that skepticism about honor was pervasive in the eighteenth century and much earlier, Falstaff's speech being a good case in point. But Mandeville's **Fable** and **Origin of Honour** were so vigorously written and so shocking to the age, that every major writer was forced to find the answers to the questions which he put to posterity. It is not within the province of this essay to show, for example, how profoundly Mandeville influenced Fielding. When, however, the Lieutenant in *Tom Jones* exclaims, "I love my religion very well, but I love my honour more" (Bk. VII, ch. xiii), it is hard to see how Fielding could not have been painfully aware of Mandeville's **Origin of Honour.** If *Tom Jones* begins with the question of what is true honor, it ends by scrapping honor altogether and replacing it with Christian goodness. One can make a strong case for one of the differences between *Tom Jones* and *Amelia* being Fielding's increasing awareness that it was a Mandevillian world, and no longer possessing the resilience to transcend that realization in style and artistic choice.[22]

It is here that we confront a complex difficulty in our understanding of Mandeville. To his contemporaries he was "man-devil," a cynical disciple of Hobbes. In answering Mandeville such writers as Fielding and Pope were forced to reinvest stale terms with earned meanings and to clarify their own ideas in significant literary ways. But if my interpretation of Mandeville's satire is valid, we are obligated as twentieth-century readers to see how much in common Mandeville had with some of his illustrious adversaries in attacking the same satiric targets. It seems to me that his contemporaries owed much to Mandeville in his refusal to allow language and experience to be censored and devitalized by the Societies for the Reformation of Manners, by the genteel "Christian Hero" ideology of Addison and Steele, and by the reifying deistic optimism of Shaftesbury and Hutcheson. Mandeville deliberately sought out key phrases that carried the semantic burden of these genteel ideologies and then proceeded to deflate their flatulences by mimicry, low burlesque, and shockingly asserted paradoxes. Insofar as Mandeville put his contemporaries on their mettle by forcing them to redefine, and thus earn the right to use, some of these key-words, his adversary role in the foreground of eighteenth-century English literature is a positive gain. But I should like to hope that ultimately Mandeville's relevance as a perceptive satirist of the genteel compromise and of the contradictions and hypocrisies of our own "liberal" compromise, shared in a common historical heritage, will allow his work to be recognized as a substantial achievement in its own right.

Notes

1. *Swift and the Satirist's Art* (Chicago: Univ. of Chicago Press, 1963), p. 25. See Phillip Harth, "The Satiric Purpose of *The Fable of the Bees,*" *ECS,* 2 (1968-69), 321-40; and "Introduction," *The Fable of the Bees,* ed. Harth (Harmondsworth, Middlesex, England: Penguin Books Ltd.), pp. 7-46. All references to *The Fable of the Bees* in this essay will be by volume and page number in the text to *The Fable of the Bees,* ed. F. B. Kaye (Oxford: Clarendon Press, 1924).

2. Elias J. Chiasson, "Bernard Mandeville: A Reappraisal," *PQ,* 49 (1970), 504.

3. *Bolingbroke and His Circle: The Politics of Nostalgia* (Cambridge: Harvard Univ. Press, 1968), p. 201,

p. 303, fn. 40. The phrase is that of P. G. M. Dickson, *The Financial Revolution in England: A Study in the Development of Public Finance* (London: Macmillan, 1967).

4. "Ideas of Nature," *TLS,* Dec. 4, 1970, p. 1421.

5. Long ago F. W. Bateson interpreted Swift's "Description of the Morning" as an implicit satire on "the *laissez-faire* individualism of urban capitalism" implying the Christian point "that we are members of one another." See *English Poetry: An Introduction* (London, 1950), p. 177. I hope to show that the phrase "possessive individualism" is both more appropriate and historically accurate than Bateson's phrase. The urban nature of this capitalism has been ably discussed by John Loftis, *Comedy and Society from Congreve to Fielding* (Stanford: Stanford Univ. Press, 1959), pp. 1-19. Swift's poem appeared in *The Tatler,* a periodical slanted towards the middle and upper classes most involved in the development of urban capitalism. As is well known, *The Spectator* attempted to effect a social compromise by improving the morals of the aristocracy and the gentry while refining the manners of a growing middle class. In its level of style, its didacticism of purpose, and its eschewal of potentially risqué or coarse subject matter and language, *The Spectator* tends in retrospect to be genteel. That is to say, it self-consciously simplifies the complexity of eigtheenth-century experience by means of a class-consciousness so that its imagination is limited by that consciousness. Addison and Steele tended to romanticize the monied interest and to emphasize only the affirmative aspects of the Financial Revolution. Mandeville satirizes this genteel consciousness by a deliberately coarse style and by stressing the negative aspects of the Financial Revolution. F. B. Kaye was struck by the literary resemblances between *The Spectator,* No. 69 and a passage in Mandeville's *The Fable of the Bees* but then noted that Addison, unlike Mandeville, had "made little attempt to deduce economic principles" (I, 357, n. 1). I believe that Mandeville's satire is directed towards the negative aspects of this social compromise including both its political and economic implications insofar as it is based upon an optimistic view of human nature.

6. I believe that Mandeville's "State of Nature" is a deliberately loaded phrase used for satirical effects, that Macpherson is the first to show an almost identical usage in Hobbes's use of the term, and that Macpherson's critics have tended to react to Macpherson's interpretation too narrowly in their interpretation of this term. If we admit that Hobbes was satirizing a growing possessive individualism in his society without necessarily providing a justification for it, as Macpherson seems to insist, Macpherson's interpretation of "State of Nature" is still valid. For examples of the spectrum of critical opinion about Macpherson's book see Christopher Hill's review, *Past & Present,* No. 24 (1963), 86-9,

and Sir Isaiah Berlin's critique, *Political Quarterly*, 35 (1964), 444-68.

7. *Vice and Luxury Publick Mischiefs*: or, *Remarks on a Book intituled, the Fable of the Bees* (London, 1724), p. 30. Dennis interprets Mandeville's usage much as Macpherson has interpreted Hobbes's usage as a logical rather than historical condition. As literary critics, we may see *both* meanings as simultaneously present in Hobbes's and Mandeville's "State of Nature."

8. See John Locke, *Two Treatises of Government*, ed. Peter Laslett, 2nd ed. (Cambridge: Cambridge Univ. Press, 1967), Bk. II, ch. ii, "Of the State of Nature," pp. 287-96. For an essay which seems to me to be directed against Macpherson's interpretation of Locke although Macpherson is never mentioned, see Hans Aarsleff, "The State of Nature and the Nature of Man in Locke," *John Locke: Problems and Perspectives*, ed. John W. Yolton (Cambridge Univ. Press, 1969), pp. 99-136. I find, like David Hume, considerable "ambiguity and circumlocution" in Locke in spite of Aarsleff's argument to the contrary.

9. *The Palace of Wisdom: Studies in Order and Energy From Dryden to Blake* (New York, 1964), p. 114.

10. *The Spectator*, ed. Donald F. Bond (Oxford: Clarendon Press, 1965), I, 296, fn. 2.

11. "The Other Face of Mercantilism," *Trans. Royal Hist. Soc.*, 5th Ser., 9 (1959), 81-101. See also David Owen, *English Philanthropy* (London: Oxford Univ. Press, 1965); and Charles Wilson, *Mercantilism*, Hist. Assoc. Pamph., No. 37 (London, 1958).

12. See M. G. Jones, *The Charity School Movement: A Study of Eighteenth-Century Puritanism in Action* (Cambridge: Cambridge Univ. Press, 1938), p. 113. This valuable study is essential for any real understanding of Mandeville's "Essay on Charity," but Miss Jones treats the "Essay" apart from *The Fable* and yokes it with the "Cato" attack on charity schools (*The British Journal*, June 15, 1723) as a two-prong Whig attack (p. 123). This is sheer conjecture and requires considerably more support to be accepted as valid.

13. In *The Guardian*, No. 79, 1713, Steele had deplored the fact that "only the middle kind of people" seemed to be concerned with teaching the young or with charity. See also Dorothy Marshall, *English People in the Eighteenth Century* (London, 1956), p. 161. Cultural historians now seem generally agreed that "middle-class" is an attitude of mind rather than a rigidly economically or quantitatively defined category. For a very commonsensical discussion of the use of "class" in historiography see the preface to E. P. Thompson, *The Making of the English Working Class* (Harmondsworth, Middlesex, England: Penguin Books Ltd., 1968), pp. 9-12.

14. *A Modest Defence of Public Stews* (London, 1724).

15. See Nathan Rosenberg, "Mandeville and Laissez-Faire," *JHI*, 24 (1963), 183-96. The late Jacob Viner rightly insisted that Mandeville, like the other major satirists of the century, accepted the "then-existing economic structure of society." "Satire and Economics in the Augustan Age of Satire," *The Augustan Milieu: Essays presented to Louis A. Landa*, ed. Henry Knight Miller, Eric Rothstein, G. S. Rousseau (Oxford: Clarendon Press, 1970), p. 95.

16. It is this proposal which for me distinguishes Mandeville from Addison and Steele and gives his "Essay on Charity Schools" an almost visionary quality.

17. "'The Wrath of the Lamb': A Study of William Blake's Conversions," *From Sensibility to Romanticism*, ed. Frederick W. Hilles and Harold Bloom (New York: Oxford Univ. Press, 1965), p. 316; and *William Blake: Poet and Painter* (Chicago: Univ. of Chicago Press, 1964), p. 84.

18. "Isaac Watts and William Blake," *RES*, 20 (1944), 214-23.

19. *The Honest Muse* (Oxford: Clarendon Press, 1967), p. 118.

20. "The Character of Swift's Satire," *Swift*, ed. C. J. Rawson, "Focus" series (London: Sphere Books, 1971), p. 44.

21. Jonathan Swift, *Irish Tracts 1720-1723 and Sermons*, ed. Herbert Davis with Introd. and Notes by Louis Landa (Oxford: Basil Blackwell, 1948), pp. 114-16.

22. For analysis of Mandeville's impact on Fielding's art see Glenn Hatfield, *Henry Fielding and the Language of Irony* (Chicago: Univ. of Chicago Press, 1969) and C. H. K. Bevan, "The Unity of Fielding's *Amelia*," *Renaissance and Modern Studies*, 14 (1970), 90-110. Both of these studies tend to accept a pejorative view of Mandeville even while recognizing his considerable influence as an adversary on Fielding.

Louis Schneider (essay date 1987)

SOURCE: Schneider, Louis. "Bernard Mandeville: Observations in Lieu of a Biography." In *Paradox and Society: The Work of Bernard Mandeville*. New Brunswick, N.J.: Transaction Books, 1987, pp. 29-66.

[*In the following essay, Schneider, provides an outline of Mandeville's life, thought, and literary activity.*]

Material for a life of Mandeville is scant and a biography of him of any considerable scale is not feasible. One may make certain inferences about his character or personal traits from his work. Although this is a somewhat precarious enterprise, it is not entirely unrewarding. The effort to discover something of his character also will suggest intellectual features that help toward the construction of a portrait of the man and thinker.

Kaye has provided a brief sketch of Mandeville's life.[1] From this it appears that Mandeville was baptized in Rotterdam on the 20th of November, 1670. He attended the Erasmian School in Rotterdam and subsequently studied at the University of Leyden, obtaining the degree of Doctor of Medicine from that institution toward the end of March of 1691. He took up the branch of medicine in which his father had been engaged, specializing in nervous and gastric disorders. He may have toured Europe. He did visit London and was apparently taken with England generally, where he settled and married in the late 1690s. Kaye records that he "died at Hackney, Sunday morning, 21 January 1732, in his sixty-third year, possibly of the prevalent influenza."[2]

Somewhat more than this bare recital is provided by Kaye but not much that we can be sure of, although it does appear likely that Mandeville was at any rate a reasonably successful physician and it is certain that he was a successful and very well known writer. It is also easy to believe from his writings that he was "neither a saint in his life nor a hermit in his diet."[3] But we must soon turn to his time and indeed to his writings to learn substantially more about him.

The years of Mandeville's maturity were years of economic and social ferment. London, inevitably of great interest to Mandeville, had been growing vastly. About one-quarter of the way into the new eighteenth century, Defoe was writing enthusiastically about the city, claiming to see "such a prodigy of buildings" that nothing ever equalled it except the Rome of Trajan—which, Defoe said, had 6.8 million inhabitants. Defoe estimated the population of London in his day at a million and one-half and wrote of "the present and past greatness of this mighty city." He even seemed to taken pride in the number of London's prisons, "perhaps as many as in all the capital cities of Europe put together."[4] He greatly overestimated the city's population, which was then probably in the neighborhood of one-half million.[5] But it is evident that London was a large and bustling place—and in process of becoming larger still. Moreover, towns generally were growing, and some twenty percent of the English population lived in towns by the early eighteenth century.[6]

London itself, particularly in the earlier part of the century in which Mandeville's literary activity falls, constituted a world in which, in the words of one writer, "violence, disorder and brutal punishment . . . were still part of the normal background of life."[7] Mandeville looked upon this scene of crime and disease and dirt, and he commented on the dirt in particular in the Preface to *The Fable.* He argues that people could well wish the streets of London considerably cleaner, but "when once they come to consider that what offends them is the result of the plenty, great traffic and opulency of that mighty city, if they have any concern in its welfare, they will hardly ever wish to see the streets of it less dirty."[8] This statement is very much in accordance with what Mandeville tells us in the same Preface is the main design of *The Fable,* which is to show "the impossibility of enjoying all the most elegant comforts of life that are to be met with in an industrious, wealthy and powerful nation and at the same time be blessed with all the virtue and innocence that can be wished for in a golden age." Mandeville wishes to expose "the unreasonableness and folly of those that, desirous of being an opulent and flourishing people, and wonderfully greedy after all the benefits they can receive as such are yet always murmuring at and exclaiming against those vices and inconveniences that from the beginning of the world to the present day have been inseparable from all kingdoms and states ever were famed for strength, riches and politeness at the same time."[9]

Mandeville was always intrigued with economic development. Important new economic organizations were arising in England. The Bank of England came into being in 1694, modelled on the Bank of Amsterdam and serving to fund the national debt. It is of possible significance as background for the motivation of Mandeville's own move to England that an element in the acceptance of the Bank was the popularization among the English of the Dutch and Dutch institutions that came with the accession of William III.[10] The South Sea Company was incorporated in 1711. The inflation of the value of its stock occasioned a great panic in the stock market in 1720 and even generated some revulsion against commerce.[11] The emergence of the East India Company as a single, united company in 1709 meant the presence of a third imposing economic enterprise. The dates indicated (1709, 1711, 1720), except for 1694, are at the very center of Mandeville's literary life.

Economic activity in the world of the early eighteenth century posed hard moral questions. The moralist was faced with a dilemma about vice that Mandeville was to explore thoroughly in his own fashion. "Vice" unequivocally brought economic benefits. English prosperity at this time was intimately related to increase of consumption. But that increase meant increase in "vice." The imbibing of more alcohol meant more drunkenness. Pride and vanity (prime manifestations of vice in Mandeville's lexicon) motivated the purchase of fine items of clothing and choice housing and furniture.[12] Less vice, less prosperity. More prosperity, more vice. (It was in *The Fable of the Bees* that Mandeville suggested his much controverted definition of vice itself.)[13] A man like Defoe might have moral qualms about a vice that was nevertheless economically valuable, but, along with Petty, Barbon, North, Carey, Mandeville, and Berkeley, he was still in fear of lowering of employment because of underconsumption.[14] (Yet vice might also mean such large demand for foreign goods as would adversely influence the balance of trade.)

To a new financial world, and a world in which vice and luxury posed serious moral problems that were being discussed in new terms, one must add a world otherwise involved in considerable social change. Old, simple demarcations of social classes or portions thereof were being confused or baffled. There was considerable social mobility. The professions were growing rapidly. Mercantile activity was making its contribution to changing older class situations. Kramnick's book, *Bolingbroke and his Circle*, pursues the thesis that Bolingbroke (1678-1751) and with him men like the great Augustan literary figures Swift and Pope saw in the England of their time a society changing for the worse as commerce and money engendered corruption. In the view of men such as these, stockjobbing and vulgarity and the disturbance of an ancient system of social rank were all too evident and the country was degenerating. The landed gentry suffered heavily from taxation levied to finance the nearly twenty years of war under William and Anne. The small gentry, indeed, ironically, exhausted themselves financially in "helping to create the class that would dispossess them," for they paid the taxes that helped the moneyed to take their land away from them. Not only did the gentry feel they were being "victimized by a conspiracy of commerce and government," but they also responded with a sense of being impersonally thrust about by a novel financial order featuring mysteries of public credit and paper transactions.[15]

The political leader Robert Walpole stood for corruption, and particularly financial corruption, in the eyes of critics like Bolingbroke and Swift (although apparently Bolingbroke himself allowed *some* measure of corruption to be needed "to maintain subordination and to carry on even good government"). Despicable new projects, unappreciative of the old and committed to novelty and immorality were increasing disconcertingly. Or so it seemed to the Bolingbrokes, the Swifts, the Popes, the John Gays, and others like them, who spoke for aristocratic and humanist and nostalgic Tory values. Mandeville is seen by Kramnick as spokesman for the new commercial and financial society. His *Fable of the Bees* appeared when Tory yearning for the social simplicities and stabilities that the Tories conceived existed before 1688 had expressed itself in demand for sumptuary laws "to curb the luxury they alleged corrupted public manners and extinguished public spirit;" and Mandeville's work undermined the Tory position. Kramnick even writes of Mandeville's "great attack on the Tory position."[16]

In line with his thesis, Kramnick simplifies somewhat. It may be questioned whether he does justice to the tensions in Mandeville's thought: tensions between "virtue" and "vice" in particular; and whether it is not too facile to say that Mandeville flatly saw "nothing wrong" with the corruption of his day that ran through various occupations. Mandeville does have a deep vein of sympathy for a society and economy that pursue worldly goods by worldly methods. Like Pierre Bayle (among others) before him, he insists that Gospel precepts make one sort of demand on humans in society while the exigencies of worldly welfare make a very different sort of demand. In this sense, he may be interpreted to be on the side of "vice" and worldliness, and we have here a powerful strain in his thought. But it is not always clear that he is really quite out of sympathy with "virtue," and some of the poignancy of effect of his work may be traceable to uneasy conscience on his part about that very corruption and hypocrisy that he does indeed regard as inseparable from a society powered by ambition and the desire for prosperity.[17] Kramnick's views have been challenged on other grounds, as on the ground that while his sense of Mandeville as a Court Whig, a defender of Walpole and his methods, has something to be said for it, it is still too narrow and limited to fit Mandeville's idiosyncratic political stance.[18] But Kramnick's "location" of Mandeville is broadly helpful. If we must see Mandeville's attitude toward the new economic order as rather more nuanced and subtle than Kramnick appears to do, there is still no denying that Mandeville was far indeed from repudiating that order.[19] It is most suggestive that John Gay, in the second volume of his *Fables* (1738), should have written an item contrasting provocatively with Mandeville's "The Grumbling Hive," the doggerel that precedes **The Fable**. The bees in Mandeville's grumbling hive individually pursued "vice" assiduously and achieved public prosperity:

> "Thus every Part was full of Vice,
> Yet the whole Mass a Paradise."[20]

In his own fable, "The Regenerate Bees," Gay wrote:

> "Know that, in selfish ends pursuing,
> You scramble for the public ruin."[21]

The opposition could hardly be more plain. But if Mandeville was appreciably partial to the new economic order and its ineluctable propensity toward "vice," there was another way in which he was much like those who had greater nostalgia than he for aristocratic, so-called Tory values and an older society and economy. Jacob Viner gives us a pertinent account of the conservatism generally shown by the Augustan satirists. After 1660, the civil strife of earlier decades became, in Viner's words, "an unpleasant memory," and the quality of this memory served to strengthen opposition to change and to criticism of current institutions. The focus here is somewhat different from that in Kramnick's work. In the Augustan age of satire, the satiric lance was not employed to get concerted action against the poverty and wretchedness of the masses. In literate and articulate England for the century or so beginning in 1660, there was no serious push toward modification of fundamental social institutions by that sort of social reform that seeks to recast those institutions and support major legislative change to this end. There might be quarrels significant enough in themselves, such as those between spokesman for aristocracy and spokesman for popular commercial and financial values, but on the whole English satire was overwhelmingly conservative in tendency before the nineteenth century.

Some special reservations may be made for Swift, on the subject of English-Irish relations and aspects of the Irish economy, but Swift hardly qualifies in general as a social reformer. There was concern with the moral reform of individuals. There was the presumption that society would be reformed through the reform of individuals. But criticisms, on moral, intellectual, religious, or other fronts, of the managers of existing institutions were not matched by criticism of institutions themselves. Wickedness was conceived essentially to emanate from humans, not from the social structures they had reared that might embody or "freeze" a variety of evils. (In France, at the same time, as Viner suggests, there was much criticism of institutions, just as there was later in nineteenth-century England.)[22] Mandeville himself was by no means a naive sort of sociologist, but at least in not launching an attack upon existing institutions with an eye to changing them fundamentally, he was at one with the Augustan satirists with whom he would have differed considerably on other matters. Rather than attacking the economic and social system that he knew, he twitted those who prospered under it while they presumed that they operated on fine moral principles.

There is certainly room for divergent views of Mandeville on a number of matters, but one of the things that is very clear about him is that he was no supporter of major social upheaval. His *Free Thoughts* advocated tolerance in religion (within limits). He was sympathetic with a king of Dutch origin and in favor of the Protestant succession. If he did indeed write *The Mischiefs that Ought Justly to be Apprehended from a Whig Government* (1714), as both Kaye and a more recent student, H. T. Dickinson, have inclined to think,[23] then it is worth noting that we find in it expectable doctrine stressing the obligation of kings to their subjects and expectable Mandevillean dislike of "Popery." Mandeville's "mercantilism" was not of a rigid variety and he was in economic matters generally "progressive," as we know. But to think of him as on the order of a social revolutionary of the left is entirely out of the question. His attitude toward the laboring poor, which we shall consider, would alone constitute a serious disqualification in this regard. He certainly did not want to upset the class order.[24] Further comment on his conservatism (which should not be exaggerated) is reserved for a later point. In the interim, our knowledge of Mandeville may be advanced by consideration of his writings, an initial overview of which will provide something of an introduction to his distinctive outlook.

MANDEVILLE'S WRITINGS

A middle class nourished on mercantile activity was important in the new social scene of Mandeville's maturity. Readers of middle class origin have been said to have been "the author's main support" in the eighteenth century.[25] According to Watt's analysis of the reading public early in the century, such a public did in fact exist among tradesmen, shopkeepers, favored apprentices, and indoor servants; and with accession to these categories from groups engaged in commerce and manufacturing, Watt suggests, the middle class as a whole may have come into "a dominating position" in the reading public at large for the first time.[26] Recent research, it is true, has cast some doubt on facile generalization about various connections of "the middle class" (the term itself is not altogether unambiguous) and eighteenth-century literature (especially as regards the novel).[27] Yet a person who wrote as

Mandeville did was bound to have a certain advantage to make an appeal to persons with sharp understanding even if with no imposing classical education. Mandeville offered "plain talk." Even the deeper aspects of his thought were presented with a certain captivating lucidity. Dobrée states of Mandeville and Shaftesbury that "they were understandable." And they addressed themselves to questions that were plausibly important, at least, to significant sectors of a "middle class" audience. "What was the basis of morality? What was the nature of conscience?"[28]

Mandeville's publications came to an end in 1732, somewhat before the time of really marked increase in English publishing activity.[29] This alone certainly suggests limitations on how far down into the class structure his writing penetrated, but it retained the advantage of plainness and cogency that has just been suggested and it clearly received very considerable attention from persons in some sense qualified to judge it. From 1723 on, the success and notoriety of *The Fable* alone were great. Kaye writes of "the enormous vogue of the book" and indicates that it "retained its celebrity for over a century." David Hume, in his *Treatise of Human Nature,* listed "Dr. Mandeville" along with Locke, Shaftesbury, Hutcheson, and Butler as one of "some late philosophers in England who have begun to put the science of man on a new footing and have engaged the attention and excited the curiosity of the public."[30]

The earliest writings in the Mandeville canon were much too specialized to "engage the attention and excite the curiosity of the public." The initial three items were published in Rotterdam and Leyden. The first of these, also Mandeville's first "authentic work,"[31] is *De Medicina Oratio Scholastica,* Rotterdam, 1685. Mandeville contended in this that the most important thing in the practice of medicine is observation or experience. It is of interest to note how early this most characteristic empirical bias is stated by him. The second work we have is a philosophical dissertation, entitled *Disputatio Philosophica de Brutorum Operationibus,* Leyden, 1689. Sakmann renders the substance of this philosophical essay thus:

> The position of the Peripatetics who assume a substantial principle of cogitation in animals but do not grant them a rational, immortal soul is untenable. With thought, rationality and immortality are given, as one can show from the Peripatetics' own examples and arguments and from the true idea of God and his decrees. The upshot is that, because of the difference between man and animal, to which we must hold firmly, the capacity to think cannot be granted to animals. Many of their vital functions may now already be explained on mechanical grounds.[32]

Mandeville's third authentic work is a medical doctoral dissertation entitled *Disputatio Medica Inauguralis de Chylosi Vitata,* Leyden, 1691. This is a work on the digestive disturbances supporting the thesis that it is fermentation rather than heat that explains the digestive process.[33] Mandeville had an abiding interest in the digestive processes. The physician who is evidently his spokesman in a later treatise on hypochondriacal and hysterical ailments holds that the stomach is the source of such ailments and Mandeville clearly believed also that the stomach is readily affected by mental disturbance.[34]

The doggerel, entitled *The Grumbling Hive: or, Knaves Turned Honest,* appeared in 1705. It tells the famous story of a beehive that prospered as a whole when its individual bees were engaged by the millions in "endeavoring to supply each other's lust and vanity" but then declined drastically when by the agency of Jupiter the individual bees had ceased to be knaves and had been rendered honest.[35] It was ultimately incorporated in Mandeville's most important work, *The Fable of the Bees,* the small fable of the hive serving as the nucleus of the much larger Fable.

The Virgin Unmask'd: or, Female Dialogues Betwixt an Elderly Maiden Lady and her Niece was published in 1709. There are ten dialogues in this, between Lucinda, the elderly maiden lady of the title, and her young, unmarried niece, Antonia. Mandeville states his purpose on the penultimate page of his Preface: "My design through the whole is to let young ladies know whatever is dreadful in marriage, and this could not be done, but by introducing one that was an enemy to it. Therefore, tho' Lucinda speaks altogether against matrimony, don't think that I do so too."[36] The design of bringing out "what is dreadful in marriage," one must acknowledge, is rather well executed. Lucinda is a sagacious woman entirely capable of instructing her niece in those ways of errant husbands that have a cruel impact on wives.

In 1711 Mandeville's *A Treatise of the Hypochondriack and Hysterick Passions* was published. (The second, enlarged edition of which—here used—appeared in 1730 under the title, *A Treatise of the Hypochondriack and Hysterick Diseases.*) This may be described as a summary of Mandeville's psychiatric views and contains much medical lore, especially as bearing on the digestive processes. It probably reveals more about Mandeville as a person than any of his other publications. It is significant that the physician in it is named Philopirio, or lover of experience, and that he is described (and speaks) in such terms that it would appear easy to justify the notion that he is a spokesman for Mandeville.[37]

The Fable of the Bees was published in 1714. This contained *The Grumbling Hive* but added "An Enquiry into the Origin of Moral Virtue" and some twenty **"Remarks"** designed to explain or expand various phrases or statements in *The Grumbling Hive.* A second edition of the *Fable* appeared in the same year, but in 1723 another "second edition" was issued with the **"Remarks"** expanded and the addition of two new essays (**"An Essay on Charity and Charity-Schools"** and **"A Search into the Nature of Society"**). This is the material (viz., *The Grumbling Hive,* the "Enquiry into the Origin of Moral Virtue," the twenty "Remars," and the two essays on charity-schools and the nature of society) that now also constitutes

the first volume of the extremely useful edition of *The Fable* that F. B. Kaye published in 1924. Kaye mentions other editions of *The Fable of the Bees,*[38] but crucial is the appearance of a new second volume with that title, issued in 1728 (with 1729 shown on its title-page), which complements the first volume by another of similar length. The *Fable* is the centerpiece of Mandeville's lifework. Its views will be discussed at length. It features Mandeville's paradoxical juxtaposition of private vices and public virtues. It presents a relatively elaborate theory of human nature. It affords acute views on economy and society and gives in its second volume a most interesting perspective on human evolution.

An interval of six years comes after 1714 before Mandeville's next book is issued. This is his *Free Thoughts on Religion, the Church, and National Happiness* of 1720. It is, broadly, a plea for religious toleration (although it does not seek to extend toleration to Roman Catholics). It conveys a chastening sense of how once-persecuted sects, when they have achieved acceptance or power, manifest an unseemly intolerance of their own. It is clearly in favor of the Protestant succession to the English throne. Perhaps it should be treated with some reservation, as a not especially characteristic product of Mandeville's, on the ground that it often merely rather mechanically repeats ideas current in his time. Sakmann contended that in large parts of this book its author writes as "no more than a complier" and that "many of the statements of the book are . . . at most interesting as contributions to knowledge of the theological common sense of the time." In *Free Thoughts,* accordingly, in Sakmann's view, Mandeville is minimally original.[39] There will be no heavy dependence on the book here but it will be assumed that it does authentically represent Mandeville's views, whether they are inordinately imitative or not.

In 1724 appeared what this writer considers to be one of Mandeville's most powerful and significant pieces of writing, *Modest Defence of Publick Stews.*[40] In this work a plan is set out for the establishment and regulations of houses of prostitution, which will have various beneficial effects, including: the preservation of the chastity of "decent" women (a theme already touched on in the *Fable* and there described as a "seeming paradox"),[41] the reduction of crime and disorder, and the initiation of young men into amatory experiences that will make them less giddily romantic in their comportment in love. This is one of the most ironic of Mandeville's productions and one of the most obviously pervaded by Mandeville's comic sense—which does not prevent it from being a most significant sociological document, with even a not altogether negligible economic argument involved in it, as will be indicated in Chapter 4.

In *An Enquiry into the Causes of the Frequent Executions at Tyburn,* published in 1725, Mandeville shows interest in theftbote or the carrying on of negotiations with thieves (or criminals connected with them) by the "law-abiding" in getting back goods stolen from the latter. As the title of the pamphlet suggests, the causes of the frequent executions at Tyburn are explored. Mandeville points out that prison evokes or intensifies criminal tendencies. He considers how drunkenness affects the manner in which the condemned take their trip to the gallows and how it affects their behavior when they are about to be executed. He is clear on the point that the main object of public execution, deterrence, is blunted or destroyed by the barbarous spectacles that public executions present.

As previously noted, the second volume of the *Fable* appeared in 1728 and was dated 1729. Three years later, in 1732, another of Mandeville's more important prose works appeared, his *An Enquiry into the Origin of Honour and the Usefulness of Christianity in War.* The book is especially significant for its expansion of the discussion of honor that had already appeared in the *Fable.* It is a subtle study of what might be called the honor motive. It explores what a sociologist might label the "functions" that honor performs, let us say briefly for now, its contributions to the sustainment of the larger social order within which it occurs. It explores as well the complexities confronting the "politician" who works with honor: as when, in the France of Louis XIV, the politician wishes to see maintained the truculence that honor-based duelling encourages but does not wish to see too much valuable military blood spilled in outright orgies of duelling.

A Letter to Dion, Occasion'd by his Book Call'd Alciphron, published in 1732, is a short apologia by Mandeville. The title refers to a work by Bishop Berkeley that showed that Berkeley had genuinely misunderstood Mandeville (quite possibly having refused to take the trouble to understand him). *Dion* is a restrained statement. Among other things, it reminds the reader of Mandeville's position (whether one considers it "sincere" or not) that when he avers that societies cannot rise to worldly wealth, power, and glory without vices, this does not mean that he himself bids men be vicious.[42]

Something may be learned about Mandeville the man from these writings, but one must proceed with a good deal of caution. It is tempting, and it may well be accurate, to assume that Lucinda, the elderly maiden aunt of *The Virgin Unmask'd,* often expresses Mandeville's views on women. But the possibility that she is a *persona,* an assumed identity, introduced for dramatic purposes and an advocate of views unlike those of the "real Mandeville" (in Monro's phrase), cannot be dismissed out of hand. Texts need to be cross-checked. We are fortunate in having the *Treatise on the Hypochondriack and Hysterick Diseases,* with its physician Philopiro evidently so close to Mandeville himself. The texts at our disposal in any case allow some exploration of certain traits of Mandeville's character, thought, and style that are of peculiar interest either because they are intimately connected with his social-science endeavors or because they have long occupied commentators on Mandeville who have seriously pondered his meaning and sought to assess the quality of his work.

SOME FEATURES OF CHARACTER, THOUGHT, AND STYLE

Mandeville has very frequently struck readers as cynical. It would hardly be possible to be more partial to him than F. B. Kaye; yet Kaye also once referred to him as "cynical Mandeville,"[43] if only in the interest of making a point casting him in a more favorable light than "the uncynical Berkeley." Hayek, who obviously has great regard for Mandeville, suggests that he had a "somewhat cynical mind."[44] In our own day, too, Dobrée refers to "the optimism of a Shaftesbury, the pessimism of a Swift, or the cynicism of a Mandeville."[45] In an older day, Leslie Stephen wrote of Mandeville (although he found much of value in him) as both "cynical" and "brutal" and could aver that he had "contempt for the human race."[46] Stephen rather outdid himself on the subject of Mandeville in his *History of English Thought* when he observed that "his brutality and his paradox revolt us as a display of cynical levity."[47] George Saintsbury wrote of Mandeville's "cynical pessimism" and called him the "Diogenes of English philosophy," asserting at the same time that he had "a great deal too much of the polecat about him."[48] But among writers reaching back roughly a century, probably none insisted on Mandeville's cynicism so vigorously as Wilhelm Hasbach, the historian of economic thought, who must be quoted in full:

> Mandeville stands before us as the man who unified in his work all the low conceptions of human nature that had gotten a distinctive stamp in the sixteenth and seventeenth centuries. Himself of French derivation, he becomes the channel through which the Epicurean-skeptical-mechanical thought of the French is definitely brought over into English ethics and politics. With the boldness of the epigonus he sharpens this thought on all fronts. With cynical enjoyment he rummages in filth. With mephistophelian laughter he seeks to lower humans in their own eyes. He knows how to convert the treasures of wisdom of the libraries into rough coins that pass quickly from hand to hand.[49]

In Mandeville's own time the *Fable* was repeatedly described as a wicked book and Mandeville himself as misanthropic. "Cynical" is certainly an apt word to convey the sense of him of many of his contemporaries. Mandeville has also often been charged with brutality (as by Stephen), heartlessness, callousness. Notoriously he objected to and wrote against charity schools for the poor, taking the position that the society in which he lived needed a plentiful supply of ignorant people willing to work for very modest compensation. Thereby he aroused much antagonism and the accusation of brutality. John M. Robertson was keenly appreciative of Mandeville's merits but observed that "it cannot be denied that there is certain aggressive callousness in his treatment of the problem of poverty."[50] Again in Mandeville's own time a critic like William Hendley, who devoted a long pamphlet to a defense of the charity schools, averred forthrightly that it is "both unjust and unnatural to make the poor always slaves to the rich and exclude them and their children forever from bettering their fortunes in this world."[51] From Hendley's entire argument it might well appear that Mandeville was thoroughly heartless in his opposition to education for the poor.

The accusations of cynicism and brutality are of considerable interest if only because they bear on traits of character intimately related to Mandeville's social thought. The "real Mandeville" is in all likelihood more complex than the accusations suggest. Cynicism and brutality can be closely connected and either might be considered first. It is well now to continue with brutality, which, as easily as cynicism would, brings us duly to a kind of holistic outlook on society that is most important in Mandeville and that it is well to note at an early point.

But to begin with, it is well to remember that Mandeville was a practicing physician with a special interest in nervous (and digestive) disorders. His attitudes as a physician are not irrelevant to the general question of his brutality or humanity. The *Treatise of the Hypochondriack and Hysterick Diseases* suggests a measure of authentic humanity. At the beginning of the first of the three dialogues that make up the book, the patient Misomedon (hater of medicine or doctors; "hater of restraint," according to Cook)[52] goes on at some length in his meeting with his doctor (Philopirio) about his history and ailments and is finally apologetic for having someone listen to so tedious a tale. But this elicits a most encouraging and friendly response from Philopirio, who assures his patient that his story is both diverting and medically valuable. Asked at a certain point by Misomedon to stay another quarter hour, Philopirio answers, "With all my Heart; half an Hour if you please."[53]

Perhaps some of this is mere professional and self-interested courtesy. But Philopirio shows much gentleness with the people he attends, at least on the representations of the *Treatise.* He evidently listened very carefully to what his patients said and reported their talk with every sign of sympathy. Misomedon's wife, Polytheca,[54] who suffers from "the vapors," says:

> I never dare speak of vapours, the very name is a joke; and the general notion that men have of them is that they are nothing but a malicious mood and contrived sullenness of willful, extravagant and imperious women, when they are denied or thwarted in their unreasonable desires; nay, even physicians, because they cannot cure them, are forced to ridicule them in their own defense, and a woman that is really troubled by vapours is pitied by none but her unhappy fellow-sufferers, that labor under the same affliction.[55]

Misomedon, as if to verify part of Polytheca's statement, states at a later point, "I can't think but the greater part of her distemper is fancy."[56] He cannot believe "it's real" either. Misomedon is indeed a harsh critic of Polytheca's views, and Philopirio points out to him that harsh criticism is hardly helpful to the sort of disorder from which she suffers.[57] Again, all this might be explained on grounds of effort at professionally appropriate and competent behavior, but it is difficult after a while to avoid an impression

of sheer compassion for his patients on Philopirio's (or Mandeville's) part. His listening with great care would have been reinforced by his powerful empirical or observational bent. He clearly understood more than a little of psychic suffering. It appears quite evident that he sought his patients' welfare.[58]

Mandeville's attitudes toward women are also of interest in relation to brutality. He remarks in the preface to the *Virgin Unmask'd* that, though the elderly maiden lady Lucinda argues strongly against matrimony, it does not follow that he would do so too. (On this point, at any rate, then, Mandeville claims that Lucinda's views differ from his own.) Nevertheless, Lucinda states various views on men and women that Mandeville may well have shared. One might conceive that Lucinda is deliberately moved by her author-creator to present a strong case for women's rights. She certainly has a powerful sense of their wrongs. Men, she contends, have "a thousand advantages beyond us [women]." Advocates of women's rights might thoroughly disapprove when Lucinda avers that "in reasoning, women can never cope with men" or that "women are shallow creatures; we may boast of prattling, and be quick at a jest, or repartee, but a sound and penetrating judgment only belongs to men, as the masters of reason and solid sense." Yet these statements do occur in the course of a paragraph in which Lucinda points, precisely, to men's advantages in education, for "it is thought sufficient, if a women can but read and write; we receive no other education, as to learning. But where we leave off, they [viz. men] start out; they are not trusted to manage their own affairs, before they are sent to schools, and universities, to have their intellectuals mended and sharpened."[59] Lucinda apparently has not the slightest notion of *changing* the social order as it pertains to the relations of the sexes, but she can certainly be interpreted to be critical of that order. Granted the hazards of this sort of presumption: still, just as Mandeville seemed sympathetic to a vaporish or "hypish" (the word "hyp" deriving from hypochondriasis) Polytheca, he appears sympathetic to Lucinda. He was evidently willing to "listen" to her sort of talk.

In the *Fable,* even the proposition that Lucinda had sustained, to the effect that "sound and penetrating judgment only belongs to men," at least if it may be supposed that Lucinda thought this an inevitable or "natural" male advantage, is directly challenged. Horatio asserts that sound judgment is a great rarity among women, to which Cleomenes (who is undoubtedly very often Mandeville's spokesman) answers that this is true "only for want of practice, application and assiduity." Cleomenes adds that there is "no labor of the brain which women are not as capable of performing, at least, as well as men, with the same assistance, if they set about, and persevere in it . . ." He even holds that "the workmanship in the make of women seems to be more elegant and better finished" and suggests that this greater refinement on the "outside" might well be continued on the "inside," with particular reference to "the formation of the brain, as to the nicety of the structure, and superior accuracy in the fabric."[60] Whatever the merits or demerits of these views, and even if it should be argued that Mandeville is here only stating "facts" as he understands them, he appears, on the basis of what has been adduced, anything but brutal or callous toward women; and it is at least plausible to presume that he would have had sympathy with the notion of better education for them—a matter to which he had obviously given some thought. In this whole area, his conservatism is subject to real strain.

It might be argued that Mandeville on the subject of prostitution reveals far less amiable attitudes toward women. *The Modest Defense of Publick Stews,* however ironic one may construe its intention to be, is clearly in support of prostitution. The argument that the chastity of women generally is preserved by the incontinence of a number of them may have seemed to some a piece of outright brutality or indeed cynicism. George Bluet plainly suggested that there was a class bias associated with Mandeville's stance on prostitution.[61] There is little doubt that Mandeville was in fact complacent toward prostitution, and he sounds as if he rather relishes it. He hardly dons the mantle of the prophet crying out against it. Many others in his time also failed to don that mantle. Defoe, for example, who hardly relished prostitution, evidently was disposed to have a controlled, carefully limited practice of it, willing to tolerate a certain amount of discreetly segregated sex for sale.[62] Here, as often elsewhere, too, what appears as brutality or cynicism may not strike one quite the same way when he takes into serious account Mandeville's holistic-functional outlook on society, as will be done shortly. (One need not condone such brutality or cynicism as may occur in Mandeville but it is important to consider them in the full light of his own outlook.)

The more amiable attitudes toward women still remain, and it is by no means implausible that Mandeville should have entertained these at the same time as the less amiable ones that his stance on prostitution might suggest. In point of the former attitudes, his conservatism, as suggested, would appear to be mitigated, although the attitudes did not lead him to reform activity on behalf of women. Questions about his brutality and cynicism are not unconnected with questions about his conservatism. If he was not a social revolutionary of the left, Monro is still justified in saying that it is hard to believe him simply a reactionary, "even by present-day standards."[63] He was certainly critical, for example, of the church of his time, in the interest of a larger tolerance and more relaxed attitude about theological differences than he saw prevailing about him. This is something that his *Free Thoughts,* whatever its precise significance in the corpus of his writings, makes quite clear. But his conservatism is very marked with respect to the laboring poor. And here too the matter of brutality again comes sharply to the fore.

It comes to the fore even because of what Mandeville writes himself. It is true that he wanted the poor to serve as a labor force doing back-breaking, unskilled jobs while they were kept in ignorance even for "their own good"—

for knowledge would only bring them gnawing dissatisfaction. They would not be tormented by better possibilities if they could not even imagine them. Their wants must be relieved but it would be folly to "cure" them. Their education must be severely restricted and they did not need the pampering of charity schools to give them the rudiments of religion they required. Mandeville condemns joint efforts of servants to improve their working conditions or wages to "abolish the low dignity of their condition," which they have already raised beyond what it would be for the general welfare.[64] With all this, Mandeville is remarkably self-conscious about his stance. He writes in the famous essay on the charity schools in which his views of the poor are expounded, "I have no design that is cruel, nor the least aim that savors of inhumanity." He then adds, as if to make this assurance concrete: "To have sufficient hospitals for sick and wounded I look upon as an indispensable duty both in peace and war: Young children without parents, old age without support, and all that are disabled from working ought to be taken care of with tenderness and alacrity." Again he tells us in the same essay: "I would not be thought cruel and am well assured, if I know anything of myself, that I abhor inhumanity." And he is not done yet, for a few pages later he tells us, "I would not advance anything that is barbarous or unhuman."[65] He did indeed get much criticism of his position on the poor and charity schools. Whatever the motivation for his repeated apologies and qualifications, they do suggest some inner uncertainty on the whole matter of his antagonism to charity schools and exploitation of the laboring poor. If Mandeville "sinned" here in the direction of brutality, callousness, or the like, he was not a man simply and unreservedly brutal or cynical about the laboring poor. Yet he was still constrained by his theoretical views on the economic necessity of a large, ignorant, and poor working population.

Kaye observes that the "gusto" of his assault on the charity schools and on "petty reverence for the poor" (Mandeville's own phrase) is likely to strike the modern reader as "incredibly brutal," but that this impression comes from judging Mandeville from a humanitarian point of view hardly existing in his own time: "Seen in historical perspective, there is nothing unusually harsh in Mandeville's position."[66] Here Kaye may be a little too generous. The relevant literature on the charity schools in Mandeville's time, as there will be occasion to note in Chapter 4, does express a measure of humanitarianism. (It is significant that it occurs within a context of acceptance of the status quo, but it is present.) Granted Mandeville's apologetic remarks about his position on the schools and the laboring poor, the position was still clearly and unambiguously stated. There was finally no doubt about the point that Mandeville was firmly "conservative" here. Horne is close to the mark when he suggests that Mandeville offers us the picture of a "strictly differentiated class-structured society," dependent for its prosperity on mass poverty.[67]

But now it becomes important to mark Mandeville's holistic outlook on society. The body politic, he suggests in a well known passage, might be compared to a bowl of punch:

> Avarice should be the souring and prodigality the sweetening of it. The water I would call the ignorance, folly and credulity of the floating insipid multitude; while wisdom, honour, fortitude and the rest of the sublime qualities of men, which separated by art from the dregs of nature the fire of glory has exalted and refined into a spiritual essence, should be an equivalent to brandy . . . A . . . dull stranger that is unacquainted with the whole composition, if he was to taste the several ingredients apart, would think it impossible they should make any tolerable liquor. The lemons would be too sour, the sugar too luscious, the brandy . . . too strong . . . Yet experience teaches us that the ingredients I named, judiciously mixed, will make an excellent liquor, liked . . . and admired by men of excellent palates.⁶⁸

The body politic or society, analogously, needs a variety of ingredients to make some sort of tolerable or "palatable" whole, even if particular ingredients abstracted from that whole should seem singularly unappealing or "unappetizing." Mandeville again gives expression to the holistic view in the following:

> Some narrow souls can never thrive because they are too stingy, while longer heads amass great wealth by spending their money freely and seeming to despite it. But the vicissitudes of fortune are necessary, and the most lamentable are not more detrimental to society than the death of the individual members of it. Christenings are a proper balance to burials. Those who immediately lose by the misfortunes of others are very sorry, complain and make a noise; but the others who get by them, as there always are such, hold their tongues, because it is odious to be thought the better for the losses and calamities of our neighbour. The various ups and downs compose a wheel that always turning round gives motion to the whole machine. Philosophers, that dare extend their thoughts beyond the narrow compass of what is immediately before them look on the alternate changes in the civil society no otherwise than they do on the rising and fallings of the lungs; the latter of which are as much a part of respiration in the more perfect animals as the first; so that the fickle breath of never-stable fortune is to the body politic the same as floating air to a living creature.⁶⁹

There are those "who extend their thought beyond the narrow compass of what is immediately before them," and in so doing inevitably regard what is before them in relation to larger contexts. "Christenings are a proper balance to burials." In the existence and maintenance of large populations and societies, one must observe that some individuals die while others get born. Seeing from this vantage point does *not* mean that when one shifts one's attention to the deaths of particular individuals one must be callous or brutal about them. But the individuals are part of a demographic flux that transcends them.

This holistic view of Mandeville's strongly suggests what is now called a "functional" analysis of society. The term *functional* is here used with particular reference to Merton's assertion regarding "the central orientation of functionalism," to the effect that that orientation is "expressed in the practice of interpreting data by establishing their consequences for larger structures in which they are implicated.⁷⁰ (Nothing can be clearer, with regard to Mandeville's punch, than that its individual ingredients are to be considered in relation to the whole.) In this sense, functional analysis is concerned with whether various social activities work "adaptively" ("or maladaptively") "positively" ("or negatively") for a system or larger whole.

The mischief of imputing to Mandeville ideas of today that he did not hold must be avoided. Certainly, he could not use the term *structures* in the sophisticated sense in which Merton does. Nor did Mandeville seek deliberately to develop his functional view as a strategic sociological "approach." And he did not introduce under the rubric of "dysfunction" the notion of "negative" consequence for a large system. In fact, on this point he may strike us today as excessively optimistic: must the ingredients of a punch or of a society always "blend" so harmoniously for the excellence of the whole?⁷¹ May not a punch have ingredients that are simply bad from the point of view of the whole mixture? And, for that matter, may not a punch itself be subject to criticism? If something is "functional" or "adaptive" for a large whole, this implies nothing whatever as to the value of that whole itself. But, all this conceded, we find ourselves faced time and again with Mandeville's holistic-functional bias. It is impossible to avoid it, no matter what we may call it, and it is part and parcel of some of his most striking and important paradoxes. He *will* say that the prostitution of some women has effects *in the larger society,* preserving the chastity of women generally. He *will* say that duelling harms individuals (it might of course kill them) and yet insist that the duel diffuses civility and courtesy throughout society at large and keeps alive a touchiness and bellicosity generally valuable to a nation engaged in military enterprise.⁷² He *will* say that (under appropriate circumstances) private vices become public benefits. These are matters at the heart of his concerns. And of course we must not forget that in his view keeping the poor ignorant and very modestly paid would work out to the larger social good. This does not necessarily mean that Mandeville was right on this point. It is, however, to note his perspective.

The holistic-functional orientation we find in Mandeville is a "theoretical" orientation that, as it happens, does not give much factual grounding for any of his particular propositions. Obviously, to consider what prostitution actually "does" within a society, for example, raises questions of fact. Those questions will be faced as best they can be in Chapter 6. But in all this one may note a persistent tension. Let us suppose that one outcome, at any rate, of the assassination of a central political figure in a nation would be to enhance and deepen "unselfish" feeling for the nation throughout its expanse. Let us further assume that this is in some important sense a "beneficent" outcome for the nation as a whole. The assassination itself thereby becomes no less cruel and savage. But neither does the "positive" or "beneficent" effect disappear. (Mandeville does *not* give this example, but it is very much in his spirit, not least in making good emerge from evil.)[73] Thus we may be repelled and at the same time persuaded of the emergence of something desirable. Possibly the modern exhortation not to "commit a social science" is well advised. But it was already too late even for Mandeville to refrain. He has already begun to "commit" a social science. And it becomes clear that the questions of his brutality (or cynicism) can get so closely involved with questions about the nature of his social science that the latter questions often must be brought up in order for us to consider the former.

Here, indeed, one confronts two problems with respect to brutality (or cynicism, as the case may be). There is of course on the one hand Mandeville's holistic-functional position. Yes—the poor have very little; but the nation thereby prospers. Yes—men die in duels; but the general tone of civil society and the general level of courtesy are greatly improved because of duelling. And so on. If at any time Mandeville should be accused of sounding insufficiently distressed about the suffering and dying, he could claim that he was merely concentrating on the holistic-functional aspect of things, and that to concentrate on such matters does not necessarily imply brutality. But there is another problem. It is plainly not always safe to make inferences about personal character or personal traits from theoretical positions. Thus, one might advance a theory asserting the thorough selfishness of humans while being personally the most unselfish of men or women. To infer an analogous personal quality from the nature of the theory would then of course be disastrously wrong. Mandeville's view of the poor might have been due to his being a victim of a faulty economic doctrine. If one should then say that the view was in some objective sense "brutal," it would yet be hazardous to infer from it a personal trait or character of brutality.

It is still possible that Mandeville had an element of brutality in his personal make-up. But in the absence of information bearing quite directly on the point, we have to assess this possibility against what clearly seems to have been his sympathetic attitudes as a physician toward patients, a measure of apparent friendliness toward women, his holistic-functional orientation as a social scientist, and the doubts that attach to inferring personal traits from theoretical positions.[74]

Insofar as we can separate cynicism from brutality, the charge of cynicism is seen to have some foundation as Mandeville's theory of human nature is considered. (He is by no means cynical about all matters.)[75] Here, too, however, it is necessary to exercise some degree of caution. Again, we must not overlook Mandeville's paradoxical bias. He tells us explicitly, "The short-sighted vulgar in the chain of causes can seldom see further than one link; but those who can enlarge their view, and will give themselves the leisure of gazing on the prospect of concat-

enated events may, in a hundred places, see good spring up and pullulate from evil as naturally as chickens do from eggs."[76] Envy and love of glory will make schoolboys do well in their studies. Mandeville goes on with his asymmetrical, paradoxical play intended precisely to exhibit the sources of good in evil. Envy will also stimulate pointers to improvement as they try to outdo their superiors. And married women, generally guilty of the "vice" of envy too, seek to arouse the same "passion" in their husbands, and, whey they have succeeded, "envy and emulation have kept more men in bounds and reformed more ill husbands from sloth, from drinking and other evil courses, than all the sermons that have been preached since the time of the apostles."[77] Is this cynicism? Or is Mandeville most perceptive on the point that "low" passions can have great value? (The point would be highly significant in psychological, sociological, and ethical perspectives.)[78] When Leslie Stephen asserted regarding Mandeville that "his brutality and his paradox revolt us as a display of cynical levity," he was saying far too much far too fast.

Mandeville nevertheless is measurelessly skeptical of imputations of high human motivation. Human conduct, generally, has to be motivated by some form of self-interest and humans are most especially liable to the desire for glory, which lurks beneath a great many unselfish facades. Mandeville's discussion of the case of Dr. John Radcliffe, who left most of his fortune of eighty thousand pounds to Oxford University, is quite typical. Whatever Dr. Radcliffe's character may have been (and Mandeville clearly found it unadmirable) and however one may actually regard the doctor's leaving "a trifle among his relations who stood in need of it and an immense treasure to an university that did not want it," in Mandeville's words, the argument that Mandeville presents about the doctor's motivation is in any case to be expected from him. The doctor was but indulging his "darling passion," catering to his own vanity, thinking of monuments and praise and the outpouring of reverence and veneration that would be his posthumous portion. The contemplation of all this homage must have thrown the doctor's ambitious soul into "vast ecstacies of pleasure" as he ruminated" on the duration of his glory and the perpetuity he would by this means procure to his name."[79] Except for a few rare souls, authentic Christians, this is how humans are likely to be motivated. This view of motivation is a matter of principle with Mandeville. Ostensible noble motivation, in any area of conduct, must be shown to be no more noble in reality than conduct no one would claim to be nobly motivated.[80]

John Hervey gave a fundamental, two-pronged criticism of this reductive bias of Mandeville's. Hervey compares Herostratus, who set fire to the temple of Diana at Ephesus for the sake of his own glory, with Decius, "who threw himself for the sake of his country into the gulf that opened in Rome." Hervey asks us in effect to consider that one might argue that both men acted from the same motive and were "equally influenced by the vanity of being mentioned in history and perpetuating their names to posterity for as long as those of Rome and Ephesus should be known." Hervey does not elaborate the point but he clearly means to cast doubt on a theory that finds a Herostratus and a Decius motivated in precisely the same way.[81] Hervey goes on immediately to the second prong of his attack, which suggests a practical question: "I would be glad to ask the author of the *Fable of the Bees* whether he thinks it would promote and encourage that virtue called the love of one's country to show that the most renowned patriot in antiquity and the most famous incendiary were in the same way of thinking and actuated by the same passions."[82]

In a special sense, humans contribute to the construction or destruction of their own virtue. The views that they hold of virtue have some power to influence that virtue itself. Hervey sees this point—as did Hutcheson.[83] It was also seen, however, by notable eighteenth-century thinkers outside the category of critics of Mandeville in his own day. Thus Hume, for one, is again relevant. He does not easily adopt the opinion that all those who have spoken ill of humans have been enemies of virtue or moved by evil intentions. Yet he contends that those who incline to think more favorably of mankind do more for virtue than those who give human nature a bad name. Inspired with "high notions" of themselves, people will endeavor to live up to them and scorn the base and vicious.[84] Kant outdoes others in the eloquence and power of the exposition of this point in his *Anthropology*: "All the human virtue in circulation is small change: one would have to be a child to take it for real gold. . . . But we are better off having small change in circulation than no money at all; and it can eventually be converted into genuine gold, though at considerable loss." Kant even goes on to say that it is "high treason against humanity to issue these coins as *mere counters* having no value at all . . ." He then quotes Swift ("Honor is a pair of shoes that have been worn out in the mind") and refers to the preacher Hofsteder's slandering of Socrates. (He might of course have quoted and referred to others. That he did not quote or refer to Mandeville in this connection, however, was not due to ignorance of the latter's work.) He suggests, further, that authentic virtue may emerge from presumptions—he even says "pretences"—of the existence of virtue among us: "We must value even the semblance of good in others; for out of this play with pretences, which win respect though they may not deserve it, something serious can finally develop."[85]

If a measure of cynicism may be imputed to Mandeville, it does not follow that one has thereby disposed of his theory of human nature. Far from it. That theory will still merit scrutiny. It is a powerfully realistic, empirically oriented theory, and "realism" and "cynicism" are not always easy to distinguish; or, we may say, in one important aspect cynicism is but realism pushed so far that it ceases to be realistic. (Leslie Stephen deeply appreciated Mandeville's realism even while repudiating his cynicism.) Labeling Mandeville cynical will finally carry us no great distance in understanding him. The question of cynicism also points to the matter of temperament, which will be further referred to in the next chapter when Mandeville is discussed in relation to Shaftesbury.

Was Mandeville "personally" cynical? Did cynicism tincture or pervade his character and affect his relations with others? There is no way to be sure. Like some others thinkers, he may have suspended his theories when he was with congenial companions.

Mandeville's empirical bent is of course something showed by others in his day, but it is so marked that it merits special attention. It has already been noted, in connection with his works as a physician, how much he was the observer. The prime medical injunction for him is always "Observe, observe, observe!" He is a firm, unswerving enemy of speculative medical systems. In the preface to the *Treatise* he already indicates that he greatly prefers the experience of painstaking practitioners to "the witty speculations of hypothetical doctors." Philopirio characteristically remarks that "the practical part of medicine"—a part not attempted by many—"is only attained by an almost everlasting attendance on the sick, unwearied patience, and judicious as well as diligent observation." He avers again, "What I am against is the speculative part of physic, as it is distinct from the practical, that teaches men to cure all manner of distempers in their closets, without ever seeing a patient."[86]

So devoted is Mandeville to observation, to the empirical, that he sometimes creates an impression of a certain crudity or naiveté of thought along this line. One may well contend that he is too depreciatively inclined to think of "reason" and "hypotheses" as consisting "only in opinion."[87] There is a tendency in him to regard theories in science as trivial, as a kind of intellectual fluff.[88] He can carry his zeal for observation and against hypothesis, speculation, and "opinion" so far that he ends with the position that "the hypotheses only make a shew, and are wholly insignificant." Philopirio does say at a later point, a few pages after he has thus spoken of hypotheses, that actually he "would not make a step without reason";[89] it is only that he wants his reasoning always firmly controlled by observation. It is perhaps not always easy to catch Mandeville's precise meaning when he refers to "hypotheses." Forbes reminds us that the word had variant meanings in the eighteenth century (as in Newton himself) and points out that one might find the same thinker scorning and, in the same breath, using "hypotheses."[90] The impression persists that Mandeville's observational bias is so strong that it can lead him to a view of science that errs in its extreme empiricism.

In what there is good reason to consider an early statement of Mandeville's opinion, the "Oxford gentlemen"—who is evidently Mandeville's spokesman in a number of the issues of the *Female Tatler*—criticizes "the abominable pride and haughtiness" of men of learning. He observes that a man be a famous general or a deep politician or an able merchant without knowing a word of Latin. This is certainly fair enough. But the Oxford gentleman unreservedly applies criteria of utility to learning at large and, in turning to medicine, avers, "They may talk of anatomy, economy, chemistry, philosophy, pathology, therapeutica, and make as many barbarous divisions of their art as they please, but it is very plain that all these branches of university learning are very unnecessary, if not frivolous, as to the cure of the patients. . . ."[91] Here it is certain that the empirical, utilitarian, and "practical" bias is overreaching itself.

Yet the *Fable* repeatedly shows that Mandeville values thinking "abstractly," as for example when he comments, "I write not to many, nor seek for any well-wishers but among the few that can think abstractly."[92] It is also plain that he was very willing to allow scope to his imagination. The determined—the too determined—empiricist is appreciably offset by a man who is effectively willing to entertain and work with numerous "hypotheses." Mandeville's *Free Thoughts* at least demonstrates that he was not uninterested in theological speculation. (Indeed, what else should one expect from a man who had been deeply influenced by Pierre Bayle?) We are not to expect from him long chains of reasoning that become very remote from some empirical base and we are not to expect much of the determined system-builder in him, but we can expect authentic efforts at probing thought.

The "real Mandeville," one must propose, is a man whose mind is strongly preoccupied with medical and biological, psychological, social, and economic phenomena. One might conceivably be "empirical" and turn one's attention to the spiritual exercise of devout men and women, which, after all, are also "real." But this sort of thing does not engage Mandeville's empirical bent. His mind dwells where women of fashion purchase clothes and poorer women seek to imitate them, where prostitutes offer their wares, where merchants seek to make profits, where the streets of a great city are piled with dirt. To say that such things alone preoccupy him would simply be wrong, but they do catch much of his interest. Here he is in the midst of discussion (very much along the lines of his interests) of what we now call conspicuous consumption, suggesting his own delight in "viewing the various scenes of low life" (and revealing his wonted psychological insight):

> Whoever takes delight in viewing the various scenes of low life, may on Easter, Whitsun, and other great holidays, meet with scores of people, especially women, of almost the lowest rank, that wear good and fashionable clothes: if coming to talk with them, you treat them more courteously and with greater respect than what they are conscious they deserve, they'll commonly be ashamed of owning what they are; and often you may, if you are a little inquisitive, discover in them a most anxious care to conceal the business they follow, and the places they live in. The reason is plain; while they receive those civilities that are not usually paid them, and which they think only due to their betters, they have the satisfaction to imagine, that they appear what they would be, which to weak minds is a pleasure almost as substantial as they could reap from the very accomplishments of their wishes: this golden dream they are unwilling to be disturbed in, and being sure that the meanness of their condition, if it is known, must sink 'em very low in your opinion, they hug

themselves in their disguise, and take all imaginable precaution not to forfeit by a useless discovery the esteem which they flatter themselves that their good clothes have drawn from you.[93]

The interest in such scenes is intimately connected with Mandeville's style, his plain talk, his bluntness, his pungency, his "down-to-earth" quality. He wants to "tell it like it is." His bluntness is part of his clarity (although it may also shade into a degree of cynicism and possibly misanthropy). The statement that we are born amid human bodily wastes ("*Inter urinas et faeces nascimur*") would hardly have disturbed him. He might have relished the description given by some diabolical character of C. S. Lewis' of a human being as "this animal, this thing begotten in a bed"; and the bluntness of description of humans (by evil spirits) in all their naked creatureliness that one may find in a popular contemporary book on exorcism like that of Malachi Martin[94] is in a way reminiscent of Mandeville's style.

There is nothing coy or roundabout in the assertion in the *Modest Defense* that "as long as it is in the nature of man . . . to have a salt itch in the breeches, the brimstone under the petticoat will be a necessary remedy to allay it."[95] It is a certainty that Mandeville did not handle human creatureliness with inordinate delicacy. He tells of St. Francis, who, in order to conquer his sexual desires (his "domestic enemy") was capable of throwing himself into an ice-filled ditch or a heap of snow (or of scourging himself). One still catches the ironic chuckle in the comment that "the fever of lust must be very high, where such violent coolers are required."[96]

Mandeville's bluntness and pungency are also suggested by a vulgar side of his makeup. Misomedon entertains Dr. Philopiro with this compact item: "I have heard of a waterologer or piss-prophet, so expert that he could tell by a man's working-day's water what trade; and by his Sunday's water, what religion he was of."[97] But Mandeville's style and a recital of some of the distinctive phenomena of human life he dwelt upon, suggestive as these may be, do not give us definitive answers to certain questions: Did he take a measure of real and robust joy in the concrete physiological detail of human existence? Or did he like to twit prudes with "the facts of life"? Or did he himself (although one could never accuse him of being prudish) have some disgust for the "darling lusts" of humans? Perhaps he was complex enough for the answers to all three questions to be in the affirmative.[98]

SOME REACTIONS TO MANDEVILLE OVER TIME

The Fable aroused much controversy in Mandeville's lifetime (controversy addressed to considerably more than cynicism or brutality). This controversy will be referred to as the "Battle of the Bees,"[99] a battle participated in by men like Berkeley, Francis Hutcheson, and William Law. It is somewhat arbitrary to confine the Battle of the Bees to British "battlers" in the years before Mandeville's death, but it is convenient to do so and of course it does not prevent consideration of subsequent discussants of Mandeville's work. Significant features of the Battle of the Bees will be covered later, and there are several writers close to the Battle in time who will also require later consideration. But a few very outstanding men, in whose work reactions to Mandeville can be noted and who will give some notion of how he fared in the eighteenth century after the Battle of the Bees, may now be briefly attended to (while a spare statement is added bringing reaction to Mandeville up to date). Hume, Adam Smith, Rousseau, and Herder, then, are considered. The relation of the first two to Mandeville is important for this study in any case, and Mandeville exercised a considerable (if not always acknowledged) influence upon them. Rousseau is obviously a significant figure in his own right and shared with Mandeville a certain interest in the primitive. Herder may be regarded as representative of early German lack of appreciation of Mandeville's thought. There can be no question of rendering only a "sample" of reactions to Mandeville, but neither are the reactions noted seriously unrepresentative (though it must yet be remembered that eighteenth-century French thought was *generally* more favorable to Mandeville than English).

Hume is perhaps the least negative in tone of the four men chosen, although (as Lindsay states), he was in matters of morals and politics "on the side of the angels" and thus had to play his role, too, in objecting to Mandeville and Hobbes, "the two Mephistopheles of the eighteenth century in morals and politics."[100] Hume repeatedly showed his reservations about views of human nature such as Mandeville's. He specifically criticized the idea that conniving politicians created morality, contending that virtue cannot simply be "talked into" humans.[101] (It is a very serious question, however, to what extent or in what sense this idea that Hume—and others before him—thus criticized was held by Mandeville.) Although Hume rarely refers to Mandeville by name, Mandeville was clearly often present to his thought, and it may well be that much of Hume's "reaction" to Mandeville is along the line of appreciable acceptance of the latter's work. Thus, Hume's discussions of pride plainly suggest much adoption of Mandeville's views.[102] It is not easy to say how far Hume may have taken over Mandeville's particular conception of the slow evolution of human institutions. When Hume writes of society that it "must be esteemed in a manner accidental and the effect of many ages" or refers (again in a context of discussion of the history of society) to "reflections . . . which, in fact, arise insensibly and by degrees,"[103] although the language is like that of Mandeville, this does not prove very much. But when we note the striking parallelism between Mandeville's and Hume's powerful statements on the evolution of the ship,[104] we are again inclined to infer that Hume took over significant Mandevillean ideas. It was noted above that Hume listed Mandeville among philosophers in England who had begun to put the science of man on a new footing.

Adam Smith's tone with respect to Mandeville is harsher than Hume's. In an early item in the *Edinburgh Review*, Smith referred to Mandeville at some length, coupling his name with those of Hobbes, Locke, Shaftesbury, Butler, Clarke and Hutcheson. He observes that anyone attentively reading Rousseau's discourse on the origin of inequality would see that the second volume of the *Fable* had "given occasion to the system of Rousseau." He asserts that in Rousseau's work Mandeville's principles were "stripped of all that tendency to corruption and licentiousness which has disgraced them in their original author."[105] Smith's *Theory of Moral Sentiments* tells us that Mandeville's system taught vice to "appear with more effrontery and to avow the corruption of its motives with a profligate audaciousness which had never been heard of before." Yet Smith did suggest that Mandeville's system, however "destructive," had in some respect bordered upon the truth."[106] It would be too much of a distraction here to trace in detail actual resemblances of *The Theory of Moral Sentiments* and the *Fable*,[107] but Smith's explicit statements about Mandeville create the impression that his views are more remote from the latter's than they actually are. The importance of Mandeville's work in relation to Smith's *The Wealth of Nations* has again been suggested very recently by the numerous references to that work by the editors of the latest edition of Smith's major economic treatise.[108] Both Kaye and Joseph Schumpeter suggest that the "respectable" Adam Smith was rather too eager to depreciate the dubious Dr. Mandeville.[109]

"I believe I need fear no contradiction in allowing man the sole natural virtue which the most extreme detractor of human virtue has been forced to recognize." Thus wrote Rousseau, referring to compassion or pity, and "the most violent detractor of human virtue" is Mandeville, who—even he!—must acknowledge man's sense of compassion.[110] Yet Rousseau avers that Mandeville did not see that from this sense flowed those very special virtues he denied to humans. (Rousseau of course develops the argument that in the state of nature man is more capable of compassion for others than he is outside that state, in the conditions of civil society.) Mandeville again gets a rather "bad press." Smith's statement that the second volume of the *Fable* occasioned the system of Rousseau is certainly not supported in numerous particulars. Like Mandeville, Rousseau shows a strong sense of the great length of time certain human achievements may well have required, notably in the case of language. Again like Mandeville, he imputes great power in human affairs to *amour-propre,* to which, in his view, we owe a great deal that is bad and a few things that are good. For Mandeville, pride is an "instinct," native to man, whereas for Rousseau it did not exist in the state of nature. Also, Rousseau looks on luxury as evil, in sharp contrast to Mandeville, who, while he may still have some qualms about luxury as "vice," nevertheless attaches great value to it as cause and concomitant of prosperity. Rousseau clearly did not react to Mandeville with any wholesale adoption of his views.[111]

Herder's *Adrastea* asks, referring to Mandeville's **Grumbling Hive,** "Where is there consistency? Where is there consistently pursued truth? The fable fits neither the beehive nor human states." Herder sees the fable as a wretchedly poor piece of work. He writes: "Who will trust himself to a rogue? What a monstrosity would be a state, not only full of rogues but entirely built on roguery and consisting of rogues! Every society is built on fidelity and honor." Again Herder writes:

> That there are in every estate [*in jedem Stande*] respectable scoundrels—who does not know this? . . . But that the welfare of the state should be built upon them and upon the trickery that they carry on [*auf die kunst die sie treiben*] is a slander upon all states. Swift at least opposed the Yahoos to his honorable Houyhnhnms: Mandeville makes all citizens into Yahoos, only with different masks and functions.

Herder goes on to say that Mandeville's affirmations were taken in England to constitute "a system of difformity" [*sic*] but this system or scheme of "deformity" Herder calls an ugly dream. Mandeville's republic of the bees amounts to "a nest of spiders, of which one eats up the other; no abode of healthy industry but a place for the sick, a *Bedlam*." Herder has some justification when he argues that every society is built on fidelity and honor, but he does not seem to have a very good understanding of Mandeville, who hardly wants or conceives of a society based *exclusively* upon vice; and Herder conveys the impression that he took the term vice as Mandeville used it too loosely to capture the latter's meaning.[112]

Kaye notes that **The Fable** retained its celebrity for over a century, until about 1835, by which time "it had apparently ceased to be a sensation."[113] Mandeville went into eclipse for much of the nineteenth century. A figure bridging the eighteenth and nineteenth centuries, like Malthus, might contend in the midst of other concerns that Mandeville's great art consisted in misusing words,[114] and Mandeville was not entirely neglected. But he does not appear to have aroused serious or extensive modern attention until about a century ago, when, Grégoire notes, a section was devoted to him by Bain in his *Mental and Moral Science*.[115] Bain's section, however, was, despite Grégoire's putting it in the category of "a complete or disinterested study," no more than a brief sketch. When Grégoire points to Leslie Stephen's essay on Mandeville in Stephen's *Essay on Freethinking and Plainspeaking,* we may well be more inclined to see this a sign of genuine revival of interest in Mandeville.[116] Also pertinent is the somewhat appreciative estimate of Mandeville that Stephen presented in his *History of English Thought in the Eighteenth Century* (originally 1876). Scholarly interest in Mandeville is alive again. There are indications of that interest over the past century, and recent decades have witnessed a regular flow of relevant material.[117]

Notes

1. F. B. Kaye, "Life of Mandeville," in Kaye's Introduction to *The Fable of the Bees* (hereafter *FB*), 2 vols. (Oxford: Clarendon Press, 1924), 1:xvii-xxx.

2. Kaye, *FB* 1, Introduction, xxix-xxx.

3. See Kaye, *FB* 1, Introduction, xxi.

4. Daniel Defoe, *A Tour Through the Whole Island of Great Britain* (originally 1724-1726). With an Introduction by G. D. H. Cole. 2 vols. (New York: Augustus M. Kelley, 1968), 1: 316, 332, 355.

5. See Peter Earle, *The World of Defoe* (New York: Atheneum, 1977), pp. 117, 165, 323, n. 76. Stone states that the population of London and its suburbs increased "from about sixty thousands in 1500 to about five hundred and fifty thousand in 1700." Lawrence Stone, *The Family, Sex and Marriage in England, 1500-1800* (New York: Harper and Row, 1977), p. 147.

6. Earle, *The World of Defoe,* p. 160.

7. M. Dorothy George, *London Life in the Eighteenth Century* (New York: Capricorn Books, 1965), p. 4.

8. Preface to *FB* 1:11.

9. Preface to *FB* 1:6-7.

10. See Isaac Kramnick, *Bolingbroke and his Circle* (Cambridge: Harvard University Press, 1968), p. 41.

11. Sherburn observes that there is considerable evidence of "the long-term chastening effects" of the bursting of the South Sea bubble and that there is evidence here even for "a revulsion from the mercantilist worship of commerce to the physiocratic idea that wealth comes basically from the soil." George Sherburn, *The Restoration and Eighteenth Century*. A Literary History of England, edited by Albert C. Baugh, vol. 3 (New York: Appleton-Century-Crofts, 1948), p. 830.

12. See Earle, *The World of Defoe,* p. 152.

13. He clearly intimated that he would agree that "everything which, without regard to the public, man should commit to gratify any of his appetites" is legitimately labeled vice (adding, "if in that action there could be observed the least prospect that it might either be injurious to any of the society or ever render himself less serviceable to others"). The name of virtue would be assignable to "every performance by which man, contrary to the impulse of nature, should endeavour the benefit of others or the conquest of his own passions out of a rational ambition of being good." *FB* 1:48-49.

14. Earle, *The World of Defoe,* pp. 152-57 and 308, n. 7.

15. Kramnick, *Bolingbroke and his Circle,* pp. 59-60.

16. Kramnick, *Bolingbroke and his Circle,* pp. 203, 304.

17. See, e.g., E. D. James, "Faith, Sincerity and Morality: Mandeville and Bayle," in Irwin Primer, ed., *Mandeville Studies* (The Hague: Martinus Nijhoff, 1975), p. 65.

18. See H. T. Dickinson, "Bernard Mandeville: An Independent Whig," in *Studies on Voltaire and the Eighteenth Century* 152 (1976): 559-70. Other reserva-

tions and pertinent sources for them are briefly indicated in Albert O. Hirschman, *The Passions and the Interests* (Princeton: Princeton University Press, 1977), p. 57, fn. w. But see also the restatement of Kramnick's theme in John Sekora, *Luxury* (Baltimore: Johns Hopkins Press, 1977), ch. 2.

19. See Kramnick, *Bolingbroke and his Circle*, p. 225.

20. *FB* 1:24.

21. John Gay, *Poetry and Prose,* ed. by Vinton A. Dearing with the assistance of Charles E. Beckwith, 2 vols. (Oxford: Clarendon Press, 1974), 2:416.

22. See Jacob Viner, "Satire and Economics in the Augustan Age of Satire," in H. K. Miller, E. Rothstein, and G. S. Rousseau, eds., *The Augustan Milieu: Essays Presented to Louis A. Landa* (Oxford: Clarendon Press, 1970), pp. 77-101. (Viner is here followed in his application of the term "satire" but whether Mandeville himself is aptly characterized as a "Satirist" is discussed in Chapter 6.) Note also the very pertinent comments in Edward A. Bloom and Lillian D. Bloom, *Joseph Addison's Sociable Animal* (Providence: Brown University Press, 1971), pp. 42-43. A more optimistic picture of social reform in the Augustan Age than Viner affords is suggested by Cecil A. Moore in "Shaftesbury and the Ethical Poets," in More, *Backgrounds of English Literature, 1600-1760* (Minneapolis: University of Minnesota Press, 1953), ch. 1.

23. Kaye, *FB* 1, Introduction, xxxi, fn. 5; H. T. Dickinson's Introduction, pp. 1-xii of the Augustan Reprint Society publication of the *Mischiefs,* William A. Clark Memorial Library, University of California at Los Angeles, 1975.

24. His defense of "vice" against the "virtuous" bent of the Societies for the Reformation of Manners should also be mentioned. See especially Horne, *The Social Thought of Bernard Mandeville,* ch. 1, and D. W. R. Bahlman, *The Moral Revolution of 1688* (New Haven: Yale University Press, 1957).

25. A. R. Humphreys, *The Augustan World* (New York: Harper and Row, 1954), p. 91.

26. Ian Watt, *The Rise of the Novel* (Berkeley and Los Angeles: University of California Press, 1965), p. 48.

27. See Monroe Berger, *Real and Imagined Worlds: The Novel and Social Science* (Cambridge: Harvard University Press, 1977), pp. 43-44.

28. See Bonany Dobrée, *English Literature in the Early Eighteenth Century* (New York: Oxford University Press, 1959), p. 261.

29. "The average annual publication of new books, excluding pamphlets, grew nearly fourfold between 1666 and 1802. From 1666 to 1756 it averaged less than 100 a year; from 1792 to 1802, it averaged 372. Illiteracy and semi-illiteracy, caused by inadequacies of education, poverty, lack of leisure and the high price of books delayed the growth in demand until the second half of the eighteenth century." Diane Laurenson in Laurenson and Alan Swingewood, *The Sociology of Literature* (London: MacGibbon and Kee, 1971), p. 121.

30. David Hume, *Treatise of Human Nature,* 2 vols. (1739; reprint ed., New York: Dutton, Everyman's Library, 1974), 1:6.

31. Kaye lists "authentic works" in his Introduction, *FB* 1:xxx-xxxi. Kaye's list is reproduced in Irwin Primer, ed., *Mandeville Studies,* p. 212, with brief but useful comments appended on the Mandeville canon since 1924 (when Kaye's edition of the *Fable* appeared), at pp. 212-13.

32. Sakmann, *Bernard de Mandeville,* pp. 9-10.

33. The information about these first three works derives from Sakmann, *Bernard de Mandeville,* pp. 8-11. (Sakmann's detailed description of Mandeville's writings is generally valuable although perforce based on information available at the end of the last century. A much briefer listing and description, the description being guided by interests rather different from the present ones, is provided in Chiaki Nishiyama, "The Theory of Self-Love," pp. 232-37.) As regards explanation of animal behavior, Kaye observes, "Mandeville had originally held the Cartesian hypothesis that animals are feelingless automatons. . . . In the *Fable,* however, he has adopted instead the position of Gassendi . . . that animals do feel." Kaye, *FB* 1:181, fn. 1.

34. See Mandeville, *A Treatise of the Hypochondriack and Hysterick Diseases.* 2nd ed. Corrected and enlarged by the author. London, 1730, pp. 94, 163-64.

35. Between the *Disputatio Medica Inauguralis* of 1691 and *The Grumbling Hive* of 1705 there had appeared *Some Fables after the Easie and Familiar Method of Monsieur de la Fontaine* (1703), *Aesop Dress'd or a Collection of Fables Writ in Familiar Verse* (1704), and *Typhon: or the Wars between the Gods and Giants: a Burlesque Poem in Imitation of the Comical Mons. Scarron* (1704). The content of *Aesop Dress'd* is precisely the same as that of *Some Fables.* (See Sakmann, *Bernard de Mandeville,* p. 11.) Also, in 1712 appeared Mandeville's *Wishes to a Godson, with Other Miscellany Poems.* It must suffice to say of *Typhon* (1704) and *Wishes to a Godson* (1712) that they attest, as does Mandeville's prose work, that he was irreverent, capable of vulgarity, and quite free of prudishness. His Aesop poetry (after La Fontaine—with two of the fables by Mandeville himself), it may be remarked, still makes amusing reading. A substantial discussion of the verse is provided in Cook's *Bernard Mandeville,* ch. 2. Thomas Horne, *The Social Thought of Bernard Mandeville,* pp. 25-28, takes La Fontaine as a significant figure in the French *moraliste* tradition that deeply influenced

Mandeville's view of human nature. In 1703, also, Mandeville wrote a short poem (not considered here) prefixed to a medical treatise by one Johannes Groeneveldt or John Greenfield. (See H. Gordon Ward, "An Unnoted Poem by Mandeville," *Review of English Studies* 7 [1931]: 73-76.) This poem is one of two attributions to be accepted into the Mandeville canon since Kaye wrote in 1924, the other being the thirty-two Lucinda-Artesia papers in *The Female Tatler* that are referred to below, fn. 42.

36. Preface, not paginated, of *The Virgin Unmask'd,* London, 1709, Facsimile Reproduction with an Introduction by Stephen H. Gord, Scholar's Facsimiles and Reprints (New York: Delmar, 1975).

37. Note the statement in the Preface, at p. xiii of *A Treatise of the Hypochondriack and Hysterick Diseases,* 2nd ed., 1730: "Philipirio is a foreigner and a physician, who, after he had finished his studies and taken his degree beyond-sea, was come to London to learn the language; in which having happened to take great delight, and in the meantime found the country and the manners of it agreeable to his humour, he has now been many years, and is like to end his days in England."

38. See his Introduction to *FB* on the "History of the Text," at pp. xxxiii-xxvii and his "Description of the Editions" in Kaye, *FB* 2: 386-400.

39. Sakmann, *Bernard de Mandeville,* pp. 158, 177-78.

40. There is substantial scholarly agreement that this is Mandeville's work and Kaye includes it in the Mandeville canon.

41. *FB* 1:100.

42. This is a convenient point at which to add a word regarding the thirty-two Lucinda-Artesia papers appearing in *The Female Tatler* between November 2, 1709 and March 31, 1710, now also included in the Mandeville canon. The papers contained early expressions of some of Mandeville's very characteristic views. (See the article by Paul B. Anderson, "Splendour out of Scandal: The Lucinda-Artesia Papers in the *Female Tatler.*" *Philological Quarterly* 15 [July, 1936]: 286-300.) M. M. Goldsmith's article, "Public Virtue and Private Vice: Bernard Mandeville and English Political Ideologies in the Early Eighteenth Century," in *Eighteenth Century Studies* 9 (1976): 477-510, provides much pertinent information for those who do not have ready access to the Lucinda-Artesia papers (Note Goldsmith's statement, p. 500: "Lucinda and Artesia were Bernard Mandeville.") The papers will be drawn upon in this study. The sole omission of items of Mandeville's prose in the present overview is of letters published in the *British Journal* for April 24 and May 1, 1725. These are of minor significance. (Note the comment on them by Gerald Howson, *Thief-Taker General: The Rise and Fall of Jonathan Wild* [London: Hutchinson, 1970], p. 294.)

43. *FB* 2: 413.

44. Friedrich A. Hayek, "Dr. Bernard Mandeville" (Lecture on a Master Mind, British Academy), *Proceedings of the British Academy* 7 (1966): 128.

45. *English Literature in the Early Eighteenth Century,* p. 19.

46. *Essays in Freethinking and Plainspeaking* (London: Smith, Elder and Co., Duckworth and Co., 1907), pp. 279, 280.

47. *History of English Thought in the Eighteenth Century,* 2:34.

48. George Saintsbury, *A Short History of English Literature* (London: Macmillan, 1913), p. 544.

49. Wilhelm Hasbach, "Larochefoucault und Mandeville," in *Schmollers Jahrbuch für Gesetzgebung, Verwaltung und Volkswritschaft im deutschen Reich* 14 (1890): 17.

50. Robertson in *Essays towards a Critical Method,* p. 218.

51. William Hendley, *A Defense of the Charity Schools,* London, 1725, p. 28.

52. Cook, *Bernard Mandeville,* p. 65

53. *Treatise,* p. 68.

54. Her name is rendered by Cook as "one with many containers—pillboxes." Cook, *Bernard Mandeville,* p. 65.

55. *Treatise,* 1730, p. 270.

56. *Treatise,* 1730, p. 353.

57. In the light of Polytheca's statement and Misomedon's later comment, it is of interest that, according to Cecil Moore, physicians in Mandeville's day were strongly of the opinion that emotional instability was very "real" and that it had a special "gusto for the female sex." Cecil A. Moore, "The English Malady," in Moore's *Backgrounds of English Literature, 1700-1760* (Minneapolis: University of Minnesota Press, 1953), p. 189.

58. Light is thrown on Mandeville's medical work or the psychiatry of his time by Moore, "The English Malady"; Cook, *Bernard Mandeville,* ch. 4 ("Mandeville as a Physician"); G. S. Rousseau, "Mandeville and Europe: Medicine and Philosophy," in Primer, ed., Mandeville studies, pp. 11-21; John Hill, *Hypochondriasis: A Practical Treatise* (1766; reprint ed., William Andrews Clark Memorial Library, University of California at Los Angeles, 1969. See also the Introduction to this edition by G. S. Rousseau.) The *Treatise,* incidentally, shows that Mandeville had no exaggerated opinion of the abilities of doctors and *The Grumbling Hive* has it that "physicians valued fame and wealth above the dropping patient's health."

59. *The Virgin Unmask'd,* p. 27.

60. *FB* 2:172-73. See also the *Treatise,* where Philopirio says he thinks women "unfit both for abstruse and elaborate thoughts, all studies of depth, coherence, and solidity, that fatigue the spirits and require a steadiness and assiduity of thinking." But where women have advantages of education and knowledge equalling those of men, they "exceed the men in sprightliness of fancy, quickness of thought, and off-hand wit." *Treatise,* p. 247. An apt passage on the different aspects of differing education in the generation of "modesty" among men and women is in *FB* 1:71-72. It is worth noting that John M. Robertson (*Essays towards Critical Method,* p. 231) saw Mandeville as "quite unique in his generation in his insistence on the intellectual capacities of women."

61. See George Bluet, *An Enquiry Whether a General Practice of Virtue Tends to the Wealth or Property, Benefit or Disadvantage of a People,* London, 1725, p. 146.

62. See Daniel Defoe, *Some Consideration Upon Street-Walkers,* London, 1726.

63. Monro, *The Ambivalence of Bernard Mandeville,* p. 99.

64. *FB* 1:306.

65. *FB* 1:267, 310, 314. See also *FB* 2:351-52.

66. Introduction to *FB* 1:lxx.

67. Horne, *The Social Thought of Bernard Mandeville,* p. 69. Horne is more cognizant of certain hard realities in Mandeville's position on the laboring poor than a writer like Robert H. Hopkins in his "The Cant of Social Compromise: Some Observations on Mandeville's Satire," in Primer, ed., *Mandeville Studies,* pp. 185-86.

68. *FB* 1:105-106.

69. *FB* 1:250.

70. Robert K. Merton, *Social Theory and Social Structure* (New York: Free Press, 1968), pp. 100-101. (It may also be important to note different consequences for different portions of a "larger structure.") See also Albert Schatz, "Bernard de Mandeville (Contribution a l'Etude des Origines du Liberalisme Economique)," in *Vierteljahrschrift für Socialund Wirtschaftsgeschichte* (Leipzig: Hirschfeld, 1903), 1:455-56. A contemporary discussion of Mandeville and functional analysis is also presented in Joseph Spengler, "Veblen and Mandeville Contrasted," *Weltwirtschaftliches Archiv* 82 (1959):35-65.

71. One may note the optimistic laissez-faire accent that appears when Cleomenes refers to "a felicity that would flow spontaneously from the nature of every large society if none were to divert or interrupt the stream." *FB* 2:353.

72. See *FB* 1:219-20, *FB* 2:102; *Origin of Honour,* London, 1732, p. 65.

73. The example is deliberately not carried beyond this point. A view of its "full" effects might make it seem to point to a less happy outcome than that suggested. While in some sense benefiting the nation as a whole, it might, for example, demoralize other leading political figures.

74. Reference should at least be made also to *FB* 1:173-81, where Mandeville eloquently expresses compassion for the animals that humans slaughter for meat and writes (p. 175) of "this barbarity of eating flesh." Another comment about Mandeville's holism is required also. The emphasis of his holism need not necessarily be in the *functional* direction, although it often is. The emphasis may rather be in the direction of order. Here a whole is looked upon as its exhibits regularity or predictability. A holistic-*orderly* outlook in Mandeville is likely to become marked when, for example, he contrasts the actions of individuals directed to their own limited economic purposes or interests and the (unanticipated or unintended) orderly outcome of those limited pursuits for a society or economy as a whole (or for some sector thereof conceived as a whole). Every part is "full of vice" as individuals strive for their own gain but an orderly (and not merely a beneficent) economic whole emerges as they strive (at least under certain circumstances). The holistic-orderly orientation in Mandeville is also extremely important and will call for attention again. Holistic-functional and holistic-orderly orientations are not incompatible, but they differ as concern turns to contribution to a whole, on one hand, or to state or degree of order exhibited by the whole itself, on the other.

75. The *Free Thoughts* is worth adducing in this connection. The book seems clearly to be the work of man who is trying (within his limitations) to be reasonable and is desirous of seeing peace and tolerance among his fellows. Here Mandeville is neither cynic nor misanthrope as he seeks to ascertain how humans may enjoy "as much happiness as the condition of mortals is susceptible of" (his very last words in *Free Thoughts,* p. 409).

76. *FB* 1:91.

77. *FB* 1:138-39.

78. Much of this paragraph is taken, with minor changes, from the writer's paper, "Mandeville as Forerunner of Modern Sociology," *Journal of the History of the Behavioral Sciences* 6 (July, 1970):229.

79. *FB* 1:263-64.

80. The view of human motivation presented undoubtedly—and quite understandably—is the source of innumerable accusations of cynicism brought against Mandeville. No attempt is made here to discuss the pertinent thought of Mandeville in relation to that of

"an Epicurean or a Hobbist," in the sense in which Hume writes, "An Epicurean or a Hobbist readily allows that there is such a thing as friendship in the world without hypocrisy or disguise, though he may attempt, by a philosophical chemistry, to resolve the elements of this passion, if I may so speak, into those of another and explain every affection to be self-love twisted and molded by a particular turn of imagination into a variety of appearances." *An Inquiry Concerning the Principles of Morals* (Indianapolis: Bobbs-Merrill, 1957), p. 114. For a contention that this "Epicurean or Hobbist" view of human nature is "subtler" than Mandeville's and much harder to refute, see John Laird, *Hume's Philosophy of Human Nature* (Hamden, Connecticut: Archon Books, 1967), p. 239. Quite possibly Laird is right. The precise value of this alternative view is another matter.

81. In Mandeville's day, Bishop Butler suggested something similar with regard to power: "For the sake of power," humans may engage in very different ways of behaving, as they may engage in charitable action, "for power"—and in mischievous action, "for power." Joseph Butler, *Fifteen Sermons* (London: G. Bell and Sons, 1953), p. 34. Hume has some cogent statements in this same general connection. He notes that the virtuous are not indifferent to praise—"and therefore they may have been represented as a set of vainglorious men who had nothing in view but the applause of others." However, "it is very unjust in the world, when they find any tincture of vanity in a laudable action, to depreciate it upon that account or ascribe it entirely to that motive. . . . Vanity is so closely allied to virtue, and to love the form of laudable actions approaches so near the love of laudable actions for their own sake, that these passions are more capable of mixture than other kinds of affection. . . ." "Of the Dignity or Meanness of Human Nature," in T. H. Green and T. H. Grose, eds., Hume's *Essays Moral, Political and Literary,* 2 vols. (New York: Longmans Green, 1912), 1:155-56. (Neither Butler nor Hume mentioned Mandeville specifically in these connections.)

82. See John Hervey, *Some Remarks on the Minute Philosopher,* London, 1732, pp. 46-47. See also Kaye in *FB* 2:412.

83. See Francis Hutcheson, *An Inquiry into the Original of Our Ideas of Beauty and Virtue* (1725; reprint ed., Hildesheim: Georg Olms Verlag, 1971). Appended "Alterations and Additions Made in the Second Edition" (1726), pp. 20-21.

84. Hume, *Essays,* 1:151.

85. Immanuel Kant, *Anthropology from a Pragmatic Point of View,* trans. Mary J. Gregor (The Hague: M. Nijhoff, 1974), p. 32.

86. *Treatise,* pp. v, 35, 59-60. See also, e.g., pp. 69, 98. Philopirio was also no friend to doctors who adorned ignorance with Latin or to those who made preten-

tious claims about what mathematics could do in the sphere of medicine. On mathematics and medicine there are some acute comments in the *Treatise,* pp. 183-84. On Medicine, mathematics and observation, see also *FB* 2:161-62, 164.

87. See *Treatise,* pp. 120-21.

88. At the same time he is most shrewd on the sociology or social psychology of scientific strife. See *Treatise,* pp. 125-26.

89. *Treatise,* pp. 123, 129-30.

90. Ducan Forbes, *Hume's Philosophical Politics* (Cambridge: Cambridge University Press, 1975), p. 61

91. *The Female Tatler,* No. 66, December 7, 1709.

92. *FB* 1:231.

93. *FB* 1:128.

94. See his *Hostage to the Devil* (New York: Reader's Digest Press, 1976), particularly p. 79. Yet one must admit that Malachi Martin's demons might be a bit too strong even for Mandeville's stomach.

95. Preface to *Modest Defence.*

96. *Free Thoughts,* pp. 216-17.

97. *Treatise,* p. 80.

98. A more circumstantial statement on Mandeville's style than the above very curtailed one would, among other things, give fair attention to his oft-encountered "verbal" or "rhetorical" ironies and attend, also, to his gift for sharp and concise statement, as in this: "To search into the real causes of things imports no ill design nor has any tendency to do harm. A man may write on poisons and be an excellent physician." *FB* 1:408.

99. The term "Battle of the Bees" has been most directly suggested by Grégoire's phrase, "La Querelle de Fable" (see Grégoire, *Bernard de Mandeville,* p. 146, and his title for the section of his book running pp. 177-94), although an older writer like Sakmann uses in the subtitle of his study of Mandeville the phrase, "die Bienenfable-Controverse."

100. See A. D. Lindsay's Introduction to Hume's *Treatise of Human Nature,* 2:v.

101. See the *Treatise of Human Nature,* 2:204; *An Inquiry Concerning the Principles of Morals,* p. 42.

102. See, e.g., the *Treatise of Human Nature,* 2:287-95. Laird, who is not excessively receptive to Mandeville, also proposes that Hume owed him a good deal in the matter of analysis of pride. John Laird, *Hume's Philosophy of Human Nature,* p. 211.

103. *Treatise of Human Nature,* 2:198, 207.

104. See *FB* 2:141-42; Hume, *Dialogues Concerning Natural Religion* (Indianapolis: Bobbs-Merrill, 1947), p. 167.

105. See *The Early Writings of Adam Smith,* ed. J. Ralph Lindgen (New York: Augustus M. Kelley, 1967), pp. 15-28, esp. 23-25.

106. *The Theory of Moral Sentiments,* eds. D. D. Raphael and A. L. Macfie (Oxford: Clarendon Press, 1967), p. 313.

107. See Kaye's interesting fn. in Introduction, *FB* 1:cxli-cxliii.

108. Adam Smith, *The Wealth of Nations,* eds. R. H. Cambell and A. S. Skinner, 2 vols. (Oxford: Clarendon Press, 1976); see Index of Authorities, vol. 2, *s. v.* Mandeville.

109. Kaye, *FB* 1, "Introduction," cxlii, fn. Schumpeter, *History of Economic Analysis* (New York: Oxford University Press, 1954), p. 184, fn. 16.

110. J. J. Rousseau, *Discours sur l'Origine et les Fondements de l'Inégalité Parmi les Hommes,* in C. E. Vaughan, ed. *The Political Writings of Jean Jacques Rousseau,* 2 vols. (Oxford: B. Blackwell, 1962), 1:125-220, p. 160.

111. Informative commentary on Mandeville in relation to eighteenth-century French thought other than that of Rousseau is given by Ellen Ross, "Mandeville, Melon, and Voltaire: The Origins of the Luxury Controversy in France," *Studies on Voltaire and the Eighteenth Century,* 155 (1976):1897-1912.

112. Johann Gotfried von Herder, *Sämmtliche Werke.* Herausgegeben von Bernhard Suphan, 33 vols. (Berlin: Wiedmannsche Buchhandlung, 1886), 24:105, 106, 119. Bernhard Fabian does not appear to see much more merit in Herder's understanding of Mandeville than does the present writer. Fabian also notes Kant's more sympathetic attitude toward *The Fable,* while noting that Kant apparently was the sole critic of Mandeville in eighteenth-century Germany who comprehended clearly the quality of the latter's thought. Bernhard Fabian, "The Reception of Bernard Mandeville in Eighteenth-Century Germany," in *Studies in Voltaire and the Eighteenth Century* 152 (1976): 693-722.

113. Introduction, *FB* 1:cxvii, fn. 5.

114. Grégoire, *Bernard de Mandeville,* p. 221, fn. 6.

115. Alexander Bain, *Mental and Moral Sciences* (London: Longmans Green, 1872), pp. 593-98; Grégoire, p. 223.

116. On Leslie Stephen as renewing interest in Mandeville, see also Walther Hübner, "Mandeville Bienenfabel und die Bergründung der praktischen Zweckethik in der englichen Aufklärung," in Paul Meissner, ed., *Grundformen der Englichen Geistesgeschichte* (Stuttgart and Berlin: W. Kohlhammer Verlag, 1941), p. 307.

117. A useful selective bibliography of items of controversy over *The Fable,* for a period of two and one-half centuries up to 1969, is afforded in *The New Cambridge Bibliography of English Literature,* ed. George Watson (Cambridge: University Press, 1971), vol. 2, 1660-1800, cols. 1096-98.

M. M. Goldsmith (essay date 1992)

SOURCE: Goldsmith, M. M. "Bernard Mandeville and the Virtues of the Dutch." *Dutch Crossing* 48 (autumn 1992): 20-38.

[*In the following essay, Goldsmith discusses the impact that Mandeville's Dutch heritage may have had on his viewpoints, literary style, and subject matter.*]

Little is known about the life of Bernard Mandeville (1670-1733), author of **The Fable of the Bees: or Private Vices, Publick Benefits.** Until recently all that was available concerning that part of his life which he spent in his native Holland was a few bald facts about his family background and his education. He was baptized in Rotterdam on 20 November 1670.[1] His background, Dutch on both sides, was from well-established medical and professional families.[2] After attending the Erasmian School in Rotterdam until 1685, he studied philosophy and medicine at the University of Leiden. Those studies left him a Cartesian.[3] Apparently, having taken his first degree in 1689, he returned to Rotterdam, spending a year there before returning briefly to Leiden to take his medical degree.[4] Following his father's example, he specialized in nervous and digestive diseases.[5]

During his absence from Leiden in 1690, as Rudolf Dekker has shown, Bernard Mandeville, along with his father, was involved in the agitation and riot against the Rotterdam bailiff, Jacob Van Zuijlen van Nievelt, which followed the trial and execution of Cornelis Costerman, a member of the city militia, for the killing of an agent of a tax farmer. Bernard's father, Michael, was connected with a faction hostile to the Bailiff. Informants suggested that Bernard had composed or helped to compose a pasquil, 'Sanctimonious Atheist', denouncing Van Zuijlen, which contributed to instigating a riot in which the Bailiff's house front was demolished. The States of Holland acted: soldiers were sent to restore order and the provincial court eventually instituted a prosecution against Van Zuijlen. However, William III intervened to remove the case to the High Council of Holland and Zealand, where the stadholder exercised greater influence. Van Zuijlen was acquitted in 1692, reinstated and compensated. The Bailiff's triumph led to a purge of the opposing faction in the course of which Michael Mandeville was banished (in 1693) and moved to Amsterdam. Indeed, this setback to the Mandevilles' rise up the social ladder may well have prompted Bernard's departure for England.[6] At some point in the 1690s then, Bernard de Mandeville moved to England, bringing with him a stock of Dutch experience which he was to find useful; by 1699 he had settled in London, for in that year he married Ruth Laurence.[7] Later he dropped the particle.

Although, it is hard to know how much of what is specifically Mandevillean about Mandeville can be attributed to his Dutch background, it is clear that some aspects of his native land provided salient examples to support his views. Certainly, he had some connections with the Dutch community in and around London, contributing a Latin poem to Groenevelt's medical work and later being the unlikely translator of a sermon.[8] Moreover, the first work he published in English defended a countryman; in 1703, *The Pamphleteers* defended the late King William against the slurs upon his achievements and character current among the recently triumphant Tories.[9] The poem celebrated the divine protection which had preserved William against assassination, reminded its readers of his providential rescue of Britain from popery and tyranny despite the risks to the Netherlands as well as the difficulties of a winter invasion, and asked what he had done to deserve being lampooned.[10] After all it was William who first, without allies, resisted French expansion. In fact, William's detractors are covert Jacobites: they complain of William's grants in order to attack Protestantism; they regret the Revolution; they call the money misspent which was employed in defending Britain; and they rail against foreigners because they wish to exclude the House of Hanover.[11] Nonetheless, William's virtues and his fame cannot be diminished by this 'toothless malice'. Finally the poem wishes for Anne 'all the Blessings that can crowd a Throne': ministerial integrity, conciliar wisdom and secrecy, military prudence and courage, clerical learning and humility, along with judicial impartiality. He also wishes that Anne may curb 'Gallick Tyranny' so that England may have peace and plenty and the divine gift 'Which we ne'er tasted yet, to be CONTENT', even if that is unlikely for 'A grumbling Nation that was ne'er at ease',[12] *The Pamphleteers,* by diagnosing the English disease as splenetic grumbling, exhibits a theme frequently repeated in his work—the verses which grew into *The Fable of the Bees* were originally published in 1705 under the title, *The Grumbling Hive.* It also strikes another familiar note with its commitment to Whig politics.[13]

Mandeville never seems to have changed his views about William, the Glorious Revolution, the grumbling of the English and the resistance to Louis XIV's tyranny. In 1714, Mandeville again deployed his Whig politics in his one known overt party tract, *The Mischiefs that ought justly to be Apprehended from a Whig-Government*; he still defended the memory of William, the war against Louis XIV and the accession of the House of Hanover. That George I is a foreigner is unimportant: most of the English derive from foreign stock; George will wish to pass on the kingdom to his descendants, who will not be foreign after a generation; the Pretender and any other Stuart candidates for the throne are equally foreign, at least to English institutions. Once again railing against foreigners is identified with Jacobitism. The same views re-appear in his *Free Thoughts on Religion* (1720). The English have every reason for happiness, yet complain. Why do they complain? because they are 'hypped'. He repeats his praise of the Dutch republic, William and all those who preserved

England's freedom, religion and tranquillity and reasserts the unimportance of the supposed foreignness of the house of Hanover.[14]

These characteristics are reiterated in another of Mandeville's early works, *The Virgin Unmask'd.*[15] The work takes the form of ten conversations between the naive, young Antonia and her 'elderly maiden aunt', Lucinda. The dialogue in which a younger woman is instructed by an older, experienced one is a stock form for pornography.[16] *The Virgin Unmask'd* exploited that commercial possibility by beginning the first dialogue with Lucinda demanding that Antonia cover her breasts. But in writing a dialogue between an older and a younger woman Mandeville may equally have been following the example of the most popular Dutch writer of the seventeenth century, the moralist Jacob Cats. Be that as it may, the conversation proceeds from its suggestive beginning to a discussion of the relations between men and women, then to the question of whether marriage is desirable for a woman, and between two exemplary tales, it turns to politics.[17] The politics of *The Virgin Unmask'd* are those of a Whig supporter of the war against France. Lucinda paints Louis XIV as an especially dangerous enemy, a master of politics who has succeeded in displacing the house of Austria as the most powerful monarchy in Europe, a 'wicked Tyrant' whose 'wonderful Atchievements' must be recognized.

> In Feats of War, he has out-done Alexander and Caesar both; in encouraging Learning, and promoting all Arts and Sciences, in embellishing his Nation, he has exceeded Augustus, and shew'd himself both at Home and Abroad, a deeper Politician than Tiberius.[18]

It is also a mistake to underestimate the wealth and power of France, which is now capable of sustaining a war against almost all of Europe, even, indeed, of losing the battle of Ramillies after Hochstedt and still resisting the allied armies. In the course of this discussion, clearly aimed at refuting the contention, increasingly put forward by Tories, that Britain's allies, especially the Dutch, were benefiting from the war while doing too little to sustain it, Lucinda slips in a mention of 'our late King, of glorious Memory' reiterating Mandeville's favourable view of William.[19]

Lucinda's instruction of Antonia in 'State-Affairs' goes beyond the mere espousal of Whig positions.

> Those that would meddle with 'em, ought to have not only read, but digested all manner of History, that they may be ready to compare what is present, with what has been; and be able, upon every Accident, allowing for the Difference of Time and Place, to judge of the Event of Things to come.

But more than history is required in order to understand politics:

> A Politician that would pretend to fore-see what shall happen, ought to be acquainted with other Countries, as well as he is with his own, to know the great Cities,

their Commerce, the Sea-ports, their Shipping, the Fortifications, Artillery, Stores, and Ammunition; all the
Towns of Note, the Number of Villages, and the People
they contain; the Soil, the Climate, the Extent and
Product of every Province; some of these things are
very difficult to be learn'd.[20]

And even that is not all, for the politician ought also to
know about the ruler, the court and the ministers and generals.

Without this detailed empirical knowledge, even those involved in decisions can only guess at what will happen.
Admittedly, these accomplishments are rare and difficult:

> they are so difficult that it is an Accomplishment to
> know the Difficulty of it. It is very hard in some Coun-
> tries to be well acquainted with the hidden Springs that
> give Life to the several Courts of Justice; the several
> Pullies, by the Help of which, the Money is hoisted up
> from the very Bottom to the Top, as well as the many
> Holes thro' which it is suffer'd to drop down again,
> with the Wheels that turn it, and all the other Parts that
> compose the Machine of Government. Travellers have
> not Time for it, and seldom troubling their Heads with
> the Inside, are commonly satisfy'd, if they can but see
> the Engine play. Those that make it their Business, and
> enquire into it, are often impos'd upon, by addressing
> themselves to People that pretend to know more than
> they do.[21]

Thus, understanding politics requires extensive information organized in a systematic, mechanical conception of
the machinery of government and society.

Not surprisingly, few of the English understand foreign
countries. Here Lucinda, and Mandeville, turn to the Dutch
example: there are many errors even in Sir William Temple's account of the Netherlands.

> The seven united Provinces are very near; there is a
> strict Alliance between them and us, and both actually
> shew, at this present Time, such an unparallel'd Confi-
> dence in one another, as never was seen before be-
> tween two such powerful Neighbours, of so different
> an Interest in Trade; an[d] yet, though we have so great
> a Commerce with them, how few People have we here,
> that exactly understand their Government!

Most people cannot identify the composition and authority
of the provincial and federal authorities; even the elite
'have no clearer Notion of 'em, tho' they are next Door to
us, than they have of the Mandarins in China'. British ignorance is so extensive that they have no idea what the
Dutch war tax, the 'hundred penny', actually involves as a
twice annual tax on wealth.[22] If the English understood
that tax, along with extensive excise taxes paid by the
Dutch, they would no longer complain that the Nether-
landers were not paying their share. They would cease to
'grumble at paying four Shillings in the Pound' in Land
Tax, a much lighter burden, and instead 'cry out, Blessed
England!'.[23]

The accurate assessment of Louis XIV and the vindication
of the Dutch are only parts of Antonia's lesson in political
science. Lucinda goes on to instruct her in comparative
politics, contrasting the situations and interests of France,
Britain and the United Provinces. It is a mistake to estimate the wealth and power of France by 'the miserable
Poverty of the lowest Rank of People' there. For,

> the Subordinations of the Degrees of People, differs in
> every Nation, according to the Degrees of Liberty they
> enjoy. As for Example; In France there is a vast Dis-
> tance between the Nobility and the Gentry; in Holland
> there is none at all, not so much as in the Language;
> with us, that are a Mixture of Monarchy and Common-
> wealth together, tho' there is a great Difference, the
> Top of the Gentry converse with the Nobility; a Gentle-
> man here, speaks to a Peer with his Hat on, goes to the
> Tavern, pays his Club; but in France there is no such
> Thing. What I say of the Nobility and Gentry, you must
> understand of all the several Degrees of People, from
> the Sovereign to the Beggar.[24]

The account deploys a conception of the relation of property, power and social relations which is derived from
civic humanism: wealth and power are relatively equally
distributed in republics; in monarchies, the hierarchy of
rank and wealth is more distinct. Thus France is a wealthy
and powerful kingdom, notwithstanding the abject slavish
condition of the lowest rank. Britain is less egalitarian
than Holland, and less hierarchical than France. The English poor are better off than the French poor, especially in
London and other prosperous areas.

It is the distribution of wealth rather than its absolute
amount which is determined by the constitutional form;
the analysis must take into account that the English 'are a
greater and richer Nation by abundance, than they'. The
wealth of the Dutch is entirely dependent on money and
trade; they have little land. Consequently, the English poor
eat better than the Dutch. The Dutch are nevertheless better clothed and housed; typically each has a 'small hoard
of Money, or Money's Worth to go to in Time of Need'.
Whereas the common people in France are obliging and
submissive, republican Holland is so egalitarian that the
'Notion they have of Liberty, makes 'em so proud, that the
ordinary Man thinks himself as good as the best in the
Land', so they pay little respect even to magistrates, except in the execution of their offices. An English porter
will call out 'Have a Care' or even 'With your Leave, Sir',

> But in Holland, a Fellow very often, without giving the
> Warning, will trundle a Wheel-barrow against your
> Legs, and afterwards scold at you for not standing out
> of the Way.

Thus Antonia learns that republics, mixed governments
and monarchies are different in their distributions of wealth
and in their manners.[25]

The discussion of politics in *The Virgin Unmask'd* uses
the Netherlands as a prime case of republican liberty. That
was far from unusual; Sir William Temple had already

characterized the Dutch as 'obstinate Lovers and Defenders of their Liberty'.[26] But Mandeville extends the usual 'civic humanist' analysis by contrasting the social condition and manners of the people under different constitutions. Moreover, the Netherlands provides a substantial empirical example of the systematic materialist and mechanical principles involved. But even in Mandeville's account something remains of the virtues usually ascribed to the Dutch. They are neater in their dress, better equipped with furniture and utensils and more provident than the English; the poor are proportionally better paid there. The Dutch virtues of cleanliness and frugality thus survive even though Mandeville recognizes that these characteristics will not make the Netherlands wealthier than France, where the frivolous fashionability of the upper classes will 'occasion an incredible Circulation of Money'. It is roughly right to regard the Dutch as covetous and careful, the French as lavish and extravagant and the English as 'not so provident as the one, and less extravagant than the other'. Nonetheless there are misers in France and spendthrifts in Holland, despite the prevailing social mores.[27]

The Dutch have another, less usual virtue. Lucinda is an independently wealthy woman who loves liberty; she therefore feels toward all men as European states do toward Louis XIV—she hates and detests them. Lucinda holds that marriage is slavery. When Antonia responds that this may be true in other countries, 'but in England, Women are treated very Respectfully, as well as Tenderly', Lucinda retorts:

> 'Tis that Respect and Tenderness I hate, when it consists only in outward shew: In Holland Women sit in their Counting-houses, and do Business, or at least are acquainted with every thing their Husbands do. But says a Rascal here, no, my Dear, that is too much Trouble; those Butter-Boxes don't know, how to treat Ladies; Men should only study, how to give 'em Pleasure.

So she is sent to the theatre, only to have the rings torn from her previously respected fingers on her return, her husband having been declared bankrupt in the meanwhile.[28] In England, women are regarded as possessions, whereas in Holland they are partners in their husbands' affairs.

The Virgin Unmask'd thus relies on the Dutch example when Mandeville wishes to emphasize and illustrate his central tenets. He is a convinced Whig, a supporter of the war against Louis XIV. The enemy of the Netherlands is also Britain's foe. Moreover, contrary to the grumbles of the Tories, the Dutch are paying their share of the war expenses. Moreover, it is to the Netherlands that Mandeville turns when he wishes to demonstrate the necessity of extensive factual information for statesmanship, describe the workings and consequences of the political system or damn the way that women are treated.

Mandeville's concern for the position of women was further shown in his next publication. From November 1709 until March 1710 he wrote about half the issues of the thrice-weekly *Female Tatler*. This journal imitated both the format and the content of Richard Steele's successful *Tatler.* Initially a 'Mrs. Crackenthorpe', who pretended to know everything, was the nominal author, writing little stories and essays and spreading supposed or actual scandal; but from the fifty-second issue the paper was written by "a Society of Ladies" which included the sisters, Lucinda and Artesia—both Bernard Mandeville.[29]

In *The Female Tatler,* Mandeville continues to espouse the cause of women. To Bickerstaff's sneer that if there were enough famous women a tea table might be set up for them, Mandeville responded by devoting eight issues of the newspaper to famous and virtuous women: rulers, philosophers and saints, learned or courageous, modern and ancient, biblical and historical, real or legendary. To *The Tatler*'s select dozen men, Lucinda and Artesia respond by naming dozens of women. Should the 'Male-Cricks' object that many of these women are obscure and that the evidence of their virtue (and hence what fame they enjoy) relies upon a few recorded incidents, Artesia has an answer prepared.

> From what I have said it is evident, that the Women, unless they had enjoy'd an equal Share of Power and Greatness with the Men, will not be found on Record for their Excellencies so much as the latter, tho' they had exceeded them in every Virtue. Since Men have enslav'd us, the greatest part of the World have always debar'd our Sex from Governing, which is the Reason that the Lives of Women have so seldom been describ'd in History; but as this is only to be impute to the Injustice and Tyranny of the Men, It ought not to be of any Disadvantage to the Women.[30]

Thus virtuous women have been unjustly denied the fame they deserve, partly because they have often been excluded from displaying their talents and also because, even when they have, male historians have neglected them.[31]

In *The Female Tatler,* Mandeville repeated his views about the position of women in England. In *Female Tatler* 88 (27 Jan. 1710), the explicit contrast with the Dutch is omitted when Artesia complains that English women were 'treated almost as if we were Irrational Creatures', denied education in Latin and the arts and sciences and laughed at for discussing any serious subject, such as politics:

> But what enrages me most is to see our Sex so stupid as to believe themselves better treated than the Women in other Nations, because we are more egregiously Cheated of our Rights and Liberties than they; a Man is call'd Prudent for not trusting anything of Moment to his Wife, and makes her believe, that to be his Co-partner in the Management of his Estate, would be an insufferable Trouble to her; while by his Neglect, Folly or Extravagancy, she is often made a Beggar at the same Time when she thinks herself a Wealthy Woman.

The criticism is reiterated by Lucinda who notes that women have now escaped some of their former servitude, having taken up learning to the extent that there are now almost as many female as male authors. But to learn practical as well as theoretical mathematics, English women have taken to gambling:

> It must be own'd, the Dutch women have a far better Method to attain that Art by counting their Gains, and confining it to Trade; but when English Husbands will give a sincere account of their Affairs, and consult with their Wives and confide in their Friendship and Diligence, I dare believe they will soon overtake their Neighbours in the use of that Commendable Science.[32]

Thus the Dutch once again provide an example of how women should be treated.

In *The Fable of the Bees* we discover even more of the virtues of the Dutch. They have proved skilful politicians, turning a 'contemptible Spot of Ground' into one of the main European powers through 'their Political Wisdom in postponing everything to Merchandize and Navigation, the unlimited Liberty of Conscience that is enjoy'd among them, and the unwearied Application with which they have always made use of the most effectual means to encourage and increase Trade in general'. National frugality generally results from the necessities of life being dear. What made the Dutch frugal was their revolt against Spain; acting with 'Fortitude and Resolution' they 'maintain'd against the greatest and best disciplin'd Nation in Europe, the most tedious and bloody War, that is to be met with in ancient or modern History'. To do so they had to devote most of their income to the struggle for a period of eighty years; thus frugality became 'Customary and Habitual to them'.[33]

The Dutch, laden with taxes, crammed into a small territory devoid of natural resources, were obliged to be saving. But that cannot make them 'a Pattern to others' who are 'more happily situated' and naturally endowed with more land. The Dutch must import everything except cheese, butter and fish; when the English eat meat they maintain their own farmers. Of course the Dutch probably have more ships and a greater quantity of money, but these are their tools.

> He that keeps three or four Stage-Coaches to get his Bread, is to a Gentleman that keeps a Coach for his Pleasure, what the Dutch are in comparison to us.[34]

In the poorer provinces where taxes are lower, the people are more generous than in Holland where daily necessities are dear. But the Hollanders spend lavishly on pictures, marbles, buildings and gardens: 'in all Europe you shall find no private Buildings so sumptuously Magnificent, as a great many of the Merchants and other Gentlemen's Houses are in Amsterdam'. Moreover things have changed since Sir William Temple lived there; the common people may remain much as they were, but 'a great Alteration has been made among the better sort of People in their Equipages, Entertainments, and whole manner of living'.

Dutch frugality, then, originated in necessity; insofar as it continues to exist it does so because of their situation. But there is no general aversion to vice and luxury. Those who write panegyrics on the Dutch point to their prudence in the administration of public affairs and ascribe it to the 'Virtue and Honesty of Ministers'. On Mandeville's account, it is the constitution which provides 'strict Regulations', consequently necessitating this type of behaviour: 'unhappy is the People, and their Constitution must ever be precarious, whose Welfare must depend upon the Virtues and Consciences of Ministers and Politicians'.[35] The Dutch thus provide no exception to Mandeville's contentions that there never was a national frugality without national necessity, and that commercial prosperity and luxury are inseparable. They also exemplify his views about government; a good system involves a complex machine composed of simple tasks which are not beyond the capacity of normal self-interested mortals, and thus require no extraordinary knowledge or virtue. This view is reiterated in *Free Thoughts on Religion*, in *The Fable of the Bees, Part II* and in *The Origin of Honour*.[36]

But since the Dutch are skilful politicians they also provide empirical support both for Mandeville's insistence that frugality is encouraged because it is usually beneficial to them and for his contention that luxury and vice are beneficial. He actually commends the wisdom of the Dutch twice in *The Fable of the Bees* for harnessing ineradicable vice to the public benefit. The 'Wise Rulers of that well-order'd City', viz., Amsterdam, exhibit their 'Prudence and Oeconomy' by tolerating 'an uncertain number of Houses, in which Women are hired as publickly as Horses at a Livery-Stable'. Thousands of sailors arrive when the East India ships come in, having spent months in all male company; 'how is it to be suppos'd that honest Women should walk the Streets unmolested, if there were no Harlots to be had at reasonable Prices?' These houses are allowed only 'in the most slovenly and unpolish'd part of the Town'; no public lewdness but only the bargains are permitted; the women are from 'the Scum of the People'. Moreover, the officials 'are always vexing, mulcting, and upon the least Complaint removing the miserable Keepers' of these houses, thereby both squeezing 'a Living out of the immoderate Gains accruing from the worst of Employments' and punishing the 'Bawds and Panders, which tho' they abominate, they desire not wholly to destroy'. Thus this trade is 'conniv'd at', allowing the 'wary Magistrates' to maintain the 'good Opinion of the weaker sort of People, who imagine that the Government is always endeavouring, tho' unable, to suppress what it actually tolerates'.[37]

On their arrival, these sailors are paid their full wages, some for seven years, others for as many as fifteen or sixteen years' work. These 'Lords of six Weeks' are encouraged to 'revel and riot with greater Licentiousnes than is customary to be allowed in others' and so squander their pay on 'Wine, Women and Musick' until they have nothing left and are ready to sign on for another long term. By this means, the Dutch are able to reemploy trained men 'inured to the hot Climates and unwholesome Air and Diet' instead of training new recruits and also to make the large sums paid to the sailors circulate through the domestic economy, a substantial amount of which returns to the treasury through taxes and excises.[38] When it serves their purpose, the Dutch can employ their political wisdom to encourage beneficial vice.

In *The Fable of the Bees, Part II,* a discussion of painting illustrates one of Mandeville's central contentions. Cleomenes, ridiculing Shaftesbury's position, denies that truth should have any part in the 'Sublime'; he ironically praises an Italian painting for its depiction of the Nativity; mean elements, like the ox and the ass, are carefully hidden in obscurity while the subject is shown in 'majestick Grandeur', complete with a colonnade of pillars of the Corinthian order. This elevated, noble presentation is contrasted with a Dutch piece which does not hesitate to show things that are 'abject, low, pitiful and mean' and in which the artist might actually violate all good taste, even 'put the Bambino into the manger'. Fulvia, no doubt with Mandeville's approval, demands, 'has good Sense ever any Share in the Judgement which your Men of true Taste form about Pictures?' She finds the false elevation of the scene more offensive than the depiction of those low things which are beneath the contemplation of members of the 'Beau Monde'. At least the Dutch picture does not affront her understanding by showing a country inn 'that might have serv'd for a great Hall or Banquetting-house to any Roman Emperor'. It aims at truth, showing nature as it is rather than 'as we would wish it to be'. Fulvia even prefers plays which show the conflict of raw human passion to the ennobling, but not natural, spectacle provided by opera.[39]

In this instance, the Dutch, this time Dutch painters, exhibit the virtue of showing things as they are rather than flattering human vanity. The presentation of the real mechanism of human passions is like that of the human body, where we have to look at the 'small trifling Films and little Pipes that are overlook'd or else seem inconsiderable to Vulgar Eyes'.[40] Dutch painters thus do in painting what the physician must do in treating disease and the moralist must do in examining society. To see things as they are, we must eschew grand speculative theories, elevated conceptions of human dignity and grandiose presentations. Instead we must carefully observe and compare particular instances, pay attention to what is low and mean and thereby construct an explanation of the mechanism by which the phenomenon, even when apparently noble and grand, is produced. That this is precisely his view about medical theory can be seen in his *Treatise of the Hypocondriack and Hysterick Diseases.*[41]

Mandeville's depreciation of human dignity in favour of a more mechanical view of human psychology may have been prompted by his medical background. At any rate it is clear that he gave up his early Cartesian views, rejecting the notion that there was a clear distinction between human beings and animals. Humans were not special, noble, upright, possessed of a soul while animals were mere mechanisms. Many animals other than man exhibit supposedly human traits of pride, envy or pity. Human beings,

supposedly compassionate, have managed to stifle their natural reaction to the extensive slaughter of animals for food. It is easy to understand how pity for the lower animals, like mollusks or fish, need not occur.

> But in such perfect Animals as Sheep and Oxen, in whom the Heart, the Brain and Nerves differ so little from ours, and in whom the Separation of the Spirits from the Blood, the Organs of Sense, and consequently Feeling it self, are the same as they are in Human Creatures; I can't imagine how a Man not hardned in Blood and Massacre, is able to see a violent Death, and the Pangs of it, without Concern.

After narrating the encounter of a Roman merchant with a lion in which human superiority and any supposed warrant to use other creatures are questioned, Mandeville describes the death of a bullock and asks, 'is there a follower of Descartes so inur'd to Blood, as not to refute, by his Commiseration, the Philosophy of that vain Reasoner?'.[42]

In rejecting Descartes, Mandeville followed the same path as another philosopher of Rotterdam, Pierre Bayle.[43] How much Mandeville learned from Bayle and when he learned it are difficult questions. He quotes Bayle's *Miscellaneous Reflections on the Comet* (London 1708) in the *Fable,* to support the contentions that it is desirable to tolerate prostitution and that human beings do not act according to their professed principles.[44] He paraphrases, quotes or uses (without acknowledgement) the *Miscellaneous Reflections* or the *Dictionary* on at least four other occasions in the *Fable* and at least another four times in the *Fable, Part II.*[45] On the other hand, in the *Female Tatler,* there are many allusions to obscure historical persons. One might have supposed the information not derived from Plutarch to have come from Bayle, yet Mandeville's source turns out to be Pierre Le Moyne.[46]

In general, Bayle is used to support doubting the reality of supposed virtue. The preface to *Free Thoughts on Religion* acknowledges the 'great use' of Bayle's *Dictionary*; but a passage added in the second edition (1729) disclaims endorsement of the views expressed in Chapter V, which discusses free will and is almost entirely cribbed from Bayle. Mandeville claims to repeat Bayle's discussion on the grounds that Bayle had shown what could plausibly be said for and against these heterodox views but denies responsibility for these views, claiming that he has not examined them.[47] Bayle is again explicitly quoted in *A Letter to Dion,* in which Mandeville asserts that he uniformly condemns vice and that Berkeley (Dion) has misread the Fable or more charitably, according to Mandeville, not read it at all.[48]

Thus Mandeville's debts to Bayle are only partly acknowledged. It seems clear that Mandeville used Bayle as support for scepticism about the rationality and virtue of human beings. As with Bayle, Mandeville's religious professions remain doubtful and disputed; so are the sincerity of Mandeville's repeated assertions of high morality.[49]

Mandeville's basic cast of mind seems to have been part of what he brought with him from the Netherlands when he emigrated. If it did not originate from his medical background, that certainly reinforced it, especially as he endeavoured systematically to explain the causes and consequences of private vices. Mandeville retained a loyalty to William III and his struggle against the power of Louis XIV's France. He was also able to discover the source of the traditional Dutch virtue, frugality, while demonstrating that this did not violate his contention that prosperity and luxury were inseparable; in this situation the Dutch could be praised for exhibiting political wisdom. Moreover, they also managed the relations between the sexes in an admirable way. Thus the Dutch provided a stock of examples as, repeatedly throughout his works, Mandeville insisted that the noble and the virtuous are to be explained as the operations of mean, low and vicious characteristics.

Notes

1. The record of his baptism is cited by F. B. Kaye in Bernard Mandeville, *The Fable of the Bees* (Oxford 1924), ed. F. B. Kaye, vol. I, p. 17, n. 4. (Kaye also records an unsupported allegation in the *Biographia Britannica* that he had been born in Dort, viz., Dordrecht, 10 miles from Rotterdam.) The records of the University of Leiden are probably incorrect (see Kaye *Fable of the Bees,* I, p. 18, n. 3). It is more likely that Mandeville left the Erasmian School at the normal age of 15 in 1685 and persuaded the university authorities and the beadle to enrol him as several years older than his actual age than that he was baptised at the unusually late age of three (or even older). I am grateful to Drs N. van der Blom formerly of that school for his informed help about the practices of that time.

2. See Rudolf Dekker, '"Private vices, public virtues" revisited: the Dutch background of Bernard Mandeville', *History of European Ideas,* 14 (1992), 481-98. Mandeville's family background is discussed on pp. 482-3, citing a genealogy of the Mandevilles: P. A. Christiaans, 'De Mandeville', *Jaarboek Centraal Bureau voor Genealogie,* 33 (1979), 18-25. This partially supplants Kaye's discussion in *Fable of the Bees,* I, pp. xvii-xx, II, pp. 80-5.

3. In both his *Disputatio Philosophica de Brutorum Operationibus* (Leiden, 1689) and his *Disputatio Medica Inauguralis de Chylosi Vitiati* (Leiden, 1691), Cartesian theses about animals are proposed for defence. But by 1714 Mandeville had abandoned those views: see Remark P *Fable of the Bees,* I, pp. 173-81. Mandeville's *De Medicina: Oratio Scholastica* (Rotterdam, 1685) documents his leaving the Erasmian School in October 1685 to proceed to the University of Leiden.

4. Mandeville was apparently away from Leiden during 1690, returning briefly to take his medical examination, as indicated by his registration at the university on 19 March and the date of his medical disputation,

Disputatio Medica Inauguralis de Chylosi Vitiata, on 30 March 1691. See Kaye, *Fable of the Bees,* I, pp. xviii-xix. For further evidence that he was away from Leiden and in Rotterdam during 1690, see Dekker, 'Private vices, public virtues revisited', pp. 483-9.

5. As indicated by his *Disputatio Medica Inauguralis de Chylosi Vitiata* and his later *A Treatise of the Hypocondriack and Hysterick Passions* (London, 1711, 1715) and its later version. *A Treatise of the Hypocondriack and Hysterick Diseases* (London, 1730).

6. See Dekker, 'Private vices, public benefits revisited', pp. 484-95. A further effect of the restoration of Van Zuijlen was the dominance of the orthodox faction in the church—a dominance which in 1699 led to Bayle's dismissal from his chair at the Illustre School.

   Although Dekker refers to the 'Sanctimonious Atheist' as a satire, the piece is a straightforward invective or libel denouncing a particular individual for various alleged crimes and vices. Dekker points out that this suggests a moral stance in which private vices are not regarded as public benefits, yet he concludes that this position is somehow retained in his later work: Mandeville is a pessimist about human nature, but remains a moralist (p. 495).

   I doubt that much about Mandeville's later views can be inferred from the Costerman incident of the 'Sanctimonious Atheist'. It is worth noting that William III's actions on behalf of Van Zuijlen do not seem to have affected Bernard Mandeville's opinions about him (see below). Perhaps the denunciation of a sanctimonious, hypocritical atheist is most consistent with Mandeville's repeated jibes at the hypocrisy of the clergy and the pious, and his own free-thinking position.

7. *Fable of the Bees,* I, p. xx.

8. Bernard Mandeville, 'In authorem de usu cantharidum scribentem' in J. Groenevelt, *Titus Cantharidum in Medicina Usus Internus* (2nd ed; London 1703); see also 'Upon the author treating of the internal use of cantharides' in J. Greenfield, *A Treatise of the Safe Internal Use of Cantharides in the Practice of Physick,* trans. J. Marten (London 1706). Mandeville was the translator of C. Shrevelius, *A Sermon Preach'd at Colchester to the Dutch Congregation,* trans. by B. M., M.D. (London 1708).

9. Bernard Mandeville, *The Pamphleteers: a Satyr* (London, 1703). For evidence of Mandeville's authorship see D. F. Foxon, *English Verse 1701-1750* (Cambridge 1975), M 72 and M. M. Goldsmith, *Private Vices, Public Benefits: Bernard Mandeville's Social and Political Thought* (Cambridge, 1985), p. 28 n. 1. If Mandeville had felt resentment against William, it is odd that he defended him so consistently, and moreover defended him after his death when it was not necessarily to his advantage to do so.

10. *Pamphleteers,* pp. 3-6.

11. *Pamphleteers,* pp. 8-10.

12. *Pamphleteers,* pp. 11-12, 6.

13. Goldsmith, *Private Vices, Public Benefits,* pp. 78-119; see also H. T. Dickinson, 'The politics of Bernard Mandeville' in *Mandeville Studies: New Explorations in the Art and Thought of Dr. Bernard Mandeville (1670-1733),* ed. I. Primer (The Hague, 1975), pp. 80-97.

14. Bernard Mandeville, *The Mischiefs that ought justly to be Apprehended from a Whig-Government* (London, 1714), pp. 3-15; Bernard Mandeville, *Free Thought on Religion, the Church and National Happiness* (London, 1729), pp. 394-5; Goldsmith, *Privat Vices, Public Benefits,* pp. 91-9.

15. *The Virgin Unmask'd* (London, 1709).

16. D. F. Foxon, 'Libertine literature in England, 1660-1745', *Book Collector,* 12 (1963), pp. 21-36, 159-77, 294-307.

17. See G. S. Vichert, 'Bernard Mandeville's *The Virgin Unmask'd* in *Mandeville Studies,* pp. 1-10; see also Goldsmith *Private Vices, Public Benefits,* pp. 80-4.

18. *The Virgin Unmask'd,* p. 140.

19. *The Virgin Unmask'd,* pp. 133, 167.

20. *The Virgin Unmask'd,* p. 133.

21. *The Virgin Unmask'd,* p. 136.

22. The 'hundreth penny' was a tax on landed wealth.

23. *The Virgin Unmask'd,* pp. 136-9; one of the main points of Mandeville's verse fable, 'The Carp', is that fish's woeful ignorance of affairs in his own as well as other countries; perhaps we may see the blunt herring, who reproves the carp, as a Dutchman. For the poem, see B. Mandeville, *Aesop Dress'd* (London n.d. [1710?]), pp. 25-27; *Female Tatler* 97 (24 February 1710); Goldsmith, *Private Vices, Public Benefits,* pp. 30-1.

24. *The Virgin Unmask'd,* p. 163.

25. *The Virgin Unmask'd,* p. 165-7; Goldsmith, *Private Vices, Public Benefits,* pp. 82-3.

26. Sir William Temple, *Observations upon the United Provinces of the Netherlands,* ed. G. N. Clark (Cambridge 1932), p. 109, see also pp. 76-8, 97-102.

27. *The Virgin Unmask'd,* pp. 165-9.

28. *The Virgin Unmask'd,* 127-8.

29. See P. B. Anderson, 'Splendor out of scandal: the Lucinda Artesia papers in *The Female Tatler',* *Philological Quarterly,* 15 (1936), pp. 286-300; Goldsmith, *Private Vices, Public Benefits,* pp. 35-46.

30. *Female Tatler* 88 (27 Jan. 1710).

31. M. M. Goldsmith, '"The Treacherous Arts of Mankind": Bernard Mandeville and Female Virtue', *History of Political Thought,* 7 (1986), pp. 93-114.

32. *Female Tatler* 111 (31 March 1710).

33. *Fable of the Bees,* I, pp. 183-7.

34. *Fable of the Bees,* I, pp. 187-8.

35. *Fable of the Bees,* I, pp. 189-90.

36. *Free Thoughts on Religion* (London 1729), pp. 331-4, 378-408; *Fable of the Bees,* II, pp. 320-37; Bernard Mandeville, *An Enquiry into the Origin of Honour and the Usefulness of Christianity in War* (London, 1732), pp. 15-6; Goldsmith, *Private Vices, Public Benefits,* pp. 94-119.

37. *Fable of the Bees,* I, pp. 95-8; Mandeville actually cited this passage in his answer to Berkeley to show that *The Fable of the Bees* disapproves of vice: *A Letter to Dion* (London, 1732), pp. 11-4.

38. *Fable of the Bees,* I, pp. 190-1.

39. *Fable of the Bees,* II, pp. 31-43.

40. *Fable of the Bees,* I, p. 3.

41. The retitled version (second and third editions, London, 1730) of *A Treatise of the Hypocondriack and Hysterick Passions* (London 1709). See Collins, R., *"Private Vices, Publick Benefits": Dr. Mandeville and the Body Politic* (unpublished D Phil, Oxford 1988) for a discussion of Mandeville's medical theories and their relation to his other views.

42. *Fable of the Bees,* I, pp. 44-5, 137, 172-81.

43. Although Bayle taught at the Illustre School in Rotterdam while Mandeville was a pupil at the Erasmian School, there is no direct evidence that they ever met. As Bayle's biographer Elisabeth Labrousse remarks, one would very much like to know; see *Pierre Bayle: Du pays de foix a la cité d' Erasme* (The Hague, 1963), vol. I, p. 177 n. 38.

44. *Fable of the Bees,* I, pp. 98-100; 167-8.

45. *Fable of the Bees,* I. pp. 5, 55, 210, 214-15; *Fable of the Bees,* pp. 55, 104, 216, 316.

46. *La Gallerie des Femmes Fortes* (Paris 1647); *The Gallery of Heroick Women,* trans. the Marquis of Winchester (London 1652); see Goldsmith, '"The Treacherous Arts of Mankind": Bernard Mandeville and Female Virtue', *History of Political Thought,* 7 (1986), p. 110.

47. *Free Thoughts on Religion,* pp. xix-xx.

48. *A Letter to Dion,* p. 34.

49. Kaye, 'Introduction', *Fable of the Bees,* esp. lxxx-lxxxiv, cii-cv; all the examples from the *Fable* and the *Fable, Part II* noted above are indicated by Kaye. See also M. R. Jack, 'Religion and Ethics in

Mandeville, in *Mandeville Studies,* pp. 34-42; E. D. James, 'Faith, Sincerity and Morality: Mandeville and Bayle', *Mandeville Studies,* pp. 43-65; Goldsmith, *Private Vices, Public Benefits,* pp. 144-59.

E. G. Hundert (essay date 1994)

SOURCE: Hundert, E. G. "A World of Goods." In *The Enlightenment's Fable: Bernard Mandeville and the Discovery of Society,* pp. 175-218. Cambridge: Cambridge University Press, 1994.

[*In the following essay, Hundert examines Mandeville's "unsettling observation" throughout his satires "that the technical operations of the market could be seen to govern even the most intimate aspects of civilized living."*]

When, early in his literary career, Mandeville wrote **The Grumbling Hive,** he satirized his contemporaries for trumpeting their commitment to classical or Christian ideals of virtue while glorying in recent English prosperity. Employing the beehive as a symbol of productive activity for his own satiric purposes, he divided the poem into two parts. The first part stresses the economic benefits that follow when a society can accommodate a certain amount of (relatively unselfconscious) moral corruption amongst its members. In the second part, Mandeville contrasts this public felicity with an imagined society in which disastrous economic consequences follow when the lives of citizens are purged of immoral and immoderate behavior. Yet even in the wealthy hive, the "knaves" populating it are hypocrites who "boast . . . of their honesty" while engaging in duplicitous social practices. Mandeville's obvious and intentionally transgressive point in the poem is that commercial societies seem naturally to entail forms of artifice and imposture which should be understood as the moral price of commercial prosperity. As we have seen, he gave theoretical expression to this common concern amongst observers of British public life in the early eighteenth century, that, as one of them noted, "Greatness is so Theatrical, and the actors change so often that really I was at a loss where to fix."[1] Mandeville later put the point starkly in the body of **The Fable**: "it is impossible we could be socialized creatures without hypocrisy," the necessary ingredient of all "civil commerce" (I, 349).

FROM HYPOCRISY TO EMULATION

In the 1723, and even more pointedly in the 1728 volume of **The Fable,** however, Mandeville altered some of his original views about moral evil. Vice he now most often associated with pride and envy rather than with avarice and greed. This shift to emphasis probably resulted from his having to defend **The Fable**'s dominant assertion of irreducible egoism by answering critics like Butler, Hutcheson and Law, who claimed to defeat Mandeville's arguments by explaining social actions through an appeal to the natural benevolence of mankind. Mandeville's critics also argued, as we have seen, that no peaceful and prosperous society could possibly be sustained by pure egoists competing for scarce satisfactions; they argued, indeed, that Mandeville could only make such an absurd claim by perversely suspecting the most obviously innocent and benevolent actors of hidden and vicious intentions. "It is a suspicion," William Law wished to convince his readers, "thus founded against all the appearances of truth, and is forced to make those the proofs of the absence of a thing, which are the natural signs of its presence."[2] Assaults like these had an immediate rhetorical design. They were meant to blunt *The Fable*'s force amongst the educated public by treating Mandeville as little more than a minor Hobbesian acolyte with a Grub Street talent for churning out conceptually nonsensical satirical wit. Hutcheson's first attacks on Mandeville, which appeared in the pages of *The Dublin Journal* in 1725, were brought together and posthumously published in 1750 under the title *Reflections on Laughter* for this polemical purpose,[3] expressing a collective hope nearly twenty years after his death that Mandeville finally could be dismissed as a wicked but ultimately risible author whose pernicious doctrines were philosophically vacuous. Hutcheson's Scots colleague, Adam Ferguson, while echoing *The Fable*'s charge that the "standard of felicity" amongst commercial moderns "flatter[s] their own imbecility under the name of *politeness,*" adopted the same tactic in the 1760s. "It is pleasant," he wrote of Mandeville,

> to find men, who, in their speculations, deny the reality of moral distinctions, forget in detail the general positions they maintain, and give loose to ridicule, indignation, and scorn, as if any of these sentiments could have place, were the actions of men indifferent; and with acrimony pretend to detect fraud by which moral restraints have been imposed, as if to censure a fraud were not already to take part on the side of morality.[4]

For his part, Mandeville seems never to have been less than secure about his own rhetorical agility. Critics who attempted to demolish with ridicule saw their own assertions effectively reduced to parody and held up for derision in the **"Vindication of the Book,"** where Mandeville mocked the "*Scribblers*" who attacked him (I, 390), and did so again in both **The Fable**'s second volume and its supplement on "Honour." Yet in addition to these purely polemical objectives, Mandeville was intensely concerned in these works to answer those critics who bracketed **The Fable** with *Leviathan,* the work of Hobbes he seems most to have admired but which he thought had exhausted the analogy between natural and political bodies.[5] Mandeville distinguished his work from Hobbes' by elaborating and refining his claim that consistent common experience confirmed that men care immeasurably more about the opinions rather than the welfare of others. *Pace* Hobbes, Mandeville argued that in polished as opposed to predatory societies envy and the hypocrisy to which it gave rise were naturally self-limiting rather than a socially destructive passions—a conception Montesquieu was known to have transposed in his discussion of the stabilizing role of noble honor in monarchies in *The Spirit of the Laws.*[6] Instead of encouraging men to engage in bouts of physical aggression and to invade the property of others, as Hobbes had claimed, Mandeville argued that in conditions of modern opulence envy would instead be directed into politically harmless and socially beneficial channels. In fine: the emergence of commerce had unintentionally contributed to the stability of the modern state.

It is important to keep in mind that Mandeville's seminal claim about communally beneficent hypocrisy in commercial settings ran counter to most informed opinion during most of the eighteenth century, not only to Hobbes.[7] Mandeville's immediate contemporaries like Hutcheson and Law, and later Ferguson, Rousseau and Smith, all worried that once the arts of dissembling, economic self-interest and envy were aroused by the informal as well as the formal institutions of commerce, these intensely self-regarding types of activity could not reasonably be expected to remain confined to economic affairs. They feared that the drive for profit, accumulation, and material superiority would corrupt and then finally dominate all other aspects of communal life. It was classically argued and still widely believed in the eighteenth century that as private interests took precedence over public duties nations largely comprised of persons consumed with self-regard in their struggle for material advantage were threatened with civil incapacity. Public morals would wither amidst an anarchic scramble for wealth as an instrument of dominance, a struggle that could only be contained, as Plato imagined in the final Book of *The Republic,* by a despot. In *The Discourse on the Origins of Inequality* Rousseau, who, as we have seen, took Mandeville's *Fable* as commercial society's most truthful and self-incriminating expression, followed this line of thought. He argued that despotism was the inevitable consequence of modernity, a conclusion in his view supported not only by classical authorities but most recently by Montesquieu's observation in *The Spirit of the Laws,* where it was argued that mere avarice threatened to supplant lofty ambition in societies circumscribed by petty commercial concerns.[8] Indeed, when Mandeville directly addressed contemporary British politics in the wake of the collapse of the South Sea Company's shares, he also assumed that talent in trade and knowledge of commercial dealings in no way prepared a person for a full civic identity. Unlike virtually the whole of his initial audience, however, Mandeville remained pointedly undisturbed by the prospect that in commercial societies, which by their nature required an intensified specialization of social functions, a man may "have good notions of *Meum* and *Teum* of private persons, and yet not be able to determine anything concerning the property of nations."[9]

Mandeville seems always to have believed that British politics could safely be left in the hands of enlightened Whig elites. He argued neither that the manipulative practices of these elites, nor the hypocrisy which characterized the commercial populations they governed, in any way threatened social peace, as the dominant strand of Western political argument had maintained. Like his critics, Mandeville understood hypocrisy as the socially constituted ensemble of techniques necessary for the fabrication

of disguises civilized persons don in order to conceal their avarice from one another. For persons inextricably bound by the web of commercial relations, hypocrisy is the requisite mask for hiding avaricious economic vanity from the moralizing gaze of one's fellows (1, 72-80 and 131-132). Mandeville repeatedly argued that *from any given individual's point of view,* hypocritical practices may correctly be seen as devices employed to conceal a person's vicious motives. This was, he knew, the point of view consistently adopted by the moralists he proposed to satirize; and it was one, moreover, whose conclusions he seldom tired of repeating himself. As he put toward at the end of his career, "[t]o make a Shew outwardly of what is not felt within, and counterfeit what is not real, is certainly Hypocrisy, whether it does good or hurt." Indeed, Mandeville went on, we can reasonably include all that comes under the headings of morality, modern manners and politeness in this category.[10]

But amongst Mandeville's most historically important theoretical achievements was the recognition that the individual's point of view, while instinctive in naturally self-regarding creatures, in fact tends often to conceal the social significance of his actions. The first-person perspective encourages the apparently obvious but false belief that what is morally good or materially beneficial for an individual actor must needs be so for society as a whole. Similarly, we unreflectively tend to believe that an individual vice must be communally vicious. Since every person is "an entire individual, a wonderful machine, endowed with thought and will independent of anything visible from without . . . every body looks upon his own dear person, as an individual, if not independent being which he is obliged in every way to gratify and take care of, very often forgetting they are members of society."[11] The scientific student of society, by contrast, is obliged to regard actions from an altered and counter-intuitive perspective, a perspective consistently alert to the ironic disjunction between the truth of a belief held by an actor—the passions from which his action may spring—and, most significantly, its social consequences. He evaluates the deeds of persons by different criteria,

> the Usefulness and dignity of their callings, their capacities, with all qualifications required for the exercise or performance of their functions . . . In this view we have no regard for the persons themselves, but only the benefit they may be of to the publick . . . they are only look'd upon as parts and members of the whole society.[12]

As Mandeville put it to Bishop Berkeley, "to understand the Nature of Civil Society, requires Study and Experience . . . They are silly People who imagine that the Good of the whole is consistent with the Good of every Individual."[13]

The Fable's conceptually significant and radical claim regarding the function of hypocrisy proceeds from this methodological insight: *from the point of view of society itself* the vice of hypocrisy in fact serves a hidden positive purpose, the familiar Mandevillian objective of pride being managed for public benefit "by playing the Passion against itself" (II, 78-79). "The more pride [men] have and the greater value they set on [gaining] the esteem of others, the more they'll make it their study to render themselves acceptable to all they converse with" (II, 65). Mandevillian pride, then, should be seen from his own dual, evolutionary perspective. Pride begins its career as the egoistic and hedonistic desire to enhance one's self-esteem. This desire initially empowers "flattery" to tame men by encouraging the internalization of elementary forms of social discipline. Then, after they have become moralized in the latter stages of the civilizing process, pride appears as the consequent desire of persons for some form of *dependence* on the approbation of others. The passion which highlights human hypocrisy and the role of theatrical appearance, the pride of polished moderns can at the same time be employed by politicians to direct individual actions into socially beneficial channels by appealing to the need of civilized egoists to gain public approval. As was the case with honor, the previous "tye of society," hypocrisy in commercial nations masks the emulative striving arising from envy. Hypocrisy, disseminated amongst all but the poorest ranks, thereby curbs rather than encourages violent and communally baneful forms of immoderate behavior. As Voltaire perceptively noted, Mandeville effectively disturbed one of his audience's most deep-seated moral intuitions by explaining in detail the positive consequences of envy. By taking emulation rather than aggression as envy's primary expression, Mandeville, so Voltaire thought, achieved his greatest insight: he "is the first who sought to prove that envy is a very good thing, a very useful passion" for society.[14] Mandeville showed how, without any formal encouragement, hypocrites discover socially useful methods of "making ourselves acceptable to others" (II, 147).

> What is chiefly aim'd at in a refined Education is to procure as much Ease and Pleasure upon Earth, as that can afford: Therefore Men are first instructed in all the various Arts of rendering their Behaviour agreeable to others, with the least Disturbance to themselves. Secondly, they are imbued with the Knowledge of all the elegant Comforts of Life, as well as the Lessons of human Prudence, to avoid Pain and Trouble, in order to enjoy as much of the World, and with as little Opposition, as it is possible: whilst thus Men study their own private Interest, in assisting each other to promote and encrease the Pleasures of Life in general, they find by Experience, that to compass those Ends, every thing ought to be banish'd from Conversation, that can have the least Tendency of making others uneasy.
>
> (II, 11)

The modish and powerful follow fashion as their chief rule. As Mandeville argued both in his attack on Shaftesbury and in the Introduction to **The Fable**'s second volume, it is from the rules of polite sociability that they acquire their notions of virtue; not, as standardly claimed, the other way round (II, 12). So the difference between being and appearing, which for Mandeville remains the most

psychologically significant characteristic of public life in commercial societies (I, 127-130), is at the same time the most visibly obvious and socially significant consequence of the spread of modern manners since the seventeenth century. A regime of polished intercourse had accompanied the growth of commercial relations and the decline of those aristocratic concepts of honor which hitherto tamed the warrior class (I, 122). The unintended social consequence of this transformation, Mandeville argued, was that just as the arts of flattery and thus hypocrisy reached new stages of perfection with the expansion of commerce in the course of recent history, so too did exceedingly subtle and efficiently self-regulating forms of social discipline. Although Hume regarded Mandeville's philosophical arguments as seriously flawed, he endorsed the practical and political implications of this insight when he argued, in the first **Enquiry,** that "those who prove or attempt to prove, that such refinements rather tend to increase industry, civility, and arts, regulate anew our moral as well as political sentiments."[15]

As we have seen, contemporaries less committed than Hume to adopting Mandeville's scientific perspective on society were often scandalized by the licentious premises of these novel assertions. But they would not have been wholly surprised by the more narrowly economic implications of Mandeville's thesis. During the first decades of the Restoration many English economic writers began to understand that material possessions beyond those necessary to sustain a frugal existence were desired more for their aesthetic effects and approbative power than for the actual material needs they satisfied. Like Mandeville, these writers examined the psychology of envy, desire and imaginary wants, extending their investigations of market relations well beyond the conventional limits of trade viewed as merely the exchange of commodities.[16] The aggregate demand for economic goods, both Nicholas Barbon and Sir William Petty reasoned, would be intensified in wealthy trading nations primarily because of the esteem they attracted and, also perhaps, the consequent self-respect they appeared to engender in their possessors. "The meaner sort," Sir Dudley North claimed in his *Discourses on Trade,*

> seeing their Fellows become rich, and great, are spurr'd up to imitate their Industry. A Tradesman sees his Neighbour keep a Coach, presently all his Endeavours is at work to do the like, and many times is beggered by it; however the extraordinary Application he made, to support his Vanity, was beneficial to the Publick, tho' not enough to answer his false Measures as to himself.[17]

John Pollexfen saw evidence of this process in London at the end of the 1690s. "From the greatest Gallants to the meanest Cook-Maids," he remarked, "nothing was thought fit, to adorn their persons, as the Fabricks of India."[18] Once the implications of such observations were accepted, a process of burgeoning consumption could be seen as in principle endless under appropriate legal and political conditions, endless since goods in the economic realm, void of lasting psychological satisfaction, would quickly lose their luster in the face of other novelties supplied by trade and manufacture.

Mandeville gave his readers little indication of having carefully studied the reflections of late seventeenth-century pamphleteers on the domestic social implications of an enlarged foreign trade. They were primarily concerned with detailed considerations of government policy, a subject to which Mandeville paid only infrequent attention. Yet, as was long ago pointed out by Marx,[19] and then in some detail in the classic study of mercantilism,[20] the amoral and proto-utilitarian assumptions of many neo-mercantilist writers, who treated the pursuit of self-interest as the sole motive required to understand economic behavior, bear a striking resemblance to Mandeville's. When *The Fable* was branded "Hobbist," it was Mandeville's affinity with the work of these writers that his critics often had in mind. Here, Mandeville's critics had an important point, although not the precise one they wished to make. Mandeville effectively incorporated the insights of his seventeenth-century predecessors into a comprehensive account of the wider social implications of modern prosperity. According to his picture, first the great and then all monied persons throughout the social spectrum do not derive their primary social satisfactions from a naked ability physically to subdue competitors. Rather, such satisfaction as they attain comes from the attention conspicuous displays of articles of consumption are able to draw from others in an economically expanding world of newly available goods. To this thesis Mandeville added a philosophically significant caveat: it is either blatantly hypocritical or simply conceptually fruitless to attempt to understand the relatively recent explosion of emulative behavior in an expanding commercial market for material marks of esteem within the terms provided by the inherited moral tradition. Instead—so he argued—envy and emulation must properly be conceived from a naturalistic perspective, as strong impulses resulting from the passion for dominance "playing" against pride, while changing "its symptoms" in a way unimagined by Hobbes. The expansion of commerce makes products available which markedly reduce the primitive powers of select individuals to compel approbation and obedience by "Looks and Gestures" backed simply by force. As it does so, "costly Equipages, Furniture, Buildings, Titles of Honour, and everything that Men can acquire" rapidly become the primary "Marks and Tokens" of esteem (II, 126). Commerce thus transforms the rules of dominion. "While . . . wallowing in a Sea of Lust and Vanity," civilized men in advanced societies remain psychologically compelled "to put a favourable Construction upon [their] most glaring Vices" (I, 149). For the first time, however, these persons are obliged to gear their public performances to the hidden imperatives of a mobile world of goods, in which relations with others are rarely brutal and immediate, but instead are commonly mediated by the unstable imaginary values embodied in their very possessions. In such a world, Mandeville's relentless critic John Brown recognized to his horror when he attacked *The Fable* some thirty years after its publication, "*moral*

Beauty and Deformity, *Virtue* and Vice, could have no other Law, that that of Fancy and Opinion."[21]

LABOR AND LUXURY

Brown, who authored the popular *Estimate of the Manners and Principles of the Times* (1757)—a veritable encyclopedia of conventional worry about contemporary immorality which was reprinted at least a dozen times within a year of its appearance—detested Mandeville's glorification of excess. His unmitigated abhorrence flowed from a realization that *The Fable* had dramatically placed into circulation the question of what happens when large numbers of individuals are required to engage with, and are powerfully moved by, the imagery produced through the display and manipulation of commodities. For Brown, the luxurious practices these fantasies encouraged signalled the imminent "destruction" of the "Desire of Rational Esteem," just as some of Mandeville's first readers, like William Law, feared that he had perversely but successfully celebrated the fact that persons in modern economic conditions could define their public identities primarily through their patterns of consumption. Mandeville forced his audience to confront the possibility that a conceptual environment had developed in which notions of moral goodness, now degenerated into mere codes of manners and politeness, are merely markers distinguishing habits which easily could be altered or discarded when they came into conflict with economic rationality.

Mandeville's interests always centered on the social dynamics of what he repeatedly styled an "opulent, flourishing and warlike state," the polity created in Britain by the financial and military revolutions at the end of the seventeenth century. Here, one's public role no longer had any necessarily official connection to the state administration; it could instead largely be constructed from the processes of economic opportunity. The desire of persons activated by self-liking to have their self-image shared by others, so he argued, could account for social cohesion in a commercial world of self-interested egoists, in a society whose habits and social hierarchies were primarily delineated by the mechanisms of fashion, public display and role distance. In this new setting, individuals *qua* individuals could achieve their social identities through the exchange of goods and ideas, practicing a secular ethos of manners "that will joyn worldly Prudence to Sensuality, and make it their chief Study to refine upon Pleasure" (II, 127). Mandeville claims, in other words, that, from the point of view of the dramatically altered intersubjective conditions which characterize commercial society, an enormous range of social actions should be understood without *any* reference to moral categories, but rather as starkly instrumental attempts to satisfy pride through the establishment of one's status. Echoing Mandeville's words, the popular moralist Erasmus Jones expressed regret that "in large and populous cities where obscure Men may hourly meet with fifty strangers, handsome Apparel is a main point . . . and People where they are not known, are generally honoured according to the Clothes, and other accountrements they have about them."[22]

Mandeville thus situated his audience as agents possessing a subjectivity at a considerable remove from any available contemporary account of the person in terms of which he may assent to society's norms as a unified, autonomous, self-reflecting member. He put it to his readers that the actual economy and polity in which they lived had insensibly given birth to a semi-autonomous region of civil society, a zone sustained by private fantasies and driven by future prospects of wealth. He extolled the fact that certain features of social power were radically unstable, and he aimed to show in some detail how emerging opportunities for the advancement of status could thereby be maximized. Social personality in Mandeville's vision became discontinuous with moral commitment; character was now an artifact crafted by role-players within contemporary forms of social exchange and inherited hierarchies of power, and had to remain so if commercial society was to survive and flourish. By highlighting the role of fantasy in modern social intercourse, Mandeville's account of social cohesion in commercial conditions struck at his readers' understanding of themselves and of the very moral foundations of society.[23] He provided an ethically subversive analysis of interest and economic action, understood as founded upon the power of hypocrites guiltlessly to meet as strangers, who each day assembled personae composed of promises and signs of display which signified the "character" of their possessors. *The Fable* described an emergent zone of human interaction notionally bereft of undivided personalities and populated by characters who threatened to dissolve and reassemble in their staged appearances before others. By identifying the "restless desire after Changes and Novelty" (II, 260) as the psychologically activating mechanism of commercial societies, Mandeville placed the issue of wealth creation within the enlarged and precarious context of markets for rapidly changing symbols of esteem, the demand for which ironically dominated the demand for articles of use. Unsurprisingly, Mandeville's thesis that social identity had come to depend upon the acquisition of things was most starkly expressed (and despised) by Rousseau, who lamented in *Emile* that "the introduction of the superfluous makes division of labour possible," and that "a society . . . of commerce [consists in] the exchange of things, that of banks in [the] exchange of money," which quickly becomes "the true bond of society."[24]

The explicitly economic dimensions of this vision should not however be exaggerated. One must keep in mind that Mandeville gave remarkably little sustained attention to the articulation of any consistently held set of economic principles, and certainly none that are adequately captured by the retrospective application of the language of classical economics.[25] The overwhelming majority of readers never understood *The Fable* as a work whose primary significance derived from its economic doctrines. For them, the text was seen as one which pointed uncomfortably to the paradoxes Mandeville insisted were unresolvable within prevailing conceptions of the moral responsibilities of wealth. *The Fable*'s discussion of wealth creation was scandalous not because of Mandeville's visionary pur-

chase on the hidden laws of economic life, nor yet because of his satiric mockery of elite patterns of consumption,[26] but, rather, because he succeeded in placing before the moral imagination of his readers an unsettling vision of a prosperous, powerful and pleasure-filled dystopia, a necessarily desacralized society sustained, as he first put it, only by pride, avarice, prodigality, luxury, envy, folly and fickleness (I, 25).

Many of Mandeville's observations about wealth creation were conventional in the context of early eighteenth-century economic understanding, while at other times his claims could be confused, uninformed or simply unimaginative. As Sir James Steuart remarked of virtually all of his immediate Augustan contemporaries who wrote on the economy, Mandeville had almost no concern for—indeed, he hardly took any notice of—the processes of investment and savings.[27] Moreover, unlike Pufendorf or Locke before him, Charles Davenant amongst his contemporaries, or particularly the Scots like Hume, Steuart, Ferguson and Smith who wrote in *The Fable*'s wake, Mandeville showed no abiding interest in the role of property in the development of justice, morals and civilization. Mandeville's great and, to his immediate contemporaries, shocking insight that national prosperity depended substantially upon an enlarged availability of consumer goods, and the consequently enlarged, but, he thought, politically harmless social power of the *nouveaux riches* who could command them, was nevertheless yoked in *The Fable* to a wholesale disregard of the economic importance of the mobility of wealth between individuals and families. Mandeville's most striking assertions clearly depend on his assumption that "[a]ll Human Creatures have a restless Desire of mending their condition,"[28] and that in commercial societies, and by contrast with previous formations bound by codes of honor, money serves as a singularly significant index of an individual's ability to satisfy his passions (II, 348-349; 353). Yet at the same time, he thought that "all the trading part of the people" are motivated by the want of unfair advantage (I, 61), seeking to conceal their costs,[29] and, moreover, often lying in order to turn a profit (I, 81-82). Mandeville accused his contemporaries of being imaginatively imprisoned by atavistic moral ideals. Still, he was quite capable of speaking in the voice of the vanishing age in whose demise he gloried. For example, Mandeville enthusiastically approved of the sumptuary law requiring the dead to be buried in wool instead of linen (I, 329), and defended the privileges of the Turkey Company's monopoly in the Near East, despite its mismanagement and declining business (I, 109). Even Mandeville's criticism of Dutch frugality could reasonably be taken as an example of his failure to understand the relationship between social discipline and national economic success. George Bluett noticed this immediately, pointing out that the example of Holland could be invoked against *The Fable*'s thesis in order to demonstrate that virtue and interest were in fact consonant. "[I]f the Necessities and Poverty of the *Dutch* made the Practice of Frugality the

Interest, and that the keeping up to that Policy, has raised them from Poverty, to the State of Wealth and Grandeur they now enjoy," Bluett inquired,

> why is it not as much the Interest of those Kingdoms to do so, who have none of those Wants to provide against? If the *Dutch* in their present Condition are oblig'd to be more frugal than their Neighbours, from the vast Experience they have at Repairing their Dykes, the Weight of other Taxes, and the Scantiness of their Dominions; would not the same Frugality in their Neighbours, who have a greater Extent of Land, and no such Demands of Expense, keep them in a Condition still proportionably above them, and continue them still proportionably richer?[30]

Mandeville's most comprehensive economic argument rests upon the assertion that in commercial societies self-interest, driven by ineradicable human passions, is at once the "cause of earthly greatness" (II, 260) and consonant with social order because of its self-regulating properties. He first developed one facet of this argument in a wholly satirical mode, seeking to infuriate contemporary moralists by praising the illegal practices of thieves who provide work for locksmiths, drunkards who benefit brewers and contribute to the duty on malt, and highwaymen who spend more freely than the cautious citizens they prey upon (I, 86-87). Still, while divines like Law were suitably outraged by this defense of vice on the grounds of public utility, the more economically educated of Mandeville's readers recognized that he had implied the absurdity that unproductive labor could in fact create wealth. "I have known an Overseer of the Poor in the Country," Bluett mockingly reported, "when a lusty Fellow has complain'd to him of his want of Work, employ him for a whole Day together in turning a Grindstone tho' nothing was all that while ground upon it. I believe it won't be said that the Parish was the richer for the Fellow's Labour."[31] Mandeville soon came to realize that in commending robbery and drunkenness as wealth-creating he had made a polemical mistake, and he was at pains in **The Fable**'s second volume to provide his audience with no opportunity to echo Bluett's effective mockery. But as with the filth in London streets produced by "the great Traffick and Opulency of that mighty City" (I, 11), and the butchered castrati who on that account sing so beautifully (II, 106), Mandeville's intention in raising these examples was not to suggest that all vice produced wealth, but to ask what inconveniences or outright damage may be the *necessary consequence* of opulence. This question Bluett, like most of **The Fable**'s immediate audience, either failed fully to understand or simply wished to elide.[32] Following Addison, and particularly Shaftesbury, Mandeville's critics were prepared to recognize rather than deny the importance of self-regarding interests, particularly "that passion . . . having for its aim the possession of wealth . . . [for] the public as well as private system is advanced by the industry which this affection excites." "But," Shaftesbury continued,

> if it grows at length into a real passion, the injury and mischief it does the public is not greater than that which

it creates to the person himself. Such a one is in reality a self-oppressor, and lies heavier on himself than he can ever do on mankind.[33]

Mandeville intended directly to challenge this attempt to moralize self-regard in the name of affluence. If some morally or materially pernicious effects necessarily accompany the causes of prosperity in commercial societies, then it is mere cant, he uncomfortably insisted, to claim that one favors the cause but despises the effect. In fact, as his criticism of the executions at Tyburn demonstrates, Mandeville neither praised all pernicious effects, nor claimed that all of these effects were necessary. "Should any of my Readers," he wrote,

> draw Conclusions *in infinitum* from my Assertions that Goods sunk or burnt are as beneficial . . . as they had been well sold and put to proper Uses, I would count him a Caviller and not worth answering: Should it always Rain and the Sun never shine, the Fruits of the Earth would soon be rotten and destroy'd; and yet it is no Paradox to affirm, that, to have Grass or Corn, Rain is as necessary as the Sunshine.
>
> (I, 364)

Mandeville intended to emphasize the consequences of the point—essentially a moral one—that prosperity cannot possibly be caused by other-regarding virtues. As Cleomenes put it, mocking Shaftesbury, it is absurd to think that the barrister toils to secure the property of others, that the doctor works day and night to secure the health of his patients, or that the clergyman who holds several livings does so in order to minister to many souls (II, 52). The primary economic conclusion Mandeville derived from this fundamentally ethical argument was this, that in commercial societies many vices were systemic features of heightened mediums of exchange, in the same way as are the "Hardships and Calamities" of dangerous commercial voyages:

> When we are acquainted with . . . and duly consider [the physical perils of the open sea] it is scarce possible to conceive a Tyrant so inhuman and void of Shame, that beholding things in the same View, he should extract such terrible services from the innocent Slaves; and at the same time dare to own, that he did it for no other Reason, than the Satisfaction a Man receives from having a Garment made of Scarlet or Crimson Cloth. But to what Height of Luxury must a Nation be arrived, where not only the King's Officers, but likewise his Guards, even the Private Soldiers should have such impudent Desires!
>
> (I, 337-338)

Mandeville never tired of repeating his fundamental point that suchlike narrow motives underlie the widest range of individual pursuits in commercial societies. The private soldier, the wealthy barrister and the grasping parson would eagerly perform prodigious feats of self-denial in the process of responding to their petty but unyielding desires for money and the ornaments of status money commanded. In so doing, they unknowingly (and uncaringly) create employment for others. In the minds of his contemporaries, *The Fable*'s analysis of these reciprocally dependent processes offered a direct challenge to the moral legitimacy of modern, opulent nations. So too did Mandeville's corollary claim that the mechanisms of commercial societies were best understood as natural artifacts of hidden, systemic social forces, properly a subject for philosophic inquiry, and a subject which promised to provide scientific foundations for social understanding. For just as physicians "write on Poisons" (I, 408) from a physiological perspective, so too

> Philosophers, that dare extend their Thoughts beyond the narrow compass of what is immediately before them, look on the alternate Changes in the Civil Society no otherwise than they do on the risings and fallings of the Lungs; the latter of which are as much a Part of Respiration in the more perfect Animals as the first; so that the fickle Breath of never-stable Fortune is to the Body Politick, the same as floating Air is to a living Creature.
>
> (I, 149)

In ways which directly bore upon issues of economic and social policy, Mandeville developed the second facet of his thesis, that is, that in modern conditions, economic self-interest is a natural, progressive and self-regulating human propensity. Thus, on the local level, he argued that "as it is folly to set up trades that are not wanted, so what is next to it is to increase in any one trade the numbers beyond what are required . . . This proportion as to numbers in every trade finds itself and is never better kept than when nobody meddles or interferes with it" (I, 299-300), while

> [i]n the compound of all nations, the different degrees of men ought to bear a certain proportion to each other, as to numbers, in order to render the whole a well proportioned mixture. And . . . this due proportion . . . is never better attained to, or preserved than when nobody meddles with it. Hence we may learn how the shortsighted wisdom of perhaps well-meaning people may rob us of a felicity that would flow spontaneously from the nature of every large society if none were to divert or interrupt that stream.
>
> (II, 353)

These arguments, however, were almost invariably confined to issues bearing upon the domestic economy rather than on problems of international commerce, a subject about which Mandeville simply repeated the conventional view regarding the need for government to ensure a positive balance of trade, believing as he did that unregulated international exchange in goods would reduce employment (I, 248-249; 312-317). Even when discussing the domestic economy, in fact, Mandeville was far from consistent. For example, he emphasized the importance of unconstrained material ambition, while praising the regulation of trades, handicrafts and occupations in London as an example of the "dextrous management" of politicians (II, 321). Indeed, the types of organizations which most aroused Mandeville's interest in both volumes of *The Fable* and its supplement on "Honour" were neither financial nor productive institutions, but churches, sects and armies. The latter were not viewed by him as bodies which provide their members or the community at large with material resources for living, but as vehicles for the management of men through the manipulation of their pride.

Only two significant regions of economic activity, labor and luxury consumption, attracted Mandeville's sustained attention. In his "Vindication" of *The Fable* (I, 383-412), addressing the attacks of those seeking to censor the book, he suggested that the main reason for the work's sudden popularity may have been the long **"Essay on Charity, and Charity Schools"** (I, 253-322), which he had appended to the second printing of the original 1723 edition. There Mandeville criticized the charity schools as ineffectual in their expressed goal of disseminating morality, and as pernicious too, since they encouraged a weakening of the established hierarchies of power, obedience and knowledge upon which the British state rested. He argued that proponents of the schools in the Societies for the Reformation of Manners were nothing but smug hypocrites who supported the schools solely in order to indulge their appetite for praise. Contemporaries expressed outrage at the "Essay" 's brutal assertions that in free and prosperous nations the labor force must be kept poor and ignorant if its members are to be efficiently exploited in heavy, dirty and low-wage work; and that, in direct consequence, the lower orders could no longer be treated within the confines of an inherited morality of protection and obedience. It was a potentially disastrous, as well as hypocritical, mistake, Mandeville thought, to accept, let alone encourage, a paternalist view of the laboring poor as quasifamilial dependents of the social superiors charged with their governance. Laborers were little more than drones in a prosperous hive, creatures whose unrelieved drudgery was a necessary, and thus acceptable, requirement for continued prosperity.

Mandeville's conception of the laboring poor was hardly novel. He allied himself with contemporary economic writers, particularly merchants, who stressed the importance of the dynamics of consumption based on expansion of demand in the domestic market, and who realized that levels of employment, rather than stores of precious metals, held the key to national prosperity (I, 197).[34] Mandeville seemed fully to accept the opinion that rich countries would be pulled into a cycle of decline unless their goverments enforced low wages by way of compelling the poor to industry (I, 286-287)—an already old-fashioned view of wealth creation which was attacked by Josiah Child, Charles Brewster, Nicholas Barbon, Dudley North, and John Cary before *The Fable* was published, and by Defoe amongst others soon after.[35] Even so implacable a foe of extravagance and licentiousness as Mandeville's enemy Bishop Berkeley flatly stated in *The Querist* that "the creating of wants is the likeliest way to produce industry in a people."[36] For unlike the elites to which his argument was directed, and the abstract "man" whose passions *The Fable* anatomized, Mandeville claimed in *The Fable*'s second edition of 1723 that the poor are "seldom powerfully influenced by pride and avarice" to exert themselves (I, 194 and 242), and that they would only work from "immediate necessity" (I, 192), usually preferring to remain idle in the most rudimentary conditions rather than work to improve their comforts. Bound by customary habits and natural sloth, laborers would attempt to support themselves in conditions of bare subsistence by downwardly adjusting their working hours to any rise in wages. "Every Body knows," he thought, "that there is a vast number of Journey-men Weavers, Tailors, Cloth-workers, and twenty other Handicrafts; who, if by four Days Labour in a Week they can maintain themselves, will hardly be persuaded to work the fifth" (I, 192). Low wages supplemented by ignorance would thus have a three-fold beneficial effect: individual employers would retain more money to meet their other costs, Britain would gain a competitive advantage for its relatively cheap finished products in the export trade, while enforced material desperation would insure a continuing supply of hands.

Now although the "Essay" on the charity schools was the most likely cause of *The Fable*'s prosecution and Mandeville's sudden rise to fame, none of its central arguments about the laboring poor, it should be noted, was seen to be of importance by Hutcheson, Butler, Hume, Rousseau or, as we shall see, Adam Smith.[37] Indeed, by the mid-eighteenth century the European discussion of work and workers began to be placed on a new conceptual footing as the intimate relationship between high wages, worker motivation and commercial prosperity began to be better understood.[38] And even in the immediate wake of the scandal initiated by the charity school "Essay," Bluett, among others, recognized that Mandeville's objections to the schools contradicted some of his own stated principles. There were obvious, indeed Mandevillian, reasons to think that able-bodied laborers wished to better themselves, and that governments exercising the intrusive powers Mandeville had advocated in order to discipline the poor would only damage the economy, in which "trades and Employments will take their natural Course where Profit directs them."[39]

As was the case with Butler's important attack upon *The Fable*'s anatomy of self-love, Mandeville carefully responded to some of his critics of the 1720s by revising his original arguments, while never openly conceding in the process that the efforts of these critics held the slightest importance for him. Thus, solely from the text of *The Fable,* it is impossible to judge the degree to which Mandeville was impressed by the telling criticisms made against the "Essay" on charity schools. Yet it nevertheless remains the case that Mandeville neither repeated nor enlarged upon his first thoughts about labor after 1723, save to mock the supposedly bruised moral sensibilities of those who sought to proscribe his work. Moreover, in *The Fable*'s second volume of 1728, not only did Mandeville dispense with any further discussion of the necessity of low wages or continue to denegrate the capacities of the poor,

but he in fact looked to the natural proclivities of "none but Men of ordinary Capacity" as a critical source of economic progress. Contemplating the classical Epicurean (and Baconian) figure of a ship at sea, as Hume was later to do in an identical context,[40] Mandeville speculated about the processes by which such technical perfection could have been attained.

> There are many Sets of Hands in the Nation, that, not wanting proper Materials, would be able in less than half a Year to produce, fit out, and navigate a First-Rate [Man of War]: yet it is certain, that this Task would be impracticable, if it were not divided and subdivided in a great Variety of different Labours; and it is certain, that none of these Labours require any other, than working Men of ordinary Capacities.
>
> (II, 142)

Even in rudimentary societies,

> if one will wholly apply himself to the making of Bows and Arrows, whilst another provides Food, a third builds Huts, a fourth makes Garments, and a fifth Utensils, they not only become more useful to one another, but the Callings and Employments themselves will in the same Number of Years receive much greater Improvements, than if all had been promiscuously follow'd by every one of the Five.
>
> (II, 284)

These examples served further to enhance the aggressively evolutionary perspective Mandeville had adopted by 1728. They further emphasize the point that "we often ascribe to the Excellency of Man's Genius . . . what is in Reality owing to . . . the experience of many Generations, all of them very little differing from one another in natural Parts and Sagacity" (II, 142), But in contrast to his earlier claim that "what we call Evil in this World . . . is the . . . solid Basis, the Life and Support of all Trades and Employments without Exception" (I, 369), in *The Fable*'s second volume Mandeville makes no reference at all to vice when discussing the division of labor. Indeed, without any moral comment, he simply treats material improvement as the necessary consequence of the unplanned development of specialized skills, a process so ubiquitous, as he later wrote in "Honour," that one could recognize its profound effects even in the organization of the Roman Church.[41]

This argument about the centrality of the division of labor Mandeville made specifically in support of an original sociological thesis, that is, that the progress of society depends upon increasing specialization, which in turn is the natural outgrowth of political stability. The entry in *The Fable*'s index of 1728, "Labour, The usefulness of dividing and subdividing it" (II, 335), directs the reader precisely to this point: "When once Men come to be govern'd by written Laws, all the rest comes on a-pace," since "[n]o number of Men, when once they enjoy Quiet, and no Man needs to his Neighbour, will be long without learning to divide and subdivide their Labour" (II, 283-284). An intensified division of labor is at once the axial productive characteristic of economically advanced communities, Mandeville claimed, and a wholly natural concomitant of civilization itself. Moralists who drew their principles from the civic tradition's ideal of self-sufficiency saw in commercial specialization a threat to personal integrity and the power of the full citizen to command his landed dependents. Mandeville countered with the startling claims that civilized living and commercial opulence entailed the liberation of large numbers of persons from previous martial dependencies, encouraged social mobility because of the increase of monied wealth at the expense of landed power, and simultaneously brought forth *new* mutual dependencies fostered by the progress of the division of "Art into many Branches" (II, 284).

When he first addressed the pretensions of London moral reformers in the charity school "Essay," Mandeville embraced the conventional view that the consumer demand of the masses was and would continue to be economically insignificant, and that enforced subsistence living amongst the poor could therefore be regarded as an economically benign instrument of social discipline. But he abandoned this view by 1728 in the face of trenchant criticism, shifting his focus to the necessary connections between the development of the division of labor and the growth of civilization. There is good reason to think that Mandeville only provisionally adopted conventional presumptions about the laboring classes in the "Essay" on charity schools for the immediate polemical purpose of heaping scorn on the pretensions of his enemies, the London moral reformers. For even in *The Fable*'s first volume of 1723, Mandeville's primary economic insight was that wealth creation in commercial society depended upon the "emulation and continual striving to out-do one another." While he here mainly referred to the conspicuous consumption of monied elites, Mandeville clearly intended to encompass all persons throughout the social hierarchy, beginning with "the poorest Labourer's Wife." His main example is worth quoting in full:

> The poorest Labourer's Wife in the Parish, who scorns to wear a strong wholesome Frize, as she might, will half starve herself and her Husband to purchase a second-hand Gown and Petticoat, that cannot do her half the Service; because forsooth, it is more genteel. The Weaver, the Shoemaker, the Tailor, the Barber, and every mean working Fellow, that can set up with little, has the Impudence with the first Money he gets, to Dress himself like a Tradesman of Substance: The ordinary Retailer in the clothing of his Wife, takes Pattern from his Neighbour, that deals in the same Commodity by Wholesale, and the Reason he gives for it is, that Twelve Years ago the other had no bigger a Shop than himself. The Druggist, Mercer, Draper, and other creditable Shopkeepers can find no difference between themselves and Merchants, and therefore dress and live like them. The Merchant's Lady, who cannot bear the Assurance of those Mechanics, flies for refuge to the other End of the Town, and scorns to follow any Fashion but what she takes from thence. This Haughtiness alarms the court, the Women of Quality are frighten'd to see Merchants Wives and Daughters dress'd like themselves: this Impudence of the City, they cry, is in-

tolerable; Mantua-makers are sent for, and the contrivance of Fashions becomes all their Study, that they may have always new Modes ready to take up, as soon as those saucy Cits shall begin to imitate those in being. The same Emulation is continued through the several degrees of Quality to an incredible Expence, till at last the Prince's great Favourites and those of the first Rank of all, having nothing else left to outstrip some of their Inferiors, are forc'd to lay out vast Estates in pompous Equipages, magnificent Furniture, sumptuous Gardens and Princely Palaces.

> To this Emulation and continual striving to out-do one another is owing, that after so many various Shiftings and Changings of Modes, in trumpting up new ones and renewing old ones, there is still a *plus ultra* left for the ingenious; it is this, or at least the consequence of it, that sets the Poor to Work, add Spurs to Industry, and encourages the skilful Artificer to search after further Improvements.

> (I, 129-130)

Some critics may have merely feigned outrage at Mandeville's hackneyed assertion in the "Essay" on charity schools that continued British prosperity depended upon the exploitation of the laboring poor. Yet most of *The Fable*'s first readers, and many others during the next generation, found this foundational claim about the crucial social significance of hyper-consumption and luxury spending both conceptually shocking and morally suspect. For if true, they sensed, the unbridled emulative propensities Mandeville described posed a threat to social stability. In such a society, Henry Fielding warned, in a virtual paraphrase of *The Fable*'s remarks, "while the Nobleman will emulate the Grandeur of a Prince and the Gentleman will aspire to the proper state of a Nobleman, the Tradesman steps from behind his Counter into the vacant place of the Gentleman. Nor doth the confusion end there: It reaches the very Dregs of the People, who aspire still to a degree beyond that which belongs to them."[42]

Seen as an excess every bit as fatal to individuals as to states, luxury was an established pejorative designator belonging both to the vocabularies of morals and politics during much of the early eighteenth century. The term retained its strong association in historical memory with the licentiousness, corruption and political enfeeblement of great states, most notably the Roman Republic.[43] Moreover, Mandeville's contemporaries had before their eyes two competing and exclusive models of modern economic history: the frugal Dutch as leaders in economic growth and the luxurious Spaniards (or most recently, the French) as exemplars of decadence accompanied by material decline. From the beginning of his literary career, Mandeville strove to subvert these defective notions about the association between inherited moral ideals and the requirements of economic advance by offering a competing account of the relationship of prosperity to social hierarchies of wealth and power in societies as diverse as republican Holland, absolutist France, and the limited monarchy of contemporary Britain. His model stressed that man was a consuming animal with boundless appetites to emulate the "Gayety and Fickleness" of the opulent, to follow the ephemeral conformity dictated by fashion and to seek social promotion through spending.

Mandeville made two important, linked claims about luxury consumption, each following from the historical thesis that if we "look back on old *Greece,* the *Roman* Empire, or the great Eastern Nations, that flourish'd before them, and we shall find, that Luxury and Politeness ever grew up together, and were never enjoy'd asunder" (II, 147). Here he developed his original discussion of modern consumption in *The Fable*'s **"Remark L"** (I, 107-123), drawing for the purpose on Bayle's observation that luxury enriches a nation through the promotion of avarice, the particular vice which encourages the manufacture and circulation of goods.[44] This argument had as its primary targets the moralizing arguments of writers like Addison, Boyer and Shaftesbury, for whom the polished habits of the expanding urban elites they sought further to refine were a vital aspect of improvement and civilization. Leisured ways of polished intercourse, so they argued, were indispensable to an expanding society, in which tolerant sociability and broadened views are the necessary concomitants of material growth. Mandeville challenged these claims. He did so not by attempting to show them as strictly false, but by exposing to view what he argued was the essential psychological reality of opulent societies—that they were driven by excess rather than moderation, and characterized by extravagance masquerading as refinement. Not only did all "great societies" rest upon "increased wants," but the satisfaction of these wants and the consequent creation of others in their stead constitute the propulsive mechanism for change in the interdependent domains of fashion and morals. Since "our Liking or Disliking of things chiefly depends on Mode and Custom, and the Precepts and Example of our Betters and such whom one way or other we think to be Superior to us,"

> In Morals there is no greater Certainty [than] . . . What Men have learned from their Infancy enslaves them, and the Force of Custom warps Nature, and at the same time imitates her in such a manner, that it is often difficult to know which of the two we are influenced by.
>
> (I, 330)

Mandeville did not simply give voice to the much-repeated Latin proverb that "fashion is more powerful than any tyrant." Nor, in pointing to an intimate connection between moral habits and prevailing tastes, did he wish merely to make satirical sport of philosophers like Locke, here in agreement with the main stream of British and continental Protestant casuistry, who regretted that "the greatest part" of mankind "govern themselves chiefly, if not solely, by the Law of Fashion" rather than "the unchangeable Rule of Right and Wrong, which the Law of God hath established."[45] Instead, Mandeville proposed a radical thesis, systematically elaborated in "A Search into the Nature of Society" (I, 323-370), that the history of the civilizing process offered conclusive evidence for thinking that moral reasoning itself was a species of fashion and, like habits of dress, a dependent feature of the search for esteem.

Mandeville's second significant point about luxury was that hyperconsumption should properly be understood as the direct consequence of social processes. The conventional moral condemnation of supposedly superfluous material indulgence rested, he argued, upon a patent absurdity—a point neatly expressed in *The Fable*'s parable of small beer, repeated in *A Letter to Dion,*[46] where a community is supposed in which

> the chief moral evil . . . was Thirst, and to quench it, a Damnable Sin; yet they unanimously agreed, that Every one was born Thirsty more or less. Small Beer in Moderation was allow'd to All; and he was counted an Hypocrite, a Cynick, or a Madman, who pretended that One could live together without it; yet those who owned they loved it, and drank it to Excess, were counted Wicked. All this while the Beer itself was reckon'd a Blessing from Heaven, and there was no Harm in the use of it; all the Enormity lay in the Abuse, the Motive of the Heart, that made them drink it. He that took the least Drop of it to quench his Thirst, committed a heinous Crime, while others drank large Quantities without any Guilt, so they did it indifferently, and for no other Reason than to mend their Complexion.
>
> (I, 235)

Luxury, Mandeville sought to show, effectively captures the behavior of individuals possessed of the ability by virtue of their command of wealth to satisfy the desires they share with others. In commercial societies these desires are decisively shaped by newly liberated emulative propensities which may be (temporarily) satisfied through the acquisition of socially esteemed goods. If correct, Mandeville recognized, this understanding of consumption would immediately throw into question the semantic force of "luxury" as conventionally understood, a point which revolted Rousseau,[47] and one Diderot emphasized to readers of the *Encyclopédie* when he proposed "luxury" as the term best exemplifying the abuses to which words have commonly been put.[48] In conventional usage, Mandeville wrote, luxury is "that not immediately necessary to make Man subsist" (I, 107). "It increases Avarice and Rapine: And where they are reigning Vices, Offices of the greatest Trust are bought and sold; the Ministers that should serve the Publick . . . corrupted, and the Countries every Moment in danger of being betray'd to the highest Bidders: And lastly, that it effeminates and enervates the people, by which the Nations become an easy Prey to the first Invaders" (I, 135). But, he added,

> If you tell me, that Men may make use of all . . . [supposedly luxurious] things with Moderation, and consequently that the Desire after them is no Vice, then I answer, that either no Degree of Luxury ought to be called a Vice, or that it is impossible to give a definition of Luxury, which Everybody will allow to be a just one . . . [for] if once we depart from calling every thing Luxury that is not absolutely necessary to keep a Man alive, then there is no Luxury at all.
>
> (I, 108)

Indeed,

> if we are to abate one Inch of this Severity [in the definition of luxury], I am afraid we shan't know where to

stop. When People tell us they only desire to keep themselves sweet and clean, there is no understanding what they would be at; if they made use of these Words in their genuine proper literal Sense, they might soon be satisfy'd without much cost or trouble, if they did not want Water; But these two little Adjectives are so comprehensive, especially in the Dialect of some Ladies, that no body can guess how far they may be stretched.

(I, 107)

Francis Hutcheson immediately recognized that Mandeville's primary intention was to displace the conventional meaning of luxury, as well as terms like intemperance and pride, in public discourse[49]—meanings which, for Hutcheson, were foundational moral concepts. Luxury, he said, was properly to be defined as

an excessive desire or use of the lowest pleasures as is consistent with discharging the offices of life . . . Luxury . . . lavishes out men's fortunes, and yet increases their keen desires, making them needy and craving. It must occasion the strongest temptations to desert their duty to their country, whenever it is inconsistent with pleasure: it must lead the citizens to betray their country, either to a tyrant at home, or to a foreign enemy . . . With the luxurious generally everything is venal.[50]

In defending Shaftesbury, Hutcheson objected to Mandeville by insisting that any "man of good sense" would immediately recognize when a superfluity of consumption would be injurious to his health or fortune.[51] He perfectly expressed the ambivalent and, in Mandeville's view, essentially incoherent contemporary attitudes to prosperity that *The Fable* intended to expose. Mandeville's most insistent scorn was always reserved for those, like Shaftesbury and Hutcheson, who sought to moralize prosperity by claiming that excessive consumption, symbolizing a loss of independence and self-control, was nothing beyond the character defect of a socially insignificant minority within progressive and polished societies.

Hutcheson focused on this point in order to refute Mandeville's main contention about the beneficial effects of vice, envisioning the common-sensical possibility that the development and expansion of commercial exchanges could be founded upon socially moderate and, in Hutcheson's view, virtuous behavior. He offered the counter-example of how the beer industry would be better supported by people who drank in moderation, and who therefore had a normal life expectancy, than the immoderate imbibers suggested by Mandeville's parable, who ran the risk of dying young.[52] What this criticism missed or, more likely, what Hutcheson wished to elide, was Mandeville's pointing out the absurdity of *any* strict definition of luxury, and thus of moderation, in which consumption above the level of subsistence could be considered an indulgence, and therefore vicious. Furthermore, Mandeville had already anticipated and roundly dismissed the heart of Hutcheson's argument when he maintained that even a looser definition of luxury than the one inher-

ited from classical and Christian ethics would offer no conceptual advantage in understanding the moral implications of large populations living in societies characterized by rapidly increasing levels of consumption. A more lax and apparently reasonable standard of moderate behavior would serve merely to rescue rhetorical space for the hypocritical jeremiads of traditional strict moralists—precisely the persons from whom both Shaftesbury and Hutcheson wished to distance themselves.

Mandeville stuck fast to his initial paradox, first developed in **"A Search Into the Nature of Society"**: the establishment of morality was conventional; and without a precise, socially agreed-upon limit between necessity and luxury, it would have been quite impossible to imagine the establishment of self-denial as the foundation of moral virtue. Although this standard could be shown to be philosophically empty, it was nevertheless a socially necessary device, since without its foundation in a putatively objective language of morals society could not safely regulate the passions of its members through the promotion of shame.

The Fable's analysis of luxury, then, follows from a consistent adherence by Mandeville to his initial rigoristic definition of morality as self-denial, which he then supported with arguments and often examples that paralleled Bayle's, as some of his initial opponents like Bluett recognized. But Mandeville approached the problem of the morality of hyper-consumption from a different perspective when considering the *public* effects of immoderate and vicious behavior. He pointed out another paradoxical and counter-intuitive disjunction between private pleasures and public policies in modern states. As with his argument about the unexpectedly self-regulating and publicly beneficial workings of hypocrisy—when, of course, this vice was considered from the perspective of the community as a whole rather than from the point of view of the individual actor—Mandeville sought to demonstrate that in commercial as opposed to antique and static societies two distinct sets of criteria were required in order to evaluate the propriety of actions. Mandeville took a thoroughly conventional line in stressing the dangers posed by indulgence to the fortunes of individuals. As he put it, "[i]t is certain that the fewer Desires a Man has and the less he covets, the more easy he is to himself; the more active he is to supply his own Wants, and the less he requires to be waited upon, the more he will be beloved and the less trouble he is in a Family" (I, 355). But he then added forthwith that the personal tragedies born of imprudent spending were of no concern to the public at large, since from the point of view of commercial prosperity it was only the aggregate gain from the mobility of goods and money that counted, and that the power of states themselves was markedly increased by the acceleration of commercial exchanges, regardless of the immediate fortunes of any given participant in them. For, "let us be Just," he said, and ask

what Benefit can these things be, or what earthly good can they do to promote the Wealth, the Glory and the worldly Greatness of Nations? It is the sensual Courtier that sets no Limits to his Luxury; the Fickle Strumpet that invents new fashions every Week; the haughty Duchess that in Equipage, Entertainments, and all her Behaviour would imitate a Princess . . . It is these that are the Prey and proper Food of a full grown Leviathan; or in other words . . . we stand in need of the Plagues and Monsters I named to have all the Variety of Labour perform'd . . . in order to procure an honest Livelihood to the vast Multitudes . . . that are required to make a large Society: And it is folly to imagine that Great and Wealthy Nations can subsist, and be at once Powerful and Polite without.

(I, 355-356)

The mobility of modern property as exemplified by the explosion of the luxury trades, Mandeville contended, had effectively amplified natural emulative propensities. These could no longer be moralized, as both traditional moralists and the followers of Shaftesbury hoped, but now had to be managed by governing elites. Unlike the ascetics of economically rudimentary ancient republics, or the culturally and materially primitive dependents of predatory feudal warriors, a commercial public could, under conditions of modern opulence, be the direct if unintended beneficiaries of personally disastrous private indulgence. On the level of the polity, moreover, the intemperance of the great, and of those who could afford to emulate them, in no way threatened public security by draining the courage and fortitude of a patriotic citizenry. The military fortunes of commercial states no longer depended upon the supposed virtues of ancient republics, "public spiritedness to one's ruin, and the contempt of death to any extreme," as Mandeville put it when defending the Whig regime. These "romantick notions" are now "laugh'd out of countenance by those who best understand the world,"[53] for the recent victories against France, solidified by the Peace of Utrecht, had amply demonstrated that the power of modern states like Britain no longer depended upon the martial virtues of citizens, but on the capacities of their treasuries to arm and support a professional soldiery.

Recent domestic and European history thus provided Mandeville with conclusive evidence of a transformation of both morals and public priorities, in the process of which the arms-bearing citizen whose stable holdings provided the foundation for his martial independence and civic identity was relegated to the realm of nostalgic romance. He argued that the social dynamics of what was commonly decried as morally degenerate luxury consumption in fact revealed the most startling example of public benefits issuing from private vice.

Required by their recently unshackled emulative propensities to live within the parameters of Mandeville's animating paradox, commercial moderns had unintentionally traversed an unbridgeable gulf, separating them irrevocably from an antique or Christian ethic of private restraint. Like Hume, following Hutcheson, a number of critics sought to deny Mandeville's paradox, since it is, as Hume said, "little less than a contradiction in terms, to talk of a vice, which is in general beneficial to society."[54] Yet *The Fa-*

ble's argument was nevertheless purveyed on the continent by Montesquieu's friend and John Law's secretary Jean-François Melon, then by Montesquieu himself in *The Spirit of the Laws,*[55] and triumphantly by Voltaire in *Le Mondain* and the entry "Luxe" in the *Philosophical Dictionary*. By mid-century a critically important segment of his European audience had been convinced that in modern commercial conditions, as Hume himself said, classical moral "principles are too disinterested and too difficult to support, [and] it is requisite to govern men by other passions, and animate them with a spirit of avarice and industry, art and luxury."[56] *The Fable*'s account of a public sphere transformed by wealth, in which the arts and sciences flourished, rapidly became conventional within a large segment of Enlightenment Europe. The assumption was as pivotal in Voltaire's account of the ascendancy of French culture in *La Siècle de Louis XIV* as in Gibbon's praise of aristocratic civility under the Antonines in *The Decline and Fall of the Roman Empire*. After Mandeville, even a pious Christian like Doctor Johnson could offer a defense of luxury on moral grounds by comparing its effects on the industry of the poor with those slothful habits induced by charity.[57] Men had to be governed by, in Mandeville's idiom, "playing" their passions against each other. Or as Hume put it in the conclusion of his essay, "Of Refinement in the Arts," "[b]y banishing *vicious* luxury, without curing sloth and an indifference to others, you only diminish industry in the state, and add nothing to men's charity or their generosity. Let us, therefore, rest contented with asserting, that two opposite vices in a state may be more advantageous than either of them alone."[58]

HOMO ECONOMICA AND HER DOUBLE

If Mandeville's striking claims about the causal relationship of abundance to refinement proved a critical point of departure in the Enlightenment's attempt to comprehend commercial modernity, *The Fable*'s discussion of luxury consumption also had embedded within it a particularly disturbing, because less easily moralized, implication regarding the psychological foundations of economic activity. In satirically trading upon the classical and Christian conceptions of luxury as a self-indulgent diversion from the exercise both of public and private responsibilities, Mandeville highlighted the paradox that the pursuit of leisure, rather than disciplined attention to work and duty, was the energizing force of contemporary prosperity. He denied, in the words preached by an Anglican divine in 1700, that "Industry, Temperance, and Frugality are most inexhaustible mines, and make the certainest, if not the most ample Returns to the Publick; whilst Luxury, Prodigality and Idleness are continually preying upon it, and dayly tending to enervate by Impoverishing it."[59] At the same time, *The Fable*'s ideal economic agent was the person whose voracious self-seeking produces materially beneficial effects in commercial societies. It is apparent that Mandeville's actor is primarily motivated not by considerations of rational economic choice, but by inconstancy and whimsy—by the frivolity of those wants whose satisfaction energizes the economy.

This celebration of perfidious desire as a signal source of economic advance followed from *The Fable*'s thorough-going attack upon frugality in **"Remark L"** (I, 181-198). Here the promotion of "prudent Oeconomy, which some people call *Saving,*" Mandeville understands in terms of what we now call the fallacy of composition. While an obvious course of action from the point of view of distressed individuals seeking to improve their family's meagre fortunes, frugal practices have ruinous consequences when understood as a principle meant to govern the economy as a whole (I, 182). And when thoroughly practiced, as by the Spartans or Dutch, Mandeville views prudence and thrift merely as consequences of impending poverty, when the "Necessaries of life [are] scarce, and consequently dear" (I, 183). For "[f]rugality is like Honesty, a mean starving Virtue, that is only fit for small Societies of good peaceable Men, who are contented to be poor so they may be easy; but in a large stirring Nation you may soon have enough of it." "Prodigality," by contrast, "has a thousand Inventions to keep People from sitting still, that Frugality would never think of; and as this must consume a prodigious Wealth, so Avarice again knows innumerable Tricks to rake it together, which Frugality would scorn to make use of" (I, 104-105).

In his early journalism in **The Female Tatler,** Mandeville had drawn a portrait of a wealthy merchant, Labourio, ever diligent "in getting a penny." Labourio explained to a friend who wondered why he would rise at five in the morning and pore over his accounts all day, rather than enjoy a life of luxury, that parsimony was his pleasure, and that the accumulation of money itself, rather than the goods it commands, was his reward. "Some never think themselves happy but in the enjoyment of a thing," Mandeville has Labourio say, "whilst the happiness of others consists in the Pursuit only . . . I am sure that I enjoy the same satisfaction in the keeping of money, that a Sovereign has in being possessed of a power which he doesn't care to exert."[60] Labourio's point, emphasized in a following number of the journal by Mandeville's Lucinda, is that since all action results from the attempt to satisfy desire, and since the strength of different passions varies amongst individuals, anybody "is happy who thinks himself so."[61] No behavioral style can be deemed superior to any other, save on the grounds of the satisfactions it brings. In commercial societies, satisfactions derived from the habit of gain rather than the demands of vanity could be seen to engender the small but significant virtues of thrift and punctuality, a view later adopted by Hume and then Smith.[62] By the time he published **The Fable,** however, Mandeville had abandoned this defense of frugality, however emotionally and socially plausible. Rather than a virtue, he relocated frugality in opulent nations within an altered psychological context, that of the indolent drone with a strong fear of shame who embraces this supposed virtue merely in order to escape contempt. By contrast, the active man with the same share of vanity would do anything rather than submit to frugality's restraints, "unless his avarice forc'd him to do it" (II, 113). In attempting to devalue both moderation and self-discipline as either moral or economic virtues, Mandeville's attack upon frugality immediately placed **The Fable** within contentious streams of ideological dispute.

As Tawney long ago pointed out, what we have come to identify as a vital feature of Weber's thesis about the development of capitalism—the ascription to different confessions of distinctive economic orientations—was by the late seventeenth century something not far from a platitude.[63] Among writers concerned with the contrasts between different post-Reformation European societies it was almost a common form of argument, as it was a standard feature occurring repeatedly in works of religious controversy. Routinely, the extravagance of Catholic ruling elites was contrasted with the indolence of their subjects on the one hand, and, on the other, to the disciplined attention paid by Protestants to the mundane economic opportunities afforded by daily life in reformed communities. The same link can be found, as we have seen, in Sir William Temple's account of the United Provinces, in which he repeats identical views of the De la Courts,[64] as well as in Petty's *Political Arithmetic.*[65] In England particularly, the explanation of economic superiority by resort to the habits promoted by Protestant churches merged with establishment Whig celebrations of trade, notably in the homilies of Addison's Sir Andrew Freeport in *The Spectator.* As Defoe attested,[66] such assumptions easily meshed with Dissenting self-assertion and anti-Catholic animus after the Revolution of 1688. Clearly aware of these ideologically charged associations, Mandeville offered an explicitly competing explanation of the modern history of economic advance. "I protest against Popery as much as ever *Luther* and *Calvin* did, or Queen *Elizabeth* herself," he said in "A Search Into the Nature of Society," "but I believe from my Heart, that the Reformation has scarce been more Instrumental in rend'ring the Kingdoms and States that have embraced it, flourishing beyond other Nations, than the silly and capricious Invention of Hoop'd and Quilted Petticoats" (I, 356).

The association of luxury with women's inconstancy and the social power of female desire was ancient. It served most potently as a standard resource in classical republican as well as Augustinian-inspired accounts of political decline, where "effeminacy" and the luxury it entailed were standardly considered integral features of moral and political corruption.[67] In this discourse, the term "virtue" itself, as Mandeville pointed out, derived from the Latin *vir*—the disciplined manliness which distinguished a genuine man.[68] At Chartres, luxury appears as a woman carrying the comb and mirror of cupidity and self-love, while in many other medieval and Renaissance depictions she holds a scepter to mark her omnipotence and sexual domination over men, several of which depictions place beneath her name the subtitle: "The Power of Woman."[69] By the late seventeenth century, however, the argument *ad feminam* against luxury consumption had significantly intensified, notably amongst economic writers who observed a rising demand by women for imported items, which these writers saw as hurting the home economy by draining money from the country as well as fostering lax morals.[70] The words "commerce," "intercourse" and "conversation" typically came to be employed equally as terms for social and sexual exchange, while the analysis of desire in the literature regarding the economy exposed sexuality as a visibly threatening and unstable feature of the market's liberation of private instinct,[71] which Dudley North called the "exorbitant appetites of man," while using women as his main examples.[72] Women were often pictured as capricious beings entirely devoted to traffic, to sexual and social human intercourse, to the unreflective and unending activities of shopping, and especially to fashion, which incessantly urges trivial shifts in custom and appearance.

By the time Mandeville added his comments on the social significance of female luxury in **The Fable**'s **"Remark T"** (I, 225-238), women made up a significant proportion of owners of Bank of England stock and subscribers to government loans.[73] They commanded earnings of their own, had access to a greater proportion of rapidly rising metropolitan incomes, and had established a burgeoning market for goods dominated by their own consumer choices, particularly for fashion accessories which, by the turn of the century, formed a significant segment of international trade.[74] An observer of British society could not help but notice the profusion of manuals of decorum, like John Gay's *Implements Proper for Female Walkers* (1716), specifically addressed to women with recently acquired disposable incomes. Both these "ladies" and their serving maids, Defoe observed in a pamphlet that went through at least five editions in 1725 alone, were thought habitually to exhibit in their costumes "an excess of pride and extravagance,"[75] a common literary observation which Mandeville noted in **The Fable** (I; 115; 117; 122) and Hogarth made part of eighteenth-century popular imagery. The heroine of Richardson's *Pamela* (1740), although the humble personal maid to a lady of the gentry, found that by assiduous application of the social niceties—dress, deportment, conversation—she was able to achieve her ambition of marrying into the family of her late mistress. Pamela's impenetrable virtue was not so attractive to the rakish Mr. B. as was her acceptability gained through the heightening of her natural virtues by applied intelligence. Clothes, Richardson knew, were the visible emblems of social standing in a society where fashions were no longer dictated at court, but were increasingly manipulated by industries catering to monied social ambitions. When Pamela dressed in her home-spun gown and petticoat with a plain muslin tucker, instead of the cast-off fine silk gown and lace which she had been given from her mistress's wardrobe, Mr. B. was literally unable to recognize his mother's servant, so accustomed was he to seeing her in clothes befitting a newly acquired gentility—a recurring theme in eighteenth-century novels and plays, where potential suitors mistake the mistress for the maid dressing up in fancy costume.

Thus feminized, attendance to fashion easily conveyed an image of masculine corruption, as in Fielding's portrait of the decadent Bellarmine in *Joseph Andrews*. Bishop Ber-

keley thought that the luxurious desires of "women of fashion . . . enslave[d] men to their private passions,"[76] while William Law, Mandeville's persistent adversary, claimed that "fictions of reason" and "fictions of behaviour" were leading characteristics of contemporary society. What is more extravagant, he asked,[77]

> than to suppose a man racking his brains, and studying night and day how to fly?—wandering from his own house and home, wearying himself with climbing in every ascent, cringing and courting everybody he meets to lift him from the ground, bruising himself with continual falls and at last breaking his neck.

Such were the deplorable effects of a public sphere dominated by feminine whimsy, a zone in which, Law observed to his horror, women might buy "two hundred suits of clothes" in ten years.[78] The pursuit of wealth itself was hardly immune to these associations. When seen to be the province of sober mercantile interests, commerce, viewed as a source of national power, posed little ideological threat to established conceptions of social order. But when conceived as driven by fashion industries catering primarily to female tastes and women's liberated incomes, commercial exchange could appear radically transfigured. Trade was "a mystery, which will never be completely discovered or understood," Defoe wrote in his *Review* of 1706. "[I]t suffers convulsive fits, hysterical disorders, and most unaccountable emotions—sometimes it is acted by the evil spirit of general vogue; tomorrow it suffers violence from the storms and vapours of human fancy—a sort of lunacy in trade attends all its circumstances, and no man can give a rational account of it."[79] A generation later, in a work modelled on Defoe's *Compleat English Tradesman*, commerce was simply assumed to require "a fruitful Fancy, to invent new Whims, to please the Changeable Foibles of the Ladies," habits of capricious consumption which had penetrated the entire social body.

> No man is ignorant that a Taylor is the Person that makes our Cloathes; to some he not only makes their Dress, but, in some measure, may be said to make themselves. There are Numbers of Beings in and about the Metropolis who have no other identical Existence than that what the Taylor, Milliner and Periwig-Maker bestow upon them. Strip them of these Distinctions, and they are a quite different Species of Beings; have no more Relation to their dressed selves, than they have to the Great Mogul, and are as insignificant in Society as Punch, deprived of his moving Wires, and hung up upon a Peg.[80]

Even Montesquieu, whose *Persian Letters* was one of the century's most prominent declarations of female rationality and moral insight,[81] took care in that work, and again in *The Spirit of the Laws,* to reassure his audience that while emulation and luxury consumption, powerfully promoted by women, were amongst the most effective spurs to prosperity, these arts of civilization in no way "make men effeminate,"[82] a claim John Brown forcefully denied in his famous *Estimate* of 1757. Condillac, perhaps alluding to **The Fable,** saw in the faculty of the imagination—"a bee that culls its treasure from the finest blooms of a flower bed"—the feminine principle lurking behind the confusions wrought by the liberation of fancy.

> It is a flirtatious woman whose only desire is to please, and who draws on her fancy rather more than on her reason. Ever obliging, she adapts herself to our tastes, passions weaknesses. One she attracts and persuades by her saucy flirting manners, the other she surprises and astonishes by her grand and noble ways . . . Although imagination changes everything it touches, it often succeeds when its meaning is merely trying to please.[83]

Mandeville's "petticoat" thesis achieves its full import when situated within these ideological contexts. In Britain particularly, Protestant, especially "vulgar Whig," associations of commerce with liberty,[84] were fed by complementary misogynist fears that were themselves exacerbated in the early eighteenth century by the explosion of the European luxury trades. In reducing to self-serving cant the attempt to moralize economic expansion by associating it with the frugal virtues of pious, independent citizens, Mandeville, while insisting that "Religion is one thing and Trade is another" (I, 336), forced his readers to confront the sheer power of their now unadorned avarice. As he put it, "nothing could make amends for the Detriment Trade would sustain, if all those of that Sex, who enjoy the happy State of Matrimony, should act and behave themselves as a sober wise Man could wish them" (I, 356). Indeed,

> a considerable Portion of what the Prosperity of *London* and Trade in general . . . and all the worldly Interest of the Nation consists in, depends entirely on the Deceit and vile Strategems of Women; and that Humility, Content, Meekness, Obedience to reasonable Husbands, Frugality, and all the Virtues together, if they were possess'd of them in the most eminent Degree, could not possibly be a thousandth Part so serviceable, to make an opulent, powerful, and what we call a flourishing Kingdom, than their most hateful Qualities.
>
> (I, 228)

Following upon this argument, Mandeville then transformed female desire from a localized force driving recent economic advance into a general principle of social explanation. His acid observation that a great society depends upon "the abominable improvement of Female Luxury" (I, 356) was meant to and succeeded in challenging one of his audience's deepest assumptions about the moral integrity of its own aspirations. Luxury, as one of the characters in *The Tryal of the Lady Allurea Luxury* bemoaned, "is the Author of all the Books that have been published these last fifty Years in Favour of . . . Gaming, Atheism, and every Kind of Vice, public as well as private." Indeed, "[s]he wrote the Fable of the Bees, and published it under the Name of Mandeville."[85] Mandeville endorsed precisely the behavior which horrified Law, observing that women, "when they have half a Score Suits of Clothes, Two or Three of them not the worse for wearing, will think it a sufficient Plea for new Ones, if they can say that they have never seen a Gown or Petticoat, but what they have been

often seen in, and are known by" (I, 226). He took information of this kind as evidence for the provocative thesis "that the worst of Women and most profligate of the Sex did contribute to the Consumption of Superfluities, as well as the Necessaries of Life, and consequently were Beneficial to . . . peaceable Drudges, that . . . have no worse design than an honest Livelihood." Indeed, "the number of Hands employ'd to gratify the Fickleness and Luxury of Women" is nothing short of "prodigious" (I, 225-226). After incorporating these passages into his own defense of luxury, Helvétius nicely caught one of Mandeville's primary implications when he attributed to the euphemistically titled "femmes Galantes" a primary role in the promotion of public welfare.[86]

The Fable's ironic arguments about the liberating economic effects of female desire derived from the established libertine literary genre within which Mandeville first began to publish. In the so-called "Querelle des Femmes" of the previous century, paradoxical elaborations of women's supposed failings had as their intended purpose the satirical exploitation of conventional misogynist sentiments in order to offer a critique of institutions like marriage, coupled with a defense of women's abilities. Many were founded upon a materialist assumption that social expressions of sexuality were historically conditioned phenomena.[87] In *The Virgin Unmask'd* (1709), as well as in his articles in *The Female Tatler* during the two following years, Mandeville exploited these conventions by speaking through female personae—one of whom, Lucinda, is "a student of medicine"[88]—in order to expose as exploitative contemporary prejudices against women. "The Men like wary Conquerors," one of his women says, "keep us Ignorant, because they are afraid of us, and that they may the easier maintain their Dominion over us, they Compliment us into Idleness, pretending those P[r]esants to be the Tokens of their Affection, which in reality are the Consequences of their Tyranny."[89] Mandeville sought to show how female avarice, inconstancy and ambition, now "at their height" as he put it,[90] were socially generated "vices" of opulent living rather than natural artifacts of femininity. He situated his main characters, like Mrs. Crackenthorpe in *The Female Tatler*, "the Lady who knows everything," as persons cognitively empowered by their sexually constituted social inferiority to voice pertinent truths to which men were blind. Lucinda brushes aside all moralized accounts of social intercourse by baldly insisting that money is "the only thing that standing by itself has any signification, to which all the vertues and good qualities are meer cyphers, that are never to be used but to advance the figure,"[91] a point whose informing principle regarding the illusions fostered by commercial life Fulvia articulated in *The Fable,* insisting that "no body can please my Eye that affronts my Understanding" (II, 33).

While Mandeville had no interest in arguing that women should have equal political rights, he thought the conventional view that women are more lustful than men because of a defect in their constitution—a view which he would have found not only in contemporary moralizing, but clearly asserted by Bayle[92]—to be physiologically absurd. "There is no Reason to imagine," as he said in *The Fable*, "that Nature should have been more neglectful of them . . . and not have taken the same Care of them in the Formation of the Brain, as to the Nicety of the Structure, and superior Accuracy in the Fabrick, which is so visible in the rest of their Frame" (II, 173). Mandeville also found derisory the attempt by followers of Shaftesbury to moralize the supposed constitutional opposition between the sexes into a higher form of cosmic harmony, presenting society as an ordered moral whole, only apparently composed, as in Addison and Steele, of discordant parts. It was nothing but self-delusion to believe with Pope that

> Each loves itself, but not itself alone,
> Each sex desires alike, till two are one.
> Nor ends the pleasure with the fierce embrace;
> They love themselves, a third time, in their race.[93]

For Mandeville, conflict and contrivance, dissimulation and deception, are elemental and necessary features of polished social life. In sexual relations particularly, self-love never finds "the private in the public good," as Pope would have it. Rather, women, less attractive "naked and unenhanced" in the state of nature than men, quickly discover that they are able to augment their beauty by the use of artifice and ornament.[94] Since all human beings strive to emulate those whom they feel are superior, women are driven to dress above their stations and enthusiastically embrace the world of fashion as they compete with one another for men's attention (II, 123-125). Women have more pride than men, and efficiently exploit it, not because of their natures, but from an education which, especially amongst the higher ranks, at once puts a premium on virginity and coquettishness.[95] Women thus have a powerful, historically constituted interest in perfecting the arts of flattery, especially in the cultivation of devices linking sexual attraction with modesty (I, 63-69), and unnaturally maintaining their virginity at the expense of their mental health (I, 46). Engendered by the sexual division of labor, enhanced female pride and the need for the attentions of men combine to produce in modern conditions an almost insatiable desire for fashionable goods amongst women of all ranks.

Once unmasked, the "modesty" of virgins can properly be understood as "the Result of Custom and Education . . . the Lessons of it, like those of *Grammar,* are taught us long before we have occasion for, or understand the Usefulness of them" (I, 69; 72). Conversely, while "Men may take greater Liberty, because in them the Appetite is more violent and ungovernable" (I, 74-75), women, as bearers of children, are more in need of "good breeding" and the arts of dissimulation to achieve their socially specified ends. So while both sexes cultivate "politeness" to enhance, rather than abridge, their sensual pleasures (I, 73), the sexual marketplace mediated by modern habits of sociability, Mandeville argued, provides an occasion to reflect on market mechanisms themselves.

In *A Modest Defence of Publick Stews,* published shortly after the charge against *The Fable*'s publisher, and elaborating upon his comments on the function of prostitution in **"Remark H"** (I, 94-100),[96] Mandeville offered his fullest technical account of how vice may lead to public benefit. He proposed the establishment of public houses of prostitution in London and market towns, above all to allay male sexual desire and to reduce overall whoring. Mandeville would have the licensed public stews maintain healthy women, who would attract men, even without penalties designed to keep them away from other prostitutes, and by so doing protect respectable ladies from male lust. "As there is constantly in the nation a certain number of young men, whose passions are too strong to brook any opposition, our business is to contrive a method how they may be gratified, with as little expense of female virtue as possible."[97] But when his project is first launched, Mandeville expects a run upon the stews, which would involve too much neglect of private whoring, "the only nursery for our courtezans," since "the whole body of our incontinent youth, like a standing army, being employ'd in constant action, there cannot well be spar'd a sufficient detachment to raise the necessary recruits."[98] Thus, while it is in the public interest to discourage private prostitution, the demands of the market require that the ranks of privately debauched women be permitted at a level acceptable for continued recruitment into public houses.

Anticipating criticism, Mandeville then argued that even if the run on the stews should not be remedied by supplies of young women from private employment, the worst that would happen would be "a gradual relapse into our former state of private whoring; and this no farther than is just necessary to recruit the stews and thereby make them retrieve their former character." The debauching of more numbers of women than are strictly necessary to allow the stews to satisfy demand will make these public houses popular, thereby curtailing private whoring which, in consequence, "must be reduced so low that there will remain just a sufficient quantity to supply the stews; which is as low as in the nature of the thing is possible." While whoring would be diminished to the lowest level possible, ample scope for male sexual drives outside of marriage would nevertheless be accommodated. The mechanism of supply and demand alone would thus work to effect maximum public benefit or, as Mandeville says of his proposal, it "necessarily executes itself."[99]

Mandeville's wry but wholly unsatirical scheme for the licensing of prostitutes followed from and was meant to supplement his initial aim of exploiting the anxiety of his readers about the intrusion of vicious desire into the heart of prosperity. In the essay on **Publick Stews** he deliberately invoked culturally threatening images of unbridled male lust and the morally undecorated acceptance of its consequences. In *The Fable* he employed images of feminine instability, where fashion reigns and even merchants are imagined as so overcome by luxury that one might expect them to "walk along the street in petticoats" (I, 118). Mandeville combined an aggressive insistence that commercial modernity heavily depended upon female desire—upon both the "fickle strumpet" and the "haughty

Dutchess" (I, 355), whose "Fickleness and Luxury" employ a "prodigious number of Hands" (I, 226)—with the unsettling observation that the technical operations of the market could be seen to govern even the most intimate aspects of civilized living. In so doing, he achieved some of the most disturbingly paradoxical of his purposes: to show first, that modern prosperity not only depended upon the emancipation of persons from their former political dependencies, but, equally important, upon the liberation of their self-regarding wants; and second, to show that the desires of these persons were rooted in the most elemental of passions, whose capricious expressions, while governable, were nevertheless the necessarily defining features of commercial society's occluded moral life. After Mandeville, particularly after the incorporation of *The Fable*'s primary arguments about luxury consumption into the heart of Enlightenment public discourse, any systematic defense of commercial society's moral legitimacy remained vulnerable to a Mandevillian critique of the substructure of viciousness and sublimated sexual license upon which it rested. This problem was nowhere more importantly confronted than in the work of Adam Smith.

Notes

1. E. Phillips, *An Appeal to Common Sense: Or, Some Considerations Offer'd to Restore Publick Credit. As Also the Means of Reviving It* (London, 1720), p. 4.

2. William Law, *Remarks,* p. 43.

3. Francis Hutcheson, *Reflections on Laughter and Remarks on The Fable of the Bees* (Glasgow, 1750).

4. Adam Ferguson, *An Essay on the History of Civil Society 1767,* ed. Duncan Forbes (Edinburgh University Press, 1966), p. 33.

5. Bernard Mandeville, *A Modest Defence of Publick Stews* (London, 1724), p. 57.

6. Montesquieu, *The Spirit of the Laws,* III.7. See Melvin Richter, *The Political Theory of Montesquieu* (Cambridge University Press, 1977), pp. 43-44.

7. A point usefully explored by Thomas Horne, "Envy in Commercial Society," *Political Theory* 9, 4 (1981), pp. 551-569.

8. Montesquieu, *The Spirit of the Laws,* III.3.

9. Bernard Mandeville, *Free Thoughts,* pp. 390-391.

10. *Honour,* p. 202.

11. Mandeville, *Free Thoughts,* pp. 282 and 285.

12. Mandeville, *Free Thoughts,* p. 282.

13. Mandeville, *A Letter to Dion,* p. 49.

14. Voltaire, "Envie," *Questions sur l'encyclopédie* (1771), in *œuvres complètes de Voltaire,* ed. Louis Moland (Paris: Garnier, 1878), II, pp. 537-538, added to all later editions of the *Dictionnaire philosophique.*

15. David Hume, *Enquiry Concerning the Principles of Morals,* ed. L. A. Selby-Bigge (Oxford University Press, 1902), p. 181.

16. Joyce Oldham Appleby, *Economic Thought and Ideology in Seventeenth-Century England* (Princeton University Press, 1978), pp. 158-198.

17. Sir Dudley North, *Discourses on Trade* (London, 1690), p. 15.

18. John Pollexfen, *A Discourse on Trade, Coyne, and Paper Credit* (London, 1697), p. 99.

19. Karl Marx, *Capital* (Moscow: Foreign Languages Publishing House, n.d.) I, p. 616, n. 2.

20. Eli F. Heckscher, *Mercantilism,* trans. Mendel Shapiro (London: Allen and Unwin, 1955), II, pp. 286-315. See, too, J. A. W. Gunn, *Politics and the Public Interest in the Seventeenth Century* (London: Routledge, 1969), pp. 205-265, p. 21, and John Brown, *Essays on the Characteristics of the Earl of Shaftesbury* (1751) (New York: Garland Reprint, 1970), p. 140.

21. John Brown, *Estimate of the Manners and Principles of the Times* (London, 1757), I, p. 173.

22. Erasmus Jones, *Luxury, Pride and Vanity the Bane of the British Nation* (London, 1736; reprinted 1750), p. 14. Compare *Fable,* I, pp. 127-128.

23. Compare J. G. A. Pocock, *The Machiavellian Moment: Florentine Political Thought and the Atlantic Republican Tradition* (Princeton University Press, 1975), pp. 465-6.

24. Jean-Jacques Rousseau, *Emile,* trans. Allan Bloom (New York: Free Press, 1979), pp. 185 and 189.

25. For the literature on this subject, primarily by historians of economic doctrine, see Goldsmith, *Private Vices, Public Benefits,* Chapter 5; Nathan Rosenberg, "Mandeville and Laissez-Faire," *Journal of the History of Ideas* 24 (1963), pp. 183-196; and Salim Rashid, "Mandeville's *Fable*: Laissez-Faire or Libertinism?," *Eighteenth-Century Studies* 18, 3 (1985), pp. 313-330.

26. Jacob Viner, "Satire and Economics in the Augustan Age of Satire," in H. K. Miller, G. Rothstein and G. S. Rousseau (eds.), *The Augustan Milieu: Essays Presented to Louis A. Landa* (Oxford: Clarendon Press, 1970), pp. 77-101.

27. Sir James Steuart, *Inquiry Into the Principles of Political œconomy* (1767), ed. Andrew Skinner (Edinburgh: Olner and Boyd, 1966), 2 volumes, II, pp. 606-607.

28. Mandeville, *Honour,* pp. 15-16.

29. Mandeville, *Free Thoughts,* p. 292.

30. Bluett, *Enquiry,* pp. 48-49.

31. Bluett, *Enquiry,* p. 5.

32. For example, see Bluett, *Enquiry,* p. 17.

33. Shaftesbury, "An Inquiry Concerning Virtue and Merit," p. 326.

34. On these writers see Jacob Viner, *Studies in the Theory of International Trade* (New York: Harper and Row, 1937), pp. 52-57, and 117-118, and William Letwin, *The Origins of Scientific Economics* (London: Methuen, 1963), pp. 59-60 and 198-201.

35. See, amongst a large literature, Charles Wilson, "The Other Face of Mercantilism," in D. C. Coleman (ed.), *Revisions in Mercantilism* (London: Methuen, 1969), pp. 118-139, and Daniel Defoe, *A Plan of the English Commerce,* in J. R. McCulloch (ed.), *A Select Collection of Scarce and Valuable Tracts on Commerce* (London: Harrison, 1859), p. 109 and *passim.*

36. See T. W. Hutchinson, "Berkeley's *Querist* and its Place in the Economic Thought of the Eighteenth Century," *British Journal for the Philosophy of Science* 4 (May 1953-February 1954), pp. 52-77.

37. They did, however, receive the approval of Voltaire. See A. Owen Aldridge, "Mandeville and Voltaire," in Irwin Primer (ed.), *Mandeville Studies* (The Hague: Nijhoff, 1975), pp. 142-156.

38. See, for example, Edgar S. Furniss, *The Position of the Laborer in a System of Nationalism* (New York: Houghton Mifflin, 1920); A.W. Coates, "Changing Attitudes Toward Labour in the Mid-Eighteenth Century," *Economic History Review* 2nd series, 11, 1 (1958), pp. 35-51; Richard C. Wiles, "The Theory of Labour in Later English Mercantilism," *Economic History Review* 2nd series, 30, 1 (1968), pp. 113-126, and E. J. Hundert, "The Achievement Motive in Hume's Political Economy," *Journal of the History of Ideas* 35 (1974), pp. 139-143.

39. Bluett, *Enquiry,* p. 181. See, too, William Hendley, *A Defence of the Charity Schools* (London, 1725), pp. 27-28.

40. David Hume, *Dialogues Concerning Natural Religion,* ed. J. V. Price (Oxford University Press, 1976), p. 167.

41. Mandeville, *Honour,* pp. 102-103.

42. Henry Fielding, *Enquiry into the . . . Recent Causes of the . . . Increase of Robbers,* in *Complete Works,* II, p. 783.

43. Ellen Ross, "Mandeville, Melon and Voltaire: The Origins of the Luxury Controversy in France," *Studies on Voltaire and the Eighteenth Century* 155 (1976), pp. 1897-1912; John Sekora, *Luxury: The Concept in Western Thought, Eden to Smollett* (Baltimore: John Hopkins University Press, 1977), especially pp. 80-88, 113-115 and 138; André Morize, *L'Apologie du luxe au XVIIIe siècle et 'Le Mondaine' de Voltaire* (Geneva: Slatkine Reprint, 1970); and Hans Kortum, "Frugalité et luxe à travers la querelle des anciens et des modernes," *Studies on Voltaire and the Eighteenth Century* 56 (1987), pp. 705-775.

44. Pierre Bayle, *Continuation des pensées divers,* in *œuvres diverses de Pierre Bayle,* ed. Pierre Des Maizeaux (The Hague, 1717-1731), III, Section 124, p. 361, and Bayle, "Ajax, fils de Telamon B," in *Dictionnaire.*

45. John Locke, *An Essay Concerning Human Understanding,* ed. Peter Niddich (Oxford: Clarendon Press, 1975), II.28.12.

46. Mandeville, *A Letter to Dion,* pp. 25-26.

47. Jean-Jacques Rousseau, *Discourse on the Origins of Inequality,* note i.

48. Diderot, "Encyclopédie," in *Encyclopédie,* IV, pp. 635-636.

49. Francis Hutcheson, *A Collection of Letters,* in *Collected Works,* pp. 146 and 386.

50. Hutcheson, *A Short Introduction to Moral Philosophy* (Glasgow, 1747), in *Collected Works,* IV, p. 321.

51. Hutcheson, *A Collection of Letters,* p. 385.

52. Hutcheson, *Reflections on Laughter,* pp. 144-156.

53. Mandeville, *Free Thoughts,* p. 285.

54. Hume "Of Refinement in the Arts," in *Essays Moral, Political and Literary* (Indianapolis: Liberty Press, 1985), p. 280.

55. See Jean François Melon, *Essai politique sur le commerce* (Bordeaux, 1734; English trans., 1735), Chapter 9, and Montesquieu, *The Spirit of the Laws,* VII.1 and IV.8.

56. Hume, "Of Commerce," *Essays,* p. 263.

57. James Boswell, *Life of Johnson,* ed. R. W. Chapman, revised by J. D. Fleeman (Oxford University Press, 1970), pp. 755-756 and 947-948.

58. Hume, "Of Refinement in the Arts," *Essays,* p. 250. The essay was originally entitled "Of Luxury."

59. Matthew Heynes, *A Sermon for the Reformation of Manners Preac'd in St. Paul's Church in Bedford at the Assizes there held March the 15th 1700* (London, 1701), pp. 7-8, quoted in M. M. Goldsmith, "Liberty, Luxury and the Pursuit of Happiness," in Anthony Pagden (ed.), *The Languages of Political Theory in Early-Modern Europe* (Cambridge University Press, 1987), pp. 225-251, p. 236.

60. *The Female Tatler,* No. 108 (misnumbered as 105), 13 March-15 March, 1710. Compare the discussion of this character in M. M. Goldsmith, "Mandeville and the Spirit of Capitalism," *Journal of British Studies* 17 (1977), pp. 63-68, and Goldsmith, *Private Vices, Public Benefits,* pp. 137-139.

61. *The Female Tatler,* No. 112 (misnumbered as 109) 22 March-24 March, 1710.

62. See, David Hume, "Of Interest," in *Essays,* pp. 300-301, and Adam Smith, *The Wealth of Nations,* III.iv.3.

63. R. H. Tawney, *Religion and the Rise of Capitalism* (1926) (New York: Harcourt, Brace, 1954), especially pp. 8-9, and 171-172.

64. *The True Interest and Political Maxims of the Republick of Holland,* Part 1, Chapter 4.

65. William Petty, *Political Arithmetic* (London, 1690), pp. 25-26.

66. Daniel Defoe, *Enquiry into Occasional Conformity* (London, 1702), pp. 18-19.

67. Hanna Fenichel Pitkin, *Fortune is a Woman: Gender and Politics in the Thought of Niccolo Machiavelli* (Berkeley: University of California Press, 1984).

68. *Honour,* iii-iv.

69. Sekora, *Luxury,* pp. 44-45.

70. Joan Thirsk, *Economic Policy and Projects* (Oxford: Clarendon Press, 1978). p. 134.

71. See J. G. A. Pocock, *The Machiavellian Moment,* pp. 452-453, and Pocock, "The Mobility of Property and the Rise of Eighteenth-Century Sociology," in *Virtue, Commerce and History* (Cambridge University Press, 1985), p. 114.

72. Dudley North, *Discourses on Trade,* pp. 14-15.

73. Dickson, *The Financial Revolution,* p. 256.

74. Neil McKendrick, John Brewer and J. H. Plumb (eds.), *The Birth of a Consumer Society* (London: Hutchinson, 1983), Chapter 2, especially p. 23.

75. Daniel Defoe, *Everybody's Business is Nobody's Business* (1725), in *Works* (London: Bohn's Classics, 1870), II, p. 504.

76. Berkeley, *The Querist,* pp. 20 and 308-309.

77. William Law, *A Serious Call to A Devout and Holy Life* (London, 1729), p. 119.

78. William Law, *A Serious Call,* p. 69.

79. Daniel Defoe, *The Review* No. 3 (1706), p. 503.

80. Richard Campbell, *The London Tradesman* (London, 1747), p. 191.

81. E. J. Hundert, "Sexual Politics and the Allegory of Identity in Montesquieu's *Persian Letters,*" *The Eighteenth Century: Theory and Society* 31, 2 (1990), pp. 99-113.

82. Montesquieu, *The Persian Letters,* Letter CVI. See, too, *The Spirit of the Laws,* VII.1 and XIX.8.

83. Condillac, "Where the Imagination Gets the Embellishments it Gives to Truth," in *Philosophical Writings of Etienne Bonnot, Abbé de Condillac,* trans. Franklin Philip (Hillsdale, New Jersey: Lawrence Erlbaum Associates, 1987), II, pp. 478-479.

84. Duncan Forbes, "Sceptical Whiggism, Commerce and Liberty," in A. S. Skinner and T. Wilson (eds.), *Essays on Adam Smith* (Oxford: Clarendon Press, 1976), pp. 179-202.

85. Anon., *The Tryal of the Lady Allurea Luxury* (London, 1757), pp. 40 and 52, quoted in James Raven, *Judging New Wealth: Popular Publishing and Responses to Commerce in England, 1750-1800* (Oxford: Clarendon Press, 1992), p. 173.

86. Helvétius, *De L'Esprit,* Discourse II, 15.

87. Rosalie L. Colie, *Paradoxia Epidemica: The Renaissance Tradition of Paradox* (Princeton University Press, 1966), pp. 53-60 and 102-107. See, too, Gordon S. Vichert, "Bernard Mandeville's *The Virgin Unmask'd,,*" in Irwin Primer (ed.), *Mandeville Studies* (The Hague: Nijhoff, 1975), pp. 1-10, M. M. Goldsmith, "'The Treacherous Arts of Mankind': Bernard Mandeville and Female Virtue," in M. M. Goldsmith and Thomas A. Horne (eds.), *The Politics of Fallen Man* (Exeter: Imprint Academic, 1986), pp. 93-114, and Carol J. Gibson, "Bernard Mandeville: The Importance of Women in the Development of Civil Societies," MA thesis, University of British Columbia, 1989.

88. *The Virgin Unmask'd,* p. 123.

89. *The Female Tatler* No. 88 (1 February 1710), p. 68.

90. *The Virgin Unmask'd,* pp. 3-4.

91. *The Virgin Unmask'd,* pp. 58-59.

92. Pierre Bayle, *Pensées diverses sur la comète,* 2 volumes ed. A. Prat (Paris: Droz, 1939), II, pp. 79-80 and 82.

93. Alexander Pope, *An Essay on Man,* Epistle III, lines 121-124.

94. Mandeville, *The Virgin Unmask'd,* pp. 10-12.

95. *The Virgin Unmask'd,* p. 27.

96. Bernard Mandeville, *A Modest Defence of Publick Stews: Or an Essay upon Whoring as it is now Practis'd in these Kingdoms,* Written by a Layman (London, 1724). See too Richard I. Cook, "The Great 'Leviathan of Lechery': Mandeville's *Modest Defence of Public Stews* (1724)," in Irwin Primer (ed.), *Mandeville Studies* (The Hague: Nijhoff, 1975), pp. 22-33.

97. Mandeville, *Publick Stews,* pp. 63-64.

98. Mandeville, *Publick Stews,* p. 64.

99. Mandeville, *Publick Stews,* pp. 64-65.

J. A. W. Gunn (essay date 2000)

SOURCE: Gunn, J. A. W. "'State Hypochondriacks' Dispraised: Mandeville versus the Active Citizen." In *Mandeville and Augustan Ideas: New Essays,* edited by Charles W. A. Prior, pp. 16-34. Victoria, Canada: English Literary Studies, University of Victoria, 2000.

[In the following essay, Gunn analyzes Mandeville's distanced and detached perspective on public affairs.]

Mandeville as a thinker has always resisted easy labelling; were this not so, his place as a continuing focus for scholarly attention would be less easy to understand. Especially susceptible to exaggeration and plain misreading is his role as the apparent advocate of individual self-seeking. As I argued in an earlier encounter with this figure,[1] the portrayal of Mandeville as an extreme individualist fails to come to terms with the fact that his famous formula of "private vices, public benefits" is dependent upon a very conventional notion of what constituted a benefit to the public. This may occasion surprise, for we have long known that much of his notoriety rested upon the studied ambiguity of his understanding of "vice." By contrast, public benefit was not conceived in terms of private satisfactions but unambiguously in holistic, society-wide, even mercantilist, terms. A full treasury, a strong navy and magnificent public buildings were what signalled a flourishing society, and these conditions might well rest upon a foundation of distress at the level of the striving individual. A certain freedom for individual self-indulgence may well have been the means of attaining the desired public gain, but that condition was not itself conceived as many true individualists saw it.

The attainment of the public weal was not, to all appearances, a spontaneous process but was somehow subject to the guidance of politicians, supposedly wise in the ways of mankind. Here too there has been ample room for pondering Mandeville's true meaning, for he expresses various sentiments about political figures, thus leading to the possibility that, sometimes at least, he was thinking less of specific human agents and more of the work of time and tradition in shaping institutions to their optimum form. About the institutions of his day, he was genuinely positive in the manner of all those who accepted the Glorious Revolution, and his Whiggish party loyalties were, at times, no less evident. What clouds the picture is Mandeville's apparent animus against Walpole, the man of the time, and his readiness to depict the task of politicians as one calling only for abilities of a second order. This allowed him to discriminate in awarding praise and left some room in the title of "statesman" to recognise those few public men who were worthy of the highest honours. For all the reservations that Mandeville allowed himself to express about the politicians of his own decades, he did tend to assume the perspective of those who viewed society from the vantage point of governors; not for him the modest station of the subject or private citizen. The reason for this presumption lies in the whole point of Mandeville's most compelling message—namely, that society worked in ways mysterious to most who lived their lives within it, and the significance of individual acts was better understood by certain others who assumed the role of observers, placed above the fray. How much credit living politicians should get for the dextrous management is a moot question, but clearly Mandeville saw himself a party to such knowledge. This alone served effectively to separate him from his fellow beings.

A New Liberty—the Background

The times added another dimension to Mandeville's relations with authority. In order to appreciate this, we need but contemplate that Britain after 1688 was a regime that proclaimed its commitment to constitutional monarchy and had therefore established the centrality of the king in parliament. There would no longer, then, be an irregular standing army with which to menace the population, nor would taxation without representation be tolerated. One might still lose one's life for seditious libel—as did one young printer of Jacobite materials during the reign of Anne—but, in the main, press, stage and pulpit were open to a great diversity of sentiment. In similar fashion, a variety of clubs provided opportunities for those of similar habits and political views to associate. The spirit of the new era was epitomised by those compromises whereby an established church was made compatible with substantial freedom of religion and the simple failure to renew the Licensing Act freed the press in a manner that avoided making any declaration of principle. Britain was slipping, almost through negligence, into a real, if limited, freedom. That dictum of the common law that deemed one free to do what was not prohibited expressed the meaning of it all.

Was there then no serpent in Eden? There was, as incessant warnings about the threat posed by the Pretender served to remind people. Further evidence of discontent lay in the principled plight of those churchmen who had refused to swear allegiance to the new sovereign. For Non-Jurors, and for many others, the hand of authority was heavy still. The emergence of the Whig oligarchy, after 1714, occasioned a good deal of comment about the resolve of Whigs in power to put all of their revolutions behind them. Passage of the Septennial Act in 1716 made it very clear that the victorious Whigs saw no incongruity in their removing from the electorate the possibility of ejecting them from office in the immediate future. An administration that so distanced itself from the wrath of subjects set the tone of a time when there would be many occasions for objecting that the free people of Britain were pressing the government too hard, and with this observation we reach the focus of this analysis. It was a complaint that made sense only in a regime that, in principle, offered its citizens—or the more substantial of them, at least—the means of redress when displeased with government. In the past, the doctrine of hereditary divine right and associated prejudices had supplied the means of reminding subjects to behave like subjects and some Whigs continued to urge variants of this position with but a subtle departure from the teaching of Stuart absolutism. This might consist only in pointing out that the supreme power that exacted obedience and non-resistance was not the king alone, as in seventeenth-century usage, but the king in parliament. This did, of course, make a difference, for whereas it made sense to attribute some divine mandate for legitimate sovereigns, it seemed to be stretching matters to attribute to God a fondness for legislatures. Even before the onset of the Hanoverian era in 1714, one heard with varying emphasis that a Whig government might not be very different from a Tory one.[2] However, coming as close as some did to preaching the doctrines of a discredited absolutism could not readily supply the everyday vocabulary for protecting those in authority, and consequently a yet more nuanced language had to be found. There is considerable evidence that Mandeville was one of the writers who sought specifically to supply these new forms of argument.

In the manner of some of Mandeville's other inspirations, this one revealed itself early in his literary career and was subject to adaptation to suit the desired emphasis. In his early dig at the pamphleteers, whose numbers and audacity were surely the infallible sign of political freedom, he had observed how William III had spent his declining years striving to gain favour with "a grumbling nation that was ne'er at ease."[3] Even at this juncture, Mandeville was no friendlier to the grumbling of a free people than to the same activity of a thriving hive. He may, indeed, already have reached the judgement that, in neither case, were the grumblers in a position to realise how well off they really were. It is perhaps worth noting too that the grumbling was often carried to the pitch of alleging, supported by not a scrap of convincing evidence, that the ministers were conspiring to sap the nation's liberties—no trivial charge.[4] The assault on an amateurish presumption to know about matters of high policy is intensified in Mandeville's rendering of La Fontaine's fable about belling the cat. Here, the moral contains a mild sarcasm about those gentlemen who, from the safety of a coffee house, "prudently . . . rule the Nation."[5] A wisdom that exacted no costs and which might be exercised quite free of any responsibility had become a target more inviting than ever it might have been under the different conditions of absolute government. When liberties were fairly new, exhilarating and so subject to misuse, they mark a new era in political thought, and they do so more obviously than modern scholars' discoveries of the articulate citizen of the sixteenth century or of that more elusive condition, in the seventeenth, called the rise of civic consciousness.[6] Mandeville's contribution to the coming to terms with liberty also, as we shall see, adds an important dimension to what has come to be known as the emergence of the "public sphere."

Mandeville developed his theme, fleetingly visible in these early works, in three separate versions. Spread over a period of some twenty years, it is not surprising that each took up, with a different emphasis, this notion of rulers being distracted or even threatened by the ambitious or the ignorant. Quite the oddest of these performances comes in *The Virgin Unmask'd,* Mandeville's entertaining dialogue of 1709, a work that saw a fourth edition as late as 1742. There, incidental to the main business of educating a young woman as to the proper ways of deporting herself in the world, both participants in the dialogue settle upon certain issues of public affairs. The two speakers agree on a number of matters, but it remains for Lucinda, the wise aunt and preceptor, to deepen the analysis in the interests of encouraging a more adequate command of the issues of the day. It all begins when the virgin of the tale objects to that

silliness whereby every cobbler and tinker talked of politics. The very example puts one in mind of the famous rebuke that James I made to his parliament: he had told them, in words originally written by Pliny the elder, "cobbler stick to your last." Clearly, that exalted conception of ruling had ceased to be in fashion, and one suspects that, in beginning thus, our artful author is making the point that the whole business is far more complex than it had been in the early seventeenth century. It is worth noting that an allusion to those who desert their lasts to invade the realm of statecraft occurs in a work contemporaneous with the outburst from King James.

This is John Melton's long-drawn-out complaint about the presumption of gossips and projectors, travellers and poets, all ambitious to gain employment in affairs of state.[7] Here was a lament for the wearing away of status and degree, made at a time when there were no new liberties to test the bounds of official tolerance. Very different was the issue in the Augustan age, and so the superficial parallels disguise the fact that Melton's concerns were not those of Mandeville. It was not given to Whig writers in the age of Anne simply to invoke divine right, yet the objections to meddling with affairs of state were heard still. Early in the century had come the crisis brought on when a Tory House of Commons was aggressively unreceptive to the Aylesbury petition. Later, in 1710 to be exact, it would be the turn of Whigs to discountenance the petitions and addresses that rained down following the impeachment of Henry Sacheverell, the High Church firebrand. So the desire to curb popular intervention continued, constrained by the new circumstances brought to the fore by the Revolution of 1688. Emphasis here is upon those new features in the Augustan era that speak to the importance of Mandeville's theme. In all ages there have been people of no importance or capacity who took a vicarious pleasure in associating themselves with their political superiors, if only in the capacity of gossip and critic. In the ancient world, Epictetus and Dio Chrysostom both had had occasion to rebuke layabouts who thought themselves able to improve the management of the Roman empire.[8] But Mandeville was responding to the more delicate matter of discouraging unwelcome attention in a regime that could hardly afford to deny to at least some private citizens a voice in their public business. It was an issue peculiar to a time of supposed political freedom such as had dawned with the Glorious Revolution.

THE PRESUMPTUOUS CITIZEN—VARIATIONS ON A
THEME

In keeping with a different age, emphasis initially was not on the divine mandate of rulers but on the extraordinary complexity of public affairs; in later versions of this theme Mandeville found different arguments. The two women of *The Virgin Unmask'd* were agreed that those who opined so readily on the fate of the nation were out of their depth, but this point had to be made without insistence on the remarkable abilities of rulers. To protect the official conductors of politics without excessively dignifying their persons was to be the hallmark of Mandeville's position, and this entailed some refinement on the claim that the line that separated competence from incompetence was the same as that between statesman and subject. The real focus of awe was the endless intricacy of politics where prediction was rendered hazardous by the "hidden springs" of events. Certainty, in the form of "mathematical demonstration" was, of course, denied to the student of politics, but so too was even that confidence that might attend the empirical knowledge of probabilities. In politics, as in gardening, unforeseen factors might easily defeat one's expectations about the outcome.[9] So far were the specialists from the privilege of grasping truth that even Sir William Temple, ambassador to Holland, had returned with some serious misconceptions about the power with which he had been accredited. Evidently Mandeville remained sufficiently close to his Dutch roots for this to matter. Pointing in the same direction but more suggestive of his future line of reasoning was the claim that, indeed, no individual could presume to know enough about all relevant issues and so the necessary information was lodged, if at all, in "all the court and the whole Government of a Nation."[10] The immediate application was transparent; if the professionals, privy to such information as was to be had, might err, what likelihood was there that those less well informed could fare better?

Missing in this argument was much by way of reference to the state of British domestic politics. Once, to be sure, there was mention of the public's unfairness in judging generals in the field. So to express oneself in 1709 could hardly be other than a reference to the current situation of the Duke of Marlborough, victorious over the French again and again but still made the victim of party politics at home. Yet the richest vein of evidence explored here related, surprisingly enough, to France and its ruler. Of this figure, on whose qualities most Britons would seem to be agreed, there were still positive things to be said, and aunt Lucinda said them. She allowed that the king—referred to in contemporary pamphlets as the "great Bastard"—was a "wicked tyrant," but that was not the whole story. For his moral stature or his political aims she had nothing good to say, but at a purely technical level, his political acumen earned more favourable words:

> if you consider the vastness of his Undertakings, the multitude of his Negotiations, it will be difficult to find a Prince of half his Standing and that has had but a quarter Part of his Business, that has committed so few errors in Politicks as himself. Besides that a great many things prove unsuccessful at the end, that were well concerted at the Beginning.

Complementing this admission that Louis XIV possessed only a relatively good record was an earlier remark to the effect that a number of his demarches had misfired. Again, ordinary talents and those in a lower station were effectively warned off without bestowing adulation upon this astute calculator. Subsequent comment on reigning misconceptions about the alleged poverty of the French nation, followed by the reminder that one could never accu-

rately judge individuals outside their own country,[11] can only have been intended to correct the notoriously insular and xenophobic propensities of an English, especially a London, public.

But why dwell at all upon the Sun King, almost universally condemned, not least by exiles from France, as trying to dominate Europe at the expense of his own nation's welfare? Perhaps Mandeville was already learning the gentle art of offending popular prejudices. But it may be true as well that immediate political circumstances dictated some caution in awarding praise or blame to the actors in British politics. The parties were, at this time, rather even in strength; indeed, the next year would see Anne tire of her Whig advisers, who were promptly defeated in the ensuing election. The case of Marlborough, a seemingly appealing example of Lucinda's thesis, was rendered complex by the fact that he was not a party man and that his waging of war had been subject to interference by both Whigs and Tories and, most recently, by the former. At this stage, the future Whig monopoly of power could not have been anticipated, and the unruly enthusiasm for Sacheverell, as it would emerge in 1710, testified to the great popularity of the Tory cause. Discretion might then have dictated not making too many influential enemies in a political struggle that might still go either way. It is perhaps significant that Mandeville's most partisan pronouncements seem to have come only after the death of Anne and the outset of the Hanoverian period, the first two reigns of which were so friendly to Whig fortunes.

But there was more afoot here than the exercising of a prudence that sought to avoid giving offence to those who might exact retribution, for there is evidence that already Mandeville saw problems in meshing the conduct of policy with the sort of public involvement that was encouraged by the partisan passions of the time. It was not just that political enemies might interfere with delicate matters for their own ends; friend and foe were equally prone to tamper in ways that might be inimical to the purposes of the administration. The guarded allusion to the travails of Marlborough had suggested as much by citing the fact that the barest hint in the daily press might cause people to involve themselves prematurely in what used to be called mysteries of state. Should this observation seem exaggerated, one must recall that the newspapers of the time used small print and had no headlines, so that any reading must be a close one. Horror at the free speculation that was so readily let loose led Lucinda to the conclusion that "a good subject ought not to . . . speak at large of what might contribute either to the shame or the grief of his country."[12] More than once in that century, the government of the day would come to feel that the work of making war or peace had been rendered more difficult by the sort of intrusive political process that Britain's enemies did not allow. Mandeville seems here to have been early in the field, but the very next year saw some intense enquiry into the prerogatives of the *vox populi,* as John Oldmixon and others sought to defuse the tumultuous support enjoyed by Sacheverell.[13] At this time, the service to be performed by a good Whig was not, as in the 1680s, to proclaim the virtues of the public voice but rather to deprive it of legitimacy.

With the accession of George I, Mandeville offered a strong statement of Whig doctrine, containing a few hints of the arguments of interest here. *The Mischiefs that Ought Justly be Apprehended from a Whig Government* (1714) makes clear one reason for his reservations about the wisdom of public judgements, as he wrote of "our Mob" and its hostility to immigrants like himself. There was also a confirmation that Mandeville was disinclined to support Whig rule by recourse to arguments about passive obedience; he actually congratulated the Whigs for their generosity in not so arguing even when they enjoyed power.[14] We must, however, look elsewhere for the next major statement. Mandeville's least ambiguous and most partisan articulation of his prejudices was reserved for 1720, a time by which the victorious Whigs were securely ensconced in office. Some themes that arose in the early 1720s have been oddly subject to neglect in the history of political ideas. What dominates accounts of the period 1720-23 is the Old-Whig teaching about virtue, simplicity and the needs of the private citizen as proclaimed in *Cato's Letters* by John Trenchard and Thomas Gordon. Unpromising as the task must have seemed, Cato's case, and that of others, against concentrated power, political and economic, had to be answered, and this was done by a number of serial publications, presumably financed by the Treasury and issued through the printer John Roberts. It is these responses that remain little known.

To appreciate the flavour of the literature of ministerial Whigs, one can do no better than to consult that lively publication called *The Commentator* which, directed against Tory and Jacobite enemies of the government, shone too briefly in 1720 (albeit too early to attack Trenchard and Gordon). Firmly partisan, no paper better displayed the Whigs' new-found impatience with the ways of a free people. With their enemies in retreat, the writers mocked those retailers of the banal who solemnly intoned that the time had come to lay aside the odious distinctions of Whig and Tory. Of course, Whigs had no incentive to end distinctions that so effectively banished part of the nation from the prospect of office. Not themselves greatly given to reassuring clichés, the authors dismissed even the liberty of the press as but one of the "second-rate Liberties" and reminded those who availed themselves to excess in this openness that, for libellers of the administration, the courts too were open. Possibly the masters of the *Commentator* came to feel that their defenders were becoming too bold when a late number grumbled that the boasted liberty of the subject was, if anything, "too well secured,"[15] and no more was heard on that score. Reminders that all governments were necessarily sovereign and potentially terrible to those who sought to oppose them had been standard fare with Whigs for some time, and Cato came to point out, with different emphasis, that Whigs in power had a very Tory-like notion of authority.[16]

Most of those publications that argued for the unruliness of the public did not have Mandeville's perspective on the relative difficulty of forming a sound judgement on government unless privy to all the information. A typical complaint from a ministerial writer said, rather, that it was the work of designing men that stirred up the populace and thus gave individuals too good an opinion of their political skills. Under such circumstances, he objected, "the Science of ruling well becomes a very cheap and familiar thing." A sermon of 1726 made much the same point and, for good measure, added that there were secrets in public policy that were not rightly to be available to subjects.[17] There is no evidence that Mandeville directly contributed to this journalism, and certainly not to the sermons, though some of the literature—such as an article that sought to demonstrate that the rational self-interest of ministers would suffice to secure the public good[18]—may have been inspired by a reading of the *Fable.*

The more threatening tones of the government press find no echo in Mandeville's writings, but he sought the same outcomes, by what seemed to be a surer path, in the milder arguments of *Free Thoughts* (1720). The general chapter **"Of Government"** contains some anticipations of the developed argument to be presented in chapter XII, **"Of National Happiness."** In the early comments, he makes it entirely clear that he disapproved of those public clamours based upon ignorance or misunderstanding.[19] Only in the more developed version did he remark upon the strange paradox whereby a nation, with much reason for contentment, should be beset by purveyors of doom. Distempered imaginations—of the same nature as those forms of hypochondria and the vapours of which he had written as a medical man in 1711—were one way of characterising the problem. Amongst a flurry of epithets, he called his quarry **"State Hypochondriacks"** whose lamentations assailed his ears daily. Even in this most ministerial of writings Mandeville shows no inclination to proclaim the personal merit of those in office. Indeed, he avowed that serving the public was an ungrateful task, unattractive to men of fortune and quality. He even offered the disconcerting thought that honest men fared the worst in such a capacity. He thus pursued the double objective of discouraging those who insisted upon the probity of politicians and, equally, those who were intent on misconstruing the actions of these public men.[20] The burden of his plea was not, then, that virtue and genius had to endure calumny, but rather that (1) the truth about matters of state remained, on the whole, opaque to most people; (2) complaints were often made in bad faith, as in the long-standing absurdity that ministers sought to enslave the nation while preserving but the forms of freedom; and (3) such acts had unfortunate consequences.

It was this last that afforded much of the detail, and that detail was in contrast to Melton's predictions about the bad end that awaited those who sought to rise too high in national counsels. In fact, Mandeville declined to contemplate disasters of any sort—a wise move, given his scorn for alarmists—and confined himself to the rather moderate inconveniences that attended the practice. In this spirit, he wondered what good to the nation was secured by complaints about the conduct of a war that Britain had won. Surely the complainers sought some good only to themselves, and one who so behaved was "an arch Politician." Of the manifestly irresponsible acts that needed checking was the bellowing of some bravo about the church being in danger or the insistence of a fellow of ruined fortune that the Pretender be brought in. The High Church and Jacobite nature of the offences is readily apparent. Examples of a more complex nature had to do with those who commented superficially on the proposed demolition of Dunkirk or on British changes of policy with respect to Gibraltar. These matters of high policy had to do with managing the balance of power, and here the views of the multitude were distinctly unwelcome. Public discussion of Gibraltar's value to Britain could only be expected to ensure Spain's efforts to regain it.[21] This was his most convincing example of the costs of conducting foreign policy in the glare of publicity.

The most divisive item in domestic politics at this time was the proposal to limit future creations of peers, a measure that pitted Whig against Whig. Mandeville assured his readers that here lay no assurance as to where the balance of wisdom should rest. He was thus neither for nor against it, "because it is above my capacity to judge of it." Only rarely did Mandeville place his own understanding at the ordinary level, and this rare show of modesty may conceal a disinclination to take issue with the views of any influential Whigs. Not that there was an obvious answer as to the wisdom of the legislation, for it raised questions about future relations among all three branches of government. Some measured the power of the lords by their number, by which reckoning more of them meant more influence. Others, by contrast, judged the importance of a peer by their rarity, and so each grew more significant as the numbers were reduced. There was also the problem that the influence of individual members of a legislative body was one thing and its corporate prerogatives quite another. The lapse in Mandeville's air of omniscience was thus aptly chosen. Covering his position here was the general observation that, when circumstances were new or subject to variation, even knowledgeable people were apt to err about outcomes.[22] With this caution applying to all, he then returned to the familiar ground of those whose ambition to appear discerning outstripped their understanding. Even with respect to them, he was careful not to deny opportunities that were best not taken, and he cleverly put in doubt the legitimacy of drawing any social line that separated insight and ignorance. The approved course of action lay in:

> forbearing to meddle with what is above, or at least foreign to us; it is ill Manners for Subjects to pry into Family Affairs of their Kings; their Pastimes, their Pleasures and Diversions, have nothing to do with the State . . .[23]

If, as seems likely, the specific source of the problem was the penchant of an unpopular king to live in his German possessions and not in England, then, of course, subjects were well advised to complain. But the state's defenders are no more on oath than are its detractors, and Mandeville had a case to make. The advice that he offered was that one should not meddle overmuch, and it applied both to a great range of public policies and to his general view of society and its workings. Though especially emphasised in the Whig ascendancy, such had also been the views of Queen Anne who had endorsed the injunction that subjects "study to be quiet."

In the final performance where Mandeville emphasised his anti-civist theme, he was somewhat less emphatic in his position, though the original argument leaves more than a trace. Two new factors may help to account for changes. The first lies in Mandeville's apparent intent, in 1729, to run down the capacities of Walpole as prime minister, probably the better to serve the interests of Lord Macclesfield, Mandeville's patron. Of grander import is that development of Mandeville's thought—one especially marked by Professor Hayek—whereby the art of the politician came increasingly to be sublimated into a social process which, acting over time, might create optimal institutions through a sort of natural selection.[24] From both of these considerations there followed an apparent resolve to downplay the difficulty of the politician's business. With the generation that had made the Glorious Revolution now passed from the scene and the new institutions performing well, it may have been entirely sensible to accord less attention to the immanent contribution of the rulers of the day. It may also be viewed as little more than a matter of building upon that remark in *Free Thoughts* that declared the wrongness both of the extremes of flattering the abilities of those in office and of presuming to criticise their every move. In the second part of *The Fable of the Bees*, Horatio puts the naive claims for a surpassing excellence that must belong to successful politicians, whereas Cleomenes speaks for Mandeville's evident scepticism.

The complex and nuanced argument here is that of Cleomenes. The firm resolve not to make much of the difficulty of ruling necessarily threatened to deprive Mandeville of that appeal to complexity that was the main weapon against a meddlesome public. His statements thus bear the appearance of being carefully phrased so as not to give away too much. When Horatio offers an encomium to the skills of the minister who must fight off jealous malcontents, Cleomenes replies so as to stress the cheekiness of too near an enquiry into the business of the great and not the impenetrability of mysteries of state. His words also nicely capture his growing tendency to find excellence more in the new political order and not in the ministrations of discernible individuals:

> I am not to judge of the Exigency of our Affairs. But as I would not pry into the Conduct, or scan the Action of our Princes and their Ministers, so I pretend to justify or defend no wisdom, but that of the Constitution itself.[25]

The persistent Horatio, to whom has clearly been assigned the role of bringing out the real afflictions suffered by ministers who become the target of those anxious to discredit them, forges ahead, while Cleomenes continues to insist that his friend entertains too sublime a notion of the skills needed to counter the stratagems of the disaffected. However, in repeating his argument that the offices in question were not as demanding as Horatio had thought, he leaves open the possibility that the political manoeuvring needed to stay in power may well make considerable demands on incumbents. This equivocal response includes the claim that the very possession of office brings advantages to men in power. For one thing, Cleomenes tells us, so many are the charges levelled against ministers that the impartial and discerning tend not to credit the stories, even when they are true![26] Here is a skilful holding of a balance between seeming too friendly to the abilities of the ministers or too insensitive to the array of devices, not all of them in their nature fair or just, that were employed to supplant them. Horatio's point about the mischievous energies devoted to misrepresenting the ministers finds its mark, but only after judicious redirection from Cleomenes. As the dialectic comes to the end of the second exchange, it has become clear that the very undiscriminating character of the malcontents' assault means that no great abilities are needed by those who would parry their thrusts. It is a formula for reducing the credibility of both sides simultaneously.

The third round opens with Horatio insisting still that the ministers must command abilities congruent with their mission and that great trust reposes in them. He instances those secret- service funds, so intimately connected with "Reasons of State" that even to mention their existence may be deemed improper. Here, indeed, was a sensitive matter, one that in the form of funds supposedly open to misuse would help eventually to hound Walpole from office. These were not small matters, for the government's sensitivity to the Jacobite threat meant that those whose loyalty was suspect might expect to have their mail opened, while an army of spies watched the plots being hatched in Europe. Unimpressed, Cleomones retorts that annual parliaments serve to keep watch on activities of the ministers and that, anyway, one could scarcely make off with money reserved for clandestine operations. Present in these parliaments, summoned annually, were those very enemies of the ministers who, in the eyes of Horatio, represented such a challenge. Here, finally, we find his agreeing with some portion of Horatio's argument, but only when presented in different form. The very fact that parliament was a check on the ministers and that it participated in securing the public welfare was one way of spelling out the earlier claim that honour should be paid to the constitution and not to individuals. Cleomones puts in thus:

> The malicious Overlookers that envy them their Places, and watch all their Motions, are a great Awe upon them: The Animosities between these Antagonists, and the Quarrels between Parties, are a considerable Part of the Nation's Security.[27]

Here, then, lay the key to the business. It was the presence, in the nation, of fairly stable associations of politicians, each side with pre-conceived views about who was fit to enjoy the king's confidence, that secured a good that belonged to the credit of neither side. So long as these persisted, it was clear that men in office would continue to be, for some, without blemish and, for others, devoid of all virtues. To close the circle with his previous arguments, Mandeville introduced once more the name of Marlborough.[28] The great contribution of "contrary Parties" was that these supplied the mechanism whereby the nation might flourish even when those entrusted with ruling it were deficient in knowledge or probity. The presence of the two parties gave the incumbents an incentive not to be caught out, for where fault might be alleged, one might be sure that it would be done. Still carrying the burden of Mandeville's message, Cleomenes readily allowed that, were virtue to be discovered, it should indeed rule. Just to emphasise his total incomprehension, Horatio, the "straight man," continues to register distress that there is to be no talent in the counsels of state. Cleomenes then brings the dialogue that ends the ***Fable*** to a close with the assurance that matters are far from being that serious.

THE PUBLIC SPHERE IN PERSPECTIVE

With the argument closed, it is clear that Mandeville has discarded none of his insights, but instead he had become one of the very few in his time to appreciate that political parties served some useful purpose even when the ambitious men who were their members remained unaware of what it was. The concern, first expressed in his work of a quarter of a century before, that irresponsible criticism of the king's ministers might do damage had met a prejudice claiming that the talents needed to rule were not extraordinary. Neither proposition had, in the event, to be set aside, for both might be reconciled with a political order in which the actors built better than they knew. Suitably qualified, the two contentions were reduced in scope. On the one side, this led to the claim that critics, even when misguided, might serve the interests of the public. This was especially so, of course, when the coffee-house politician assumed the more impressive guise of a member of parliament anxious to display his fitness to replace those in office. The disconcerting claim about the capacities of ministers had also been trimmed to usable proportions. It did not consign government to the protection of knaves or fools, but made the much more modest point that the available pool of talent was ranged in competing parties and that the interaction of the two sides did better for the nation than would either side ruling unopposed. No longer need one sigh in vain for wisdom and virtue clothed in power, nor were the Cassandra-like cries of the mongers of national decline to be accepted at face value. Instead, the two sides—each imperfect—together might supply a rough approximation of that rule which was beyond either to create by itself. The very structure of the dialogue itself mirrors the sense of the argument, for the undiscerning Horatio does, all considered, contribute to spelling out a complex insight of which he himself was not the master.

It is fitting that the supposed originator of the concept of the division of labour should have toiled so well in applying to the political competition of the time the insight that the interaction of several contributors might do better than all the available knowledge and virtue combined in a single set of hands. So to argue was a *tour de force* that dated for all time rationalistic appeals to a lawgiver or vain incitements to virtue as with Trenchard and Gordon. Others, in their various ways, had seen comparable virtues in political parties, but the sources are few and obscure.[29] In this case, there can be little reason to suppose that Mandeville depended upon antecedent texts; rather, this insight was a natural development of the modes of reasoning which had already made for him his reputation. The future was another matter. It can fairly be said that Mandeville was one of those pro-administration writers who first found some effective alternative to fulminating against liberty or joining in the dark threats of the authoritarian Whigs of the early 1720s. The denigration of the liberties of the subject was not the wave of the future and, by the 1730s, Walpole's writers had learned to expect systematic opposition and justified their own use of "influence" as the legitimate means of defence. This did not rule out condemning the malcontents for their want of knowledge or principle, but it successfully discouraged any wholesale resurrection of the language of absolutism. Admirers of Mandevillean subtlety may add to his accomplishments his having come early to an awareness of the costs that accompanied individual and constitutional liberty. The voice of the "state hypochondriack" was indeed heard in the land and brought with it certain difficulties that are endemic within a free society. To Mandeville's great credit, he applied his usual cleverness to analysing the complaint and then came to suggest that already present in the mode of government existed a form of self-correction which, far from needing implementation, had only, in some quarters, to be recognised. Throughout, he never strayed from his initial assumption that social actors could not, on the whole, be expected to comprehend the outcomes linked to their activity.

It has been fashionable for some time now to refer to the growth of civism in terms of the emergence of a public sphere, a concept that we owe to Jürgen Habermas.[30] The exact hallmarks of this aspect of modernity are subject to scholarly debate, and there has been discussion as well as to whether the expression refers to a specific epoch in the European Enlightenment, whether it is a stage in the modernisation of societies in general or, indeed, an ideal not necessarily revealed at all in reality. Among the criteria that might identify such a moment in the appearance of modernity are an emphasis upon public opinion—here Habermas was inclined to accept the currency of the term as coterminous with the condition—and a middle-class challenge to the powers established. Those now using the concept would seem too to conceive of the process as one where the levers of influence had to be wrested from the privileged orders and, in addition, the interpreters have been prone to make a positive evaluation of the process. Departing from the eighteenth-century focus employed by Habermas, some now purport to find a public sphere in England of the Civil War. In this version, the public sphere's arrival would share some of the lustre previously

claimed for "civic consciousness." However, the enthusiastic migration of the public sphere has also encountered some severe checks for its unconvincing use of historical evidence.[31] It is also true, of course, that efforts to impose categories made in the twentieth century on an earlier age—though not in themselves illegitimate—must be undertaken with some care. In both Habermas's original and in the numerous works influenced by it, the scope for misinterpreting the past looms large. In hailing the relative newness of a large public ready to debate national issues and in seeing here the birth of a modern ideal, talk of a public sphere takes on a certain amount of baggage from the Whig theory of history. That is to say, it too readily discovers a past bearing the flags that announce our own world; consequently, it may well distort that past in the name of modern prejudices.

Mandeville affords us a vantage point useful for assessing the usefulness of the notion of a public sphere in eighteenth-century Britain. He serves to remind us that the rational discourse admired by Habermas was attained in practice only with difficulty and, far from earning our uncritical admiration, was very much a two-way street. Mandeville must have been one of the first to note, within the institutions of parliamentary government, that subjecting public figures to the critical scrutiny of a large and indiscriminate public might have the effect of depriving the political realm of some of the ablest participants. It was not a point that need arise with comparable significance under absolute rule. Far from emphasising the rational character of the ensuing discourse, Mandeville saw it, at its best, as affording an opportunity to counter exaggerations of one sort with those of another. In his brilliant move of translating the public voice into the point and counter-point of the party struggle, Mandeville manages as well to depict the new era as one where those enjoying authority and others challenging it both contributed to the process of creating a dialectic. This is in keeping with the finding that, most often in the first half of the eighteenth century, it was the spokesmen for power that made more than their share of contributions to appreciating the nature of public opinion and party competition as the significant institutions for securing a stable freedom.[32] Looking at the same facts that are now identified as a public sphere, Mandeville's very undeceived sort of Whiggism first made the practical and telling point that there might seem to be too much public discourse for the good of the nation and that what would come, in time, to be known as public opinion was all too often incompetent, even a bit dangerous. From this plateau, his analysis grew to embrace the emerging cacophony, but only with the proviso that one not expect too much. His was not the only way of bringing a measure of realism to expectations about the governance of a free society, but his refusal to discover truth either in the language of the friends of administration or that of its foes was a significant corrective to enthusiastic misconceptions about the *vox populi*. Because of an absence of such a perspective, French thought—which served of course as the evidence upon which Habermas chiefly relied—was subject to the rationalist view that public opinion was the opinion of a single unanimous entity.[33] Mandeville's scepticism effectively dissolved the public voice into opposed claims and so more readily approximates the twentieth-century understanding.

By his characteristic refusal either to commit himself to the praise of ministers or to join the coffee-house politicians in their presumption, Mandeville managed, as usual, to define a position that bore the stamp of his remarkably original mind. In so doing, he taught some of his contemporaries to expect to discover those institutions that work well in that no-man's-land beyond human intention. It is a landscape peopled neither with heroes nor with villains and where even the state hypochondriac gains a stature that was no part of his intention or design.

Notes

1. J. A. W. Gunn, "Mandeville and Wither: Individualism and the Workings of Providence," in *Mandeville Studies: New Explorations in the Art and Thought of Dr. Bernard Mandeville,* ed. Irwin Primer (The Hague, 1975), 98-118 at 114-15.

2. See, with a positive emphasis, Daniel Defoe, *Whigs turn'd Tories, and Hanoverian Tories . . . prov'd Whigs* (London, 1713), 18. More commonly, such comments were intended as anti-Whiggish: see Anon., *The Reconciler* (London, 1716), 27-28; *Weekly Journal or Saturday's Post* 202 (29 September 1722), and various publications by the Jacobite Matthias Earbery.

3. [Mandeville], *The Pamphleteers: A Satyr* (London, 1703), 6. I owe this reference to Charles Prior.

4. See J. A. W. Gunn, "Parliament and the Caesars: Legal Tyranny in the Political Rhetoric of Eighteenth-Century England," in *Beyond Liberty and Property* (Kingston & Montreal, 1983), 7-42.

5. *Aesop dress'd, or a Collection of Fables writ in Familiar Verse* (London, 1704), 35.

6. Arthur B. Ferguson, *The Articulate Citizen and the English Renaissance* (Durham, N. C., 1967) and C. B. Hanson, *From Kingdom to Commonwealth: The Development of Civic Consciousness in English Political Thought* (Cambridge, Mass., 1970).

7. John Melton, *A Sixe-folde Politician, together with a Sixe-folde Precept of Policy* (London, 1609), 5-6.

8. Epictetus, *The Discourses,* trans. W. A. Oldfather, (London & New York, 1928), 3:4.7 at II, 39 in the Loeb edition; *Dio Chrysostom,* 5 vols., trans. J. W. Cohoon (Cambridge, Mass. & London, 1961), discourse 20.3 at II, 249 in the Loeb edition.

9. Mandeville, *The Virgin Unmask'd* [1709], intro. Stephen H. Good (New York, 1975), 136, 147, 160.

10. Ibid., 137-38, 139.

11. Ibid., 163, 167, 168.

12. Ibid., 148, 152.

13. See Gunn, *Beyond Liberty and Property,* 77-78.

14. Bernard Mandeville, *The Mischiefs that Ought Justly to be Apprehended from a Whig Government* (London, 1714), 12, 38.

15. *The Commentator,* 3 (8 January 1720); 8 (25 January 1720) and 33 (22 April 1720). This periodical seems not to be held in the Burney collection at the British Library but is in the Bodleian. See Rev. Frederick William Hope, *Catalogue of a Collection of early Newspapers and Essayists . . . presented to the Bodleian Library* (Oxford, 1865), 42. The writers have not, it seems, been identified.

16. *The Patriot* (printed by Roberts and also to be found in the Hope collection), 57 (14-17 August 1714). See too *Beyond Liberty and Property,* 102, where I cite other sources. For Cato's judgment, see *The British Journal* 1 (22 September 1722).

17. *St. James's Journal* 14 (2 August 1722). The editor seems to have been one Thomas Robe. Here is the only one of this neglected set of publications that has been reprinted in the series *Early English Newspapers* (Woodbridge, Conn.: Research Publications). The sermon in question is Edward Oliver, *The Relative Duties of Magistrates and People* (London, 1726), 4.

18. *The Whitehall Journal* 47 (April, 1723). This is to be found in the Nichols collection, Bodleian.

19. Bernard Mandeville, *Free Thoughts on Religion, the Church and National Happiness* (London, 1720), 318, 321-22.

20. Ibid., 340, 344.

21. Ibid., 348.

22. Ibid., 345-46.

23. Ibid., 350.

24. See "Dr. Bernard Mandeville" in F. A. Hayek, *New Studies in Philosophy, Politics, Economics and the History of Ideas* (Chicago & London, 1978), 249-66 at 260-61.

25. [Bernard Mandeville] *The Fable of the Bees; or, Private Vices, Publick Benefits,* ed. F. B. Kaye, 2 vols. (Oxford, 1924), II, 328.

26. Ibid., 330, 332.

27. Ibid., 334.

28. Ibid., 337.

29. For an essay, probably by Defoe, that may be inspired by Mandeville's earlier work, see *Applebee's Original Weekly Journal* (27 April 1723), 2579. For an earlier source where the views on party can owe nothing to Mandeville, see J. A. W. Gunn, "Party before Burke: Shute Barrington" in *Government and Opposition* 3 (Spring 1968), 223-40.

30. Habermas, *The Structural Transformation of the Public Sphere* [1962], trans. Thomas Burger (Cambridge, Mass., 1989).

31. See especially criticisms by Keith Baker, "Defining the Public Sphere in Eighteenth-Century France: Variations on a Theme by Habermas," in *Habermas and the Public Sphere,* ed. Craig Calhoun (Cambridge, Mass., 1992), 181-211 at 188.

32. I argue this at length in "Court Whiggery—Justifying Innovation," in *Politics, Politeness and Patriotism,* ed. Gordon J. Schochet (Washington, D.C., 1993), 125-56.

33. See J. A. W. Gunn, *Queen of the World: Opinion in the Public Life of France from the Renaissance to the Revolution* (Oxford, 1995), esp. 387-92.

M. M. Goldsmith (essay date 2000)

SOURCE: Goldsmith, M. M. "Mandeville's Pernicious System." In *Mandeville and Augustan Ideas: New Essays,* edited by Charles W. A. Prior, pp. 71-84. Victoria, Canada: English Literary Studies, University of Victoria, 2000.

[*In the following essay, Goldsmith analyzes the validity of the claims by his detractors that Mandeville was promoting immorality and irreligion in* The Fable of the Bees.]

Bernard Mandeville's **The Fable of the Bees** caught the attention of virtually every thinker of note in the eighteenth century.[1] The book was widely attacked for irreligion and immorality; contemporary periodicals commented on the stir it made.[2] When Adam Smith, in his *Theory of Moral Sentiments,*[3] denounced Mandeville's views as "wholly pernicious," he joined such critics as William Law, Francis Hutcheson, George Berkeley and David Hume.

In fact, the *Fable* became famous because it was denounced. The first edition of 1714, apart from the modest success of achieving two printings, went unnoticed.[4] In the second edition of 1723, Mandeville enlarged the **"Remarks"** on *The Grumbling Hive: or, Knaves turn'd Honest,* the poem which formed the basis of the work and which had first been published separately in 1705, and added two essays: **"An Essay on Charity and Charity-Schools"** and **"A Search into the Nature of Society."** In the second of these essays, Mandeville criticised Shaftesbury's views and further explained his own. But it was the first of the essays which seems to have triggered the public reaction.

On 8 July 1723, the book's printer, Edmund Parker, was presented by the Middlesex Grand Jury as the publisher of principles which had "a direct Tendency to the Subversion of all Religion and Civil Government" on the grounds that the *Fable* denigrated the clergy, encouraged libertinism and immorality, maliciously attacked education that inculcated Christian principles, ran down religion and virtue as prejudicial to society and the state, recommended luxury, pride, avarice and other vices as necessary to public good and even praised houses of prostitution.[5] On 27 July, the *London Journal* published a letter addressed to "Lord C." by "Theophilus Philo-Britannus" which similarly denounced the *Fable.*[6] Mandeville responded with **"A Vindication of the Book,"** in which both the Grand Jury's presentment and Theophilus's letter were incorporated. The **"Vindication"** was first published in the *London Journal* (10 August 1723) and then in a format suitable for binding with the *Fable.* It was included in subsequent editions of that work.

The **"Vindication"** was thus Mandeville's continued as well as his earliest explicit reply to the repeated accusations that the *Fable* promoted immorality and irreligion. In the end, Mandeville produced one other explicit response to those hostile allegations: his **A Letter to Dion** (1732), specifically countering Berkeley's attack on apparent adherents of the *Fable* in *Alciphron,* again claims to rebut the charges that the *Fable* "is a wicked Book, wrote for the Encouragement of Vice, and to debauch the Nation."[7] The purpose of this essay is to examine Mandeville's defence of the *Fable.* Firstly, I shall set out and refine a version of the attack on Mandeville. I shall then state and examine his arguments against that attack. I shall attempt to ascertain whether those arguments are valid and sound. After all, if they are not valid and sound we shall be able to conclude that Mandeville had no adequate defence of the *Fable* against those condemnations. Finally, I shall consider whether we should accept Mandeville's defence.

I

The standard case against Mandeville is succinctly put in the "Abusive Letter to Lord C." by "Theophilus Philo-Britannus" which Mandeville reprinted, along with the Grand Jury's presentment.[8] Theophilus accused Mandeville of assisting "Cato" (i.e., John Trenchard and Thomas Gordon, authors of *Cato's Letters*) in opposing Christianity and of endeavouring "to tear up the very Foundations of *Moral Virtue* and establish *Vice* in its Room." The evidence to support this charge is a quotation from **The Fable of the Bees** itself: neither the natural "Friendly Qualities and kind Affections," "nor the real Virtues," which can be acquired by "Reason and Self-Denial," are the foundation of society and of the arts and sciences. It is instead moral and natural evil which makes humans social creatures: "the Moment Evil ceases, the Society must be spoiled, if not totally dissolved."[9]

Let me flesh out Theophilus's argument a bit. Natural evil includes all the aspects of the environment which may harm humans, causing death and suffering, for example, disease, storms, floods, meteors, fires.[10] Although Mandeville does give examples of natural evils which result in benefits to humans and society, these are not his main concern. He is more interested in connecting public benefits to "Private Vices," that is, to moral rather than natural evil. So, for the moment at least, the question of whether natural evil is essential to society can be set aside.

Moral evils originate from wrong human action. Wrong actions may be of several types. Traditionally, sin is itself morally evil and so too are its consequences. But not all sins need be socially prohibited; it may be impractical or undesirable to attempt to discover and punish all sins or even all sinful actions. Nevertheless, if humans are to live together, at least some actions must be prohibited by social rules, laws and mores. Many social rules will prohibit actions which do (or tend to) harm others or the society (and many of these actions will be sinful or morally wrong ones). Other social rules may proscribe actions which are not otherwise wrong (examples might include conventions about proper eating manners and parking restrictions). At least some of these prohibitions are likely to promote social convenience. Thus, society requires morality. Moral virtues prescribe the ways in which humans should act and especially act toward others. They restrain human conduct. Without some restraints, humans could not live together.

But Theophilus is mainly concerned to defend religion, especially Christianity. On his line of thought, that defence is necessary, for religion is an essential support of morality. It is all very well to rely on social enforcement of the rules of right behaviour insofar as that behaviour is observable. But what can induce "men" to obey the rules when they are not observed? to refrain from violence to others, from stealing their goods, from breaking their contracts and their promises to them when they can get away with these actions? Where the fear of detection and punishment by other humans is absent, what can induce humans not to cheat, lie, steal or kill? The standard answer is that they will abstain from prohibited actions if they believe that there is a God, aware of their otherwise unseen actions, committed to rewarding the good and punishing the evil, and capable of doing so.[11] Therefore, if they do not hold those beliefs, morality is a matter of mere policy, a matter of prudence. Humans will restrain their actions when they fear retribution or expect some benefit by so doing. Otherwise they will act out their rapacious desires. No more than Mandeville does Theophilus believe that humans are naturally good.

The standard position is thus that vice produces evil, harming other individuals and human society, whereas virtue restrains evil, producing "publick benefits": it is good for society and for other individuals.[12]

The case that Mandeville advocates, the substitution of vice for virtue, requires the premise that "publick benefits" are good. But it also requires something more, namely the proposition that if public benefits are good, then the means which produce them are also good. Mandeville's detractors claim that if Mandeville's position is that private vices produce public benefits, then it follows that Mandeville holds that private vices are good.

Mandeville sets out two defences of his views: the first is that he holds a severely restricted version of how private vices produce public benefits, namely that the vices are turned into benefits by the "dextrous management of skilful Politicians"; the second defence is that holding that the consequences are good does not imply that the means are good.

II

Let us look at Mandeville's first defence: he claims that he holds a severely restricted version of the seeming paradox, "Private Vices, Publick Benefits."

The case that Mandeville advocates vice requires some refinement. It is not necessary either to argue that Mandeville's position is that all private vices always produce public benefits or that only private vices produce public benefits (and so that virtues never produce public benefits). It is only asserted that he holds that some private vices sometimes, perhaps even usually, produce public benefits.[13] That is a limited, or moderate version of the relation between vice and public good. However, there are occasions on which Mandeville restricts his subtitular "seeming Paradox" even more sharply. For example, at the very end of **"A Search into the Nature of Society,"** he states that he is claiming "that Private Vices by the dextrous Management of a skilful Politician may be turned into publick Benefits."[14] The severely restricted version of the paradox Mandeville here claims to hold involves a double limitation: firstly, only some vices sometimes produce public benefits; secondly, these vices produce benefits by dint of the actions of a "skilful Politician."

Mandeville's suggestion that his contention is so severely constrained looks difficult to sustain. It is at least clear that Mandeville does not hold that all private vices always result in public benefits. However, the second limitation is contentious. Are vices only beneficial through their management by individual political leaders or even political institutions? There is some support for his severely restricted version of his thesis. For example, in ***The Grumbling Hive*** itself, he says

> *So Vice is beneficial found,*
> *When it's by Justice lopt and bound.*[15]

Those lines seem to stringently qualify the circumstances in which vice is beneficial.

The role of the "skilful Politician" is perhaps most evident in Mandeville's discussion in the *Fable*'s **"Remark H"** of the prudent arrangements of the Amsterdam magistrates in tolerating a "red-light" district with "Temples of Venus" to accommodate sexual urges which cannot be eliminated.[16] The sin of "uncleanness" cannot be extirpated. Since it is impossible to eliminate it completely, other courses of action must be considered. Tolerating establishments which cater to it is good policy; it limits the evil.

Mandeville also contends that politicians should not curb international trade which results in the importing of luxury goods. Restricting those imports will have the consequence of reducing exports to the partner countries, and so of reducing trade and its benefits. Nevertheless, he still finds a role for the politician, who will "keep a watchful Eye over the Balance of Trade in general," making sure that the total value imported does not exceed that exported, that trade is maximised, and that it is directed by customs duties and import prohibitions toward countries which will allow specie to be exported and which will not refuse to trade except for money.[17]

Both of the above instances seem to support Mandeville's severely restricted version of the meaning of his paradox. They are instances in which policies are adopted by identifiable public officials. But Mandeville also insists that "The *Meum* and *Tuum* must be secur'd, Crimes punish'd, and all other Laws concerning the Administration of Justice, wisely contriv'd, and strictly executed."[18] This edges away from taking the "dextrous Politicians" as identifiable individuals acting in particular instances, moving toward regarding them as the symbol of a system of institutions. And while the security of property and the strict administration of justice look like a mixture of institutional arrangements and individual actions by magistrates, Mandeville gives many examples of vice producing public benefits without there being any imaginable manipulation by individual politicians. Not only do thieves and burglars provide employment for smiths and locksmiths, the eighteenth-century security experts, but, were a thousand guineas stolen from a miser, "it is certain that as soon as this Money should come to circulate, the Nation would be the better for the Robbery."[19] These benefits are not produced by the actions of "skilful Politicians," nor even by vice being limited by the administration of justice.[20]

Mandeville also finds benefits being produced by other vices. Pride, luxury, envy, emulation—all the vices which involve desires for more than one has—activate the wheels of trade, producing employment for millions and making the country prosperous and powerful.[21] The beneficial consequences of these vices are unintended; they are not produced by the vices being dexterously managed by skilful politicians but rather by an "invisible hand." Given Mandeville's willingness to adduce examples of vices having beneficial consequences which are produced without the "dextrous Management" of an actual politician, the restricted version he proposed of his paradox seems at least to be undermined. It looks as if Mandeville's first defence fails; he did not hold a severely restricted, but rather a less restricted, version of his thesis.

III

Nonetheless, Mandeville still has his second defence against Theophilus and other accusers to rely on. They suppose that what is a means or a cause of good is itself good and therefore that Mandeville implies that vices, because they produce public benefits, are good. The accusation thus depends upon a consequentialist criterion of the goodness of means. Actions are to be judged on their consequences, which fully justify the action. The consequences do not merely make an action the most eligible—the best choice—under the circumstances. If something produces a good result, then it is good. If private vices always produced public benefits, then those vices would always be good. At least they are good to the extent that they produce (or tend to produce) benefits—and Mandeville seems to hold that they normally do produce benefits. He certainly holds that some benefits cannot be produced without private vices: the vices of pride and luxury are necessary conditions of the opulence and power of a wealthy commercial society. But Mandeville does not have to embrace consequentialism. It is open to him to reject it, and if consequentialism is rejected, then one may deny that an evil that is a necessary condition, or even a cause, of good cannot really be an evil. In discussing the problem of evil, anti-consequentialists insist that such causes or necessary conditions, although they may be good as means, nevertheless remain evil in themselves. For instance, William Rowe has argued:

> Intense human and animal suffering, for example, occurs daily and in great plenitude in our world. Such intense suffering is a clear case of evil. Of course, if the intense suffering leads to some greater good, a good we could not have obtained without undergoing the suffering in question, we might conclude that the suffering is justified, but it remains an evil nevertheless. For we must not confuse the intense suffering in and of itself with the good things to which it sometimes leads or of which it may be a necessary part. Intense human or animal suffering is in itself bad, an evil, even though it may sometimes be justified by virtue of being a part of, or leading to, some good which is unobtainable without it. What is evil in itself may sometimes be good as a means because it leads to something that is good in itself. In such a case, while remaining an evil in itself, the intense human or animal suffering is, nevertheless, an evil which someone might be morally justified in permitting.[22]

In the passage quoted above, Rowe argues that it may be justifiable in some circumstances to permit something which is an evil. In criticising utilitarianism, Bernard Williams has suggested that in some circumstances it may be justifiable not merely to permit an evil but to do one. He gives the example of the visitor who arrives in the central square of a South American village just as the captain of a body of troops is about to order the execution of a number of peasants in reprisal for local anti-governmental activities. In honour of this arrival, the captain offers the visitor the opportunity to execute any one of the condemned peasants. If the visitor accepts, the rest will be reprieved. The visitor has no chance of succeeding in such amateur heroics as shooting the captain instead; should the visitor refuse, the captain will proceed with the execution of the whole group. It may be that the visitor's accepting the captain's offer will produce the best outcome. Williams accepts that. His point is that utilitarianism and other forms of consequentialism, by using the best outcome under the circumstances as the criterion of what is good, offend against our notions that killing an innocent person is nevertheless a bad action—an evil to be regretted—even if it is the best action available under the circumstances.[23]

So, Mandeville's second defence seems to hold.

IV

It is thus open to Mandeville to claim that his position is only a "seeming Paradox": the vices remain evil despite their producing public benefits which are good. In the **"Vindication,"** he claims that the passage from **"A Search into the Nature of Society"** cited above is "both innocent and true."[24] Had he been writing for the vulgar he would have explained that every want is an evil, and further "that on the Multiplicity of those Wants depended all those mutual Services which the individual Members of a Society pay to each other." Moreover, "[t]he many Hands that are employ'd to supply our natural Wants, that are really such, as Hunger, Thirst, and Nakedness, are inconsiderable to the vast Numbers that are all innocently gratifying the Depravity of our corrupt Nature."[25] It is those who take "Sollicitous Care . . . of their Backs and Bellies, [who] make Money Circulate, and are the real Encouragers of every useful Art and Science." They are "very Useful and Beneficial to the Publick," indeed "they are the very Springs that turn all the Wheels of Trade."[26] Unfortunately, the book has been misunderstood by persons who must lack "candour" or "capacity"; whilst the former have a motive for distorting the meaning, presumably some of the latter are among the "short-sighted Vulgar" who fail to see far enough in the "Chain of Causes" to perceive "the Prospect of concatenated Events" and so "see *Good* spring up and pullulate from *Evil,* as naturally as Chickens do from Eggs."[27] In *A Letter to Dion,* he explicitly asserts, citing Pierre Bayle, that "Vice is always bad, whatever benefit we receive from it."[28]

In that work, Mandeville repeats his claims about the morality of the *Fable.* Firstly, it is a "vulgar Error" that the *Fable* is a "wicked Book, wrote for the Encouragement of Vice, and to debauch the Nation."[29] He goes on to claim that it is a book of severe and exalted morality. Secondly, he reiterates verbatim the denial in the **"Vindication"** that it contains encomiums on stews. The accusation misinterprets what is merely a political dissertation giving policy advice in a situation in which there is a choice between two evils.[30] (So Mandeville can avail himself of the Williams position that choosing the better of the evils is not choosing a good.) Thirdly, Mandeville repeats his denial in **"Remark T"**: in contending that societies cannot be prosperous without human vices, he is not recommending that individuals be vicious or even that what applies to a society also applies to individuals:

> I lay down as a first Principle, that in all Societies, great or small, it is the Duty of every Member of it to be good, that Virtue ought to be encourag'd, Vice discountenanc'd, the Laws obey'd, and the Transgressors punish'd . . . I never said nor imagin'd that Man could not be virtuous as well in a rich and mighty Kingdom, as in the most pitiful Commonwealth; but I own it is my Sense that no Society can be rais'd into such a rich and mighty Kingdom, or so rais'd, subsist in their Wealth and Power for any considerable Time, without the Vices of Man.[31]

Fourthly, there is no attack on religion. Christ's kingdom is not of this world. Following its precepts will not lead to worldly wealth and power. The *Fable* is concerned with the "world," the fashionable world, the "*beau monde*" and with the inherent hypocrisy of claiming to be virtuous and religious while pursuing the goods of that world.[32]

Thus Mandeville has a defence against the charge that the *Fable* substitutes vice for virtue. He is even prepared to assert that he believes that "Dion" and others could not have attacked the book as they have, had they read it. Those who have denounced it either have not read it or have found it in their interest to misrepresent its contents or have been misled by the book's reputation as established by its detractors. Yes, vice does result in public benefits—without wants people would have no need for others; without vices there would be less consumption. A general frugality would lead to a small, poor society; those who would restore the "Golden Age" had best be willing to live on acorns. Hutcheson's fantasy that people could choose to consume as many goods without luxury or pride may be a logical possibility but it is not a practical one because it takes no account of normal human motivation.[33]

V

At this point it may seem that I have arrived at a position which falls foul of supposed methodological strictures against interpretations contrary to the way that a thinker's contemporaries understood him.[34] Actually all I have done is to show that Mandeville has a good defence against a crude version of the attack on the *Fable.* This defence is both logically valid and historically plausible; it uses positions available at the time and known to Mandeville. However, I do need to explain why so many, if not all, contemporaries did not regard the *Fable* as a book of exalted morality.

At least some of Mandeville's critics had good reasons for wishing to distinguish their own views from his. Both Hume and Smith were engaged in examining human motivation and behaviour, and analysing and explaining moral belief and action. Their enterprises were akin to the Mandevillean anatomisation of motivation, and their theories involved revising some traditional moral assessments, revisions which might look Mandevillean. Distancing themselves from Mandeville and his reputation was in their interests.[35]

But what of Mandeville's other critics? Why should they have maintained their refusal to accept Mandeville's defence of his views? Despite Mandeville's claims, it seems to me that their view of the *Fable* is not mistaken. Firstly, the book does not read like a book that maintains morality and religion. Mandeville would apparently have us believe that he is sermonising against sin or satirising vice. Neither sermons nor satires revel, as does the *Fable,* in the beneficial consequences of these evils or describe with such evident relish various examples of beneficial evil. To read that good springs up "and pulluates" as naturally from evil as chickens do from eggs at least hints that the author intends rather to annoy the preachers of morality than to convert the sinner or to ridicule the vicious. The parable of small beer is one never heard from the pulpit.[36] The tone of the book is not that of a denunciation of wrong-doing. It is hard to believe that Mandeville's professions are not ironic. Secondly, look at Mandeville's responses to his accusers and critics. A sermonising author, and perhaps even a satirising one, might attempt to correct the critics' misapprehension by withdrawing passages and expressions which were regarded as objectionable. Mandeville claims to have been misunderstood, it is true, but what he does is not only to defend what he has written but also to reiterate the offensive passages.

Moreover, thirdly, Mandeville's definition of virtue and his account of human motivation undermine the contention that he is denouncing sin or castigating vice. In the **Fable,** virtue is defined as "every Performance, by which Man, contrary to the impulse of Nature, should endeavour the Benefit of others or the Conquest of his own Passions out of a Rational Ambition of being good."[37] The definition requires (1) that actions be morally motivated and (2) undertaken either to improve oneself or to benefit others. Actions which are intended to benefit others may be aimed at benefiting individuals or the "the public"—the whole society or some unspecified members of it. Actions naturally motivated, viz., those motivated by natural inclination, desire or "passion," cannot be virtuous actions. By this definition virtuous actions are formally possible, but when Mandeville examines any alleged example of a virtuous action, he always discovers a natural motivation.

Consider how "Savage Man was broke" and how children are trained into sociable behaviour, that is, into restraining their impulses toward immediate gratification of their desires. In exchange for that restraint they are offered gratification of other desires, namely "pride" and "vanity": the desires for the good opinion and praises of others and not to be thought badly of and dispraised (approbativeness), and the desire to have a high rather than a low opinion of oneself.[38] Do we restrain ourselves from taking all we can get? That is motivated by pride or by the natural satisfaction we get from having a good opinion of ourselves. Moreover, should someone act directly for immediate gratification, that person is likely both to give social offence and to hinder others seeking their own gratification. Maintaining the social restraints on others' gratification thus turns out to be in each person's self-interest. Indirect routes toward satisfying one's desires tend to work better than direct ones.

Pity may well lead humans to act beneficially to others or society. But, although it "bears the greatest Resemblance to Virtue," it is not virtue, but "an Impulse of Nature." So, "There is no Merit in saving an innocent Babe ready to drop into the Fire." Such actions are neither good nor bad; they prevent an anticipated mental pain.[39] A mother's self-sacrificing care for her child results from a (developed) natural inclination, not from an intention to perform actions beneficial to society. It may even be harmful to the child.[40] Mandeville even makes the point in general terms

in *An Enquiry into the Origin of Honour*: all humans follow their passions; even those "who act suitably to their Knowledge, and strictly follow the Dictates of their Reason" are as compelled to do so by some passion as those "whom we call Slaves to their Passions."[41]

I think that one might further strengthen the argument that Mandeville is not merely opposing the hypocrisy of enjoying the world while pretending to practice the classical and Christian virtues, but also making the case that those virtues are never actually practised by human beings, by looking at his comments on the virtues. It turns out that practising them would be at least insignificant and sometimes possibly disastrous. Moreover, virtue and reason are believed to be peculiar to humans, yet animals exhibit many qualities which are praised as virtues, and humans exhibit, but take no notice of, vicious qualities.

So, it seems to me that Mandeville's opponents did have good reason for objecting to his views. Perhaps Adam Smith was the most percipient of these opponents. He regarded Mandeville's system as pernicious because it eliminated the distinction between virtue and vice. It did this by taking all actions as motivated by some passion or other, and blurring the distinction between, for example, actions which aimed at gaining approbation and those which aimed at what ought to be approved.[42]

Notes

1. See F. B. Kaye's discussion of Mandeville's "influence" in *The Fable of the Bees: or, Private Vices, Publick Benefits,* ed. F. B. Kaye, 2 vols. (Oxford, 1924; rpt. Indianapolis, 1988), I, cxiv-cxlvi. All subsequent references to *The Fable of the Bees* are to Kaye's edition. Kaye also provides an extensive list of references to Mandeville's works, ibid., II, 418-53. E. J. Hundert's *The Enlightenment's "Fable": Bernard Mandeville and the Discovery of Society* (Cambridge, 1994) centres on the eighteenth-century responses to Mandeville.

2. *Fable of the Bees,* I, civ, n. 4.

3. *The Theory of Moral Sentiments,* Part VII, Sect. 2, Chap. 4, ed. D. D. Raphael and A. L. Macfie (Oxford, 1976), 306-14.

4. Kaye, *Fable of the Bees,* II, 419, found no references to the *Fable* earlier than 1723. J. A. W. Gunn, *Beyond Liberty and Property: The Process of Self-Recognition in Eighteenth-Century Political Thought* (Kingston & Montreal, 1983), 106-7, identifies references to Mandeville in Matthew Tindal's *A Defence of Our Present Happy Establishment* (London, 1722) and by Defoe in *Mist's Weekly Journal* from 1719 on.

5. *Fable of the Bees,* I, 383-86. (I have extracted the points in the Grand Jury's presentment most likely to have been directed at the *Fable.*) The *Fable* was presented, along with some contributions of "Cato"

(John Trenchard and Thomas Gordon), to the *British Journal.* See W. A. Speck, "Bernard Mandeville and the Middlesex Grand Jury," *Eighteenth Century Studies* 11 (1978), 362-74, who argues for a political interpretation of the presentment: the Grand Jury was predominantly Tory, and perhaps Jacobite; it had on 3 July already presented "Cato," a Country Whig; in presenting the *Fable,* which was Court Whig, the Grand Jury could affirm its Hanoverian loyalty while uniting Tories and Country Whigs in attacking Walpole. Unfortunately part of Speck's case for identifying the *Fable* as Court Whig depends on the Grand Jury's knowing that Mandeville was also the author of the far more evidently Hanoverian and Court Whig, *Free Thoughts on Religion, the Church and National Happiness* (London 1720) by "B. M." Did they know this? It is possible that they did. *Free Thoughts* actually quotes the *Fable;* moreover there was a reissue of *Free Thoughts* in 1723 which identifies the work as "by the Author of the *Fable of the Bees.*" (However I suspect that the reissue was subsequent to the presentment.) For a fuller discussion of Mandeville's political views in the *Fable* and in *Free Thoughts,* see M. M. Goldsmith, *Private Vices, Public Benefits: Bernard Mandeville's Social and Political Thought* (Cambridge, 1985), 78-119.

6. According to Kaye, Mandeville appears to have believed that "Lord *C.*" was John, Baron Carteret and first Earl of Granville: *Fable of the Bees,* I, 15, n. 1. As a Whig minister and Privy Councillor, close to the King while hostile to Walpole, he would be an obvious candidate for dedicatee of the letter.

7. *A Letter to Dion,* intro. by Jacob Viner, Augustan Reprint Society Publication no. 41 (Los Angeles, 1953), 1. See George Berkeley, *Alciphron: or the Minute Philosopher* (1732), ed. T. E. Jessop, in *The Works of George Berkeley* (London, 1950), III, esp. Dialogue 2, pp. 65-111. Mandeville's elaborations of his views in *The Fable of the Bees. Part II* (1729; reprinted as *The Fable of the Bees,* ed. F. B. Kaye, vol. 2) and in *An Enquiry into the Origin of Honour, and the Usefulness of Christianity in War* (London, 1732; London, 1971) are not here considered as explicit replies to these attacks.

8. *Fable of the Bees,* I, 381-412.

9. *Fable of the Bees,* I, 397, quoting "A Search into the Nature of Society," ibid., 369.

10. See "A Search into the Nature of Society," *Fable of the Bees,* I, 334-59 where Mandeville points out that many aspects of the world can harm humans and these stimulate the development of arts which benefit humanity. He mentions the benefits which resulted from the fire of London. Note how the activities resulting from natural disasters increase gross domestic production of goods and services.

11. Mandeville cites this standard position in "An Enquiry into the Origin of Moral Virtue," *Fable of the Bees,* I, 50-51 and argues against it. Having dis-

claimed referring to Jews or Christians societies to which truth had been revealed, he contends that the ridiculous religions of other nations were not capable of exciting them to virtue. Their virtues, which involved self-denial, resulted from flattering human pride not from religion. In *A Letter to Dion,* 56, Mandeville suggests that most people "are not more influenced by what they believe of a Future State, than they are by the Name of the Street they live in." Cleomenes, usually Mandeville's mouthpiece, expounds the standard view in the *Origin of Honour,* 23-24. In *Alciphron,* Dialogue 2, Lysicles, Berkeley's Mandevillean, describes the standard view as a vulgar error, *Works,* III, 65.

12. I use the term "public benefit" here in a broad, non-technical sense to include things which are beneficial for the society as a whole, or for a large number of individuals in the society and/or for unspecified individuals in the society. The discussion is confined to "publick benefits": I have put aside the question of whether vice is harmful and virtue beneficial to their possessors.

13. See M. J. Scott-Taggart, "Mandeville: Cynic or Fool?" *Philosophical Quarterly* 16 (1966), 221-33, esp. 221-23.

14. *Fable of the Bees,* I, 369; reiterated in the "Vindication," 411-12.

15. *Fable of the Bees,* I, 37.

16. *Fable of the Bees,* I, 95-98.

17. *Fable of the Bees* (Remark "L"), I, 109-16.

18. *Fable of the Bees* (Remark "L"), I, 116.

19. *Fable of the Bees* (Remark "G"), I, 86-87.

20. Thus Mandeville uses the "skilful Politician" for a wide range of purposes: as individual office holders acting or refraining from acting in specific ways; more generally as established government policies and institutional arrangements; still more generally as social processes, sometimes involving unintended consequences. See Goldsmith, *Private Vices, Public Benefits,* 47-77, where it is argued that Mandeville also uses the "skilful Politician" as a placeholder for gradual developments of institutions and practices—a use which is more evident in *The Fable of the Bees, Part II.*

21. See for example *Fable of the Bees* (Remark "M"), I, 124-30 (pride and emulation); (Remark "N"), I, 134-36 (envy).

22. William L. Rowe, "The Problem of Evil and Some Varieties of Atheism," *American Philosophical Quarterly* 16 (1979), 335-41 at 335. Note that the evil means are "justified" as means in the sense of "permitted" or "tolerated"; they are not made good. It is, nonetheless, a common explanation of evil in eighteenth-century theodicy, that evil is allowed by

God, who arranges the world so that good (at a higher level or overall) results. Some evil is thus "absorbed" as a necessary condition for good, e.g., pain and distress are necessary if compassion is to be displayed. The most common English eighteenth-century discussion is William King, *De originali mali* (London, 1701), translated with extensive annotation by William Law as *An Essay on the Origin of Evil* (London, 1731). See also Alexander Pope, *An Essay on Man*, II, 237-40. For a modern discussion see J. L. Mackie, *The Miracle of Theism* (Oxford, 1982), I, 150-76. Note that Mandeville's "skilful Politician" plays the role of God in transmuting evil into good. (I am grateful for the help of my colleague, Ken Perszyk, on these matters.)

23. See Bernard Williams's essay in *Utilitarianism: For and Against*, by J. J. C. Smart and B. A. O. Williams (Cambridge, 1973), 98-100, and Bernard Williams, *Morality: An Introduction to Ethics* (Cambridge, 1972), 99-100.

24. *Fable of the Bees*, "Vindication," I, 402, referring to "A Search into the Nature of Society," ibid., 369.

25. *Fable of the Bees*, "Vindication," I, 402-03.

26. *Female Tatler* 64 (30 November to 2 December 1709), in Bernard Mandeville, *"By a Society of Ladies": Essays in "The Female Tattler,"* ed. M. M. Goldsmith (Bristol, 1999), 104-05.

27. *Fable of the Bees* (Remark "G"), I, 91, quoted in the "Vindication," ibid., 403-04.

28. *A Letter to Dion*, 34.

29. *A Letter to Dion*, 1.

30. *A Letter to Dion*, 11-14; "Vindication," *Fable of the Bees*, I, 404-405.

31. *Fable of the Bees* (Remark "T"), I, 229, 231; *A Letter to Dion*, 16.

32. *A Letter to Dion*, 18-32.

33. See Francis Hutcheson, *Dublin Journal* 46 (Saturday, 12 February 1726). Part of Hutcheson's argument, that a temperate man will live over a longer period and consequently consume more food and drink than a drunkard or glutton who ruins his health, reappears in George Berkeley, *Alciphron*, Dialogue 2, in *Works*, III, 71-72.

34. See Quentin Skinner, "Meaning and Understanding in the History of Ideas," *History and Theory* 8 (1969), 3-53; "Some Problems in the Analysis of Political Thought and Action," *Political Theory* 2 (1974), 277-301.

35. See Dario Castiglione, "Considering Things Minutely: Reflections on Mandeville and the Eighteenth-Century Science of Man," *History of Political Thought* 7 (1986), 463-88; M. M. Goldsmith, "Regulating Anew the Moral and Political Sentiments of Mankind: Bernard Mandeville and the Scottish Enlightenment," *Journal of the History of Ideas* 49 (1988), 587-606.

36. *Fable of the Bees* (Remark "T"), I, 235-38; repeated in *A Letter to Dion*, 25-29.

37. *Fable of the Bees*, "Origin of Moral Virtue," I, 48-49.

38. *Fable of the Bees*, "Origin of Moral Virtue," I, 41-55. See A. O. Lovejoy, *Reflections on Human Nature* (Baltimore, 1961).

39. *Fable of the Bees*, "Origin of Moral Virtue," I, 56.

40. *Fable of the Bees* (Remark "C"), I, 76.

41. *Origin of Honour*, 31-33.

42. See Adam Smith, *Theory of Moral Sentiments*, Part VII, Sect. 2, Chap. 4, 310. See also E. J. Hundert's extensive discussion of Smith and Mandeville, *The Enlightenment's "Fable,"* 219-36.

M. M. Goldsmith (essay date 2002)

SOURCE: Goldsmith, M. M. "Private Vices." In *Private Vices, Public Benefits: Bernard Mandeville's Social and Political Thought*, second ed., pp. 33-49. Cybereditions, 2002.

[*In the following excerpt, Goldsmith analyzes Mandeville's theory of society, which "justified the activities of those who sought only their private good or pleasure—what many called vice."*]

But something could be said against the ideology of public virtue. And it was, by Bernard Mandeville, an immigrant Dutch physician who had settled in London.[1]

Mandeville began his literary career writing verses. His first published work seems to have been **The Pamphleteers**, a work which defended William's character and the policies pursued under his rule against those who alleged that millions had been misspent and who called for resumption of the grants that had been made.[2] He soon turned to verse fables. **Some Fables after the Easie and Familiar Method of Monsieur de la Fontaine** appeared in 1703; originally it contained twenty-nine fables and appeared anonymously. They show but few signs of the distinctive views he was to publish in **The Fable of the Bees**. A new version enlarged by ten more translations and acknowledging its author was soon issued under the title **Aesop Dress'd**.[3] Among the fables Mandeville chose to translate were some that debunk vain pretensions to wisdom or virtue and others that illustrate connections between low, even vicious activities and those which are respectable and admirable. In his version of the **'Council held by the rats'**, Mandeville added a moral which shifts the tale about belling the cat away from La Fontaine's target—cowardly courtiers. Instead Mandeville pokes fun at coffee-house pundits:

The Cits advise what's to be done,
This way they should attack the Town;
Now here, now there, why don't they come?
So, often in a Coffee-room,
Where prudently they rule the Nation,
I've heard some Men of Reputation
Propose things which they dare as well
Perform, as Rats to tie the Bell.[4]

Mandeville characteristically made La Fontaine's fables more explicit, often by extending the moral, sometimes by appending morals to fables which lacked them. He also tended to lengthen the fables, usually by adding descriptive details. Where La Fontaine's touch is light and elegant, the right word and tone placing his characters socially and psychologically, Mandeville is more explicit and heavy-handed. Moreover, La Fontaine addressed an audience of courtly aristocrats—and even the king; unquestionably, Mandeville wrote for an audience whose acquaintance with kings and courts was rather more remote. In 'The bat and two weasels' La Fontaine recommended diplomatic hypocrisy; it is wise to claim to be bird or mouse as the occasion suggests:

Le Sage dit, selon les gens:
Vive le roi! vive la Ligue!

The moral is 'accommodate to the circumstances'—and the circumstances are historically distant. Mandeville's moral never suggests that the practice is a wise one, and the circumstances are utterly contemporary:

The Trimmer that will side with none,
Is forc'd to side with eve'ry one;
And with his Comp'ny change his story,
Long live the Whig, long live the Tory.[5]

Typically Mandevillean characteristics are evident in some of the fables Mandeville added to the second issue. In **'The hands, feet, and belly'**, the hands and feet rebel. Like La Fontaine's plebeian members they refuse to work for the benefit of the belly. But Mandeville's strikers have specific vulgar objections to their conditions of employment: the feet complain that they've marched in 'Shoes that let the Water in' and

We rais'd four Blisters th' other Night,
And yet got not a farthing by 't.

While the hands reply that they not only work every day but, however weary, 'are forced to serve at every meal':

And often, whilst you're set at ease,
Drudge to the Knucles up in Grease.[6]

One cannot imagine La Fontaine describing plebeian woes in this explicit fashion; Mandeville's plebeians are not Romans complaining about their rights, but labourers on strike. His moral to this tale is somewhat more general than the original one; it is not simply the king's but the government's concern for the interests of all that justifies its greater pomp, power and wealth. The moral may even glance at the same target as *The Pamphleteers* or indeed at Country ideology in declaring that the vulgar think themselves slaves burdened with taxes and wars and the courts 'But Seats of Sloth and Luxury'.

Another fable Mandeville added was **'The frog'**, which describes that creature's vain attempts to expand to the size of an ox. Here again Mandeville lengthened the moral and applied it closer to home. Where La Fontaine remarked that townsmen built like 'grands seigneurs', petty princes sent ambassadors and every marquis wished to have pages, Mandeville's citizens have pages, tradesmen's children have governors and:

A Fellow, that i'n't worth a Louse,
Still keeps his Coach and Country-house.[7]

By far the most interesting of the fables are two of Mandeville's 'own Invention'. **'The carp'** has been 'genteely bred' but goes off on the grand tour knowing only his own language and not 'the Language of the Main' which all the sea fish speak. Eventually encountering a herring 'vers'd in Languages', the carp is quizzed about affairs at home:

. . . what News of Late?
Which are your Ministers of State?
. . .
What Laws, what Form of Government?
Are Taxes rais'd without consent
of Parliament? . . .

Ridiculed for travelling to learn what's done in other countries while so ignorant of his own by the plain-spoken herring, he falls into the company of a pike who introduces him to debauchery. The carp returns home no wiser, having acquired from his foreign travels only disease.[8] **'The carp'** is thus a critique of the provincialism of the English—and it is more than likely that the herring is a Netherlander. The Dutch were known as herring eaters and reputed to be blunt.

Mandeville's **'The nightingale and the owl'** is another tale of vanity. The nightingale is so sure of court appointment as a night watchman who proves his wakefulness by singing that he waits to be begged to accept the position. The humbler owl simply offers his services. When the nightingale presents himself to claim the appointment he finds he must share it with the owl. Incensed by being thus disparaged he bursts into disloyal remarks. Thus, we are told, vanity and haughtiness may deprive able men of their chance to use their abilities in the state's service.[9]

Mandeville's collections of fables exhibited no startling new ideas. As he told his readers in the preface, they need expect neither instruction nor anything to puzzle their brains, but merely some amusement for their idle hours. These readers at least would not be constantly striving to improve themselves or acting for the public good. The translations are fairly close to La Fontaine's originals, given Mandeville's tendency to be cruder and more explicit. Perhaps in the choice of fables and in the differences from La Fontaine, one can perceive an interest in pride, folly, hypocrisy and vanity—and perhaps even the notion of a connection between the individual's good and that of the public.[10] In the closing sentence of the preface, Mandeville offered his readers more fables if they liked these. Perhaps a mild success with **Some Fables** had induced the publication of the enlarged **Aesop Dress'd.**

Mandeville's next work was an imitation of Scarron's burlesque epic, *Typhon.* In the preface he informs us that 'I presented you some time ago with a Dish of *Fables,* but *Wel——ton* says, *They went down with* you *like chopt Hay.*' Since the ingredients were good, Mandeville admitted that he had spoiled them in the cooking. 'I told you then, that if you did not like them, you should be troubled with no more of 'em, and I have been as good as my word; for I have made no more *Fables* since, than I have built Churches.'[11] Instead the reader is offered **Typhon** as a sort of French ragout. In fact, it is more of an English (or perhaps Dutch) stew—a bit coarse in its description of drunken and lecherous gods. In the scene described the gods are lounging in the dining room in an inebriated slumber. Venus is awake. (But what is she doing with her right hand?) Their peace is disturbed by a hail of ninepins flung about by Typhon, who had been painfully struck on the ankle by a bowl. The befuddled gods speculate on what is happening—one thinks it might be a meteor, a star that has escaped from a vortex:

> Which may, according to *Descartes,*
> Happen if near the Poles . . . a Fart is,
> Quoth Jove, I'm sure that such a plenty
> *Materia primi Elementi*
> Had burnt us when the vortex broke
> And I see neither Fire nor Smoke.[12]

Thus **Typhon** did little to recommend piety, sobriety and public spirit. It is dedicated 'To the Serenissime the numerous society of F——ls in London and Westminster' in what looks like a hit at the Societies for the Reformation of Manners in London and Westminster, for Mandeville specifically announced that the action of the poem occurred in:

> An Age, that spoil'd by Peace and Plenty,
> Had no Reformers, under Banners
> Of holy Thirst-encountering Manners;
> Those Champions of Sobriety,
> That watch to keep the World adry;
> Whose Drummers teach one day in seven
> That the tap-too's the March of Heaven.[13]

Later in the poem, because mortals have been so ungrateful, Jove loads punishments upon them: discord, fear, impotence, wives, lawyers, twenty-five kinds of doctors and poets. His anger had been evoked by Athena's report that men have been improving in knowledge but growing worse in all other ways.[14]

In 1705, Mandeville broke his promise and produced another fable. It might be one after the manner of La Fontaine but for its gargantuan size—some 433 lines.[15]

Eventually it was to swell into **The Fable of the Bees,** not by the addition of further verses but by the incorporation of an introduction, an inquiry and a substantial annotation of **'Remarks'**. While the mortals in **Typhon** are punished for their vices and corruptions—an outcome consistent with the prevalent ideology of public and private virtue—this seems to have been an aberration for Mandeville. In **The Grumbling Hive,** the bees are punished by Jove simply by his granting their desire for reformation of manners, much as the frogs are punished in **'The frogs asking for a king'** in **Aesop Dress'd.** Neither the frogs nor the bees are contented with their lot. The frogs have grown weary of democracy and ask for a king. Jove supplies them with a log but the frogs find him too supine; they soon grow contemptuous of his good-natured, passive somnolence. They petition again and Jove, exasperated, gives them a crane who devours them. Mandeville tells us that this fable of the evils of divine right monarchy is not meant for Englishmen, for

> . . . they are content,
> And hate to change their Government.[16]

Nevertheless, it may have a slight anti-Jacobite edge—Mandeville hardly regarded Englishmen as content. More interesting are the parallels to **The Grumbling Hive**: both the frogs and the bees are discontented and both receive divine retribution by having their wishes granted.

But where the frogs are unhappy about their government, the bees in **The Grumbling Hive** are Englishmen.

> They were not Slaves to Tyranny,
> Nor rul'd by wild *Democracy*;
> But Kings, that could not wrong, because
> Their Power was circumscrib'd by Laws.[17]

Although content with its constitution, the hive does grumble about politicians, the army, the fleet, avarice, cheating, prodigality, luxury and corruption. In the bees' society flourish stockjobbers, sharpers, pimps, actors, quacks and fortune tellers along with other frauds and fakers. However, the respectable and industrious bourgeoisie are no better: lawyers split cases and fees and oppose reforms which would reduce their practice; doctors are more interested in fame and wealth than in curing their patients and they curry favour with apothecaries; priests dissimulate their vices and ignorance; prelates live in plenty while working curates starve; the king's ministers call their peculations 'perquisites' or emoluments. The poor get justice; the rich escape it by bribery.

Mandeville makes his attitude to any reformation of manners quite clear:

> Thus every Part was full of Vice,
> Yet the whole Mass a Paradise.

He tells us that the bees' very crimes contributed to their prosperity and the power that made them the balance of all other hives. Virtue, having been reconciled to vice by political cunning, arranged things so that:

The worst of all the Multitude
Did something for the Common Good.

The beneficial consequences are remarkable.

Thus Vice nurs'd Ingenuity,
Which joined with Time and Industry,
Had carry'd Life's conveniencies,
It's real Pleasures, Comforts, Ease,
To such a Height, the very Poor
Liv'd better than the Rich before.

But instead of accepting their comfortable circumstances and enjoying them, the bees deprecate the pride, luxury, vanity, vice and other corruptions which are its causes or necessary conditions. Jove, eventually annoyed by their continued supplication, gives them what they pray for—a reformation of manners. The result is private and public virtue, but in the process the hive is dispossessed of its wealth and power; defeated and impoverished, the bees go and live in primitive simplicity in a hollow tree,

. . . as free,
For Acorns as for Honesty.[18]

The Grumbling Hive relies upon the ideology of public and private virtue in order to make its point; if luxury, vice and corruption are connected with wealth and power and so with prosperity, then the converse is also true: virtue is accompanied by simplicity, poverty and primitive conditions. The doggerel poem cleverly suggested that men's professed moral judgments condemn rather more than they suspect and that 'vice' in its various aspects is closely related to the sort of society that these critics live in and expect to live in. Far more than Mandeville's other early verse works, which at most hint at an interest in the themes that Mandeville was later to discuss and which show no greater penetration than the verses of other hacks, *The Grumbling Hive* foreshadows *The Fable of the Bees*. Nevertheless, despite the hints of Mandevillean doctrine in it, *The Grumbling Hive* was not *The Fable of the Bees*; it was not an argued attack on the current ideology of public and private virtue. Yet Mandeville did turn to such an attack in 1709-10 in response to the version of that ideology put forward by Squire Bickerstaff.

The success of the Squire's lucubrations inspired many imitators who hoped to exploit the market that Steele had discovered. Like him they aimed to be sufficiently polite to be present at the ladies' tea table as well as in the coffee-house. Among them were the *Visions of Sir Heister Ryley*, the *Gazette à la Mode* or *Tom Brown's Ghost* written by 'Sir Thomas Whipstaff', a *Whisperer* by 'Mrs Jenny Distaff' and *Titt for Tatt* written by a supposed John Partridge getting his own back. There were also a *Tatling Harlot*, a *Tory Tatler*, a *North Tatler* and, most significantly, *The Female Tatler*.[19] Most of these papers copied *The Tatler*'s format of four columns on a half-sheet and its formula of not confining itself to news and politics, or even to serious examination of the theatre and literature, but including both serious and frivolous discussions of a variety of topics, describing different social characters, printing letters from actual or supposed correspondents, rehearsing conversations, filling up with snippets of classical literature and so on. Bickerstaff expatiated on the evils of duelling, attacked sharpers, considered canes, recommended Charles Lilly and pronounced on petticoats. Many of his little social fictions must have been spicier versions of situations familiar to his readers, pictures of characteristics they too had observed or stereotypes which could be used to sort out their acquaintances—such as Miss Molly, the scolding wife, and her drinking husband, Sir John (*Tatler* 2) or Cynthio who eventually dies of unrequited love for the devastating Clarissa (*Tatler* 1, 4, 5, 22, 35, 58, 85), not to mention the procession of rakes, fools, coxcombs, platonnes, toasts and very pretty fellows. Nor was Steele above salting his columns with scandalous tales about real people, identifiable by circumstantial descriptions but thinly disguised under pseudonyms. This was bound to lend verisimilitude to his fictitious accounts of individuals illustrating a characteristic or a type.

In November 1709, *The Female Tatler* was taken over by a 'society of ladies'. Previously it had been written by 'Mrs Crackenthorpe', 'a Lady that knows every thing', and told it thrice weekly. Two ladies of the society, the sisters Lucinda and Artesia, were Bernard Mandeville.[20] He immediately encroached on one of Bickerstaff's favourite subjects, for in Lucinda's sitting room the conversation turned to honour and duelling. Bickerstaff had argued for the abolition of duelling and speculated about ways of suppressing it. When the example of the Greeks and Romans is adduced as one of courage without duels, 'Colonel Worthy' points out that in those days society was less refined. 'He added, that he had duely weigh'd whatever had been said against Duelling, but that he cou'd not conceive how the Conversation, as is now establish'd among the better sort of People, could be upheld if the Customs of it was totally abolish'd.' The Colonel urges that duelling is no more sinful than drinking a man to death—which is far more common. It being early November, Mandeville makes the Colonel remark 'that more were killed by the Gluttony and Drunkenness of one Lord Mayor's Day in the City of *London* only, than by Duelling in a whole Twelvemonth throughout *Great Britain*'. The Colonel clinches his argument with a particularly Mandevillean reflection: 'The strict Observation of the point of Honour, said he, is a necessary Evil, and a large Nation can no more be call'd Polite without it, than it can be Rich and Flourishing without Pride or Luxury.'[21] Yet the Colonel disapproves of duelling. Therefore he regrets that duellists are frequently pardoned and suggests that whenever one combatant dies his opponent should invariably be executed. In that way the laws of honour can be made serviceable to a polite and warlike nation and yet giving offence be prevented.

Thus in his first *Female Tatler*, Mandeville had a thrust at Steele. And he continued to jab at Bickerstaff: no fewer than fifteen of his *Female Tatlers* mention him or take up a topic initiated in *The Tatler*. The most devastatingly hilarious of these anti-Tatlers is Mandeville's ridicule of the cure of blindness by the grand oculist, Roger Grant. Bickerstaff had related the affecting story of a young gentleman cured at Newington. 'Happy are they', quipped Mandeville, 'that can see to read it!'[22]

This kind of thing in Mandeville's pungent prose would have made *The Female Tatler* a parasite, albeit an amusing one. But Mandeville seems to have been stung by Steele into expounding a general account of society contrary to the theory of public and private virtue which Bickerstaff advocated as Censor of Great Britain and adherent of the Societies for the Reformation of Manners. In his self-exalted role of Censor, Bickerstaff declared many inhabitants of Britain dead even though they walked, talked, ate their meals, smoked their pipes and sipped their coffees.

> In short, whoever resides in the World without having any Business in it, and passes away an Age without even thinking on the Errand for which he was sent hither, is to me a Dead Man to all Intents and Purposes; and I desire that he may be so reputed. The Living are only those that are in some way or other laudably employed in the Improvement of their own Minds, or for the Advantage of others.[23]

And just a week later *Tatler* 99 (26 November 1709) peremptorily announced:

> I have already taken great Pains to inspire Notions of Honour and Virtue into the People of this Kingdom, and used all gentle Methods imaginable, to bring those who are dead in Idleness, Folly, and Pleasure into Life by applying themselves to Learning, Wisdom, and Industry. But since fair Means are ineffectual, I must proceed to Extremities, and shall give my good Friends, the Company of Upholders, full Power to bury all such Dead as they meet with, who are within my former Descriptions of deceased Persons.

This Bickerstaffian proclamation precedes a facetious remonstrance from the undertakers. They complain that vast numbers of the unburied dead have not turned themselves in and that they go putrefying about the streets. And citing a number of other inconveniences they petition for the power that Bickerstaff grants.

The Tatler's campaign against the walking dead only made sense on the basis of the ideology of public and private virtue. Society existed, improved and flourished because human beings devoted themselves to the public good or to learning; they self-sacrificingly sought to improve the material and moral conditions of life. Those who did not consciously dedicate themselves to these ends were useless; they went about consuming resources which could be devoted to good purposes; they might as well be dead and buried.

Mandeville immediately responded in a series of *Female Tatlers*. Number 62 appeared on 28 November, just two days after *Tatler* 99. In it Artesia reported a conversation which supposedly occurred on the afternoon of the 26th—

the very day on which that issue of *The Tatler* appeared. Arsinoe interrupted Emilia as she was rhapsodizing on the happiness of a well-governed nation. She wonders why 'Man' is the only 'Sociable Creature' when 'not only the Herds and Flocks of the Field, but likewise the Shoals both of the Air and the Deep' seem temperamentally better fitted for society, since they associate 'without design' simply 'for the Love of each other's Company' whereas among human beings there are 'Feuds, Frauds, Enmities, and Depredations, against and upon one another . . . not only between different Nations, but Cities, Corporations, Societies and private Persons, under the same Government, and seemingly of the same interest'. It follows that 'there is no Animal that is naturally inclined so little to be Sociable as Man, and consequently, that without Government and the Rigour of the Laws, it would be impossible that a Dozen of them should ever spend one day together in Peace'. But Arsinoe's opinion, with its Hobbesian or Augustinian overtones, is immediately rejected by Lucinda. She holds that men are not less sociable than beasts, which will clash when their appetites for food or sex conflict. Man, being endowed with reason and condemned to work, has improved his condition.

> It is to this only, that all Arts and Sciences are Subservient; when I think on this, and compare the Meanness as well as Ignorance of the Infant World, and yet unpolish'd Nations of *Africa* and *America* to the Knowledge and Comforts of Human Life, which the more Civilised Countries, and more especially the politer Parts of *Christendom*, enjoy, I can never forbear thinking how infinitely we are indebted to all those who ever invented anything for the Publick Good: It is they that have actually meliorated their kind, and from that groveling State and despicable Condition in which we now see the *Negroes* and other Savages, raised their Posterity to the Enjoyment of these Blessings we have among us. To all the rest of our Ancestors and Predecessors, we are no more beholden, than if they never had been born; And I am of the Ingenious Mr. *Bickerstaff*'s Opinion that none are to be counted Alive, but such as, setting aside all private Interest and Personal Pleasure, are Generous enough to labour and exert themselves for the benefit of others.

Thus, according to Lucinda, the human condition has improved over time. Savagery has become civilization by the beneficial effects of those who have acted for the public good. This view is accepted by those assembled—Lucinda found 'in most of us, what by her Looks she seem'd to demand, *a tacit* Applause'. But this Bickerstaffian view is challenged by an 'Oxford Gentleman' who denies that the virtuous, the learned and the public-spirited have improved the human condition:

> *Madam,* said he, it is unquestionable, that the greatest and most immediate Benefactors to Human Society, are the idle Favourites of blind Fortune, that having more Money left to them than they know what to do with, take no other Care than to please themselves, and studying as well to create new Appetites as to gratify those they feel already, are given over to all Sensuality, and value neither Health nor Estate in the purchase of Delight.

Not the virtuous and public-spirited but the selfish hedonists have been the motive power of history.[24]

Whereas Lucinda and Bickerstaff could see changes in man's conditions of life, Mandeville and the Oxford gentleman recognized a different type of development. It is not merely that humans have modified their situation; they have also developed their needs and wants. Indeed men are not sociable because they instinctively love other humans. They are sociable because, being biologically capable of society, that is, having the capacity for speech along with certain other physical characteristics, such as arms and hands, and having many wants and appetites along with some other psychological characteristics, they can be organized into quite large social groups. Although each individual has a certain interest in being virtuous— since virtue will be rewarded in heaven even if it is not always rewarded on earth—many virtues (like temperance, humility, contentedness and frugality) are insignificant for society; 'and so far from making a Country Flourish, that no Nation ever yet enjoy'd the most ordinary Comforts of Life, if they were not Counter-ballanc'd by the opposite Vices'.[25]

Mandeville contends that vice produces not only prosperity but civilization as well. 'Vice' is essential to a flourishing society in two senses of the word: firstly, vice in the sense of physical deficiency, privation and need makes society necessary for human survival; secondly, vice in the sense of moral defect (greed, vanity, pride, selfishness, lust, luxury and envy) stimulates production and improvement. Needs and appetites make social cooperation desirable in conditions where it will increase the available benefits and resources. But what human beings consume is not restricted to what is necessary for biological survival. The standard of necessity as well as that of comfort is a social standard; the consumption of the rich, so beneficial, is stimulated by pride and vanity, that is, the human characteristics of wishing for the approval of others, desiring to have a good opinion of oneself and seeking superiority and recognition of that superiority—the characteristics of approbativeness, self-esteem and emulation.[26]

It is these vices that we must thank for the development of the arts and the sciences: 'They are all come to the Perfection they are in by very slow Degrees, and the first Rudiments of most of them have been so small, that the Authors are hardly worth naming.'[27]

In denigrating Bickerstaff's self-righteous puff for virtue and learning, Mandeville extended his earlier hints into a theory of society which emphasized the functional relationship between human characteristics and societal consequences and which also required that existing societies should be the product of a long genesis.[28] That the views put into the mouth of the Oxford gentleman amount to something more than a passing joke at Steele's expense is shown by their further discussion in the next two numbers of *The Female Tatler* written by Mandeville, 64 and 66. For the Oxford gentleman is not permitted simply to assert these outrageous opinions; in *Female Tatler* 64 he is challenged. Lucinda reports a second meeting of the same company. Emilia and Camilla ridicule the Oxford gentleman's views by saying 'a hundred Things in praise of *Calligula, Heliogabalus, Sardanapalus,* and all the King and Emperors they could think on, that had been Infamous for Luxury and Extravagancy'. On these grounds Vitellius (corrected in no. 66 from Tiberius) must have been the best emperor because at one supper he had three thousand fishes and seven thousand birds served. How could: 'so Wise a Senate as theirs, that was so watchful for the Publick Welfare, . . . suffer the pernitious Tenets of the *Cato*'s, the *Seneca*'s, and other Moral-Mongers that extolled Content and Frugality, and preach'd against Gluttony, Drunkenness and the rest of the Supporters of the Common Wealth'?[29] Arsinoe suggests the reverse of a sumptuary law: the well-off should be obliged to buy new clothes every month and new furniture every year; good subjects would eat four meals a day, those who did not take tobacco would be treated as recusants and gentlemen who went to bed without having drunk four bottles would be taxed double.

Responding to this appeal to the authority of the Catos and the other 'Moral-Mongers', the Oxford gentleman proceeds with a direct attack on the Censor of Great Britain:

> I confess, I cannot be of the Opinion, that all those People that take no other Worldly Care than how to Dress, Eat, Drink and Sleep well, are so useless to Human Society, that they ought to be reckon'd among the Dead. The Comical Remonstrance of the Upholders Company, is very Witty and Diverting, and what I read some Days ago about their Interment, pleased me exceedingly, as long as I knew that the Ingenious Author of them was only in Jest, and had no design to bring it in Fashion, and make *Funerals a la Mode* of them; but if we may be Serious, and reflect upon all the different Parts, of which a Potent and Flourishing Society must unavoidably consist, I doubt the Banter will lose its Force.[30]

According to the Oxford gentleman, princes are educated from infancy to be motivated by what A. O. Lovejoy called emulativeness rather than sensuality. Nonetheless hedonism in private citizens is also quite acceptable:

> to be always Clean, and wear Cloaths that are Sumptuously Fashionable, to have Pompous Equipages, and be well attended, to live in Stately Dwellings, adorn'd with Rich and Modish Furniture, both for use and Magnificence, to Eat and Drink Deliciously, Treat Profusely, and have a plentiful Variety of what either Art or Nature can contribute, not only to the Ease and Comfort only, but likewise the Joy and Splendor of Life, is without doubt to be very Useful and Beneficial to the Publick; nay I am so far from allowing these to be Dead, that I think they are the very Springs that turn all the Wheels of Trade, and if the Metaphor is ever to be used, it is much more applicable to Men of Letters.[31]

Private pleasures thus produce public benefits.

No doubt Bernard Mandeville with the Oxford gentleman is commending the good things of life. Worldly enjoyment, the pleasures of the senses including aesthetic delight and the pleasure of treating our friends, are here wholeheartedly accepted. Those who take 'Sollicitous Care' of 'their Backs and Bellies' are not dead; it is they who 'make money Circulate'. Those whom *The Tatler* condemns as dead need not excuse themselves or apologize for their neglect of others. They need not constantly try to improve themselves or act for the public good. They do good unwittingly by being as they are and without consciously intending to do it.

The learned on the other hand, if not actually harmful, are quite useless. Those who study Latin and Greek for their use in theology, law and medicine are despised as drudges by the true '*Litterati*':

> that illustrious Title is only due to Men of Polite Learning, that is, such as by reading the same Books twenty times over and over, become Critically versed in Classick Authors, and without Expectation, or Possibility of ever being a Farthing the better for it, pursue an endless Study, that is of no manner of use to Human Society.[31]

Men of letters deserve to be called dead if anyone does.

Mandeville, himself a learned man, perhaps even somewhat versed in the classics, as well as a physician—the most academically respectable branch of medicine—thus deflated the pretensions of learning as expounded by the learned Bickerstaff. The instrument he employs is an 'Oxford Gentleman'. Like his creator he is no ignorant clot but rather someone who handles deftly the ordinary paraphernalia of bookishness, not hesitating to throw in an occasional Latin tag. Surely the identification of the gentleman suggests a connection with learning and the university; no one can imagine that the gentleman from Oxford is a merchant from the town or some country squire—Mandeville's version of the as yet uninvented Sir Roger de Coverley. No, the Oxford gentleman, despite his denigration of scholarship, certainly smells of the book and the midnight oil. He seems an intellectual far more likely to engage in lucubrations than is Isaac Bickerstaff, Esq. It is needless to say that Mandeville's fetching this wit from Oxford was another hit at Bickerstaff; for the Censor himself had established connections with Oxford. In *Tatler* 30 (18 June 1709), he announced his decision that his ward, Will, should go to Oxford, where if he did not become a man of sense he should at least learn that he was a coxcomb: 'There is in that Place such a true Spirit of Raillery and Humour, that if they can't make you a wise Man, they will certainly let you know you are a Fool.' Is not his spirit exhibited by our Oxford gentleman? (And is his target not Bickerstaff?) Moreover, in *Tatler* 31 Bickerstaff announced that he had taken the universities under his protection and, judging them impartially, he would rank the tutors and pupils according to their merits. By number 39 (9 July 1709) Bickerstaff had visited Oxford. His 'warm Inclination . . . to stem the . . . prevailing Torrent of Vice and Ignorance' leads him to see there the highest lustre of virtue and knowledge. In Oxford, deference is accorded to wisdom and learning. So taken is Bickerstaff

that he adopts the Oxford almanac even when torn from that 'noble Society by the Business of this dirty mean World'. What could be more appropriate than that a gentleman possessed of the 'true Spirit of Raillery and Humour' should let Bickerstaff know that he is nothing like as wise as he supposes himself?[33]

The Oxford gentleman, like Mandeville himself, is far more tolerant of this dirty mean world and the variety of ways of living in it than is the supposedly genial Censor of Great Britain. Were the learned not disposed to look down on the rest of mankind, the Oxford gentleman would not have so low an opinion of them. In *Female Tatler* 66, he deplores the prestige accorded to university education and the consequent tendency of the successful tradesmen to disable their children from useful activities by educating them. What good does learning do? It disqualifies its possessor from trade. People pity a young scholar who receives ten pounds a year for living in a well-off family and saying grace before dinners he shares, but not his uneducated brother who gets sixpence per day as a soldier. Latin has delightful characteristics, but 'a Man may be a famous General, a deep Politician, or an accomplish'd Merchant, and not understand a word of it; the least of these requires a more particular Genius, greater Abilities, and more various Qualifications than any of the Three Faculties, where the learned Languages are counted necessary.'[34]

The crucial test of Bickerstaff's version of the ideology of public and private virtue is whether those who have devoted themselves to the public good have improved their arts and thereby improved the condition of mankind. The Oxford gentleman contends that there has been no progress in divinity, 'whose purpose is to teach us how to live well here and Happy hereafter'. A thousand years ago there were clerics notably virtuous and others notably vicious: 'the good ones preach'd Peace, and the others Sedition'. Things are as they were among the clergy except that their divisions are worse while their followers are no better for a thousand years of effort.[35]

Having subjected the divines to this crude and perhaps anti-clerical examination, Mandeville turned next to the remaining learned professions. Lawyers provide no more certainty than they did in antiquity—nevertheless they, and their dependants, benefit the nation by their numbers, wealth and consequent consumption. Even medicine gets short shrift from the Oxford gentleman. Despite the abundance of systems and new cures, actual success in curing the ill remains uncertain; diseases incurable in antiquity are so still. Moreover, university learning is irrelevant to curing patients. Any decent apothecary can look up the various medicines once he knows the simples and reads enough Latin to follow the recipes.

Here one may doubt that the opinions of the Oxford gentleman coincide exactly with Mandeville's own. Although both were sceptical about medical theories and systems, Mandeville continued to practise medicine. Indeed, he soon published a book under his own name, surely intended, at least in part, to publicize his own practice: some versions of the imprint include the information that the book may be obtained from the author at his own address. These medical dialogues show that Mandeville favoured an empirical approach to curing the diseases in which he specialized and warned against relying upon the prescriptions of the unsupervised apothecary—not quite the wholesale rejection of physicians in favour of apothecaries suggested by the Oxford gentleman.[36]

But if the Oxford gentleman's strictures on the achievements of the learned are rhetorically exaggerated, they nevertheless express Mandeville's conviction that 'it is evident, how Insignificant the Lucubrations as well as the Day-light Labours of the Learned have been in the main to Human Society'.[37] It is also evident that the arrogant claims of Bickerstaff for the learned and the public-spirited ought to be rejected. On the contrary, the Oxford gentleman, with Mandeville, turns to praise improvements in the everyday comforts of life provided by useful and quite humble things: for example, clocks and watches have lately been much improved. And setting aside the larger works of mechanical industry, the works of shipbuilders, millwrights and engineers, he points to the notable improvements in household furniture. 'In what Palace would you have found Thirty Years ago a Seat so Judiciously contriv'd for the Ease and Repose of the Body, in almost every Position, as the Easy Chair in which you Sit?' Any other type of cane chair would spoil the cream-painted wainscot. And to clinch the point there is that most beneficial of new inventions, both for the silk it uses and the labour it employs—the furbelowed scarf.[38]

Thus Mandeville caps his attack on Isaac Bickerstaff, Richard Steele and the ideology of private and public virtue with the paradoxical praise of things small, humble, domestic and useful—chairs, watches and scarves.[39] To arrive at this overturning of the high-minded and righteous, Mandeville invented a theory of society that justified such paradoxical praise. Comfortable chairs, elegant creampainted wainscots and fashionable scarves were just the sort of things which attracted the attention of those useful members of society who thought of nothing but their backs and their bellies. Mandeville's new theory of society justified the activities of those who sought only their private good or pleasure—what many called vice. He thus gave a new twist to the discussion of pride and vanity. But it was not *The Female Tatler* which made Mandeville's views widely known. That journal may have had its readers but it never attracted the notoriety achieved by Mandeville's later works, especially **The Fable of the Bees.**

Notes

1. For Mandeville's life, see 'Bernard Mandeville', *New Dictionary of National Biography* (forthcoming); Bernard Mandeville, *The Fable of the Bees; or Private Vices, Publick Benefits,* ed. F. B. Kaye (2 vols., Oxford, 1924), vol. 1 pp. xvii-xxx; vol. 2, pp. 380–5. Kaye's account has been supplemented by Rudolf Dekker, '"Private Vices, public benefits" revisited: the Dutch background of Bernard Mandeville', *History of European Ideas,* 14 (1992), 481–98. Dekker gives an account of the 'Costerman Riot' in Rotterdam in 1690 that implicates Bernard Mandeville and his father in composing and posting a satirical poem, the 'Sanctimonious Atheist', against the bailiff, Van Zuijlen. The bailiff was reinstated in October 1692; Michael Mandeville was banished at the beginning of 1693, resettling in Amsterdam. In November 1693, Bernard was summoned by the London College of Physicians for practising medicine without a license: see Harold J. Cook, 'Materialism and the passions: Dr Bernard Mandeville and the therapy of "the clever politician"', *Journal of the History of Ideas,* 60 (1999) 101–24. On 1 February 1699, he married Ruth Elizabeth Laurence at St Giles-in-the-Fields (Westminster). Their first child, Michael, was born on 1 March 1699.

2. *The Pamphleteers: a Satyr* (London, 1703). Luttrell dated his copy 9 March; it was advertised in the *Flying Post* on 17 June 1703 as 'by the author of Some Fables after the Familiar Method of Mr. de la Fontaine'; see D. F. Foxon, *English Verse 1701-1750: a Catalogue of Separately Printed Poems with Notes on Contemporary Collected Editions* (2 vols., Cambridge, 1975), M 72; and see below, Chapter 4.

3. There were three issues of these verse fables. The first (Foxon M 73) was published by Richard Wellington; although there is no imprint on the title page, a list of books published by Wellington is appended on pp. 82-4; listed in the *History of the Works of the Learned* in May 1703. The second, retitled *Aesop Dress'd* (Foxon M 74), must have appeared soon after, for it was made up by adding a new title page and new signatures both at the beginning and the end of the sheets of the first issue (signatures, B, C, M completed and N). The text is joined in the middle of 'The countryman and the knight', substituting pp. 15-16 for the original pp. 1-2 (B and Bv); listed in the *Post Man* on 18 January 1704.

A second, reset version of *Aesop Dress'd,* the third issue (Foxon M 75), bears the imprint, 'London: Sold at Lock's-Head adjoyning to Ludgate'. It is undated; the British Library assigned it to 1710. Foxon notes it as listed in the *Post Man* in 1727. This issue has been reprinted by the Augustan Reprint Society and is cited here.

4. *Aesop Dress'd,* p. 35 (italics reversed); La Fontaine, book II, 2.

5. *Aesop Dress'd,* p. 37 (italics reversed); La Fontaine, II, 5.

6. *Aesop Dress'd,* pp. 7-10; La Fontaine, III, 2.

7. *Aesop Dress'd,* pp. 4-5; La Fontaine, I, 3.

8. *Aesop Dress'd,* pp. 25-7.

9. *Ibid.,* pp. 27-33.

10. For further discussion see John S. Shea's introduction to the Augustan Reprint Society's edition of *Aesop Dress'd* (Augustan Reprint Society Publication no. 120, Los Angeles, 1966); Hector Monro, *The Ambivalence of Bernard Mandeville* (Oxford, 1975), pp. 26-30; Thomas A. Horne, *The Social Thought of Bernard Mandeville: Virtue and Commerce in Early Eighteenth-Century England* (New York and London, 1978), pp. 26-8 and Stephen H. Daniel, 'Political and philosophical uses of fables in eighteenth-century England', *Eighteenth Century,* 28 (1982), 151-71.

11. *Typhon: or The Wars Between the Gods and Giants: a Burlesque Poem in Imitation of the Comical Mons. Scarron* (London, 1704), preface. Foxon M 76; advertised in the *Daily Courant* on 15 April 1704.

12. *Ibid.,* p. 18.

13. *Ibid.,* p. 6. See W. A. Speck, 'Mandeville and the Eutopia seated in the brain', in *Mandeville Studies: New Explorations in the Art and Thought of Dr. Bernard Mandeville (1670-1733),* International Archives of the History of Ideas, 81, ed. Irwin Primer (The Hague, 1975), pp. 66-79.

14. *Typhon,* pp. 24-5.

15. *The Grumbling Hive: or Knaves Turn'd Honest* (London, 1705).

16. *Aesop Dress'd,* pp. 62-4 (italics reversed).

17. *The Grumbling Hive,* lines 9-12.

18. *Ibid.,* lines 155-6, 167-8, 197-202, 432-3 (italics reversed).

19. See *Contemporaries of the Tatler and the Spectator,* ed., with intro., Richmond P. Bond, Augustan Reprint Society Publication no. 47 (Los Angeles, 1954).

20. Issues of the *Female Tattlers* are cited by number and date with page numbers from Bernard Mandeville, *By a Society of Ladies: Essays in the Female Tattler,* ed. M. M. Goldsmith (Bristol, 1999). Irregularities in issue numbers occur after no. 88, viz., there are three issues numbered 88, two numbered 94, 98 and 110 and some numbers omitted; they are numbered here as they are in *By a Society of Ladies,* which is cited as *Female tattler.*

Mandeville's contributions were first identified by Paul Bunyan Anderson, 'Splendor out of scandal: the Lucinda-Artesia papers in the *Female Tatler*', *Philological Quarterly,* 15 (1935), 286-300; see Gordon S. Vichert, 'Some recent Mandeville attributions', *Philological Quarterly,* 45 (1966), 459-63 and Francis McKee, 'The Early Works of Bernard Mandeville, 1685–1715', PhD Thesis, University of Glasgow, 1993. The evidence is conclusive for Mandeville's being the author of the Lucinda-Artesia papers. Apart from the similarity of style and content to Mandeville's other works, *Female Tatler* 97 (24 February 1710), pp. 206-8, prints one of Mandeville's own fables, 'The carp', from *Aesop Dress'd; Female Tatler* 98* (1 March 1710) includes 'The wolves and sheep'; *Female Tatler* 100 (6 March 1710), 'The hands, feet, and belly' and *Female Tatler* 78 (4 January 1710) concludes with a poem, 'Grinning Honour', which was later included in Mandeville's *Wishes to a Godson, with other Miscellany Poems* (London, 1712). Mandeville also used the name 'Lucinda' for the sagacious bluestocking aunt in *The Virgin Unmask'd* (London, 1709; reprinted Delmar, NY, 1975).

The authorship of the other papers in *The Female Tatler* not by Mandeville has not been established. The most likely 'Mrs Crackenthorpe' is Thomas Baker (writer of numbers 1-18 for Benjamin Bragg and 19-51 for Abigail Baldwin). The evidence for Baker's being 'Mrs Crackenthorpe' is given by Robert B. White, 'A study of the Female Tattler (1709-1710)', PhD Thesis, University of North Carolina, 1966, p. 98. The rival 'Mrs Crackenthorpe' (Bragg 19-44) is unknown. The identities of the other members of the 'Society of Ladies' has not been established. Suggested authors include Susanna Centlivre and Mary Delariviere Manley. It seems to me that one person wrote the papers by Emilia (16) and Rosella (10) whilst those by Arabella (3) and Sophronia (3) were written by two others. For a fuller discussion, see Mandeville, *Female Tattler,* pp. 41-8. where I also discuss Mandeville's long connection with Abigail Baldwin and her son-in-law, James Roberts.

21. *Female Tatler* 52 (4 November 1709). Duelling was discussed in *Tatlers* 25-9, 31, 38. Problems about honour occupied Bickerstaff and were taken up by Mandeville in *Female Tatlers* 77, 78, 80, 84 (2, 4, 9, 11 January 1710), *The Fable of the Bees,* Remark C, vol. 1, pp. 63-80; and in *An Enquiry into the Origin of Honour, and the Usefulness of Christianity in War* (London, 1732; reprinted 1971). See my introduction to the 1971 reprint.

22. *Tatler* 55 (16 August 1709); *Female Tatler* 58 (18 November 1709). Roger Grant was a frequent advertiser of his cure; see *Female Tatler* 62 (28 November 1709). Sir William Read, the Queen's oculist, advertised in *Female Tatler* 72 (21 December 1709). The advertising columns of *The Tatler* and *The Female Tatler* were stuffed with cures for asthma, coughs, colds, eye trouble, dropsy, toothache and most other common diseases as well as purges, cordials, breath-sweeteners and elixirs for wind.

For a fuller discussion of the relations between *The Tatler* and *The Female Tatler,* see Mandeville, *Female Tattler,* pp. 63–72. There I suggest several instances where Steele may have been responding to *The Female Tattler.*

23. *Tatler* 96 (19 November 1709).

24. *Female Tatler* 62 (28 November 1709), pp. 96–9.

25. *Ibid.,* pp. 99–100.

26. For the best account of eighteenth-century views on these traits, see A. O. Lovejoy, *Reflections on Human Nature* (Baltimore, 1961), especially pp. 88-117, 129 and on Mandeville, pp. 170-9.

27. *Female Tatler* 62 (28 November 1709). See F. A. Hayek, 'Dr. Bernard Mandeville', Lecture on a Master Mind, British Academy, 1966, *Proceedings of the British Academy,* 52 (1967), 125-41; Hayek's case for Mandeville's contribution to the appreciation that social institutions are the unintended consequences of a large number of individual actions over a long period of time rather than something planned would have been strengthened had he known that Mandeville explicitly expressed this view in *The Female Tatler.*

28. See below, Chapter 3.

29. *Female Tatler* 64 (2 December 1709), pp. 102–3.

30. *Ibid.,* p. 104.

31. *Ibid.,* pp. 104-5.

32. *Ibid.,* p. 105.

33. The Oxford gentleman first appears in number 62, where we are told that he came in with Emilia. Whenever he appears he takes a characteristically Mandevillean attitude. Colonel Worthy, his predecessor in this role in *Female Tatler* 52, reappears as a more conventional military proponent of honour in *Female Tatler* 80 (9 January 1710), pp. 151–2. The Oxford gentleman's status is never clearly indicated, but a connection with the university is surely intended. Part of the joke is that he should be a member of the corporation so highly lauded by Bickerstaff and yet profess opinions scoffing at that gentleman. But there is no indication that the Oxford gentleman is a student as suggested by H. T. Dickinson, 'The politics of Bernard Mandeville', in *Mandeville Studies,* p. 89.

34. *Female Tatler* 66 (7 December 1709), pp. 109–10. The 'Three Faculties' are the traditional university faculties of law, medicine and theology.

35. *Ibid.,* pp. 110-1. The accusation of sedition is aimed at Dr Sacheverell and his recent notorious sermon, *The Perils of False Brethren.* There is also an anti-Sacheverell squib in this issue announcing the publication of a sermon on passive obedience preached in the 'Chief Mosque of Constantinople'.

36. *Ibid.,* pp. 111–2. On Mandeville's medical views, see Cook, 'Materialism and the Passions', 101–24 and *A Treatise of the Hypocondriack and Hysterick Passions, vulgarly call'd the Hypo in Men and Vapours in Women* (London, 1711). The book obviously had some success since it was reissued (with a new title page) in 1715 and went into a revised second edition in 1730 which was reissued as a third edition in the same year; see Bibliography, Section I. Mandeville originally owned the copyright; it was entered against his name in Stationers' Hall, 27 February 1711. A copy in the Bodleian (0 151.n.102) contains the following note: 'The Copy of this Book is mine, I having bought it of the Author D^r. Mandeville, in the year 1711. M^r. Leach, Printer, has offer'd me several times Ten Guineas for the Copy, but I refus'd it, it being worth fifty Guineas, and will sell well if Printed again. May 31st. 1728'. The note is signed with initials which could be J.M. or J.W.

On the profession of medicine see Geoffrey Holmes, *Augustan England: Professions, State and Society, 1680–1730* (London, 1982), pp. 166–235, esp. pp. 166–84, who suggests that the attempt of the College of Physicians to maintain a restrictive hold on the practice of medicine was failing. See also G. S. Rousseau, 'Mandeville and Europe: medicine and philosophy', in *Mandeville Studies,* p. 11 and Francis McKee, 'Honeyed words: Bernard Mandeville and medical discourse', in *Medicine in the Enlightenment,* ed. Roy Porter (Amsterdam, 1995), pp. 223–54.

37. *Female Tatler* 66 p. 112. Lucubrations was one of Bickerstaff's favourite words.

38. *Ibid.,* pp. 112-3.

39. Praise of mean, obscure or humble things is typical of Renaissance paradox; see Rosalie L. Colie, *Paradoxia Epidemica: the Renaissance Tradition of Paradox* (Princeton, NJ, 1966).

FURTHER READING

Biography

Cook, Richard I. *Bernard Mandeville.* New York: Twayne Publishers, 1974, 174 p.
  Valuable biographical and critical study.

Criticism

Daniel, Stephen H. "Myth and Rationality in Mandeville." *Journal of the History of Ideas* 47, no. 4 (October-December 1986): 595-609.
  Argues that Mandeville's works can be understood only when the author's use of myth is considered.

Dykstal, Timothy. "Commerce, Conversation, and Contradiction in Mandeville's *Fable.*" *Studies in Eighteenth-Century Culture* 23 (1994): 93-110.
  Detailed analysis of Mandeville's *Fable of the Bees.*

Farrell, William J. "The Role of Mandeville's Bee Analogy in 'The Grumbling Hive'." *Studies in English Literature, 1500-1900* 25, no. 3 (summer 1985): 511-27.

Analyzes why Mandeville used the analogy between a bee hive and human society in *The Grumbling Hive.*

Hjort, Anne Mette. "Mandeville's Ambivalent Modernity." *Modern Language Notes* 106, no. 5 (December 1991): 951-66.
    Considers the intent of *The Fable of the Bees.*

Horne, Thomas A. *The Social Thought of Bernard Mandeville.* London: The Macmillan Press, 1978, 123 p.
    Provides commentary and criticism on Mandeville and his works from a variety of perspectives.

Hundert, E. J. "Bernard Mandeville and the Enlightenment's Maxims of Modernity." *Journal of the History of Ideas* 56, no. 4 (October 1995): 577-93.
    Discusses Mandeville's *Fable of the Bees.*

———. "Performing the Passions in Commercial Society: Bernard Mandeville and the Theatricality of Eighteenth-Century Thought." In *Refiguring Revolutions: Aesthetics and Politics from the English Revolution to the Romantic Revolution,* edited by Kevin Sharpe and Steven N. Zwicker, pp. 141-72. Berkeley: University of California Press, 1998.
    Investigates Mandeville as partaking in "an aesthetic of theatricality," which "functioned in the eighteenth century discourse of morals as a form of anxious uncertainty about stable ethical norms and a unitary personal identity."

Jack, Malcolm. "Bernard Mandeville: The Progress of Public Benefits." In *Corruption & Progress: The Eighteenth-Century Debate,* pp. 18-62. New York: A M S Press, 1989.
    Reflects on Mandeville's interpretation of human nature and society in his writings.

Kramnick, Jonathan Brody. "'Unwilling to be Short, or Plain, in any Thing Concerning Gain': Bernard Mandeville and the Dialectic of Charity." *Eighteenth Century: Theory and Interpretation* 33, no. 2 (summer 1992): 148-75.
    Examines the reaction to Mandeville's works that dealt with public and private life.

Peereboom, J. J. "A Common Language: Mandeville as a Contemporary of Pope." *DQR: Studies in Literature* 8 (1988): 97-110.
    Considers the value of a revived study of Mandeville and his works.

Primer, Irwin. "Erasmus and Bernard Mandeville: A Reconsideration." *Philological Quarterly* 72, no. 3 (summer 1993): 313-35.
    Discusses the influence of Erasmus on Mandeville and his writings.

Additional coverage of Mandeville's life and career is contained in the following source published by the Gale Group: *Dictionary of Literary Biography,* **Vol. 101.**

Thomas Warton
1728-1790

English poet, critic, biographer, and nonfiction writer.

The following entry provides an overview of Warton's life and works. For additional information on his career, see *LC,* Volume 15.

INTRODUCTION

Warton is best known as a critic whose writings, especially the three-volume *History of English Poetry, from the Close of the Eleventh to the Commencement of the Eighteenth Century* (1774-81?), were influential for their consideration of literary works in a broad historical context. Warton also wrote poetry, most notably *The Pleasures of Melancholy* (1747), an early work that exemplifies what commentators describe as the author's "Gothic" sensibility.

BIOGRAPHICAL INFORMATION

Warton was born on January 9, 1728, in Basingstoke, Hampshire, to Thomas Warton, the Elder, a poet and schoolmaster, and his wife, Elizabeth Richardson Warton. At the time, Warton the Elder was headmaster of Basingstoke Grammar School. Warton's elder brother, Joseph, also became a poet and academic and collaborated with his sibling on occasion. Warton received much of his early education from his father and in 1744 entered Trinity College, Oxford. It was at this time that Warton began writing poetry as a serious pursuit, producing, among other works, his famous *The Pleasures of Melancholy.* He also submitted several works to collections published by his brother and father, sometimes under their names. After earning his undergraduate degree in 1747, Warton remained at Oxford to continue his studies and became more involved in literary activities at the university. Warton earned his M.A. in 1750 and was elected a probationary fellow of Trinity College in 1752. He became a full fellow the following year. While continuing to work on his own poetry and fulfilling his academic duties, Warton also assembled several poetry anthologies as well editions and studies of the works of noted poets. One important study was *Observations on the Faerie Queene of Spenser* (1754). In 1756, Warton was elected as professor of poetry at Oxford, a position he held for ten years. In addition to the scholarly works Warton published during this period, he also wrote biographies, comic verse, and travel books. After his poetry professorship ended in 1766, Warton was given a bachelor of divinity degree the following year but was afterward passed over for significant positions at the university. For example, in 1776, although Warton was arguably the most respected fellow at Trinity, he was not chosen to serve as its president. By then, Warton was publishing the initial volumes of what many consider his most important work, *The History of English Poetry.* Primarily a literary historian and academic by this point in his life, he continued to write poetry that was highly regarded. In 1785, he was appointed poet laureate; the same year, he was elected Camden Professor of Ancient History at Oxford. In the last decade of his life, Warton acted as a mentor to many young poets. He died on May 21, 1790.

MAJOR WORKS

As David Fairer has written: "Warton's literary achievement was certainly many-sided: poet, literary historian, classical scholar, Gothic enthusiast, humorist, biographer, editor. He was a man in whom so many strands of cultural life of the eighteenth century met." While Warton indeed produced a varied body of works, critics often emphasize a quality common to many of them that is generally described as "Gothic." As applied to Warton's writings, the term Gothic signifies a profound sense of the influence of the past upon the present as well as a taste for gloomy natural landscapes, medieval architecture, and ruins. The dour imagery and pensive mood of *The Pleasures of Melancholy,* written when the author was only seventeen years old, well illustrates the Gothicism that many critics observe in much of Warton's work. A vivid sense of the past, especially the period of the Middle Ages, informed Warton's critical writings and distinguished them among literary criticism theretofore published in English. In *Observations on the Faerie Queene of Spenser,* Warton took on a new approach to critical study by demonstrating the manner in which the past was embodied in and influenced Edmund Spenser's epic poem, as well as placing it in the historical context of its own time. This idea was expanded in Warton's most ambitious project, *The History of English Poetry, from the Close of the Eleventh to the Commencement of the Eighteenth.* In the three volumes Warton completed—a fourth volume was published in its uncompleted form—he studied the history of England's literature from the Norman Conquest to his own day.

CRITICAL RECEPTION

Many critics credit Warton with redefining literary criticism. From the time of its first publication, *Observations on the Faerie Queene of Spenser* was recognized as a benchmark in the history of English literature. Warton is believed to be the first to look at a work in relation to its time, cultural influences, and earlier literature. Critics note that Warton accomplished this on a greater scale in *The History of English Poetry*. Although commentators have often faulted this study as sometimes difficult to follow—in part because of its ambitiously all-inclusive but unsystematic scheme—and have discovered it to be riddled with errors of fact, it is nonetheless regarded as a seminal work in the history of English literary criticism. With this work, Warton helped define periods and styles in literature for the first time, an achievement that alone justifies his place among prominent writers of the eighteenth century.

PRINCIPAL WORKS

The Pleasures of Melancholy: A Poem (poetry) 1747

A Description of the City, College, and Cathedral of Winchester (nonfiction) 1750; revised edition, 1760; third edition published as *The Winchester Guide*, 1796

The Triumph of Isis: A Poem. Occasioned by Isis: An Elegy (poetry) 1750

New-market, A Satire (poetry) 1751

Observations on the Faerie Queene of Spenser (criticism) 1754; revised and enlarged edition, 1762

A Description of the City, College, and Cathedral of Winchester (nonfiction) 1760

The Life and Literary Remains of Ralph Bathurst. 2 vols. (biography) 1761

A Companion to the Guide, and a Guide to the Companion: Being a Complete Supplement to All the Accounts of Oxford Hitherto Published (nonfiction) 1760; revised and enlarged edition, 1762?

The Life of Sir Thomas Pope (biography) 1772; expanded edition, 1780

*The History of English Poetry, from the Close of the Eleventh to the Commencement of the Eighteenth Century. 4 vols. (criticism) 1774-81?

Poems: A New Edition, with Additions (poetry) 1777; enlarged as *Poems: A New Edition* 1777; enlarged as *Poems on Various Subjects of Thomas Warton: Now First Collected*, 1791

An Enquiry into the Authenticity of the Poems Attributed to Thomas Rowley (criticism) 1782

Specimen of a Parochial History of Oxfordshire (history) 1782; enlarged as *Specimen of a History of Oxfordshire*, 1783; published as *The History and Antiquities of Kiddington*, 1815

Verses on Sir Joshua Reynold's Painted Window at New-College Oxford (poetry) 1782

The Poetical Works of the Late Thomas Warton, B.D. 2 vols. [edited by Richard Mant] (poetry) 1802

*The fourth volume of this work was left incomplete and was issued without a publication date.

CRITICISM

Clarissa Rinaker (essay date 1916)

SOURCE: Rinaker, Clarissa. "Criticism: The *Observations on the Fairie Queene of Spenser*, 1754-1762." In *Thomas Warton: A Biographical and Critical Study*, pp. 37-58. Urbana: University of Illinois Studies in Language and Literature, 1916.

[*In the following excerpt, Rinaker regards* Observations on the Faerie Queene of Spenser *as an important work of English literary criticism for having revived interest in Edmund Spenser.*]

The hand of the poet is as evident as that of the scholar in the ***Observations on the Faerie Queene of Spenser.***[1] Warton's love for Spenser and his poetical enthusiasm were here first turned to criticism, but of a sort unknown before. And the secret of the new quality is to be found in this poetical enthusiasm of the writer which enabled him to study the poem from its own point of view, not hampered by artificial, pseudo-classical standards of which the poet had known nothing, but with a sympathetic appreciation of his literary models, the spirit of his age, his heritage of romance and chivalry, and the whole many-coloured life of the middle ages. These things Warton was able to see and to reveal not with the eighteenth century prejudice against, and ignorance of, the Gothic, but with the understanding and long familiarity of the real lover of Spenser.

The result of Warton's combined poetical enthusiasm and scholarly study of Spenser was that he produced in the ***Observations on the Faerie Queene*** the first important piece of modern historical criticism in the field of English literature. By the variety of its new tenets and the definitiveness of its revolt against the pseudo-classical criticism by rule, it marks the beginning of a new school. Out of the turmoil of the quarrel between the 'ancients' and the 'moderns' the pseudo-classical compromise had emerged. The 'moderns', by admitting and apologizing for a degree of barbarity and uncouthness in even their greatest poets, had established their right to a secure and reputable place in the assembly of immortals, although on the very questionable ground of conformity with the ancients and by submitting to be judged by rules which had not determined their development. It was thus by comparisons with the ancients that Dryden had found Spenser's verse harmonious but his design imperfect;[2] it was in the light of the classical rules for epic poetry that Addison had praised *Paradise Lost*,[3] and that Steele had wished an 'Encomium of Spenser'[4] also.

Impossible as was the task of reconciling literature partly romantic and modern with classical and ancient standards, the critics of a rationalistic age did not hesitate to accomplish it; common sense was the pseudo-classical handmaiden that justified the rules, methodized nature, standardized critical taste, and restrained the 'Enthusiastick Spirit' and the *je ne sais quoi* of the school of taste. The task was a hard one, and the pseudo-classical position dangerous and ultimately untenable. A more extended study of literary history—innocuously begun by Rymer[5]—and an enlightened freedom from prejudice would show at the same time the inadequacy of the rules and the possibility of arriving at sounder critical standards.

These are the two principal gifts that Thomas Warton had with which he revolutionized criticism: intelligent independence to throw off the bondage of the rules, and broad knowledge to supply material for juster criteria. When he said, 'It is absurd to think of judging either Ariosto or Spenser by precepts which they did not attend to,'[6] he not merely asserted their right to be judged by Gothic or 'romantic', as opposed to pseudo-classical, standards, but sounded the death-knell of criticism by rule, and the bugle-note of the modern school. When, in the same critical work, and even more impressively in two later ones,[7] he brought to bear upon the subject in hand a rich store of ideas and illustrations drawn from many literatures—Latin, Greek, Italian, French, and English in its obscure as well as its more familiar eras,—he rendered an even more important service on the side of constructive criticism.

Warton's **Observations** is connected not only with the history of critical theory in the eighteenth century but also with what is called the Spenserian revival. It was partly the culmination of one of several related movements tending toward the restoration of the older English classics. While Chaucer was slowly winning a small circle of appreciators; Shakespeare, from ignorantly apologetic admiration and garbled staging, through serious study and intelligent comprehension, was coming into his own; and Milton was attaining a vogue that left its mark on the new poetry; the Spenserian revival was simultaneously preparing to exert an even greater influence. Although Spenser was never without a select circle of readers, that circle was small and coldly critical during the pseudo-classical period when his principal charm was that which his moral afforded readers who held that the purpose of poetry was to instruct. Most readers assented to Jonson's dictum that Spenser 'writ no language' without attending to the caveat that followed, 'Yet I would have him read for his matter.' The difficulties of his language, the tiresomeness of his stanza,[8] the unclassical imperfection of his design, and the extravagance of the adventures too often obscured even the beauty of his moral. Therefore it was after a pretty general neglect of his poetry that the eighteenth century saw a species of Spenserian imitation arise which showed to what low ebb the study of Spenser had sunk. The first of these imitators either ignorantly fancied that any arrangement of from six to ten iambic pentameter lines capped with an Alexandrine, with distinctly Popeian cadence and a sprinkling of 'I ween', 'I weet' and 'whilom' by way of antiquated diction, could pass for Spenserian verse,[9] or followed the letter of the stanza closely enough, but failed to take their model seriously, and misapplied it

to vulgar burlesque, social and political satire, and mere moralizing.[10] Their ignorance of the poet whom they professed to imitate is marked. Often they knew him only through Prior's imitations; usually their attempts at antiquated diction betray them.[11] Occasionally, as in the case of Shenstone, a study of Spenser followed imitation of him, and led to a new attitude, changes in the imitation, and finally, apparently, to an admiration that he neither understood nor cared to admit.[12]

Of course by far the best of the Spenserian imitators was James Thomson, whose work was the first to rise above the merely imitative and to have an independent value as creative poetry. Although his *Advertisement* and a few burlesque touches throughout the poem are evidence of the influence of the *Schoolmistress* and of the prevailing attitude toward Spenser, Thomson went further than mere external imitation and reproduced something of the melody and atmosphere of the *Fairy Queen*. Thus poetical enthusiasm began the Spenserian revival; it remained for a great critical enthusiasm to vindicate the source of this inspiration and to establish it on the firm basis of scholarly study and intelligent appreciation.

The first attempt at anything like an extended criticism of the *Fairy Queen* was in the two essays *On Allegorical Poetry* and *Remarks on the Fairy Queen* which prefaced John Hughes's edition of Spenser's works in 1715, the first eighteenth century edition.[13] Steele, in the 540th *Spectator,* three years before, had desired an 'Encomium of Spencer', 'that charming author', like Addison's Milton papers, but nothing further than his own meagre hints was forthcoming. And Hughes's attitude, like that of the imitators, was wholly apologetic.

Hughes seems almost to have caught a glimpse of the promised land when he refused to examine the *Fairy Queen* by the classical rules for epic poetry, saying: 'As it is plain the Author never design'd it by those Rules, I think it ought rather to be consider'd as a Poem of a particular kind, describing in a Series of Allegorical Adventures or Episodes the most noted Virtues and Vices: to compare it therefore with the Models of Antiquity, wou'd be like drawing a Parallel between the *Roman* and the *Gothick* Architecture.'[14] At first sight one is inclined to think this very near to Warton's revolutionary dictum, but the bungling way in which he spoiled the effect of this striking statement by preparing in advance a set of pseudo-classical and misfit standards to apply as he exposed the unsuitability of the old, merely by the substitution of allegory for epic, shows that he was a true pseudo-classicist after all. He could not, nor would, throw off his allegiance to the ancients. If the *Fairy Queen* could not be considered as an epic, it could be judged as an allegory, the rules of which, though not described by the ancients, were easily determinable. And in attempting to set forth the rules for allegorical poetry, he tried to conform to the spirit of the classical critics as he understood it, and to illustrate his subject by examples from classical poets. Nevertheless he felt some reluctance in introducing a subject which was 'something out of the way, and not expressly treated upon by those who have laid down Rules for the Art of Poetry.'[15] Hughes's ideas of what should constitute successful allegory were therefore embodied in his *Essay on Allegorical Poetry,* by the uncertain light of which the critic hoped 'not only to discover many Beauties in the *Fairy Queen,* but likewise to excuse some of its Irregularities.'[16]

Hughes did not, however, yield to the spell of 'magic Spenser's wildly-warbled song.' While he admitted that his fable gave 'the greatest Scope to that Range of Fancy which was so remarkably his Talent'[17] and that his plan, though not well chosen, was at least well executed and adapted to his talent, he apologized for and excused both fable and plan on the score of the Italian models which he followed, and the remnants of the 'old Gothic Chivalry' which yet survived. The only praise he could give the poem was wholly pseudo-classical,—for the moral and didactic bent which the poet had contrived to give the allegory,[18] and for some fine passages where the author 'rises above himself' and imitates the ancients.[19] In spite of his statement that the *Fairy Queen* was not to be examined by the strict rules of epic poetry, he could not free himself from that bondage, and the most of his essay is taken up with a discussion of the poem in the light of the rules. Moreover Hughes was but ill-equipped for his task; he failed even to realize that a great field of literary history must be thoroughly explored before the task of elucidating Spenser could be intelligently undertaken, and that genuine enthusiasm for the poet could alone arouse much interest in him. These are the reasons why nearly forty years elapsed before the edition was reprinted, and why it failed to give a tremendous impetus to the Spenserian revival. Yet, notwithstanding its defects, it is extremely important that Hughes should have undertaken at all the editing of so neglected a poet.[20] It is a straw that points the direction of the wind.

The next attempt at Spenserian criticism was a small volume of *Remarks on Spenser's Poems and on Milton's Paradise Regained,* published anonymously in 1734, and soon recognized as the work of Dr. Jortin, a classical scholar of some repute. This is practically valueless as a piece of criticism. But Jortin was at least partly conscious of his failure and of a reason for it, though he was more anxious to have the exact text determined by a 'collation of Editions, and by comparing the Author with himself' than to furnish an interpretive criticism; and he acknowledged himself unwilling to bestow the necessary time and application for the work,[21]—a gratifying acknowledgement of the fact that no valuable work could be done in this field without special preparation for it.

And when Thomas Warton was able to bring this special preparation for the first time to the study of the *Fairy Queen,* he produced a revolution in criticism. Freed from the tyranny of the rules by the perception of their limitations, he substituted untried avenues of approach and juster standards of criticism, and revealed beauties which could never have been discovered with the old restrictions. That

he should be without trace of pseudo-classicism is something we cannot expect; but that his general critical method and principles are ultimately irreconcilable with even the most generous interpretation of that term is a conclusion one cannot escape after a careful study of the *Observations on the Fairy Queen.*

Briefly, the causes of Warton's superiority over all previous critics of Spenser, the reasons why he became through this piece of critical writing the founder of a new kind of criticism, are four. First, he recognized the inadequacy of the classical rules, as interpreted by Boileau and other modern commentators, as standards for judging modern literature, and declared his independence of them and his intention of following new methods based upon the belief that the author's purpose is at least as important a subject for critical study as the critic's theories and that imagination is as important a factor in creative literature as reason. Second, he introduced the modern historical method of criticism by recognizing that no work of art could be independently judged, isolated from the conditions under which it was produced, without reference to the influences which determined its character, and without considering its relation to other literatures. In taking this broad view of his subject, Warton was, of course, recognizing the necessity for a comparative study of literature. In the third place, and as a consequence of this independence and this greater breadth of view, Warton understood more fully than his contemporaries the true relation between classical and modern literature, understood that the English writers of the boasted Augustan age, in renouncing their heritage from the middle ages, had deprived themselves of the qualities which alone could have redeemed their desiccated pseudo-classicism. And last, Warton made a place in criticism for the reader's spontaneous delight and enthusiasm.

Few critics of the eighteenth century recognized any difference between their own rules and practice and those of the ancients, or saw the need for modern standards for judging modern poems. Just here comes the important and irreparable break between Warton and his contemporaries. While Hughes and the rest attempted to justify Spenser by pointing out conformities to the rules[22] where they existed or might be fancied, and condemned his practice when they failed to find any, Warton was at some pains to show that Hughes failed and that such critics must fail because their critical method was wrong.[23] He pointed out that the *Fairy Queen* cannot be judged by rule, that the 'plan and conduct' of Spenser's poem 'is highly exceptionable', 'is confused and irregular', and has 'no general unity';[24] it fails completely when examined by the rules. To Warton this clearly showed the existence of another standard of criticism—not the Aristotelian, but the poet's: Spenser had not tried to write like Homer, but like Ariosto; his standard was romantic, not classical; and he was to be judged by what he tried to do.

Warton's declaration of independence of pseudo-classical criticism was a conscious revolt; yet it was one to which he made some effort to win the assent of his contemporaries by conceding that Spenser's frequent extravagances[25] did violate the rules approved by an age that took pride in its critical taste. His desire to engage their interest, however, neither succeeded in that purpose nor persuaded him that those rules were properly applied to poems written in ignorance of them. There is no uncertainty, no compromise with pseudo-classical criticism in the flat defiance, 'it is absurd to think of judging either Ariosto or Spenser by precepts which they did not attend to.'[26]

Having thus condemned the accepted standards as inadequate for a just criticism of the *Fairy Queen,* Warton's next purpose was to find those by which it could be properly judged: not the rules of which the poet was ignorant, but the literature with which he was familiar. He recognized quite clearly a distinction between a classical and a romantic poet, and accounted for it by a difference of circumstances. Warton's even then extensive knowledge of the neglected periods of earlier English literature gave him a power that most of his contemporaries lacked and enabled him to see that Spenser's peculiarities were those of his age, that the 'knights and damsels, the tournaments and enchantments, of Spenser' were not oddities but the familiar and admired features of romance, a prevailing literary form of the age, and that 'the fashion of the times' determined Spenser's purpose of becoming a *'romantic Poet.'*[27]

Warton determined therefore not only to judge but to praise Spenser as a romantic[28] poet. He found that as the characteristic appeal of pseudo-classical poetry was to the intellect, to the reason, romantic poetry addressed itself to the feelings, to the imagination. Its excellence, therefore, consisted not in design and proportion, but in interest and variety of detail. The poet's business was 'to engage the fancy, and interest the attention by bold and striking images, in the formation, and the disposition of which, little labour or art was applied. The various and marvelous were the chief sources of delight'.[29] Hence Spenser had ransacked 'reality and romance', 'truth and fiction' to adorn his 'fairy structure', and Warton revelled in the result, in its very formlessness and richness, which he thought preferable, in a romantic poem, to exactness. 'Exactness in his poem,' he said, 'would have been like the cornice which a painter introduced in the grotto of Calypso. Spenser's beauties are like the flowers in Paradise.'[30]

When beauties thus transcend nature, delight goes beyond reason. Warton did not shrink from the logical result of giving rein to imagination; he was willing to recognize the romantic quest for beauties beyond the reach of art, to sacrifice reason and 'nature methodiz'd' in an exaltation of a higher quality which rewarded the reader with a higher kind of enjoyment. 'If the Fairy Queen,' he said, 'be destitute of that arrangement and æconomy which epic severity requires, yet we scarcely regret the loss of these, while their place is so amply supplied by something which more powerfully attracts us: something which engages the affections, the feelings of the heart, rather than the cold approbation of the head. If there be any poem whose graces

please, because they are situated beyond the reach of art, and where the force and faculties of creative imagination[31] delight, because they are unassisted and unrestrained by those of deliberate judgment, it is this. In reading Spenser, if the critic is not satisfied, yet the reader is transported.'[32]

When Warton thus made a place for transport in a critical discourse, he had parted company with his contemporaries and opened the way for the whole romantic exaltation of feeling. He had turned from Dr. Johnson, who condemned 'all power of fancy over reason' as a 'degree of insanity',[33] and faced toward Blake, who exalted the imagination and called reason the only evil.[34] Every propriety of Queen Anne criticism had now been violated. Not satisfied with condemning all previous Spenserian criticism as all but nonsense, Warton dared to place the uncritical reader's delight above the critic's deliberate disapproval, and then to commend that enthusiasm and the beauties that aroused it. In repudiating the pseudo-classical rules, Warton enunciated two revolutionary dicta: there are other critical standards than those of Boileau and the ancients (save the mark!); there are other poetical beauties than those of Pope and 'nature methodiz'd.'

Revolutionary as he was in his enjoyment of Spenser's fable, Warton had not at the time he wrote the ***Observations*** freed himself from the pseudo-classical theories of versification and he agreed with his predecessors in his discussion of this subject. Altough he did not feel the nineteenth century romanticist's enthusiasm for Spenser's versification, he was nevertheless sufficiently the poet to appreciate and to enjoy his success with it. 'It is indeed surprising,' he said, 'that Spenser should execute a poem of uncommon length, with so much spirit and ease, laden as he was with so many shackles, and embarrassed with so complicated a *bondage* of *riming*. . . . His sense and sound are equally flowing and uninterrupted.'[35] Similarly, with respect to language, we neither expect nor find enthusiasm. Warton thought Jonson 'perhaps unreasonable,'[36] and found the origin of his language in the language of his age, as he found the origin of his design in its romances. Long acquaintance enabled him to read the *Fairy Queen* with ease; he denied that Spenser's language was either so affected or so obsolete as it was generally supposed, and asserted that 'For many stanzas together we may frequently read him with as much facility as we can the same number of lines in Shakespeare.'[37] In his approval and appreciation of Spenser's moral purpose Warton was, of course, nearer to his pseudo-classical predecessors than to his romantic followers; however, without relinquishing that prime virtue of the old school, the solidity which comes from well-established principles, he attained to new virtues, greater catholicity of taste and flexibility of judgment.

In seeking in the literature of and before the sixteenth century and in the manners and customs of the 'spacious times of great Elizabeth' for the explanation of Spenser's poem—so far as explanation of genius is possible—Warton was, as has been said, laying the foundations of modern historical criticism. Some slight progress had been made in this direction before, but without important results. Warton was by no means original in recognizing Spenser's debt to the Italian romances which were so popular in his day, and to Ariosto in particular. And many critics agreed that he was 'led by the prevailing notions of his age to write an irregular and romantic poem.' They, however, regarded his age as one of barbarity and ignorance of the rules, and its literature as unworthy of study and destitute of intrinsic value. No critic before Warton had realized the importance of supplementing an absolute by an historical criticism, of reconstructing, so far as possible, a poet's environment and the conditions under which he worked, in order to judge his poetry. 'In reading the works of a poet who lived in a remote age,' he said, 'it is necessary that we should look back upon the customs and manners which prevailed in that age. We should endeavour to place ourselves in the writer's situation and circumstances. Hence we shall become better enabled to discover how his turn of thinking, and manner of composing, were influenced by familiar appearances and established objects, which are utterly different from those with which we are at present surrounded.'[38] And, realizing that the neglect of these details was fatal to good criticism, that the 'commentator[39] whose critical enquiries are employed on Spenser, Jonson, and the rest of our elder poets, will in vain give specimens of his classical erudition, unless, at the same time, he brings to his work a mind intimately acquainted with those books, which though now forgotten, were yet in common use and high repute about the time in which his authors respectively wrote, and which they consequently must have read,'[40] he resolutely reformed his own practice.

Warton not only perceived the necessity of the historical method of studying the older poets, but he had acquired what very few of his contemporaries had attained, sufficient knowledge of the earlier English literature to undertake such a study of Spenser. He embarked upon the study of the *Fairy Queen,* its sources and literary background, with a fund of knowledge which, however much later scholars, who have taken up large holdings in the territory charted by that pioneer, may unjustly scorn its superficiality or inexactness, was for that time quite exceptional, and which could not fail to illuminate the poem to the point of transfiguration. Every reader of Spenser had accepted his statement that he took Ariosto as his model, but no one before Warton had remarked another model, one closer in respect of matter, which the poet no doubt thought too obvious to mention, the old romances of chivalry. Warton observed that where Spenser's plan is least like Ariosto's, it most resembles the romances; that, although he 'formed his Faerie Queene upon the fanciful plan of Ariosto', he formed the particular adventures of his knight upon the romances. 'Spenser's first book is,' he said, 'a regular and precise imitation of such a series of action as we frequently find in books of chivalry.'[41]

In proof of Spenser's indebtedness to the romances Warton cited the prevalence of romances of chivalry in his day, and pointed out particular borrowings from this popular poetry. In the first place he insisted again and again not only that the 'encounters of chivalry' which appeared extraordinary to modern eyes were familiar to readers in Spenser's day,[42] but that the practices of chivalry were even continued to some extent.[43] Warton's close acquaintance with the literature of the sixteenth century and before showed him that the matter of the romances was common property and had permeated other works than those of mediæval poets. He discovered that the story of Arthur, from which Spenser borrowed most, was so generally known and so great a favourite that incidents from it were made the basis for entertainment of Elizabeth at Kenilworth,[44] and that Arthur and his knights were alluded to by writers so various as Caxton, Ascham, Sidney, Puttenham, Bacon, and Jonson;[45] that even Ariosto[46] himself borrowed from the story of Arthur. At the same time his first-hand knowledge of the romances enabled him to point out among those which most directly influenced the *Fairy Queen* Malory's *Morte Arthur,* the largest contributor, of course, from which such details as the story of Sir Tristram, King Ryence and the Mantle of Beards, the Holy Grail, and the Blatant Beast were drawn;[47] *Bevis of Southampton,* which furnished the incident of the well of marvelous healing power;[48] the ballad of the Boy and the Mantle, from the French romance, *Le Court Mantel,* which suggested Spenser's conceit of Florimel's girdle.[49] Warton also carefully discussed Spenser's fairy mythology, which supplanted the classical mythology as his romantic adventures replaced those of antiquity, ascribing its origin to romance and folk-lore of Celtic and ultimately Oriental origin.[50]

As in the case of mediæval romance, Warton was the first critic to consider in any detail Spenser's indebtedness to Chaucer. Antiquarians and a few poets had been mildly interested in Chaucer, but his importance for the study of the origins of English poetry had been ignored in the prevalent delusion that the classics were the ultimate sources of poetry. Dryden, to be sure, had remarked that Spenser imitated Chaucer's language,[51] and subsequent readers, including Warton, concurred. But it still remained for Warton to point out that Spenser was also indebted to Chaucer for ideas, and to show the extent and nature of his debt by collecting 'specimens of Spenser's imitations from Chaucer, both of language and sentiment.'[52] Without, of course, attempting to exhaust the subject, Warton collected enough parallel passages to prove that Spenser was not only an 'attentive reader and professed admirer', but also an imitator of Chaucer. For example, he pointed out that the list of trees in the wood of error was more like Chaucer's in the *Assembly of Fowls* than like similar passages in classical poets mentioned by Jortin;[53] that he had borrowed the magic mirror which Merlin gave Ryence from the *Squire's Tale,*[54] and from the *Romance of the Rose,* the conceit of Cupid dressed in flowers.[55] By a careful comparison with Chaucer's language, Warton was able to explain some doubtful passages as well as to show Spenser's draughts from 'the well of English undefiled.'

One can scarcely overestimate the importance of Warton's evident first-hand knowledge of Chaucer in an age when he was principally known only through Dryden's and Pope's garbled modernizations, or Milton's reference to him who

> . . . 'left half-told
> The story of Cambuscan bold.'

Warton was not satisfied that Chaucer should be studied merely to illustrate Spenser; he recognized his intrinsic value as well, and suffered his enthusiasm for Chaucer to interrupt the thread of his criticism of Spenser, while he lauded and recommended to his neglectful age the charms of the older poet.[56] To be sure his reasons for admiring Chaucer were somewhat too romantic to convince an age that preferred regular beauties; his 'romantic arguments', 'wildness of painting', 'simplicity and antiquity of expression', though 'pleasing to the imagination' and calculated to 'transport us into some fairy region', were certainly not the qualities to attract Upton or Hughes or Dr. Johnson. Unlike the pseudo-classical admirers of Chaucer, Warton held that to read modern imitations was not to know Chaucer; that to provide such substitutes was to contribute rather to the neglect than to the popularity of the original. With characteristic soundness of scholarship he condemned the prevalence of translations because they encouraged 'indolence and illiteracy', displaced the originals and thus gradually vitiated public taste.[57]

The study of Spenser's age yielded the third element which Warton introduced into Spenserian criticism—the influence of the mediæval moralities and allegorical masques. Warton's study of Spenser's allegory is of quite another sort than Hughes's essay. Instead of trying to concoct a set of *a priori* rules for a kind of epic which should find its justification in its moral, Warton, as usual, was concerned with forms of allegory as they actually existed and were familiar to his poet, and with the history of allegorical poetry in England. Without denying the important influence of Ariosto, he pointed out that his predecessors had erred in thinking the *Orlando Furioso* a sufficient model; he saw that the characters of Spenser's allegory much more resembled the 'emblematical personages, visibly decorated with their proper attributes, and actually endued with speech, motion and life',[58] with which Spenser was familiar upon the stage, than the less symbolical characters of Ariosto. Warton could support his position by quoting references in the *Fairy Queen* to masques and dumb shows,[59] and by tracing somewhat the progress of allegory in English poetry before Spenser.[60] It is characteristic that he should not have been satisfied to observe that allegory was popular in Spenser's age, but that he should wish to explain it by a 'retrospect of English poetry from the age of Spenser.'[61] Superficial and hasty as this survey is, it must have confirmed Warton's opinion that a thorough exploration of early English poetry was needed, and so anticipated his *magnum opus*. And we can find little fault with its conclusions, even when he says that this poetry 'principally consisted in visions and allegories', when he could add as a matter of information, 'there are, indeed, the writings of some English poets now remaining, who wrote before Gower or Chaucer.'

In rejecting the conclusions of pseudo-classical criticism, in regarding Spenser as the heir of the middle ages, Warton did not by any means overlook the influence of the renaissance, of the classical revival, upon his poetry. His study of the classical sources from which Spenser embellished his plan[62] is as careful and as suggestive as his study of the mediæval sources; it is not only so strikingly new. His attack on Scaliger, who subordinated a comparative method to the demonstration of *a priori* conclusions, shows that he was a sounder classicist than that pseudo-classical leader. Scaliger, he said, more than once 'betrayed his ignorance of the nature of ancient poetry';[63] he 'had no notion of simple and genuine beauty; nor had ever considered the manners and customs which prevailed in early times.'[64] Warton was a true classicist in his admiration for Homer and Aristotle, and in his recognition of them as 'the genuine and uncorrupted sources of ancient poetry and ancient criticism';[65] but, as has been said, he did not make the mistake of supposing them the sources of modern poetry and criticism as well.

Warton shows in this essay an extraordinarily clear recognition of the relation between classical, mediæval and modern literatures, and a corresponding adaptation of criticism to it. By a wide application of the historical method he saw that English poetry was the joint product of two principal strains, the ancient or classical, and the mediæval or romantic; and that the poet or critic who neglected either disclaimed half his birthright. The poetry of Spenser's age, Warton perceived, drew from both sources. Although the study of the ancient models was renewed, the 'romantic manner of poetical composition introduced and established by the Provencial bards' was not superseded by a 'new and more legitimate taste of writing.' And Warton as a critic accepted—as Scaliger would not—the results of his historical study: he admired and desired the characteristic merits of classical poetry, 'justness of thought and design', 'decorum', 'uniformity',[66] he 'so far conformed to the reigning maxims of modern criticism, as . . . to recommend classical propriety';[67] but he wished them completed and adorned with the peculiar imaginative beauties of the 'dark ages', those fictions which 'rouse and invigorate all the powers of imagination [and] store the fancy with those sublime and charming images, which true poetry best delights to display.'[68]

The inevitable result of recognizing the relation between the classical and romantic sources of literature was contempt for pseudo-classicism, for those poets and critics who rejected the beauties of romance for the less natural perfections approved by the classical and French theorists, who aped the ancients without knowing them and despised their own romantic ancestry. The greatest English poets, Warton perceived, were those who combined both elements in their poetry; those who rejected either fell short of the highest rank. And therefore he perceived the loss to English poetry when, after the decline of romance and allegory, 'a poetry succeeded, in which imagination gave way to correctness, sublimity of description to delicacy of sentiment, and majestic imagery to conceit and epigram.'

Warton's brief summary of this poetry points out its weakness. 'Poets began now to be more attentive to words, than to things and objects. The nicer beauties of happy expression were preferred to the daring strokes of great conception. Satire, that bane of the sublime, was imported from France. The muses were debauched at court; and polite life, and familiar manners, became their only themes. The simple dignity of Milton[69] was either entirely neglected, or mistaken for bombast and insipidity, by the refined readers of a dissolute age, whose taste and morals were equally vitiated.'[70]

The culmination—perhaps the crowning—glory of Warton's first piece of critical writing is his keen delight in the task. Addison had praised and popularized criticism.[71] but with reservations; and most people—even until recent times (if indeed the idea has now wholly disappeared from the earth)—would agree with Warton that the 'business of criticism is commonly laborious and dry.' Yet he affirms that his work 'has proved a most agreeable task;' that it has 'more frequently amused than fatigued (his) attention,' and that 'much of the pleasure that Spenser experienced in composing the Fairy Queen, must, in some measure, be shared by his commentator; and the critic, on this occasion, may speak in the words, and with the rapture, of the poet,—

> The wayes through which my weary steppes I guyde
> In this *delightfull land* of *faerie,*
> Are so exceeding spacious and wyde,
> And sprinkled with such sweet varietie
> Of all that pleasant is to ear or eye,
> That I nigh ravisht with rare thoughts delight,
> *My tedious travel* do forgett thereby:
> And when I gin to feele decay of might,
> It strength to me supplies, and cheares my dulled spright.

Warton's real classicism and his endeavours to carry his contemporaries with him by emphasizing wherever possible his accord with them blinded them for a time to the strongly revolutionary import of the **Observations on the Fairy Queen,** and the book was well received by pseudo-classical readers. Its scholarly merits and the impulse it gave to the study of literature were generously praised by Dr. Johnson,[72] who could partly appreciate the merits of the historical method, but would not emulate them. This is however scarcely a fair test, for the 'watch-dog of classicism', although an indifferent scholar when compared with Warton, had an almost omnivorous thirst for knowledge, and although he despised research for its own sake, his nearest sympathy with the romantic movement was when its researches tended to increase the sum of human knowledge. Warburton was delighted with the **Observations,** and told Warton so.[73] Walpole complimented the author upon it, though he had no fondness for Spenser.[74] The reviewer for the *Monthly Review*[75] showed little critical perception. Although he discussed the book section by section, he discovered nothing extraordinary in it, nothing but the usual influence of Ariosto, defects of the language, parallel passage and learned citation; and he reached the

height of inadequacy when he thus commended Warton's learning: 'Upon the whole, Mr. *Warton* seems to have studied his author with much attention, and has obliged us with no bad prelude for the edition, of which he advises us.[76] His acquaintance with our earliest writers must have qualified him with such a relish of the *Anglo-Saxon* dialect, as few poets, since *Prior,* seem to have imbibed.' A scurrilous anonymous pamphlet, *The Observer Observ'd, or Remarks on a certain curious Tract, intitl'd, Observations on the Faiere Queen of Spencer, by Thomas Warton, A. M.,* etc, which appeared two years after the **Observations,** deserved the harsh treatment it received at the hands of the reviewers.[77] The immediate results on the side of Spenserian criticism were not striking. Two editions of the *Fairy Queen,* by John Upton and Ralph Church, appeared in 1758. Of these, the first was accused at once of borrowing without acknowledgment from Warton's **Observations**;[78] the second is described as having notes little enlightening;[79] both editors were still measuring Spenser by the ancients.[80]

From this time the Spenserian movement was poetical. Warton's essay put a new seal of critical approval upon the *Fairy Queen* and Spenser's position as the poet's poet was established with the new school. He was no longer regarded judicially as an admirable poet who unfortunately chose inferior models for verse and fable with which to present his moral; he was enthusiastically adopted as an inexhaustible source of poetic inspiration, of imagination, of charming imagery, of rich colour, of elusive mystery, of melodious verse.

Although Warton's pseudo-classical contemporaries did not perceive the full significance of his study of Spenser, his general programme began to be accepted and followed; and his encouragement of the study of mediæval institutions and literature gave a great impetus to the new romantic movement. His followers were, however, often credited with the originality of their master, and their work was apt to arouse stronger protest from the pseudo-classicists.[81] When Hurd's very romantic *Letters on Chivalry and Romance* appeared, they were credited with having influenced Warton to greater tolerance of romance and chivalry.[82] This unjust conclusion was derived no doubt from the tone of greater confidence that Hurd was able to assume. Following both the Wartons, he sharpened the distinction between the prevailing pseudo-classical school of poetry and what he called the Gothic; insisted upon the independence of its standards; and even maintained the superiority of its subjects.[83] In all this however he made no real departure from Warton, the difference being one of emphasis; Hurd gave an important impetus to the movement his master had begun. But with all his modernity, his admiration for the growing school of imaginative poets, he lacked Warton's faith in his school; he had no forward view, but looked back on the past with regret, and toward the future without hope.[84]

On the side of pure literary criticism Warton's first and most important follower was his elder brother, Joseph, whose *Essay on Pope* was a further application of his critical theories to the reigning favourite. This very remarkable book was the first extensive and serious attack upon Pope's supremacy as a poet, and it is credited with two very important contributions to the romantic movement: the overthrow of Pope and his school; and the substitution of new models, Spenser, Shakespeare, Milton, and the modern school;[85] it contained the first explicit statement of the new poetic theories.[86]

Warton's **Observations on the Faerie Queene** thus wrought so great and so salutary a change in literary criticism that it is hardly possible to exaggerate its importance. Here first the historical method was appreciated and extensively employed. Here first the pseudo-classicism of the age of Pope was exposed. Here first is maintained a nice and difficult balance between classical and romantic criticism: without underestimating the influence of classical literature upon the development of English poetry, Warton first insisted that due attention be paid the neglected literature of the Middle Ages, which with quite independent but equally legitimate traditions contributed richly not only to the poetry of Spenser but to all great poetry since. His strength lies in the solidity and the inclusiveness of his critical principles. Without being carried away by romantic enthusiasm to disregard the classics, he saw and accounted for a difference between modern and ancient poetry and adapted his criticism to poetry as he found it instead of trying to conform poetry to rules which were foreign to it. This new criticism exposed the fatal weakness in the prevailing pseudo-classical poetry and criticism; it showed the folly of judging either single poems or national literatures as independent and detached, and the necessity of considering them in relation to the national life and literature to which they belong. Thus Warton's freedom from prejudice and preconceived standards, his interest in the human being who writes poetry, and the influences both social and literary which surround him, his—for that day—extraordinary knowledge of all those conditions, enabled him to become the founder of a new school of criticism.

Notes

1. London, 1754. Second edition, corrected and enlarged, 2 vols. 1762. References are to the third edition, 2 vols., 1807.

2. *Essay on Satire.*

3. *Spectator,* Jan. to May, 1712.

4. *Spectator,* No. 540.

5. *A Short View of Tragedy,* 1693. See Chapter V.

6. *Observations.* I, p. 21.

7. *Hist. Eng. Poetry,* 1774, 1778, 1781. Milton's *Poems upon Several Occasions.* 1785.

8. Hughes, *Remarks on the Fairy Queen* prefixed to Spenser's *Works,* 2nd. ed. 1750. I, p. lxvii.

9. Prior: *Ode to the Queen, written in imitation of Spenser's Style.* 1706. Preface. Whitehead: *Vision of Solomon,* 1739, and two *Odes to the Hon. Charles Townsend.* Boyse: *The Olives an Heroic Ode, etc. in the stanza of Spenser* (ababcdcdee) 1736-7. *Vision of Patience: an Allegorical Poem; Psalm XLII: In imitation of the Style of Spenser* (ababcc, no Alexandrine) 1740. Blacklock: *Hymn to Divine Love,* and *Philantheus* (ababbcc) 1746. T. Warton, Sr.: *Philander* (ababcc) 1748. Lloyd: *Progress of Envy* (ababcdcdd) 1751. Smith: *Thales* (ababbccc) 1751. See W. L. Phelps: *Beginnings of the English Romantic Movement.* Boston, 1902. Ch. on Spenserian Revival, and Appendix I, for a more complete list.

10. Pope: *The Alley,* date unknown, an exercise in versification, and ill-natured burlesque. Croxall: *Two Original Cantos of the Fairy Queen.* 1713 and 1714. Akenside: *The Virtuoso,* 1737, mild satire. G. West: *Abuse of Travelling,* 1739, satire. Cambridge: *Archimage,* 1742-50, a clever parody. Shenstone: *The School-mistress,* 1742, satirical. Pitt: *The Jordan,* 1747, vulgar burlesque. Ridley: *Psyche,* 1747, moral allegory. Mendez: *The Seasons,* 1751, *Squire of Dames,* 1748-58. Thomson: *Castle of Indolence,* 1748. See also Phelps, as above.

11. Such slips as 'nor ceasen he from study' and 'he would oft ypine' in Akenside's *Virtuoso* and even Thomson's note. 'The letter *y* is frequently placed in the beginning of a word by Spenser to lengthen it a syllable; and *en* at the end of a word for the same reason.' Glossary to the *Castle of Indolence.*

12. I cannot agree with Professor Phelps that, 'as people persisted in admiring *The Schoolmistress* for its own sake, he finally consented to agree with them, and in later editions omitted the commentary explaining that the whole thing was done in jest'. *The Beginning of the English Romantic Movement,* p. 66. On the contrary, it seems pretty clear that although Shenstone had probably not come to any very profound appreciation of the older poet, his admiration for him became more and more serious, but that he lacked the courage of his convictions, and conformed outwardly with a public opinion wholly ignorant of Spenser. Two later letters of Shenstone's indicate pretty clearly that it was he, and not 'the people', whose taste for Spenser had developed. In November, 1745, he wrote to Graves (to whom he had written of his early contempt) that he had read Spenser once again and 'added full as much more to my *School-mistress,* in regard to *number of lines; something in* point of *matter* (or *manner* rather), *which* does not displease me. I would be glad if Mr.————were, upon your request, to give his opinion of particulars,' etc. Evidently the judgment was unfavorable, for he wrote the next year, 'I thank you for your perusal of that trivial poem. If I were going to print it, I should give way to your remarks *implicitly,* and would not *dare* to do otherwise. But so long as I keep it in manuscript, you will pardon my silly prejudices, if I chuse to read and shew it with the addition of most of my new stanzas. I own, I have a fondness for several, imagining them to be *more* in Spenser's way, yet

more independent on the antique phrase, than any part of the poem; and, on that account, I cannot yet prevail on myself to banish *them* entirely; but were I to print, I should (with *some* reluctance) give way to your sentiments.' Shenstone's *Works.* 1777. III, pp. 105-6.

13. And the first attempt at an annotated edition. *Spenser's Works, to which is prefix'd . . . an Essay on Allegorical Poetry* by Mr. Hughes. 6 vols. London, 1715. Second edition, 1750. There is a second preface, *Remarks on the Fairy Queen.* References are to the second edition.

14. *Remarks on the Fairy Queen.* I, p. xliii.

15. *Essay on Allegorical Poetry,* I, p. xxi.

16. *Remarks on the Fairy Queen,* I, p. xlii.

17. *Ibid.* I, p. xliv.

18. *Ibid.* I, p. xl. *Essay on Allegorical Poetry.*

19. *Ibid.* I, p. l.

20. The neglect of Spenser is best shown by the few editions of either the *Fairy Queen* or the complete works which had appeared since the first three books of the former were published in 1590. *Faerie Queene,* 1st. ed. 4to. 1590-6; 2nd, 1596; 3rd, fol., 1609; Birch ed. 3 vols. 4to. 1751. *Poetical Works.* 1st fol. ed. 1611; 2nd, 1617-18; 3rd, 1679. Hughes, 1st ed. 1715, 2nd, 1750.

21. Jortin's conclusion quoted in Nichols's *Literary Anecdotes,* II, p. 53. H. E. Cory says nothing of Jortin's *Remarks* in his monograph, *The Critics of Edmund Spenser,* Univ. of California *Pub. in Mod. Phil.* II; 2, pp. 71-182.

22. Dryden had done the same thing in the *Dedication to the Translation of Juvenal* by pointing out how the character of Prince Arthur 'shines throughout the whole poem,' and Warton took issue squarely with him on the point and denied any such unity. See *Observations,* I, p. 10-11. Addison used the same method in his papers on *Paradise Lost.* Beni was probably the originator of this sort of misapplied criticism in his comparison of Tasso with Homer and Virgil. I, p. 3.

23. *Ibid.* I, p. 11 ff.

24. *Ibid.* I, p. 17.

25. *Ibid.* I, p. 18.

26. *Ibid,* I, p. 21.

27. *Ibid.* II, p. 72.

28. Warton used the word *romantic* as a derivative of *romance,* implying the characteristics of the mediæval romances, and I have used the word frequently in this chapter with that meaning.

29. *Ibid.* I, p. 22.

30. *Ibid.* I, p. 23.

31. Without the same precision in nomenclature but with equal clearness of idea Warton distinguished between creative and imaginative power in exactly the same way that Coleridge differentiated imagination and fancy. He did not compose exact philosophical definitions of the two qualities, but in a careful contrast between the poetic faculties of Spenser and Ariosto, he made the same distinction. Spenser's power, imagination, he described as creative, vital; it endeavours to body forth the unsubstantial, to represent by visible and external symbols the ideal and abstracted. (II, p. 77.) Ariosto's faculty, fancy, he called imitative, lacking in inventive power. (I, p. 308; II, p. 78.) Although Warton at times applied the term *imagination* loosely to both, there was no confusion of ideas; when he used both terms it was with the difference in meaning just described. In speaking of the effect of the marvels of romance upon the poetic faculty he said they 'rouse and invigorate all the powers of imagination' and 'store the fancy with . . . images.' (II, p. 323.)

32. *Ibid.* I, p. 24.

33. *Rasselas.* Ch. XLIV.

34. H. C. Robinson: *Diary.* Ed. Sadler, Boston 1870, II, p. 43.

35. *Obs.* I, pp. 168-170.

36. In his opinion that 'Spenser, in affecting the ancients, writ no language'. I, p. 184.

37. *Ibid.* I, p. 185. This parallel does not greatly help the case in an age when Atterbury could write to Pope that he found 'the hardest part of Chaucer . . . more intelligible' than some parts of Shakespeare and that 'not merely through the faults of the edition, but the obscurity of the writer.' Pope's *Works,* Elwin-Courthope ed. IX, p. 26.

38. *Obs.* II, p. 71.

39. Warton ably and sharply met Pope's attack on Theobald for including in his edition of Shakespeare a sample of his sources, of '"———All such reading as never was read",' and concluded 'If Shakespeare is worth reading, he is worth explaining; and the researches used for so valuable and elegant a purpose, merit the thanks of genius and candour, not the satire of prejudice and ignorance.' II, p. 319. In similar vein he rebuked such of his own critics as found his quotations from the romances 'trifling and uninteresting': 'such readers can have no taste for Spenser.' I, p. 91.

40. *Ibid.* II, pp. 317-18.

41. *Ibid.* I, p. 26.

42. And even later to the time of Milton. Warton found Milton's 'mind deeply tinctured with romance reading' and his imagination and poetry affected

thereby. I, p. 257 and p. 350. Even Dryden wanted to write an epic about Arthur or the Black Prince but on the model of Virgil and Spenser, not Spenser and the romances. *Essay on Satire.*

43. *Obs.* I, p. 27 and II, pp. 71-72. Warton cited Holinshed's Chronicles (Stowe's contin.) where is an account of a tourney for the entertainment of Queen Elizabeth, in which Fulke Greville and Sir Philip Sidney, among others, entered the lists. Holin. *Chronicles,* ed. 1808. IV, p. 437 ff.

44. Warton quotes Laneham's '*Letter wherein part of the Entertainment untoo the Queen's Majesty at Killinworth Castl in Warwicksheer in this Soomer's progress, 1575, is signified,*' and Gascoigne's *Pleasures of Kenilworth Castle, Works,* 1576. *Obs.* I, pp. 41, 43.

45. *Ibid.* I, pp. 50-74.

46. *Ibid.* I, pp. 53-57.

47. *Ibid.* I, pp. 27-57.

48. *Ibid.* I, pp. 69-71.

49. *Ibid.* I, p. 76. Warton says an 'ingenious correspondent communicated' to him this 'old ballad or metrical romance.' Part of *Le Court Mantel* he found in Sainte Palaye's *Memoires sur l'ancienne Chevalerie,* 1760. Other details, which could not be traced to particular romances, Warton attributed to 'a mind strongly tinctured with romantic ideas.' One of these, the custom of knights swearing on their swords, Upton had explained as derived from the custom of the Huns and Goths, related by Jornandes and Ammianus Marcellinus, but Warton pointed out that it was much more probably derived from the more familiar romances. II, p. 65. A Bodleian MS. containing *Sir Degore* and other romances is quoted from and described, II, pp. 5-9.

50. *Ibid.* I, pp. 77-89. Warton often used the terms Celtic and Norse very loosely without recognizing the difference. Like Huet and Mallet and other students of romance he was misled by the absurd and fanciful ethnologies in vogue in the 17th and 18th centuries. For his theory of romance see his dissertation 'On the Origin of Romantic Fiction in Europe' prefixed to the first volume of his *History of English Poetry,* 1774.

51. *Essay on Satire.* Dryden frequently referred to Chaucer as Spenser's master, meaning in the matter of language. See also *Dedication of the Pastorals* and *Preface to the Fables.*

52. Section V 'Of Spenser's Imitations from Chaucer.'

53. In his *Remarks on Spenser's Poems.* See *Observations* I, p. 190.

54. *Ibid.* I, p. 205. Warton showed many instances of Spenser's interest in Cambuscan, including his continuation of part of the story. See also pp. 210 ff.

55. *Ibid.* I, p. 221.

56. Warton found opportunity to express more fully his enthusiasm for Chaucer in a detailed study comparable to this of Spenser, in his *History of English Poetry* twenty years later.

57. *Obs.* I, pp. 269-71. Warton extended his criticism to translations of classical authors as well. Of course the greatest of the classicists, Dryden and Johnson, realized the limits of translation, that it was only a makeshift. See *Preface* to translation of Ovid's epistle, to *Sylvæ* and to the *Fables,* and Boswell's *Johnson,* Hill ed. III, p. 36. But the popularity of Dryden's translations and the large number of translations and imitations that appeared during his and succeeding generations, justified Warton's criticism.

58. *Obs.* II, p. 78.

59. *Ibid.* II, pp. 78-81. 'Spenser expressly denominates his most exquisite groupe of allegorical figures, the *Maske of Cupid.* Thus, without recurring to conjecture, his own words evidently demonstrate that he sometimes had representations of this sort in his eye.'

60. *Ibid.* II, pp. 93-103. Beginning with Adam Davy and the author of *Piers Plowman.* Like Spence, Warton recognized in Sackville's *Induction* the nearest approach to Spenser, and a probable source of influence upon him.

61. *Ibid.* II, p. 92.

62. *Ibid.* I, pp. 92-156.

63. *Ibid.* I, p. 147.

64. *Ibid.* I, p. 133.

65. *Ibid.* I, p. 1.

66. *Ibid.* I, p. 2.

67. *Ibid.* II, pp. 324-5.

68. *Ibid.* II, pp. 322-3.

69. There is a digression on Milton in the *Observations* (I, pp. 335-351), the prelude to his edition of Milton, 1785 and 1791.

70. *Ibid.* II, pp. 106-8.

71. In his critical essays in the *Spectator.*

72. July 16, 1754. 'I now pay you a very honest acknowledgement, for the advancement of the literature of our native country. You have shewn to all, who shall hereafter attempt the study of our ancient authours, the way to success; by directing them to the perusal of the books which those authours had read. Of this method, Hughes and men much greater than Hughes, seem never to have thought. The reason why the authours, which are yet read, of the sixteenth century, are so little understood, is, that they are read alone; and no help is borrowed from those who lived with them, or before them.' Boswell's *Johnson,* Hill ed. I, p. 270.

73. Warburton's *Letters,* No. CLVII, Nov. 30, 1762. *Works,* London, 1809. XIII, p. 338.

74. Walpole to Warton, October 30, 1767. Walpole's *Letters,* ed. cit. VII, p. 144.

75. August, 1754, XI, pp. 112-124.

76. Perhaps Upton's Edition of the *Fairy Queen,* which is frequently referred to in the second edition of the *Observations.* There is ample evidence in Johnson's letters and Warton's comments upon them, as well as in his own manuscript notes in his copy of Spenser's *Works* that he intended a companion work of remarks on the best of Spenser's works, but this made so little progress that it cannot have been generally known. See Boswell's *Johnson,* I, p. 276, and Warton's copy of Spenser's *Works,* ed. 1617. This quarto volume, which I have examined in the British Museum, contains copious notes which subsequently formed the basis for the *Observations.* The notes continue partly through the shorter poems as well as the *Fairy Queen.* Some of them were evidently made for the second edition, for they contain references to Upton's edition.

77. *Mon. Rev.* July, 1756, XV, p. 90. *Crit. Rev.* May, 1756, I, p. 374.

78. *An impartial Estimate of the Rev. Mr. Upton's notes on the Fairy Queen,* reviewed in *Crit. Rev.* VIII, p. 82 ff.

79. *Crit. Rev.* VII, p. 106.

80. H. E. Cory,: Op. cit., pp. 149-50.

81. While even Dr. Johnson had only praise for the *Observations,* Joseph Warton's *Essay on Pope,* on the whole a less revolutionary piece of criticism, touched a more sensitive point. He found the essay instructive, and recommended it as a 'just specimen of literary moderation.' Johnson's *Works,* ed. 1825, V, p. 670. But as an attack on the reputation of the favourite Augustan poet, its drift was evident, and pernicious. This heresy was for him an explanation of Warton's delay in continuing it. 'I suppose he finds himself a little disappointed, in not having been able to persuade the world to be of his opinion as to Pope.' Boswell's *Johnson,* I, p. 448.

82. *Crit. Rev.* XVI, p. 220. It is perfectly evident however that the debt does not lie on that side. Hurd's *Letters* and the second edition of the *Observations* appeared in the same year, which would almost conclusively preclude any borrowings from the first for the second. But Warton's first edition, eight years before, had enough of chivalry and romance to kindle a mind in sympathy. Hurd was a less thorough student of the old romances themselves than Warton was. He seems to have known them through a French work, probably Sainte Palaye's *Memoires sur l'Ancienne Chevalerie* (1750), for he said, 'Not that I shall make

a merit with you in having perused these barbarous volumes myself. . . . Thanks to the curiosity of certain painful collectors, this knowledge may be obtained at a cheaper rate. And I think it sufficient to refer you to a learned and very elaborate memoir of a *French* writer.' *Letters on Chivalry and Romance.* Letter IV, Hurd's *Works,* ed. 1811, IV, p. 260. Warton also knew this French work (Ste. Palaye's at least) and quoted from it, *Observations,* I, p. 76, and frequently in his *History of English Poetry.*

83. 'May there not be something in the *Gothic* Romance peculiarly suited to the views of a genius, and to the ends of poetry?' Hurd, IV, p. 239. 'Under this idea then of a Gothic, not classical poem, the *Fairy Queen* is to be read and criticized.' IV, p. 292. 'So far as the heroic and *Gothic* manners are the same, the pictures of each, . . . must be equally entertaining. But I go further, and maintain that the circumstances, in which they differ, are clearly to the advantage of the *Gothic* designers . . .' could Homer 'have seen . . . the manners of the feudal ages, I make no doubt but he would certainly have preferred the latter,' because of '"*the improved gallantry of the Gothic Knights*; and the *superior solemnity of their superstitions*".' IV, p. 280.

84. Hurd's *Letters,* IV, p. 350.

85. Joseph Warton placed Spenser, Shakespeare, Milton, 'our only three sublime and pathetic poets,' in the first class, at the head of English poets. The object of the essay was to determine Pope's place in the list. 'I revere the memory of POPE,' he said, 'I respect and honour his abilities; but I do not think him at the head of his profession. In other words, in that species of poetry wherein POPE excelled, he is superior to all mankind; and I only say, that this species of poetry is not the most excellent one of the art.' Dedication, pp. i-ii. 'The sublime and pathetic are the two chief nerves of all genuine poetry. What is there transcendently sublime or pathetic in POPE?' Ded., p. vi. After a careful examination of all Pope's works Joseph Warton assigned him the highest place in the second class, below Milton and above Dryden. He was given a place above other modern English poets because of the 'excellencies of his works *in general,* and *taken all together*; for there are *parts* and *passages* in other modern authors, in *Young* and in *Thomson,* for instance, equal to any of POPE, and he has written nothing in a strain so truly sublime, as the *Bard of Gray.*' II, p. 405. References are to the fifth edition, 2 vols. 1806.

86. The first volume of Joseph Warton's *Essay on Pope* appeared in 1756, two years after the *Observations.* Though its iconoclasm was more apparent, the later essay made little advance in the way of new theory upon the earlier one, and there is rather more of hedging in the discussion of Pope than in that of Spenser.

Joan Pittock (essay date 1973)

SOURCE: Pittock, Joan. "The Taste for the Gothic: Thomas Warton and the History of English Poetry." In *The Ascendancy of Taste: The Achievement of Joseph and Thomas Warton*, pp. 176-214. London: Routledge and Kegan Paul, 1973.

[*In the following essay, Pittock traces influences on "Gothic" poems by Warton and others and critiques his* History of English Poetry.]

I

When [Samuel] Johnson's *Dictionary* appeared in 1755 it contained no reference to the word 'Gothic'. Yet Horace Walpole had succumbed to the spell of Gothic architecture in building his castle at Strawberry Hill in 1750, and the vogue for Gothic as well as Chinese in design is attested by Robert Lloyd in his description of 'The Cit's County Box' (1757):

The traveller with amazement sees
A temple, Gothic or Chinese,
With many a bell or tawdry rag on
And crested with a sprawling dragon,
A ditch of water four foot wide . . .
With angles, curves, and zig-zag lines . . .

The taste for the nebulously exotic, wild or fanciful could be localised to best effect for several reasons in those periods of history which might be thought to have produced Gothic buildings. When Walpole published his *Castle of Otranto* in 1764 he subtitled it 'A Gothic Tale'. And as the Gothic novel developed in the work of Clara Reeve, Charlotte Smith, Ann Radcliffe and 'Monk' Lewis it held spellbound a reading public wider and more heterogeneous than ever before. So in *Northanger Abbey* (written in 1798) even the judicious Henry Tilney confesses himself incapable of leaving *The Mysteries of Udolpho* half-finished, while the story affords his girlish heroine not only 'the luxury of a raised, restless, and frightened imagination' but an inability to control her state of mind when she at last encounters an authentic abbey.

II

Clearly Gothic architecture was of less significance, culturally speaking, than the emotions it aroused by its associations, its suggestions of the manners and trappings of what was supposed to have been the medieval way of life. But the cultivation of a taste for the Gothic in the novel was to a considerable extent a continuation, at a culturally more sophisticated level, of the tales of heroic deeds, bloody murders and supernatural horrors which had been the fiction of the unrefined reading public as far back as the sixteenth century.

In the later seventeenth century 'Gothic' had become equivalent to rude, barbarous and uncouth: its primary connection after all was with the race of vandals which had overrun and demolished the civilisation of ancient Rome. For this reason it was inherently opposed to classicism, while the 'Gothic' in relation to the architecture and literature of the medieval period was likewise associated with whatever was extravagant, fanciful, wild and uncontrolled by the overall sense of design and function which was so pre-eminently the virtue of the buildings and literary forms of classical antiquity.

The difficulties of providing a definition for so potentially ambivalent a word are best illustrated by Addison. In the *Spectator*, no. 415, he compares the two types of architecture in terms of their effect on the mind:

Let any one reflect on the Disposition of Mind he finds in himself, at his first Entrance into the *Pantheon* at *Rome,* and how his Imagination is filled with something Great and Amazing; and, at the same time, consider how little, in proportion, he is affected with the inside of a *Gothick* Cathedral, tho' it be five times larger than the other; which can arise from nothing else but the Greatness of the Manner in the one, and the Meanness in the other.

But, somewhat paradoxically, in defending his admiration for the ballad of Chevy Chase, he removes the ballad from its historical context and employs it as a neoclassical touchstone of true taste:

I know nothing which more shews essential and inherent Perfection of Simplicity of Thought, above that which I call the Gothick Manner in Writing, than this, that the first pleases all Kinds of Palates, and the latter only such as have formed to themselves a wrong artificial Taste upon little fanciful Authors and Writers of Epigram. *Homer, Virgil, or Milton,* so far as the language of their poems is understood, will please a Reader of plain common Sense, who would neither relish nor comprehend an Epigram of *Martial,* or a Poem of *Cowley:* So, on the contrary, an ordinary Song or Ballad that is the Delight of the common People, cannot fail to please all such Readers as are not unqualified for the Entertainment by their Affectation or Ignorance; and the Reason is plain, because the same Paintings of Nature which recommend it to the most ordinary Reader, will appear Beautiful to the most refined.

(no. 70)

Cowley and Martial are, then, Gothic in their artificiality and fancifulness. But this was inevitably an ephemeral distinction, only sustained by the familiar Gothic-Grecian antithesis. More generally acceptable is the verdict on contemporary taste which I cited in chapter 1:

I look upon those writers as Goths in Poetry, who, like those in Architecture, not being able to come up to the Beautiful Simplicity of the old *Greeks* and *Romans,* have endeavoured to supply its Place with all the Extravagancies of an irregular Fancy. . . . The Taste of most of our *English* Poets, as well as Readers, is extremely *Gothick.*

To set the classical against the English tradition in this way is to associate the violations committed by Spenser and Shakespeare, for example, against the classical modes of composition in epic and tragedy, with the wild and fan-ciful exuberance of Gothic architecture. And so indeed John Hughes attempted to defend Spenser's *Faerie Queene* three years later, by suggesting that in structure it resembled a Gothic rather than a Grecian edifice. Pope employed the same analogy in expressing his appreciation of Shakespeare in 1725: Gothic architecture is 'more strong and solemn' than neat modern buildings; 'Nor does the whole fail to strike us with greater reverence, though many of the parts are childish, ill placed and unequal to its grandeur.'

III

In his account of *The Gothic Revival* Sir Kenneth Clark quoted the analogy employed by Hughes and Pope to show that although[1]

> These two passages have been much quoted by histori-ans of literature to prove that Gothic architecture influ-enced literary taste. . . . I think the reverse is true. We accept as almost axiomatic the generalisation that in England a love and understanding of literature greatly exceeds, and indeed swamps, appreciation of the visual arts; and a new current of taste is likely to be first felt in a literary channel. Shakespeare and Spenser would be appreciated before a Gothic cathedral; and in fact it was the analogous forms of these great writers which shed lustre on the despised architectural style. Above all it was Shakespeare, so unmistakably great in defi-ance of all the rules of Aristotle, who broke the back of classical prejudice. If Aristotle's rules could be defied with success, why not those of Vitruvius too? Gothic architecture crept in through a literary analogy.

But the experience derived from the poetry of Spenser or the plays of Shakespeare could not be justified seriously enough to counter criticisms of defects in structure and tone merely in terms of an architectural analogy. Sir Ken-neth Clark himself concluded that the writers of the Gothic novel:

> have their place in the Gothic Revival because they show the frame of mind in which the multitude of novel-readers looked at medieval buildings. But if we search the second half of the eighteenth century for lit-erary influences on the Gothic Revival we need not spend time on the *Castle of Otranto*'s offspring, but on those books which show a real interest in the middle age, a veneration for its arts and manners, and a serious study of its monuments.

We are in the province not only of imaginative response to literature but of antiquarianism and scholarship:

> When antiquarianism reappears as a vital interest it is in the persons of Gray and Warton. Now Gray and Warton were poets. Their enthusiasm for Gothic springs from a literary impulse which first made itself felt as antiquarianism was beginning to decline. This literary impulse, if anything, can be called the true starting-point of the Gothic revival.

IV

If indeed there was a decline in antiquarianism—though the Society of Antiquarians was incorporated in 1751—it was chiefly in terms of its social acceptability. The study of the abstruse and recondite to no socially useful end had been pilloried by Pope when he placed Thomas Hearne in the third book of his 'Dunciad' (1728):

> 'But who is he, in closet close y-pent,
> Of sober face, with learned dust besprent?'
> 'Right well mine eyes arede the myster wight,
> On parchment scraps y-fed, and Wormius hight.
> To future ages may thy dulness last,
> As thou preserv'st the dulness of the past!
> 'There, dim in clouds, the poring Scholiasts mark,
> Wits, who like Owls, see only in the dark,
> A Lumberhouse of Books in ev'ry head,
> For ever reading, never to be read!'

(185-94)

The cultural gap between the antiquarian and the man of taste narrowed as the study of registers and chronicles be-came essential to the work of the scholar and critic. The work of editors like Warton, Percy and Ritson was only made possible by the perseverance of those whom Pope had so lightly dismissed. Hearne's editions of the chronicles of Robert of Gloucester (1724) and Peter Langtoft (1725), Ames's *Typographical Antiquities* (1749), with its description of the contents of Malory's *Morte Darthur,* Walpole's *Catalogue of Royal and Noble Authors* (1758) augmented the earlier work of Bale, Camden, Leland, A Wood, and their successors, Oldys, Wanley and Hickes. New areas of literary enquiry were opened up by the cataloguing of manuscript collections. Oxford Univer-sity published a catalogue of manuscripts in 1697; Wanley's catalogue of the Harleian collection, published by order of the trustees of the British Museum in 1759, contained substantial extracts from some of the entries; and in 1767 the Oxford University published a catalogue of the manuscripts held by the Oxford and Cambridge col-leges. Abroad St Palaye published his *Mémoires de l'Ancienne Chévalerie* in 1759.

The publication of early literature, whether in the reprint-ing of *England's Helicon,* or *Tottel's Miscellany,* Dodsley's *Select Collection of Old Plays* (1744), or in contemporary collections like those of Ramsay, met a demand not from scholars so much as from the general public. So Shenstone wrote to Percy in 1760 urging him to publish the manu-script ballad, song and romance material which he had dis-covered, but not without making certain alterations and improvements which would adapt the original material to the taste of the general reader, for[2]

> All People of Taste throu'out the Kingdom will rejoice to see a judicious, a correct and elegant collection of such Pieces. For after all, 'tis such Pieces that contain ye true Chemical Spirit or Essence of Poetry, a little of which properly mingled is sufficient to strengthen and keep alive very considerable Quantities of the kind. 'Tis ye voice of Sentiment rather y^n the the Language of Reflection, and adapted peculiarly to strike ye Pas-sions, which is the only Merit of Poetry that has ob-tained my regard of late.

Shenstone was proved right. And after all it was Macpherson who by decking out legendary scraps with biblical cadences and contemporary sentiments achieved so great a success with *Ossian.* The cultivation of the public taste had never blended more happily with the growth of a sense of historical perspectives and an illuminating and revivifying range of imaginative expression in earlier literature. When Warton discovered James I's *Kingis Quair* Percy wrote to him at Oxford:[3]

> Were I at the fountain head of literature, as you are, I should be tempted to transcribe some of the curiosities that lie mouldering in your libraries for publication—I am persuaded this of James would be acceptable to the public, both to the Antiquarians and men of taste:—this and two or three other such pieces would make an additional volume to the *Ever green* or Collection of ancient Scots poems of which a second Edition has lately been called for.

There was a general uneasiness felt among scholars lest they should appear to their potential public as too pedantic, though their keen interest in exact scholarly enquiry is illustrated in the mid-century correspondence between Percy and his collaborators—Warton, Evans, Farmer, Malone, Shenstone and Johnson. So Warton explains to his readers the need for the investigation into the use of romance, allegory and legend by Spenser in writing the *Faerie Queene*:

> In reading the works of an author who lived in a remote age, it is necessary, that we should look back upon the customs and manners which prevailed in his age; that we should place ourselves in his situation, and circumstances; that so we may be the better enabled to judge and discern how his turn of thinking, and manner of composing were biass'd, influenc'd, and, as it were, tinctur'd, by very familiar and reigning appearances, which are utterly different from those with which we are at present surrounded. For want of this caution, too many readers view the knights and damsels, the turnaments and enchantments of Spenser with modern eyes, never considering that the encounters of Chivalry subsisted in an author's age, as as has been before hinted; that romances were then most eagerly and universally read; and that thus, Spenser from the fashion of his age, was naturally dispos'd to undertake a recital of Chivalrous achievements, and to become, in short, a Romantic Poet.

> (p. 217)

Spenser was, then, a poet conditioned by his environment as much as Blackwell and Wood had shown Homer to have been, and in the same way as Lowth had demonstrated the relationship between the style and subject-matter of the Scriptures and the customs and environment of the Hebrews.

As he shows in his use of terms in the 1765 *Preface* Johnson was quick to see the potentialities of this approach as a way out of the stalemate at which criticism seem to have arrived in working according to the requirements of ideal forms. He wrote to congratulate Warton on his achievement in a well-known letter:

> You have shewn to all, who shall hereafter attempt the study of our ancient authors, the way to success; by directing them to the perusal of the books which these

authors had read. Of this method, Hughes and men much greater than Hughes, seem never to have thought. The reason why the authours, which are yet read, of the sixteenth century, are so little understood, is, that they are read alone; and no help is borrowed from those who lived with them, or before them.

> (*Life,* p. 190)

A second enlarged edition of the ***Observations*** came out in two volumes in 1762, in the same year as Hurd's *Letters on Chivalry and Romance.* Warton had, then, eight years earlier, already suggested what Hurd specifically undertook, a defence of the manners of chivalry as the most promising subject-matter for poetry; though he does not imply as Hurd does that the classical authors might have benefited from an acquaintance with chivalry and romance: the myths and legends of antiquity had, after all, afforded a similar repository of superstition and fancy. In the ***Observations*** of 1754 he wrote:

> Though the Faerie Queene does not exhibit that economy of plan, and exact arrangement of parts which Epic severity requires, yet we scarcely regret the loss of these, while their place is so amply supplied, by something which more powerfully attracts us, as it engages the affection of the heart, rather than the applause of the head; and if there be any poem whose graces please, because they are situated beyond the reach of art, and where the faculties of creative imagination delight us, because they are unassisted and unrestrained by those of deliberate judgment, it is in this of which we are now speaking. To sum up all in a few words; tho' in the Faerie Queene we are not satisfied as critics, yet we are transported as readers.

> (pp. 12-13)

The distinction Warton makes here between the reader and the critic is one which he shows applies equally to the poet and the critic. He concludes his postscript to the work with a quotation from Spenser in which the critic identifies himself with the statements of the poet:

> The waies thro' which my weary steps I guide,
> In this Delightful Land of Faery,
> Are so exceeding spacious and wide,
> And sprinkled with such sweet varietie
> Of all that pleasant is to ear or eye
> That I nigh ravisht with rare thought's delight,
> My tedious travel do forgett thereby,
> And when I gin to feel decay of might,
> It strength to me supplies, and cheares my dulled spright.

The same reaction to Spenser was expressed by Goldsmith in the *Critical Review* for February 1759:

> There is a pleasing tranquillity of mind which ever attends the reading of this ancient poet. We leave the ways of the present world, and all the ages of primeval innocence and happiness rise to our view. . . . The imagination of his reader leaves reason behind, pursues the tale without considering the allegory, and upon the whole, is charmed without instruction.

Gray told Nicholls that 'he never sat down to compose poetry without reading Spenser for a considerable time previously',[4] and it was Gray whose odes, published at Strawberry Hill by Walpole in 1757, were a deliberate attempt to recreate the tone and subject-matter of Gothic poetry.

The enriching of the poet's imagination as well as the illumination and pleasure of the general reader were effected by Spenser, and these two ends were those which Shenstone had referred to as the impression created by the early poetry which he was encouraging Percy to publish in the letter I quoted earlier. With Thomas Warton's work we move into more clearly defined areas of Gothic inspiration where the colleges of Oxford, and cathedrals, abbeys and castles alike summon up the visions, which were for him the province of true poetry, while through an omnivorous appetite for antiquities and a real sensitivity to the romantic elements in the poetry of Spenser and Milton he evolves for the first time an interpretation of the development of a history of English poetry.

V

In 1748 William Mason published 'Isis', an elegy attacking the political principles and the dissipation of Oxford. The following year Thomas Warton, then aged twenty-one, replied in **'The Triumph of Isis',** acclaiming Oxford as a bastion of enlightenment and a haunt of the Muses:

> Green as of old each olived portal smiles,
> And still the Graces build my Grecian piles:
> My Gothic spires in ancient glory rise,
> And dare with wonted pride to rush into the skies.
>
> (77-80)

It is the Gothic aspect of Oxford rather than the Grecian which is seen as the stimulus to reflection which awakens the poetic sensibility:

> Ye fretted pinnacles, ye fanes sublime,
> Ye towers that wear the mossy vest of time;
> Ye massy piles of old munificence,
> At once the pride of learning and defence;
> Ye cloisters pale, that, lengthening to the sight,
> To contemplation, step by step, invite;
> Ye high-arch'd walks, where oft the whispers clear
> Of harps unseen have swept the poet's ear;
> Ye temples dim, where pious duty pays
> Her holy hymns of ever-echoing praise;
> Lo! your loved Isis, from the bordering vale,
> With all a mother's fondness bids you hail!
>
> (149-60)

The poet's dedication to his vision connects Spenser's *Faerie Queene* with Milton's minor poems—there is the poet's awareness of his vocation in 'Lycidas' and the indulgence in contemplation as a means of gaining access to a variety of worlds in 'Il Penseroso'. Of Milton's description of the 'embowed roof' in this last poem Warton writes in the second edition of the ***Observations***:

Impressions made in earliest youth, are ever afterwards most strongly felt; and I am inclin'd to think, that Milton was first affected with, and often indulged the pensive pleasure, which the awful solemnity of a Gothic church conveys to the mind, and which is here so feelingly described, while he was a schoolboy at St. Paul's. The church was then in its original Gothic state, and one of the noblest patterns of that kind of architecture.

> (ii, 135)

Such solemn glooms were congenial to the youthful Warton's soul (his first poem of note, written when he was only seventeen, is **'The Pleasures of Melancholy'**) as they were, he thought, to the poets he loved best.

But Warton shows, too, an awareness of the danger inherent in prolonged introspection on the part of the poet. In **'The Suicide',** for example, which Goethe mentions as influencing the sensibility of young Werther, the Muse is responsible for filling the poet's 'soft ingenious mind / With many a feeling too refined' so that

> More wounds than Nature gave he knew,
> While Misery's form his fancy drew
> In dark ideal hues, and sorrows not its own.
>
> (46-7, 52-4)

Later Warton made what has been regarded as a repudiation of his allegiance to the Gothic in his **'Verses on Sir Joshua Reynold's Painted Window at New College, Oxford'** (1778). He describes himself as having been:

> A faithless truant to the classic page,—
> Long have I lov'd to catch the simple chime
> Of minstrel harps, and spell the fabling rime.
>
> (8-10)

He dwells on the attractions of the Gothic at length, whilst assigning a controlling role to those of the Grecian:

> . . . chief, enraptured have I loved to roam,
> A lingering votary, the vaulted dome,
> Where the tall shafts, that mount in massy pride,
> Their mingling branches shoot from side to side;
> Where elfin sculptors with fantastic clue,
> O'er the long roof their wild embroidery drew;
> Where Superstition, with capricious hand,
> In many a maze the wreathed window plann'd,
> With hues romantic tinged the gorgeous pane.
>
> (17-25)

But as he looks at Reynolds's window he acknowledges the power of formal design and lucidity of colour:

> Sudden, the sombrous imagery is fled,
> Which late my visionary rapture fed;
> Thy powerful hand has broke the Gothic chain,
> And brought my bosom back to truth again;
> To truth by no peculiar taste confined,
> Whose universal pattern strikes mankind;
> To truth, whose bold and unresisted aim
> Checks frail caprice, and Fashion's fickle claim;

To truth, whose charms deception's magic quell,
And bind coy Fancy in a stronger spell.

(61-70)

In Reynolds's window the Graces are wedded to 'the Gothic pile'. The Grecian is necessary to ensure permanence of appeal in checking the subjective waywardness of individual fancy. One might perhaps see this as reflecting the two aspects of taste at this time: the public and social taste which is a matter for critical discrimination and assessment according to recognisable and generally acknowledged principles, that taste which operates to establish standards and to 'improve opinion into knowledge'; and secondly, in the taste for the Gothic, that encouragement of an actively responsive sensibility, necessary to arouse in the reader, essential to stimulate the creative energy of the poet.

But to Warton the Grecian also was a source of poetical delight. He devoted his lectures in his two terms as Professor of Poetry at Oxford (1756-66) to Greek poetry. In his inaugural lecture he shows a sensitive awareness of what is traditionally a vitally important but at this time neglected function of poetry.

In itself, he says, the reading of poetry nourishes the faculties of man and enlarges his potentialities for assimilating different kinds of wisdom:[5]

> the man who has spent his leisure for a time on these more polite and refined letters will thereafter follow up the more exacting and abstruse literature with greater acumen and with a mind more nimble and more ready to tackle any study you wish; he has also prepared for himself this pleasure in which he can withdraw into a tranquil haven from the tension of thought, and in which, exhausted and over-whelmed by over-work he can take refuge and find rest.

This, he concludes, is because:

> We humans are so shaped in our inner selves, there exists in us such a kind of delicate and fastidious feeling, that we are by no means content with things as they in fact are, suffering as we do from a certain dryness (to confess the truth) and poverty. . . . In all things . . . we strive for an outward beauty and charm. And human nature seems to seek out this end, that somewhere there may be accorded a place to that which we call refined and tasteful.

So he enlarges on the beauties of natural scenery as the divine provision made for this end, and, as he makes clear in his edition of Theocritus (comparing the pastorals of Theocritus with those of Virgil) it is the particular selection of detail which alerts the reader to an imaginative participation in the experience evoked by such a scene. This use of detail accounts to Warton for the superiority of Theocritus. 'Virgil becomes thin and meagre where Theocritus, treating the same matter, becomes fuller, copious and richer, because Theocritus describes things fully whereas Virgil only hints at them.' The pastorals of

Theocritus as compared with those of Virgil exemplify beauty as opposed to mere symmetry and refinement. 'They (the pastorals of Theocritus) were beautiful precisely because they preserved the unevenness of actual life.' (preface). Of the description of the cup in the first idyll Warton comments: 'the work [on the cup] consists of pastoral images, beautiful and brilliant. In selecting these the taste of the poet is seen no less than his invention. . . . I easily prefer the fulness of Theocritus to the dryness and sparseness of Virgil' (i, 5n. line 27).

And in much of his own poetry he evokes the beauty of the natural scene with what is essentially an attempt at a similar delicacy and exactness. Although he begins his **'Ode on the First of April'** with the conventional classical personae:

> With dalliance rude young Zephyr woos
> Coy May,

he explores their significance on a different note: Spring creeps timidly upon the land:

> Scant along the ridgy land
> The beans their new-born ranks expand:
> The fresh-turn'd soil with tender blades
> Thinly the sprouting barley shades:
> Fringing the forest's devious edge,
> half robed appears the hawthorn hedge;
> Or to the distant eye displays
> Weakly green its budding sprays.

(27-34)

VI

The interests which have been traced so far account for the pattern of Warton's work. He spent his life in Oxford, where he became Fellow of Trinity in 1750, Professor of Poetry in 1756 and Camden Professor of Ancient History in 1785; he occupied his leisure with his brother in Winchester College or travelling round the country examining buildings and landmarks of architectural, historical or legendary interest. His observations on these fill several notebooks and are still unpublished, though some of this work was used (in illustrating places mentioned by poets) in **The History of English Poetry** and in his edition of Milton's *Poems on Several Occasions*.

His work falls under three main heads. First, there is the working out of an English poetic tradition which he explored in the **Observations on the Faerie Queene** (1754); the **History** (1774, 1778 and 1781); his **Enquiry into the Authenticity of the Poems attributed to Thomas Rowley** (1782), and lastly his edition of Milton's minor poems (1785). The second group consists of work in classical literature: his edition of the *Inscriptionum Romanarum Metricarum Delectus* (1758) accompanied the delivery of his still unpublished lectures on the Greek writers to which I have already referred; the *Anthologia Graeca* appeared in 1766; and in 1770, with a prefatory essay which was an enlarged version of his lecture on pastoral poetry, his edition of Theocritus. Into the third group falls his antiquarian or topographical work: his *Description of Winchester* (1750), his *Specimen of a History of Oxfordshire* (1782), and the essay on Gothic architecture which originally appeared as part of the two-volume second edition of *Observations* (1762). The bulk of the material of the *Life and Literary Remains of Ralph Bathurst* (in two volumes, 1761), and of the *Life of Sir Thomas Pope* (1772), fall into this category, as they are closely connected with the history of the university and were produced by Warton as Fellow of Trinity under the spur of desire for preferment. There are, apart from these, odd contributions to the *Idler*—merely of entertainment value—and his popular and still amusing burlesque of the antiquarian pedantry of the language of guidebooks, *A Companion to the Guide and a Guide to the Companion* (1760). He became Camden Professor of Ancient History in 1785 and Poet Laureate in the same year. As laureate Warton is chiefly remarkable for contriving, as Peter Pindar noted, to slide off the Royal Occasion into Gothic inspiration with a happy and congenial irrelevance.

In *The New Rolliad* (no. 1, 1785) Warton is described as approaching the King with a 'certain hasty spasmodic mumbling, together with two or three prompt quotations from Virgil', and as associating the efficacy of his talent as laureate with 'mist, darkness, and obscurity' in connection with 'the sublime and mysterious topics' he touches on in his odes (pp. 284, 206-7). Throughout his career there is a continual intermingling of his different interests so that the sensitivity of the poet often guides the researches of the antiquarian and the concern for the standards of taste and exactness of scholarship augments the delight in the exuberance of fancy.

VII

Having given a retrospective account of English poetry before Spenser in *Observations* Warton adds: 'from the age of Spenser, we shall find, that it (poetry) principally consisted in visions and allegories. Fancy was a greater friend to the dark ages, as they are called, than is commonly supposed' (ii, 101-2). He appends a note: 'This subject may, probably, be one day considered more at large in a regular history.'

His work on the Greek poets, and his researches into manuscript material, collating texts or consulting editions on Percy's behalf as well as his own—in a letter to Shenstone of 1762 Percy refers to Warton's sparing no pains in pursuing this kind of research—encouraged this ambition. In a letter to Percy in 1765 Warton expresses his intention of writing the history, and asserts that his materials for it are 'almost ready'.

In 1766 Warton informs Percy that he has had to lay the work aside to prepare the edition of Theocritus which had been commenced in 1758, but in July 1768 he declares the publication of the edition imminent and promises himself 'another Excursion into Fairy Land'. In the following year

he declares: 'I am sitting down in good Earnest to write the History of English Poetry. It will be a large work; but as variety of materials have been long collected, it will be soon completed.'[6]

The preface to the *History* itself suggests that Warton's intention is eminently orthodox:

> In an age advanced to the highest degrees of refinement, that species of curiosity commences, which is busied in contemplating the progress of social life, in displaying the gradations of science, and in tracing the transitions from barbarism to civility.

Warton proceeds to insist on the sense of achievement which this must necessarily encourage, but apart from this social purpose there is another:

> In the mean time, the manners, monuments, customs, practices, and opinions of antiquity, by forming so strong a contrast with those of our own times, and by exhibiting human nature and human inventions in new lights, in unexpected appearances, and in various forms, are objects which forcibly strike a feeling imagination.

This development in the argument is immediately checked, however: 'Nor does this spectacle afford nothing more than a fruitless gratification to the fancy.' The element of delight in the fancy and exuberance of earlier poetry is to be kept under the control of the social purpose of the history—to educate the public taste.

But the end of the third volume, published in 1781, saw Warton embarking on a 'general View and Character of the Poetry of Queen Elisabeth's age' and the few sheets of the fourth volume printed in his lifetime contained only an account of the satires of Marston and Hall. Other manuscript material was found to contain an account of the Elizabethan sonnet, but it seems a reasonable conclusion that Warton had little inclination to bring the historical account of English poetry beyond the Elizabethan period. His biographer, Richard Mant, considers the nature of the task remaining to be completed:

> The next part of his employment was to have been a particular examination of this, our Augustan age of Poetry; and having, like Aeneas, surmounted the difficulties, and escaped from the obscurity, of Tartarus, he was now about to enter on the Elysian fields . . . But notwithstanding the enjoyment of these scenes must have been so congenial to his mind; though in his first edition of Milton's juvenile poems in 1785 he announces that speedily will be published the fourth and last volume of the History of English Poetry; and though four years had elapsed since the publication of the third volume, and five years afterwards elapsed between this notice and his death, the work (from what cause it does not appear) was never completed: whether it was that the long duration of the same employment had in the end occasioned disgust; or whether his subsequent attention was nearly engrossed by Milton, and thus diverted from the masters to their greater disciple . . . Certain . . . it is, that the work was never brought

to a conclusion, though the completion of it would
have entitled him to the receipt of a considerable sum:
and there is reason to believe, that not much was written beyond what is in the possession of the public.

(pp. l-li)

It was, in fact (as the reviewer of Mant's biography in the
Edinburgh Review to some extent realised), Warton's last
work, the edition of Milton's minor poems, which provided some kind of conclusion—and indeed the only one
which was logical—to the massive undertaking of the *History*. Referring to the edition of Milton's poems, the reviewer concludes: 'These commentaries and his observations on Spenser, may now be regarded as in some degree
supplemental to his great unfinished work on English
poetry' (ii, 258).

The drift of Warton's comments on these poems reveals a
preoccupation with Milton as a neglected old English poet,
the inheritor of the fictions and fable of his predecessors,
of the story of 'Cambuscan bold, Of Camball and of
Algarsife', of 'masque and antique pageantry'. It was this
which attracted Warton in the poetry of Milton, and it was
almost certainly through these early poems that part at
least of the magic and enchantment which were for Warton
associated with the literature of the age of chivalry and superstition made its appeal. Warton's emphasis on the way
in which Gothic and classical myth and legend go side by
side in Milton's poetry is a continuation of and a fitting
chronological conclusion to the interpretation of the nature
of poetry which emerges from the three completed volumes of the *History.*

VIII

This is to some degree confirmed by the way in which
Warton insisted on seeing the history of poetry evolve, a
way which, as he knew, ran counter to the interpretations
of Pope and Gray.

Outlines for the *History* exist in four different forms: the
first is a brief sketch among Warton's manuscript annotations to his copy of the *Faerie Queene*; the second is the
general survey of the development of poetry to the eighteenth century given in the *Observations*; the third was
printed from the Trinity College MSS. by Clarissa Rinaker;
and the fourth occurs in Warton's reply to a letter from
Hurd which had contained Gray's plan for a history.

The first is a note in Warton's hand on the blank leaf facing the title page of 'Prothalamion':

> The Rise and Progress of Allegoric Poetry in England
> 'till it's Consummation in Spenser, & it's Decline after
> him. We have the visionary Poet, or personification be-
> fore P. Plowman, who drew it from the Troubadours.
> After him came Chaucer, Gower, Lidgate, (Harding)
> Barclay, Hawes, Skelton bad. Sackville, Spenser and
> effects ended with Fletcher.

The account in the *Observations* begins:

> If we take a retrospect of english poetry from the age
> of Spenser, we shall find that it principally consisted in

the allegoric species; but that this species never received its absolute consummation till it appeared with
new lustre in the Faerie Queene . . .

(ii, 101)

Chaucer's invention and humour, Lydgate's improvements
in versification are considered; then Warton comes to
Stephen Hawes—'a name generally unknown, and not
mentioned by any compiler of the lives of english poets':

> This author was at this period the restorer of invention,
> which seems to have suffered a gradual degeneracy
> from the days of Chaucer. He not only revived, but im-
> proved, the antient allegoric vein, which Hardyng had
> almost entirely banished. Instead of that dryness of de-
> scription, so remarkably disgusting in many of his pre-
> decessors, we are by this poet often entertained with
> the luxuriant effusions of Spenser.

(ii, 104)

The rise of classical studies in the reign of Henry VIII is
related to a group of scholars 'and the Greek language, in
which are reposited the treasures of true learning now began to be taught and admir'd'; with Skelton poetry made
no advances in versification, nor was his allegorical poetry
remarkable. Reference is made to the allegorising successes of Lindsay and Dunbar, and to those of Sackville as
the precursor of Spenser. But:

> After the Fairy Queen, allegory began to decline, and
> by degrees gave way to a species of poetry whose im-
> ages were of the metaphysical and abstracted kind.
> This fashion evidently took it's rise from the predomi-
> nant studies of the times.
>
> Allegory, notwithstanding, unexpectedly rekindled
> some faint sparks of its native splendor, in the Purple
> Island of Fletcher, with whom it almost as soon disap-
> peared: when a poetry succeeded, in which imagination
> gave way to correctness, sublimity of description to
> delicacy of sentiment, and majestic imagery to conceit
> and epigram.

And he diagnoses the situation as it has affected the poetry
of his contemporaries:

> Poets began now to be more attentive to words than to
> things and objects. The nicer beauties of happy expres-
> sion were preferred to the daring strokes of great con-
> ception. Satire, that bane of the sublime, was imported
> from France. . . . The muses were debauched at court,
> and polite life, and familiar manners, became their only
> themes . . . The simple dignity of Milton was either
> entirely neglected, or mistaken for bombast and insi-
> pidity by the refined readers of a dissolute age, whose
> taste and morals were equally vitiated.

(ii, 110-12)

It is in the second edition, in which Warton had clearly become more confident of his own taste, that he explicitly
associates the rise of satire with this decline. After 'daring
strokes of great conception', Warton adds 'Satire, that
bane of the sublime, was imported from France'. He omits

from the opening pages of the second edition a reference to the 'bad taste' which prevailed when Spenser began to write the *Faerie Queene,* and he softens his earlier condemnation of Spenser's choosing to model his work on that of Ariosto rather than Tasso—Ariosto's superior in 'conduct and decorum'. Between 1754 and 1762 the attitude towards things Gothic, strange or fanciful had clearly moved from a condemnation of its uncouth barbarism to what was at least an interested curiosity.

The structuring of each account in terms of allegorical poetry is the most obvious feature too of the third sketch—a plan which was probably drafted some time in the 'fifties, as it repeats the reference to bad taste prevailing before Spenser which was rephrased to indicate a more neutral approach in the 1762 edition. Clarissa Rinaker comments that this draft is probably for the first volume as it was originally planned. The first item—the plan is again chronological in outline—refers to the Druids and Bards; the second to 'Pierce Plowman' as 'the first Allegorical Poem in our Tongue'; in the third Warton describes how 'The Allegoric inventive Vein seem'd in a little time to be lost'; fourth comes the revival of learning and the rise of polished verse with Wyatt and Surrey; lastly, 'A fine harvest of Poësy now shew'd itself in Q. Elizabeth's reign'.

IX

In 1770 Gray wrote, at Hurd's request, to Warton, who was by this time far advanced in his preparation of the first volume, offering his own sketch of a history and enquiring whether it corresponded with anything in Warton's own approach:[7]

> few of your friends have been better pleased than I, to find this subject, surely neither unentertaining nor unuseful, had fallen into hands so likely to do it justice; few have felt a higher esteem for your talents, your taste, and industry.

Gray's scheme is based on Pope's, which had appeared in Ruffhead's *Life* in 1769. It introduces the subject with a survey of Gothic and Saxon poetry. Gray bases his account on the assumption that there were different schools of poets, first, that of Provence to which Chaucer and his successors belonged; the second, the Italian school, which in turn influenced the lyric poetry of Surrey and his contemporaries. Next, in a fourth section, he deals with

> Spenser, his character: subject of his poem, allegoric and romantic, or Provençal invention; but his manner of tracing it borrowed from the second Italian School.— Drayton, Fairfax, Phineas Fletcher, Golding, Phaer, &c. This school ends in Milton.—A third Italian school, full of conceit, begun in Queen Elizabeth's reign, continued under James and Charles the First, by Donne, Crashaw, Cleveland, carried to its height by Cowley, and ending perhaps in Sprat.

Part V

> School of France, introduced after the Restoration— Waller, Dryden, Addison, Prior, and Pope—which has continued to our own times.

Walpole felt after reading Warton's *History* that Gray's plan had not been superseded and would have been far superior; and although Warton is writing after completing only the first volume it is obvious that this more systematic approach in terms of schools, influences and kinds of writing might have produced a more satisfactory treatment of the ways in which writing poetry in English had developed. Warton replied in a letter which raises points of considerable interest, while revealing his complete lack of grasp of the overall structuring his material would require:[8]

> Although I have not followed the plan, yet it is of great service to me, and throws light on many of my periods by giving connected views and details. I begin with such an introduction or general dissertation as you had intended, viz. on the Northern Poetry, with its introduction into England by the Danes and Saxons, and its duration. I then begin my history of the Conquest, which I write chronologically in sections, and continue as matter successively offers itself, in a series of regular annals, down to and beyond the Restoration. I think with you that dramatic poetry is detached from the idea of my work, that it requires a separate consideration and will swell the size of my book beyond all bounds. One of my sections, a very large one, is entirely on Chaucer, and will almost make my first volume, for I design two volumes in quarto. This first volume will soon be in the press. I should have said before that though I proceed chronologically, yet I often stand still to give some general view, as perhaps of a particular species of poetry, etc., and even anticipate sometimes for this purpose. These views often form one section, yet are interwoven with the tenor of the work, without interrupting my historical series. In this respect some of my sections have the effect of your parts or divisions.

The first three outlines of his survey show that what the letter to Gray implies has indeed happened. Warton is not so much concerned with historical developments in poetry, but with charting the fortunes of a type of poetry—that allegorical and inventive vein—which had for him the greatest appeal. His grounds for not employing the schemes of Pope or Gray he later enlarged on:

> To confess the real truth, upon examination and experiment, I soon discovered their mode of treating my subject, plausible as it is and brilliant in theory, to be attended with difficulties and inconveniences. . . . Like other ingenious systems, it sacrifices much useful intelligence to the observance of arrangement; and in the place of that satisfaction, which arises from a clearness and a fulness of information, seemed only to substitute the merit of disposition, and the praise of contrivance. The constraint imposed by a mechanical attention to this distribution, appeared to me to destroy that free exertion of research, with which such a history ought to be executed, and not easily reconcileable with that complication, variety, and extent of materials, which it ought to comprehend.
>
> (*Mant* [*The Poetical Works of the Late Thomas Warton, B.D.,* edited by Richard Mant], i, lxii-iii)

Warton's chief concern is not with standards or theories, but with research into, and making his readers acquainted with, the chief elements in that vein of poetic inspiration which had helped to produce England's greatest national poets. And this in consequence would improve the taste of his time.

X

Warton's plan for the *Observations* is based on an acceptance of current tools of analysis—the ways in which the author to be considered has imitated the work of his predecessors; the relationship between his style and his subject; and the chief characteristics of his poetry—in this case the allegorical. Spenser's indebtedness to the classical and Italian poets had received consideration from Warton's predecessors, Hughes and Upton. But, as Johnson noted in the letter I quoted earlier, Warton realised that a mass of popular romance and ballad material had been accessible to the poet. Employing therefore, an already accepted method of investigation Warton opened fresh perspectives of knowledge and established a new kind of relevance for popular literature and for the researches of the antiquarians.

For after establishing Spenser's indebtedness to the manners of chivalry and the literature of romance in section 10, 'Of Spenser's Allegorical Character', Warton goes on to mention the effects of public entertainments of his time on the invention of the allegory:

> Nor is it sufficiently consider'd, that a prevalent practice of Spenser's age contributed in a very considerable degree to make him an ALLEGORICAL POET. It should be remember'd that, in the age of which we are speaking, allegory was the subject and foundation of public shews and spectacles, which were then exhibited with a magnificence superior to that of former times; that the vices and virtues personify'd and represented by living actors, distinguish'd with their representative emblematical types, were generally introduc'd to constitute PAGEANTRIES, which were then the principal entertainments, and shewn not only in private, and upon the stage, but very frequently in the open streets, for solemnising any public occasion.

> (pp. 217-18)

Warton refers to Holinshed's description of the 'SHEW OF MANHOOD AND DESERT' at Norwich, and of a 'TURNEY' at Westminster. He draws the conclusion that 'Spenser's manner of allegorizing seems to have rather resulted from some of the spectacles just-mention'd, than from what he had red in Ariosto'. The researches of the antiquarian are demonstrated as necessary to a true understanding of the fabric of what was becoming more clearly recognisable as a complex and broad national literary heritage.

Warton points out that Spenser uses the allegory as a moral vehicle in the manner of Ariosto in book 1, but that his characteristic method is different from Ariosto's:

> In fact, Ariosto's species of Allegory does not so much consist in impersonating the virtues, vices, and affections of the mind, as in the adumbration of moral doc-

trine, under the actions of men and women. On this plan Spenser's allegories are sometimes formed: as in the first book, where the Red-crosse Knight or a TRUE CHRISTIAN . . . defeats the wiles of Archimago, or the DEVIL, &c.

> (pp. 219-20)

And he adds a footnote:

> It is observed by Plutarch, that 'Allegory is that, in which one thing is *related* and another *understood*'. Thus Ariosto RELATES the adventures of Orlando, Rogero, Bradamante, &c. by which is UNDERSTOOD the conquest of the passions, the importance of virtue, and other moral doctrines; on which account we may call the ORLANDO a MORAL poem; but can we call the FAIRY QUEEN upon the whole a MORAL poem? is it not equally an HISTORICAL or POLITICAL poem? For though it may be, according to it's author's words, an ALLEGORY or DARK CONCEIT, yet that which is couched or understood under this allegory is the history, and intrigues, of queen Elizabeth's courtiers; which however are introduced with a Moral design.

> (p. 219 n.)

For Warton the allegory of Spenser is peculiarly rich and abundant: it is not merely a narration which can be given interpretative gloss—as Plutarch had defined allegory and as Ariosto had practised it. Nourished on the pageantry and romance literature of his time, Spenser's imagination, peculiarly susceptible, like that of all great artists, to the dominant modes of statement of his age, became steeped in symbolic forms of expression so that his poetry was not a direct representation but an imaginative transformation of the experience available to him. In this Warton's approach to Spenser resembles his observations on the excellence of Theocritus as compared to Virgil in the pastoral. The details of either allegory or pastoral are so presented that an ideal world is rendered real to the imagination of the reader. The tension between form and subject is resolved without, as in Ariosto or Virgil, the importance of the formal concerns dominating the experience offered by the poem. This is achieved by combining the natural representation of particularised and concrete detail to suggest the texture of real life to the reader with the formal structuring of that experience to produce a significant whole. And as the very use of allegorical form guarantees the intention on the poet's part of conveying to the reader some general, abstract truth, so the form or forms in which the allegory is cast may employ all the fantastic and beguiling creativity of the poet without the validity of a central theme being undermined, any more than the ebullient fantastic forms of Gothic architecture detracted from the awareness of the intention with which the building had been erected. The mind is led to ponder on the general theme by being alerted to responsiveness by local and specific details which the poet depicts.

It will be remembered that Warton sees a decline in poetry as 'Poets began . . . to be more attentive to words than to things and objects'. Following on the references to the indebtedness of Spenser to the spectacles and entertainments he saw for his allegory, Warton makes an important statement about the relationship between poetry and reality, beginning, it is true, conventionally enough:

> he [Spenser] has shewn himself a much more ingenious allegorist, where his IMAGINATION BODIES forth unsubstantial things, TURNS THEM TO SHAPE, and marks out the nature, powers, and effects of that which is ideal and abstracted, by visible and external symbols; as in his delineation of FEAR, ENVY, FANCY, DESPAIR, and the like. Ariosto gives us but few of these symbolical beings, in comparison of Spenser; and those which he has given us, are by no means drawn with that fullness and distinctness with which they are painted by the latter. And that Spenser painted these figures so fully and distinctly, may we not reasonably attribute it, to his being so frequently habituated to the sight of these symbolical beings, distinguished with their proper emblems, and actually endued with speech, motion, and life?

> (p. 220)

The principle is the same as that employed when he referred to the impact of Gothic architecture on the youthful imagination of Milton. It follows that Spenser's failures and inconsistencies—to which an entire section of the *Observations* is devoted—are not Warton's central concern. His chief interest is in showing how the poet's mind was so furnished that it could excel in true poetry. And it was the conditions in the age of Elizabeth which had produced the fine harvest of poetry to which he refers in his outline sketch for *History*.

XI

In his account of *Early English Stages, 1300-1576* (1959), Glynne Wickham considers the modes of statement inherent in experience offered by the pageant theatres which were erected in the streets of a city to welcome a royal visitor:

> The nature of their content was sermon, spectacular and dramatic, the significance of which was specifically directed at the visitor but which the occasion caused author, actors and audience to share alike. In consequence of all these facts, thematic content took precedence over everything else in the construction of both text and spectacle. Where topical subject matter was inevitably of so personal a kind, courtesy, if nothing else, forbade bald statement. Instead, it suggested allegorical treatment. This could be scriptural, historical, mythological or whatever best fitted the occasion and justifies the remarks which Warton made in his *History of English Poetry* and which I quote in full since they appear to have sustained such unwarrantable neglect from subsequent historians of our drama:

> 'It seems probable that the PAGEANTS, which being shown on civil occasions, derived great part of their decoration and actors from historical fact, and consequently made profane characters the subject of public exhibition, dictated ideas of a regular drama much sooner that the MYSTERIES; which being confined to scripture stories, or rather the legendary miracles of

sainted martyrs, and the no less ideal personifications of the christian virtues, were not calculated to make so quick and easy a transition to the representations of real life and rational action.'

> (pp. 62-3)

The variety of allegorical modes available, to which Professor Wickham refers, was related to Spenser's allegorising by Warton in the passage which I have already quoted from the *Observations*. The closer the parallel to actual existence for the reader, the more flexible the modes of treatment of that reality available to the writer. It was historical fact that mattered:

> Witches were thought really to exist in the age of Queen Elizabeth, and our author had, probably, been struck with seeing such a cottage as this, in which a witch was supposed to live. Those who have perus'd Mr. Blackwall's Enquiry into the Life and Writings of Homer, will be best qualified to judge how much better enabled that poet is to describe, who copies from living objects, than he who describes, in a later age, from tradition.

> (p. 267)

Warton's motivation in assembling the 'mass of raw materials which Scott saw as preliminary to writing a history' rather than as itself constituting the *History of English Poetry*, is, then, to accumulate evidences of a tradition of true poetry and the conditions of the ages from which it emerged. So in the second edition of the *Observations* he concludes an account of the decorations of various buildings with the sudden remark:

> Taste and imagination make more antiquarians, than the world is willing to allow. One looks back with romantic pleasure on the arts and fashions of an age, which

> Employ'd the power of fairy hands.

> (ii, 234)

—a quotation from Gray which emphasises the bond of antiquarian enthusiasm which they shared.

XII

It is characteristic of Warton that from an apparently commonplace standpoint he arrives at a surprising delicacy and subtlety of insight. The material available to the poet is of course modified by his characteristic responses to his environment. So in the section rather unpromisingly headed 'Of Spenser's Imitations of Himself', we have first the commonsense assertion that while the tracing of borrowings from other authors which Warton had dealt with so far is

> a business which proceeds upon an uncertain foundation, affording the amusement of conjecture rather than the satisfaction of truth; it may perhaps be a more serviceable undertaking, to produce an author's IMITATIONS OF HIMSELF: and this will be more particularly useful in

the three following respects, viz. It will discover the FAVORITE IMAGES of an author; it will teach us how VARIOUSLY he expresses the same thought; and it will often EXPLAIN DIFFICULT passages, and words.

(p. 181)

From a discussion of various passages he concludes that Spenser 'particularly excels in painting affright, confusion, and astonishment'. But Warton does not rest content with this generalisation. The poetry of Spenser conveys to him a certain quality of mind of the author, providing indeed a clue to that bent of disposition which causes the poet to dwell on certain kinds of experience and intensities of feeling. Of the account of Despair in book 1 Warton remarks:

It is a trite observation, that we paint that best, which we have felt most. Spenser's whole life seems to have consisted of disappointments and distress; so that he probably was not unacquainted with the bitter agonies of a despairing mind, which the warmth of his imagination, and, what was its consequence, his sensibility of temper contributed to render doubly severe. Unmerited and unpitied indigence ever struggles hardest with true genius; and a good taste, for the same reasons that it enhances the pleasures of life, sustains with uncommon tortures the miseries of that state, in which (says an incomparable moralist) 'every virtue is obscured, and in which no conduct can avoid reproach; a state in which cheerfulness is insensibility, and dejection sullenness, of which the hardships are without honour, and the labours without reward'.

(pp. 193-4)

But while each bent of the creative mind is different, and poets may suffer in a variety of ways, the prospects offered by antiquarianism are limitless and, given Warton's assumptions, invariably rewarding. For him the unfolding of a *History of Poetry* will inevitably be an investigation into the records of the past combined with responsiveness to that poetry which delights him most and this will be intermingled with antiquarian digression and extensive transcription.

XIII

In the preface to his **History** Warton shows above all a sense of his obligation to his public:

We look back on the savage conditions of our ancestors with the triumph of superiority; we are pleased to mark the steps by which we have been raised from rudeness to elegance: and our reflections on this subject are accompanied with a conscious pride, arising in great measure from a tacit comparison between the feeble efforts of remote ages, and our present improvements in knowledge.

But, none the less, to appreciate present achievements it is necessary to gain insight into the manners of the past:

to develop the dawnings of genius, and to pursue the progress of our national poetry, from a rude origin and obscure beginnings, to its perfection in a polished age,

must prove an interesting and instructive investigation. But a history of poetry, for another reason, yet on the same principles, must be more especially productive of entertainment and utility. I mean, as it is an art, whose object is human society: as it has the peculiar merit, in its operations on that object, of faithfully recording the features of the times, and of preserving the most picturesque and expressive representations of manners.

(pp. ii-iii)

So although the overt aim of the work is to improve his readers' knowledge of the past, and extend their awareness of present achievements and past ways of life, of different modes of thinking and feeling, Warton soon discloses in discussing his plan where the main emphasis of his work is to lie. He refers to his decision not to employ the schemes of Gray or Pope on the grounds that:

The constraint imposed by a mechanical attention to this distribution (of materials in Schools) appeared to me to destroy that free exertion of research with which such a history ought to be executed, and not easily reconcilable with that complication, variety, and extent of materials, which it ought to comprehend.

The method I have pursued, on one account at least, seems preferable to all others. My performance, in its present form, exhibits without transposition the gradual improvements of our poetry, at the same time as it uniformly presents the progression of our language.

(p. v)

Unlike Gray he feels that the drama cannot properly be excluded: though it can only of necessity be given a subordinate place in his account, yet 'I flatter myself . . . that from evidences hitherto unexplored, I have recovered hints which may facilitate the labours of those, who shall hereafter be inclined to investigate the antient state of dramatic exhibition in this country, with due comprehension and accuracy' (p. vii). He defends himself in advance against accusations of prolixity in quotation: 'it should be remembered, that most of these are extracted from antient manuscript poems never before printed, and hitherto but little known. Nor was it easy to illustrate the darker and more distant period of our poetry without producing ample specimens.'

In the mean time, I hope to merit the thanks of the antiquarian, for enriching the stock of our early literature by these new accessions: and I trust I shall gratify the reader of taste, in having so frequently rescued from oblivion the rude inventions and irregular beauties of the heroic tale, or the romantic legend.

(p. viii)

The purpose of the **History** as he sees it at the beginning is to unearth discoveries, not to pursue an overall interpretation. It is not surprising that over a quarter of the first volume (the pages are not numbered) should consist of the two digressions which Warton asserts will consider 'some material points of a general and preliminary nature', and will at the same time 'endeavour to establish certain fundamental principles to which frequent appeals might occasionally be made, and to clear the way for various observations arising in the course of my future enquiries'. The two digressions are 'On the Origin of Romantic Fiction in Europe' and 'On the Introduction of Learning into England'. These two topics serve to indicate, as Warton claims, his main lines of investigation.

XIV

Whereas Percy had opened the *Reliques* with an account of the importance of the minstrels, Warton is concerned with the ways in which the fantasies of the romantic imagination reached Europe. The interpretation offered by Warburton, which had relied on the impact of the Saracens on the Spanish culture, was undermined by Percy's investigations into the dating of Spanish romance material. Warton quickly arrives at the fund of legend held in common by Celtic speakers: the stories of Wales and Brittany strongly resemble one another. Consequently on the fourth page of his Dissertation he observes that Milton 'mentions indiscriminately' the knights of Wales and Armorica as the customary retinue of king Arthur:

> —What resounds
> In fable or romance, of Uther's son
> Begirt with BRITISH and ARMORIC knights'.

He refers to *Ossian* as evidence of the intermingling of different influences:

> It is indeed very remarkable, that in these poems the terrible graces, which so naturally characterise, and so generally constitute, the early poetry of barbarous people, should so frequently give way to a gentler set of manners, to the social sensibilities of polished life, and a more civilised and elegant species of imagination. Nor is this circumstance, which disarranges all our established ideas concerning the savage stages of society, easily to be accounted for, unless we suppose, that the Celtic tribes, who were so strongly addicted to poetical composition, and who made it so much their duty from the earliest times, might by degrees have attained a higher vein of poetical refinement, than could at first sight or on common principles be expected among nations, whom we are accustomed to call barbarous; that some few instances of an elevated strain of friendship, of love, and other sentimental feelings, existing in such nations, might lay the foundations for introducing a set of manners among the bards, more refined and exalted than the real manners of the country; and that panegyrics on those virtues, transmitted with improvements from bard to bard, must at length have formed characters of ideal excellence, which might propagate among the people real manners bordering on the poetical.

He cites Blair's defence of *Ossian,* and refers (in a note) with some respect to Macpherson's. But Warton is mainly concerned with establishing relationships between early literatures in which a love of the marvellous and supernatural is manifested. So he proceeds:

> These poems, however, notwithstanding the difference between the Gothic and the Celtic rituals, contain many visible vestiges of Scandinavian superstition. The allu-

sions in the songs of Ossian to spirits, who preside over the different parts and direct the various operations of nature . . . entirely correspond with the Runic system, and breathe the spirit of its poetry.

In support of this he cites instances from Olaus Wormius and Olaus Magnus, as well as from Bartholin's *De Contemptu Mortis apud Daniis,* and the 'HERVARER SAGA'. Tacitus joins Diodorus Siculus and Joannes Aventinus, Posidonius and Aelian in notes to support Warton's assertions concerning the subject matter of Scandinavian poetry. The giants, dragons and fairies on the other hand are attributed to Arabian influence, and their absence from the poems of Ossian is for Warton 'a striking proof of their antiquity'. The work of Evans is cited in confirmation of the absence of fantastic marvels of this kind from the productions of the ancient Welsh bards. And so he comes to his conclusion:

> Amid the gloom of superstition, in an age of the grossest ignorance and credulity, a taste for the wonders of Oriental fiction was introduced by the Arabians into Europe, many countries of which were already seasoned to a reception of its extravagancies, by means of the poetry of the Gothic scalds, who perhaps originally derived their ideas from the same fruitful region of invention. These fictions, coinciding with the reigning manners, and perpetually kept up and improved in the tales of troubadours and ministrels, seem to have centred about the eleventh century in the ideal histories of Turpin and Geoffrey of Monmouth, which record the suppositious achievements of Charlemagne and King Arthur, where they formed the ground-work of that species of fabulous narrative called romance. And from these beginnings, or causes, afterwards enlarged and enriched by kindred fancies fetched from the crusades, that singular and capricious mode of imagination arose, which at length composed the marvellous machineries of the more sublime Italian poets, and of their disciple Spenser.

The climax of fine fablings is exemplified in Spenser, so that control of the imagination by the judgment which is necessitated for the advance of society and the improvement of civilised life is achieved through the acquisition of wisdom. Hence the second dissertation deals, sequentially, with the introduction of learning into England.

Warton traces here the impact of the barbarian invasions on the Roman civilisation, the incursion of the Gothic disorder into Roman 'peace and civility'. But not only did the Goths have the opportunity to acquire some degree of wisdom from their conquests: Warton observes that

> Their enemies have been their historians, who naturally painted these violent disturbers of the general repose in the warmest colours. It is not easy to conceive, that the success of their amazing enterprizes was merely the effect of numbers and tumultuary depredation. . . . Superior strength and courage must have contributed in a considerable degree to their rapid and extensive conquests; but at the same time, such mighty achievements could not have been planned and executed without some extraordinary vigour of mind, uniform principles of conduct, and no common talents of political sagacity.

Meantime Latin poetry had lapsed into barbarism—'From the growing increase of christianity, it was deprived of its old fabulous embellishments, and chiefly employed in composing ecclesiastical hymns.' In monasteries, however, the spark of knowledge was kept alive, and with increasing stability libraries began to grow and learning again to flourish. Warton's attitude towards his material is shown when he considers the work of Bede: 'It is diverting', he writes, referring to the *Mélanges d'Histoire et de Littérature* (Paris, 1725) of 'Monsieur de Vigneul Marville',

> to see the French critics censuring Bede for credulity: they might as well have accused him of superstition. . . . He has recorded but few civil transactions: but besides that his history professedly considers ecclesiastical affairs, we should remember, that the building of a church, the preferment of an abbot, the canonisation of a martyr, and the importation into England of the shinbone of an apostle, were necessarily matters of much more importance in Bede's conceptions than histories or revolutions. He is fond of minute descriptions; but particularities are the fault and often the merit of early historians.

And earlier:

> His knowledge, if we consider his age, was extensive and profound: and it is amazing, in so rude a period, and during a life of no considerable length, he should have made so successful a progress, and such rapid improvements, in scientific and philological studies, and have composed so many elaborate treatises on different subjects.

The deployment of an historical imagination is characteristic of Warton's best work. Again, in the conclusion to the Dissertation, he insists on the ways in which civilising influences may not necessarily foster the growth of a civilising literature. In the medieval period he sees in the growth of civil and canonical laws an encouragement to pedantry and casuistry in the universities, where jurisprudence 'was treated with the same spirit of idle speculation which had been carried into philosophy and theology, it was overwhelmed with endless commentaries which disclaimed all elegance of language, and served only to exercise genius, as it afforded materials for framing the flimsy labyrinths of casuistry.' But, in any case, in spite of an increase of learning:

> The habits of superstition and ignorance were as yet too powerful for a reformation of this kind to be affected by a few polite scholars. It was necessary that many circumstances and events, yet in the womb of time, should take place, before the minds of men could be so far enlightened as to receive these improvements.

And he returns to his main theme before beginning the *History* proper:

> But perhaps inventive poetry lost nothing by this relapse. Had classical taste and judgment been now established, imagination would have suffered, and too early a check would have been given to the beautiful extravagancies of romantic fabling. In a word, truth and reason would have chased before their time those spectres of illusive fancy, so pleasing to the imagination, which delight to hover in the gloom of ignorance and superstition, and which form so considerable a part of the poetry of the succeeding centuries.

XV

The experience of reading the *History* has been variously described as 'wading rather than reading' and as being guided by the 'torch of genius through ruins in which he [Warton] loves to wander'. The grounds for such apparently conflicting verdicts should by now have become clear. For Gibbon the *History* combined 'the taste of a poet with the minute diligence of an antiquarian':[9] and whereas the concern of the poet is with that poetry of the past which advanced the art of verse and at the same time awakened the imaginative response of the modern reader, the business of the antiquarian is with the reproduction of obscure material which illuminated the life of the past in which those poets wrote. It is the critic or man of taste who attempts to unite both interests, and this role of Warton's as professor and Poet Laureate is too often forgotten. Warton places his concern with poetry and manners, however, before any questioning of critical assumptions. It is on this account that his work suffers from a lack of discrimination between poets of very different levels of achievement but at the same time and for the same reason benefits from what is essentially a free exertion of research. In the infancy of historical accounts of poetry it was of greater importance to extend the imaginative awareness of the reader than to utter precepts and demarcate schools and influences and traditions.

Warton employs the greater part of his first volume in quoting from various romances of chivalry, and in giving accounts of contemporary pageants and miracle plays. He proceeds to *Piers Plowman* and Langland's use of personification and allegory, then to Chaucer, whose work marks at once the advent of pathos into literature and of some elegance and refinement into the vernacular. The lengthy appreciation devoted to Chaucer and the comparison of his work with that of his originals serves to emphasise the national genius of the poet and offers the best criticism of his work since Dryden.

But the expectations which were aroused by the first volume were not answered by the second. Although he begins with a valuable account of Gower, Occleve and Lydgate, emphasising considerations of style, dwelling appreciatively on passages of natural description and noting any indebtedness to romance material, Warton goes on to a protracted and detailed account of fifteenth-century translations from the classics into French and English, from Harding and the Lives of the Saints to Hawes, Skelton, the Scottish poets and the moralities and mysteries, with a digression on the acting of plays in schools and universities. It is disappointing that the Renaissance is described almost entirely in terms of the revival of learning, the increase in translations, the endowment of schools and colleges (material which Warton had employed in his lives of Pope and Bathurst), so that any element of exposition is buried beneath a mass of recorded detail. Vast tracts of this volume disappointed Warton's contemporaries by their dullness:

> The learned and ingenious Writer [comments the *Monthly* reviewer] has prosecuted his respectable labours with great assiduity, but, possibly, with too much prolixity. On that account only it is to be feared that his valuable book may become the solitary inhabitant of *consulted* libraries . . . there is to certain minds a charm in the investigation of antiquity, which is not easily dissolved: and it is no wonder if, in tracing the progress of ancient genius, a writer whose pursuits have been congenial with his subject, should loiter in the fairy region through which he passes.
>
> (lix, 132)

XVI

The principal interest of this volume, however, was the lengthy dissertation on the Rowley poems. For although Warton goes so far as to say that if they were indeed authentic they might be considered to have redeemed the poetic reputation of the fifteenth century, he states at the beginning of his account that 'there are some circumstances which incline us to suspect these pieces to be a modern forgery' (p. 139). The sensitivity to different poetic modes of statement which was present in the comments on *Ossian* quoted earlier, is now brought to bear on the different aspects of Chatterton's forgeries. The Epistle prefixed to *The Tragedy of Aella* commends 'SOME GREAT STORY OF HUMAN MANNERS', as most suitable for theatrical presentation. But, says Warton:

> this idea is the result of that taste and discrimination, which could only belong to a more advanced period of society.
>
> But, above all, the cast of thought, the complexion of the sentiments, and the structure of the composition evidently prove these pieces not antient.
>
> (pp. 155-6)

And if the obsolete language be offered as proof:

> As to his knowledge of the old English literature, which is rarely the study of a young poet, a sufficient quantity of obsolete words and phrases were readily attainable from the glossary to Chaucer, and to Percy's Ballads. It is confessed, that this youth wrote the *Execution of Sir Charles Bawdwin*: and he who could forge that poem, might easily forge all the rest.
>
> (p. 157)

Warton does not allow his sensibility to the poetry to distract him from the application of standards of scholarship. He concludes:

> It is with regret that I find myself obliged to pronounce Rowlie's poems to be spurious. Antient remains of English poetry, unexpectedly discovered, and fortunately

rescued from a long oblivion, are contemplated with a degree of fond enthusiasm: exclusive of any real or intrinsic excellence, they afford those pleasures, arising from the idea of antiquity which deeply interest the imagination. With these pleasures we are unwilling to part. But there is a more solid satisfaction, resulting from the detection of artifice and imposture.

> (p. 164)

Warton's *Enquiry into the Authenticity of the Rowley Poems* was published in 1782, and here his rigorous analysis of their forgeries was part of a defence of his standards of scholarship against the attacks of Joseph Ritson and others. He affirms roundly that if the Rowley poems are not established finally as forgeries 'the entire system that has hitherto been framed concerning the progression of poetical composition, and every theory that has been established on the gradual improvements of taste, style, and language, will be shaken and disarranged' (p. 8).

Earlier in the *Enquiry* Warton discusses the charges levelled against his scholarship by his critics, and compares them to 'the unexpected retort of Curll the bookseller, who being stigmatised by Pope for having been ignominiously tossed in a blanket, seriously declared he was not tossed in a blanket but in a rug' (p. 5). In his edition of Pope's *Works* Bowles remarks of Thomas Warton: 'So sweet was his temper, and so remote from pageantry and all affectation was his conduct, that when even Ritson's scurrilous abuse came out, in which he asserted that his [Warton's] back was "*broad enough,* and his heart *hard enough*" to bear any thing Ritson could lay on it, he only said, with his usual smile, "*A black letter'd* dog, sir"' (vi, 325).

Although Warton did not question the authenticity of Ossian in print, there is some suggestion in the manner of his references to the poems in the Dissertation that their authenticity is not beyond all doubt. And among the Trinity College MSS. is a fragment headed 'Doubts &c. about Ossian'. Under this heading are arranged the following items: '1. That there should be no religious Idea or Image—2. That there should be such Sentiments of Humanity—3. Such Taste of Beauty.—4. Similes—5. General imagery. 6. Savages are not so struck with their wild scenes— . . . as to describe them [MS. in part indecipherable] and to think them strange—To persons accustomed to politer life they are only *strange*. 7. Tradition in *all* Countries imperfect.' Professor Wellek judged the comments on Ossian in the Dissertation to be an unfortunate lapse on Warton's part, but the MS. goes a long way to supporting Walpole's assumption that Warton was here being merely civil—probably to Blair whose Dissertation in defence of the poems had appeared in 1763.

XVII

Warton's *History* was edited twice in the nineteenth century; by Price in 1824 and by William Carew Hazlitt, the grandson of the essayist and critic in 1871. His editors find the *History* deficient not only in its lack of plan, but in its omission of authors who should have been included, and in its textual inaccuracies: Carew Hazlitt remarks: 'From a careful comparison of many of Warton's quotations with the very originals to which he refers, one can only draw the conclusion that he considered the faithful representation of texts as a matter of very subordinate consequence' (pp. x-xi). The books which Warton has conveniently seen in the library of 'the late Mr. William Collins' have 'been dispersed'—never to be located more. The account of a Christmas feast given by Queen Mary and King Philip of Spain for Princess Elizabeth which enlivened Warton's *Life of Sir Thomas Pope* was probably a more serious lapse from scholarly standards, as it seems possible that Warton forged the document from which he is supposed to have derived the information or that he took its authenticity too easily for granted.[10] But as Warton's methods of work were spasmodic and slovenly—as his brother found when seeking material for the completion of the *History* after his death—errors both trivial and serious were likely to have occurred when Warton was dealing with such areas of material.

The structural weaknesses in the *History* reach their climax in the third volume. Here a dissertation on the *Gesta Romanorum* as the origin of many of the tales and legends of English romance fiction heralds consideration of the work of Surrey. An account of More is interrupted for a twenty-five-page quotation from the romance of *Ywain and Gawain*; and Warton seems to find a certain relief in quoting at length the drinking song from *Gammer Gurton's Needle* at the conclusion of a section on the versifying of the Psalms. The allegorical effectiveness of Sackville's *Induction* to the *Mirror for Magistrates* is dwelt on at some length. The *History* ends with a general view of the reign of Elizabeth 'as the most POETICAL age of these annals' (p. 490), stressing the abundance of fable, fiction and fancy not only in native literature but also in translation from the classical and Italian writers: these are related to the spirit and manners of the times. Learning was beginning to advance, so that:

> On the whole, we were now arrived at that period, propitious to the operations of original and true poetry, when the coyness of fancy was not always proof against the approaches of reason, when genius was rather directed than governed by judgment, and when taste and learning had so far only disciplined imagination, as to suffer its excesses to pass without censure or control, for the sake of the beauties to which they were allied.
>
> (p. 501)

It is a conventional enough ending, and its tone is more final than Warton's plan, 'a conspectus of poetry from the Conquest to the Revolution', would have implied. Warton had appeared to Percy to be fatigued with his researches in the 'sixties, and the various undertakings, classical, antiquarian and local historical, find their place in the *History* itself, accounting for some at least of the otherwise irresponsibly digressive pattern of the work. Indeed parts of the *Life of Bathurst* were to be used to eke out the notes on Milton's minor poems. Passages in the third volume of the *History* are taken, often word for word and quite irrelevantly, from the text of the *Life of Sir Thomas Pope*.

XVIII

But against these weaknesses in Warton's *History* must be set its status as a pioneering work in taste and criticism, and one which bears the authenticity of a sensitively apprehended view of poetry. He shows himself aware of treading much of the ground for the first time, and, as he supposed, the last. Of the *Pricke of Conscience* he remarked, 'I prophecy that I am its last transcriber' (i, 256). Conscious of his too frequent and copious use of quotation he wrote:

> It is neither my inclination nor intention to write a catalogue, or compile a miscellany. It is not to be expected that this work should be a general repository of our ancient poetry: I cannot, however, help observing, that English literature and English poetry suffer, while so many pieces of this kind [he is referring to *Sir Bevys*] still remain concealed and forgotten in our manuscript libraries.
>
> (i, 207-8)

He was reading many of the manuscripts for the first time for centuries: it is no wonder that his treatment of them was unequal. Ker pointed out that Warton had unfortunately missed the *Gawain* and *Pearl* MSS; but in fact, although *Gawain* is not dealt with in the *History,* an extract from *Pearl* is quoted as if it had been transcribed and inserted from the catalogue description (iii, 107n). Errors in transcription might be numerous, and glossing faulty, but when one looks at his appreciation of Gavin Douglas's prologue to the sixth book of his translation of the *Aeneid,* one sees in his selection a critical attitude of permanent value. 'The several books', he says, 'are introduced with metrical prologues, which are often highly poetical; and shew that Douglas's proper walk was original poetry' (p. 282). He quotes for nearly seven pages the charming description of May, and observes:

> The poetical beauties of this specimen will be relished by every reader who is fond of lively touches of fancy, and rural imagery. But the verses will have another merit with those critics who love to contemplate the progress of composition, and to mark the original workings of genuine nature; as they are the effusion of a mind not overlaid by the descriptions of other poets, but operating, by its own force and bias, in the delineation of a vernal landscape, on such subjects as really occurred.

So he renders the passage into modern English. Again, there is the admiration for Sackville's *Induction*:

> These shadowy inhabitants of hell-gate are conceived with the vigour of a creative imagination, and described with great force of expression. They are delineated with that fulness of proportion, that invention of picturesque attributes, distinctness, animation, and amplitude, of which Spenser is commonly supposed to have given the first specimens in our language, and which are characteristical of his poetry.
>
> (p. 233)

The influence of Dante, hitherto generally regarded as a 'Gothic' poet, is seen in the greater licence given to extravagances of description; comparing Dante with Virgil:

> It must be allowed, that the scenes of Virgil's sixth book have many fine strokes of the terrible. But Dante's colouring is of a more gloomy temperature. There is a sombrous cast in his imagination: and he has given new shades of horror to the classical hell. We may say of Dante, that
>
> Hell
> Grows DARKER at his FROWN.—
>
> The sensations of fear impressed by the Roman poet are less harrassing to the repose of the mind: they have a more equable and placid effect. The terror of Virgil's tremendous objects is diminished by correctness of composition and elegance of style. We are reconciled to his Gorgons and Hydras, by the grace of expression, and the charms of versification.
>
> (p. 254)

The repudiation of formal statement as in itself a desirable end for the artist to perfect is here given concrete expression in criticism; the responsiveness of reader and poet alike is roused more by Dante than Virgil: 'the Charms which we so much admire in Dante, do not belong to the Greeks and Romans. They are derived from another origin and must be traced back to a different stock' (p. 255). So the characters over the gate of brass in the Inferno, quoted and translated by Warton, impress by the 'severe solemnity in these abrupt and comprehensive sentences, and they are a striking preparation to the scenes that follow. But the idea of such an inscription on the brazen portal of hell, was suggested to Dante by books of chivalry; in which the gate of an impregnable enchanted castle, is often inscribed with words importing the dangers or wonders to be found within' (p. 239).

XIX

The ease and breadth of reference, the absence of any prejudice and preconception to impede the responsiveness of the writer to the poetry he is discovering to his public, remain Warton's major contribution to the writing of literary history. As Chalmers observed, the magnitude of the undertaking exceeded the original idea. He praised the digressions for the wealth of information they contained. Warton, he wrote:

> was the first who taught the true method of acquiring a taste for the excellencies of our ancient poets, and of rescuing their writings from obscurity and oblivion. Of Warton it may be said as of Addison; 'he is now despised by some who perhaps would never have seen his defects, but by the lights which he afforded them'. His erudition was extensive, and his industry must have been at one time incessant. The references in his History of Poetry only, indicate a course of varied reading, collation, and transcription, to which the common life of man seems insufficient. He was one of those scholars who have happily rescued the study of antiquities

from the reproaches of the frivolous or indolent. Amidst the most rugged tracks of ancient lore, he produces cultivated spots, flowery paths, and gay prospects.

> (p. 85)

His successor, Courthope, deplored that Warton set about his work in the spirit of an antiquary, though he allowed that 'his reading was wide, his scholarship sound, his taste fine and discriminating; and though he had no pretensions to be called a great poet, his verse is at least marked by genuine poetic sensibility' (ix, xii). But these qualities enabled Warton to keep the relationship between the reader and the writer paramount when discussing poetry, and to widen the historical approach and the perspectives of the imagination accordingly in opening up tracts of early literature and manners to his contemporaries. And when Eliot could write, not so very long ago, about alliteration 'as primitive as that of *Piers Plowman*', Warton's subtler approach to medieval literature retains an intrinsic importance even in the twentieth century.

XX

Of all the attempts which have been made to express the essential character of Warton's achievement, that which regards him as a precursor of Romanticism is plainly inadequate, as, indeed, is that which sees him, conversely, as an essentially Augustan figure. Nichol Smith's suggestion that Warton found in the romances a relief from the classics fails to explain why Warton was so preoccupied with early literature, and, more important, the critical standpoint which dominated the greater part of his writings. R. D. Havens saw Warton as a transitional figure of purely historical significance:[11]

> The truth of Warton's opinions does not matter but their inconsistencies and other limitations do. We read the ***Observations*** and the **'Verses on Reynolds's Window',** not for light on the *Faerie Queene* or on Gothic architecture, but on a subject about which we know much less,—the mid eighteenth century. If we are ever to understand this period, it will be through a careful study of such typical figures as Thomas Warton, a study, not only of their successes, but of their failures, a study which does not overlook their conventionality and conservatism in its search for originality and liberalism. Such a study will convince us of the impossibility of tagging the writers of the time as 'romantic' or 'classic'.

The statement is a just one, but in the assumption on which it rests it defeats the true end of studying literary history—the only one which makes it of living interest—that, namely, to attempt, however imperfectly, to interpret the spirit in which the Wartons approached the problems and responsibilities of interpreting and assessing their literary inheritance.

In his last work, that on Milton's minor poems, Warton wrote of his subject:

> Smit with the deplorable polemics of puritanism, he suddenly ceased to gaze on *such sights as youthful poets dream* . . . instead of embellishing original tales of

chivalry, of cloathing the fabulous atchievements of the early British kings and champions in the gorgeous trappings of epic attire, he wrote SMECTYMNUUS and TETRACHORDON, apologies for fanatical preachers and the doctrine of divorce. . . . Yet in this chaos of controversy . . . he sometimes seems to have heaved a sigh for the peaceable enjoyments of lettered solitude, for his congenial pursuits, and the more mild and ingenuous exercises of the muse. In one of his prose tracts, he says, 'I may one day hope to have ye again in a still time, when there shall be no Chiding. . . .' When Milton wrote these poems Romances and fabulous narratives were still in fashion, and not yet driven away by puritans and usurpers. . . . Milton, at least in these poems, may be reckoned an old English poet; and therefore here requires that illustration, without which no old English poet can be well illustrated.

(Preface, pp. xi-xii and xx-xxi)

These early poems of Milton seem to Warton the last emanation of those flights of fancy which had figuratively and inventively bodied forth the experiences of life itself, to transmute mundane existence into an artificial but poetical ideal. This faculty has departed with the new insistence on the importance of everyday life and manners. He illustrates his point with reference to Elizabethan love poetry. When the Elizabethan lover praises his mistress;

She is complimented in strains neither polite nor pathetic, without elegance, and without affection: she is described, not in the address of intelligible yet artful panegyric, not in the real colours, and with the genuine accomplishments of nature, but as an eccentric ideal being of another system, and as inspiring sentiments equally unmeaning, hyperbolical and unnatural.

(iii, 501)

All or most of these circumstances contributed to give a descriptive, a picturesque, and a figurative cast to the poetical language. This effect appears even in the prose compositions of the reign of Elizabeth I. In the subsequent age, prose became the language of poetry.

Thomas Warton does not localise the problems of the poets of his time merely in terms of a reaction against Pope, but attempts with reference to a rich diversity of literary contexts to ascertain the nature of the experience offered by true poetry. In so far as his particular concern is with English poetry he locates its origins in the highly fictionalised renderings of past modes and bygone ideals of that allegorical and romance tradition which flowered in the natural genius of Spenser, Shakespeare and Milton.

Notes

1. *The Gothic Revival* (Pelican; London, 1962), 21-2, 33, 16.

2. Arthur Johnston, *Enchanted Ground* (London, 1964), 79-80.

3. The Percy Letters, *The Correspondence of Thomas Percy and Thomas Warton,* ed. M. G. Robinson and Leah Dennis (Louisiana State U.P., 1951), 69-70.

4. *The Poems of Gray, Collins and Goldsmith,* ed. Roger Lonsdale (London, 1969), p. xvii.

5. Thomas Warton's Inaugural Lecture as Professor of Poetry, delivered 1757; unpublished MS., translated by Professor W. S. Watt.

6. *The Correspondence of Thomas Percy and Thomas Warton,* pp. xxii, 123, 130, 133.

7. *Mant,* i, lviii-lxi.

8. W. J. Courthope, *A History of English Poetry,* 6 vols (London, 1926), i, x-xi.

9. Mason to Walpole, 1772, in *Horace Walpole's Correspondence with William Mason,* ed. W. S. Lewis, G. Cronin Jr., and C. H. Bennett (Yale ed. *Walpole's Correspondence,* vols 28-9; London, 1955), i, 148; 'Thomas Warton', *D.N.B.,* ed. Sir Leslie Stephen and Sidney Lee, 63 vols (London 1899), lix; cf. Chalmers, 'Life of Thomas Warton', in *The Works of the English Poets.*

10. See H. E. D. Blakiston, 'Thomas Warton and Machyn's Diary', *E.H.R.,* xi (1896), 282-300.

11. R. D. Havens, 'Thomas Warton and the Eighteenth Century Dilemma', *S.P.,* xxv (1928), 50.

Pat Rogers (essay date 1987)

SOURCE: Rogers, Pat. "Thomas Warton and the Waxing of the Middle Ages." In *Medieval Literature and Antiquities: Studies in Honour of Basil Cottle,* edited by Myra Stokes and T. L. Burton, pp. 175-86. Cambridge: D. S. Brewer, 1987.

[*In the following essay, Rogers contends that Warton's* History of English Poetry *played a significant role in the codifying of historical eras in literature.*]

In any age, Basil Cottle would have been a notable scholar. But it is only within the last century and a half that he could possibly have held a distinguished post in Medieval English. The prime reason for this has nothing to do with the belated appearance of departments of English within universities (Dr Cottle could, in any case, have survived happily under the aegis of 'classical studies' (to use an anachronistic form), such are his attainments in the ancient languages). But the middle ages, as a linguistic entity, were not fully to dawn until the nineteenth century. Prior to 1800, anyone who wished to specialize in, say, Middle English (not many did) would have had to describe himself or herself as a Goth of one kind or another.

The lexical history of terms such as 'middle age' and 'medieval' has been explored on a few occasions, although never for the purposes I shall adopt in this essay. When the original [*Oxford English Dictionary*; hereafter cited as *OED*] reached the letter M in about 1905, the editors were unable to find any examples of *middle age(s)* earlier than

1722, with two further citations from the eighteenth century—the more interesting from Chambers's *Cyclopaedia* (1753 edition). The illustrations show that the usage took off properly in the next century, and it was probably Henry Hallam's work entitled *A View of the State of Europe during the Middle Ages* (1818) which confirmed the currency of the phrase as a historiographical marker. The recent supplement to *OED* has found earlier citations, from a Donne sermon and from the historian Henry Spelman: both date from the first quarter of the seventeenth century, but neither seems to be the easy use of a widely recognizable or accepted label. The locution existed, but it did not trip off the tongue: it had still to acquire the force of a technical term. As for the entry *mediæval, medieval, OED* finds nothing prior to 1827. The second instance given is dated 1856, and comes from Ruskin; he provides the first example for both *mediævalist* (1874) and *mediævalism* (1853). The supplement cannot antedate these cases: so recent is the adoption of expressions which seem so necessary and natural in the scholarly world today.

In a recent essay in *Speculum*, Fred C. Robinson has considered both these key terms, though in a highly personal manner. His article has two centres of interest: first, the earliest appearance of the terms in major European languages, and second, their current linguistic fate. Robinson ends by deploring the 'sorry semantic state of *medieval* and *Middle Ages*' today—by this he means such distorted usages as 'medieval torture'. His complaint is ostensibly on grounds of historical accuracy (medieval warfare was not conducted with the ferocity which careless modern speakers and writers assume). But on a deeper level it can be seen as part of a long campaign to distance these words from associations of barbarity and uncivilized crudity. This 'anti-medieval mischief' has been going on in the language for centuries, and it is a pity that Robinson's account leaps over a truly crucial phase in the evolution of both expressions. What he says about the emergence of the terms is highly important; Robinson shows, for example, that there was a separate development of the phrase 'Middle Age' (and its equivalents) in modern languages, independently of the supposed root form *medium aevum*. Alongside this neo-Latin version there were competing expressions such as *media aetas*. In addition, Robinson has some useful comments on such matters as the preference in various languages for singular or plural in the noun *age/s*: and he even has time to say something about the Anglo-American split on the medial vowel in *mediæval/ medieval*. It is, in short, a stimulating discussion of an intrinsically important topic.[1]

But there is a black hole at the centre of this cosmography. One cannot understand the current semantic state of the keywords under review, whether it be sorry or otherwise, without some understanding of what happened to them in their lexical adolescence. As far as English goes, this is intimately tied up with a complex set of historical, political, cultural and social factors. The story carries a sub-plot, in the form of the fortunes of the Gothic. Our neutral and technical use of *medieval* in the present century, just as

much as our casual or journalistic application of the word as a loosely condemnatory term, goes back to developments in the language two hundred years ago. It was the eighteenth century which institutionalized the study of Old and Middle English, though it did not invent such study. For its own purposes the age increasingly came to feel the need for labels and descriptive terminology: the shorthand of historical analysis. In my submission, it was the intellectual needs which manifested themselves around the 1770s which explain, more than any other comparable data, the course which *middle ages* and (indirectly) *medieval* have taken in subsequent use. According to this view of the matter, it was that curious marriage between old and new, the enlightenment and the antiquarian movement, which produced the first literary history and the first ideological typing of the medieval. The key figure in this process is Thomas Warton, though he must be seen in a context which displays to view Samuel Johnson, Thomas Gray, Richard Hurd, Thomas Percy, Warton's own brother Joseph, and others.

I

Thomas Warton is celebrated as the author of what is generally considered the first major work of literary history in the language: the **History of English Poetry, from the Close of the Eleventh to the Commencement of the Eighteenth Century,** which appeared in three volumes between 1774 and 1781. Part of a fourth volume was left incomplete at Warton's death in 1790, and was printed in subsequent editions, notably that of Richard Price in 1824. Two dissertations were placed in the first volume, a third, on the *Gesta Romanorum*, followed in the third. Price puts all three at the head of the entire work.[2] Warton had corresponded with Gray in 1769-70, at a time when the poet was finally resigning himself to the fact that his own planned history would never go beyond 'fragments, or sketches of a design'. Through the intercession of Hurd and William Mason, Warton sought to discover what Gray's 'scheme' for his work had been. After some delay Gray sent Warton his outline of the history of English poetry, 'in some measure taken from a scribbled paper of *Pope*'. The only relevant feature of this draft for our present purposes is that it is divided into 'schools', but has no term remotely corresponding to *medieval*. There is a reference to the poetry 'of the Goths', but this is a loose racial categorization, not any sort of cultural marker and not really a period designation as such.[3]

Warton's plan is different in significant ways. After the dissertations, it is almost entirely a chronological account; the notorious digressive quality of the text does not affect that fact. The narrative is chiefly organized under reigns of the various English monarchs, even where Warton can find nothing specially characteristic in the writing of that reign. A typical opening to a chapter will take the form, 'We have seen, in the preceding section, that the character of our poetical composition began to be changed about the reign of the first Edward' (I. 111). Warton is not seeking to create wholly discrete phases of 'Edwardian' and

'Ricardian' poetry and the like, but his method does directly involve a mode of periodization which is central to the development of literary history. Such temporal organization is so natural to us that it takes an effort to appreciate how avoidable such a course was for Warton. In the vogue work of criticism from the previous decade, Warton's friend Richard Hurd had set out his ideas in a series of *Letters on Chivalry and Romance* (1762). Similarly, Edward Young had offered *Conjectures on Original Composition,* 'in a letter to the author of *Sir Charles Grandison*' (1759). Such forms of words indicate that the discursive will prevail over the temporal. Literature will be viewed *sub specie aeternitatis,* or at least under aspects which only incidentally correspond with time divisions. Warton made a celebrated claim to the effect that he was undertaking something unattempted yet, a history 'at large, and in form'. The claim is justified in more than a purely formal sense. Few books, as a matter of fact, had actually specified their subject matter by reference to 'centuries': the word, as applied to a period such as 1500-1600, did not enter English until the 1630s and was quite rare until Warton's time (Adam Smith employs it in *The Wealth of Nations*). And no treatment of literature had been on a wide enough scale to make an overarching concept such as the middle ages fully intelligible between a single pair of covers. This concept was later adopted in the service of various Whig versions of literary history; Warton helped to initiate the Whig versions, not because of the specific teleology which his argument enshrines (although there is one), but because he laid foundations large enough for others to construct their own intellectual edifices on.

There are two seminal modern accounts of the nature of Warton's achievement. One is the culminating chapter in René Wellek's magisterial *Rise of English Literary History* (1941; 2nd edn, 1966). The other is the section devoted to the *History* in Lawrence Lipking's *The Ordering of the Arts in Eighteenth-Century England* (1970): this brilliant panoptic volume sets Warton alongside the historical surveys and summations of men like Johnson, Horace Walpole, Reynolds, John Hawkins and Charles Burney. Both are remarkably illuminating, and deserve careful study.[4] But Lipking seems to me to exaggerate the 'thoroughly compromised' form of the *History.* He speaks of a 'surrender' by Warton to the materials, the blurring of 'any clear line of interpretation', the inability to contrive any 'permanent order for English poetry'. According to Lipking, Warton was defeated by his vacillation on the issue of progress:

> Earlier historians of poetry like Pope and Spence and even Gray could believe in a progress of poetry that had led to their own times; later historians could believe that all great poets join in a single community of genius which acknowledges no progress or division. Warton could believe both, or neither. At times he applies the idea of progress dogmatically, at times he dogmatically contradicts it.

As a result, Warton has no true principle guiding his work: 'Politely turning his back on schools and systems, [he] opens his history to the full complicated play of illimitable

information.' But Lipking's last observation is based on what Warton says in his preface, and the subsequent text does not altogether bear out that statement of intent.

Though not systematic, Warton's historicism is endemic to his book. It is seen as clearly as anywhere at the start of the dissertation on the *Gesta Romanorum*:

> Tales are the learning of a rude age. In the progress of letters, speculation and enquiry commence with refinement of manners. Literature becomes sentimental and discursive, in proportion as a people is polished: and men must be instructed by facts, either real or imaginary, before they can apprehend the subtleties of argument, and the force of reflection.
>
> (I.clxxvii)

What is apparent here, and it is a crucial quality which Lipking and others have missed, is a strong tincture of enlightenment thought and jargon (especially seen in words such as 'refinement of manners', 'sentimental', 'polished'). Warton is indeed writing the progress of romance, a decade before Clara Reeve undertook that task. Later on, we find Warton remarking of minstrelsy, 'as the minstrel profession became a science, and the audience grew more civilised, refinements began to be studied, and the romantic poet sought to gain new attention, and to recommend his story, by giving it the advantage of a plan' (II. 14-15). Later still, the narrative reaches Stephen Hawes, and Warton controverts the opinion of Antony Wood regarding the *Passetyme of Pleasure*:

> Wood, with the zeal of a true antiquary, laments, that 'such is the fate of poetry, that this book, which in the time of Henry the Seventh and Eighth was taken into the hands of all ingenious men, is now thought but worthy of a ballad-monger's stall!' The truth is, such is the good fortune of poetry, and such the improvement of taste, that much better books are become fashionable.
>
> (III. 54)

The received view of Warton would place him as one actuated by 'the zeal of a true antiquary'. What such passages show is that he could take a more independent line. The entire work is studded with comments along these lines:

> The antiquaries of former times overlooked or rejected these valuable remains ['fables of chivalry']. . . . But in the present age we are beginning to make ample amends: in which the curiosity of the antiquarian is connected with taste and genius, and his researches tend to display the progress of human manners, and to illustrate the history of society.
>
> (II. 41-2)

The key word here, along with 'progress', is obviously 'taste'. A sentence like the last one quoted could hardly have been written without the tutelary presence of Hume. And indeed the Scottish enlightenment underlines the entire work—not surprising for any book entitled a 'history' in the 1770s, but a totally disregarded fact up till now. A long shadow is cast over the work by a classic text of the previous decade: Adam Ferguson's *Essay on the History of Civil Society* (1767), with its seminal discussion of the nature of a 'polished' society. Ferguson considers the use of such expressions as 'barbarian' in the light of conquest and colonization; he anatomizes the idea of progress in terms of organic metaphor; and he plots the stages by which civilizations move from the 'rude' to the 'refined'. I do not know whether Warton read this actual work, but its currency was sufficient for its message to spread through to him by osmosis. Warton can hardly have missed the ideas of Hume, or those of Adam Smith—even though what appears to have been Smith's classic statement of the four stages of human development remained in the form of unpublished lecture notes until recently, and did its work through the advocacy of Smith's pupils and acolytes.[5]

This is, needless to say, not an attempt to recruit Warton to the ranks of the Edinburgh literati. But no one writing at this precise juncture, on issues of historical evolution, could fail to be influenced at some level by the ferment of thought in this area. Even a timid Oxford don would have gleaned from his literary contacts something of what had been happening in ideas. Warton was not so blinkered as to have avoided reading and citing, several times, the historical work of Voltaire. Meetings with Burke at the Club, not to mention the appearance of *The Wealth of Nations* and the first part of the *Decline and Fall* in 1776, would further have opened his mind. The source of such contamination of an old-style antiquarian sensibility by fashionable philosophic history can only be a matter of conjecture, in the absence of published records of Warton's reading at the time he was engaged on writing the ***History***. But the fact of this influence is visible throughout: an example occurs in the discussion of the effect of the 'cultivation of an English style' during the Renaissance—another omnipresent modern term not available to Warton, who speaks of 'the general restoration of knowledge and taste' (IV. 154). Few later generations would specify 'taste' in delimiting this epoch. Warton's idiom at such moments is often close to that in which Johnson contemplates raw nature in the Hebrides and places it in the scale of values against 'civilization'. The idea of literacy is central to both authors. But the point of making such collocations is not to give Warton a precise intellectual ancestry; it is rather to indicate that Warton's novel enterprise had its parallels among the social and political enquiries of the time. Ragged as its final effect may sometimes be, Warton's book is far more than a thoughtless accumulation of detail (a fault he imputes to the early chroniclers). It is in fact an attempt to *range* facts, to make sense of a series of events by imputing connection, contrast, development. Warton is constantly explaining features of literature by reference to its historically determined quality: thus, 'It is in vain to apologise for the coarseness, obscenity, and scurrility of Skelton, by saying that his poetry is tinctured with the manners of his age. Skelton would have been a writer without decorum at any period' (III. 167).

Warton seeks 'a general literary history of Britain' (III. 161), and to this end follows 'the progress of modern letters in the fifteenth century' (III. 257). His habit of periodization results at times in what may now seem a blatant kind of historicism: 'I consider Chaucer, as a genial day in an English spring. . . . But winter returns with redoubled horrors . . . and those tender buds . . . which were called forth by the transient gleam of a temporary sun-shine, are nipped by frosts' (II. 361). In other words, 'most of the poets that immediately succeeded Chaucer seem . . . relapsing into barbarism'. The point is not how persuasive such views are, but how intelligible they make history. I wish to suggest that Warton, more than anyone else, gave a shape and entelechy to the course of literature. Johnson's *Lives of the Poets* (1779-81) could not do this, since they began in the seventeenth century. Gray had characteristically ducked out. Percy could editorialize, Mason could biographicize, Hurd and Joseph Warton could criticize—but none of these was able to realign the great historical categories. It took a maggoty old fellow to construct a usable past. Like another seemingly credulous guardian of a cabinet of curiosities, John Aubrey, he was to show that what looked like antiquarian jottings could lay the groundwork of a serious and organized human science.

II

'The progress of romance and the state of learning in the middle ages', wrote Gibbon in the *Decline and Fall*, 'are illustrated by Mr Thomas Warton with the taste of a poet, and the minute diligence of an antiquarian.'[6] This is one of Gibbon's very infrequent uses of the term at the centre of this inquiry. It was by no means a familiar or natural expression, even at the height of a decade which saw unparalleled activity in historiography. For example, it scarcely ever occurs in Charles Burney's *General History of Music*: I have noted a fitful instance, in the second volume (1782): 'With respect to the music of the middle ages in Italy. . . .' Burney, of course, has the standard concerns of the age; his attitudes are made manifest in a passage earlier in this same volume:

> If it be true that the progress of music in every country depends on the degrees of civilization and culture of other arts and sciences among its inhabitants, and on the languages which they speak . . . great perfection cannot be expected in the music of Europe during the middle ages, when the Goths, Vandals, Huns, Germans, Franks, and Gauls, whose ideas were savage, and language harsh and insolent, had seized on its most fertile provinces.

The role of Italy was to 'civilize and polish [its] conquerors'; whereas it is inconceivable that the Welsh, 'a rude, and uncivilized people, . . . without commerce or communication with the rest of Europe, should *invent counterpoint*'. Burney also refers to a 'dark and Gothic period'.[7]

A rapid scan suggests that Joshua Reynolds's *Discourses* contrive, not surprisingly, to get by without any mention of the middle ages. But the term is also rare, more unexpectedly, in William Robertson's *History of the Reign of the Emperor Charles V* (1769). This work enjoyed great celebrity in its day, and was at the peak of its renown when Thomas Warton was engaged on his *magnum opus*. Robertson begins with 'A View of the Progress of Society in Europe, from the Subversion of the Roman Empire, to the Beginning of the Sixteenth Century' (note the parallel in form to Warton's title). He makes reference to 'the martial spirit of Europe, during the middle ages', and to 'the first literary efforts . . . of the European nations in the middle ages'. But his concern is avowedly philosophical, that is, analytic rather than chronological; it is a review of such matters as feudalism, rather than a century-by-century chronicle of the dark ages.[8] This is very different from Warton, who organizes his work on narrative rather than discursive lines. The discursive episodes are, formally speaking, inadvertent.

A comparison might also be drawn with Percy's *Reliques*. The very first sentence of the 'Essay on the Ancient Minstrels in England', which Thomas Percy set at the head of his *Reliques of Ancient Poetry* (1765), states that 'The Minstrels were an order of men in the middle ages, who subsisted by the arts of poetry and music'. But the concept of the middle ages drops from attention as Percy goes on to compile a 'slight history' of minstrelsy from the 'scanty materials' available. In his Preface, Percy evinces the usual desire to 'exhibit the progress of popular opinions', and seeks to display the 'many artless graces' of primitive poetry for the delight of 'a polished age, like the present'.[9] Five years later, Percy wrote a preface to the translation of Paul-Henri Mallet's *Introduction à l'histoire du Danemarck,* entitled *Northern Antiquities*. This is mainly devoted to dispelling the confusion which had arisen concerning the notions 'Gothic' and 'Celtic', and although it reveals the usual preoccupations ('refinement of manners' as a source of linguistic change, for example), it does not reach the medieval era proper.[10]

None of these writers, whatever his contribution, seems to me to have foregrounded the 'medieval' as Warton does, though he cannot yet do this *eo nomine*. His employment of the expression 'middle ages', though more regular than that of his colleagues, is equally casual and unemphatic on most occasions. Thus we are told that 'Statius was a favourite writer with the poets of the middle ages' (II. 197). *Confessio Amantis* is a miscellany of the tales which delighted 'readers of the middle age' (Warton makes no distinction between singular and plural forms). Just over the page, there is mention of collections of the marvellous 'which in the middle ages multiplied to an excessive degree' (II. 313, 315). But on at least one occasion the defining role of the term is crucial, for it is precisely on its 'historical' function that this characteristic passage of the *History* relies:

> We are apt to form romantic and exaggerated notions about the moral innocence of our ancestors. Ages of ignorance and simplicity are thought to be ages of purity. The direct contrary, I believe, is the case. Rude periods have that grossness of manners which is not less

friendly to virtue than luxury itself. In the middle ages, not only the most flagrant violations of modesty were frequently practised and permitted, but the most infamous vices. Men are less ashamed as they are less polished.

All this derives from the belief that 'Chaucer's obscenity', in the fabliaux naturally, 'is in great measure to be imputed to his age' (II. 266-7). We need not enter here into the question of how much—if any—historical understanding Warton actually commands when writing in this vein. The point is that he seeks to make sense of the past specifically by allowing for the situation of earlier writers. The evolution of a definable 'middle age' was essential to his purposes. Sometimes he can make do with a more narrowly delimited temporal span: 'Many classic authors were known in the thirteenth century, but the scholars of that period wanted taste to read and admire them' (II. 175).

But the sweep of the *History* is such that Warton often feels the need for broader categories. It is the 'age' at large, not a temporary fashion, which explains the lack of any 'just idea of decorum' in the miracle plays (II. 76). Even in his moments of near-Gibbonian irony, Warton is especially prone to the word 'age' to adumbrate historical change. On the subject of Stonehenge, he remarks, 'That the Druids constructed this stupendous pile for a place of worship, was a discovery reserved for the sagacity of a wiser age, and the laborious discussion of modern antiquaries' (II. 466). Irony is perhaps not the right word here: Warton does not doubt for a minute that his is a wiser age, and his faint self-mocking amusement rests on a clearcut view of the 'progress' from one age to another. No previous generation of writers had such constant occasion for the terminology of ages, eras, epochs. A self-consciously 'refined' culture needs to naturalize its prejudices, and the ideological function of 'middle ages' is to give essentially normative terms the force of neutral historic markers. Warton's book is the most important single document in the literary sphere to perform this task.

III

The question may well be asked, were there no preceding terms which the new expressions came to supplant? The answer is yes and no. None of the possible synonyms or alternative concepts could fill exactly the same role as 'middle ages'. Expressions like 'our feudal ancestry' or 'the spirit of chivalry', used by Warton's editor Price, are too specialized for general use.[11] The fact is that the commonest epithets in the eighteenth century are simply 'ancient' writers, 'older' literature, and the like. Warton himself has 'our elder English classics' (II. 41). But words like 'older' have a double ambiguity. First of all, they can lead to confusion with a quite different group of ancient writers, that is, those of classical antiquity. Second, the usage works in opposition to the common verbal habit which alludes to the 'infancy of society', a key notion in the enlightenment critique (as in Smith and Ferguson), explicitly or implicitly. People of Warton's generation saw their own culture as mature and developed; they did not really want expressions which suggested that their predecessors were older than themselves. There is a bit of an ambiguity with 'middle age', but it was a less worrying one for Warton and his friends.

This is to leave aside the other key term, 'Gothic', which is a topic too large to enter upon in any detail. It is enough to say that Warton uses the expression a dozen or more times in his *History,* but generally in a 'neutral' fashion. The word is employed sometimes in an architectural or artistic sense (e.g. III. 394, 462). Sometimes it is quasi-ethnological, used in the sense Percy attempted to make distinctive. But sometimes it does appear to be a kind of historical label, as when Warton says, 'The very devotion of the Gothic times was romantic' (III. 285). The commonest usage is 'Gothic romance' or 'Gothic fiction', an indeterminate form.

Plainly, the overtones of the word were so complex, and for the most part so obviously hostile, that it could not seriously hope to survive as a bland historical term. One student has distinguished three principal senses of 'Gothic' in the period.[12] The first is the opprobrious expression meaning barbarous or uncivilized. The second, in time, is the plain sense 'medieval' (neither is in the first edition of Johnson's *Dictionary* in 1755, though the former appears in the 1773 revision). A third and more specialized sense is the one found in 'Gothic novel', that is, 'grotesque' or 'supernatural'. The student argues that the first two senses 'marched on' their separate ways, without any mutual influence. He suggests that it was Hurd who neutralized the term for general historical use, in his famous *Letters on Chivalry and Romance.* But the term is as much an aesthetic categorizer as a simple temporal marker; when Hurd distinguishes a Gothic poem from a classical one, he is not really pointing to any closely defined epoch. Hurd speaks without any embarrassment of the 'Gothic language and ideas' in *Paradise Regained,* and this is more like the third sense than the second. It was only with the *History* of Warton, in my judgment, that the expression loses all its emotional overtones. Famously, in his poem on Reynolds's window at New College, Oxford (1782), Thomas Warton frees himself of 'visionary rapture' and with the help of Reynolds's classic art breaks the 'Gothic chain'. In fact, most commentators believe that his fundamental adherences remained unaffected up to his death.[13] But it could be said that in the *History* he had done much to break the Gothic chain, in the sense of supplying an alternative model of cultural development, which meant there was less need for an overtly normative term such as 'Gothic' had always been, in Hurd as much as anywhere else. (That Hurd approves where others had disapproved does not affect the point.)

Warton was never to complete the task he set himself. In 1790, as Isaac D'Israeli rather heartlessly put it, he expired amid his volumes.[14] But he had done much already to codify, as well as to chronicle, English poetry. There are two passages of surpassing eloquence which stuck in the English mind for generations: all the major Romantic po-

ets knew these paragraphs. One concerns the reign of Elizabeth, in Section LXI: here Warton asserts that the reformation did not manage to 'disenchant all the strong holds of superstition':

> A few dim characters were yet legible in the mouldering creed of tradition. Every goblin of ignorance did not vanish at the first glimmerings of the morning of science. Reason suffered a few demons still to linger, which she chose to retain in her service under the guidance of poetry.
>
> (IV. 327)

And there is a still more plangent threnody for the poetic world which had been lost in the account of Henry VIII's reign (III. 284-5), where Warton describes the pageants and ceremonies of earlier times as 'friendly to imagery . . . and allegory'. His basic idea is that 'the customs, institutions, traditions, and religion, of the middle ages, were favorable to poetry'. What may strike us most today is not the truth or otherwise of the picture he draws, but the sheer fact of a period designated as 'middle ages' for Warton to dilate upon. The jargon of our schools owes an unsuspected debt to Thomas Warton.

Notes

1. Fred C. Robinson, 'Medieval, the Middle Ages', *Speculum* 59 (1984) 745-56.

2. Thomas Warton, *History of English Poetry,* ed. [Richard Price], 4 vols (London, 1824). All references are to this edition. Subsequent quotations are given in the text within parentheses.

3. *Correspondence of Thomas Gray,* ed. P. Toynbee and L. Whibley, rev. H. W. Starr (Oxford, 1971), III. 1092-3, 1125-7.

4. R. Wellek, *The Rise of English Literary History* (1941; rptd. New York, 1966), pp. 166-201; L. Lipking, *The Ordering of the Arts in Eighteenth-Century England* (Princeton, 1970), pp. 352-404 (quotations which follow are from pp. 354-5, 371, 395-6). A more specialized but informative treatment will be found in Joan Pittock, *The Ascendancy of Taste: The Achievement of Joseph and Thomas Warton* (London, 1973), pp. 167-214.

5. Smith's lecture notes are printed in *The Origins of the Scottish Enlightenment 1707-1776,* ed. Jane Rendall (London, 1978), pp. 141-3. Quotations from Ferguson relevant to my argument appear on pp. 137-9, 187-9, 201-3; for Hume, Robertson, John Millar *et al.* see Rendall, *passim.*

6. Cited by Price, *History of Poetry,* I. i[n].

7. C. Burney, *A General History of Music,* ed. F. Mercer (London, 1935), 2 vols: I. 457, 458, 487, 622, 631.

8. W. Robertson, *The History of the Reign of the Emperor Charles V,* 7th edn (London, 1792), I. 61, 87.

9. T. Percy, *Reliques of Ancient English Poetry* (London, 1857), I. xvi, xxv, xxxv.

10. P.-H. Mallet, *Northern Antiquities,* tr. T. Percy [*et al.*], ed. I. A. Blackwell (London, 1847), pp. 1-21.

11. Price, ed., *History of Poetry,* I. 12-13.

12. Alfred E. Longueil, 'The Word "Gothic" in Eighteenth Century Criticism', *MLN* 38 (1923) 453-60.

13. See the discusion in Lipking, pp. 396-401.

14. Cited by James Ogden, *Isaac D'Israeli* (Oxford, 1969), p. 174.

Joseph M. P. Donatelli (essay date 1991)

SOURCE: Donatelli, Joseph M. P. "The Medieval Fictions of Thomas Warton and Thomas Percy." *University of Toronto Quarterly* 60, No. 4 (summer 1991): 435-51.

[*In the following essay, Donatelli argues that Warton and Percy were leaders in a movement that inspired a popular fascination with the Middle Ages.*]

The enthusiasm for the culture of the Middle Ages during the latter half of the eighteenth century finds various forms of expression. Yet the visitors who flocked to Walpole's Strawberry Hill instead of Glastonbury Abbey, the readers who purchased Thomas Percy's *Reliques of Ancient English Poetry* instead of Joseph Ritson's scholarly editions, and the antiquarians who preferred Matthew Prior's prettified and sentimental version of 'The Nut-Brown Maid' to the original remind us that the pseudo-medieval was often more attractive than the genuine article. For the past was invested with a significance that might prove offensive to contemporary beliefs, tastes, and values: a medieval building carried an objectionable taint of Catholicism,[1] and medieval poems were considered to be ill-formed compositions of 'wild fancy' and 'rude meter.' These are but two of the qualities that offended an age which, as William Shenstone had repeatedly advised Thomas Percy, had little taste for 'unadulterated antiquity.'[2] One writer expressed this predilection when he declared that 'a happy imitation is of much more value than a defective original.'[3]

Yet eighteenth-century scholars, let alone the public, were often hard put to discriminate between imitations and originals. For instance, George Steevens, the Shakespeare scholar, settled a score with Richard Gough, who was then director of the Society for Antiquaries, by fabricating an inscribed stone in commemoration of Hardicanute, an Anglo-Saxon king whose name had been immortalized, appropriately enough, in Lady Wardlaw's ballad forgery.[4] The inscription, in Anglo-Saxon letters, declared that Hardicanute had expired by drinking too much at the wedding of a Danish lord. Gough was convinced of the authenticity of this monument, and at his instigation the inscription immediately became the subject of a learned disquisition by the well-respected antiquary Dr Samuel Pegge, who confidently identified the stone as the work of the eleventh century. Steevens then exposed the hoax in the *General Evening Post,* and Gough was pilloried in the *Gentleman's Magazine* for his credulity. Cruel, yes, but Steevens's revelation might also be viewed as an act of mercy, for other controversies about originals and forgeries raged on, and they admitted no such easy solution.

Thomas Percy's *Reliques of Ancient English Poetry,* first published in 1765, and Thomas Warton's **History of English Poetry,** the first volume of which appeared in 1774, are pre-eminent among the works of literary scholarship which catered to, and promoted, this fascination with the Middle Ages. In doing so, these works directed their attention to the medieval and pseudo-medieval alike, and their authors, both knowingly and unknowingly, often turned one into the other. The *Reliques* and the **History** won large audiences not because of their scholarly accuracy, which few were in any position to judge,[5] but because they presented coherent and seamless accounts of a distant past for audiences which had little taste for ancient poetry. As has often been noted, the narratives which these scholars fashioned have much in common with the fictionalized accounts of the past found in the Gothic novel. This essay will consider precisely how these widely read texts conditioned the expectations of readers about the Middle Ages in a way that corroborated, if not encouraged, the fabrication of pseudo-medieval backdrops of Gothic fiction, for the blending of fact and fiction, the historical anachronisms, and the skewed view of the past were to be found in those authoritative scholarly works which stood closest to genuine medieval sources.

Before examining the medieval scholarship of the eighteenth century, we should consider briefly the remarkable achievement of the seventeenth century, which produced what David Douglas has termed 'the longest and most prolific movement of medieval research which [England] has ever seen.'[6] The 'revival' of interest in medieval institutions and culture certainly does not begin with Hurd, Walpole, the Wartons, or Percy. The groundwork for later scholars was laid by men such as Sir Edward Coke, John Selden, William Dugdale, and Thomas Hearne, as well as Anglo-Saxonists such as George Hickes and Edward Thwaites. Although a scholar like Anthony Wood might pursue his antiquarian studies to indulge 'the humour of making discoveries for a man's own private information,' the researches of these scholars were largely purposive and utilitarian. They scrutinized Latin, Anglo-Saxon, and Anglo-Norman documents of the past for the light which they shed on the contentious ecclesiastical, political, and legal issues of the Civil War and Restoration. Since matters of polity and church depended upon these texts, scholars took a sober and grave attitude towards their research. Textual accuracy was valued highly, and close study of the lexicon was promoted by a pressing concern with minutiae. The cast of these studies is considerably different from the eighteenth-century scholarship which we are about to consider: the ponderous tomes of Dugdale's great *Monasticon Anglicanum* and the Anglo-Saxon editions of

Hickes were forbidding and largely inaccessible to those who did not have the competence to deal with the primary texts.

Except for the notice of a few antiquaries, these scholarly volumes gathered dust during the latter half of the eighteenth century.[7] These studies had lost their topical relevance, for the crises of church and polity which had brought these texts into being had long since been resolved. Without that impetus, few had the competence or patience to wade through such trying and weighty scholarship. We are therefore correct in identifying the reception of medieval culture in the middle of the eighteenth century not as the first expression of interest in the Middle Ages, but rather as a new development and direction. Warton's comment in the *History* is instructive, for it indicates the scorn that was heaped on the projects of earlier scholars: 'The antiquaries of former times overlooked or rejected these valuable remains ['fables of chivalry'], which they despised as false and frivolous; and employed their industry in reviving obscure fragments of uninstructive morality or uninteresting history.'[8] The researches of a Dugdale or Hickes (which, we might note, Warton had relied upon in the *History*) were directed to serious ends; therefore, these scholars had little use for the romance materials which so fascinated Percy and Warton, yet Warton's smug attitude is ironic, for these seventeenth-century editions and compilations continued to be useful to students of the Middle Ages long after eighteenth-century efforts, including Warton's own *History,* had been superseded and exploded.[9]

The goals of Percy's *Reliques* and Warton's *History* were entirely different from those of the scholarship of the previous century. Although these works provided scholarly discussions of the history of literature for the serious student of antiquities, they were equally, if not primarily, addressed to 'readers of taste' who did not have, nor did they wish to have, first-hand knowledge of medieval texts. In his preface to the *History,* Warton had addressed himself to both classes of readers: 'I hope to merit the thanks of the antiquarian, for enriching the stock of our early literature by these new accessions; and I trust I shall gratify the reader of taste, in having so frequently rescued from oblivion the rude inventions and irregular beauties of the heroic tale, or the romantic legend' (***History of English Poetry***; hereafter cited as *HEP* 1:viii). The rhetoric of this statement is noteworthy: Warton speaks of his bibliographic achievement when addressing the antiquarian, but he appeals to the imagination of the 'reader of taste' by evoking the image of his noble rescue of 'heroic tale' and 'romantic legend' from oblivion, much as a knight might rescue a damsel. The antiquary did not have to be persuaded of the merits of the subject, but a general readership had to be encouraged to appreciate its value. The remarkable public success of both works, especially Percy's *Reliques* which went through four editions during his lifetime, would indicate that Percy and Warton succeeded in widening and broadening the appeal of the Middle Ages.[10] As the cantankerous but scholarly Joseph Ritson pointed out, with some justice, in his vicious attacks on both authors, such renown

was won by the sacrifice of, or lack of interest in, painstaking scholarship, and by the invention of a 'tissue of falsehood' about the Middle Ages.[11]

Both Percy and Warton were well aware of the burdens which their works placed on the reader. Percy expressed his concerns to Richard Farmer prior to the publication of his anthology: 'When I consider what strange old stuff I have raked together, I tremble for its reception with a fastidious public. What rare hacking and hewing will there be for Mess.[rs] the Reviewers!'[12] In the Preface to the *Reliques,* Percy anticipates such attacks by adopting an apologetic tone: 'In a polished age, like the present, I am sensible that many of these reliques of antiquity will require great allowances to be made for them.'[13] Although individual compositions might tax the reader because of their 'rudeness,' both authors counselled patience to their audience, for they insisted that the value of such poetry was teleological: with these 'reliques,' one could appreciate 'the gradual improvements of the English language and poetry from the earliest ages down to the present' (*Reliques* 1:8). Warton promised his reader that he would experience 'a conscious pride, arising in great measure from a tacit comparison of the infinite disproportion between the feeble efforts of remote ages, and our present improvements in knowledge' (*HEP* 1:i). Nevertheless, despite such excuses, Percy and Warton were convinced that the images and customs depicted in medieval literature had intrinsic value, for this literature exerted a power to 'forcibly strike a feeling imagination' (*HEP* 1:ii) with its potent mix of the fabulous and the heroic. These two strains—one apologetic, the other enthusiastic—run throughout both works.[14] They might be compared to similar cross-currents in the Gothic novel: in her Preface to the *Old English Baron,* Clara Reeve recognizes that it is 'the business of romance . . . to excite attention,' but she stipulates that it must be 'directed to some useful, or at least innocent, end.'[15] In Ann Radcliffe's *Gaston de Blondeville* (which was written in 1802 but remained unpublished until 1826, after her death), Willoughton, while reading a medieval manuscript which he has acquired, is alternately amused and repelled by the absurdity of medieval superstition and lore, yet 'he sometimes found his attention seized, in spite of himself, by the marvellous narratives before him.'[16]

Since the *Reliques* and the *History* sought to address a general readership, both Percy and Warton devised strategies for putting the reader who had little taste for ancient poetry at ease. This was accomplished by bridging and foreshortening the vast historical distance between a barbaric past and an elegant, refined present. In the *Reliques,* Percy sought to atone 'for the rudeness of the more obsolete poems,' by concluding each of the three volumes 'with a few modern attempts in the same kind of writing,' which were offered as a palliative for the reader who had struggled through the 'ancient' ballads (*Reliques* 1:8). Of course, the ballads themselves were not nearly as old as Percy considered them to be. Creating a wonderfully evocative image that was to have a long history in Romantic poetry, Percy claimed that his ballads had originally been composed by noble bards and minstrels who had performed at the houses of great nobles, and that these 'reliques of antiquity' preserved 'the customs and opinions of remote ages' from before Chaucer's time.[17] The dating of ballads continues to be a vexed question, of course, but Percy overestimated the antiquity of his texts by centuries. Moreover, the oldest ballads, such as *Sir Cauline* and *The Marriage of Sir Gawaine,* were those which Percy had completely rewritten, not only to mitigate the 'rudeness' of the language and metre, as Percy had openly avowed, but also to reshape plots extensively so that these works would appeal to the sentimental and neoclassical tastes of eighteenth-century readers.[18] These 'reliques' then, which had been offered with such profuse apologies, were simply not that old, but a reader of the anthology who had little or nothing to compare them to would be left with the impression that he had read ancient songs and poems, which, for all their 'rudeness,' were not only remarkably lucid, but similar in conception and sentiment to contemporary literature.

In the prefaces which Percy provided for each poem or ballad, he produced a hotchpotch of information, with strange historical conflations and juxtapositions. In the introduction to *Sir Cauline* (*Reliques* 1:61-2), for example, Percy discusses both the origin of the Round Table and the association of women with the art of healing. Having planted the image of the Round Table in the poem himself in a lengthy interpolation, Percy glosses his own fiction by explaining in his preface that 'the Round Table was not peculiar to the reign of King Arthur but was common in all ages of chivalry,' and he cites Dugdale's description of a 'torneament' held at Kenilworth during Edward I's time as evidence. While the image of a lady as a 'leeche' who ministers to a knight does appear briefly in the original text ('Fetche me downe my daughter deere, / She is a leeche fulle fine' [*Reliques* 1:63, lines 29-30]), Percy makes much of this image, devoting half his preface to the subject. He declares that the association of women with the art of healing is 'a practice derived from the earliest times among all the Gothic and Celtic nations,' and that women 'even of the highest rank' continued to practice the art of surgery even as late as the reign of Queen Elizabeth. This informed discussion, wherein he cites Dugdale, Ste-Palaye, Mallet, and Harrison's preface to Holinshed, covers a span of over a thousand years in a few sentences, thereby foreshortening the historical distance between the contemporary reader and the past, and creating a jumble of earlier periods in which Goths and Celts, Arthur, Edward I, and Elizabeth are invoked, and, in some sense, coexist on one page together. There is little depth or contour to this historical discussion, but the parade of these great names results in a highly evocative short narrative, which competes, I would suggest, with the ballad itself (which was largely Percy's own composition) for attention. This impressive collection of historical personages in a fictional context is analogous to the historical casts which are assembled in novels such as Sophia Lee's *The Recess.*[19]

Whereas Percy's prefaces address individual works, in the first volume of the *History of English Poetry,* Warton composes an extended narrative about the medieval period, which I would like to consider here as remarkably similar in form and content to a work of fiction. While the *History* could not match the popularity of the *Reliques,* it claimed a readership which extended well beyond the small circle of antiquaries and scholars: we know that the work was read by Horace Walpole, Clara Reeve, and Ann Radcliffe.[20] One reviewer praised the 'graces and ornaments' which this 'poetical historian' had brought to the study of antiquity.[21] Upon opening the first volume, Walpole remarked that the *History* seemed 'delightfully full of things I love,' yet he (as well as other readers) became increasingly disenchanted with subsequent volumes, which had less to offer the dilettant and aesthete.[22]

Warton rejected Pope's and Gray's schemes for histories of English poetry, which would have grouped works according to various types and schools, choosing instead to construct a continuous, chronological narrative whose shape was determined by what Warton termed the 'free exertion of research.'[23] This design was tantamount to granting himself poetic licence, and it led to the baggy and digressive structure of the *History,* a failing which Ritson pointed out when he uncharitably described the *History* as 'an injudicious *farrago,* a *gallimawfry* of things which both do and do not belong to the subject.'[24] Since David Fairer's invaluable study of Warton's notebooks, the earlier view that Warton's *History of English Poetry* is a fuller execution of the plan and method of the earlier *Observations on the Faerie Queene* can no longer be held.[25] It is clear that Warton had been 'laying in materials for this work' as early as 1752-4, and that, during the long interval between his conception of the project and its publication, he had repeatedly cast about in order to find the proper format for his research.[26] Since Warton's work was without precedent, we should not underestimate the difficulties which Warton faced in composing a chronological survey of English verse.[27] When the *History* was finally launched, the narrative was constructed around bits and pieces of texts which Warton had encountered (and copied) during years of reading in medieval manuscripts and early printed editions. In elucidating these texts, the *History* draws upon a wide range of sources, and the work therefore serves as a clearing house for the earlier scholarship which had become so unfashionable. References to sources as varied as Du Cange, Ste-Palaye, Froissart, Dugdale, Hickes, Wormius, Mabillon, and Geoffrey of Monmouth are woven together, with some skill, into a collection of seamless narrative vignettes in the footnotes.[28] Warton is primarily interested in extracting memorable anecdotes and striking images from these authors. The 'plot,' if you will, consists of Warton's selection from his vast fund of primary and secondary materials. Just how skewed Warton's selection might be is indicated by his peremptory dismissal of the Anglo-Saxons as an 'unformed and unsettled race' and of their poetry as unworthy of notice:

> But besides that a legitimate illustration of that jejune and intricate subject would have almost doubled my labour, that the Saxon language is familiar only to a few learned antiquaries, that our Saxon poems are for

the most part little more than religious rhapsodies, and that scarce any compositions remain marked with the native images of that people in their pagan state, every reader that reflects but for a moment on our political establishment must perceive, that the Saxon poetry has no connection with the nature and purpose of my present undertaking.

(*HEP* 1:vi)

Undoubtedly, part of the 'intricacy' of the subject was owing to Warton's ignorance of Anglo-Saxon,[29] a testimony to the decline of scholarship from the high-water mark of the seventeenth century, a state of affairs which was not to be remedied until the revival of Anglo-Saxon studies at Oxford with the establishment of the Rawlinson Chair.[30] But Warton has also taken the measure of his audience, and he shows that he is perfectly willing to sacrifice a subject (although in this case he had little choice) if it means holding the reader's interest, for the success of the *History* demanded that 'the curiosity of the antiquarian' be connected 'with taste and genius' (*HEP* 1:209). In place of the Anglo-Saxon past, Warton offers a study of the origin of romances which reviews fashionable theories about the Eastern origin of romances, and their transmission through Spain or, as Percy had suggested after reading Mallet, through Scandinavia.[31] Hence, the *History* begins with oriental fantasies and ruminations on the migration of the Asiatic Goths to the northern climes of Scandinavia. With its mixture of the exotic and the sublime, sections of Warton's text work powerfully on the imagination in a way that is reminiscent of the Ossianic poems and of the settings of Gothic fiction: 'In the mean time, we may suppose, that the new situation of these people in Scandinavia, might have added a darker shade and a more savage complexion to their former fictions and superstitions; and that the formidable objects of nature to which they became familiarized in those northern solitudes, the piny precipices, the frozen mountains, and the gloomy forests, acted on their imaginations, and gave a tincture of horror to their imagery' (*HEP* 1:diss I, sig d4). Elsewhere, we read assertions that recall the potent mix of orientalism and medievalism in Beckford's *Vathek*: 'The books of the Arabians and Persians abound with extravagant traditions about the giants Gog and Magog. These they call Jagiouge and Magiouge; and the Caucasian wall, said to be built by Alexander the Great from the Caspian to the Black Sea, in order to cover the frontiers of his dominion, and to prevent the incursions of the Sythians, is called by the orientals the WALL of GOG and MAGOG' (*HEP* 1:diss I, sig b3r-v). Sensational pronouncements (e.g. 'Dragons are a sure mark of orientalism' [*HEP* 1:diss I, sig c1]) abound. Indeed, Warton seems to disapprove of Anglo-Saxon poetry because it does not contain that which he and others treasured in the Ossianic poems—hopelessly romanticized 'native images of that people in their pagan state' which were remarkably free of the 'religious rhapsodies' (and Catholic, at that) which Warton and other readers apparently found offensive. One might say that his cursory readings in the origins of English poetry do not serve his 'plot,' and that they were therefore jettisoned in favour of more exotic and sensational materials. Warton's decision not to

begin at the beginning was probably determined as much by aesthetics as by scholarship.[32]

Warton's dismissal of Anglo-Saxons and their literature results in a radical historical foreshortening so that a reader who was guided solely by Warton would come away with the impression that the history of English literature began with the Norman Conquest. Yet Warton's historical displacement of Anglo-Saxon literature also meant that the genesis of this 'epoch of chivalry' could be traced to a distant past which evoked images of oriental dragons, dramatic continental migrations, and primitive 'Celtic tribes, who were strongly addicted to poetical compositions.' A large part of the *History* is devoted to romance, the literature of this 'epoch of chivalry.' Again, the technique was to quote liberally from the romances, but the selections frequently emphasized the pageantry of court life (especially individual contests in the lists), the superstitions which had been imported from the East during the Crusades, the gallantry which knights extended towards ladies, and the ubiquitous presence of bards and minstrels who, since Warton knew Percy's views well, sang at houses of the great.[33] These are, of course, the very scenes that serve as commonplaces in the medieval settings of Gothic fiction. In a few later works, Warton's *History* has obviously played a role in disseminating these images.[34] However, it would appear that scholarship did not serve as a source for fiction, but rather that scholarly and fictional works shared this imagery because these texts were conceived in a similar cultural matrix and were aimed at similar audiences: in both *Longsword* and *The Old English Baron* (both of which were published prior to the *History*), meagre historical sources have been amplified with individual combats in the lists, minstrels who sing 'native lays about Arthur' before nobles, gallant knights who defer to ladies, and colourful pageants and tournaments.

The language of the original texts which Warton had collected presented severe challenges to the reader. The reviewer for the *Gentleman's Magazine* declared that the specimens of Norman-Saxon poems in the *History* were 'curious only as antiquities,' for they were scarcely readable.[35] Another reviewer, commenting generally on editions of ancient poems, declared that 'the labour of reading was not repaid by the pleasures which were communicated by the poetry.'[36] 'A refined age,' he noted, 'must have all its amusements, without the labour of attainment.' The hit-and-miss glossing of the *History* reveals that even Warton himself was not always in command of the Middle English, and one can well imagine that readers (who are perhaps not that different from those today who read the *History* without adequate preparation in Middle English, Scots, Old French, Italian, and Latin) looked only at Warton's comments rather than reading the excerpt. It was therefore possible to ignore these inset quotations from manuscripts, and to pay attention solely to Warton's synopsis. Indeed, the above-mentioned reviewer for the *Gentleman's Magazine* praised the 'skill and taste' of Warton's commentary while dismissing the poetry itself as 'dross': 'the dross of these old bards . . . has here received both lustre and value from the skill and taste with which they have been refined and illustrated.'[37]

Warton's commentary contained idealized portraits of medieval society and institutions, especially since Warton followed his contemporaries in regarding romances as historical documents which provided accurate descriptions of ancient manners and times, with exception being taken only to their accounts of the fabulous. The quotations themselves are composed of graphic and detailed imagery; Warton's comments produced a highly abbreviated, though attractive, portrait, one which approaches the level of abstraction and generalization that one finds in the Gothic novel's medieval veneer. For example, most of Warton's observations about Richard I were drawn from the romance *Richard Cœur de Lyon.* Thus we read that the 'first of our hero's achievements in chivalry is at a splendid tournament held at Salisbury' (*HEP* 1:153), and 'Richard arming himself is a curious Gothic picture' (*HEP* 1:166). In commenting upon a passage from this romance, Warton mistranslates *faucon,* that is 'falchion' or 'sword,' as 'falcon.'[38] Citing various learned sources as well as corroborating evidence from tapestries, he unhesitatingly asserts that 'in the feudal times . . . no gentleman appeared on horseback, unless going to battle, without a hawk on his fist' (*HEP* 1:166). This lexical error provides the occasion for a lengthy footnote on the practice of hawking, but it also leads to a reading of the action of the romance which is Warton's fiction, rather than the medieval poet's: 'The soldan is represented as meeting Richard with a hawk on his fist, to shew indifference, or a contempt of his adversary; and that he came rather prepared for the chace, than the combat' (*HEP* 1:166). When discussing Edward III's foundation of the Order of the Garter, Warton describes Edward as a 'romantic monarch' who venerated his predecessor, Arthur, and established 'this most antient and revered institution of chivalry' in his honour (1:252). Edward's court 'was the theatre of romantic elegance.' Elsewhere, in commenting on a passage from the romance *Ipomedon,* Warton draws a picture of court life that resembles the parlour-rooms of eighteenth-century polite society: 'In the feudal castles, where many persons of both sexes were assembled, and who did not know how to spend the time, it is natural to suppose that different parties were formed, and different schemes of amusement invented' (1:199, *n.* x).

If Warton's *History* may be read as a fiction, we can identify both a narrative persona and voice. Warton delivers his pronouncements on medieval texts and culture with a voice that is authoritative, sensible, informed, urbane, and at times reverential. Having cultivated this persona in his poetry and in *Observations on the Faerie Queene,* Warton presents himself as a genial guide who is there to escort his readers as they wander through ancient times.[39] One reader of the *History* spoke of being guided by the 'torch of genius through ruins in which he [Warton] loves to wander,' a metaphor which evokes images of the dimly lit corridors in the fiction of the period.[40] Warton seeks to bridge historical distance while still allowing the reader to

appreciate the strangeness of ancient times and beliefs. Despite his enthusiasm, Warton's point of view remains that of one who is firmly convinced of the advantages of his own period. Although he reads Bede, for example, he comes to the text with expectations conditioned by Gibbon. He reminds us that for Bede 'the importation into England of the shin-bone of an apostle' was more significant than victories or revolutions (*HEP* 1:diss II, sig e1). Warton also invites the reader to enjoy historical vistas, which are not unlike the prospects of Radcliffe's novels, but instead of looking out over space, we look over time. In a letter to Gray, Warton declared his intention to include such 'terraces' from which readers might survey the past: 'I should have said before, that although I proceed chronologically, yet I often stand still to give some general view.'[41] Warton's remarks prior to introducing Chaucer (who does not appear until the end of the first volume) provide such a panoramic vista as we reach one of the many 'summits' in the *History*:

> As we are approaching to Chaucer, let us here stand still, and take a retrospect of the general manners. The tournaments and carousals of our antient princes, by forming splendid assemblies of both sexes, while they inculcated the most liberal sentiments of honour and heroism, undoubtedly contributed to introduce ideas of courtesy, and to encourage decorum.
>
> (*HEP* 1:339)

Chaucer's achievement was largely made possible by this 'politeness and propriety,' but Warton, using figurative language, makes it clear that this advance in the growth of manners and literature, which seem to march hand in hand, was only temporary:

> I consider Chaucer as a genial day in an English spring. A brilliant sun enlivens the face of nature with an unusual lustre: the sudden appearance of cloudless skies, and the unexpected warmth of a tepid atmosphere, after the gloom and the inclemencies of a tedious winter, fill our hearts with the visionary prospect of a speedy summer: and we fondly anticipate a long continuance of gentle gales and vernal serenity. But winter returns with redoubled horrors: the clouds condense more formidably than before; and those tender buds, and early blossoms, which were called forth by the transient gleam of a temporary sun-shine, are nipped by frosts, and torn by tempests.
>
> (2:51)[42]

Clearly, Chaucer's achievement is being judged in terms of Warton's present. The fifteenth century, which had provided Horace Walpole with such little amusement, is roundly condemned because the literature of this period failed to appeal to the fancy of Warton or his eighteenth-century audience. Warton, I would suggest, found it infinitely more difficult to shape a self-contained imaginative narrative, with sensational and evocative images, from the disparate materials of fifteenth-century and sixteenth-century verse. As has often been noted, Warton's enthusiasm is dampened at a certain point in the *History*[43]: one of the reasons, I would suggest, is that as Warton approached his own period, and discussed literature that was more widely known, it became increasingly difficult for him to compose the kinds of fictions which had so engaged readers of the first volume. Paradoxically, as the **History** became more scholarly, it proved less attractive to contemporary readers.

Percy's *Reliques* and Warton's **History** may also help to explain the popularity of the recovered manuscript as a narrative convention in Gothic fiction.[44] The first edition of *The Castle of Otranto* purports to be William Marshal's English translation of an original black-letter edition printed at Naples in 1529, which recounts events that occurred during the Crusades.[45] Appropriately enough, the volume was found in the library of an ancient Catholic family in the north of England. In the first edition of the *Old English Baron,* Reeve claims that the tale is preserved in a manuscript written in Old English. The novel breaks off repeatedly in places where the manuscript is discontinuous, illegible, or damaged. Radcliffe uses the device in several novels: although it serves merely as a device to introduce the narrative in *The Italian* and *A Sicilian Romance,* in *Gaston de Blondeville* Radcliffe elaborates the description of the manuscript. Willoughton, an antiquarian of sorts, obtains a manuscript, 'written on vellum and richly illuminated,' which contains an English translation of an original Norman account dating from the time of Henry III.[46] Conveniently for eighteenth-century readers, the narrative is a modernized copy, which Willoughton has written for a friend 'who was fond of the subjects it touched upon, but had not industry enough to work his way through the obstructions of the original.'[47] In the novel, Radcliffe reproduces the title page of this manuscript, which announces, in appropriate but improbable archaic spellings and black letter, that this account, originally dated 1261, has been 'changed out of the Norman tongue by Grymbald, Monk of Seӡnt Marie Priori in Killingworth.'[48] Charles Maturin also uses the device in *Melmoth the Wanderer.* The manuscript which John Melmoth discovers in his uncle's closet is 'discoloured, obliterated, and mutilated beyond any that ever before exercised the patience of a reader.'[49] Walpole, the bibliophile, had owned such black-letter editions and manuscripts, and Maturin, a clergyman who took a degree at Trinity College, Dublin, was conversant with textual studies.[50] It seems less likely, however, that Reeve or Radcliffe, any more than many other novelists who used the device, had ever seen, let alone read, the kind of manuscript which they describe in their fiction.[51]

Although this narrative device was in vogue because of the popularity of French historical and epistolary novels, works such as Percy's *Reliques* and Warton's **History** had given manuscripts a prominence which they had not previously had. Readers had been primed for this kind of archival digging by the very public controversies concerning the forged manuscripts of Macpherson's Ossian poems and Chatterton's Rowley poems, and some readers undoubtedly turned to the *Reliques* and the **History** in hope of finding more of the kind of poetry that they had read

there. Moreover, the manuscripts which had contributed to the *Reliques* and the **History** were described colourfully: Percy gave himself a heroic role when he described how he had rescued the manuscript containing his 'ancient reliques' from under a bureau at the house of one of his friends, where it was being used by the maids to light the fire.[52] When a controversy erupted about whether the manuscript existed or not, Sir Joshua Reynolds painted a portrait of Percy, with the famous folio manuscript under the bishop's arm. The **History** conveys Warton's excitement as he sifts through hundreds of manuscripts which have lain unread for many years. Warton's scholarly persona comes alive, in a way that reminds one of Alonzo copying Adonijah's manuscript in *Melmoth the Wanderer,* when he poignantly states about the *Pricke of Conscience*: 'I prophesy that I am its last transcriber' (**HEP** 1:256). The remarks of a reviewer demonstrate the association of this kind of scholarship with the sensational and lurid imagery which describes manuscripts in the fiction of the period: 'The laudable desire of examining the antiquities of our country, has occasioned many works of our old poets to be emancipated from the dust and obscurity of musty libraries . . . poems, really ancient, have been recovered from the cobwebs by which they were concealed, and from worms, which had already commenced their depredations.'[53]

Hence, the manuscripts which commanded public attention allowed readers to appreciate a distant past, but they were remarkably free of the lexical and conceptual difficulties which had taxed even a Thomas Warton. This was accomplished either by the mediation of scholarly works, such as those of Percy and Warton, whose commentaries provided 'texts' which readers could follow even if they could not read the original materials,[54] or by forged or doctored texts, which had been designed so that they would appeal directly to eighteenth-century sensibilities. Moreover, the idealized views of the Middle Ages which these manuscripts conveyed repeatedly invited comparison and identification with the mores and values of contemporary society. Warton, who was at first convinced by the Ossian poems, marvelled that 'the early poetry of a barbarous people, should so frequently give place to a gentler set of manners, to the social sensibilities of polished life, and a more civilised and elegant species of imagination' (**HEP** 1:diss I, sig g2v). Elsewhere, Warton had noted that the institutions of chivalry had 'salutary consequences in assisting the general growth of refinement' and in 'teaching modes of decorum' (**HEP** 1:diss I, sig 13v). Similar confusion of the past and present is evident in Clara Reeve's *Progress of Romance,* which described medieval romance as 'an Epic in prose,' and considers the genre as 'the *polite literature* of those early ages.'[55] She envisions a readership for these works which mirrors contemporary concerns about the effect of Gothic fiction on impressionable young minds: 'In the days of Gothic ignorance, these Romances might perhaps, be read by many young persons as true Histories, and might therefore more easily affect their manners.'[56] Is it odd then that the manuscripts of Gothic novels set in the past should speak so directly and coherently to the present, except for the occasional archaic form?

The point has often been made that what eighteenth-century readers saw in the Middle Ages was a mirror of their own values, society, and taste, and that once the slender trappings of chivalry have been put aside, the characters of novels like *The Old English Baron* and *Longsword* behave as eighteenth-century ladies and gentlemen. However, it would be incorrect to consider that novelists made informed choices between fact and fiction, since both were intermingled in the authoritative scholarly accounts of the period. By reading Percy and Warton, we become aware that these highly influential works created a hall of mirrors down which both readers and novelists looked when they considered the Middle Ages. Those scholarly sources which stood closest to original medieval texts were themselves full of the pseudo-medieval; indeed, their success depended upon the creation of 'fictions' about the Middle Ages that would cater to the 'reader of taste.'

Notes

1. Kenneth Clark, *The Gothic Revival: An Essay in the History of Taste*, 4th ed (London: John Murray 1974), 99-107.

2. *The Correspondence of Thomas Percy and William Shenstone*, ed Cleanth Brooks, vol 7 of *The Percy Letters* (New Haven: Yale University Press 1977), 51, 72-3, 118, 136-7.

3. James Dallaway, *Anecdotes of the Arts in England* (London: T. Cadell and W. Davies 1800), 159.

4. For an account of this hoax, see B. Sprague Allen, *Tides in English Taste (1519-1800)* (Cambridge, Mass: Harvard University Press 1937), 2:91; a drawing of the stone was published in the *Gentleman's Magazine* 67 (1790), 217; see also 290-2.

5. Their contemporary, Joseph Ritson, was a notable exception because of his painstaking and careful scholarship. In *Observations on the Three First Volumes of the History of English Poetry* (London: J. Stockdale and R. Faulder 1782; repr New York 1971), a scathing critique of the *History of English Poetry*, Ritson sneered at both men, declaring that Percy's 'knowledge in these matters seems pretty much upon a level with your own' (4). For his critique of the *Reliques*, to which Percy felt himself obligated to respond in the fourth edition (which appeared in 1794), see *Ancient English Metrical Romances*, rev E. Goldsmid (Edinburgh: E. and G. Goldsmid 1884-6), 1:58.

6. David C. Douglas, *English Scholars* (London: Jonathan Cape 1939), 16; I am indebted to Douglas for the following brief survey of seventeenth-century scholarship; see also *Anglo-Saxon Scholarship: The First Three Centuries*, ed Carl T. Berkhout and Milton McC. Gatch (Boston: G.K. Hall and Co 1982).

7. Douglas, 354-67.

8. Thomas Warton, *History of English Poetry*, with an introduction by René Wellek, 4 vols (1774-81; repr New York 1968), 1:209; hereafter abbreviated as *HEP*. In elucidating 'fables of chivalry,' eighteenth-century scholars supplemented the meagre information they gleaned from the English tradition by turning to continental sources, such as J. B. de la Curne de Sainte-Palaye's *Mémoires sur l'ancienne chevalerie* (1759-81) and Paul-Henri Mallet's *Introduction à l'Histoire de Dannemarc* (1755), for there had been a continuous tradition of the study of early French literature (see Arthur Johnston, *Enchanted Ground: The Study of Medieval Romance in the Eighteenth Century* [London: Athlone Press 1964], 22-4).

9. See, for example, the apologies and corrections offered by Richard Price in his edition of the *History* (London: Thomas Tegg 1824). William Carew Hazlitt condemned Warton's 'whole narrative' as 'emphatically *slipshod*' (x) in the preface to his edition of the *History* (1871; repr New York 1970). He nevertheless thought it worthwhile to publish a new edition, albeit with extensive corrections.

10. The works of these popularizers may be compared with similar efforts by classicists to aim at a wider polite market. See Penelope Wilson's essay 'Classical Poetry and the Eighteenth-Century Reader,' in *Books and Their Readers in Eighteenth-Century England*, ed Isabel Rivers (New York: St Martin's Press 1982), esp 83-90.

11. *Observations*, 48.

12. Percy to Farmer, 10 Feb 1765; *The Correspondence of Thomas Percy and Richard Farmer*, ed Cleanth Brooks (Baton Rouge: Louisiana State University Press 1946), vol 2 of *The Percy Letters*, 82.

13. *Reliques of Ancient English Poetry*, ed Henry B. Wheatley (1886; repr New York 1966), 1:8. All references are to this edition.

14. Previous critics have called attention to conflicting voices in Warton's *History*. In *The Ordering of the Arts in Eighteenth-Century England* (Princeton: Princeton University Press 1970), Lawrence Lipking views the conflict as a dialectic between imagination and reason (375-6 and 392-404). See also R. D. Havens, 'Thomas Warton and the Eighteenth-Century Dilemma,' *Studies in Philology* 25 (1928), 36-50.

15. Clara Reeve, *The Old English Baron with the Castle of Otranto* (London: J.C. Nimms and Bain 1883), 12.

16. Ann Radcliffe, *Gaston de Blondeville or the Court of Henry III Keeping Festival in Ardenne* (1826; repr New York 1972), 1:74.

17. For a recent discussion of this image in Romantic poetry, see Kathryn Sutherland, 'The Native Poet: The Influence of Percy's Minstrel from Beattie to Wordsworth,' *Review of English Studies* ns 33 (1982), 414-33.

18. On Percy's revisions to the ballads, see Joseph M. P. Donatelli, 'Thomas Percy's Use of the Metrical Romances in the *Reliques*,' in *Hermeneutics and Medieval Culture,* ed Patrick J. Gallacher and Helen Damico (Albany: SUNY Press 1989), 225-35; Albert B. Friedman, *The Ballad Revival* (Chicago: University of Chicago Press 1961), 203-12; Walter Jackson Bate, 'Percy's Use of His Folio-Manuscript,' *Journal of English and Germanic Philology* 43 (1944), 337-48.

19. On the responses of eighteenth-century readers to historical fiction, see James R. Foster, *History of the Pre-Romantic Novel in England* (New York: Modern Language Association 1949), 186-224; and J. M. S. Tompkins, *The Popular Novel in England 1770-1800* (London: Methuen and Co, 1932), 232-42.

20. Horace Walpole's letters to William Mason, dated 23 March 1774 and 7 April 1774 in *Horace Walpole's Correspondence with William Mason,* ed W. S. Lewis, Grover Cronin Jr, and Charles H. Bennett, vols 28-9 of *The Yale Edition of Horace Walpole's Correspondence* (New Haven: Yale University Press 1955), 1:140, 143; Clara Reeve, *The Progress of Romance* (1785; repr New York 1970), vii-xi; *Gaston de Blondeville,* 1:61-2.

21. *Gentleman's Magazine* 44 (1774), 370.

22. 'He has dipped into an incredible ocean of dry and obsolete authors of the dark ages, and has brought up more rubbish than riches . . . it is very fatiguing to wade through the muddy poetry of three or four centuries that had never a poet.' Walpole to Mason, 18 April 1778, *Correspondence,* 1:385. See also a reviewer's remarks on the second volume: 'The learned and ingenious Writer has prosecuted his respectable labours with great assiduity, but possibly, with too much prolixity. On that account only it is to be feared that his valuable book may become the solitary inhabitant of *consulted* libraries' (*Monthly Review* 59 [1778], 132).

23. *HEP,* 1:iv-v; See René Wellek, *The Rise of English Literary History* (Chapel Hill: University of North Carolina Press 1941), 162-5.

24. Ritson, *Observations,* 48.

25. 'The Origin of Warton's *History of English Poetry,*' *Review of English Studies* ns 32 (1981), 37-63.

26. Fairer, 40-5.

27. On the precursors to the *HEP,* see Wellek, chap 5.

28. On Warton's use of sources in the *HEP,* see Clarissa Rinaker, *Thomas Warton: A Bibliographic and Critical Study* (Urbana: University of Illinois Press 1916), 121-3, 177-232.

29. For considerably less shrill assessments of Warton's philological competence than Ritson's (see below n 32), see David Nichol Smith, 'Warton's History of

English Poetry,' *Proceedings of the British Academy* 15 (1929), 77-9, and A. M. Kinghorn, 'Warton's History and Early English Poetry,' *English Studies* 44 (1963), 197-204.

30. See Richard C. Payne, 'The Rediscovery of Old English Poetry in the English Literary Tradition,' in Berkhout and Gatch, 156-9.

31. For a discussion of these theories of romance origin, see Johnston, 13-31.

32. Ritson again stands alone among Warton's contemporaries in calling attention to this gross historical distortion: 'You, Sir, have sometimes been a biographer; and did you ever find it necessary to commence the story of your hero at the 15th or 16th year of his age, and to assert that the time of his birth and infancy had no connection with the story of his life, because, forsooth, he was become a very different person when grown up and sent to college, from what he was when born, breeched, and sent to school?' (*Observations,* 2).

33. *HEP* 1:diss I, sig c3v-c4v.

34. In *Literary Hours* (3rd ed, London 1804), Dr Nathan Drake refers to Warton when describing the production of 'Legendary and Romantic fiction' in Britain (3:257-8); in *Gaston de Blondeville* (1:141), 'Maister Henry,' the versifier, sings the ballad of the Giant of Cornwall before Henry III—he is none other than Warton's Henry of Avranches (*HEP* 1:46-8).

35. *Gentleman's Magazine* 44 (1774), 373.

36. *Critical Review* 61 (1786), 172.

37. *Gentleman's Magazine* 44 (1774), 429.

38. This lexical error, as well as many others, had not escaped Ritson's notice: 'Though such unparalleled ignorance, such matchless effrontery, is not, Mr. Warton, in my humble opinion, worthy of any thing but castigation or contempt, yet, should there be a single person, beside yourself, who can mistake the meaning of so plain, so obvious a passage (which I much suspect to have been corrupted in coming through your hands) I shall beg leave to inform him that a FAUCON BRODE is nothing more or less than a BROAD FAUCHION' (*Observations,* 9).

39. On the close connection between Warton's creative corpus and his scholarly efforts, see John A. Vance, *Joseph and Thomas Warton* (Boston: Twayne Publishers 1983), 37-40; Joan Pittock, *The Ascendancy of Taste: The Achievement of Joseph and Thomas Warton* (London: Routledge and Kegan Paul 1973), 176ff; Lipking, 377-84; and Frances Schouler Miller, 'The Historic Sense of Thomas Warton, Junior,' *ELH* 5 (1938), 71-92.

40. Quoted by Pittock, 203.

41. Warton's letter to Gray, 20 April 1770, *Correspondence of Thomas Gray,* ed. P. Toynbee and L. Whibley (Oxford 1935), 3:1129.

42. According to Warton, this kind of 'night' had fallen before when a budding interest in the liberal arts during the twelfth century was overwhelmed by 'the barbarous and barren subtleties of scholastic divines': 'this promising dawn of polite letters and rational knowledge was soon obscured. The temporary gleam of light did not arrive to perfect day' [*HEP* 1:diss II, sig k3].

43. Vance, 115-21; Pittock, 203-8; Lipking, 392-6.

44. For previous discussions of this convention, see Elizabeth MacAndrew, *The Gothic Tradition in Fiction* (New York: Columbia University Press 1979), 10-11, 35-6; and Montague Summers, *The Gothic Quest* (1938; repr New York 1964), 169-70.

45. Horace Walpole, *The Castle of Otranto,* ed W. S. Lewis (Oxford: Oxford University Press 1964), 3.

46. *Gaston de Blondeville* 1:49.

47. Ibid, 1:75.

48. Ibid, 1:76.

49. Charles Maturin, *Melmoth the Wanderer,* ed William F. Axton (Lincoln: University of Nebraska Press 1961), 21.

50. Maturin graduated with honours in classics: see Robert E. Lougy, *Charles Robert Maturin* (Lewisburg: Bucknell University Press 1975), 14. In *Melmoth,* Maturin alludes to the biblical scholar Johann Michaelis 'scrutinizing into the pretended autograph of St. Mark at Venice' (21).

51. However, Radcliffe apparently looked for old books when she visited Belvedere House, the seat of Lord Eardely. See 'Memoir of the Life and Writings of Mrs. Radcliffe,' in *Gaston de Blondeville* 1:68.

52. John W. Hales and Frederick J. Furnivall, *Bishop Percy's Folio Manuscript: Ballads and Romances* (London: N. Trübner and Co 1867-8), 1: lxxiv.

53. *Critical Review* 61 (1786), 169-70.

54. When speaking of original texts, one should keep in mind that most editors smoothed over orthographic problems silently: Warton, for example, declared himself unwilling to reproduce the 'capricious peculiarities and even ignorance of transcribers' (*HEP* 1:220).

55. *Progress of Romance,* 1:13, 38.

56. Ibid, 1:57.

Edward J. Rielly (essay date 1991)

SOURCE: Rielly, Edward J. "Thomas Warton's Gothic Sensibility." In *Man and Nature/L'Homme et La Nature,* 10 (1991): 147-58.

[*In the following essay, Rielly illustrates how Warton's writings and other scholarly interests reveal his Gothic sensibility.*]

Thomas Warton was an ardent antiquarian who contributed significantly to the late eighteenth century fusion of the antiquarian and the man of taste (the latter the discerning critic or editor whose successful enterprises depend on the former's diligence and judgment).[1] Warton, of course, was also much more than an antiquarian, even more than an antiquarian of taste. He was a poet, literary historian, critic, and editor. This paper is concerned not only with Warton's antiquarianism, but also with what bound together Warton's many activities. This common, synthesizing link was his abiding love for the distant past, more specifically his Gothic sensibility; and virtually all of his interests, personal and professional, manifested that sensibility. His study of literature reflected this attitude, as in the famous passage from the first edition of ***Observations on the Faerie Queene of Spenser,*** in which he emphasized his conviction that an adequate understanding of earlier literature (which on the whole he much preferred to contemporary literature) depends on a careful study of the past:

> In reading the works of an author who lived in a remote age, it is necessary, that we should look back upon the customs and manners which prevailed in his age; that we should place ourselves in his situation, and circumstances; that so we may be the better enabled to judge and discern how his turn of thinking, and manner of composition were biass'd by . . . familiar and reigning appearances, which are utterly different from those with which we are at present surrounded.[2]

Warton happily lived out this concept of self-placement in the past. Oxford, where he dwelt from the age of sixteen until his death over forty-five years later, gave him an ideal setting for this effort, with its Gothic architecture and illustrious history, extending through legend back to King Alfred.[3] For Warton, vocation and avocation coalesced, even during summer vacations when he traveled the countryside visiting ancient buildings, often urging owners to preserve their old edifices from destruction.[4]

Buildings (and, of course, poems) were the ancient monuments Warton most valued. **'The Pleasures of Melancholy,'** which he wrote at about the age of seventeen, includes generalized references to Gothic architecture: a 'ruin'd abbey's moss-grown piles' and 'Gothic vaults' (11. 28, 204).[5] Although most of the poem is the sentimental posturing of a talented but immature poet, the interest in Gothic architecture would endure. Only a few years later, in 1750, Thomas Warton published ***A Description of the City, College, and Cathedral of Winchester.***[6] Portions of the book are almost unreadable, particularly the lengthy accounts of Latin inscriptions from urns, brass floor plates, marble tables, monuments, and doors in the college chapels (28-43, 46-61). Nonetheless, Warton exhibits a keen observer's eye and an antiquarian's heart in the volume, even if he has not yet become very discriminating in his antiquarianism. There is also that interest in windows about which Warton's editor, Richard Mant, asserts, 'It may be difficult to mention any distinguishing feature in that branch of Gothic architecture ["the Gothic window"], which Warton has not noticed' (1: 133-34n.).[7]

Warton would go on to write much more about Gothic architecture. He added an essay on the history of Gothic architecture to the second edition of the **Observations on the Fairy Queen,**[8] a survey that offers little of importance today on the subject but was well respected in its time.[9] Warton openly admits his inadequate preparation for such a survey, citing unfamiliarity 'with the terms and principles of architecture' (2: 198).

Warton's many poems that refer to Gothic structures include **'The Triumph of Isis,' 'The Grave of King Arthur,' 'Newmarket, A Satire,' 'On the Birth of the Prince of Wales,' 'Ode for the New Year, 1788,' 'Ode Written at Vale-Royal Abbey in Cheshire,' 'Ode for Music,'** and the sonnet **'On King Arthur's Round Table.'** Warton planned to write a substantial work entitled **Observations, Critical and Historical, on Churches, Monasteries, Castles and Other Monuments of Antiquity,** even announcing in his **History of English Poetry** that the work was nearly ready for publication.[10] Unfortunately, the manuscript was either lost or never written.

Specimen of a History of Oxfordshire is yet another reflection of Warton's Gothic interests. It initially appeared as a pamphlet in 1782, with only twenty copies issued,[11] followed in 1783 by an enlarged edition.[12] The **Specimen** is a history of the parish of Kiddington, assigned to Warton as a living in 1771. The **Specimen,** which Warton hoped to see become part of a comprehensive history of Oxfordshire,[13] is much better written than the earlier **Description of . . . Winchester.** As a contribution toward Warton's antiquarian views, the work is especially important for its preface, in which Warton offers his opinions on local histories and, by extension, on antiquarian writings. Warton cites 'the prevailing opinion of the world, that these performances are solely fabricated on the petty diligence of those unaspiring antiquaries, who employ their time in collecting coats of arms, poring over parish-registers, and transcribing tombstones' (iii). Warton could have been thinking of himself at an earlier age, though instead he implicitly places himself in a far different rank with the opinion that 'in the hands of a sensible and judicious examiner, they are the histories of antient manners, arts and customs' (iii). Warton goes on to offer a rationale for antiquarian efforts, 'that general knowledge is to be drawn from particularities' (iv); and this 'general knowledge,' to repeat Warton's words, is of 'antient manners, arts, and customs.' In short, antiquarian efforts should be productive and useful. Not an end in itself, antiquarianism should serve the larger purpose of demonstrating how earlier people lived, thought, and created works of art.

A prominent example of the usefulness of Warton's type of antiquarianism (and a testimony to his critical integrity) occurs when he puts his knowledge of 'antient manners, arts, and customs' to use in attempting a solution to the Chatterton controversy.[14] Warton's passion for the past caused him to wish that the poems were genuine, but his fidelity to historical truth compelled him, after a detailed study of the poems, to acknowledge in **An Enquiry into the Authenticity of the Poems Attributed to Thomas Rowley** that they were spurious.[15] In the conclusion to his **Enquiry,** Warton offers a convincing exposition of the need to join strictly antiquarian efforts to taste, judgment, and understanding:

> I could mention many other circumstantial evidences relating to the process and management of this forgery. But I do not wish to rest my proof on evidences of this nature. It is not from the complexion of ink or of parchment, from the information of cotemporaries, the tales of relations, the recollection of apprentices, and the prejudices of friends, nor even from doomsday-book, pedigrees in the herald's office, armorial bearings, parliamentary rolls, inquisitions, indentures, episcopal registers, epitaphs, tomb-stones, and brass-plates, that this controversy is to be finally and effectually adjusted. Our arguments should be drawn from principles of taste, from analogical experiment, from a familiarity with antient poetry, and from the gradations of composition. Such a proof, excluding all imposition, liable to no deception, and proceeding upon abstracted truth, will be the surest demonstration.
>
> (124)

Thomas Warton observed, of course, that not all antiquarian efforts are useful; many wander into the trivial, some into the absurd. One of Warton's most delightful compositions, **A Companion to the Guide and a Guide to the Companion: Being a Complete Supplement to all the Accounts of Oxford Hitherto Published,** parodies antiquarian writings and travel guides while also having some fun at the expense of Oxford itself.[16] The **Companion,** for example, spoofs antiquarian etymological debates, including the quest for the origin of the name *Oxford,* settling finally on *bullositum* as the original name for the city. Warton offers as evidence:

> that there are many *kindred appellations* in and about *Oxford,* which conduce to illustrate and confirm my hypothesis. Need I mention *Bullington* Hundred, in which *Oxford* is situated, *Bullock's Lane,* and *Bullstock Bridge?*—Are not our frequent Bullbaitings in *Oxford* standing memorials of this *original* Denomination?
>
> (6)

Bull, then as now, had the meaning of nonsense; it also meant a jest. In fact, an earlier antiquary well known to Warton, Anthony à Wood, used the term this way in his *Oxoniana* ('Every one in order was to . . . make a jest or bull, or speake some eloquent nonsense, to make company laugh').[17]

Warton then refers to an observation by Thomas Hearne concerning an old Oxford custom '"of blowing with, and drinking, horns"'; and mentions a ford near Oxford referred to by Hearne as a popular passage for oxen (6-7). Warton claims that Hearne was alluding to the issue at hand (presumably implying that 'oxen's ford' was the original for 'Oxford') and offers a conciliatory suggestion:

> Why may we not suppose, by way of reconciling both opinions, that the Ford was common to *horned* cattle in

general? Nay that even *Cows* had more concern in this case than is commonly supposed, seems very probable from the name of the neighbouring village, *Cowley.*

(6-7)

After this *reductio ad absurdum,* Warton shares other findings, like his discovery of twelve Oxford halls never before described, among them Cabbage Hall, Caterpillar Hall, Lemon Hall, Tripe Hall, and Kidney Hall (8). He explores a number of ancient edifices, including the remnants of a 'Pennyless-Bench' upon which 'many eminent Poets have been Benchers' (15); and a mysterious water pump with two heads on top and one spout. Warton conjectures that the pump may be a 'genuine Roman Priapus,' but suspects that most likely it 'is a just Matrimonial Emblem; as it plainly exhibits the Faces of a Man and Woman, but of a very *sour Aspect,* and *reverted from* each other' (19).

Warton returns several times to Hearne, including Hearne's statement concerning an almanac, '"It is rude, and very little is to be gathered from it: Yet 'Tis a Curiosity"' (30). The statement, with its acknowledgment of indiscriminate and pointless hunting after old things, expresses the potential folly of antiquarians that Warton mentions in the preface to his *Specimen of a History of Oxfordshire* as the 'petty diligence of those unaspiring antiquaries . . .' (iii). In the *Observations on the Fairy Queen,* Warton refers to 'That laborious antiquary Thomas Hearne' and his 'extreme thirst after antient things,' while letting the antiquarian's own words ridicule him: '"But tho' I have taken so much pleasure in perusing the English bible of the year 1541, yet 'tis nothing equal to that I should take, in turning over that of the year 1539"' (2: 102n.).

Hearne, of course, is the Wormius satirized by Pope in the third book of *The Dunciad:*

> 'But who is he, in closet close y-pent,
> Of sober face, with learned dust besprent?'
> 'Right well mine eyes arede the myster wight,
> On parchment scraps y-fed, and Wormius hight.
> To future ages may thy dulness last,
> As thou preserv'st the dulness of the past!'[18]

As *The Dictionary of National Biography* points out, Hearne lacked the 'power to distinguish the relative value of what fell in his way; it seemed to him enough that a document was old to induce him to publish it.'[19] The complaint against Hearne recalls Warton's reference in his *History of English Poetry* to those 'antiquaries of former times' who 'employed their industry in reviving obscure fragments of uninstructive morality or uninteresting history' rather than in displaying 'the progress of human manners' and illustrating 'the history of society' (1: 209).

After publication of the *Companion,* Joseph Warton contributed to *The Oxford Sausage,* which Thomas edited, a poem entitled 'Epistle from Thomas Hearne, Antiquary, to the Author of The Companion to the Oxford Guide.'[20] The poem has Hearne describing Thomas Warton as a former 'Friend of the moss-grown Spire and crumbling Arch' (1.1), and wondering

> What malignant Fiend
> Thy cloyster-loving Mind, from antient Lore,
> Hath base seduc'd? Urg'd thy apostate Pen
> To trench deep Wounds on *Antiquaries* sage,
> And drag the venerable Fathers forth,
> Victims to Laughter!

(11. 3-8)

The poem concludes with an extended curse on the apostate Warton, cleverly hitting him where it hurts most—his love for Gothic buildings:

> But now may Curses every Search attend
> That seems inviting! May'st thou pore in vain
> For dubious Door-ways! May revengeful Moths
> Thy Ledgers eat! May chronologic Spouts
> Retain no Cypher legible! May crypts
> Lurk undiscern'd! Nor may'st thou spell the Names
> Of Saints in storied Windows! Nor the Dates
> Of Bells discover! Nor the genuine Site
> Of Abbot's Pantries! And may *Godstowe* veil,
> Deep from Thy Eyes profane, her Gothic Charms!

(11. 18-27)

Being essentially good-natured, Thomas Warton could laugh at his own inclinations as well as mock the excesses and failures of misguided antiquarianism in others. However, he recognized, as he says in the sonnet **'Written in a Blank Leaf of Dugdale's Monasticon,'** that 'the winding ways / Of hoar Antiquity' are 'strown with flowers' (11. 13-14). These flowers—the exhibition of 'ancient manners, arts, and customs'—blossom in the same garden that produced the poetry of England's past. Warton consistently believed that literature reflects the manners and values of the age that produced it. In the *History of English Poetry,* Warton goes so far as to claim that the 'chief source of entertainment which we seek in antient poetry' is 'the representation of antient manners' (2: 264; also 1: 208-09 and *Observations* 1: 156; 2: 267-68).

Warton intended his *History of English Poetry* not only as a history of poetry but also as a history of the national genius and character of England, as manifested in its literary productions.[21] He speaks, for example, of developing 'the dawnings of genius' and pursuing 'the progress of our national poetry . . .' (1: ii). Warton deserves criticism for his omission of Old English poetry, and certainly his remark that 'Saxon poems are for the most part little more than religious rhapsodies' (1: vi) indicates insufficient knowledge about poetry of that period. Yet his primary reason for eliminating the 'Saxon poetry' from his history was that he believed it had little effect on the British national character. He writes in the *History* that the Norman accession 'obliterated almost all relation to the former inhabitants of this island; and produced that signal change in our policy, constitution, and public manners, the effects of which have reached modern times' (1: vi). Seen in this light, the omission at least reflects method, not just ignorance. Further, the position is consistent with Warton's survey of Gothic architecture in *Observations on the Fairy Queen,* where Warton also begins with the Normans, who, he states, 'introduced arts and civility' into England (2: 185).

Warton draws this national character in his *History* through three primary manifestations: poetry, manners, and language. He considers poetry, of course, as art; but he also studies poetry for its 'faithfully recording the features of the times, and of preserving the most picturesque and expressive representations of manners: and,' he writes, 'because the first monuments of composition in every nation are those of the poet, as it possesses the additional advantage of transmitting to posterity genuine delineations of life in its simplest stages' (1: ii-iii). He adds, 'My performance, in its present form . . . represents the progression of our language' (1: v). The explicit point of reference is poetry, but the actual subject of his *History* is multifaceted.

There is insufficient space in this paper to consider Warton's discussion of language development or his extensive treatment of a wide range of literary topics, among them his important analysis of the periods of English poetry.[22] It is important, however, to recall here that *The History of English Poetry* was a monumental undertaking that, regardless of how one evaluates its level of success, was possible because Warton was an antiquarian who also was a scholar, critic, and editor. The editor in Warton is clearly visible in the many long quotations that give the *History* its near-anthology character. At a time when a great many of the works cited in the *History* were difficult to come by, that dimension of the study was of great practical value.

It is also worth remembering at this point that Warton's scholarly interest in early poetry and his antiquarianism (most importantly his love for Gothic structures and his explorations into ancient behavior and attitudes) run along parallel lines, both illustrating Warton's love for the past and his interest in ancient compositions as conveyers of ancient manners. Which came first in Warton's life, his fondness for literature or for medieval castles and ruins, is impossible to say. As a child, Thomas Warton spent considerable time exploring in both books and fields. As a clergyman and former Poetry Professor at Oxford, the father, Thomas Warton the Elder, certainly had a ready library for his children.[23] In addition, the young Thomas visited a range of historic sites with his father, among them Windsor Castle and possibly Stonehenge, as well as various ruins, such as the Chapel of the Holy Ghost in their village of Basingstoke and the nearby Basing House at the site of a battle between Danes and Saxons.[24] There was no lack of influences to wed young Warton to the past.

It is not surprising, then, that the famous 'recantation' in Warton's **'Verses on Sir Joshua Reynolds's Painted Window at New College, Oxford'** appears less than sincere. It did not convince Reynolds, although the artist greatly admired the poem. He even wrote to Warton praising the **'Verses'** and gently chiding Warton for not using his name in the first edition. Warton subsequently replaced 'artist' near the end of the poem with 'Reynolds' (1. 101).

In the first forty lines, Warton laments that the beauty of the new window has 'ravish'd' him from his earlier love, Gothic architecture and sculpture. He realizes that he has been 'A faithless truant to the classic page,' but nonetheless loved

> To catch the simple chime
> Of minstrel-harps, and spell the fabling rime;
> To view the festive rites, the knightly play,
> That deck'd heroic Albion's elder day;
> To mark the mouldering halls of barons bold,
> And the rough castle, cast in giant mould;
> With Gothic manners Gothics arts explore,
> And muse on the magnificence of yore.
>
> (119-16)

He adds that he chiefly loved to examine the 'vaulted dome,' the 'fretted shrines,' the 'nooks profound,' and 'Where SUPERSTITION with capricious hand / In many a maze the wreathed window plann'd . . .' (11. 23-24). The first section of the poem ends with the poet imploring the classical artist to

> spare the weakness of a lover's heart!
> Chase not the phantoms of my fairy dream,
> Phantoms that shrink at Reason's painful gleam.
>
> (11. 36-38)

In the second movement of the poem, beginning at line forty-one, the poet accepts his ravishment by Attic art and acknowledges his earlier complaint to have been mistaken (11. 41-44). He commends the design, colors, and figures of the painted window, and adds that

> Sudden, the sombrous imagery is fled,
> Which late my visionary rapture fed:
> Thy powerful hand has broke the Gothic chain,
> And brought my bosom back to truth again.
>
> (11. 61-64)

As the poem progresses, Warton fuses aesthetic truth to religious truth, which by its nature he sees as eternal and immutable. He describes this truth to which he has returned:

> To truth, by no peculiar taste confin'd,
> Whose universal pattern strikes mankind;
> To truth, whose bold and unresisted aim
> Checks frail caprice, and fashion's fickle claim;
> To truth, whose charms deception's magic quell,
> And bind coy Fancy in a stronger spell.
>
> (11.65-70)

The old windows created by Superstition yield to a new window by a Protestant artist. The old figures and the stories that they convey—the rich prophets, proud saints, false miracles, and 'Martyrdoms of unenlighten'd days'—no more disgrace the sacred window, but yield to 'Grecian groupes' and the 'warm enamel' in which 'Nature lives' (11. 71-100).

Warton has identified nature with truth, and both with the rational, eternal, and immutable. Of course, Warton believed that Anglican Christianity embodies this eternal truth. Gothic art, on the other hand, as a product of medieval superstition, is based on falsehood. And because falsehood is transitory rather than eternal, the Gothic aesthetic could have only a temporary acceptance. A modern critic must reject it in favor of the productions rooted in truth, such as the painted window by a Christian classicist. The choice ultimately seems dictated more by religious factors than by Gothic and neoclassic aesthetics.

Most of the poem, however, is concerned with aesthetics, and it is that aspect of the poem to which Reynolds responded with gratitude but disbelief:

> I owe you great obligations for the sacrifice which you have made, or pretend to have made, to modern art: I say pretend; for though it is allowed that you have, like a true poet, feigned marvellously well, and have opposed the two different styles with the skill of a Connoisseur, yet I may be allowed to entertain some doubts of the sincerity of your conversion. I have no great confidence in the recantation of such an old offender.[25]

A more accurate statement of Warton's views on Gothic structures occurs approximately three years after the **'Verses'** in a passage not encumbered with the need to make proper religious choices. The statement concerns Milton and appears in Warton's edition of Milton's *Poems Upon Several Occasions*:

> Milton was educated at saint Paul's school, contiguous to the church; and thus became impressed with an early reverence for the solemnities of the antient ecclesiastical architecture, its vaults, shrines, iles, pillars, and painted glass, rendered yet more aweful by the accompaniment of the choral service. Does the present modern church convey these feelings? Certainly not. We justly admire and approve sir Christopher Wren's Grecian proportions. Truth and propriety gratify the judgment, but they do not affect the imagination.[26]

In fact, Thomas Warton could not renounce his love for Gothic architecture without disavowing his life's work, his Oxford home, even his summer tours. All of these efforts and experiences were too closely joined by Warton's great love for the past to permit the removal of any one part. He was an indefatigable explorer of the past who, throughout his life, expressed both his knowledge of the past and his Gothic sensibility in his wide range of activities—as poet, critic, editor, and literary historian.

Notes

1. Joan Pittock, *The Ascendancy of Taste: The Achievement of Joseph and Thomas Warton* (London: Routledge and Kegan Paul, 1973), 170-73.

2. Thomas Warton. *Observations on the Faerie Queene of Spenser* (London, 1754), 217. For Warton's contributions toward historical criticism, see Frances Schouler Miller, 'The Historic Sense of Thomas Warton, Junior,' *English Literacy History*, 5 (1938): 71-92. The belief that the past is significantly different from the present was not nearly as commonly held in the eighteenth century as a twentieth-century reader might think. In fact, belief in the uniformity of human nature through time was still widespread. It is now clear that Warton's departure from this principle was an important step in the rise of historical study in the century. For a discussion of uniform nature and eighteenth-century history, see R. N. Stromberg, 'History in the Eighteenth Century,' *Journal of the History of Ideas,* 12 (1951), 295-304.

3. Warton uses this legend of Alfred as the founder of Oxford University in his 'Ode for Music,' 11. 88-99. For Warton's poetry I have used the most definitive edition, *The Poetical Works of the Late Thomas Warton,* ed. Richard Mant, 2 vols. (Oxford, 1802).

4. Clarissa Rinaker, *Thomas Warton: A Biographical and Critical Study,* University of Illinois Studies in Language and Literature, 2.1 (Urbana: University of Illinois, 1916), 148-51. A more recent biography is John A Vance, *Joseph and Thomas Warton,* Twayne's English Authors Series 380 (Boston: Twayne Publishers, 1983). Vance also has produced the very useful *Joseph and Thomas Warton: An Annotated Bibliography* (New York: Garland Publishing, 1983).

5. A relevant study of the poem is Arthur Fenner, Jr., 'The Wartons "Romanticize" Their Verse,' *Studies in Philology,* 53 (1956): 501-08.

6. Thomas Warton, *A Description of the City, College, and Cathedral of Winchester* (London, 1750).

7. Mant is quite right. See, for example, Warton's consideration of Gothic windows in *A Description of . . . Winchester,* 18, 21, 27-28, 45, 75, 77, 80-81, 85, 94.

8. Thomas Warton, *Observations on the Fairy Queen of Spenser,* 2nd ed., 2 vols. (London, 1762), 2: 184-98.

9. For recent evaluation of Thomas Warton's competence in Gothic architecture, consult Kenneth Clark, *The Gothic Revival,* 3rd ed. (New York: Holt, Rinehart & Winston, 1962), 39-41.

10. Thomas Warton, *The History of English Poetry,* 3 vols. (London, 1774, 1778, 1781), 3: xxii. Also see Rinaker, 146-147. Useful accounts of Gothic architecture in England include William Anderson, *The Rise of the Gothic* (Salem, N.H.: Salem House, 1985); and Agnes Eleanor Addison, *Romanticism and the Gothic Revival* (New York: R.R. Smith, 1938). Clark's book, of course, should be mentioned again here.

11. Thomas Warton, *Specimen of A History of Oxfordshire* (privately printed, 1782).

12. *Specimen of a History of Oxfordshire,* 2nd ed, (London, 1783). Subsequent references are to this edition.

13. Warton makes it clear in the preface (vii) that he does not intend to write this history himself.

14. The controversy concerned whether the poems attributed to a fifteenth-century Thomas Rowley were written by Rowley or by the teen-ager, Thomas Chatterton, who claimed to have discovered the poems. The poems were published as *Poems, Supposed to Have Been Written at Bristol, by Thomas Rowley, and Others, in the Fifteenth Century* (London, 1777).

15. Thomas Warton, *An Enquiry into the Authenticity of the Poems Attributed to Thomas Rowley* (London, 1782).

16. Thomas Warton, *A Companion to the Guide, and a Guide to the Companion* (London, 1760).

17. Wood's statement from his *Oxoniana,* 2: 23; is quoted in *The Compact Edition of the Oxford English Dictionary,* 2 vols. (New York: Oxford University Press, 1971), 1: 292. Warton's involvement with *The Lives of Those Eminent Antiquaries John Leland, Thomas Hearne, and Anthony a Wood,* 2 vols. (Oxford, 1772) is examined in Edward J. Rielly, 'Thomas Warton and Other Contributors to *The Lives of Those Eminent Antiquaries,'* *Notes and Queries,* N.S. 35 (1988): 188-90. An account of Oxford that remains valuable is A. D. Godley, *Oxford in the Eighteenth Century* (London: Methuen, 1908).

18. I have used the short Twickenham Text, *The Poems of Alexander Pope,* ed. John Butt (New Haven: Yale University Press, 1966).

19. *The Dictionary of National Biography,* ed. Leslie Stephen and Sidney Lee, 66 vols. (1885-1901; London: Oxford University Press, 1949-50), 9: 337.

20. *The Oxford Sausage,* ed. Thomas Warton, 3rd ed. (Oxford, 1772).

21. Recent examinations of Warton's *History* include David Fairer, 'The Origins of Warton's *History of English Poetry,'* *Review of English Studies,* N.S. 32 (1981): 37-63; portions of ch. 3 in Joel Weinsheimer, *Imitation* (Boston: Routledge & Kegan Paul, 1984), 93-172; and Pittock's *Ascendancy of Taste,* especially ch. 5, 167-214. Slightly earlier is Lawrence Lipking, *The Ordering of the Arts* (Princeton: Princeton University Press, 1970), 352-404.

22. These issues are addressed in Edward J. Rielly, 'An Ideational Study of Joseph and Thomas Warton,' diss. University of Notre Dame, 1974.

23. Thomas Warton the Elder's poetic reputation has declined in recent years, especially in light of David Fairer's articles showing that many poems previously believed to be his, and published as his in Thomas Warton [the Elder], *Poems on Several Occasions* (London, 1748); actually were written by his sons Thomas and Joseph. See David Fairer, 'The Poems of Thomas Warton the Elder?' *Review of English Studies,* N.S. 26 (1975): 287-300, 395-406; and 'The Poems of Thomas Warton the Elder? A Postscript,' *Review of English Studies,* 29 (1978): 61-65.

24. See Rinaker for a summary of Warton's childhood influences, 12-14.

25. The letter is reprinted in Mant, 1: 1xxx-1xxxi.

26. Thomas Warton, ed., *Poems Upon Several Occasions* (London, 1785), 90-91n.

Robert J. Griffin (essay date 1992)

SOURCE: Griffin, Robert J. "The Eighteenth-Century Construction of Romanticism: Thomas Warton and the Pleasures of Melancholy." *ELH* 59, no. 4 (winter 1992): 799-815.

[*In the following essay, Griffin explores the idea that Warton is a romantic poet by analyzing his poem* The Pleasures of Melancholy.]

> The great merit of this writer appears to us to consist in the boldness and originality of his composition, and in the fortunate audacity with which he has carried the dominion of poetry into regions that had been considered as inaccessible to her ambition. The gradual refinement of taste had, for nearly a century, been weakening the force of original genius. Our poets had become timid and fastidious, and circumscribed themselves both in the choice and management of their subjects, by the observance of a limited number of models, who were thought to have exhausted all the legitimate resources of the art. ———was one of the first who crossed this enchanted circle; who reclaimed the natural liberty, and walked abroad in the open field of observation as freely as those by whom it was originally trodden. He passed from the imitation of poets to the imitation of nature.

This quotation expresses many of the essentials of the "romantic" version of literary history. The chain of associations—boldness, original genius, break from a refined taste, natural liberty, direct observation, and imitation of nature—would lead most readers, I suggest, to complete the chain and fill in the space I have left blank with the name "Wordsworth." Pressed to identify the author of the passage, one might reasonably guess it was Arnold, or some other Victorian influenced by Wordsworth, surveying the revolution in taste that occurred at the beginning of his/her century. In actual fact, this is an appreciation of William Cowper written in 1803 by the critic generally recognized to be Wordsworth's mortal enemy, Francis Jeffrey.[1] The feeling of disorientation that comes over one upon realizing this is caused by certainties rapidly dissolving. How is it that in 1803 Jeffrey writes in these terms? And if his subject is Cowper, why do we expect it to be Wordsworth?

It's certainly possible to argue that Jeffrey owes his critical orientation to Wordsworth's Preface to *Lyrical Ballads* published a few years earlier. But this response misses the broader cultural context: both Wordsworth and Jeffrey participate in a discourse that was formulated in the 1740s and 1750s, twenty years before they were born in the early 1770s, primarily by Joseph and Thomas Warton, and by Edward Young. Jeffrey's placing of Cowper, for instance, which one easily mistakes for a much later critic's placing of Wordsworth using Wordsworthian terms, reads like a summary of the main points of Joseph Warton's *Essay on Pope* (1756) and Young's *Conjectures on Original Composition* (1759). Similarly, it was Joseph Warton who first argued that Pope was the "poet of reason." To the extent that we give assent to the "wordsworthian" version of the eighteenth century, or agree with Arnold that the century was an age of reason and prose, we continue to participate uncritically in the master narrative established by Pope's rivals in the decade after his death. Students of the eighteenth century have long abandoned such terminology, but they have been talking mostly to themselves. The romantic paradigm continues to dominate the way critics think about literature generally, as several recent studies have confirmed.

The critical paradigm that prepared poets like Cowper, Bowles, and Wordsworth to challenge Pope was already in place by 1760, though it was not widely accepted. Romantic literary history, in other words, existed *before* there was such a thing as romantic poetry, or rather, before a great romantic poet appeared.[2] The romantic paradigm, moreover, is shared by those who divide sharply over the value of Wordsworth, as my opening citation of Jeffrey should make clear. "Romantic" literary history, as I argue here, originates with, and continues to function in relation to, an anxiety about Pope. It begins in the mid-eighteenth century and develops through the early nineteenth century as a polemical construction of Pope's place in English literary history. Pope's considerable influence throughout this period, even when construed as purely negative, is brought home by Byron's sardonic remark about his contemporaries in 1821: "The attempt of the poetical populace of the present day to obtain an ostracism against Pope is as easily accounted for as the Athenian's shell against Aristides; they are tired of hearing him always called 'the Just'. They are also fighting for life; for, if he maintains his station, they will reach their own—by falling."[3]

The Wartons and Young are usually defined as minor, pre-romantic poets, stock figures in a "Whig" history of ideas in which progress leads to a magic year, 1798. The teleological fallacy inherent in the notion "pre-romanticism" has often been noticed, most recently by Douglas Lane Patey in a review of a book by James Engell.[4] My perspective, however, defines romanticism not positively according to the very varied forms its takes—Marilyn Butler uses the word "protean"—but negatively as a phenomenon that is intimately bound up in what it dislikes. The unity of romanticism, that is to say, is discovered in the agreement over what it rejects. From this perspective, the

Wartons and Young are key figures, for they, in conscious but ambivalent rebellion against Pope, helped create the new paradigm out of old materials—such as the hierarchy of genres and the distinction between art and nature. For me, then, "pre-romanticism" disappears entirely as a category: the Wartons and Young are simply the first "romantics." Critics from at least the 1930s to the present have argued that "romanticism" is something that happened to Wordsworth or to Blake at a certain stage of their career, which is to say that before that they were pre-romantic.[5] This makes no sense to me because I see what is generally called romanticism as neither a particular style (attention to details of nature, symbol, lyric expression, etc.), nor a particular content, but rather as a discourse that arises in response to a psychological dilemma in relation to modernity in general, and modern poetry, which is to say "Pope," in particular.

Though discredited as a concept by many, the point of view implied by the notion of "pre-romanticism" continues to function as a mode of understanding literary history from Wordsworth's and Coleridge's point of view. This is only one example of the way that criticism, and with it literary history, tends to become simply a satellite orbiting around the attractive power of "great writers." Since Wordsworth writes the poetry that is taken, retrospectively, to be the true alternative to Pope, criticism simply subsumes under his name a movement that had been gathering force for a half a century, labeling it "pre-". This leads to strange formulations that seem to corroborate Harold Bloom's notion of the way that strong poets are able to reverse chronological priority. Edith Morley, for example, cites Joseph Warton on the need to see the object steady and whole, and on the need for a simpler poetic diction. Rather than suggest that Wordsworth was influenced, or indeed shaped by Warton's discourse, Morley actually compliments Warton for agreeing with Wordsworth: "Wordsworth himself could say no more."[6]

The same dynamic is at work in the fate of Cowper, for Wordsworth would eventually assume the place in the romantic paradigm that had once been held by the earlier poet. Chalmers, in 1810, wrote that Cowper, "above all poets of recent times, has become the universal favourite of his nation." Jeffrey, in 1811, repeated his estimate of 1803: "Cowper is, and is likely to continue, the most popular of all who have written for the present or the last generation." Coleridge in 1817 named the most recent era of English poetry, "from Cowper to the present day."[7] But already by 1852 Wordsworth's reputation appears to have eclipsed Cowper's with the consequence that Cowper's priority was eclipsed as well. A reviewer thus protests against distortions of literary history:

> It is constantly asserted that he [that is, Wordsworth] effected a reform in the language of poetry, that he found the public bigoted to a vicious and flowery diction which seemed to mean a great deal and really meant nothing, and that he led them back to sense and simplicity. The claim appears to us to be a fanciful assumption, refuted by the facts of literary history. Fee-

bler poetasters were no doubt read when Wordsworth began to write than would now command an audience, however small, but they had no real hold on the public, and Cowper was the only *popular* bard of the day. His masculine and unadorned English was relished in every cultivated circle in the land, and Wordsworth was the child, and not the father of the reaction, which after all, has been greatly exaggerated.[8]

My interest in the genealogy of literary values, in telling the story of "the story"—telling, that is, not how mirror became lamp, but how this particular episode of literary history came to be constructed in that way—focuses on the disjunction between today's dominant understanding of the relation between the Romantics and the eighteenth century, and the very different perspective that historical reconstruction opens up. In turning to the Wartons, it is useful to recall that Francis Jeffrey, writing in the early nineteenth century, took their place in history for granted: "The Whartons [*sic*], both as critics and as poets, were of considerable service in discrediting the high pretensions of the former race [that is, the Augustans], and in bringing back to public notice the great stores and treasures of poetry which lay hid in the records of our older literature."[9] The exposure of the pretenders to the throne, Dryden-Addison-Pope, and the reinstatement of the "true" line of inheritance is, in fact, the constitutive gesture of that narrative of history we call romanticism. Everything follows from this.

In this essay I focus on Thomas Warton's **"The Pleasures of Melancholy"** for the insights it gives into the genesis of a romantic construction of literary history. The relegation of Thomas Warton to the category of "pre-" by our standard literary histories is richly suggestive. From a more oblique angle, the prefix conjures up an archaeological level of romantic consciousness that has been labeled in order to be forgotten because it is meant to serve as a foundation we can confidently build upon in our discussions of what really matters. The uncanny, as defined by Freud, involves a confrontation with something strange, yet familiar, something that awakens in us something we thought was long put to rest. The notable obscurity of a figure like Thomas Warton holds forth the possibility of moments of uncanny recognition on the margin—uncanny not simply because they appear so often as repressed doubles of our own discourse, but also because of the way they repeat Pope in the very act of displacing him.

I

Thomas Warton's **"The Pleasures of Melancholy,"** written in 1745, a year after Pope's death, is a poem referred to more often than read. In the last forty years it has been addressed infrequently, twice as a rough draft for Keats's "Ode on Melancholy."[10] Dismissing pre-romanticism as the logic of the contradictions inherent in romanticism proper, I find that nowhere is the genesis of romanticism better studied than in Warton's poem.

Drawing upon "Il Penseroso" (and implicitly "L'Allegro") for its structure, **"The Pleasures of Melancholy"** constructs itself around the allegorical opposition between

Day and Night, Mirth and Melancholy. The noise of the city is opposed to the quiet of nature, vice to virtue, summer to winter, bright sunshine to fogs, gloom, and rain. The speaker's preference for solitude and night, emblems for "virtue," expresses itself further in his choice between fictional women, emblems for their authors. In this erotics of reading, Warton prefers Spenser's Una, alone in the wilderness, to Pope's Belinda, launched at noon on the silver Thames.

> Thro' POPE'S soft song though all the Graces breathe,
> And happiest art adorn his Attic page;
> Yet does my mind with sweeter transport glow,
> As at the root of mossy trunk reclin'd,
> In magic SPENSER'S wildy-warbled song
> I see deserted UNA wander wide
> Through wasteful solitudes, and lurid heaths
> Weary, forlorn; than when the fated fair,
> Upon the bright bosom of silver Thames,
> Launches in all the lustre of brocade,
> Amid the splendors of the laughing Sun.
> The gay description palls upon the sense,
> And coldly strikes the mind with feeble bliss.
>   Oh, wrap me then in shades of darksome pine,
> Bear me to caves of desolation brown,
> To dusky vales and hermit-haunted rocks!

(153-68)[11]

To identify Pope with his ironic heroine, Belinda, is rather tendentious because it collapses the distance signaled by Pope's satire. But if we read the poem simply as a statement of preference for *The Fairie Queene* over *The Rape of the Lock,* there is no point in quibbling, nor are standards of taste here the real issue. What is more to the point is an examination of the evidence the poem provides for the grounds of evaluation. Warton's poem is intensely interesting because it reveals the contradictions at the very heart of the ideological construction we recognize as romanticism. For the poem cannot sustain its own dichotomy between a sunny classicism that is attractive but superficial—Pope, Belinda, "Attic" art—and a melancholy Gothicism that offers deeper pleasures—Spenser's Una, Milton's Penseroso. The poem itself gives evidence that Pope, master of classic forms, is also the primary revivalist and transmitter of Gothic gloom.

Structured as it is by opposing Mirth to Melancholy, Day to Night, and Spenser-Milton to Pope, the logic of the poem breaks down in several places. First of all, Pope is represented not just by Belinda, but also by his Eloisa and the Unfortunate Lady, both of whom are recruited to the side of pensive Melancholy. It is worth noting that these two figures were the ones Blake, too, recalled when representing Pope for a series of English authors. The opening lines of Pope's "Elegy to the Memory of an Unfortunate Lady" (1717) read as follows:

> What beck'ning ghost, along the moonlight shade
> Invites my steps, and points to yonder glade?
> 'Tis she!—but why the bleeding bosom gor'd,
> Why dimly gleams the visionary sword?[12]

The ghost appears with sword and bleeding bosom, we discover, because she is the spirit of a principled young woman who chose death rather than marry against her wishes in order to enrich her guardian. Thomas Warton, apparently, saw the same ghost during his own imagined midnight vigils:

> But when the world
> Is clad in Midnight's raven-color'd robe,
> In hollow charnel let me watch the flame
> Of taper dim, while airy voices talk
> Along the glimmering walls, *or ghostly shape*
> *At distance seen, invites with beck'ning hand.*
>
> (44-49, emphasis added)

Eloisa, unlike the Unfortunate Lady, is named explicitly, but before turning to that passage it is useful to reread the much-admired set piece on Melancholy from Pope's "Eloisa to Abelard" (1717):

> The darksome pines that o'er yon rocks reclin'd
> Wave high, and murmur to the hollow wind,
> The wand'ring streams that shine between the hills,
> The grots that echo to the tinkling rills,
> The dying gales that pant upon the trees,
> The lakes that quiver to the curling breeze;
> No more these scenes my meditation aid,
> Or lull to rest the visionary maid.
> But o'er the twilight groves and dusky caves,
> Long-sounding isles, and intermingled graves,
> Black Melancholy sits, and round her throws
> A death-like silence, and a dread repose:
> Her gloomy presence saddens all the scene,
> Shades ev'ry flower, and darkens ev'ry green,
> Deepens the murmur of the falling floods,
> And breathes a browner horror on the woods.
>
> (155-70)

Here is Warton, 28 years later:

> Few know the elegance of soul refin'd,
> Whose soft sensation feels a quicker joy
> From Melancholy's scenes, than the dull pride
> Of tasteless splendor and magnificence
> Can e'er afford. Thus Eloise, whose mind
> Had languish'd to the pangs of melting love,
> More genuine transport found, as on some tomb
> Reclin'd, she watch'd the tapers of the dead;
> Or through the pillar'd iles, amid pale shrines
> Of imag'd saints, and intermingled graves,
> Mus'd a veil'd votaress; than Flavia feels,
> As through the mazes of festive balls,
> Proud of her conquering charms, and beauty's blaze,
> She floats amid the silken sons of dress,
> And shines the fairest of the fair.
>
> (2nd ed., 93-106)

Warton's allusion to Eloisa imbeds her within an opposition to a Belinda-like coquette, picking up verbal echoes from both poems. Notice that the thematic structure in this passage is the same as in the lines preferring Una-Spenser to Belinda-Pope. If we follow Warton's synecdochal method of associating characters with their authors, the explicit opposition Eloisa/Flavia signifies the implicit opposition of Pope to himself, Pope/Pope. Since this passage (Pope/Pope) occurs some fifty lines *before* the one in which authors are openly named and evaluated (Spenser/Pope), and since the thematic content of the two passages is identical, the difference between them, the substitution of Una for Eloisa in the second passage, is highly significant. For it is this substitution that allows Warton to displace Pope altogether. When Pope/Pope becomes Spenser/Pope, the preference expressed between two characters in Pope has been transformed into a preference for Spenser over a Pope now wholly identified with one of his own satiric creations.

The internal contradiction by which Pope is dissociated from Eloisa but identified with Belinda is the crucial, foundational move. For it is in the disjunctive space created by that substitution and displacement, and indeed by the dissociation of "Pope" from himself, that the ideology of what later will be called "romanticism" grows and flourishes.[13] In "Eloisa" Pope drew upon Ovid's *Heroides* for a genre of the woman's lament, but he transposed it to the Gothic Middle Ages. Thomas Warton, however, separates out the gothic and the classical strands in Pope, and then attributes what is valued more highly, in this case gothic, to someone else. This constitutive contradiction and displacement, of course, is a symptom of Warton's intense identification with Pope, who is apparently both Muse and rival. The misrecognition that brings romanticism into being is, at bottom, a response to the anxiety of Pope's influence.

In this erotics of reading that substitutes the female character as object of desire for the male author as inspiring muse, Warton's identification with, his desire to be, Pope is made quite clear in his subsequent use of Eloisa. After claiming that Pope's description of Belinda "coldly strikes the mind with feeble bliss," Warton turns away and cries, in lines I've cited above: "Oh, wrap me then in shades of darksome pine. . . ." The darksome pines, of course, are those with which Pope surrounded Eloisa's convent in the other passage already cited: "The darksome pines that o'er yon rock reclin'd. . . ." Thus, Warton turns coldly from Belinda to rush into the arms of Eloisa. In the continuation of these lines Warton's use of Eloisa is revealing.

Gothic settings are congenial to ghosts and phantoms, and these poems are no exception. Pope's "Unfortunate Lady" opens, as we noted, with an apparition; in "Eloisa," too, the heroine's desire for Abelard produces in her the delusion of his presence. She rushes after the phantom, only to be returned abruptly to her forlorn condition. Eloisa:

> Sudden you mount! you beckon from the skies;
> Clouds interpose, waves roar, and winds arise.
> I shriek, start up, the same sad prospect find,
> And wake to all the griefs I left behind.
>
> (254-58)

Warton rewrites this incident, but in his version the "you" refers reflexively to the speaker who recounts his experience of waking from delusion:

Sudden you start—the imagined joys recede,
The same sad prospect opens on your sense.

(186-87)

The close verbal repetitions suggest that the narrator writes from the place of Eloisa. The ghost he chases, however, is not Abelard, but one Sapphira, and the experience, unlike the painful awakening of Eloisa, is for Warton one of the pleasures of melancholy:

These are delights that absence drear has made
Familiar to my soul, ere since the form
Of young Sapphira, beauteous as the Spring,
When from her violet-woven couch awaked
By frolic Zephyr's hand, her tender cheek
Graceful she lifts, and blushing from her bower,
Issues to clothe in gladsome-glistering green
The genial globe, first met my dazzled sight.

(191-98)

According to the logic of the poem, Sapphira should not really be attractive to Warton because she so clearly personifies the L'Allegro chain of associations that he shuns (day, sunshine, greenness, spring-summer). Not just "beauteous as the Spring," she actually embodies the Spring's power for it is she who "issues to clothe in gladsome-glistering green / The genial globe." But the speaker had already told us: "I choose the pale December's foggy glooms" (74). Now we see that he was driven to melancholy by his love for Sapphira, that, indeed, one of its pleasures is the contemplation of her glad, green, spring-dayness from his retreat. Penseroso, so far from holding Allegr[a] in contempt, has been dazzled by her and nurses his wound in solitude; the Penseroso character is, in Warton's version, brought into being simultaneously with his desire for Allegra.

If we correlate this section with Warton's literary historical allegory, the contempt he displays for Belinda is the defensive reaction-formation of his desire for her. The explicit aggression against Pope-Belinda in the earlier passage suggests, in the light of this later one, a parallel between Warton and the Baron who plots to clip Belinda's lock, and whose only wish in battling her is to "die" upon his foe. For surely, Sapphira, as goddess and power of nature, is a pastoralized, or rather pasteurized form of Belinda, launched forth on the Thames and shining brighter than the sun, in that her "toxic" elements have been neutralized.

This episode rehearses Eloisa's hallucinatory sorrow over Abelard's absence (and ultimately, of course, over the crucial absence signified by his castration), but with a difference, for now we have a male Eloisa contemplating in retreat a sublimated, idealized, and thus more acceptable image of Belinda, duly transferred from a social to a pastoral garden. The contradictions in Warton's text suggest that the poem accomplishes for him the first stages of a disengagement from Pope, while the fact that he retreats into Eloisa's role at all reveals the strength of the original attachment. Out of this double bind, he clears a space for himself by creating a structure that fragments Pope, and then opposes part to part.

Warton's original identification with Pope, we may conclude, gave rise to an ambivalence that produced a series of corresponding images: the negative values attached to Belinda and her double, Flavia, little better than tarts, are matched symmetrically by the positive values attached to Eloisa, the holy, and Sapphira, the light of life. The text of the father-as-muse has been first feminized and then fragmented into a saint on one hand and a whore on the other. Warton's double-headed synecdoche, representing Pope as Eloisa-Belinda, distances Pope from his work, and thus allows Warton to appropriate that work in an oedipal exchange.[14]

"The Pleasures of Melancholy" is both useful and fascinating because it manifests the influence of Pope *before* it has been fully repressed and transformed. Here we see the very process by which the text of Pope is divided, alienated from itself, and assigned to "Pope" on the one hand, and to "Spenser-Milton" on the other. Warton's poem is "pre"-romantic only in the limited sense that a "fully" romantic text would be self-conscious enough of its own origins to efface any explicit trace of Eloisa while retaining her poetic value in the name of the gothic. But then we must remember that Warton was seventeen; in his revision of the poem ten years later, he in fact did edit out several verbatim echoes of "Eloisa," including the "darksome pine" passage, but could not eradicate her completely without destroying the fabric of the poem.

Romanticism, therefore, originates in a two-fold strategy: arising from a primal reading of Pope, it misrepresents him on a doctrinal level, while transposing him into a less threatening, pastoral version of himself on the level of imagery. The doctrinal necessity of opposing Pope to Spenser, or to Milton, ensures that explicit references to Eloisa will eventually drop out. Thus, although Pope's mediation of the early Milton in "Eloisa to Abelard" leads to the valorization of the penseroso figure as the characteristic romantic protagonist, Pope's role as transmitter of gothic alienation (and this describes "Eloisa" more appropriately than it does Milton's poem) will nonetheless be gradually forgotten, even though it remains open to be read in Warton's poem.

II

Both Wartons quickly became jealously possessive of Milton and began to consider Pope as a usurper of the poetic tradition. They came to construct Pope as no more than the poet of witty rhyme and polished couplet whose dominance actually prevented Milton's "Il Penseroso" from being appreciated. They, of course, revived the "true" line, and thus, as Thomas said in his 1785 Preface to an edition of Milton's minor poems, "the school of Milton rose in emulation of the school of Pope."[15] An anecdote told by both brothers about the relation of Pope's Eloisa to Milton's Penseroso takes us to the heart of romantic literary history.

According to the Wartons, Pope owed his knowledge of Milton's minor poems to their father, Thomas Warton the Elder, who brought them to his attention through Digby, a mutual acquaintance. Very shortly after, Pope's "Eloisa" appeared with passages, Tom Warton claims,

> pilfered from *COMUS* and the *PENSEROSO*. He was however conscious, that he might borrow from a book then scarcely remembered, without the hazard of discovery, or the imputation of plagiarism.

Having made the accusation, Warton backs off a little:

> Yet the theft was so slight, as hardly to deserve the name: and it must be allowed, that the experiment was happily and judiciously applied, in delineating the sombrous scenes of the pensive Eloisa's convent, the solitary Paraclete.[16]

Whether Pope's troping upon Milton deserves the name of theft or not, it is curious that the charge comes from the writer who drew so liberally upon Pope when writing **"The Pleasures of Melancholy."** It is odd also that it appears in an edition of Milton, the overstuffed notes of which call our attention to "parallel passages" in authors ancient and modern.

Tom Warton recurs to this story in his discussion of *Comus,* and manages to insinuate that it is an odd thing altogether that Pope's poem ever came into existence because it isn't like him:

> It is strange that Pope, by no means of a congenial spirit, should be the first who copied *Comus* and *Il Penseroso*. But Pope was a gleaner of Old English poets; and he was pilfering from *obsolete* English poetry, without the least fear or danger of being detected.[17]

The problem with such a narrative, of course, is that it is false, not just in its larger claims, but also in the very details of the transmission. In actual fact Pope possessed an edition of Milton's minor poems (1645) at least as early as 1705, when he was seventeen, some twelve years before "Eloisa," and before the Elder Warton is supposed to have mentioned the volume to Digby. We know this because William Trumball, former secretary of state under William III and Pope's neighbor, sent Pope a letter, dated 19 October 1705, thanking him for the loan of the book. Internal evidence, furthermore, shows that influences of "Penseroso" appear as early as Pope's first published work, *The Pastorals* (1709), as the Twickenham edition records. The elder Warton, apparently, lent Pope a rare copy of *Gorbuduc* in the summer of 1717, but the probability is that Warton came to the early Milton through Pope, not the other way around.[18]

There are two conclusions I draw from these facts. First, Milton's minor poems were rarely read, but Pope assimilated them and transmitted their strain in his work. Second, the Wartons cannot give Pope credit for this; instead they transfer the source of proper taste to their father, while accusing Pope of being both an alien ("uncongenial," literally, not of the same spirit) and a thief. While the Wartons are defenders of true poetry, Pope is the usurper who came to the early Milton through the Elder Warton and stole from it shamelessly. This anecdote, in fact, encodes in miniature the paradigm of romantic literary history operative in Francis Jeffrey and many others, according to which it is the Wartons who revived Milton in opposition to Pope.[19] Francis Jeffrey simply repeats the Wartons, as others will repeat Jeffrey. Wordsworth recalls the anecdote when he comments on Milton's early poems, which, he says, "though on their first appearance they were praised by a few of the judicious, were afterwards neglected to that degree, that Pope in his youth could borrow from them without risk of its being known."[20] Gosse retells this story in the early twentieth century, but adds, extraordinarily, that "Eloisa" never was a favorite among Pope's admirers, probably, he speculates, because of its "horror." The only thing missing, but found elsewhere in the Wartons, Jeffrey, Coleridge and others, is the corollary that Pope's line is a French deviation from English stock. Northrop Frye echoes this essentially eighteenth-century Wartonian view, but in a different context, when he says in 1963 that criticism, having recognized its true lineage in romanticism, has returned to its proper channel.[21]

III

The denials that work themselves out in the foundation of the Wartonian version of literary history need, perhaps, no further explanation. But some ironies are too rare, too significant, and too representative, to let pass. One of these involves, again, the elder Warton, who, as it happens, was born in the same year as Pope, 1688. A few years after their father's death in 1745, the dutiful sons, pressed for funds, hit upon the idea of publishing a collection of their father's verse by subscription to friends and relatives as a kind of memorial. Occasionally, scholars have looked into the collection to discover signs of pre-romanticism and found them. But it also possible to find there a poem like "The Ode to Taste," which pays tribute to Pope. The opening stanza, addressed to Taste, reads as follows:

> Leave not Brittania's Isle; since Pope is fled
> 　To meet his Homer in Elysian Bowers,
> 　　What Bard shall dare presume
> 　　His various-sounding Harp?
> Let not resistless Dulness o'er us spread
> 　Deep Gothic night; for lo! the Fiend appears
> 　　To blast each blooming Bay
> 　　That decks our barren Shores.[22]

Pope, according to this stanza, was the last bulwark of Taste against the spread of Dulness's "Gothic night." Now that he is gone, Britain appears to be in bad way, for no worthy successor has appeared to take up his instrument, so that the loss threatens an apocalyptic breach with true standards. The poem, in fact, constructs Pope in the very terms he had fashioned for himself in *The Dunciad*. It is fair to assume he would have been pleased. Since Pope fled to Elysian Bowers in 1744, this clearly had to have been written in the final year of the Elder Warton's life.

However, the most remarkable thing about this poem is that it was not written by the Elder Warton at all, but by Thomas, Jr. roughly about the same time that he wrote **"The Pleasures of Melancholy."** David Fairer, by examining the manuscripts, determined that, since the father's corpus was not large enough to make up a volume, his pious sons contributed about ten poems of their own, generously donating them in their father's name. Subsequent investigations by Christina Le Prevost led her to conclude that nineteen poems were certainly by the brothers, and probably fourteen others, leaving the father with less than a third of the volume, not even counting the fact that some of those were revised by Joseph.[23]

Fairer concludes from his evidence that, since poems showing pre-romantic tendencies (whatever that might mean) were actually written by the sons, the Elder Warton can no longer be legitimately considered a lone pre-romantic voice in Pope's generation. He does not deal with "The Ode to Taste" except to identify it as Thomas, Jr.'s. But Fairer's scholarship, and Le Prevost's even more so, adds evidence to my own thesis that romanticism begins in a love-hate relation to Pope. When Warton assigned his ode to his father, he simply transferred his own earlier self, one cathected to Pope, to the previous generation, and then began a series of polemics against it.

Notes

1. Review of William Hayley's *Life of Cowper* in *Edinburgh Review* (April 1803), in Francis Jeffrey, *Contributions to the Edinburgh Review,* 4 vols. (London, 1844), 1:411. Jeffrey's "this-will-never-do" review of *The Excursion* is the infamous and standard example of the forces Wordsworth had to overcome in order to obtain recognition.

2. I wrote this sentence before I discovered that my words echo Marlon Ross's similar formulation: "In other words, romantic ideology began to dominate the literary establishment *before* the romantic canon, as we know it, was established" (54). Two differences: first, my phrase refers to "literary history" rather than "ideology" because I assume throughout that ideological values require a narrative framework for their expression; second, Ross's statement occurs in a discussion of Wordsworth's reputation circa 1820, whereas the burden of my argument is that we find essentially the same "romantic" paradigm operative in literary history before Wordsworth was born. For Ross's very rich and wide-ranging book see *The Contours of Masculine Desire: Romanticism and the Rise of Women's Poetry* (New York: Oxford Univ. Press, 1989).

3. Lord Byron, *Selected Prose,* ed. Peter Gunn (Harmondsworth: Penguin, 1972), 406.

4. See Douglas Lane Patey, review of *Forming the Critical Mind: Dryden to Coledrige,* by James Engell, *Eighteenth Century Studies* 23 (1989-90): 205-211. See also Henry Knight Miller, "The 'Whig

Interpretation' of Literary History," *Eighteenth Century Studies* 6 (1972): 60-84, especially 78. Marshall Brown defends the notion of teleology in a new book, *Preromanticism* (Stanford: Stanford Univ. Press, 1991). He offers a reading of Young's *Night Thoughts,* but does not address the Wartons at all.

5. Edwin Stein, commenting on Wordsworth's early long poems, exemplifies the general application of this conceptual frame: "The mixture of naturalism and vision in these poems is evident in its cruder pre-Romantic form"; see *Wordsworth's Art of Allusion* (University Park: Pennsylvania State Univ. Press, 1988), 194. Stein, of course, is in good company, for very few critics of the Romantics have seriously questioned the term. Ernest Bernbaum provides the crudest, most naive example of the logic of pre-romanticism when he gives us a "Chronological Table of the Chief Pre-Romantic Works." The list begins with 1696 and includes *all* of the major and minor eighteenth-century writers of every possible genre—the only exceptions are Dryden, Pope, Swift, Fielding, and Johnson (*Guide through the Romantic Movement,* 2nd ed. [New York: Ronald Press, 1949], 6-7).

6. Edith Morley, "Joseph Warton: A Comparison of His *Essay on the Genius and Writings of Pope* with His Edition of Pope's *Works,*" *Essays and Studies,* vol. 9, ed. W. P. Ker (Oxford: Clarendon Press, 1924), 102.

7. See Chalmers' "Life of Cowper" in *The Works of the English Poets from Chaucer to Cowper,* ed. Alexander Chalmers, 21 vols. (London: J. Johnson, 1810), 17:602. For Jeffrey see his review of John Ford, *Edinburgh Review* (August 1811), in Jeffrey (note 1), 2:294. Coleridge's comment appears in *Biographia Literaria, The Collected Works of Samuel Taylor Coleridge, Vol. 7,* ed. James Engell and W. Jackson Bate (Princeton: Princeton Univ. Press, 1983), 7:54.

8. Within the last few years a scholar has concluded, oddly from my point of view, that "the review itself is of minor interest in the history of Wordsworth scholarship"; see Thomas C. Richardson, "Lockhart and Elwin on Wordsworth," *Wordsworth Circle* 20 (1989): 156. Richardson traces the influence of Lockhart on Whitwell Elwin, the author of the review in the *Quarterly Review* (December 1852): 182-236. My citation is taken from page 233.

9. Jeffrey's review of Scott's edition of Swift, *Edinburgh Review* (September 1816), (note 1), 1:166.

10. See Oliver Ferguson, "Warton and Keats: Two Views of Melancholy," *Keats and Shelley Journal* 18 (1969): 12-15; and Nathaniel Teich, "A Comparative Approach to Periodization: Forms of Self-Consciousness in Warton's 'The Pleasures of Melancholy' and Keats's 'Ode on Melancholy,'" in *Proceedings of the Xth Congress of the International Comparative Literature Association, Vol. 1: General Problems of Literary History* (New York: Garland,

1982): 158-63. This volume provides much evidence that romantic literary history continues to thrive. In relation to Teich, I would only suggest that it may be more useful to compare "forms of self-consciousness" in two major poets, rather than pitting a major one against a minor one, especially in this case since Warton's poem was raw material for Keats. The best overview of both Wartons, and the place to begin, is Lawrence Lipking's *The Ordering of the Arts in Eighteenth-Century England* (Princeton: Princeton Univ. Press, 1970). For a selection of scholarship, see John A. Vance, *Joseph and Thomas Warton: An Annotated Bibliography* (New York: Garland, 1983).

11. Although written in 1745, the poem was first published in 1747; a revised version was printed by Dodsley in 1755. The first edition is reprinted in *Eighteenth Century Poetry and Prose,* ed. Louis I. Bredvold, Alan D. McKillop, and Lois Whitney (New York: Ronald Press, 1939), 565-70. I quote from this anthology except where I indicate the 2nd edition, which I cite from Dodsley's *A Collection of Poems, in Six Volumes, by Several Hands, with Notes,* (London, 1782), 4:224-35.

12. My text for "Eloisa" and "The Unfortunate Lady" is *Twickenham Edition: The Poems of Alexander Pope,* ed. John Butt (New Haven: Yale Univ. Press, 1963), 252-61, 262-64.

13. It may be useful here to cite Freud on the mechanism of repression: "In this connection it becomes comprehensible that those objects to which men give their preference, that is, their ideals, originate in the same perceptions and experiences as those objects of which they have the most abhorrence, and that the two originally differed from one another only by slight modifications. Indeed, . . . it is possible for the original instinct-presentation to be split into two, one part undergoing repression, while the remainder, just on account of its intimate association with the other undergoes idealization" ("Repression" [1915], in *General Psychological Theory: Papers on Metapsychology,* ed. Philip Rieff [New York: Collier, 1963], 108).

14. My analysis here draws directly upon Patricinio Schweickart's observations on Joyce: "Relevant here is Levi-Strauss's theory that woman functions as currency exchanged between men. The woman in the text converts the text into a woman, and the circulation of this text/woman becomes the central ritual that establishes the bond between the author and his male readers." See Patricinio Schweickart, "Reading Ourselves: Toward a Feminist Theory of Reading," in *Gender and Reading: Essays on Readers, Texts, and Contexts,* ed. Elizabeth A. Flynn and Patricinio P. Schweickart (Baltimore: Johns Hopkins Univ. Press, 1986), 31-62. The quotation is taken from the reprint of this article in *Contemporary Literary Criticism: Literary and Cultural Studies,* ed. Robert Con Davis and Ronald Schleifer, 2nd ed. (New York: Longman, 1989), 126.

15. John Milton, *Poems upon Several Occasions,* ed. Thomas Warton (London: Dodsley, 1785), xi.

16. Warton introduces the anecdote by saying, "My brother remembers to have heard my father say. . . ." (Milton [note 15], viii-ix).

17. Milton, 186.

18. Arthur H. Scouten discusses this incident in "The Warton Forgeries and the Concept of Preromanticism in English Literature," *Etudes Anglaises* 40 (1987): 438.

19. After the establishment of "romanticism" in the nineteenth century, the Wartons were forgotten until, at the end of the century, scholars began to search for precursors to the "romantic movement." Phelps (1893), Beers (1898), and Courthope (1905) are some of the literary historians who call attention to the Wartons. Courthope wrote that Joseph and Thomas were "the pioneers of the Romantic Movement." Shortly afterwards the concept of "pre-romanticism," part of a certain politicized version of French history, was applied to the literary history of Europe by Van Tieghem (1924), and to English literary history by Legouis and Cazamian (1924). A few years later, Bernbaum's *Guide Through the Romantic Movement* (1930) provided an extensive discussion of preromanticism. For details see Arthur H. Scouten, "The Warton Forgeries and the Concept of Preromanticism in English Literature," *Etudes Anglaises* 40 (1987): 434-47.

20. Wordsworth, "Essay, Supplementary to the Preface," in *The Prose Works of William Wordsworth,* ed. W. J. B. Owen and Jane Worthington Smyser, 3 vols. (Oxford: Clarendon Press, 1974), 3:70.

21. "The anti-Romantic movement in criticism, which in Britain and America followed the Hulme-Eliot-Pound broadsides of the early twenties, is now over and done with, and criticism has got its sense of literary tradition properly in focus again" (Foreword to the collection of English Institute essays, *Romanticism Reconsidered,* ed. Nothrop Frye [New York: Columbia Univ. Press, 1963], v). It is here that Frye simply takes for granted the standard construction of romantic literary history: "It is a datum of literary experience that when we cross the divide of 1798 we find ourselves in a different kind of poetic world, darker in color, so to speak, than what has preceded it" (v-vi).

22. Thomas Warton the Elder, *Poems on Several Occasions* (1748) (New York: Facsimile Text Society, 1930), 180.

23. See David Fairer, "The Poems of Thomas Warton the Elder?" *Review of English Studies* 26 (1975): 287-300, 395-406; together with "The Poems of Thomas Warton the Elder?—A Postscript," *Review of English Studies* 29 (1978): 61-65. For Christina Le Prevost, see "More Unacknowledged Verse by Joseph Warton," *Review of English Studies* 37 (1986): 314-47.

Gwin J. Kolb and Robert DeMaria, Jr. (essay date 1995)

SOURCE: Kolb, Gwin J. and Robert DeMaria, Jr. "Thomas Warton's *Observations on the 'Faerie Queene' of Spenser,* Samuel Johnson's 'History of the English Language,' and Warton's *History of English Poetry*: Reciprocal Indebtedness?" *Philological Quarterly* 74, no. 3 (1995): 327-35.

[*In the following essay, Kolb and DeMaria analyze the relationship between Warton and Samuel Johnson, arguing that the two writers influenced and borrowed from each other.*]

Several commentators have discussed in varying detail the long, sometimes troubled friendship of Samuel Johnson and Thomas Warton, which began in the early 1750s (when Johnson was in his forties and Warton in his twenties) and apparently lasted until the former's death in 1784; and the same investigators have usually treated some of the numerous literary relationships obtaining between the two men.[1] But no one, so far as we are aware, has pointed out the possible connections between Warton's **Observations on the "Faerie Queene" of Spenser** (1754) and Johnson's "History of the English Language" (in his *Dictionary of the English Language,* 1755); and only one person has touched on the possible affiliations between Johnson's History and Warton's three-volume **History of English Poetry** (1774, 1778, 1781).[2] In this article, we present the results of a fresh examination, which, while admittedly not conclusive, pose new circumstances of composition, and new causes of specific parts, of the two latter works, especially Warton's.

1

Extant evidence suggests that the putative relationships originated in 1754, when Warton sent Johnson a copy of his recently published **Observations** and Johnson responded with a letter, dated July 16, 1754, praising the study for its disclosure of the books which "our ancient authours" "had read." He proceeds to express the hope that his forthcoming *Dictionary* (presumably including the "History of the English Language") will reduce the "ignorance" regarding such authors. Then he states his intention of "visiting the libraries of Oxford . . . in about a fortnight" in order to "finish" the *Dictionary*[3]—mainly the preliminaries (the Preface, History, and Grammar), researchers have plausibly inferred, since the bulk of the wordlist had been completed by the summer of 1754 and since none of the preliminaries was "yet begun" as of April 3, 1753.[4]

If he was indeed thinking seriously about composing the Preface, History, and Grammar during the spring and summer of 1754, Johnson must have paid unusual attention to the section of Warton's **Observations** (pp. 227-39) casting a backward glance at English poetry "from Spenser's age thro' the state of poesy in this kingdom." For, whatever their affiliation, it is noteworthy that the **Observations** and

Johnson's History, both referring to earlier English poets as "bards," select for comment—in the same order—Robert of Gloucester, John Gower, Chaucer, John Lydgate, Sir Thomas More, and John Skelton.

Moreover, portions of Warton's and Johnson's remarks about these authors are comparable, though far from identical. First, in Warton's opinion, the rhyming "chronicle of Robert of Glocester [*sic*], who wrote . . . about the year 1280," is an example of "the last dregs of that kind of composition which was practic'd by the British bards . . ." (p. 227). Likewise, Johnson says that *"Robert of Gloucester,"* who employed rhyme and "is placed by the criticks in the thirteenth century, seems to have used a kind of intermediate diction, neither *Saxon* nor *English*; in his work therefore we see the transition exhibited" (first ed., sig. E2r).

Second, Warton comments that "Gower and Chaucer were reputed the first English poets because they first introduc'd INVENTION into our poetry; they MORALIZED THEIR SONG. . . ." He adds, "Chaucer . . . deserves to be rank'd as one of the first English poets, on another account; his admirable artifice in painting the manners . . . ; and it should be remember'd to his honour, that he was the first who gave the English nation, in its own language, an idea of HUMOUR" (p. 228). For Johnson, Gower, "the first of our authours, who can be properly said to have written *English*" and who "calls *Chaucer* his disciple, . . . may . . . be considered as the father of our poetry." Of Chaucer, Johnson remarks in part, "The history of our language is now brought to the point at which the history of our poetry is generally supposed to commence, the time of the illustrious *Geoffry Chaucer,* who may perhaps, with great justice, be stiled the first of our versifyers who wrote poetically" (sig. F1v).

Third, in his relatively extended discussion of Lydgate, Warton says, among other things, that the poet "succeeded" Gower, Chaucer, and the writer of *Piers Plowman*; that "his principal performances" were "the FALL of PRINCES, and STORY OF THEBES"; that he was a "Monk of Bury"; and that he "is the first English poet, who can be red [*sic*] without hesitation and difficulty" (pp. 228-29, 230, 232). Johnson states that *"Lydgate* was a monk of *Bury,* who wrote about the same time with *Chaucer.* Out of his prologue to his third book of the *Fall of Princes* a few stanzas are selected, which, being compared with the style of his two contemporaries [Gower and Chaucer], will show that our language was then not written by caprice, but was in a settled state" (sig. G2r).

Fourth, Warton merely lists "Sir Thomas More" as one of the "great names" ("Colet, dean of St. Paul's, Cheke," and Ascham are also mentioned) affording luster to the age of Henry VIII, "perhaps the first which England ever saw, that may with propriety be styled classical . . ." (p. 234). Johnson introduces excerpts from More's compositions by remarking, "Of the works of Sir *Thomas More* it was necessary to give a larger specimen [than that by Sir John

Fortescue], both because our language was then in a great degree formed and settled, and because it appears from *Ben Johnson,* that his works were considered as models of pure and elegant style. The tale, which is placed first ['A merry iest how a sergeant would learne to playe the frere'], . . . will show what an attentive reader will, in perusing our old writers, often remark, that the familiar and colloquial part of our language, being [diffused][5] among those classes who had no ambition of refinement, or affectation of novelty, has suffered very little change" (sig. G2v).

Fifth, of John Skelton, Warton writes, "In this age [of Henry VIII] flourish'd John Skelton, who . . . contributed not the least share of improvement to what his ancestors had left him; nor do I perceive that his versification is in any degree more polish'd than that of his immediate predecessor [Stephen Hawes]. His best pieces . . . are, his CROWNE of LAURELL, and BOWGE of COURT. But the genius of this author seems little better qualify'd for picturesque, than for satyrical poetry; in the former, he wants invention, grace, and dignity; in the latter, wit, and good manners" (p. 234). Johnson devotes a single sentence to Skelton: "At the same time with Sir *Thomas More* lived *Skelton,* the poet laureate of *Henry* VIII. from whose works it seems proper to insert a few stanzas, though he cannot be said to have attained great elegance of language." The "few stanzas" are taken from Skelton's "prologue to the Bouge of Courte" (sig. I2v).

Summing up and making explicit what has already been intimated, we are led to conjecture that the creation of Johnson's History was indebted to Warton's *Observations.* Specifically, Johnson's choice of authors to be quoted, and his remarks about these authors, may have been influenced—even if only slightly—by Warton's "backward glance" at English poetry. More than this, we think, cannot be validly concluded. One is also led to wonder whether, during his visit to Oxford mentioned in the letter of July 16, 1754 cited above, Johnson received from Warton any assistance on the History. Many years later, Warton recalled numerous details about Johnson's visit, but none which suggested his contribution to any part of the *Dictionary.*[6] Although it seems certain that he and Johnson discussed the latter's massive undertaking—the cause, after all, of Johnson's trip—the help (if any) he afforded Johnson will just as certainly never be known. We guess that the two men's talks sometimes encompassed Warton's "Plan of the History of English Poetry" (see footnote 2 above) and pertinent remarks in his *Observations,* and we have considered—but rejected—the possibility that Warton's aid extended to phrasing and the choice of illustrative passages in Johnson's History. This hypothesis strikes us as unconvincing for several reasons, among them our doubt that in 1754 Warton would, or could, have provided Johnson with the detailed materials which comprise the evidence adduced below.

2

Johnson's *Dictionary* was published, of course, only months after his visit to Oxford—on April 15, 1755. As indicated above, the first volume of Warton's **History of English Poetry** appeared in 1774 (and a second edition in 1775), the second in 1778, and the third in 1781.[7] Warton's acquaintance with Johnson's "History of the English Language" is made explicit in Volume 1 of his work.[8] There, beginning his treatment of Chaucer, Warton declares: "The most illustrious ornament of the reign of Edward the third, and of his successor Richard the second, was Jeffrey Chaucer; a poet with whom the history of our poetry is by many supposed to have commenced; and who has been pronounced, by a critic of unquestionable taste and discernment, to be the first English versifier who wrote poetically" (p. 341). A footnote names the discerning critic and the location of his remark, "Johnson's DICTION. Pref. p. 1"—but mistakes Johnson's Preface for his History.

In his Preface, Warton states that his "performance" simultaneously "exhibits . . . the gradual improvements of our poetry" and "uniformly represents the progression of our language" (p. v). The attainment of these goals probably caused him, so the following pieces of evidence suggest in varying degrees, to increase his debt to Johnson's History well beyond the instance he acknowledges.

We present first the three passages which exhibit the strongest signs of Warton's borrowings.

(1) In Volume 1, Dissertation 2 (sig. c3r), Warton writes: "The Anglo-Saxons were converted to christianity about the year 570. *In consequence of this event, they soon acquired civility and learning* [our italics]. Hence they necessarily established a communication with Rome, and acquired a familiarity with the Latin language." The comparable passage in Johnson's History reads: "[In] the year 570 . . . *Augustine* came from *Rome* to convert them [the Anglo-Saxons] to Christianity. *The Christian religion always implies or produces a certain degree of civility and learning* [our italics]; they then became by degrees acquainted with the *Roman* language . . ." (sig. D1r).

(2) In Volume 2 (p. 32) Warton labels King Alfred "the father of learning and civility [cf. Warton's and Johnson's earlier use of the phrase] in the midst of a rude and intractable people."

(3) On pages 8-9 of Volume 1, Warton writes: "[George] Hickes has printed [in his *Thesaurus*] a satire on the monastic profession; *which clearly exemplifies the Saxon adulterated by the Norman* [our italics] . . ."; and he goes on to transcribe the first twelve lines of the "satire," an anonymous lyric entitled "The Land of Cockayne." Soon afterwards (pp. 12-13), he turns to "another Norman Saxon poem cited by" Hickes, "entitled THE LIFE OF SAINT MARGARET," the versification of which "*is like the French Alexandrines* [our italics]." Repeating his procedure for "The Land of Cockayne," he also transcribes the first twelve lines of the "Life," whose title in Hickes is "Vita Santae Maragaretae."

In his History, Johnson observes that these two poems display "the adulteration of the *Saxon* tongue, by a mixture of the *Norman*" and that the "Vita" "taught the way to the

Alexandrines of the *French* poetry." He transcribes the first forty-eight lines of "The Land of Cockayne" (including, of course, the twelve quoted by Warton) and the first twenty of the "Vita" (including, of course, the twelve quoted by Warton (sig. E2r). However, although the resemblances are marked between Johnson's and Warton's treatments of the works, the quoted lines common to both treatments are decidedly different (Johnson's are much closer than Warton's to the texts in the first edition of Hickes's *Thesaurus*). Nevertheless, it is quite possible, we think, that Warton, while not copying Johnson's transcriptions, decided to follow Johnson in his choice of extracts from "The Land of Cockayne" and the "Vita."

This group, evincing accord of ideas and phrasing, virtually proves, we conclude, Warton's indebtedness—admittedly small—to Johnson's History.

Next we complete the list begun above of Warton's full or partial repetition of quotations cited by Johnson.

(2) On page 390 of Volume 1, Warton, discussing Chaucer's *House of Fame,* quotes lines 121-27 of the first book of the poem. In his History (sig. G1v), Johnson quotes lines 109-218 (including, of course, those cited by Warton). It is possible that Warton's selection of his lines was prompted by Johnson's choice of his.

(3) On pages 19-20 of Volume 3, Warton, without titling the poem (in *Tottel's Miscellany*), reproduces the first twelve lines of "Description of Spring, wherin eche thing renewes saue onelie the louer." In his History, the initial piece Johnson cites (sig. 12v) by the Earl of Surrey is "Description of Spring" (including, of course, the lines quoted by Warton). It is possible, although unlikely, that Warton's selection, of his lines was prompted by Johnson's quotation of the poem.[9]

(4) On pages 47-49 of Volume 3, Warton, again drawing on *Tottel's Miscellany,* quotes, with the omission of three stanzas, "A praise of his Ladye," which he identifies as "nameless stanzas." In his History (sig. K1r), Johnson reproduces 28 lines from the same poem, including 24 also cited by Warton. It is possible, although unlikely, that Warton's selection of his extracts was prompted by Johnson's choice of his lines.[10]

(5) On pages 63-65 of Volume 3, Warton, again drawing on *Tottel's Miscellany,* cites four passages from "The Death of Zoroas, an Egiptian Astronomer, in the first fight, that Alexander had with the Persians" by Nicholas Grimald. In his History (sig. K1v), Johnson quotes the same passages, plus others. It is possible, although unlikely, that Warton's choice of his passages was caused by Johnson's choice of his.[11]

(6) On pages 97-98 of Volume 3, Warton quotes some of the opening and closing stanzas of the youthful More's "A MERY JEST *how a* SERGEANT *would learne to play the* FREERE,*" the "story" of which, Warton remarks, "is too

dull and too long to be told here." In his History (sigs. G2v-H2r), Johnson reproduces the whole (minus six lines) of "A MERY JEST," including, of course, the passages cited by Warton. It is possible that Warton's choice of his passages was prompted by Johnson's selection of the poem for quotation.

(7) On pages 99-101 of Volume 3, Warton quotes two passages from More's "RUFULL LAMENTATION on the death of queen Elizabeth, wife of Henry the seventh . . . ," saying at the end, "I have been prolix in my citation from this forgotten poem: but I am of opinion, that some of the stanzas have strokes of nature and pathos, and deserved to be rescued from total oblivion." In his History (sig. H2r), Johnson reproduces the entire poem (including, of course, the passages cited by Warton). It is possible, although perhaps unlikely (note Warton's comment about "total oblivion"), that Warton's choice of his passages was caused by Johnson's selection of the poem for quotation.

Like the first two, the texts of the remainder of Warton's illustrative quotations differ markedly from Johnson's texts of the same quotations. Moreover, Warton sometimes indicates the specific sources of his texts.[12] Consequently, the chances that Warton's choices of authors and/or passages consciously followed Johnson's never rise, as we have noted, above the level of possibility.

Lastly, in five other instances Warton and Johnson comment on the same authors and works—namely, King Alfred's translation of Boethius's *Of the Consolation of Philosophy* (Warton, Vol. 1, sig. d1v, Vol. 2, p. 32; Johnson, sig. D1r), Sir John Mandeville's *Travels* (Warton, Vol. 1, p. 102; Johnson, sig. F1r), Alexander Barclay's *Ship of Fooles* (Warton, Vol. 2, pp. 240-56; Johnson, sig. K1v)[13], Thomas Wilson's *Arte of Rhetorique* (Warton, Vol. 2, p. 453, Vol. 3, p. 331; Johnson, sig. K2r), and Sir Thomas More's *History of King Richard III* (Warton, Vol. 3, p. 329; Johnson, sig. G2r). It is possible, although (in the absence of relevant evidence) not likely, that one or more of Warton's selections resulted from Johnson's. Summing up, we repeat our conclusion that Warton's ***History of English Poetry*** almost certainly owes three small debts to Johnson's "History of the English Language" and that its total number of debts may—but only may—be larger than three.[14]

Notes

1. The fullest, most illuminating discussion of the Johnson-Warton friendship is John A. Vance's essay, "Samuel Johnson and Thomas Warton," *Biography* 9 (1986): 95-111. Other treatments of the friendship—and of selected literary relationships—include: *Boswell's Life of Johnson,* ed. G. B. Hill, rev. L. F. Powell (Oxford: Clarendon Press, 1934), 1:271-74, 335-36; vol. 1-4, *passim* (cited hereafter as *Life*); Richard Mant, *Memoirs* of Warton prefixed to Mant's edition of *The Poetical Works of Thomas Warton* (Oxford, 1802), 1:xxvii-xxviii, xxxv-xl, lxxxii; Clarissa Rinaker, *Thomas Warton: A Biographical*

and Critical Study (U. of Illinois Press, 1916), pp. 35, 68-70, 139-40, 169-70, *passim*; John Wain, *Samuel Johnson* (New York, 1974), pp. 171-74, *passim*; John A. Vance, *Joseph and Thomas Warton* (Boston, 1983), pp. 8, 9-11, 54-56, 94-95.

2. In his *Johnson the Philologist* (Osaka: Intercultural Research Institute, Kansai University of Foreign Studies, 1988), Daisuke Nagashima discerns what he calls "a good deal of agreement . . . if not in detail at least in broad historical perspectives" (p. 73) between Johnson's History and Warton's short outline "Plan of the History of English Poetry," which was written in the early 1750s (see David Fairer, "The Origins of Warton's *History of English Poetry*," *RES*, n. s., 32 [1981]: 37-63, esp. 42-45). Like Fairer (p. 42), Nagashima reproduces the "Plan" and then goes on to imply that Warton may have communicated its substance to Johnson during the latter's visit to Oxford in the summer of 1754. Nagashima does not note the fact that Warton's "Plan" shares with Johnson's History the same sequential mention of British "bards," Robert of Gloucester, John Gower, Chaucer, John Lydgate, John Skelton, and Sir Thomas Wyatt and the Earl of Surrey. However, as we observe below, Johnson had earlier found the same sequence (without Wyatt and Surrey but with Sir Thomas More, between Lydgate and Skelton) and longer descriptive comments in Warton's *Observations*. As we also point out below, although Johnson and Warton surely discussed the *Dictionary* (presumably including the History of the Language) during Johnson's visit to Oxford, it seems impossible to ascertain the help Warton gave Johnson on the project.

3. *The Letters of Samuel Johnson*, ed. Bruce Redford (Princeton U. Press, 1992), 1:81-82.

4. See James H. Sledd and Gwin J. Kolb, *Dr. Johnson's Dictionary* (U. of Chicago, 1955), 109-10; Allen Reddick, *The Making of Johnson's Dictionary, 1746-1773* (Cambridge U. Press, 1990), 72-75; Samuel Johnson, *Diaries, Prayers, and Annals*, ed. E. L. McAdam, Jr., with Donald and Mary Hyde, Yale Edition of the Works of Samuel Johnson, vol. 1 (Yale U. Press, 1958), 50.

5. We have emended the first (folio) edition reading of "disused" to the second (folio) edition reading of "diffused." See Gwin J. Kolb and Robert DeMaria, Jr., "The Preliminaries to Dr. Johnson's *Dictionary*: Authorial Revisions and the Establishment of the Texts," *Studies in Bibliography* 48 (1995): 131.

6. *Life*, 1:270, n. 5, 271-74.

7. Our references in the text below cite the first editions of the three volumes.

8. Warton's knowledge of Johnson's History is also apparent when, in a letter to his brother Joseph, he describes the History as "pretty full;" see John Wooll, *Biographical Memoirs of the Late Revd. Joseph Warton* (London, 1806), 230.

9. David Fairer points out that Warton was familiar with the contents of Tottel's *Miscellany* long before the publication of his *History* and that in a letter of April 5, 1763, Thomas Percy asked Warton's opinion of a proposed emendation in "Description of Spring." See Fairer's edition of *The Correspondence of Thomas Warton* (U. of Georgia Press, 1995), 158.

10. See the preceding note.

11. See n. 9 above.

12. For example, Warton implies that he has drawn the passages in (3) above from George Hickes's *Thesaurus*, he provides "folio" references (in footnotes) for the selections from Tottel's *Miscellany*, and in a footnote he specifies More's "WORKES, Lond. 1557. in folio" (3:97) as the source of his excerpts from Sir Thomas More.

13. David Fairer reminds us that Johnson drew Warton's attention to Barclay's *Ship of Fooles* in a letter of December 21, 1754, that Warton used Johnson's information in the second edition (1762) of his *Observations* (2:106), and that he devoted a chapter to Barclay in his *History* (2:240-56). See Fairer's edition of *The Correspondence of Thomas Warton*, pp. 33-34.

14. We express our warm thanks to David Fairer for his searching comments on an earlier draft of this article, and to John Vance for reading the same draft. Gwin Kolb also expresses his lasting gratitude to the Beinecke Library (Yale University) for the award, during the fall of 1993, of the Frederick and Marion Pottle Fellowship, which enabled him to collect some of the material contained herein.

David Fairer (essay date 1995)

SOURCE: Fairer, David. Introduction to *The Correspondence of Thomas Warton*, edited by David Fairer, pp. xvii-xxxvi. Athens: The University of Georgia Press, 1995.

[In the following essay, Fairer describes Warton's importance as a literary figure.]

On the evening of 20 March 1776 Dr. Johnson and Boswell, who were on a visit to Oxford together, went round to Trinity College to call on Johnson's friend of over twenty years' standing, Thomas Warton: "We went to Mr. Thomas Warton of Trinity, whom I had long wished to see. We found him in a very elegant apartment ornamented with good prints, and with wax or spermaceti candles before him. All this surprised me, because I had heard that Tom kept low drunken company, and I expected to see a confused dusty room and a little, fat, laughing fellow. In place of which I found a good, sizable man, with most decent clothes and darkish periwig, one who might figure as a canon."[1] Caught between expectation and reality, Boswell finds Warton hard to pin down. The confused dusty room is obviously the place where *The History of English Poetry* was written; the little, fat, laughing fellow is Tom Warton of *The Oxford Sausage*; but instead Boswell seems to have found, in his elegant apartment, Professor Warton, the editor of Theocritus.

Warton's literary achievement was certainly many-sided: poet, literary historian, classical scholar, Gothic enthusiast, humorist, biographer, editor. He was a man in whom so many strands of the cultural life of the eighteenth century met. He represented, too, something of the capaciousness of the "literary" in an age when it subsumed classical studies and historical research and scholarship generally, before the post-romantic contraction of literature within confined notions of creativity. It is important to recognize that in his wide range of works Warton was addressing one public. His edition of Latin inscriptions was received as eagerly as a new volume of the *History,* Professor Dalzel of Edinburgh used *Theocritus* and *Newmarket: A Satire* in the same lesson, and Gibbon owned not only the *History* but the *Life of Bathurst* too.[2] It is perhaps inevitable that such a widely based achievement should fragment once this omnivorous readership declined.

If modern criticism cannot reinstate Warton to his former greatness, it can at least recognize what René Wellek has called his "immense historical importance"[3] and attempt to appreciate him as the eighteenth century did, by viewing him as a whole. An edition of his correspondence will perhaps encourage this by showing him at work not just on *The History of English Poetry* but on many of his less familiar works. By bringing Thomas Warton into sharper focus among his friends and contemporaries it may be possible to renew critical interest in a significant feature of the eighteenth-century literary landscape, and to understand how it was possible for Sir Samuel Egerton Brydges (by no means an uncritical admirer of Warton's work) to say of him in 1800: "Perhaps there was no one, by whose death the literature of England could have sustained a greater chasm."[4]

At the time of his death in 1790 as Poet Laureate and Camden Professor of History at Oxford, Warton was at the head of his profession and occupied a unique and somewhat contradictory place in the nation's affections. On the one hand he represented the nostalgic spirit of the old antiquarians, bookish and devoted to curious inquiry, and yet, far from being an out-of-touch figure from a previous age, he was in his later years surrounded by a band of admiring young poets who were speaking and developing his own poetic voice and placing it at the forefront of literary tastes. Henry Headley, Thomas Russell, and William Lisle Bowles (to name only three) were Wartonians steeped in the spirit of their mentor, and the poetry produced during the 1790s by Coleridge, Southey, and Wordsworth was rooted in the work of Warton and his followers. In 1825, casting his eye backwards, Robert Southey wrote of the poetic scene: "If any man may be called the father of the present race, it is Thomas Warton," and he spoke of the School of Warton as "the true English school."[5]

Warton's greatest achievement, *The History of English Poetry,* was similarly both retrospective and a generator of new literary trends. What the neo-Gothic Horace Walpole had regarded as an inelegant trudge through "the muddy poetry of three or four centuries that had never a poet,"[6] Sir Walter Scott was to welcome in 1804 as an "immense common-place-book," a mine "inexhaustible in its treasures" which Warton had recovered and fed into the literary consciousness of his country.[7] It would be an exaggeration to say that Warton gave Britain its literary past, but none at all to argue that he helped shape the nation's awareness of it. To a great storyteller like Scott the Wartonian narrative was too crowded with incident and too unsorted to be a satisfactory history, and so his response to it was that of a poet finding a hoard of precious source materials "from the perusal of which we rise, our fancy delighted with beautiful imagery, and with the happy analysis of ancient tale and song."

The significance of Warton's *History* for the next generation lay also in what it was *not.* In the 1770s, when some in the literary establishment were looking for a classical work of polite learning in which literary history was regulated into periods and schools, Warton rejected the taxonomic patterns of Pope and Gray.[8] Where some might have expected the narrative to be one of incremental improvement culminating in the elegance and correctness of the Restoration period, 1660-88, Warton's story sets this in tension with another movement—a retrospect, which is continually reaching back through its footnotes and digressions to a world that has been lost, to old customs and images that fascinated Warton the antiquarian. During its writing the *History* began turning round on itself, pursuing the retrospect rather than the official pattern of improvement and progress.

The key to what is only an apparent contradiction lies in the notion of the recovery of the past, a process of literary archaeology, or unlayering, in which personal conviction combined with a deep knowledge of the remains of former ages in an attempt to locate and reanimate hidden sources of poetic inspiration. This aim set Warton at variance with his great contemporary, Dr. Johnson. Their principles of literary value were opposed and their canons incompatible, and some of the complexity of the intellectual scene during the second half of the eighteenth century is lost if the dubious term "the Age of Johnson" is allowed to conceal the fact that the Wartonian pattern of literary history was in the ascendant.

From 1750, when he began reading in the Bodleian Library, Warton steeped himself in the literature of the medieval and Renaissance past, and he established a kind of native line of descent, working back through the early Milton to his beloved Spenser, and back through him to the world of Malory, Chaucer, and the medieval romances of chivalry. Warton's three important works of literary history, *Observations on the Faerie Queene* (1754), *The History of English Poetry* (1774-81), and the edition of Milton's minor poems (1785), are part of a single enterprise to establish and explore the root system of the native verse tradition. The age, 1660-1740, which for Johnson had seen the culmination of literary achievement, was for Warton an interlude, an elegant and artificial interruption into the continuum that was English poetry. Where Johnson's *Lives of the Poets* (1779-81) placed Pope's *Homer* as the climax of his story and considered that any attempts at improving on Pope's versification would be "dangerous,"[9] the Wartonian reversal involved the demotion of Pope to the secondary branch of didactic rather than imaginative poetry. In this way Joseph Warton's *Essay on Pope* (1756, 1782) had its part to play in the Wartonian project.[10] Johnson's *Lives* can be seen to have been directed at the literary tastes and principles represented by the Warton brothers: if Johnson wished to establish 1660-1740 as the great age of English poetry, he had to demote the work of the early Milton at one end and that of Gray and the poetry of "Sensibility" at the other. But the *Lives* could not of course engage directly with the Wartons' work. In conversation Johnson mocked, only half jokingly, the "Ode and Elegy and Sonnet" of Thomas's 1777 volume (a text that was to have a marked influence on the direction poetry took during the next generation), not knowing that he was quoting what would be the subtitle of Southey's first collection of verse.[11] To the degree that Johnson's *Lives of the Poets* attempted to correct and divert the literary developments of his day, the period 1740-90 was, if anything, more truly the Age of Warton than the Age of Johnson. It is this fact that makes the reinstatement of Warton as a significant literary figure a useful counterweight to the "Augustan Pantheon" view of the eighteenth century.

The future Laureate was born on 9 January 1728 in the small market town of Basingstoke, Hampshire, where his father was Vicar and Headmaster of the local grammar school. Thomas Warton the Elder had moved there from Oxford where he had been fellow of Magdalen College, and in that same year he was ending his tenure as the University's Professor of Poetry. Unlike his elder brother Joseph, who was sent to Winchester College, Thomas remained at home in Basingstoke under his father's care, and from him he picked up a thorough knowledge of the classical languages, a fascination for antiquity, a tinge of Jacobitism, and the habit of writing verse.

Between his entering Trinity College Oxford as a sixteen-year-old in 1744 and his appointment to a fellowship there in 1752, Warton's poetic output was considerable. He published six volumes of verse, the most influential of which was **"The Pleasures of Melancholy,"** written at the age of seventeen and published by Dodsley in 1747.[12] Warton's world of solitude, darkness, and eerie suggestion, now and again broken by glimpses of a contrasting scene of glitter and artifice, became part of the poetic currency of the age. By 1750 he had also become known in the literary world as the University's poetic champion: his *Triumph of Isis,* written in response to William Mason's attack on the University's morals and patriotism, routed the opposition and celebrated Oxford in terms that inaugurated its myth of dreaming spires and unfashionable ideals.

In many early twentieth-century narratives of literary history "the Wartons" were given a strategic role as "pioneers of romanticism,"[13] and certainly in the mid-1740s Thomas and his brother Joseph regarded themselves as part of a movement to change public taste and reinstate vision and imagination as the primary poetic qualities. Joseph's words in the advertisement to his *Odes* of 1746 ("the following Odes may be look'd upon as an attempt to bring back Poetry into its right channel") were in fact anticipated by Thomas's draft preface to **Five Pastoral Eclogues,** 1745 ("The taste of Poetry in England begins to amend . . ."), and by his sketch for **"An Essay on Romantic Poetry"** dateable to the same year ("Several modern authors have employed a manner of poetry . . . which perhaps it would not be improper to call a Romantic Kind of Poetry, as it is altogether conceived in the spirit . . . & affects the Imagination in the same Manner, with the old Romances").[14] The letters between the brothers during these early years breathe the excitement of two young men reveling in being at the forefront of poetic trends. We are given tantalizing glimpses of some of their projects, especially Joseph's, and the correspondence conveys an infectious enthusiasm for the literary scene.

When Thomas Warton the Elder died leaving some worrying debts and a collection of unpublished verse, it seemed natural enough that the brothers should publish a subscription volume of their father's poetry. *Poems on Several Occasions. By the Reverend Mr. Thomas Warton,* when it appeared in 1748, was a landmark in literary taste, but it was so because his sons secretly contributed at least nineteen poems of their own.[15] The precedent for such family "co-operation" had been set two years earlier when Thomas anonymously contributed two odes to Joseph's 1746 collection.[16]

We are fortunate in having forty-nine letters between the two brothers, more than enough to convey a sense of their lifelong devotion to each other, but the gaps are considerable (there is nothing surviving from the 1770s, for example) and so we shall probably never know how extensive their collaboration may have been. The existing letters, however, give an interesting picture of the two men exchanging hints and guidance on each other's work. Joseph advises Thomas on the structure of **The Triumph of Isis,** suggests an outline for an important sermon his brother is about to preach, or boasts about a fine new couplet for his *Ode to Fancy,*[17] while Thomas sends **"Ode to a Gentleman"** to be included in his brother's 1746 *Odes,* helps out with the "Z" papers of *The Adventurer,* and oversees the printing of Joseph's *Essay on Pope,* attempting to bring some shape to material that was being written while the presses were running.[18] Two significant survivals from 1786[19] reveal that Thomas submitted his laureate odes in draft form to his brother for correction and improvement, and the **New Year Ode** for 1787 clearly benefited from Joseph's mastery of the well-turned phrase. In literary history "The Wartons" have often been treated as a single phenomenon and their correspondence confirms their closeness, but it also highlights their respective characters, which were as distinctive as their handwriting. Joseph's hand became increasingly flowing and rapid, full of breathless dashes, while Thomas's was ever more crabbed, scratchy, and laconic. Joseph's role as Headmaster of Winchester and head of a large and extended family contrasts with Thomas's bachelor life in his Oxford college. Where Joseph unfailingly charmed the ladies, Thomas was awkward in polite company and preferred to unwind among the boys of his brother's school, or in the company of soldiers and sailors or the tavern wits.[20] In their work, too, the emphases are differently placed: the sensational primitivism in *The Enthusiast* (1744) is as characteristic of Joseph as the melancholy nostalgia in **"Ode Written at Vale-Royal Abbey"** is of Thomas. Where Joseph's *Essay on Pope* shows its author's mastery of the latest French theories and, though a corrective, is essentially an engagement with current tastes,[21] Thomas's *Observations on the Faerie Queene* is an act of scholarly archaeology, the fruit of his historical researches in the Bodleian Library and the Ashmolean Museum.

Before he entered Trinity in 1744, his maternal grandfather, Joseph Richardson, gave him his copy of the 1617 folio of Spenser's works[22] and this volume proved a catalyst for the young man's reading. The margins of the book became crowded with annotations for what was being planned as an edition of Spenser but instead grew into the ***Observations on the Faerie Queene*** (1754), whose capacious format allowed him to use a lot of analogical material that had developed from footnotes into miniature essays. Working in the Oxford libraries, Warton soon discovered a wealth of older literature. It has been calculated from the Bodleian's records that in 1753 alone roughly one ninth of all orders for books and manuscripts were made by him, most being collections of older English literature and especially Elizabethan poetry and medieval romances.[23] His discovery of the 1634 edition of Malory (which he began reading on 7 May 1753) was a breakthrough and revealed how much Spenser had drawn from a stock of older romance motifs and episodes from the Arthurian story.

This aspect of the ***Observations*** was of particular interest to Thomas Percy, who was able to supply Warton with material for the expanded second edition (1762), and at the same time enlist his new friend's help in gathering material from the Oxford libraries for the *Reliques* and his editions of Buckingham and Surrey. Their correspondence during the 1760s is an absorbing example of the opportunities and difficulties that confronted the eighteenth-century literary scholar. But Percy's aims and principles were quite distinct from Warton's. Where Percy worked to accommodate his ballad material to the present by a kind of gentrification that adapted the past to the polite sensibilities of his own age, Warton's material somehow always resisted accommodation, and in spite of his occasional gestures towards smoothness and elegance, it is usually the curious or exotic that stirs his interest. The voluminous double-columned footnotes in the ***History*** have an effect equivalent to opening long-closed secret drawers and peering in at their slightly musty contents.

Observations on the Faerie Queene marked a change in literary history towards a more relativist, source-based approach that saw literature in organic terms as developing from a common stock of poetic language. Warton's innovation in this field was something for which Samuel Johnson was ready to give generous praise, and letter 25 inaugurated a warm friendship between the Rambler and the young Oxford don. In the letters of 1754-55, as M.A. of Oxford and author of the great *Dictionary,* Johnson grows conscious of being accepted into an academic community, and we see him attempting a range of literary reference that he sometimes has difficulty in getting right. By 1757 the relationship shows signs of strain, and Johnson's remark, "Professors forget their Friends,"[24] suggests he was feeling a little distanced from the successful young man.

Warton's election to the Oxford Professorship of Poetry in 1756 brought a shift in his career towards official university duties and an increasing commitment to classical literature. The ancient writers could never be far from the mind of any Oxford tutor, but the discipline of lecturing four times a year over a decade on the poetry of the Greeks allowed him to range through the topics of epic, tragedy, comedy, lyric, epigram, didactic, and pastoral verse, and something of the Greek spirit began to find its way into his own poetry, as several later critics noticed.[25] But it would be wrong to see this as a deviation from his other literary studies. On the contrary, the same principle drove him: the uncovering of purer sources of literary inspiration. This was partly why he chose Ancient Greek literature, and why the fundamental principle he repeatedly stressed was that of simplicity. This had been the subject of a projected **"Essay on the Simplicity of the Ancients"** (dated 28 February 1745) and of a brief advertisement prefixed to the "Three Epigrams Translated from the Greek" in his father's 1748 *Poems* (the translations were probably also by him). In praising Warton's 1758 collection of classical and modern Latin inscriptions, James "Hermes" Harris must have delighted his correspondent by differentiating his Athenian good taste from "that phantom bearing its name, imported by Petit Maitres from France."[26] The aims of Warton's youthful campaign (for so it must be called) were the re-establishing in English poetry of both the native tradition and the principles of true Greek classicism. Each could give modern poetry a new immediacy, whether through simplicity of style or a direct appeal to the imagination. It is important for an understanding of Warton's character and works to see that he was able, from his early years, to bring these two traditions into some sort of reconciliation. In the ***History*** Warton can define and appreciate the classical qualities in the poetry of Lord Surrey (the smoothness of his verse, the elegance of his transitions, the balance of thought and feeling) while at the same time appreciating the imaginative qualities of less polished Tudor poetry. Warton's love of classical literature widened his sympathies as a critic and also affected his poetry. An interesting text in this regard is his translation of the famous "Dirge for Bion," which occupied twelve pages of his father's *Poems* and shows the young man's skill in assimilating the language of the original Greek into the tones of Spenser and the early Milton.

Warton's attitude to the classics is intimately related to the principles behind his English literary history, and one significant feature of his correspondence is that it serves to remind us of Warton the classical scholar. We see him acting officially as a Delegate of the Clarendon Press, negotiating with Samuel Musgrave for the Oxford Euripides, and most fascinatingly we view him at work on all stages of his major project, the two-volume *Theocritus* (1770). The correspondence with Jonathan Toup is notable in that it was the latter's contributions to Warton's work that gave the edition a degree of scholarly importance. Warton's priorities were not textual (the text of the idylls had in fact been printed off in 1758, the year the contract was signed), whereas Toup's contributions to the textual study of Theocritus remain significant to this day, and Warton perhaps recognized that diplomatic handling of the prickly Cornish clergyman would pay dividends. During the period of their correspondence we can see Toup's *Appendicula* take shape as we follow the "magnific" edition through to the dilemma of its dedication and the drama of its publication, when a storm blew up around Warton's head and Toup finally lost his equilibrium. The scandal of the "obscene" note drew in those other battle-hardened adversaries, Lowth and Warburton, to the embarrassment of Warton, who wanted to remain on good terms with both. The affair made considerable demands on his tact and his usually irrepressible good humor.

Fortunately the correspondence offers some characteristic glimpses of that aspect of Warton which delighted many of his contemporaries—and unsettled a few. The Warton of *The Oxford Sausage* (1764)[27] occasionally shows through to remind the reader that the good-natured humorist never lies far beneath the surface of his work. Warton's popular anthology of Oxford verse was designed as a burlesque work of "Taste," whose ingredients were *"highly seasoned . . . carefully selected and happily blended,"* and it exemplifies the spirit of Oxford "waggery" that was a feature of the University's literary life.[28]

Boswell's sketch, quoted at the beginning of this introduction, places Warton within a set of contradictory terms: the elegant and the low, order and confusion, sobriety and drunkenness, solemnity and laughter, even the "sizable" and the "little." It is the material out of which the eighteenth century fashioned the burlesque, or shaped the antitheses of the heroic couplet, and such contradictions are at the heart of Warton's character and literary output. But in him they coexist amicably rather than work against each other. Boswell's diary entry does not banish the Warton of his expectations, but keeps it hovering in sight as a ghostly twin, and there is a similar unkempt and laughing presence haunting the Warton correspondence.

To put it in more formal terms, Warton's social range was considerable. The Poet Laureate at the Court of George III, whose sphere was aristocratic house parties, private

theatricals at Blenheim, and foxhunting with the Duke of Beaufort,[29] was as likely to be found in Captain Jolly's Tavern, where porter was fourpence a quart and Ben Tyrrell's mutton pies could be had for threepence. The University Professor was a stalwart of the Jelly-Bag Society, a group who would meet for drink and puns at secret venues in Oxford.[30] Warton's humorous poems, some contributed anonymously to *Jackson's Oxford Journal* and *The Student* (1750-51), were generously represented in Warton's anthology, *The Union* (as by **"A Gentleman formerly of the University of Aberdeen"**), and later in the *Sausage*. His best-known comic poem, **"The Progress of Discontent,"** was quoted back at him by Johnson in letter 37, and one of its couplets came into Lord Byron's mind as he sailed away from England in 1811.[31] **"A Panegyric on Oxford Ale," "Ode to a Grizzle Wig,"** and **"Prologue on the Old Winchester Playhouse, Over the Butcher's Shambles"** all have a verbal relish that interweaves mock pomposity and lyric fancy until the two tones fuse. The effect is subtle, as innocence and experience meet in a humorous nostalgia.[32]

A similarly complex tone characterizes *A Companion to the Guide, and a Guide to the Companion* (1760). This prose pamphlet, with a title suggested by Ovid, is both a burlesque upon, and supplement to, the official Oxford Guide. It provides a tour of neglected places of interest such as the tennis courts, the racetracks, and the unofficial University Libraries run by coffee-house proprietors. But the pamphlet is at the same time the work of Warton the antiquarian. He describes with affectionate detail the old pillory in the Cornmarket, the down-and-outs' bench beneath Carfax clock-tower, and the two-faced pump in the High Street. He records amusing epitaphs, gives a woodcut of the Carfax clock, and in discussing the Boar's Head Ceremony at Queen's he prints the original carol from the unique Bodleian fragment. The message is that conveyed by one of the grotesque figures overlooking Magdalen College cloisters, which is "significantly situated . . . to admonish strangers, and particularly the Young Student, that Science is not inconsistent with Good-Humour, and that Scholars are a *merrier* Sett of People than the World is apt to imagine."[33]

Letter 166, which Warton sent anonymously to *Jackson's Oxford Journal*, has the same combination of good-humored satire and a genuine fondness for Oxford's old buildings, and it adds significantly to our appreciation of Warton's architectural interests and his uneasiness with contemporary elegance. Beneath the playful humor can be glimpsed a genuine distaste for the process of modernization that was spoiling the character of his beloved medieval city.

From 1744 until the moment of his death (sitting in his chair in the common room while enjoying a convivial evening with friends) Trinity College Oxford was the center of Warton's life. Unrewarded by any substantial college benefice and overlooked for its Presidency, he nevertheless served it faithfully for forty years. He gave much time to the troublesome rotation of college offices during his years of writing the *History,*[34] and an awareness of his college duties can only increase our respect for a life characterized throughout by a fund of physical and mental energy. The official side of his college duties has been happily preserved in a group of letters exchanged, in his role as Bursar, with Lord Guilford, the college's most important tenant. These, along with records among the Trinity Archives of audits and college visitations, confirm that Warton's amusing contribution to Johnson's *Idler* (no. 33, 2 December 1758), the **"Journal of a Senior Fellow,"** is a young man's benign laughter at a lazy old don, and neither a portrait nor a prophecy of Warton's own daily routine.

Warton's fascination for sources and foundations shows through in the fact that he traced the origins of each institution with which he was connected. Here again it is evident that his work in literary history is intimately bound up with his other concerns. Winchester, the place where he spent most vacations in the company of Joseph's family and the boys of the school, was the subject of his historical guidebook, *A Description of the City, College and Cathedral of Winchester* (1760), and he prepared for the press an edition of Wykeham's Roll, a venerable manuscript of the household expenses of the college's founder that he had come across in the muniment room.[35] When Warton was given the Rectory of Kiddington by the Chancellor of Oxford University, Lord Lichfield, he inevitably began working on the history of the parish, published in 1781 as *Specimen of a Parochial History of Oxfordshire.* Above all, Trinity College was the focus of Warton's passion for a kind of localized history that could work back to the past through his own experience and strengthen a relationship by recovering its sources and influences. His *Life and Literary Remains of Ralph Bathurst* (1761) took as its subject Trinity's greatest President who had built its reputation and its chapel, and the *Life of Sir Thomas Pope* (1772) traced not merely the life of the college's founder but gathered into a lengthy appendix many interesting historical documents, one of which found its way to him from a helpful clergyman.[36] The correspondence can help fill out our view of Warton's scholarly studies by showing him at work on these less familiar achievements that helped build up his reputation as a historian.

Warton in fact came very near to being appointed Oxford's Regius Professor of History. The story during the years 1768-71 of his oft-kindled hopes and ultimate failure is an absorbing one.[37] Where Warton had failed to enlist either Horace Walpole or Bishop Shipley to his cause,[38] the doughty William Warburton strode into battle on his behalf. Not merely do the bishop's letters reveal Warton's attitudes and tactics in his bid for office, but they also convey a sharply drawn picture of Warburton himself, who saw in his younger friend a standard-bearer for integrity and merit amid the encroaching gloom of an age of place-fixing and moral compromise. Warburton's often moving letters show him recapturing a Popean ethical fervor, especially in letter 263 when he quotes with feeling from the

apocalyptic close of *The Dunciad* as though he were wishing his own former friend and patron back to life. Warton's failure to become Regius Professor may have confirmed his patron's views of a corrupt age, but it is clear that bad luck and Warton's own eventual diffidence also played a part. In 1785, however, the university recognized his achievements in the historical field by making him its Camden Professor.

Historical researches were Warton's great love, which becomes abundantly clear from the correspondence. Many letters in this volume are concerned with antiquarian matters, and his works in literary history, as well as the historical cast of much of his poetry, are here given their context in Warton's concern for the retrieval of the past. We see him attributing a coat of arms in a painting in Winchester Cathedral and conjecturing about the date of the Salisbury spire in a letter that found its way into the local guidebook.[39] He identifies a coin found during an excavation, offers his interpretation of the reliefs on the Winchester font, and explains an unusual gesture in a stained-glass window.[40] He is always ready to inspect and report on the state of historic buildings: the Hospital of St. John Baptist at Basingstoke, Sir Thomas Pope's wainscot at Luton Hoo, or the remains of Titchfield House associated with the Earls of Southampton.[41] Warton appears never happier than when engaged in the retrieval and preservation of the past. In 1865 Henry Boyle Lee (Warton's great-nephew) drew on family papers and locally preserved anecdotes to draw a vivid picture of Warton exploring architectural antiquities:

> On such occasions Warton was in all his glory; and, whether alone or in company, he was equally busy and delighted. Note-book in hand, he would mark, and measure, and speculate, and admire; or, if an audience should improvise itself around him, then would he, like Captain Clutterbuck, "expatiate to their astonished minds upon crypts, and chancels, and naves, Gothic and Saxon architectures, mullions, and flying buttresses." In this way he passed the summer vacations during many years of his life; storing up facts, searching out records, consulting authorities, and noting references, all with the ultimate view of producing a complete and systematic work on the subject of Gothic architecture, the study of which he pursued up to the time of his death with a love which admitted of no engrossing rivalry, except in that which he bore to his brother and sister, his writing-desk, his old books, and his old college ale.[42]

Lee also describes, through the recollections of Warton's niece, probably his own mother, Harriet Lee (1775-1863), examples of his intervening to save remnants of medieval craftsmanship: "[She] could well remember having witnessed, in her early days, her uncle's self-congratulations on the subject of his efforts in that direction. He would relate with glee how often he had stopped some pursy vicar riding with his wife stuck behind him . . . , and how he had scolded, and argued, and almost shed tears, rather than fail to enlist their sympathies in favour of some tomb or niche, which he had heard of as being doomed to destruction." Warton's delight in the Gothic was no mere aesthetic preference, but a zealous commitment to preserving the monuments of former ages. All Warton's works were the result of his passion for the past; the poems on Stonehenge, the Crusades, and King Arthur's Round Table, and the nostalgic descriptions of loved scenes left or revisited are two poetic aspects of the impulse that filled the footnotes of the *History* with wardrobe-lists and records of forgotten customs.

Warton gained a national reputation as an expert on Gothic architecture from a fourteen-page account added for the second edition of *Observations on the Fairy Queen.*[43] This example of Wartonian digression (offered as a note on the "stately pillours" of Venus's temple in book 4, canto 10) was praised by Horace Walpole as the first successful attempt to distinguish the successive periods of Gothic,[44] and it was being reprinted as a separate essay into the nineteenth century.[45] Each style is characterized and discussed; dated examples from specific churches are presented from Warton's own observations, supported by ecclesiastical records and evidence from the seals of medieval monarchs. The scholarly world waited in vain for the advertised *History of Gothic Architecture in England.* After Warton's death John Price possessed the manuscript written out for the press, but this has disappeared.[46] However, the work for which it was to serve as a preface still survives at Winchester: *Observations Critical and Historical, on Castles, Churches, Monasteries, and other Monuments of Antiquity in Various Parts of England.* This work, containing dated accounts of some of the buildings he visited written out fairly into notebooks, was the fruit of Warton's summer rambles.

It is useful to be reminded that *The History of English Poetry* was the brain-child of a poet, classical scholar, humorist, historian, and Gothic enthusiast. The many sides of Warton's personality evident in his correspondence all have a bearing on the complex character of the *History*: the poet retrieved striking images and beautiful phrases from the obscurest texts; the classical scholar traced the spread of Greek and Latin learning into England and noted the virtues of smooth phrasing and elegant simplicity; the humorist could enliven the dullest catalog with an ironic smile; the historian traced literary influences through an intricate narrative of progress and deterioration, occasionally stepping back to characterize a period or take stock of his project; meanwhile, the Gothic enthusiast delighted in accumulating the bric-a-brac of the past to illustrate ancient customs and manners. The *History* is the sum of all these aspects of Warton's life and personality.

The *magnum opus* had germinated in Warton's mind as early as 1754, but it was the encouragement of Richard Hurd in 1762, reinforced by brother Joseph's enthusiastic support, that was decisive.[47] Warton had already done considerable research but was unsure of how to order his material, and in the early years he toyed with a number of projects. There was no precedent for a single unfolding narrative of English literary history. After a century of ten-

tative efforts in the guise of anecdotes, catalogs, chronologies, and prefaces, it was Warton who first accepted the challenge of narrating the progress of English literature from the Norman Conquest. Before his work there prevailed even among scholars a surprising ignorance of medieval and early Tudor poetry, to an extent that is difficult for us now to appreciate. To take an example two years before the publication of Warton's first volume: William Barrett, the Bristol Antiquary, had commented to his friend Andrew Coltee Ducarel[48] that there was generally held to be no writer between Chaucer and Spenser entitled to the name of "poet." The Keeper of the Lambeth Library replied: "who knows that? who hath particularly looked into this branch of literature? The world is indeed much obliged to the learned Dr. Percy for his Reliques of Antient Poetry. But is there nothing else left amongst us of that kind? have all the old MSS on that subject in the libraries of the two universities, in the Cotton, Harleian, &c. &c. been examined? The contrary is known to be true; and, till that is done, the question must remain undecided."[49] This was the challenge that Warton took up, and he did so in a chronological, though digressive, narrative that encompassed not only poetry but also translation, prose, history, and drama. Clarissa Rinaker's bibliography of printed sources for the *History* gives a selected list of more than eight hundred titles (many of them foreign), which she admits to be about half the full figure.[50] Warton also used some seven hundred manuscripts, printing for the first time the important lyrics in British Library MS Harley 2253, many extracts from romances, the Bodleian Vernon manuscript, John Gower's *Balades,* and *The Kingis Quair* of James I of Scotland.[51] He also gave the first full discussion of the origins of the English drama, the first critical survey of the Scottish Chaucerians, Gower, John Lydgate, Thomas Hoccleve, and Stephen Hawes, as well as many selections from the minor poetry of the sixteenth century. Ducarel's letter could not have been written after 1774.

In pursuing his task Warton explored numerous libraries in colleges, museums, cathedrals, and private houses, and he was fortunate in the number of catalogs available to help him—the dedicated work of Ames, Tanner, Wanley, and others. But his greatest advantage was the proximity of the Bodleian Library, just across Broad Street from Trinity College, and he was also fortunate in having as his close friend Bodley's Librarian, John Price, who was a valuable man to know during the years when the *History* was taking shape. When the library was closed Price would admit Warton "behind the scenes,"[52] and while he was away in Winchester Price kept him in touch with the library by dispatching information by post.[53] Practical help was also forthcoming from other friends: David Garrick generously loaned two volumes of metrical romances and several old plays from his collection.[54] Less helpfully perhaps, Warton was also the recipient of a friend's theories: the well-intentioned Hans Stanley thought he had discovered a Greek source for Boccaccio's *Teseida* and bombarded him with his proofs. But Warton's early skepticism proved justified and Stanley eventually had to concede that his poem was in fact a Greek translation of the Italian.[55]

Such were in these early years the perils of literary history, when error and confusion hovered behind every confident statement, and new facts lurked somewhere to disprove any too hasty conclusion. In October 1782 Warton became a notable victim of a scholarly castigator with the publication of Joseph Ritson's *Observations on the Three First Volumes of the History of English Poetry*. Besides gleefully pointing out errors in the *History,* Ritson made a vicious personal attack on the author's character and scholarly credentials. Warton had many eloquent defenders in the magazines, but one of the most effective replies was actually by Warton himself, signed "Verax" and sent to Nichols for publication in the *Gentleman's Magazine.*[56]

Certainly Warton fell below modern standards of accuracy and his work is at times rambling, but his adversary could choose his ground and it was not difficult to spotlight specific errors among the 1,765 pages of the *History.* Like a Blakean Devourer, Ritson received the excess of Warton's prolific delights. Warton's faults, however, should be set in context by an appreciation of the conditions under which he worked. Because he had been collecting materials since the early 1750s, he often found himself relying on old memoranda in pocketbooks kept at Winchester and Trinity, where entries from Bishops' Registers jostled with pressmarks and illegible shorthand. Each published volume also brought fresh information from correspondents, some giving their names, others writing anonymously, and as the work went on Warton chose to disrupt his chronology rather than omit any significant new item. After publication of the second volume, for example, he received two anonymous letters from someone with a wide knowledge of Spanish troubadour literature,[57] and so in volume 3, during a discussion of Tudor books of rhetoric, he introduced a digressive footnote containing a long extract from one of them, "from an ingenious correspondent, who has not given me the honour of his name."[58] Another instance of a late influx of new material causing problems is John Watson Reed's transcriptions from MS Cotton Galba E ix.[59] Warton thought these too important to ignore, and therefore turned aside from the poetry of Sir Thomas More to introduce twenty-seven pages of extracts from *Ywain and Gawain* with the naive explanation that it was "to recall the reader's attention to the poetry and language of the last century."[60] In a similar way, Minot's poems were introduced rather awkwardly into both text and footnotes.[61] Unfortunately for Warton, this happened to be his helper's "first Essay in transcribing" and was not very neat or very accurate. It is no surprise, therefore, to find Ritson condemning Warton's inaccurate text of Minot. Mistakes and organizational lapses could sometimes be a result of the inchoateness of the field in which he worked, and this is something his scholarly correspondence may help us to appreciate.

In the wake of Ritson's attack the impetus behind the writing of the *History* seems to have slackened. Warton never gave up the project, but by the following year he had begun editing the "minor" poems of Milton, a work that clearly impinged on the *History*'s future territory. Through many letters of the 1780s we can see the edition grow. What was to have been a work of Taste, a justification of the early Milton against the "specious" criticisms of Johnson,[62] becomes much more. Warton the antiquarian and topographer will not rest until he has found the poet's will and traced his dwellings. The correspondence offers a fascinating picture of the scholarly network within which Warton worked: Sir John Hawkins offered him notes on music,[63] Charles Burney wrote a whole appendix on the poet's Greek verse,[64] Sir William Scott found legal documents detailing the dispute between Milton's widow and daughters over the poet's property,[65] John "Don" Bowle lent books and sent notes on *Comus,*[66] William Julius Mickle looked for papers and Josiah Dornford searched for Milton's house,[67] and both George Steevens and Joseph Warton wrote with corrections and additions later incorporated into the second edition.[68] At Warton's death this manuscript had been delivered to the printers, and he was working on a second volume to include *Paradise Regained* and *Samson Agonistes.*[69]

Another distraction from Warton's work on the *History* was his involvement in the Chatterton controversy. The recently discovered poems of the Bristol monk, Thomas Rowley, seemed at a stroke to redeem the literature of the fifteenth century. But Warton was not convinced and devoted a section of volume 2 of the *History* to exposing them as forgeries. He recognized Chatterton as a "prodigy of genius" who "would have proved the first of English poets, had he reached a maturer age,"[70] and he quoted generously from the texts in question; but his wide scholarly experience left him in no doubt that they were modern productions. The Chatterton controversy reached its climax in 1782 when Jeremiah Milles produced an edition of Rowley that supported their genuineness. Warton's weighty *Enquiry into the Authenticity of the Poems Attributed to Thomas Rowley* published in March that year (with a second edition in June) showed common sense and scholarship in a debate that was frequently short of both.[71] Along with contributions by Tyrwhitt and Malone, it was decisive in proving the Rowley poems fabrications. While Warton worked on his second edition, the effervescent George Steevens helped keep the controversy bubbling away in the newspapers and supplied his friend with the latest London gossip and morsels for his "lion."[72] Steevens's letters to Warton during 1782 catch the playful mood of the anti-Rowleians, for whom scholarship and satirical fun could be combined.

It was Warton's Shakespeare studies that had brought Steevens into correspondence with him. In November 1773 he accepted Warton's suggested emendation of *Othello*, 2.1.297 ("trash"), a widely accepted reading that is attributed in modern editions to Steevens. In fact, Warton's substantial and detailed Shakespeare notes (offering analogues, explanations, and emendations) have been overlooked since they became embedded in the "Variorum" edition.[73] Warton also influenced Shakespearean scholarship indirectly through the work of Edmond Malone, with whom he corresponded during the 1780s. Malone's 1780 *Supple-*

ment had printed Warton's extended note on Shakespeare, the D'Avenant family, and the Crown Inn,[74] and in preparing his ground-breaking 1790 edition Malone relied on Warton for regular help. Throughout the forty-nine surviving letters the assistance is almost wholly one way. Warton supplied Malone with transcripts from John Aubrey's "brief lives," which had become known to scholars thanks to one of his own footnotes,[75] and he sent the younger scholar copies of the 1596 edition of *Venus and Adonis* and Chettle's *Kind-Harts Dreame* with its apology to Shakespeare. Malone's "Historical Account of the English Stage" (whose sections on mysteries and moralities are packed with quotations from Warton's *History*) was extended by nineteen pages to accommodate material discussed with Warton during 1789.

The Warton-Malone correspondence is significant because it shows the old ways of scholarship at the service of the new. Warton's rummaging curiosity and fascination for the past encounter Malone's more analytical and objective approach. When Warton sends him a transcript of Aubrey's "life" of Ben Jonson, he is bombarded with questions: is there any other source that places Jonson's birth in Warwickshire? Can Warton add to Malone's list of Aubrey's friends? What did Wood and Aubrey quarrel about, and when? How can he find the poems of "Jonson Junior"? When were Aubrey's accounts of Shakespeare and Jonson written? Did Wood jot down any queries in the margin?[76] This is curiosity too, but the kind bred in someone who knows what he is looking for. At moments like this we glimpse the older generation of antiquarian-scholar being superseded. Building on Warton's historical approach, Malone brought something more to scholarship: an objectivity, a sense of disciplined inquiry, and a mind with a firm grasp of the problems in hand.

In this relationship we have in prosaic terms the dynamics of Warton's later poetry, where indulgence and discipline, fancy and judgment, meet. *Poems: A New Edition, with Additions* (first and second editions, 1777; third edition, 1779) marked a clear break with his work of the 1740s. The poems collected in this volume have a subtle verbal music, occasional echoes of older bardic invocation, moments of personal meditation and mood-painting, and visual images invoking nostalgia and fancy. Of the odes, the companion pieces **"The Crusade"** and **"The Grave of King Arthur"** have the incantatory fervor of the old bards; quite different are **"On the First of April"** and **"The Hamlet,"** which celebrate the English countryside in a wealth of atmospheric detail, using octosyllabic couplets to subtle effect; the stanzaic ode **"The Suicide"** has a lurid sublimity that proved popular in its time but has perhaps worn less well.

Probably the most influential poems in the collection are the sonnets, which did much to re-establish the popularity of this distinctive Renaissance form.[77] Warton uses them for meditations on a lost world of the past, a personal bereavement only his imagination can allay. Stonehenge, Wilton House, Dugdale's *Monasticon,* King Arthur's

Round Table at Winchester, and his own "native stream" of the Loddon are some of the contexts for Warton's thoughts on the mind's craving to recapture a lost delight. Sometimes in these later poems he places the pull of the past in tension with the claims of the present, in a struggle between imagination and reason or judgment. Again the key is to be found in Warton the literary historian, to whom the Elizabethan Age was the most conducive to great poetry. He speaks of it in the *History* as "that period, propitious to the operations of original and true poetry, when the coyness of fancy was not always proof against the approaches of reason, when genius was rather directed than governed by judgement."[78]

Such tensions form the subject of *Verses on Sir Joshua Reynold's Painted Window at New-College Oxford* (1782), published a few months after Reynolds had proposed his friend for membership of The Club. It is often seen as a recantation by Warton of his renegade delight in the Gothic:

> Sudden, the sombrous imagery is fled,
> Which late my visionary rapture fed:
> Thy powerful hand has broke the Gothic chain,
> And brought my bosom back to truth again.

But the victory is won by Decorum and Truth, two of the fundamental principles of Reynolds's *Discourses on Art* (1769-90), and the whole poem is really Warton's graceful compliment to his friend and patron. Reynolds jokingly remarked that he had "no great confidence in the recantation of such an old offender,"[79] and indeed when the *east* end of New College Chapel was dismantled to reveal the original Gothic stonework, one observer reported that "Poor Thomas fetched such sighs as I could not have thought he could breathe."[80]

Reynolds was certainly a good friend. His 1784 portrait of Warton still looks down on diners in the Senior Common Room at Trinity, and it was to him that Warton owed his appointment in 1785 to the Poet Laureateship, with its twice-yearly duty of composing a formal ode to be set to music for performance at court. Warton's first ode (for the King's birthday in 1785) had to be hurriedly written, leading to good-humored mockery in the volume *Probationary Odes* (1785),[81] in which the burlesque offerings of various "candidates" were placed, with little incongruity, alongside Warton's own. By all accounts, Warton enjoyed the joke. His later laureate odes, however, were effective and dignified, and in them he took the opportunity to explore both historical and descriptive subjects, including the tradition of the Laureateship itself. It was generally held that Warton, whose tenure fell between those of William Whitehead and Henry James Pye, raised the reputation of the post at a difficult moment in its history.[82]

In the 1780s Warton gathered around him a group of young poets, many of whom were former schoolboys at Winchester. The best remembered disciples are three Trinity friends and contemporaries: Henry Headley, William Benwell, and William Lisle Bowles, whose 1789 volume of sonnets had such a powerful effect on the young Coleridge.[83] Sir Herbert Croft wrote to John Nichols on 15 May 1786: "The magnetism of Tom Warton draws many a youth into rhymes and loose stockings, who had better be thinking of prose and propriety."[84] Croft's hinting at student radicalism in the Warton circle might seem surprising, given the Laureate's obvious loyalty to tradition and monarchy. But there is an ironic twist here: the Wartonian project of recovering purer voices from the past, unencumbered by the structures of contemporary society and speaking a primal language of nature and the imagination, can be shown to have set the agenda for the radical young poets of the 1790s. These poets of sensibility were viciously attacked in the *Anti-Jacobin,* for whom Sensibility herself (the "Sweet Child of sickly fancy") was a democrat goddess. Warton's rediscovery of a root system of poetic language helped supply a radical discourse for the next generation.[85]

Much of Warton's poetry is about the location and recovery of texts, of authentic voices; they are revived not as something curious and dead, but as a resource that can feed into the work of the modern poet. Likewise in his **History** he reached back into the past to explore continuities and re-establish a tradition of which he felt himself a part. Thomas Warton's achievement across so many aspects of literary studies is one that itself deserves to be recovered. The editor hopes that this edition of Warton's correspondence will make him more accessible to present-day scholars and will bring his achievement into focus. At a time when the traditional canon of eighteenth-century literature has expanded in exciting ways, Warton's is a voice that needs to be more widely heard.

Notes

1. *Boswell: The Ominous Years, 1774-1776,* ed. Charles Ryskamp and Frederick A. Pottle (London, 1963), p. 281.

2. See letters 64 and 353 [in the present volume]. Gibbon's copy of the *Life of Bathurst* is in Trinity College Library. For his praise of Warton's *History,* see *Decline and Fall of the Roman Empire,* ed. J. B. Bury, 7 vols. (1909-14), 4:163 (chap. 38, note 148).

3. René Wellek, *The Rise of English Literary History* (Chapel Hill, 1941), p. 199.

4. Edward Phillips's *Theatrum Poetarum Anglicanorum,* ed. Sir Samuel Egerton Brydges (1800), p. lxi.

5. Review of Hayley's *Memoirs,* in *Quarterly Review* 31 (1824-25): 289.

6. Horace Walpole to William Mason, 18 April 1778. *The Yale Edition of Horace Walpole's Correspondence,* ed. W. S. Lewis, 28:385.

7. Review of George Ellis's *Specimens of the Early English Poets,* in *Edinburgh Review* 7 (April 1804): 151-63, p. 153.

8. See letters 133, 251, and 253.

9. "Life of Pope," in *Lives of the English Poets,* ed. George Birkbeck Hill (Oxford, 1905), 3:251.

10. See letter 54, note 3.

11. *Thraliana. The Diary of Mrs. Hester Lynch Thrale,* ed. Katharine C. Balderston, 2d ed. (Oxford, 1951), 1:209. Southey's volume (with Robert Lovell) was *Poems: containing the Retrospect, Odes, Elegies, Sonnets &c.* (Bath, 1795).

12. Letter 14.

13. See, for example, Edmund Gosse, "Two Pioneers of Romanticism: Joseph and Thomas Warton," *Proceedings of the British Academy* 7 (1915-16): 145-63.

14. See Fairer 1975, pp. 401-2.

15. See Fairer 1975, also Christina le Prevost, "More Unacknowledged Verse by Joseph Warton," *RES* 37 (1986): 317-47, and Arthur H. Scouten, "The Warton Forgeries and the Concept of Preromanticism in English Literature," *Études Anglaises* 40 (1987): 434-47.

16. Letter 13.

17. Letters 16, 43, and 10.

18. Letters 13, 21, and 54.

19. Letters 523 and 525.

20. In letter 220, after apologizing to Garrick for not attending the Stratford Jubilee, Warton confesses to having slipped off to Spithead to see the Russian sailors. At the close of their 1776 visit, Johnson remarked to Boswell about Warton's shyness: "all men who have that love of low company are also timid" (*The Ominous Years,* p. 281).

21. See Douglas Lane Patey, "'Aesthetics' and the Rise of Lyric in the Eighteenth Century," *SEL,* 33 (1993): 587-608.

22. Now BL C.28m.7.

23. See Fairer 1981, p. 41.

24. Letter 59.

25. The writer of an article in the *London Magazine* for 1821 considered that some of Warton's odes "might more properly be termed idylliums" (p. 126), and Coleridge noted: "The greater part of Warton's Sonnets are severe and masterly likenesses of the Greek ἐπιγράμματα" (*Complete Poetical Works,* ed. E. H. Coleridge [Oxford, 1912], 2:1139).

26. Letter 65.

27. See letter 143.

28. See David Fairer, "Oxford and the Literary World," in *The History of the University of Oxford,* vol. 5, ed. L. S. Sutherland and L. G. Mitchell (Oxford, 1986), pp. 779-805, pp. 793-96.

29. Letters 556 and 529.

30. See Francis Newbery's anecdote in Charles Welsh, *A Bookseller of the Last Century* (London, 1885), pp. 67-68.

31. Byron to Hodgson, 29 June 1811, *Byron's Letters and Journals,* ed. Leslie A. Marchand, 2:54.

32. Section 43 of the *History* ("General view and character of the poetry of queen Elisabeth's age") is close at times to the Warton of the humorous poems.

33. *Companion to the Guide,* pp. 31-32.

34. See letter 290, note 1.

35. Letter 367.

36. Letter 136. Both figures were the subject of Warton poems: "Sacellum Coll. SS. Trin. Oxon. Instauratum" (Mant, 2:230-44), and the unpublished "Ode. On the Monument of Sir Thomas Pope," Bodleian MS Dep. c. 638, ff. 51 and 118.

37. See Appendix C.

38. Letters 194 and 198.

39. Letters 459 and 527.

40. Letters 351, 490, 521, 532.

41. Letters 292, 302, 549, 531, 533, 535.

42. *Cornhill Magazine* 11 (January-June 1865): 734-35.

43. 1762 *Observations,* 2:184-98.

44. Letter 99.

45. It was reprinted in *Essays on Gothic Architecture, by the Rev. T. Warton, Rev. J. Bentham, Captain Grose, and the Rev. J. Milner* (London, 1800; 2d ed., 1802).

46. Mant, 1:xxxii. Warton refers to it in the third volume (1781) of the *History*: "But, with the careless haste of a lover, I am anticipating what I have to say of it in my HISTORY OF GOTHIC ARCHITECTURE IN ENGLAND" (3:xxii).

47. Letters 103, 105, 106, and 109. See Fairer 1981, pp. 38-41.

48. Warton corresponded with Barrett in 1774 about the Rowley poems (see Appendix B). For Warton's correspondence with Ducarel, see Calendar.

49. Ducarel to Barrett, 18 March 1772, printed in *GM* 56 (1786): 461.

50. Rinaker, pp. 177-232.

51. Discovered thanks to Percy's inquiries. See letter 107, note 2.

52. Letter 312.

53. Letter 388.

54. Letters 212 and 213.

55. Letter 364.

56. Letters 420 and 421.

57. Letters 368 and 370.

58. *History,* 3:349.

59. Letters 372 and 374.

60. *History,* 3:107-8.

61. *History,* 3:103-4, 107, 146-51.

62. Letter 476.

63. Letters 456 and 457.

64. Letter 565.

65. Letter 572.

66. Letters 441, 444, 447, and 450.

67. Letters 451 and 580.

68. Letters 467 and 477.

69. See letter 476, note 1.

70. *History,* 2:157.

71. Though Warton upset the Rowleian George Catcott. See letter 412.

72. Letter 406.

73. Nineteen first appeared in Johnson's 1765 appendix, and forty-nine were printed in the Oxford edition of 1770-71. These were included by Steevens in his 1773 edition. See letter 303, note 5, and letter 209, note 3.

74. Letter 369.

75. In a digressive footnote in his *Life of Bathurst* (pp. 153-55) Warton had quoted extracts from Aubrey's jottings on Spenser and Shakespeare "as a specimen" of a manuscript "very little known, but valuable." This caused Richard Farmer to make use of Aubrey in his *Essay on the Learning of Shakespeare* (1767).

76. Letter 592.

77. William Hazlitt often praised Warton's sonnets: "Thomas Warton was a man of taste and genius. His SONNETS I cannot help preferring to any in the language" (*Select British Poets,* 1824. *Complete Works,* ed. P. P. Howe, 9:242). He quoted three of them in full in his sixth lecture, *On the English Poets,* 1818 (Howe, 5:120-22).

78. *History,* 3:501.

79. Letter 409.

80. Nichols, *Anecdotes,* 3:699.

81. Letter 495.

82. Robert Southey, having been commissioned to write a birthday ode for the King, wrote: "as for making anything good of a birthday ode, I might as well at-

tempt to manufacture silk purses from sows' ears. Like Warton, I shall give the poem an historical character; but I shall not do this as well as Warton, who has done it very well" (Southey to May, 4 March 1821, *Life and Correspondence,* ed. C. C. Southey [London, 1850] 5:63).

83. *Biographia Literaria,* chapter 1.

84. Nichols, *Illustrations,* 5:210. Two other significant disciples were the Wykehamists Thomas Russell (1762-88) and John Bampfylde (1754-97). For a discussion of the Warton School of poets, see J. B. Bamborough, "William Lisle Bowles and the Riparian Muse," in *Essays and Poems Presented to Lord David Cecil,* ed. W. W. Robson (London, 1970), pp. 93-108.

85. See David Fairer, "Baby Language and Revolution: The Early Poetry of Charles Lloyd and Charles Lamb," *Charles Lamb Bulletin,* no. 74 (April 1991): 33-52.

FURTHER READING

Bibliography

Vance, John A. *Joseph and Thomas Warton: An Annotated Bibliography.* New York: Garland Publishing, 1983, 190 p.
> Primary and secondary bibliography devoted to Warton's writings as well as those of his brother, Joseph.

Biography

Gilfillan, George. "The Life of Thomas Warton." In *The Poetical Works of Goldsmith, Collins, and T. Warton* pp. 145-54. Edinburgh: James Nichol, 1854.
> Overview of Warton's life and works.

Vance, John. "Samuel Johnson and Thomas Warton." *Biography* 9, no. 2 (spring 1986): 95-111.
> Analyzes the complex professional and personal relationship between Johnson and Warton.

Criticism

Fairer, David. "Historical Criticism and the English Canon: A Spenserian Dispute in the 1750s." *Eighteenth-Century Life* 24 (spring 2000): 43-64.
> Uses Warton's *Observations on the Faerie Queene of Spenser* as part of a larger argument about the formation of the English literary canon.

Teich, Nathaniel. "A Comparative Approach to Periodization: Forms of Self-Consciousness in Warton's 'The Pleasures of Melancholy' and Keat's 'Ode on Melancholy.'" In *Proceedings of the Xth Congress of the International Comparative Literature Association/Actes Du Xe Congres de l'Assocation Internationale de Literature Comparee New York 1982,* edited by Anna Balakian and James J. Wilhelm, pp. 158-63. New York: Garland Publishing, 1985.
> Compares poems by Warton and John Keats on similar themes.

Vance, John A. *Joseph and Thomas Warton.* Boston: Twayne Publishers, 1983, 152 p.
> Provides a biographical and critical study of the Wartons.

How to Use This Index

The main references

Calvino, Italo
    1923-1985 .... CLC **5, 8, 11, 22, 33, 39,
                                73; SSC 3**

---

list all author entries in the following Gale Literary Criticism series:

BLC = *Black Literature Criticism*
CLC = *Contemporary Literary Criticism*
CLR = *Children's Literature Review*
CMLC = *Classical and Medieval Literature Criticism*
DA = *DISCovering Authors*
DAB = *DISCovering Authors: British*
DAC = *DISCovering Authors: Canadian*
DAM = *DISCovering Authors: Modules*
    DRAM: *Dramatists Module;* *MST:* *Most-Studied Authors Module;*
    MULT: *Multicultural Authors Module;* *NOV:* *Novelists Module;*
    POET: *Poets Module;* *POP:* *Popular Fiction and Genre Authors Module*
DC = *Drama Criticism*
HLC = *Hispanic Literature Criticism*
LC = *Literature Criticism from 1400 to 1800*
NCLC = *Nineteenth-Century Literature Criticism*
NNAL = *Native North American Literature*
PC = *Poetry Criticism*
SSC = *Short Story Criticism*
TCLC = *Twentieth-Century Literary Criticism*
WLC = *World Literature Criticism, 1500 to the Present*

The cross-references

See also CANR 23; CA 85-88;
obituary CA116

---

list all author entries in the following Gale biographical and literary sources:

AAYA = *Authors & Artists for Young Adults*
AITN = *Authors in the News*
BEST = *Bestsellers*
BW = *Black Writers*
CA = *Contemporary Authors*
CAAS = *Contemporary Authors Autobiography Series*
CABS = *Contemporary Authors Bibliographical Series*
CANR = *Contemporary Authors New Revision Series*
CAP = *Contemporary Authors Permanent Series*
CDALB = *Concise Dictionary of American Literary Biography*
CDBLB = *Concise Dictionary of British Literary Biography*
DLB = *Dictionary of Literary Biography*
DLBD = *Dictionary of Literary Biography Documentary Series*
DLBY = *Dictionary of Literary Biography Yearbook*
HW = *Hispanic Writers*
JRDA = *Junior DISCovering Authors*
MAICYA = *Major Authors and Illustrators for Children and Young Adults*
MTCW = *Major 20th-Century Writers*
SAAS = *Something about the Author Autobiography Series*
SATA = *Something about the Author*
YABC = *Yesterday's Authors of Books for Children*

Literary Criticism Series
Cumulative Author Index

Aherne, Owen
See Cassill, R(onald) V(erlin)

Ai 1947- .... CLC **4, 14, 69**
See also CA 85-88; CAAS 13; CANR 70; DLB 120

Aickman, Robert (Fordyce)
1914-1981 .... CLC **57**
See also CA 5-8R; CANR 3, 72, 100; DLB 261; HGG; SUFW

Aiken, Conrad (Potter) 1889-1973 .... CLC **1, 3, 5, 10, 52; PC 26; SSC 9**
See also AMW; CA 5-8R; 45-48; CANR 4, 60; CDALB 1929-1941; DAM NOV, POET; DLB 9, 45, 102; EXPS; HGG; MTCW 1, 2; RGAL 4; RGSF 2; SATA 3, 30; SSFS 8; TUS

Aiken, Joan (Delano) 1924- .... CLC **35**
See also AAYA 1, 25; CA 9-12R; 182; CAAE 182; CANR 4, 23, 34, 64; CLR 1, 19; DLB 161; FANT; HGG; JRDA; MAICYA 1, 2; MTCW 1; RHW; SAAS 1; SATA 2, 30, 73; SATA-Essay 109; WYA; YAW

Ainsworth, William Harrison
1805-1882 .... NCLC **13**
See also DLB 21; HGG; RGEL 2; SATA 24; SUFW

Aitmatov, Chingiz (Torekulovich)
1928- .... CLC **71**
See also CA 103; CANR 38; MTCW 1; RGSF 2; SATA 56

Akers, Floyd
See Baum, L(yman) Frank

Akhmadulina, Bella Akhatovna
1937- .... CLC **53; PC 43**
See also CA 65-68; CWP; CWW 2; DAM POET

Akhmatova, Anna 1888-1966 ..... CLC **11, 25, 64, 126; PC 2**
See also CA 19-20; 25-28R; CANR 35; CAP 1; DA3; DAM POET; EW 10; MTCW 1, 2; RGWL 2

Aksakov, Sergei Timofeyvich
1791-1859 .... NCLC **2**
See also DLB 198

Aksenov, Vassily
See Aksyonov, Vassily (Pavlovich)

Akst, Daniel 1956- .... CLC **109**
See also CA 161; CANR 110

Aksyonov, Vassily (Pavlovich)
1932- .... CLC **22, 37, 101**
See also CA 53-56; CANR 12, 48, 77; CWW 2

Akutagawa Ryunosuke
1892-1927 .... TCLC **16; SSC 44**
See also CA 117; 154; DLB 180; MJW; RGSF 2; RGWL 2

Alain 1868-1951 .... TCLC **41**
See also CA 163; GFL 1789 to the Present

Alain de Lille c. 1116-c. 1203 .... CMLC **53**
See also DLB 208

Alain-Fournier .... TCLC **6**
See also Fournier, Henri Alban
See also DLB 65; GFL 1789 to the Present; RGWL 2

Alanus de Insluis
See Alain de Lille

Alarcon, Pedro Antonio de
1833-1891 .... NCLC **1**

Alas (y Urena), Leopoldo (Enrique Garcia)
1852-1901 .... TCLC **29**
See also CA 113; 131; HW 1; RGSF 2

Albee, Edward (Franklin III) 1928- . CLC **1, 2, 3, 5, 9, 11, 13, 25, 53, 86, 113; DC 11; WLC**
See also AITN 1; AMW; CA 5-8R; CABS 3; CAD; CANR 8, 54, 74; CD 5; CDALB 1941-1968; DA; DA3; DAB; DAC; DAM DRAM, MST; DFS 2, 3, 8, 10, 13, 14; DLB 7, 266; INT CANR-8; LAIT 4; MTCW 1, 2; RGAL 4; TUS

Alberti, Rafael 1902-1999 .... CLC **7**
See also CA 85-88; 185; CANR 81; DLB 108; HW 2; RGWL 2

Albert the Great 1193(?)-1280 ...... CMLC **16**
See also DLB 115

Alcala-Galiano, Juan Valera y
See Valera y Alcala-Galiano, Juan

Alcayaga, Lucila Godoy
See Godoy Alcayaga, Lucila

Alcott, Amos Bronson 1799-1888 .... NCLC **1**
See also DLB 1, 223

Alcott, Louisa May 1832-1888 . NCLC **6, 58, 83; SSC 27; WLC**
See also AAYA 20; AMWS 1; BPFB 1; BYA 2; CDALB 1865-1917; CLR 1, 38; DA; DA3; DAB; DAM MST, NOV; DLB 1, 42, 79, 223, 239, 242; DLBD 14; FW; JRDA; LAIT 2; MAICYA 1, 2; NFS 12; RGAL 4; SATA 100; TUS; WCH; WYA; YABC 1; YAW

Aldanov, M. A.
See Aldanov, Mark (Alexandrovich)

Aldanov, Mark (Alexandrovich)
1886(?)-1957 .... TCLC **23**
See also CA 118; 181

Aldington, Richard 1892-1962 .... CLC **49**
See also CA 85-88; CANR 45; DLB 20, 36, 100, 149; RGEL 2

Aldiss, Brian W(ilson) 1925- . CLC **5, 14, 40; SSC 36**
See also AAYA 42; CA 5-8R; CAAE 190; CAAS 2; CANR 5, 28, 64; CN 7; DAM NOV; DLB 14, 261; MTCW 1, 2; SATA 34; SFW 4

Aldrich, Bess Streeter
1881-1954 .... TCLC **125**
See also CLR 70

Alegria, Claribel 1924- .... CLC **75; HLCS 1; PC 26**
See also CA 131; CAAS 15; CANR 66, 94; CWW 2; DAM MULT; DLB 145; HW 1; MTCW 1

Alegria, Fernando 1918- .... CLC **57**
See also CA 9-12R; CANR 5, 32, 72; HW 1, 2

Aleichem, Sholom .... TCLC **1, 35; SSC 33**
See also Rabinovitch, Sholem
See also TWA

Aleixandre, Vicente 1898-1984 ... TCLC **113; HLCS 1**
See also CANR 81; DLB 108; HW 2; RGWL 2

Aleman, Mateo 1547-1615(?) .... LC **81**

Alencon, Marguerite d'
See de Navarre, Marguerite

Alepoudelis, Odysseus
See Elytis, Odysseus
See also CWW 2

Aleshkovsky, Joseph 1929-
See Aleshkovsky, Yuz
See also CA 121; 128

Aleshkovsky, Yuz .... CLC **44**
See also Aleshkovsky, Joseph

Alexander, Lloyd (Chudley) 1924- ... CLC **35**
See also AAYA 1, 27; BPFB 1; BYA 5, 6, 7, 9, 10, 11; CA 1-4R; CANR 1, 24, 38, 55; CLR 1, 5, 48; CWRI 5; DLB 52; FANT; JRDA; MAICYA 1, 2; MAICYAS 1; MTCW 1; SAAS 19; SATA 3, 49, 81, 129, 135; SUFW; TUS; WYA; YAW

Alexander, Meena 1951- .... CLC **121**
See also CA 115; CANR 38, 70; CP 7; CWP; FW

Alexander, Samuel 1859-1938 .... TCLC **77**

Alexie, Sherman (Joseph, Jr.)
1966- .... CLC **96, 154**
See also AAYA 28; CA 138; CANR 95; DA3; DAM MULT; DLB 175, 206; MTCW 1; NNAL

Alfau, Felipe 1902-1999 .... CLC **66**
See also CA 137

Alfieri, Vittorio 1749-1803 .... NCLC **101**
See also EW 4; RGWL 2

Alfred, Jean Gaston
See Ponge, Francis

Alger, Horatio, Jr. 1832-1899 .... NCLC **8, 83**
See also DLB 42; LAIT 2; RGAL 4; SATA 16; TUS

Al-Ghazali, Muhammad ibn Muhammad
1058-1111 .... CMLC **50**
See also DLB 115

Algren, Nelson 1909-1981 ..... CLC **4, 10, 33; SSC 33**
See also AMWS 9; BPFB 1; CA 13-16R; 103; CANR 20, 61; CDALB 1941-1968; DLB 9; DLBY 1981, 1982, 2000; MTCW 1, 2; RGAL 4; RGSF 2

Ali, Ahmed 1908-1998 .... CLC **69**
See also CA 25-28R; CANR 15, 34

Alighieri, Dante
See Dante

Allan, John B.
See Westlake, Donald E(dwin)

Allan, Sidney
See Hartmann, Sadakichi

Allan, Sydney
See Hartmann, Sadakichi

Allard, Janet .... CLC **59**

Allen, Edward 1948- .... CLC **59**

Allen, Fred 1894-1956 .... TCLC **87**

Allen, Paula Gunn 1939- .... CLC **84**
See also AMWS 4; CA 112; 143; CANR 63; CWP; DA3; DAM MULT; DLB 175; FW; MTCW 1; NNAL; RGAL 4

Allen, Roland
See Ayckbourn, Alan

Allen, Sarah A.
See Hopkins, Pauline Elizabeth

Allen, Sidney H.
See Hartmann, Sadakichi

Allen, Woody 1935- .... CLC **16, 52**
See also AAYA 10; CA 33-36R; CANR 27, 38, 63; DAM POP; DLB 44; MTCW 1

Allende, Isabel 1942- . CLC **39, 57, 97; HLC 1; WLCS**
See also AAYA 18; CA 125; 130; CANR 51, 74; CDWLB 3; CWW 2; DA3; DAM MULT, NOV; DLB 145; DNFS 1; FW; HW 1, 2; INT CA-130; LAIT 5; LAWS 1; MTCW 1, 2; NCFS 1; NFS 6; RGSF 2; SSFS 11; WLIT 1

Alleyn, Ellen
See Rossetti, Christina (Georgina)

Alleyne, Carla D. .... CLC **65**

Allingham, Margery (Louise)
1904-1966 .... CLC **19**
See also CA 5-8R; 25-28R; CANR 4, 58; CMW 4; DLB 77; MSW; MTCW 1, 2

Allingham, William 1824-1889 ...... NCLC **25**
See also DLB 35; RGEL 2

Allison, Dorothy E. 1949- .... CLC **78, 153**
See also CA 140; CANR 66, 107; CSW; DA3; FW; MTCW 1; NFS 11; RGAL 4

Alloula, Malek .... CLC **65**

Allston, Washington 1779-1843 .... NCLC **2**
See also DLB 1, 235

Almedingen, E. M. .... CLC **12**
See also Almedingen, Martha Edith von
See also SATA 3

Astley, William 1855-1911
See Warung, Price

Aston, James
See White, T(erence) H(anbury)

Asturias, Miguel Angel 1899-1974 .... **CLC 3, 8, 13; HLC 1**
See also CA 25-28; 49-52; CANR 32; CAP 2; CDWLB 3; DA3; DAM MULT, NOV; DLB 113; HW 1; LAW; MTCW 1, 2; RGWL 2; WLIT 1

Atares, Carlos Saura
See Saura (Atares), Carlos

Athanasius c. 295-c. 373 .... **CMLC 48**

Atheling, William
See Pound, Ezra (Weston Loomis)

Atheling, William, Jr.
See Blish, James (Benjamin)

Atherton, Gertrude (Franklin Horn)
1857-1948 .... **TCLC 2**
See also CA 104; 155; DLB 9, 78, 186; HGG; RGAL 4; SUFW; TCWW 2

Atherton, Lucius
See Masters, Edgar Lee

Atkins, Jack
See Harris, Mark

Atkinson, Kate 1951- .... **CLC 99**
See also CA 166; CANR 101; DLB 267

Attaway, William (Alexander)
1911-1986 .... **CLC 92; BLC 1**
See also BW 2, 3; CA 143; CANR 82; DAM MULT; DLB 76

Atticus
See Fleming, Ian (Lancaster); Wilson, (Thomas) Woodrow

Atwood, Margaret (Eleanor) 1939- ... **CLC 2, 3, 4, 8, 13, 15, 25, 44, 84, 135; PC 8; SSC 2, 46; WLC**
See also AAYA 12; BEST 89:2; BPFB 1; CA 49-52; CANR 3, 24, 33, 59, 95; CN 7; CP 7; CWP; DA; DA3; DAB; DAC; DAM MST, NOV, POET; DLB 53, 251; EXPN; FW; INT CANR-24; LAIT 5; MTCW 1, 2; NFS 4, 12, 13, 14; PFS 7; RGSF 2; SATA 50; SSFS 3, 13; TWA; YAW

Aubigny, Pierre d'
See Mencken, H(enry) L(ouis)

Aubin, Penelope 1685-1731(?) .... **LC 9**
See also DLB 39

Auchincloss, Louis (Stanton) 1917- .. **CLC 4, 6, 9, 18, 45; SSC 22**
See also AMWS 4; CA 1-4R; CANR 6, 29, 55, 87; CN 7; DAM NOV; DLB 2, 244; DLBY 1980; INT CANR-29; MTCW 1; RGAL 4

Auden, W(ystan) H(ugh) 1907-1973 . **CLC 1, 2, 3, 4, 6, 9, 11, 14, 43, 123; PC 1; WLC**
See also AAYA 18; AMWS 2; BRW 7; BRWR 1; CA 9-12R; 45-48; CANR 5, 61, 105; CDBLB 1914-1945; DA; DA3; DAB; DAC; DAM DRAM, MST, POET; DLB 10, 20; EXPP; MTCW 1, 2; PAB; PFS 1, 3, 4, 10; TUS; WP

Audiberti, Jacques 1900-1965 .... **CLC 38**
See also CA 25-28R; DAM DRAM

Audubon, John James 1785-1851 . **NCLC 47**
See also ANW; DLB 248

Auel, Jean M(arie) 1936- .... **CLC 31, 107**
See also AAYA 7; BEST 90:4; BPFB 1; CA 103; CANR 21, 64; CPW; DA3; DAM POP; INT CANR-21; NFS 11; RHW; SATA 91

Auerbach, Erich 1892-1957 .... **TCLC 43**
See also CA 118; 155

Augier, Emile 1820-1889 .... **NCLC 31**
See also DLB 192; GFL 1789 to the Present

August, John
See De Voto, Bernard (Augustine)

Augustine, St. 354-430 .... **CMLC 6; WLCS**
See also DA; DA3; DAB; DAC; DAM MST; DLB 115; EW 1; RGWL 2

Aunt Belinda
See Braddon, Mary Elizabeth

Aunt Weedy
See Alcott, Louisa May

Aurelius
See Bourne, Randolph S(illiman)

Aurelius, Marcus 121-180 .... **CMLC 45**
See also Marcus Aurelius
See also RGWL 2

Aurobindo, Sri
See Ghose, Aurabinda

Austen, Jane 1775-1817 ...... **NCLC 1, 13, 19, 33, 51, 81, 95; WLC**
See also AAYA 19; BRW 4; BRWR 2; BYA 3; CDBLB 1789-1832; DA; DA3; DAB; DAC; DAM MST, NOV; DLB 116; EXPN; LAIT 2; NFS 1, 14; TEA; WLIT 3; WYAS 1

Auster, Paul 1947- .... **CLC 47, 131**
See also CA 69-72; CANR 23, 52, 75; CMW 4; CN 7; DA3; DLB 227; MTCW 1

Austin, Frank
See Faust, Frederick (Schiller)
See also TCWW 2

Austin, Mary (Hunter) 1868-1934 . **TCLC 25**
See also Stairs, Gordon
See also ANW; CA 109; 178; DLB 9, 78, 206, 221; FW; TCWW 2

Averroes 1126-1198 .... **CMLC 7**
See also DLB 115

Avicenna 980-1037 .... **CMLC 16**
See also DLB 115

Avison, Margaret 1918- .... **CLC 2, 4, 97**
See also CA 17-20R; CP 7; DAC; DAM POET; DLB 53; MTCW 1

Axton, David
See Koontz, Dean R(ay)

Ayckbourn, Alan 1939- ...... **CLC 5, 8, 18, 33, 74; DC 13**
See also BRWS 5; CA 21-24R; CANR 31, 59; CBD; CD 5; DAB; DAM DRAM; DFS 7; DLB 13, 245; MTCW 1, 2

Aydy, Catherine
See Tennant, Emma (Christina)

Ayme, Marcel (Andre) 1902-1967 ... **CLC 11; SSC 41**
See also CA 89-92; CANR 67; CLR 25; DLB 72; EW 12; GFL 1789 to the Present; RGSF 2; RGWL 2; SATA 91

Ayrton, Michael 1921-1975 .... **CLC 7**
See also CA 5-8R; 61-64; CANR 9, 21

Azorin .... **CLC 11**
See also Martinez Ruiz, Jose
See also EW 9

Azuela, Mariano 1873-1952 .. **TCLC 3; HLC 1**
See also CA 104; 131; CANR 81; DAM MULT; HW 1, 2; LAW; MTCW 1, 2

Baastad, Babbis Friis
See Friis-Baastad, Babbis Ellinor

Bab
See Gilbert, W(illiam) S(chwenck)

Babbis, Eleanor
See Friis-Baastad, Babbis Ellinor

Babel, Isaac
See Babel, Isaak (Emmanuilovich)
See also EW 11; SSFS 10

Babel, Isaak (Emmanuilovich)
1894-1941(?) .... **TCLC 2, 13; SSC 16**
See also Babel, Isaac
See also CA 104; 155; MTCW 1; RGSF 2; RGWL 2; TWA

Babits, Mihaly 1883-1941 .... **TCLC 14**
See also CA 114; CDWLB 4; DLB 215

Babur 1483-1530 .... **LC 18**

Babylas 1898-1962
See Ghelderode, Michel de

Baca, Jimmy Santiago 1952- .... **PC 41**
See also CA 131; CANR 81, 90; CP 7; DAM MULT; DLB 122; HLC 1; HW 1, 2

Baca, Jose Santiago
See Baca, Jimmy Santiago

Bacchelli, Riccardo 1891-1985 .... **CLC 19**
See also CA 29-32R; 117; DLB 264

Bach, Richard (David) 1936- .... **CLC 14**
See also AITN 1; BEST 89:2; BPFB 1; BYA 5; CA 9-12R; CANR 18, 93; CPW; DAM NOV, POP; FANT; MTCW 1; SATA 13

Bache, Benjamin Franklin
1769-1798 .... **LC 74**
See also DLB 43

Bachman, Richard
See King, Stephen (Edwin)

Bachmann, Ingeborg 1926-1973 .... **CLC 69**
See also CA 93-96; 45-48; CANR 69; DLB 85; RGWL 2

Bacon, Francis 1561-1626 .... **LC 18, 32**
See also BRW 1; CDBLB Before 1660; DLB 151, 236, 252; RGEL 2; TEA

Bacon, Roger 1214(?)-1294 .... **CMLC 14**
See also DLB 115

Bacovia, George 1881-1957 .... **TCLC 24**
See also Vasiliu, Gheorghe
See also CDWLB 4; DLB 220

Badanes, Jerome 1937- .... **CLC 59**

Bagehot, Walter 1826-1877 .... **NCLC 10**
See also DLB 55

Bagnold, Enid 1889-1981 .... **CLC 25**
See also BYA 2; CA 5-8R; 103; CANR 5, 40; CBD; CWD; CWRI 5; DAM DRAM; DLB 13, 160, 191, 245; FW; MAICYA 1, 2; RGEL 2; SATA 1, 25

Bagritsky, Eduard 1895-1934 .... **TCLC 60**

Bagrjana, Elisaveta
See Belcheva, Elisaveta Lyubomirova

Bagryana, Elisaveta -1991 .... **CLC 10**
See also Belcheva, Elisaveta Lyubomirova
See also CA 178; CDWLB 4; DLB 147

Bailey, Paul 1937- .... **CLC 45**
See also CA 21-24R; CANR 16, 62; CN 7; DLB 14; GLL 2

Baillie, Joanna 1762-1851 .... **NCLC 71**
See also DLB 93; RGEL 2

Bainbridge, Beryl (Margaret) 1934- . **CLC 4, 5, 8, 10, 14, 18, 22, 62, 130**
See also BRWS 6; CA 21-24R; CANR 24, 55, 75, 88; CN 7; DAM NOV; DLB 14, 231; MTCW 1, 2

Baker, Carlos (Heard)
1909-1987 .... **TCLC 119**
See also CA 5-8R; 122; CANR 3, 63; DLB 103

Baker, Elliott 1922- .... **CLC 8**
See also CA 45-48; CANR 2, 63; CN 7

Baker, Jean H. .... **TCLC 3, 10**
See also Russell, George William

Baker, Nicholson 1957- .... **CLC 61**
See also CA 135; CANR 63; CN 7; CPW; DA3; DAM POP; DLB 227

Baker, Ray Stannard 1870-1946 .... **TCLC 47**
See also CA 118

Baker, Russell (Wayne) 1925- .... **CLC 31**
See also BEST 89:4; CA 57-60; CANR 11, 41, 59; MTCW 1, 2

Bakhtin, M.
See Bakhtin, Mikhail Mikhailovich

Bakhtin, M. M.
See Bakhtin, Mikhail Mikhailovich

Bakhtin, Mikhail
See Bakhtin, Mikhail Mikhailovich

Barthes, Roland (Gerard)
1915-1980 .... **CLC 24, 83**
See also CA 130; 97-100; CANR 66; EW 13; GFL 1789 to the Present; MTCW 1, 2; TWA

Barzun, Jacques (Martin) 1907- ..... **CLC 51, 145**
See also CA 61-64; CANR 22, 95

Bashevis, Isaac
See Singer, Isaac Bashevis

Bashkirtseff, Marie 1859-1884 .... **NCLC 27**

Basho, Matsuo
See Matsuo Basho
See also RGWL 2; WP

Basil of Caesaria c. 330-379 .... **CMLC 35**

Bass, Kingsley B., Jr.
See Bullins, Ed

Bass, Rick 1958- .... **CLC 79, 143**
See also ANW; CA 126; CANR 53, 93; CSW; DLB 212

Bassani, Giorgio 1916-2000 .... **CLC 9**
See also CA 65-68; 190; CANR 33; CWW 2; DLB 128, 177; MTCW 1; RGWL 2

Bastian, Ann .... **CLC 70**

Bastos, Augusto (Antonio) Roa
See Roa Bastos, Augusto (Antonio)

Bataille, Georges 1897-1962 .... **CLC 29**
See also CA 101; 89-92

Bates, H(erbert) E(rnest)
1905-1974 .... **CLC 46; SSC 10**
See also CA 93-96; 45-48; CANR 34; DA3; DAB; DAM POP; DLB 162, 191; EXPS; MTCW 1, 2; RGSF 2; SSFS 7

Bauchart
See Camus, Albert

Baudelaire, Charles 1821-1867 . **NCLC 6, 29, 55; PC 1; SSC 18; WLC**
See also DA; DA3; DAB; DAC; DAM MST, POET; DLB 217; EW 7; GFL 1789 to the Present; RGWL 2; TWA

Baudouin, Marcel
See Peguy, Charles (Pierre)

Baudouin, Pierre
See Peguy, Charles (Pierre)

Baudrillard, Jean 1929- .... **CLC 60**

Baum, L(yman) Frank 1856-1919 ... **TCLC 7**
See also CA 108; 133; CLR 15; CWRI 5; DLB 22; FANT; JRDA; MAICYA 1, 2; MTCW 1, 2; NFS 13; RGAL 4; SATA 18, 100; WCH

Baum, Louis F.
See Baum, L(yman) Frank

Baumbach, Jonathan 1933- .... **CLC 6, 23**
See also CA 13-16R; CAAS 5; CANR 12, 66; CN 7; DLBY 1980; INT CANR-12; MTCW 1

Bausch, Richard (Carl) 1945- .... **CLC 51**
See also AMWS 7; CA 101; CAAS 14; CANR 43, 61, 87; CSW; DLB 130

Baxter, Charles (Morley) 1947- . **CLC 45, 78**
See also CA 57-60; CANR 40, 64, 104; CPW; DAM POP; DLB 130; MTCW 2

Baxter, George Owen
See Faust, Frederick (Schiller)

Baxter, James K(eir) 1926-1972 .... **CLC 14**
See also CA 77-80

Baxter, John
See Hunt, E(verette) Howard, (Jr.)

Bayer, Sylvia
See Glassco, John

Baynton, Barbara 1857-1929 .... **TCLC 57**
See also DLB 230; RGSF 2

Beagle, Peter S(oyer) 1939- .... **CLC 7, 104**
See also BPFB 1; BYA 9, 10; CA 9-12R; CANR 4, 51, 73, 110; DA3; DLBY 1980; FANT; INT CANR-4; MTCW 1; SATA 60, 130; SUFW; YAW

Bean, Normal
See Burroughs, Edgar Rice

Beard, Charles A(ustin)
1874-1948 .... **TCLC 15**
See also CA 115; 189; DLB 17; SATA 18

Beardsley, Aubrey 1872-1898 .... **NCLC 6**

Beattie, Ann 1947- ..... **CLC 8, 13, 18, 40, 63, 146; SSC 11**
See also AMWS 5; BEST 90:2; BPFB 1; CA 81-84; CANR 53, 73; CN 7; CPW; DA3; DAM NOV, POP; DLB 218; DLBY 1982; MTCW 1, 2; RGAL 4; RGSF 2; SSFS 9; TUS

Beattie, James 1735-1803 .... **NCLC 25**
See also DLB 109

Beauchamp, Kathleen Mansfield 1888-1923
See Mansfield, Katherine
See also CA 104; 134; DA; DA3; DAC; DAM MST; MTCW 2; TEA

Beaumarchais, Pierre-Augustin Caron de
1732-1799 .... **LC 61; DC 4**
See also DAM DRAM; DFS 14; EW 4; GFL Beginnings to 1789; RGWL 2

Beaumont, Francis 1584(?)-1616 .... **LC 33; DC 6**
See also BRW 2; CDBLB Before 1660; DLB 58; TEA

Beauvoir, Simone (Lucie Ernestine Marie Bertrand) de 1908-1986 .... **CLC 1, 2, 4, 8, 14, 31, 44, 50, 71, 124; SSC 35; WLC**
See also BPFB 1; CA 9-12R; 118; CANR 28, 61; DA; DA3; DAB; DAC; DAM MST, NOV; DLB 72; DLBY 1986; EW 12; FW; GFL 1789 to the Present; MTCW 1, 2; RGSF 2; RGWL 2; TWA

Becker, Carl (Lotus) 1873-1945 ..... **TCLC 63**
See also CA 157; DLB 17

Becker, Jurek 1937-1997 .... **CLC 7, 19**
See also CA 85-88; 157; CANR 60; CWW 2; DLB 75

Becker, Walter 1950- .... **CLC 26**

Beckett, Samuel (Barclay)
1906-1989 .. **CLC 1, 2, 3, 4, 6, 9, 10, 11, 14, 18, 29, 57, 59, 83; SSC 16; WLC**
See also BRWR 1; BRWS 1; CA 5-8R; 130; CANR 33, 61; CBD; CDBLB 1945-1960; DA; DA3; DAB; DAC; DAM DRAM, MST, NOV; DFS 2, 7; DLB 13, 15, 233; DLBY 1990; GFL 1789 to the Present; MTCW 1, 2; RGSF 2; RGWL 2; SSFS 15; TEA; WLIT 4

Beckford, William 1760-1844 .... **NCLC 16**
See also BRW 3; DLB 39, 213; HGG; SUFW

Beckman, Gunnel 1910- .... **CLC 26**
See also CA 33-36R; CANR 15; CLR 25; MAICYA 1, 2; SAAS 9; SATA 6

Becque, Henri 1837-1899 .... **NCLC 3**
See also DLB 192; GFL 1789 to the Present

Becquer, Gustavo Adolfo
1836-1870 .... **NCLC 106; HLCS 1**
See also DAM MULT

Beddoes, Thomas Lovell
1803-1849 .... **NCLC 3; DC 15**
See also DLB 96

Bede c. 673-735 .... **CMLC 20**
See also DLB 146; TEA

Bedford, Donald F.
See Fearing, Kenneth (Flexner)

Beecher, Catharine Esther
1800-1878 .... **NCLC 30**
See also DLB 1, 243

Beecher, John 1904-1980 .... **CLC 6**
See also AITN 1; CA 5-8R; 105; CANR 8

Beer, Johann 1655-1700 .... **LC 5**
See also DLB 168

Beer, Patricia 1924- .... **CLC 58**
See also CA 61-64; 183; CANR 13, 46; CP 7; CWP; DLB 40; FW

Beerbohm, Max
See Beerbohm, (Henry) Max(imilian)

Beerbohm, (Henry) Max(imilian)
1872-1956 .... **TCLC 1, 24**
See also BRWS 2; CA 104; 154; CANR 79; DLB 34, 100; FANT

Beer-Hofmann, Richard
1866-1945 .... **TCLC 60**
See also CA 160; DLB 81

Beg, Shemus
See Stephens, James

Begiebing, Robert J(ohn) 1946- .... **CLC 70**
See also CA 122; CANR 40, 88

Behan, Brendan 1923-1964 ...... **CLC 1, 8, 11, 15, 79**
See also BRWS 2; CA 73-76; CANR 33; CBD; CDBLB 1945-1960; DAM DRAM; DFS 7; DLB 13, 233; MTCW 1, 2

Behn, Aphra 1640(?)-1689 .... **LC 1, 30, 42; DC 4; PC 13; WLC**
See also BRWS 3; DA; DA3; DAB; DAC; DAM DRAM, MST, NOV, POET; DLB 39, 80, 131; FW; TEA; WLIT 3

Behrman, S(amuel) N(athaniel)
1893-1973 .... **CLC 40**
See also CA 13-16; 45-48; CAD; CAP 1; DLB 7, 44; IDFW 3; RGAL 4

Belasco, David 1853-1931 .... **TCLC 3**
See also CA 104; 168; DLB 7; RGAL 4

Belcheva, Elisaveta Lyubomirova
1893-1991 .... **CLC 10**
See also Bagryana, Elisaveta

Beldone, Phil "Cheech"
See Ellison, Harlan (Jay)

Beleno
See Azuela, Mariano

Belinski, Vissarion Grigoryevich
1811-1848 .... **NCLC 5**
See also DLB 198

Belitt, Ben 1911- .... **CLC 22**
See also CA 13-16R; CAAS 4; CANR 7, 77; CP 7; DLB 5

Bell, Gertrude (Margaret Lowthian)
1868-1926 .... **TCLC 67**
See also CA 167; CANR 110; DLB 174

Bell, J. Freeman
See Zangwill, Israel

Bell, James Madison 1826-1902 ... **TCLC 43; BLC 1**
See also BW 1; CA 122; 124; DAM MULT; DLB 50

Bell, Madison Smartt 1957- ...... **CLC 41, 102**
See also AMWS 10; BPFB 1; CA 111, 183; CAAE 183; CANR 28, 54, 73; CN 7; CSW; DLB 218; MTCW 1

Bell, Marvin (Hartley) 1937- .... **CLC 8, 31**
See also CA 21-24R; CAAS 14; CANR 59, 102; CP 7; DAM POET; DLB 5; MTCW 1

Bell, W. L. D.
See Mencken, H(enry) L(ouis)

Bellamy, Atwood C.
See Mencken, H(enry) L(ouis)

Bellamy, Edward 1850-1898 ...... **NCLC 4, 86**
See also DLB 12; NFS 15; RGAL 4; SFW 4

Belli, Gioconda 1949-
See also CA 152; CWW 2; HLCS 1

Bellin, Edward J.
See Kuttner, Henry

Belloc, (Joseph) Hilaire (Pierre Sebastien Rene Swanton) 1870-1953 ...... **TCLC 7, 18; PC 24**
See also CA 106; 152; CWRI 5; DAM POET; DLB 19, 100, 141, 174; MTCW 1; SATA 112; WCH; YABC 1

Belloc, Joseph Peter Rene Hilaire
See Belloc, (Joseph) Hilaire (Pierre Sebastien Rene Swanton)
Belloc, Joseph Pierre Hilaire
See Belloc, (Joseph) Hilaire (Pierre Sebastien Rene Swanton)
Belloc, M. A.
See Lowndes, Marie Adelaide (Belloc)
Bellow, Saul 1915- . **CLC 1, 2, 3, 6, 8, 10, 13, 15, 25, 33, 34, 63, 79; SSC 14; WLC**
See also AITN 2; AMW; BEST 89:3; BPFB 1; CA 5-8R; CABS 1; CANR 29, 53, 95; CDALB 1941-1968; CN 7; DA; DA3; DAB; DAC; DAM MST, NOV, POP; DLB 2, 28; DLBD 3; DLBY 1982; MTCW 1, 2; NFS 4, 14; RGAL 4; RGSF 2; SSFS 12; TUS
Belser, Reimond Karel Maria de 1929-
See Ruyslinck, Ward
See also CA 152
Bely, Andrey .... **TCLC 7; PC 11**
See also Bugayev, Boris Nikolayevich
See also EW 9; MTCW 1
Belyi, Andrei
See Bugayev, Boris Nikolayevich
See also RGWL 2
Bembo, Pietro 1470-1547 .... **LC 79**
See also RGWL 2
Benary, Margot
See Benary-Isbert, Margot
Benary-Isbert, Margot 1889-1979 .... **CLC 12**
See also CA 5-8R; 89-92; CANR 4, 72; CLR 12; MAICYA 1, 2; SATA 2; SATA-Obit 21
Benavente (y Martinez), Jacinto 1866-1954 .... **TCLC 3; HLCS 1**
See also CA 106; 131; CANR 81; DAM DRAM, MULT; GLL 2; HW 1, 2; MTCW 1, 2
Benchley, Peter (Bradford) 1940- .. **CLC 4, 8**
See also AAYA 14; AITN 2; BPFB 1; CA 17-20R; CANR 12, 35, 66; CPW; DAM NOV, POP; HGG; MTCW 1, 2; SATA 3, 89
Benchley, Robert (Charles) 1889-1945 .... **TCLC 1, 55**
See also CA 105; 153; DLB 11; RGAL 4
Benda, Julien 1867-1956 .... **TCLC 60**
See also CA 120; 154; GFL 1789 to the Present
Benedict, Ruth (Fulton) 1887-1948 .... **TCLC 60**
See also CA 158; DLB 246
Benedikt, Michael 1935- .... **CLC 4, 14**
See also CA 13-16R; CANR 7; CP 7; DLB 5
Benet, Juan 1927-1993 .... **CLC 28**
See also CA 143
Benet, Stephen Vincent 1898-1943 . **TCLC 7; SSC 10**
See also AMWS 11; CA 104; 152; DA3; DAM POET; DLB 4, 48, 102, 249; DLBY 1997; HGG; MTCW 1; RGAL 4; RGSF 2; SUFW; WP; YABC 1
Benet, William Rose 1886-1950 ..... **TCLC 28**
See also CA 118; 152; DAM POET; DLB 45; RGAL 4
Benford, Gregory (Albert) 1941- ..... **CLC 52**
See also BPFB 1; CA 69-72, 175; CAAE 175; CAAS 27; CANR 12, 24, 49, 95; CSW; DLBY 1982; SCFW 2; SFW 4
Bengtsson, Frans (Gunnar) 1894-1954 .... **TCLC 48**
See also CA 170
Benjamin, David
See Slavitt, David R(ytman)
Benjamin, Lois
See Gould, Lois

Benjamin, Walter 1892-1940 .... **TCLC 39**
See also CA 164; DLB 242; EW 11
Benn, Gottfried 1886-1956 .. **TCLC 3; PC 35**
See also CA 106; 153; DLB 56; RGWL 2
Bennett, Alan 1934- .... **CLC 45, 77**
See also BRWS 8; CA 103; CANR 35, 55, 106; CBD; CD 5; DAB; DAM MST; MTCW 1, 2
Bennett, (Enoch) Arnold 1867-1931 .... **TCLC 5, 20**
See also BRW 6; CA 106; 155; CDBLB 1890-1914; DLB 10, 34, 98, 135; MTCW 2
Bennett, Elizabeth
See Mitchell, Margaret (Munnerlyn)
Bennett, George Harold 1930-
See Bennett, Hal
See also BW 1; CA 97-100; CANR 87
Bennett, Hal .... **CLC 5**
See also Bennett, George Harold
See also DLB 33
Bennett, Jay 1912- .... **CLC 35**
See also AAYA 10; CA 69-72; CANR 11, 42, 79; JRDA; SAAS 4; SATA 41, 87; SATA-Brief 27; WYA; YAW
Bennett, Louise (Simone) 1919- ...... **CLC 28; BLC 1**
See also BW 2, 3; CA 151; CDWLB 3; CP 7; DAM MULT; DLB 117
Benson, A. C. 1862-1925 .... **TCLC 123**
See also DLB 98
Benson, E(dward) F(rederic) 1867-1940 .... **TCLC 27**
See also CA 114; 157; DLB 135, 153; HGG; SUFW
Benson, Jackson J. 1930- .... **CLC 34**
See also CA 25-28R; DLB 111
Benson, Sally 1900-1972 .... **CLC 17**
See also CA 19-20; 37-40R; CAP 1; SATA 1, 35; SATA-Obit 27
Benson, Stella 1892-1933 .... **TCLC 17**
See also CA 117; 154, 155; DLB 36, 162; FANT; TEA
Bentham, Jeremy 1748-1832 .... **NCLC 38**
See also DLB 107, 158, 252
Bentley, E(dmund) C(lerihew) 1875-1956 .... **TCLC 12**
See also CA 108; DLB 70; MSW
Bentley, Eric (Russell) 1916- .... **CLC 24**
See also CA 5-8R; CAD; CANR 6, 67; CBD; CD 5; INT CANR-6
Beranger, Pierre Jean de 1780-1857 .... **NCLC 34**
Berdyaev, Nicolas
See Berdyaev, Nikolai (Aleksandrovich)
Berdyaev, Nikolai (Aleksandrovich) 1874-1948 .... **TCLC 67**
See also CA 120; 157
Berdyayev, Nikolai (Aleksandrovich)
See Berdyaev, Nikolai (Aleksandrovich)
Berendt, John (Lawrence) 1939- ...... **CLC 86**
See also CA 146; CANR 75, 93; DA3; MTCW 1
Beresford, J(ohn) D(avys) 1873-1947 .... **TCLC 81**
See also CA 112; 155; DLB 162, 178, 197; SFW 4; SUFW
Bergelson, David 1884-1952 .... **TCLC 81**
Berger, Colonel
See Malraux, (Georges-)Andre
Berger, John (Peter) 1926- .... **CLC 2, 19**
See also BRWS 4; CA 81-84; CANR 51, 78; CN 7; DLB 14, 207
Berger, Melvin H. 1927- .... **CLC 12**
See also CA 5-8R; CANR 4; CLR 32; SAAS 2; SATA 5, 88; SATA-Essay 124

Berger, Thomas (Louis) 1924- .. **CLC 3, 5, 8, 11, 18, 38**
See also BPFB 1; CA 1-4R; CANR 5, 28, 51; CN 7; DAM NOV; DLB 2; DLBY 1980; FANT; INT CANR-28; MTCW 1, 2; RHW; TCWW 2
Bergman, (Ernst) Ingmar 1918- ...... **CLC 16, 72**
See also CA 81-84; CANR 33, 70; DLB 257; MTCW 2
Bergson, Henri(-Louis) 1859-1941 . **TCLC 32**
See also CA 164; EW 8; GFL 1789 to the Present
Bergstein, Eleanor 1938- .... **CLC 4**
See also CA 53-56; CANR 5
Berkeley, George 1685-1753 .... **LC 65**
See also DLB 31, 101, 252
Berkoff, Steven 1937- .... **CLC 56**
See also CA 104; CANR 72; CBD; CD 5
Berlin, Isaiah 1909-1997 .... **TCLC 105**
See also CA 85-88; 162
Bermant, Chaim (Icyk) 1929-1998 ... **CLC 40**
See also CA 57-60; CANR 6, 31, 57, 105; CN 7
Bern, Victoria
See Fisher, M(ary) F(rances) K(ennedy)
Bernanos, (Paul Louis) Georges 1888-1948 .... **TCLC 3**
See also CA 104; 130; CANR 94; DLB 72; GFL 1789 to the Present; RGWL 2
Bernard, April 1956- .... **CLC 59**
See also CA 131
Berne, Victoria
See Fisher, M(ary) F(rances) K(ennedy)
Bernhard, Thomas 1931-1989 ..... **CLC 3, 32, 61; DC 14**
See also CA 85-88; 127; CANR 32, 57; CDWLB 2; DLB 85, 124; MTCW 1; RGWL 2
Bernhardt, Sarah (Henriette Rosine) 1844-1923 .... **TCLC 75**
See also CA 157
Bernstein, Charles 1950- .... **CLC 142,**
See also CA 129; CAAS 24; CANR 90; CP 7; DLB 169
Berriault, Gina 1926-1999 .... **CLC 54, 109; SSC 30**
See also CA 116; 129; 185; CANR 66; DLB 130; SSFS 7,11
Berrigan, Daniel 1921- .... **CLC 4**
See also CA 33-36R; CAAE 187; CAAS 1; CANR 11, 43, 78; CP 7; DLB 5
Berrigan, Edmund Joseph Michael, Jr. 1934-1983
See Berrigan, Ted
See also CA 61-64; 110; CANR 14, 102
Berrigan, Ted .... **CLC 37**
See also Berrigan, Edmund Joseph Michael, Jr.
See also DLB 5, 169; WP
Berry, Charles Edward Anderson 1931-
See Berry, Chuck
See also CA 115
Berry, Chuck .... **CLC 17**
See also Berry, Charles Edward Anderson
Berry, Jonas
See Ashbery, John (Lawrence)
See also GLL 1
Berry, Wendell (Erdman) 1934- ... **CLC 4, 6, 8, 27, 46; PC 28**
See also AITN 1; AMWS 10; ANW; CA 73-76; CANR 50, 73, 101; CP 7; CSW; DAM POET; DLB 5, 6, 234; MTCW 1
Berryman, John 1914-1972 ... **CLC 1, 2, 3, 4, 6, 8, 10, 13, 25, 62**
See also AMW; CA 13-16; 33-36R; CABS 2; CANR 35; CAP 1; CDALB 1941-1968; DAM POET; DLB 48; MTCW 1, 2; PAB; RGAL 4; WP

Boyle, Kay 1902-1992 .... **CLC 1, 5, 19, 58, 121; SSC 5**
See also CA 13-16R; 140; CAAS 1; CANR 29, 61, 110; DLB 4, 9, 48, 86; DLBY 1993; MTCW 1, 2; RGAL 4; RGSF 2; SSFS 10, 13, 14

Boyle, Mark
See Kienzle, William X(avier)

Boyle, Patrick 1905-1982 .... **CLC 19**
See also CA 127

Boyle, T. C.
See Boyle, T(homas) Coraghessan
See also AMWS 8

Boyle, T(homas) Coraghessan
1948- .... **CLC 36, 55, 90; SSC 16**
See also Boyle, T. C.
See also BEST 90:4; BPFB 1; CA 120; CANR 44, 76, 89; CN 7; CPW; DA3; DAM POP; DLB 218; DLBY 1986; MTCW 2; SSFS 13

Boz
See Dickens, Charles (John Huffam)

Brackenridge, Hugh Henry
1748-1816 .... **NCLC 7**
See also DLB 11, 37; RGAL 4

Bradbury, Edward P.
See Moorcock, Michael (John)
See also MTCW 2

Bradbury, Malcolm (Stanley)
1932-2000 .... **CLC 32, 61**
See also CA 1-4R; CANR 1, 33, 91, 98; CN 7; DA3; DAM NOV; DLB 14, 207; MTCW 1, 2

Bradbury, Ray (Douglas) 1920- .... **CLC 1, 3, 10, 15, 42, 98; SSC 29, 53; WLC**
See also AAYA 15; AITN 1, 2; AMWS 4; BPFB 1; BYA 4, 5, 11; CA 1-4R; CANR 2, 30, 75; CDALB 1968-1988; CN 7; CPW; DA; DA3; DAB; DAC; DAM MST, NOV, POP; DLB 2, 8; EXPN; EXPS; HGG; LAIT 3, 5; MTCW 1, 2; NFS 1; RGAL 4; RGSF 2; SATA 11, 64, 123; SCFW 2; SFW 4; SSFS 1; SUFW; TUS; YAW

Braddon, Mary Elizabeth
1837-1915 .... **TCLC 111**
See also Aunt Belinda
See also BRWS 8; CA 108; 179; CMW 4; DLB 18, 70, 156; HGG

Bradford, Gamaliel 1863-1932 .... **TCLC 36**
See also CA 160; DLB 17

Bradford, William 1590-1657 .... **LC 64**
See also DLB 24, 30; RGAL 4

Bradley, David (Henry), Jr. 1950- ... **CLC 23, 118; BLC 1**
See also BW 1, 3; CA 104; CANR 26, 81; CN 7; DAM MULT; DLB 33

Bradley, John Ed(mund, Jr.) 1958- . **CLC 55**
See also CA 139; CANR 99; CN 7; CSW

Bradley, Marion Zimmer
1930-1999 .... **CLC 30**
See also Chapman, Lee; Dexter, John; Gardner, Miriam; Ives, Morgan; Rivers, Elfrida
See also AAYA 40; BPFB 1; CA 57-60; 185; CAAS 10; CANR 7, 31, 51, 75, 107; CPW; DA3; DAM POP; DLB 8; FANT; FW; MTCW 1, 2; SATA 90; SATA-Obit 116; SFW 4; YAW

Bradshaw, John 1933- .... **CLC 70**
See also CA 138; CANR 61

Bradstreet, Anne 1612(?)-1672 ...... **LC 4, 30; PC 10**
See also AMWS 1; CDALB 1640-1865; DA; DA3; DAC; DAM MST, POET; DLB 24; EXPP; FW; PFS 6; RGAL 4; TUS; WP

Brady, Joan 1939- .... **CLC 86**
See also CA 141

Bragg, Melvyn 1939- .... **CLC 10**
See also BEST 89:3; CA 57-60; CANR 10, 48, 89; CN 7; DLB 14; RHW

Brahe, Tycho 1546-1601 .... **LC 45**

Braine, John (Gerard) 1922-1986 . **CLC 1, 3, 41**
See also CA 1-4R; 120; CANR 1, 33; CD-BLB 1945-1960; DLB 15; DLBY 1986; MTCW 1

Bramah, Ernest 1868-1942 .... **TCLC 72**
See also CA 156; CMW 4; DLB 70; FANT

Brammer, William 1930(?)-1978 ...... **CLC 31**
See also CA 77-80

Brancati, Vitaliano 1907-1954 .... **TCLC 12**
See also CA 109; DLB 264

Brancato, Robin F(idler) 1936- .... **CLC 35**
See also AAYA 9; BYA 6; CA 69-72; CANR 11, 45; CLR 32; JRDA; MAICYA 2; MAICYAS 1; SAAS 9; SATA 97; WYA; YAW

Brand, Max
See Faust, Frederick (Schiller)
See also BPFB 1; TCWW 2

Brand, Millen 1906-1980 .... **CLC 7**
See also CA 21-24R; 97-100; CANR 72

Branden, Barbara .... **CLC 44**
See also CA 148

Brandes, Georg (Morris Cohen)
1842-1927 .... **TCLC 10**
See also CA 105; 189

Brandys, Kazimierz 1916-2000 .... **CLC 62**

Branley, Franklyn M(ansfield)
1915- .... **CLC 21**
See also CA 33-36R; CANR 14, 39; CLR 13; MAICYA 1, 2; SAAS 16; SATA 4, 68

Brathwaite, Edward Kamau 1930- . **CLC 11; BLCS**
See also BW 2, 3; CA 25-28R; CANR 11, 26, 47, 107; CDWLB 3; CP 7; DAM POET; DLB 125

Brathwaite, Kamau
See Brathwaite, Edward Kamau

Brautigan, Richard (Gary)
1935-1984 ..... **CLC 1, 3, 5, 9, 12, 34, 42**
See also BPFB 1; CA 53-56; 113; CANR 34; DA3; DAM NOV; DLB 2, 5, 206; DLBY 1980, 1984; FANT; MTCW 1; RGAL 4; SATA 56

Brave Bird, Mary
See Crow Dog, Mary (Ellen)
See also NNAL

Braverman, Kate 1950- .... **CLC 67**
See also CA 89-92

Brecht, (Eugen) Bertolt (Friedrich)
1898-1956 ..... **TCLC 1, 6, 13, 35; DC 3; WLC**
See also CA 104; 133; CANR 62; CDWLB 2; DA; DA3; DAB; DAC; DAM DRAM, MST; DFS 4, 5, 9; DLB 56, 124; EW 11; IDTP; MTCW 1, 2; RGWL 2; TWA

Brecht, Eugen Berthold Friedrich
See Brecht, (Eugen) Bertolt (Friedrich)

Bremer, Fredrika 1801-1865 .... **NCLC 11**
See also DLB 254

Brennan, Christopher John
1870-1932 .... **TCLC 17**
See also CA 117; 188; DLB 230

Brennan, Maeve 1917-1993 .... **CLC 5**
See also CA 81-84; CANR 72, 100; TCLC 124

Brent, Linda
See Jacobs, Harriet A(nn)

Brentano, Clemens (Maria)
1778-1842 .... **NCLC 1**
See also DLB 90; RGWL 2

Brent of Bin Bin
See Franklin, (Stella Maria Sarah) Miles (Lampe)

Brenton, Howard 1942- .... **CLC 31**
See also CA 69-72; CANR 33, 67; CBD; CD 5; DLB 13; MTCW 1

Breslin, James 1930-
See Breslin, Jimmy
See also CA 73-76; CANR 31, 75; DAM NOV; MTCW 1, 2

Breslin, Jimmy .... **CLC 4, 43**
See also Breslin, James
See also AITN 1; DLB 185; MTCW 2

Bresson, Robert 1901(?)-1999 .... **CLC 16**
See also CA 110; 187; CANR 49

Breton, Andre 1896-1966 .. **CLC 2, 9, 15, 54; PC 15**
See also CA 19-20; 25-28R; CANR 40, 60; CAP 2; DLB 65, 258; EW 11; GFL 1789 to the Present; MTCW 1, 2; RGWL 2; TWA; WP

Breytenbach, Breyten 1939(?)- .. **CLC 23, 37, 126**
See also CA 113; 129; CANR 61; CWW 2; DAM POET; DLB 225

Bridgers, Sue Ellen 1942- .... **CLC 26**
See also AAYA 8; BYA 7, 8; CA 65-68; CANR 11, 36; CLR 18; DLB 52; JRDA; MAICYA 1, 2; SAAS 1; SATA 22, 90; SATA-Essay 109; WYA; YAW

Bridges, Robert (Seymour)
1844-1930 .... **TCLC 1; PC 28**
See also BRW 6; CA 104; 152; CDBLB 1890-1914; DAM POET; DLB 19, 98

Bridie, James .... **TCLC 3**
See also Mavor, Osborne Henry
See also DLB 10

Brin, David 1950- .... **CLC 34**
See also AAYA 21; CA 102; CANR 24, 70; INT CANR-24; SATA 65; SCFW 2; SFW 4

Brink, Andre (Philippus) 1935- . **CLC 18, 36, 106**
See also AFW; BRWS 6; CA 104; CANR 39, 62, 109; CN 7; DLB 225; INT CA-103; MTCW 1, 2; WLIT 2

Brinsmead, H. F.
See Brinsmead, H(esba) F(ay)

Brinsmead, H. F(ay)
See Brinsmead, H(esba) F(ay)

Brinsmead, H(esba) F(ay) 1922- ...... **CLC 21**
See also CA 21-24R; CANR 10; CLR 47; CWRI 5; MAICYA 1, 2; SAAS 5; SATA 18, 78

Brittain, Vera (Mary) 1893(?)-1970 . **CLC 23**
See also CA 13-16; 25-28R; CANR 58; CAP 1; DLB 191; FW; MTCW 1, 2

Broch, Hermann 1886-1951 .... **TCLC 20**
See also CA 117; CDWLB 2; DLB 85, 124; EW 10; RGWL 2

Brock, Rose
See Hansen, Joseph
See also GLL 1

Brod, Max 1884-1968 .... **TCLC 115**
See also CA 5-8R; 25-28R; CANR 7; DLB 81

Brodkey, Harold (Roy) 1930-1996 ... **CLC 56**
See also CA 111; 151; CANR 71; CN 7; DLB 130; TCLC 123

Brodskii, Iosif
See Brodsky, Joseph
See also RGWL 2

Brodsky, Iosif Alexandrovich 1940-1996
See Brodsky, Joseph
See also AITN 1; CA 41-44R; 151; CANR 37, 106; DA3; DAM POET; MTCW 1, 2

Brodsky, Joseph . **CLC 4, 6, 13, 36, 100; PC 9**
See also Brodsky, Iosif Alexandrovich
See also AMWS 8; CWW 2; MTCW 1

Brodsky, Michael (Mark) 1948- .... **CLC 19**
See also CA 102; CANR 18, 41, 58; DLB 244

Brodzki, Bella ed. .... **CLC 65**

Brome, Richard 1590(?)-1652 .... **LC 61**
See also DLB 58

Bromell, Henry 1947- .... **CLC 5**
See also CA 53-56; CANR 9

Bromfield, Louis (Brucker)
1896-1956 .... **TCLC 11**
See also CA 107; 155; DLB 4, 9, 86; RGAL 4; RHW

Broner, E(sther) M(asserman)
1930- .... **CLC 19**
See also CA 17-20R; CANR 8, 25, 72; CN 7; DLB 28

Bronk, William (M.) 1918-1999 .... **CLC 10**
See also CA 89-92; 177; CANR 23; CP 7; DLB 165

Bronstein, Lev Davidovich
See Trotsky, Leon

Bronte, Anne 1820-1849 ..... **NCLC 4, 71, 102**
See also BRW 5; BRWR 1; DA3; DLB 21, 199; TEA

Bronte, (Patrick) Branwell
1817-1848 .... **NCLC 109**

Bronte, Charlotte 1816-1855 ...... **NCLC 3, 8, 33, 58, 105; WLC**
See also AAYA 17; BRW 5; BRWR 1; BYA 2; CDBLB 1832-1890; DA; DA3; DAB; DAC; DAM MST, NOV; DLB 21, 159, 199; EXPN; LAIT; NFS 4; TEA; WLIT 4

Bronte, Emily (Jane) 1818-1848 ... **NCLC 16, 35; PC 8; WLC**
See also AAYA 17; BPFB 1; BRW 5; BRWR 1; BYA 3; CDBLB 1832-1890; DA; DA3; DAB; DAC; DAM MST, NOV, POET; DLB 21, 32, 199; EXPN; LAIT 1; TEA; WLIT 3

Brontes
See Bronte, Anne; Bronte, Charlotte; Bronte, Emily (Jane)

Brooke, Frances 1724-1789 .... **LC 6, 48**
See also DLB 39, 99

Brooke, Henry 1703(?)-1783 .... **LC 1**
See also DLB 39

Brooke, Rupert (Chawner)
1887-1915 ..... **TCLC 2, 7; PC 24; WLC**
See also BRWS 3; CA 104; 132; CANR 61; CDBLB 1914-1945; DA; DAB; DAC; DAM MST, POET; DLB 19, 216; EXPP; GLL 2; MTCW 1, 2; PFS 7; TEA

Brooke-Haven, P.
See Wodehouse, P(elham) G(renville)

Brooke-Rose, Christine 1926(?)- ...... **CLC 40**
See also BRWS 4; CA 13-16R; CANR 58; CN 7; DLB 14, 231; SFW 4

Brookner, Anita 1928- .. **CLC 32, 34, 51, 136**
See also BRWS 4; CA 114; 120; CANR 37, 56, 87; CN 7; CPW; DA3; DAB; DAM POP; DLB 194; DLBY 1987; MTCW 1, 2; TEA

Brooks, Cleanth 1906-1994 . **CLC 24, 86, 110**
See also CA 17-20R; 145; CANR 33, 35; CSW; DLB 63; DLBY 1994; INT CANR-35; MTCW 1, 2

Brooks, George
See Baum, L(yman) Frank

Brooks, Gwendolyn (Elizabeth)
1917-2000 .. **CLC 1, 2, 4, 5, 15, 49, 125; BLC 1; PC 7; WLC**
See also AAYA 20; AFAW 1, 2; AITN 1; AMWS 3; BW 2, 3; CA 1-4R; 190; CANR 1, 27, 52, 75; CDALB 1941-1968; CLR 27; CP 7; CWP; DA; DA3; DAC; DAM

MST, MULT, POET; DLB 5, 76, 165; EXPP; MAWW; MTCW 1, 2; PFS 1, 2, 4, 6; RGAL 4; SATA 6; SATA-Obit 123; TUS; WP

Brooks, Mel .... **CLC 12**
See also Kaminsky, Melvin
See also AAYA 13; DLB 26

Brooks, Peter (Preston) 1938- .... **CLC 34**
See also CA 45-48; CANR 1, 107

Brooks, Van Wyck 1886-1963 .... **CLC 29**
See also AMW; CA 1-4R; CANR 6; DLB 45, 63, 103; TUS

Brophy, Brigid (Antonia)
1929-1995 .... **CLC 6, 11, 29, 105**
See also CA 5-8R; 149; CAAS 4; CANR 25, 53; CBD; CN 7; CWD; DA3; DLB 14; MTCW 1, 2

Brosman, Catharine Savage 1934- ..... **CLC 9**
See also CA 61-64; CANR 21, 46

Brossard, Nicole 1943- .... **CLC 115**
See also CA 122; CAAS 16; CCA 1; CWP; CWW 2; DLB 53; FW; GLL 2

Brother Antoninus
See Everson, William (Oliver)

The Brothers Quay
See Quay, Stephen; Quay, Timothy

Broughton, T(homas) Alan 1936- ..... **CLC 19**
See also CA 45-48; CANR 2, 23, 48, 111

Broumas, Olga 1949- .... **CLC 10, 73**
See also CA 85-88; CANR 20, 69, 110; CP 7; CWP; GLL 2

Broun, Heywood 1888-1939 .... **TCLC 104**
See also DLB 29, 171

Brown, Alan 1950- .... **CLC 99**
See also CA 156

Brown, Charles Brockden
1771-1810 .... **NCLC 22, 74**
See also AMWS 1; CDALB 1640-1865; DLB 37, 59, 73; FW; HGG; RGAL 4; TUS

Brown, Christy 1932-1981 .... **CLC 63**
See also BYA 13; CA 105; 104; CANR 72; DLB 14

Brown, Claude 1937-2002 ... **CLC 30; BLC 1**
See also AAYA 7; BW 1, 3; CA 73-76; CANR 81; DAM MULT

Brown, Dee (Alexander) 1908- ... **CLC 18, 47**
See also AAYA 30; CA 13-16R; CAAS 6; CANR 11, 45, 60; CPW; CSW; DA3; DAM POP; DLBY 1980; LAIT 2; MTCW 1, 2; SATA 5, 110; TCWW 2

Brown, George
See Wertmueller, Lina

Brown, George Douglas
1869-1902 .... **TCLC 28**
See also Douglas, George
See also CA 162

Brown, George Mackay 1921-1996 ... **CLC 5, 48, 100**
See also BRWS 6; CA 21-24R; 151; CAAS 6; CANR 12, 37, 67; CN 7; CP 7; DLB 14, 27, 139; MTCW 1; RGSF 2; SATA 35

Brown, (William) Larry 1951- .... **CLC 73**
See also CA 130; 134; CSW; DLB 234; INT 133

Brown, Moses
See Barrett, William (Christopher)

Brown, Rita Mae 1944- .... **CLC 18, 43, 79**
See also BPFB 1; CA 45-48; CANR 2, 11, 35, 62, 95; CN 7; CPW; CSW; DA3; DAM NOV, POP; FW; INT CANR-11; MTCW 1, 2; NFS 9; RGAL 4; TUS

Brown, Roderick (Langmere) Haig-
See Haig-Brown, Roderick (Langmere)

Brown, Rosellen 1939- .... **CLC 32**
See also CA 77-80; CAAS 10; CANR 14, 44, 98; CN 7

Brown, Sterling Allen 1901-1989 ...... **CLC 1, 23, 59; BLC 1**
See also AFAW 1, 2; BW 1, 3; CA 85-88; 127; CANR 26; DA3; DAM MULT, POET; DLB 48, 51, 63; MTCW 1, 2; RGAL 4; WP

Brown, Will
See Ainsworth, William Harrison

Brown, William Wells 1815-1884 ... **NCLC 2, 89; BLC 1; DC 1**
See also DAM MULT; DLB 3, 50, 183, 248; RGAL 4

Browne, (Clyde) Jackson 1948(?)- ... **CLC 21**
See also CA 120

Browning, Elizabeth Barrett
1806-1861 ... **NCLC 1, 16, 61, 66; PC 6; WLC**
See also BRW 4; CDBLB 1832-1890; DA; DA3; DAB; DAC; DAM MST, POET; DLB 32, 199; EXPP; PAB; PFS 2; TEA; WLIT 4; WP

Browning, Robert 1812-1889 . **NCLC 19, 79; PC 2; WLCS**
See also BRW 4; BRWR 2; CDBLB 1832-1890; DA; DA3; DAB; DAC; DAM MST, POET; DLB 32, 163; EXPP; PAB; PFS 1, 15; RGEL 2; TEA; WLIT 4; WP; YABC 1

Browning, Tod 1882-1962 .... **CLC 16**
See also CA 141; 117

Brownmiller, Susan 1935- .... **CLC 159**
See also CA 103; CANR 35, 75; DAM NOV; FW; MTCW 1, 2

Brownson, Orestes Augustus
1803-1876 .... **NCLC 50**
See also DLB 1, 59, 73, 243

Bruccoli, Matthew J(oseph) 1931- ... **CLC 34**
See also CA 9-12R; CANR 7, 87; DLB 103

Bruce, Lenny .... **CLC 21**
See also Schneider, Leonard Alfred

Bruin, John
See Brutus, Dennis

Brulard, Henri
See Stendhal

Brulls, Christian
See Simenon, Georges (Jacques Christian)

Brunner, John (Kilian Houston)
1934-1995 .... **CLC 8, 10**
See also CA 1-4R; 149; CAAS 8; CANR 2, 37; CPW; DAM POP; DLB 261; MTCW 1, 2; SCFW 2; SFW 4

Bruno, Giordano 1548-1600 .... **LC 27**
See also RGWL 2

Brutus, Dennis 1924- ... **CLC 43; BLC 1; PC 24**
See also AFW; BW 2, 3; CA 49-52; CAAS 14; CANR 2, 27, 42, 81; CDWLB 3; CP 7; DAM MULT, POET; DLB 117, 225

Bryan, C(ourtlandt) D(ixon) B(arnes)
1936- .... **CLC 29**
See also CA 73-76; CANR 13, 68; DLB 185; INT CANR-13

Bryan, Michael
See Moore, Brian
See also CCA 1

Bryan, William Jennings
1860-1925 .... **TCLC 99**

Bryant, William Cullen 1794-1878 . **NCLC 6, 46; PC 20**
See also AMWS 1; CDALB 1640-1865; DA; DAB; DAC; DAM MST, POET; DLB 3, 43, 59, 189, 250; EXPP; PAB; RGAL 4; TUS

Bryusov, Valery Yakovlevich
1873-1924 .... **TCLC 10**
See also CA 107; 155; SFW 4

Carlson, Ron(ald F.) 1947- .... **CLC 54**
See also CA 105; CAAE 189; CANR 27;
DLB 244

Carlyle, Thomas 1795-1881 ..... **NCLC 22, 70**
See also BRW 4; CDBLB 1789-1832; DA;
DAB; DAC; DAM MST; DLB 55, 144,
254; RGEL 2; TEA

Carman, (William) Bliss
1861-1929 .... **TCLC 7; PC 34**
See also CA 104; 152; DAC; DLB 92;
RGEL 2

Carnegie, Dale 1888-1955 .... **TCLC 53**

Carossa, Hans 1878-1956 .... **TCLC 48**
See also CA 170; DLB 66

Carpenter, Don(ald Richard)
1931-1995 .... **CLC 41**
See also CA 45-48; 149; CANR 1, 71

Carpenter, Edward 1844-1929 .... **TCLC 88**
See also CA 163; GLL 1

Carpenter, John (Howard) 1948- ... **CLC 161**
See also AAYA 2; CA 134; SATA 58

Carpentier (y Valmont), Alejo
1904-1980 . **CLC 8, 11, 38, 110; HLC 1;
SSC 35**
See also CA 65-68; 97-100; CANR 11, 70;
CDWLB 3; DAM MULT; DLB 113; HW
1, 2; LAW; RGSF 2; RGWL 2; WLIT 1

Carr, Caleb 1955(?)- .... **CLC 86**
See also CA 147; CANR 73; DA3

Carr, Emily 1871-1945 .... **TCLC 32**
See also CA 159; DLB 68; FW; GLL 2

Carr, John Dickson 1906-1977 .... **CLC 3**
See also Fairbairn, Roger
See also CA 49-52; 69-72; CANR 3, 33,
60; CMW 4; MSW; MTCW 1, 2

Carr, Philippa
See Hibbert, Eleanor Alice Burford

Carr, Virginia Spencer 1929- .... **CLC 34**
See also CA 61-64; DLB 111

Carrere, Emmanuel 1957- .... **CLC 89**
See also CA 200

Carrier, Roch 1937- .... **CLC 13, 78**
See also CA 130; CANR 61; CCA 1; DAC;
DAM MST; DLB 53; SATA 105

Carroll, James P. 1943(?)- .... **CLC 38**
See also CA 81-84; CANR 73; MTCW 1

Carroll, Jim 1951- .... **CLC 35, 143**
See also AAYA 17; CA 45-48; CANR 42

Carroll, Lewis ... **NCLC 2, 53; PC 18; WLC**
See also Dodgson, Charles L(utwidge)
See also AAYA 39; BRW 5; BYA 5, 13; CD-
BLB 1832-1890; CLR 2, 18; DLB 18,
163, 178; DLBY 1998; EXPN; EXPP;
FANT; JRDA; LAIT 1; NFS 7; PFS 11;
RGEL 2; SUFW; TEA; WCH

Carroll, Paul Vincent 1900-1968 ...... **CLC 10**
See also CA 9-12R; 25-28R; DLB 10;
RGEL 2

Carruth, Hayden 1921- ..... **CLC 4, 7, 10, 18,
84; PC 10**
See also CA 9-12R; CANR 4, 38, 59, 110;
CP 7; DLB 5, 165; INT CANR-4; MTCW
1, 2; SATA 47

Carson, Rachel Louise 1907-1964 .... **CLC 71**
See also AMWS 9; ANW; CA 77-80; CANR
35; DA3; DAM POP; FW; LAIT 4;
MTCW 1, 2; NCFS 1; SATA 23

Carter, Angela (Olive) 1940-1992 ...... **CLC 5,
41, 76; SSC 13**
See also BRWS 3; CA 53-56; 136; CANR
12, 36, 61, 106; DA3; DLB 14, 207, 261;
EXPS; FANT; FW; MTCW 1, 2; RGSF 2;
SATA 66; SATA-Obit 70; SFW 4; SSFS
4, 12; WLIT 4

Carter, Nick
See Smith, Martin Cruz

Carver, Raymond 1938-1988 ..... **CLC 22, 36,
53, 55, 126; SSC 8, 51**
See also AMWS 3; BPFB 1; CA 33-36R;
126; CANR 17, 34, 61, 103; CPW; DA3;
DAM NOV; DLB 130; DLBY 1984,
1988; MTCW 1, 2; RGAL 4; RGSF 2;
SSFS 3, 6, 12, 13; TCWW 2; TUS

Cary, Elizabeth, Lady Falkland
1585-1639 .... **LC 30**

Cary, (Arthur) Joyce (Lunel)
1888-1957 .... **TCLC 1, 29**
See also BRW 7; CA 104; 164; CDBLB
1914-1945; DLB 15, 100; MTCW 2;
RGEL 2; TEA

Casanova de Seingalt, Giovanni Jacopo
1725-1798 .... **LC 13**

Casares, Adolfo Bioy
See Bioy Casares, Adolfo
See also RGSF 2

Casas, Bartolome de las 1474-1566
See Las Casas, Bartolome de
See also WLIT 1

Casely-Hayford, J(oseph) E(phraim)
1866-1903 .... **TCLC 24; BLC 1**
See also BW 2; CA 123; 152; DAM MULT

Casey, John (Dudley) 1939- .... **CLC 59**
See also BEST 90:2; CA 69-72; CANR 23,
100

Casey, Michael 1947- .... **CLC 2**
See also CA 65-68; CANR 109; DLB 5

Casey, Patrick
See Thurman, Wallace (Henry)

Casey, Warren (Peter) 1935-1988 .... **CLC 12**
See also CA 101; 127; INT 101

Casona, Alejandro .... **CLC 49**
See also Alvarez, Alejandro Rodriguez

Cassavetes, John 1929-1989 .... **CLC 20**
See also CA 85-88; 127; CANR 82

Cassian, Nina 1924- .... **PC 17**
See also CWP; CWW 2

Cassill, R(onald) V(erlin) 1919- ... **CLC 4, 23**
See also CA 9-12R; CAAS 1; CANR 7, 45;
CN 7; DLB 6, 218

Cassiodorus, Flavius Magnus c. 490(?)-c.
583(?) .... **CMLC 43**

Cassirer, Ernst 1874-1945 .... **TCLC 61**
See also CA 157

Cassity, (Allen) Turner 1929- .... **CLC 6, 42**
See also CA 17-20R; CAAS 8; CANR 11;
CSW; DLB 105

Castaneda, Carlos (Cesar Aranha)
1931(?)-1998 .... **CLC 12, 119**
See also CA 25-28R; CANR 32, 66, 105;
DNFS 1; HW 1; MTCW 1

Castedo, Elena 1937- .... **CLC 65**
See also CA 132

Castedo-Ellerman, Elena
See Castedo, Elena

Castellanos, Rosario 1925-1974 .... **CLC 66;
HLC 1; SSC 39**
See also CA 131; 53-56; CANR 58; CD-
WLB 3; DAM MULT; DLB 113; FW;
HW 1; LAW; MTCW 1; RGSF 2; RGWL
2

Castelvetro, Lodovico 1505-1571 .... **LC 12**

Castiglione, Baldassare 1478-1529 ...... **LC 12**
See also Castiglione, Baldesar
See also RGWL 2

Castiglione, Baldesar
See Castiglione, Baldassare
See also EW 2

Castillo, Ana (Hernandez Del)
1953- .... **CLC 151**
See also AAYA 42; CA 131; CANR 51, 86;
CWP; DLB 122, 227; DNFS 2; FW; HW
1

Castle, Robert
See Hamilton, Edmond

Castro (Ruz), Fidel 1926(?)-
See also CA 110; 129; CANR 81; DAM
MULT; HLC 1; HW 2

Castro, Guillen de 1569-1631 .... **LC 19**

Castro, Rosalia de 1837-1885 ... **NCLC 3, 78;
PC 41**
See also DAM MULT

Cather, Willa (Sibert) 1873-1947 .... **TCLC 1,
11, 31, 99, 125; SSC 2, 50; WLC**
See also AAYA 24; AMW; AMWR 1; BPFB
1; CA 104; 128; CDALB 1865-1917; DA;
DA3; DAB; DAC; DAM MST, NOV;
DLB 9, 54, 78, 256; DLBD 1; EXPN;
EXPS; LAIT 3; MAWW; MTCW 1, 2;
NFS 2; RGAL 4; RGSF 2; RHW; SATA
30; SSFS 2, 7; TCWW 2; TUS

Catherine II
See Catherine the Great
See also DLB 150

Catherine the Great 1729-1796 .... **LC 69**
See also Catherine II

Cato, Marcus Porcius 234 B.C.-149
B.C. .... **CMLC 21**
See also Cato the Elder

Cato, Marcus Porcius, the Elder
See Cato, Marcus Porcius

Cato the Elder
See Cato, Marcus Porcius
See also DLB 211

Catton, (Charles) Bruce 1899-1978 . **CLC 35**
See also AITN 1; CA 5-8R; 81-84; CANR
7, 74; DLB 17; SATA 2; SATA-Obit 24

Catullus c. 84 B.C.-54 B.C. .... **CMLC 18**
See also AW 2; CDWLB 1; DLB 211;
RGWL 2

Cauldwell, Frank
See King, Francis (Henry)

Caunitz, William J. 1933-1996 .... **CLC 34**
See also BEST 89:3; CA 125; 130; 152;
CANR 73; INT 130

Causley, Charles (Stanley) 1917- .... **CLC 7**
See also CA 9-12R; CANR 5, 35, 94; CLR
30; CWRI 5; DLB 27; MTCW 1; SATA
3, 66

Caute, (John) David 1936- .... **CLC 29**
See also CA 1-4R; CAAS 4; CANR 1, 33,
64; CBD; CD 5; CN 7; DAM NOV; DLB
14, 231

Cavafy, C(onstantine) P(eter) ... **TCLC 2, 7;
PC 36**
See also Kavafis, Konstantinos Petrou
See also CA 148; DA3; DAM POET; EW
8; MTCW 1; RGWL 2; WP

Cavalcanti, Guido c. 1250-c.
1300 .... **CMLC 54**

Cavallo, Evelyn
See Spark, Muriel (Sarah)

Cavanna, Betty .... **CLC 12**
See also Harrison, Elizabeth (Allen) Ca-
vanna
See also JRDA; MAICYA 1; SAAS 4;
SATA 1, 30

Cavendish, Margaret Lucas
1623-1673 .... **LC 30**
See also DLB 131, 252; RGEL 2

Caxton, William 1421(?)-1491(?) .... **LC 17**
See also DLB 170

Cayer, D. M.
See Duffy, Maureen

Cayrol, Jean 1911- .... **CLC 11**
See also CA 89-92; DLB 83

Cela, Camilo Jose 1916-2002 .... **CLC 4, 13,
59, 122; HLC 1**
See also BEST 90:2; CA 21-24R; CAAS
10; CANR 21, 32, 76; DAM MULT;
DLBY 1989; EW 13; HW 1; MTCW 1, 2;
RGSF 2; RGWL 2

Chiang, Pin-chin 1904-1986
See Ding Ling
See also CA 118

Ch'ien, Chung-shu 1910-1998 .... **CLC 22**
See also CA 130; CANR 73; MTCW 1, 2

Chikamatsu Monzaemon 1653-1724 ... **LC 66**
See also RGWL 2

Child, L. Maria
See Child, Lydia Maria

Child, Lydia Maria 1802-1880 .. **NCLC 6, 73**
See also DLB 1, 74, 243; RGAL 4; SATA 67

Child, Mrs.
See Child, Lydia Maria

Child, Philip 1898-1978 .... **CLC 19, 68**
See also CA 13-14; CAP 1; DLB 68; RHW; SATA 47

Childers, (Robert) Erskine
1870-1922 .... **TCLC 65**
See also CA 113; 153; DLB 70

Childress, Alice 1920-1994 .. **CLC 12, 15, 86, 96; BLC 1; DC 4**
See also AAYA 8; BW 2, 3; BYA 2; CA 45-48; 146; CAD; CANR 3, 27, 50, 74; CLR 14; CWD; DA3; DAM DRAM, MULT, NOV; DFS 2, 8, 14; DLB 7, 38, 249; JRDA; LAIT 5; MAICYA 1, 2; MAIC-YAS 1; MTCW 1, 2; RGAL 4; SATA 7, 48, 81; TCLC 116; TUS; WYA; YAW

Chin, Frank (Chew, Jr.) 1940- ...... **CLC 135; DC 7**
See also CA 33-36R; CANR 71; CD 5; DAM MULT; DLB 206; LAIT 5; RGAL 4

Chin, Marilyn (Mei Ling) 1955- .... **PC 40**
See also CA 129; CANR 70; CWP

Chislett, (Margaret) Anne 1943- ...... **CLC 34**
See also CA 151

Chitty, Thomas Willes 1926- .... **CLC 11**
See also Hinde, Thomas
See also CA 5-8R; CN 7

Chivers, Thomas Holley
1809-1858 .... **NCLC 49**
See also DLB 3, 248; RGAL 4

Choi, Susan .... **CLC 119**

Chomette, Rene Lucien 1898-1981
See Clair, Rene
See also CA 103

Chomsky, (Avram) Noam 1928- ..... **CLC 132**
See also CA 17-20R; CANR 28, 62, 110; DA3; DLB 246; MTCW 1, 2

Chopin, Kate 1851-1904 ... **TCLC 5, 14, 127; SSC 8; WLCS**
See also Chopin, Katherine
See also AAYA 33; AMWS 1; CDALB 1865-1917; DA; DAB; DLB 12, 78; EXPN; EXPS; FW; LAIT 3; MAWW; NFS 3; RGAL 4; RGSF 2; SSFS 2, 13; TUS

Chopin, Katherine
See also Chopin, Kate
See also CA 104; 122; DA3; DAC; DAM MST, NOV

Chretien de Troyes c. 12th cent. - . **CMLC 10**
See also DLB 208; EW 1; RGWL 2; TWA

Christie
See Ichikawa, Kon

Christie, Agatha (Mary Clarissa)
1890-1976 .. **CLC 1, 6, 8, 12, 39, 48, 110**
See also AAYA 9; AITN 1, 2; BPFB 1; BRWS 2; CA 17-20R; 61-64; CANR 10, 37, 108; CBD; CDBLB 1914-1945; CMW 4; CPW; CWD; DA3; DAB; DAC; DAM NOV; DFS 2; DLB 13, 77, 245; MSW; MTCW 1, 2; NFS 8; RGEL 2; RHW; SATA 36; TEA; YAW

Christie, Philippa .... **CLC 21**
See also Pearce, Philippa
See also BYA 5; CANR 109; CLR 9; DLB 161; MAICYA 1; SATA 1, 67, 129

Christine de Pizan 1365(?)-1431(?) .... **LC 9**
See also DLB 208; RGWL 2

Chubb, Elmer
See Masters, Edgar Lee

Chulkov, Mikhail Dmitrievich
1743-1792 .... **LC 2**
See also DLB 150

Churchill, Caryl 1938- .... **CLC 31, 55, 157; DC 5**
See also BRWS 4; CA 102; CANR 22, 46, 108; CBD; CWD; DFS 12; DLB 13; FW; MTCW 1; RGEL 2

Churchill, Charles 1731-1764 .... **LC 3**
See also DLB 109; RGEL 2

Churchill, Sir Winston (Leonard Spencer)
1874-1965 .... **TCLC 113**
See also BRW 6; CA 97-100; CDBLB 1890-1914; DA3; DLB 100; DLBD 16; LAIT 4; MTCW 1, 2

Chute, Carolyn 1947- .... **CLC 39**
See also CA 123

Ciardi, John (Anthony) 1916-1986 . **CLC 10, 40, 44, 129**
See also CA 5-8R; 118; CAAS 2; CANR 5, 33; CLR 19; CWRI 5; DAM POET; DLB 5; DLBY 1986; INT CANR-5; MAICYA 1, 2; MTCW 1, 2; RGAL 4; SAAS 26; SATA 1, 65; SATA-Obit 46

Cibber, Colley 1671-1757 .... **LC 66**
See also DLB 84; RGEL 2

Cicero, Marcus Tullius 106 B.C.-43
B.C. .... **CMLC 3**
See also AW 1; CDWLB 1; DLB 211; RGWL 2

Cimino, Michael 1943- .... **CLC 16**
See also CA 105

Cioran, E(mil) M. 1911-1995 .... **CLC 64**
See also CA 25-28R; 149; CANR 91; DLB 220

Cisneros, Sandra 1954- .. **CLC 69, 118; HLC 1; SSC 32**
See also AAYA 9; AMWS 7; CA 131; CANR 64; CWP; DA3; DAM MULT; DLB 122, 152; EXPN; FW; HW 1, 2; LAIT 5; MAICYA 2; MTCW 2; NFS 2; RGAL 4; RGSF 2; SSFS 3, 13; WLIT 1; YAW

Cixous, Helene 1937- .... **CLC 92**
See also CA 126; CANR 55; CWW 2; DLB 83, 242; FW; GLL 2; MTCW 1, 2; TWA

Clair, Rene .... **CLC 20**
See also Chomette, Rene Lucien

Clampitt, Amy 1920-1994 .... **CLC 32; PC 19**
See also AMWS 9; CA 110; 146; CANR 29, 79; DLB 105

Clancy, Thomas L., Jr. 1947-
See Clancy, Tom
See also CA 125; 131; CANR 62, 105; DA3; INT CA-131; MTCW 1, 2

Clancy, Tom .... **CLC 45, 112**
See also Clancy, Thomas L., Jr.
See also AAYA 9; BEST 89:1, 90:1; BPFB 1; BYA 10, 11; CMW 4; CPW; DAM NOV, POP; DLB 227

Clare, John 1793-1864 .. **NCLC 9, 86; PC 23**
See also DAB; DAM POET; DLB 55, 96; RGEL 2

Clarin
See Alas (y Urena), Leopoldo (Enrique Garcia)

Clark, Al C.
See Goines, Donald

Clark, (Robert) Brian 1932- .... **CLC 29**
See also CA 41-44R; CANR 67; CBD; CD 5

Clark, Curt
See Westlake, Donald E(dwin)

Clark, Eleanor 1913-1996 .... **CLC 5, 19**
See also CA 9-12R; 151; CANR 41; CN 7; DLB 6

Clark, J. P.
See Clark Bekederemo, J(ohnson) P(epper)
See also CDWLB 3; DLB 117

Clark, John Pepper
See Clark Bekederemo, J(ohnson) P(epper)
See also AFW; CD 5; CP 7; RGEL 2

Clark, M. R.
See Clark, Mavis Thorpe

Clark, Mavis Thorpe 1909-1999 ...... **CLC 12**
See also CA 57-60; CANR 8, 37, 107; CLR 30; CWRI 5; MAICYA 1, 2; SAAS 5; SATA 8, 74

Clark, Walter Van Tilburg
1909-1971 .... **CLC 28**
See also CA 9-12R; 33-36R; CANR 63; DLB 9, 206; LAIT 2; RGAL 4; SATA 8

Clark Bekederemo, J(ohnson) P(epper)
1935- .... **CLC 38; BLC 1; DC 5**
See also Clark, J. P.; Clark, John Pepper
See also BW 1; CA 65-68; CANR 16, 72; DAM DRAM, MULT; DFS 13; MTCW 1

Clarke, Arthur C(harles) 1917- .... **CLC 1, 4, 13, 18, 35, 136; SSC 3**
See also AAYA 4, 33; BPFB 1; BYA 13; CA 1-4R; CANR 2, 28, 55, 74; CN 7; CPW; DA3; DAM POP; DLB 261; JRDA; LAIT 5; MAICYA 1, 2; MTCW 1, 2; SATA 13, 70, 115; SCFW; SFW 4; SSFS 4; YAW

Clarke, Austin 1896-1974 .... **CLC 6, 9**
See also CA 29-32; 49-52; CAP 2; DAM POET; DLB 10, 20; RGEL 2

Clarke, Austin C(hesterfield) 1934- .. **CLC 8, 53; BLC 1; SSC 45**
See also BW 1; CA 25-28R; CAAS 16; CANR 14, 32, 68; CN 7; DAC; DAM MULT; DLB 53, 125; DNFS 2; RGSF 2

Clarke, Gillian 1937- .... **CLC 61**
See also CA 106; CP 7; CWP; DLB 40

Clarke, Marcus (Andrew Hislop)
1846-1881 .... **NCLC 19**
See also DLB 230; RGEL 2; RGSF 2

Clarke, Shirley 1925-1997 .... **CLC 16**
See also CA 189

Clash, The
See Headon, (Nicky) Topper; Jones, Mick; Simonon, Paul; Strummer, Joe

Claudel, Paul (Louis Charles Marie)
1868-1955 .... **TCLC 2, 10**
See also CA 104; 165; DLB 192, 258; EW 8; GFL 1789 to the Present; RGWL 2; TWA

Claudian 370(?)-404(?) .... **CMLC 46**
See also RGWL 2

Claudius, Matthias 1740-1815 .... **NCLC 75**
See also DLB 97

Clavell, James (duMaresq)
1925-1994 .... **CLC 6, 25, 87**
See also BPFB 1; CA 25-28R; 146; CANR 26, 48; CPW; DA3; DAM NOV, POP; MTCW 1, 2; NFS 10; RHW

Clayman, Gregory .... **CLC 65**

Cleaver, (Leroy) Eldridge
1935-1998 .... **CLC 30, 119; BLC 1**
See also BW 1, 3; CA 21-24R; 167; CANR 16, 75; DA3; DAM MULT; MTCW 2; YAW

Cleese, John (Marwood) 1939- .... **CLC 21**
See also Monty Python
See also CA 112; 116; CANR 35; MTCW 1

Cleishbotham, Jebediah
See Scott, Sir Walter

Cleland, John 1710-1789 .... **LC 2, 48**
See also DLB 39; RGEL 2

Clemens, Samuel Langhorne 1835-1910
See Twain, Mark
See also CA 104; 135; CDALB 1865-1917;
DA; DA3; DAB; DAC; DAM MST, NOV;
DLB 12, 23, 64, 74, 186, 189; JRDA;
MAICYA 1, 2; NCFS 4; SATA 100; YABC
2

Clement of Alexandria
150(?)-215(?) .... **CMLC 41**

Cleophil
See Congreve, William

Clerihew, E.
See Bentley, E(dmund) C(lerihew)

Clerk, N. W.
See Lewis, C(live) S(taples)

Cliff, Jimmy .... **CLC 21**
See also Chambers, James
See also CA 193

Cliff, Michelle 1946- .... **CLC 120; BLCS**
See also BW 2; CA 116; CANR 39, 72; CD-
WLB 3; DLB 157; FW; GLL 2

Clifford, Lady Anne 1590-1676 .... **LC 76**
See also DLB 151

Clifton, (Thelma) Lucille 1936- . **CLC 19, 66,
162; BLC 1; PC 17**
See also AFAW 2; BW 2, 3; CA 49-52;
CANR 2, 24, 42, 76, 97; CLR 5; CP 7;
CSW; CWP; CWRI 5; DA3; DAM MULT,
POET; DLB 5, 41; EXPP; MAICYA 1, 2;
MTCW 1, 2; PFS 1, 14; SATA 20, 69,
128; WP

Clinton, Dirk
See Silverberg, Robert

Clough, Arthur Hugh 1819-1861 ... **NCLC 27**
See also BRW 5; DLB 32; RGEL 2

Clutha, Janet Paterson Frame 1924-
See Frame, Janet
See also CA 1-4R; CANR 2, 36, 76; MTCW
1, 2; SATA 119

Clyne, Terence
See Blatty, William Peter

Cobalt, Martin
See Mayne, William (James Carter)

Cobb, Irvin S(hrewsbury)
1876-1944 .... **TCLC 77**
See also CA 175; DLB 11, 25, 86

Cobbett, William 1763-1835 .... **NCLC 49**
See also DLB 43, 107, 158; RGEL 2

Coburn, D(onald) L(ee) 1938- .... **CLC 10**
See also CA 89-92

Cocteau, Jean (Maurice Eugene Clement)
1889-1963 ...... **CLC 1, 8, 15, 16, 43; DC
17; WLC**
See also CA 25-28; CANR 40; CAP 2; DA;
DA3; DAB; DAC; DAM DRAM, MST,
NOV; DLB 65, 258; EW 10; GFL 1789 to
the Present; MTCW 1, 2; RGWL 2; TCLC
119; TWA

Codrescu, Andrei 1946- .... **CLC 46, 121**
See also CA 33-36R; CAAS 19; CANR 13,
34, 53, 76; DA3; DAM POET; MTCW 2

Coe, Max
See Bourne, Randolph S(illiman)

Coe, Tucker
See Westlake, Donald E(dwin)

Coen, Ethan 1958- .... **CLC 108**
See also CA 126; CANR 85

Coen, Joel 1955- .... **CLC 108**
See also CA 126

The Coen Brothers
See Coen, Ethan; Coen, Joel

Coetzee, J(ohn) M(ichael) 1940- ...... **CLC 23,
33, 66, 117, 161, 162**
See also AAYA 37; AFW; BRWS 6; CA 77-
80; CANR 41, 54, 74; CN 7; DA3; DAM
NOV; DLB 225; MTCW 1, 2; WLIT 2

Coffey, Brian
See Koontz, Dean R(ay)

Coffin, Robert P(eter) Tristram
1892-1955 .... **TCLC 95**
See also CA 123; 169; DLB 45

Cohan, George M(ichael)
1878-1942 .... **TCLC 60**
See also CA 157; DLB 249; RGAL 4

Cohen, Arthur A(llen) 1928-1986 ...... **CLC 7,
31**
See also CA 1-4R; 120; CANR 1, 17, 42;
DLB 28

Cohen, Leonard (Norman) 1934- ...... **CLC 3,
38**
See also CA 21-24R; CANR 14, 69; CN 7;
CP 7; DAC; DAM MST; DLB 53; MTCW
1

Cohen, Matt(hew) 1942-1999 .... **CLC 19**
See also CA 61-64; 187; CAAS 18; CANR
40; CN 7; DAC; DLB 53

Cohen-Solal, Annie 19(?)- .... **CLC 50**

Colegate, Isabel 1931- .... **CLC 36**
See also CA 17-20R; CANR 8, 22, 74; CN
7; DLB 14, 231; INT CANR-22; MTCW
1

Coleman, Emmett
See Reed, Ishmael

Coleridge, Hartley 1796-1849 .... **NCLC 90**
See also DLB 96

Coleridge, M. E.
See Coleridge, Mary E(lizabeth)

Coleridge, Mary E(lizabeth)
1861-1907 .... **TCLC 73**
See also CA 116; 166; DLB 19, 98

Coleridge, Samuel Taylor
1772-1834 ...... **NCLC 9, 54, 99, 111; PC
11, 39; WLC**
See also BRW 4; BRWR 2; BYA 4; CD-
BLB 1789-1832; DA; DA3; DAB; DAC;
DAM MST, POET; DLB 93, 107; EXPP;
PAB; PFS 4, 5; RGEL 2; TEA; WLIT 3;
WP

Coleridge, Sara 1802-1852 .... **NCLC 31**
See also DLB 199

Coles, Don 1928- .... **CLC 46**
See also CA 115; CANR 38; CP 7

Coles, Robert (Martin) 1929- .... **CLC 108**
See also CA 45-48; CANR 3, 32, 66, 70;
INT CANR-32; SATA 23

Colette, (Sidonie-Gabrielle)
1873-1954 .... **TCLC 1, 5, 16; SSC 10**
See also Willy, Colette
See also CA 104; 131; DA3; DAM NOV;
DLB 65; EW 9; GFL 1789 to the Present;
MTCW 1, 2; RGWL 2; TWA

Collett, (Jacobine) Camilla (Wergeland)
1813-1895 .... **NCLC 22**

Collier, Christopher 1930- .... **CLC 30**
See also AAYA 13; BYA 2; CA 33-36R;
CANR 13, 33, 102; JRDA; MAICYA 1,
2; SATA 16, 70; WYA; YAW 1

Collier, James Lincoln 1928- .... **CLC 30**
See also AAYA 13; BYA 2; CA 9-12R;
CANR 4, 33, 60, 102; CLR 3; DAM POP;
JRDA; MAICYA 1, 2; SAAS 21; SATA 8,
70; WYA; YAW 1

Collier, Jeremy 1650-1726 .... **LC 6**

Collier, John 1901-1980 . **TCLC 127; SSC 19**
See also CA 65-68; 97-100; CANR 10;
DLB 77, 255; FANT; SUFW

Collingwood, R(obin) G(eorge)
1889(?)-1943 .... **TCLC 67**
See also CA 117; 155; DLB 262

Collins, Hunt
See Hunter, Evan

Collins, Linda 1931- .... **CLC 44**
See also CA 125

Collins, (William) Wilkie
1824-1889 .... **NCLC 1, 18, 93**
See also BRWS 6; CDBLB 1832-1890;
CMW 4; DLB 18, 70, 159; MSW; RGEL
2; RGSF 2; SUFW; WLIT 4

Collins, William 1721-1759 .... **LC 4, 40**
See also BRW 3; DAM POET; DLB 109;
RGEL 2

Collodi, Carlo .... **NCLC 54**
See also Lorenzini, Carlo
See also CLR 5; WCH

Colman, George
See Glassco, John

Colonna, Vittoria 1492-1547 .... **LC 71**
See also RGWL 2

Colt, Winchester Remington
See Hubbard, L(afayette) Ron(ald)

Colter, Cyrus 1910-2002 .... **CLC 58**
See also BW 1; CA 65-68; CANR 10, 66;
CN 7; DLB 33

Colton, James
See Hansen, Joseph
See also GLL 1

Colum, Padraic 1881-1972 .... **CLC 28**
See also BYA 4; CA 73-76; 33-36R; CANR
35; CLR 36; CWRI 5; DLB 19; MAICYA
1, 2; MTCW 1; RGEL 2; SATA 15; WCH

Colvin, James
See Moorcock, Michael (John)

Colwin, Laurie (E.) 1944-1992 .... **CLC 5, 13,
23, 84**
See also CA 89-92; 139; CANR 20, 46;
DLB 218; DLBY 1980; MTCW 1

Comfort, Alex(ander) 1920-2000 .... **CLC 7**
See also CA 1-4R; 190; CANR 1, 45; CP 7;
DAM POP; MTCW 1

Comfort, Montgomery
See Campbell, (John) Ramsey

Compton-Burnett, I(vy)
1892(?)-1969 .... **CLC 1, 3, 10, 15, 34**
See also BRW 7; CA 1-4R; 25-28R; CANR
4; DAM NOV; DLB 36; MTCW 1; RGEL
2

Comstock, Anthony 1844-1915 ...... **TCLC 13**
See also CA 110; 169

Comte, Auguste 1798-1857 .... **NCLC 54**

Conan Doyle, Arthur
See Doyle, Sir Arthur Conan
See also BPFB 1; BYA 4, 5, 11

Conde (Abellan), Carmen 1901-1996
See also CA 177; DLB 108; HLCS 1; HW
2

Conde, Maryse 1937- ..... **CLC 52, 92; BLCS**
See also BW 2, 3; CA 110; CAAE 190;
CANR 30, 53, 76; CWW 2; DAM MULT;
MTCW 1

Condillac, Etienne Bonnot de
1714-1780 .... **LC 26**

Condon, Richard (Thomas)
1915-1996 .... **CLC 4, 6, 8, 10, 45, 100**
See also BEST 90:3; BPFB 1; CA 1-4R;
151; CAAS 1; CANR 2, 23; CMW 4; CN
7; DAM NOV; INT CANR-23; MTCW 1,
2

Confucius 551 B.C.-479 B.C. .... **CMLC 19;
WLCS**
See also DA; DA3; DAB; DAC; DAM
MST

Congreve, William 1670-1729 . **LC 5, 21; DC
2; WLC**
See also BRW 2; CDBLB 1660-1789; DA;
DAB; DAC; DAM DRAM, MST, POET;
DFS 15; DLB 39, 84; RGEL 2; WLIT 3

Connell, Evan S(helby), Jr. 1924- . **CLC 4, 6,
45**
See also AAYA 7; CA 1-4R; CAAS 2;
CANR 2, 39, 76, 97; CN 7; DAM NOV;
DLB 2; DLBY 1981; MTCW 1, 2

Crabbe, George 1754-1832 .... **NCLC 26**
See also BRW 3; DLB 93; RGEL 2
Crace, Jim 1946- .... **CLC 157**
See also CA 128; 135; CANR 55, 70; CN
7; DLB 231; INT CA-135
Craddock, Charles Egbert
See Murfree, Mary Noailles
Craig, A. A.
See Anderson, Poul (William)
Craik, Mrs.
See Craik, Dinah Maria (Mulock)
See also RGEL 2
Craik, Dinah Maria (Mulock)
1826-1887 .... **NCLC 38**
See also Craik, Mrs.; Mulock, Dinah Maria
See also DLB 35, 163; MAICYA 1, 2;
SATA 34
Cram, Ralph Adams 1863-1942 ..... **TCLC 45**
See also CA 160
Cranch, Christopher Pearse
1813-1892 .... **NCLC 115**
See also DLB 1, 42, 243
Crane, (Harold) Hart 1899-1932 .... **TCLC 2,
5, 80; PC 3; WLC**
See also AMW; CA 104; 127; CDALB
1917-1929; DA; DA3; DAB; DAC; DAM
MST, POET; DLB 4, 48; MTCW 1, 2;
RGAL 4; TUS
Crane, R(onald) S(almon)
1886-1967 .... **CLC 27**
See also CA 85-88; DLB 63
Cranshaw, Stanley
See Fisher, Dorothy (Frances) Canfield
Crase, Douglas 1944- .... **CLC 58**
See also CA 106
Crashaw, Richard 1612(?)-1649 .... **LC 24**
See also BRW 2; DLB 126; PAB; RGEL 2
Cratinus c. 519 B.C.-c. 422 B.C. ... **CMLC 54**
Craven, Margaret 1901-1980 .... **CLC 17**
See also BYA 2; CA 103; CCA 1; DAC;
LAIT 5
Crawford, F(rancis) Marion
1854-1909 .... **TCLC 10**
See also CA 107; 168; DLB 71; HGG;
RGAL 4; SUFW
Crawford, Isabella Valancy
1850-1887 .... **NCLC 12**
See also DLB 92; RGEL 2
Crayon, Geoffrey
See Irving, Washington
Creasey, John 1908-1973 .... **CLC 11**
See also Marric, J. J.
See also CA 5-8R; 41-44R; CANR 8, 59;
CMW 4; DLB 77; MTCW 1
Crebillon, Claude Prosper Jolyot de (fils)
1707-1777 .... **LC 1, 28**
See also GFL Beginnings to 1789
Credo
See Creasey, John
Credo, Alvaro J. de
See Prado (Calvo), Pedro
Creeley, Robert (White) 1926- .. **CLC 1, 2, 4,
8, 11, 15, 36, 78**
See also AMWS 4; CA 1-4R; CAAS 10;
CANR 23, 43, 89; CP 7; DA3; DAM
POET; DLB 5, 16, 169; DLBD 17;
MTCW 1, 2; RGAL 4; WP
Crevecoeur, Hector St. John de
See Crevecoeur, Michel Guillaume Jean de
See also ANW
Crevecoeur, Michel Guillaume Jean de
1735-1813 .... **NCLC 105**
See also Crevecoeur, Hector St. John de
See also AMWS 1; DLB 37
Crevel, Rene 1900-1935 .... **TCLC 112**
See also GLL 2

Crews, Harry (Eugene) 1935- ..... **CLC 6, 23,
49**
See also AITN 1; AMWS 11; BPFB 1; CA
25-28R; CANR 20, 57; CN 7; CSW; DA3;
DLB 6, 143, 185; MTCW 1, 2; RGAL 4
Crichton, (John) Michael 1942- .... **CLC 2, 6,
54, 90**
See also AAYA 10; AITN 2; BPFB 1; CA
25-28R; CANR 13, 40, 54, 76; CMW 4;
CN 7; CPW; DA3; DAM NOV, POP;
DLBY 1981; INT CANR-13; JRDA;
MTCW 1, 2; SATA 9, 88; SFW 4; YAW
Crispin, Edmund .... **CLC 22**
See also Montgomery, (Robert) Bruce
See also DLB 87; MSW
Cristofer, Michael 1945(?)- .... **CLC 28**
See also CA 110; 152; CAD; CD 5; DAM
DRAM; DFS 15; DLB 7
Croce, Benedetto 1866-1952 .... **TCLC 37**
See also CA 120; 155; EW 8
Crockett, David 1786-1836 .... **NCLC 8**
See also DLB 3, 11, 183, 248
Crockett, Davy
See Crockett, David
Crofts, Freeman Wills 1879-1957 .. **TCLC 55**
See also CA 115; 195; CMW 4; DLB 77;
MSW
Croker, John Wilson 1780-1857 .... **NCLC 10**
See also DLB 110
Crommelynck, Fernand 1885-1970 .. **CLC 75**
See also CA 189; 89-92
Cromwell, Oliver 1599-1658 .... **LC 43**
Cronenberg, David 1943- .... **CLC 143**
See also CA 138; CCA 1
Cronin, A(rchibald) J(oseph)
1896-1981 .... **CLC 32**
See also BPFB 1; CA 1-4R; 102; CANR 5;
DLB 191; SATA 47; SATA-Obit 25
Cross, Amanda
See Heilbrun, Carolyn G(old)
See also BPFB 1; CMW; CPW; MSW
Crothers, Rachel 1878-1958 .... **TCLC 19**
See also CA 113; 194; CAD; CWD; DLB
7, 266; RGAL 4
Croves, Hal
See Traven, B.
Crow Dog, Mary (Ellen) (?)- .... **CLC 93**
See also Brave Bird, Mary
See also CA 154
Crowfield, Christopher
See Stowe, Harriet (Elizabeth) Beecher
Crowley, Aleister .... **TCLC 7**
See also Crowley, Edward Alexander
See also GLL 1
Crowley, Edward Alexander 1875-1947
See Crowley, Aleister
See also CA 104; HGG
Crowley, John 1942- .... **CLC 57**
See also BPFB 1; CA 61-64; CANR 43, 98;
DLBY 1982; SATA 65; SFW 4
Crud
See Crumb, R(obert)
Crumarums
See Crumb, R(obert)
Crumb, R(obert) 1943- .... **CLC 17**
See also CA 106; CANR 107
Crumbum
See Crumb, R(obert)
Crumski
See Crumb, R(obert)
Crum the Bum
See Crumb, R(obert)
Crunk
See Crumb, R(obert)
Crustt
See Crumb, R(obert)
Crutchfield, Les
See Trumbo, Dalton

Cruz, Victor Hernandez 1949- .... **PC 37**
See also BW 2; CA 65-68; CAAS 17;
CANR 14, 32, 74; CP 7; DAM MULT,
POET; DLB 41; DNFS 1; EXPP; HLC 1;
HW 1, 2; MTCW 1; WP
Cryer, Gretchen (Kiger) 1935- .... **CLC 21**
See also CA 114; 123
Csath, Geza 1887-1919 .... **TCLC 13**
See also CA 111
Cudlip, David R(ockwell) 1933- .... **CLC 34**
See also CA 177
Cullen, Countee 1903-1946 .... **TCLC 4, 37;
BLC 1; PC 20; WLCS**
See also AFAW 2; AMWS 4; BW 1; CA
108; 124; CDALB 1917-1929; DA; DA3;
DAC; DAM MST, MULT, POET; DLB 4,
48, 51; EXPP; MTCW 1, 2; PFS 3; RGAL
4; SATA 18; WP
Cum, R.
See Crumb, R(obert)
Cummings, Bruce F(rederick) 1889-1919
See Barbellion, W. N. P.
See also CA 123
Cummings, E(dward) E(stlin)
1894-1962 .. **CLC 1, 3, 8, 12, 15, 68; PC
5; WLC**
See also AAYA 41; AMW; CA 73-76;
CANR 31; CDALB 1929-1941; DA;
DA3; DAB; DAC; DAM MST, POET;
DLB 4, 48; EXPP; MTCW 1, 2; PAB;
PFS 1, 3, 12, 13; RGAL 4; TUS; WP
Cunha, Euclides (Rodrigues Pimenta) da
1866-1909 .... **TCLC 24**
See also CA 123; LAW; WLIT 1
Cunningham, E. V.
See Fast, Howard (Melvin)
Cunningham, J(ames) V(incent)
1911-1985 .... **CLC 3, 31**
See also CA 1-4R; 115; CANR 1, 72; DLB
5
Cunningham, Julia (Woolfolk)
1916- .... **CLC 12**
See also CA 9-12R; CANR 4, 19, 36; CWRI
5; JRDA; MAICYA 1, 2; SAAS 2; SATA
1, 26, 132
Cunningham, Michael 1952- .... **CLC 34**
See also CA 136; CANR 96; GLL 2
Cunninghame Graham, R. B.
See Cunninghame Graham, Robert
(Gallnigad) Bontine
**Cunninghame Graham, Robert (Gallnigad)
Bontine** 1852-1936 .... **TCLC 19**
See also Graham, R(obert) B(ontine) Cun-
ninghame
See also CA 119; 184
Currie, Ellen 19(?)- .... **CLC 44**
Curtin, Philip
See Lowndes, Marie Adelaide (Belloc)
Curtis, Price
See Ellison, Harlan (Jay)
Cusanus, Nicolaus 1401-1464 .... **LC 80**
See also Nicholas of Cusa
Cutrate, Joe
See Spiegelman, Art
Cynewulf c. 770- .... **CMLC 23**
See also DLB 146; RGEL 2
Cyrano de Bergerac, Savinien de
1619-1655 .... **LC 65**
See also DLB 268; GFL Beginnings to
1789; RGWL 2
Czaczkes, Shmuel Yosef Halevi
See Agnon, S(hmuel) Y(osef Halevi)
Dabrowska, Maria (Szumska)
1889-1965 .... **CLC 15**
See also CA 106; CDWLB 4; DLB 215
Dabydeen, David 1955- .... **CLC 34**
See also BW 1; CA 125; CANR 56, 92; CN
7; CP 7

Dexter, John
See Bradley, Marion Zimmer
See also GLL 1

Dexter, Martin
See Faust, Frederick (Schiller)
See also TCWW 2

Dexter, Pete 1943- .... **CLC 34, 55**
See also BEST 89:2; CA 127; 131; CPW; DAM POP; INT 131; MTCW 1

Diamano, Silmang
See Senghor, Leopold Sedar

Diamond, Neil 1941- .... **CLC 30**
See also CA 108

Diaz del Castillo, Bernal 1496-1584 .. **LC 31; HLCS 1**
See also LAW

di Bassetto, Corno
See Shaw, George Bernard

Dick, Philip K(indred) 1928-1982 ... **CLC 10, 30, 72**
See also AAYA 24; BPFB 1; BYA 11; CA 49-52; 106; CANR 2, 16; CPW; DA3; DAM NOV, POP; DLB 8; MTCW 1, 2; NFS 5; SCFW; SFW 4

Dickens, Charles (John Huffam) 1812-1870 .... **NCLC 3, 8, 18, 26, 37, 50, 86, 105, 113; SSC 17, 49; WLC**
See also AAYA 23; BRW 5; BYA 1, 2, 3, 13, 14; CDBLB 1832-1890; CMW 4; DA; DA3; DAB; DAC; DAM MST, NOV; DLB 21, 55, 70, 159, 166; EXPN; HGG; JRDA; LAIT 1, 2; MAICYA 1, 2; NFS 4, 5, 10, 14; RGEL 2; RGSF 2; SATA 15; SUFW; TEA; WCH; WLIT 4; WYA

Dickey, James (Lafayette) 1923-1997 .... **CLC 1, 2, 4, 7, 10, 15, 47, 109; PC 40**
See also AITN 1, 2; AMWS 4; BPFB 1; CA 9-12R; 156; CABS 2; CANR 10, 48, 61, 105; CDALB 1968-1988; CP 7; CPW; CSW; DA3; DAM NOV, POET, POP; DLB 5, 193; DLBD 7; DLBY 1982, 1993, 1996, 1997, 1998; INT CANR-10; MTCW 1, 2; NFS 9; PFS 6, 11; RGAL 4; TUS

Dickey, William 1928-1994 .... **CLC 3, 28**
See also CA 9-12R; 145; CANR 24, 79; DLB 5

Dickinson, Charles 1951- .... **CLC 49**
See also CA 128

Dickinson, Emily (Elizabeth) 1830-1886 ... **NCLC 21, 77; PC 1; WLC**
See also AAYA 22; AMW; AMWR 1; CDALB 1865-1917; DA; DA3; DAB; DAC; DAM MST, POET; DLB 1, 243; EXPP; MAWW; PAB; PFS 1, 2, 3, 4, 5, 6, 8, 10, 11, 13; RGAL 4; SATA 29; TUS; WP; WYA

Dickinson, Mrs. Herbert Ward
See Phelps, Elizabeth Stuart

Dickinson, Peter (Malcolm) 1927- .. **CLC 12, 35**
See also AAYA 9; BYA 5; CA 41-44R; CANR 31, 58, 88; CLR 29; CMW 4; DLB 87, 161; JRDA; MAICYA 1, 2; SATA 5, 62, 95; SFW 4; WYA; YAW

Dickson, Carr
See Carr, John Dickson

Dickson, Carter
See Carr, John Dickson

Diderot, Denis 1713-1784 .... **LC 26**
See also EW 4; GFL Beginnings to 1789; RGWL 2

Didion, Joan 1934- . **CLC 1, 3, 8, 14, 32, 129**
See also AITN 1; AMWS 4; CA 5-8R; CANR 14, 52, 76; CDALB 1968-1988; CN 7; DA3; DAM NOV; DLB 2, 173, 185; DLBY 1981, 1986; MAWW; MTCW 1, 2; NFS 3; RGAL 4; TCWW 2; TUS

Dietrich, Robert
See Hunt, E(verette) Howard, (Jr.)

Difusa, Pati
See Almodovar, Pedro

Dillard, Annie 1945- .... **CLC 9, 60, 115**
See also AAYA 6, 43; AMWS 6; ANW; CA 49-52; CANR 3, 43, 62, 90; DA3; DAM NOV; DLBY 1980; LAIT 4, 5; MTCW 1, 2; NCFS 1; RGAL 4; SATA 10; TUS

Dillard, R(ichard) H(enry) W(ilde) 1937- .... **CLC 5**
See also CA 21-24R; CAAS 7; CANR 10; CP 7; CSW; DLB 5, 244

Dillon, Eilis 1920-1994 .... **CLC 17**
See also CA 9-12R, 182; 147; CAAE 182; CAAS 3; CANR 4, 38, 78; CLR 26; MAICYA 1, 2; MAICYAS 1; SATA 2, 74; SATA-Essay 105; SATA-Obit 83; YAW

Dimont, Penelope
See Mortimer, Penelope (Ruth)

Dinesen, Isak .... **CLC 10, 29, 95; SSC 7**
See also Blixen, Karen (Christentze Dinesen)
See also EW 10; EXPS; FW; HGG; LAIT 3; MTCW 1; NCFS 2; NFS 9; RGSF 2; RGWL 2; SSFS 3, 6, 13; WLIT 2

Ding Ling .... **CLC 68**
See also Chiang, Pin-chin

Diphusa, Patty
See Almodovar, Pedro

Disch, Thomas M(ichael) 1940- ... **CLC 7, 36**
See also AAYA 17; BPFB 1; CA 21-24R; CAAS 4; CANR 17, 36, 54, 89; CLR 18; CP 7; DA3; DLB 8; HGG; MAICYA 1, 2; MTCW 1, 2; SAAS 15; SATA 92; SCFW; SFW 4

Disch, Tom
See Disch, Thomas M(ichael)

d'Isly, Georges
See Simenon, Georges (Jacques Christian)

Disraeli, Benjamin 1804-1881 ... **NCLC 2, 39, 79**
See also BRW 4; DLB 21, 55; RGEL 2

Ditcum, Steve
See Crumb, R(obert)

Dixon, Paige
See Corcoran, Barbara (Asenath)

Dixon, Stephen 1936- .... **CLC 52; SSC 16**
See also CA 89-92; CANR 17, 40, 54, 91; CN 7; DLB 130

Doak, Annie
See Dillard, Annie

Dobell, Sydney Thompson 1824-1874 .... **NCLC 43**
See also DLB 32; RGEL 2

Doblin, Alfred .... **TCLC 13**
See also Doeblin, Alfred
See also CDWLB 2; RGWL 2

Dobrolyubov, Nikolai Alexandrovich 1836-1861 .... **NCLC 5**

Dobson, Austin 1840-1921 .... **TCLC 79**
See also DLB 35, 144

Dobyns, Stephen 1941- .... **CLC 37**
See also CA 45-48; CANR 2, 18, 99; CMW 4; CP 7

Doctorow, E(dgar) L(aurence) 1931- .... **CLC 6, 11, 15, 18, 37, 44, 65, 113**
See also AAYA 22; AITN 2; AMWS 4; BEST 89:3; BPFB 1; CA 45-48; CANR 2, 33, 51, 76, 97; CDALB 1968-1988; CN 7; CPW; DA3; DAM NOV, POP; DLB 2, 28, 173; DLBY 1980; LAIT 3; MTCW 1, 2; NFS 6; RGAL 4; RHW; TUS

Dodgson, Charles L(utwidge) 1832-1898
See Carroll, Lewis
See also CLR 2; DA; DA3; DAB; DAC; DAM MST, NOV, POET; MAICYA 1, 2; SATA 100; YABC 2

Dodson, Owen (Vincent) 1914-1983 .... **CLC 79; BLC 1**
See also BW 1; CA 65-68; 110; CANR 24; DAM MULT; DLB 76

Doeblin, Alfred 1878-1957 .... **TCLC 13**
See also Doblin, Alfred
See also CA 110; 141; DLB 66

Doerr, Harriet 1910- .... **CLC 34**
See also CA 117; 122; CANR 47; INT 122

Domecq, H(onorio Bustos)
See Bioy Casares, Adolfo

Domecq, H(onorio) Bustos
See Bioy Casares, Adolfo; Borges, Jorge Luis

Domini, Rey
See Lorde, Audre (Geraldine)
See also GLL 1

Dominique
See Proust, (Valentin-Louis-George-Eugene-)Marcel

Don, A
See Stephen, Sir Leslie

Donaldson, Stephen R(eeder) 1947- .... **CLC 46, 138**
See also AAYA 36; BPFB 1; CA 89-92; CANR 13, 55, 99; CPW; DAM POP; FANT; INT CANR-13; SATA 121; SFW 4; SUFW

Donleavy, J(ames) P(atrick) 1926- .... **CLC 1, 4, 6, 10, 45**
See also AITN 2; BPFB 1; CA 9-12R; CANR 24, 49, 62, 80; CBD; CD 5; CN 7; DLB 6, 173; INT CANR-24; MTCW 1, 2; RGAL 4

Donne, John 1572-1631 ..... **LC 10, 24; PC 1, 43; WLC**
See also BRW 1; BRWR 2; CDBLB Before 1660; DA; DAB; DAC; DAM MST, POET; DLB 121, 151; EXPP; PAB; PFS 2, 11; RGEL 2; TEA; WLIT 3; WP

Donnell, David 1939(?)- .... **CLC 34**
See also CA 197

Donoghue, P. S.
See Hunt, E(verette) Howard, (Jr.)

Donoso (Yanez), Jose 1924-1996 ... **CLC 4, 8, 11, 32, 99; HLC 1; SSC 34**
See also CA 81-84; 155; CANR 32, 73; CD-WLB 3; DAM MULT; DLB 113; HW 1, 2; LAW; LAWS 1; MTCW 1, 2; RGSF 2; WLIT 1

Donovan, John 1928-1992 .... **CLC 35**
See also AAYA 20; CA 97-100; 137; CLR 3; MAICYA 1, 2; SATA 72; SATA-Brief 29; YAW

Don Roberto
See Cunninghame Graham, Robert (Gallnigad) Bontine

Doolittle, Hilda 1886-1961 . **CLC 3, 8, 14, 31, 34, 73; PC 5; WLC**
See also H. D.
See also AMWS 1; CA 97-100; CANR 35; DA; DAC; DAM MST, POET; DLB 4, 45; FW; GLL 1; MAWW; MTCW 1, 2; PFS 6; RGAL 4

Doppo, Kunikida .... **TCLC 99**
See also Kunikida Doppo

Dorfman, Ariel 1942- .... **CLC 48, 77; HLC 1**
See also CA 124; 130; CANR 67, 70; CWW 2; DAM MULT; DFS 4; HW 1, 2; INT CA-130; WLIT 1

Dorn, Edward (Merton) 1929-1999 .... **CLC 10, 18**
See also CA 93-96; 187; CANR 42, 79; CP 7; DLB 5; INT 93-96; WP

Dor-Ner, Zvi .... **CLC 70**

Dorris, Michael (Anthony) 1945-1997 .... **CLC 109**
See also AAYA 20; BEST 90:1; BYA 12; CA 102; 157; CANR 19, 46, 75; CLR 58;

DA3; DAM MULT, NOV; DLB 175;
LAIT 5; MTCW 2; NFS 3; NNAL; RGAL
4; SATA 75; SATA-Obit 94; TCWW 2;
YAW
Dorris, Michael A.
See Dorris, Michael (Anthony)
Dorsan, Luc
See Simenon, Georges (Jacques Christian)
Dorsange, Jean
See Simenon, Georges (Jacques Christian)
Dos Passos, John (Roderigo)
1896-1970 ... **CLC 1, 4, 8, 11, 15, 25, 34,
82; WLC**
See also AMW; BPFB 1; CA 1-4R; 29-32R;
CANR 3; CDALB 1929-1941; DA; DA3;
DAB; DAC; DAM MST, NOV; DLB 4,
9; DLBD 1, 15; DLBY 1996; MTCW 1,
2; NFS 14; RGAL 4; TUS
Dossage, Jean
See Simenon, Georges (Jacques Christian)
Dostoevsky, Fedor Mikhailovich
1821-1881 . **NCLC 2, 7, 21, 33, 43; SSC
2, 33, 44; WLC**
See also Dostoevsky, Fyodor
See also AAYA 40; DA; DA3; DAB; DAC;
DAM MST, NOV; EW 7; EXPN; NFS 3,
8; RGSF 2; RGWL 2; SSFS 8; TWA
Dostoevsky, Fyodor
See Dostoevsky, Fedor Mikhailovich
See also DLB 238
Doughty, Charles M(ontagu)
1843-1926 .... **TCLC 27**
See also CA 115; 178; DLB 19, 57, 174
Douglas, Ellen .... **CLC 73**
See also Haxton, Josephine Ayres; William-
son, Ellen Douglas
See also CN 7; CSW
Douglas, Gavin 1475(?)-1522 .... **LC 20**
See also DLB 132; RGEL 2
Douglas, George
See Brown, George Douglas
See also RGEL 2
Douglas, Keith (Castellain)
1920-1944 .... **TCLC 40**
See also BRW 7; CA 160; DLB 27; PAB;
RGEL 2
Douglas, Leonard
See Bradbury, Ray (Douglas)
Douglas, Michael
See Crichton, (John) Michael
Douglas, (George) Norman
1868-1952 .... **TCLC 68**
See also BRW 6; CA 119; 157; DLB 34,
195; RGEL 2
Douglas, William
See Brown, George Douglas
Douglass, Frederick 1817(?)-1895 .. **NCLC 7,
55; BLC 1; WLC**
See also AFAW 1, 2; AMWS 3; CDALB
1640-1865; DA; DA3; DAC; DAM MST,
MULT; DLB 1, 43, 50, 79, 243; FW;
LAIT 2; NCFS 2; RGAL 4; SATA 29
Dourado, (Waldomiro Freitas) Autran
1926- .... **CLC 23, 60**
See also CA 25-28R; 179; CANR 34, 81;
DLB 145; HW 2
Dourado, Waldomiro Autran
See Dourado, (Waldomiro Freitas) Autran
See also CA 179
Dove, Rita (Frances) 1952- .... **CLC 50, 81;
BLCS; PC 6**
See also AMWS 4; BW 2; CA 109; CAAS
19; CANR 27, 42, 68, 76, 97; CDALBS;
CP 7; CSW; CWP; DA3; DAM MULT,
POET; DLB 120; EXPP; MTCW 1; PFS
1, 15; RGAL 4
Doveglion
See Villa, Jose Garcia

Dowell, Coleman 1925-1985 .... **CLC 60**
See also CA 25-28R; 117; CANR 10; DLB
130; GLL 2
Dowson, Ernest (Christopher)
1867-1900 .... **TCLC 4**
See also CA 105; 150; DLB 19, 135; RGEL
2
Doyle, A. Conan
See Doyle, Sir Arthur Conan
Doyle, Sir Arthur Conan
1859-1930 .... **TCLC 7; SSC 12; WLC**
See also Conan Doyle, Arthur
See also AAYA 14; BRWS 2; CA 104; 122;
CDBLB 1890-1914; CMW 4; DA; DA3;
DAB; DAC; DAM MST, NOV; DLB 18,
70, 156, 178; EXPS; HGG; LAIT 2;
MSW; MTCW 1, 2; RGEL 2; RGSF 2;
RHW; SATA 24; SCFW 2; SFW 4; SSFS
2; TEA; WCH; WLIT 4; WYA; YAW
Doyle, Conan
See Doyle, Sir Arthur Conan
Doyle, John
See Graves, Robert (von Ranke)
Doyle, Roddy 1958(?)- .... **CLC 81**
See also AAYA 14; BRWS 5; CA 143;
CANR 73; CN 7; DA3; DLB 194
Doyle, Sir A. Conan
See Doyle, Sir Arthur Conan
Dr. A
See Asimov, Isaac; Silverstein, Alvin; Sil-
verstein, Virginia B(arbara Opshelor)
Drabble, Margaret 1939- ...... **CLC 2, 3, 5, 8,
10, 22, 53, 129**
See also BRWS 4; CA 13-16R; CANR 18,
35, 63; CDBLB 1960 to Present; CN 7;
CPW; DA3; DAB; DAC; DAM MST,
NOV, POP; DLB 14, 155, 231; FW;
MTCW 1, 2; RGEL 2; SATA 48; TEA
Drapier, M. B.
See Swift, Jonathan
Drayham, James
See Mencken, H(enry) L(ouis)
Drayton, Michael 1563-1631 .... **LC 8**
See also DAM POET; DLB 121; RGEL 2
Dreadstone, Carl
See Campbell, (John) Ramsey
Dreiser, Theodore (Herman Albert)
1871-1945 .... **TCLC 10, 18, 35, 83; SSC
30; WLC**
See also AMW; CA 106; 132; CDALB
1865-1917; DA; DA3; DAC; DAM MST,
NOV; DLB 9, 12, 102, 137; DLBD 1;
LAIT 2; MTCW 1, 2; NFS 8; RGAL 4;
TUS
Drexler, Rosalyn 1926- .... **CLC 2, 6**
See also CA 81-84; CAD; CANR 68; CD
5; CWD
Dreyer, Carl Theodor 1889-1968 ...... **CLC 16**
See also CA 116
Drieu la Rochelle, Pierre(-Eugene)
1893-1945 .... **TCLC 21**
See also CA 117; DLB 72; GFL 1789 to the
Present
Drinkwater, John 1882-1937 .... **TCLC 57**
See also CA 109; 149; DLB 10, 19, 149;
RGEL 2
Drop Shot
See Cable, George Washington
Droste-Hulshoff, Annette Freiin von
1797-1848 .... **NCLC 3**
See also CDWLB 2; DLB 133; RGSF 2;
RGWL 2
Drummond, Walter
See Silverberg, Robert
Drummond, William Henry
1854-1907 .... **TCLC 25**
See also CA 160; DLB 92

Drummond de Andrade, Carlos
1902-1987 .... **CLC 18**
See also Andrade, Carlos Drummond de
See also CA 132; 123; LAW
Drury, Allen (Stuart) 1918-1998 .... **CLC 37**
See also CA 57-60; 170; CANR 18, 52; CN
7; INT CANR-18
Dryden, John 1631-1700 ..... **LC 3, 21; DC 3;
PC 25; WLC**
See also BRW 2; CDBLB 1660-1789; DA;
DAB; DAC; DAM DRAM, MST, POET;
DLB 80, 101, 131; EXPP; IDTP; RGEL
2; TEA; WLIT 3
Duberman, Martin (Bauml) 1930- ..... **CLC 8**
See also CA 1-4R; CAD; CANR 2, 63; CD
5
Dubie, Norman (Evans) 1945- .... **CLC 36**
See also CA 69-72; CANR 12; CP 7; DLB
120; PFS 12
Du Bois, W(illiam) E(dward) B(urghardt)
1868-1963 ... **CLC 1, 2, 13, 64, 96; BLC
1; WLC**
See also AAYA 40; AFAW 1, 2; AMWS 2;
BW 1, 3; CA 85-88; CANR 34, 82;
CDALB 1865-1917; DA; DA3; DAC;
DAM MST, MULT, NOV; DLB 47, 50,
91, 246; EXPP; LAIT 2; MTCW 1, 2;
NCFS 1; PFS 13; RGAL 4; SATA 42
Dubus, Andre 1936-1999 ..... **CLC 13, 36, 97;
SSC 15**
See also AMWS 7; CA 21-24R; 177; CANR
17; CN 7; CSW; DLB 130; INT CANR-
17; RGAL 4; SSFS 10
Duca Minimo
See D'Annunzio, Gabriele
Ducharme, Rejean 1941- .... **CLC 74**
See also CA 165; DLB 60
Duchen, Claire .... **CLC 65**
Duclos, Charles Pinot- 1704-1772 .... **LC 1**
See also GFL Beginnings to 1789
Dudek, Louis 1918- .... **CLC 11, 19**
See also CA 45-48; CAAS 14; CANR 1;
CP 7; DLB 88
Duerrenmatt, Friedrich 1921-1990 ... **CLC 1,
4, 8, 11, 15, 43, 102**
See also Durrenmatt, Friedrich
See also CA 17-20R; CANR 33; CMW 4;
DAM DRAM; DLB 69, 124; MTCW 1, 2
Duffy, Bruce 1953(?)- .... **CLC 50**
See also CA 172
Duffy, Maureen 1933- .... **CLC 37**
See also CA 25-28R; CANR 33, 68; CBD;
CN 7; CP 7; CWD; CWP; DFS 15; DLB
14; FW; MTCW 1
Du Fu
See Tu Fu
See also RGWL 2
Dugan, Alan 1923- .... **CLC 2, 6**
See also CA 81-84; CP 7; DLB 5; PFS 10
du Gard, Roger Martin
See Martin du Gard, Roger
Duhamel, Georges 1884-1966 .... **CLC 8**
See also CA 81-84; 25-28R; CANR 35;
DLB 65; GFL 1789 to the Present; MTCW
1
Dujardin, Edouard (Emile Louis)
1861-1949 .... **TCLC 13**
See also CA 109; DLB 123
Duke, Raoul
See Thompson, Hunter S(tockton)
Dulles, John Foster 1888-1959 .... **TCLC 72**
See also CA 115; 149
Dumas, Alexandre (pere)
1802-1870 .... **NCLC 11, 71; WLC**
See also AAYA 22; BYA 3; DA; DA3;
DAB; DAC; DAM MST, NOV; DLB 119,
192; EW 6; GFL 1789 to the Present;
LAIT 1, 2; NFS 14; RGWL 2; SATA 18;
TWA; WCH

Dumas, Alexandre (fils)
1824-1895 .... **NCLC 9; DC 1**
See also DLB 192; GFL 1789 to the Present;
RGWL 2

Dumas, Claudine
See Malzberg, Barry N(athaniel)

Dumas, Henry L. 1934-1968 .... **CLC 6, 62**
See also BW 1; CA 85-88; DLB 41; RGAL
4

du Maurier, Daphne 1907-1989 .. **CLC 6, 11, 59; SSC 18**
See also AAYA 37; BPFB 1; BRWS 3; CA
5-8R; 128; CANR 6, 55; CMW 4; CPW;
DA3; DAB; DAC; DAM MST, POP;
DLB 191; HGG; LAIT 3; MSW; MTCW
1, 2; NFS 12; RGEL 2; RGSF 2; RHW;
SATA 27; SATA-Obit 60; SSFS 14; TEA

Du Maurier, George 1834-1896 ..... **NCLC 86**
See also DLB 153, 178; RGEL 2

Dunbar, Paul Laurence 1872-1906 . **TCLC 2, 12; BLC 1; PC 5; SSC 8; WLC**
See also AFAW 1, 2; AMWS 2; BW 1, 3;
CA 104; 124; CANR 79; CDALB 1865-
1917; DA; DA3; DAC; DAM MST,
MULT, POET; DLB 50, 54, 78; EXPP;
RGAL 4; SATA 34

Dunbar, William 1460(?)-1520(?) .... **LC 20**
See also BRWS 8; DLB 132, 146; RGEL 2

Duncan, Dora Angela
See Duncan, Isadora

Duncan, Isadora 1877(?)-1927 .... **TCLC 68**
See also CA 118; 149

Duncan, Lois 1934- .... **CLC 26**
See also AAYA 4, 34; BYA 6, 8; CA 1-4R;
CANR 2, 23, 36; CLR 29; JRDA;
MAICYA 1, 2; MAICYAS 1; SAAS 2;
SATA 1, 36, 75, 133; WYA; YAW

Duncan, Robert (Edward)
1919-1988 .... **CLC 1, 2, 4, 7, 15, 41, 55; PC 2**
See also CA 9-12R; 124; CANR 28, 62;
DAM POET; DLB 5, 16, 193; MTCW 1,
2; PFS 13; RGAL 4; WP

Duncan, Sara Jeannette
1861-1922 .... **TCLC 60**
See also CA 157; DLB 92

Dunlap, William 1766-1839 .... **NCLC 2**
See also DLB 30, 37, 59; RGAL 4

Dunn, Douglas (Eaglesham) 1942- .... **CLC 6, 40**
See also CA 45-48; CANR 2, 33; CP 7;
DLB 40; MTCW 1

Dunn, Katherine (Karen) 1945- .... **CLC 71**
See also CA 33-36R; CANR 72; HGG;
MTCW 1

Dunn, Stephen (Elliott) 1939- .... **CLC 36**
See also AMWS 11; CA 33-36R; CANR
12, 48, 53, 105; CP 7; DLB 105

Dunne, Finley Peter 1867-1936 ...... **TCLC 28**
See also CA 108; 178; DLB 11, 23; RGAL
4

Dunne, John Gregory 1932- .... **CLC 28**
See also CA 25-28R; CANR 14, 50; CN 7;
DLBY 1980

Dunsany, Lord .... **TCLC 2, 59**
See also Dunsany, Edward John Moreton
Drax Plunkett
See also DLB 77, 153, 156, 255; FANT;
IDTP; RGEL 2; SFW 4; SUFW

**Dunsany, Edward John Moreton Drax
Plunkett** 1878-1957
See Dunsany, Lord
See also CA 104; 148; DLB 10; MTCW 1

du Perry, Jean
See Simenon, Georges (Jacques Christian)

Durang, Christopher (Ferdinand)
1949- .... **CLC 27, 38**
See also CA 105; CAD; CANR 50, 76; CD
5; MTCW 1

Duras, Marguerite 1914-1996 . **CLC 3, 6, 11, 20, 34, 40, 68, 100; SSC 40**
See also BPFB 1; CA 25-28R; 151; CANR
50; CWW 2; DLB 83; GFL 1789 to the
Present; IDFW 4; MTCW 1, 2; RGWL 2;
TWA

Durban, (Rosa) Pam 1947- .... **CLC 39**
See also CA 123; CANR 98; CSW

Durcan, Paul 1944- .... **CLC 43, 70**
See also CA 134; CP 7; DAM POET

Durkheim, Emile 1858-1917 .... **TCLC 55**

Durrell, Lawrence (George)
1912-1990 ..... **CLC 1, 4, 6, 8, 13, 27, 41**
See also BPFB 1; BRWS 1; CA 9-12R; 132;
CANR 40, 77; CDBLB 1945-1960; DAM
NOV; DLB 15, 27, 204; DLBY 1990;
MTCW 1, 2; RGEL 2; SFW 4; TEA

Durrenmatt, Friedrich
See Duerrenmatt, Friedrich
See also CDWLB 2; EW 13; RGWL 2

Dutt, Toru 1856-1877 .... **NCLC 29**
See also DLB 240

Dwight, Timothy 1752-1817 .... **NCLC 13**
See also DLB 37; RGAL 4

Dworkin, Andrea 1946- .... **CLC 43, 123**
See also CA 77-80; CAAS 21; CANR 16,
39, 76, 96; FW; GLL 1; INT CANR-16;
MTCW 1, 2

Dwyer, Deanna
See Koontz, Dean R(ay)

Dwyer, K. R.
See Koontz, Dean R(ay)

Dwyer, Thomas A. 1923- .... **CLC 114**
See also CA 115

Dybek, Stuart 1942- .... **CLC 114; SSC 55**
See also CA 97-100; CANR 39; DLB 130

Dye, Richard
See De Voto, Bernard (Augustine)

Dyer, Geoff 1958- .... **CLC 149**
See also CA 125; CANR 88

Dylan, Bob 1941- .... **CLC 3, 4, 6, 12, 77; PC 37**
See also CA 41-44R; CANR 108; CP 7;
DLB 16

Dyson, John 1943- .... **CLC 70**
See also CA 144

E. V. L.
See Lucas, E(dward) V(errall)

Eagleton, Terence (Francis) 1943- .. **CLC 63, 132**
See also CA 57-60; CANR 7, 23, 68; DLB
242; MTCW 1, 2

Eagleton, Terry
See Eagleton, Terence (Francis)

Early, Jack
See Scoppettone, Sandra
See also GLL 1

East, Michael
See West, Morris L(anglo)

Eastaway, Edward
See Thomas, (Philip) Edward

Eastlake, William (Derry)
1917-1997 .... **CLC 8**
See also CA 5-8R; 158; CAAS 1; CANR 5,
63; CN 7; DLB 6, 206; INT CANR-5;
TCWW 2

Eastman, Charles A(lexander)
1858-1939 .... **TCLC 55**
See also CA 179; CANR 91; DAM MULT;
DLB 175; NNAL; YABC 1

Eberhart, Richard (Ghormley)
1904- .... **CLC 3, 11, 19, 56**
See also AMW; CA 1-4R; CANR 2;
CDALB 1941-1968; CP 7; DAM POET;
DLB 48; MTCW 1; RGAL 4

Eberstadt, Fernanda 1960- .... **CLC 39**
See also CA 136; CANR 69

**Echegaray (y Eizaguirre), Jose (Maria
Waldo)** 1832-1916 .... **TCLC 4; HLCS 1**
See also CA 104; CANR 32; HW 1; MTCW
1

Echeverria, (Jose) Esteban (Antonino)
1805-1851 .... **NCLC 18**
See also LAW

Echo
See Proust, (Valentin-Louis-George-Eugene-
)Marcel

Eckert, Allan W. 1931- .... **CLC 17**
See also AAYA 18; BYA 2; CA 13-16R;
CANR 14, 45; INT CANR-14; MAICYA
2; MAICYAS 1; SAAS 21; SATA 29, 91;
SATA-Brief 27

Eckhart, Meister 1260(?)-1327(?) ... **CMLC 9**
See also DLB 115

Eckmar, F. R.
See de Hartog, Jan

Eco, Umberto 1932- .... **CLC 28, 60, 142**
See also BEST 90:1; BPFB 1; CA 77-80;
CANR 12, 33, 55, 110; CPW; CWW 2;
DA3; DAM NOV, POP; DLB 196, 242;
MSW; MTCW 1, 2

Eddison, E(ric) R(ucker)
1882-1945 .... **TCLC 15**
See also CA 109; 156; DLB 255; FANT;
SFW 4; SUFW

Eddy, Mary (Ann Morse) Baker
1821-1910 .... **TCLC 71**
See also CA 113; 174

Edel, (Joseph) Leon 1907-1997 .. **CLC 29, 34**
See also CA 1-4R; 161; CANR 1, 22; DLB
103; INT CANR-22

Eden, Emily 1797-1869 .... **NCLC 10**

Edgar, David 1948- .... **CLC 42**
See also CA 57-60; CANR 12, 61; CBD;
CD 5; DAM DRAM; DFS 15; DLB 13,
233; MTCW 1

Edgerton, Clyde (Carlyle) 1944- ...... **CLC 39**
See also AAYA 17; CA 118; 134; CANR
64; CSW; INT 134; YAW

Edgeworth, Maria 1768-1849 .... **NCLC 1, 51**
See also BRWS 3; DLB 116, 159, 163; FW;
RGEL 2; SATA 21; TEA; WLIT 3

Edmonds, Paul
See Kuttner, Henry

Edmonds, Walter D(umaux)
1903-1998 .... **CLC 35**
See also BYA 2; CA 5-8R; CANR 2; CWRI
5; DLB 9; LAIT 1; MAICYA 1, 2; RHW;
SAAS 4; SATA 1, 27; SATA-Obit 99

Edmondson, Wallace
See Ellison, Harlan (Jay)

Edson, Russell 1935- .... **CLC 13**
See also CA 33-36R; DLB 244; WP

Edwards, Bronwen Elizabeth
See Rose, Wendy

Edwards, G(erald) B(asil)
1899-1976 .... **CLC 25**
See also CA 201; 110

Edwards, Gus 1939- .... **CLC 43**
See also CA 108; INT 108

Edwards, Jonathan 1703-1758 .... **LC 7, 54**
See also AMW; DA; DAC; DAM MST;
DLB 24; RGAL 4; TUS

Efron, Marina Ivanovna Tsvetaeva
See Tsvetaeva (Efron), Marina (Ivanovna)

Egoyan, Atom 1960- .... **CLC 151**
See also CA 157

Ehle, John (Marsden, Jr.) 1925- ...... **CLC 27**
See also CA 9-12R; CSW

Ehrenbourg, Ilya (Grigoryevich)
See Ehrenburg, Ilya (Grigoryevich)

Ehrenburg, Ilya (Grigoryevich)
1891-1967 .... **CLC 18, 34, 62**
See also CA 102; 25-28R

Ehrenburg, Ilyo (Grigoryevich)
See Ehrenburg, Ilya (Grigoryevich)

Fitzgerald, Zelda (Sayre)
1900-1948 .... **TCLC 52**
See also AMWS 9; CA 117; 126; DLBY
1984

Flanagan, Thomas (James Bonner)
1923- .... **CLC 25, 52**
See also CA 108; CANR 55; CN 7; DLBY
1980; INT 108; MTCW 1; RHW

Flaubert, Gustave 1821-1880 .... **NCLC 2, 10,**
19, 62, 66; SSC 11; WLC
See also DA; DA3; DAB; DAC; DAM
MST, NOV; DLB 119; EW 7; EXPS; GFL
1789 to the Present; LAIT 2; NFS 14;
RGSF 2; RGWL 2; SSFS 6; TWA

Flavius Josephus
See Josephus, Flavius

Flecker, Herman Elroy
See Flecker, (Herman) James Elroy

Flecker, (Herman) James Elroy
1884-1915 .... **TCLC 43**
See also CA 109; 150; DLB 10, 19; RGEL
2

Fleming, Ian (Lancaster) 1908-1964 . **CLC 3,**
30
See also AAYA 26; BPFB 1; CA 5-8R;
CANR 59; CDBLB 1945-1960; CMW 4;
CPW; DA3; DAM POP; DLB 87, 201;
MSW; MTCW 1, 2; RGEL 2; SATA 9;
TEA; YAW

Fleming, Thomas (James) 1927- ...... **CLC 37**
See also CA 5-8R; CANR 10, 102; INT
CANR-10; SATA 8

Fletcher, John 1579-1625 .... **LC 33; DC 6**
See also BRW 2; CDBLB Before 1660;
DLB 58; RGEL 2; TEA

Fletcher, John Gould 1886-1950 .... **TCLC 35**
See also CA 107; 167; DLB 4, 45; RGAL 4

Fleur, Paul
See Pohl, Frederik

Flooglebuckle, Al
See Spiegelman, Art

Flora, Fletcher 1914-1969
See Queen, Ellery
See also CA 1-4R; CANR 3, 85

Flying Officer X
See Bates, H(erbert) E(rnest)

Fo, Dario 1926- .... **CLC 32, 109; DC 10**
See also CA 116; 128; CANR 68; CWW 2;
DA3; DAM DRAM; DLBY 1997; MTCW
1, 2

Fogarty, Jonathan Titulescu Esq.
See Farrell, James T(homas)

Follett, Ken(neth Martin) 1949- .... **CLC 18**
See also AAYA 6; BEST 89:4; BPFB 1; CA
81-84; CANR 13, 33, 54, 102; CMW 4;
CPW; DA3; DAM NOV, POP; DLB 87;
DLBY 1981; INT CANR-33; MTCW 1

Fontane, Theodor 1819-1898 .... **NCLC 26**
See also CDWLB 2; DLB 129; EW 6;
RGWL 2; TWA

Fontenot, Chester .... **CLC 65**

Fonvizin, Denis Ivanovich
1744(?)-1792 .... **LC 81**
See also DLB 150; RGWL 2

Foote, Horton 1916- .... **CLC 51, 91**
See also CA 73-76; CAD; CANR 34, 51,
110; CD 5; CSW; DA3; DAM DRAM;
DLB 26, 266; INT CANR-34

Foote, Mary Hallock 1847-1938 .. **TCLC 108**
See also DLB 186, 188, 202, 221

Foote, Shelby 1916- .... **CLC 75**
See also AAYA 40; CA 5-8R; CANR 3, 45,
74; CN 7; CPW; CSW; DA3; DAM NOV,
POP; DLB 2, 17; MTCW 2; RHW

Forbes, Cosmo
See Lewton, Val

Forbes, Esther 1891-1967 .... **CLC 12**
See also AAYA 17; BYA 2; CA 13-14; 25-
28R; CAP 1; CLR 27; DLB 22; JRDA;
MAICYA 1, 2; RHW; SATA 2, 100; YAW

Forche, Carolyn (Louise) 1950- .... **CLC 25,**
83, 86; PC 10
See also CA 109; 117; CANR 50, 74; CP 7;
CWP; DA3; DAM POET; DLB 5, 193;
INT CA-117; MTCW 1; RGAL 4

Ford, Elbur
See Hibbert, Eleanor Alice Burford

Ford, Ford Madox 1873-1939 ... **TCLC 1, 15,**
39, 57
See Chaucer, Daniel
See also BRW 6; CA 104; 132; CANR 74;
CDBLB 1914-1945; DA3; DAM NOV;
DLB 34, 98, 162; MTCW 1, 2; RGEL 2;
TEA

Ford, Henry 1863-1947 .... **TCLC 73**
See also CA 115; 148

Ford, John 1586-1639 .... **LC 68; DC 8**
See also BRW 2; CDBLB Before 1660;
DA3; DAM DRAM; DFS 7; DLB 58;
IDTP; RGEL 2

Ford, John 1895-1973 .... **CLC 16**
See also CA 187; 45-48

Ford, Richard 1944- ..... **CLC 46, 99; SSC 57**
See also AMWS 5; CA 69-72; CANR 11,
47, 86; CN 7; CSW; DLB 227; MTCW 1;
RGAL 4; RGSF 2

Ford, Webster
See Masters, Edgar Lee

Foreman, Richard 1937- .... **CLC 50**
See also CA 65-68; CAD; CANR 32, 63;
CD 5

Forester, C(ecil) S(cott) 1899-1966 ... **CLC 35**
See also CA 73-76; 25-28R; CANR 83;
DLB 191; RGEL 2; RHW; SATA 13

Forez
See Mauriac, Francois (Charles)

Forman, James
See Forman, James D(ouglas)

Forman, James D(ouglas) 1932- .... **CLC 21**
See also AAYA 17; CA 9-12R; CANR 4,
19, 42; JRDA; MAICYA 1, 2; SATA 8,
70; YAW

Forman, Milos 1932- .... **CLC 164**
See also CA 109

Fornes, Maria Irene 1930- . **CLC 39, 61; DC**
10; HLCS 1
See also CA 25-28R; CAD; CANR 28, 81;
CD 5; CWD; DLB 7; HW 1, 2; INT
CANR-28; MTCW 1; RGAL 4

Forrest, Leon (Richard) 1937-1997 .. **CLC 4;**
BLCS
See also AFAW 2; BW 2; CA 89-92; 162;
CAAS 7; CANR 25, 52, 87; CN 7; DLB
33

Forster, E(dward) M(organ)
1879-1970 ...... **CLC 1, 2, 3, 4, 9, 10, 13,**
15, 22, 45, 77; SSC 27; WLC
See also AAYA 2, 37; BRW 6; BRWR 2;
CA 13-14; 25-28R; CANR 45; CAP 1;
CDBLB 1914-1945; DA; DA3; DAB;
DAC; DAM MST, NOV; DLB 34, 98,
162, 178, 195; DLBD 10; EXPN; LAIT
3; MTCW 1, 2; NCFS 1; NFS 3, 10, 11;
RGEL 2; RGSF 2; SATA 57; SUFW;
TCLC 125; TEA; WLIT 4

Forster, John 1812-1876 .... **NCLC 11**
See also DLB 144, 184

Forster, Margaret 1938- .... **CLC 149**
See also CA 133; CANR 62; CN 7; DLB
155

Forsyth, Frederick 1938- .... **CLC 2, 5, 36**
See also BEST 89:4; CA 85-88; CANR 38,
62; CMW 4; CN 7; CPW; DAM NOV,
POP; DLB 87; MTCW 1, 2

Forten, Charlotte L. 1837-1914 .... **TCLC 16;**
BLC 2
See also Grimke, Charlotte L(ottie) Forten
See also DLB 50, 239

Foscolo, Ugo 1778-1827 .... **NCLC 8, 97**
See also EW 5

Fosse, Bob .... **CLC 20**
See also Fosse, Robert Louis

Fosse, Robert Louis 1927-1987
See Fosse, Bob
See also CA 110; 123

Foster, Hannah Webster
1758-1840 .... **NCLC 99**
See also DLB 37, 200; RGAL 4

Foster, Stephen Collins
1826-1864 .... **NCLC 26**
See also RGAL 4

Foucault, Michel 1926-1984 . **CLC 31, 34, 69**
See also CA 105; 113; CANR 34; DLB 242;
EW 13; GFL 1789 to the Present; GLL 1;
MTCW 1, 2; TWA

Fouque, Friedrich (Heinrich Karl) de la
Motte 1777-1843 .... **NCLC 2**
See also DLB 90; RGWL 2; SUFW

Fourier, Charles 1772-1837 .... **NCLC 51**

Fournier, Henri Alban 1886-1914
See Alain-Fournier
See also CA 104; 179

Fournier, Pierre 1916- .... **CLC 11**
See also Gascar, Pierre
See also CA 89-92; CANR 16, 40

Fowles, John (Robert) 1926- . **CLC 1, 2, 3, 4,**
6, 9, 10, 15, 33, 87; SSC 33
See also BPFB 1; BRWS 1; CA 5-8R;
CANR 25, 71, 103; CDBLB 1960 to
Present; CN 7; DA3; DAB; DAC; DAM
MST; DLB 14, 139, 207; HGG; MTCW
1, 2; RGEL 2; RHW; SATA 22; TEA;
WLIT 4

Fox, Paula 1923- .... **CLC 2, 8, 121**
See also AAYA 3, 37; BYA 3, 8; CA 73-76;
CANR 20, 36, 62, 105; CLR 1, 44; DLB
52; JRDA; MAICYA 1, 2; MTCW 1; NFS
12; SATA 17, 60, 120; WYA; YAW

Fox, William Price (Jr.) 1926- .... **CLC 22**
See also CA 17-20R; CAAS 19; CANR 11;
CSW; DLB 2; DLBY 1981

Foxe, John 1517(?)-1587 .... **LC 14**
See also DLB 132

Frame, Janet .. **CLC 2, 3, 6, 22, 66, 96; SSC**
29
See also Clutha, Janet Paterson Frame
See also CN 7; CWP; RGEL 2; RGSF 2;
TWA

France, Anatole .... **TCLC 9**
See also Thibault, Jacques Anatole Francois
See also DLB 123; GFL 1789 to the Present;
MTCW 1; RGWL 2; SUFW

Francis, Claude .... **CLC 50**
See also CA 192

Francis, Dick 1920- .... **CLC 2, 22, 42, 102**
See also AAYA 5, 21; BEST 89:3; BPFB 1;
CA 5-8R; CANR 9, 42, 68, 100; CDBLB
1960 to Present; CMW 4; CN 7; DA3;
DAM POP; DLB 87; INT CANR-9;
MSW; MTCW 1, 2

Francis, Robert (Churchill)
1901-1987 .... **CLC 15; PC 34**
See also AMWS 9; CA 1-4R; 123; CANR
1; EXPP; PFS 12

Francis, Lord Jeffrey
See Jeffrey, Francis
See also DLB 107

Frank, Anne(lies Marie)
1929-1945 .... **TCLC 17; WLC**
See also AAYA 12; BYA 1; CA 113; 133;
CANR 68; DA; DA3; DAB; DAC; DAM
MST; LAIT 4; MAICYA 2; MAICYAS 1;
MTCW 1, 2; NCFS 2; SATA 87; SATA-
Brief 42; WYA; YAW

Griffith, Lawrence
See Griffith, D(avid Lewelyn) W(ark)

Griffiths, Trevor 1935- .... **CLC 13, 52**
See also CA 97-100; CANR 45; CBD; CD 5; DLB 13, 245

Griggs, Sutton (Elbert)
1872-1930 .... **TCLC 77**
See also CA 123; 186; DLB 50

Grigson, Geoffrey (Edward Harvey)
1905-1985 .... **CLC 7, 39**
See also CA 25-28R; 118; CANR 20, 33; DLB 27; MTCW 1, 2

Grillparzer, Franz 1791-1872 . **NCLC 1, 102; DC 14; SSC 37**
See also CDWLB 2; DLB 133; EW 5; RGWL 2; TWA

Grimble, Reverend Charles James
See Eliot, T(homas) S(tearns)

Grimke, Charlotte L(ottie) Forten
1837(?)-1914
See Forten, Charlotte L.
See also BW 1; CA 117; 124; DAM MULT, POET

Grimm, Jacob Ludwig Karl
1785-1863 .... **NCLC 3, 77; SSC 36**
See also DLB 90; MAICYA 1, 2; RGSF 2; RGWL 2; SATA 22; WCH

Grimm, Wilhelm Karl 1786-1859 .. **NCLC 3, 77; SSC 36**
See also CDWLB 2; DLB 90; MAICYA 1, 2; RGSF 2; RGWL 2; SATA 22; WCH

Grimmelshausen, Hans Jakob Christoffel von
See Grimmelshausen, Johann Jakob Christoffel von
See also RGWL 2

Grimmelshausen, Johann Jakob Christoffel von 1621-1676 .... **LC 6**
See also Grimmelshausen, Hans Jakob Christoffel von
See also CDWLB 2; DLB 168

Grindel, Eugene 1895-1952
See Eluard, Paul
See also CA 104; 193

Grisham, John 1955- .... **CLC 84**
See also AAYA 14; BPFB 2; CA 138; CANR 47, 69; CMW 4; CN 7; CPW; CSW; DA3; DAM POP; MSW; MTCW 2

Grossman, David 1954- .... **CLC 67**
See also CA 138; CWW 2

Grossman, Vasily (Semenovich)
1905-1964 .... **CLC 41**
See also CA 124; 130; MTCW 1

Grove, Frederick Philip .... **TCLC 4**
See also Greve, Felix Paul (Berthold Friedrich)
See also DLB 92; RGEL 2

Grubb
See Crumb, R(obert)

Grumbach, Doris (Isaac) 1918- . **CLC 13, 22, 64**
See also CA 5-8R; CAAS 2; CANR 9, 42, 70; CN 7; INT CANR-9; MTCW 2

Grundtvig, Nicolai Frederik Severin
1783-1872 .... **NCLC 1**

Grunge
See Crumb, R(obert)

Grunwald, Lisa 1959- .... **CLC 44**
See also CA 120

Guare, John 1938- .... **CLC 8, 14, 29, 67**
See also CA 73-76; CAD; CANR 21, 69; CD 5; DAM DRAM; DFS 8, 13; DLB 7, 249; MTCW 1, 2; RGAL 4

Gubar, Susan (David) 1944- .... **CLC 145**
See also CA 108; CANR 45, 70; FW; MTCW 1; RGAL 4

Gudjonsson, Halldor Kiljan 1902-1998
See Laxness, Halldor
See also CA 103; 164; CWW 2

Guenter, Erich
See Eich, Guenter

Guest, Barbara 1920- .... **CLC 34**
See also CA 25-28R; CANR 11, 44, 84; CP 7; CWP; DLB 5, 193

Guest, Edgar A(lbert) 1881-1959 ... **TCLC 95**
See also CA 112; 168

Guest, Judith (Ann) 1936- .... **CLC 8, 30**
See also AAYA 7; CA 77-80; CANR 15, 75; DA3; DAM NOV, POP; EXPN; INT CANR-15; LAIT 5; MTCW 1, 2; NFS 1

Guevara, Che .... **CLC 87; HLC 1**
See also Guevara (Serna), Ernesto

Guevara (Serna), Ernesto
1928-1967 .... **CLC 87; HLC 1**
See also Guevara, Che
See also CA 127; 111; CANR 56; DAM MULT; HW 1

Guicciardini, Francesco 1483-1540 ..... **LC 49**

Guild, Nicholas M. 1944- .... **CLC 33**
See also CA 93-96

Guillemin, Jacques
See Sartre, Jean-Paul

Guillen, Jorge 1893-1984 . **CLC 11; HLCS 1; PC 35**
See also CA 89-92; 112; DAM MULT, POET; DLB 108; HW 1; RGWL 2

Guillen, Nicolas (Cristobal)
1902-1989 .... **CLC 48, 79; BLC 2; HLC 1; PC 23**
See also BW 2; CA 116; 125; 129; CANR 84; DAM MST, MULT, POET; HW 1; LAW; RGWL 2; WP

Guillen y Alvarez, Jorge
See Guillen, Jorge

Guillevic, (Eugene) 1907-1997 .... **CLC 33**
See also CA 93-96; CWW 2

Guillois
See Desnos, Robert

Guillois, Valentin
See Desnos, Robert

Guimaraes Rosa, Joao
See Rosa, Joao Guimaraes
See also LAW

Guimaraes Rosa, Joao 1908-1967
See also CA 175; HLCS 2; LAW; RGSF 2; RGWL 2

Guiney, Louise Imogen
1861-1920 .... **TCLC 41**
See also CA 160; DLB 54; RGAL 4

Guinizelli, Guido c. 1230-1276 ...... **CMLC 49**

Guiraldes, Ricardo (Guillermo)
1886-1927 .... **TCLC 39**
See also CA 131; HW 1; LAW; MTCW 1

Gumilev, Nikolai (Stepanovich)
1886-1921 .... **TCLC 60**
See also CA 165

Gunesekera, Romesh 1954- .... **CLC 91**
See also CA 159; CN 7; DLB 267

Gunn, Bill .... **CLC 5**
See also Gunn, William Harrison
See also DLB 38

Gunn, Thom(son William) 1929- .. **CLC 3, 6, 18, 32, 81; PC 26**
See also BRWS 4; CA 17-20R; CANR 9, 33; CDBLB 1960 to Present; CP 7; DAM POET; DLB 27; INT CANR-33; MTCW 1; PFS 9; RGEL 2

Gunn, William Harrison 1934(?)-1989
See Gunn, Bill
See also AITN 1; BW 1, 3; CA 13-16R; 128; CANR 12, 25, 76

Gunn Allen, Paula
See Allen, Paula Gunn

Gunnars, Kristjana 1948- .... **CLC 69**
See also CA 113; CCA 1; CP 7; CWP; DLB 60

Gunter, Erich
See Eich, Guenter

Gurdjieff, G(eorgei) I(vanovich)
1877(?)-1949 .... **TCLC 71**
See also CA 157

Gurganus, Allan 1947- .... **CLC 70**
See also BEST 90:1; CA 135; CN 7; CPW; CSW; DAM POP; GLL 1

Gurney, A. R.
See Gurney, A(lbert) R(amsdell), Jr.
See also DLB 266

Gurney, A(lbert) R(amsdell), Jr.
1930- .... **CLC 32, 50, 54**
See also Gurney, A. R.
See also AMWS 5; CA 77-80; CAD; CANR 32, 64; CD 5; DAM DRAM

Gurney, Ivor (Bertie) 1890-1937 ... **TCLC 33**
See also BRW 6; CA 167; PAB; RGEL 2

Gurney, Peter
See Gurney, A(lbert) R(amsdell), Jr.

Guro, Elena 1877-1913 .... **TCLC 56**

Gustafson, James M(oody) 1925- ... **CLC 100**
See also CA 25-28R; CANR 37

Gustafson, Ralph (Barker)
1909-1995 .... **CLC 36**
See also CA 21-24R; CANR 8, 45, 84; CP 7; DLB 88; RGEL 2

Gut, Gom
See Simenon, Georges (Jacques Christian)

Guterson, David 1956- .... **CLC 91**
See also CA 132; CANR 73; MTCW 2; NFS 13

Guthrie, A(lfred) B(ertram), Jr.
1901-1991 .... **CLC 23**
See also CA 57-60; 134; CANR 24; DLB 6, 212; SATA 62; SATA-Obit 67

Guthrie, Isobel
See Grieve, C(hristopher) M(urray)

Guthrie, Woodrow Wilson 1912-1967
See Guthrie, Woody
See also CA 113; 93-96

Guthrie, Woody .... **CLC 35**
See also Guthrie, Woodrow Wilson
See also LAIT 3

Gutierrez Najera, Manuel 1859-1895
See also HLCS 2; LAW

Guy, Rosa (Cuthbert) 1925- .... **CLC 26**
See also AAYA 4, 37; BW 2; CA 17-20R; CANR 14, 34, 83; CLR 13; DLB 33; DNFS 1; JRDA; MAICYA 1, 2; SATA 14, 62, 122; YAW

Gwendolyn
See Bennett, (Enoch) Arnold

H. D. .... **CLC 3, 8, 14, 31, 34, 73; PC 5**
See also Doolittle, Hilda

H. de V.
See Buchan, John

Haavikko, Paavo Juhani 1931- .. **CLC 18, 34**
See also CA 106

Habbema, Koos
See Heijermans, Herman

Habermas, Juergen 1929- .... **CLC 104**
See also CA 109; CANR 85; DLB 242

Habermas, Jurgen
See Habermas, Juergen

Hacker, Marilyn 1942- . **CLC 5, 9, 23, 72, 91**
See also CA 77-80; CANR 68; CP 7; CWP; DAM POET; DLB 120; FW; GLL 2

Hadrian 76-138 .... **CMLC 52**

Haeckel, Ernst Heinrich (Philipp August)
1834-1919 .... **TCLC 83**
See also CA 157

Hafiz c. 1326-1389(?) .... **CMLC 34**
See also RGWL 2

Haggard, H(enry) Rider
1856-1925 .... **TCLC 11**
See also BRWS 3; BYA 4, 5; CA 108; 148; DLB 70, 156, 174, 178; FANT; MTCW 2; RGEL 2; RHW; SATA 16; SCFW; SFW 4; SUFW; WLIT 4

Heyward, (Edwin) DuBose
1885-1940 .... **TCLC 59**
See also CA 108; 157; DLB 7, 9, 45, 249;
SATA 21

Heywood, John 1497(?)-1580(?) .... **LC 65**
See also DLB 136; RGEL 2

Hibbert, Eleanor Alice Burford
1906-1993 .... **CLC 7**
See also Holt, Victoria
See also BEST 90:4; CA 17-20R; 140;
CANR 9, 28, 59; CMW 4; CPW; DAM
POP; MTCW 2; RHW; SATA 2; SATA-
Obit 74

Hichens, Robert (Smythe)
1864-1950 .... **TCLC 64**
See also CA 162; DLB 153; HGG; RHW;
SUFW

Higgins, George V(incent)
1939-1999 .... **CLC 4, 7, 10, 18**
See also BPFB 2; CA 77-80; 186; CAAS 5;
CANR 17, 51, 89, 96; CMW 4; CN 7;
DLB 2; DLBY 1981, 1998; INT CANR-
17; MSW; MTCW 1

Higginson, Thomas Wentworth
1823-1911 .... **TCLC 36**
See also CA 162; DLB 1, 64, 243

Higgonet, Margaret ed. .... **CLC 65**

Highet, Helen
See MacInnes, Helen (Clark)

Highsmith, (Mary) Patricia
1921-1995 .... **CLC 2, 4, 14, 42, 102**
See also Morgan, Claire
See also BRWS 5; CA 1-4R; 147; CANR 1,
20, 48, 62, 108; CMW 4; CPW; DA3;
DAM NOV, POP; MSW; MTCW 1, 2

Highwater, Jamake (Mamake)
1942(?)-2001 .... **CLC 12**
See also AAYA 7; BPFB 2; BYA 4; CA 65-
68; 199; CAAS 7; CANR 10, 34, 84; CLR
17; CWRI 5; DLB 52; DLBY 1985;
JRDA; MAICYA 1, 2; SATA 32, 69;
SATA-Brief 30

Highway, Tomson 1951- .... **CLC 92**
See also CA 151; CANR 75; CCA 1; CD 5;
DAC; DAM MULT; DFS 2; MTCW 2;
NNAL

Hijuelos, Oscar 1951- .... **CLC 65; HLC 1**
See also AAYA 25; AMWS 8; BEST 90:1;
CA 123; CANR 50, 75; CPW; DA3; DAM
MULT, POP; DLB 145; HW 1, 2; MTCW
2; RGAL 4; WLIT 1

Hikmet, Nazim 1902(?)-1963 .... **CLC 40**
See also CA 141; 93-96

Hildegard von Bingen 1098-1179 . **CMLC 20**
See also DLB 148

Hildesheimer, Wolfgang 1916-1991 .. **CLC 49**
See also CA 101; 135; DLB 69, 124

Hill, Geoffrey (William) 1932- ...... **CLC 5, 8, 18, 45**
See also BRWS 5; CA 81-84; CANR 21,
89; CDBLB 1960 to Present; CP 7; DAM
POET; DLB 40; MTCW 1; RGEL 2

Hill, George Roy 1921- .... **CLC 26**
See also CA 110; 122

Hill, John
See Koontz, Dean R(ay)

Hill, Susan (Elizabeth) 1942- ...... **CLC 4, 113**
See also CA 33-36R; CANR 29, 69; CN 7;
DAB; DAM MST, NOV; DLB 14, 139;
HGG; MTCW 1; RHW

Hillard, Asa G. III .... **CLC 70**

Hillerman, Tony 1925- .... **CLC 62**
See also AAYA 40; BEST 89:1; BPFB 2;
CA 29-32R; CANR 21, 42, 65, 97; CMW
4; CPW; DA3; DAM POP; DLB 206;
MSW; RGAL 4; SATA 6; TCWW 2; YAW

Hillesum, Etty 1914-1943 .... **TCLC 49**
See also CA 137

Hilliard, Noel (Harvey) 1929-1996 ... **CLC 15**
See also CA 9-12R; CANR 7, 69; CN 7

Hillis, Rick 1956- .... **CLC 66**
See also CA 134

Hilton, James 1900-1954 .... **TCLC 21**
See also CA 108; 169; DLB 34, 77; FANT;
SATA 34

Himes, Chester (Bomar) 1909-1984 .. **CLC 2, 4, 7, 18, 58, 108; BLC 2**
See also AFAW 2; BPFB 2; BW 2; CA 25-
28R; 114; CANR 22, 89; CMW 4; DAM
MULT; DLB 2, 76, 143, 226; MSW;
MTCW 1, 2; RGAL 4

Hinde, Thomas .... **CLC 6, 11**
See also Chitty, Thomas Willes

Hine, (William) Daryl 1936- .... **CLC 15**
See also CA 1-4R; CAAS 15; CANR 1, 20;
CP 7; DLB 60

Hinkson, Katharine Tynan
See Tynan, Katharine

Hinojosa(-Smith), Rolando (R.) 1929-
See also CA 131; CAAS 16; CANR 62;
DAM MULT; DLB 82; HLC 1; HW 1, 2;
MTCW 2; RGAL 4

Hinton, S(usan) E(loise) 1950- .. **CLC 30, 111**
See also AAYA 2, 33; BPFB 2; BYA 2, 3;
CA 81-84; CANR 32, 62, 92; CDALBS;
CLR 3, 23; CPW; DA; DA3; DAB; DAC;
DAM MST, NOV; JRDA; LAIT 5; MAI-
CYA 1, 2; MTCW 1, 2; NFS 5, 9, 15;
SATA 19, 58, 115; WYA; YAW

Hippius, Zinaida .... **TCLC 9**
See also Gippius, Zinaida (Nikolayevna)

Hiraoka, Kimitake 1925-1970
See Mishima, Yukio
See also CA 97-100; 29-32R; DA3; DAM
DRAM; MTCW 1, 2

Hirsch, E(ric) D(onald), Jr. 1928- .... **CLC 79**
See also CA 25-28R; CANR 27, 51; DLB
67; INT CANR-27; MTCW 1

Hirsch, Edward 1950- .... **CLC 31, 50**
See also CA 104; CANR 20, 42, 102; CP 7;
DLB 120

Hitchcock, Alfred (Joseph)
1899-1980 .... **CLC 16**
See also AAYA 22; CA 159; 97-100; SATA
27; SATA-Obit 24

Hitchens, Christopher (Eric)
1949- .... **CLC 157**
See also CA 152; CANR 89

Hitler, Adolf 1889-1945 .... **TCLC 53**
See also CA 117; 147

Hoagland, Edward 1932- .... **CLC 28**
See also ANW; CA 1-4R; CANR 2, 31, 57,
107; CN 7; DLB 6; SATA 51; TCWW 2

Hoban, Russell (Conwell) 1925- .... **CLC 7, 25**
See also BPFB 2; CA 5-8R; CANR 23, 37,
66; CLR 3, 69; CN 7; CWRI 5; DAM
NOV; DLB 52; FANT; MAICYA 1, 2;
MTCW 1, 2; SATA 1, 40, 78; SFW 4

Hobbes, Thomas 1588-1679 .... **LC 36**
See also DLB 151, 252; RGEL 2

Hobbs, Perry
See Blackmur, R(ichard) P(almer)

Hobson, Laura Z(ametkin)
1900-1986 .... **CLC 7, 25**
See also Field, Peter
See also BPFB 2; CA 17-20R; 118; CANR
55; DLB 28; SATA 52

Hoccleve, Thomas c. 1368-c. 1437 ...... **LC 75**
See also DLB 146; RGEL 2

Hoch, Edward D(entinger) 1930-
See Queen, Ellery
See also CA 29-32R; CANR 11, 27, 51, 97;
CMW 4; SFW 4

Hochhuth, Rolf 1931- .... **CLC 4, 11, 18**
See also CA 5-8R; CANR 33, 75; CWW 2;
DAM DRAM; DLB 124; MTCW 1, 2

Hochman, Sandra 1936- .... **CLC 3, 8**
See also CA 5-8R; DLB 5

Hochwaelder, Fritz 1911-1986 .... **CLC 36**
See also Hochwalder, Fritz
See also CA 29-32R; 120; CANR 42; DAM
DRAM; MTCW 1

Hochwalder, Fritz
See Hochwaelder, Fritz
See also RGWL 2

Hocking, Mary (Eunice) 1921- .... **CLC 13**
See also CA 101; CANR 18, 40

Hodgins, Jack 1938- .... **CLC 23**
See also CA 93-96; CN 7; DLB 60

Hodgson, William Hope
1877(?)-1918 .... **TCLC 13**
See also CA 111; 164; CMW 4; DLB 70,
153, 156, 178; HGG; MTCW 2; SFW 4;
SUFW

Hoeg, Peter 1957- .... **CLC 95, 156**
See also CA 151; CANR 75; CMW 4; DA3;
DLB 214; MTCW 2

Hoffman, Alice 1952- .... **CLC 51**
See also AAYA 37; AMWS 10; CA 77-80;
CANR 34, 66, 100; CN 7; CPW; DAM
NOV; MTCW 1, 2

Hoffman, Daniel (Gerard) 1923- . **CLC 6, 13, 23**
See also CA 1-4R; CANR 4; CP 7; DLB 5

Hoffman, Stanley 1944- .... **CLC 5**
See also CA 77-80

Hoffman, William 1925- .... **CLC 141**
See also CA 21-24R; CANR 9, 103; CSW;
DLB 234

Hoffman, William M(oses) 1939- ..... **CLC 40**
See also CA 57-60; CANR 11, 71

Hoffmann, E(rnst) T(heodor) A(madeus)
1776-1822 .... **NCLC 2; SSC 13**
See also CDWLB 2; DLB 90; EW 5; RGSF
2; RGWL 2; SATA 27; SUFW; WCH

Hofmann, Gert 1931- .... **CLC 54**
See also CA 128

Hofmannsthal, Hugo von
1874-1929 .... **TCLC 11; DC 4**
See also CA 106; 153; CDWLB 2; DAM
DRAM; DFS 12; DLB 81, 118; EW 9;
RGWL 2

Hogan, Linda 1947- .... **CLC 73; PC 35**
See also AMWS 4; ANW; BYA 12; CA 120;
CANR 45, 73; CWP; DAM MULT; DLB
175; NNAL; SATA 132; TCWW 2

Hogarth, Charles
See Creasey, John

Hogarth, Emmett
See Polonsky, Abraham (Lincoln)

Hogg, James 1770-1835 .... **NCLC 4, 109**
See also DLB 93, 116, 159; HGG; RGEL 2;
SUFW

Holbach, Paul Henri Thiry Baron
1723-1789 .... **LC 14**

Holberg, Ludvig 1684-1754 .... **LC 6**
See also RGWL 2

Holcroft, Thomas 1745-1809 .... **NCLC 85**
See also DLB 39, 89, 158; RGEL 2

Holden, Ursula 1921- .... **CLC 18**
See also CA 101; CAAS 8; CANR 22

Holderlin, (Johann Christian) Friedrich
1770-1843 .... **NCLC 16; PC 4**
See also CDWLB 2; DLB 90; EW 5; RGWL
2

Holdstock, Robert
See Holdstock, Robert P.

Holdstock, Robert P. 1948- .... **CLC 39**
See also CA 131; CANR 81; DLB 261;
FANT; HGG; SFW 4

Holinshed, Raphael fl. 1580- .... **LC 69**
See also DLB 167; RGEL 2

Hueffer, Ford Madox
  See Ford, Ford Madox
Hughart, Barry 1934- .... **CLC 39**
  See also CA 137; FANT; SFW 4
Hughes, Colin
  See Creasey, John
Hughes, David (John) 1930- .... **CLC 48**
  See also CA 116; 129; CN 7; DLB 14
Hughes, Edward James
  See Hughes, Ted
  See also DA3; DAM MST, POET
Hughes, (James Mercer) Langston
  1902-1967 .... **CLC 1, 5, 10, 15, 35, 44,
  108; BLC 2; DC 3; PC 1; SSC 6; WLC**
  See also AAYA 12; AFAW 1, 2; AMWR 1;
  AMWS 1; BW 1, 3; CA 1-4R; 25-28R;
  CANR 1, 34, 82; CDALB 1929-1941;
  CLR 17; DA; DA3; DAB; DAC; DAM
  DRAM, MST, MULT, POET; DLB 4, 7,
  48, 51, 86, 228; EXPP; EXPS; JRDA;
  LAIT 3; MAICYA 1, 2; MTCW 1, 2;
  PAB; PFS 1, 3, 6, 10, 15; RGAL 4; RGSF
  2; SATA 33; SSFS 4, 7; TUS; WCH;
  WP; YAW
Hughes, Richard (Arthur Warren)
  1900-1976 .... **CLC 1, 11**
  See also CA 5-8R; 65-68; CANR 4; DAM
  NOV; DLB 15, 161; MTCW 1; RGEL 2;
  SATA 8; SATA-Obit 25
Hughes, Ted 1930-1998 . **CLC 2, 4, 9, 14, 37,
  119; PC 7**
  See also Hughes, Edward James
  See also BRWR 2; BRWS 1; CA 1-4R; 171;
  CANR 1, 33, 66, 108; CLR 3; CP 7;
  DAB; DAC; DLB 40, 161; EXPP; MAI-
  CYA 1, 2; MTCW 1, 2; PAB; PFS 4;
  RGEL 2; SATA 49; SATA-Brief 27;
  SATA-Obit 107; TEA; YAW
Hugo, Richard
  See Huch, Ricarda (Octavia)
Hugo, Richard F(ranklin)
  1923-1982 .... **CLC 6, 18, 32**
  See also AMWS 6; CA 49-52; 108; CANR
  3; DAM POET; DLB 5, 206; RGAL 4
Hugo, Victor (Marie) 1802-1885 .... **NCLC 3,
  10, 21; PC 17; WLC**
  See also AAYA 28; DA; DA3; DAB; DAC;
  DAM DRAM, MST, NOV, POET; DLB
  119, 192, 217; EFS 2; EW 6; EXPN; GFL
  1789 to the Present; LAIT 1, 2; NFS 5;
  RGWL 2; SATA 47; TWA
Huidobro, Vicente
  See Huidobro Fernandez, Vicente Garcia
  See also LAW
Huidobro Fernandez, Vicente Garcia
  1893-1948 .... **TCLC 31**
  See also Huidobro, Vicente
  See also CA 131; HW 1
Hulme, Keri 1947- .... **CLC 39, 130**
  See also CA 125; CANR 69; CN 7; CP 7;
  CWP; FW; INT 125
Hulme, T(homas) E(rnest)
  1883-1917 .... **TCLC 21**
  See also BRWS 6; CA 117; 203; DLB 19
Hume, David 1711-1776 .... **LC 7, 56**
  See also BRWS 3; DLB 104, 252; TEA
Humphrey, William 1924-1997 .... **CLC 45**
  See also AMWS 9; CA 77-80; 160; CANR
  68; CN 7; CSW; DLB 6, 212, 234;
  TCWW 2
Humphreys, Emyr Owen 1919- .... **CLC 47**
  See also CA 5-8R; CANR 3, 24; CN 7;
  DLB 15
Humphreys, Josephine 1945- ..... **CLC 34, 57**
  See also CA 121; 127; CANR 97; CSW;
  INT 127
Huneker, James Gibbons
  1860-1921 .... **TCLC 65**
  See also CA 193; DLB 71; RGAL 4

Hungerford, Hesba Fay
  See Brinsmead, H(esba) F(ay)
Hungerford, Pixie
  See Brinsmead, H(esba) F(ay)
Hunt, E(verette) Howard, (Jr.)
  1918- .... **CLC 3**
  See also AITN 1; CA 45-48; CANR 2, 47,
  103; CMW 4
Hunt, Francesca
  See Holland, Isabelle (Christian)
Hunt, Howard
  See Hunt, E(verette) Howard, (Jr.)
Hunt, Kyle
  See Creasey, John
Hunt, (James Henry) Leigh
  1784-1859 .... **NCLC 1, 70**
  See also DAM POET; DLB 96, 110, 144;
  RGEL 2; TEA
Hunt, Marsha 1946- .... **CLC 70**
  See also BW 2, 3; CA 143; CANR 79
Hunt, Violet 1866(?)-1942 .... **TCLC 53**
  See also CA 184; DLB 162, 197
Hunter, E. Waldo
  See Sturgeon, Theodore (Hamilton)
Hunter, Evan 1926- .... **CLC 11, 31**
  See also McBain, Ed
  See also AAYA 39; BPFB 2; CA 5-8R;
  CANR 5, 38, 62, 97; CMW 4; CN 7;
  CPW; DAM POP; DLBY 1982; INT
  CANR-5; MSW; MTCW 1; SATA 25;
  SFW 4
Hunter, Kristin 1931-
  See Lattany, Kristin (Elaine Eggleston)
  Hunter
Hunter, Mary
  See Austin, Mary (Hunter)
Hunter, Mollie 1922- .... **CLC 21**
  See also McIlwraith, Maureen Mollie
  Hunter
  See also AAYA 13; BYA 6; CANR 37, 78;
  CLR 25; DLB 161; JRDA; MAICYA 1,
  2; SAAS 7; SATA 54, 106; WYA; YAW
Hunter, Robert (?)-1734 .... **LC 7**
Hurston, Zora Neale 1891-1960 .. **CLC 7, 30,
  61; BLC 2; DC 12; SSC 4; WLCS**
  See also AAYA 15; AFAW 1, 2; AMWS 6;
  BW 1, 3; BYA 12; CA 85-88; CANR 61;
  CDALBS; DA; DA3; DAC; DAM MST,
  MULT, NOV; DFS 6; DLB 51, 86; EXPN;
  EXPS; FW; LAIT 3; MAWW; MTCW 1,
  2; NFS 3; RGAL 4; RGSF 2; SSFS 1, 6,
  11; TCLC 121; TUS; YAW
Husserl, E. G.
  See Husserl, Edmund (Gustav Albrecht)
Husserl, Edmund (Gustav Albrecht)
  1859-1938 .... **TCLC 100**
  See also CA 116; 133
Huston, John (Marcellus)
  1906-1987 .... **CLC 20**
  See also CA 73-76; 123; CANR 34; DLB
  26
Hustvedt, Siri 1955- .... **CLC 76**
  See also CA 137
Hutten, Ulrich von 1488-1523 .... **LC 16**
  See also DLB 179
Huxley, Aldous (Leonard)
  1894-1963 .... **CLC 1, 3, 4, 5, 8, 11, 18,
  35, 79; SSC 39; WLC**
  See also AAYA 11; BPFB 2; BRW 7; CA
  85-88; CANR 44, 99; CDBLB 1914-1945;
  DA; DA3; DAB; DAC; DAM MST, NOV,
  DLB 36, 100, 162, 195, 255; EXPN;
  LAIT 5; MTCW 1, 2; NFS 6; RGEL 2;
  SATA 63; SCFW 2; SFW 4; TEA; YAW
Huxley, T(homas) H(enry)
  1825-1895 .... **NCLC 67**
  See also DLB 57; TEA

Huysmans, Joris-Karl 1848-1907 ... **TCLC 7,
  69**
  See also CA 104; 165; DLB 123; EW 7;
  GFL 1789 to the Present; RGWL 2
Hwang, David Henry 1957- .. **CLC 55; DC 4**
  See also CA 127; 132; CAD; CANR 76;
  CD 5; DA3; DAM DRAM; DFS 11; DLB
  212, 228; INT CA-132; MTCW 2; RGAL
  4
Hyde, Anthony 1946- .... **CLC 42**
  See also Chase, Nicholas
  See also CA 136; CCA 1
Hyde, Margaret O(ldroyd) 1917- ..... **CLC 21**
  See also CA 1-4R; CANR 1, 36; CLR 23;
  JRDA; MAICYA 1, 2; SAAS 8; SATA 1,
  42, 76
Hynes, James 1956(?)- .... **CLC 65**
  See also CA 164; CANR 105
Hypatia c. 370-415 .... **CMLC 35**
Ian, Janis 1951- .... **CLC 21**
  See also CA 105; 187
Ibanez, Vicente Blasco
  See Blasco Ibanez, Vicente
Ibarbourou, Juana de 1895-1979
  See also HLCS 2; HW 1; LAW
Ibarguengoitia, Jorge 1928-1983 ...... **CLC 37**
  See also CA 124; 113; HW 1
Ibsen, Henrik (Johan) 1828-1906 ... **TCLC 2,
  8, 16, 37, 52; DC 2; WLC**
  See also CA 104; 141; DA; DA3; DAB;
  DAC; DAM DRAM, MST; DFS 15; EW
  7; LAIT 2; RGWL 2
Ibuse, Masuji 1898-1993 .... **CLC 22**
  See also Ibuse Masuji
  See also CA 127; 141; MJW
Ibuse Masuji
  See Ibuse, Masuji
  See also DLB 180
Ichikawa, Kon 1915- .... **CLC 20**
  See also CA 121
Ichiyo, Higuchi 1872-1896 .... **NCLC 49**
  See also MJW
Idle, Eric 1943-2000 .... **CLC 21**
  See also Monty Python
  See also CA 116; CANR 35, 91
Ignatow, David 1914-1997 .... **CLC 4, 7, 14,
  40; PC 34**
  See also CA 9-12R; 162; CAAS 3; CANR
  31, 57, 96; CP 7; DLB 5
Ignotus
  See Strachey, (Giles) Lytton
Ihimaera, Witi 1944- .... **CLC 46**
  See also CA 77-80; CN 7; RGSF 2
Ilf, Ilya .... **TCLC 21**
  See also Fainzilberg, Ilya Arnoldovich
Illyes, Gyula 1902-1983 .... **PC 16**
  See also CA 114; 109; CDWLB 4; DLB
  215; RGWL 2
Immermann, Karl (Lebrecht)
  1796-1840 .... **NCLC 4, 49**
  See also DLB 133
Ince, Thomas H. 1882-1924 .... **TCLC 89**
  See also IDFW 3, 4
Inchbald, Elizabeth 1753-1821 ...... **NCLC 62**
  See also DLB 39, 89; RGEL 2
Inclan, Ramon (Maria) del Valle
  See Valle-Inclan, Ramon (Maria) del
Infante, G(uillermo) Cabrera
  See Cabrera Infante, G(uillermo)
Ingalls, Rachel (Holmes) 1940- .... **CLC 42**
  See also CA 123; 127
Ingamells, Reginald Charles
  See Ingamells, Rex
Ingamells, Rex 1913-1955 .... **TCLC 35**
  See also CA 167; DLB 260

Inge, William (Motter) 1913-1973 ..... **CLC 1, 8, 19**
See also CA 9-12R; CDALB 1941-1968; DA3; DAM DRAM; DFS 1, 5, 8; DLB 7, 249; MTCW 1, 2; RGAL 4; TUS

Ingelow, Jean 1820-1897 .... **NCLC 39, 107**
See also DLB 35, 163; FANT; SATA 33

Ingram, Willis J.
See Harris, Mark

Innaurato, Albert (F.) 1948(?)- ... **CLC 21, 60**
See also CA 115; 122; CAD; CANR 78; CD 5; INT CA-122

Innes, Michael
See Stewart, J(ohn) I(nnes) M(ackintosh)
See also MSW

Innis, Harold Adams 1894-1952 .... **TCLC 77**
See also CA 181; DLB 88

Insluis, Alanus de
See Alain de Lille

Iola
See Wells-Barnett, Ida B(ell)

Ionesco, Eugene 1912-1994 ... **CLC 1, 4, 6, 9, 11, 15, 41, 86; DC 12; WLC**
See also CA 9-12R; 144; CANR 55; CWW 2; DA; DA3; DAB; DAC; DAM DRAM, MST; DFS 4, 9; EW 13; GFL 1789 to the Present; MTCW 1, 2; RGWL 2; SATA 7; SATA-Obit 79; TWA

Iqbal, Muhammad 1877-1938 .... **TCLC 28**

Ireland, Patrick
See O'Doherty, Brian

Irenaeus St. 130- .... **CMLC 42**

Irigaray, Luce 1930- .... **CLC 164**
See also CA 154; FW

Iron, Ralph
See Schreiner, Olive (Emilie Albertina)

Irving, John (Winslow) 1942- ... **CLC 13, 23, 38, 112**
See also AAYA 8; AMWS 6; BEST 89:3; BPFB 2; CA 25-28R; CANR 28, 73; CN 7; CPW; DA3; DAM NOV, POP; DLB 6; DLBY 1982; MTCW 1, 2; NFS 12, 14; RGAL 4; TUS

Irving, Washington 1783-1859 . **NCLC 2, 19, 95; SSC 2, 37; WLC**
See also AMW; CDALB 1640-1865; DA; DA3; DAB; DAC; DAM MST; DLB 3, 11, 30, 59, 73, 74, 183, 186, 250, 254; EXPS; LAIT 1; RGAL 4; RGSF 2; SSFS 1, 8; SUFW; TUS; WCH; YABC 2

Irwin, P. K.
See Page, P(atricia) K(athleen)

Isaacs, Jorge Ricardo 1837-1895 ... **NCLC 70**
See also LAW

Isaacs, Susan 1943- .... **CLC 32**
See also BEST 89:1; BPFB 2; CA 89-92; CANR 20, 41, 65; CPW; DA3; DAM POP; INT CANR-20; MTCW 1, 2

Isherwood, Christopher (William Bradshaw) 1904-1986 .... **CLC 1, 9, 11, 14, 44; SSC 56**
See also BRW 7; CA 13-16R; 117; CANR 35, 97; DA3; DAM DRAM, NOV; DLB 15, 195; DLBY 1986; IDTP; MTCW 1, 2; RGAL 4; RGEL 2; TUS; WLIT 4

Ishiguro, Kazuo 1954- .. **CLC 27, 56, 59, 110**
See also BEST 90:2; BPFB 2; BRWS 4; CA 120; CANR 49, 95; CN 7; DA3; DAM NOV; DLB 194; MTCW 1, 2; NFS 13; WLIT 4

Ishikawa, Hakuhin
See Ishikawa, Takuboku

Ishikawa, Takuboku 1886(?)-1912 .... **TCLC 15; PC 10**
See also CA 113; 153; DAM POET

Iskander, Fazil 1929- .... **CLC 47**
See also CA 102

Isler, Alan (David) 1934- .... **CLC 91**
See also CA 156; CANR 105

Ivan IV 1530-1584 .... **LC 17**

Ivanov, Vyacheslav Ivanovich 1866-1949 .... **TCLC 33**
See also CA 122

Ivask, Ivar Vidrik 1927-1992 .... **CLC 14**
See also CA 37-40R; 139; CANR 24

Ives, Morgan
See Bradley, Marion Zimmer
See also GLL 1

Izumi Shikibu c. 973-c. 1034 .... **CMLC 33**

J .... **TCLC 11, 17, 32; SSC 7, 56; WLC**
See also AAYA 21; AMW; BPFB 1; BYA 3; CA 109; 140; CANR 86; CDALB 1865-1917; DA; DA3; DAB; DAC; DAM MST, NOV, POET; DLB 12, 54, 78; EXPN; EXPS; LAIT 2; NFS 4; PFS 9; RGAL 4; RGSF 2; SSFS 4; TUS; WYA; YABC 2

J. R. S.
See Gogarty, Oliver St. John

Jabran, Kahlil
See Gibran, Kahlil

Jabran, Khalil
See Gibran, Kahlil

Jackson, Daniel
See Wingrove, David (John)

Jackson, Helen Hunt 1830-1885 .... **NCLC 90**
See also DLB 42, 47, 186, 189; RGAL 4

Jackson, Jesse 1908-1983 .... **CLC 12**
See also BW 1; CA 25-28R; 109; CANR 27; CLR 28; CWRI 5; MAICYA 1, 2; SATA 2, 29; SATA-Obit 48

Jackson, Laura (Riding) 1901-1991 .... **PC 44**
See Riding, Laura
See also CA 65-68; 135; CANR 28, 89; DLB 48

Jackson, Sam
See Trumbo, Dalton

Jackson, Sara
See Wingrove, David (John)

Jackson, Shirley 1919-1965 . **CLC 11, 60, 87; SSC 9, 39; WLC**
See also AAYA 9; AMWS 9; BPFB 2; CA 1-4R; 25-28R; CANR 4, 52; CDALB 1941-1968; DA; DA3; DAC; DAM MST; DLB 6, 234; EXPS; HGG; LAIT 4; MTCW 2; RGAL 4; RGSF 2; SATA 2; SSFS 1; SUFW

Jacob, (Cyprien-)Max 1876-1944 .... **TCLC 6**
See also CA 104; 193; DLB 258; GFL 1789 to the Present; GLL 2; RGWL 2

Jacobs, Harriet A(nn) 1813(?)-1897 .... **NCLC 67**
See also AFAW 1, 2; DLB 239; FW; LAIT 2; RGAL 4

Jacobs, Jim 1942- .... **CLC 12**
See also CA 97-100; INT 97-100

Jacobs, W(illiam) W(ymark) 1863-1943 .... **TCLC 22**
See also CA 121; 167; DLB 135; EXPS; HGG; RGEL 2; RGSF 2; SSFS 2; SUFW

Jacobsen, Jens Peter 1847-1885 .... **NCLC 34**

Jacobsen, Josephine 1908- .... **CLC 48, 102**
See also CA 33-36R; CAAS 18; CANR 23, 48; CCA 1; CP 7; DLB 244

Jacobson, Dan 1929- .... **CLC 4, 14**
See also AFW; CA 1-4R; CANR 2, 25, 66; CN 7; DLB 14, 207, 225; MTCW 1; RGSF 2

Jacqueline
See Carpentier (y Valmont), Alejo

Jagger, Mick 1944- .... **CLC 17**

Jahiz, al- c. 780-c. 869 .... **CMLC 25**

Jakes, John (William) 1932- .... **CLC 29**
See also AAYA 32; BEST 89:4; BPFB 2; CA 57-60; CANR 10, 43, 66, 111; CPW; CSW; DA3; DAM NOV, POP; DLBY 1983; FANT; INT CANR-10; MTCW 1, 2; RHW; SATA 62; SFW 4; TCWW 2

James I 1394-1437 .... **LC 20**
See also RGEL 2

James, Andrew
See Kirkup, James

James, C(yril) L(ionel) R(obert) 1901-1989 .... **CLC 33; BLCS**
See also BW 2; CA 117; 125; 128; CANR 62; DLB 125; MTCW 1

James, Daniel (Lewis) 1911-1988
See Santiago, Danny
See also CA 174; 125

James, Dynely
See Mayne, William (James Carter)

James, Henry Sr. 1811-1882 .... **NCLC 53**

James, Henry 1843-1916 ..... **TCLC 2, 11, 24, 40, 47, 64; SSC 8, 32, 47; WLC**
See also AMW; AMWR 1; BPFB 2; BRW 6; CA 104; 132; CDALB 1865-1917; DA; DA3; DAB; DAC; DAM MST, NOV; DLB 12, 71, 74, 189; DLBD 13; EXPS; HGG; LAIT 2; MTCW 1, 2; NFS 12; RGAL 4; RGEL 2; RGSF 2; SSFS 9; SUFW; TUS

James, M. R.
See James, Montague (Rhodes)
See also DLB 156, 201

James, Montague (Rhodes) 1862-1936 .... **TCLC 6; SSC 16**
See also James, M. R.
See also CA 104; HGG; RGEL 2; RGSF 2; SUFW

James, P. D. .... **CLC 18, 46, 122**
See also White, Phyllis Dorothy James
See also BEST 90:2; BPFB 2; BRWS 4; CDBLB 1960 to Present; DLB 87; DLBD 17; MSW

James, Philip
See Moorcock, Michael (John)

James, Samuel
See Stephens, James

James, Seumas
See Stephens, James

James, Stephen
See Stephens, James

James, William 1842-1910 .... **TCLC 15, 32**
See also AMW; CA 109; 193; RGAL 4

Jameson, Anna 1794-1860 .... **NCLC 43**
See also DLB 99, 166

Jameson, Fredric (R.) 1934- .... **CLC 142**
See also CA 196; DLB 67

Jami, Nur al-Din 'Abd al-Rahman 1414-1492 .... **LC 9**

Jammes, Francis 1868-1938 .... **TCLC 75**
See also CA 198; GFL 1789 to the Present

Jandl, Ernst 1925-2000 .... **CLC 34**
See also CA 200

Janowitz, Tama 1957- .... **CLC 43, 145**
See also CA 106; CANR 52, 89; CN 7; CPW; DAM POP

Japrisot, Sebastien 1931- .... **CLC 90**
See also Rossi, Jean Baptiste
See also CMW 4

Jarrell, Randall 1914-1965 .... **CLC 1, 2, 6, 9, 13, 49; PC 41**
See also AMW; BYA 5; CA 5-8R; 25-28R; CABS 2; CANR 6, 34; CDALB 1941-1968; CLR 6; CWRI 5; DAM POET; DLB 48, 52; EXPP; MAICYA 1, 2; MTCW 1, 2; PAB; PFS 2; RGAL 4; SATA 7

Jarry, Alfred 1873-1907 .... **TCLC 2, 14; SSC 20**
See also CA 104; 153; DA3; DAM DRAM; DFS 8; DLB 192, 258; EW 9; GFL 1789 to the Present; RGWL 2; TWA

Jarvis, E. K.
See Silverberg, Robert

Jawien, Andrzej
See John Paul II, Pope

Jaynes, Roderick
   See Coen, Ethan

Jeake, Samuel, Jr.
   See Aiken, Conrad (Potter)

Jean Paul 1763-1825 .... **NCLC 7**

Jefferies, (John) Richard
   1848-1887 .... **NCLC 47**
   See also DLB 98, 141; RGEL 2; SATA 16;
   SFW 4

Jeffers, (John) Robinson 1887-1962 .. **CLC 2,**
   3, 11, 15, 54; PC 17; WLC
   See also AMWS 2; CA 85-88; CANR 35;
   CDALB 1917-1929; DA; DAC; DAM
   MST, POET; DLB 45, 212; MTCW 1, 2;
   PAB; PFS 3, 4; RGAL 4

Jefferson, Janet
   See Mencken, H(enry) L(ouis)

Jefferson, Thomas 1743-1826 . **NCLC 11, 103**
   See also ANW; CDALB 1640-1865; DA3;
   DLB 31, 183; LAIT 1; RGAL 4

Jeffrey, Francis 1773-1850 .... **NCLC 33**
   See also Francis, Lord Jeffrey

Jelakowitch, Ivan
   See Heijermans, Herman

Jellicoe, (Patricia) Ann 1927- .... **CLC 27**
   See also CA 85-88; CBD; CD 5; CWD;
   CWRI 5; DLB 13, 233; FW

Jemyma
   See Holley, Marietta

Jen, Gish .... **CLC 70**
   See also Jen, Lillian

Jen, Lillian 1956(?)-
   See Jen, Gish
   See also CA 135; CANR 89

Jenkins, (John) Robin 1912- .... **CLC 52**
   See also CA 1-4R; CANR 1; CN 7; DLB
   14

Jennings, Elizabeth (Joan)
   1926-2001 .... **CLC 5, 14, 131**
   See also BRWS 5; CA 61-64; 200; CAAS
   5; CANR 8, 39, 66; CP 7; CWP; DLB 27;
   MTCW 1; SATA 66

Jennings, Waylon 1937- .... **CLC 21**

Jensen, Johannes V. 1873-1950 ...... **TCLC 41**
   See also CA 170; DLB 214

Jensen, Laura (Linnea) 1948- .... **CLC 37**
   See also CA 103

Jerome, Jerome K(lapka)
   1859-1927 .... **TCLC 23**
   See also CA 119; 177; DLB 10, 34, 135;
   RGEL 2

Jerrold, Douglas William
   1803-1857 .... **NCLC 2**
   See also DLB 158, 159; RGEL 2

Jewett, (Theodora) Sarah Orne
   1849-1909 .... **TCLC 1, 22; SSC 6, 44**
   See also AMW; CA 108; 127; CANR 71;
   DLB 12, 74, 221; EXPS; FW; MAWW;
   NFS 15; RGAL 4; RGSF 2; SATA 15;
   SSFS 4

Jewsbury, Geraldine (Endsor)
   1812-1880 .... **NCLC 22**
   See also DLB 21

Jhabvala, Ruth Prawer 1927- . **CLC 4, 8, 29,**
   94, 138
   See also BRWS 5; CA 1-4R; CANR 2, 29,
   51, 74, 91; CN 7; DAB; DAM NOV; DLB
   139, 194; IDFW 3, 4; INT CANR-29;
   MTCW 1, 2; RGSF 2; RGWL 2; RHW;
   TEA

Jibran, Kahlil
   See Gibran, Kahlil

Jibran, Khalil
   See Gibran, Kahlil

Jiles, Paulette 1943- .... **CLC 13, 58**
   See also CA 101; CANR 70; CWP

Jimenez (Mantecon), Juan Ramon
   1881-1958 .... **TCLC 4; HLC 1; PC 7**
   See also CA 104; 131; CANR 74; DAM
   MULT, POET; DLB 134; EW 9; HW 1;
   MTCW 1, 2; RGWL 2

Jimenez, Ramon
   See Jimenez (Mantecon), Juan Ramon

Jimenez Mantecon, Juan
   See Jimenez (Mantecon), Juan Ramon

Jin, Ha .... **CLC 109**
   See also Jin, Xuefei
   See also CA 152; DLB 244

Jin, Xuefei 1956-
   See Jin, Ha
   See also CANR 91

Joel, Billy .... **CLC 26**
   See also Joel, William Martin

Joel, William Martin 1949-
   See Joel, Billy
   See also CA 108

John, Saint 107th cent. -100 .... **CMLC 27**

John of the Cross, St. 1542-1591 .... **LC 18**
   See also RGWL 2

John Paul II, Pope 1920- .... **CLC 128**
   See also CA 106; 133

Johnson, B(ryan) S(tanley William)
   1933-1973 .... **CLC 6, 9**
   See also CA 9-12R; 53-56; CANR 9; DLB
   14, 40; RGEL 2

Johnson, Benjamin F., of Boone
   See Riley, James Whitcomb

Johnson, Charles (Richard) 1948- .... **CLC 7,**
   51, 65, 163; BLC 2
   See also AFAW 2; AMWS 6; BW 2, 3; CA
   116; CAAS 18; CANR 42, 66, 82; CN 7;
   DAM MULT; DLB 33; MTCW 2; RGAL
   4

Johnson, Denis 1949- . **CLC 52, 160; SSC 56**
   See also CA 117; 121; CANR 71, 99; CN
   7; DLB 120

Johnson, Diane 1934- .... **CLC 5, 13, 48**
   See also BPFB 2; CA 41-44R; CANR 17,
   40, 62, 95; CN 7; DLBY 1980; INT
   CANR-17; MTCW 1

Johnson, Eyvind (Olof Verner)
   1900-1976 .... **CLC 14**
   See also CA 73-76; 69-72; CANR 34, 101;
   DLB 259; EW 12

Johnson, J. R.
   See James, C(yril) L(ionel) R(obert)

Johnson, James Weldon
   1871-1938 . **TCLC 3, 19; BLC 2; PC 24**
   See also AFAW 1, 2; BW 1, 3; CA 104;
   125; CANR 82; CDALB 1917-1929; CLR
   32; DA3; DAM MULT, POET; DLB 51;
   EXPP; MTCW 1, 2; PFS 1; RGAL 4;
   SATA 31; TUS

Johnson, Joyce 1935- .... **CLC 58**
   See also CA 125; 129; CANR 102

Johnson, Judith (Emlyn) 1936- ... **CLC 7, 15**
   See also Sherwin, Judith Johnson
   See also CA 25-28R, 153; CANR 34

Johnson, Lionel (Pigot)
   1867-1902 .... **TCLC 19**
   See also CA 117; DLB 19; RGEL 2

Johnson, Marguerite (Annie)
   See Angelou, Maya

Johnson, Mel
   See Malzberg, Barry N(athaniel)

Johnson, Pamela Hansford
   1912-1981 .... **CLC 1, 7, 27**
   See also CA 1-4R; 104; CANR 2, 28; DLB
   15; MTCW 1, 2; RGEL 2

Johnson, Paul (Bede) 1928- .... **CLC 147**
   See also BEST 89:4; CA 17-20R; CANR
   34, 62, 100

Johnson, Robert .... **CLC 70**

Johnson, Robert 1911(?)-1938 .... **TCLC 69**
   See also BW 3; CA 174

Johnson, Samuel 1709-1784 .... **LC 15, 52;**
   WLC
   See also BRW 3; BRWR 1; CDBLB 1660-
   1789; DA; DAB; DAC; DAM MST; DLB
   39, 95, 104, 142, 213; RGEL 2; TEA

Johnson, Uwe 1934-1984 .. **CLC 5, 10, 15, 40**
   See also CA 1-4R; 112; CANR 1, 39; CD-
   WLB 2; DLB 75; MTCW 1; RGWL 2

Johnston, George (Benson) 1913- .... **CLC 51**
   See also CA 1-4R; CANR 5, 20; CP 7; DLB
   88

Johnston, Jennifer (Prudence)
   1930- .... **CLC 7, 150**
   See also CA 85-88; CANR 92; CN 7; DLB
   14

Joinville, Jean de 1224(?)-1317 ..... **CMLC 38**

Jolley, (Monica) Elizabeth 1923- ..... **CLC 46;**
   SSC 19
   See also CA 127; CAAS 13; CANR 59; CN
   7; RGSF 2

Jones, Arthur Llewellyn 1863-1947
   See Machen, Arthur
   See also CA 104; 179; HGG

Jones, D(ouglas) G(ordon) 1929- ..... **CLC 10**
   See also CA 29-32R; CANR 13, 90; CP 7;
   DLB 53

Jones, David (Michael) 1895-1974 .... **CLC 2,**
   4, 7, 13, 42
   See also BRW 6; BRWS 7; CA 9-12R; 53-
   56; CANR 28; CDBLB 1945-1960; DLB
   20, 100; MTCW 1; PAB; RGEL 2

Jones, David Robert 1947-
   See Bowie, David
   See also CA 103; CANR 104

Jones, Diana Wynne 1934- .... **CLC 26**
   See also AAYA 12; BYA 6, 7, 9, 11, 13; CA
   49-52; CANR 4, 26, 56; CLR 23; DLB
   161; FANT; JRDA; MAICYA 1, 2; SAAS
   7; SATA 9, 70, 108; SFW 4; YAW

Jones, Edward P. 1950- .... **CLC 76**
   See also BW 2, 3; CA 142; CANR 79; CSW

Jones, Gayl 1949- ...... **CLC 6, 9, 131; BLC 2**
   See also AFAW 1, 2; BW 2, 3; CA 77-80;
   CANR 27, 66; CN 7; CSW; DA3; DAM
   MULT; DLB 33; MTCW 1, 2; RGAL 4

Jones, James 1921-1977 ...... **CLC 1, 3, 10, 39**
   See also AITN 1, 2; AMWS 11; BPFB 2;
   CA 1-4R; 69-72; CANR 6; DLB 2, 143;
   DLBD 17; DLBY 1998; MTCW 1; RGAL
   4

Jones, John J.
   See Lovecraft, H(oward) P(hillips)

Jones, LeRoi .... **CLC 1, 2, 3, 5, 10, 14**
   See also Baraka, Amiri
   See also MTCW 2

Jones, Louis B. 1953- .... **CLC 65**
   See also CA 141; CANR 73

Jones, Madison (Percy, Jr.) 1925- ...... **CLC 4**
   See also CA 13-16R; CAAS 11; CANR 7,
   54, 83; CN 7; CSW; DLB 152

Jones, Mervyn 1922- .... **CLC 10, 52**
   See also CA 45-48; CAAS 5; CANR 1, 91;
   CN 7; MTCW 1

Jones, Mick 1956(?)- .... **CLC 30**

Jones, Nettie (Pearl) 1941- .... **CLC 34**
   See also BW 2; CA 137; CAAS 20; CANR
   88

Jones, Preston 1936-1979 .... **CLC 10**
   See also CA 73-76; 89-92; DLB 7

Jones, Robert F(rancis) 1934- .... **CLC 7**
   See also CA 49-52; CANR 2, 61

Jones, Rod 1953- .... **CLC 50**
   See also CA 128

Jones, Terence Graham Parry
   1942- .... **CLC 21**
   See also Jones, Terry; Monty Python
   See also CA 112; 116; CANR 35, 93; INT
   116; SATA 127

Lazarus, Emma 1849-1887 ...... NCLC 8, 109

Lazarus, Felix
See Cable, George Washington

Lazarus, Henry
See Slavitt, David R(ytman)

Lea, Joan
See Neufeld, John (Arthur)

Leacock, Stephen (Butler)
1869-1944 .... TCLC 2; SSC 39
See also CA 104; 141; CANR 80; DAC;
DAM MST; DLB 92; MTCW 2; RGEL 2;
RGSF 2

Lead, Jane Ward 1623-1704 .... LC 72
See also DLB 131

Leapor, Mary 1722-1746 .... LC 80
See also DLB 109

Lear, Edward 1812-1888 .... NCLC 3
See also BRW 5; CLR 1, 75; DLB 32, 163,
166; MAICYA 1, 2; RGEL 2; SATA 18,
100; WCH; WP

Lear, Norman (Milton) 1922- .... CLC 12
See also CA 73-76

Leautaud, Paul 1872-1956 .... TCLC 83
See also CA 203; DLB 65; GFL 1789 to the
Present

Leavis, F(rank) R(aymond)
1895-1978 .... CLC 24
See also BRW 7; CA 21-24R; 77-80; CANR
44; DLB 242; MTCW 1, 2; RGEL 2

Leavitt, David 1961- .... CLC 34
See also CA 116; 122; CANR 50, 62, 101;
CPW; DA3; DAM POP; DLB 130; GLL
1; INT 122; MTCW 2

Leblanc, Maurice (Marie Emile)
1864-1941 .... TCLC 49
See also CA 110; CMW 4

Lebowitz, Fran(ces Ann) 1951(?)- ... CLC 11,
36
See also CA 81-84; CANR 14, 60, 70; INT
CANR-14; MTCW 1

Lebrecht, Peter
See Tieck, (Johann) Ludwig

le Carre, John .... CLC 3, 5, 9, 15, 28
See also Cornwell, David (John Moore)
See also AAYA 42; BEST 89:4; BPFB 2;
BRWS 2; CDBLB 1960 to Present; CMW
4; CN 7; CPW; DLB 87; MSW; MTCW
2; RGEL 2; TEA

Le Clezio, J(ean) M(arie) G(ustave)
1940- .... CLC 31, 155
See also CA 116; 128; DLB 83; GFL 1789
to the Present; RGSF 2

Leconte de Lisle, Charles-Marie-Rene
1818-1894 .... NCLC 29
See also DLB 217; EW 6; GFL 1789 to the
Present

Le Coq, Monsieur
See Simenon, Georges (Jacques Christian)

Leduc, Violette 1907-1972 .... CLC 22
See also CA 13-14; 33-36R; CANR 69;
CAP 1; GFL 1789 to the Present; GLL 1

Ledwidge, Francis 1887(?)-1917 .... TCLC 23
See also CA 123; 203; DLB 20

Lee, Andrea 1953- .... CLC 36; BLC 2
See also BW 1, 3; CA 125; CANR 82;
DAM MULT

Lee, Andrew
See Auchincloss, Louis (Stanton)

Lee, Chang-rae 1965- .... CLC 91
See also CA 148; CANR 89

Lee, Don L. .... CLC 2
See also Madhubuti, Haki R.

Lee, George W(ashington)
1894-1976 .... CLC 52; BLC 2
See also BW 1; CA 125; CANR 83; DAM
MULT; DLB 51

Lee, (Nelle) Harper 1926- .... CLC 12, 60;
WLC
See also AAYA 13; AMWS 8; BPFB 2;
BYA 3; CA 13-16R; CANR 51; CDALB
1941-1968; CSW; DA; DA3; DAB; DAC;
DAM MST, NOV; DLB 6; EXPN; LAIT
3; MTCW 1, 2; NFS 2; SATA 11; WYA;
YAW

Lee, Helen Elaine 1959(?)- .... CLC 86
See also CA 148

Lee, John .... CLC 70

Lee, Julian
See Latham, Jean Lee

Lee, Larry
See Lee, Lawrence

Lee, Laurie 1914-1997 .... CLC 90
See also CA 77-80; 158; CANR 33, 73; CP
7; CPW; DAB; DAM POP; DLB 27;
MTCW 1; RGEL 2

Lee, Lawrence 1941-1990 .... CLC 34
See also CA 131; CANR 43

Lee, Li-Young 1957- .... CLC 164; PC 24
See also CA 153; CP 7; DLB 165; PFS 11,
15

Lee, Manfred B(ennington)
1905-1971 .... CLC 11
See also Queen, Ellery
See also CA 1-4R; 29-32R; CANR 2; CMW
4; DLB 137

Lee, Shelton Jackson 1957(?)- .... CLC 105;
BLCS
See also Lee, Spike
See also BW 2, 3; CA 125; CANR 42;
DAM MULT

Lee, Spike
See Lee, Shelton Jackson
See also AAYA 4, 29

Lee, Stan 1922- .... CLC 17
See also AAYA 5; CA 108; 111; INT 111

Lee, Tanith 1947- .... CLC 46
See also AAYA 15; CA 37-40R; CANR 53,
102; DLB 261; FANT; SATA 8, 88, 134;
SFW 4; SUFW; YAW

Lee, Vernon .... TCLC 5; SSC 33
See also Paget, Violet
See also DLB 57, 153, 156, 174, 178; GLL
1; SUFW

Lee, William
See Burroughs, William S(eward)
See also GLL 1

Lee, Willy
See Burroughs, William S(eward)
See also GLL 1

Lee-Hamilton, Eugene (Jacob)
1845-1907 .... TCLC 22
See also CA 117

Leet, Judith 1935- .... CLC 11
See also CA 187

Le Fanu, Joseph Sheridan
1814-1873 .... NCLC 9, 58; SSC 14
See also CMW 4; DA3; DAM POP; DLB
21, 70, 159, 178; HGG; RGEL 2; RGSF
2; SUFW

Leffland, Ella 1931- .... CLC 19
See also CA 29-32R; CANR 35, 78, 82;
DLBY 1984; INT CANR-35; SATA 65

Leger, Alexis
See Leger, (Marie-Rene Auguste) Alexis
Saint-Leger

Leger, (Marie-Rene Auguste) Alexis
Saint-Leger 1887-1975 .. CLC 4, 11, 46;
PC 23
See also Perse, Saint-John; Saint-John Perse
See also CA 13-16R; 61-64; CANR 43;
DAM POET; MTCW 1

Leger, Saintleger
See Leger, (Marie-Rene Auguste) Alexis
Saint-Leger

Le Guin, Ursula K(roeber) 1929- ..... CLC 8,
13, 22, 45, 71, 136; SSC 12
See also AAYA 9, 27; AITN 1; BPFB 2;
BYA 5, 8, 11, 14; CA 21-24R; CANR 9,
32, 52, 74; CDALB 1968-1988; CLR 3,
28; CN 7; CPW; DA3; DAB; DAC; DAM
MST, POP; DLB 8, 52, 256; EXPS;
FANT; FW; INT CANR-32; JRDA; LAIT
5; MAICYA 1, 2; MTCW 1, 2; NFS 6, 9;
SATA 4, 52, 99; SCFW; SFW 4; SSFS 2;
SUFW; WYA; YAW

Lehmann, Rosamond (Nina)
1901-1990 .... CLC 5
See also CA 77-80; 131; CANR 8, 73; DLB
15; MTCW 2; RGEL 2; RHW

Leiber, Fritz (Reuter, Jr.)
1910-1992 .... CLC 25
See also BPFB 2; CA 45-48; 139; CANR 2,
40, 86; DLB 8; FANT; HGG; MTCW 1,
2; SATA 45; SATA-Obit 73; SCFW 2;
SFW 4; SUFW

Leibniz, Gottfried Wilhelm von
1646-1716 .... LC 35
See also DLB 168

Leimbach, Martha 1963-
See Leimbach, Marti
See also CA 130

Leimbach, Marti .... CLC 65
See also Leimbach, Martha

Leino, Eino .... TCLC 24
See also Loennbohm, Armas Eino Leopold

Leiris, Michel (Julien) 1901-1990 ..... CLC 61
See also CA 119; 128; 132; GFL 1789 to
the Present

Leithauser, Brad 1953- .... CLC 27
See also CA 107; CANR 27, 81; CP 7; DLB
120

Lelchuk, Alan 1938- .... CLC 5
See also CA 45-48; CAAS 20; CANR 1,
70; CN 7

Lem, Stanislaw 1921- ...... CLC 8, 15, 40, 149
See also CA 105; CAAS 1; CANR 32;
CWW 2; MTCW 1; SCFW 2; SFW 4

Lemann, Nancy 1956- .... CLC 39
See also CA 118; 136

Lemonnier, (Antoine Louis) Camille
1844-1913 .... TCLC 22
See also CA 121

Lenau, Nikolaus 1802-1850 .... NCLC 16

L'Engle, Madeleine (Camp Franklin)
1918- .... CLC 12
See also AAYA 28; AITN 2; BPFB 2; BYA
2, 4, 5, 7; CA 1-4R; CANR 3, 21, 39, 66,
107; CLR 1, 14, 57; CPW; CWRI 5; DA3;
DAM POP; DLB 52; JRDA; MAICYA 1,
2; MTCW 1, 2; SAAS 15; SATA 1, 27,
75, 128; SFW 4; WYA; YAW

Lengyel, Jozsef 1896-1975 .... CLC 7
See also CA 85-88; 57-60; CANR 71;
RGSF 2

Lenin 1870-1924
See Lenin, V. I.
See also CA 121; 168

Lenin, V. I. .... TCLC 67
See also Lenin

Lennon, John (Ono) 1940-1980 .. CLC 12, 35
See also CA 102; SATA 114

Lennox, Charlotte Ramsay
1729(?)-1804 .... NCLC 23
See also DLB 39; RGEL 2

Lentricchia, Frank, (Jr.) 1940- .... CLC 34
See also CA 25-28R; CANR 19, 106; DLB
246

Lenz, Gunter .... CLC 65

Lenz, Siegfried 1926- .... CLC 27; SSC 33
See also CA 89-92; CANR 80; CWW 2;
DLB 75; RGSF 2; RGWL 2

Leon, David
See Jacob, (Cyprien-)Max

Lindsay, David 1878(?)-1945 .... **TCLC 15**
See also CA 113; 187; DLB 255; FANT;
SFW 4; SUFW

Lindsay, (Nicholas) Vachel
1879-1931 .... **TCLC 17; PC 23; WLC**
See also AMWS 1; CA 114; 135; CANR
79; CDALB 1865-1917; DA; DA3; DAC;
DAM MST, POET; DLB 54; EXPP;
RGAL 4; SATA 40; WP

Linke-Poot
See Doeblin, Alfred

Linney, Romulus 1930- .... **CLC 51**
See also CA 1-4R; CAD; CANR 40, 44,
79; CD 5; CSW; RGAL 4

Linton, Eliza Lynn 1822-1898 .... **NCLC 41**
See also DLB 18

Li Po 701-763 .... **CMLC 2; PC 29**
See also WP

Lipsius, Justus 1547-1606 .... **LC 16**

Lipsyte, Robert (Michael) 1938- ...... **CLC 21**
See also AAYA 7; CA 17-20R; CANR 8,
57; CLR 23, 76; DA; DAC; DAM MST,
NOV; JRDA; LAIT 5; MAICYA 1, 2;
SATA 5, 68, 113; WYA; YAW

Lish, Gordon (Jay) 1934- ... **CLC 45; SSC 18**
See also CA 113; 117; CANR 79; DLB 130;
INT 117

Lispector, Clarice 1925(?)-1977 .... **CLC 43;**
HLCS 2; SSC 34
See also CA 139; 116; CANR 71; CDWLB
3; DLB 113; DNFS 1; FW; HW 2; LAW;
RGSF 2; RGWL 2; WLIT 1

Littell, Robert 1935(?)- .... **CLC 42**
See also CA 109; 112; CANR 64; CMW 4

Little, Malcolm 1925-1965
See Malcolm X
See also BW 1, 3; CA 125; 111; CANR 82;
DA; DA3; DAB; DAC; DAM MST,
MULT; MTCW 1, 2; NCFS 3

Littlewit, Humphrey Gent.
See Lovecraft, H(oward) P(hillips)

Litwos
See Sienkiewicz, Henryk (Adam Alexander
Pius)

Liu, E. 1857-1909 .... **TCLC 15**
See also CA 115; 190

Lively, Penelope (Margaret) 1933- .. **CLC 32,**
50
See also BPFB 2; CA 41-44R; CANR 29,
67, 79; CLR 7; CN 7; CWRI 5; DAM
NOV; DLB 14, 161, 207; FANT; JRDA;
MAICYA 1, 2; MTCW 1, 2; SATA 7, 60,
101; TEA

Livesay, Dorothy (Kathleen)
1909-1996 .... **CLC 4, 15, 79**
See also AITN 2; CA 25-28R; CAAS 8;
CANR 36, 67; DAC; DAM MST, POET;
DLB 68; FW; MTCW 1; RGEL 2; TWA

Livy c. 59 B.C.-c. 12 .... **CMLC 11**
See also AW 2; CDWLB 1; DLB 211;
RGWL 2

Lizardi, Jose Joaquin Fernandez de
1776-1827 .... **NCLC 30**
See also LAW

Llewellyn, Richard
See Llewellyn Lloyd, Richard Dafydd Viv-
ian
See also DLB 15

Llewellyn Lloyd, Richard Dafydd Vivian
1906-1983 .... **CLC 7, 80**
See also Llewellyn, Richard
See also CA 53-56; 111; CANR 7, 71;
SATA 11; SATA-Obit 37

Llosa, (Jorge) Mario (Pedro) Vargas
See Vargas Llosa, (Jorge) Mario (Pedro)

Lloyd, Manda
See Mander, (Mary) Jane

Lloyd Webber, Andrew 1948-
See Webber, Andrew Lloyd
See also AAYA 1, 38; CA 116; 149; DAM
DRAM; SATA 56

Llull, Ramon c. 1235-c. 1316 .... **CMLC 12**

Lobb, Ebenezer
See Upward, Allen

Locke, Alain (Le Roy) 1886-1954 . **TCLC 43;**
BLCS
See also BW 1, 3; CA 106; 124; CANR 79;
RGAL 4

Locke, John 1632-1704 .... **LC 7, 35**
See also DLB 31, 101, 213, 252; RGEL 2;
WLIT 3

Locke-Elliott, Sumner
See Elliott, Sumner Locke

Lockhart, John Gibson 1794-1854 .. **NCLC 6**
See also DLB 110, 116, 144

Lockridge, Ross (Franklin), Jr.
1914-1948 .... **TCLC 111**
See also CA 108; 145; CANR 79; DLB 143;
DLBY 1980; RGAL 4; RHW

Lodge, David (John) 1935- ...... **CLC 36, 141**
See also BEST 90:1; BRWS 4; CA 17-20R;
CANR 19, 53, 92; CN 7; CPW; DAM
POP; DLB 14, 194; INT CANR-19;
MTCW 1, 2

Lodge, Thomas 1558-1625 .... **LC 41**
See also DLB 172; RGEL 2

Loewinsohn, Ron(ald William)
1937- .... **CLC 52**
See also CA 25-28R; CANR 71

Logan, Jake
See Smith, Martin Cruz

Logan, John (Burton) 1923-1987 .... **CLC 5**
See also CA 77-80; 124; CANR 45; DLB 5

Lo Kuan-chung 1330(?)-1400(?) .... **LC 12**

Lombard, Nap
See Johnson, Pamela Hansford

Lomotey (editor), Kofi .... **CLC 70**

London, Jack 1876-1916 ..... **TCLC 9, 15, 39;**
SSC 4, 49; WLC
See also London, John Griffith
See also AAYA 13; AITN 2; AMW; BPFB
2; BYA 4, 13; CDALB 1865-1917; DLB
8, 12, 78, 212; EXPS; LAIT 3; NFS 8;
RGAL 4; RGSF 2; SATA 18; SFW 4;
SSFS 7; TCWW 2; TUS; WYA; YAW

London, John Griffith 1876-1916
See London, Jack
See also CA 110; 119; CANR 73; DA; DA3;
DAB; DAC; DAM MST, NOV; JRDA;
MAICYA 1, 2; MTCW 1, 2

Long, Emmett
See Leonard, Elmore (John, Jr.)

Longbaugh, Harry
See Goldman, William (W.)

Longfellow, Henry Wadsworth
1807-1882 .... **NCLC 2, 45, 101, 103; PC**
30; WLCS
See also AMW; CDALB 1640-1865; DA;
DA3; DAB; DAC; DAM MST, POET;
DLB 1, 59, 235; EXPP; PAB; PFS 2, 7;
RGAL 4; SATA 19; TUS; WP

Longinus c. 1st cent. - .... **CMLC 27**
See also AW 2; DLB 176

Longley, Michael 1939- .... **CLC 29**
See also BRWS 8; CA 102; CP 7; DLB 40

Longus fl. c. 2nd cent. - .... **CMLC 7**

Longway, A. Hugh
See Lang, Andrew

Lonnrot, Elias 1802-1884 .... **NCLC 53**
See also EFS 1

Lonsdale, Roger ed. .... **CLC 65**

Lopate, Phillip 1943- .... **CLC 29**
See also CA 97-100; CANR 88; DLBY
1980; INT 97-100

Lopez, Barry (Holstun) 1945- .... **CLC 70**
See also AAYA 9; ANW; CA 65-68; CANR
7, 23, 47, 68, 92; DLB 256; INT CANR-7,
-23; MTCW 1; RGAL 4; SATA 67

Lopez Portillo (y Pacheco), Jose
1920- .... **CLC 46**
See also CA 129; HW 1

Lopez y Fuentes, Gregorio
1897(?)-1966 .... **CLC 32**
See also CA 131; HW 1

Lorca, Federico Garcia
See Garcia Lorca, Federico
See also DFS 4; EW 11; RGWL 2; WP

Lord, Bette Bao 1938- .... **CLC 23; AAL**
See also BEST 90:3; BPFB 2; CA 107;
CANR 41, 79; INT CA-107; SATA 58

Lord Auch
See Bataille, Georges

Lord Brooke
See Greville, Fulke

Lord Byron
See Byron, George Gordon (Noel)

Lorde, Audre (Geraldine)
1934-1992 .. **CLC 18, 71; BLC 2; PC 12**
See also Domini, Rey
See also AFAW 1, 2; BW 1, 3; CA 25-28R;
142; CANR 16, 26, 46, 82; DA3; DAM
MULT, POET; DLB 41; FW; MTCW 1,
2; RGAL 4

Lord Houghton
See Milnes, Richard Monckton

Lord Jeffrey
See Jeffrey, Francis

Loreaux, Nichol .... **CLC 65**

Lorenzini, Carlo 1826-1890
See Collodi, Carlo
See also MAICYA 1, 2; SATA 29, 100

Lorenzo, Heberto Padilla
See Padilla (Lorenzo), Heberto

Loris
See Hofmannsthal, Hugo von

Loti, Pierre .... **TCLC 11**
See also Viaud, (Louis Marie) Julien
See also DLB 123; GFL 1789 to the Present

Lou, Henri
See Andreas-Salome, Lou

Louie, David Wong 1954- .... **CLC 70**
See also CA 139

Louis, Father M.
See Merton, Thomas (James)

Lovecraft, H(oward) P(hillips)
1890-1937 .... **TCLC 4, 22; SSC 3, 52**
See also AAYA 14; BPFB 2; CA 104; 133;
CANR 106; DA3; DAM POP; HGG;
MTCW 1, 2; RGAL 4; SCFW; SFW 4;
SUFW

Lovelace, Earl 1935- .... **CLC 51**
See also BW 2; CA 77-80; CANR 41, 72;
CD 5; CDWLB 3; CN 7; DLB 125;
MTCW 1

Lovelace, Richard 1618-1657 .... **LC 24**
See also BRW 2; DLB 131; EXPP; PAB;
RGEL 2

Lowell, Amy 1874-1925 ... **TCLC 1, 8; PC 13**
See also AMW; CA 104; 151; DAM POET;
DLB 54, 140; EXPP; MAWW; MTCW 2;
RGAL 4; TUS

Lowell, James Russell 1819-1891 ... **NCLC 2,**
90
See also AMWS 1; CDALB 1640-1865;
DLB 1, 11, 64, 79, 189, 235; RGAL 4

Lowell, Robert (Traill Spence, Jr.)
1917-1977 .... **CLC 1, 2, 3, 4, 5, 8, 9, 11,**
15, 37, 124; PC 3; WLC
See also AMW; CA 9-12R; 73-76; CABS
2; CANR 26, 60; CDALBS; DA; DA3;
DAB; DAC; DAM MST, NOV; DLB 5,
169; MTCW 1, 2; PAB; PFS 6, 7; RGAL
4; WP

MacLean, Alistair (Stuart)
1922(?)-1987 .... **CLC 3, 13, 50, 63**
See also CA 57-60; 121; CANR 28, 61;
CMW 4; CPW; DAM POP; MTCW 1;
SATA 23; SATA-Obit 50; TCWW 2

Maclean, Norman (Fitzroy)
1902-1990 .... **CLC 78; SSC 13**
See also CA 102; 132; CANR 49; CPW;
DAM POP; DLB 206; TCWW 2

MacLeish, Archibald 1892-1982 ... **CLC 3, 8,
14, 68**
See also AMW; CA 9-12R; 106; CAD;
CANR 33, 63; CDALBS; DAM POET;
DFS 15; DLB 4, 7, 45; DLBY 1982;
EXPP; MTCW 1, 2; PAB; PFS 5; RGAL
4; TUS

MacLennan, (John) Hugh
1907-1990 .... **CLC 2, 14, 92**
See also CA 5-8R; 142; CANR 33; DAC;
DAM MST; DLB 68; MTCW 1, 2; RGEL
2; TWA

MacLeod, Alistair 1936- .... **CLC 56**
See also CA 123; CCA 1; DAC; DAM
MST; DLB 60; MTCW 2; RGSF 2

Macleod, Fiona
See Sharp, William
See also RGEL 2; SUFW

MacNeice, (Frederick) Louis
1907-1963 .... **CLC 1, 4, 10, 53**
See also BRW 7; CA 85-88; CANR 61;
DAB; DAM POET; DLB 10, 20; MTCW
1, 2; RGEL 2

MacNeill, Dand
See Fraser, George MacDonald

Macpherson, James 1736-1796 .... **LC 29**
See also Ossian
See also BRWS 8; DLB 109; RGEL 2

Macpherson, (Jean) Jay 1931- .... **CLC 14**
See also CA 5-8R; CANR 90; CP 7; CWP;
DLB 53

Macrobius fl. 430- .... **CMLC 48**

MacShane, Frank 1927-1999 .... **CLC 39**
See also CA 9-12R; 186; CANR 3, 33; DLB
111

Macumber, Mari
See Sandoz, Mari(e Susette)

Madach, Imre 1823-1864 .... **NCLC 19**

Madden, (Jerry) David 1933- .... **CLC 5, 15**
See also CA 1-4R; CAAS 3; CANR 4, 45;
CN 7; CSW; DLB 6; MTCW 1

Maddern, Al(an)
See Ellison, Harlan (Jay)

Madhubuti, Haki R. 1942- . **CLC 6, 73; BLC
2; PC 5**
See also Lee, Don L.
See also BW 2, 3; CA 73-76; CANR 24,
51, 73; CP 7; CSW; DAM MULT, POET;
DLB 5, 41; DLBD 8; MTCW 2; RGAL 4

Maepenn, Hugh
See Kuttner, Henry

Maepenn, K. H.
See Kuttner, Henry

Maeterlinck, Maurice 1862-1949 ..... **TCLC 3**
See also CA 104; 136; CANR 80; DAM
DRAM; DLB 192; EW 8; GFL 1789 to
the Present; RGWL 2; SATA 66; TWA

Maginn, William 1794-1842 .... **NCLC 8**
See also DLB 110, 159

Mahapatra, Jayanta 1928- .... **CLC 33**
See also CA 73-76; CAAS 9; CANR 15,
33, 66, 87; CP 7; DAM MULT

Mahfouz, Naguib (Abdel Aziz Al-Sabilgi)
1911(?)- .... **CLC 153**
See also Mahfuz, Najib (Abdel Aziz al-
Sabilgi)
See also BEST 89:2; CA 128; CANR 55,
101; CWW 2; DA3; DAM NOV; MTCW
1, 2; RGWL 2; SSFS 9

Mahfuz, Najib (Abdel Aziz al-Sabilgi)
.... **CLC 52, 55**
See also Mahfouz, Naguib (Abdel Aziz Al-
Sabilgi)
See also AFW; DLBY 1988; RGSF 2;
WLIT 2

Mahon, Derek 1941- .... **CLC 27**
See also BRWS 6; CA 113; 128; CANR 88;
CP 7; DLB 40

Maiakovskii, Vladimir
See Mayakovski, Vladimir (Vladimirovich)
See also IDTP; RGWL 2

Mailer, Norman 1923- ... **CLC 1, 2, 3, 4, 5, 8,
11, 14, 28, 39, 74, 111**
See also AAYA 31; AITN 2; AMW; BPFB
2; CA 9-12R; CABS 1; CANR 28, 74, 77;
CDALB 1968-1988; CN 7; CPW; DA;
DA3; DAB; DAC; DAM MST, NOV,
POP; DLB 2, 16, 28, 185; DLBD 3;
DLBY 1980, 1983; MTCW 1, 2; NFS 10;
RGAL 4; TUS

Maillet, Antonine 1929- .... **CLC 54, 118**
See also CA 115; 120; CANR 46, 74, 77;
CCA 1; CWW 2; DAC; DLB 60; INT
120; MTCW 2

Mais, Roger 1905-1955 .... **TCLC 8**
See also BW 1, 3; CA 105; 124; CANR 82;
CDWLB 3; DLB 125; MTCW 1; RGEL 2

Maistre, Joseph 1753-1821 .... **NCLC 37**
See also GFL 1789 to the Present

Maitland, Frederic William
1850-1906 .... **TCLC 65**

Maitland, Sara (Louise) 1950- .... **CLC 49**
See also CA 69-72; CANR 13, 59; FW

Major, Clarence 1936- . **CLC 3, 19, 48; BLC
2**
See also AFAW 2; BW 2, 3; CA 21-24R;
CAAS 6; CANR 13, 25, 53, 82; CN 7;
CP 7; CSW; DAM MULT; DLB 33; MSW

Major, Kevin (Gerald) 1949- .... **CLC 26**
See also AAYA 16; CA 97-100; CANR 21,
38; CLR 11; DAC; DLB 60; INT CANR-
21; JRDA; MAICYA 1, 2; MAICYAS 1;
SATA 32, 82, 134; WYA; YAW

Maki, James
See Ozu, Yasujiro

Malabaila, Damiano
See Levi, Primo

Malamud, Bernard 1914-1986 .. **CLC 1, 2, 3,
5, 8, 9, 11, 18, 27, 44, 78, 85; SSC 15;
WLC**
See also AAYA 16; AMWS 1; BPFB 2; CA
5-8R; 118; CABS 1; CANR 28, 62;
CDALB 1941-1968; CPW; DA; DA3;
DAB; DAC; DAM MST, NOV, POP;
DLB 2, 28, 152; DLBY 1980, 1986;
EXPS; LAIT 4; MTCW 1, 2; NFS 4, 9;
RGAL 4; RGSF 2; SSFS 8, 13; TUS

Malan, Herman
See Bosman, Herman Charles; Bosman,
Herman Charles

Malaparte, Curzio 1898-1957 .... **TCLC 52**
See also DLB 264

Malcolm, Dan
See Silverberg, Robert

Malcolm X .... **CLC 82, 117; BLC 2; WLCS**
See also Little, Malcolm
See also LAIT 5

Malherbe, Francois de 1555-1628 .... **LC 5**
See also GFL Beginnings to 1789

Mallarme, Stephane 1842-1898 ...... **NCLC 4,
41; PC 4**
See also DAM POET; DLB 217; EW 7;
GFL 1789 to the Present; RGWL 2; TWA

Mallet-Joris, Francoise 1930- .... **CLC 11**
See also CA 65-68; CANR 17; DLB 83;
GFL 1789 to the Present

Malley, Ern
See McAuley, James Phillip

Mallowan, Agatha Christie
See Christie, Agatha (Mary Clarissa)

Maloff, Saul 1922- .... **CLC 5**
See also CA 33-36R

Malone, Louis
See MacNeice, (Frederick) Louis

Malone, Michael (Christopher)
1942- .... **CLC 43**
See also CA 77-80; CANR 14, 32, 57

Malory, Sir Thomas 1410(?)-1471(?) . **LC 11;
WLCS**
See also BRW 1; BRWR 2; CDBLB Before
1660; DA; DAB; DAC; DAM MST; DLB
146; EFS 2; RGEL 2; SATA 59; SATA-
Brief 33; TEA; WLIT 3

Malouf, (George Joseph) David
1934- .... **CLC 28, 86**
See also CA 124; CANR 50, 76; CN 7; CP
7; MTCW 2

Malraux, (Georges-)Andre
1901-1976 .... **CLC 1, 4, 9, 13, 15, 57**
See also BPFB 2; CA 21-22; 69-72; CANR
34, 58; CAP 2; DA3; DAM NOV; DLB
72; EW 12; GFL 1789 to the Present;
MTCW 1, 2; RGWL 2; TWA

Malzberg, Barry N(athaniel) 1939- ... **CLC 7**
See also CA 61-64; CAAS 4; CANR 16;
CMW 4; DLB 8; SFW 4

Mamet, David (Alan) 1947- .. **CLC 9, 15, 34,
46, 91; DC 4**
See also AAYA 3; CA 81-84; CABS 3;
CANR 15, 41, 67, 72; CD 5; DA3; DAM
DRAM; DFS 15; DLB 7; IDFW 4;
MTCW 1, 2; RGAL 4

Mamoulian, Rouben (Zachary)
1897-1987 .... **CLC 16**
See also CA 25-28R; 124; CANR 85

Mandelshtam, Osip
See Mandelstam, Osip (Emilievich)
See also EW 10; RGWL 2

Mandelstam, Osip (Emilievich)
1891(?)-1943(?) .... **TCLC 2, 6; PC 14**
See also Mandelshtam, Osip
See also CA 104; 150; MTCW 2; TWA

Mander, (Mary) Jane 1877-1949 ... **TCLC 31**
See also CA 162; RGEL 2

Mandeville, Bernard 1670-1733 .... **LC 82**
See also DLB 101

Mandeville, Sir John fl. 1350- ...... **CMLC 19**
See also DLB 146

Mandiargues, Andre Pieyre de .... **CLC 41**
See also Pieyre de Mandiargues, Andre
See also DLB 83

Mandrake, Ethel Belle
See Thurman, Wallace (Henry)

Mangan, James Clarence
1803-1849 .... **NCLC 27**
See also RGEL 2

Maniere, J.-E.
See Giraudoux, Jean(-Hippolyte)

Mankiewicz, Herman (Jacob)
1897-1953 .... **TCLC 85**
See also CA 120; 169; DLB 26; IDFW 3, 4

Manley, (Mary) Delariviere
1672(?)-1724 .... **LC 1, 42**
See also DLB 39, 80; RGEL 2

Mann, Abel
See Creasey, John

Mann, Emily 1952- .... **DC 7**
See also CA 130; CAD; CANR 55; CD 5;
CWD; DLB 266

Mann, (Luiz) Heinrich 1871-1950 ... **TCLC 9**
See also CA 106; 164, 181; DLB 66, 118;
EW 8; RGWL 2

Masefield, John (Edward)
1878-1967 .... **CLC 11, 47**
See also CA 19-20; 25-28R; CANR 33;
CAP 2; CDBLB 1890-1914; DAM POET;
DLB 10, 19, 153, 160; EXPP; FANT;
MTCW 1, 2; PFS 5; RGEL 2; SATA 19
Maso, Carole 19(?)- .... **CLC 44**
See also CA 170; GLL 2; RGAL 4
Mason, Bobbie Ann 1940- ... **CLC 28, 43, 82,
154; SSC 4**
See also AAYA 5, 42; AMWS 8; BPFB 2;
CA 53-56; CANR 11, 31, 58, 83;
CDALBS; CN 7; CSW; DA3; DLB 173;
DLBY 1987; EXPS; INT CANR-31;
MTCW 1, 2; NFS 4; RGAL 4; RGSF 2;
SSFS 3,8; YAW
Mason, Ernst
See Pohl, Frederik
Mason, Hunni B.
See Sternheim, (William Adolf) Carl
Mason, Lee W.
See Malzberg, Barry N(athaniel)
Mason, Nick 1945- .... **CLC 35**
Mason, Tally
See Derleth, August (William)
Mass, Anna .... **CLC 59**
Mass, William
See Gibson, William
Massinger, Philip 1583-1640 .... **LC 70**
See also DLB 58; RGEL 2
Master Lao
See Lao Tzu
Masters, Edgar Lee 1868-1950 .... **TCLC 2,
25; PC 1, 36; WLCS**
See also AMWS 1; CA 104; 133; CDALB
1865-1917; DA; DAC; DAM MST,
POET; DLB 54; EXPP; MTCW 1, 2;
RGAL 4; TUS; WP
Masters, Hilary 1928- .... **CLC 48**
See also CA 25-28R; CANR 13, 47, 97; CN
7; DLB 244
Mastrosimone, William 19(?)- .... **CLC 36**
See also CA 186; CAD; CD 5
Mathe, Albert
See Camus, Albert
Mather, Cotton 1663-1728 .... **LC 38**
See also AMWS 2; CDALB 1640-1865;
DLB 24, 30, 140; RGAL 4; TUS
Mather, Increase 1639-1723 .... **LC 38**
See also DLB 24
Matheson, Richard (Burton) 1926- .. **CLC 37**
See also AAYA 31; CA 97-100; CANR 88,
99; DLB 8, 44; HGG; INT 97-100; SCFW
2; SFW 4
Mathews, Harry 1930- .... **CLC 6, 52**
See also CA 21-24R; CAAS 6; CANR 18,
40, 98; CN 7
Mathews, John Joseph 1894-1979 .... **CLC 84**
See also CA 19-20; 142; CANR 45; CAP 2;
DAM MULT; DLB 175; NNAL
Mathias, Roland (Glyn) 1915- .... **CLC 45**
See also CA 97-100; CANR 19, 41; CP 7;
DLB 27
Matsuo Basho 1644-1694 .... **LC 62; PC 3**
See also Basho, Matsuo
See also DAM POET; PFS 2, 7
Mattheson, Rodney
See Creasey, John
Matthews, (James) Brander
1852-1929 .... **TCLC 95**
See also DLB 71, 78; DLBD 13
Matthews, Greg 1949- .... **CLC 45**
See also CA 135
Matthews, William (Procter III)
1942-1997 .... **CLC 40**
See also AMWS 9; CA 29-32R; 162; CAAS
18; CANR 12, 57; CP 7; DLB 5
Matthias, John (Edward) 1941- .... **CLC 9**
See also CA 33-36R; CANR 56; CP 7

Matthiessen, F(rancis) O(tto)
1902-1950 .... **TCLC 100**
See also CA 185; DLB 63
Matthiessen, Peter 1927- ... **CLC 5, 7, 11, 32,
64**
See also AAYA 6, 40; AMWS 5; ANW;
BEST 90:4; BPFB 2; CA 9-12R; CANR
21, 50, 73, 100; CN 7; DA3; DAM NOV;
DLB 6, 173; MTCW 1, 2; SATA 27
Maturin, Charles Robert
1780(?)-1824 .... **NCLC 6**
See also BRWS 8; DLB 178; HGG; RGEL
2; SUFW
Matute (Ausejo), Ana Maria 1925- .. **CLC 11**
See also CA 89-92; MTCW 1; RGSF 2
Maugham, W. S.
See Maugham, W(illiam) Somerset
Maugham, W(illiam) Somerset
1874-1965 .. **CLC 1, 11, 15, 67, 93; SSC
8; WLC**
See also BPFB 2; BRW 6; CA 5-8R; 25-
28R; CANR 40; CDBLB 1914-1945;
CMW 4; DA; DA3; DAB; DAC; DAM
DRAM, MST, NOV; DLB 10, 36, 77, 100,
162, 195; LAIT 3; MTCW 1, 2; RGEL 2;
RGSF 2; SATA 54
Maugham, William Somerset
See Maugham, W(illiam) Somerset
Maupassant, (Henri Rene Albert) Guy de
1850-1893 .... **NCLC 1, 42, 83; SSC 1;
WLC**
See also BYA 14; DA; DA3; DAB; DAC;
DAM MST; DLB 123; EW 7; EXPS; GFL
1789 to the Present; LAIT 2; RGSF 2;
RGWL 2; SSFS 4; SUFW; TWA
Maupin, Armistead (Jones, Jr.)
1944- .... **CLC 95**
See also CA 125; 130; CANR 58, 101;
CPW; DA3; DAM POP; GLL 1; INT 130;
MTCW 2
Maurhut, Richard
See Traven, B.
Mauriac, Claude 1914-1996 .... **CLC 9**
See also CA 89-92; 152; CWW 2; DLB 83;
GFL 1789 to the Present
Mauriac, Francois (Charles)
1885-1970 .... **CLC 4, 9, 56; SSC 24**
See also CA 25-28; CAP 2; DLB 65; EW
10; GFL 1789 to the Present; MTCW 1,
2; RGWL 2; TWA
Mavor, Osborne Henry 1888-1951
See Bridie, James
See also CA 104
Maxwell, William (Keepers, Jr.)
1908-2000 .... **CLC 19**
See also AMWS 8; CA 93-96; 189; CANR
54, 95; CN 7; DLB 218; DLBY 1980; INT
CA-93-96; SATA-Obit 128
May, Elaine 1932- .... **CLC 16**
See also CA 124; 142; CAD; CWD; DLB
44
Mayakovski, Vladimir (Vladimirovich)
1893-1930 .... **TCLC 4, 18**
See also Maiakovskii, Vladimir; Mayak-
ovsky, Vladimir
See also CA 104; 158; MTCW 2; SFW 4;
TWA
Mayakovsky, Vladimir
See Mayakovski, Vladimir (Vladimirovich)
See also EW 11; WP
Mayhew, Henry 1812-1887 .... **NCLC 31**
See also DLB 18, 55, 190
Mayle, Peter 1939(?)- .... **CLC 89**
See also CA 139; CANR 64, 109
Maynard, Joyce 1953- .... **CLC 23**
See also CA 111; 129; CANR 64

Mayne, William (James Carter)
1928- .... **CLC 12**
See also AAYA 20; CA 9-12R; CANR 37,
80, 100; CLR 25; FANT; JRDA; MAI-
CYA 1, 2; MAICYAS 1; SAAS 11; SATA
6, 68, 122; YAW
Mayo, Jim
See L'Amour, Louis (Dearborn)
See also TCWW 2
Maysles, Albert 1926- .... **CLC 16**
See also CA 29-32R
Maysles, David 1932-1987 .... **CLC 16**
See also CA 191
Mazer, Norma Fox 1931- .... **CLC 26**
See also AAYA 5, 36; BYA 1, 8; CA 69-72;
CANR 12, 32, 66; CLR 23; JRDA; MAI-
CYA 1, 2; SAAS 1; SATA 24, 67, 105;
WYA; YAW
Mazzini, Guiseppe 1805-1872 .... **NCLC 34**
McAlmon, Robert (Menzies)
1895-1956 .... **TCLC 97**
See also CA 107; 168; DLB 4, 45; DLBD
15; GLL 1
McAuley, James Phillip 1917-1976 .. **CLC 45**
See also CA 97-100; DLB 260; RGEL 2
McBain, Ed
See Hunter, Evan
See also MSW
McBrien, William (Augustine)
1930- .... **CLC 44**
See also CA 107; CANR 90
McCabe, Patrick 1955- .... **CLC 133**
See also CA 130; CANR 50, 90; CN 7;
DLB 194
McCaffrey, Anne (Inez) 1926- .... **CLC 17**
See also AAYA 6, 34; AITN 2; BEST 89:2;
BPFB 2; BYA 5; CA 25-28R; CANR 15,
35, 55, 96; CLR 49; CPW; DA3; DAM
NOV, POP; DLB 8; JRDA; MAICYA 1,
2; MTCW 1, 2; SAAS 11; SATA 8, 70,
116; SFW 4; WYA; YAW
McCall, Nathan 1955(?)- .... **CLC 86**
See also BW 3; CA 146; CANR 88
McCann, Arthur
See Campbell, John W(ood, Jr.)
McCann, Edson
See Pohl, Frederik
McCarthy, Charles, Jr. 1933-
See McCarthy, Cormac
See also CANR 42, 69, 101; CN 7; CPW;
CSW; DA3; DAM POP; MTCW 2
McCarthy, Cormac .... **CLC 4, 57, 59, 101**
See also McCarthy, Charles, Jr.
See also AAYA 41; AMWS 8; BPFB 2; CA
13-16R; CANR 10; DLB 6, 143, 256;
TCWW 2
McCarthy, Mary (Therese)
1912-1989 .. **CLC 1, 3, 5, 14, 24, 39, 59;
SSC 24**
See also AMW; BPFB 2; CA 5-8R; 129;
CANR 16, 50, 64; DA3; DLB 2; DLBY
1981; FW; INT CANR-16; MAWW;
MTCW 1, 2; RGAL 4; TUS
McCartney, (James) Paul 1942- . **CLC 12, 35**
See also CA 146; CANR 111
McCauley, Stephen (D.) 1955- .... **CLC 50**
See also CA 141
McClaren, Peter .... **CLC 70**
McClure, Michael (Thomas) 1932- ... **CLC 6,
10**
See also CA 21-24R; CAD; CANR 17, 46,
77; CD 5; CP 7; DLB 16; WP
McCorkle, Jill (Collins) 1958- .... **CLC 51**
See also CA 121; CSW; DLB 234; DLBY
1987
McCourt, Frank 1930- .... **CLC 109**
See also CA 157; CANR 97; NCFS 1
McCourt, James 1941- .... **CLC 5**
See also CA 57-60; CANR 98

McCourt, Malachy 1932- .... **CLC 119**
See also SATA 126

McCoy, Horace (Stanley)
1897-1955 .... **TCLC 28**
See also CA 108; 155; CMW 4; DLB 9

McCrae, John 1872-1918 .... **TCLC 12**
See also CA 109; DLB 92; PFS 5

McCreigh, James
See Pohl, Frederik

McCullers, (Lula) Carson (Smith)
1917-1967 .... **CLC 1, 4, 10, 12, 48, 100;**
SSC 9, 24; WLC
See also AAYA 21; AMW; BPFB 2; CA
5-8R; 25-28R; CABS 1, 3; CANR 18;
CDALB 1941-1968; DA; DA3; DAB;
DAC; DAM MST, NOV; DFS 5; DLB 2,
7, 173, 228; EXPS; FW; GLL 1; LAIT 3,
4; MAWW; MTCW 1, 2; NFS 6, 13;
RGAL 4; RGSF 2; SATA 27; SSFS 5;
TUS; YAW

McCulloch, John Tyler
See Burroughs, Edgar Rice

McCullough, Colleen 1938(?)- .. **CLC 27, 107**
See also AAYA 36; BPFB 2; CA 81-84;
CANR 17, 46, 67, 98; CPW; DA3; DAM
NOV, POP; MTCW 1, 2; RHW

McDermott, Alice 1953- .... **CLC 90**
See also CA 109; CANR 40, 90

McElroy, Joseph 1930- .... **CLC 5, 47**
See also CA 17-20R; CN 7

McEwan, Ian (Russell) 1948- ..... **CLC 13, 66**
See also BEST 90:4; BRWS 4; CA 61-64;
CANR 14, 41, 69, 87; CN 7; DAM NOV;
DLB 14, 194; HGG; MTCW 1, 2; RGSF
2; TEA

McFadden, David 1940- .... **CLC 48**
See also CA 104; CP 7; DLB 60; INT 104

McFarland, Dennis 1950- .... **CLC 65**
See also CA 165; CANR 110

McGahern, John 1934- ... **CLC 5, 9, 48, 156;**
SSC 17
See also CA 17-20R; CANR 29, 68; CN 7;
DLB 14, 231; MTCW 1

McGinley, Patrick (Anthony) 1937- . **CLC 41**
See also CA 120; 127; CANR 56; INT 127

McGinley, Phyllis 1905-1978 .... **CLC 14**
See also CA 9-12R; 77-80; CANR 19;
CWRI 5; DLB 11, 48; PFS 9, 13; SATA
2, 44; SATA-Obit 24

McGinniss, Joe 1942- .... **CLC 32**
See also AITN 2; BEST 89:2; CA 25-28R;
CANR 26, 70; CPW; DLB 185; INT
CANR-26

McGivern, Maureen Daly
See Daly, Maureen

McGrath, Patrick 1950- .... **CLC 55**
See also CA 136; CANR 65; CN 7; DLB
231; HGG

McGrath, Thomas (Matthew)
1916-1990 .... **CLC 28, 59**
See also AMWS 10; CA 9-12R; 132; CANR
6, 33, 95; DAM POET; MTCW 1; SATA
41; SATA-Obit 66

McGuane, Thomas (Francis III)
1939- .... **CLC 3, 7, 18, 45, 127**
See also AITN 2; BPFB 2; CA 49-52;
CANR 5, 24, 49, 94; CN 7; DLB 2, 212;
DLBY 1980; INT CANR-24; MTCW 1;
TCWW 2

McGuckian, Medbh 1950- ... **CLC 48; PC 27**
See also BRWS 5; CA 143; CP 7; CWP;
DAM POET; DLB 40

McHale, Tom 1942(?)-1982 .... **CLC 3, 5**
See also AITN 1; CA 77-80; 106

McIlvanney, William 1936- .... **CLC 42**
See also CA 25-28R; CANR 61; CMW 4;
DLB 14, 207

McIlwraith, Maureen Mollie Hunter
See Hunter, Mollie
See also SATA 2

McInerney, Jay 1955- .... **CLC 34, 112**
See also AAYA 18; BPFB 2; CA 116; 123;
CANR 45, 68; CN 7; CPW; DA3; DAM
POP; INT 123; MTCW 2

McIntyre, Vonda N(eel) 1948- .... **CLC 18**
See also CA 81-84; CANR 17, 34, 69;
MTCW 1; SFW 4; YAW

McKay, Claude .... **TCLC 7, 41; BLC 3; PC**
2; WLC
See also McKay, Festus Claudius
See also AFAW 1, 2; AMWS 10; DAB;
DLB 4, 45, 51, 117; EXPP; GLL 2; LAIT
3; PAB; PFS 4; RGAL 4; WP

McKay, Festus Claudius 1889-1948
See McKay, Claude
See also BW 1, 3; CA 104; 124; CANR 73;
DA; DAC; DAM MST, MULT, NOV,
POET; MTCW 1, 2; TUS

McKuen, Rod 1933- .... **CLC 1, 3**
See also AITN 1; CA 41-44R; CANR 40

McLoughlin, R. B.
See Mencken, H(enry) L(ouis)

McLuhan, (Herbert) Marshall
1911-1980 .... **CLC 37, 83**
See also CA 9-12R; 102; CANR 12, 34, 61;
DLB 88; INT CANR-12; MTCW 1, 2

McMillan, Terry (L.) 1951- .... **CLC 50, 61,**
112; BLCS
See also AAYA 21; BPFB 2; BW 2, 3; CA
140; CANR 60, 104; CPW; DA3; DAM
MULT, NOV, POP; MTCW 2; RGAL 4;
YAW

McMurtry, Larry (Jeff) 1936- .. **CLC 2, 3, 7,**
11, 27, 44, 127
See also AAYA 15; AITN 2; AMWS 5;
BEST 89:2; BPFB 2; CA 5-8R; CANR
19, 43, 64, 103; CDALB 1968-1988; CN
7; CPW; CSW; DA3; DAM NOV, POP;
DLB 2, 143, 256; DLBY 1980, 1987;
MTCW 1, 2; RGAL 4; TCWW 2

McNally, T. M. 1961- .... **CLC 82**

McNally, Terrence 1939- .... **CLC 4, 7, 41, 91**
See also CA 45-48; CAD; CANR 2, 56; CD
5; DA3; DAM DRAM; DLB 7, 249; GLL
1; MTCW 2

McNamer, Deirdre 1950- .... **CLC 70**

McNeal, Tom .... **CLC 119**

McNeile, Herman Cyril 1888-1937
See Sapper
See also CA 184; CMW 4; DLB 77

McNickle, (William) D'Arcy
1904-1977 .... **CLC 89**
See also CA 9-12R; 85-88; CANR 5, 45;
DAM MULT; DLB 175, 212; NNAL;
RGAL 4; SATA-Obit 22

McPhee, John (Angus) 1931- .... **CLC 36**
See also AMWS 3; ANW; BEST 90:1; CA
65-68; CANR 20, 46, 64, 69; CPW; DLB
185; MTCW 1, 2; TUS

McPherson, James Alan 1943- .. **CLC 19, 77;**
BLCS
See also BW 1, 3; CA 25-28R; CAAS 17;
CANR 24, 74; CN 7; CSW; DLB 38, 244;
MTCW 1, 2; RGAL 4; RGSF 2

McPherson, William (Alexander)
1933- .... **CLC 34**
See also CA 69-72; CANR 28; INT
CANR-28

McTaggart, J. McT. Ellis
See McTaggart, John McTaggart Ellis

McTaggart, John McTaggart Ellis
1866-1925 .... **TCLC 105**
See also CA 120; DLB 262

Mead, George Herbert 1873-1958 . **TCLC 89**

Mead, Margaret 1901-1978 .... **CLC 37**
See also AITN 1; CA 1-4R; 81-84; CANR
4; DA3; FW; MTCW 1, 2; SATA-Obit 20

Meaker, Marijane (Agnes) 1927-
See Kerr, M. E.
See also CA 107; CANR 37, 63; INT 107;
JRDA; MAICYA 1, 2; MAICYAS 1;
MTCW 1; SATA 20, 61, 99; SATA-Essay
111; YAW

Medoff, Mark (Howard) 1940- .... **CLC 6, 23**
See also AITN 1; CA 53-56; CAD; CANR
5; CD 5; DAM DRAM; DFS 4; DLB 7;
INT CANR-5

Medvedev, P. N.
See Bakhtin, Mikhail Mikhailovich

Meged, Aharon
See Megged, Aharon

Meged, Aron
See Megged, Aharon

Megged, Aharon 1920- .... **CLC 9**
See also CA 49-52; CAAS 13; CANR 1

Mehta, Ved (Parkash) 1934- .... **CLC 37**
See also CA 1-4R; CANR 2, 23, 69; MTCW
1

Melanter
See Blackmore, R(ichard) D(oddridge)

Meleager c. 140 B.C.-c. 70 B.C. .... **CMLC 53**

Melies, Georges 1861-1938 .... **TCLC 81**

Melikow, Loris
See Hofmannsthal, Hugo von

Melmoth, Sebastian
See Wilde, Oscar (Fingal O'Flahertie Wills)

Meltzer, Milton 1915- .... **CLC 26**
See also AAYA 8; BYA 2, 6; CA 13-16R;
CANR 38, 92, 107; CLR 13; DLB 61;
JRDA; MAICYA 1, 2; SAAS 1; SATA 1,
50, 80, 128; SATA-Essay 124; WYA;
YAW

Melville, Herman 1819-1891 ..... **NCLC 3, 12,**
29, 45, 49, 91, 93; SSC 1, 17, 46; WLC
See also AAYA 25; AMW; AMWR 1;
CDALB 1640-1865; DA; DA3; DAB;
DAC; DAM MST, NOV; DLB 3, 74, 250,
254; EXPN; EXPS; LAIT 1, 2; NFS 7, 9;
RGAL 4; RGSF 2; SATA 59; SSFS 3;
TUS

Members, Mark
See Powell, Anthony (Dymoke)

Membreno, Alejandro .... **CLC 59**

Menander c. 342 B.C.-c. 293 B.C. . **CMLC 9,**
51; DC 3
See also AW 1; CDWLB 1; DAM DRAM;
DLB 176; RGWL 2

Menchu, Rigoberta 1959- .. **CLC 160; HLCS**
2
See also CA 175; DNFS 1; WLIT 1

Mencken, H(enry) L(ouis)
1880-1956 .... **TCLC 13**
See also AMW; CA 105; 125; CDALB
1917-1929; DLB 11, 29, 63, 137, 222;
MTCW 1, 2; NCFS 4; RGAL 4; TUS

Mendelsohn, Jane 1965- .... **CLC 99**
See also CA 154; CANR 94

Menton, Francisco de
See Chin, Frank (Chew, Jr.)

Mercer, David 1928-1980 .... **CLC 5**
See also CA 9-12R; 102; CANR 23; CBD;
DAM DRAM; DLB 13; MTCW 1; RGEL
2

Merchant, Paul
See Ellison, Harlan (Jay)

Meredith, George 1828-1909 ... **TCLC 17, 43**
See also CA 117; 153; CANR 80; CDBLB
1832-1890; DAM POET; DLB 18, 35, 57,
159; RGEL 2; TEA

Meredith, William (Morris) 1919- .... **CLC 4, 13, 22, 55; PC 28**
See also CA 9-12R; CAAS 14; CANR 6, 40; CP 7; DAM POET; DLB 5

Merezhkovsky, Dmitry Sergeyevich 1865-1941 .... **TCLC 29**
See also CA 169

Merimee, Prosper 1803-1870 ... **NCLC 6, 65; SSC 7**
See also DLB 119, 192; EW 6; EXPS; GFL 1789 to the Present; RGSF 2; RGWL 2; SSFS 8; SUFW

Merkin, Daphne 1954- .... **CLC 44**
See also CA 123

Merlin, Arthur
See Blish, James (Benjamin)

Merrill, James (Ingram) 1926-1995 .. **CLC 2, 3, 6, 8, 13, 18, 34, 91; PC 28**
See also AMWS 3; CA 13-16R; 147; CANR 10, 49, 63, 108; DA3; DAM POET; DLB 5, 165; DLBY 1985; INT CANR-10; MTCW 1, 2; PAB; RGAL 4

Merriman, Alex
See Silverberg, Robert

Merriman, Brian 1747-1805 .... **NCLC 70**

Merritt, E. B.
See Waddington, Miriam

Merton, Thomas (James) 1915-1968 . **CLC 1, 3, 11, 34, 83; PC 10**
See also AMWS 8; CA 5-8R; 25-28R; CANR 22, 53, 111; DA3; DLB 48; DLBY 1981; MTCW 1, 2

Merwin, W(illiam) S(tanley) 1927- ... **CLC 1, 2, 3, 5, 8, 13, 18, 45, 88**
See also AMWS 3; CA 13-16R; CANR 15, 51; CP 7; DA3; DAM POET; DLB 5, 169; INT CANR-15; MTCW 1, 2; PAB; PFS 5, 15; RGAL 4

Metcalf, John 1938- .... **CLC 37; SSC 43**
See also CA 113; CN 7; DLB 60; RGSF 2; TWA

Metcalf, Suzanne
See Baum, L(yman) Frank

Mew, Charlotte (Mary) 1870-1928 .. **TCLC 8**
See also CA 105; 189; DLB 19, 135; RGEL 2

Mewshaw, Michael 1943- .... **CLC 9**
See also CA 53-56; CANR 7, 47; DLBY 1980

Meyer, Conrad Ferdinand 1825-1905 .... **NCLC 81**
See also DLB 129; EW; RGWL 2

Meyer, Gustav 1868-1932
See Meyrink, Gustav
See also CA 117; 190

Meyer, June
See Jordan, June
See also GLL 2

Meyer, Lynn
See Slavitt, David R(ytman)

Meyers, Jeffrey 1939- .... **CLC 39**
See also CA 73-76; CAAE 186; CANR 54, 102; DLB 111

Meynell, Alice (Christina Gertrude Thompson) 1847-1922 .... **TCLC 6**
See also CA 104; 177; DLB 19, 98; RGEL 2

Meyrink, Gustav .... **TCLC 21**
See also Meyer, Gustav
See also DLB 81

Michaels, Leonard 1933- .... **CLC 6, 25; SSC 16**
See also CA 61-64; CANR 21, 62; CN 7; DLB 130; MTCW 1

Michaux, Henri 1899-1984 .... **CLC 8, 19**
See also CA 85-88; 114; DLB 258; GFL 1789 to the Present; RGWL 2

Micheaux, Oscar (Devereaux) 1884-1951 .... **TCLC 76**
See also BW 3; CA 174; DLB 50; TCWW 2

Michelangelo 1475-1564 .... **LC 12**
See also AAYA 43

Michelet, Jules 1798-1874 .... **NCLC 31**
See also EW 5; GFL 1789 to the Present

Michels, Robert 1876-1936 .... **TCLC 88**

Michener, James A(lbert) 1907(?)-1997 .. **CLC 1, 5, 11, 29, 60, 109**
See also AAYA 27; AITN 1; BEST 90:1; BPFB 2; CA 5-8R; 161; CANR 21, 45, 68; CN 7; CPW; DA3; DAM NOV, POP; DLB 6; MTCW 1, 2; RHW

Mickiewicz, Adam 1798-1855 . **NCLC 3, 101; PC 38**
See also EW 5; RGWL 2

Middleton, Christopher 1926- .... **CLC 13**
See also CA 13-16R; CANR 29, 54; CP 7; DLB 40

Middleton, Richard (Barham) 1882-1911 .... **TCLC 56**
See also CA 187; DLB 156; HGG

Middleton, Stanley 1919- .... **CLC 7, 38**
See also CA 25-28R; CAAS 23; CANR 21, 46, 81; CN 7; DLB 14

Middleton, Thomas 1580-1627 .... **LC 33; DC 5**
See also BRW 2; DAM DRAM, MST; DLB 58; RGEL 2

Migueis, Jose Rodrigues 1901- .... **CLC 10**

Mikszath, Kalman 1847-1910 .... **TCLC 31**
See also CA 170

Miles, Jack .... **CLC 100**
See also CA 200

Miles, John Russiano
See Miles, Jack

Miles, Josephine (Louise) 1911-1985 .... **CLC 1, 2, 14, 34, 39**
See also CA 1-4R; 116; CANR 2, 55; DAM POET; DLB 48

Militant
See Sandburg, Carl (August)

Mill, Harriet (Hardy) Taylor 1807-1858 .... **NCLC 102**
See also FW

Mill, John Stuart 1806-1873 .... **NCLC 11, 58**
See also CDBLB 1832-1890; DLB 55, 190, 262; FW 1; RGEL 2; TEA

Millar, Kenneth 1915-1983 .... **CLC 14**
See also Macdonald, Ross
See also CA 9-12R; 110; CANR 16, 63, 107; CMW 4; CPW; DA3; DAM POP; DLB 2, 226; DLBD 6; DLBY 1983; MTCW 1, 2

Millay, E. Vincent
See Millay, Edna St. Vincent

Millay, Edna St. Vincent 1892-1950 ... **TCLC 4, 49; PC 6; WLCS**
See also Boyd, Nancy
See also AMW; CA 104; 130; CDALB 1917-1929; DA; DA3; DAB; DAC; DAM MST, POET; DLB 45, 249; EXPP; MAWW; MTCW 1, 2; PAB; PFS 3; RGAL 4; TUS; WP

Miller, Arthur 1915- ...... **CLC 1, 2, 6, 10, 15, 26, 47, 78; DC 1; WLC**
See also AAYA 15; AITN 1; AMW; CA 1-4R; CABS 3; CAD; CANR 2, 30, 54, 76; CD 5; CDALB 1941-1968; DA; DA3; DAB; DAC; DAM DRAM, MST; DFS 1, 3; DLB 7, 266; LAIT 1, 4; MTCW 1, 2; RGAL 4; TUS; WYAS 1

Miller, Henry (Valentine) 1891-1980 .... **CLC 1, 2, 4, 9, 14, 43, 84; WLC**
See also AMW; BPFB 2; CA 9-12R; 97-100; CANR 33, 64; CDALB 1929-1941;

DA; DA3; DAB; DAC; DAM MST, NOV; DLB 4, 9; DLBY 1980; MTCW 1, 2; RGAL 4; TUS

Miller, Jason 1939(?)-2001 .... **CLC 2**
See also AITN 1; CA 73-76; 197; CAD; DFS 12; DLB 7

Miller, Sue 1943- .... **CLC 44**
See also BEST 90:3; CA 139; CANR 59, 91; DA3; DAM POP; DLB 143

Miller, Walter M(ichael, Jr.) 1923-1996 .... **CLC 4, 30**
See also BPFB 2; CA 85-88; CANR 108; DLB 8; SCFW 1; SFW 4

Millett, Kate 1934- .... **CLC 67**
See also AITN 1; CA 73-76; CANR 32, 53, 76, 110; DA3; DLB 246; FW; GLL 1; MTCW 1, 2

Millhauser, Steven (Lewis) 1943- .... **CLC 21, 54, 109**
See also CA 110; 111; CANR 63; CN 7; DA3; DLB 2; FANT; INT CA-111; MTCW 2

Millin, Sarah Gertrude 1889-1968 ... **CLC 49**
See also CA 102; 93-96; DLB 225

Milne, A(lan) A(lexander) 1882-1956 .... **TCLC 6, 88**
See also BRWS 5; CA 104; 133; CLR 1, 26; CMW 4; CWRI 5; DA3; DAB; DAC; DAM MST; DLB 10, 77, 100, 160; FANT; MAICYA 1, 2; MTCW 1, 2; RGEL 2; SATA 100; WCH; YABC 1

Milner, Ron(ald) 1938- .... **CLC 56; BLC 3**
See also AITN 1; BW 1; CA 73-76; CAD; CANR 24, 81; CD 5; DAM MULT; DLB 38; MTCW 1

Milnes, Richard Monckton 1809-1885 .... **NCLC 61**
See also DLB 32, 184

Milosz, Czeslaw 1911- ...... **CLC 5, 11, 22, 31, 56, 82; PC 8; WLCS**
See also CA 81-84; CANR 23, 51, 91; CDWLB 4; CWW 2; DA3; DAM MST, POET; DLB 215; EW 13; MTCW 1, 2; RGWL 2

Milton, John 1608-1674 ..... **LC 9, 43; PC 19, 29; WLC**
See also BRW 2; BRWR 2; CDBLB 1660-1789; DA; DA3; DAB; DAC; DAM MST, POET; DLB 131, 151; EFS 1; EXPP; LAIT 1; PAB; PFS 3; RGEL 2; TEA; WLIT 3; WP

Min, Anchee 1957- .... **CLC 86**
See also CA 146; CANR 94

Minehaha, Cornelius
See Wedekind, (Benjamin) Frank(lin)

Miner, Valerie 1947- .... **CLC 40**
See also CA 97-100; CANR 59; FW; GLL 2

Minimo, Duca
See D'Annunzio, Gabriele

Minot, Susan 1956- .... **CLC 44, 159**
See also AMWS 6; CA 134; CN 7

Minus, Ed 1938- .... **CLC 39**
See also CA 185

Miranda, Javier
See Bioy Casares, Adolfo
See also CWW 2

Mirbeau, Octave 1848-1917 .... **TCLC 55**
See also DLB 123, 192; GFL 1789 to the Present

Miro (Ferrer), Gabriel (Francisco Victor) 1879-1930 .... **TCLC 5**
See also CA 104; 185

Misharin, Alexandr .... **CLC 59**

Mishima, Yukio ... **CLC 2, 4, 6, 9, 27; DC 1; SSC 4**
See also Hiraoka, Kimitake
See also BPFB 2; GLL 1; MJW; MTCW 2; RGSF 2; RGWL 2; SSFS 5, 12

Moreas, Jean .... TCLC **18**
See also Papadiamantopoulos, Johannes
See also GFL 1789 to the Present
Moreton, Andrew Esq.
See Defoe, Daniel
Morgan, Berry 1919- .... CLC **6**
See also CA 49-52; DLB 6
Morgan, Claire
See Highsmith, (Mary) Patricia
See also GLL 1
Morgan, Edwin (George) 1920- .... CLC **31**
See also CA 5-8R; CANR 3, 43, 90; CP 7;
DLB 27
Morgan, (George) Frederick 1922- .. CLC **23**
See also CA 17-20R; CANR 21; CP 7
Morgan, Harriet
See Mencken, H(enry) L(ouis)
Morgan, Jane
See Cooper, James Fenimore
Morgan, Janet 1945- .... CLC **39**
See also CA 65-68
Morgan, Lady 1776(?)-1859 .... NCLC **29**
See also DLB 116, 158; RGEL 2
Morgan, Robin (Evonne) 1941- .... CLC **2**
See also CA 69-72; CANR 29, 68; FW;
GLL 2; MTCW 1; SATA 80
Morgan, Scott
See Kuttner, Henry
Morgan, Seth 1949(?)-1990 .... CLC **65**
See also CA 185; 132
**Morgenstern, Christian (Otto Josef
Wolfgang)** 1871-1914 .... TCLC **8**
See also CA 105; 191
Morgenstern, S.
See Goldman, William (W.)
Mori, Rintaro
See Mori Ogai
See also CA 110
Moricz, Zsigmond 1879-1942 .... TCLC **33**
See also CA 165; DLB 215
Morike, Eduard (Friedrich)
1804-1875 .... NCLC **10**
See also DLB 133; RGWL 2
Mori Ogai 1862-1922 .... TCLC **14**
See also Ogai
See also CA 164; DLB 180; TWA
Moritz, Karl Philipp 1756-1793 .... LC **2**
See also DLB 94
Morland, Peter Henry
See Faust, Frederick (Schiller)
Morley, Christopher (Darlington)
1890-1957 .... TCLC **87**
See also CA 112; DLB 9; RGAL 4
Morren, Theophil
See Hofmannsthal, Hugo von
Morris, Bill 1952- .... CLC **76**
Morris, Julian
See West, Morris L(anglo)
Morris, Steveland Judkins 1950(?)-
See Wonder, Stevie
See also CA 111
Morris, William 1834-1896 .... NCLC **4**
See also BRW 5; CDBLB 1832-1890; DLB
18, 35, 57, 156, 178, 184; FANT; RGEL
2; SFW 4; SUFW
Morris, Wright 1910-1998 .. CLC **1, 3, 7, 18,
37**
See also AMW; CA 9-12R; 167; CANR 21,
81; CN 7; DLB 2, 206, 218; DLBY 1981;
MTCW 1, 2; RGAL 4; TCLC 107;
TCWW 2
Morrison, Arthur 1863-1945 .... TCLC **72;
SSC 40**
See also CA 120; 157; CMW 4; DLB 70,
135, 197; RGEL 2
Morrison, Chloe Anthony Wofford
See Morrison, Toni

Morrison, James Douglas 1943-1971
See Morrison, Jim
See also CA 73-76; CANR 40
Morrison, Jim .... CLC **17**
See also Morrison, James Douglas
Morrison, Toni 1931- . CLC **4, 10, 22, 55, 81,
87; BLC 3**
See also AAYA 1, 22; AFAW 1, 2; AMWS
3; BPFB 2; BW 2, 3; CA 29-32R; CANR
27, 42, 67; CDALB 1968-1988; CN 7;
CPW; DA; DA3; DAB; DAC; DAM MST,
MULT, NOV, POP; DLB 6, 33, 143;
DLBY 1981; EXPN; FW; LAIT 2, 4;
MAWW; MTCW 1, 2; NFS 1, 6, 8, 14;
RGAL 4; RHW; SATA 57; SSFS 5; TUS;
YAW
Morrison, Van 1945- .... CLC **21**
See also CA 116; 168
Morrissy, Mary 1957- .... CLC **99**
See also DLB 267
Mortimer, John (Clifford) 1923- ..... CLC **28,
43**
See also CA 13-16R; CANR 21, 69, 109;
CD 5; CDBLB 1960 to Present; CMW 4;
CN 7; CPW; DA3; DAM DRAM, POP;
DLB 13, 245; INT CANR-21; MSW;
MTCW 1, 2; RGEL 2
Mortimer, Penelope (Ruth)
1918-1999 .... CLC **5**
See also CA 57-60; 187; CANR 45, 88; CN
7
Mortimer, Sir John
See Mortimer, John (Clifford)
Morton, Anthony
See Creasey, John
Morton, Thomas 1579(?)-1647(?) .... LC **72**
See also DLB 24; RGEL 2
Mosca, Gaetano 1858-1941 .... TCLC **75**
Mosher, Howard Frank 1943- .... CLC **62**
See also CA 139; CANR 65
Mosley, Nicholas 1923- .... CLC **43, 70**
See also CA 69-72; CANR 41, 60, 108; CN
7; DLB 14, 207
Mosley, Walter 1952- .... CLC **97; BLCS**
See also AAYA 17; BPFB 2; BW 2; CA
142; CANR 57, 92; CMW 4; CPW; DA3;
DAM MULT, POP; MSW; MTCW 2
Moss, Howard 1922-1987 . CLC **7, 14, 45, 50**
See also CA 1-4R; 123; CANR 1, 44; DAM
POET; DLB 5
Mossgiel, Rab
See Burns, Robert
Motion, Andrew (Peter) 1952- .... CLC **47**
See also BRWS 7; CA 146; CANR 90; CP
7; DLB 40
Motley, Willard (Francis)
1912-1965 .... CLC **18**
See also BW 1; CA 117; 106; CANR 88;
DLB 76, 143
Motoori, Norinaga 1730-1801 .... NCLC **45**
Mott, Michael (Charles Alston)
1930- .... CLC **15, 34**
See also CA 5-8R; CAAS 7; CANR 7, 29
Mountain Wolf Woman 1884-1960 .. CLC **92**
See also CA 144; CANR 90; NNAL
Moure, Erin 1955- .... CLC **88**
See also CA 113; CP 7; CWP; DLB 60
Mowat, Farley (McGill) 1921- .... CLC **26**
See also AAYA 1; BYA 2; CA 1-4R; CANR
4, 24, 42, 68, 108; CLR 20; CPW; DAC;
DAM MST; DLB 68; INT CANR-24;
JRDA; MAICYA 1, 2; MTCW 1, 2; SATA
3, 55; YAW
Mowatt, Anna Cora 1819-1870 ..... NCLC **74**
See also RGAL 2
Moyers, Bill 1934- .... CLC **74**
See also AITN 2; CA 61-64; CANR 31, 52

Mphahlele, Es'kia
See Mphahlele, Ezekiel
See also AFW; CDWLB 3; DLB 125, 225;
RGSF 2; SSFS 11
Mphahlele, Ezekiel 1919- .... CLC **25, 133;
BLC 3**
See also Mphahlele, Es'kia
See also BW 2, 3; CA 81-84; CANR 26,
76; CN 7; DA3; DAM MULT; MTCW 2;
SATA 119
Mqhayi, S(amuel) E(dward) K(rune Loliwe)
1875-1945 .... TCLC **25; BLC 3**
See also CA 153; CANR 87; DAM MULT
Mrozek, Slawomir 1930- .... CLC **3, 13**
See also CA 13-16R; CAAS 10; CANR 29;
CDWLB 4; CWW 2; DLB 232; MTCW 1
Mrs. Belloc-Lowndes
See Lowndes, Marie Adelaide (Belloc)
M'Taggart, John M'Taggart Ellis
See McTaggart, John McTaggart Ellis
Mtwa, Percy (?)- .... CLC **47**
Mueller, Lisel 1924- .... CLC **13, 51; PC 33**
See also CA 93-96; CP 7; DLB 105; PFS 9,
13
Muggeridge, Malcolm (Thomas)
1903-1990 .... TCLC **120**
See also AITN 1; CA 101; CANR 33, 63;
MTCW 1, 2
Muir, Edwin 1887-1959 .... TCLC **2, 87**
See also Moore, Edward
See also BRWS 6; CA 104; 193; DLB 20,
100, 191; RGEL 2
Muir, John 1838-1914 .... TCLC **28**
See also AMWS 9; ANW; CA 165; DLB
186
Mujica Lainez, Manuel 1910-1984 ... CLC **31**
See also Lainez, Manuel Mujica
See also CA 81-84; 112; CANR 32; HW 1
Mukherjee, Bharati 1940- .... CLC **53, 115;
AAL; SSC 38**
See also BEST 89:2; CA 107; CANR 45,
72; CN 7; DAM NOV; DLB 60, 218;
DNFS 1, 2; FW; MTCW 1, 2; RGAL 4;
RGSF 2; SSFS 7; TUS
Muldoon, Paul 1951- .... CLC **32, 72**
See also BRWS 4; CA 113; 129; CANR 52,
91; CP 7; DAM POET; DLB 40; INT 129;
PFS 7
Mulisch, Harry 1927- .... CLC **42**
See also CA 9-12R; CANR 6, 26, 56, 110
Mull, Martin 1943- .... CLC **17**
See also CA 105
Muller, Wilhelm .... NCLC **73**
Mulock, Dinah Maria
See Craik, Dinah Maria (Mulock)
See also RGEL 2
Munford, Robert 1737(?)-1783 .... LC **5**
See also DLB 31
Mungo, Raymond 1946- .... CLC **72**
See also CA 49-52; CANR 2
Munro, Alice 1931- .... CLC **6, 10, 19, 50, 95;
SSC 3; WLCS**
See also AITN 2; BPFB 2; CA 33-36R;
CANR 33, 53, 75; CCA 1; CN 7; DA3;
DAC; DAM MST, NOV; DLB 53; MTCW
1, 2; RGEL 2; RGSF 2; SATA 29; SSFS
5, 13
Munro, H(ector) H(ugh) 1870-1916
See Saki
See also CA 104; 130; CANR 104; CDBLB
1890-1914; DA; DA3; DAB; DAC; DAM
MST, NOV; DLB 34, 162; EXPS; MTCW
1, 2; RGEL 2; SSFS 15; WLC
Murakami, Haruki 1949- .... CLC **150**
See also Murakami Haruki
See also CA 165; CANR 102; MJW; SFW 4

New York Dept. of Ed. .... CLC 70

Nexo, Martin Andersen
1869-1954 .... TCLC 43
See also CA 202; DLB 214

Nezval, Vitezslav 1900-1958 .... TCLC 44
See also CA 123; CDWLB 4; DLB 215

Ng, Fae Myenne 1957(?)- .... CLC 81
See also CA 146

Ngema, Mbongeni 1955- .... CLC 57
See also BW 2; CA 143; CANR 84; CD 5

Ngugi, James T(hiong'o) .... CLC 3, 7, 13
See also Ngugi wa Thiong'o

Ngugi wa Thiong'o
See Ngugi wa Thiong'o
See also DLB 125

Ngugi wa Thiong'o 1938-.... CLC 36; BLC 3
See also Ngugi, James T(hiong'o); Ngugi
wa Thiong'o
See also AFW; BRWS 8; BW 2; CA 81-84;
CANR 27, 58; CDWLB 3; DAM MULT,
NOV; DNFS 2; MTCW 1, 2; RGEL 2

Nichol, B(arrie) P(hillip) 1944-1988 . CLC 18
See also CA 53-56; DLB 53; SATA 66

Nicholas of Cusa 1401-1464 .... LC 80
See also DLB 115

Nichols, John (Treadwell) 1940- .... CLC 38
See also CA 9-12R; CAAE 190; CAAS 2;
CANR 6, 70; DLBY 1982; TCWW 2

Nichols, Leigh
See Koontz, Dean R(ay)

Nichols, Peter (Richard) 1927- .... CLC 5, 36,
65
See also CA 104; CANR 33, 86; CBD; CD
5; DLB 13, 245; MTCW 1

Nicholson, Linda ed. .... CLC 65

Ni Chuilleanain, Eilean 1942- .... PC 34
See also CA 126; CANR 53, 83; CP 7;
CWP; DLB 40

Nicolas, F. R. E.
See Freeling, Nicolas

Niedecker, Lorine 1903-1970 ..... CLC 10, 42;
PC 42
See also CA 25-28; CAP 2; DAM POET;
DLB 48

Nietzsche, Friedrich (Wilhelm)
1844-1900 .... TCLC 10, 18, 55
See also CA 107; 121; CDWLB 2; DLB
129; EW 7; RGWL 2; TWA

Nievo, Ippolito 1831-1861 .... NCLC 22

Nightingale, Anne Redmon 1943-
See Redmon, Anne
See also CA 103

Nightingale, Florence 1820-1910 ... TCLC 85
See also CA 188; DLB 166

Nijo Yoshimoto 1320-1388 .... CMLC 49
See also DLB 203

Nik. T. O.
See Annensky, Innokenty (Fyodorovich)

Nin, Anais 1903-1977 ..... CLC 1, 4, 8, 11, 14,
60, 127; SSC 10
See also AITN 2; AMWS 10; BPFB 2; CA
13-16R; 69-72; CANR 22, 53; DAM
NOV, POP; DLB 2, 4, 152; GLL 2;
MAWW; MTCW 1, 2; RGAL 4; RGSF 2

Nisbet, Robert A(lexander)
1913-1996 .... TCLC 117
See also CA 25-28R; 153; CANR 17; INT
CANR-17

Nishida, Kitaro 1870-1945 .... TCLC 83

Nishiwaki, Junzaburo 1894-1982 .... PC 15
See also Nishiwaki, Junzaburo
See also CA 194; 107; MJW

Nishiwaki, Junzaburo 1894-1982
See Nishiwaki, Junzaburo
See also CA 194

Nissenson, Hugh 1933- .... CLC 4, 9
See also CA 17-20R; CANR 27, 108; CN
7; DLB 28

Niven, Larry .... CLC 8
See also Niven, Laurence Van Cott
See also AAYA 27; BPFB 2; BYA 10; DLB
8; SCFW 2

Niven, Laurence Van Cott 1938-
See Niven, Larry
See also CA 21-24R; CAAS 12; CANR 14,
44, 66; CPW; DAM POP; MTCW 1, 2;
SATA 95; SFW 4

Nixon, Agnes Eckhardt 1927- .... CLC 21
See also CA 110

Nizan, Paul 1905-1940 .... TCLC 40
See also CA 161; DLB 72; GFL 1789 to the
Present

Nkosi, Lewis 1936- .... CLC 45; BLC 3
See also BW 1, 3; CA 65-68; CANR 27,
81; CBD; CD 5; DAM MULT; DLB 157,
225

Nodier, (Jean) Charles (Emmanuel)
1780-1844 .... NCLC 19
See also DLB 119; GFL 1789 to the Present

Noguchi, Yone 1875-1947 .... TCLC 80

Nolan, Christopher 1965- .... CLC 58
See also CA 111; CANR 88

Noon, Jeff 1957- .... CLC 91
See also CA 148; CANR 83; DLB 267;
SFW 4

Norden, Charles
See Durrell, Lawrence (George)

Nordhoff, Charles (Bernard)
1887-1947 .... TCLC 23
See also CA 108; DLB 9; LAIT 1; RHW 1;
SATA 23

Norfolk, Lawrence 1963- .... CLC 76
See also CA 144; CANR 85; CN 7; DLB
267

Norman, Marsha 1947- .... CLC 28; DC 8
See also CA 105; CABS 3; CAD; CANR
41; CD 5; CSW; CWD; DAM DRAM;
DFS 2; DLB 266; DLBY 1984; FW

Normyx
See Douglas, (George) Norman

Norris, (Benjamin) Frank(lin, Jr.)
1870-1902 .... TCLC 24; SSC 28
See also AMW; BPFB 2; CA 110; 160;
CDALB 1865-1917; DLB 12, 71, 186;
NFS 12; RGAL 4; TCWW 2; TUS

Norris, Leslie 1921- .... CLC 14
See also CA 11-12; CANR 14; CAP 1; CP
7; DLB 27, 256

North, Andrew
See Norton, Andre

North, Anthony
See Koontz, Dean R(ay)

North, Captain George
See Stevenson, Robert Louis (Balfour)

North, Captain George
See Stevenson, Robert Louis (Balfour)

North, Milou
See Erdrich, Louise

Northrup, B. A.
See Hubbard, L(afayette) Ron(ald)

North Staffs
See Hulme, T(homas) E(rnest)

Northup, Solomon 1808-1863 ...... NCLC 105

Norton, Alice Mary
See Norton, Andre
See also MAICYA 1; SATA 1, 43

Norton, Andre 1912- .... CLC 12
See also Norton, Alice Mary
See also AAYA 14; BPFB 2; BYA 4, 10,
12; CA 1-4R; CANR 68; CLR 50; DLB
8, 52; JRDA; MAICYA 2; MTCW 1;
SATA 91; SUFW; YAW

Norton, Caroline 1808-1877 .... NCLC 47
See also DLB 21, 159, 199

Norway, Nevil Shute 1899-1960
See Shute, Nevil
See also CA 102; 93-96; CANR 85; MTCW
2

Norwid, Cyprian Kamil
1821-1883 .... NCLC 17

Nosille, Nabrah
See Ellison, Harlan (Jay)

Nossack, Hans Erich 1901-1978 .... CLC 6
See also CA 93-96; 85-88; DLB 69

Nostradamus 1503-1566 .... LC 27

Nosu, Chuji
See Ozu, Yasujiro

Notenburg, Eleanora (Genrikhovna) von
See Guro, Elena

Nova, Craig 1945- .... CLC 7, 31
See also CA 45-48; CANR 2, 53

Novak, Joseph
See Kosinski, Jerzy (Nikodem)

Novalis 1772-1801 .... NCLC 13
See also CDWLB 2; DLB 90; EW 5; RGWL
2

Novick, Peter 1934- .... CLC 164
See also CA 188

Novis, Emile
See Weil, Simone (Adolphine)

Nowlan, Alden (Albert) 1933-1983 ... CLC 15
See also CA 9-12R; CANR 5; DAC; DAM
MST; DLB 53; PFS 12

Noyes, Alfred 1880-1958 ...... TCLC 7; PC 27
See also CA 104; 188; DLB 20; EXPP;
FANT; PFS 4; RGEL 2

Nunn, Kem .... CLC 34
See also CA 159

Nwapa, Flora 1931-1993 .... CLC 133; BLCS
See also BW 2; CA 143; CANR 83; CD-
WLB 3; CWRI 5; DLB 125; WLIT 2

Nye, Robert 1939- .... CLC 13, 42
See also CA 33-36R; CANR 29, 67, 107;
CN 7; CP 7; CWRI 5; DAM NOV; DLB
14; FANT; HGG; MTCW 1; RHW; SATA
6

Nyro, Laura 1947-1997 .... CLC 17
See also CA 194

Oates, Joyce Carol 1938- .. CLC 1, 2, 3, 6, 9,
11, 15, 19, 33, 52, 108, 134; SSC 6;
WLC
See also AAYA 15; AITN 1; AMWS 2;
BEST 89:2; BPFB 2; BYA 11; CA 5-8R;
CANR 25, 45, 74; CDALB 1968-1988;
CN 7; CP 7; CPW; CWP; DA; DA3;
DAB; DAC; DAM MST, NOV, POP;
DLB 2, 5, 130; DLBY 1981; EXPS; FW;
HGG; INT CANR-25; LAIT 4; MAWW;
MTCW 1, 2; NFS 8; RGAL 4; RGSF 2;
SSFS 1, 8; TUS

O'Brian, E. G.
See Clarke, Arthur C(harles)

O'Brian, Patrick 1914-2000 .... CLC 152
See also CA 144; 187; CANR 74; CPW;
MTCW 2; RHW

O'Brien, Darcy 1939-1998 .... CLC 11
See also CA 21-24R; 167; CANR 8, 59

O'Brien, Edna 1936- ..... CLC 3, 5, 8, 13, 36,
65, 116; SSC 10
See also BRWS 5; CA 1-4R; CANR 6, 41,
65, 102; CDBLB 1960 to Present; CN 7;
DA3; DAM NOV; DLB 14, 231; FW;
MTCW 1, 2; RGSF 2; WLIT 4

O'Brien, Fitz-James 1828-1862 ..... NCLC 21
See also DLB 74; RGAL 4; SUFW

O'Brien, Flann .... CLC 1, 4, 5, 7, 10, 47
See also O Nuallain, Brian
See also BRWS 2; DLB 231; RGEL 2

O'Brien, Richard 1942- .... CLC 17
See also CA 124

Perse, St.-John
See Leger, (Marie-Rene Auguste) Alexis Saint-Leger

Perse, Saint-John
See Leger, (Marie-Rene Auguste) Alexis Saint-Leger
See also DLB 258

Perutz, Leo(pold) 1882-1957 .... **TCLC 60**
See also CA 147; DLB 81

Peseenz, Tulio F.
See Lopez y Fuentes, Gregorio

Pesetsky, Bette 1932- .... **CLC 28**
See also CA 133; DLB 130

Peshkov, Alexei Maximovich 1868-1936
See Gorky, Maxim
See also CA 105; 141; CANR 83; DA; DAC; DAM DRAM, MST, NOV; MTCW 2

Pessoa, Fernando (Antonio Nogueira)
1898-1935 ..... **TCLC 27; HLC 2; PC 20**
See also CA 125; 183; DAM MULT; EW 10; RGWL 2; WP

Peterkin, Julia Mood 1880-1961 ...... **CLC 31**
See also CA 102; DLB 9

Peters, Joan K(aren) 1945- .... **CLC 39**
See also CA 158; CANR 109

Peters, Robert L(ouis) 1924- .... **CLC 7**
See also CA 13-16R; CAAS 8; CP 7; DLB 105

Petofi, Sandor 1823-1849 .... **NCLC 21**
See also RGWL 2

Petrakis, Harry Mark 1923- .... **CLC 3**
See also CA 9-12R; CANR 4, 30, 85; CN 7

Petrarch 1304-1374 .... **CMLC 20; PC 8**
See also DA3; DAM POET; EW 2; RGWL 2

Petronius c. 20-66 .... **CMLC 34**
See also AW 2; CDWLB 1; DLB 211; RGWL 2

Petrov, Evgeny .... **TCLC 21**
See also Kataev, Evgeny Petrovich

Petry, Ann (Lane) 1908-1997 ... **CLC 1, 7, 18**
See also AFAW 1, 2; BPFB 3; BW 1, 3; BYA 2; CA 5-8R; 157; CAAS 6; CANR 4, 46; CLR 12; CN 7; DLB 76; JRDA; LAIT 1; MAICYA 1, 2; MAICYAS 1; MTCW 1; RGAL 4; SATA 5; SATA-Obit 94; TCLC 112; TUS

Petursson, Halligrimur 1614-1674 .... **LC 8**

Peychinovich
See Vazov, Ivan (Minchov)

Phaedrus c. 15 B.C.-c. 50 .... **CMLC 25**
See also DLB 211

Phelps (Ward), Elizabeth Stuart
See Phelps, Elizabeth Stuart
See also FW

Phelps, Elizabeth Stuart
1844-1911 .... **TCLC 113**
See also Phelps (Ward), Elizabeth Stuart
See also DLB 74

Philips, Katherine 1632-1664 . **LC 30; PC 40**
See also DLB 131; RGEL 2

Philipson, Morris H. 1926- .... **CLC 53**
See also CA 1-4R; CANR 4

Phillips, Caryl 1958- .... **CLC 96; BLCS**
See also BRWS 5; BW 2; CA 141; CANR 63, 104; CBD; CD 5; CN 7; DA3; DAM MULT; DLB 157; MTCW 2; WLIT 4

Phillips, David Graham
1867-1911 .... **TCLC 44**
See also CA 108; 176; DLB 9, 12; RGAL 4

Phillips, Jack
See Sandburg, Carl (August)

Phillips, Jayne Anne 1952- .... **CLC 15, 33, 139; SSC 16**
See also BPFB 3; CA 101; CANR 24, 50, 96; CN 7; CSW; DLBY 1980; INT CANR-24; MTCW 1, 2; RGAL 4; RGSF 2; SSFS 4

Phillips, Richard
See Dick, Philip K(indred)

Phillips, Robert (Schaeffer) 1938- .... **CLC 28**
See also CA 17-20R; CAAS 13; CANR 8; DLB 105

Phillips, Ward
See Lovecraft, H(oward) P(hillips)

Piccolo, Lucio 1901-1969 .... **CLC 13**
See also CA 97-100; DLB 114

Pickthall, Marjorie L(owry) C(hristie)
1883-1922 .... **TCLC 21**
See also CA 107; DLB 92

Pico della Mirandola, Giovanni
1463-1494 .... **LC 15**

Piercy, Marge 1936- .... **CLC 3, 6, 14, 18, 27, 62, 128; PC 29**
See also BPFB 3; CA 21-24R; CAAE 187; CAAS 1; CANR 13, 43, 66, 111; CN 7; CP 7; CWP; DLB 120, 227; EXPP; FW; MTCW 1, 2; PFS 9; SFW 4

Piers, Robert
See Anthony, Piers

Pieyre de Mandiargues, Andre 1909-1991
See Mandiargues, Andre Pieyre de
See also CA 103; 136; CANR 22, 82; GFL 1789 to the Present

Pilnyak, Boris 1894-1938 . **TCLC 23; SSC 48**
See also Vogau, Boris Andreyevich

Pinchback, Eugene
See Toomer, Jean

Pincherle, Alberto 1907-1990 ...... **CLC 11, 18**
See also Moravia, Alberto
See also CA 25-28R; 132; CANR 33, 63; DAM NOV; MTCW 1

Pinckney, Darryl 1953- .... **CLC 76**
See also BW 2, 3; CA 143; CANR 79

Pindar 518(?) B.C.-438(?) B.C. .... **CMLC 12; PC 19**
See also AW 1; CDWLB 1; DLB 176; RGWL 2

Pineda, Cecile 1942- .... **CLC 39**
See also CA 118; DLB 209

Pinero, Arthur Wing 1855-1934 .... **TCLC 32**
See also CA 110; 153; DAM DRAM; DLB 10; RGEL 2

Pinero, Miguel (Antonio Gomez)
1946-1988 .... **CLC 4, 55**
See also CA 61-64; 125; CAD; CANR 29, 90; DLB 266; HW 1

Pinget, Robert 1919-1997 .... **CLC 7, 13, 37**
See also CA 85-88; 160; CWW 2; DLB 83; GFL 1789 to the Present

Pink Floyd
See Barrett, (Roger) Syd; Gilmour, David; Mason, Nick; Waters, Roger; Wright, Rick

Pinkney, Edward 1802-1828 .... **NCLC 31**
See also DLB 248

Pinkwater, Daniel
See Pinkwater, Daniel Manus

Pinkwater, Daniel Manus 1941- .... **CLC 35**
See also AAYA 1; BYA 9; CA 29-32R; CANR 12, 38, 89; CLR 4; CSW; FANT; JRDA; MAICYA 1, 2; SAAS 3; SATA 8, 46, 76, 114; SFW 4; YAW

Pinkwater, Manus
See Pinkwater, Daniel Manus

Pinsky, Robert 1940- .... **CLC 9, 19, 38, 94, 121; PC 27**
See also AMWS 6; CA 29-32R; CAAS 4; CANR 58, 97; CP 7; DA3; DAM POET; DLBY 1982, 1998; MTCW 2; RGAL 4

Pinta, Harold
See Pinter, Harold

Pinter, Harold 1930- .. **CLC 1, 3, 6, 9, 11, 15, 27, 58, 73; DC 15; WLC**
See also BRWR 1; BRWS 1; CA 5-8R; CANR 33, 65; CBD; CD 5; CDBLB 1960 to Present; DA; DA3; DAB; DAC; DAM DRAM, MST; DFS 3, 5, 7, 14; DLB 13; IDFW 3, 4; MTCW 1, 2; RGEL 2; TEA

Piozzi, Hester Lynch (Thrale)
1741-1821 .... **NCLC 57**
See also DLB 104, 142

Pirandello, Luigi 1867-1936 ...... **TCLC 4, 29; DC 5; SSC 22; WLC**
See also CA 104; 153; CANR 103; DA; DA3; DAB; DAC; DAM DRAM, MST; DFS 4, 9; DLB 264; EW 8; MTCW 2; RGSF 2; RGWL 2

Pirsig, Robert M(aynard) 1928- ... **CLC 4, 6, 73**
See also CA 53-56; CANR 42, 74; CPW 1; DA3; DAM POP; MTCW 1, 2; SATA 39

Pisarev, Dmitry Ivanovich
1840-1868 .... **NCLC 25**

Pix, Mary (Griffith) 1666-1709 .... **LC 8**
See also DLB 80

Pixerecourt, (Rene Charles) Guilbert de
1773-1844 .... **NCLC 39**
See also DLB 192; GFL 1789 to the Present

Plaatje, Sol(omon) T(shekisho)
1878-1932 .... **TCLC 73; BLCS**
See also BW 2, 3; CA 141; CANR 79; DLB 125, 225

Plaidy, Jean
See Hibbert, Eleanor Alice Burford

Planche, James Robinson
1796-1880 .... **NCLC 42**
See also RGEL 2

Plant, Robert 1948- .... **CLC 12**

Plante, David (Robert) 1940- . **CLC 7, 23, 38**
See also CA 37-40R; CANR 12, 36, 58, 82; CN 7; DAM NOV; DLBY 1983; INT CANR-12; MTCW 1

Plath, Sylvia 1932-1963 ..... **CLC 1, 2, 3, 5, 9, 11, 14, 17, 50, 51, 62, 111; PC 1, 37; WLC**
See also AAYA 13; AMWS 1; BPFB 3; CA 19-20; CANR 34, 101; CAP 2; CDALB 1941-1968; DA; DA3; DAB; DAC; DAM MST, POET; DLB 5, 6, 152; EXPN; EXPP; FW; LAIT 4; MAWW; MTCW 1, 2; NFS 1; PAB; PFS 1, 15; RGAL 4; SATA 96; TUS; WP; YAW

Plato c. 428 B.C.-347 B.C. . **CMLC 8; WLCS**
See also AW 1; CDWLB 1; DA; DA3; DAB; DAC; DAM MST; DLB 176; LAIT 1; RGWL 2

Platonov, Andrei
See Klimentov, Andrei Platonovich

Platt, Kin 1911- .... **CLC 26**
See also AAYA 11; CA 17-20R; CANR 11; JRDA; SAAS 17; SATA 21, 86; WYA

Plautus c. 254 B.C.-c. 184 B.C. .... **CMLC 24; DC 6**
See also AW 1; CDWLB 1; DLB 211; RGWL 2

Plick et Plock
See Simenon, Georges (Jacques Christian)

Plieksans, Janis
See Rainis, Janis

Plimpton, George (Ames) 1927- .... **CLC 36**
See also AITN 1; CA 21-24R; CANR 32, 70, 103; DLB 185, 241; MTCW 1, 2; SATA 10

Pliny the Elder c. 23-79 .... **CMLC 23**
See also DLB 211

Plomer, William Charles Franklin
1903-1973 .... **CLC 4, 8**
See also AFW; CA 21-22; CANR 34; CAP 2; DLB 20, 162, 191, 225; MTCW 1; RGEL 2; RGSF 2; SATA 24

Plotinus 204-270 .... **CMLC 46**
See also CDWLB 1; DLB 176

Plowman, Piers
See Kavanagh, Patrick (Joseph)

Plum, J.
See Wodehouse, P(elham) G(renville)

Pritchett, V(ictor) S(awdon)
1900-1997 ... CLC 5, 13, 15, 41; SSC 14
See also BPFB 3; BRWS 3; CA 61-64; 157;
CANR 31, 63; CN 7; DA3; DAM NOV;
DLB 15, 139; MTCW 1, 2; RGEL 2;
RGSF 2; TEA

Private 19022
See Manning, Frederic

Probst, Mark 1925- .... CLC 59
See also CA 130

Prokosch, Frederic 1908-1989 ...... CLC 4, 48
See also CA 73-76; 128; CANR 82; DLB
48; MTCW 2

Propertius, Sextus c. 50 B.C.-c. 16
B.C. .... CMLC 32
See also AW 2; CDWLB 1; DLB 211;
RGWL 2

Prophet, The
See Dreiser, Theodore (Herman Albert)

Prose, Francine 1947- .... CLC 45
See also CA 109; 112; CANR 46, 95; DLB
234; SATA 101

Proudhon
See Cunha, Euclides (Rodrigues Pimenta)
da

Proulx, Annie
See Proulx, E(dna) Annie

Proulx, E(dna) Annie 1935- ...... CLC 81, 158
See also AMWS 7; BPFB 3; CA 145;
CANR 65, 110; CN 7; CPW 1; DA3;
DAM POP; MTCW 2

Proust,
(Valentin-Louis-George-Eugene-)Marcel
1871-1922 .... TCLC 7, 13, 33; WLC
See also BPFB 3; CA 104; 120; CANR 110;
DA; DA3; DAB; DAC; DAM MST, NOV;
DLB 65; EW 8; GFL 1789 to the Present;
MTCW 1, 2; RGWL 2; TWA

Prowler, Harley
See Masters, Edgar Lee

Prus, Boleslaw 1845-1912 .... TCLC 48
See also RGWL 2

Pryor, Richard (Franklin Lenox Thomas)
1940- .... CLC 26
See also CA 122; 152

Przybyszewski, Stanislaw
1868-1927 .... TCLC 36
See also CA 160; DLB 66

Pteleon
See Grieve, C(hristopher) M(urray)
See also DAM POET

Puckett, Lute
See Masters, Edgar Lee

Puig, Manuel 1932-1990 .... CLC 3, 5, 10, 28,
65, 133; HLC 2
See also BPFB 3; CA 45-48; CANR 2, 32,
63; CDWLB 3; DA3; DAM MULT; DLB
113; DNFS 1; GLL 1; HW 1, 2; LAW;
MTCW 1, 2; RGWL 2; TWA; WLIT 1

Pulitzer, Joseph 1847-1911 .... TCLC 76
See also CA 114; DLB 23

Purchas, Samuel 1577(?)-1626 .... LC 70
See also DLB 151

Purdy, A(lfred) W(ellington)
1918-2000 .... CLC 3, 6, 14, 50
See also CA 81-84; 189; CAAS 17; CANR
42, 66; CP 7; DAC; DAM MST, POET;
DLB 88; PFS 5; RGEL 2

Purdy, James (Amos) 1923- .... CLC 2, 4, 10,
28, 52
See also AMWS 7; CA 33-36R; CAAS 1;
CANR 19, 51; CN 7; DLB 2, 218; INT
CANR-19; MTCW 1; RGAL 4

Pure, Simon
See Swinnerton, Frank Arthur

Pushkin, Aleksandr Sergeevich
See Pushkin, Alexander (Sergeyevich)
See also DLB 205

Pushkin, Alexander (Sergeyevich)
1799-1837 .... NCLC 3, 27, 83; PC 10;
SSC 27, 55; WLC
See also Pushkin, Aleksandr Sergeevich
See also DA; DA3; DAB; DAC; DAM
DRAM, MST, POET; EW 5; EXPS; RGSF
2; RGWL 2; SATA 61; SSFS 9; TWA

P'u Sung-ling 1640-1715 .... LC 49; SSC 31

Putnam, Arthur Lee
See Alger, Horatio, Jr.

Puzo, Mario 1920-1999 .... CLC 1, 2, 6, 36,
107
See also BPFB 3; CA 65-68; 185; CANR 4,
42, 65, 99; CN 7; CPW; DA3; DAM
NOV, POP; DLB 6; MTCW 1, 2; RGAL
4

Pygge, Edward
See Barnes, Julian (Patrick)

Pyle, Ernest Taylor 1900-1945
See Pyle, Ernie
See also CA 115; 160

Pyle, Ernie .... TCLC 75
See also Pyle, Ernest Taylor
See also DLB 29; MTCW 2

Pyle, Howard 1853-1911 .... TCLC 81
See also BYA 2, 4; CA 109; 137; CLR 22;
DLB 42, 188; DLBD 13; LAIT 1; MAI-
CYA 1, 2; SATA 16, 100; WCH; YAW

Pym, Barbara (Mary Crampton)
1913-1980 .... CLC 13, 19, 37, 111
See also BPFB 3; BRWS 2; CA 13-14; 97-
100; CANR 13, 34; CAP 1; DLB 14, 207;
DLBY 1987; MTCW 1, 2; RGEL 2; TEA

Pynchon, Thomas (Ruggles, Jr.)
1937- ...... CLC 2, 3, 6, 9, 11, 18, 33, 62,
72, 123; SSC 14; WLC
See also AMWS 2; BEST 90:2; BPFB 3;
CA 17-20R; CANR 22, 46, 73; CN 7;
CPW 1; DA; DA3; DAB; DAC; DAM
MST, NOV, POP; DLB 2, 173; MTCW 1,
2; RGAL 4; SFW 4; TUS

Pythagoras c. 582 B.C.-c. 507
B.C. .... CMLC 22
See also DLB 176

Q
See Quiller-Couch, Sir Arthur (Thomas)

Qian, Chongzhu
See Ch'ien, Chung-shu

Qian Zhongshu
See Ch'ien, Chung-shu

Qroll
See Dagerman, Stig (Halvard)

Quarrington, Paul (Lewis) 1953- ..... CLC 65
See also CA 129; CANR 62, 95

Quasimodo, Salvatore 1901-1968 ..... CLC 10
See also CA 13-16; 25-28R; CAP 1; DLB
114; EW 12; MTCW 1; RGWL 2

Quatermass, Martin
See Carpenter, John (Howard)

Quay, Stephen 1947- .... CLC 95
See also CA 189

Quay, Timothy 1947- .... CLC 95
See also CA 189

Queen, Ellery .... CLC 3, 11
See also Dannay, Frederic; Davidson,
Avram (James); Deming, Richard; Fair-
man, Paul W.; Flora, Fletcher; Hoch,
Edward D(entinger); Kane, Henry; Lee,
Manfred B(ennington); Marlowe, Stephen;
Powell, (Oval) Talmage; Sheldon, Walter
J(ames); Sturgeon, Theodore (Hamilton);
Tracy, Don(ald Fiske); Vance, John Hol-
brook
See also BPFB 3; CMW 4; MSW; RGAL 4

Queen, Ellery, Jr.
See Dannay, Frederic; Lee, Manfred
B(ennington)

Queneau, Raymond 1903-1976 ..... CLC 2, 5,
10, 42
See also CA 77-80; 69-72; CANR 32; DLB
72, 258; EW 12; GFL 1789 to the Present;
MTCW 1, 2; RGWL 2

Quevedo, Francisco de 1580-1645 .... LC 23

Quiller-Couch, Sir Arthur (Thomas)
1863-1944 .... TCLC 53
See also CA 118; 166; DLB 135, 153, 190;
HGG; RGEL 2; SUFW

Quin, Ann (Marie) 1936-1973 .... CLC 6
See also CA 9-12R; 45-48; DLB 14, 231

Quinn, Martin
See Smith, Martin Cruz

Quinn, Peter 1947- .... CLC 91
See also CA 197

Quinn, Simon
See Smith, Martin Cruz

Quintana, Leroy V. 1944- .... PC 36
See also CA 131; CANR 65; DAM MULT;
DLB 82; HLC 2; HW 1, 2

Quiroga, Horacio (Sylvestre)
1878-1937 .... TCLC 20; HLC 2
See also CA 117; 131; DAM MULT; HW
1; LAW; MTCW 1; RGSF 2; WLIT 1

Quoirez, Francoise 1935- .... CLC 9
See also Sagan, Francoise
See also CA 49-52; CANR 6, 39, 73; CWW
2; MTCW 1, 2; TWA

Raabe, Wilhelm (Karl) 1831-1910 . TCLC 45
See also CA 167; DLB 129

Rabe, David (William) 1940- .. CLC 4, 8, 33;
DC 16
See also CA 85-88; CABS 3; CAD; CANR
59; CD 5; DAM DRAM; DFS 3, 8, 13;
DLB 7, 228

Rabelais, Francois 1494-1553 .... LC 5, 60;
WLC
See also DA; DAB; DAC; DAM MST; EW
2; GFL Beginnings to 1789; RGWL 2;
TWA

Rabinovitch, Sholem 1859-1916
See Aleichem, Sholom
See also CA 104

Rabinyan, Dorit 1972- .... CLC 119
See also CA 170

Rachilde
See Vallette, Marguerite Eymery

Racine, Jean 1639-1699 .... LC 28
See also DA3; DAB; DAM MST; DLB 268;
EW 3; GFL Beginnings to 1789; RGWL
2; TWA

Radcliffe, Ann (Ward) 1764-1823 ... NCLC 6,
55, 106
See also DLB 39, 178; HGG; RGEL 2;
SUFW; WLIT 3

Radclyffe-Hall, Marguerite
See Hall, (Marguerite) Radclyffe

Radiguet, Raymond 1903-1923 ...... TCLC 29
See also CA 162; DLB 65; GFL 1789 to the
Present; RGWL 2

Radnoti, Miklos 1909-1944 .... TCLC 16
See also CA 118; CDWLB 4; DLB 215;
RGWL 2

Rado, James 1939- .... CLC 17
See also CA 105

Radvanyi, Netty 1900-1983
See Seghers, Anna
See also CA 85-88; 110; CANR 82

Rae, Ben
See Griffiths, Trevor

Raeburn, John (Hay) 1941- .... CLC 34
See also CA 57-60

Ragni, Gerome 1942-1991 .... CLC 17
See also CA 105; 134

Rahv, Philip .... CLC 24
See also Greenberg, Ivan
See also DLB 137

Raimund, Ferdinand Jakob
1790-1836 .... **NCLC 69**
See also DLB 90
Raine, Craig (Anthony) 1944- .. **CLC 32, 103**
See also CA 108; CANR 29, 51, 103; CP 7;
DLB 40; PFS 7
Raine, Kathleen (Jessie) 1908- ..... **CLC 7, 45**
See also CA 85-88; CANR 46, 109; CP 7;
DLB 20; MTCW 1; RGEL 2
Rainis, Janis 1865-1929 .... **TCLC 29**
See also CA 170; CDWLB 4; DLB 220
Rakosi, Carl .... **CLC 47**
See also Rawley, Callman
See also CAAS 5; CP 7; DLB 193
Ralegh, Sir Walter
See Raleigh, Sir Walter
See also BRW 1; RGEL 2; WP
Raleigh, Richard
See Lovecraft, H(oward) P(hillips)
Raleigh, Sir Walter 1554(?)-1618 .... **LC 31,
39; PC 31**
See also Ralegh, Sir Walter
See also CDBLB Before 1660; DLB 172;
EXPP; PFS 14; TEA
Rallentando, H. P.
See Sayers, Dorothy L(eigh)
Ramal, Walter
See de la Mare, Walter (John)
Ramana Maharshi 1879-1950 .... **TCLC 84**
Ramoacn y Cajal, Santiago
1852-1934 .... **TCLC 93**
Ramon, Juan
See Jimenez (Mantecon), Juan Ramon
Ramos, Graciliano 1892-1953 .... **TCLC 32**
See also CA 167; HW 2; LAW; WLIT 1
Rampersad, Arnold 1941- .... **CLC 44**
See also BW 2, 3; CA 127; 133; CANR 81;
DLB 111; INT 133
Rampling, Anne
See Rice, Anne
See also GLL 2
Ramsay, Allan 1686(?)-1758 .... **LC 29**
See also DLB 95; RGEL 2
Ramsay, Jay
See Campbell, (John) Ramsey
Ramuz, Charles-Ferdinand
1878-1947 .... **TCLC 33**
See also CA 165
Rand, Ayn 1905-1982 ...... **CLC 3, 30, 44, 79;
WLC**
See also AAYA 10; AMWS 4; BPFB 3;
BYA 12; CA 13-16R; 105; CANR 27, 73;
CDALBS; CPW; DA; DA3; DAC; DAM
MST, NOV, POP; DLB 227; MTCW 1, 2;
NFS 10; RGAL 4; SFW 4; TUS; YAW
Randall, Dudley (Felker) 1914-2000 . **CLC 1,
135; BLC 3**
See also BW 1, 3; CA 25-28R; 189; CANR
23, 82; DAM MULT; DLB 41; PFS 5
Randall, Robert
See Silverberg, Robert
Ranger, Ken
See Creasey, John
Rank, Otto 1884-1939 .... **TCLC 115**
Ransom, John Crowe 1888-1974 .. **CLC 2, 4,
5, 11, 24**
See also AMW; CA 5-8R; 49-52; CANR 6,
34; CDALBS; DA3; DAM POET; DLB
45, 63; EXPP; MTCW 1, 2; RGAL 4;
TUS
Rao, Raja 1909- .... **CLC 25, 56**
See also CA 73-76; CANR 51; CN 7; DAM
NOV; MTCW 1, 2; RGEL 2; RGSF 2
Raphael, Frederic (Michael) 1931- ... **CLC 2,
14**
See also CA 1-4R; CANR 1, 86; CN 7;
DLB 14
Ratcliffe, James P.
See Mencken, H(enry) L(ouis)

Rathbone, Julian 1935- .... **CLC 41**
See also CA 101; CANR 34, 73
Rattigan, Terence (Mervyn)
1911-1977 .... **CLC 7; DC 18**
See also BRWS 7; CA 85-88; 73-76; CBD;
CDBLB 1945-1960; DAM DRAM; DFS
8; DLB 13; IDFW 3, 4; MTCW 1, 2;
RGEL 2
Ratushinskaya, Irina 1954- .... **CLC 54**
See also CA 129; CANR 68; CWW 2
Raven, Simon (Arthur Noel)
1927-2001 .... **CLC 14**
See also CA 81-84; 197; CANR 86; CN 7
Ravenna, Michael
See Welty, Eudora (Alice)
Rawley, Callman 1903-
See Rakosi, Carl
See also CA 21-24R; CANR 12, 32, 91
Rawlings, Marjorie Kinnan
1896-1953 .... **TCLC 4**
See also AAYA 20; AMWS 10; ANW;
BPFB 3; BYA 3; CA 104; 137; CANR 74;
CLR 63; DLB 9, 22, 102; DLBD 17;
JRDA; MAICYA 1, 2; MTCW 2; RGAL
4; SATA 100; WCH; YABC 1; YAW
Ray, Satyajit 1921-1992 .... **CLC 16, 76**
See also CA 114; 137; DAM MULT
Read, Herbert Edward 1893-1968 ..... **CLC 4**
See also BRW 6; CA 85-88; 25-28R; DLB
20, 149; PAB; RGEL 2
Read, Piers Paul 1941- .... **CLC 4, 10, 25**
See also CA 21-24R; CANR 38, 86; CN 7;
DLB 14; SATA 21
Reade, Charles 1814-1884 .... **NCLC 2, 74**
See also DLB 21; RGEL 2
Reade, Hamish
See Gray, Simon (James Holliday)
Reading, Peter 1946- .... **CLC 47**
See also BRWS 8; CA 103; CANR 46, 96;
CP 7; DLB 40
Reaney, James 1926- .... **CLC 13**
See also CA 41-44R; CAAS 15; CANR 42;
CD 5; CP 7; DAC; DAM MST; DLB 68;
RGEL 2; SATA 43
Rebreanu, Liviu 1885-1944 .... **TCLC 28**
See also CA 165; DLB 220
Rechy, John (Francisco) 1934- ...... **CLC 1, 7,
14, 18, 107; HLC 2**
See also CA 5-8R; CAAE 195; CAAS 4;
CANR 6, 32, 64; CN 7; DAM MULT;
DLB 122; DLBY 1982; HW 1, 2; INT
CANR-6; RGAL 4
Redcam, Tom 1870-1933 .... **TCLC 25**
Reddin, Keith .... **CLC 67**
See also CAD
Redgrove, Peter (William) 1932- . **CLC 6, 41**
See also BRWS 6; CA 1-4R; CANR 3, 39,
77; CP 7; DLB 40
Redmon, Anne .... **CLC 22**
See also Nightingale, Anne Redmon
See also DLBY 1986
Reed, Eliot
See Ambler, Eric
Reed, Ishmael 1938- .. **CLC 2, 3, 5, 6, 13, 32,
60; BLC 3**
See also AFAW 1, 2; AMWS 10; BPFB 3;
BW 2, 3; CA 21-24R; CANR 25, 48, 74;
CN 7; CP 7; CSW; DA3; DAM MULT;
DLB 2, 5, 33, 169, 227; DLBD 8; MSW;
MTCW 1, 2; PFS 6; RGAL 4; TCWW 2
Reed, John (Silas) 1887-1920 .... **TCLC 9**
See also CA 106; 195; TUS
Reed, Lou .... **CLC 21**
See also Firbank, Louis
Reese, Lizette Woodworth 1856-1935 . **PC 29**
See also CA 180; DLB 54
Reeve, Clara 1729-1807 .... **NCLC 19**
See also DLB 39; RGEL 2

Reich, Wilhelm 1897-1957 .... **TCLC 57**
See also CA 199
Reid, Christopher (John) 1949- .... **CLC 33**
See also CA 140; CANR 89; CP 7; DLB 40
Reid, Desmond
See Moorcock, Michael (John)
Reid Banks, Lynne 1929-
See Banks, Lynne Reid
See also CA 1-4R; CANR 6, 22, 38, 87;
CLR 24; CN 7; JRDA; MAICYA 1, 2;
SATA 22, 75, 111; YAW
Reilly, William K.
See Creasey, John
Reiner, Max
See Caldwell, (Janet Miriam) Taylor
(Holland)
Reis, Ricardo
See Pessoa, Fernando (Antonio Nogueira)
Remarque, Erich Maria 1898-1970 . **CLC 21**
See also AAYA 27; BPFB 3; CA 77-80; 29-
32R; CDWLB 2; DA; DA3; DAB; DAC;
DAM MST, NOV; DLB 56; EXPN; LAIT
3; MTCW 1, 2; NFS 4; RGWL 2
Remington, Frederic 1861-1909 ..... **TCLC 89**
See also CA 108; 169; DLB 12, 186, 188;
SATA 41
Remizov, A.
See Remizov, Aleksei (Mikhailovich)
Remizov, A. M.
See Remizov, Aleksei (Mikhailovich)
Remizov, Aleksei (Mikhailovich)
1877-1957 .... **TCLC 27**
See also CA 125; 133
Renan, Joseph Ernest 1823-1892 .. **NCLC 26**
See also GFL 1789 to the Present
Renard, Jules(-Pierre) 1864-1910 .. **TCLC 17**
See also CA 117; 202; GFL 1789 to the
Present
Renault, Mary .... **CLC 3, 11, 17**
See also Challans, Mary
See also BPFB 3; BYA 2; DLBY 1983;
GLL 1; LAIT 1; MTCW 2; RGEL 2;
RHW
Rendell, Ruth (Barbara) 1930- .. **CLC 28, 48**
See also Vine, Barbara
See also BPFB 3; CA 109; CANR 32, 52,
74; CN 7; CPW; DAM POP; DLB 87;
INT CANR-32; MSW; MTCW 1, 2
Renoir, Jean 1894-1979 .... **CLC 20**
See also CA 129; 85-88
Resnais, Alain 1922- .... **CLC 16**
Reverdy, Pierre 1889-1960 .... **CLC 53**
See also CA 97-100; 89-92; DLB 258; GFL
1789 to the Present
Rexroth, Kenneth 1905-1982 .... **CLC 1, 2, 6,
11, 22, 49, 112; PC 20**
See also CA 5-8R; 107; CANR 14, 34, 63;
CDALB 1941-1968; DAM POET; DLB
16, 48, 165, 212; DLBY 1982; INT
CANR-14; MTCW 1, 2; RGAL 4
Reyes, Alfonso 1889-1959 .. **TCLC 33; HLCS
2**
See also CA 131; HW 1; LAW
Reyes y Basoalto, Ricardo Eliecer Neftali
See Neruda, Pablo
Reymont, Wladyslaw (Stanislaw)
1868(?)-1925 .... **TCLC 5**
See also CA 104
Reynolds, Jonathan 1942- .... **CLC 6, 38**
See also CA 65-68; CANR 28
Reynolds, Joshua 1723-1792 .... **LC 15**
See also DLB 104
Reynolds, Michael S(hane)
1937-2000 .... **CLC 44**
See also CA 65-68; 189; CANR 9, 89, 97
Reznikoff, Charles 1894-1976 .... **CLC 9**
See also CA 33-36; 61-64; CAP 2; DLB 28,
45; WP

Rezzori (d'Arezzo), Gregor von
1914-1998 .... **CLC 25**
See also CA 122; 136; 167

Rhine, Richard
See Silverstein, Alvin; Silverstein, Virginia
B(arbara Opshelor)

Rhodes, Eugene Manlove
1869-1934 .... **TCLC 53**
See also CA 198; DLB 256

R'hoone, Lord
See Balzac, Honore de

Rhys, Jean 1894(?)-1979 ...... **CLC 2, 4, 6, 14,
19, 51, 124; SSC 21**
See also BRWS 2; CA 25-28R; 85-88;
CANR 35, 62; CDBLB 1945-1960; CD-
WLB 3; DA3; DAM NOV; DLB 36, 117,
162; DNFS 2; MTCW 1, 2; RGEL 2;
RGSF 2; RHW; TEA

Ribeiro, Darcy 1922-1997 .... **CLC 34**
See also CA 33-36R; 156

Ribeiro, Joao Ubaldo (Osorio Pimentel)
1941- .... **CLC 10, 67**
See also CA 81-84

Ribman, Ronald (Burt) 1932- .... **CLC 7**
See also CA 21-24R; CAD; CANR 46, 80;
CD 5

Ricci, Nino 1959- .... **CLC 70**
See also CA 137; CCA 1

Rice, Anne 1941- .... **CLC 41, 128**
See also Rampling, Anne
See also AAYA 9; AMWS 7; BEST 89:2;
BPFB 3; CA 65-68; CANR 12, 36, 53,
74, 100; CN 7; CPW; CSW; DA3; DAM
POP; GLL 2; HGG; MTCW 2; YAW

Rice, Elmer (Leopold) 1892-1967 ...... **CLC 7,
49**
See also CA 21-22; 25-28R; CAP 2; DAM
DRAM; DFS 12; DLB 4, 7; MTCW 1, 2;
RGAL 4

Rice, Tim(othy Miles Bindon)
1944- .... **CLC 21**
See also CA 103; CANR 46; DFS 7

Rich, Adrienne (Cecile) 1929- ... **CLC 3, 6, 7,
11, 18, 36, 73, 76, 125; PC 5**
See also AMWS 1; CA 9-12R; CANR 20,
53, 74; CDALBS; CP 7; CSW; CWP;
DA3; DAM POET; DLB 5, 67; EXPP;
FW; MAWW; MTCW 1, 2; PAB; PFS 15;
RGAL 4; WP

Rich, Barbara
See Graves, Robert (von Ranke)

Rich, Robert
See Trumbo, Dalton

Richard, Keith .... **CLC 17**
See also Richards, Keith

Richards, David Adams 1950- .... **CLC 59**
See also CA 93-96; CANR 60, 110; DAC;
DLB 53

Richards, I(vor) A(rmstrong)
1893-1979 .... **CLC 14, 24**
See also BRWS 2; CA 41-44R; 89-92;
CANR 34, 74; DLB 27; MTCW 2; RGEL
2

Richards, Keith 1943-
See Richard, Keith
See also CA 107; CANR 77

Richardson, Anne
See Roiphe, Anne (Richardson)

Richardson, Dorothy Miller
1873-1957 .... **TCLC 3**
See also CA 104; 192; DLB 36; FW; RGEL
2

**Richardson (Robertson), Ethel Florence
Lindesay** 1870-1946
See Richardson, Henry Handel
See also CA 105; 190; DLB 230; RHW

Richardson, Henry Handel .... **TCLC 4**
See also Richardson (Robertson), Ethel Flo-
rence Lindesay
See also DLB 197; RGEL 2; RGSF 2

Richardson, John 1796-1852 .... **NCLC 55**
See also CCA 1; DAC; DLB 99

Richardson, Samuel 1689-1761 ...... **LC 1, 44;
WLC**
See also BRW 3; CDBLB 1660-1789; DA;
DAB; DAC; DAM MST, NOV; DLB 39;
RGEL 2; TEA; WLIT 3

Richler, Mordecai 1931-2001 .... **CLC 3, 5, 9,
13, 18, 46, 70**
See also AITN 1; CA 65-68; 201; CANR
31, 62, 111; CCA 1; CLR 17; CWRI 5;
DAC; DAM MST, NOV; DLB 53; MAI-
CYA 1, 2; MTCW 1, 2; RGEL 2; SATA
44, 98; SATA-Brief 27; TWA

Richter, Conrad (Michael)
1890-1968 .... **CLC 30**
See also AAYA 21; BYA 2; CA 5-8R; 25-
28R; CANR 23; DLB 9, 212; LAIT 1;
MTCW 1, 2; RGAL 4; SATA 3; TCWW
2; TUS; YAW

Ricostranza, Tom
See Ellis, Trey

Riddell, Charlotte 1832-1906 .... **TCLC 40**
See also Riddell, Mrs. J. H.
See also CA 165; DLB 156

Riddell, Mrs. J. H.
See Riddell, Charlotte
See also HGG; SUFW

Ridge, John Rollin 1827-1867 .... **NCLC 82**
See also CA 144; DAM MULT; DLB 175;
NNAL

Ridgeway, Jason
See Marlowe, Stephen

Ridgway, Keith 1965- .... **CLC 119**
See also CA 172

Riding, Laura .... **CLC 3, 7**
See also Jackson, Laura (Riding)
See also RGAL 4

Riefenstahl, Berta Helene Amalia 1902-
See Riefenstahl, Leni
See also CA 108

Riefenstahl, Leni .... **CLC 16**
See also Riefenstahl, Berta Helene Amalia

Riffe, Ernest
See Bergman, (Ernst) Ingmar

Riggs, (Rolla) Lynn 1899-1954 .... **TCLC 56**
See also CA 144; DAM MULT; DLB 175;
NNAL

Riis, Jacob A(ugust) 1849-1914 ..... **TCLC 80**
See also CA 113; 168; DLB 23

Riley, James Whitcomb
1849-1916 .... **TCLC 51**
See also CA 118; 137; DAM POET; MAI-
CYA 1, 2; RGAL 4; SATA 17

Riley, Tex
See Creasey, John

Rilke, Rainer Maria 1875-1926 .. **TCLC 1, 6,
19; PC 2**
See also CA 104; 132; CANR 62, 99; CD-
WLB 2; DA3; DAM POET; DLB 81; EW
9; MTCW 1, 2; RGWL 2; TWA; WP

Rimbaud, (Jean Nicolas) Arthur
1854-1891 .... **NCLC 4, 35, 82; PC 3;
WLC**
See also DA; DA3; DAB; DAC; DAM
MST, POET; DLB 217; EW 7; GFL 1789
to the Present; RGWL 2; TWA; WP

Rinehart, Mary Roberts
1876-1958 .... **TCLC 52**
See also BPFB 3; CA 108; 166; RGAL 4;
RHW

Ringmaster, The
See Mencken, H(enry) L(ouis)

Ringwood, Gwen(dolyn Margaret) Pharis
1910-1984 .... **CLC 48**
See also CA 148; 112; DLB 88

Rio, Michel 1945(?)- .... **CLC 43**
See also CA 201

Ritsos, Giannes
See Ritsos, Yannis

Ritsos, Yannis 1909-1990 .... **CLC 6, 13, 31**
See also CA 77-80; 133; CANR 39, 61; EW
12; MTCW 1; RGWL 2

Ritter, Erika 1948(?)- .... **CLC 52**
See also CD 5; CWD

Rivera, Jose Eustasio 1889-1928 ... **TCLC 35**
See also CA 162; HW 1, 2; LAW

Rivera, Tomas 1935-1984
See also CA 49-52; CANR 32; DLB 82;
HLCS 2; HW 1; RGAL 4; SSFS 15;
TCWW 2; WLIT 1

Rivers, Conrad Kent 1933-1968 .... **CLC 1**
See also BW 1; CA 85-88; DLB 41

Rivers, Elfrida
See Bradley, Marion Zimmer
See also GLL 1

Riverside, John
See Heinlein, Robert A(nson)

Rizal, Jose 1861-1896 .... **NCLC 27**

Roa Bastos, Augusto (Antonio)
1917- .... **CLC 45; HLC 2**
See also CA 131; DAM MULT; DLB 113;
HW 1; LAW; RGSF 2; WLIT 1

Robbe-Grillet, Alain 1922- .... **CLC 1, 2, 4, 6,
8, 10, 14, 43, 128**
See also BPFB 3; CA 9-12R; CANR 33,
65; DLB 83; EW 13; GFL 1789 to the
Present; IDFW 3, 4; MTCW 1, 2; RGWL
2; SSFS 15

Robbins, Harold 1916-1997 .... **CLC 5**
See also BPFB 3; CA 73-76; 162; CANR
26, 54; DA3; DAM NOV; MTCW 1, 2

Robbins, Thomas Eugene 1936-
See Robbins, Tom
See also CA 81-84; CANR 29, 59, 95; CN
7; CPW; CSW; DA3; DAM NOV, POP;
MTCW 1, 2

Robbins, Tom .... **CLC 9, 32, 64**
See also Robbins, Thomas Eugene
See also AAYA 32; AMWS 10; BEST 90:3;
BPFB 3; DLBY 1980; MTCW 2

Robbins, Trina 1938- .... **CLC 21**
See also CA 128

Roberts, Charles G(eorge) D(ouglas)
1860-1943 .... **TCLC 8**
See also CA 105; 188; CLR 33; CWRI 5;
DLB 92; RGEL 2; RGSF 2; SATA 88;
SATA-Brief 29

Roberts, Elizabeth Madox
1886-1941 .... **TCLC 68**
See also CA 111; 166; CWRI 5; DLB 9, 54,
102; RGAL 4; RHW; SATA 33; SATA-
Brief 27; WCH

Roberts, Kate 1891-1985 .... **CLC 15**
See also CA 107; 116

Roberts, Keith (John Kingston)
1935-2000 .... **CLC 14**
See also CA 25-28R; CANR 46; DLB 261;
SFW 4

Roberts, Kenneth (Lewis)
1885-1957 .... **TCLC 23**
See also CA 109; 199; DLB 9; RGAL 4;
RHW

Roberts, Michele (Brigitte) 1949- ..... **CLC 48**
See also CA 115; CANR 58; CN 7; DLB
231; FW

Robertson, Ellis
See Ellison, Harlan (Jay); Silverberg, Robert

Robertson, Thomas William
1829-1871 .... **NCLC 35**
See also Robertson, Tom
See also DAM DRAM

Rothenberg, Jerome 1931- .... **CLC 6, 57**
　　See also CA 45-48; CANR 1, 106; CP 7;
　　DLB 5, 193
Rotter, Pat ed. .... **CLC 65**
Roumain, Jacques (Jean Baptiste)
　　1907-1944 .... **TCLC 19; BLC 3**
　　See also BW 1; CA 117; 125; DAM MULT
Rourke, Constance (Mayfield)
　　1885-1941 .... **TCLC 12**
　　See also CA 107; YABC 1
Rousseau, Jean-Baptiste 1671-1741 ...... **LC 9**
Rousseau, Jean-Jacques 1712-1778 .... **LC 14,**
　　36; WLC
　　See also DA; DA3; DAB; DAC; DAM
　　MST; EW 4; GFL Beginnings to 1789;
　　RGWL 2; TWA
Roussel, Raymond 1877-1933 .... **TCLC 20**
　　See also CA 117; 201; GFL 1789 to the
　　Present
Rovit, Earl (Herbert) 1927- .... **CLC 7**
　　See also CA 5-8R; CANR 12
Rowe, Elizabeth Singer 1674-1737 ..... **LC 44**
　　See also DLB 39, 95
Rowe, Nicholas 1674-1718 .... **LC 8**
　　See also DLB 84; RGEL 2
Rowlandson, Mary 1637(?)-1678 .... **LC 66**
　　See also DLB 24, 200; RGAL 4
Rowley, Ames Dorrance
　　See Lovecraft, H(oward) P(hillips)
Rowling, J(oanne) K(athleen)
　　1965- .... **CLC 137**
　　See also AAYA 34; BYA 13, 14; CA 173;
　　CLR 66, 80; SATA 109
Rowson, Susanna Haswell
　　1762(?)-1824 .... **NCLC 5, 69**
　　See also DLB 37, 200; RGAL 4
Roy, Arundhati 1960(?)- .... **CLC 109**
　　See also CA 163; CANR 90; DLBY 1997
Roy, Gabrielle 1909-1983 .... **CLC 10, 14**
　　See also CA 53-56; 110; CANR 5, 61; CCA
　　1; DAB; DAC; DAM MST; DLB 68;
　　MTCW 1; RGWL 2; SATA 104
Royko, Mike 1932-1997 .... **CLC 109**
　　See also CA 89-92; 157; CANR 26, 111;
　　CPW
Rozanov, Vassili 1856-1919 .... **TCLC 104**
Rozewicz, Tadeusz 1921- ..... **CLC 9, 23, 139**
　　See also CA 108; CANR 36, 66; CWW 2;
　　DA3; DAM POET; DLB 232; MTCW 1,
　　2
Ruark, Gibbons 1941- .... **CLC 3**
　　See also CA 33-36R; CAAS 23; CANR 14,
　　31, 57; DLB 120
Rubens, Bernice (Ruth) 1923- .... **CLC 19, 31**
　　See also CA 25-28R; CANR 33, 65; CN 7;
　　DLB 14, 207; MTCW 1
Rubin, Harold
　　See Robbins, Harold
Rudkin, (James) David 1936- .... **CLC 14**
　　See also CA 89-92; CBD; CD 5; DLB 13
Rudnik, Raphael 1933- .... **CLC 7**
　　See also CA 29-32R
Ruffian, M.
　　See Hasek, Jaroslav (Matej Frantisek)
Ruiz, Jose Martinez .... **CLC 11**
　　See also Martinez Ruiz, Jose
Rukeyser, Muriel 1913-1980 . **CLC 6, 10, 15,**
　　27; PC 12
　　See also AMWS 6; CA 5-8R; 93-96; CANR
　　26, 60; DA3; DAM POET; DLB 48; FW;
　　GLL 1; MTCW 1, 2; PFS 10; RGAL 4;
　　SATA-Obit 22
Rule, Jane (Vance) 1931- .... **CLC 27**
　　See also CA 25-28R; CAAS 18; CANR 12,
　　87; CN 7; DLB 60; FW

Rulfo, Juan 1918-1986 .. **CLC 8, 80; HLC 2;**
　　SSC 25
　　See also CA 85-88; 118; CANR 26; CD-
　　WLB 3; DAM MULT; DLB 113; HW 1,
　　2; LAW; MTCW 1, 2; RGSF 2; RGWL 2;
　　WLIT 1
Rumi, Jalal al-Din 1207-1273 .... **CMLC 20**
　　See also RGWL 2; WP
Runeberg, Johan 1804-1877 .... **NCLC 41**
Runyon, (Alfred) Damon
　　1884(?)-1946 .... **TCLC 10**
　　See also CA 107; 165; DLB 11, 86, 171;
　　MTCW 2; RGAL 4
Rush, Norman 1933- .... **CLC 44**
　　See also CA 121; 126; INT 126
Rushdie, (Ahmed) Salman 1947- .... **CLC 23,**
　　31, 55, 100; WLCS
　　See also BEST 89:3; BPFB 3; BRWS 4;
　　CA 108; 111; CANR 33, 56, 108; CN 7;
　　CPW 1; DA3; DAB; DAC; DAM MST,
　　NOV, POP; DLB 194; FANT; INT CA-
　　111; MTCW 1, 2; RGEL 2; RGSF 2;
　　TEA; WLIT 4
Rushforth, Peter (Scott) 1945- .... **CLC 19**
　　See also CA 101
Ruskin, John 1819-1900 .... **TCLC 63**
　　See also BRW 5; BYA 5; CA 114; 129; CD-
　　BLB 1832-1890; DLB 55, 163, 190;
　　RGEL 2; SATA 24; TEA; WCH
Russ, Joanna 1937- .... **CLC 15**
　　See also BPFB 3; CA 5-28R; CANR 11,
　　31, 65; CN 7; DLB 8; FW; GLL 1;
　　MTCW 1; SCFW 2; SFW 4
Russell, George William 1867-1935
　　See A.E.; Baker, Jean H.
　　See also BRWS 8; CA 104; 153; CDBLB
　　1890-1914; DAM POET; RGEL 2
Russell, Jeffrey Burton 1934- .... **CLC 70**
　　See also CA 25-28R; CANR 11, 28, 52
Russell, (Henry) Ken(neth Alfred)
　　1927- .... **CLC 16**
　　See also CA 105
Russell, William Martin 1947-
　　See Russell, Willy
　　See also CA 164; CANR 107
Russell, Willy .... **CLC 60**
　　See also Russell, William Martin
　　See also CBD; CD 5; DLB 233
Rutherford, Mark .... **TCLC 25**
　　See also White, William Hale
　　See also DLB 18; RGEL 2
Ruyslinck, Ward .... **CLC 14**
　　See also Belser, Reimond Karel Maria de
Ryan, Cornelius (John) 1920-1974 ..... **CLC 7**
　　See also CA 69-72; 53-56; CANR 38
Ryan, Michael 1946- .... **CLC 65**
　　See also CA 49-52; CANR 109; DLBY
　　1982
Ryan, Tim
　　See Dent, Lester
Rybakov, Anatoli (Naumovich)
　　1911-1998 .... **CLC 23, 53**
　　See also CA 126; 135; 172; SATA 79;
　　SATA-Obit 108
Ryder, Jonathan
　　See Ludlum, Robert
Ryga, George 1932-1987 .... **CLC 14**
　　See also CA 101; 124; CANR 43, 90; CCA
　　1; DAC; DAM MST; DLB 60
S. H.
　　See Hartmann, Sadakichi
S. S.
　　See Sassoon, Siegfried (Lorraine)
Saba, Umberto 1883-1957 .... **TCLC 33**
　　See also CA 144; CANR 79; DLB 114;
　　RGWL 2
Sabatini, Rafael 1875-1950 .... **TCLC 47**
　　See also BPFB 3; CA 162; RHW

Sabato, Ernesto (R.) 1911- .... **CLC 10, 23;**
　　HLC 2
　　See also CA 97-100; CANR 32, 65; CD-
　　WLB 3; DAM MULT; DLB 145; HW 1,
　　2; LAW; MTCW 1, 2
Sa-Carniero, Mario de 1890-1916 . **TCLC 83**
Sacastru, Martin
　　See Bioy Casares, Adolfo
　　See also CWW 2
Sacher-Masoch, Leopold von
　　1836(?)-1895 .... **NCLC 31**
Sachs, Marilyn (Stickle) 1927- .... **CLC 35**
　　See also AAYA 2; BYA 6; CA 17-20R;
　　CANR 13, 47; CLR 2; JRDA; MAICYA
　　1, 2; SAAS 2; SATA 3, 68; SATA-Essay
　　110; WYA; YAW
Sachs, Nelly 1891-1970 .... **CLC 14, 98**
　　See also CA 17-18; 25-28R; CANR 87;
　　CAP 2; MTCW 2; RGWL 2
Sackler, Howard (Oliver)
　　1929-1982 .... **CLC 14**
　　See also CA 61-64; 108; CAD; CANR 30;
　　DFS 15; DLB 7
Sacks, Oliver (Wolf) 1933- .... **CLC 67**
　　See also CA 53-56; CANR 28, 50, 76;
　　CPW; DA3; INT CANR-28; MTCW 1, 2
Sadakichi
　　See Hartmann, Sadakichi
Sade, Donatien Alphonse Francois
　　1740-1814 .... **NCLC 3, 47**
　　See also EW 4; GFL Beginnings to 1789;
　　RGWL 2
Sadoff, Ira 1945- .... **CLC 9**
　　See also CA 53-56; CANR 5, 21, 109; DLB
　　120
Saetone
　　See Camus, Albert
Safire, William 1929- .... **CLC 10**
　　See also CA 17-20R; CANR 31, 54, 91
Sagan, Carl (Edward) 1934-1996 .... **CLC 30,**
　　112
　　See also AAYA 2; CA 25-28R; 155; CANR
　　11, 36, 74; CPW; DA3; MTCW 1, 2;
　　SATA 58; SATA-Obit 94
Sagan, Francoise .... **CLC 3, 6, 9, 17, 36**
　　See also Quoirez, Francoise
　　See also CWW 2; DLB 83; GFL 1789 to
　　the Present; MTCW 2
Sahgal, Nayantara (Pandit) 1927- .... **CLC 41**
　　See also CA 9-12R; CANR 11, 88; CN 7
Said, Edward W. 1935- .... **CLC 123**
　　See also CA 21-24R; CANR 45, 74, 107;
　　DLB 67; MTCW 2
Saint, H(arry) F. 1941- .... **CLC 50**
　　See also CA 127
St. Aubin de Teran, Lisa 1953-
　　See Teran, Lisa St. Aubin de
　　See also CA 118; 126; CN 7; INT 126
Saint Birgitta of Sweden c.
　　1303-1373 .... **CMLC 24**
Sainte-Beuve, Charles Augustin
　　1804-1869 .... **NCLC 5**
　　See also DLB 217; EW 6; GFL 1789 to the
　　Present
Saint-Exupery, Antoine (Jean Baptiste
　　Marie Roger) de 1900-1944 .... **TCLC 2,**
　　56; WLC
　　See also BPFB 3; BYA 3; CA 108; 132;
　　CLR 10; DA3; DAM NOV; DLB 72; EW
　　12; GFL 1789 to the Present; LAIT 3;
　　MAICYA 1, 2; MTCW 1, 2; RGWL 2;
　　SATA 20; TWA
St. John, David
　　See Hunt, E(verette) Howard, (Jr.)
St. John, J. Hector
　　See Crevecoeur, Michel Guillaume Jean de

Scammell, Michael 1935- .... **CLC 34**
  See also CA 156
Scannell, Vernon 1922- .... **CLC 49**
  See also CA 5-8R; CANR 8, 24, 57; CP 7;
  CWRI 5; DLB 27; SATA 59
Scarlett, Susan
  See Streatfeild, (Mary) Noel
Scarron 1847-1910
  See Mikszath, Kalman
Schaeffer, Susan Fromberg 1941- ..... **CLC 6,**
  11, 22
  See also CA 49-52; CANR 18, 65; CN 7;
  DLB 28; MTCW 1, 2; SATA 22
Schama, Simon (Michael) 1945- ..... **CLC 150**
  See also BEST 89:4; CA 105; CANR 39,
  91
Schary, Jill
  See Robinson, Jill
Schell, Jonathan 1943- .... **CLC 35**
  See also CA 73-76; CANR 12
Schelling, Friedrich Wilhelm Joseph von
  1775-1854 .... **NCLC 30**
  See also DLB 90
Scherer, Jean-Marie Maurice 1920-
  See Rohmer, Eric
  See also CA 110
Schevill, James (Erwin) 1920- .... **CLC 7**
  See also CA 5-8R; CAAS 12; CAD; CD 5
Schiller, Friedrich von
  1759-1805 .... **NCLC 39, 69; DC 12**
  See also CDWLB 2; DAM DRAM; DLB
  94; EW 5; RGWL 2; TWA
Schisgal, Murray (Joseph) 1926- .... **CLC 6**
  See also CA 21-24R; CAD; CANR 48, 86;
  CD 5
Schlee, Ann 1934- .... **CLC 35**
  See also CA 101; CANR 29, 88; SATA 44;
  SATA-Brief 36
Schlegel, August Wilhelm von
  1767-1845 .... **NCLC 15**
  See also DLB 94; RGWL 2
Schlegel, Friedrich 1772-1829 .... **NCLC 45**
  See also DLB 90; EW 5; RGWL 2; TWA
Schlegel, Johann Elias (von)
  1719(?)-1749 .... **LC 5**
Schleiermacher, Friedrich
  1768-1834 .... **NCLC 107**
  See also DLB 90
Schlesinger, Arthur M(eier), Jr.
  1917- .... **CLC 84**
  See also AITN 1; CA 1-4R; CANR 1, 28,
  58, 105; DLB 17; INT CANR-28; MTCW
  1, 2; SATA 61
Schmidt, Arno (Otto) 1914-1979 ...... **CLC 56**
  See also CA 128; 109; DLB 69
Schmitz, Aron Hector 1861-1928
  See Svevo, Italo
  See also CA 104; 122; MTCW 1
Schnackenberg, Gjertrud (Cecelia)
  1953- .... **CLC 40**
  See also CA 116; CANR 100; CP 7; CWP;
  DLB 120; PFS 13
Schneider, Leonard Alfred 1925-1966
  See Bruce, Lenny
  See also CA 89-92
Schnitzler, Arthur 1862-1931 ... **TCLC 4; DC**
  17; SSC 15
  See also CA 104; CDWLB 2; DLB 81, 118;
  EW 8; RGSF 2; RGWL 2
Schoenberg, Arnold Franz Walter
  1874-1951 .... **TCLC 75**
  See also CA 109; 188
Schonberg, Arnold
  See Schoenberg, Arnold Franz Walter
Schopenhauer, Arthur 1788-1860 .. **NCLC 51**
  See also DLB 90; EW 5
Schor, Sandra (M.) 1932(?)-1990 ..... **CLC 65**
  See also CA 132

Schorer, Mark 1908-1977 .... **CLC 9**
  See also CA 5-8R; 73-76; CANR 7; DLB
  103
Schrader, Paul (Joseph) 1946- .... **CLC 26**
  See also CA 37-40R; CANR 41; DLB 44
Schreber, Daniel 1842-1911 .... **TCLC 123**
Schreiner, Olive (Emilie Albertina)
  1855-1920 .... **TCLC 9**
  See also AFW; BRWS 2; CA 105; 154;
  DLB 18, 156, 190, 225; FW; RGEL 2;
  TWA; WLIT 2
Schulberg, Budd (Wilson) 1914- .. **CLC 7, 48**
  See also BPFB 3; CA 25-28R; CANR 19,
  87; CN 7; DLB 6, 26, 28; DLBY 1981,
  2001
Schulman, Arnold
  See Trumbo, Dalton
Schulz, Bruno 1892-1942 .. **TCLC 5, 51; SSC**
  13
  See also CA 115; 123; CANR 86; CDWLB
  4; DLB 215; MTCW 2; RGSF 2; RGWL
  2
Schulz, Charles M(onroe)
  1922-2000 .... **CLC 12**
  See also AAYA 39; CA 9-12R; 187; CANR
  6; INT CANR-6; SATA 10; SATA-Obit
  118
Schumacher, E(rnst) F(riedrich)
  1911-1977 .... **CLC 80**
  See also CA 81-84; 73-76; CANR 34, 85
Schuyler, James Marcus 1923-1991 .. **CLC 5,**
  23
  See also CA 101; 134; DAM POET; DLB
  5, 169; INT 101; WP
Schwartz, Delmore (David)
  1913-1966 ... **CLC 2, 4, 10, 45, 87; PC 8**
  See also AMWS 2; CA 17-18; 25-28R;
  CANR 35; CAP 2; DLB 28, 48; MTCW
  1, 2; PAB; RGAL 4; TUS
Schwartz, Ernst
  See Ozu, Yasujiro
Schwartz, John Burnham 1965- .... **CLC 59**
  See also CA 132
Schwartz, Lynne Sharon 1939- .... **CLC 31**
  See also CA 103; CANR 44, 89; DLB 218;
  MTCW 2
Schwartz, Muriel A.
  See Eliot, T(homas) S(tearns)
Schwarz-Bart, Andre 1928- .... **CLC 2, 4**
  See also CA 89-92; CANR 109
Schwarz-Bart, Simone 1938- . **CLC 7; BLCS**
  See also BW 2; CA 97-100
Schwerner, Armand 1927-1999 .... **PC 42**
  See also CA 9-12R; 179; CANR 50, 85; CP
  7; DLB 165
Schwitters, Kurt (Hermann Edward Karl
  Julius) 1887-1948 .... **TCLC 95**
  See also CA 158
Schwob, Marcel (Mayer Andre)
  1867-1905 .... **TCLC 20**
  See also CA 117; 168; DLB 123; GFL 1789
  to the Present
Sciascia, Leonardo 1921-1989 .. **CLC 8, 9, 41**
  See also CA 85-88; 130; CANR 35; DLB
  177; MTCW 1; RGWL 2
Scoppettone, Sandra 1936- .... **CLC 26**
  See also Early, Jack
  See also AAYA 11; BYA 8; CA 5-8R;
  CANR 41, 73; GLL 1; MAICYA 2; MAI-
  CYAS 1; SATA 9, 92; WYA; YAW
Scorsese, Martin 1942- .... **CLC 20, 89**
  See also AAYA 38; CA 110; 114; CANR
  46, 85
Scotland, Jay
  See Jakes, John (William)
Scott, Duncan Campbell
  1862-1947 .... **TCLC 6**
  See also CA 104; 153; DAC; DLB 92;
  RGEL 2

Scott, Evelyn 1893-1963 .... **CLC 43**
  See also CA 104; 112; CANR 64; DLB 9,
  48; RHW
Scott, F(rancis) R(eginald)
  1899-1985 .... **CLC 22**
  See also CA 101; 114; CANR 87; DLB 88;
  INT CA-101; RGEL 2
Scott, Frank
  See Scott, F(rancis) R(eginald)
Scott, Joan .... **CLC 65**
Scott, Joanna 1960- .... **CLC 50**
  See also CA 126; CANR 53, 92
Scott, Paul (Mark) 1920-1978 .... **CLC 9, 60**
  See also BRWS 1; CA 81-84; 77-80; CANR
  33; DLB 14, 207; MTCW 1; RGEL 2;
  RHW
Scott, Sarah 1723-1795 .... **LC 44**
  See also DLB 39
Scott, Sir Walter 1771-1832 .... **NCLC 15, 69,**
  110; PC 13; SSC 32; WLC
  See also AAYA 22; BRW 4; BYA 2; CD-
  BLB 1789-1832; DA; DAB; DAC; DAM
  MST, NOV, POET; DLB 93, 107, 116,
  144, 159; HGG; LAIT 1; RGEL 2; RGSF
  2; SSFS 10; SUFW; TEA; WLIT 3; YABC
  2
Scribe, (Augustin) Eugene
  1791-1861 .... **NCLC 16; DC 5**
  See also DAM DRAM; DLB 192; GFL
  1789 to the Present; RGWL 2
Scrum, R.
  See Crumb, R(obert)
Scudery, Georges de 1601-1667 .... **LC 75**
  See also GFL Beginnings to 1789
Scudery, Madeleine de 1607-1701 .. **LC 2, 58**
  See also DLB 268; GFL Beginnings to 1789
Scum
  See Crumb, R(obert)
Scumbag, Little Bobby
  See Crumb, R(obert)
Seabrook, John
  See Hubbard, L(afayette) Ron(ald)
Sealy, I(rwin) Allan 1951- .... **CLC 55**
  See also CA 136; CN 7
Search, Alexander
  See Pessoa, Fernando (Antonio Nogueira)
Sebastian, Lee
  See Silverberg, Robert
Sebastian Owl
  See Thompson, Hunter S(tockton)
Sebestyen, Igen
  See Sebestyen, Ouida
Sebestyen, Ouida 1924- .... **CLC 30**
  See also AAYA 8; BYA 7; CA 107; CANR
  40; CLR 17; JRDA; MAICYA 1, 2; SAAS
  10; SATA 39; WYA; YAW
Secundus, H. Scriblerus
  See Fielding, Henry
Sedges, John
  See Buck, Pearl S(ydenstricker)
Sedgwick, Catharine Maria
  1789-1867 .... **NCLC 19, 98**
  See also DLB 1, 74, 183, 239, 243, 254;
  RGAL 4
Seelye, John (Douglas) 1931- .... **CLC 7**
  See also CA 97-100; CANR 70; INT 97-
  100; TCWW 2
Seferiades, Giorgos Stylianou 1900-1971
  See Seferis, George
  See also CA 5-8R; 33-36R; CANR 5, 36;
  MTCW 1
Seferis, George .... **CLC 5, 11**
  See also Seferiades, Giorgos Stylianou
  See also EW 12; RGWL 2
Segal, Erich (Wolf) 1937- .... **CLC 3, 10**
  See also BEST 89:1; BPFB 3; CA 25-28R;
  CANR 20, 36, 65; CPW; DAM POP;
  DLBY 1986; INT CANR-20; MTCW 1

Shepherd, Michael
See Ludlum, Robert

Sherburne, Zoa (Lillian Morin)
1912-1995 .... **CLC 30**
See also AAYA 13; CA 1-4R; 176; CANR 3, 37; MAICYA 1, 2; SAAS 18; SATA 3; YAW

Sheridan, Frances 1724-1766 .... **LC 7**
See also DLB 39, 84

Sheridan, Richard Brinsley
1751-1816 .... **NCLC 5, 91; DC 1; WLC**
See also BRW 3; CDBLB 1660-1789; DA; DAB; DAC; DAM DRAM, MST; DFS 15; DLB 89; WLIT 3

Sherman, Jonathan Marc .... **CLC 55**

Sherman, Martin 1941(?)- .... **CLC 19**
See also CA 116; 123; CANR 86

Sherwin, Judith Johnson
See Johnson, Judith (Emlyn)
See also CANR 85; CP 7; CWP

Sherwood, Frances 1940- .... **CLC 81**
See also CA 146

Sherwood, Robert E(mmet)
1896-1955 .... **TCLC 3**
See also CA 104; 153; CANR 86; DAM DRAM; DFS 15; DLB 7, 26, 249; IDFW 3, 4; RGAL 4

Shestov, Lev 1866-1938 .... **TCLC 56**

Shevchenko, Taras 1814-1861 .... **NCLC 54**

Shiel, M(atthew) P(hipps)
1865-1947 .... **TCLC 8**
See also Holmes, Gordon
See also CA 106; 160; DLB 153; HGG; MTCW 2; SFW 4; SUFW

Shields, Carol 1935- .... **CLC 91, 113**
See also AMWS 7; CA 81-84; CANR 51, 74, 98; CCA 1; CN 7; CPW; DA3; DAC; MTCW 2

Shields, David 1956- .... **CLC 97**
See also CA 124; CANR 48, 99

Shiga, Naoya 1883-1971 ..... **CLC 33; SSC 23**
See also Shiga Naoya
See also CA 101; 33-36R; MJW

Shiga Naoya
See Shiga, Naoya
See also DLB 180

Shilts, Randy 1951-1994 .... **CLC 85**
See also AAYA 19; CA 115; 127; 144; CANR 45; DA3; GLL 1; INT 127; MTCW 2

Shimazaki, Haruki 1872-1943
See Shimazaki Toson
See also CA 105; 134; CANR 84

Shimazaki Toson .... **TCLC 5**
See also Shimazaki, Haruki
See also DLB 180

Sholokhov, Mikhail (Aleksandrovich)
1905-1984 .... **CLC 7, 15**
See also CA 101; 112; MTCW 1, 2; RGWL 2; SATA-Obit 36

Shone, Patric
See Hanley, James

Shreve, Susan Richards 1939- .... **CLC 23**
See also CA 49-52; CAAS 5; CANR 5, 38, 69, 100; MAICYA 1, 2; SATA 46, 95; SATA-Brief 41

Shue, Larry 1946-1985 .... **CLC 52**
See also CA 145; 117; DAM DRAM; DFS 7

Shu-Jen, Chou 1881-1936
See Lu Hsun
See also CA 104

Shulman, Alix Kates 1932- .... **CLC 2, 10**
See also CA 29-32R; CANR 43; FW; SATA 7

Shusaku, Endo
See Endo, Shusaku

Shuster, Joe 1914-1992 .... **CLC 21**

Shute, Nevil .... **CLC 30**
See also Norway, Nevil Shute
See also BPFB 3; DLB 255; NFS 9; RHW; SFW 4

Shuttle, Penelope (Diane) 1947- .... **CLC 7**
See also CA 93-96; CANR 39, 84, 92, 108; CP 7; CWP; DLB 14, 40

Sidney, Mary 1561-1621 .... **LC 19, 39**
See also Sidney Herbert, Mary

Sidney, Sir Philip 1554-1586 . **LC 19, 39; PC 32**
See also BRW 1; BRWR 2; CDBLB Before 1660; DA; DA3; DAB; DAC; DAM MST, POET; DLB 167; EXPP; PAB; RGEL 2; TEA; WP

Sidney Herbert, Mary
See Sidney, Mary
See also DLB 167

Siegel, Jerome 1914-1996 .... **CLC 21**
See also CA 116; 169; 151

Siegel, Jerry
See Siegel, Jerome

Sienkiewicz, Henryk (Adam Alexander Pius)
1846-1916 .... **TCLC 3**
See also CA 104; 134; CANR 84; RGSF 2; RGWL 2

Sierra, Gregorio Martinez
See Martinez Sierra, Gregorio

Sierra, Maria (de la O'LeJarraga) Martinez
See Martinez Sierra, Maria (de la O'LeJarraga)

Sigal, Clancy 1926- .... **CLC 7**
See also CA 1-4R; CANR 85; CN 7

Sigourney, Lydia H.
See Sigourney, Lydia Howard (Huntley)
See also DLB 73, 183

Sigourney, Lydia Howard (Huntley)
1791-1865 .... **NCLC 21, 87**
See also Sigourney, Lydia H.; Sigourney, Lydia Huntley
See also DLB 1

Sigourney, Lydia Huntley
See Sigourney, Lydia Howard (Huntley)
See also DLB 42, 239, 243

Siguenza y Gongora, Carlos de
1645-1700 .... **LC 8; HLCS 2**
See also LAW

Sigurjonsson, Johann 1880-1919 ... **TCLC 27**
See also CA 170

Sikelianos, Angelos 1884-1951 ...... **TCLC 39; PC 29**
See also RGWL 2

Silkin, Jon 1930-1997 .... **CLC 2, 6, 43**
See also CA 5-8R; CAAS 5; CANR 89; CP 7; DLB 27

Silko, Leslie (Marmon) 1948- .... **CLC 23, 74, 114; SSC 37; WLCS**
See also AAYA 14; AMWS 4; ANW; BYA 12; CA 115; 122; CANR 45, 65; CN 7; CP 7; CPW; CWP; DA; DA3; DAC; DAM MST, MULT, POP; DLB 143, 175, 256; EXPP; EXPS; LAIT 4; MTCW 2; NFS 4; NNAL; PFS 9; RGAL 4; RGSF 2; SSFS 4, 8, 10, 11

Sillanpaa, Frans Eemil 1888-1964 ... **CLC 19**
See also CA 129; 93-96; MTCW 1

Sillitoe, Alan 1928- .. **CLC 1, 3, 6, 10, 19, 57, 148**
See also AITN 1; BRWS 5; CA 9-12R; CAAE 191; CAAS 2; CANR 8, 26, 55; CDBLB 1960 to Present; CN 7; DLB 14, 139; MTCW 1, 2; RGEL 2; RGSF 2; SATA 61

Silone, Ignazio 1900-1978 .... **CLC 4**
See also CA 25-28; 81-84; CANR 34; CAP 2; DLB 264; EW 12; MTCW 1; RGSF 2; RGWL 2

Silone, Ignazione
See Silone, Ignazio

Silva, Jose Asuncion
See da Silva, Antonio Jose
See also LAW

Silver, Joan Micklin 1935- .... **CLC 20**
See also CA 114; 121; INT 121

Silver, Nicholas
See Faust, Frederick (Schiller)
See also TCWW 2

Silverberg, Robert 1935- .... **CLC 7, 140**
See also AAYA 24; BPFB 3; BYA 7, 9; CA 1-4R; 186; CAAE 186; CAAS 3; CANR 1, 20, 36, 85; CLR 59; CN 7; CPW; DAM POP; DLB 8; INT CANR-20; MAICYA 1, 2; MTCW 1, 2; SATA 13, 91; SATA-Essay 104; SCFW 2; SFW 4

Silverstein, Alvin 1933- .... **CLC 17**
See also CA 49-52; CANR 2; CLR 25; JRDA; MAICYA 1, 2; SATA 8, 69, 124

Silverstein, Virginia B(arbara Opshelor)
1937- .... **CLC 17**
See also CA 49-52; CANR 2; CLR 25; JRDA; MAICYA 1, 2; SATA 8, 69, 124

Sim, Georges
See Simenon, Georges (Jacques Christian)

Simak, Clifford D(onald) 1904-1988 . **CLC 1, 55**
See also CA 1-4R; 125; CANR 1, 35; DLB 8; MTCW 1; SATA-Obit 56; SFW 4

Simenon, Georges (Jacques Christian)
1903-1989 .... **CLC 1, 2, 3, 8, 18, 47**
See also BPFB 3; CA 85-88; 129; CANR 35; CMW 4; DA3; DAM POP; DLB 72; DLBY 1989; EW 12; GFL 1789 to the Present; MSW; MTCW 1, 2; RGWL 2

Simic, Charles 1938- .... **CLC 6, 9, 22, 49, 68, 130**
See also AMWS 8; CA 29-32R; CAAS 4; CANR 12, 33, 52, 61, 96; CP 7; DA3; DAM POET; DLB 105; MTCW 2; PFS 7; RGAL 4; WP

Simmel, Georg 1858-1918 .... **TCLC 64**
See also CA 157

Simmons, Charles (Paul) 1924- .... **CLC 57**
See also CA 89-92; INT 89-92

Simmons, Dan 1948- .... **CLC 44**
See also AAYA 16; CA 138; CANR 53, 81; CPW; DAM POP; HGG

Simmons, James (Stewart Alexander)
1933- .... **CLC 43**
See also CA 105; CAAS 21; CP 7; DLB 40

Simms, William Gilmore
1806-1870 .... **NCLC 3**
See also DLB 3, 30, 59, 73, 248, 254; RGAL 4

Simon, Carly 1945- .... **CLC 26**
See also CA 105

Simon, Claude 1913-1984 ... **CLC 4, 9, 15, 39**
See also CA 89-92; CANR 33; DAM NOV; DLB 83; EW 13; GFL 1789 to the Present; MTCW 1

Simon, Myles
See Follett, Ken(neth Martin)

Simon, (Marvin) Neil 1927- ... **CLC 6, 11, 31, 39, 70; DC 14**
See also AAYA 32; AITN 1; AMWS 4; CA 21-24R; CANR 26, 54, 87; CD 5; DA3; DAM DRAM; DFS 2, 6, 12; DLB 7, 266; LAIT 4; MTCW 1, 2; RGAL 4; TUS

Simon, Paul (Frederick) 1941(?)- ..... **CLC 17**
See also CA 116; 153

Simonon, Paul 1956(?)- .... **CLC 30**

Simonson, Rick ed. .... **CLC 70**

Simpson, Harriette
See Arnow, Harriette (Louisa) Simpson

Simpson, Louis (Aston Marantz)
1923- .... **CLC 4, 7, 9, 32, 149**
See also AMWS 9; CA 1-4R; CAAS 4;
CANR 1, 61; CP 7; DAM POET; DLB 5;
MTCW 1, 2; PFS 7, 11, 14; RGAL 4

Simpson, Mona (Elizabeth) 1957- ... **CLC 44, 146**
See also CA 122; 135; CANR 68, 103; CN 7

Simpson, N(orman) F(rederick)
1919- .... **CLC 29**
See also CA 13-16R; CBD; DLB 13; RGEL 2

Sinclair, Andrew (Annandale) 1935- . **CLC 2, 14**
See also CA 9-12R; CAAS 5; CANR 14, 38, 91; CN 7; DLB 14; FANT; MTCW 1

Sinclair, Emil
See Hesse, Hermann

Sinclair, Iain 1943- .... **CLC 76**
See also CA 132; CANR 81; CP 7; HGG

Sinclair, Iain MacGregor
See Sinclair, Iain

Sinclair, Irene
See Griffith, D(avid Lewelyn) W(ark)

Sinclair, Mary Amelia St. Clair 1865(?)-1946
See Sinclair, May
See also CA 104; HGG; RHW

Sinclair, May .... **TCLC 3, 11**
See also Sinclair, Mary Amelia St. Clair
See also CA 166; DLB 36, 135; RGEL 2; SUFW

Sinclair, Roy
See Griffith, D(avid Lewelyn) W(ark)

Sinclair, Upton (Beall) 1878-1968 ..... **CLC 1, 11, 15, 63; WLC**
See also AMWS 5; BPFB 3; BYA 2; CA 5-8R; 25-28R; CANR 7; CDALB 1929-1941; DA; DA3; DAB; DAC; DAM MST, NOV; DLB 9; INT CANR-7; LAIT 3; MTCW 1, 2; NFS 6; RGAL 4; SATA 9; TUS; YAW

Singer, Isaac
See Singer, Isaac Bashevis

Singer, Isaac Bashevis 1904-1991 .. **CLC 1, 3, 6, 9, 11, 15, 23, 38, 69, 111; SSC 3, 53; WLC**
See also AAYA 32; AITN 1, 2; AMW; BPFB 3; BYA 1, 4; CA 1-4R; 134; CANR 1, 39, 106; CDALB 1941-1968; CLR 1; CWRI 5; DA; DA3; DAB; DAC; DAM MST, NOV; DLB 6, 28, 52; DLBY 1991; EXPS; HGG; JRDA; LAIT 3; MAICYA 1, 2; MTCW 1, 2; RGAL 4; RGSF 2; SATA 3, 27; SATA-Obit 68; SSFS 2, 12; TUS; TWA

Singer, Israel Joshua 1893-1944 .... **TCLC 33**
See also CA 169

Singh, Khushwant 1915- .... **CLC 11**
See also CA 9-12R; CAAS 9; CANR 6, 84; CN 7; RGEL 2

Singleton, Ann
See Benedict, Ruth (Fulton)

Singleton, John 1968(?)- .... **CLC 156**
See also BW 2, 3; CA 138; CANR 67, 82; DAM MULT

Sinjohn, John
See Galsworthy, John

Sinyavsky, Andrei (Donatevich)
1925-1997 .... **CLC 8**
See Tertz, Abram
See also CA 85-88; 159

Sirin, V.
See Nabokov, Vladimir (Vladimirovich)

Sissman, L(ouis) E(dward)
1928-1976 .... **CLC 9, 18**
See also CA 21-24R; 65-68; CANR 13; DLB 5

Sisson, C(harles) H(ubert) 1914- .... **CLC 8**
See also CA 1-4R; CAAS 3; CANR 3, 48, 84; CP 7; DLB 27

Sitwell, Dame Edith 1887-1964 ..... **CLC 2, 9, 67; PC 3**
See also BRW 7; CA 9-12R; CANR 35; CDBLB 1945-1960; DAM POET; DLB 20; MTCW 1, 2; RGEL 2; TEA

Siwaarmill, H. P.
See Sharp, William

Sjoewall, Maj 1935- .... **CLC 7**
See also Sjowall, Maj
See also CA 65-68; CANR 73

Sjowall, Maj
See Sjoewall, Maj
See also BPFB 3; CMW 4; MSW

Skelton, John 1460(?)-1529 ..... **LC 71; PC 25**
See also BRW 1; DLB 136; RGEL 2

Skelton, Robin 1925-1997 .... **CLC 13**
See also Zuk, Georges
See also AITN 2; CA 5-8R; 160; CAAS 5; CANR 28, 89; CCA 1; CP 7; DLB 27, 53

Skolimowski, Jerzy 1938- .... **CLC 20**
See also CA 128

Skram, Amalie (Bertha)
1847-1905 .... **TCLC 25**
See also CA 165

Skvorecky, Josef (Vaclav) 1924- ...... **CLC 15, 39, 69, 152**
See also CA 61-64; CAAS 1; CANR 10, 34, 63, 108; CDWLB 4; DA3; DAC; DAM NOV; DLB 232; MTCW 1, 2

Slade, Bernard .... **CLC 11, 46**
See also Newbound, Bernard Slade
See also CAAS 9; CCA 1; DLB 53

Slaughter, Carolyn 1946- .... **CLC 56**
See also CA 85-88; CANR 85; CN 7

Slaughter, Frank G(ill) 1908-2001 ... **CLC 29**
See also AITN 2; CA 5-8R; 197; CANR 5, 85; INT CANR-5; RHW

Slavitt, David R(ytman) 1935- ..... **CLC 5, 14**
See also CA 21-24R; CAAS 3; CANR 41, 83; CP 7; DLB 5, 6

Slesinger, Tess 1905-1945 .... **TCLC 10**
See also CA 107; 199; DLB 102

Slessor, Kenneth 1901-1971 .... **CLC 14**
See also CA 102; 89-92; DLB 260; RGEL 2

Slowacki, Juliusz 1809-1849 .... **NCLC 15**

Smart, Christopher 1722-1771 . **LC 3; PC 13**
See also DAM POET; DLB 109; RGEL 2

Smart, Elizabeth 1913-1986 .... **CLC 54**
See also CA 81-84; 118; DLB 88

Smiley, Jane (Graves) 1949- ...... **CLC 53, 76, 144**
See also AMWS 6; BPFB 3; CA 104; CANR 30, 50, 74, 96; CN 7; CPW 1; DA3; DAM POP; DLB 227, 234; INT CANR-30

Smith, A(rthur) J(ames) M(arshall)
1902-1980 .... **CLC 15**
See also CA 1-4R; 102; CANR 4; DAC; DLB 88; RGEL 2

Smith, Adam 1723(?)-1790 .... **LC 36**
See also DLB 104, 252; RGEL 2

Smith, Alexander 1829-1867 .... **NCLC 59**
See also DLB 32, 55

Smith, Anna Deavere 1950- .... **CLC 86**
See also CA 133; CANR 103; CD 5; DFS 2

Smith, Betty (Wehner) 1904-1972 .... **CLC 19**
See also BPFB 3; BYA 3; CA 5-8R; 33-36R; DLBY 1982; LAIT 3; RGAL 4; SATA 6

Smith, Charlotte (Turner)
1749-1806 .... **NCLC 23, 115**
See also DLB 39, 109; RGEL 2; TEA

Smith, Clark Ashton 1893-1961 .... **CLC 43**
See also CA 143; CANR 81; FANT; HGG; MTCW 2; SCFW 2; SFW 4; SUFW

Smith, Dave .... **CLC 22, 42**
See also Smith, David (Jeddie)
See also CAAS 7; DLB 5

Smith, David (Jeddie) 1942-
See Smith, Dave
See also CA 49-52; CANR 1, 59; CP 7; CSW; DAM POET

Smith, Florence Margaret 1902-1971
See Smith, Stevie
See also CA 17-18; 29-32R; CANR 35; CAP 2; DAM POET; MTCW 1, 2; TEA

Smith, Iain Crichton 1928-1998 .... **CLC 64**
See also CA 21-24R; 171; CN 7; CP 7; DLB 40, 139; RGSF 2

Smith, John 1580(?)-1631 .... **LC 9**
See also DLB 24, 30; TUS

Smith, Johnston
See J

Smith, Joseph, Jr. 1805-1844 .... **NCLC 53**

Smith, Lee 1944- .... **CLC 25, 73**
See also CA 114; 119; CANR 46; CSW; DLB 143; DLBY 1983; INT CA-119; RGAL 4

Smith, Martin
See Smith, Martin Cruz

Smith, Martin Cruz 1942- .... **CLC 25**
See also BEST 89:4; BPFB 3; CA 85-88; CANR 6, 23, 43, 65; CMW 4; CPW; DAM MULT, POP; HGG; INT CANR-23; MTCW 2; NNAL; RGAL 4

Smith, Mary-Ann Tirone 1944- .... **CLC 39**
See also CA 118; 136

Smith, Patti 1946- .... **CLC 12**
See also CA 93-96; CANR 63

Smith, Pauline (Urmson)
1882-1959 .... **TCLC 25**
See also DLB 225

Smith, Rosamond
See Oates, Joyce Carol

Smith, Sheila Kaye
See Kaye-Smith, Sheila

Smith, Stevie .... **CLC 3, 8, 25, 44; PC 12**
See also Smith, Florence Margaret
See also BRWS 2; DLB 20; MTCW 2; PAB; PFS 3; RGEL 2

Smith, Wilbur (Addison) 1933- .... **CLC 33**
See also CA 13-16R; CANR 7, 46, 66; CPW; MTCW 1, 2

Smith, William Jay 1918- .... **CLC 6**
See also CA 5-8R; CANR 44, 106; CP 7; CSW; CWRI 5; DLB 5; MAICYA 1, 2; SAAS 22; SATA 2, 68

Smith, Woodrow Wilson
See Kuttner, Henry

Smith, Zadie 1976- .... **CLC 158**
See also CA 193

Smolenskin, Peretz 1842-1885 .... **NCLC 30**

Smollett, Tobias (George) 1721-1771 ... **LC 2, 46**
See also BRW 3; CDBLB 1660-1789; DLB 39, 104; RGEL 2; TEA

Snodgrass, W(illiam) D(e Witt)
1926- .... **CLC 2, 6, 10, 18, 68**
See also AMWS 6; CA 1-4R; CANR 6, 36, 65, 85; CP 7; DAM POET; DLB 5; MTCW 1, 2; RGAL 4

Snow, C(harles) P(ercy) 1905-1980 ... **CLC 1, 4, 6, 9, 13, 19**
See also BRW 7; CA 5-8R; 101; CANR 28; CDBLB 1945-1960; DAM NOV; DLB 15, 77; DLBD 17; MTCW 1, 2; RGEL 2; TEA

Snow, Frances Compton
See Adams, Henry (Brooks)

Snyder, Gary (Sherman) 1930- . **CLC 1, 2, 5, 9, 32, 120; PC 21**
See also AMWS 8; ANW; CA 17-20R; CANR 30, 60; CP 7; DA3; DAM POET; DLB 5, 16, 165, 212, 237; MTCW 2; PFS 9; RGAL 4; WP

Snyder, Zilpha Keatley 1927- .... **CLC 17**
See also AAYA 15; BYA 1; CA 9-12R; CANR 38; CLR 31; JRDA; MAICYA 1, 2; SAAS 2; SATA 1, 28, 75, 110; SATA-Essay 112; YAW

Soares, Bernardo
See Pessoa, Fernando (Antonio Nogueira)

Sobh, A.
See Shamlu, Ahmad

Sobol, Joshua 1939- .... **CLC 60**
See also Sobol, Yehoshua
See also CA 200; CWW 2

Sobol, Yehoshua 1939-
See Sobol, Joshua
See also CWW 2

Socrates 470 B.C.-399 B.C. .... **CMLC 27**

Soderberg, Hjalmar 1869-1941 ...... **TCLC 39**
See also DLB 259; RGSF 2

Soderbergh, Steven 1963- .... **CLC 154**
See also AAYA 43

Sodergran, Edith (Irene) 1892-1923
See Soedergran, Edith (Irene)
See also CA 202; DLB 259; EW 11; RGWL 2

Soedergran, Edith (Irene)
1892-1923 .... **TCLC 31**
See also Sodergran, Edith (Irene)

Softly, Edgar
See Lovecraft, H(oward) P(hillips)

Softly, Edward
See Lovecraft, H(oward) P(hillips)

Sokolov, Raymond 1941- .... **CLC 7**
See also CA 85-88

Sokolov, Sasha .... **CLC 59**

Solo, Jay
See Ellison, Harlan (Jay)

Sologub, Fyodor .... **TCLC 9**
See also Teternikov, Fyodor Kuzmich

Solomons, Ikey Esquir
See Thackeray, William Makepeace

Solomos, Dionysios 1798-1857 .... **NCLC 15**

Solwoska, Mara
See French, Marilyn

Solzhenitsyn, Aleksandr I(sayevich)
1918- .. **CLC 1, 2, 4, 7, 9, 10, 18, 26, 34, 78, 134; SSC 32; WLC**
See also AITN 1; BPFB 3; CA 69-72; CANR 40, 65; DA; DA3; DAB; DAC; DAM MST, NOV; EW 13; EXPS; LAIT 4; MTCW 1, 2; NFS 6; RGSF 2; RGWL 2; SSFS 9; TWA

Somers, Jane
See Lessing, Doris (May)

Somerville, Edith Oenone
1858-1949 .... **TCLC 51**
See also CA 196; DLB 135; RGEL 2; RGSF 2

Somerville & Ross
See Martin, Violet Florence; Somerville, Edith Oenone

Sommer, Scott 1951- .... **CLC 25**
See also CA 106

Sondheim, Stephen (Joshua) 1930- . **CLC 30, 39, 147**
See also AAYA 11; CA 103; CANR 47, 67; DAM DRAM; LAIT 4

Song, Cathy 1955- .... **PC 21**
See also AAL; CA 154; CWP; DLB 169; EXPP; FW; PFS 5

Sontag, Susan 1933- .... **CLC 1, 2, 10, 13, 31, 105**
See also AMWS 3; CA 17-20R; CANR 25, 51, 74, 97; CN 7; CPW; DA3; DAM POP; DLB 2, 67; MAWW; MTCW 1, 2; RGAL 4; RHW; SSFS 10

Sophocles 496(?) B.C.-406(?) B.C. . **CMLC 2, 47, 51; DC 1; WLCS**
See also AW 1; CDWLB 1; DA; DA3; DAB; DAC; DAM DRAM, MST; DFS 1, 4, 8; DLB 176; LAIT 1; RGWL 2; TWA

Sordello 1189-1269 .... **CMLC 15**

Sorel, Georges 1847-1922 .... **TCLC 91**
See also CA 118; 188

Sorel, Julia
See Drexler, Rosalyn

Sorokin, Vladimir .... **CLC 59**

Sorrentino, Gilbert 1929- .. **CLC 3, 7, 14, 22, 40**
See also CA 77-80; CANR 14, 33; CN 7; CP 7; DLB 5, 173; DLBY 1980; INT CANR-14

Soseki
See Natsume, Soseki
See also MJW

Soto, Gary 1952- ... **CLC 32, 80; HLC 2; PC 28**
See also AAYA 10, 37; BYA 11; CA 119; 125; CANR 50, 74, 107; CLR 38; CP 7; DAM MULT; DLB 82; EXPP; HW 1, 2; INT CA-125; JRDA; MAICYA 2; MAIC-YAS 1; MTCW 2; PFS 7; RGAL 4; SATA 80, 120; WYA; YAW

Soupault, Philippe 1897-1990 .... **CLC 68**
See also CA 116; 147; 131; GFL 1789 to the Present

Souster, (Holmes) Raymond 1921- .... **CLC 5, 14**
See also CA 13-16R; CAAS 14; CANR 13, 29, 53; CP 7; DA3; DAC; DAM POET; DLB 88; RGEL 2; SATA 63

Southern, Terry 1924(?)-1995 .... **CLC 7**
See also AMWS 11; BPFB 3; CA 1-4R; 150; CANR 1, 55, 107; CN 7; DLB 2; IDFW 3, 4

Southey, Robert 1774-1843 .... **NCLC 8, 97**
See also BRW 4; DLB 93, 107, 142; RGEL 2; SATA 54

Southworth, Emma Dorothy Eliza Nevitte
1819-1899 .... **NCLC 26**
See also DLB 239

Souza, Ernest
See Scott, Evelyn

Soyinka, Wole 1934- .... **CLC 3, 5, 14, 36, 44; BLC 3; DC 2; WLC**
See also AFW; BW 2, 3; CA 13-16R; CANR 27, 39, 82; CD 5; CDWLB 3; CN 7; CP 7; DA; DA3; DAB; DAC; DAM DRAM, MST, MULT; DFS 10; DLB 125; MTCW 1, 2; RGEL 2; TWA; WLIT 2

Spackman, W(illiam) M(ode)
1905-1990 .... **CLC 46**
See also CA 81-84; 132

Spacks, Barry (Bernard) 1931- .... **CLC 14**
See also CA 154; CANR 33, 109; CP 7; DLB 105

Spanidou, Irini 1946- .... **CLC 44**
See also CA 185

Spark, Muriel (Sarah) 1918- ..... **CLC 2, 3, 5, 8, 13, 18, 40, 94; SSC 10**
See also BRWS 1; CA 5-8R; CANR 12, 36, 76, 89; CDBLB 1945-1960; CN 7; CP 7; DA3; DAB; DAC; DAM MST, NOV; DLB 15, 139; FW; INT CANR-12; LAIT 4; MTCW 1, 2; RGEL 2; TEA; WLIT 4; YAW

Spaulding, Douglas
See Bradbury, Ray (Douglas)

Spaulding, Leonard
See Bradbury, Ray (Douglas)

Spelman, Elizabeth .... **CLC 65**

Spence, J. A. D.
See Eliot, T(homas) S(tearns)

Spencer, Elizabeth 1921- .... **CLC 22**
See also CA 13-16R; CANR 32, 65, 87; CN 7; CSW; DLB 6, 218; MTCW 1; RGAL 4; SATA 14

Spencer, Leonard G.
See Silverberg, Robert

Spencer, Scott 1945- .... **CLC 30**
See also CA 113; CANR 51; DLBY 1986

Spender, Stephen (Harold)
1909-1995 .... **CLC 1, 2, 5, 10, 41, 91**
See also BRWS 2; CA 9-12R; 149; CANR 31, 54; CDBLB 1945-1960; CP 7; DA3; DAM POET; DLB 20; MTCW 1, 2; PAB; RGEL 2; TEA

Spengler, Oswald (Arnold Gottfried)
1880-1936 .... **TCLC 25**
See also CA 118; 189

Spenser, Edmund 1552(?)-1599 ..... **LC 5, 39; PC 8, 42; WLC**
See also BRW 1; CDBLB Before 1660; DA; DA3; DAB; DAC; DAM MST, POET; DLB 167; EFS 2; EXPP; PAB; RGEL 2; TEA; WLIT 3; WP

Spicer, Jack 1925-1965 .... **CLC 8, 18, 72**
See also CA 85-88; DAM POET; DLB 5, 16, 193; GLL 1; WP

Spiegelman, Art 1948- .... **CLC 76**
See also AAYA 10; CA 125; CANR 41, 55, 74; MTCW 2; SATA 109; YAW

Spielberg, Peter 1929- .... **CLC 6**
See also CA 5-8R; CANR 4, 48; DLBY 1981

Spielberg, Steven 1947- .... **CLC 20**
See also AAYA 8, 24; CA 77-80; CANR 32; SATA 32

Spillane, Frank Morrison 1918-
See Spillane, Mickey
See also CA 25-28R; CANR 28, 63; DA3; MTCW 1, 2; SATA 66

Spillane, Mickey .... **CLC 3, 13**
See also Spillane, Frank Morrison
See also BPFB 3; CMW 4; DLB 226; MSW; MTCW 2

Spinoza, Benedictus de 1632-1677 .. **LC 9, 58**

Spinrad, Norman (Richard) 1940- ... **CLC 46**
See also BPFB 3; CA 37-40R; CAAS 19; CANR 20, 91; DLB 8; INT CANR-20; SFW 4

Spitteler, Carl (Friedrich Georg)
1845-1924 .... **TCLC 12**
See also CA 109; DLB 129

Spivack, Kathleen (Romola Drucker)
1938- .... **CLC 6**
See also CA 49-52

Spoto, Donald 1941- .... **CLC 39**
See also CA 65-68; CANR 11, 57, 93

Springsteen, Bruce (F.) 1949- .... **CLC 17**
See also CA 111

Spurling, Hilary 1940- .... **CLC 34**
See also CA 104; CANR 25, 52, 94

Spyker, John Howland
See Elman, Richard (Martin)

Squires, (James) Radcliffe
1917-1993 .... **CLC 51**
See also CA 1-4R; 140; CANR 6, 21

Srivastava, Dhanpat Rai 1880(?)-1936
See Premchand
See also CA 118; 197

Stacy, Donald
See Pohl, Frederik

Stael
See Stael-Holstein, Anne Louise Germaine Necker
See also EW 5; RGWL 2

Stael, Germaine de
  See Stael-Holstein, Anne Louise Germaine Necker
  See also DLB 119, 192; FW; GFL 1789 to the Present; TWA

Stael-Holstein, Anne Louise Germaine Necker 1766-1817 .... **NCLC 3, 91**
  See also Stael; Stael, Germaine de

Stafford, Jean 1915-1979 .. **CLC 4, 7, 19, 68; SSC 26**
  See also CA 1-4R; 85-88; CANR 3, 65; DLB 2, 173; MTCW 1, 2; RGAL 4; RGSF 2; SATA-Obit 22; TCWW 2; TUS

Stafford, William (Edgar) 1914-1993 .... **CLC 4, 7, 29**
  See also AMWS 11; CA 5-8R; 142; CAAS 3; CANR 5, 22; DAM POET; DLB 5, 206; EXPP; INT CANR-22; PFS 2, 8; RGAL 4; WP

Stagnelius, Eric Johan 1793-1823 . **NCLC 61**

Staines, Trevor
  See Brunner, John (Kilian Houston)

Stairs, Gordon
  See Austin, Mary (Hunter)
  See also TCWW 2

Stalin, Joseph 1879-1953 .... **TCLC 92**

Stampa, Gaspara c. 1524-1554 .... **PC 43**
  See also RGWL 2

Stancykowna
  See Szymborska, Wislawa

Stannard, Martin 1947- .... **CLC 44**
  See also CA 142; DLB 155

Stanton, Elizabeth Cady 1815-1902 .... **TCLC 73**
  See also CA 171; DLB 79; FW

Stanton, Maura 1946- .... **CLC 9**
  See also CA 89-92; CANR 15; DLB 120

Stanton, Schuyler
  See Baum, L(yman) Frank

Stapledon, (William) Olaf 1886-1950 .... **TCLC 22**
  See also CA 111; 162; DLB 15, 255; SFW 4

Starbuck, George (Edwin) 1931-1996 .... **CLC 53**
  See also CA 21-24R; 153; CANR 23; DAM POET

Stark, Richard
  See Westlake, Donald E(dwin)

Staunton, Schuyler
  See Baum, L(yman) Frank

Stead, Christina (Ellen) 1902-1983 ... **CLC 2, 5, 8, 32, 80**
  See also BRWS 4; CA 13-16R; 109; CANR 33, 40; DLB 260; FW; MTCW 1, 2; RGEL 2; RGSF 2

Stead, William Thomas 1849-1912 .... **TCLC 48**
  See also CA 167

Stebnitsky, M.
  See Leskov, Nikolai (Semyonovich)

Steele, Sir Richard 1672-1729 .... **LC 18**
  See also BRW 3; CDBLB 1660-1789; DLB 84, 101; RGEL 2; WLIT 3

Steele, Timothy (Reid) 1948- .... **CLC 45**
  See also CA 93-96; CANR 16, 50, 92; CP 7; DLB 120

Steffens, (Joseph) Lincoln 1866-1936 .... **TCLC 20**
  See also CA 117

Stegner, Wallace (Earle) 1909-1993 .. **CLC 9, 49, 81; SSC 27**
  See also AITN 1; AMWS 4; ANW; BEST 90:3; BPFB 3; CA 1-4R; 141; CAAS 9; CANR 1, 21, 46; DAM NOV; DLB 9, 206; DLBY 1993; MTCW 1, 2; RGAL 4; TCWW 2; TUS

Stein, Gertrude 1874-1946 .... **TCLC 1, 6, 28, 48; PC 18; SSC 42; WLC**
  See also AMW; CA 104; 132; CANR 108; CDALB 1917-1929; DA; DA3; DAB; DAC; DAM MST, NOV, POET; DLB 4, 54, 86, 228; DLBD 15; EXPS; GLL 1; MAWW; MTCW 1, 2; NCFS 4; RGAL 4; RGSF 2; SSFS 5; TUS; WP

Steinbeck, John (Ernst) 1902-1968 ... **CLC 1, 5, 9, 13, 21, 34, 45, 75, 124; SSC 11, 37; WLC**
  See also AAYA 12; AMW; BPFB 3; BYA 2, 3, 13; CA 1-4R; 25-28R; CANR 1, 35; CDALB 1929-1941; DA; DA3; DAB; DAC; DAM DRAM, MST, NOV; DLB 7, 9, 212; DLBD 2; EXPS; LAIT 3; MTCW 1, 2; NFS 1, 5, 7; RGAL 4; RGSF 2; RHW; SATA 9; SSFS 3, 6; TCWW 2; TUS; WYA; YAW

Steinem, Gloria 1934- .... **CLC 63**
  See also CA 53-56; CANR 28, 51; DLB 246; FW; MTCW 1, 2

Steiner, George 1929- .... **CLC 24**
  See also CA 73-76; CANR 31, 67, 108; DAM NOV; DLB 67; MTCW 1, 2; SATA 62

Steiner, K. Leslie
  See Delany, Samuel R(ay), Jr.

Steiner, Rudolf 1861-1925 .... **TCLC 13**
  See also CA 107

Stendhal 1783-1842 .. **NCLC 23, 46; SSC 27; WLC**
  See also DA; DA3; DAB; DAC; DAM MST, NOV; DLB 119; EW 5; GFL 1789 to the Present; RGWL 2; TWA

Stephen, Adeline Virginia
  See Woolf, (Adeline) Virginia

Stephen, Sir Leslie 1832-1904 .... **TCLC 23**
  See also BRW 5; CA 123; DLB 57, 144, 190

Stephen, Sir Leslie
  See Stephen, Sir Leslie

Stephen, Virginia
  See Woolf, (Adeline) Virginia

Stephens, James 1882(?)-1950 .... **TCLC 4; SSC 50**
  See also CA 104; 192; DLB 19, 153, 162; FANT; RGEL 2; SUFW

Stephens, Reed
  See Donaldson, Stephen R(eeder)

Steptoe, Lydia
  See Barnes, Djuna
  See also GLL 1

Sterchi, Beat 1949- .... **CLC 65**
  See also CA 203

Sterling, Brett
  See Bradbury, Ray (Douglas); Hamilton, Edmond

Sterling, Bruce 1954- .... **CLC 72**
  See also CA 119; CANR 44; SCFW 2; SFW 4

Sterling, George 1869-1926 .... **TCLC 20**
  See also CA 117; 165; DLB 54

Stern, Gerald 1925- .... **CLC 40, 100**
  See also AMWS 9; CA 81-84; CANR 28, 94; CP 7; DLB 105; RGAL 4

Stern, Richard (Gustave) 1928- ... **CLC 4, 39**
  See also CA 1-4R; CANR 1, 25, 52; CN 7; DLB 218; DLBY 1987; INT CANR-25

Sternberg, Josef von 1894-1969 .... **CLC 20**
  See also CA 81-84

Sterne, Laurence 1713-1768 .... **LC 2, 48; WLC**
  See also BRW 3; CDBLB 1660-1789; DA; DAB; DAC; DAM MST, NOV; DLB 39; RGEL 2; TEA

Sternheim, (William Adolf) Carl 1878-1942 .... **TCLC 8**
  See also CA 105; 193; DLB 56, 118; RGWL 2

Stevens, Mark 1951- .... **CLC 34**
  See also CA 122

Stevens, Wallace 1879-1955 ...... **TCLC 3, 12, 45; PC 6; WLC**
  See also AMW; AMWR 1; CA 104; 124; CDALB 1929-1941; DA; DA3; DAB; DAC; DAM MST, POET; DLB 54; EXPP; MTCW 1, 2; PAB; PFS 13; RGAL 4; TUS; WP

Stevenson, Anne (Katharine) 1933- .. **CLC 7, 33**
  See also BRWS 6; CA 17-20R; CAAS 9; CANR 9, 33; CP 7; CWP; DLB 40; MTCW 1; RHW

Stevenson, Robert Louis (Balfour) 1850-1894 ...... **NCLC 5, 14, 63; SSC 11, 51; WLC**
  See also AAYA 24; BPFB 3; BRW 5; BRWR 1; BYA 1, 2, 4, 13; CDBLB 1890-1914; CLR 10, 11; DA; DA3; DAB; DAC; DAM MST, NOV; DLB 18, 57, 141, 156, 174; DLBD 13; HGG; JRDA; LAIT 1, 3; MAICYA 1, 2; NFS 11; RGEL 2; RGSF 2; SATA 100; SUFW; TEA; WCH; WLIT 4; WYA; YABC 2; YAW

Stewart, J(ohn) I(nnes) M(ackintosh) 1906-1994 .... **CLC 7, 14, 32**
  See also Innes, Michael
  See also CA 85-88; 147; CAAS 3; CANR 47; CMW 4; MTCW 1, 2

Stewart, Mary (Florence Elinor) 1916- .... **CLC 7, 35, 117**
  See also AAYA 29; BPFB 3; CA 1-4R; CANR 1, 59; CMW 4; CPW; DAB; FANT; RHW; SATA 12; YAW

Stewart, Mary Rainbow
  See Stewart, Mary (Florence Elinor)

Stifle, June
  See Campbell, Maria

Stifter, Adalbert 1805-1868 .. **NCLC 41; SSC 28**
  See also CDWLB 2; DLB 133; RGSF 2; RGWL 2

Still, James 1906-2001 .... **CLC 49**
  See also CA 65-68; 195; CAAS 17; CANR 10, 26; CSW; DLB 9; DLBY 01; SATA 29; SATA-Obit 127

Sting 1951-
  See Sumner, Gordon Matthew
  See also CA 167

Stirling, Arthur
  See Sinclair, Upton (Beall)

Stitt, Milan 1941- .... **CLC 29**
  See also CA 69-72

Stockton, Francis Richard 1834-1902
  See Stockton, Frank R.
  See also CA 108; 137; MAICYA 1, 2; SATA 44; SFW 4

Stockton, Frank R. .... **TCLC 47**
  See also Stockton, Francis Richard
  See also BYA 4, 13; DLB 42, 74; DLBD 13; EXPS; SATA-Brief 32; SSFS 3; SUFW; WCH

Stoddard, Charles
  See Kuttner, Henry

Stoker, Abraham 1847-1912 .... **SSC 55, 56**
  See Stoker, Bram
  See also CA 105; 150; DA; DA3; DAC; DAM MST, NOV; HGG; SATA 29

Stoker, Bram .... **TCLC 8; WLC**
  See also Stoker, Abraham
  See also AAYA 23; BPFB 3; BRWS 3; BYA 5; CDBLB 1890-1914; DAB; DLB 36, 70, 178; RGEL 2; SUFW; TEA; WLIT 4

Stolz, Mary (Slattery) 1920- .... **CLC 12**
See also AAYA 8; AITN 1; CA 5-8R; CANR 13, 41; JRDA; MAICYA 1, 2; SAAS 3; SATA 10, 71, 133; YAW

Stone, Irving 1903-1989 .... **CLC 7**
See also AITN 1; BPFB 3; CA 1-4R; 129; CAAS 3; CANR 1, 23; CPW; DA3; DAM POP; INT CANR-23; MTCW 1, 2; RHW; SATA 3; SATA-Obit 64

Stone, Oliver (William) 1946- .... **CLC 73**
See also AAYA 15; CA 110; CANR 55

Stone, Robert (Anthony) 1937- ... **CLC 5, 23, 42**
See also AMWS 5; BPFB 3; CA 85-88; CANR 23, 66, 95; CN 7; DLB 152; INT CANR-23; MTCW 1

Stone, Zachary
See Follett, Ken(neth Martin)

Stoppard, Tom 1937- ... **CLC 1, 3, 4, 5, 8, 15, 29, 34, 63, 91; DC 6; WLC**
See also BRWR 2; BRWS 1; CA 81-84; CANR 39, 67; CBD; CD 5; CDBLB 1960 to Present; DA; DA3; DAB; DAC; DAM DRAM, MST; DFS 2, 5, 8, 11, 13; DLB 13, 233; DLBY 1985; MTCW 1, 2; RGEL 2; TEA; WLIT 4

Storey, David (Malcolm) 1933- . **CLC 2, 4, 5, 8**
See also BRWS 1; CA 81-84; CANR 36; CBD; CD 5; CN 7; DAM DRAM; DLB 13, 14, 207, 245; MTCW 1; RGEL 2

Storm, Hyemeyohsts 1935- .... **CLC 3**
See also CA 81-84; CANR 45; DAM MULT; NNAL

Storm, (Hans) Theodor (Woldsen) 1817-1888 .... **NCLC 1; SSC 27**
See also DLB 129; EW

Storm, Theodor 1817-1888 .... **SSC 27**
See also CDWLB 2; RGSF 2; RGWL 2

Storni, Alfonsina 1892-1938 .. **TCLC 5; HLC 2; PC 33**
See also CA 104; 131; DAM MULT; HW 1; LAW

Stoughton, William 1631-1701 .... **LC 38**
See also DLB 24

Stout, Rex (Todhunter) 1886-1975 ..... **CLC 3**
See also AITN 2; BPFB 3; CA 61-64; CANR 71; CMW 4; MSW; RGAL 4

Stow, (Julian) Randolph 1935- ... **CLC 23, 48**
See also CA 13-16R; CANR 33; CN 7; DLB 260; MTCW 1; RGEL 2

Stowe, Harriet (Elizabeth) Beecher 1811-1896 .... **NCLC 3, 50; WLC**
See also AMWS 1; CDALB 1865-1917; DA; DA3; DAB; DAC; DAM MST, NOV; DLB 1, 12, 42, 74, 189, 239, 243; EXPN; JRDA; LAIT 2; MAICYA 1, 2; NFS 6; RGAL 4; TUS; YABC 1

Strabo c. 64 B.C.-c. 25 .... **CMLC 37**
See also DLB 176

Strachey, (Giles) Lytton 1880-1932 .... **TCLC 12**
See also BRWS 2; CA 110; 178; DLB 149; DLBD 10; MTCW 2; NCFS 4

Strand, Mark 1934- .... **CLC 6, 18, 41, 71**
See also AMWS 4; CA 21-24R; CANR 40, 65, 100; CP 7; DAM POET; DLB 5; PAB; PFS 9; RGAL 4; SATA 41

Stratton-Porter, Gene(va Grace) 1863-1924
See Porter, Gene(va Grace) Stratton
See also ANW; CA 137; DLB 221; DLBD 14; MAICYA 1, 2; SATA 15

Straub, Peter (Francis) 1943- ... **CLC 28, 107**
See also BEST 89:1; BPFB 3; CA 85-88; CANR 28, 65, 109; CPW; DAM POP; DLBY 1984; HGG; MTCW 1, 2

Strauss, Botho 1944- .... **CLC 22**
See also CA 157; CWW 2; DLB 124

Streatfeild, (Mary) Noel 1897(?)-1986 .... **CLC 21**
See also CA 81-84; 120; CANR 31; CLR 17, 83; CWRI 5; DLB 160; MAICYA 1, 2; SATA 20; SATA-Obit 48

Stribling, T(homas) S(igismund) 1881-1965 .... **CLC 23**
See also CA 189; 107; CMW 4; DLB 9; RGAL 4

Strindberg, (Johan) August 1849-1912 ... **TCLC 1, 8, 21, 47; DC 18; WLC**
See also CA 104; 135; DA; DA3; DAB; DAC; DAM DRAM, MST; DFS 4, 9; DLB 259; EW 7; IDTP; MTCW 2; RGWL 2; TWA

Stringer, Arthur 1874-1950 .... **TCLC 37**
See also CA 161; DLB 92

Stringer, David
See Roberts, Keith (John Kingston)

Stroheim, Erich von 1885-1957 ..... **TCLC 71**

Strugatskii, Arkadii (Natanovich) 1925-1991 .... **CLC 27**
See also CA 106; 135; SFW 4

Strugatskii, Boris (Natanovich) 1933- .... **CLC 27**
See also CA 106; SFW 4

Strummer, Joe 1953(?)- .... **CLC 30**

Strunk, William, Jr. 1869-1946 ...... **TCLC 92**
See also CA 118; 164

Stryk, Lucien 1924- .... **PC 27**
See also CA 13-16R; CANR 10, 28, 55, 110; CP 7

Stuart, Don A.
See Campbell, John W(ood, Jr.)

Stuart, Ian
See MacLean, Alistair (Stuart)

Stuart, Jesse (Hilton) 1906-1984 ... **CLC 1, 8, 11, 14, 34; SSC 31**
See also CA 5-8R; 112; CANR 31; DLB 9, 48, 102; DLBY 1984; SATA 2; SATA-Obit 36

Stubblefield, Sally
See Trumbo, Dalton

Sturgeon, Theodore (Hamilton) 1918-1985 .... **CLC 22, 39**
See also Queen, Ellery
See also BPFB 3; BYA 9, 10; CA 81-84; 116; CANR 32, 103; DLB 8; DLBY 1985; HGG; MTCW 1, 2; SCFW; SFW 4; SUFW

Sturges, Preston 1898-1959 .... **TCLC 48**
See also CA 114; 149; DLB 26

Styron, William 1925- .... **CLC 1, 3, 5, 11, 15, 60; SSC 25**
See also AMW; BEST 90:4; BPFB 3; CA 5-8R; CANR 6, 33, 74; CDALB 1968-1988; CN 7; CPW; CSW; DA3; DAM NOV, POP; DLB 2, 143; DLBY 1980; INT CANR-6; LAIT 2; MTCW 1, 2; NCFS 1; RGAL 4; RHW; TUS

Su, Chien 1884-1918
See Su Man-shu
See also CA 123

Suarez Lynch, B.
See Bioy Casares, Adolfo; Borges, Jorge Luis

Suassuna, Ariano Vilar 1927-
See also CA 178; HLCS 1; HW 2; LAW

Suckert, Kurt Erich
See Malaparte, Curzio

Suckling, Sir John 1609-1642 . **LC 75; PC 30**
See also BRW 2; DAM POET; DLB 58, 126; EXPP; PAB; RGEL 2

Suckow, Ruth 1892-1960 .... **SSC 18**
See also CA 193; 113; DLB 9, 102; RGAL 4; TCWW 2

Sudermann, Hermann 1857-1928 .. **TCLC 15**
See also CA 107; 201; DLB 118

Sue, Eugene 1804-1857 .... **NCLC 1**
See also DLB 119

Sueskind, Patrick 1949- .... **CLC 44**
See also Suskind, Patrick

Sukenick, Ronald 1932- .... **CLC 3, 4, 6, 48**
See also CA 25-28R; CAAS 8; CANR 32, 89; CN 7; DLB 173; DLBY 1981

Suknaski, Andrew 1942- .... **CLC 19**
See also CA 101; CP 7; DLB 53

Sullivan, Vernon
See Vian, Boris

Sully Prudhomme, Rene-Francois-Armand 1839-1907 .... **TCLC 31**
See also GFL 1789 to the Present

Su Man-shu .... **TCLC 24**
See also Su, Chien

Summerforest, Ivy B.
See Kirkup, James

Summers, Andrew James 1942- .... **CLC 26**

Summers, Andy
See Summers, Andrew James

Summers, Hollis (Spurgeon, Jr.) 1916- .... **CLC 10**
See also CA 5-8R; CANR 3; DLB 6

Summers, (Alphonsus Joseph-Mary Augustus) Montague 1880-1948 .... **TCLC 16**
See also CA 118; 163

Sumner, Gordon Matthew .... **CLC 26**
See also Police, The; Sting

Surtees, Robert Smith 1805-1864 .. **NCLC 14**
See also DLB 21; RGEL 2

Susann, Jacqueline 1921-1974 .... **CLC 3**
See also AITN 1; BPFB 3; CA 65-68; 53-56; MTCW 1, 2

Su Shi
See Su Shih
See also RGWL 2

Su Shih 1036-1101 .... **CMLC 15**
See also Su Shi

Suskind, Patrick
See Sueskind, Patrick
See also BPFB 3; CA 145; CWW 2

Sutcliff, Rosemary 1920-1992 .... **CLC 26**
See also AAYA 10; BYA 1, 4; CA 5-8R; 139; CANR 37; CLR 1, 37; CPW; DAB; DAC; DAM MST, POP; JRDA; MAICYA 1, 2; MAICYAS 1; RHW; SATA 6, 44, 78; SATA-Obit 73; WYA; YAW

Sutro, Alfred 1863-1933 .... **TCLC 6**
See also CA 105; 185; DLB 10; RGEL 2

Sutton, Henry
See Slavitt, David R(ytman)

Suzuki, D. T.
See Suzuki, Daisetz Teitaro

Suzuki, Daisetz T.
See Suzuki, Daisetz Teitaro

Suzuki, Daisetz Teitaro 1870-1966 .... **TCLC 109**
See also CA 121; 111; MTCW 1, 2

Suzuki, Teitaro
See Suzuki, Daisetz Teitaro

Svevo, Italo .... **TCLC 2, 35; SSC 25**
See also Schmitz, Aron Hector
See also DLB 264; EW 8; RGWL 2

Swados, Elizabeth (A.) 1951- .... **CLC 12**
See also CA 97-100; CANR 49; INT 97-100

Swados, Harvey 1920-1972 .... **CLC 5**
See also CA 5-8R; 37-40R; CANR 6; DLB 2

Swan, Gladys 1934- .... **CLC 69**
See also CA 101; CANR 17, 39

Swanson, Logan
See Matheson, Richard (Burton)

Tryon, Thomas 1926-1991 .... **CLC 3, 11**
　　See also AITN 1; BPFB 3; CA 29-32R; 135;
　　CANR 32, 77; CPW; DA3; DAM POP;
　　HGG; MTCW 1
Tryon, Tom
　　See Tryon, Thomas
Ts'ao Hsueh-ch'in 1715(?)-1763 .... **LC 1**
Tsushima, Shuji 1909-1948
　　See Dazai Osamu
　　See also CA 107
Tsvetaeva (Efron), Marina (Ivanovna)
　　1892-1941 .... **TCLC 7, 35; PC 14**
　　See also CA 104; 128; CANR 73; EW 11;
　　MTCW 1, 2; RGWL 2
Tuck, Lily 1938- .... **CLC 70**
　　See also CA 139; CANR 90
Tu Fu 712-770 .... **PC 9**
　　See also Du Fu
　　See also DAM MULT; TWA; WP
Tunis, John R(oberts) 1889-1975 ..... **CLC 12**
　　See also BYA 1; CA 61-64; CANR 62; DLB
　　22, 171; JRDA; MAICYA 1, 2; SATA 37;
　　SATA-Brief 30; YAW
Tuohy, Frank .... **CLC 37**
　　See also Tuohy, John Francis
　　See also DLB 14, 139
Tuohy, John Francis 1925-
　　See Tuohy, Frank
　　See also CA 5-8R; 178; CANR 3, 47; CN 7
Turco, Lewis (Putnam) 1934- ..... **CLC 11, 63**
　　See also CA 13-16R; CAAS 22; CANR 24,
　　51; CP 7; DLBY 1984
Turgenev, Ivan (Sergeevich)
　　1818-1883 .... **NCLC 21, 37; DC 7; SSC
　　7; WLC**
　　See also DA; DAB; DAC; DAM MST,
　　NOV; DFS 6; DLB 238; EW 6; RGSF 2;
　　RGWL 2; TWA
Turgot, Anne-Robert-Jacques
　　1727-1781 .... **LC 26**
Turner, Frederick 1943- .... **CLC 48**
　　See also CA 73-76; CAAS 10; CANR 12,
　　30, 56; DLB 40
Turton, James
　　See Crace, Jim
Tutu, Desmond M(pilo) 1931- .... **CLC 80;
　　BLC 3**
　　See also BW 1, 3; CA 125; CANR 67, 81;
　　DAM MULT
Tutuola, Amos 1920-1997 ...... **CLC 5, 14, 29;
　　BLC 3**
　　See also AFW; BW 2, 3; CA 9-12R; 159;
　　CANR 27, 66; CDWLB 3; CN 7; DA3;
　　DAM MULT; DLB 125; DNFS 2; MTCW
　　1, 2; RGEL 2; WLIT 2
Twain, Mark .... **TCLC 6, 12, 19, 36, 48, 59;
　　SSC 34; WLC**
　　See also Clemens, Samuel Langhorne
　　See also AAYA 20; AMW; BPFB 3; BYA 2,
　　3, 11, 14; CLR 58, 60, 66; DLB 11;
　　EXPN; EXPS; FANT; LAIT 2; NFS 1, 6;
　　RGAL 4; RGSF 2; SFW 4; SSFS 1, 7;
　　SUFW; TUS; WCH; WYA; YAW
Tyler, Anne 1941- . **CLC 7, 11, 18, 28, 44, 59,
　　103**
　　See also AAYA 18; AMWS 4; BEST 89:1;
　　BPFB 3; BYA 12; CA 9-12R; CANR 11,
　　33, 53, 109; CDALBS; CN 7; CPW;
　　CSW; DAM NOV, POP; DLB 6, 143;
　　DLBY 1982; EXPN; MAWW; MTCW 1,
　　2; NFS 2, 7, 10; RGAL 4; SATA 7, 90;
　　TUS; YAW
Tyler, Royall 1757-1826 .... **NCLC 3**
　　See also DLB 37; RGAL 4
Tynan, Katharine 1861-1931 .... **TCLC 3**
　　See also CA 104; 167; DLB 153, 240; FW

Tyutchev, Fyodor 1803-1873 .... **NCLC 34**
Tzara, Tristan 1896-1963 ..... **CLC 47; PC 27**
　　See also CA 153; 89-92; DAM POET;
　　MTCW 2
Uhry, Alfred 1936- .... **CLC 55**
　　See also CA 127; 133; CAD; CD 5; CSW;
　　DA3; DAM DRAM, POP; DFS 15; INT
　　CA-133
Ulf, Haerved
　　See Strindberg, (Johan) August
Ulf, Harved
　　See Strindberg, (Johan) August
Ulibarri, Sabine R(eyes) 1919- .... **CLC 83;
　　HLCS 2**
　　See also CA 131; CANR 81; DAM MULT;
　　DLB 82; HW 1, 2; RGSF 2
Unamuno (y Jugo), Miguel de
　　1864-1936 . **TCLC 2, 9; HLC 2; SSC 11**
　　See also CA 104; 131; CANR 81; DAM
　　MULT, NOV; DLB 108; EW 8; HW 1, 2;
　　MTCW 1, 2; RGSF 2; RGWL 2; TWA
Undercliffe, Errol
　　See Campbell, (John) Ramsey
Underwood, Miles
　　See Glassco, John
Undset, Sigrid 1882-1949 ..... **TCLC 3; WLC**
　　See also CA 104; 129; DA; DA3; DAB;
　　DAC; DAM MST, NOV; EW 9; FW;
　　MTCW 1, 2; RGWL 2
Ungaretti, Giuseppe 1888-1970 ... **CLC 7, 11,
　　15**
　　See also CA 19-20; 25-28R; CAP 2; DLB
　　114; EW 10; RGWL 2
Unger, Douglas 1952- .... **CLC 34**
　　See also CA 130; CANR 94
Unsworth, Barry (Forster) 1930- .... **CLC 76,
　　127**
　　See also BRWS 7; CA 25-28R; CANR 30,
　　54; CN 7; DLB 194
Updike, John (Hoyer) 1932- . **CLC 1, 2, 3, 5,
　　7, 9, 13, 15, 23, 34, 43, 70, 139; SSC 13,
　　27; WLC**
　　See also AAYA 36; AMW; AMWR 1; BPFB
　　3; BYA 12; CA 1-4R; CABS 1; CANR 4,
　　33, 51, 94; CDALB 1968-1988; CN 7;
　　CP 7; CPW 1; DA; DA3; DAB; DAC;
　　DAM MST, NOV, POET, POP; DLB 2, 5,
　　143, 218, 227; DLBD 3; DLBY 1980,
　　1982, 1997; EXPP; HGG; MTCW 1, 2;
　　NFS 12; RGAL 4; RGSF 2; SSFS 3; TUS
Upshaw, Margaret Mitchell
　　See Mitchell, Margaret (Munnerlyn)
Upton, Mark
　　See Sanders, Lawrence
Upward, Allen 1863-1926 .... **TCLC 85**
　　See also CA 117; 187; DLB 36
Urdang, Constance (Henriette)
　　1922-1996 .... **CLC 47**
　　See also CA 21-24R; CANR 9, 24; CP 7;
　　CWP
Uriel, Henry
　　See Faust, Frederick (Schiller)
Uris, Leon (Marcus) 1924- .... **CLC 7, 32**
　　See also AITN 1, 2; BEST 89:2; BPFB 3;
　　CA 1-4R; CANR 1, 40, 65; CN 7; CPW
　　1; DA3; DAM NOV, POP; MTCW 1, 2;
　　SATA 49
Urista, Alberto H. 1947- .... **PC 34**
　　See also Alurista
　　See also CA 45-48, 182; CANR 2, 32;
　　HLCS 1; HW 1
Urmuz
　　See Codrescu, Andrei
Urquhart, Guy
　　See McAlmon, Robert (Menzies)
Urquhart, Jane 1949- .... **CLC 90**
　　See also CA 113; CANR 32, 68; CCA 1;
　　DAC

Usigli, Rodolfo 1905-1979
　　See also CA 131; HLCS 1; HW 1; LAW
Ustinov, Peter (Alexander) 1921- .... **CLC 1**
　　See also AITN 1; CA 13-16R; CANR 25,
　　51; CBD; CD 5; DLB 13; MTCW 2
U Tam'si, Gerald Felix Tchicaya
　　See Tchicaya, Gerald Felix
U Tam'si, Tchicaya
　　See Tchicaya, Gerald Felix
Vachss, Andrew (Henry) 1942- .... **CLC 106**
　　See also CA 118; CANR 44, 95; CMW 4
Vachss, Andrew H.
　　See Vachss, Andrew (Henry)
Vaculik, Ludvik 1926- .... **CLC 7**
　　See also CA 53-56; CANR 72; CWW 2;
　　DLB 232
Vaihinger, Hans 1852-1933 .... **TCLC 71**
　　See also CA 116; 166
Valdez, Luis (Miguel) 1940- ..... **CLC 84; DC
　　10; HLC 2**
　　See also CA 101; CAD; CANR 32, 81; CD
　　5; DAM MULT; DFS 5; DLB 122; HW
　　1; LAIT 4
Valenzuela, Luisa 1938- .... **CLC 31, 104;
　　HLCS 2; SSC 14**
　　See also CA 101; CANR 32, 65; CDWLB
　　3; CWW 2; DAM MULT; DLB 113; FW;
　　HW 1, 2; LAW; RGSF 2
Valera y Alcala-Galiano, Juan
　　1824-1905 .... **TCLC 10**
　　See also CA 106
Valery, (Ambroise) Paul (Toussaint Jules)
　　1871-1945 .... **TCLC 4, 15; PC 9**
　　See also CA 104; 122; DA3; DAM POET;
　　DLB 258; EW 8; GFL 1789 to the Present;
　　MTCW 1, 2; RGWL 2; TWA
Valle-Inclan, Ramon (Maria) del
　　1866-1936 .... **TCLC 5; HLC 2**
　　See also CA 106; 153; CANR 80; DAM
　　MULT; DLB 134; EW 8; HW 2; RGSF 2;
　　RGWL 2
Vallejo, Antonio Buero
　　See Buero Vallejo, Antonio
Vallejo, Cesar (Abraham)
　　1892-1938 .... **TCLC 3, 56; HLC 2**
　　See also CA 105; 153; DAM MULT; HW
　　1; LAW; RGWL 2
Valles, Jules 1832-1885 .... **NCLC 71**
　　See also DLB 123; GFL 1789 to the Present
Vallette, Marguerite Eymery
　　1860-1953 .... **TCLC 67**
　　See also CA 182; DLB 123, 192
Valle Y Pena, Ramon del
　　See Valle-Inclan, Ramon (Maria) del
Van Ash, Cay 1918- .... **CLC 34**
Vanbrugh, Sir John 1664-1726 .... **LC 21**
　　See also BRW 2; DAM DRAM; DLB 80;
　　IDTP; RGEL 2
Van Campen, Karl
　　See Campbell, John W(ood, Jr.)
Vance, Gerald
　　See Silverberg, Robert
Vance, Jack .... **CLC 35**
　　See also Vance, John Holbrook
　　See also DLB 8; FANT; SCFW 2; SFW 4;
　　SUFW
Vance, John Holbrook 1916-
　　See Queen, Ellery; Vance, Jack
　　See also CA 29-32R; CANR 17, 65; CMW
　　4; MTCW 1
**Van Den Bogarde, Derek Jules Gaspard
　　Ulric Niven** 1921-1999 .... **CLC 14**
　　See also Bogarde, Dirk
　　See also CA 77-80; 179
Vandenburgh, Jane .... **CLC 59**
　　See also CA 168
Vanderhaeghe, Guy 1951- .... **CLC 41**
　　See also BPFB 3; CA 113; CANR 72

von Daniken, Erich
See von Daeniken, Erich
von Hartmann, Eduard
1842-1906 .... **TCLC 96**
von Hayek, Friedrich August
See Hayek, F(riedrich) A(ugust von)
von Heidenstam, (Carl Gustaf) Verner
See Heidenstam, (Carl Gustaf) Verner von
von Heyse, Paul (Johann Ludwig)
See Heyse, Paul (Johann Ludwig von)
von Hofmannsthal, Hugo
See Hofmannsthal, Hugo von
von Horvath, Odon
See von Horvath, Odon
von Horvath, Odon
See von Horvath, Odon
von Horvath, Odon 1901-1938 .... **TCLC 45**
See also von Horvath, Oedoen
See also CA 118; 194; DLB 85, 124; RGWL
2
von Horvath, Oedoen
See von Horvath, Odon
See also CA 184
von Liliencron, (Friedrich Adolf Axel)
Detlev
See Liliencron, (Friedrich Adolf Axel) De-
tlev von
Vonnegut, Kurt, Jr. 1922- . **CLC 1, 2, 3, 4, 5,**
8, 12, 22, 40, 60, 111; SSC 8; WLC
See also AAYA 6; AITN 1; AMWS 2; BEST
90:4; BPFB 3; BYA 3, 14; CA 1-4R;
CANR 1, 25, 49, 75, 92; CDALB 1968-
1988; CN 7; CPW 1; DA; DA3; DAB;
DAC; DAM MST, NOV, POP; DLB 2, 8,
152; DLBD 3; DLBY 1980; EXPN;
EXPS; LAIT 4; MTCW 1, 2; NFS 3;
RGAL 4; SCFW; SFW 4; SSFS 5; TUS;
YAW
Von Rachen, Kurt
See Hubbard, L(afayette) Ron(ald)
von Rezzori (d'Arezzo), Gregor
See Rezzori (d'Arezzo), Gregor von
von Sternberg, Josef
See Sternberg, Josef von
Vorster, Gordon 1924- .... **CLC 34**
See also CA 133
Vosce, Trudie
See Ozick, Cynthia
Voznesensky, Andrei (Andreievich)
1933- .... **CLC 1, 15, 57**
See also CA 89-92; CANR 37; CWW 2;
DAM POET; MTCW 1
Wace, Robert c. 1100-c. 1175 .... **CMLC 55**
See also DLB 146
Waddington, Miriam 1917- .... **CLC 28**
See also CA 21-24R; CANR 12, 30; CCA
1; CP 7; DLB 68
Wagman, Fredrica 1937- .... **CLC 7**
See also CA 97-100; INT 97-100
Wagner, Linda W.
See Wagner-Martin, Linda (C.)
Wagner, Linda Welshimer
See Wagner-Martin, Linda (C.)
Wagner, Richard 1813-1883 .... **NCLC 9**
See also DLB 129; EW 6
Wagner-Martin, Linda (C.) 1936- .... **CLC 50**
See also CA 159
Wagoner, David (Russell) 1926- .... **CLC 3, 5,**
15; PC 33
See also AMWS 9; CA 1-4R; CAAS 3;
CANR 2, 71; CN 7; CP 7; DLB 5, 256;
SATA 14; TCWW 2
Wah, Fred(erick James) 1939- .... **CLC 44**
See also CA 107; 141; CP 7; DLB 60
Wahloo, Per 1926-1975 .... **CLC 7**
See also BPFB 3; CA 61-64; CANR 73;
CMW 4; MSW
Wahloo, Peter
See Wahloo, Per

Wain, John (Barrington) 1925-1994 . **CLC 2,**
11, 15, 46
See also CA 5-8R; 145; CAAS 4; CANR
23, 54; CDBLB 1960 to Present; DLB 15,
27, 139, 155; MTCW 1, 2
Wajda, Andrzej 1926- .... **CLC 16**
See also CA 102
Wakefield, Dan 1932- .... **CLC 7**
See also CA 21-24R; CAAS 7; CN 7
Wakefield, Herbert Russell
1888-1965 .... **TCLC 120**
See also CA 5-8R; CANR 77; HGG; SUFW
Wakoski, Diane 1937- ...... **CLC 2, 4, 7, 9, 11,**
40; PC 15
See also CA 13-16R; CAAS 1; CANR 9,
60, 106; CP 7; CWP; DAM POET; DLB
5; INT CANR-9; MTCW 2
Wakoski-Sherbell, Diane
See Wakoski, Diane
Walcott, Derek (Alton) 1930- .... **CLC 2, 4, 9,**
14, 25, 42, 67, 76, 160; BLC 3; DC 7
See also BW 2; CA 89-92; CANR 26, 47,
75, 80; CBD; CD 5; CDWLB 3; CP 7;
DA3; DAB; DAC; DAM MST, MULT,
POET; DLB 117; DLBY 1981; DNFS 1;
EFS 1; MTCW 1, 2; PFS 6; RGEL 2;
TWA
Waldman, Anne (Lesley) 1945- .... **CLC 7**
See also CA 37-40R; CAAS 17; CANR 34,
69; CP 7; CWP; DLB 16
Waldo, E. Hunter
See Sturgeon, Theodore (Hamilton)
Waldo, Edward Hamilton
See Sturgeon, Theodore (Hamilton)
Walker, Alice (Malsenior) 1944- ... **CLC 5, 6,**
9, 19, 27, 46, 58, 103; BLC 3; PC 30;
SSC 5; WLCS
See also AAYA 3, 33; AFAW 1, 2; AMWS
3; BEST 89:4; BPFB 3; BW 2, 3; CA 37-
40R; CANR 9, 27, 49, 66, 82; CDALB
1968-1988; CN 7; CPW; CSW; DA; DA3;
DAB; DAC; DAM MST, MULT, NOV,
POET, POP; DLB 6, 33, 143; EXPN;
EXPS; FW; INT CANR-27; LAIT 3;
MAWW; MTCW 1, 2; NFS 5; RGAL 4;
RGSF 2; SATA 31; SSFS 2, 11; TUS;
YAW
Walker, David Harry 1911-1992 ...... **CLC 14**
See also CA 1-4R; 137; CANR 1; CWRI 5;
SATA 8; SATA-Obit 71
Walker, Edward Joseph 1934-
See Walker, Ted
See also CA 21-24R; CANR 12, 28, 53; CP
7
Walker, George F. 1947- .... **CLC 44, 61**
See also CA 103; CANR 21, 43, 59; CD 5;
DAB; DAC; DAM MST; DLB 60
Walker, Joseph A. 1935- .... **CLC 19**
See also BW 1, 3; CA 89-92; CAD; CANR
26; CD 5; DAM DRAM, MST; DFS 12;
DLB 38
Walker, Margaret (Abigail)
1915-1998 .... **CLC 1, 6; BLC; PC 20**
See also AFAW 1, 2; BW 2, 3; CA 73-76;
172; CANR 26, 54, 76; CN 7; CP 7;
CSW; DAM MULT; DLB 76, 152; EXPP;
FW; MTCW 1, 2; RGAL 4; RHW
Walker, Ted .... **CLC 13**
See also Walker, Edward Joseph
See also DLB 40
Wallace, David Foster 1962- ..... **CLC 50, 114**
See also AMWS 10; CA 132; CANR 59;
DA3; MTCW 2
Wallace, Dexter
See Masters, Edgar Lee
Wallace, (Richard Horatio) Edgar
1875-1932 .... **TCLC 57**
See also CA 115; CMW 4; DLB 70; MSW;
RGEL 2

Wallace, Irving 1916-1990 .... **CLC 7, 13**
See also AITN 1; BPFB 3; CA 1-4R; 132;
CAAS 1; CANR 1, 27; CPW; DAM NOV,
POP; INT CANR-27; MTCW 1, 2
Wallant, Edward Lewis 1926-1962 ... **CLC 5,**
10
See also CA 1-4R; CANR 22; DLB 2, 28,
143; MTCW 1, 2; RGAL 4
Wallas, Graham 1858-1932 .... **TCLC 91**
Walley, Byron
See Card, Orson Scott
Walpole, Horace 1717-1797 .... **LC 2, 49**
See also BRW 3; DLB 39, 104, 213; HGG;
RGEL 2; SUFW; TEA
Walpole, Hugh (Seymour)
1884-1941 .... **TCLC 5**
See also CA 104; 165; DLB 34; HGG;
MTCW 2; RGEL 2; RHW
Walser, Martin 1927- .... **CLC 27**
See also CA 57-60; CANR 8, 46; CWW 2;
DLB 75, 124
Walser, Robert 1878-1956 .... **TCLC 18; SSC**
20
See also CA 118; 165; CANR 100; DLB 66
Walsh, Gillian Paton
See Paton Walsh, Gillian
Walsh, Jill Paton .... **CLC 35**
See also Paton Walsh, Gillian
See also CLR 2, 65; WYA
Walter, William Christian
See Andersen, Hans Christian
Walton, Izaak 1593-1683 .... **LC 72**
See also BRW 2; CDBLB Before 1660;
DLB 151, 213; RGEL 2
Wambaugh, Joseph (Aloysius, Jr.)
1937- .... **CLC 3, 18**
See also AITN 1; BEST 89:3; BPFB 3; CA
33-36R; CANR 42, 65; CMW 4; CPW 1;
DA3; DAM NOV, POP; DLB 6; DLBY
1983; MSW; MTCW 1, 2
Wang Wei 699(?)-761(?) .... **PC 18**
See also TWA
Ward, Arthur Henry Sarsfield 1883-1959
See Rohmer, Sax
See also CA 108; 173; CMW 4; HGG
Ward, Douglas Turner 1930- .... **CLC 19**
See also BW 1; CA 81-84; CAD; CANR
27; CD 5; DLB 7, 38
Ward, E. D.
See Lucas, E(dward) V(errall)
Ward, Mrs. Humphry 1851-1920
See Ward, Mary Augusta
See also RGEL 2
Ward, Mary Augusta 1851-1920 ... **TCLC 55**
See also Ward, Mrs. Humphry
See also DLB 18
Ward, Peter
See Faust, Frederick (Schiller)
Warhol, Andy 1928(?)-1987 .... **CLC 20**
See also AAYA 12; BEST 89:4; CA 89-92;
121; CANR 34
Warner, Francis (Robert le Plastrier)
1937- .... **CLC 14**
See also CA 53-56; CANR 11
Warner, Marina 1946- .... **CLC 59**
See also CA 65-68; CANR 21, 55; CN 7;
DLB 194
Warner, Rex (Ernest) 1905-1986 ...... **CLC 45**
See also CA 89-92; 119; DLB 15; RGEL 2;
RHW
Warner, Susan (Bogert)
1819-1885 .... **NCLC 31**
See also DLB 3, 42, 239, 250, 254
Warner, Sylvia (Constance) Ashton
See Ashton-Warner, Sylvia (Constance)

CLR 3, 78; DLB 52; JRDA; MAICYA 1,
2; SAAS 2; SATA 1, 58; SATA-Essay 103;
WYA; YAW

Wertmueller, Lina 1928- .... **CLC 16**
See also CA 97-100; CANR 39, 78

Wescott, Glenway 1901-1987 .. **CLC 13; SSC
35**
See also CA 13-16R; 121; CANR 23, 70;
DLB 4, 9, 102; RGAL 4

Wesker, Arnold 1932- .... **CLC 3, 5, 42**
See also CA 1-4R; CAAS 7; CANR 1, 33;
CBD; CD 5; CDBLB 1960 to Present;
DAB; DAM DRAM; DLB 13; MTCW 1;
RGEL 2; TEA

Wesley, Richard (Errol) 1945- .... **CLC 7**
See also BW 1; CA 57-60; CAD; CANR
27; CD 5; DLB 38

Wessel, Johan Herman 1742-1785 .... **LC 7**

West, Anthony (Panther)
1914-1987 .... **CLC 50**
See also CA 45-48; 124; CANR 3, 19; DLB
15

West, C. P.
See Wodehouse, P(elham) G(renville)

West, Cornel (Ronald) 1953- .... **CLC 134;
BLCS**
See also CA 144; CANR 91; DLB 246

West, Delno C(loyde), Jr. 1936- .... **CLC 70**
See also CA 57-60

West, Dorothy 1907-1998 .... **TCLC 108**
See also BW 2; CA 143; 169; DLB 76

West, (Mary) Jessamyn 1902-1984 ... **CLC 7,
17**
See also CA 9-12R; 112; CANR 27; DLB
6; DLBY 1984; MTCW 1, 2; RHW;
SATA-Obit 37; TUS; YAW

West, Morris L(anglo) 1916-1999 ..... **CLC 6,
33**
See also BPFB 3; CA 5-8R; 187; CANR
24, 49, 64; CN 7; CPW; MTCW 1, 2

West, Nathanael 1903-1940 .... **TCLC 1, 14,
44; SSC 16**
See also AMW; BPFB 3; CA 104; 125;
CDALB 1929-1941; DA3; DLB 4, 9, 28;
MTCW 1, 2; RGAL 4; TUS

West, Owen
See Koontz, Dean R(ay)

West, Paul 1930- .... **CLC 7, 14, 96**
See also CA 13-16R; CAAS 7; CANR 22,
53, 76, 89; CN 7; DLB 14; INT CANR-
22; MTCW 2

West, Rebecca 1892-1983 ... **CLC 7, 9, 31, 50**
See also BPFB 3; BRWS 3; CA 5-8R; 109;
CANR 19; DLB 36; DLBY 1983; FW;
MTCW 1, 2; NCFS 4; RGEL 2; TEA

Westall, Robert (Atkinson)
1929-1993 .... **CLC 17**
See also AAYA 12; BYA 2, 6, 7, 8, 9; CA
69-72; 141; CANR 18, 68; CLR 13;
FANT; JRDA; MAICYA 1, 2; MAICYAS
1; SAAS 2; SATA 23, 69; SATA-Obit 75;
WYA; YAW

Westermarck, Edward 1862-1939 . **TCLC 87**

Westlake, Donald E(dwin) 1933- . **CLC 7, 33**
See also BPFB 3; CA 17-20R; CAAS 13;
CANR 16, 44, 65, 94; CMW 4; CPW;
DAM POP; INT CANR-16; MSW;
MTCW 2

Westmacott, Mary
See Christie, Agatha (Mary Clarissa)

Weston, Allen
See Norton, Andre

Wetcheek, J. L.
See Feuchtwanger, Lion

Wetering, Janwillem van de
See van de Wetering, Janwillem

Wetherald, Agnes Ethelwyn
1857-1940 .... **TCLC 81**
See also CA 202; DLB 99

Wetherell, Elizabeth
See Warner, Susan (Bogert)

Whale, James 1889-1957 .... **TCLC 63**

Whalen, Philip 1923- .... **CLC 6, 29**
See also CA 9-12R; CANR 5, 39; CP 7;
DLB 16; WP

Wharton, Edith (Newbold Jones)
1862-1937 ... **TCLC 3, 9, 27, 53; SSC 6;
WLC**
See also AAYA 25; AMW; AMWR 1; BPFB
3; CA 104; 132; CDALB 1865-1917; DA;
DA3; DAB; DAC; DAM MST, NOV;
DLB 4, 9, 12, 78, 189; DLBD 13; EXPS;
HGG; LAIT 2, 3; MAWW; MTCW 1, 2;
NFS 5, 11, 15; RGAL 4; RGSF 2; RHW;
SSFS 6, 7; SUFW; TUS

Wharton, James
See Mencken, H(enry) L(ouis)

Wharton, William (a pseudonym) . **CLC 18,
37**
See also CA 93-96; DLBY 1980; INT 93-96

Wheatley (Peters), Phillis
1753(?)-1784 ... **LC 3, 50; BLC 3; PC 3;
WLC**
See also AFAW 1, 2; CDALB 1640-1865;
DA; DA3; DAC; DAM MST, MULT,
POET; DLB 31, 50; EXPP; PFS 13;
RGAL 4

Wheelock, John Hall 1886-1978 .... **CLC 14**
See also CA 13-16R; 77-80; CANR 14;
DLB 45

White, Babington
See Braddon, Mary Elizabeth

White, E(lwyn) B(rooks)
1899-1985 .... **CLC 10, 34, 39**
See also AITN 2; AMWS 1; CA 13-16R;
116; CANR 16, 37; CDALBS; CLR 1, 21;
CPW; DA3; DAM POP; DLB 11, 22;
FANT; MAICYA 1, 2; MTCW 1, 2;
RGAL 4; SATA 2, 29, 100; SATA-Obit
44; TUS

White, Edmund (Valentine III)
1940- .... **CLC 27, 110**
See also AAYA 7; CA 45-48; CANR 3, 19,
36, 62, 107; CN 7; DA3; DAM POP; DLB
227; MTCW 1, 2

White, Hayden V. 1928- .... **CLC 148**
See also CA 128; DLB 246

White, Patrick (Victor Martindale)
1912-1990 ...... **CLC 3, 4, 5, 7, 9, 18, 65,
69; SSC 39**
See also BRWS 1; CA 81-84; 132; CANR
43; DLB 260; MTCW 1; RGEL 2; RGSF
2; RHW; TWA

White, Phyllis Dorothy James 1920-
See James, P. D.
See also CA 21-24R; CANR 17, 43, 65;
CMW 4; CN 7; CPW; DA3; DAM POP;
MTCW 1, 2; TEA

White, T(erence) H(anbury)
1906-1964 .... **CLC 30**
See also AAYA 22; BPFB 3; BYA 4, 5; CA
73-76; CANR 37; DLB 160; FANT;
JRDA; LAIT 1; MAICYA 1, 2; RGEL 2;
SATA 12; SUFW; YAW

White, Terence de Vere 1912-1994 ... **CLC 49**
See also CA 49-52; 145; CANR 3

White, Walter
See White, Walter F(rancis)

White, Walter F(rancis)
1893-1955 .... **TCLC 15; BLC 3**
See also BW 1; CA 115; 124; DAM MULT;
DLB 51

White, William Hale 1831-1913
See Rutherford, Mark
See also CA 121; 189

Whitehead, Alfred North
1861-1947 .... **TCLC 97**
See also CA 117; 165; DLB 100, 262

Whitehead, E(dward) A(nthony)
1933- .... **CLC 5**
See also CA 65-68; CANR 58; CBD; CD 5

Whitehead, Ted
See Whitehead, E(dward) A(nthony)

Whitemore, Hugh (John) 1936- .... **CLC 37**
See also CA 132; CANR 77; CBD; CD 5;
INT CA-132

Whitman, Sarah Helen (Power)
1803-1878 .... **NCLC 19**
See also DLB 1, 243

Whitman, Walt(er) 1819-1892 .. **NCLC 4, 31,
81; PC 3; WLC**
See also AAYA 42; AMW; AMWR 1;
CDALB 1640-1865; DA; DA3; DAB;
DAC; DAM MST, POET; DLB 3, 64,
224, 250; EXPP; LAIT 2; PAB; PFS 2, 3,
13; RGAL 4; SATA 20; TUS; WP; WYAS
1

Whitney, Phyllis A(yame) 1903- .... **CLC 42**
See also AAYA 36; AITN 2; BEST 90:3;
CA 1-4R; CANR 3, 25, 38, 60; CLR 59;
CMW 4; CPW; DA3; DAM POP; JRDA;
MAICYA 1, 2; MTCW 2; RHW; SATA 1,
30; YAW

Whittemore, (Edward) Reed (Jr.)
1919- .... **CLC 4**
See also CA 9-12R; CAAS 8; CANR 4; CP
7; DLB 5

Whittier, John Greenleaf
1807-1892 .... **NCLC 8, 59**
See also AMWS 1; DLB 1, 243; RGAL 4

Whittlebot, Hernia
See Coward, Noel (Peirce)

Wicker, Thomas Grey 1926-
See Wicker, Tom
See also CA 65-68; CANR 21, 46

Wicker, Tom .... **CLC 7**
See also Wicker, Thomas Grey

Wideman, John Edgar 1941- ...... **CLC 5, 34,
36, 67, 122; BLC 3**
See also AFAW 1, 2; AMWS 10; BPFB 4;
BW 2, 3; CA 85-88; CANR 14, 42, 67,
109; CN 7; DAM MULT; DLB 33, 143;
MTCW 2; RGAL 4; RGSF 2; SSFS 6, 12

Wiebe, Rudy (Henry) 1934- .. **CLC 6, 11, 14,
138**
See also CA 37-40R; CANR 42, 67; CN 7;
DAC; DAM MST; DLB 60; RHW

Wieland, Christoph Martin
1733-1813 .... **NCLC 17**
See also DLB 97; EW 4; RGWL 2

Wiene, Robert 1881-1938 .... **TCLC 56**

Wieners, John 1934- .... **CLC 7**
See also CA 13-16R; CP 7; DLB 16; WP

Wiesel, Elie(zer) 1928- .... **CLC 3, 5, 11, 37;
WLCS**
See also AAYA 7; AITN 1; CA 5-8R; CAAS
4; CANR 8, 40, 65; CDALBS; DA; DA3;
DAB; DAC; DAM MST, NOV; DLB 83;
DLBY 1987; INT CANR-8; LAIT 4;
MTCW 1, 2; NCFS 4; NFS 4; SATA 56;
YAW

Wiggins, Marianne 1947- .... **CLC 57**
See also BEST 89:3; CA 130; CANR 60

Wiggs, Susan .... **CLC 70**
See also CA 201

Wight, James Alfred 1916-1995
See Herriot, James
See also CA 77-80; SATA 55; SATA-Brief
44

Wilbur, Richard (Purdy) 1921- ..... **CLC 3, 6,
9, 14, 53, 110**
See also AMWS 3; CA 1-4R; CABS 2;
CANR 2, 29, 76, 93; CDALBS; CP 7;
DA; DAB; DAC; DAM MST, POET;
DLB 5, 169; EXPP; INT CANR-29;
MTCW 1, 2; PAB; PFS 11, 12; RGAL 4;
SATA 9, 108; WP

Wirth, Louis 1897-1952 .... **TCLC 92**

Wiseman, Frederick 1930- .... **CLC 20**
  See also CA 159

Wister, Owen 1860-1938 .... **TCLC 21**
  See also BPFB 3; CA 108; 162; DLB 9, 78,
  186; RGAL 4; SATA 62; TCWW 2

Witkacy
  See Witkiewicz, Stanislaw Ignacy

Witkiewicz, Stanislaw Ignacy
  1885-1939 .... **TCLC 8**
  See also CA 105; 162; CDWLB 4; DLB
  215; EW 10; RGWL 2; SFW 4

Wittgenstein, Ludwig (Josef Johann)
  1889-1951 .... **TCLC 59**
  See also CA 113; 164; DLB 262; MTCW 2

Wittig, Monique 1935(?)- .... **CLC 22**
  See also CA 116; 135; CWW 2; DLB 83;
  FW; GLL 1

Wittlin, Jozef 1896-1976 .... **CLC 25**
  See also CA 49-52; 65-68; CANR 3

Wodehouse, P(elham) G(renville)
  1881-1975 ... **CLC 1, 2, 5, 10, 22; SSC 2**
  See also AITN 2; BRWS 3; CA 45-48; 57-
  60; CANR 3, 33; CDBLB 1914-1945;
  CPW 1; DA3; DAB; DAC; DAM NOV;
  DLB 34, 162; MTCW 1, 2; RGEL 2;
  RGSF 2; SATA 22; SSFS 10; TCLC 108

Woiwode, L.
  See Woiwode, Larry (Alfred)

Woiwode, Larry (Alfred) 1941- ... **CLC 6, 10**
  See also CA 73-76; CANR 16, 94; CN 7;
  DLB 6; INT CANR-16

Wojciechowska, Maia (Teresa)
  1927-2002 .... **CLC 26**
  See also AAYA 8; BYA 3; CA 9-12R; 183;
  CAAE 183; CANR 4, 41; CLR 1; JRDA;
  MAICYA 1, 2; SAAS 1; SATA 1, 28, 83;
  SATA-Essay 104; SATA-Obit 134; YAW

Wojtyla, Karol
  See John Paul II, Pope

Wolf, Christa 1929- .... **CLC 14, 29, 58, 150**
  See also CA 85-88; CANR 45; CDWLB 2;
  CWW 2; DLB 75; FW; MTCW 1; RGWL
  2; SSFS 14

Wolf, Naomi 1962- .... **CLC 157**
  See also CA 141; CANR 110; FW

Wolfe, Gene (Rodman) 1931- .... **CLC 25**
  See also AAYA 35; CA 57-60; CAAS 9;
  CANR 6, 32, 60; CPW; DAM POP; DLB
  8; FANT; MTCW 2; SATA 118; SCFW 2;
  SFW 4

Wolfe, George C. 1954- .... **CLC 49; BLCS**
  See also CA 149; CAD; CD 5

Wolfe, Thomas (Clayton)
  1900-1938 ...... **TCLC 4, 13, 29, 61; SSC
  33; WLC**
  See also AMW; BPFB 3; CA 104; 132;
  CANR 102; CDALB 1929-1941; DA;
  DA3; DAB; DAC; DAM MST, NOV;
  DLB 9, 102, 229; DLBD 2, 16; DLBY
  1985, 1997; MTCW 1, 2; RGAL 4; TUS

Wolfe, Thomas Kennerly, Jr.
  1930- .... **CLC 147**
  See also Wolfe, Tom
  See also CA 13-16R; CANR 9, 33, 70, 104;
  DA3; DAM POP; DLB 185; INT
  CANR-9; MTCW 1, 2; TUS

Wolfe, Tom .... **CLC 1, 2, 9, 15, 35, 51**
  See also Wolfe, Thomas Kennerly, Jr.
  See also AAYA 8; AITN 2; AMWS 3; BEST
  89:1; BPFB 3; CN 7; CPW; CSW; DLB
  152; LAIT 5; RGAL 4

Wolff, Geoffrey (Ansell) 1937- .... **CLC 41**
  See also CA 29-32R; CANR 29, 43, 78

Wolff, Sonia
  See Levitin, Sonia (Wolff)

Wolff, Tobias (Jonathan Ansell)
  1945- .... **CLC 39, 64**
  See also AAYA 16; AMWS 7; BEST 90:2;
  BYA 12; CA 114; 117; CAAS 22; CANR
  54, 76, 96; CN 7; CSW; DA3; DLB 130;
  INT CA-117; MTCW 2; RGAL 4; RGSF
  2; SSFS 4, 11

Wolfram von Eschenbach c. 1170-c.
  1220 .... **CMLC 5**
  See also CDWLB 2; DLB 138; EW 1;
  RGWL 2

Wolitzer, Hilma 1930- .... **CLC 17**
  See also CA 65-68; CANR 18, 40; INT
  CANR-18; SATA 31; YAW

Wollstonecraft, Mary 1759-1797 ..... **LC 5, 50**
  See also BRWS 3; CDBLB 1789-1832;
  DLB 39, 104, 158, 252; FW; LAIT 1;
  RGEL 2; TEA; WLIT 3

Wonder, Stevie .... **CLC 12**
  See also Morris, Steveland Judkins

Wong, Jade Snow 1922- .... **CLC 17**
  See also CA 109; CANR 91; SATA 112

Woodberry, George Edward
  1855-1930 .... **TCLC 73**
  See also CA 165; DLB 71, 103

Woodcott, Keith
  See Brunner, John (Kilian Houston)

Woodruff, Robert W.
  See Mencken, H(enry) L(ouis)

Woolf, (Adeline) Virginia
  1882-1941 .. **TCLC 1, 5, 20, 43, 56, 101,
  123; SSC 7; WLC**
  See also BPFB 3; BRW 7; BRWR 1; CA
  104; 130; CANR 64; CDBLB 1914-1945;
  DA; DA3; DAB; DAC; DAM MST, NOV;
  DLB 36, 100, 162; DLBD 10; EXPS; FW;
  LAIT 3; MTCW 1, 2; NCFS 2; NFS 8,
  12; RGEL 2; RGSF 2; SSFS 4, 12; TEA;
  WLIT 4

Woollcott, Alexander (Humphreys)
  1887-1943 .... **TCLC 5**
  See also CA 105; 161; DLB 29

Woolrich, Cornell .... **CLC 77**
  See also Hopley-Woolrich, Cornell George
  See also MSW

Woolson, Constance Fenimore
  1840-1894 .... **NCLC 82**
  See also DLB 12, 74, 189, 221; RGAL 4

Wordsworth, Dorothy 1771-1855 .. **NCLC 25**
  See also DLB 107

Wordsworth, William 1770-1850 .. **NCLC 12,
  38, 111; PC 4; WLC**
  See also BRW 4; CDBLB 1789-1832; DA;
  DA3; DAB; DAC; DAM MST, POET;
  DLB 93, 107; EXPP; PAB; PFS 2; RGEL
  2; TEA; WLIT 3; WP

Wotton, Sir Henry 1568-1639 .... **LC 68**
  See also DLB 121; RGEL 2

Wouk, Herman 1915- .... **CLC 1, 9, 38**
  See also BPFB 2, 3; CA 5-8R; CANR 6,
  33, 67; CDALBS; CN 7; CPW; DA3;
  DAM NOV, POP; DLBY 1982; INT
  CANR-6; LAIT 4; MTCW 1, 2; NFS 7;
  TUS

Wright, Charles (Penzel, Jr.) 1935- .. **CLC 6,
  13, 28, 119, 146**
  See also AMWS 5; CA 29-32R; CAAS 7;
  CANR 23, 36, 62, 88; CP 7; DLB 165;
  DLBY 1982; MTCW 1, 2; PFS 10

Wright, Charles Stevenson 1932- ... **CLC 49;
  BLC 3**
  See also BW 1; CA 9-12R; CANR 26; CN
  7; DAM MULT, POET; DLB 33

Wright, Frances 1795-1852 .... **NCLC 74**
  See also DLB 73

Wright, Frank Lloyd 1867-1959 .... **TCLC 95**
  See also AAYA 33; CA 174

Wright, Jack R.
  See Harris, Mark

Wright, James (Arlington)
  1927-1980 .... **CLC 3, 5, 10, 28; PC 36**
  See also AITN 2; AMWS 3; CA 49-52; 97-
  100; CANR 4, 34, 64; CDALBS; DAM
  POET; DLB 5, 169; EXPP; MTCW 1, 2;
  PFS 7, 8; RGAL 4; TUS; WP

Wright, Judith (Arundell)
  1915-2000 .... **CLC 11, 53; PC 14**
  See also CA 13-16R; 188; CANR 31, 76,
  93; CP 7; CWP; DLB 260; MTCW 1, 2;
  PFS 8; RGEL 2; SATA 14; SATA-Obit
  121

Wright, L(aurali) R. 1939- .... **CLC 44**
  See also CA 138; CMW 4

Wright, Richard (Nathaniel)
  1908-1960 .... **CLC 1, 3, 4, 9, 14, 21, 48,
  74; BLC 3; SSC 2; WLC**
  See also AAYA 5, 42; AFAW 1, 2; AMW;
  BPFB 3; BW 1; BYA 2; CA 108; CANR
  64; CDALB 1929-1941; DA; DA3; DAB;
  DAC; DAM MST, MULT, NOV; DLB 76,
  102; DLBD 2; EXPN; LAIT 3, 4; MTCW
  1, 2; NCFS 1; NFS 1, 7; RGAL 4; RGSF
  2; SSFS 3, 9, 15; TUS; YAW

Wright, Richard B(ruce) 1937- .... **CLC 6**
  See also CA 85-88; DLB 53

Wright, Rick 1945- .... **CLC 35**

Wright, Rowland
  See Wells, Carolyn

Wright, Stephen 1946- .... **CLC 33**

Wright, Willard Huntington 1888-1939
  See Van Dine, S. S.
  See also CA 115; 189; CMW 4; DLBD 16

Wright, William 1930- .... **CLC 44**
  See also CA 53-56; CANR 7, 23

Wroth, Lady Mary 1587-1653(?) .... **LC 30;
  PC 38**
  See also DLB 121

Wu Ch'eng-en 1500(?)-1582(?) .... **LC 7**

Wu Ching-tzu 1701-1754 .... **LC 2**

Wurlitzer, Rudolph 1938(?)- .... **CLC 2, 4, 15**
  See also CA 85-88; CN 7; DLB 173

Wyatt, Sir Thomas c. 1503-1542 . **LC 70; PC
  27**
  See also BRW 1; DLB 132; EXPP; RGEL
  2; TEA

Wycherley, William 1640-1716 .... **LC 8, 21**
  See also BRW 2; CDBLB 1660-1789; DAM
  DRAM; DLB 80; RGEL 2

Wylie, Elinor (Morton Hoyt)
  1885-1928 .... **TCLC 8; PC 23**
  See also AMWS 1; CA 105; 162; DLB 9,
  45; EXPP; RGAL 4

Wylie, Philip (Gordon) 1902-1971 ... **CLC 43**
  See also CA 21-22; 33-36R; CAP 2; DLB
  9; SFW 4

Wyndham, John .... **CLC 19**
  See also Harris, John (Wyndham Parkes
  Lucas) Beynon
  See also DLB 255; SCFW 2

Wyss, Johann David Von
  1743-1818 .... **NCLC 10**
  See also JRDA; MAICYA 1, 2; SATA 29;
  SATA-Brief 27

Xenophon c. 430 B.C.-c. 354
  B.C. .... **CMLC 17**
  See also AW 1; DLB 176; RGWL 2

Yakumo Koizumi
  See Hearn, (Patricio) Lafcadio (Tessima
  Carlos)

Yamada, Mitsuye (May) 1923- .... **PC 44**
  See also CA 77-80

Yamamoto, Hisaye 1921- .... **SSC 34; AAL**
  See also DAM MULT; LAIT 4; SSFS 14

Yanez, Jose Donoso
  See Donoso (Yanez), Jose

Yanovsky, Basile S.
  See Yanovsky, V(assily) S(emenovich)

Literary Criticism Series
Cumulative Topic Index

This index lists all topic entries in Gale's *Classical and Medieval Literature Criticism, Contemporary Literary Criticism, Drama Criticism, Literature Criticism from 1400 to 1800, Nineteenth-Century Literature Criticism,* and *Twentieth-Century Literary Criticism.*

Topic Index

Topic Index

Topic Index

LC Cumulative Nationality Index

AFGHAN

Babur **18**

AMERICAN

Bache, Benjamin Franklin **74**
Bradford, William **64**
Bradstreet, Anne **4, 30**
Edwards, Jonathan **7, 54**
Eliot, John **5**
Franklin, Benjamin **25**
Hathorne, John **38**
Henry, Patrick **25**
Hopkinson, Francis **25**
Knight, Sarah Kemble **7**
Mather, Cotton **38**
Mather, Increase **38**
Morton, Thomas **72**
Munford, Robert **5**
Occom, Samson **60**
Penn, William **25**
Rowlandson, Mary **66**
Sewall, Samuel **38**
Stoughton, William **38**
Taylor, Edward **11**
Washington, George **25**
Wheatley (Peters), Phillis **3, 50**
Winthrop, John **31**

BENINESE

Equiano, Olaudah **16**

CANADIAN

Marie de l'Incarnation **10**

CHINESE

Lo Kuan-chung **12**
P'u Sung-ling **3, 49**
Ts'ao Hsueh-ch'in **1**
Wu Ch'eng-en **7**
Wu Ching-tzu **2**

DANISH

Holberg, Ludvig **6**
Wessel, Johan Herman **7**

DUTCH

Erasmus, Desiderius **16**
Lipsius, Justus **16**
Spinoza, Benedictus de **9, 58**

ENGLISH

Addison, Joseph **18**
Amory, Thomas **48**
Andrewes, Lancelot **5**
Arbuthnot, John **1**
Askew, Anne **81**
Astell, Mary **68**
Aubin, Penelope **9**
Bacon, Francis **18, 32**
Bale, John **62**

Barker, Jane **42, 82**
Beaumont, Francis **33**
Behn, Aphra **1, 30, 42**
Boswell, James **4, 50**
Bradstreet, Anne **4, 30**
Brome, Richard **61**
Brooke, Frances **6, 48**
Bunyan, John **4, 69**
Burke, Edmund **7, 36**
Burton, Robert **74**
Butler, Samuel **16, 43**
Camden, William **77**
Campion, Thomas **78**
Carew, Thomas **13**
Cary, Elizabeth, Lady Falkland **30**
Cavendish, Margaret Lucas **30**
Caxton, William **17**
Centlivre, Susanna **65**
Chapman, George **22**
Charles I **13**
Chatterton, Thomas **3, 54**
Chaucer, Geoffrey **17, 56**
Churchill, Charles **3**
Cibber, Colley **66**
Cleland, John **2, 48**
Clifford, Anne **76**
Collier, Jeremy **6**
Collins, William **4, 40**
Congreve, William **5, 21**
Coventry, Francis **46**
Coverdale, Myles **77**
Crashaw, Richard **24**
Daniel, Samuel **24**
Davenant, William **13**
Davys, Mary **1, 46**
Day, John **70**
Day, Thomas **1**
Dee, John **20**
Defoe, Daniel **1, 42**
Dekker, Thomas **22**
Delany, Mary (Granville Pendarves) **12**
Deloney, Thomas **41**
Denham, John **73**
Dennis, John **11**
Devenant, William **13**
Donne, John **10, 24**
Drayton, Michael **8**
Dryden, John **3, 21**
Elyot, Thomas **11**
Equiano, Olaudah **16**
Etherege, George **78**
Fanshawe, Ann **11**
Farquhar, George **21**
Fielding, Henry **1, 46**
Fielding, Sarah **1, 44**
Finch, Anne **3**
Fletcher, John **33**
Ford, John **68**
Foxe, John **14**
Garrick, David **15**
Gay, John **49**
Gower, John **76**
Gray, Thomas **4, 40**

Greene, Robert **41**
Greville, Fulke **79**
Hakluyt, Richard **31**
Hawes, Stephen **17**
Haywood, Eliza (Fowler) **1, 44**
Henry VIII **10**
Herbert, George **24**
Herrick, Robert **13**
Heywood, John **65**
Hobbes, Thomas **36**
Hoccleve, Thomas **75**
Holinshed, Raphael **69**
Howell, James **13**
Hunter, Robert **7**
Johnson, Samuel **15, 52**
Jonson, Ben(jamin) **6, 33**
Julian of Norwich **6, 52**
Kempe, Margery **6, 56**
Killigrew, Anne **4, 73**
Killigrew, Thomas **57**
Kyd, Thomas **22**
Langland, William **19**
Lanyer, Aemilia **10, 30**
Lead, Jane Ward **72**
Leapor, Mary **80**
Lilly, William **27**
Locke, John **7, 35**
Lodge, Thomas **41**
Lovelace, Richard **24**
Lydgate, John **81**
Lyly, John **41**
Lyttelton, George **10**
Macaulay, Catherine **64**
Malory, Thomas **11**
Mandeville, Bernard **82**
Manley, (Mary) Delariviere **1, 42**
Marlowe, Christopher **22, 47**
Marston, John **33**
Marvell, Andrew **4, 43**
Massinger, Philip **70**
Middleton, Thomas **33**
Milton, John **9, 43**
Montagu, Mary (Pierrepont) Wortley **9, 57**
More, Henry **9**
More, Thomas **10, 32**
Nashe, Thomas **41**
Newton, Isaac **35, 52**
Parnell, Thomas **3**
Pepys, Samuel **11, 58**
Philips, Katherine **30**
Pix, Mary (Griffith) **8**
Pope, Alexander **3, 58, 60, 64**
Prior, Matthew **4**
Purchas, Samuel **70**
Raleigh, Walter **31, 39**
Reynolds, Joshua **15**
Richardson, Samuel **1, 44**
Roper, William **10**
Rowe, Nicholas **8**
Sandys, George **80**
Sheridan, Frances **7**
Sidney, Mary **19, 39**
Sidney, Philip **19, 39**

ISBN 0-7876-5996-7